INVESTMENTS

INVESTMENTS: ANALYSIS, SELECTION, AND MANAGEMENT

EDWARD A. MOSES

UNIVERSITY OF NORTH FLORIDA

JOHN M. CHENEY

UNIVERSITY OF CENTRAL FLORIDA

WEST PUBLISHING COMPANY

ST. PAUL   NEW YORK   LOS ANGELES   SAN FRANCISCO

PRODUCTION CREDITS

Interior Design: Judith Fletcher Getman
Copyeditor: Robert K. Burdette
Artwork: Rolin Graphics
Composition: Syntax International
Cover Image: *Work No. 25, Red Wing, 1949* by Charles Biederman

COPYRIGHT © 1989 BY WEST PUBLISHING COMPANY
50 W. Kellogg Boulevard
P.O. Box 64526
St. Paul, MN 55164-1003

Printed in the United States of America
96 95 94 93 92 91 90 89   8 7 6 5 4 3 2 1 0

Library of Congress Cataloging-in-Publication Data

Moses, Edward A.
   Investments: analysis, selection, and management/Edward A. Moses, John M. Cheney.
   p. cm.
   Includes indexes.
   ISBN 0-314-48127-3
   1. Investments. 2. Portfolio management. 3. Stocks. 4. Bonds.
I. Cheney, John M. II. Title.
HG4521.M8536 1989
332, 6--dc 19   88-28264 CIP

TO MY MOTHER, CAROLYN MOSES

TO THE MEMORY OF MY PARENTS, JOHN M. AND EVELYN D. CHENEY

BRIEF CONTENTS

CONTENTS

---

3   SECURITIES MARKETS: OPERATIONS AND REGULATIONS 48

---

8 ANALYSIS OF PORTFOLIO PERFORMANCE   **190**

**PART FOUR
ANALYSIS OF BONDS**   **385**

18   CONVERTIBLE SECURITIES   510

**PART SIX
PROFESSIONAL AND PERSONAL
PORTFOLIO MANAGEMENT   639**

23   INVESTING INTERNATIONALLY   641

PREFACE

Security markets have undergone dramatic changes in recent years adding significantly to the complexities of institutional and personal investment management. These changes include a proliferation of new investment products, such as traded options on stocks, indices, debt, currencies, commodities, as well as interest rate and stock index futures. In addition, specialized mutual funds, innovative insurance products, and the emergence of international financial markets have added to the alternatives available to investors. Increasing volatility in the securities markets, as evidenced by the stock market "crash" of October 19, 1987, and the continuing changes in the Tax Code represent examples of additional factors investors must consider in developing and implementing investment strategies.

Accompanying the changes in security markets has been the development and empirical testing of investment theories and techniques. These include hypotheses related to the efficiency of financial markets, portfolio and capital market theory, arbitrage pricing theory, option pricing models, program trading, and portfolio insurance, just to name a few. These developments, along with the need to have an understanding of investment basics, create quite a challenge for the student of investments, the professor, and, we might add, the authors of investments books.

The purpose of this book is to provide information and procedures that will enable individual investors to make informed investment decisions. The information contained in appropriate chapters combines the results from theoretical and empirical investment research with the practical aspects for the investor. The techniques and procedures for active investment strategies presented in this book recognize that there is strong evidence that financial markets are efficient. An underlying proposition throughout the book is that investors should appreciate the pitfalls and complications that occur in pursuing an active investment strategy in an efficient market.

Investments: Analysis, Selection, and Management is intended for use in advanced undergraduate and MBA investment courses. While the topics are covered in a comprehensive manner, with specific references to empirical studies, the book presents material requiring quantitative analysis in an easily understandable manner. The intended prerequisites for an investments course using this book are courses in managerial finance and statistics.

DISTINGUISHING FEATURES

Students usually begin an investments class with great expectations and are excited and interested in the subject matter. It is the responsibility of the professor and the selected textbook not to disappoint the student. An overriding objective in writing *Investments: Analysis, Selection, and Management* was to provide the student and professor with a comprehensive book that is readable, presents difficult concepts in an understandable manner, incorporates the latest advances in theory and practice, and is organized in such a way that the student's expectations of gaining insightful and usable investment information are met.

The distinguishing features include the following:

TIMELINESS   During the 1980s, significant advances in investment theory and empirical investigations have occurred. In addition, factors, such as the Tax Reform Act of 1986 and the October 19, 1987 stock market "crash," impact the investment decision process. These developments are presented in appropriate areas throughout the book.

INVESTMENT STRATEGIES   There appears to be little doubt that capital markets are efficient. The controversial and unresolved issue, however, is the degree of market efficiency. In a perfectly efficient market, a passive strategy which does not attempt to outperform the market on a risk-adjusted basis is appropriate. A less than perfectly efficient market may justify an active strategy that attempts to earn risk-adjusted excess returns. Throughout the book, the efficiency of the market for different types of securities is examined and appropriate investment strategies are suggested.

INVESTING INTERNATIONALLY   The growth of international markets has increased significantly in the decade of the 1980s. The 24-hour financial market is a reality and the opportunities, and risks, of international diversification are important considerations in the investment decision process. International investments are covered in Appendix 4C of Chapter 4 and in Chapter 23.

INVESTMENT INFORMATION AND THE PERSONAL COMPUTER   The investor can create a system that provides significant financial information through the use of a computer, modem, software, and an on-line data service. Investors can research and analyze individual securities, receive news on companies, monitor stock prices, place buy and sell orders, and manage portfolios through their personal computers. Information about such a system is provided in Appendix 4A of Chapter 4. In addition, the software that accompanies this book can be used on IBM PCs and compatibles to perform investment analysis.

TREATMENT OF TAXES   While brief overviews of taxes are given in Chapters 1 and 5, the impact of taxes on specific types of investments and investment techniques are treated in the appropriate chapters throughout the book. This approach has the advantage of relating the specific tax implications of an investment decision to the chapter in which the investment instrument or technique is presented.

ORGANIZATION The book is designed to combine the results from investment research with the practical aspects for individual investors. The organization of the book reflects the overriding importance of the portfolio effect on asset selection. This is the reason for including the material on portfolio theory and analysis in Chapters 2, 6, and 7.

This book contains twenty-six chapters, divided into six parts. Part One covers the investment fundamentals and the institutional aspects of investing. While this part contains introductory material on investment fundamentals and the institutional aspects of investing, additional details are provided in the appropriate chapters throughout the book. For those students with a previous course in investments, this part need only be briefly reviewed. Part Two, Portfolio Theory and Analysis, presents in separate chapters, portfolio and capital market theory, the assumptions, tests, and other models of asset pricing, such as Arbitrage Pricing Theory, and the use of capital market theory and the capital asset pricing model in risk-adjusted performance analysis. Much of the book builds on Part Two. Thus, while the other parts of the book are self-contained and may be selected in a sequence preferred by the professor, Part Two should be included early in the course.

Part Three presents the analysis of common stocks, including economic, industry and company analysis. Common stock valuation models, technical analysis, and market efficiency are included as chapters in this part. Part Four, Analysis of Bonds, contains three chapters, including an introductory chapter on bond fundamentals, a chapter on bond valuation and a chapter on bond investment and portfolio strategies. Heavy emphasis is given to bond analysis because of the increasing investor interest towards bonds.

Part Five provides an analysis of investment alternatives. While this part contains chapters on preferred stocks, convertible securities, precious metals, real estate and collectibles, it also includes extensive coverage of options, commodity futures and financial futures. Part Six, Professional and Personal Portfolio Management, describes international investing, mutual funds and other types of investment companies, pension funds and insurance products, and a concluding chapter on personal investment management. This final chapter provides an illustration of personal financial planning based on a case example introduced in Chapter 1.

EDUCATIONAL AIDS AND SUPPLEMENTS

Investments: Analysis, Selection, and Management and its ancillary materials are designed to maximize the learning experience of the student and assist the professor in using the book. These educational aids and supplements include:

EXAMPLES, FIGURES AND TABLES Important concepts are illustrated with examples throughout the book. In most instances the examples are numerical and presented as separate tables. Quite often, several examples are provided while a concept is being developed to insure that the student comprehends each part of the concept. Numerous figures and tables are used to illustrate important points in each chapter. Many of these examples, figures, and tables are based on actual securities using market data.

CHAPTER FOOTNOTES AND END-OF-CHAPTER REFERENCES Many chapters in the book include a significant number of reference footnotes and end-of-chapter references. These range from the popular press (e.g., *Wall Street Journal* and *Business Week*), practitioners' journals (e.g. *Journal of Portfolio Management* and *Financial Analysts Journal*) to the more theoretical, academic journals (e.g., *Financial Review, Journal of Financial Research, Journal of Financial and Quantitative Analysis, Journal of Finance*, and *Journal of Financial Economics*). These references are included to allow students at different levels of academic background to pursue further reading or research in areas of interest.

SOFTWARE At the end of appropriate chapters, there is a computer applications section. This section describes the templates that are on the floppy disks that accompany the book. The software, written by Carol Billingham of Central Michigan University, consists of templates for Lotus 123 and can be used with IBM PCs and compatibles. The disks contain templates that can be used to solve most of the end-of-chapter problems and can be used by the students for a wide range of investment related analysis and management.

NEW TERM IDENTIFICATION When an important term or word is first introduced, it is italicized and defined. This allows for quick referral by the student until the meaning of the term or word is understood.

END-OF-CHAPTER QUESTIONS AND PROBLEMS Extensive questions and problems are included at the end of each chapter. These questions and problems relate to the key concepts in the chapter and allow the students to test their understanding of the contents of the chapter. In certain chapters, the number of end-of-chapter problems is extensive in order to allow the professor flexibility in making assignments and because we feel problems represent good pedagogy. Many of the problems use data from security markets.

APPENDICES There are three appendices designed to aid the student. Appendix A1 presents the time value of money formulas and examples of calculating effective holding period returns and annualizing holding period returns. In addition, this appendix contains compound and present value tables. Appendix A2 has an explanation and table of the standard normal cumulative probability function. Appendix A3 contains mathematical terms, symbols, and key formulas used in the book.

INDICES There are three indices at the end of the book. These indices are designed to provide the student with quick page references to subjects, authors, and corporations and organizations referred to in the book.

INSTRUCTOR'S MANUAL The Instructor's Manual, IM, is designed to help professors prepare and teach a course in investments using *Investments: Analysis, Selection, and Management*. The IM contains suggested course syllabi for undergraduate and graduate level classes taught in the quarter or semester system.

Outlines for possible class projects on economic, industry, and security analysis are also included. Each chapter in the IM includes a detailed outline for the corresponding chapter in the book, teaching suggestions with appropriate class discussion questions, suggested answers to end-of-chapter questions and solutions to end-of-chapter problems. The IM also contains a test bank prepared by Richard E. White of the University of North Florida. The test bank consists of questions and problems with multiple-choice answers.

TRANSPARENCY MASTERS A separate pack of transparency masters of key tables and figures in the book, as well as additional figures, is available on a complimentary basis to adopters of the book.

ACKNOWLEDGEMENTS

The authors wish to gratefully acknowledge the significant efforts of the many contributors to this book. Without their expertise, suggestions, and support this book would not be possible.

Working from first draft to final manuscript requires the help of reviewers who not only have expertise in the area of investments but also have the classroom experience to improve the clarity of the presentation for the students. We are deeply indebted for the excellent reviews provided by the following individuals:

Scott Besley, University of South Florida; Carol Billingham, Central Michigan University; Randall S. Billingsley, Virginia Polytechnic Institute; Gerald A. Blum, University of Nevada–Reno; Paul Bolster, Northeastern University; Rosita Chang, University of Rhode Island; Mike Devaney, Memphis State University; Eugene Drzycimski, University of Wisconsin–Oshkosh; John W. Ellis, Colorado State University; James Feller, Middle Tennessee State University; Thomas Fetherston, University of Alabama–Birmingham; Albert Fredman, California State University; Jim Greenleaf, Lehigh University; Elizabeth Hennigar, Santa Clara University; A. James Ifflander, University of Arizona; David Ketcham, University of Tennessee; Robert Kleiman, Babson College; David Krause, Marquette University; Dennis J. Lasser, University of Miami; Beni Lauterbach, University of Illinois–Chicago; Christopher K. Ma, University of Pittsburgh; Naval Modani, University of Central Florida; Art Neustel, University of Central Florida; James Overdahl, University of Texas–Dallas; Daniel E. Page, Auburn University; David Peterson, Florida State University; Philip Pfaff, Canisius College; Bruce L. Rubin, Old Dominion University; Louis Scott, University of Illinois; Michael Solt, University of Santa Clara; Pochara Theerathorn, Wichita State University; David Upton, Virginia Commonwealth University; Howard Van Auken, Iowa State University; Bill Weaver, University of Central Florida; Herbert J. Weinraub, University of Toledo; Richard Williams, Wright State University; Glenda Wenchi Wong, DePaul University; Colin Young, Bentley College.

We are especially indebted to Sharon Graham for her help in developing the concept for the book and assistance in developing the chapters on An Overview of Investments and Investment Fundamentals. Stan Atkinson was extremely helpful in preparing the chapter on Options, Warrants and Rights. Charles Jones provided us with his expertise in the insurance area. Richard White deserves special thanks for preparing the chapters on Security Markets and Investment Information. He also did an excellent job in preparing the test bank for the Instructor's Manual. We are also indebted to Jeff Madura for his preparation of the chapter on Investing Internationally. Wallace Reiff deserves special mention for his efforts in preparing the chapter on Technical Analysis. We also wish to thank Carol Billingham for developing the software for the Computer Applications accompanying the book. We are deeply appreciative of the expertise and loving care for details demonstrated by Florence Rendulic in typing the entire manuscript and Instructors Manual.

The professionals at West Publishing Company, Richard Fenton, Nancy Roth, Esther Craig, and Francine DeZiel deserve special mention, not only for their expertise but also for their encouragement and tremendous effort put forth in bringing this book to life.

Our wives, Susan and Anne, and children, Lynne, Daniel and Cheryl, deserve special thanks for their understanding while this book was being prepared. Their support and encouragement played a major role in our being able to make this book a reality.

Edward A. Moses
John M. Cheney

INVESTMENTS: FUNDAMENTALS AND ENVIRONMENT

AN OVERVIEW OF INVESTMENTS

INTRODUCTION

The word *investments* brings forth visions of profit, risk, speculation, and wealth. For the uninformed, investing may result in disaster. For the knowledgeable, the investment process can be financially rewarding and exciting. This chapter introduces the basic concepts of investing and the myriad decisions facing the individual investor. A brief overview is presented of the many investment alternatives available to individual investors, including references to the chapters in which these alternatives are discussed. The investment environment has been changing rapidly since the 1950s, and this chapter examines the changing characteristics of this environment. Specific attention is given to the stock market crash of October 19, 1987, and the overall increase in stock market volatility that occurred during late 1987 and early 1988. The chapter concludes with a brief discussion of the organization and some features of the book.

The following hypothetical case illustrates many of the issues that are addressed in this book. While the case is somewhat abbreviated, it presents many of the complex problems facing investors in today's environment.

THE DECISION TO INVEST—A CASE EXAMPLE

Bob and Barbara Drane, both forty-nine years old, are concerned about their financial security for retirement. They were married 25 years ago, shortly after graduating from college. They have three children: Doug, aged twenty; Marsha, seventeen, and Todd, fifteen. Doug is currently a senior finance major at the state university. Marsha and Todd plan to go to college. Bob and Barbara currently have savings of $62,000. They are concerned that after they pay for all three college educations, they will have very little left in savings for their retirement years.

The Drane's principal asset is their "dream" home that they bought three years ago. While the house has an estimated fair market value of $130,000 and is mortgaged for twenty-two more years, with a balance of $83,000, the Dranes really like their home and have no plans to sell it.

Bob and Barbara also own 50 percent of a small retail carpet company which employs fourteen people. They started the business twenty years ago with Bob's brother. The business has been reasonably successful, and Bob and Barbara's current share of the earnings is about $68,000 per year. It appears that the company will continue its modest growth. Bob and Barbara save approximately $6,000 per year after living expenses and taxes.

Bob and Barbara have never considered selling their share of the business. They always hoped that one of their children would come into the business with them so that they could spend less time at work. They realize that their income from the business would probably decline if one of the children came into the business, but they have always wanted to travel. If one of the children came into the business, then they would realize two dreams: they could travel, and they could leave the business to one of their children.

Bob and Barbara know that they need to plan for their retirement. As small business owners, they never established a company retirement plan, and they realize that their retirement income, other than Social Security income, is their responsibility. They are also considering whether they should change the amount of their life insurance coverage. Currently, Bob has $200,000 of decreasing term life insurance on himself, and Barbara has $100,000 of decreasing term.

In an effort to begin a financial plan, Bob and Barbara have created a list of questions:

1. If they decide to retire from the business when they are both 60, how much income is needed to maintain their desired life-style? How much should they be saving and investing per year toward retirement?

2. Where should they invest their savings? Should they explore mutual funds, bonds, common stocks, real estate, and other investment alternatives, or should they seek out a professional for financial advice?

3. Where can they find information about investment alternatives?

4. Once they have identified the investment alternatives, how can the investments be analyzed and combined into a portfolio? What is the impact of selection, of timing, and of diversification (including international investments) on their investment decisions?

5. How much risk are they willing to assume? How are expected risk and return calculated? How are expected risk and return related?

6. How can they assess the performance of their investments?

7. Should the savings program be through the family-owned company, or should Bob and Barbara set up their own tax-sheltered retirement plan?

8. What should they do about their life insurance? Can insurance be used as an investment alternative?

Many of these questions require complex answers. More importantly, the answers are interrelated. Each of the questions points to two issues: (1) How much wealth do Bob and Barbara need before they retire? and (2) How can Bob and Barbara create the maximum amount of wealth, consistent with their risk preference, before retirement? Part of the wealth will be created by their annual savings and could be increased by increasing salary income or reducing living expenses. Wealth could be increased by increasing the earnings from invested funds, which may require increased risk. Finally, since the government taxes most sources of income, reducing taxes will always add wealth.

Most individuals have a desire or need to create enough wealth to permit them to satisfy their personal life-styles and objectives. Frequently, these desires require expenditures in a given period that exceed income for the same period. For example, the Drane's annual income is probably not large enough to pay for all living expenses and to support two or three children in college in one year. They also realize that their income during the retirement years may not be large enough to support their planned retirement life-style. Because of this mismatch between income and expenses, individuals frequently plan ahead for activities which will require significant expenditures. Hopefully, proper planning will permit them to create the necessary wealth by the time they plan to spend the money. When per-period income is less than current expenses, the needed funds are provided from the individual's assets or from borrowing.

Investments play two roles in this situation. First, the investment medium or vehicle must ensure that money will be available when it is needed. Second, the invested money should grow because a dollar's real value today is greater than a dollar's value tomorrow in a world of inflation.

OVERVIEW OF INVESTMENT ALTERNATIVES

A wide range of investment alternatives is available to individual investors. In addition to the traditional common stock and bond alternatives, other financial assets—such as options on individual common stocks, commodity futures, and financial futures—are examined in this book. In addition, *real* asset alternatives— such as real estate, precious metals, and collectibles—are considered.

Table 1.1 provides an overview of the investment alternatives discussed in this book. Each alternative is classified among the following major categories: (1) equity securities; (2) short-term debt securities; (3) intermediate and long-term debt securities; (4) hybrid securities; (5) derivative securities; (6) real assets; (7) international investments; and (8) other investment alternatives. A brief definition of each category is provided.

Table 1.1 also briefly defines each type of investment alternative. For each of these individual alternatives, the market or method of trading is indicated. The organized exchanges indicated in the table include the New York Stock Exchange, American Stock Exchange, and the regional exchanges. The other major market is the Over-the-Counter, OTC, market where numerous stocks, bonds, and other types of securities are traded.

Short-term debt securities are traded in the money market, which consists of a communications network between security dealers and market makers. Some investment alternatives are not traded in the traditional securities markets. Alternatives such as real estate and insurance products must be bought through individual brokers and dealers.

The last column in Table 1.1 indicates the chapter(s) that provide the major coverage of the investment. However, for a number of alternatives, such as common stocks, numerous discussions occur throughout the book. The subject index should be consulted to determine where specific details about each alternative are presented.

FACTORS TO CONSIDER IN CHOOSING AMONG INVESTMENT ALTERNATIVES

The major factors that should be considered in making investment decisions include (1) basic investment objective, (2) expected rate of return, (3) expected risk, (4) taxes, (5) investment horizon, and (6) investment strategies.

Investment Objective

The *investment objective* is to increase systematically the individual's wealth, defined as assets minus liabilities. Investing requires that an individual invest money in assets which will create the necessary wealth when that wealth is needed. Consequently, most investments are undertaken to provide an increase in wealth.

TABLE 1.1   OVERVIEW OF INVESTMENT ALTERNATIVES

	BRIEF DESCRIPTION	MARKET OR METHOD OF TRADING	COVERAGE IN TEXT
I. EQUITY SECURITIES			
A. Common Stock	Represents ownership interest in issuing corporation.		
1. Class A	Nonvoting common stock entitled to receive dividends.	Organized exchanges and OTC Market	Chapters 9–13
2. Class B	Voting common stock not entitled to receive dividends.	Organized exchanges and OTC Market	Chapters 9–13
B. Preferred Stock	Usually nonvoting but has priority over common stock in dividend and liquidation rights.	Organized exchanges and OTC Market	Chapter 17
II. SHORT-TERM DEBT SECURITIES	Obligations that mature in one year or less.		
A. Negotiable Certificates of Deposit	Issued by federally insured commercial bank with a minimum face value of $100,000.	Money Market	Chapter 3
B. Commercial Paper	Promissory negotiable notes issued by larger well-known corporations.	Money Market	Chapter 3
C. Banker's Acceptances	Used by importers to secure trade credit from exporter; The accepting bank guarantees payment by borrower.	Money Market	Chapter 3
D. Treasury Bills	Obligations issued by U.S. Treasury, sold at a discount from face value.	Money Market	Chapters 14 & 21
III. INTERMEDIATE AND LONG-TERM DEBT SECURITIES	Obligations that mature in more than one year.		
A. U.S. Government Securities			
1. Treasury Notes	Issued by U.S. Treasury with maturities between one and ten years; sold at face value with a specified interest payment.	OTC Market	Chapters 14 & 21
2. Treasury Bonds	U.S. Treasury securities with maturities over ten years.	OTC Market	Chapter 14
3. Savings Bonds	Non-negotiable savings instruments issued by U.S. Treasury.	—	Chapter 14
B. U.S. Agency Securities			
1. Government National Mortgage Association	Mortgage-backed, pass-through debt security.	OTC Market	Chapter 14
2. Federal Home Loan Mortgage Corporation	Mortgage-backed, pass-through debt security.	OTC Market	Chapter 14
3. Federal National Mortgage Association	Mortgage-backed, pass-through debt security.	OTC Market	Chapter 14

(continued)

TABLE 1.1 (*Continued*)

	BRIEF DESCRIPTION	MARKET OR METHOD OF TRADING	COVERAGE IN TEXT
C. Municipal Securities	Debt obligations issued by state or local governments and agencies.		
1. Revenue Bonds	Issued to obtain financing for specific projects such as sewerage facilities and hospitals. Revenues from these projects are earmarked to meet interest and principal payments.	OTC Market	Chapter 14
2. General Obligation Bonds	The general revenues (tax receipts) of the issuer provide funds to meet interest and principal payments.	OTC Market	Chapter 14
D. Corporate Bonds	Debt obligations issued by corporations. There are many different types of corporate bonds because of differences in how principal and interest payments are made and the collateral used to back the bonds.	Organized exchanges and OTC Market	Chapters 14–16
IV. HYBRID SECURITIES	Securities that have characteristics of both equity and debt.		
A. Convertible Preferred Stock	The convertible feature allows the investor to convert the preferred stock to a specified number of shares of common stock.	Organized exchanges and OTC Market	Chapter 18
B. Convertible Bonds	The convertible feature allows the investor to convert the bond to a specified number of shares of common stock.	Organized exchanges and OTC Market	Chapter 18
V. DERIVATIVE SECURITIES	Securities that derive their value from the value of an underlying asset.		
A. Options	Provide the right to buy or sell shares of common stock of a specific corporation within a limited period of time at a designated price.	Chicago Board of Trade; American Stock Exchange; other exchanges and markets	Chapter 19
B. Commodity Futures	Provide the contract holder the right to sell a specified amount of an agricultural or natural resources commodity at a designated price within a specified period of time.	Chicago Board of Trade; Kansas City Board of Trade; other markets	Chapter 20
C. Financial Futures	Provide the contract holder the right to sell a specified amount of a common stock index, bonds, or foreign currencies at a designated price within a specified period of time.	International Monetary Market; Chicago Board of Trade; other exchanges	Chapter 21

D. Options on Futures	Provide the right to buy or sell a specified commodity or financial future within a limited period of time at a designated price.	Chicago Board of Trade; Chicago Mercantile Exchange; other exchanges	Chapters 19 & 21
E. Rights	Issued by a corporation to existing common stockholders in connection with the sale of additional shares of stock.	Organized exchanges and OTC Market	Chapter 19
F. Warrants	Issued by a corporation; provides holder the right or option to purchase additional bonds or common stocks from the issuing corporation at a specified price within a designated period of time.	Organized exchanges and OTC Market	Chapter 19
VI. REAL ASSETS			
A. Precious Metals	Nonfinancial assets. Includes gold, silver, platinum, and others in the form of coins, bullion, or depository certificates.	Individual dealers	Chapter 22
B. Real Estate	Includes single- and multi-family residences, undeveloped land, commercial property, and farm land.	Individual brokers	Chapter 22
C. Collectibles	Includes diamonds, prints, fine art, numismatic coins, stamps, and other categories.	Individual dealers	Chapter 22
VII. INTERNATIONAL INVESTMENTS	Investments by individuals in debt or equity securities issued by organizations outside the country of residency of the investor.		
A. Multinational Corporations	Stocks and bonds issued by large corporations with significant business interests in more than one country.	Organized exchanges and OTC Market	Chapter 23
B. Foreign Stocks Traded on a Local Exchange	Stocks of large firms that have established trading for their securities on domestic as well as foreign exchanges.	Organized exchanges and OTC Market	Chapter 23
C. American Depository Receipts	Securities issued by large international banks that represent ownership of foreign securities held by their foreign branches.	Organized exchanges and OTC Market	Chapter 23
VIII. OTHER INVESTMENT ALTERNATIVES			
A. Pension Funds	Public or private investment funds that provide retirement and other benefits to eligible employees.	Not marketable	Chapter 25
B. Insurance Products	Products offered by insurance companies that involve investment features and provide life insurance.	Purchased from agents; usually not marketable	Chapter 25
C. Mutual Funds	Investment companies that sell shares of common stock that represent an ownership interest in a portfolio of securities.	OTC Market and direct transactions with individual funds	Chapter 24

The higher the level of desired wealth, the higher the return that must be received. An investor seeking higher returns must be willing to face higher levels of risk. While wealth maximization may remain an investor's investment objective over a lifetime, the age or family circumstances of an investor will necessarily force the investor to change his or her investment approach. Consider further the example of Bob and Barbara Drane. Twenty-five years ago, when they were first married and had no children, their investment objective should logically have been wealth maximization, just as it is today. However, in their earlier years they would have been willing to face high levels of risk to achieve this objective. Today, with children to educate and concerns about retirement, they cannot afford to expose themselves to the high levels of risk they were willing to face in their earlier years. They still desire to maximize their wealth, but only at a level of risk consistent with their current circumstances. The Dranes are more risk-averse today than they were early in their careers. However, even as the acceptable level of risk decreases, they desire to maximize their return (wealth) at any given level of risk.

Rate of Return

When selecting investment alternatives, the easiest task is to identify the amount or *rate of return* that you want—you always want the most you can get. With most investments, however, the forecast return may or may not be absolutely accurate. Since it is a forecast, there is usually some variability about the precise amount of the return. This variability requires an analysis of risk.

Rates of return can vary greatly between investment alternatives and over time. Figure 1.1 provides a vivid illustration of this point. This chart provides the average annual rates of return on fourteen alternatives calculated for the period June 1982 to June 1987. The rate of inflation, as indicated by the Consumer Price Index, CPI, is also provided. Notice that financial assets provided much higher returns than did real assets over this five-year period of relatively low inflation.

The lower panel in Figure 1.1 indicates the returns for the one-year period ending June 1, 1987. Notice that real assets, such as silver and gold, provided much higher returns than did financial assets over this one-year period.

The large differences in returns among investment alternatives and the changing ranking of returns over time indicate the importance of a careful analysis of alternatives. The returns shown in Figure 1.1 do not necessarily reflect what will occur in the future.

Risk

Risk can be defined as the variability of possible returns around the expected return of an investment. For some investments, this variability can be quite small. For example, the short-term debt securities described in Table 1.1 have very little variability around their expected return because of their relatively short term to maturity (very low interest rate risk), and the issuer has a very low probability of defaulting. On the other hand, commodity futures are an example of a high-risk investment alternative because of the high variability in prices of the underlying agricultural or natural resources commodities.

Each investor has his or her own attitude about risk and how much he or she can tolerate. Since investment alternatives have different types of risks associated with them (e.g., interest rate risk, purchasing power risk, default risk, and

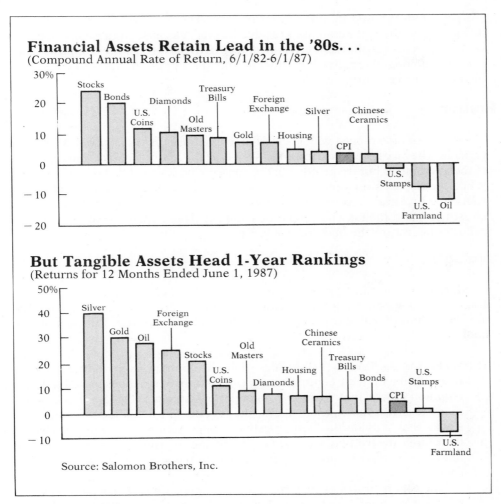

FIGURE 1.1   Rates of return on investment alternatives
Source: *The Price Report,* T. Rowe Price, Baltimore (Fall 1987): p. 2.
Reprinted by permission of T. Rowe Price Associates, Inc.

business risk), the investor must determine which combination of alternatives match his or her particular risk tolerances.

Most investors know that there is no free lunch; that is, the return you can expect is a function of the risk you take. Those investors who can tolerate higher levels of risk should be rewarded with higher levels of return. Most empirical studies of historical risk-return relationships support this statement. Choosing among investment alternatives requires finding the alternative, or combination of alternatives, that offers a fair return for the risk that you are willing to assume.

Taxes

While risk and return are the primary considerations when choosing investments, other factors must be considered. Since the government taxes most sources of income, the *tax consequences* must be considered. In the United States, tax rates are progressive, based upon levels of income. The tax laws also provide many deductions in the computation of taxable income. Because of these features, the tax consequences of different investment alternatives can be quite complex. When choosing among alternative investments, the appropriate number to consider is the net after-tax return.

Investment Horizon

The length of time money will be invested, or the *investment horizon*, is a critical variable. The investment horizon affects not only the return and risk characteristics of the alternatives but frequently the tax consequences associated with the return. While the tax laws no longer differentiate between ordinary income and capital gains, the investor's income level could change dramatically over the life of the investment, and the tax code could be changed. These changes would affect the net after-tax return the investor will receive.

Investment Strategies

In addition to selecting appropriate investment alternatives, an investor needs to consider strategies dealing with selection, timing, and diversification. These ideas are briefly introduced in this section and are more fully discussed throughout the book.

1. SELECTION As Table 1.1 illustrates, there are numerous investment alternatives. Even within the common stock category there are thousands of different common stocks that represent potential investments. Once the decision is made to invest in common stocks, the investor must still identify individual stocks that provide the best investment opportunities. *Selection* decisions, therefore, involve two aspects: (1) identifying appropriate investment alternatives or categories and (2) selecting individual securities or assets in each category.

    Selection strategies may use different approaches. For example, in the selection of common stocks technical and/or fundamental analysis can be employed. These strategies and the impact of an efficient market on these strategies are discussed in more detail in Chapters 5, 12, and 13.

2. TIMING *Investment timing*, another critical variable in the selection of any investment alternative, refers to purchasing an asset just before it is likely to increase in value and selling the asset just before it is likely to decrease in value. This decision assumes, of course, that there is some pattern in the way prices of assets change and that the investor can accurately forecast the change in prices. Forecasting the change in prices can be quite difficult. However, employing a timing strategy does not necessarily mean that you have to be a mathematician. For example, consider the purchase of a home. Real estate prices tend to reflect the level of inflation. If inflation is quite high, real estate prices tend to go up. Consequently, deciding to purchase a home as economists forecast increases in inflation may be a good timing strategy.

    The potential rewards and risks from timing decisions using financial assets are illustrated in Figure 1.2. The top panel in the figure shows average annual rates of return, calculated over the period 1926–1983, for market

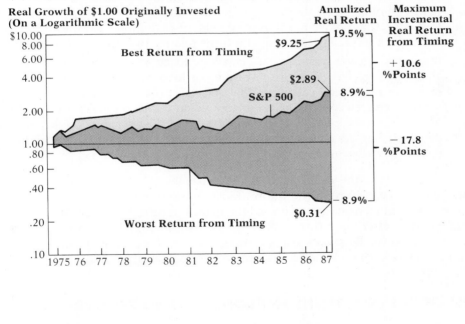

Market Timing Vs. Buy-and-Hold*
(1926-1983)

% Average Annual Return

- 100%: 18.2%
- 70%: 12.1%
- Buy-and-Hold: No Timing Decisions: 11.8%
- 50%: 8.1%

Market Timing Accuracy

*Assumes annual timing intervals between stocks and Treasury bills and a 1% commission on each transaction. Market timing returns are simulated based on historical data.

Maximum Impact of Market Timing on S & P 500 Real Return
1/1/75-6/30/87 (Using Quarterly Timing Intervals Between Stocks and Treasury Bills)

Real Growth of $1.00 Originally Invested (On a Logarithmic Scale)

Best Return from Timing — $9.25

$2.89

S&P 500

1.00

Worst Return from Timing — $0.31

Annualized Real Return
- 19.5%
- 8.9%
- 8.9%

Maximum Incremental Real Return from Timing
- +10.6 %Points
- −17.8 %Points

FIGURE 1.2 Market timing using financial assets

Source: *The Price Report,* T. Rowe Price, Baltimore (Fall 1987): pp. 1 and 5.
Reprinted by permission of T. Rowe Price Associates, Inc.

timing versus a buy-and-hold strategy. Market timing in this example consists of transferring funds between common stocks and Treasury bills. ''Perfect'' market timing occurs when all funds are invested in common stocks prior to a ''bull'' (increasing) market and all funds are invested in Treasury bills prior to a ''bear'' (decreasing) market. Figure 1.2 shows that if an investor correctly forecast each bull and bear market over the period 1926–1983 and used this information to move funds between common stocks and Treasury bills, the average annual rate of return would have been 18.2 percent. On the other hand, if only 50 percent of the bull and bear markets were correctly forecast, the average annual rate of return would have been 8.1 percent. This rate is significantly below the rate of 11.8 percent that resulted from a simple buy-and-hold strategy using only common stocks.

The lower panel in Figure 1.2 provides additional information about market timing using common stocks and Treasury bills. This graph indicates the changes in the dollar value of an investment made in 1975 using the best, worst, and no timing strategies. The ''best'' strategy is defined as correctly forecasting stock market movements and switching funds quarterly into or out of common stocks. The ''best'' strategy provided an average annual real (inflation-adjusted) rate of return of 19.5 percent. The ''worst'' strategy consists of holding common stocks over bear markets and Treasury bills during bull markets. This strategy produced an annualized real rate of return of −8.9 percent.

Figure 1.2 illustrates the potential rewards and risks associated with market timing. To be successful at market timing, an investor must correctly forecast market movements over 50 percent of the time. Less accurate forecasts result in greatly diminished returns relative to a buy-and-hold strategy.

3.   DIVERSIFICATION   Investment risk can be reduced by including more than one alternative or category of assets in the portfolio and by including more than one asset from each category. This naive form of diversification may significantly reduce risk without a corresponding reduction in the expected rate of return on the portfolio. The importance of diversification is discussed in detail in Chapters 6 and 7, and diversification considerations for each investment alternative are discussed in the applicable chapters.

In summary, the decision to invest is usually related to some planned or unplanned expenditure in the future. Most investors prefer the invested money to be placed in an asset that will yield the highest return. However, other factors, such as risk, after-tax return relative to the risk, investment horizon, selection, timing, and diversification must also be considered. Frequently, these factors are all interrelated. These issues are addressed throughout the book.

THE EVOLUTION OF THE INVESTMENT ENVIRONMENT AND PROCESS

The 1950s and 1960s

During the 1950s and early 1960s, the typical young adult got married, had children, purchased whole life insurance, bought a house, and perhaps purchased a few stocks or bonds for retirement when there was extra discretionary income.

Most people planned to pay for their home within ten to twenty years and planned to retire and live on their income from their few stocks and bonds as well as their Social Security income. During the late 1960s, an individual's lifetime consumption increased dramatically. More money was spent for the children's education as the cost of a college education increased. Companies increased the number and size of their pension plans. Pension plans provided a supplemental income for the retiree's Social Security income. Most individuals still saved some money to invest in a few good long-term stocks or bonds.

The 1970s

The investment environment began to change dramatically in the 1970s. The rate of inflation grew dramatically. The impact of rapidly increasing wages and prices, as well as the restructuring of the relationships between wages and prices, was particularly felt in the financial community. In response to these changing patterns of return, risk, and prices, individuals began to realize that certain investments, such as real estate, might be a good investment in an inflationary environment. Other investments, however, were not as likely to provide a return sufficient to offset inflation. The response of the financial community was the creation of a multitude of new investment products. Investments in money market alternatives grew significantly during this period and yielded 15 percent or more. Individual investors realized that the savings and loan associations could not compete and shifted much of their money to the higher-yielding money market instruments. Insurance companies also saw a drain on their capital as individuals borrowed against their whole life insurance policies at very low rates of interest and invested the proceeds in money market alternatives. Real estate partnerships began to form. The traditional stock and bond investment alternatives did not appear to promise the same rate of return as other new, exciting products.

Interest rates on borrowed money also changed. In response, the mortgage market invented *adjustable rate mortgages*, which frequently had interest rates below those of fixed rate mortgages, but carried the risk of higher interest rates and thus higher monthly payments. The world struggled to invent new ways to deal with an inflationary environment not fully understood. Many individual investors tended to move out of the traditional stock and bond markets and into other markets such as precious metals, real estate, and money market securities. This shift left institutional investors, like insurance companies or pension funds, dominant in the traditional financial markets.

The 1980s

While the rate of inflation decreased significantly by the mid-1980s, interest rates continued to fluctuate. Rates on money market securities declined significantly to reflect the lower rates of inflation. Real estate prices did not rise as rapidly as before and actually declined in some geographic areas. Investors, however, were used to high rates of return. The stock market provided the opportunity to obtain those rates. The stock market began a long period of rising prices that continued until August 1987. The world, however, was more complex than it had been before the inflationary period. The stock and bond markets were still dominated by large institutional investors. The response was once again the creation of new products with different patterns of return and risk. Mutual funds grew rapidly during this period, both in dollar size and number of funds. Insurance companies created new products such as universal life insurance with both insurance and investment features. Additional complexity was added by the Tax Reform Act of 1986. Technological change also added to the complexities. The widespread use of the microcomputer permitted information to flow faster and to be analyzed better and quicker. Investment decisions could now be made almost instantaneously with the arrival of new information.

Even with these environmental changes, the individual investor still has the same basic objective: save money from current income so that more money can be spent in later years. This same investor still wants the highest level of return possible for the risk that he or she must assume. The difference is that the investment-choice set has grown substantially. This change has created an investment environment that is more complex and challenging than ever before.

This new financial environment has been a major catalyst in the creation of new industries as well as the reformation of some old industries. The *financial services industry*, for example, is just now beginning to mature. Professional financial planners help investors plan for the college education of their children or their retirement. While the financial planner can help, frequently tax accountants are also needed to sort through the complex tax consequences of these plans. Many investors rely on a professional portfolio manager. This manager may be associated with a brokerage house or may manage the mutual fund where your money is invested. The efficient transfer of wealth from one generation to another may now require not only a lawyer but a tax planner, a financial planner, and an insurance broker. The individual investor, however, cannot leave the decisions to the advisors. Rather, the investor must seek good advice about alternative investments, analyze the alternatives, invest the money, and periodically review the performance of the investments (i.e., compare the actual performance of the investments with the planned performance).

The Stock Market Crash of 1987

The stock market experienced a bull market during the 1980s that ranked as the strongest market over the four decades beginning with the 1950s. Figure 1.3 indicates the movement in stock prices over the period 1949–1987. In addition to the trend, Figure 1.3 provides percentage changes for bull and bear markets that occurred over this period. For example, the bull market beginning in August 1982 and ending in August 1987 resulted in a 228.8 percent increase in common stock prices.

Beginning on August 25, 1987, however, the stock market experienced the second worst bear market since World War II. The market declined 33.2 percent in approximately two months. Declines of this magnitude typically take six to twenty one months. Even more amazing than the 33.2 percent decline is the market behavior on October 19, 1987, or ''Black Monday.''

On Black Monday, the Dow Jones Industrial Average declined 508 points (22 percent), and the Standard & Poor's 500 Stock Composite Index declined 57.6 points (20.5 percent), on record trading volume. This decline is significantly

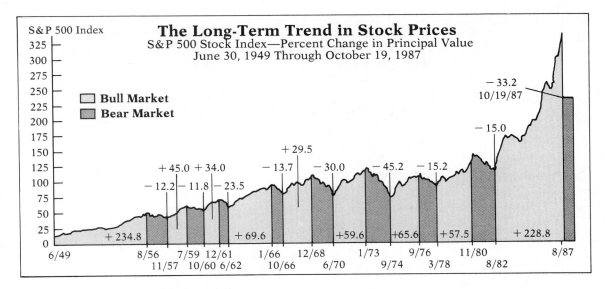

FIGURE 1.3 Bull and bear stock markets
Source: *The Price Report,* T. Rowe Price, Baltimore (Winter 1987): p. 1.
Reprinted by permission of T. Rowe Price Associates, Inc.

greater than the 12.8 percent decline that occurred on "Black Tuesday," October 29, 1929.

The volatility of the stock market during late 1987 caused many investors to sell common stocks and to reassess their investment strategies. In addition to the domestic stock markets, foreign markets experienced increased volatility. Other investment alternatives, such as long-term bonds and precious metals, also demonstrated volatile prices.

The month of October 1987 was one of the most volatile months, in terms of stock price movements, in recent history. According to the Center for Research on Security Prices at the University of Chicago, October 1987 had the eighth largest monthly percent change (-21.9 percent), as measured by the NYSE Composite Index, since January 1926. April 1933, with a 37.4 percent change, ranks the highest over the January 1926 through October 1987 period.

What has caused this recent increase in volatility? While it is possible that shifts in fundamental factors may be the underlying cause, the investigations into the cause have usually centered around computer-generated program trading. Although program trading may take several forms, the most common involves taking a position in a stock-index futures contract and an opposite position in a group of stocks that replicates the movement of the underlying stock index. When a sufficient "spread" exists between the index and the futures contract, a risk-free opportunity exists to take advantage of the price differences. These arbitrage opportunities involve computerized buying and selling of a large number of stocks.

Investigations of the role played by program trading in the increased volatility of stock prices are being undertaken by Congress, the Securities Exchange Commission, and the Commodity Futures Trading Commission. In the meantime, the futures exchanges have put price limits on the movement of stock-index futures, and the New York Stock Exchange has suspended program trading whenever the Dow Jones Industrial Average moves more than fifty points in one day. These temporary restraints will likely stay in place until the investigations of the stock market crash of October 19, 1987, are completed.

The investment environment of the late 1980s and early 1990s may offer a frightening but challenging opportunity for individual investors. This environment suggests a strategy of careful and informed investment decisions.

ORGANIZATION OF THE BOOK

While reading and studying this book may not make you wealthy, studying it seriously should enable you to make wiser and more-informed investment decisions. The information contained in each chapter tries to combine the results from investment research with the practical aspects for individual investors. Each chapter presents the theoretical framework and then applies that framework to investment decisions faced by individuals.

The text is organized into six sections. Part 1 (Chapters 1 through 5) introduces the fundamental aspects of investing and the investment environment. Part 2 (Chapters 6 through 8) presents portfolio and capital market theory, and portfolio performance analysis. Part 3 (Chapters 9 through 13) examines in detail the analysis of common stocks; Part 4 (Chapters 14 through 16) details bond fundamentals, valuation, and investment strategies. Part 5 (Chapters 17 through 22) provides information on other investment opportunities, including preferred stock, convertible securities, options, commodities, financial futures, and real assets such as precious metals, real estate, and collectibles. Portfolio management, both professional and personal, and international investing are discussed in Part 6 (Chapters 23 through 26). Finally, in Chapter 26 the Drane case introduced in this chapter is used to illustrate financial planning.

This text also considers the expanding use of the microcomputer in the management of portfolios. A section at the end of several chapters indicates software that is available to analyze the types of investments discussed in the chapter. Many of the end-of-chapter problems can be solved using the software accompanying this book.

SUMMARY

Bob and Barbara Drane's desire to provide for their children's education and their retirement years is not based on "get-rich-quick" schemes. They have the same investment objectives that most individuals would choose in the late 1980s and early 1990s. While their past investment strategy in the business has enabled them to reach one of their financial goals, they recognize that the second goal will have to be realized in a more complex environment. The reality of the situation is that they will probably need to get financial advice from a variety of sources, including a financial planner, a tax accountant, a lawyer, and an insurance broker.

1. Briefly define selection, timing, and diversification. In your opinion, is one of these three decisions more important to an individual investor?

2. Explain why many individuals are willing to save rather than consume some of their current income.

3. What are some of the advantages of including real assets as investment alternatives for individuals?

4. Briefly compare and contrast the money market with the organized security exchanges.

5. Use Figure 1.1 to indicate the best and worst investment alternative in terms of return over the 1982–1987 period. What were the best and worst alternatives for the year ending June 1, 1987? How many of the alternatives provided a rate of return greater than the rate of inflation over the two time periods?

6. Define the investment horizon and indicate why it is an important factor to consider in choosing among investment alternatives.

7. Use Figure 1.2 to indicate the potential risks and rewards associated with market timing using common stocks and Treasury bills. In your opinion, is market timing a viable strategy for individual investors?

8. Explain how an individual investor can diversify a portfolio. What are the advantages of diversification?

9. Compare and contrast the investment environment of the 1970s with that of the 1980s. What are the implications of this changing environment for individual investors?

10. Briefly discuss the impact of the stock market crash of 1987 on individual investors. What are some of the likely short-term and long-term consequences of this crash?

CHAPTER 2

INVESTMENT FUNDAMENTALS

INTRODUCTION

Most individuals need to earn enough money to satisfy their consumption desires and long-run objectives. Frequently, their desired life-style requires expenditures that exceed their income for a given time period. During other income periods, expenditures might be less than their income. This imbalance between current income and consumption will cause most individuals sometimes to be *net savers* and at other times to be *net consumers* of accumulated wealth.

While one could bury savings in the yard, the financial system allows an individual to earn additional income on money set aside for future consumption or other purposes. This trade-off between foregoing current consumption for higher levels of future consumption is the essence of the investment process. If asked, "How much future consumption do you want?" most individuals would respond, "As much as I can have." Unfortunately, the amount of future consumption is affected by several factors, including

- How long will the savings be invested?
- How much will be saved or consumed in future income periods?
- What are the tax consequences associated with the money saved?
- How much will the invested income earn after taxes?
- Is the investment income guaranteed, or is there some uncertainty regarding the amount of future income?

The length of time the savings are invested, called the *investment horizon*, is usually stated in terms of months, years, or some other period of time. Horizons of less than one year are considered very short; periods of twenty or thirty years are very long horizons.

The amount that invested money will earn is called the *investment return*. Because the tax code requires investors to pay taxes on income and capital gains generated by most types of investments, the investment return is usually measured on an after-tax basis. The specific income-tax effect for different types of investments should always be identified.

If the investment after-tax rate of return is not guaranteed, then there is *uncertainty* about the rate of return. The uncertainty is frequently called *risk*. Although uncertainty and risk are technically different, most investors tend to use the two words interchangeably. The discussion in this book will not differentiate between risk and uncertainty.

The major factors in the decision to consume now or to invest and consume later can be summarized by considering the after-tax return relative to the risk over the investment horizon. Rational investors believe that the expected return from an investment should increase as risk increases and that return should increase as the investment horizon increases since there is more uncertainty for long horizons.

MEASURES OF RETURN

While the rate of return is intuitively easy to understand, the time horizon can make the computation complex. Therefore, it is necessary to examine the measurement of rate of return over different periods of time.

Single-Period Measure of Return

The *investment return* is defined as the after-tax increase in the value of the initial investment. The increase in value can come from two sources: a direct cash payment to the investor or an increase in the market value of the investment relative to the original purchase price. For example, suppose you own shares of common stock which you bought one year ago for $20,000. Under the Tax Reform Act of 1986, no distinction is made, for tax purposes, between cash dividends and capital gains. If during the year you received $500 in cash dividends on an after-tax basis and the stock could be sold today for a net after-tax receipt of $25,000, then your total $5,500 after-tax return would be calculated by

$$\$500 + (\$25,000 - \$20,000) = \$5,500 \tag{2.1}$$

Because the dollar amount of the return is related to the dollar amount of the initial investment, investors prefer to express return as a percentage. This is calculated by comparing the return to the amount initially invested. The *rate of return*, or holding period return, *HPR*, over the holding period is computed as

$$HPR = \frac{\text{cash receipts} + (\text{ending price} - \text{beginning price})}{\text{beginning price}} \tag{2.2}$$

Applying Equation 2.2 to the common stock example gives a *HPR* over the one-year period:

$$HPR = \frac{500 + (25,000 - 20,000)}{20,000} = 27.5\% \tag{2.3}$$

The after-tax *HPR* of 27.5 percent has two components: 25 percent increase in price or capital appreciation (5,000 ÷ 20,000), and a 2.5 percent dividend return (500 ÷ 20,000).

Holding period returns are often calculated for periods other than one year; for this reason, the length of the holding period must always be indicated for a specific *HPR*. Many *HPRs* over periods shorter or longer than one year are "annualized." In general, if the length of the holding period is not specified, it is assumed to be one year. *HPRs* calculated for holding periods of various lengths are discussed in more detail later in this chapter and in the analysis of portfolio performance in Chapter 8.

The calculation of the *HPR*, once each of the components is known, is quite easy. An investor knows the beginning (purchase) price and must estimate the cash payment to be received and the ending (selling) price. The investor must estimate these numbers to compute the *expected* return to compare with the *required* rate of return.

Required Rate of Return

When setting the *required rate of return* on an investment, an investor must consider the real rate of return, expected inflation, and risk. Because of foregoing consumption today, the investor is entitled to a rate of return that compensates for this deferred consumption. Since the investor expects to receive an increase in the *real* goods purchased later, the required rate is called the *real rate of return* and represents the pure time value of money. The capital markets determine this rate based upon the supply of money to be invested relative to the demand for borrowed money.

For example, if an investor plans to loan $500 today, in exchange for consumption at some later date, then the lender may expect to receive $515 at the expected time of consumption. The $15 return on the investment of $500 represents the pure time value of money, the real return paid to compensate the investor for deferred consumption.

If the investor expects that the prices of the goods to be consumed will increase by the time the investment provides a return, then the investor will also require that the return be adjusted for those price increases. An investor is entitled to be compensated for the rate of inflation in addition to the real return. For example, if the investor expects inflation to be 5 percent over the period of the loan, then he or she would expect to receive a total of $540, which includes $15 for the real return and $25 (.05 × $500) to compensate for the 5 percent rate of inflation.

Investment returns are usually not guaranteed. If an investor is uncertain about future returns, he or she will expect to be compensated for that uncertainty and will require an additional return from the borrower. In the example, the investor may want to add a 2 percent additional return for risk. Then the rate of return required by the investor would be 10 percent. The total 10 percent required return pays the investor 3 percent for the time value of money, 5 percent for inflation, and 2 percent for risk. The return for inflation and risk, or 7 percent, is called the *risk premium*.

Measure of Return over Several Periods

Over extended time horizons, rates of return may change because of changes in the component rates. For example, the real rate of return may change because of supply and demand of investment funds relative to borrowed funds. Or expectations about inflation and other sources of risk may change, causing risk premiums to change. This changing environment causes investors' required rates of return to change. For example, an investor may expect that the credit union will pay a 5.5 percent return during 1989, but will probably increase this rate to 6 percent in 1990 and will even increase the rate again in 1991 to 6.25 percent. An investor with a three-year investment horizon must analyze the decision to invest the money in the credit union by determining the expected rate of return over the three years.

There are a number of ways to determine the single required rate of return over multiple periods.[1] First, the investor can calculate a simple arithmetic average of the individual required annual rates of return. The simple arithmetic average required rate of return, $\overline{HPR}$, is computed by

$$\overline{HPR} = \left[\sum_{j=1}^{n} (HPR_j) \right] \Big/ n \tag{2.4}$$

---

[1] Other techniques that involve compounding and discounting procedures are discussed in Chapter 8.

The arithmetic required rate of return, $\overline{HPR}$, for our credit union example would be 5.917 percent and would be calculated as

$$(.055 + .06 + .0625)/3 = 5.917\% \tag{2.5}$$

The result of an arithmetic average return can be distorted if there are large differences in the rates of return across time periods. A rather extreme example will illustrate the problem. Suppose rental property is expected to increase 300 percent in the first year but will lose 75 percent of its value in the second year. The arithmetic average is computed as

$$\overline{HPR} = [3.00 + (-.75)]/2 = 112.5\% \tag{2.6}$$

If you initially invested $50,000 in the property, at the end of the first year the investment would be worth $200,000 [50,000 + (50,000)(3)], and by the end of the second year, your property would be worth the original $50,000 [200,000 + (200,000)(−.75)]. While the arithmetic rate of return is 112.5 percent, this investment really generates zero return over the two-year holding period.

Although the example may be extreme, large differences in the periodic rates of return over longer investment horizons will cause the arithmetic rate of return to be misleading.

The *geometric mean* required rate of return does not suffer from this flaw. The geometric mean required rate of return, HPR_g, is defined as that rate of return which would make the initial investment equal the ending investment value. In our example above, the geometric mean rate of return would be 0 percent since a 0 rate of return makes the initial investment equal to the ending investment value.

The HPR_g is calculated by taking the nth root of the product of one plus the individual required rates of return. The formula for the geometric rate of return is

$$HPR_g = [\pi(1 + HPR_j)]^{1/n} - 1 \tag{2.7}$$

where π represents the product (the result of multiplying). The individual required rates of return, represented by HPR_j, are expressed as 1 plus the individual rate of return. For example, a 10 percent HPR would be 1.10, and a loss of 20 percent would be represented by .80 $[1 + (-.20)]$. The exponent, $1/n$, represents the number of equal interval periods over the investment horizon.

The calculation of the 0 percent HPR_g from the rental property example is as follows:

$$
\begin{aligned}
HPR_g &= [(1 + 3)(1 + (-.75)]^{1/2} - 1 \\
&= [(4)(.25)]^{1/2} - 1 \\
&= (1)^{1/2} - 1 \\
&= \sqrt{1} - 1 \\
&= 1 - 1 \\
&= 0\%
\end{aligned}
\tag{2.8}
$$

A second example, with less extreme HPRs, may help to clarify the geometric mean rate of return. Consider the following example, using annual required rates of return for a three-year investment horizon.

YEAR	HPR_j	1 PLUS HPR_j
1	8.0%	$(1 + .08) = 1.08$
2	−5.0%	$(1 − .05) = .95$
3	20.0%	$(1 + .20) = 1.20$

$$\text{Arithmetic Mean} = \overline{HPR} = \left[\sum_{j=1}^{n} (HPR_j) \right] \bigg/ n \qquad (2.9)$$
$$= .23/3 = 7.667\%$$

$$\text{Geometric Mean} = HPR_g = [\pi(1 + HPR_j)]^{1/n} - 1 = 1.2312^{1/3} - 1 \qquad (2.10)$$
$$= \sqrt[3]{1.2312} - 1$$
$$= 1.0718 - 1$$
$$= 7.18\%$$

The arithmetic mean is larger than the geometric mean. Due to the inherent bias in the arithmetic mean, the geometric mean will always be equal to or less than the arithmetic mean. The arithmetic and geometric means will only be equal when the *HPRs* over the investment horizon are constant. By considering the compound rate of return during the time intervals composing the investment horizon, the geometric mean rate of return is similar to the rate of interest used in compound interest calculations.

Expected Rate of Return

If an investment is to be made, the *expected rate of return* should be equal to or greater than the *required rate of return* for that investment. The expected rate of return is based upon the expected cash receipts (dividends or interest) over the holding period and the expected ending, or selling, price. As indicated earlier, the required rate of return indicates the minimum return the investor is willing to accept, given expectations about the real rate of return, inflation, and other sources of risk that determine the risk premium for the investment. Unless the rate of return is guaranteed, most investors recognize that several rates of return are possible. Investors summarize these possible rates of return into a single number called the expected rate of return. Three techniques for calculating expected return are examined in the remainder of this section.

If the investor can describe the possible variables that will influence each of the possible rates of return and assign probabilities to these outcomes, then the expected rate of return should equal the weighted average of the various possibilities. Listing the possible investment results and assigning probabilities to each of these outcomes is the same as creating a probability distribution in statistics. Probability distributions are used to describe possible outcomes and to assign individual probabilities, from zero (no chance of occurring) to one (full certainty that the outcome will happen), to each possible outcome.

For example, a probability distribution for investment returns might be given by an investor who believes that an investment will provide different rates of return under different economic conditions. If there is a strong economy, defined by strong real economic growth, the investment might yield a 20 percent rate of return. The investor may think that if the economy shows moderate real growth, the investment will yield a 10 percent rate of return. Finally, the investor may forecast that if the economy weakens, the investment will provide a negative return of 10 percent. The estimated probabilities for each of these economic scenarios: 30 percent chance of a strong economy, 40 percent chance of a moderate economy, and 30 percent chance of a weakened economy. The information is summarized by the following:

STATE OF THE ECONOMY	PROBABILITY	EXPECTED RATE OF RETURN
Strong Growth	.30	20%
Moderate Growth	.40	10
Weak Growth	.30	−10
	1.00	

This example illustrates a forecast of three possible outcomes, each based upon a possible state of the economy. Each economic state will result in a different expected rate of return. Subjective probabilities, P_j, were assigned to each outcome. The overall expected rate of return, $E(HPR)$, can be calculated as a weighted average of the three forecasts:

$$E(HPR) = \sum_{j=1}^{n} P_j HPR_j \qquad (2.11)$$

In the example, $E(HPR)$ can be estimated as

$$E(HPR) = (.3)(.20) + (.4)(.1) + (.3)(-.1)$$
$$= .06 + .04 - .03$$
$$= 7.0\%$$

In this example, the investor assigned probabilities to each of the three possible economic conditions and estimated the expected rate of return under each of the economic conditions. This task is usually quite difficult. The investor is attempting to forecast accurately uncertain economic events and rates of return that will result under each economic environment.

Often, forecast probabilities are measured by using statistical sampling techniques from historical data. In this second approach, actual historical or *ex-post* rates of return are collected. Then the percentage of observations which represents each of the economic conditions is computed. For example, assume that 100 historical rates of return were collected and categorized as occurring during strong, moderate, or weak economic conditions. If 30 observations occurred during strong economic conditions, 40 occurred during moderate economic conditions, and the rest occurred during weak economic conditions, then the forecaster, based on historical observations, could estimate the probabilities of a strong, moderate, or weak economy as 30 percent, 40 percent, and 30 percent, respectively.

The corresponding rates of return could then be estimated from the ex-post rates of return in each category (i.e., the average rate of return for all observations categorized as strong economic conditions might be 20 percent). While this technique of using historical relationships to forecast the future possibilities has its limitations, it does at least provide an initial forecast which the investor can use as a guide in the creation of a forecast. Another advantage is that the technique is relatively straightforward and easy to use.

A third technique for estimating the expected rate of return is to collect a sampled number of ex-post rates of return which represent the distribution of the rates of return over the forecast horizon. Then, assuming that the observations have equal probabilities of occurring, compute the statistical average. For example, consider an investor who has collected quarterly rates of return for the past five years. By assuming that each observed rate of return has an equal chance of occurring next quarter, the investor can calculate the expected return by using a simple arithmetic average. Table 2.1 provides the data that would be needed for this calculation.

Assuming that each of the ex-post rates of return has an equal probability of occurring during the forecast period, the probability of each return is 5 percent. The expected rate of return, $E(HPR)$, can then be calculated using Equation 2.11. Alternatively, since each of the outcomes has equal probabilities, the $E(HPR)$ can be calculated using a simple arithmetic average. This calculation would result in the following expected quarterly rate of return, using Equation 2.4 and the information in Table 2.1:

$$E(\overline{HPR}) = 1.3065/20$$
$$= 6.53\%$$

TABLE 2.1 QUARTERLY EX-POST HOLDING PERIOD RETURNS

QUARTER	QUARTERLY EX-POST HPRs
1	15.87%
2	5.38
3	4.84
4	6.07
5	−4.44
6	6.20
7	0.19
8	2.73
9	−1.93
10	11.46
11	11.65
12	−2.03
13	10.05
14	5.61
15	10.57
16	3.03
17	−1.08
18	16.38
19	14.15
20	15.95
Total	130.65%

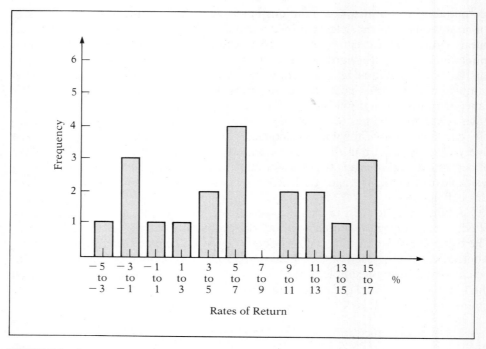

FIGURE 2.1   Frequency Distribution

The three estimation techniques discussed above are relatively simple fore-casting tools. There are more-sophisticated forecasting techniques which could also be used to derive the estimated probability distribution. Regardless of the forecasting technique used, the goal is the same. The investor is attempting to describe the possible events which could influence the expected rate of return. The process helps the investor to accomplish two objectives: to compute the expected rate of return from the distribution of possible outcomes and simulta-neously to describe the uncertainty or risk associated with the investment. For example, Figure 2.1 describes the distribution associated with the data from Table 2.1. Because of the wide dispersion of historical returns, as shown in Figure 2.1, there is a great uncertainty associated with the expected return estimated from the quarterly holding period returns.

MEASURES OF RISK

Sources of Risk

Investors would agree that an investment's expected return should increase as the risk of the investment increases.[2] Most investors would also agree on how the expected rate of return should be calculated. But when the discussion turns to risk, the debate begins.

---

[2] This point is discussed in detail in Chapter 6.

A risk-free investment will provide a rate of return to compensate the investor for the time value of money. To this rate of return should be added an additional rate of return to provide for expected inflation and other types of risk. But how much additional return should be added to this rate to compensate the investor for risk? This relationship can be illustrated as

$$E(R_j) = R_f + RP_j \qquad\qquad (2.12)$$

where $E(R_j)$ = expected rate of return for asset j
R_f = risk-free rate of return
RP_j = risk premium for asset j

A single risk premium must compensate the investor for all the uncertainty associated with the investment, yet there are several major sources of investment uncertainty. The four usually mentioned with respect to marketable securities are business risk, financial risk, liquidity risk, and default risk.

1. BUSINESS RISK Business risk refers to the uncertainty about the rate of return caused by the nature of the business. The most frequently discussed causes of business risk are uncertainty about the firm's sales and operating expenses. Clearly, the firm's sales are not guaranteed and will fluctuate as the economy fluctuates or the nature of the industry changes. A firm's income is also related to its operating expenses. If all operating expenses are variable, then sales volatility will be passed directly to operating income. Most firms, however, have some fixed operating expenses (for example, depreciation, rent, salaries). These fixed expenses cause the operating income to be more volatile than sales. If a firm is operating below its break-even point, decreases in sales will cause a greater decrease in operating income. Sales levels above the break-even point will cause operating income to increase faster than sales. Business risk is related to sales volatility as well as the operating leverage of the firm caused by fixed operating expenses.[3]

2. FINANCIAL RISK The firm's capital structure or sources of financing determine financial risk. If the firm is all equity financed, then any variability in operating income is passed directly, on an equal percentage basis, to net income. If a firm is partially financed by debt that requires fixed interest payments or by preferred stock that requires fixed preferred dividend payments, then these fixed charges introduce financial "leverage." This leverage causes net income to vary more than operating income. The introduction of financial leverage causes the firm's lenders and its stockholders to view their income streams as having additional uncertainty. As a result of financial leverage, both investment groups would increase the risk premiums that they require for investing in the firm.[4]

---

[3] The degree of operating leverage at a particular sales level can be measured as (Sales − Variable Operating Costs)/(Sales − Variable Operating Costs − Fixed Operating Costs).

[4] The degree of financial leverage at a particular level of operating income can be estimated as Operating Income/(Operating Income − Interest Expense − Before-tax Equivalent of Preferred Dividends). The before-tax equivalent of preferred dividends can be estimated by dividing the preferred dividends by one minus the marginal tax rate. As can be seen, in the estimation of the degree of operating leverage and the degree of financial leverage, the higher the fixed operating costs and fixed financing costs, the larger will be the impact of a change in sales on operating income and earnings.

3. LIQUIDITY RISK Liquidity risk is associated with the uncertainty created by the inability to sell the investment for cash quickly. An investor assumes that the investment can be sold at the expected price when future consumption is planned. As the investor considers the sale of the investment, there are two uncertainties: (1) What price will be received? (2) How long will it take to sell the asset? An example of an illiquid asset is a house in a market with an abundance of homes relative to the number of potential buyers. This investment may not sell for several months or even years. Finally, if the price is reduced sufficiently, the real estate will sell. A selling price concession must be made in order for the transaction to occur.

    In contrast, a U.S. Treasury bill can be sold almost immediately with very little concession on selling price. Such an investment can be converted to cash almost at will and for a price very close to the price the investor expected. Investors considering the purchase of illiquid investments, ones which have no ready market, will demand a rate that compensates for the liquidity risk.

    A third example involves an indication of liquidity risk for common stocks. Because of organized and active markets, common stocks can be quickly sold. Some common stocks, however, have greater liquidity risk than others because of a *thin* market. A thin market occurs when there are relatively few shares outstanding and investor trading interest is limited. The thin market results in a large price *spread* (the difference in the *bid* price buyers are willing to pay and the *ask* price sellers are willing to accept). A large spread increases the cost of trading to the investor and thus represents liquidity risk.

4. DEFAULT RISK Default risk is related to the probability that some or all of the initial investment will not be returned. The degree of default risk is closely related to the financial condition of the company issuing the security and the security's rank in claims on assets in the event of default or bankruptcy. For example, if a bankruptcy occurs, creditors, including bondholders, have a claim on assets prior to the claim of common stockholders.

    While most investors would agree that business, financial, liquidity, default, inflation, and other risks are basic risks associated with investment decisions, most would not agree on how to convert these sources of risk into a single risk-premium measure.

Potential Measures of Risk

Measurement of risk has always been debated in the investment industry. This disagreement stems primarily from the multitude of investors' perceptions of risk. Many investors, such as banks, might view the major risk as the uncertainty whether the money they loan will be returned. These investors define a major source of risk as the risk of bankruptcy or default. A stockholder of a firm considers not only bankruptcy risk but also the risk that the firm will yield a rate of return below some targeted rate of return. While both of these measurement ideas are intuitively appealing, the conversion of the sources of risk into a single statistical measure is quite difficult.

This section briefly introduces two traditional measures of risk: *range* (maximum return − minimum return) and the *standard deviation*. As the discussion expands from individual securities to portfolios of securities, other risk measures are introduced in this and other chapters.

While the range communicates the difference between the best possible return and the worst possible return, it does not provide any information about the distribution of rates of return between the extremes. The standard deviation provides more information about the risk of the asset; its advantage is that the uncertainties of returns can be summarized into a single number, easily calculated. Its major disadvantage is that the standard deviation considers possible returns above the expected value as risky as returns below the expected value.

Standard Deviation as a Measure of Risk

The standard deviation of a distribution is the square root of the variance of the returns around the mean, HPR. This measure considers both the rate of return, HPR_j, and the probability, P_j, associated with the return. The variance of a *historical* distribution of holding period returns is computed by

$$\sigma_j^2 = \sum_{j=1}^{n} (P_j)(HPR_j - \overline{HPR_j})^2 \tag{2.13}$$

Table 2.2 summarizes the calculations required for a distribution with equal probabilities of outcomes. Table 2.3 summarizes the necessary calculations if the HPR probabilities are unequal.

Relating Risk and Return

The standard deviation as a measure of risk has one distinct advantage over all other proposed statistical measures. The investment community would agree that expected return should increase as risk increases. If risk is measured by the standard deviation, then risk per unit of expected return can be measured by the *coefficient of variation*. The coefficient of variation is defined by

$$CV_j = \frac{\sigma_j}{\overline{HPR_j}} \tag{2.14}$$

The example from Table 2.2 yields a coefficient of variation of

$$CV_j = \frac{6.35\%}{6.53\%} = .97 \tag{2.15}$$

For the example illustrated in Table 2.3, the coefficient of variation is

$$CV_j = \frac{11.87\%}{7.00\%} = 1.70 \tag{2.16}$$

If investors believe that the rate of return should increase as the risk increases, then CV_j provides a quick summary of the relative trade-off between expected return and risk. Consider two investments. Investment **A** has an expected return

TABLE 2.2 COMPUTATION OF STANDARD DEVIATION: Equal Probabilities of Outcomes

QUARTER	HPR	$HPR_j - \overline{HPR}_j$	$(HPR_j - \overline{HPR}_j)^2$
1	15.87%	9.34%	87.2356*
2	5.38	−1.15	1.3225
3	4.84	−1.69	2.8561
4	6.07	−0.46	0.2116
5	−4.44	−10.97	120.3409
6	6.20	−0.33	0.1089
7	0.19	−6.34	40.1956
8	2.73	−3.80	14.4400
9	−1.93	−8.46	71.5716
10	11.46	4.93	24.3049
11	11.65	5.12	26.2144
12	−2.03	−8.56	73.2736
13	10.05	3.52	12.3904
14	5.61	−0.92	0.8464
15	10.57	4.04	16.3216
16	3.03	−3.50	12.2500
17	−1.08	−7.61	57.9121
18	16.38	9.85	97.0225
19	14.15	7.62	58.0644
20	15.95	9.42	88.7364
Total	130.65%		805.6195

$$\sigma_j^2 = 805.6195/20 = 40.2810$$

$$\overline{HPR}_j = 130.65\%/20 \qquad \sigma_j = \sqrt{40.2810}$$

$$= 6.53\% \qquad \sigma_j = 6.35\%$$

* Note that the unit of measurement for these numbers is percentage squared units.

TABLE 2.3 COMPUTATION OF STANDARD DEVIATION: Unequal Probabilities of Outcome

STATE OF ECONOMY	PROBABILITY (P_j)	HPR_j	$(P_j)(HPR_j)$
Strong Growth	.3	20%	6.0%
Moderate Growth	.4	10	4.0
Weak Growth	.3	−10	−3.0
	1.0		$\overline{HPR}_j = 7.0\%$

STATE OF ECONOMY	PROBABILITY	HPR_j	$(HPR_j - \overline{HPR}_j)^2$	$P_j(HPR_j - \overline{HPR}_j)^2$
Strong Growth	.3	20%	169.0*	50.70
Moderate Growth	.4	10	9.0	3.60
Weak Growth	.3	−10	289.0	86.70
	1.0			$\sigma_j^2 = 141.00$
				$\sigma_j = \sqrt{141.00}$
				$\sigma_j = 11.87\%$

* Note that the unit of measurement for these numbers is percentage squared units.

of 10 percent and a standard deviation of 2 percent. Investment B has an expected return of 11 percent and a standard deviation of 3 percent. The coefficients of variation for the two investments are

	INVESTMENT A	INVESTMENT B
Expected Return	10%	11%
Standard Deviation	2%	3%
Coefficient of Variation	2%/10% = .2	3%/11% = .2727

The coefficient of variations indicates that investment A might be preferred by investors since the risk per unit of return is less than that for investment B. The use of the coefficient of variation to rank investments assumes that the trade-off between risk and return is linear. Its use for ranking purposes may therefore result in suboptimal investment decisions.

THE PORTFOLIO CONCEPT—AN INTRODUCTION

Portfolio Expected Return

If all investment returns were guaranteed, then investors would simply invest all of their money in the asset with the highest rate of return. Because rates of return are not guaranteed and are viewed as risky, investors seek to reduce risk by diversifying, or placing portions of their savings in different investment vehicles.

Investment assets respond to economic conditions in different ways. For example, during inflationary environments real estate investments may yield a higher rate of return than assets with fixed cash-flow returns such as bonds with fixed coupon rates. If the investor is uncertain about the economic environment over the investment horizon, he or she may elect to invest a portion of savings in real estate and the remaining savings in bonds.

The investor is attempting to diversify the portfolio, so that if a particular economic event occurs, the portfolio will be protected from extreme fluctuations. The portfolio will generate returns which reflect the returns from the individual assets held in the portfolio. Consider the portfolio returns provided in Table 2.4. The investor has selected two assets, Security A and Security B. Each of their possible returns is estimated based on the four possible states of the economy.

TABLE 2.4 PORTFOLIO RETURNS ASSUMING EQUAL DOLLAR INVESTMENTS IN EACH SECURITY

STATE OF ECONOMY	EXPECTED RATES OF RETURN, $E(HPR)$		EXPECTED PORTFOLIO RETURN, $E(R_p)$
	SECURITY A	SECURITY B	
Strong Growth	18%	12%	15.0%
Moderate Growth	12	6	9.0
Weak Growth	4	8	6.0
Recession	−8	14	3.0

The investor initially plans to place 50 percent of investable wealth in Security A and 50 percent in Security B. The four possible portfolio returns are created by weighting each security's return by its proportional investment in the portfolio.

A portfolio's expected return is a weighted average of the expected returns of each security included in the portfolio:

$$E(R_p) = \sum_{j=1}^{n} X_j E(R_j) \tag{2.17}$$

where X_j is the proportion of funds invested in asset j, and $E(R_j)$ is the expected return on asset j.

For example, the expected portfolio return, $E(R_p)$, for a period with strong growth in the economy is computed as

$$E(R_p) = (.5)(18\%) + (.5)(12\%) \tag{2.18}$$
$$= 9\% + 6\%$$
$$= 15.0\%$$

The remaining three returns are computed using the same technique. The $E(R_p)$ is based upon the returns of the component investments as well as the percentage of the portfolio invested in each asset.

Table 2.5 illustrates the calculation of the expected returns, standard deviations, and coefficients of variation for Security A, Security B, and the equally

TABLE 2.5   EXPECTED RETURN, STANDARD DEVIATION, AND COEFFICIENT OF VARIATION

STATE OF ECONOMY	E(HPR) SECURITY A	SECURITY B	EQUAL WEIGHTED PORTFOLIO $E(R_p)$	$(HPR_A - \overline{HPR_A})^2$	$(HPR_B - \overline{HPR_B})^2$	$(HPR_P - \overline{HPR_P})^2$
Strong growth	18%	12%	15.0%	132.25	4.00	45.56
Moderate growth	12	6	9.0	30.25	16.00	0.56
Weak growth	4	8	6.0	6.25	4.00	5.06
Recession	−8	14	3.0	210.25	16.00	27.56
Total	26.0%	40.0%	33.0%	379.00	40.00	78.74

$$E(\overline{HPR}) = \left[\sum_{j=1}^{n} HPR_j \right] \Big/ n$$

$E(\overline{HPR})$	6.50%	10.00%	8.25%

$$\sigma_j^2 \text{ (assuming equal probabilities)} = \left[\sum_{j=1}^{n} (HPR_j - \overline{HPR_j})^2 \right] \Big/ n$$

$$\sigma_j^2 = 94.75 \qquad 10.00 \qquad 19.68$$
$$\sigma_j = \sqrt{\sigma_j^2}$$
$$\sigma_j = 9.73\% \qquad 3.16\% \qquad 4.44\%$$

$$CV_j = \frac{\sigma_j}{HPR_j}$$

$$CV_j = 1.50 \qquad 0.32 \qquad 0.54$$

weighted portfolio. The combination of securities in a portfolio can reduce or diversify some of the risk of either security. Consequently, the variance (standard deviation) of the portfolio is not a simple weighted average of the variances (standard deviations) of the individual securities. For example, the weighted average of the standard deviations of securities A and B in Table 2.5 is 6.44 percent $[(.5)(9.73\%) + (.5)(3.16\%)]$, but the calculated portfolio standard deviation is 4.44 percent. Before this concept can be developed further, the correlation coefficient and covariance relationships need to be introduced.

Portfolio Risk

The *correlation* coefficient is a relative number which measures the degree to which two variables move together. As you may recall from statistics, the correlation coefficient lies between $+1.0$ and -1.0. Perfectly positive correlation, $+1.0$, indicates that two variables move together perfectly; that is, as one variable moves above (below) its mean, the second variable moves above (below) its mean in the same proportion. If two variables are perfectly negatively correlated, then as one variable moves above (below) its mean, the second variable moves below (above) its mean in the same proportion. A correlation of zero indicates no relationship between the movements of the two sets of variables. The correlation coefficient, using historical data, can be calculated as follows:

$$\rho_{ij} = \frac{1/n \sum_{t=1}^{n} (HPR_{it} - \overline{HPR_i})(HPR_{jt} - \overline{HPR_j})}{\sigma_i \sigma_j} \tag{2.19}$$

where ρ_{ij} = correlation coefficient between assets i and j

n = number of observations or time periods

HPR_{it} = return for asset i in period t

HPR_{jt} = return for asset j in period t

σ_i = standard deviation of asset i

σ_j = standard deviation of asset j

$\overline{HPR_i}$ = mean return for asset i

$\overline{HPR_j}$ = mean return for asset j

This formulation assumes that each observation or time period has an equal probability.

Statistically, the correlation coefficient is related to the *covariance*. Covariance is an absolute number that reflects the correlation between two sets of numbers as well as the individual standard deviations of the variables. The covariance is defined by

$$Cov_{ij} = \rho_{ij}\sigma_i\sigma_j \tag{2.20}$$

where ρ represents the correlation coefficient, σ represents the standard deviation, and i and j indicate the two securities.

Often the covariance between two sets of numbers is calculated first, and the correlation coefficient is then computed using Equation 2.20. Covariance is calculated by

$$Cov_{ij} = 1/n \sum_{t=1}^{n} (HPR_{it} - \overline{HPR}_i)(HPR_{jt} - \overline{HPR}_j) \qquad (2.21)$$

where i and j represent the two securities, $\overline{HPR}_i$ and $\overline{HPR}_j$ represent the mean returns, HPR_{it} and HPR_{jt} represent the returns for each period, and n represents the number of observations or periods of time. It should be noted that Equation 2.21 is the numerator of Equation 2.19.

Table 2.6 illustrates the calculations necessary to compute the covariance and correlation between the two individual securities, A and B, from the data in Table 2.5. The covariance is -13.00, and the correlation coefficient between the two securities is -0.423.

The correlation between Securities A and B is quite low. Consequently, the combination of these two securities into an equal-weighted portfolio causes the risk of the portfolio to be reduced. While the portfolio return is a simple weighted average of the expected individual security returns, the portfolio's variance and standard deviation for a two-securities portfolio is

$$\sigma_p^2 = X_A^2 \sigma_A^2 + X_B^2 \sigma_B^2 + 2 X_A X_B Cov_{A,B} \qquad (2.22)$$
$$\sigma_p = \sqrt{\sigma_p^2}$$

where X_A is the weight (proportional investment) of security 1, and X_B is the weight (proportional investment) of security 2. From the calculations in Table 2.6

TABLE 2.6 CALCULATION OF COVARIANCE AND CORRELATION

STATE OF ECONOMY	E(HPR) SECURITY A	E(HPR) SECURITY B	$(HPR_{At} - \overline{HPR}_A)$	$(HPR_{Bt} - \overline{HPR}_B)$	$(HPR_{At} - \overline{HPR}_A)(HPR_{Bt} - \overline{HPR}_B)$
Strong Growth	18%	12%	11.50%	2.00%	23.00
Moderate Growth	12	6	5.50	-4.00	-22.00
Weak Growth	4	8	-2.50	-2.00	5.00
Recession	-8	14	-14.50	4.00	-58.00
					-52.00
$E(\overline{HPR}_j)$	6.50%	10.00%			
σ_j	9.73%	3.16%			

$$\text{Covariance} = 1/n \sum_{t=1}^{n} (HPR_{At} - \overline{HPR}_A)(HPR_{Bt} - \overline{HPR}_B)$$

$$\text{Covariance} = 1/4(-52.00) = -13.00$$

$$\text{Correlation coefficient} = \frac{Cov_{AB}}{\sigma_A \sigma_B}$$

$$= \frac{-13.00}{(9.73)(3.16)}$$

$$= -.423$$

and using Equation 2.22, the portfolio standard deviation can be calculated as

$$\sigma_p^2 = (.5)^2(9.73\%)^2 + (.5)^2(3.16\%)^2 + 2(.5)(.5)(-13.00) \tag{2.23}$$
$$= 23.67 + 2.50 - 6.50$$
$$= 19.67$$
$$\sigma_p = \sqrt{\sigma_p^2} = 4.44\%$$

The calculation of σ_p illustrates that combining two assets that have very low positive or even negative correlation coefficients will significantly reduce the risk of the portfolio. Risk reduction occurs as long as the correlation is less than perfectly positive ($+1$).

While this concept of portfolio expected return and risk is discussed in greater detail in Chapter 6, it should be noted that the portfolio standard deviation calculation becomes more complicated as the number of assets in the portfolio increases. This complication arises because the covariance between each pair of securities must be included in the calculation of the portfolio standard deviation. For example, if just three securities—A, B, and C—are included in the portfolio, then the portfolio expected return is calculated by the weighted average of the three individual expected returns:

$$E(\overline{HPR}_p) = X_A E(\overline{HPR}_A) + X_B E(\overline{HPR}_B) + X_C E(\overline{HPR}_C) \tag{2.24}$$

The portfolio standard deviation, however, is calculated by

$$\sigma_p^2 = X_A^2 \sigma_A^2 + X_B^2 \sigma_B^2 + X_C^2 \sigma_C^2 + 2X_A X_B Cov_{A,B} \tag{2.25}$$
$$+ 2X_B X_C Cov_{B,C} + 2X_A X_C Cov_{A,C}$$
$$\sigma_p = \sqrt{\sigma_p^2}$$

CAPITAL MARKET THEORY—AN INTRODUCTION

Systematic and Unsystematic Risk

Risk has been defined as the standard deviation of the possible returns from an investment. This risk measure, as noted previously, is influenced by a number of sources, including business, financial, default, and liquidity risks. An alternative approach to defining investment risk has been developed.[5] This definition extends from the portfolio concept. While this theory is detailed in Chapters 6 and 7, a brief overview follows.

It has been shown that in most cases, by combining assets into a portfolio, the risk of the portfolio will be different from the weighted-average risk of the individual assets in the portfolio. While a portfolio made up of risky assets will normally contain some risk, a portion of the individual assets' risk can be diversified away if the returns of the assets in the portfolio are not perfectly positively correlated.

---

[5] See, for example, William F. Sharpe, "Capital Asset Prices: A Theory of Market Equilibrium under Conditions of Risk," *Journal of Finance* (September 1964): pp. 425–42.

The ability of an investor to diversify away a portion of the risk allows for a distinction to be drawn between *diversifiable* and *nondiversifiable* risk. Diversifiable risk, also known as *unsystematic* risk, is that risk which has as its source company or industry factors. For example, the unexpected movement of a discount grocery chain, such as Food Lion, into a market dominated by a traditional grocery chain, such as Winn-Dixie, may have a significant effect on the earnings and price of Winn-Dixie's common stock. This impact on the common stock of Winn-Dixie is not caused by a factor common to all marketable securities but rather to a factor that is company- or industry-specific. This source of risk can be diversified away by combining the asset with a portfolio of other assets. Thus, investors should not expect any additional return for facing this portion of total risk.

Nondiversifiable risk, also referred to as *systematic* risk, has as its source factors that affect all marketable assets and thus cannot be diversified away. For example, a change in expectations about the rate of inflation is pervasive; it will have an influence on all marketable assets and cannot be avoided by diversification. This risk cannot be diversified away, and investors should expect to receive additional returns associated with systematic risk.

How can systematic risk be measured, and what is the relationship between this measure of risk and expected return? Since the sources of systematic risk are market-pervasive, it is logical to measure systematic risk as the covariance between the return of an individual asset or portfolio and the returns of the "market" portfolio. The market portfolio would include a composite of all risky assets, which is very difficult to measure. Thus, a proxy for the market portfolio, such as the Dow Jones Industrial Average or the Standard & Poor's Composite 500 Stocks Average, is used as a substitute for the market portfolio. This measure of systematic risk is represented by *beta*, β_j and can be calculated by

$$\beta_j = \frac{Cov_{jM}}{\sigma_M^2} \tag{2.26}$$

where j indicates the individual asset or portfolio, and M indicates the market portfolio. A β_j value less than 1.0 indicates that the asset is less risky than the market.

The measure of systematic risk permits an investor to evaluate an asset's expected return relative to the systematic risk of the asset. In general, the *Capital Asset Pricing Model*, CAPM, indicates that an asset's expected return should be related to the risk-free rate of return plus a risk premium based on the beta of the asset. The expected return for an asset is given by

$$E(R_j) = R_f + \beta_j[E(R_M) - R_f] \tag{2.27}$$

where $E(R_j)$ represents the expected return of asset j, R_f represents the nominal risk-free rate of return (the real risk-free rate of return plus a risk premium for inflation), β_j represents asset j's beta, and $E(R_M)$ represents the expected return on the market portfolio.[6]

---

[6] For a more detailed explanation, see Oldrich A. Vasicek and John A. McQuown, "The Efficient Market Model," *Financial Analysts Journal* 28, no. 5 (September/October 1972): pp. 71–84. This concept is fully developed in Chapter 6.

Portfolio Systematic Risk

The concept of systematic risk simplifies the calculation of portfolio risk. Unlike portfolio variance, which considers all of the combinations of the assets' covariances as well as the variances of each of the assets, the systematic risk of the portfolio uses the covariance of the portfolio returns with the market portfolio. A portfolio's systematic risk is a simple weighted average of the systematic risks of all assets included in the portfolio, where the weights are the proportion of the asset's values to the total value of the portfolio. Table 2.7 illustrates the computation of a portfolio's expected return, systematic risk, and total risk.

The expected return and systematic risk of the portfolio are both simple weighted averages of the individual securities' expected returns and systematic risks. The portfolio expected return is 6.90 percent, and the portfolio beta or systematic risk is 1.13, which yields an expected return of 6.1 percent per unit of systematic risk (6.9%/1.13).

The portfolio total risk is a function of the standard deviation of each security plus the covariance terms for each of the three pairs of assets. The portfolio total risk or standard deviation is 4.56 percent, and the return per unit of total risk is 1.5 (6.90%/4.56%). If the portfolio is sufficiently diversified, then only the portfolio's systematic risk need be considered. If the portfolio is not highly diversified, then the investor must consider the total risk, or variance, of the portfolio. Several

TABLE 2.7 PORTFOLIO EXPECTED RETURN, SYSTEMATIC RISK, AND TOTAL RISK FOR THREE SECURITIES

	PORTFOLIO WEIGHT	EXPECTED $\overline{HPR}$	STANDARD DEVIATION	BETA
Security A	33.33%	4.60%	5.62%	0.8
Security B	33.33%	8.50%	6.33%	1.4
Security C	33.33%	7.60%	5.83%	1.2

Correlation between A and B = $\rho_{AB} = 0.132$

Correlation between A and C = $\rho_{AC} = 0.246$

Correlation between B and C = $\rho_{BC} = 0.756$

Portfolio Expected Return = $E(\overline{HPR}_p) = X_A E(\overline{HPR}_A) + X_B E(\overline{HPR}_B) + X_C E(\overline{HPR}_C)$

$\quad E(\overline{HPR}_p) = (.3333)(4.60\%) + (.3333)(8.50\%) + (.3333)(7.60\%) = 6.90\%$

Portfolio Systematic Risk = $\beta_p = \sum_{j=1}^{n} X_j \beta_j$

$\quad \beta_p = (.3333)(.8) + (.3333)(1.4) + (.3333)(1.2) = 1.13$

Portfolio Total Risk = $\sigma_p^2 = X_A^2 \sigma_A^2 + X_B^2 \sigma_B^2 + X_C^2 \sigma_C^2 + 2X_A X_B Cov_{AB}$
$\quad\quad\quad + 2X_A X_C Cov_{AC} + 2X_B X_C Cov_{BC}$

$\quad \sigma_p^2 = (.3333)^2(5.62\%)^2 + (.333)^2(6.33\%)^2 + (.3333)^2(5.83\%)^2$

$\quad\quad + 2(.3333)(.3333)(.132)(5.62\%)(6.33\%)$

$\quad\quad + 2(.3333)(.3333)(.246)(5.62\%)(5.83\%)$

$\quad\quad + 2(.3333)(.3333)(.756)(6.33\%)(5.83\%)$

$\quad\quad = 20.7696$

$\quad \sigma_p = \sqrt{20.7696} = 4.56\%$

studies indicate that on average, a portfolio which contains 10 to 15 common stocks eliminates most of the diversifiable risk.[7]

APPLICATION: THE YOUNG INVESTORS

Mike and Sue O'Brian have been married for three years. They have been saving toward the purchase of their first home. Currently, they have $12,500 invested in a certificate of deposit, CD, which will mature in a few days. If they reinvest the $12,500 in a new one-year CD, the bank will guarantee a 7 percent rate of return.

The mortgage company estimates that they can afford payments on a $70,000 house, assuming that they make a 20 percent down payment and finance the house for twenty-five years. In addition to the $14,000 down payment, closing costs for the loan are estimated at approximately $3,500, for a total cash requirement of $17,500.

Based on their budget for next year, Sue thinks they can save $3,500. If the current savings of $12,500 are reinvested in a one-year CD, they will earn $875 and will bring their total savings to $16,875. They would still lack $625 and would have to postpone the purchase of the home for several months.

Mike discussed the situation with his parents. His father suggested that perhaps they could earn the necessary money by investing their current savings in higher-yielding securities. Although Mike's parents are not wealthy, they agreed to give Mike and Sue the money to cover the taxes and transaction costs from their investment. Thus, Mike and Sue could concentrate on the investment's gross return.

Mike called his friend John, a stockbroker. John suggested two possible investments. One was a mutual fund that had yielded a rate of return of 12 percent (dividends and capital appreciation) during the most recent period of strong economic growth. The alternative investment was a common stock that John thought would be a great performer over the next year. The stock could earn as much as 15 percent if the strong economy continued. John cautioned Mike that either investment might not provide the indicated return if economic growth weakened, since both alternatives involved risk. John sent Mike and Sue some basic information on the two investment alternatives.

Sue recalled from her college investments course that they needed to compare the expected returns and risk of the three alternative investments. Upon receiving the information from John, she identified the possible returns for each of the investments. She had difficulty estimating the probabilities for each of the possible economic states, so she gave each of the economic scenarios an equal weight. With the aid of her old investments book, Sue calculated the beta coefficients, expected returns, standard deviations, coefficients of variation, and expected return per unit of systematic risk for each of the three investments. She also estimated the dollar return for each alternative under each economic scenario. Table 2.8 provides the results of Sue's calculations.

---

[7] See James H. Lorie and Lawrence Fisher, "Some Studies of Variability of Returns on Investment in Common Stocks," *Journal of Business* (April 1970). This point is also discussed in more detail in Chapter 6.

TABLE 2.8   CHOICES FOR THE YOUNG INVESTORS

Current Savings	$12,500			
Additional Savings	3,500			
	$16,000			
Down Payment on House	$14,000			
Closing Costs	3,500			
	$17,500			
Additional Funds Needed	$1,500			

STATE OF ECONOMY	PROBABILITY	MUTUAL FUND	COMMON STOCK	CERTIFICATE OF DEPOSIT
Weak Growth	33%	8.00%	6.00%	7.00%
Moderate Growth	33%	10.00%	12.00%	7.00%
Strong Growth	33%	12.00%	15.00%	7.00%
Beta		1.0	1.2	0.00
Expected Return		10.00%	11.00%	7.00%
Standard Deviation		1.63%	3.74%	0.00%
Coefficient of Variation		0.16	0.34	0.00
Expected Return/ Systematic Risk (Beta)		10.00%	9.17%	

Portfolio Dollar Returns for One Year, Based on an Initial Investment of $12,500

STATE OF ECONOMY	PROBABILITY	MUTUAL FUND	COMMON STOCK	CERTIFICATE OF DEPOSIT
Weak Growth	33%	$1,000	$ 750	$875
Moderate Growth	33%	1,250	1,500	875
Strong Growth	33%	1,500	1,875	875

Mike was impressed by Sue's knowledge of investments but still did not know which alternative to select. Sue explained that although the common stock had an expected return of 11 percent, which was greater than the expected return of the mutual fund, the stock was more risky. The standard deviation of the stock was 3.74 percent, compared to the 1.63 percent standard deviation of the mutual fund. On a relative basis, the mutual fund provided a much better risk-return trade-off since the coefficient of variation for the mutual fund was only 0.16, compared to the common stock's 0.34 coefficient of variation. The mutual fund also provided a higher return per unit of systematic risk (10.0 percent) than the common stock (9.17 percent). Sue concluded that the common stock would be a good investment for a diversified portfolio, but as a single investment, it was too risky for her. She preferred the mutual fund, based on the return per unit of risk, both total risk (coefficient of variation) and systematic risk.

Mike kept looking at the projected cash value of the returns. He could not help but notice that the mutual fund investment would provide them the $1,500 only if the economy was strong. The common stock would provide them the necessary money even if the economy slowed to moderate growth. The return on the common stock was below the return on the CD, however, if the economy weakened, as some economists were predicting. Mike decided that he preferred the common stock. He thought the CD should be eliminated from consideration because it would not provide the needed return and because the mutual fund provided a higher expected return than the CD, regardless of the economic state.

Sue recalled her finance professor's discussing portfolio diversification. She suggested that perhaps they could compromise and invest in both the mutual fund and common stock. She calculated the possible portfolio returns, based upon several dollar allocation schemes between the alternatives. Table 2.9 provides the possible portfolio returns, the expected portfolio returns, the risk measures, and the portfolio cash value returns.

A comparison of the risk and return measures in Tables 2.8 and 2.9 reveals some interesting relationships. First, the standard deviations of the three portfolios in Table 2.9 are essentially a weighted average of the standard deviation of the individual assets. This occurs because the correlation coefficient between the mutual fund and common stock is 0.97. This almost perfectly positive correlation eliminates most of the potential benefits of diversification. Second, the expected returns on the portfolios are a simple weighted average of the mutual fund and common stock expected returns. Finally, the coefficient of variation for the mutual fund is lower than those for the three portfolios in Table 2.9. The mutual fund, therefore, appears to offer the lowest risk per unit of expected return.

Mike still preferred to investigate the portfolio cash returns. As he examined each of the portfolios, Mike discovered that the worst-case returns for the portfolios were always less than the mutual fund worst case of $1,000. Even his initial guess of a fifty-fifty compromise portfolio seemed risky if the economy slowed

TABLE 2.9 PORTFOLIO RETURN AND RISK

STATE OF ECONOMY	PROBABILITY	PORTFOLIOS OF MUTUAL FUND (MF) AND COMMON STOCK (S)		
		$X_{MF} = .75$ $X_S = .25$	$X_{MF} = .5$ $X_S = .5$	$X_{MF} = .25$ $X_S = .75$
Weak Growth	33%	7.50%	7.00%	6.50%
Moderate Growth	33%	10.50%	11.00%	11.50%
Strong Growth	33%	12.75%	13.50%	14.25%
Beta of Portfolio = $\beta_p = \sum_{j=1}^{n} X_j \beta_j$		1.05	1.10	1.15
Expected Return		10.25%	10.50%	10.75%
Standard Deviation		2.14%	2.68%	3.21%
Coefficient of Variation		0.21	0.26	0.30
Expected Return/Systematic Risk		9.76%	9.55%	9.35%

Covariances:

$$Cov_{MF,S} = 5.91, \quad Cov_{MF,CD} = 0, \quad Cov_{S,CD} = 0$$

Correlation Coefficients:

$$\rho_{MF,S} = .97, \quad \rho_{MF,CD} = 0, \quad \rho_{S,CD} = 0$$

Portfolio Dollar Returns for One Year, Based on an Initial Investment of $12,500

STATE OF ECONOMY	PROBABILITY	$X_{MF} = .75$ $X_S = .25$	$X_{MF} = .5$ $X_S = .5$	$X_{MF} = .25$ $X_S = .75$
Weak Growth	33%	$ 938	$ 875	$ 813
Moderate Growth	33%	1,313	1,375	1,438
Strong Growth	33%	1,594	1,688	1,781

to weak growth, since the cash return would be only $875. After all of Sue's hard work, Mike agreed that perhaps the best investment was the mutual fund. Clearly, the mutual fund exhibited the best risk-return trade-off—a beta of 1.0 and a coefficient variation of 0.16. Mike promised to call the stockbroker the next morning. Mike and Sue were aware that if the economy worsened, the mutual fund was expected to generate only $1,000 of the $1,500 they needed to buy the home next year. Both promised to monitor the mutual fund's performance during the next year, so that they could plan the purchase of their new home.

SUMMARY

The investment process serves to help individuals match the timing of their income with the timing of their consumption and investment decisions. Net savers, investors, expect net borrowers not to only repay the money borrowed but also to pay a rate of return that compensates investors for the time value of money, inflation, and risk. The risk premium must compensate investors for business, financial, liquidity, default, and other sources of risk. These risks are often measured by the standard deviation of the expected return, which indicates the total risk of the security. If investors are willing to diversify some of the risk by investing in a portfolio of securities, the appropriate measure of risk is the systematic risk of the portfolio. When selecting among alternative investments, investors will want to consider the risk-return trade-off for each investment.

The young investors' case illustrates a number of basic investment principles. Mike and Sue O'Brian are attempting to determine an appropriate risk-return trade-off. Mike appears to be willing to assume higher levels of risk, while Sue is more risk averse. The estimates of risk and rates of return provide useful information for the O'Brian's analysis. Since they have a one-year investment horizon and require a minimum investment return of $1,500, the dollar returns from each alternative for each possible state of the economy are also useful.

The O'Brians recognize the potential benefits of diversification and the insights that a portfolio perspective can provide. The potential benefits from diversification in this case are relatively minor, however, because of the almost perfect correlation between the common stock and mutual fund alternatives. Based on their available information, the mutual fund appears to be their best investment. Because of an uncertain economic environment, however, the O'Brians recognize the need to monitor the fund's performance closely during the next year.

QUESTIONS

1. Explain how financial markets can be used to facilitate decisions concerning consumption versus savings.
2. Compare and contrast the arithmetic and geometric means. Which "average" is more appropriate for analyzing rates of return over a number of holding periods?
3. In subjective terms, how do individuals usually define the concept of "risk"? Do empirical measures of risk match the subjective definition of risk?

4. Explain why the length of the investment horizon is related to the risk of the investment.

5. Compare and contrast the required rate of return with the expected rate of return. How are these two return measures used in making investment decisions?

6. Briefly discuss the three components of the required rate of return.

7. Explain how ex-post holding period returns can be used to forecast expected or ex-ante holding period returns. Do you think that this approach is a viable alternative to an investment analysis directed at providing an estimate of the expected return of an investment alternative?

8. Explain why probabilities for each investment outcome are useful in estimating the expected rate of return for an investment. What techniques can be used to estimate probabilities?

9. Compare and contrast business, financial, default, and liquidity risks. Compare these sources of risk for common stocks and corporate bonds.

10. Does the standard deviation of ex-post holding period returns reflect default risk for a common stock? Explain how default risk might be incorporated into an estimate of the expected return for a common stock.

11. Explain how the correlation coefficient influences the degree of diversification that can be achieved by combining two assets in a portfolio.

12. How are the covariance and correlation coefficient related?

13. Distinguish between total, systematic, and unsystematic risks. When is it appropriate to use the systematic risk of an individual security as a risk measure?

14. Explain how the capital asset pricing model can be used to specify a risk premium for an individual security.

15. The example of the young investors illustrated how the concepts of risk and return can be applied to individual investment alternatives and to portfolios constructed from the alternatives. Explain why the analysis indicated that an investment in a single asset (mutual fund) appeared to be more attractive than the portfolio alternatives.

PROBLEMS

1. An investor purchased 100 shares of common stock at $20 per share one year ago. The company declared and paid a dividend of $2 per share during the year. The investor sold the stock for $21 per share after the one-year holding period.

   a. Calculate the dollar return from this investment.

   b. Calculate the *HPR* for this investment.

   c. Partition the *HPR* into the dividend and capital appreciation components.

2. Consider the following ex-post *HPR*s:

	INVESTMENT	
YEAR	A	B
1	10%	14%
2	15	−10
3	8	30

a. Calculate the arithmetic mean *HPR* for each investment.

b. Calculate the geometric mean *HPR* for each investment.

c. Explain why the arithmetic and geometric means are different.

d. Assume that investments A and B have equal risk. Which investment provides the "best" return performance? (Hint: Assume that a $10,000 investment was made in each alternative and then calculate the dollar value of the investment at the end of year 3, using the geometric means.)

3. Consider the following subjective probability distribution for a potential investment:

STATE OF THE ECONOMY	PROBABILITY	ESTIMATED RATE OF RETURN
Strong growth	.1	25%
Moderate growth	.4	15
Weak growth	.4	10
Recession	.1	− 12

a. Calculate the expected rate of return.

b. Calculate the variance.

c. Calculate the standard deviation.

d. Calculate the coefficient of variation.

4. Consider the following ex-post quarterly *HPRs* provided by a common stock:

QUARTER	QUARTERLY HPR
1	− 4.3%
2	− 1.0
3	1.5
4	3.0
5	6.0
6	2.0
7	0.0
8	− 2.5

a. Assuming that each of the ex-post quarterly returns has an equal probability of occurrence, calculate the *expected HPR* for quarter 9.

b. Using the assumption in part a, calculate the variance and standard deviation.

c. Assume that the *HPRs* for quarters 1, 2, and 8 occurred during a recessionary environment and that the *HPR* for quarters 4 and 5 occurred during a period of rapid economic growth. The remaining *HPRs* occurred during quarters of moderate economic growth. Calculate the probability that quarter 9 will be (1) a period of rapid economic growth, (2) a recessionary period, (3) a period of moderate economic growth.

d. Use the probabilities calculated in part c to calculate the expected return, variance, and standard deviation.

e. What are the weaknesses of the forecasting techniques used in parts a and c above?

5. Consider the following return and risk measures for two investment alternatives:

	INVESTMENT ALTERNATIVE	
	A	B
Expected rate of return	15%	10%
Variance	9	4
Standard deviation	3%	2%

a. Assume that the correlation coefficient between the two investments is 0.6. Calculate the expected return and standard deviation of a portfolio consisting of equal dollar investments in each alternative.

b. Assume the correlation coefficient between the two investments is -0.4. Calculate the expected return and standard deviation of a portfolio consisting of equal investments in each alternative.

c. Explain any differences in the expected returns and standard deviations calculated in parts a and b.

6. Suppose an investor is analyzing the following two alternatives in terms of possibly combining them to form a portfolio.

	HOLDING PERIOD RETURNS FOR INVESTMENT ALTERNATIVES	
STATE OF NATURE	A	B
1	-10%	12%
2	5	5
3	15	0
4	20	-8

Assume that each state of nature (economy) has an equal probability of occurrence.

a. Calculate the expected return and variance for each investment alternative.

b. Calculate the covariance between A and B.

c. Calculate the correlation coefficient between A and B.

d. Do your answers to b and c indicate that there may be advantages to combining these two investment alternatives in a portfolio? Why?

e. Using your answer to the above questions, calculate the expected return and variance of a portfolio consisting of 60% of the funds invested in Alternative A and 40% in Alternative B.

7. Assume the beta of two common stocks are: $\beta_1 = 0.9$, $\beta_2 = 1.3$. If the risk-free rate of return is 10% and the expected return on the market portfolio is 12%, calculate the expected returns for the common stocks using the capital asset pricing model. Do the expected returns so calculated include a return to compensate for unsystematic risk? Explain.

COMPUTER APPLICATIONS

The floppy disk includes programs that can be used to calculate the following:

1. HPR;
2. Arithmetic and geometric means;
3. Expected rate of return;
4. Variance, standard deviation, and coefficient of variation;
5. Covariance; and
6. Correlation coefficient.

These programs can be used to solve some of the problems in this chapter. Instructions and illustrations are provided on the disk.

REFERENCES

Arditti, Fred D. "Risk and the Required Return on Equity." *Journal of Finance* 22, no. 1 (March 1967): pp. 19–36.

Babcock, Guilford C. "A Note on Justifying Beta as a Measure of Risk." *Journal of Finance* 27, no. 3 (June 1972): pp. 699–702.

Beaver, William, and James Manegold. "The Association Between Market Determined and Accounting Determined Measures of Systematic Risk: Some Further Evidence." *Journal of Financial and Quantitative Analysis* 10, no. 2 (June 1975): pp. 231–84.

Beja, Avraham. "On Systematic and Unsystematic Components of Financial Risk." *Journal of Finance* 17, no. 1 (March 1972): pp. 37–45.

Elton, Edwin J., Martin J. Gruber, and Thomas J. Urich. "Are Betas Best?" *Journal of Finance* 33, no. 5 (December 1978): pp. 1375–84.

Fouse, William L. "Risk and Liquidity Revisited." *Financial Analysts Journal* (January-February 1977): pp. 40–45.

Hamada, Robert. "The Effect of the Firm's Capital Structure on the Systematic Risk of Common Stocks." *Journal of Finance* 27, no. 3 (May 1972): pp. 435–52.

Hogan, William, and James Warren. "Toward the Development of an Equilibrium Capital Market Model Based on Semivariance." *Journal of Financial and Quantitative Analysis* 9, no. 1 (January 1974): pp. 1–11.

Lee, Cheng F. "On the Relationship between the Systematic Risk and the Investment Horizon," *Journal of Financial and Quantitative Analysis* 11, no. 5 (December 1976): pp. 803–15.

Lev, Baruch. "On the Association between Operating Leverage and Risk." *Journal of Financial and Quantitative Analysis* 9, no. 3 (June 1974): pp. 627–41.

Robichek, Alexander, and Richard A. Cohn. "The Economic Determinants of Systematic Risk." *Journal of Finance* 29, no. 2 (May 1974): pp. 439–47.

Rosenberg, Barr, and James Guy. "Prediction of Beta from Investment Fundamentals." *Financial Analyst Journal* (May-June 1976): pp. 60–72.

Rubinstein, Mark E. "A Mean-Variance Synthesis of Financial Theory." *Journal of Finance* 28, no. 1 (March 1973): pp. 167–81.

CHAPTER 3

SECURITIES MARKETS: OPERATIONS AND REGULATIONS

INTRODUCTION

The growth of the U.S. economy has been due in large part to the strength and efficiency of the securities markets. This chapter will discuss the functions, structure, operation, and regulations of the major securities markets. Security markets can be classfied in several ways. Markets may be classified by the maturity of securities traded in the market. The *money market* is made up of securities that mature in one year or less. In Table 1.1 of Chapter 1, it was shown that short-term debt securities are traded in the money market. Securities that mature in more than a year are traded in the *capital market.* While both money and capital markets provide liquidity for the investor, money market securities have little or no risk of default and do not contain significant price risk because of their short maturities. For these reasons, money market securities represent attractive opportunities for corporations to invest their temporary excess cash balances. Because of the large, minimum denominations of most money market securities, individual investors generally invest in money market mutual funds rather than directly in money market securities.

Another way of classifying security markets is to determine whether new securities are being sold (the *primary markets*) or already-issued securities are being bought and sold (the *secondary markets*). The above markets could be further segmented into stock, corporate bond, government bond, municipal bond, futures, commodities, options, and other types of markets.

PRIMARY MARKETS

As mentioned above, *primary market* is used to denote the market for the original sale of securities by an issuer to the public. The use of the words *original sale* may be somewhat misleading. For example, the issuer may initially have sold common stock to the public several years ago and has now decided to issue additional shares of common stock. The sale of these additional shares would take place in the primary market, and once the sale is completed, the new shares will be indistinguishable from the shares sold in the initial public offering. The issuer receives cash which may then be invested in productive assets, or the net proceeds from the sale may be used for other purposes. For example, the proceeds from the sale of common stock may be used to retire outstanding debt. The public receives the newly issued securities for the cash invested.

Role of the Investment Banker

Investment bankers are responsible each year for the placement of billions of dollars worth of new securities. The term *investment banker* is something of a misnomer since investment bankers are not bankers in the traditional sense of taking deposits and making loans. Although commercial banks may have investment banking divisions, the vast majority of investment banking "deals" are usually executed by brokerage firms such as Merrill Lynch; Shearson Lehman Brothers, Inc.; Goldman, Sachs & Co.; Drexel Burnham Lambert, Inc.; The First Boston Corp.; Paine Webber Inc.; and others. Brokerage firms are ideally suited to the investment banking function since they already have a large base of security holders as clients as well as a nationwide infrastructure to sell securities at any time. This allows the investment banker to offer its services at a relatively low cost to a firm desiring to raise money through a new security offering. Investment bankers offer three basic services: (1) advice and counsel, (2) underwriting, and (3) distribution.

1. ADVICE AND COUNSEL In addition to corporations, governmental units and not-for-profit organizations go to the market place to raise money. Since they issue securities so infrequently, they do not have the "in-house" expertise to undertake the considerable paperwork associated with a new issue. In addition, the issuer of securities needs investment bankers to evaluate market conditions in order to determine whether an offering can be made; at what price the security can be sold; whether the security should be debt or equity; and any special characteristics that must be considered, such as convertibility, callability, coupon rate, and maturity.

2. UNDERWRITING Once the investment banker has determined the type of security, price, issue date, and any special features, the issue is ready to market. If the investment banker *underwrites* the issue, he agrees to purchase the securities in the hope of reselling them at a higher price to the public. The investment banker has assumed the *price risk*. This difference is known as the *spread*, and the size of the spread varies with the type of issue (e.g., bonds have a smaller spread than common stocks) and the perceived difficulty of marketing the issue. The size of the spread also varies with the dollar value of the new issue. Because of the large fixed costs associated with bringing a new issue to market, larger issues have smaller spreads than smaller issues.

   If the investment banker acts only as an agent, he assumes no obligation to purchase any of the securities. This is known as a *best-efforts* sale. Under the best-efforts offering, the investment banker does not underwrite the issue but merely uses his best efforts to sell the issue to the public. All unsold securities are returned to the issuer. Best-efforts offerings are usually made for small, unknown firms, where the risk of underwriting is too great, or for well-known firms who have confidence that the public will purchase their securities.

3. DISTRIBUTION The investment banking firm that obtains a commitment from the issuer to sell the new security is called the *originator*. The originator, as managing underwriter, will form an *underwriting group*, to spread the price risk if market conditions suddenly change and to reduce the amount of cash that must be raised by any one investment banking firm to purchase the issue. Finally, a *selling group* is created comprising both members of the underwriting group and other retail brokerage houses. Each of the brokerage houses will then be alloted a portion of the new issue to sell.

   The originating investment banker must file a *registration statement* with the Securities and Exchange Commission, SEC, that provides information on the firm, the type and amount of the security being offered, and the proposed use of the proceeds from the sale. While the registration statement is being evaluated by the SEC, the investment banking firm may issue a *preliminary prospectus*, also known as a *red herring* because of the red ink on its cover. The red herring states that the information in the prospectus is being reviewed by the SEC and that the propectus is not a solicitation to sell. The difference between between the preliminary prospectus and the prospectus is that the preliminary prospectus does not state the price or the date of the offering. The offering price is determined immediately prior to the sale; since market conditions can change dramatically, it is not feasible to establish a price until the day of the offering.

In late 1983, the SEC adopted *Rule 415* which allows larger firms contemplating a future issue of stocks or bonds to bypass investment bankers' involvement in the registration process. Under Rule 415, issuers can register securities with the SEC up to two years prior to the securities being issued. This "shelf registration" allows the issuer the opportunity to issue the securities at an advantageous time (both in terms of the market price of the securities being offered and the timing of the cash needs of the issuer) and reduces the cost of the underwriting since the issuer, not the investment banker, handles the registration process.

Once the registration statement has been approved, the final prospectus is printed—with the price, offering date, underwriting discount, and any new financial information—and delivered to potential investors. The SEC requires that all investors receive a copy of the prospectus before they purchase new securities. The SEC does not approve or disapprove the investment value of the issue. Its approval means merely that sufficient information has been provided for an intelligent investor to make a rational decision on the investment merits of the issue. Table 3.1 illustrates the front page of a final prospectus.

The pricing of new issues involves the security valuation procedures described in later chapters of this book. However, other elements are involved in pricing new issues as opposed to issues already traded in the market. The underwriter is concerned about price risk, and the issuer is interested in netting the maximum proceeds from the new issue. The issuer does not want to leave too much "on the table," while the underwriter does not want to face resistance from investors marketing the new issue. An additional pricing problem is related to the fact that the new issue is untested, in the sense that market participants have not independently set a price for the security through the market process. While the financial fundamentals of publicly traded securities of comparable companies will be used in setting the price, the fact remains that there is an uncertainty about the market's acceptance of the price.

The pricing problem extends to the investor in new issues, particularly common stock. If the price set by the underwriter is perceived by the market to be too low, the issue will be oversubscribed, and the availability to the small individual investor may be quite limited. Often in these instances the first price in the secondary market may be substantially above the offering price. If, on the other, the original price is believed to be too high by the market, the new issue will be made abundantly available to all investors by the members of the selling group. Unless the underwriter has indicated to the SEC its intent to stabilize the price by buying back the newly issued securities at or near the offering price, the investor in a new issue may find that the price set by the market is below that of the the initial offering price.

TABLE 3.1   AN EXAMPLE OF A FINAL PROSPECTUS

<u>PROSPECTUS</u>

2,000,000 Shares

Holiday RV Superstores, Incorporated

Common Stock
Offering Price $2.25 Per Share

Prior to this Offering (the "Offering"), there has been no public market for shares ("Shares") of the common stock, $.01 par value, (the "Common Stock") of Holiday RV Superstores, Incorporated (the "Company"), and there can be no assurance that an active market will develop. The initial public offering price for the Shares has been determined by negotiations between the Company and Thomas James Associates, Inc., (the "Underwriter"). For information with respect to the method of determining the initial public offering price, see "Underwriting — Pricing of the Offering."

THESE SECURITIES HAVE NOT BEEN APPROVED OR DISAPPROVED BY THE SECURITIES AND EXCHANGE COMMISSION OR THE SECURITIES AUTHORITIES OF ANY STATE, NOR HAS THE COMMISSION OR ANY SUCH AUTHORITY PASSED UPON THE ACCURACY OR ADEQUACY OF THIS PROSPECTUS. ANY REPRESENTATION TO THE CONTRARY IS A CRIMINAL OFFENSE.

	Price to Public	Underwriting Discounts and Commissions(1)	Proceeds to Company(2)
Per Share	$2.25	$.225	$2.025
Total(3)	$4,500,000	$450,000	$4,050,000

(1) Does not include additional compensation to be received by the Underwriter in the form of (i) a non-accountable expense allowance equal to 2.144% of the gross proceeds of the offering or $96,500 and 3% of the gross proceeds of the offering in excess of $4,500,000 or $116,750, if the Underwriter exercises the over allotment option in full; (ii) a warrant issued to the Underwriter for nominal consideration from the effective date, to purchase 200,000 Shares, which warrant is exercisable over a period of four years, commencing twelve months after the effective date of this Prospectus, at a price equal to 125% of the initial public offering price per share; (iii) various preferential rights in connection with certain future activities of the Company; and, (iv) the right of the Underwriter to appoint an adviser to the Company's Board of Directors. In addition, the Company and the Underwriter have agreed to indemnify each other against certain liabilities under the Security Act of 1933. See "Underwriting" and "Description of Securities."

(2) Before deducting expenses of this offering, estimated at $225,000, including the Underwriter's non-accountable expense allowance.

(3) The Company has granted to the Underwriter a thirty (30) day option to purchase an additional number of shares equal to up to fifteen percent (15%) of the shares being offered, or 300,000 shares, to cover over-allotments, on the same terms and conditions as the other shares offered in this Prospectus. If the over-allotment is exercised in full, the total Price to the Public, Underwriting Discounts and Commissions, and Proceeds to Company would be $5,175,000, $517,500, and $4,657,500, respectively. See "Underwriting."

The Shares are offered by the Underwriter on a "firm commitment" basis, when, as and if delivered to and accepted by the Underwriter, subject to prior sale, withdrawal, cancellation or modification of the offer without notice; and subject to approval of legal matters by counsel for the Company and the Underwriter. The Underwriter reserves its right to reject any orders for the purchase of Shares, in whole or in part. Delivery of the Shares to the Underwriter will be made at the offices of Thomas James Associates, Inc., Suite 200, 339 East Avenue, Rochester, New York 14604 on or about November 9, 1987.

Investment Bankers in the 1980s

The investment banking industry has experienced tremendous change during the 1980s and is now viewed as the most dominant force in the securities business.[1] For example, in 1986 the Securities Industry Association estimated that investment bankers represented 2 percent of the New York Stock Exchange member firms dealing with the public but accounted for 50 percent of the total pre-tax profit of the entire U.S. securites business. In addition, the ten largest investment banking firms earned one-third of the total revenue of all securities firms.

Investment banking firms still provide the traditional underwriting services. Their tremendous growth, however, is due to their involvement in mergers, acquisitions, corporate takeovers, and securities trading. In 1986 these activities produced revenues of approximately $13 billion, compared to $2.6 billion in 1980.[2]

The growth in employment in the investment banking industry has also been phenomenal. The total number of employees for the ten largest firms was less than five thousand in the late 1970s.[3] From 1980 to 1987, employment more than doubled in the ten largest firms. This rate of employment growth is much faster than those for other sectors of the securities industry. Employment growth has been profitable to investment banking firms. In 1985, revenues per employee were estimated to be $.5 million, with pre-tax profits per employee in excess of $65,000.

Because of the 1987 market crash, the entire securities industry was forced to reduce employment levels drastically. Wall Street firms are no longer actively recruiting new M.B.A.s' or finance professors. The cyclical nature of the securities industry and its excessive rate of growth in the 1980s are likely to result in limited job opportunities for a number of years.[4]

Historically, the investment banking business was built on close personal relationships between a limited number of key investment bankers and corporate executives. The industry had a reputation of hiring only a limited number of individuals with the "right" family and educational background. Beginning in the early 1980s, however, investment banking firms began to hire many new M.B.A.s', primarily from prestigious business schools such as Harvard, Wharton, Chicago, and Stanford. These graduates viewed Wall Street, and especially investment banking firms, as some of the most desirable employers. Glamour, top starting salaries, and prospects for rapid promotion provided ample incentives. As an illustration, one large mutual fund listed three top portfolio managers who were all twenty-six years old. Each was a 1986 Harvard M.B.A. graduate and therefore had approximately ten months of experience before becoming a portfolio manager.[5]

---

[1] Benjamin J. Stein, "Not Worthy of the Name? Investment Banking Isn't What It Used to Be," *Barron's*, 13 July 1987, pp. 6, 7, 26, 28, 30, 32.

[2] Ibid, p. 6.

[3] Ibid, p. 6.

[4] For a discussion of the implications of the market crash for business schools and job opportunities in finance, see William Broesamle, "An Interview with Professor James C. Van Horne," *Selections* (Spring 1988): pp. 7–12.

[5] Jonathan R. Laing, "Muckraking Money Managers," *Barron's*, 20 July, 1987, pp. 6–7, 28, 30–31.

One of the investment banking/brokerage firms that helped to revolutionlize the industry was Drexel Burnham Lambert, Inc. This firm pioneered the use of "junk" or low-quality bonds to finance leveraged buyouts and takeovers. The profitability of merger and takeover activities can be much greater than that of traditional underwriting activities because the firm can collect a fee for advising its client, earn commissions on the publicly or privately placed junk bonds, and earn brokerage commissions by providing a secondary market for the junk bonds. If the takeover is successful, corporate assets may be liquidated to help pay off some of the debt and provide profits for the acquiring group. The investment banking firm may be involved in providing financing for the purchaser of the assets and earn additional fees and commissions.[6]

Investment banking firms have been accused of charging excessive fees for their involvement in mergers and takeovers. An interesting case involves the takeover attempt by The Limited, Inc. of Carter Hawley Stores, Inc.[7] Morgan Stanley & Co. was retained by the management of Carter Hawley to help fight the takeover. Morgan Stanley's fee is estimated to have been in excess of $50 million plus expenses that exceeded an "eight-figure range." The fee (ignoring expenses) "exceeds the total net profit of Carter Hawley Stores, Inc. for all of 1985" and represents more than 3 percent of the firm's total capitalization.[8] Morgan Stanley estimated that it spent ten thousand hours working on the project, suggesting a fee in excess of $5,000 per hour. Not only were the fees criticized as excessive but they were also questioned in terms of the benefit to the stockholders. Stockholder wealth was used to fight a takeover that might have been in the best interest of stockholders.

In addition to criticisms about their fees, a number of well-known investment banking firms have been accused of participating in illegal insider-trading activities involving mergers and takeover attempts. The most highly publicized case involved Ivan F. Boesky and Drexel Burnham Lambert, Inc. Boesky was convicted of violating security laws in 1986 and 1987 by trading on insider information provided by Dennis Levine of Drexel Burnham Lambert, Inc. Boesky agreed to pay a record $100 million in civil penalties and was sentenced to three years in prison. He cooperated with the investigation, and his testimony resulted in an announcement in June 1988 that charges would be filed against Drexel, Burnham, Lambert, Inc.[9]

Mr. Boesky has also accused the Los Angeles brokerage firm Jefferies & Co. and former investment bankers associated with Goldman Sachs, Kidder Peabody, and Merrill Lynch of providing illegal insider information.[10] In June 1987, Kidder Peabody reached a settlement with the SEC by agreeing to pay a fine of $25.3 million and to disband its arbitrage department.

---

[6] For a discussion of these arrangements, see "Travail at Drexel Burnham," *Fortune*, 22 December 1986, pp. 31–37.

[7] Benjamin J. Stein, "A Saga of Shareholder Neglect: Whose Interest Was This Management Protecting?" *Barron's*, 4 May, 1987, pp. 8–9, 70–75.

[8] Ibid, p. 74.

[9] James B. Steward and Daniel Hartzberg, "SEC Approves Charges against Drexel, Michael Milken, but Delays Filing Them," *Wall Street Journal*, 9 June, 1988, pp. 2, 14.

[10] William M. Alpert, "Judgment Day: Ivan Boesky Draws Three-Year Jail Term," *Barron's*, 21 Dec., 1987, pp. 24–25.

The investment banking industry has been very creative and successful in developing new services and entering new businesses. The controversy concerning the economic benefit of takeovers and leveraged buyouts, combined with the possible involvement of some firms in illegal activities, has damaged the reputation of the industry. The market crash in 1987 and its effects on secondary trading, mergers, and takeover activities may halt the rapid growth of the industry. There is also considerable debate concerning the need for additional regulation and control of the securities industry.

SECONDARY MARKETS

After securities have been purchased in the primary markets, they can be traded in the *secondary markets*. The secondary markets comprise the organized securities exchanges and the Over-the-Counter, OTC, markets. The majority of all capital market transactions occur in the secondary markets. The proceeds from sales of securities in the secondary markets do not go to the issuer but to the owners (sellers) of the securities.

The function of the secondary market is to provide liquidity for securities purchased in the primary markets. Once investors have purchased securities in the primary markets, they need a place to sell those securities. Without the liquidity of the secondary markets, firms would have difficulty raising funds for productive purposes in the primary markets.

New York Stock Exchange

The New York Stock Exchange, NYSE, is the largest of the organized securities exchanges in the United States. It was established in 1817 and was originally called the New York Stock and Exchange Board. Its current name was adopted in 1863. Securities of over 1,500 companies are currently traded on the NYSE, with approximately 2,300 common and preferred stocks and 3,600 bonds listed. Listing requirements for the NYSE are given in Table 3.2. The "Big Board," as the NYSE is known, accounts for approximately 80 percent of all shares traded on the organized exchanges. The volume of trading on the NYSE has grown rapidly in the past twenty years. In 1967, the average daily volume was 10 million shares. By 1977, the average volume had doubled to 21 million, and by 1987, the average daily volume had risen to approximately 170 million shares.[11] On October 19, 1987, the volume on the NYSE was over 604 million shares.

1.   MEMBERSHIP The NYSE is a corporation with 1,366 members, each of whom owns a "seat." Most of the seats are owned by brokerage firms. The cost of a seat fluctuates with the volume of trading activity on the exchange. Seats have sold for as little as $17,000, in 1942, and for as much as $650,000, in 1987. Members are classified into four categories, as follows:

   a.   COMMISSION BROKERS They are employees of a member brokerage firm who execute buy and sell orders for the firm's clients. Major brokerage firms have more than one commission broker.

---

[11] *The NYSE Fact Book 1987*, The New York Stock Exchange p. 70.

TABLE 3.2 LISTING REQUIREMENTS FOR THE NYSE

I. Initial Listing Requirements
  1. Earning power
     a. Minimum of $2.5 million earnings before taxes for most recent year
     b. Minimum of $2.0 million earnings for each of the preceding two years, or an aggregate for the last three fiscal years of $6.5 million with a minimum in the most recent year of $4.5 million (all three years must be profitable)
  2. Minimum net tangible assets: $18 million
  3. Minimum market value of publicly held shares: $18 million (as of 12/31/86)
  4. Minimum shares publicly held: 1,100,000 shares
  5. Either a minimum 2,000 holders of 100 shares or more, or 2,200 total stockholders together with average monthly trading volume of 100,000 shares

II. Continued Listing Requirements
  1. At least 1,200 round-lot stockholders
  2. At least 600,000 shares in public hands
  3. Aggregate market value of publicly held shares of $5 million or more

III. Alternate Listing Standards for Foreign Companies
  1. Pre-tax income: $100 million cumulative in the latest three years with a minimum of $25 million in any one of the three years
  2. Minimum net tangible assets of $100 million worldwide
  3. Minimum aggregate market value of publicly held shares of $100 million worldwide
  4. Minimum number of publicly held shares: 2.5 million shares
  5. Minimum 5,000 holders of 100 shares or more

SOURCE: *The NYSE Fact Book 1987*, The New York Stock Exchange, pp. 21–22.

b. FLOOR BROKERS They own their own seats on the exchange. The floor broker is also known as a ''broker's broker.'' When trading activity is high, they accept and execute orders for the commission brokers and receive a fee in return.

c. FLOOR TRADERS Floor traders are members of the NYSE who buy and sell solely for their own accounts. They can react quickly to changes in exchange activity and information on securities since they are located on the floor of the exchange. Small price changes in securities can generate profits for them since they pay no commissions.

d. SPECIALISTS Probably the most important members of the exchange, they are responsible for maintaining a ''fair and orderly market'' in the securities to which they are assigned. There are approximately fifty specialist firms, and each listed stock is assigned to one or more specialists. Specialists perform two functions. First, as *brokers*, they must handle ''limit'' and other special orders entered in their book for commission brokers. Second, they act as *dealers*, by buying and selling the stocks they are assigned in order to maintain an orderly market.

American Stock Exchange

The American Stock Exchange, AMEX, is the other major national exchange. It is often referred to as ''the Curb.'' Listing requirements for the AMEX, less stringent than those for the NYSE, are shown in Table 3.3. The approximately eight hundred firms listed on the AMEX tend to be smaller and less seasoned than the firms listed on the NYSE. As the firms grow in size and strength, they often move their listings to the NYSE because of the increased prestige.

TABLE 3.3 LISTING REQUIREMENTS FOR THE AMEX

I. Minimum Initial Listing Requirements
  1. Pre-tax income: $750,000 latest fiscal year or two of the last three fiscal years
  2. Minimum stockholders' equity: $4,000,000
  3. Minimum shares publicly held: 500,000
  4. Minimum market value of publicly held shares/price per share: $3,000,000/$3.00
  5. Number of stockholders: 800 holders of round lots if public float is less than 1 million shares, 400 if float is at least 1 million shares

II. Minimum Requirements For Continued Listing
  1. Shares publicly held: 200,000
  2. Market value of publicly held shares: $1,000,000
  3. Number of round-lot holders: 300
  The Exchange may also consider the listing of a company's securities if the company has a minimum of 500,000 shares publicly held, a minimum of 400 shareholders and the daily volume of trading in the issue has been approximately 2,000 shares or more for the six months preceding the date of application.

SOURCE: *The American Stock Exchange Fact Book 1987,* The American Stock Exchange, p. 11.

The AMEX has a number of features that differentiate it from the NYSE. The first is the smaller size of the firms listed on the AMEX due to the lesser listing requirements. Second, prior to August 1976, stocks listed on the NYSE could not also be listed on the AMEX. The "New York Stock Rule," as it was known, was abolished at the request of the AMEX, and a number of firms on the AMEX applied for and received dual listing. The AMEX demonstrated innovativeness and aggressiveness by trading warrants before they were allowed to be traded on the NYSE. It was also first to trade American Depository Receipts, ADRs, a security issued by banks which represents holdings of shares in foreign companies.

Regional Exchanges

There are several regional exchanges, including the Pacific Stock Exchange (San Francisco–Los Angeles), the Philadelphia Exchange (Philadelphia–Pittsburgh), the Midwest Stock Exchange (Chicago), and the Boston Stock Exchange (Boston). The regional exchanges operate in basically the same manner as the national exchanges, although their listing requirements are more lenient.

The regional exchanges provide two basic functions. First, they list the securities of firms that are too small to meet the listing requirements of the national exchanges. Second, they list dually the securities of firms on the national exchanges. Dual listing allows small brokerage firms, that cannot afford a seat on the national exchanges but can afford membership in a regional exchange, to buy and sell stock in the dually listed firms. The majority of the regional exchanges' equity volume is in the dually listed securities.

Over-the-Counter Market

The *Over-the-Counter market*, OTC, refers to all security transactions not taking place on the organized exchanges. The OTC has no central location, as the major and regional exchanges do; it is a network of brokers-dealers who deal (negotiate) for their own accounts with each other over the telephone or through computer terminals. For this reason, the OTC market is a "negotiated market" in contrast to the auction markets of the organized exchanges. In an auction market a third party, in this case a specialist, facilitates the transaction.

Most of the securities traded in the OTC market tend to be those of small regional businesses, banks, finance companies, and mutual funds. Also, most corporate, municipal, and United States Government bonds are traded OTC. There are a number of large firms—for example, Apple Computer—that could qualify for listing on the NYSE, but have elected for their stock to be traded OTC.

All brokers and dealers in the OTC market must belong to the National Association of Security Dealers, NASD. The NASD has developed the National Association of Security Dealers Automated Quotation, NASDAQ, system, a computerized network for obtaining bid and ask quotes on NASDAQ securities. To be included in the NASDAQ system, a security must have at least two market makers who are willing to trade a minimum number of shares and meet certain requirements regarding capital and assets. Most OTC-traded stocks have fewer than ten market makers. The NASDAQ has three levels. Level I allows a broker to get only a bid and an ask quote. At level II, brokers can find all quotes as well as the market makers in the security. Level III allows market makers to enter bid and ask quotes. The NASDAQ carries over 4,400 companies and over 5,200 issues. In 1986, the average daily trading volume was 114 million shares; the annual share volume for NASDAQ was 28.7 billion shares versus 35.7 billion shares on the NYSE.[12]

Third and Fourth Markets

The *third market* refers to OTC transactions in securities listed on the organized exchanges. It was composed primarily of large institutional investors that disliked having to pay set commissions when trading large blocks of stocks on the NYSE. To reduce the commission costs, they began to trade blocks of securities in the OTC market where they could negotiate the transaction costs. The third market flourished during the 1960s and early 1970s, but it has gradually declined with the onset of negotiated commissions in 1975.

The *fourth market* refers to security transactions directly between a buyer and seller. The broker-dealer is eliminated from the transactions, which are usually between large institutions trading big blocks of stocks, although the term would also apply to the small investor selling a hundred shares of stock to a friend. The number and size of the transactions in the fourth market is unknown.

TRADING MECHANICS

Overview

The first step in investing in securities is usually the selection of a brokerage firm. The investor must decide between a *full-service* brokerage firm and a *discount* brokerage firm. The full-service brokerage firm, such as Merrill Lynch, not only

---

[12] *The NASD Fact Book 1987*, National Association of Securities Dealers, Washington, D.C., p. 6.

executes orders but also maintains a research staff that provides economic reports and information on industries and firms to their customers. Many full-service brokerage firms not only trade in stocks and bonds but also offer a variety of other services such as mutual funds, limited partnerships, life insurance, and estate planning.

The discount brokerage firm is essentially only an order taker. These firms normally do not provide research information for customers. Since they do not have the overhead for research and other services, they charge a smaller commission than the full-service broker. Table 3.4 shows commission costs for a full-service versus discount brokers, for various transactions. Even the discount brokers have substantial differences in their commissions, as seen in Table 3.4. It should also be noted that all brokerage commissions can be negotiated.

Two other types of brokerage firms deserve mention. Regional brokerage firms are often the only source of research information on small regional companies. Some of these regional companies may have excellent growth and financial characteristics but are simply too small for the major brokerage firms to spend time analyzing them. Secondly, there has been an increase in "penny stock" brokerage firms in recent years. These firms deal in very small, high-risk firms that trade for only pennies a share. Commission rates at some penny stock firms are as high as 50 percent of the value of the transaction. Thus, it may be difficult to make a profit when trading at one of these firms.

After selecting a brokerage firm, the next step is selecting a broker (also called an account executive or financial consultant). The potential investor can ask other investors for recommendations, as a person who is new to an area would select a doctor, a dentist, or an attorney. Investors should select brokers who have a risk orientation similar to their own. For example, a retired couple seeking income from their retirement funds may not relate well to a broker who feels that active management of a stock portfolio is the best investment approach. The investor should also remember that the broker makes his or her living through buying and selling securities for customers. This creates a potential conflict of interest and can cause complications between the broker and the investor.

Opening an account at a brokerage firm is very simple. The investor must fill out an application that asks for personal information (name, address, telephone number, and social security number); financial information (salary, assets, liabilities, other investments); and investment objectives (income, appreciation, preservation of principal, tax savings).

TABLE 3.4 A COMPARISON OF COMMISSION COSTS BETWEEN A FULL-SERVICE BROKER AND TWO DISCOUNT BROKERS

TRANSACTION	MERRILL LYNCH (FULL-SERVICE)	CHARLES SCHWAB (DISCOUNT)	STOCK CROSS (DISCOUNT)
100 shares @ $35 per share	$ 93	$ 49	$ 34
500 shares @ $35 per share	305	114	68
1,000 shares @ $35 per share	488	154	110
100 shares @ $60 per share	97	49	34
500 shares @ $60 per share	435	144	68
1,000 shares @ $60 per share	625	194	110

SOURCE: *Barron's*, 4 January, 1988, p. 13.

There are two types of accounts available to the customer: cash and margin. The basic account is the cash account, in which the customer pays the full price of any securities purchased. A margin account allows the customer to pay 50 percent (currently) of the price of the securities purchased, borrowing the rest from the brokerage firm. Brokerage firms try to determine that investors have sufficient knowledge of the securities markets and the risks involved before allowing customers to open margin accounts. The risk and return characteristics of margin trading are discussed in connection with basic investment strategies in Chapter 5.

Types of Orders

1. ORDER SIZE   Stock orders are normally placed in *round lots*—100 shares. A transaction of less than 100 shares is referred to as an *odd-lot transaction*. The commission cost per share for odd lots is higher than that for round lots. Generally, an odd-lot transaction will cost the investor an eighth of a point, or 12.5 cents, per share more than a round-lot transaction. The odd-lot transaction cost does not apply for very high-priced stocks.

2. MARKET ORDER   The most common order is a *market order*. A market order indicates that the customer has requested the order be transacted at the best available price when the order reaches the floor of the exchange. The advantage of a market order is that it will be executed immediately. The disadvantage is that the investor does not know exactly what price he or she will get for the transaction. Market orders are normally *day orders* which expire at the end of the day. If there is a chance that the order cannot be executed, the investor may leave the expiration date of the order open by making the order a *good-till-cancelled order*, GTC.

3. LIMIT ORDER   A *limit order* requires that the order will be transacted at the limit price or at a better price. For example, assume that you want to buy a stock that is currently selling for $20 a share, but you want to pay only $18 a share. You call your broker and place a limit buy order at $18. The order is sent to the firm's commission broker on the floor of the exchange. The order is then taken to the "post" where the stock is being traded. If the order cannot be transacted, the commission broker will leave the order with the specialist, who puts it in the book. If the price of the stock drops to $18 or lower, the specialist will transact the order. If you want to sell a stock, the limit order is placed above the current price of the stock. Assume that you own 100 shares of IBM, which is currently trading at $120 a share. You think that the stock will rise at least $10 a share over the next few weeks. In an attempt to maximize your profit, you place a limit sell order at $130. If the stock sells for $130 or higher, your order will be executed.

    It is possible that a limit order will not be executed when the price is reached. When the specialist enters the limit order in the book, the order enters a queue. In the above example, there may already have been an order to sell 400 shares of IBM at $130 a share in the book. If only 400 shares transact at $130 a share, your order will not be executed, but it will now move to the top of the list, and the next buy order at $130 a share will cause the order to be executed.

The major disadvantage in using limit orders is that you may miss the market. If IBM stock rose to $129⅞ a share and then dropped to $100 a share, your order would not be executed, and for one-eighth of a point you suffered a significant decrease in net worth. Likewise, placing a limit buy order below the market price when a stock is rising may mean that you miss the price move that you would have gotten if you had placed a market order.

4. STOP ORDER A *stop order*, also called a *stop-loss* order, is also a special order that is placed in the specialist's book. There are two differences between stop orders and limit orders. First, the stop is placed on the opposite end (above purchase price or below selling price) of the market price on which the limit order is placed. Second, a stop order becomes a market order when the price is reached. Assume that you bought a stock at $20 per share, and the stock price has risen to $30. Your profit will be $10 a share if you sell the stock. To protect yourself against a drop in the price, you enter a stop-loss order at $27. If the price drops to $27 a share, the stop order will become a market order and will be executed at the highest bid available on the specialist's book. Although you suffered a slight decline from the $30 price, you also protected a portion of the price appreciation in the stock (approximately $7 gain). Of course, there is no guarantee that you would receive $27 per share. If the stock declines rapidly (remember October 19, 1987), the market order may be transacted at less than $27. The major disadvantage of a stop order is that if the stock was merely fluctuating within a price range but was still in an uptrend, you sold the stock because of a temporary decline in the stock's price.

Limit buy and stop-loss orders are normally reduced in price on the date the stock goes ex-dividend. This is logical since the value of the stock is reduced by the amount of the per-share cash dividend on the ex-dividend date. The amount of price reduction is rounded to the nearest eighth of a point. For example, a limit buy at $18 for Baxter Corp. GTC is placed with the specialist. The next week the stock goes ex-dividend by $.50 per share. The limit buy order would be changed to $17½. If the dividend had been $.34, the order price would have declined three-eighths of a point ($.375). Orders may be marked "DNR" (do not reduce) if desired.

5. MISCELLANEOUS ORDERS There are a number of miscellaneous orders that can be used by large investors. *Fill or Kill*, FOK, means to fill the order immediately in one trade, or cancel the order completely. An *All or None*, AON, order means fill the order in one day, or cancel the order completely. The *Immediate or Cancel*, IOC, order means that the broker must immediately fill as much of the order as possible in one trade and then cancel the remainder of the order. A *Not Held*, NH, order grants some discretion to be registered representative (and hence the commission broker) to do as he or she sees fit. The specialist will not receive the order. When the commission broker arrives at the post where the stock is traded, he can immediately try to trade the security, or he can wait if he thinks the price will become more favorable.

REGULATION OF SECURITIES MARKETS

There was very little regulation of the securities markets in the United States prior to 1933. The 1920s was a time of fraudulent trading practices, speculative excesses with borrowed funds, dissemination of fraudulent security information, and trading on inside information. These undesirable practices contributed to the market crash of 1929 and the subsequent enactment of legislation governing the securities industry.

Securities Act of 1933

This act is also known as the "truth in securities act." The act requires registration with the federal government of all new securities issues and certain secondary offerings. Offerings exempt from the law include government and municipal issues; intrastate offerings (and secondary sales out of state after nine months); Regulation A offerings (issues of less than $1.5 million); issues covered by the Interstate Commerce Commission, such as those of railroads, airlines, and trucking companies; and private placements to a small number of investors.

The primary purpose of the act is to provide full disclosure about the securities, so that rational investors can make intelligent investment decisions. The law requires that a registration statement must be filed, including information about the firm, a list of its officers and directors, audited financial statements, and the proposed use of the funds to be raised by the offering. The firm has a twenty-day waiting period before it can issue the new securities. While the federal government is evaluating the registration statement, the firm may publish a "tombstone" advertisement (see Table 3.5) and send a preliminary prospectus to potential investors. The final prospectus must be provided to all purchasers of the new security.

The act also provides for civil and criminal penalties for fraud or misrepresentation. If an investor suffers a monetary loss due to fraudulent information or misrepresentation in a security offering, the purchaser may sue to recover the lost funds.

Securities Exchange Act of 1934

A number of factors make this act important to the investor. It extends disclosure requirements to securities traded in the secondary markets (NYSE, AMEX, OTC, and regional exchanges). A firm is required to file an annual registration statement (called a 10-K report), as well as other periodic reports, with the SEC. The act was amended in 1964 to include the filing of registration statements by large OTC firms.

The act also established the Securities and Exchange Commission, SEC. The SEC is charged with the regulation of securities markets and establishing trading policies for the exchanges. It may penalize those exchanges that do not conform to its guidelines. All organized exchanges are required to register with the SEC.

The SEC also sets regulations for proxy solicitations and insider information. *Insiders* of a firm are defined as officers, directors, and individuals who own more than 10 percent of the firm's outstanding shares. All insiders are required to file reports on their trading activities with the SEC. The SEC also prohibits manipulation of stock prices through the use of pools (individuals banding together to

TABLE 3.5 A TOMBSTONE ADVERTISEMENT

5,500,000 Shares

 # Avondale Industries, Inc.

Common Stock
(par value $1.00 per share)

Price $15 Per Share

Upon request, a copy of the Prospectus describing these securities and the business of the Company may be obtained within any State from any Underwriter who may legally distribute it within such State. The securities are offered only by means of the Prospectus, and this announcement is neither an offer to sell nor a solicitation of any offer to buy

4,400,000 Shares
This portion of the offering is being offered in the United States by the undersigned.

Goldman, Sachs & Co.   Tucker, Anthony & R. L. Day, Inc.

Bear, Stearns & Co. Inc.   The First Boston Corporation   Alex. Brown & Sons   Dillon, Read & Co. Inc.
Donaldson, Lufkin & Jenrette   Drexel Burnham Lambert   Kidder, Peabody & Co.   Lazard Frères & Co.
PaineWebber Incorporated   Prudential-Bache Capital Funding   L.F. Rothschild & Co.
Salomon Brothers Inc   Shearson Lehman Hutton Inc.   Smith Barney, Harris Upham & Co.
Wertheim Schroder & Co.   Dean Witter Capital Markets   William Blair & Company   J. C. Bradford & Co.
A. G. Edwards & Sons, Inc.   Howard, Weil, Labouisse, Friedrichs   McDonald & Company
Oppenheimer & Co., Inc.   Piper, Jaffray & Hopwood   Prescott, Ball & Turben, Inc.
Thomson McKinnon Securities Inc.   Wheat, First Securities, Inc.   Advest, Inc.   Arnhold and S. Bleichroeder, Inc.
Bateman Eichler, Hill Richards   Butcher & Singer Inc.   Cable, Howse & Ragen   Cowen & Co.
Eppler, Guerin & Turner, Inc.   First Southwest Company   Furman Selz Mager Dietz & Birney
Interstate Securities Corporation   Janney Montgomery Scott Inc.   Johnson, Lane, Space, Smith & Co., Inc.
Johnston, Lemon & Co.   C.J. Lawrence, Morgan Grenfell Inc.   Morgan Keegan & Company, Inc.
Needham & Company, Inc.   Neuberger & Berman   The Ohio Company   Rauscher Pierce Refsnes, Inc.
Raymond James & Associates, Inc.   The Robinson-Humphrey Company, Inc.   Rotan Mosle Inc.
Stephens Inc.   Sutro & Co.   Underwood, Neuhaus & Co.   Volpe & Covington
The Chicago Corporation   Doley Govan Securities, Inc.   J. J. B. Hilliard, W. L. Lyons, Inc.
Investment Corporation of Virginia   Scharff & Jones   Seidler Amdec Securities Inc.

1,100,000 Shares
This portion of the offering is being offered outside the United States by the undersigned.

Goldman Sachs International Corp.   Tucker, Anthony & R. L. Day, Inc.

Banque Paribas Capital Markets Limited   Deutsche Bank Capital Markets Limited
Dresdner Bank Aktiengesellschaft   Morgan Stanley International   Nomura International Limited
Salomon Brothers International Limited   Shearson Lehman Brothers International
SBCI Swiss Bank Corporation Investment banking   S. G. Warburg Securities

SOURCE: *Wall Street Journal*, 31 March 1988, p. 37. Reprinted by permission.

profit from the manipulation of stock prices), wash sales (the buying and selling of the same security to affect the price or give the impression of activity in the stock), and other practices that could destabilize stock prices.

Maloney Act of 1936

The Maloney Act provides for the establishment of self-regulatory associations in the OTC market. The only organization to register with the SEC is the National Association of Securities Dealers, NASD. The NASD requires all potential brokers to pass a proficiency test (Series 7 Exam) before they can trade securities. The NASD may also penalize members, with fines or suspension, for misconduct.

Other Regulations

The Investiment Company Act of 1940 requires investment companies to register with the SEC and provide information to potential investors. This act is discussed in more detail in Chapter 24. The Investment Advisors Act of 1940 requires individuals and firms that sell advice about investments to register with the SEC. The Securities Investor Protection Act of 1970 provides for the establishment of the Securities Investor Protection Corporation, SIPC, which provides insurance to protect investors from brokerage firms that fail. Customer accounts are insured for up to $500,000. Only $100,000 of the amount applies to cash balances.

SUMMARY

This chapter discussed the structure and operation of securities markets. Primary markets trade initial issues of securities. Investment bankers play a critical role in the primary market by (1) advice and counsel, (2) underwriting, and (3) distribution of securities. The secondary market trades securities that are already issued. Trading of securities in the secondary market takes place on the organized security exchanges and the OTC. The NYSE and AMEX are the primary organized exchanges. The OTC market, dealing with security transactions away from the organized exchanges, is an informal network of brokers and dealers who trade through the NASDAQ system.

It is important that investors have an understanding of the mechanics of trading. Investors may use cash or borrow through margin accounts. Investors must also know the difference between market orders, limit orders, and stop orders.

The fraudulent trading practices in the securities markets during the 1920s led to the legislation regulating the securities market in effect today. The primary laws are the Securities Act of 1933, which required full disclosure of information, and the Securities Exchange Act of 1934, which created the SEC, required disclosure of information on issued securities, and prohibited fraudulent practices. Other laws include the Maloney Act of 1936, from which the NASD was created, the Investment Company Act of 1940, the Investment Advisors Act of 1940, and Securities Investor Protection Act of 1970.

1. How does the primary market differ from the secondary market?
2. What roles does the investment banker play in the primary market? What is a best-efforts offering?
3. What are the differences between the listing requirements of the NYSE and AMEX?
4. What is the OTC market? Differentiate the NASDAQ, third market, and fourth market.
5. Under what conditions would you want to go to a full-service broker instead of a discount broker?
6. Explain the role of the specialist.
7. Discuss the advantages and disadvantages of using a market order and a limit order.
8. How do limit orders and stop orders differ?
9. Why are certain securities exempt from registration under the Securities Act of 1933?
10. What are the major features of the Securities Exchange Act of 1934?
11. A customer of a failed brokerage firm had $300,000 worth of common stock and $200,000 in the cash account, for a total of $500,000. How much of the account value will be covered by SIPC?
12. Explain the differences between a commission broker and a floor broker.
13. How did the traditional activities of investment banking firms differ from their activities in the 1980s?

REFERENCES

Alpert, William M. "Judgement Day: Ivan Boesky Draws Three-Year Jail Term." *Barron's*, 21 December 1987, pp. 24–25.

American Stock Exchange Fact Book. New York: American Stock Exchange, 1987.

Broesamle, William. "An Interview with Professor James C. Van Horne." *Selections* (Spring 1988): pp. 7–12.

C.F.A. Study Guide I. Charlottesville, Va.: Institute of Chartered Financial Analysts, 1982, pp. 50–61.

Laing, Jonathan R. "Muckraking Money Managers." *Barron's*, 20 July 1987, pp. 6–7, 28, 30–31.

NASD Fact Book 1987. Washington, D.C: National Association of Security Dealers, 1987.

New York Stock Exchange Fact Book. New York: New York Stock Exchange, 1987.

Stein, Benjamin J. "A Saga of Shareholder Neglect: Whose Interest Was This Management Protecting?" *Barron's*, 4 May 1987, pp. 8–9, 70–75.

———. "Not Worthy of the Name? Investment Banking Isn't What It Used to Be." *Barron's*, 13 July 1987, pp. 6, 7, 26, 28, 30, 32.

Steward, James B., and Daniel Hartzberg. "SEC Approves Charges against Drexel, Michael Milken, but Delays Filing Them." *Wall Street Journal*, 9 June 1988, pp. 2, 14.

"Travail at Drexel Burnham." *Fortune*, 22 December 1986, pp. 31–37.

CHAPTER 4

INVESTMENT INFORMATION

INTRODUCTION

Good investment decisions are made through the careful evaluation of available information. Investors cannot make good investment decisions if they lack sufficient information to evaluate the potential risk and return associated with the investments.

The problem for many investors is failing to find information and to determine what information is useful to the investment decision. This chapter will discuss and illustrate a variety of investment information sources that are available to investors, including investment advisory services, computerized data bases, and Appendix 4A on investment information and the personal computer. Much of the information can be obtained free or at a nominal charge. Some of the information is fairly expensive, such as the *Value Line Investment Survey*. However, the more costly information may be available free at a public or university library.

The investor should remember that there is a trade-off in the time and cost of obtaining investment information and the potential increased return and/or risk reduction to be derived from the effort. Additionally, the quality of investment information can be good or bad. High cost does not guarantee good information.

A discussion of market indices is also included in this chapter. These are a variety of measures of market movement, and the more widely used indices are discussed. Market indices are used for (1) evaluating portfolio performance, (2) establishing the relationships between economic variables and overall market movements, (3) forecasting future market movements, and (4) measuring of stock or portfolio systematic risk. Therefore, an understanding of market indices is important. Appendix 4B compares the various domestic market indices over time, and Appendix 4C briefly examines the investment characteristics of the world's stock markets. (Chapter 23 discusses in detail the various aspects of international investing.)

ANALYSIS OF ECONOMIC CONDITIONS

The federal government is the primary source of raw economic data. The two major government publications are the *Federal Reserve Bulletin* and the *Survey of Current Business*. The *Federal Reserve Bulletin* is a monthly publication of the Board of Governors of the Federal Reserve System. It provides statistical data on monetary aggregates, interest rates, gross national product, credit, labor, and output. Often, graphs present data more clearly than looking at a series of numbers. The *Federal Reserve Monthly Chart Book* graphically depicts monetary and economic information from the *Federal Reserve Bulletin*. The *Historical Chart Book*, also published by the Federal Reserve, contains long-run business and financial charts.

The federal reserve banks also publish information on economic conditions. The St. Louis Federal Reserve Bank publishes weekly and monthly economic reports that are free and contain some of the best economic analyses available. The *Survey of Current Business* is a monthly publication of the U.S. Department of Commerce. It provides an excellent source of information on all segments of industrial production in the economy as well as statistics on prices, wages, interest rates, and national income.

Business Conditions Digest is a monthly publication of the Department of Commerce. It publishes the findings of the National Bureau of Economic Research

TABLE 4.1   HOW TO READ CHARTS IN BUSINESS CONDITIONS DIGEST

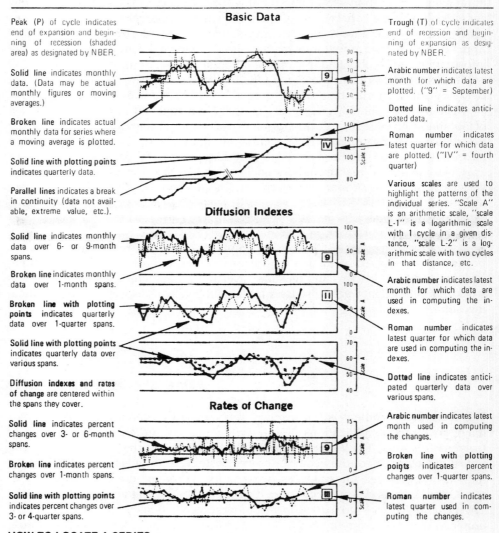

Peak (P) of cycle indicates end of expansion and beginning of recession (shaded area) as designated by NBER.

Solid line indicates monthly data. (Data may be actual monthly figures or moving averages.)

Broken line indicates actual monthly data for series where a moving average is plotted.

Solid line with plotting points indicates quarterly data.

Parallel lines indicates a break in continuity (data not available, extreme value, etc.).

Solid line indicates monthly data over 6- or 9-month spans.

Broken line indicates monthly data over 1-month spans.

Broken line with plotting points indicates quarterly data over 1-quarter spans.

Solid line with plotting points indicates quarterly data over various spans.

Diffusion indexes and rates of change are centered within the spans they cover.

Solid line indicates percent changes over 3- or 6-month spans.

Broken line indicates percent changes over 1-month spans.

Solid line with plotting points indicates percent changes over 3- or 4-quarter spans.

Trough (T) of cycle indicates end of recession and beginning of expansion as designated by NBER.

Arabic number indicates latest month for which data are plotted. ("9" = September)

Dotted line indicates anticipated data.

Roman number indicates latest quarter for which data are plotted. ("IV" = fourth quarter)

Various scales are used to highlight the patterns of the individual series. "Scale A" is an arithmetic scale, "scale L-1" is a logarithmic scale with 1 cycle in a given distance, "scale L-2" is a logarithmic scale with two cycles in that distance, etc.

Arabic number indicates latest month for which data are used in computing the indexes.

Roman number indicates latest quarter for which data are used in computing the indexes.

Dotted line indicates anticipated quarterly data over various spans.

Arabic number indicates latest month used in computing the changes.

Broken line with plotting points indicates percent changes over 1-quarter spans.

Roman number indicates latest quarter used in computing the changes.

HOW TO LOCATE A SERIES

1. See ALPHABETICAL INDEX–SERIES FINDING GUIDE at the back of the report where series are arranged alphabetically according to subject matter and key words and phrases of the series titles, or—

2. See TITLES AND SOURCES OF SERIES at the back of the report where series are listed numerically according to series numbers within each of the report's sections.

SOURCE: Business Conditions Digest, March 1988, p. 5., Washington D.C.: U.S. Department of Commerce, Bureau of Economic Analysis.

(NBER). The NBER's time series are closely followed by the investment industry. These series are used to indicate the future trend of the economy by studying leading, coincident, and lagging indicators. Table 4.1 provides a key designed to illustrate the charts published by *Business Conditions Digest.*

Other government publications include the *Economic Report of the President,* an annual report that discusses past economic events and forthcoming economic problems, and *The Statistical Abstract of the United States,* an annual publication of the Bureau of Census containing summary statistics from public and private sources on industrial, economic, political, and social trends.

INDUSTRY ANALYSIS

Once investors have achieved an understanding of current economic conditions and formulated an opinion of future economic activity, they can focus on specific industries. Information for industry analysis is available from a number of sources. Federal government publications, such as *The Quarterly Financial Report* published by the Federal Trade Commission, present aggregate financial information for all manufacturing companies. The information is broken down by industry and asset size. Business and financial publications, such as *Business Week, Forbes, Fortune, Barron's, Investor's Daily,* and *The Wall Street Journal,* also contain a great deal of information about particular industries.

Most industries have trade associations that publish statistical information about conditions in their industry. Such organizations include the American Iron and Steel Institute, the American Petroleum Institute, The National Paper Trade Association, and the Rubber Manufacturers Association.

Trade journals are also excellent sources of industry information. Examples of trade journals include *Chemical Week, Iron Age, Management News* (the National Paper Trade Association), *Oil and Gas Journal, Public Utilities Fortnightly, Rubber Age,* and *Steel.*

Standard & Poor's *Industry Survey* provides considerable information on various industries. The information is divided into a current and a basic analysis. The current analysis section discusses the latest industry developments and prospects for the industry; it also includes statistical data for the industry. The basic analysis looks at the trends and prospects of the industry from a historical perspective.

The *Value Line Investment Survey* provides industry reports on ninety-three industries. The reports include an evaluation of prospects for the industry as well as composite statistics. Table 4.2 provides an example of one page of an industry report. Value Line also prepares recommendations on individual stocks which will be discussed later in the chapter.

Excellent sources of current industry analysis are the industry reports published by the full-service brokerage firms. These research reports are generally available to customers of the brokerage firms on request. Finally, *The Wall Street Transcript* usually discusses two industries each week. The paper does in-depth interviews with CEOs and security analysts in the highlighted industries. The cost of the paper is currently $1,300 per year, putting it beyond the availability of the average investor.

TABLE 4.2 AN INDUSTRY REPORT FROM *VALUE LINE INVESTMENT SURVEY*

Dec. 11, 1987

PUBLISHING INDUSTRY

1787

Publishing stocks fared as poorly as most others during the recent market plunge. The typical issue in this group is down more than 30% since our review three months ago.

The publishing industry ranks just outside the upper third (34 out of 93) for probable year-ahead performance among the Value Line industry groupings.

Some of the stocks in this group—particularly those of companies that are heavily involved in education-related businesses—are good defensive additions to most portfolios as fears of an economic slump persist.

Takeover activity continues to influence the price performance of several issues. Two stocks in the group have had their Timeliness ranks removed pending resolution of active buyout offers.

No stock in this group ranks Highest for probable performance in the year ahead. However eight rank in the second tier, and a handful of those show substantial 3- to 5-year appreciation potential.

INDUSTRY TIMELINESS: 34 (of 93)

shown support for increased spending on education.

The renewed emphasis on education is good news for textbook publishers. Demographics indicate that the strongest sales gains are likely to come in the elementary-high school levels, as the "baby boomlet" grows up. *Bell & Howell* (through its Merrill Publishing subsidiary), *Houghton Mifflin, Macmillan, Harcourt Brace Jovanovich* and *Time* (through Scott-Foresman) are all strong in that area. Of those stocks, *Macmillan* and *Time* are ranked to outperform the market in the year ahead.

Demographic trends are not as favorable for the college textbook market. However, *McGraw-Hill*, with its emphasis on engineering and "hard" science subject areas, is likely to show consistent gains.

Adult education and training is another area that is likely to enjoy strong growth under most economic scenarios. The retraining segment, in fact, tends to benefit from business upheavals, as unemployed workers take advantage of government grants to obtain retraining in newly in-demand specialties. The biggest entrant in this segment is *National Education*, whose stock is favorably ranked for the year ahead and whose longer-term prospects are equally attractive. *Nat Ed* is slated to acquire *Advanced Systems* (rank suspended), a leading competitor, at yearend.

The Advertising Angle

Some of the companies covered here—*Time, Meredith, McGraw-Hill*, and *Playboy* on the publishing and broadcast side and *R.R. Donnelley* and *W.A. Krueger* on the printing side—are heavily dependent on the advertising market. All have suffered to some extent because of an unusually weak ad environment this year. We're expecting some firming up of the ad market in 1988 as the Olympics and the presidential campaign provide a boost. But the extent of that recovery is likely to fall short of earlier expectations if consumer spending slows down.

The magazine publishers are becoming increasingly innovative and aggressive in trying to expand their respective shares of the advertising pie. The traditional "rate card" seems in danger of becoming a relic as publishers show a willingness to negotiate individual deals. The most aggressive of these combatants is suddenly *Time*, which is now offering package deals on its several magazines.

More Takeover Talk

As mentioned above, *Bell & Howell* is the subject of a takeover battle. So far, only one offer has materialized, that from the Robert Bass group that includes the company's president. We think *Macmillan*, which has accumulated a 7.9% stake in *Bell & Howell*, will take its profits and withdraw. After the *Bell & Howell* case is resolved, the takeover frenzy that has engulfed the publishing industry for most of the year will likely ease up for a while.

Investment Considerations

Bowne, Dun & Bradstreet, John Harland, IMS Inter-

(Continued on page 1906)

COMPOSITE STATISTICS: PUBLISHING INDUSTRY							
1983	1984	1985	1986	1987	1988	© VALUE LINE, INC	90-92E
12489	14644	16265	18136	21500	24000	Sales ($mill)	32000
15.9%	17.2%	17.7%	18.2%	18.0%	18.0%	Operating Margin	18.5%
429.0	527.4	641.3	826.4	875	975	Depreciation ($mill)	1400
828.5	1120.4	1261.9	1378.5	1700	2000	Net Profit ($mill)	3100
47.1%	45.5%	44.9%	43.2%	42%	36%	Income Tax Rate	36%
6.6%	7.7%	7.8%	7.6%	7.8%	8.3%	Net Profit Margin	9.5%
2431.2	2846.8	2721.8	3034.3	4775	5350	Working Cap'l ($mill)	7400
1043.8	1092.6	1422.7	2644.4	2250	2250	Long-Term Debt ($mill)	2400
4761.9	5881.7	6782.6	7777.7	9000	10300	Net Worth ($mill)	16000
15.1%	16.9%	16.2%	14.0%	16.0%	16.5%	% Earned Total Cap'l	17.5%
17.4%	19.1%	18.6%	17.7%	18.0%	19.5%	% Earned Net Worth	19.5%
10.5%	12.5%	11.6%	10.9%	11.0%	11.5%	% Retained to Comm Eq	12.0%
41%	35%	38%	39%	40%	40%	% All Div'ds to Net Prof	40%
18.4	13.7	16.3	20.8	Bold figures are Value Line estimates		Avg Ann'l P/E Ratio	15.0
1.56	1.28	1.32	1.41			Relative P/E Ratio	1.25
2.2%	2.5%	2.3%	1.9%			Avg Ann'l Div'd Yield	2.3%

Picking Up the Pieces

Publishing stocks, despite their traditional defensive characteristics, could not hold their values during the market plunge. With the single exception of *Bell & Howell* (a takeover target), all stocks in this group are down at double-digit percentage levels from the time of our last report three months ago. Most, in fact, are down more than 25%. Given the magnitude of the Black Monday debacle, the failure of these stocks to validate their defensive reputation is understandable. In fact, the market drop did affect the fundamentals of certain companies in the publishing group: Those are the companies engaged in the specialized area of securities- and financial document-printing. Two of those stocks, *Bowne* and *International Banknote*, were hit especially hard, each losing more than half its former value. However, we think the fears for those companies' performance are exaggerated. Both stocks show above-average appreciation potential to 1990-92.

Getting an Education

Despite the aforementioned failure of publishing stocks to hold up against the recent tide, we still feel several companies in the industry are situated to do well even in less-than-ideal economic circumstances. Of particular interest here are stocks of companies whose business is education-related. Broadly, the reason for optimism here is a discernible change in the national climate. Trade deficits and shutdowns of industrial capacity have produced a feeling that America is losing its "competitive edge". The education system is getting much of the blame, as evidenced by the success of such books as *The Closing of the American Mind* and *What 17-Year Olds Know*. In fact, all of the current presidential candidates, including those considered fiscally conservative, have

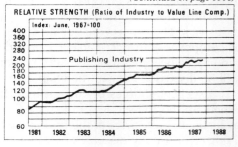

RELATIVE STRENGTH (Ratio of Industry to Value Line Comp.)

Index: June, 1967=100

Publishing Industry

STOCK INFORMATION

After the investor determines the likely industries for investment, the next step is to analyze specific firms within each industry.

Annual Report

An important source of information about a firm is the firm itself. All publicly traded firms must publish and distribute an annual report to their stockholders. Nonstockholders can obtain a copy of the annual report by writing to the firm. Annual reports may also be found in libraries and at brokerage firms.

The annual report contains audited financial information including the balance sheet, income statement, and statement of changes in financial position for the most recent and earlier periods. Footnotes to the financial statements provide important additional information in evaluating the financial condition of the firm. The annual report also discusses the operations of the firm over the preceding year and the future prospects for the business. The quality and amount of specific financial information in annual reports varies. If the firm's annual report does not contain sufficient financial information, the investor can request from the firm a copy of the annual registration statement (10-K report) filed with the Securities and Exchange Commission.

Quarterly Report

During the year, publicly traded firms publish quarterly financial reports. They show sales and earnings figures for the previous quarter and for the same period of the previous year. These reports are unaudited and do not contain the detail of the financial statements in the annual report. Many of the figures in the quarterly report must be adjusted at the end of the year.

INVESTMENT ADVISORY SERVICES

A variety of investment advisory services and newsletters provide information on specific industries and firms. The annual cost of these services varies from a few dollars to several thousand dollars. Investors may want to check with local libraries since the cost of these services may not be justified, given the size of most portfolios.

Since there are so many advisory services and letters, only the three major investment advisory services will be discussed here. A brief mention of some other advisory services will be given at the end of this section.

Standard & Poor's Corporation

Standard & Poor's Corporation publishes several financial reports and services:

1. CORPORATE RECORDS Reports are contained in six volumes, with updates in a seventh volume, ''Daily News.'' Each report contains detailed financial information on publicly traded firms under the following headings: Capitalization,

TABLE 4.3 A SAMPLE REPORT FROM STANDARD & POOR'S *STOCK REPORTS*

Wal-Mart Stores

2413

NYSE Symbol WMT Options on CBOE (Mar-Jun-Sep-Dec) In S&P 500

Price	Range	P-E Ratio	Dividend	Yield	S&P Ranking	Beta
Nov. 16'87	1987					
28½	42⅞-22	28	0.12	0.4%	A+	1.25

Summary

Wal-Mart operates a chain of discount department stores in an area spanning the Sunbelt from South Carolina through Texas, with locations generally in smaller communities. Strong base expansion and an aggressive pricing posture should facilitate market share gains in the Wal-Mart division, while the improving profitability of the wholesale clubs and contributions from a planned "hypermarket" joint venture with food retailer, Cullum Cos., enhance longer-term prospects.

Current Outlook

Per-share earnings for the fiscal year ending January 31, 1989 are projected at $1.35 a share, versus an estimated $1.10 in fiscal 1987-8.

The quarterly dividend should remain at $0.03.

Sales in 1988-9 should reflect gains in the Wal-Mart stores and growing contributions from high-volume wholesale clubs. Continuing efforts to pare operating and distribution costs coupled with savings generated by tax reform should accommodate an aggressive price posture, facilitating market share gains. Development of the hypermarket joint venture should provide a third long-term growth vehicle.

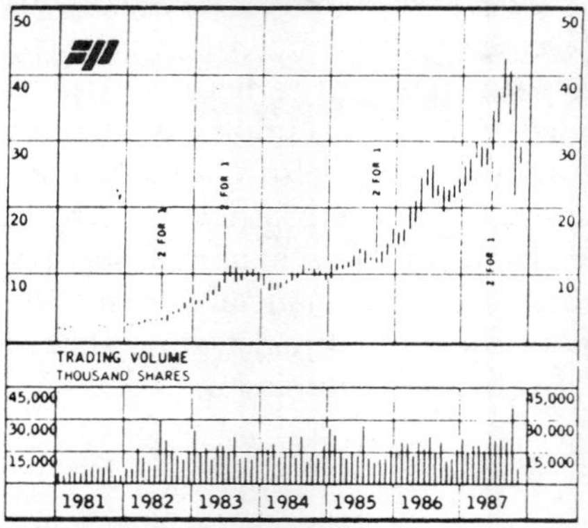

Net Sales (Billion $)

Quarter:	1987-8	1986-7	1985-6	1984-5
Apr.	3.21	2.34	1.66	1.24
Jul.	3.73	2.77	1.93	1.51
Oct.	4.02	2.95	2.09	1.58
Jan.	---	3.85	2.77	2.07
	---	11.91	8.45	6.40

Sales for the nine months ended October 31, 1987 rose 36%, year to year. Net income advanced 43%, to $0.67 a share from $0.47 (adjusted).

Common Share Earnings ($)

Quarter:	1987-8	1986-7	1985-6	1984-5
Apr.	0.20	0.13	0.10	0.08
Jul.	0.24	0.17	0.13	0.11
Oct.	0.24	0.17	0.13	0.11
Jan.	E0.42	0.33	0.24	0.19
	E1.10	0.80	0.58	0.48

Important Developments

Nov. '87—WMT said that at October 31 it had 1,091 Wal-Mart stores, 79 Sam's Wholesale Clubs and 12 dot Discount Drug stores in operation.

Jan. '87—Plans for 1987-8 call for the opening of some 125 Wal-Marts and 20 Sam's, and the testing of a potentially significant third format, a hypermarket, to be operated initially as a joint venture with Dallas-based grocery operator, Cullum Cos. The 150,000 sq. ft. outlets would stock general merchandise similar to that carried in a Wal-Mart store as well as a full selection of groceries at sharply discounted prices. The first units would open late in calendar 1987.

Next earnings report expected in mid-February.

Per Share Data ($)

Yr. End Jan. 31	1987	1986	1985	1984	1983	[1]1982	1981	1980	[1]1979	1978
Book Value	**3.00**	2.28	1.76	1.32	0.91	0.63	0.48	0.35	0.27	0.21
Earnings	**0.80**	0.58	0.48	0.35	0.23	0.16	0.11	0.09	0.07	0.05
Dividends	**0.08½**	0.07	0.05⅜	0.03½	0.02⅜	0.01¾	0.01⅜	0.01	0.00¾	0.00½
Payout Ratio	**11%**	12%	11%	10%	10%	10%	12%	11%	11%	11%
Calendar Years	**1986**	1985	1984	1983	1982	1981	1980	1979	1978	1977
Prices—High	**26⅞**	17⅜	11⅞	11¾	6⅞	2⅞	2	1¼	1	¾
Low	**14⅝**	9½	7⅝	5½	2½	1¾	⅞	⅞	⅝	½
P/E Ratio—	**34-18**	30-16	25-16	33-16	30-11	18-11	18-8	14-8	15-9	13-8

Data as orig. reptd. Adj. for stk. div(s). of 100% Jul. 1987, 100% Oct. 1985, 100% Jul. 1983, 100% Jul. 1982, 100% Dec. 1980. 1. Reflects merger or acquisition. E-Estimated.

Standard NYSE Stock Reports
Vol. 54/No. 229/Sec. 28

December 1, 1987

Copyright © 1987 Standard & Poor's Corp. All Rights Reserved

Standard & Poor's Corp.
25 Broadway, NY, NY 10004

SOURCE: *Stock Reports*, Standard & Poor's 1 Dec. 1987, p. 2413. Reprinted by permission.

TABLE 4.3 (Continued)

2413

Wal-Mart Stores, Inc.

Income Data (Million $)

Year Ended Jan. 31	Revs.	Oper. Inc.	% Oper. Inc. of Revs.	Cap. Exp.	Depr.	Int. Exp.	Net Bef. Taxes	Eff. Tax Rate	Net Inc.	% Net Inc. of Revs.
1987	11,909	972	8.2%	587	124	90.3	846	46.8%	450	3.8%
1986	8,451	695	8.2%	532	90	60.9	604	45.7%	327	3.9%
1985	6,401	563	8.8%	325	66	48.7	501	46.0%	271	4.2%
1984	4,667	405	8.7%	229	49	35.4	357	45.1%	196	4.2%
1983	3,376	278	8.2%	166	37	40.5	225	44.7%	124	3.7%
1982	2,445	189	7.7%	102	26	32.3	149	44.3%	83	3.4%
1981	1,643	122	7.4%	92	18	17.0	99	43.9%	56	3.4%
1980	1,248	90	7.2%	89	13	13.9	74	44.6%	41	3.3%
1979	900	60	6.7%	43	9	3.8	57	48.1%	29	3.3%
1978	678	41	6.1%	28	5	2.3	42	48.1%	22	3.2%

Balance Sheet Data (Million $)

Jan. 31	Cash	Current Assets	Current Liab.	Ratio	Total Assets	Ret. on Assets	Long Term Debt	Common Equity	Total Cap.	% LT Debt of Cap.	Ret. on Equity
1987	166	2,353	1,340	1.8	4,049	12.6%	943	1,690	2,709	34.8%	30.3%
1986	174	1,784	993	1.8	3,104	12.3%	776	1,278	2,111	36.8%	28.9%
1985	2	1,303	689	1.9	2,205	14.0%	491	984	1,516	32.4%	31.4%
1984	157	1,006	503	2.0	1,652	13.6%	381	737	1,149	33.1%	31.4%
1983	33	721	347	2.1	1,187	11.5%	329	488	840	39.2%	30.0%
1982	9	589	340	1.7	938	10.8%	259	323	598	43.3%	28.9%
1981	19	345	178	1.9	592	10.3%	165	248	415	39.8%	26.2%
1980	5	267	170	1.6	458	10.5%	122	165	288	42.4%	28.1%
1979	12	192	99	1.9	325	11.0%	98	127	226	43.5%	25.9%
1978	8	151	73	2.1	207	12.4%	32	99	134	24.2%	25.6%

Data as orig. reptd. 1. Reflects merger or acquisition.

Business Summary

Wal-Mart is a discount retailer, primarily operating a chain of 980 Wal-Mart discount department stores in 23 Southern, Southwestern and Midwestern states. Wal-Mart entered the wholesale club business in 1983 (49 Sam's Wholesale Clubs in operation at January 31, 1987), and operates 6 dot deep-discount drug stores and three full-line crafts stores.

The average Wal-Mart store is 59,000 sq. ft. in size (90% selling area), located primarily in small towns. Each store features nationally advertised merchandise, as well as private label items, in some 36 departments, including family apparel, automotive, housewares, sporting goods, hardware, health and beauty aids, toys, etc. Softlines generally account for about 30% of sales. The 980 Wal-Mart stores in operation at the end of 1986-7, compared with 859 at the end of fiscal 1985-6.

The first Sam's Wholesale Club was opened in April, 1983. Twenty-six stores were added in 1986-7, versus 12 in 1985-6. Sam's is a membership-only, cash and carry wholesale warehouse operating in metropolitan areas.

Ten distribution centers supplied the stores with some 77% of their merchandise needs in fiscal 1986-7.

Dividend Data

Dividends were initiated in 1973.

Amt. of Divd. $	Date Decl.	Ex-divd. Date	Stock of Record	Payment Date
0.06	Mar. 12	Mar. 17	Mar. 23	Apr. 10'87
0.06	Jun. 4	Jun. 15	Jul. 1	Jul. 10'87
2-for-1	Jun. 4	Jul. 13	Jun. 19	Jul. 10'87
0.03	Aug. 13	Aug. 27	Sep. 2	Oct. 2'87
0.03	Nov. 12	Dec. 7	Dec. 11	Jan. 4'88

Finances

Capital expenditures for 1986-7 were $404 million, excluding leased properties, compared with $351 million in 1985-6, with expenditures financed internally.

Capitalization

Long Term Debt: $1,013,618,000, incl. $825 million of capital lease obligations.

Common Stock: 564,474,000 shs. ($0.10 par). Walton family interests own about 39%. Institutions hold approximately 37%. Shareholders of record: 21,828.

Office—702 Southwest 8th St. (P.O. Box 116), Bentonville, Ark. 72712. Tel—(501) 273-4000. Chrmn & CEO—S. M. Walton. Pres—D. D. Glass. Vice-Chrmn—J. C. Shewmaker. VP-Secy—S. R. Walton. Treas—C. Ratcliff. Dirs—D. R. Banks, H. R. Clinton, J. A. Cooper, Jr., D. D. Glass, A. L. Johnson, J. H. Jones, R. Kahn, C. Lazarus, W. H. Seay, J. Shewmaker, D. G. Soderquist, J. T. Stephens, J. L. Walton, S. M. Walton, S. R. Walton. Transfer Agent & Registrar—Centerre Trust Co., St. Louis, Mo. Incorporated in Delaware in 1969.

Karen J. Sack

TABLE 4.4 A SAMPLE PAGE FROM STANDARD & POOR'S *STOCK GUIDE*

84 **Equ-Exp** Standard & Poor's Corporation

¶S&P 500 •Options Index	Ticker Symbol	Name of Issue (Call Price of Pfd. Stocks)	Market	Com. Rank. & Pfd. Rating	Par Val.	Inst.Hold Cos	Inst.Hold Shs. (000)	Principal Business	Price Range 1971-86 High	1971-86 Low	1987 High	1987 Low	1988 High	1988 Low	Feb. Sales in 100s	February, 1988 Last Sale Or Bid High	Low	Last	%Div. Yield	P-E Ratio
1	EQUI	Equion Corp	OTC	NR	1¢	7	425	Auto air condit'g,heat'g eqp	8⅞	⅛	8⅜	4	5⅞	5	444	5⅞	5	5⅝B	...	9
2	EBNC	Equitable Bancorp	OTC	A—	5	35	3871	Multi-bank hldg: Baltimore	29⅞	2½	29	15¼	24½	18⅞	1249	24½	19½	22B	s4.2	10
3	EQICB	Equitable of Iowa Cl'B'[51]	OTC	B	No	35	3721	Life insurance: dept strs	23¾	4⅜	27	15	19¼	17¼	705	19¼	18½	19B	4.8	15
4	EQM	Equitable R.E.Shop'g[52]	NY,M	NR	No	3	133	Real estate investments	10¾	10	10⅞	6⅞	9⅜	7⅜	1491	9⅜	8⅞	9⅛	11.0	..
5	EQT	Equitable Resources	NY,B,M,Ph	A	No	136	10807	Nat'l gas dstr,Pa,W.Va.&Ky	37⅛	3⅛	46⅞	27¼	36¼	31½	4500	33⅞	31½	33⅝	3.6	18
6	EFG	Equitec Fin'l Group	NY,M	NR	1¢	13	966	Diversified financial svcs	17	6	10	5¼	5⅞	5	744	5⅝	5	5⅜	3.0	d
7	EQTX	Equitex Inc	OTC	NR	0.001	4	1539	Business dvlpm & mgmt	⅛	1/16	¼	1/16	¼	⅛	87261	¼	¼	¼B	...	..
8	ATF	Equity Income Fund[55]	AS,P	NR	No	25	216	1st exch series-AT&T shrs	41⅜	19⅜	44½	30¼	41⅛	35¾	2387	41⅛	39⅜	40¼	5.1	..
9	EQTY	Equity Oil	OTC	B—	1	27	4288	Expl & prod crude oil & gas	27	1	7⅛	3⅜	4¾	3⅝	1524	4¾	4⅛	4¾B	1.1	68
10	EGS	EquityGuard Stock Fund	AS	NR	1¢	1	.6	Closed-end investment co	10⅞	8½	10⅛	7	9	7⅝	1106	9	8	9	1.8	..
11	ERB	Erbamont N.V.	NY,B,M,P	NR	4	45	3710	Int'l pharmaceutical co.	34⅜	8⅞	35	15½	27	18	33036	27	22¾	25⅞	2.3	12
12	ERC	ERC Int'l	NY,B,M	B	5¢	21	1381	Provides engin'g tech svcs	16¾	3	16½	6½	11¾	8⅝	2023	10⅜	8⅝	10⅛	...	9
13	ERICY	Ericsson(LM)Tel'B'ADR	OTC	NR	j50	38	3232	Worldwide telecommunic'ns	64	16⅜	47½	25¼	35	26⅝	6922	35	31⅞	33⅜B	3.6	13
14	ERLY	ERLY Indus	OTC	C	1	5	149	Rice,wine:agric chem	14⅞	⅞	16⅛	5½	8	5⅞	47	7¼	6½	6¾B	...	d
15	ERO	Ero Indus	AS	B	1	16	592	Outdoor sporting goods	12¾	⅛	16⅜	6½	11⅜	7½	658	11⅜	8¼	11¼	...	11

Common and Preferred Stocks **Equ-Exp** 85

Splits ◆ Index	Cash Divs. Ea. Yr. Since	Dividends Latest Payment Per$	Date	Ex. Div.	Total $ So Far 1988	Ind. Rate	Paid 1987	Financial Position Mil-$ Cash& Equiv.	Curr. Assets	Curr. Liab.	Balance Sheet Date	Capitalization Lg Trm Debt Mil-$	Shs. 000 Pfd.	Com.	Earnings $ Per Shr. Years End	1983	1984	1985	1986	1987	Last 12 Mos.	Interim Earnings Period	$ Per Shr. 1986	1987	Index
1	.....	None Paid			....	Nil	....	8.88	41.7	12.2	10-31-87	21.9	8	4194	Jl	d0.01	0.34	•1.08	•△0.52	•0.53	0.61	3 Mo Oct	•0.07	•0.15	1
2◆	1916	Q0.23	3-31-88	3-10	s0.420	0.92	s0.733	Book Value $12.73			12-31-86	p54.5	p2272	±14615	Dc	■0.70	■1.48	▲1.91	2.13	P2.19	2.19				2
3◆	1889	Q0.23	3-9-88	2-17	0.23	0.92	0.91	Equity per shr $29.45			6-30-87	p55.3	...	±8972	Dc	△2.05	1.33	△1.19	△2.60	....	1.23	9 Mo Sep	△2.40	△1.03	3
4	1987	0.25	2-12-88	12-24	0.25	1.00	[53]0.75	Equity per shr $8.59			9-30-87	40.9	...	10700	Dc	....	....	....	....		....	9 Mo Sep		0.18	4
5◆	1950	Q0.30	3-1-88	2-2	0.30	1.20	1.20	5.15	111.	72.0	9-30-87	243.	...	20592	Dc	2.89	4.13	2.85	[54]2.67	E1.90	1.82	12 Mo Sep	2.92	△1.82	5
6◆	1977	Q0.04	12-21-87	12-1	....	0.16	0.16	Equity per shr Neg			7-31-87	42.1	...	4897	Ap	0.54	1.30	1.53	0.76	0.95	d0.72	8 Mo Dec	0.75	d0.92	6
7◆	.....	None Since Public			....	Nil	....	Net Asset Val $0.07			9-30-87	....	...	146004	Dc	§0.02	§0.04	§0.06	§0.06	....	....				7
8◆	1983	0.17	3-1-88	2-10	0.51	2.04	2.04	Net Asset Val $44.74			9-30-87	....	...	25643	Dc	....	§24.55	§31.91	§37.92	....	....				8
9◆	1948	0.05	11-1-87	10-30	....	0.05	1.87	6.15	10.5	2.18	9-30-87	....	...	12265	Dc	0.46	0.35	0.32	d0.06	P△0.07	0.07				9
10	1987	0.04	1-25-88	12-23	0.04	0.16	0.72	Net Asset Val $9.20			2-26-88	....	...	2135	Je	....	....	....	....	§10.33	....				10
11	1984	Q0.15	3-25-88	3-7	0.15	0.60	0.52	608.	1062	685.	9-30-87	229.	...	44261	Dc	0.76	0.76	1.32	1.75	P2.10	2.10				11
12◆	.....	None Since Public			....	Nil	....	2.39	40.0	23.7	9-30-87	14.4	...	4363	Dc	0.36	0.39	0.56	0.08	P1.13	1.13				12
13	1967	1.198	7-1-87	5-18	....	1.20	1.198	2775	24250	12630	j12-31-86	2780	...	±41891	Dc	2.75	2.23	1.99	2.19	....	2.57	9 Mo Sep	0.63	1.01	13
14◆	.....	5% Stk	8-15-64		....	Nil	....	3.94	113.	106.	9-30-87	65.7	...	2146	Mr	d1.14	d2.15	•4.26	•1.45	....	d1.45	9 Mo Dec	1.97	d0.93	14
15◆	.....	0.014	1-16-61	12-22	....	Nil	....	0.12	19.9	7.11	9-30-87	1.05	...	3100	Dc	0.39	0.53	0.60	0.80	P0.98	0.98				15

SOURCE: *Stock Guide*, Standard & Poor's, March 1988. Reprinted by permission.

Corporate Background, Bond Description, Stock Data, Earnings and Finances, and Annual Report with income statements for three years and balance sheets for two years.

2. STOCK REPORT This publication contains information on recent developments in the firm as well as a ten-year summary of income, balance sheet, and share data. The reports also present a price chart and a summary of business activities. Reports are prepared on the more active NYSE, AMEX, and OTC stocks. An example of a stock report is presented in Table 4.3.

3. STOCK GUIDE This is a pocket-sized monthly publication containing basic financial information on over five thousand common and preferred stocks and mutual funds. The guide gives information on price, earnings, dividends, debt, industry classification, institutional holdings, and quality rankings for each security. Two partial pages from the *Stock Guide* are shown in Table 4.4. Notice that the lower panel in Table 4.4 provides additional information about the fifteen companies identified in the upper panel.

4. BOND GUIDE Also a monthly publication, it contains financial information on over four thousand corporate bonds, municipal bonds, and foreign bonds. Table 4.5 shows a page from the *Bond Guide*.

TABLE 4.5 A SAMPLE PAGE FROM STANDARD & POOR'S *BOND GUIDE*

58 Eth-Fid — STANDARD & POOR'S CORPORATION

Title-Industry Code & Co. Finances (In Italics) / Individual Issue Statistics, Exchange	*Ind* / Interest Dates	*Chgs. 1984* / S&P Quality rating	Eligible	*Times Earn. 1985* / Bond Form	*1986 Yr. End* / Legality (Ma NH NY)	*Cash & Eqv* / Redemption Provisions: Refund Earliest/Other	*Current Assets* / Call Price For S.F.	*Liabs Date* / Call Price Regular	*L. Term Debt (Mil $)* / Out-st'd'g (Mil $)	*Debt % Prop* / Underwriter Firm	Year	Price Range 1972-86 High	1972-86 Low	1987 High	1987 Low	1988 High	1988 Low	Mo. End Price Sale(s) or Bid	Curr Yield	Yield to Mat.
Ethyl Nts 11s '95	mN	BBB+	X	R	- - -	....	....	[1]100	100	F2	'85	111⅝	100	112	102⅝	107½	105⅞	107½	10.23	9.59
Exide Corp.	*8*	*1.18*		*1.12*	*0.87 Mr*	*1.43*	*295*	*125 9-87*	*301*	*269*										
SrSubNts[2] 12⅞s '97	Jd15	B-	Y	R	- - -	[3]105	[4]100	[5]107	135	D8	'87	....	....	100	92	105½	99	105½	12.20	11.88
Exxon Capital	*26*	*Subsid of & gtd by Exxon Corp,see*																		
Gtd Nts 6½s '89	mN	AAA	X	R	- ✓ -	....	....	NC	250	M3	'86	99⅞	99¼	100	94⅝	99½	96¾	98¾	6.58	7.31
Exxon Corp	*49c*	*16.78*		*10.45*	*9.01 Dc*	*3020*	*15438*	*14238 9-87*	*4536*	*6.10*										
• SF Deb 6s '97	mN	AAA	X	R	✓ ✓ ✓	....	100	±101	127	M6	'67	93¾	47	89¾	72¼	85	79	s84¼	7.12	8.41
• SF Deb 6½s '98	jJ15	AAA	X	R	✓ ✓ ✓	....	100	±101½	151	M6	'68	99⅛	47¼	93¾	72	86¾	81½	s86	7.56	8.56
Exxon Pipeline	*49*	*Subsid of & gtd by Exxon Corp,see*																		
• Gtd Deb 8¼s 2001	Ms	AAA	X	R	✓ ✓ -	....	100	±103.10	245	M6	'76	106⅝	54⅞	103	81⅞	97	90⅛	95¾	8.62	8.80
• SF Deb[6] 5⅝s '97	Jd	AAA	X	R	- ✓ ✓	....	*100	±101	11.5	M6	'67	92	45	89	79	91	83	82⅝	6.81	8.35
• SF Deb[6] 6⅝s '98	jD	AAA	X	R	✓ ✓ -	....	100	±101½	37.0	M6	'68	95½	47	91	82	No Sale		87	7.61	8.49
Fairchild Indus.	*2b*	*0.69*		*d7.71*	*1.49 Dc*	*125*	*296*	*131 9-87*	*121*	*153*										
• Sub SF Deb 9¾s '98	Ao	B+	X	R	- - -	....	100	100	11.6	Exch	'78	99½	55⅛	94½	82¾	85⅛	83	83½	11.68	12.69
Fairfield Acceptance	*26e*	*1.49*		*1.57*	*1.68 Dc*				*90.5*											
Sr Sub Nts 13½s '92	Jj15	B	Y	R	- - -	....	100	±103¾	26.0	D8	'83	105½	86⅝	100	85	91	88½	88½	15.25	17.73
Fairfield Communities	*38*	*1.69*		*[7]1.20*	*[8]0.28 Dc*	*6.24*		*9-87*	*317*											
• SrSubNts 13¼s '92	aO31	B	Y	R	- - -	[9]103.786	....	[10]±107.571	46.0	D8	'85	103⅛	100	101	90	92	85⅛	s88	15.06	17.08
• SubNts 14¼s '89	jD31	B	Y	R	- - -	[11]...	....	±105.70	35.0	D8	'85	105	96⅜	102	99	No Sale		102½	13.90	12.67
◆SubSFDeb 15⅛s '97	Fa15	B	Y	R	- - -	....	[12]100	100	[13]20.0	D8	'82	102¼	77	102½	102½	No Sale		102½	14.76	14.61
Family Finance	*26a*	*Now Aristar, Inc, see*																		
• Sr Deb 4¾s '90	Mn15	A	X	CR	- - -	z100	....	100	5.87	G2	'65	85	28	92	84⅛	93⅛	88⅛	93⅛	5.09	8.09
Fay's Drug	*58e*	*6.32*		*1.47*	*1.96 Ja*	*N/A*	*108*	*64.1 10-87*	*51.9*	*89.3*										
Sub Deb 13¾s 2005	Mn15	B+	Y	R	- - -	....	[14]100	[15]105	35.0	K1	'85	121⅞	98¾	108¾	101¾	108	104½	108	12.73	12.60
Federal Express	*70b*	*△2.02*		*△3.40*	*△6.42 My*	*66.6*	*617*	*575 11-87*	*★775*	*38.1*										
SrNts 9s '91	Fa	A+	X	R	- ✓ -	....	....	[16]100	100	K1	'86	103⅞	99⅝	104⅛	98¼	101⅛	100⅛	101⅛	8.88	8.45
SrNts 8⅛s '93	Fa15	A+	X	R	- ✓ -	....	....	NC	100	K1	'88	....	....	....	....	99⅝	98¾	99	8.21	8.37
SrNts 10⅝s '95	fA15	A+	X	R	- ✓ -	....	....	[17]100	100	K1	'85	113⅝	99⅛	112⅛	103¼	108⅜	105⅛	108⅛	9.80	9.05
Federal Mogul	*8*	*5.63*		*5.82*	*3.70 Dc*	*10.0*	*391*	*197 9-87*	*163*	*50.0*										
• SF Deb 7½s '98	Jj15	A	X	R	- ✓ -	....	100	±101⅞	5.29	G2	'73	No Sale		89½	81	90	85½	88¾	8.45	9.26
• SF Deb 13s 2005	fA15	A	X	R	- ✓ -	[18]106½	[19]100	±108.45	30.4	G2	'80	113	92¾	No Sale		No Sale		108	12.04	11.90
• Nts 8⅜s '93	aO	A	X	R	- ✓ -	....	....	NC	100	P1	'86	100	100	92½	92½	No Sale		100	8.38	8.38
Federal Paper Board	*16c*	*3.14*		*1.28*	*2.11 Dc*	*2.72*	*238*	*133 9-87*	*344*	*38.6*										
• SF Deb 7.85s '97	Jd	BB+	Y	R	- - -	....	100	±101.96	18.8	G2	'72	No Sale		91¾	80	82	82	82½	9.52	10.90
Federal Realty Inv Tr	*56*	*2.40*		*2.19*	*1.50 Dc*				*282*											
Sr Nts 8.65s '96	Ao	BBB+	X	R	- - -	....	....	[20]101	50.0	S1	'86	100	92½	102	82	87½	84⅛	87½	9.89	11.02
Federated Dept Stores[21]	*58f*	*5.75*		*7.24*	*8.11 Ja*	*96.4*	*3547*	*2106 10-87*	*973*	*38.2*										
• SF Deb 8⅜s '95	mS15	AA-	X	R	- ✓ -	....	100	±101.14	20.0	L4	'70	109	60⅛	102⅛	95	95¾	90	92¾	9.03	9.75
• SF Deb 7⅛s 2002	Ms15	AA-	X	R	- ✓ -	....	100	102.138	37.3	L4	'72	101½	50	93	87¼	No Sale		91⅛	7.82	8.20
• SF Deb 10¼s 2010	Jd15	AA-	X	R	✓ ✓ -	[22]105⅝	[23]100	±106¾	39.7	L4	'80	107¾	67	104	101	96⅝	96	s96	10.68	10.72
• SF Deb 10⅝s 2013	Mn	AA-	X	R	- ✓ -	[24]105.188	[25]100	±108.30	13.9	L4	'83	108	87¼	107½	105	No Sale		106¾	9.95	9.89
SF Deb 9½s 2016	Ms	AA-	X	R	- ✓ -	[26]104¾	[27]100	±108.55	100	S3	'86	106¾	99	105⅛	89¾	100½	88½	88½	10.73	10.81
Nts 9⅜s '92	mN	AA-	X	R	- ✓ -	....	....	NC	200	S3	'87	....	....	101⅛	100	101⅛	101	101	9.28	9.10
Nts 7⅞s '96	jD15	AA-	X	R	- ✓ -	....	....	[28]100	200	G2	'86	99¼	99¼	100⅝	85¾	90⅜	85⅞	86½	9.10	10.24
Ferro Corp	*14*	*3.18*		*2.54*	*2.36 Dc*	*46.1*	*314*	*163 9-87*	*63.3*	*38.7*										
Deb 11¾s 2000	aO15	BBB+	X	R	- - -	....	....	[29]100	49.9	F2	'85	115⅛	100	112	104	107⅞	104⅛	107⅞	10.89	10.60
Fidelcor&Inc[30]	*10a*	*1.68*		*1.87*	*1.97 Dc*				*185*											
F/R[31]Sub Nts[32] 7.062s '97	QMy2	BBB+	X	R	- - -	....	....	[33]100	75.0	B11	'85	100	97	100	90	95	90	95	7.43	....

Uniform Footnote Explanations—See Page 1. Other: [1]Fr 11-1-92. [2]Red at 100 if Net Worth levels not net. [3]Red rest'n(13%)to 6-15-92. [4]Fr 6-15-95. [5]Fr 6-15-90. [6]Was Humble P.L. [7]Fiscal Feb'86 & prior. [8]10 Mo Dec,'86. [9]Red rest'n(13 1/4%)to 10-31-90. [10]Fr 10-31-88. [11]Red rest'n(14 1/4%). [12]Fr 2-15-90. [13]Incl disc. [14]Fr 5-15-95. [15]Fr 5-15-90. [16]Fr 2-1-89. [17]Fr 8-15-92. [18]Red rest'n(13%)to 8-15-90. [19]Fr 8-15-91. [20]Fr 4-1-93. [21]See Rich's Inc. [22]Red rest'n(10.345%)to 6-15-90. [23]Fr 6-15-91. [24]Red rest'n(10.65%)to 5-1-93. [25]Fr 5-1-94. [26]Red rest'n(9.53%)to 3-1-96. [27]Fr 3-1-97. [28]Fr 12-15-93. [29]Fr 10-15-95. [30]See Fidelity Bank. [31]Int min 5 1/4%. [32]To 5-5-88,adj aft as defined. [33]Fr 5-2-89.

SOURCE: *Bond Guide*, Standard & Poor's, March 1988. Reprinted by permission.

5. OUTLOOK This publication presents a weekly commentary on the stock market, recommendations on particular industries and firms, and a market forecast.

Moody's Investor Service

Moody's Investor Service publishes a number of manuals and reports:

1. MANUAL Moody's publishes an annual set of volumes entitled *Moody's Manuals*: *Municipal and Government*; *Industrial*; *Bank and Finance*; *Transportation*; *Public Utility*; *Transportation*; *OTC–Industrials*; *International*. The manuals contain information on thousands of firms. For each firm, there is a brief history, a business summary, financial statements for two years, and a description of the firm's financial structure. All manuals are updated twice a week in separate binders. The information in *Moody's Manuals* is similar to but more complete than that published in *Standard & Poor's Corporate Records*.

2. HANDBOOK OF WIDELY HELD COMMON STOCK This handbook is issued four times per year and gives a one-page write-up on more than one thousand common stocks. The *Handbook* gives a stock price chart, financial statistics, recent developments, and prospects for each common stock. A page from the *Handbook* is shown in Table 4.6.

3. BOND SURVEY This is a weekly publication that provides information on bond market trends, prospective issues, and investment recommendations. It also provides ratings on new preferred stocks, bank ratings, and commercial paper, and a listing of Prospective Offering—Shelf Registrations under SEC Rule 415.

4. BOND RECORD The *Bond Record* covers over 48,200 issues and situations, with detailed information on approximately 9,100 corporate, municipal, and foreign bonds. The *Record* also rates preferred stocks, commercial paper, and shelf registrations, as well as industrial development revenue bonds and pollution and environmental control revenue bonds.

Value Line

The *Value Line Investment Survey* is one of the most popular advisory services used by individual investors. It is published each week and reports on over 1,700 stocks in ninety-three industries. Each stock is covered once a quarter (see Table 4.7), and "Ratings and Reports" provides a weekly stock update to keep the reports current. The "Summary and Index" provides a weekly update of the ratings on each stock.

Each week Value Line evaluates specific industries and the major firms within the industries. Every report gives a brief discussion of business prospects, financial and operating statistics, and a graph of stock-prices-to-cash-flow. Value Line also gives projections of the firm's financial and operating ratios as well as a three- to five-year estimate of price performance. A unique feature of the *Investment Survey* is its scoring system. Each stock is ranked from 1 to 5 for timeliness (relative price performance in the next twelve months) and for safety. A score of 5 presents the lowest expected performance or safety, and a score of 1 represents the highest

TABLE 4.6 A SAMPLE PAGE FROM MOODY'S *HANDBOOK*

CASTLE & COOKE, INC.

LISTED	SYM.	LTPS•	STPS•	IND. DIV.	REC. PRICE	RANGE (52-WKS.)	YLD.
NYSE	CKE	100.6	94.6	...	18	27 - 12	...

SPECULATIVE GRADE. IRREGULAR EARNINGS CONTINUE AS A RESULT OF THE VOLATILE PRICES OF BANANAS.

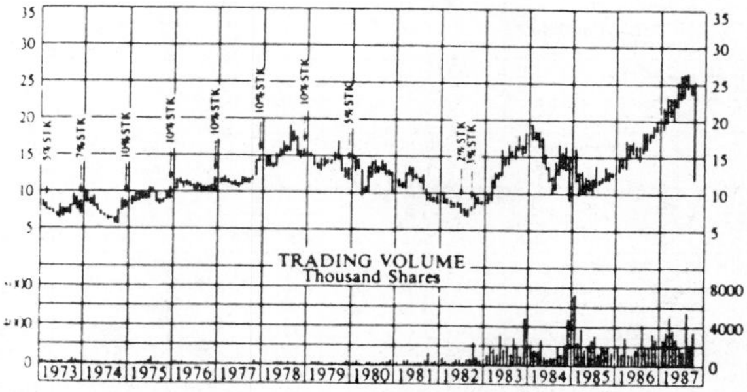

CAPITALIZATION: (1/3/87)

	(000)	(%)
Long-Term Debt	m$384,962	32.6
Redeem Pfd.	117,015	9.9
Pfd.	37,500	3.2
Defer. Inc. Tax	148,585	12.6
Minority Int.	22,751	1.9
Com. & Surp.	469,937	39.8
Total	$1,180,750	100.0

Shs. (np)-47,117,965

INTERIM EARNINGS:

Qtr.	Sept.	Dec.	Mar.	June
1985-86e	d0.03	d0.21	...	...
Qtr.	**3/31**	**6/30**	**9/30**	**12/31**
1986j	0.23	0.80	0.36	d0.06
1987	0.37	0.52	...	...

INTERIM DIVIDENDS:

Amt.	Dec.	Ex.	Rec.	Pay.
2.5%	4/30/82	6/7/82	6/11/82	7/5/82
2.5%	8/13	9/3	9/10	10/4
stk. (b)	...	7/23/85	7/1/85	7/22/85

BACKGROUND:

Castle & Cooke operates in three industry segments: food products, transportation equipment leasing, and real estate development. Food products operates through Dole Food Company which is the world's largest producer of pineapples and the second largest marketer of bananas. The Company also supplies other fresh and processed fruit and fresh vegetables. Operations are in North America, Latin America, and the Far East. Real estate development activities are conducted through CKE's wholly owned nonconsolidated subsidiary, Oceanic Properties, Inc. D.H. Murdock, the Company's chairman and chief executive officer holds 25.3% of the outstanding shares of CKE stock.

RECENT DEVELOPMENTS:

In October, Castle & Cooke completed the sale of Flexi-Van Corporation for $164.0 million, to holders of CKE. In September, CKE agreed to acquire the operations of Tenneco West, Inc. from Tenneco Inc. for $236.0 million. Tenneco West owns farmland and fruit and nut businesses. Also, CKE agreed to acquire Apache Corp.'s California agricultural properties for $68.0 million and the assumption of $24.0 million in debt. For the twelve weeks ended 6/20/87, income from continuing operations declined 26%. Revenues were 1% lower.

PROSPECTS:

Near-term results should show improvement. New products are performing well and favorable foreign exchange rates should aid earnings. Dole Foods intends on expanding further into more fresh fruits and vegetables as demand, particularly in the United States, is increasing. Dole packaged foods is experiencing higher processed pineapple volume. Worldwide distribution costs have declined. Banana prices have shown signs of recovering.

STATISTICS:

YEAR	GROSS REVS. ($mil.)	OPER. PROFIT MARGIN %	RET. ON EQUITY %	NET INCOME ($mil.)	WORK CAP. ($mil.)	SENIOR CAPITAL ($mil.)	SHARES (000)	EARN. PER SH.$	DIV. PER SH.$	DIV. PAY. %	PRICE RANGE	P/E RATIO	AVG. YIELD %
6/30													
78	1,329.6	7.8	11.4	47.6	291.9	328.0	26,527	1.81	0.66	37	19⅜ - 11⅞	9.0	4.0
79	1,593.4	5.6	7.2	31.0	301.9	345.8	27,947	1.31	0.72	64	15 - 9⅝	12.8	5.0
80	1,733.0	5.2	6.8	32.1	354.0	397.4	26,742	1.06	0.76	71	13¾ - 8⅝	11.6	6.2
81	c892.5	8.4	6.1	c30.3	356.4	364.1	26,826	c1.04	0.58	55	14⅛ - 8¾	10.7	5.1
82	1,823.0	1.7	2.0	n9.7	356.6	299.0	27,993	n0.18	0.38	—	10¾ - 7	49.3	4.3
83	1,551.7	1.5	—	d39.0	304.3	320.2	28,007	d1.57	Nil	—	18½ - 8⅝	—	—
84	1,520.1	1.9	0.3	a1.1	273.8	384.6	25,618	ad0.31	Nil	—	19⅝ - 9⅛	—	—
85	1,600.6	2.9	3.3	ad9.6	201.9	336.4	25,725	ad0.73	Nil	—	16⅜ - 9⅞	—	—
e85	803.5	—	—	d9.8	—	—	—	d0.24	—	—	-	—	—
86	**1,737.9**	**7.6**	**16.1**	**j75.6**	**184.9**	**539.5**	**47,118**	**j1.28**	**Nil**	**—**	**20¼ - 13**	**13.0**	**—**

•Long-Term Price Score — Short-Term Price Score; See page 4a. STATISTICS ARE AS ORIGINALLY REPORTED. Adjusted for all stock dividends up to 10/82. a-From continuing operations. b-0.032 share of common & 0.111 share of $0.90 conv. pref. for each share held. c-For the 24 weeks ended 6/20/81. e-Results for six months as fiscal year changed to end 12/31. j-Bef. loss from disc. opers. of $31.7 mil. m-Includes capital lease obligations. n-Before extraordinary items: 1982, cr$2.8 million (10c a sh.).

INCORPORATED:
Dec. 29, 1894 — Hawaii

PRINCIPAL OFFICE:
10900 Wilshire Blvd.
Los Angeles, CA 90024
Tel: (213) 842-1500

ANNUAL MEETING:
In May

NUMBER OF STOCKHOLDERS:
21,000

TRANSFER AGENT(S):
Morgan Shareholder Services Trust Co., N Y
Manufacturers Hanover Trust Co. of S.F., CA
Hawaiian Trust Co., Ltd., Honolulu

REGISTRAR(S):

INSTITUTIONAL HOLDINGS:
No. of Institutions: 144
Shares Held: 27,725,087

OFFICERS:
Chairman & C.E.O.
D.H. Murdock
Sr. V.P. & C.F.O.
W.H. Frank
V.P. & Sec.
A.B. Sellers
Treasurer
D.B. Cooper, Jr.

SOURCE: *Moody's Handbook of Widely Held Common Stocks*, Moody's, Winter 1987–88. Reprinted by permission.

TABLE 4.7   A SAMPLE STOCK REPORT FROM VALUE LINE *INVESTMENT SURVEY*

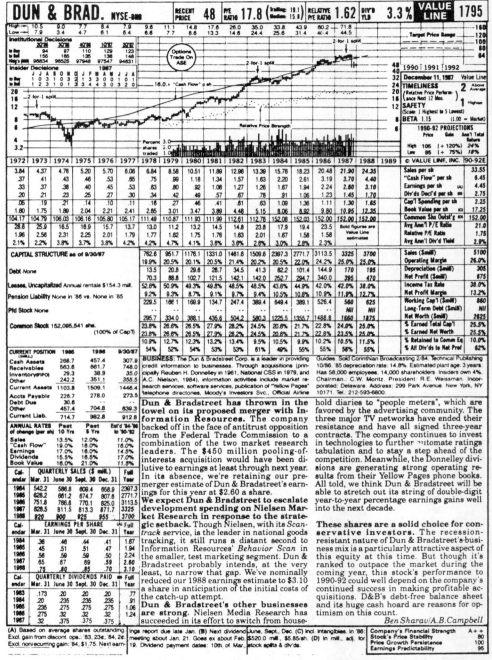

Factual material is obtained from sources believed to be reliable, but the publisher is not responsible for any errors or omissions contained herein.

SOURCE: *Value Line Investment Survey,* "Ratings and Reports," vol. 43, no. 2, Value Line, 11 December 1987, p. 1795. © 1988 by Value Line, Inc., used by permission of Value Line, Inc.

performance or safety. Value Line also publishes *Value Line Options* and *Value Line Convertibles* and reports on OTC situations.

Other Advisory Services

In addition to Standard & Poor's, Moody's, and Value Line, there are a number of specialized advisory services. Some of the more popular services include *The Astute Investor, Dow Theory Letters, The Elliott Wave Theorist, The Holt Investment Advisory, The Independent Investor, The Professional Tape Reader, United and Babson Investment Report*, and the *Zweig Forecast*. Advertisements for advisory services frequently appear in such publications as *Barron's* and *The Wall Street Journal*. Often these advisory services offer inexpensive trial subscriptions.

For the technician who feels that insights into future price movements can be obtained from past price movements, there are a number of chart services. A few of the better-known services are *Daily Graphs, Technical Trends*, and Trendline's *Daily Action Charts*.

COMPUTERIZED DATA BASES

Overview

In addition to the published financial information discussed above, a number of firms sell computerized information. Large data bases are available on tape and are processed on mainframe computers. Smaller data bases are available for the personal computer, on floppy disks. Some sources provide both versions of the data. In addition, large amounts of data are available on CD disks which, with a CD reader, can be accessed by the personal computer.

Compustat

Compustat tapes are produced by Standard & Poor's Corporation. The tapes are segmented into industrials, OTC companies, banks, utilities, bankrupt companies, and Canadian companies. Data is provided in annual and quarterly formats. The 175-item annual and 100-item quarterly data tapes cover twenty years of company financial data as well as stock price and trading volume information on approximately 10,000 companies, including 6,400 actively traded companies on the OTC, regional, and national exchanges. The data is updated monthly. Compustat also produces a price-dividend-earnings, PDE, tape for over 5,700 stocks, beginning in 1962. Smaller versions of the Compustat tapes are available on floppy disk for the personal computer.

CRSP

The Center for Research in Security Prices, CRSP, tape is produced by the University of Chicago. The CRSP tapes provide monthly stock price, dividend, and return information for every stock on the NYSE, from 1926 to the present. Daily tapes provide the same information from 1962 to the present. Tapes are also available for market indices on a monthly and daily basis.

ISL

The ISL tapes, produced quarterly by Interactive Data Corporation, provide daily price and volume data on all NYSE and AMEX stocks and some OTC stocks. Quarterly earnings and dividends are also included.

Value Line Data Base

Data Base provides information on the 1,700 companies covered by Value Line Investment Services, consisting of financial and market data, on an annual and quarterly basis. In addition to the historical data, Data Base provides forecasts of various financial and market items for the coming year. Value Line also provides data disks for personal computers.

MARKET INDICES

"What did the market do today?" is possibly the question most asked by investors every day. Why should investors be concerned with a market index or the aggregate movement of stock prices?

First, market indicators are used as a measure of performance. Investors use a market index as a base measure of how well their portfolio has performed. Since security prices tend to move together, investors feel that their portfolio should perform, on a risk-adjusted basis, at least as well as the market index.

Second, market indices are used to determine if there is a relationship between historical price movements and economic variables. By analyzing market indices and economic variables over time, the analyst can determine relationships between the market and such variables as interest rates, money supply, and GNP. The market index may be used for forecasting since it has been found to be a leading indicator of the economy.

Third, market indices are used to determine future price movements. Technical analysts believe that stock prices move in identifiable patterns. By identifying patterns in stock price movements, technicians use past price movements to predict future movements.

Finally, market indices are used to determine systematic risk for individual securities and portfolios. Systematic risk measures the relationship of the security return to the return of the market. By regressing security or portfolio returns to market returns over a period of time, the analyst can determine the systematic risk, or beta, for the security or portfolio. This concept will be fully developed in Chapter 6.

Although market indicators tend to move up and down together, there may be substantial differences in the magnitudes of the movements. It is therefore important to understand how market indicators are constructed in order to understand why the movements of the indicators are different. The factors that affect market indicators are the population from which the indicator is drawn, the

TABLE 4.8   MAJOR INDICES AS OF FEBRUARY 5, 1988

	12-MONTH HIGH	12-MONTH LOW		WEEKLY HIGH	WEEKLY LOW	FRIDAY CLOSE	FRIDAY CHG.	WEEKLY % CHG.	12-MONTH CHG.	12-MONTH % CHG.	CHANGE FROM 12/31	CHANGE FROM % CHG.
Dow Jones Averages												
30 Indus	2722.42	1738.74		1952.92	1910.48	1910.48	(47.74)	(2.44)	(276.39)	(12.64)	28.35	1.46
20 Transp	1101.16	661.00		771.16	758.57	758.57	(5.72)	(0.75)	(165.61)	(17.92)	9.71	1.30
15 Utilities	227.49	160.98		188.77	185.57	186.28	(3.74)	(1.97)	(39.88)	(17.63)	11.20	6.40
65 Comp	992.21	653.76		731.22	717.36	717.36	(14.04)	(1.92)	(124.60)	(14.80)	3.09	0.43
New York Stock Exchange												
Comp	187.99	125.91		143.61	141.35	141.35	(2.78)	(1.93)	(18.58)	(11.62)	3.12	2.26
Indus	231.05	149.43		170.34	167.51	167.51	(3.69)	(2.16)	(20.66)	(10.98)	0.47	0.28
Utilities	80.22	61.63		73.70	72.88	72.88	(1.09)	(1.47)	(6.62)	(8.33)	5.57	8.28
Transp	168.20	104.76		123.52	121.16	121.16	(1.72)	(1.40)	(15.21)	(11.15)	2.59	2.18
Finan	165.36	107.39		125.91	123.91	123.91	(1.43)	(1.14)	(33.46)	(21.26)	9.34	8.15
Standard & Poor's Indexes												
500 Index	336.77	223.92		255.57	250.96	250.96	(6.11)	(2.38)	(29.08)	(10.38)	3.88	1.57
400 Indus	393.17	255.43		291.83	286.47	286.47	(7.23)	(2.46)	(29.82)	(9.43)	0.61	0.21
20 Transp	274.20	167.59		195.92	192.24	192.24	(2.18)	(1.12)	(33.75)	(14.93)	2.07	1.09
40 Utilities	121.82	91.80		112.46	110.73	110.89	(2.38)	(2.10)	(10.93)	(8.97)	8.77	8.59
40 Finan	32.56	20.39		23.75	23.20	23.20	(0.56)	(2.36)	(6.77)	(22.59)	1.57	7.26
NASDAQ												
OTC Comp	455.26	291.88		347.19	343.71	345.75	1.09	0.32	(61.16)	(15.03)	15.28	4.62
Indus	488.92	288.30		345.08	340.44	341.73	(3.24)	(0.94)	(79.93)	(18.96)	2.79	0.82
Insur	475.78	333.66		402.83	396.61	402.83	8.98	2.28	(50.74)	(11.19)	51.77	14.75
Banks	526.64	365.63		433.64	429.31	433.64	7.97	1.87	(58.55)	(11.90)	42.98	11.00
NMS Comp	195.36	124.98		149.87	148.32	149.25	0.54	0.36	(24.99)	(14.34)	6.66	4.67
NMS Indus	187.94	110.21		133.15	131.28	131.83	(1.22)	(0.92)	(28.99)	(18.03)	0.72	0.55
Others												
AMEX	365.01	231.90		270.14	268.96	270.11	1.01	0.38	(46.62)	(14.72)	9.76	3.75
Value-Line	289.02	181.09		211.58	210.49	210.92	0.19	0.09	(48.78)	(18.78)	9.30	4.61
Wilshire 5000	3299.44	2188.11		2513.58	2478.57	2478.57	(39.24)	(1.56)	(339.91)	(12.06)	61.45	2.54
Russell 1000	176.22	117.65		135.16	133.05	133.05	(2.50)	(1.84)	(16.88)	(11.26)	3.03	2.33
Russell 2000	174.44	106.07		125.94	125.38	125.77	0.53	0.42	(31.97)	(20.27)	5.35	4.44
Russell 3000	188.97	125.26		142.22	142.14	142.14	(2.40)	(1.66)	(19.49)	(12.06)	3.47	2.50

SOURCE: *Barron's*, 8 Feb. 1988, p. 138. Reprinted courtesy of *Barron's Weekly*.

method of weighting the components of the indicator, and the method of computing the indicator.

Table 4.8 shows the major stock market indices, as reported in *Barron's*.

The Dow Jones Averages

The Dow Jones Industrial Average, DJIA, is the oldest and best known of the market indicators. The answer to "What did the market do today?" is usually based on the change in the DJIA, or "the Dow." The DJIA was begun in 1896, with twelve stocks in the average. Today, the Dow comprises thirty common stocks whose identities change from time to time because of bankruptcy, merger, or lack of trading. Of the original twelve stocks in the DJIA, only one remains: General Electric. The thirty stocks currently in the DJIA are large, well-known industrial stocks that are among the leaders of their respective industries (see Table 4.9).

The DJIA is a price-weighted series computed by adding the prices of the thirty stocks and dividing by a divisor that is adjusted for stock splits and stock dividends in excess of 10 percent. A simple example will help explain the divisor adjustment technique. Assume that each of the thirty stocks has a price of $2 per share. The average would have a value of 2 (60 ÷ 30). If one of the stocks had a two-for-one split and no other prices changed except for the impact of the split stock, going from $2 per share to $1 per share, then the average should remain at 2. By adjusting the divisor from 30 to 29.5 (59 ÷ $x = 2$; $x = 29.5$), the average remains at 2.

The method of calculating the average has resulted in several criticisms. First, high-priced stocks carry more weight than low-priced stocks in the average. As shown in Table 4.10, a 10 percent increase in Alpha common stock causes a 6.1 percent change in the average, but a 10 percent increase in the lower priced Gamma stock results in only a 0.8 percent increase in the value of the average. Thus, price changes in high-priced stocks cause the average to move more than

TABLE 4.9 THE THIRTY DOW JONES
INDUSTRIAL STOCKS AS OF APRIL 1988

Allied-Signal	International Paper
Aluminum Co.	McDonald's
American Express	Merck & Co.
AT&T	Minnesota M & M
Bethlehem Steel	Navistar
Boeing	Phillip Morris
Chevron	Primerica
Coca-Cola	Procter & Gamble
DuPont	Sears Roebuck
Eastman Kodak	Texaco
Exxon	USX Corp.
General Electric	Union Carbide
General Motors	United Technology
Goodyear	Westinghouse
IBM	Woolworth

SOURCE: *Barron's*.

TABLE 4.10 EFFECT OF 10 PERCENT CHANGE IN HIGH-PRICED VS. LOW-PRICED STOCKS ON PRICE-WEIGHTED AVERAGE

| STOCK | ORIGINAL VALUE | 10 PERCENT CHANGE IN VALUE | |
		HIGH-PRICED STOCK	LOW-PRICED STOCK
Alpha	$160	$176	$160
Beta	80	80	80
Gamma	20	20	22
Sum	$260	$276	$262
Divisor	3.0	3.0	3.0
Average	86.67	92.0	87.33
Percentage Change		6.1%	0.8%

may be indicated by a change in the overall market. In like manner, when high-priced stocks split, they create a downward bias in the average. Table 4.11 shows that when Alpha splits two for one, a new divisor must be calculated to keep the average constant. Now a ten percent increase in Alpha increases the average by only 4.4 percent instead of 6.1 percent. It should be pointed out that the best-performing stocks are those that rise in price and have a high probability of splitting with a resulting downward bias in the average.

Another criticism of the DJIA is that the divisor is not adjusted for stock dividends smaller than 10 percent. This also creates a downward bias in the value of the average since the numerator (price) is reduced by small stock dividends, with no corresponding adjustment in the divisor.

The final criticism is that the average comprises only thirty large industrial stocks. The use of only thirty stocks to represent the entire stock market is questionable. Since the average reflects the price changes of only large firms, it is claimed that the DJIA is not representative of price changes in the broader stock market.

The Dow Jones Company also compiles the Dow Jones Transportation Average, DJTA, which is composed of twenty stocks in the transportation industry; the Dow Jones Utility Average, DJUA, composed of fifteen utility stocks; and a composite average of the sixty-five stocks. These averages are also price-weighted measures.

TABLE 4.11 EFFECT OF TWO-FOR-ONE STOCK SPLIT ON PRICE-WEIGHTED AVERAGE

STOCK	ORIGINAL VALUE	AFTER SPLIT	10% CHANGE IN ALPHA VALUE
Alpha	$160	$ 80	$ 88
Beta	80	80	80
Gamma	20	20	20
Sum	$260	$180	$188
Divisor	3.0	2.077	2.077
Average	86.67	86.67	90.52
Percentage Change			4.4%

Standard & Poor's Stock Indices

Standard & Poor's Corporation computes five indices: a 400-stock industrial index, a 40-stock utility index, a 20-stock transportation index, a 40-stock financial index, and a 500-stock composite index. S&P must occasionally replace stocks in its indices as is done in the Dow Averages. As of April 6, 1988, S&P announced that it would vary the number of stocks included in the subindices. This change will allow more "flexibility" in constructing the indices.

The S&P indices overcome many of the disadvantages of the Dow Jones averages. First, the S&P indices are value weighted rather than price weighted. A value-weighted index is computed by summing the market value of all stocks in the index and dividing by the aggregate market value of the stocks in the base period. Market value (capitalization) is computed by multiplying the current price of the stock by the number of shares outstanding. The S&P 500 Index is calculated as shown in Equation 4.1. The base period value for the index was initially set at 10; thus, the ratio of current market value to base period market value is multiplied by 10.

$$\text{S\&P 500 Index} = \frac{\sum\limits_{i=1}^{500} P_{ic} \times Q_{ic}}{\sum\limits_{i=1}^{500} P_{io} \times Q_{io}} \times 10 \tag{4.1}$$

where P_{ic} = Current price of the ith stock

Q_{ic} = Current number of shares outstanding for the ith stock

P_{io} = Original price of the ith stock in the base period, 1941–43

Q_{io} = Original number of shares outstanding for the ith stock in the base period, 1941–43

TABLE 4.12   CALCULATION OF A VALUE-WEIGHTED INDEX

STOCK	PRICE	BASE YEAR NUMBER OF SHARES OUTSTANDING	TOTAL MARKET VALUE (CAPITALIZATION)
Alpha	$160	1,000,000	$160,000,000
Beta	80	40,000,000	3,200,000,000
Gamma	20	20,000,000	400,000,000
			$3,760,000,000

STOCK	PRICE	ONE YEAR LATER NUMBER OF SHARES OUTSTANDING	TOTAL MARKET VALUE (CAPITALIZATION)
Alpha	$90	2,000,000	$ 180,000,000 (2-for-1 split)
Beta	75	40,000,000	3,000,000,000
Gamma	25	22,000,000	550,000,000 (10% stock dividend)
			$3,730,000,000

$$\text{Index} = \frac{\$3,730,000,000}{\$3,760,000,000} \times 10 = .9920 \times 10 = 9.920$$

An illustration of the computation of a three-stock, value-weighted index with a base period value of 10 is shown in Table 4.12.

The second advantage of a value-weighted index is that stock splits and dividends do not affect the index value since the adjusted price and the new number of shares outstanding are used in the calculations. High-captialization stocks will have a major effect on the index value. Thus, although the S&P indices eliminate the small-sample problem of the DJIA, they are still dominated by the larger firms.

New York Stock Exchange Indices

In 1966, the New York Stock Exchange, NYSE, established the NYSE Common Stock Indices. The indices consist of a Composite Index, composed of *all* stocks listed on the NYSE, and four subindices: Industrial, Transportation, Utility, and Financial. The base value of the index is 50 (the base year ended December 31, 1965). The NYSE indices are value weighted and thus suffer from the effects of the price movements of large firms. However, the index is not subject to the small-sample criticism since it covers all stocks listed on the NYSE.

American Stock Exchange Indices

On September 4, 1973, the American Stock Exchange introduced a market value index which replaced a price change index used since April 1966. As of July 1983, the base level of the index was 50. The index is composed of common stocks, American Depository Receipts (ADRs), and warrants. The AMEX also computes sixteen subindices, including eight industrial and eight geographic groupings.

NASDAQ Indices

The National Association of Security Dealers produces ten indices. The NASDAQ/NMS Composite index contains over 4,200 securities. The National Market System, NMS, has developed since 1979 and consists of actively traded issues with a number of market makers for each security. The subindices include Industrial, Bank, Other Financial, Insurance, Utility, Transportation, NASDAQ/NMS Industrial, NASDAQ-100, and the NASDAQ-Financial Index. The indices are computed in a manner similar to that of the S&P and NYSE indices. The base period value for the indices is 100.

Value Line Index

The *Value Line Investment Survey* began publishing its Composite Index in 1963. The index is an equally weighted geometric average of stock prices. As discussed in Chapter 2, there is a downward bias to geometric averages relative to arithmetic averages. An index using a geometric average will rise more slowly and decrease more rapidly than an index that uses arithmetic averaging. However, because the index is geometric, low-priced stocks have the same effect as high-priced stocks on the index. These differences in equally weighted arithmetic and geometric stock averages are illustrated in Table 4.13.

TABLE 4.13   ARITHMETIC VERSUS GEOMETRIC STOCK AVERAGES

STOCK	LOWER PRICES	BASE PERIOD PRICES	HIGHER PRICES
Alpha	$90	$100	$110
Beta	95	100	105
Gamma	85	100	118
Arithmetic Average	$90	$100	$111
Percentage Change from Base Period Price	−10.00%	—	+11.00%
Geometric Average*	$89.87	$100	$110.82
Percentage Change from Base Period Price	−10.13%	—	+10.82%

* Calculated as the 3rd root of the product of the three stock prices, or $[(P_1)(P_2)(P_3)]^{.333}$

The Wilshire 5000

The Wilshire 5000 Index is a value-weighted index published by Wilshire Associates. The index represents the market value of all NYSE and AMEX stocks, as well as the most active OTC stocks.

SUMMARY

This chapter discussed the major sources of investment information on the economy, an industry, and an individual firm.

The United States government is the primary source of information on economic activity. Three major sources of government information are *The Federal Reserve Bulletin*, *Survey of Current Business*, and *Business Conditions Digest*.

A number of sources provide information for evaluating specific industries. Various government publications provide aggregate information on industries. In addition, business and financial publications such as *The Wall Street Journal*, *Forbes*, and *Business Week* provide industry information. Trade journals are also excellent sources of information on industries. Financial services such as Value Line and Standard & Poor's provide information on industries and individual firms.

Corporate annual reports are an important source of information about individual firms. A variety of advisory services and newsletters provide information on specific industries and firms. Moody's, Standard & Poor's, and Value Line are the major advisory services.

In addition to published financial information, a number of services provide computerized data bases. Data bases are available on tape for mainframes and on floppy disk and CDs for the personal computer. Individual investors also have access to on-line financial services, such as the Dow Jones News Retrieval Service, and computer programs to assist in security analysis and portfolio management.

Lastly, the chapter discussed the importance of market indices, how they are calculated, and their strengths and weaknesses.

QUESTIONS

1. Where can you find graphical representation of key economic variables?
2. Name two sources of information on the chemical industry.
3. What publications would be useful in forecasting economic activity?
4. Explain how the Dow Jones averages and the Standard & Poor's indices are constructed. In what way are the S&P indices superior to the Dow Jones averages?
5. What does the Value Line Investment Survey rating of "5" mean?
6. What source of information provides quality ratings for common stocks and bonds?
7. You want to determine the relationship between stock returns and the S&P 500 index. Where would you find the information?
8. What information does Value Line provide that is not provided by S&P and Moodys?
9. You want to determine the relationship between GNP and the toy industry. What sources of information would help you make this determination?
10. Where could an investor obtain historical daily stock prices for all NYSE stocks?
11. Using the stock report for Dun and Bradstreet (Table 4.7), what is the stock's timeliness and safety? Expected growth rate of earnings to 1990–1992? Projected price for 1990–1992?
12. Using Table 4.4, what stock has the highest quality rating according to Standard & Poor's? When was its most recent dividend paid? Does the company have preferred stock?

REFERENCES

Barron's: Dow Jones & Co., Inc., Chicopee, MA.

Business Conditions Digest: Department of Commerce, Washington, DC.

Daily Graphs: William O'Neil & Co., Los Angeles, CA.

Dow Jones News/Retrieval: Princeton, NJ.

Economic Report of the President: United States Government Printing Office, Washington, DC.

Federal Reserve Bulletin: Division of Administration Services, Board of Governors of the Federal Reserve System, Washington, DC.

Interactive Data Corporation: New York, NY.

Media General Financial Services: Richmond, VA.

Moody's *Handbook of Widely Held Common Stocks*: Moody's Investor Services, Inc., New York, NY.

Standard & Poor's *Bond Guide*: Standard & Poor's Corporation, New York, NY.

Standard & Poor's *Stock Guide*: Standard & Poor's Corporation, New York, NY.

Standard & Poor's *Stock Reports*: Standard & Poor's Corporation, New York, NY.

Value Line Investment Survey, "Ratings and Reports," New York, NY.

Wall Street Journal: Dow Jones & Co., Inc., Chicopee, MA.

The Wall Street Transcript: New York, NY.

APPENDIX 4A

INVESTMENT INFORMATION AND THE PERSONAL COMPUTER

The investor can create a system that provides considerable financial information through the use of a computer, modem, software, and an on-line service. Investors can research and analyze individual securities, receive news on companies, monitor stock prices, place buy and sell orders, and perform portfolio management all through the screens of their personal computers, PCs.

While the use of a PC makes it easier to gather information and track security prices, it does not ensure that your investments will be more profitable. To be successful in investing, you must have a good knowledge of investment techniques and be willing to spend time to stay informed of market developments and changes in economic activity. The remainder of this appendix will look at each of the components of a personal investment system.

HARDWARE   The hardware for your system comprises the computer, monitor, modem, and printer. The computer and monitor normally come as a single unit. The computer should be fully IBM compatible since much of the better software can be run only on an IBM PC. The computer memory should be at least 512K and have a double disk drive. Larger data bases, such as *Compustat II*, require a hard disk. A monochrome monitor is normally sufficient, although some software creates graphs that are easier to view on a color monitor. A modem is necessary to connect the computer to an information source via the telephone lines. The modem should be able to transmit information at either 300 baud or 1200 baud. Substantial savings can be achieved by transmitting information at the higher rate. The printer should be able to print text and graphics, especially if you want to do technical analysis.

SOFTWARE   Software refers to the programs used to tell the computer what functions it is to perform. In this area programs are available to maintain records, gather information, screen data, chart stocks, buy and sell securities, and manage portfolios.

Any system will probably include a portfolio management program. This can be done with existing spreadsheet software or programs developed specifically for investments. This software can be used in numerous ways, including tracking your existing portfolio, the prices you paid for the securities in the portfolio, and their current value; graphics showing the portfolio's composition; and calculations of rate of return for individual securities and the portfolio. A number of the programs allow for direct linkage to national information systems for instantaneous updates on your portfolio holdings. Some of the better-known portfolio management programs are Andrew Tobias' *Managing Your Money*, Micro Education Corp. of America, and the Isgur Portfolio System from Batteries Included.

Three national information systems—CompuServe, the Dow Jones News/Retrieval, and The Source—provide the tools to evaluate potential investments. Research reports from brokerage firms and SEC filings are available on-line from many sources. An example of an analytical program is the Dow Jones *Market Analyzer Plus* from Dow Jones Software. The program creates bar and point-and-figure charts, tracks up to forty-five portfolios with up to 1,500 transactions, creates reports, and automatically updates charts and portfolios.

The *Value/Screen Plus* program provides essentially the same information as the Value Line Investment Survey. Information on over 1,600 companies is provided on floppy disks, monthly or quarterly. OTC data can be obtained from Market Base, which provides current financial and market data on over 2,300 OTC companies. Monthly floppy disks allow you to evaluate performance figures according to various criteria.

You can subscribe to news-tracking services available on CompuServe or Dow Jones News/Retrieval. Special news-search services provided by these services automatically route stories, identified by keywords, to electronic mailboxes. One can also access 320 specialty newsletters covering thirty-five industries through News-Net, a news information data base.

On-line brokerage services are also available through CompuServe, Dow Jones News/Retrieval, and The Source. These data base services contract with discount brokerage services. CompuServe subscribers can use Quick and Reilly; Dow Jones News/Retrieval subscribers trade on-line through Fidelity Brokerage Services; and The Source subscribers trade through Spear Securities. You can also trade on-line through Charles Schwab and Co. On-line portfolio management capabilities similar to the stand-alone portfolio management software is also offered by CompuServe, The Source, and other services through Charles Schwab, Fidelity Brokerage Services, and Quick and Reilly. The advantage of the on-line service is that there is no need to enter data manually to update your portfolio.

COST   The cost of a personal investment system has declined dramatically over the past five years. Clones of name-brand products have made it possible for more individuals to acquire systems that were previously limited to professionals with large budgets. Table 4A.1 shows a cost of $1,355 for hardware and $597 for two software programs. The Dow Jones News/Retrieval service is available at $.90 per minute.

TABLE 4A.1   COST OF HARDWARE AND SOFTWARE FOR A PC SYSTEM TO MANAGE INVESTMENTS AS OF APRIL 1988

Hardware		
PC A/T Clone (dual disk drive, 640K with monochrome monitor)	$795	
Upgrade to color monitor	200	
Okidata 92 printer (with graphics)	210	
Modem (300/1200 baud)	150	
Total Cost of Hardware		$1,355
Software		
Dow Jones Market Analyzer Plus	$249	
Value/Screen Plus	348	
Total Cost of Software		$ 597
Total Cost of Hardware and Software		$1,952

Is the investment worth the cost? The answer depends on the size of your portfolio, how often you buy and sell stocks, and how successful you are at improving your return using the system. An investor with a $10,000 portfolio could not justify the cost. A large portfolio which is actively managed would probably justify spending $1,952 for the hardware and software.

COMPARISON OF MARKET INDICES OVER TIME

Table 4B.1 shows year-end prices for five major stock indices between 1972 and 1987. Table 4B.2 presents the annual percentage change in index values for each of the indices.

TABLE 4B.1   MAJOR STOCK INDICES 1972–1987

YEAR END	S&P COMPOSITE	DJIA	NYSE COMPOSITE	AMEX	NASDAQ COMPOSITE
1987	247.08	1938.83	138.23	260	330.47
1986	242.17	1895.95	138.58	263	348.83
1985	211.28	1546.67	121.58	246	324.93
1984	167.24	1211.00	96.38	204	247.35
1983	165.34	1258.00	95.18	223	278.60
1982	141.24	1046.00	81.03	170	232.41
1981	122.30	875.00	71.11	160	195.84
1980	135.76	963.00	77.86	174	202.34
1979	107.94	838.00	61.95	123	150.83
1978	96.11	805.00	53.62	75	117.98
1977	95.10	831.00	52.50	64	105.05
1976	107.46	1004.00	87.88	55	97.88
1975	80.19	852.00	47.64	42	77.62
1974	68.56	616.00	36.13	30	59.82
1973	97.55	850.00	51.82	45	92.19
1972	118.05	1020.00	64.48	64	133.72

CORRELATION MATRIX					
	S&P COMPOSITE	DJIA	NYSE COMPOSITE	AMEX	NASDAQ COMPOSITE
S&P Composite	1.000				
DJIA	0.977	1.000			
NYSE Composite	0.975	0.966	1.000		
AMEX	0.929	0.841	0.894	1.000	
NASDAQ Composite	0.962	0.893	0.926	0.988	1.000

TABLE 4B.2   ANNUAL CHANGE IN STOCK INDICES 1972–1987

YEAR END	S&P COMPOSITE	DJIA	NYSE COMPOSITE	AMEX	NASDAQ COMPOSITE
1987	2.03%	2.26%	−0.25%	−1.11%	−5.26%
1986	14.62	22.58	14.00	6.96	7.36
1985	26.33	27.72	26.10	20.65	31.36
1984	1.15	−3.74	1.26	−8.52	−11.22
1983	17.06	20.27	17.46	31.18	19.87
1982	15.49	16.69	13.95	6.25	18.67
1981	−9.91	−9.14	−8.67	−8.05	−3.21
1980	25.77	14.92	25.68	41.46	34.15
1979	12.31	4.10	15.54	64.00	27.84
1978	1.05	−3.13	2.13	17.19	12.31
1977	−11.49	−17.23	−9.30	16.36	7.33
1976	34.01	17.84	21.49	30.95	26.10
1975	16.96	38.31	31.86	40.00	29.76
1974	−29.72	−27.53	−30.28	−33.33	−35.11
1973	−17.37	−16.67	−19.63	−29.69	−31.06
1972	15.63	14.61	14.27	10.34	17.17
Arithmetic mean	7.12%	6.37%	7.23%	12.79%	9.13%
Geometric mean	5.68%	4.83%	5.76%	9.84%	6.87%
Standard Deviation	17.42%	18.26%	17.50%	25.87%	21.32%
Five-Year Annual Change					
1987–82	74.94%	85.36%	70.59%	52.94%	42.19%
1982–77	48.52%	25.87%	54.34%	165.63%	121.24%
1977–72	−19.44%	−18.53%	−18.58%	0.00%	−21.44%

The DJIA has the lowest arithmetic and geometric mean annual rates of return when compared with the four other indices. This is to be expected since it is made up of the largest companies in their respective industries. The standard deviations of the indices representing stocks on the NYSE, however, tend to be similar.

It would be expected that the AMEX Index would produce higher returns and have a higher risk than the NYSE Composite Index since AMEX companies tend to be smaller and more risky than NYSE companies. The statistics show that the AMEX has the highest arithmetic and geometric mean annual rates of return and the highest standard deviation of all the indices.

The NASDAQ Composite Index produced an annual rate of return between that of the NYSE Composite and the AMEX indices. The standard deviation is greater than that of the NYSE Composite, S&P Composite, and DJIA. The high standard deviation is due to the smaller size of companies used in the index.

The correlation matrix in Table 4B.1 shows that the five indices are highly correlated. The highest correlation is between the AMEX and NASDAQ composite indices. The lowest correlation is between the AMEX and DJIA indices.

INTERNATIONAL STOCK MARKETS

Table 4C.1 shows the market value of U.S. and foreign equity markets at the end of 1986. The total market capitalization of the international equity markets was $5,610 billion. The U.S. equity markets accounted for 39 percent of the total market value of all security markets. This is a decline from over 50 percent of all markets in 1985. The second largest market is Japan at 31 percent, with the western European countries of the United Kingdom, Germany, France, Switzerland, and Italy representing about 20 percent of the world total. Except for Canada, the other countries do not constitute a significant percentage of the world total.

When investing in foreign equity markets, one needs to consider the political and economic risks of the country, the inability to get relevant information about companies, and the returns on the securities. A letter grade is given for each country to rate its political and economic risk. The United States rates only an A− because of the weakness of the dollar and the huge budget deficit. South Africa receives a D−, the lowest rating, because of its political instability and the weakness of its currency.

The information ratings tell how easy it is to get research on foreign stocks and economic activity. A 10 is the highest rating.

One easy way to invest in foreign securities is to purchase American Depository Receipts, ADRs. ADRs trade in the U.S. equity markets as if they were U.S. stocks. Table 4C.1 shows 651 ADRs from thirteen countries are traded in the U.S. Another way to invest conveniently in foreign stock markets is to purchase shares of internationally diversified mutual funds traded in the United States. Other techniques for investing in foreign securities are presented in Chapter 23.

The lower far right columns of Table 4C.1 show the major index for each foreign stock market and the returns for those indices in local currencies and U.S. dollars. Americans must consider not only the potential returns of foreign securities but how those returns will be affected by currency fluctuations. For example,

TABLE 4C.1   INVESTMENT CHARACTERISTICS OF THE WORLD'S STOCK MARKETS

COUNTRY (POLITICAL AND ECONOMIC RISK RATING)	MARKET CAPITALIZATION (IN BILLIONS)	ECONOMIC GROWTH		INFLATION		INTEREST RATES		NUMBER OF ADRS
		1986	EST. 1987	1986	EST. 1987	1986	EST. 1987	
Australia (C)	$ 66	1.1%	1.8%	9.1%	7.9%	13.6%	13.0%	167
Canada (B−)	166	3.0	2.4	4.2	4.0	9.5	8.8	0
Denmark (A)	11	3.3	−0.5	1.4	2.5	6.8	8.0	2
France (B−)	178	2.4	2.0	2.5	2.3	9.1	8.8	17
Germany (A)	246	2.5	1.5	−0.2	0.0	5.9	5.0	23
Hong Kong (C+)	63	6.9	6.4	2.8	3.8	9.5	10.0	25
Italy (C)	140	2.5	3.0	6.5	4.5	11.5	9.1	16
Japan (A)	1,746	2.3	1.5	0.6	0.3	4.9	4.5	141
Korea (D+)	13	12.3	8.0	2.6	2.6	10.3	10.3	0
Netherlands (B+)	74	1.5	2.0	−2.0	−1.5	6.3	5.5	18
South Africa (D−)	35	1.0	−1.0	18.6	20.5	13.0	16.0	95
Spain (C)	47	3.0	3.3	8.3	6.6	11.7	9.8	2
Sweden (C+)	49	1.6	1.8	4.2	4.0	10.3	9.0	14
Switzerland (A+)	133	2.6	2.1	0.8	1.3	4.0	4.0	1
United Kingdom (B)	440	2.0	2.8	3.4	4.3	9.9	9.6	130
United States (A−)	2,203	2.5	1.7	1.9	2.9	8.1	7.0	—

COUNTRY (POLITICAL AND ECONOMIC RISK RATING)	SINGLE-COUNTRY FUNDS	INFORMATION RATING	NAME OF MAJOR MARKET INDEX	INDEX		
				GAIN 1986	GAIN ($US)	DIVIDEND YIELD
Australia (C)	Yes	9	ASE All Ordinaries	46.5%	38.5%	3.4%
Canada (B−)	No	9	Toronto Composite	4.7	7.0	2.9
Denmark (A)	No	7	Copenhagen SE	−19.2	−2.0	2.5
France (B−)	Yes	7	CAC General	49.7	76.3	2.5
Germany (A)	Yes	7	Commerzbank	4.9	33.4	2.8
Hong Kong (C+)	No	6	Hang Seng	46.6	46.9	3.1
Italy (C)	Yes	4	Banca Commerciale	58.1	96.9	1.7
Japan (A)	Yes	10	Nikkei Average	42.6	80.7	0.7
Korea (D+)	Yes	3	Korea Composite SPI	66.9	72.7	3.1
Netherlands (B+)	No	7	ANP CBS General	8.9	38.0	4.7
South Africa (D−)	Yes	8	RDM Golds	59.0	31.0	13.1
Spain (C)	No	4	Madrid SE	108.3	143.3	4.0
Sweden (C+)	Yes	7	Jacobsen & P.	41.5	58.2	2.1
Switzerland (A+)	No	7	SBC Industrials	0.2	28.3	1.9
United Kingdom (B)	No	9	Financial Times	16.1	19.2	4.2
United States (A−)	Yes	10	S&P 500	14.6	14.6	3.6

SOURCE: *Money Magazine*, vol. 16, no. 5, (May 1987): pp. 70–71. Reprinted by permission.

the Swiss market rose only 0.2 percent in 1986, but the decline in the dollar multiplied the return to 28.3 percent. South Africa shows the reveerse. Its market index rose 59.0 percent in 1986, but would have produced a return of only 31.0 percent when adjusted for currency fluctuations.

The stock markets of the world performed poorly in 1987, as seen in Table 4C.2. The U.S. stock market performed worse than all foreign stock markets,

TABLE 4C.2   RETURNS ON FOREIGN STOCK MARKET INDICES FOR 1987

INDEX THE WORLD	IN LOCAL CURRENCIES			IN. U.S. DOLLARS[1]		
	% CHANGE −3.1	12/30 308.1	52-WEEK RANGE 410.2–300.7	% CHANGE −1.6	12/30 405.9	52-WEEK RANGE 495.9–351.8
E.A.F.E.[2]	−3.8	431.7	574.5–423.9	−1.4	749.9	876.1–585.5
Australia	+0.8	254.2	433.2–222.2	+1.7	163.3	285.3–135.4
Austria	+0.8	214.7	270.2–197.8	+3.6	497.0	532.2–421.6
Belgium	+2.3	260.2	395.0–248.2	+5.1	388.0	514.1–357.6
Canada	−1.3	352.3	460.4–316.3	−1.2	291.9	374.5–257.0
Denmark	−1.1	336.6	417.5–331.9	+1.4	410.2	463.5–354.1
France	−3.1	292.3	467.6–278.3	−0.8	299.4	427.4–271.9
Germany	−3.7	156.6	264.0–147.3	−1.2	358.9	505.4–326.7
Hong Kong	−1.7	1632.7	2803.4–1348.7	−1.5	1168.5	1994.1–926.0
Italy	−3.5	378.7	591.5–370.4	−1.5	201.0	290.0–187.8
Japan	−5.0	1022.3	1360.1–899.5	−2.4	2983.8	3439.2–2001.5
Mexico	+8.8	25476.3	78086.7–9153.3	+9.9	143.5	618.2–130.6
Netherlands	−2.7	215.9	332.5–198.8	−0.0	435.5	567.3–389.8
Norway	−0.5	393.5	728.5–370.4	+1.4	448.0	784.3–417.6
Sing/Malays	−0.3	473.1	848.3–405.6	−0.0	729.9	1236.4–612.5
Spain	−4.0	209.5	284.6–176.1	−2.2	134.6	163.7–93.8
Sweden	−3.0	694.6	1058.3–655.2	−1.1	615.8	857.3–560.7
Switzerland	−2.9	140.6	220.7–137.2	+0.2	467.8	619.6–432.4
U.K.	−0.7	529.7	736.2–469.5	+1.3	409.8	500.7–285.1
U.S.A.	−2.0	230.3	313.9–208.8	−2.0	230.3	313.9–208.8

Base: Jan. 1, 1970 = 100
[1] Adjusted for foreign exchange fluctuations relative to the U.S. dollar.
[2] Europe, Australia, Far East Index.
SOURCE: *Barron's*, 4, January 1988, p. 59. Reprinted courtesy of *Barron's Weekly*.

with the exception of Japan and Spain, on an exchange-rate-adjusted basis. The sharp decline in the U.S. dollar offset many of the losses in the foreign stock market indices during 1987. For example, Switzerland showed a −2.9 percent change in its index in local currencies and a +.2 percent change in U.S. dollars.

CHAPTER 5

INVESTMENT STRATEGIES

INTRODUCTION

Investment Philosophy

Investment decisions, like any other decision, are made on the basis of the individual's beliefs and attitudes. Attitudes about consuming rather than saving income and about risk and return are important factors. The influences of these and other factors combine to produce an individual's investment philosophy. The philosophy can be observed in the style of investment decision making. Styles are often categorized by such phrases as "conservative versus aggressive" or "cautious versus impulsive."

It may be difficult to clearly define or quantify an individual's investment philosophy. However, it is important for an individual to consider his or her personal feelings about investment decisions. Generally, if an individual feels uncomfortable about an investment, the investment may not be appropriate in terms of his or her investment philosophy. In addition to influencing alternative investments, the investment philosophy is important in selecting an appropriate investment strategy.

The purpose of this chapter is to discuss major factors that determine an investment philosophy and the external factors, such as taxes, that may modify the investor's philosophy. In addition, traditional and newer approaches to investing are introduced. These approaches are further developed in detail in the chapters that follow.

Taxes

All investment decisions should include a careful analysis of the tax consequences, both in terms of the initial investment and the investment returns. A major problem in tax analysis, however, is the recent numerous changes in the U.S. tax code. For example, the Tax Reform Act of 1986 made changes in the Tax Code that have major consequences for investment decisions.

One major change is the elimination of the favorable treatment given long-term capital gains. Because of this change, individuals have less incentive to make investments that stress long-term gains rather than current income. Without the tax advantage, it is likely that investments that produce current income, in the form of interest or dividends, will become more popular at the expense of capital-gains-oriented investments. As of January 1, 1988, long-term and short-term capital gains are taxed at a maximum rate of 28 percent. This is also the maximum tax rate on other forms of investment income, such as interest and dividends. Capital gains, however, still retain the advantage of occurring at the investor's discretion, whereas dividend and interest payments are paid on a regular basis not controlled by the investor. Table 5.1 summarizes the tax rates for individuals and corporations under the Tax Reform Act of 1986.

Other major provisions affecting investments include elimination of the $100 dividend exclusion for individuals ($200 for married couples, filing jointly), restrictions on the deduction for investment interest, and more stringent requirements for tax shelters.

In addition to changes affecting individuals, major changes were made that affect corporations. Effective July 1, 1987, the maximum tax rate for corporations

TABLE 5.1   INDIVIDUAL AND CORPORATE TAX RATES

INDIVIDUALS' 1988 MARGINAL RATES				CORPORATIONS' 1988 RATES	
MARRIED FILING JOINTLY		UNMARRIED TAXPAYERS			
TAXABLE INCOME	RATE	TAXABLE INCOME	RATE	TAXABLE INCOME	RATE
$0–29,750	15.0%	$0–17,850	15.0%	$0–50,000	15%
$29,750–71,900	28.0	$17,850–43,150	28.0	$50,000–75,000	25
$71,900–149,250	33.0*	$43,150–89,560	33.0*	Over $75,000	34
Over $149,250	28.0**	Over $89,560	28.0**		

* Reflects first 5% surtax. ** Plus lesser of: (a) 28% of sum of personal and dependency exemption or (b) 5% of taxable income less $149,250 for married filing jointly or $89,560 for unmarried taxpayers.

was reduced to 34 percent from 46 percent. Because of the elimination of favorable tax treatment for long-term capital gains, less liberal depreciation allowances, and elimination of the investment tax credit, it is likely that the new code will result in higher taxes for many businesses.

The tax code also includes major changes that affect investments in real property such as real estate. In addition to depreciation changes and limitations on interest deductions, changes in the definition of "passive losses" and in the "at-risk" rules affect limited partnerships and investment trusts, often formed for the purpose of investing in real estate. For example, prior to the act of 1986, limited partners in highly leveraged real estate deals could benefit from very large tax write-offs generated through depreciation. These passive losses are no longer allowed as deductions.

This section provided a very general overview of taxes. In the chapters that follow, specific tax aspects of each type of investment will be discussed.

Speculation versus Investing

The distinction between speculation and investing is often difficult to make. Generally, *speculation* is viewed as making investments that have more risk than would be involved in *investing*. Another criterion often used to distinguish between speculation and investing is the time horizon; speculation is typically associated with a short time horizon, while investing is for a longer period of time. A third criterion distinguishing the two is the amount of information available and time spent on the analysis of investment alternatives. Speculation is usually viewed as making a decision based on limited information and analysis.

The growing popularity of financial futures (Chapter 21) and options (Chapter 19), however, challenges the traditional distinction between speculation and investing. Options and futures are risky relative to common stocks and bonds, and the investment horizon is often three months or less. Is an individual who purchases an option with a three-month maturity speculating or investing? Since the rate of return on an option can be −100 percent (total loss) or quite large (over 100 percent), the option has considerable risk. In a portfolio sense, however, the option may reduce the overall risk of the portfolio since the option can be used to reduce the risk of the stock portfolio.

For each investment alternative covered in this book, techniques of investment analysis and investment strategies are presented. This approach emphasizes careful and informed investment decisions rather than speculative decisions.

BASIC STRATEGIES

Long versus Short Position

The markets for most financial assets allow an investor to take a long or short position in the security. A *long* position is simply a purchase of the security. A *short* position, however, is the sale of a security that the investor does not presently own. This is accomplished by borrowing the security from a brokerage firm. Since many investors who have long positions use the brokerage firm for registration and for safekeeping, brokerage firms have a large inventory of certificates. This practice is referred to as registering the securities in a "street name." For example, a brokerage firm may have thousands of shares of IBM common stock in its vault that actually are owned by their customers but are registered in one street name. It is perfectly legal, however, for the brokerage firm to allow another customer to borrow the certificates that are needed for a short sale. The short seller must replace ("cover") the borrowed securities at a later date. The brokerage firm is protected, since the short seller has an established account with the firm and must keep the proceeds from the sale on deposit with the firm until the borrowed shares are replaced.

A long position in a security is appropriate in anticipation of a rising price. However, if an investor anticipates a decline in price, a *short* position is appropriate. By shorting the security, the investor hopes to make a profit by selling the stock now and buying it at a lower price later to replace the borrowed shares. The advantage of taking both long and short positions is that investors can earn returns in an increasing or a decreasing market. It should be pointed out, however, that the New York Stock Exchange has an "up-tick" and "zero puls up-tick" rule for short sales; that is, the most recent trade on the stock which an investor wishes to sell short must be at a price above the previous transaction or, if there was no change in price on the previous trade, the trade prior to it was on an up-tick. This rule helps stabilize the market. For example, if the up-tick rule did not exist, the steep decline in the market on October 19, 1987, might have been even more severe[1].

The risks of long and short positions are quite different. A short position has more risk than a long position in the same security. This occurs because the maximum loss on a long position is −100 percent, which would occur if the price declined to zero. Theoretically, however, there is no limit to the possible loss on a short position because there is no upper limit on the stock's price. If the price continues to increase, the potential loss to the short seller grows because of the

---

[1] There has been an ongoing investigation of violations of the up-tick rule on October 19, 1987, and other days of significant market declines, both before and after "Black Monday."

obligation to replace the borrowed shares. For example, if the price increased 200 percent, the loss to the short seller would be −200 percent (plus commissions) if shares were purchased to cover the short position at that point.

Table 5.2 provides an illustration of the rates of return (without considering trading commissions and taxes) that are possible on a long and a short position. A long position results in positive returns if the price of the stock increases, while negative returns occur for the short position.

Another important difference in long and short positions is the influence of cash dividends. Dividends increase the rate of return on a long position but decrease the rate of return on a short position. This occurs because the short seller must pay dividends to the brokerage firm so that they can be credited to the account from which the shares were borrowed.

It is also possible for an individual's portfolio to have both long and short positions at the same time. Long positions would be in securities that are expected to increase in price, while short positions would be in securities that are expected to decline in price. With the rapid development of the options and futures markets, however, it is now possible to duplicate most long and short positions in these markets. For example, a short position can be duplicated by taking a long position in a *put option* (the right to sell shares to the option seller at a specified price for a certain period of time), or a short position in a *call option* (the right to buy

TABLE 5.2   RATES OF RETURN ON LONG AND SHORT POSITIONS
(IGNORING COMMISSIONS AND TAXES)

I. **Long Position:** Assume that 100 shares of common stock are purchased for $50/share and sold one year later. Assume that no dividends are received on the stock.

$$\text{Rate of Return} = \frac{\text{Ending Price} - \text{Beginning Price}}{\text{Beginning Price}}$$

ENDING PRICE	BEGINNING PRICE	RATE OF RETURN
$30	$50	−40.0%
40	50	−20.0
50	50	0.0
60	50	20.0
70	50	40.0

II. **Short Position:** Assume that 100 shares of common stock are sold short for $50/share, and the position is covered (shares purchased and returned to broker) one year later. Assume that no dividends are declared on the stock.

$$\text{Rate of Return} = \frac{\text{Beginning Price} - \text{Ending Price}}{\text{Beginning Price}}$$

ENDING PRICE	BEGINNING PRICE	RATE OF RETURN
$30	$50	40.0%
40	50	20.0
50	50	0.0
60	50	−20.0
70	50	−40.0

shares from the option seller at a specified price for a certain period of time).[2] Stock options are discussed in Chapter 19.

Margin Trading

Margin trading allows investors to borrow part of the funds needed to take a position in a security. The maximum amount that can be borrowed for stock purchases is presently 50 percent. The Federal Reserve Board's Regulation T sets the margin requirement and provides the authority to raise or lower the maximum percentage that can be borrowed. Historically, margin requirements have ranged from 40 to 100 percent. Setting higher margin requirements has been seen as a means of controlling speculation in the market. The higher the margin requirements, the more cash or other assets in the customer's account required to undertake margin transactions. After the severe market decline in October 1987, consideration was given to raising margin requirements above the 50 percent level. To date, no action has been taken by the Federal Reserve to increase margin requirements.

The Federal Reserve requirement deals with the *initial margin* on the long position. Once the securities are purchased, however, the *maintenance margin* is regulated by the stock exchanges and individual brokerage firms. For example, if the price of the securities purchased on margin declines by a significant amount, the investor is required to maintain a minimum equity in the account. Since the decline in price has reduced the value of the equity, additional cash and/or securities must be deposited into the account with the brokerage firm. The price decline necessary before an additional deposit is required is explained below.

The New York Stock Exchange, NYSE, requires a minimum maintenance margin of 25 percent, but most brokerage firms usually impose 30 percent. These lower maintenance margins allow for a decline in the value of securities before the brokerage firm is required to make a *maintenance call.* For example, a maintenance call will not be made until the maintenance margin falls below 30 percent. If the investor does not have the necessary cash and/or securities to meet the maintenance call, the broker is required to liquidate enough of the customer's holdings to provide the funds to meet the maintenance call.

It is important to realize that trading on margin significantly changes the risk-return characteristics of the investment. Margin trading is simply using *financial leverage* to purchase securities. The possibility of a maintenance call also increases uncertainty about future cash requirements.

Table 5.3 provides an illustration of how to calculate the price that will trigger a maintenance call. In this illustration, the stock is purchased for $50 per share, using an initial margin of 50 percent. The remaining funds needed to purchase 100 shares are borrowed from the brokerage firm at a 10 percent annual interest rate. As the calculation indicates, with a maintenance margin of 30 percent, the price must fall below $35.71 before a maintenance call occurs.

The lower half of Table 5.3 illustrates the impact of margin trading on the possible rates of return from a long position. Notice that the rates of return with

---

[2] For examples, see Richard A. Brealey, ''How to Combine Active Management with Index Funds,'' *Journal of Portfolio Management* (Winter 1986): pp. 4–10.

TABLE 5.3 ILLUSTRATION OF MARGIN TRADING FOR A LONG POSITION

Purchase 100 shares on margin, at $50/share	$5,000
Initial margin (50%) required of investor	$2,500
Amount borrowed from brokerage firm, at 10% interest per year	$2,500
Maintenance margin required by brokerage firm	30%

1. Price of stock that will trigger a maintenance call:

$$\text{Price of Stock} = \frac{1 - \text{Initial Margin}}{1 - \text{Maintenance Margin}} \times \text{Purchase Price}$$

$$= \frac{1 - .5}{1 - .3} \times 50 = \$35.71$$

Thus, if the price falls below $35.71, a maintenance call will be made.

2. Calculation of rate of return, using indicated ending stock prices for margin trading versus using no margin: Assume that the holding period is one year, with dividends, trading commissions, and taxes ignored. For purposes of illustrating the rate of return, the maintenance call requirement is ignored when the price declines below $35.71 per share.

$$\frac{\text{Rate of Return}}{\text{without Margin}} = \frac{\text{Ending Price} - \text{Beginning Price}}{\text{Beginning Price}}$$

$$\frac{\text{Rate of Return}}{\text{with Margin}} = \frac{\text{Ending Price} - \text{Beginning Price} - \text{Interest Expense per Share}}{\text{Beginning Equity}}$$

ENDING PRICE	BEGINNING PRICE	BEGINNING EQUITY	INTEREST EXPENSE PER SHARE	RATES OF RETURN	
				WITHOUT MARGIN	WITH MARGIN
$20	$50	$25	$2.50	−60.0%	−130.0%
30	50	25	2.50	−40.0	−90.0
40	50	25	2.50	−20.0	−50.0
50	50	25	2.50	0.0	−10.0
60	50	25	2.50	20.0	30.0
70	50	25	2.50	40.0	70.0
80	50	25	2.50	60.0	110.0

margin trading are significantly smaller and larger than the corresponding returns without a margin. This illustrates the leverage resulting from margin trading.

Margin is also used for short sales, but this practice does not require interest payments by the investor. Brokerage firms typically require a minimum deposit of $2,000 to open a margin account and require a higher maintenance margin for short positions. In a short sale on margin, maintenance calls occur if the stock price increases by a certain amount. Large amounts of additional investment might be needed because, theoretically, there is no upper limit to a stock's price. Table 5.4 provides an illustration of using margin for short sales. Note that there is no interest expense in the return calculation in Table 5.4. There are no borrowed funds with marginal short sales; the initial margin indicates the minimum initial equity deposit that must be made by the investor.

An excellent article by Professors Grauer and Hakansson demonstrates the impact of using leverage (margin) to invest in portfolios consisting of common stocks, bonds, and Treasury bills over the period 1934–1983.[3] Not surprisingly,

---

[3] Robert R. Grauer and Nils H. Hakansson, ''Return on Levered, Actively Managed Long-Run Portfolios of Stocks, Bonds and Bills, 1934–1983,'' *Financial Analysts Journal* (September-October 1985): pp. 24–43.

TABLE 5.4 ILLUSTRATION OF MARGIN TRADING FOR A SHORT POSITION

Sold (shorted) 100 shares, for $50/share (proceeds from sale)	$5,000
Initial margin of 50% (equity deposit) required of investor	$2,500
Maintenance margin required by brokerage firm	30%

1. Price of stock that will trigger a maintenance call:

$$\text{Price of Stock} = \frac{1 + \text{Initial Margin}}{1 + \text{Maintenance Margin}} \times \text{Selling Price}$$

$$= \frac{1 + .5}{1 + .3} \times \$50 = \$57.69$$

Thus, if the price increases above $57.69, a maintenance call will be made.

2. Calculation of rate of return using indicated ending stock prices for 50% initial margin versus 100% initial margin: Assume that the holding period is one year, with dividends, trading commissions, and taxes ignored. For purposes of illustrating the rate of return, the maintenance call requirement is ignored when the price exceeds $57.69 per share.

$$\text{Rate of Return} = \frac{\text{Beginning Price} - \text{Ending Price}}{\text{Equity Deposit}}$$

ENDING PRICE	BEGINNING PRICE	EQUITY DEPOSIT (50% INITIAL MARGIN)	EQUITY DEPOSIT (100% INITIAL MARGIN)	RATES OF RETURN	
				50% INITIAL MARGIN	100% INITIAL MARGIN
$20	$50	$25	$50.0	120.0%	60.0%
30	50	25	50.0	80.0	40.0
40	50	25	50.0	40.0	20.0
50	50	25	50.0	0.0	0.0
60	50	25	50.0	−40.0	−20.0
70	50	25	50.0	−50.0	−40.0
80	50	25	50.0	−120.0	−60.0

the article indicates that the use of leverage increases both the return and variability of the return as the degree of leverage increases.

Hedging

Hedging activities are designed to modify or eliminate risk by undertaking such investment positions that the gain on one investment will counterbalance the loss on another. For example, it is commonly believed that investments in real assets such as real estate can be used to hedge against unexpected inflation. This implies that real estate prices may increase rapidly during, or in anticipation of, inflationary periods, while financial assets may not. If this occurs, the gains on the real asset portion of the portfolio may protect, or hedge, the portfolio against purchasing-power risk. The empirical evidence concerning the ability of a class of investments to provide an inflation hedge is discussed in detail in the applicable chapters. For example, Chapter 22 discusses the hedging potential of real estate, and Chapter 20 reviews the evidence for commodities.

Hedging strategies can also be developed to protect an investment from possible downside price risk. As previously discussed, a long position in common stock is appropriate in anticipation of a price increase. After the stock is purchased, however, the price may decline because of some unanticipated event or because the forecast was incorrect. A hedge could be formed to protect against this possible price decline. One hedge would be to buy a put option on the stock. As explained in detail in Chapter 19, the put option allows the holder to sell the stock at a designated price. The price of the put would therefore increase if the price of the stock declined. The gain on the put would partially or completely offset the loss on the stock.

A third example of a hedge deals with protecting a short position from a price increase. This risk can be hedged by purchasing a call option that allows the holder to purchase the stock at a specified price. If the stock price increased, the call could be used to cover the borrowed shares, or the profit on the call would offset some or all of the loss on the short position.

Hedging activities involve transaction and information costs. In many cases, the hedge may limit the upside potential of an investment in addition to protecting against downside risk. As is the case with other investment strategies, the costs versus the benefits should be carefully considered.

Arbitrage

Another trading strategy that is discussed in various chapters in the book is *arbitrage* trading. An arbitrage strategy is designed to profit from imperfections in security markets. For example, an arbitrageur may buy a stock in one market and immediately sell the stock at a higher price in another market. If markets are inefficient, a stock may sell simultaneously at different prices in different markets. The arbitrageur looks for trading opportunities that exploit these market imperfections. Their actions, however, tend to eliminate any price discrepancies.

A second example of arbitrage deals with attempts to exploit price differentials for companies involved in takeover efforts. For example, an arbitrageur may take a long position in the common stock of a firm being taken over and simultaneously short the common stock of the acquiring firm. This strategy is based on the expectation that the stock of the acquired firm will increase in price and the acquirer's stock will decrease in price. This often occurs because the acquirer is usually forced to pay a ''premium'' to obtain the number of shares needed to gain control.

TRADITIONAL APPROACHES TO INVESTING

The purpose of this section is to review briefly the two traditional approaches to investing—''technical'' and ''fundamental.'' The next section introduces the Efficient Market Hypothesis, EMH, and its implications for investment strategies.

Technical Analysis

Technical analysis dates back to the 1800s. It essentially involves an analysis of historical price and volume data. Often technicians are referred to as chartists since much of their analysis takes the form of graphs or charts. Technicians believe that there are recurring patterns in stock prices. Once these patterns are discovered, they can be used to forecast the direction and perhaps the magnitude of future price changes.

Technical analysis has now become much more complex because of advances in communication technology and data processing. These technological developments allow technicians almost instantaneously to obtain data and to use a variety of analytical procedures to analyze the data. Chapter 12 presents a detailed discussion of traditional techniques of technical analysis and some of the newer and more advanced procedures.

Fundamental Analysis

Fundamental analysis developed after the passage of the Securities Act of 1933 and the Securities Exchange Act of 1934. The primary purpose of these two laws was to require that publicly traded corporations provide "full disclosure" of financial and other information that could influence the price of their securities. Prior to this time, corporations were not required to provide a complete set of financial statements.

When detailed financial information became available, the techniques and procedures of fundamental analysis began to emerge. Benjamin Graham is recognized as the father of fundamental analysis. The first edition of *Security Analysis* was published by Graham and David L. Dodd in 1934. This was a widely used textbook and the fourth edition was published in 1962. Graham also obtained considerable fame from the publication in 1948 of *The Intelligent Investor*, that is essentially a layman's version of the earlier text. The last edition of this book was published in 1974 prior to Graham's death in 1976.

Graham advocated the use of mathematics and quantitative procedures in the analysis of investments. This approach allowed Graham to estimate the *intrinsic value* of a stock, which is determined independently of the market price. Intrinsic value was defined as the value that is justified by financial facts such as asset value, earnings, dividends, and other fundamentals. This approach is referred to as fundamental analysis since it stresses the major (or fundamental) factors that determine a stock's value.

Many of the early techniques and procedures developed and advocated by Graham are still in use. Chapters 9–11 of this book incorporate Graham's principles of fundamental analysis. There is evidence that Graham's procedure can still be used to select undervalued stocks.[4]

Despite the popularity and apparent success of Graham's approach, he was constantly developing and testing new techniques and procedures. Graham recognized that techniques successful in the past may not work in the future. Prior to his death, Graham expressed the view that the markets were becoming more efficient, in the sense that it was difficult to identify undervalued securities. He believed that institutional investors dominated the market but concentrated their investments in the major issues on the NYSE and AMEX. A possible strategy, therefore, was to discover "pockets of inefficiency" in the smaller and less-analyzed

---

[4] Henry R. Oppenheimer, "A Test of Benjamin Graham's Stock Selection Criteria," *Financial Analysts Journal* (September-October 1984): pp. 68–74.

companies and to avoid the radical swings in market cycles that occur because of excessive optimism and pessimism.

INVESTMENT STRATEGIES IN AN EFFICIENT MARKET

Overview

Beginning in the 1950s, a number of empirical studies suggested that changes in stock prices appear to be random.[5] These early studies encouraged additional research that finally resulted in the "random walk" theory about stock price behavior. During the 1960s, additional empirical research indicated that stock prices adjust very rapidly to information and that professional investors, such as mutual fund managers, do not appear to outperform the market. The results from all of these empirical tests are the foundation for the Efficient Market Hypothesis (EMH). The development of the EMH is discussed in detail in Chapter 13. For purposes of this chapter, however, a basic understanding of the EMH is appropriate.

The financial markets in the United States are extremely competitive, in the sense that many individual and institutional investors are attemtping to maximize the performance of their portfolios. Exceptional performance for one investor, however, comes at the expense of other investors.[6] To illustrate, assume that an investor earned risk-adjusted excess returns on a long position because the security was purchased at a price below its intrinsic value. The bargain purchase was possible because the seller did not realize that the security was undervalued. The success of the buyer was therefore at the expense of the seller.

Because of the competitiveness of the markets, naive and uninformed investors eventually realize that they will not be able to earn risk-adjusted excess returns. They have a competitive disadvantage. The remaining investors and traders represent the survival of the fittest and are likely to be the more knowledgeable and skilled players. In this type of market, security prices are likely to reflect accurately available information and to respond very rapidly to new information; prices reflect technical and fundamental factors and are unbiased indicators of intrinsic values.

Given this competitiveness and the resulting efficiency at correctly pricing securities, what investment strategies are appropriate? Is it reasonable to assume that strategies based on traditional technical and fundamental analyses can outperform the market? If the market is perfectly efficient, then no strategy will be able to beat the market. If the market is less than perfectly efficient, some strategies may result in risk-adjusted excess returns. The critical question, therefore, is the *degree* of market efficiency.

---

[5] For example, see Maurice G. Kendall, "The Analysis of Economic Time-Series, Part I: Prices," *Journal of Royal Statistical Society* (Part 1, 1953): pp. 11–25, and Harry V. Roberts, "Stock Market 'Patterns' and Financial Analysis: Methodological Suggestions," *Journal of Finance* (March 1959): pp. 1–10.

[6] For a discussion of traders and strategies, see Jack L. Treynor, "What Does It Take to Win the Trading Game?" *Financial Analysts Journal* (January-February 1981): pp. 55–60.

The degree of market efficiency is the subject of considerable debate. Academics tend to argue that markets are highly efficient, while practitioners tend to feel that there are inefficiencies. The evidence and debate are inconclusive because, "the case for all forms of the EMH seems to us to be neither as strong as most academics assume nor as weak as most professional investors like to believe."[7]

The debate has resulted in two classifications for investment strategies: *passive strategies* and *active strategies*. Efficient markets suggest passive strategies, while market inefficiencies suggest active strategies.

Passive Strategies

A passive strategy does not attempt to outperform the market or to earn risk-adjusted excess returns; the objective is to do as well as the market. At the extreme, stocks could be randomly selected since in a perfectly efficient market, the selected stocks would be correctly valued. To reduce the risk of possible unexpected company-or industry-specific developments, an adequate number of securities would be included in the portfolio.

The investment horizon would be long-term, with little, if any, portfolio revision from efforts at security selection or market timing. An advantage of passive management is that the transaction costs of the portfolio are minimized. The cost of trading or of acquiring and analyzing information is avoided. The task of the portfolio manager is limited to record keeping and tax planning.

Figure 5.1 provides some interesting statistics on the growth of passive equity investment funds that primarily manage retirement funds. These passive funds emerged during the early 1970s and by 1980 represented 7 percent of the $210 billion in retirement funds. By 1985, their share of the market increased to 19 percent and is forecast to be 34 percent by 1990. The figure also indicates that a third category of funds may evolve that stresses "actively managed universes." This category would be a compromise between active and passive management since it would engage in market timing by shifting assets in response to forecasts of the investment environment.

1. INDEXING One approach to implementing a passive investment strategy is to invest in an indexed portfolio that is designed to duplicate precisely the performance of a market index such as the S&P 500. A growing number of pension funds are indexed portfolios (see Chapter 25). For individuals, however, it is necessary to construct an indexed portfolio or to invest in an indexed mutual fund. A number of articles provide discussions of the advantages of indexing and how to construct an individual indexed portfolio.[8] The advantages and disadvantages of indexed mutual funds are discussed in Chapter 24.

---

[7] Bob L. Boldt and Hal L. Arbit, "Efficient Markets and the Professional Investor," *Financial Analysts Journal* (July-August 1984): p. 33.

[8] For example, see Robert G. Kirby, "The Coffee Can Portfolio," *Journal of Portfolio Management* (Fall 1984): pp. 76–80.

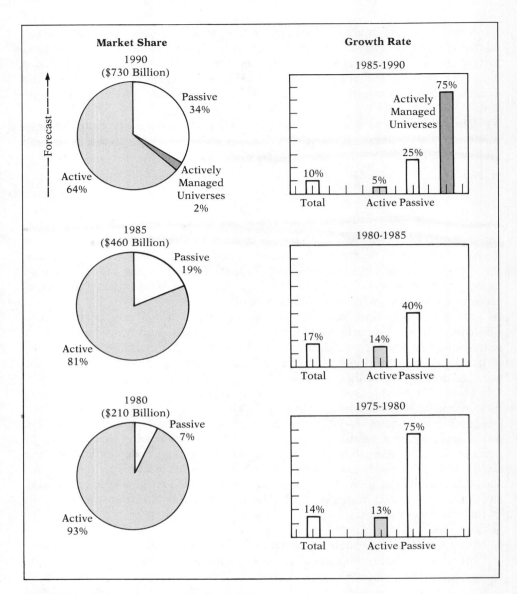

FIGURE 5.1   Active versus passive strategies

Source: Walter R. Good, Roy W. Hermansen, and T. Kirkham Barneby, "Opportunity: Actively Managed Investment Universes," *Financial Analysts Journal* (January-February 1986) p. 50.

2.   COMBINATION STRATEGY   An alternative to a completely passive strategy such as indexing is to divide the portfolio into active and passive components. In-dexed funds can be used for the passive component; selection and timing activities can be used for the active component. The division depends on the skill of the portfolio manager. A manager who can accurately forecast stocks or other securities that offer high returns should exploit these opportunities by increasing the size of the active component of the portfolio. It can also be

shown that if the portfolio manager has forecasting skill, the appropriate strategy would use stock-index futures rather than using an indexed component.[9]

In summary, efficient markets and large transaction costs suggest passive investment strategies. Evidence also indicates that the popularity of passive strategies has grown over the period 1975–1985 for both institutional and individual investors. There are also forecasts that the popularity of passive strategies will continue to grow. These forecasts are often based on the feeling that active management is usually not successful.

> *I think that professors of finance and even money managers looking back will be amazed that so many people were fooled so badly and for so long about the advisability and feasibility of trying to beat the market with high cost, conventional management.*[10]

Active Strategies

Many of the techniques and procedures presented in this book can be used in active investment strategies. The orientation of the book is toward individual investors. The primary purpose of the book is therefore to provide information and procedures that can assist individuals in making informed investment decisions. As previously discussed, however, there is strong evidence that financial markets are efficient. Informed investors should appreciate the pitfalls and complications that occur in pursuing an active investment strategy in an efficient market.

Although detailed discussions about efficient markets and their impact on investment strategies will occur throughout the book, some initial observations can be made concerning active strategies for individuals.

First, what are some basic arguments in support of the idea that market inefficiencies exist to the extent that an active strategy is rational? Essentially, this idea requires the assumption that some investors have an advantage over others. Four possible advantages are

1. information advantage;
2. analytical advantage;
3. judgmental advantage; and
4. idiosyncratic behavior advantage.[11]

The first three of these advantages are self-explanatory. The fourth, however, deserves a brief discussion. This advantage results because certain individuals or groups of investors have a particular temperament, peculiar mannerisms, or institutional requirements that influence investment decisions. An obvious example

---

[9] Richard A. Brealey, "How to Combine Active Management with Index Funds," *Journal of Portfolio Management* (Winter 1986): pp. 4–10.

[10] Jeremy Grantham, "You Can't Fool All of the People All of the Time," *Journal of Portfolio Management* (Winter 1986): p. 11.

[11] Robert Ferguson, "An Efficient Stock Market? Ridiculous!" *Journal of Portfolio Management* (Summer 1983): pp. 31–38.

of institutional requirements are "prudent man rules" that apply to fiduciaries. These rules limit investments to certain types of assets. A second example would be regulatory requirements that prohibit insurance companies from making investments in companies that do not meet certain financial criteria. The existence of these idiosyncrasies limit the investment universe and consequently the flexibility of investment decisions for certain types of investors. Individuals without idiosyncrasies may therefore have an advantage.

A second popular argument supporting active strategies for individuals is that they have advantages over institutions and professional investors. Commonly cited advantages include

1. small trades that can be executed quickly;
2. flexibility to invest in small companies;
3. ability to put all or more of their eggs in one basket; and
4. flexibility to use short sales and margin trading.

These possible advantages and a belief that active strategies for individuals are justified are the premises behind the founding of the American Association of Individual Investors, AAII.[12] The AAII was founded in 1979 as a nonprofit organization to educate and encourage individuals to make their own investment decisions. By becoming a member, an individual can attend local chapter meetings in many cities in the United States, attend educational seminars, and receive educational materials including the *AAII Journal*. This journal provides practical information about developments in investment theory and research. AAII advances the idea that individuals need to be knowledgeable in order to make rational investment decisions.

1. DO-IT-YOURSELF STRATEGIES FOR INDIVIDUAL INVESTORS Individuals who elect to pursue an active investment strategy can also perform all the necessary tasks themselves. Essentially, these individuals are their own portfolio managers. Once this decision is made, the individual is faced with the task of identifying specific investment strategies that can accomplish the objectives of the portfolio. Possible strategies are discussed in detail throughout the book. As an introduction, however, the following strategies have been suggested:

    a. Invest in stocks selling below liquidation value.[13]

    b. Invest in new issues of stocks or in stocks moving from the OTC to the NYSE.[14]

    c. Form a portfolio of stocks selling for "low" P/E ratios.[15]

---

[12] Additional information can be obtained by writing to the AAII: 625 N. Michigan Avenue, Chicago, IL 60611.

[13] Joel M. Greenblatt, Richard Pzena, and Bruce L. Newberg, "How the Small Investor Can Beat the Market," *Journal of Portfolio Management* (Summer 1981): pp. 48–52.

[14] John J. McConnell and Gary C. Sanger, "A Trading Strategy for New Listings on the NYSE," *Financial Analysts Journal* (January-February 1984): pp. 34–38, and Ben Branch,"Special Offerings and Market Efficiency," *Financial Review* (March 1984): pp. 26–35.

[15] Clinton M. Bidwell III, "SUE/PE Revista," *Journal of Portfolio Management* (Winter 1981): pp. 85–87, and John W. Peavy III and David A. Goodman, "The Significance of P/Es for Portfolio Returns," *Journal of Portfolio Management* (Winter 1983): pp. 43–47.

d.   Invest in "small" companies.[16]

e.   Buy stocks that have a high ratio of book value to stock price.[17]

Most of these strategies are based on *market anomalies* that may represent market inefficiencies and therefore provide risk-adjusted excess returns. These strategies are discussed in more detail in Chapter 13. In addition to the common stock strategies listed above, each chapter on an investment alternative discusses active strategies that are appropriate for that particular alternative.

2.   USE AN EXPERT Rather than attempting a complete do-it-yourself approach, individuals may elect to use a professional for part or all of the portfolio tasks (see Chapter 26). For example, an individual may decide to rely on investment research performed by a brokerage firm or by an investment advisory service. There is some evidence that some of this research can identify securities that can outperform the market.[18]

An individual may also decide to invest in a mutual fund (see Chapter 24) that is actively managed. With the exception of indexed mutual funds, the majority of funds are actively managed. The task facing the individual is to select the mutual fund with the appropriate objective which is most likely to achieve the best performance. Once the selection is made, the mutual fund manager performs the tasks of security selection, market timing, and diversification.

Another alternative in using professional help is to invest in one of the many new alternatives that are now offered by financial institutions such as insurance companies. Investing in new products such as bullet annuities or variable annuities shifts the investment management decision to the company. These new investment alternatives are discussed in Chapter 25.

Conclusions

The decision to pursue a passive or an active investment strategy in an efficient market is a key decision for individual investors. Much of this book is devoted to providing information that can be used to make this decision.

Once the passive-versus-active decision is made, a particular investment strategy must be selected. It is important to realize that there is no optimal investment strategy and that risks and returns can vary widely from strategy to strategy.[19]

Markets are also dynamic in the sense that new products are emerging and the important decision variables and relationships between variables are unstable. In a dynamic market, successful investors must also change; techniques and

---

[16] Marc R. Reinganum, "Portfolio Strategies for Small CAPs versus Large," *Journal of Portfolio Management* (Winter 1983): pp. 29–36.

[17] Barr Rosenberg, Kenneth Reid, and Ronald Lanstein, "Persuasive Evidence of Market Inefficiency," *Journal of Portfolio Management* (Spring 1985): pp. 9–16.

[18] For example, see C. Holloway, "A Note on Testing the Aggressive Investment Strategy Using Value Line Ranks," *Journal of Finance* (June 1981): pp. 711–19.

[19] For example, see Robert Ferguson, "A Comparison of the Mean-Variance and Long-Term Return Characteristics of Three Investment Strategies," *Financial Analysts Journal* (July-August 1987): pp. 55–66, and Eugene M. Lerner and Pochara Theerathorn, "The Returns of Different Investment Strategies," *Journal of Portfolio Management* (Summer 1983): pp. 26–28.

strategies that have been successful in the past may not be successful in the future.[20] This dynamic environment increases the difficulty of making successful investment decisions but also provides a challenge to investors inclined to question the efficiency of the markets.

SUMMARY

This chapter has provided an introduction to investment strategies. This topic is a central theme that is discussed in detail throughout the book.

The beginning of the chapter stressed the importance of developing an investment philosophy. An attempt was also made to distinguish between speculation and investing. The distinction is difficult because of differences in feelings among individuals about the risk-return trade-offs and viewing the alternative independently or in the context of the portfolio. Certain alternatives are quite risky and may be considered as speculative when viewed independently, but they can also reduce the risk of a portfolio. The orientation of the book is making investments rather than speculative decisions

The strong evidence in support of the Efficient Market Hypothesis, EMH, has generated considerable debate concerning the appropriateness of *active* versus *passive* investment strategies. If markets are highly or perfectly efficient, passive strategies are justified. Market inefficiencies, however, suggest that active strategies directed at exploiting the inefficiencies are justified. A key question facing investors is the *degree* of market efficiency.

The chapter concluded with a discussion of passive and active investment strategies in an efficient market. It should also be noted that there are considerable differences in the risk-return characteristics of different investment strategies. In a dynamic market it is also likely that successful strategies are not stable. Strategies that have been successful in the past may not work in the future.

QUESTIONS

1. Compare and contrast speculation and investing. Do all investors use the same criteria to classify an opportunity as a speculative opportunity versus an investment opportunity?

2. Compare and contrast technical analysis with fundamental analysis.

3. Individual investors may elect to pursue passive or active investment strategies. Discuss the advantages and disadvantages of these two approaches.

4. Explain why a short position in a common stock has more risk than a long position in the same stock.

5. Explain why a margined common stock investment has the potential to provide higher returns but involves more risk than an unmargined position.

---

[20] Peter L. Bernstein, "How Stable Are Successful Strategies?" *Journal of Portfolio Management* (Spring 1986): p. 1.

6. How can hedging strategies be used to modify the risk-return characteristics of a portfolio?

7. Prior to control by the Federal Reserve, margin requirements were below 30 percent in 1929, and it has been estimated that individual investors borrowed in excess of $9 billion for margin trading. Explain how these factors contributed to the 1929 stock market crash.

8. Can arbitrage opportunities exist in an efficient market? In your opinion, should individual investors attempt to identify and exploit arbitrage opportunities?

9. Explain why the degree of market efficiency should be considered in comparing active and passive investment strategies.

10. It can be argued that individuals should not attempt active investment strategies unless certain criteria can be satisfied. Discuss the criteria or conditions that justify an active strategy.

11. Should individual investors select either a passive or active strategy, or should a combination of the two approaches be considered?

PROBLEMS

1. An arbitrageur notices that XYZ common stock is selling for $29 per share on the NYSE and at $28 on the Philadelphia Stock Exchange. Assume that brokerage commissions are 2 percent on each transaction. Does this situation offer a profitable arbitrage opportunity?

2. Assume that an individual is considering an investment in the common stock of IBM Corporation. The common stock is currently selling for $115 per share with a $4.40 annual cash dividend. The investor anticipates a one-year holding period. Ignoring transaction costs and taxes,

   a. Calculate the rate of return on a long position in the stock for each of the following ending stock prices: $100, $110, $120, $130.

   b. Calculate the rate of return on a short position for each of the ending stock prices given in part a.

3. Consider the following information:

Stock price per share	$60
Margin requirement	50%
Interest rate on margin accounts	9%
Maintenance margin	30%

   Ignoring transaction costs and taxes,

   a. Assume that an investor takes a long position without using margin.
   Calculate the rate of return if the stock is sold for $70 per share after one year.

   b. Assume that an investor takes a long position using margin.

      (1) Calculate the stock price that will trigger a margin call.

      (2) Calculate the rate of return if the stock is sold for $70 per share after one year.

    c.   Explain why the rate of return using margin is different from the rate of return without margin.

4.   Consider the following information:

Stock price per share	$25
Margin requirement	50%
Maintenance margin	30%

Ignoring transaction costs and taxes,

    a.   Assume that an investor takes a short position with an equity deposit equal to 100 percent of the initial margin. Calculate the rate of return if the investor covers (purchases) the stock at $20 after one year.

    b.   Assume that an investor takes a short position with an equity deposit equal to 50 percent of the initial margin.

        (1) Calculate the stock price that will trigger a margin call.

        (2) Calculate the rate of return if the investor covers (purchases) the stock at $20 after one year.

    c.   Explain why the rate of return in parts a and b are different.

5.   A portfolio manager makes the following rate of return forecasts for the next three years:

	ONE YEAR TREASURY BILLS	COMMON STOCKS
1989	9%	15%
1990	10%	−20%
1991	8%	+10%

Assume that the portfolio manager is considering a passive versus an active investment strategy using Treasury bills and common stocks.

    a.   An example of a passive strategy would be to invest 50 percent of the portfolio funds in Treasury bills and 50 percent in common stock in each of the next three years. Calculate the annual rates of return for the portfolio.

    b.   An example of an active strategy would be to shift funds between Treasury bills and common stocks. Assume that the portfolio manager has the flexibility to hold all Treasury bills (100 percent of funds in Treasury bills) or all common stocks.

        (1) Indicate the optimal proportion of portfolio funds that should be invested in Treasury bills and common stocks each year based on the forecast rates of return.

        (2) Calculate the annual rates of return for the portfolio using the portfolio proportions calculated in b-1.

    c.   Discuss the advantages and disadvantages of the passive and active strategies described above. Describe the impact of transaction costs and income taxes on each of these strategies. In your opinion, which portfolio strategy involves more risk?

REFERENCES

Bernstein, Peter L. "How Stable are Successful Strategies?" *Journal of Portfolio Management* (Spring 1986): p. 1.

Bidwell, Clinton M. III. "SUE/PE Revista." *Journal of Portfolio Management* (Winter 1981): pp. 85–87.

Block, Stanley B. "Efficient Markets: Buzz Word of the '60s Gets Stung." *AAII Journal* (September 1984): pp. 9–13.

Boldt, Bob L., and Hal L. Arbit. "Efficient Markets and the Professional Investor." *Financial Analysts Journal* (July-August 1984): pp. 22–34.

Branch, Ben. "Special Offerings and Market Efficiency." *Financial Review* (March 1984): pp. 26–35.

Brealey, Richard A. "How to Combine Active Management with Index Funds." *Journal of Portfolio Management* (Winter 1986): pp. 4–10.

Ferguson, Robert. "An Efficient Stock Market? Ridiculous!" *Journal of Portfolio Management* (Summer 1983): pp. 31–38.

———. "A Comparison of the Mean-Variance and Long-Term Return Characteristics of Three Investment Strategies." *Financial Analysts Journal* (July-August 1987): pp. 55–66.

Graham, Benjamin. *The Intelligent Investor.* 3d ed. New York: Harper and Row, 1959.

Graham, Benjamin, and David L. Dodd. *Security Analysis: Principles and Techniques.* 4th ed. New York: McGraw-Hill, 1974.

Good, Walter R., Roy W. Hermansen, and T. Kirkham Barneby. "Opportunity: Actively Managed Investment Universes." *Financial Analysts Journal* (January-February 1986): pp. 49–57.

Grantham, Jeremy. "You Can't Fool All of the People All of the Time." *Journal of Portfolio Management* (Winter 1986): pp. 11–15.

Grauer, Robert R., and Nils H. Hakansson. "Returns on Levered, Actively Managed Long-Run Portfolios of Stocks, Bonds and Bills, 1934–1983." *Financial Analysts Journal* (September-October 1985): pp. 24–43.

Greenblatt, Joel M., Richard Pzena, and Bruce L. Newberg. "How the Small Investor Can Beat the Market." *Journal of Portfolio Management* (Summer 1981): pp. 48–52.

Holloway, C. "A Note on Testing the Aggressive Investment Strategy Using Value Line Ranks." *Journal of Finance* (June 1981): pp. 711–19.

Jobson, J. D., and Bob Korkie. "Putting Markowitz Theory to Work." *Journal of Portfolio Management* (Summer 1981): pp. 70–74.

Keane, Simon M. "The Efficient Market Hypothesis on Trial." *Financial Analysts Journal* (March-April 1986): pp. 58–63.

Kendall, Maurice G. "The Analysis of Economic Time Series, Part I: Prices." *Journal of Royal Statistical Society* (Part 1, 1953): pp. 11–25.

Kirby, Robert G. "The Coffee Can Portfolio." *Journal of Portfolio Management* (Fall 1984): pp. 76–80.

Lerner, Eugene M., and Pochara Theerathorn. "The Returns of Different Investment Strategies." *Journal of Portfolio Management* (Summer 1983): pp. 26–28.

Malkiel, Burton G. *A Random Walk Down Wall Street.* 4th ed. New York: Norton, 1985.

McConnell, John J., and Gary C. Sanger. "A Trading Strategy for New Listings on the NYSE." *Financial Analysts Journal* (January-February 1984): pp. 34–38.

Oppenheimer, Henry R. "A Test of Benjamin Graham's Stock Selection Criteria." *Financial Analysts Journal* (September-October 1984): pp. 68–74.

Peavy, John W. III, and David A. Goodman. "The Significance of P/Es for Portfolio Returns." *Journal of Portfolio Management* (Winter 1983): pp. 43–47.

Reinganum, Marc R. "Portfolio Strategies for Small CAPs Versus Large." *Journal of Portfolio Management* (Winter 1983): pp. 29–36.

Roberts, Harry V. "Stock Market 'Patterns' and Financial Analysis: Methodological Suggestions." *Journal of Finance* (March 1959): pp. 1–10.

Rosenberg, Barr, Kenneth Reid, and Ronald Lanstein. "Persuasive Evidence of Market Inefficiency." *Journal of Portfolio Management* (Spring 1985): pp. 9–16.

Sorensen, Eric H., and Terry Burke. "Portfolio Returns from Active Industry Group Rotation." *Financial Analysts Journal* (September-October 1986): pp. 43–50.

Sorensen, Roy A. "An 'Essential Reservation' about the EMH." *Journal of Portfolio Management* (Summer 1983): pp. 29–30.

Treynor, Jack L. "What Does It Take to Win the Trading Game?" *Financial Analysts Journal* (January-February 1981): pp. 55–60.

PORTFOLIO
THEORY
AND
ANALYSIS

CHAPTER 6

PORTFOLIO AND CAPITAL MARKET THEORY

INTRODUCTION

Overview

In discussing investment strategies in Chapter 1, selection, timing, and diversification were identified as the three major components of the investment decision process. This chapter develops the concepts and logic underlying portfolio and capital market theory, and the importance of diversification will become apparent. Further, an understanding of these theories will provide the investor with an understanding of how risk is measured, the relationship between expected return and risk, and a framework for the theory underlying portfolio performance measurement. This last topic is the subject of Chapter 8.

Portfolio theory is concerned with the selection of optimal portfolios by rational investors. A rational investor is defined as one who attempts to maximize expected return for any given level of expected risk or minimize expected risk for any given level of expected return. *Capital market theory* deals with the relationship between security returns and risk. These theories are intertwined and are treated together in this chapter.

Portfolio theory was originally proposed by Harry M. Markowitz in 1952.[1] Markowitz, William F. Sharpe, John Lintner, and Jack L. Treynor are credited with extending portfolio theory by developing what has come to be known as capital market theory.[2] Since their introduction, the models have stimulated extensive research examining the underpinnings of the theories and extending them. We have elected to defer consideration of this research until Chapter 7 in order not to distract the reader from the presentation of portfolio and capital market theory. Suffice it to say at this point that the empirical evidence has not been one-sided. However, relaxing the assumptions of the models to make them more realistic does not appear to jeopardize seriously the underlying concepts.

Investor Expectations

Other things being equal, a risk-averse investor will prefer less risk to more risk. In other words, as risk increases, the value or *utility* of a given expected return decreases. It is possible for an investor to determine the various combinations of expected returns and risks that provide a constant utility. For example, the portfolios shown below have been determined by an investor to have the following risk levels:

---

[1] Harry M. Markowitz, "Portfolio Selection," *Journal of Finance* (March 1952): pp. 77–91.

[2] Harry M. Markowitz, *Portfolio Selection*, New York: (Wiley, 1959); William F. Sharpe, "A Simplified Model for Portfolio Analysis," *Management Science* (January 1963): pp. 277–93; John Lintner, "Security Prices, Risk and Maximal Gains from Diversification," *Journal of Finance* (December 1965): pp. 587–615; and Jack L. Treynor, "How to Rate Management of Investment Funds," *Harvard Business Review* (January-Feburary 1965): pp. 63–75.

INVESMENT	RISK	EXPECTED RETURN
Portfolio A	1 (low)	?
Portfolio B	2	?
Portfolio C	3	?
Portfolio D	4	?
Portfolio E	5 (high)	?

By filling in the expected returns so that the investor maintains a constant utility for each portfolio, an *indifference curve* can be constructed. Figure 6.1 illustrates several possible indifference curves. For each indifference curve, utility is constant along the curve. The investor whose indifference curve is represented by I_1 has a very high tolerance for risk. This investor's expected or required return does not rise substantially with increasing levels or risk. On the other hand, the investor represented by indifference curve I_4 has a relatively high aversion to risk. In order for this investor to remain indifferent (utility remains constant) among investment alternatives of increasing risk, the returns on the higher-risk portfolios must increase substantially.

All of the indifference curves in Figure 6.1 show that as risk increases, the required return rises. This assumes that rational investors are risk averse. It is hard to imagine that any investor would be a "risk lover" (i.e., willing to accept lower levels of expected return for higher levels of risk). If "risk lovers" do exist, the actions of risk-averse individuals should offset their influence in pricing financial assets.

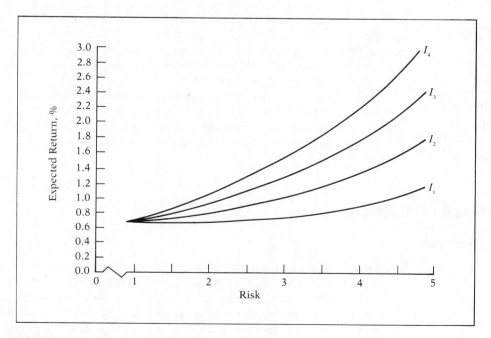

FIGURE 6.1 Indifference curves

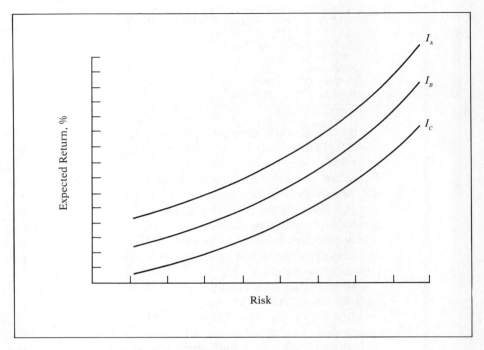

FIGURE 6.2 Investor's family of indifference curves

Each investor has a family of indifference curves, as shown in Figure 6.2. An investor should desire to be on indifference curve I_A since, for any given level of expected return, the expected risk is the lowest for I_A relative to I_B and I_C. Alternatively, for any given level of expected risk, the expected return is highest for I_A relative to I_B and I_C. Of the three indifference curves shown, indifference curve I_A provides maximum investor utility.

As the next section demonstrates, the investor should select the portfolio providing the highest utility. Not every portfolio is a candidate for selection; only those portfolios that are efficient in a risk-return sense should be considered. The determination of efficient portfolios is considered in the next section, on portfolio theory.

PORTFOLIO THEORY

Overview

Investors often define their investment portfolio as consisting only of common stocks, bonds, and other marketable securities. Further, investment portfolios are generally created piece by piece. A home is purchased; collectibles such as coins and stamps are acquired; common stocks, bonds, and other marketable securities are purchased. Each of these assets is treated as a separate investment, with little consideration given to the interaction of these assets within the investor's portfolio.

Portfolio theory warns us that defining an investment portfolio as consisting of only marketable securities is wrong. Further, making a decision to add or delete an asset based solely on the individual asset's expected risk and return characteristics will result in less than an optimum portfolio. Each asset's expected risk and return, along with the expected risk and return for other assets and their interrelationships, provide the data for portfolio analysis. Using this information, an *efficient portfolio*, defined as a portfolio that maximizes the expected rate of return at any given level of expected risk, can be identified. This portfolio is said to *dominate* all other portfolios with the same level of expected risk.

Portfolio Theory Assumptions

In order to construct an efficient portfolio, the investor must be able to quantify the portfolio's expected rate of return and an expected risk statistic. Markowitz developed the basic model which defined the expected rate of return of a portfolio as a weighted average of the expected returns of the individual assets in the portfolio.[3] The weights, X_j, are defined as the portion of the investor's wealth invested in a particular asset.

The measure of expected risk introduced by Markowitz was the variance of the expected rate of return. The risk of the portfolio is not the weighted average of the variances of the expected rate of return of the individual assets in the portfolio. To estimate portfolio risk in this way would obscure the effect of combining assets in a portfolio with different return patterns. Portfolio expected return and risk will be defined and illustrated in the next two sections.

The portfolio model developed by Markowitz is based on the following assumptions:

1. The expected rate of return from an asset is the mean value of a probability distribution of future expected returns over some holding period.

2. The risk of an individual asset or portfolio is based on the variability of expected returns (i.e., the standard deviation or variance).

3. Investors depend solely on their estimates of expected return and risk in making their investment decisions. This assumption means that an investor's utility curve is a function of expected return and risk.

4. Investors adhere to the *dominance principle*. That is, for any given level of risk, investors prefer assets with a higher expected rate of return to assets with a lower expected rate of return; for assets with same rate of expected return, investors prefer lower to higher risk.

Portfolio Return

As presented in Chapter 2, the single-period expected rate of return or holding period return, $E(HPR)$, is defined as

$$E(HPR) = \frac{\text{expected cash receipts} + (\text{expected ending price} - \text{beginning price})}{\text{beginning price}}$$

[3] Harry M. Markowitz, "Portfolio Selection," *Journal of Finance* (March 1952): pp. 77–91, and *Portfolio Selection* New York: (Wiley, 1959).

TABLE 6.1   PORTFOLIO EXPECTED RETURN

ASSET	ASSET WEIGHT (X_j)	ASSET EXPECTED RETURN (R_j)	PORTFOLIO EXPECTED RETURN $\left[E(R_p) = \sum_{j=1}^{n} X_j R_j \right]$
1	.30	12%	3.6%
2	.70	15	10.5
			$E(R_p) = \overline{14.1\%}$

For a share of common stock this measure of expected return, $E(HPR)$, can be expressed as

$$E(HPR) = \frac{D_{t+1} + P_{t+1} - P_t}{P_t} \tag{6.1}$$

where D_{t+1} is the expected cash dividends per share paid over the time interval t to $t + 1$, and P_t and P_{t+1} represent the price per share at the beginning and end of the period, respectively. Equation 6.1 expresses the rate of return in terms of the total return per dollar invested at the beginning of the period.

The expected rate of return of a portfolio is the weighted average of the expected returns of the individual assets in the portfolio. The weights are the proportion of the investor's wealth invested in each asset, X_j, and the sum of the weights must equal 1 (i.e., $\sum_{j=1}^{n} X_j = 1$). Assume that the expected rate of returns (R_j) and weights for a two-asset portfolio are as shown in Table 6.1. In this example, 30 percent of the portfolio's value is invested in asset 1, and 70 percent in asset 2. The expected returns for assets 1 and 2 are 12 percent and 15 percent, respectively. The expected return of the portfolio is calculated as follows:

$$
\begin{aligned}
E(R_p) &= \sum_{j=1}^{n} X_j R_j \\
&= (.30)(.12) + (.70)(.15) \\
&= 14.1\%
\end{aligned}
\tag{6.2}
$$

Equation 6.2 holds for any number, n, of assets in a portfolio.

Portfolio Risk

The calculation of a portfolio's risk is not as straightforward as the calculation of a portfolio's expected return. In order to calculate the risk of a portfolio, consideration must be given not only to the measure of risk of the individual assets in the portfolio and their relative weights but also to the degree to which there is comovement of the assets' returns. We measure the risk of an individual asset by the variance of returns or its square root, the standard deviation. The comovement of the assets' returns is measured by the covariance statistic. By combining the measures of individual asset risk (variance or standard deviation), relative asset weights, and the comovement of assets' returns (covariance), the risk of the portfolio can be estimated.

1. VARIANCE AND STANDARD DEVIATION It is tempting to measure the risk of an asset by considering the variability of its price changes. This is not appropriate, for several reasons. First, the calculated risk measure would depend on the level of the price of the asset. It is logical to assume that higher-priced assets would have higher absolute movements in price than lower-priced assets.

In addition to the scaling problem associated with price, the use of price data alone in determining risk ignores cash receipts such as dividends. In order to avoid these problems with the measurement of risk, an asset's expected holding period return $E(HPR)$ is used to determine risk.

The variance of an asset's returns around its expected value or its square root, the standard deviation, is used to define an asset's risk. The use of these measures is based on the assumption that the risk of an asset is a function of the degree to which the future return may deviate from its expected return. Equation 6.3 defines the variance of an asset's HPR, σ_j^2, as follows:

$$\sigma_j^2 = \sum_{j=1}^{n} [R_j - E(R_j)]^2 P_j \qquad (6.3)$$

where R_j is a possible HPR, P_j is the probability of the possible HPR, and $E(R_j)$ is the expected rate of return.

It is often convenient to measure risk by the square root of the variance or the standard deviation, σ_j, defined as

$$\sigma_j = \sqrt{\sigma_j^2} \qquad (6.4)$$

The computation of the variance and standard deviation as shown in Equations 6.3 and 6.4 requires the estimation of an asset's future possible returns and the probability associated with each of these returns. Since risk has been defined as the dispersion of future returns, this approach to measuring risk is logical.

Although we are interested in *ex-ante* or future uncertainty, risk or variance can also be calculated using historical HPRs:

$$\sigma_j^2 = \frac{1}{n} \sum_{t=1}^{n} (R_t - \bar{R}_j)^2 \qquad (6.5)$$

where n is the number of historically observed returns, R_t, and $\bar{R}_j$ is the mean of the historical returns.

The use of Equation 6.5 to estimate an *ex-ante* measure of risk is dependent on one's confidence that the *ex-post* or historical volatility of return accurately reflects *ex-ante* uncertainty. It has been shown that in most cases the rate of change in asset return volatility is quite slow.[4] If there is reason

---

[4] Marshall Blume, "On the Assessment of Risk," *Journal of Finance* (March 1971): pp. 1–10.

to believe that the historical return pattern will not reflect the future (e.g., a company has changed its business operations as a result of a major acquisition), then Equation 6.3 may be more appropriate to estimate *ex-ante* risk.

2. COVARIANCE AND CORRELATION According to portfolio theory, consideration must be given not only to the risk of the individual assets in the portfolio but also to the degree to which the returns of the assets covary or move together. Consider the return patterns shown in Figure 6.3. In the top portion of Figure 6.3 the returns on assets A and B appear to move in opposite directions each month. That is, in a particular month, if asset A's return is up from the previous month, asset B's return is down, and vice versa. This pattern indicates a negative correlation and covariance of returns between assets A and B.

In contrast, the lower portion of Figure 6.3 exhibits a different pattern in returns, for assets C and D. The returns move together from month to month; this would indicate a positive correlation and covariance of returns.

By combining assets A and B in a portfolio, the volatility of the returns of portfolio AB is reduced relative to the volatility in returns of the individual assets A and B. On the other hand, combining assets C and D does not significantly reduce the volatility of the returns of portfolio CD relative to the volatility of the individual assets. Figure 6.3 illustrates what is called the *portfolio effect* and demonstrates why the correlation or covariance between assets must be considered in determining the risk of a portfolio.

Using historical rates of return, the ex-post covariance for two assets, A and B, is defined as

$$Cov_{AB} = \frac{1}{n} \sum_{t=1}^{n} (R_{At} - \bar{R}_A)(R_{Bt} - \bar{R}_B) \qquad (6.6)$$

where R_{At} and R_{Bt} are the rates of return on the two assets, $\bar{R}_A$ and $\bar{R}_B$ are the average returns of assets A and B over the historical period, and n is the number of observations.

Equation 6.6 illustrates that, over time, if the returns on two assets are simultaneously above or below their respective means, the covariance will be positive (e.g., see assets C and D in Figure 6.3). Conversely, when the return on one asset is above its mean and the return on another asset is simultaneously below its mean, the covariance will be negative (e.g., see assets A and B in Figure 6.3). The examples in Figure 6.3 are designed to illustrate extreme negative and positive covariances. It is highly unlikely that in the real world comparative asset returns would move in the patterns shown in Figure 6.3. In some periods the returns from two assets may both be above their means, while in other periods the return from one asset may be above its mean and the return from the other asset below its mean.

The calculated value of the covariance measure is not easily interpreted. A covariance value such as +30 tells us only that the returns of the two assets tend to move together. Just as we used the *HPR* measure, as opposed to asset prices, to standardize for differences in the level of prices of assets, we can use the correlation coefficient to standardize the covariance measure. The

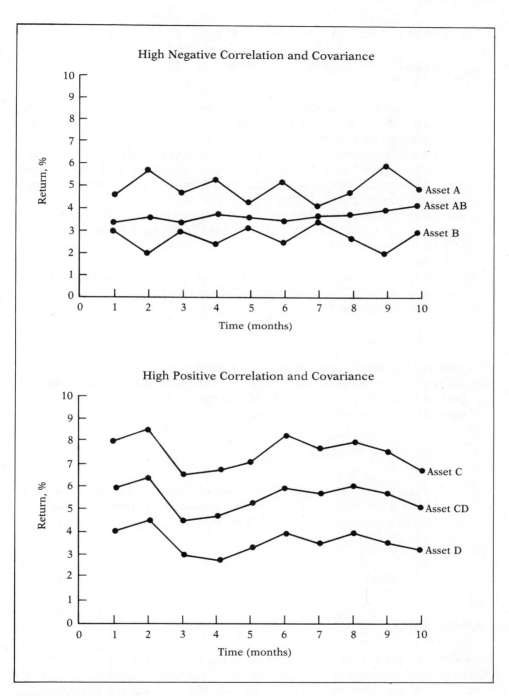

FIGURE 6.3   Return patterns

correlation coefficient, ρ_{AB}, is defined as

$$\rho_{AB} = \frac{Cov_{AB}}{\sigma_A \sigma_B} \tag{6.7}$$

The correlation statistic is a relative number which measures the degree to which two sets of numbers move together. As you may recall from statistics, the correlation statistic can take on a range of values between $+1.0$ and -1.0. Perfectly positive correlation, $+1.0$, indicates that the two sets of numbers move together perfectly (i.e., as one set of numbers moves above (below) the set's mean, the second set of numbers also moves above (below) the mean in the same proportion). If the two sets of numbers are perfectly negatively correlated, -1.0, then as one set of numbers moves above (below) its mean, the second set of numbers moves below (above) its mean. A correlation statistic of 0.0 indicates no consistent relationship between the movements of the two sets.

Solving Equation 6.7 for covariance allows us to express the covariance statistic in terms of the correlation coefficient and the standard deviations of the individual assets.

$$Cov_{AB} = \rho_{AB}\sigma_A\sigma_B \tag{6.8}$$

3. PORTFOLIO STANDARD DEVIATION Earlier we discussed the fact that the risk of the portfolio must consider not only the risk of the individual assets in the portfolio but their covariance. Markowitz included both of these statistics for measuring portfolio risk, as follows:

$$\sigma_p^2 = \sum_{i=1}^{n} \sum_{j=1}^{n} X_i X_j \, Cov_{ij} \tag{6.9}$$

Taking the square root of both sides of Equation 6.9 and substituting Equation 6.8 for the covariance measure allows us to express the risk of the portfolio in terms of its standard deviation, σ_p:

$$\sigma_p = \sqrt{\sum_{i=1}^{n} \sum_{j=1}^{n} X_i X_j \rho_{ij} \sigma_i \sigma_j} \tag{6.10}$$

Portfolio Risk: An Example

Equation 6.10 defines the measure of portfolio risk for n assets. It is useful to illustrate the calculation of portfolio risk for a portfolio comprising two assets rather than a large number of assets. The use of two assets not only simplifies the example; the two-asset portfolio also plays a central role in capital market theory.

1. THE TWO-ASSET CASE Table 6.2 uses historical returns for assets A and B (columns (2) and (3)) to illustrate the calculation of each asset's expected

TABLE 6.2 EXPECTED RETURN, VARIANCE, STANDARD DEVIATION, COVARIANCE, AND CORRELATION COEFFICIENT CALCULATION

YEAR (1)	ASSET A RETURNS, R_A (2)	ASSET B RETURNS, R_B (3)	$(R_{At} - \bar{R}_A)^2$ (4)	$(R_{Bt} - \bar{R}_B)^2$ (5)	$(R_{At} - \bar{R}_A)(R_{Bt} - \bar{R}_B)$ (6)
1979	16%	12%	129.96	12.25	39.90
1980	5	(2)	0.16	110.25	−4.20
1981	5	10	0.16	2.25	0.60
1982	6	6	1.96	6.25	−3.50
1983	(4)	11	73.96	6.25	−21.50
1984	6	3	1.96	30.25	−7.70
1985	0	(1)	21.16	90.25	43.70
1986	3	16	2.56	56.25	−12.00
1987	(2)	14	43.56	30.25	−36.30
1988	11	16	40.96	56.25	48.00
Total	46%	85%	316.40	400.50	47.00

STATISTICS

1. Mean, $\bar{R} = \dfrac{1}{n}\sum(R)$

$$\bar{R}_A = \frac{1}{10}(46\%) = 4.60\%$$

$$\bar{R}_B = \frac{1}{10}(85\%) = 8.50\%$$

2. Variance, $\sigma_j^2 = \dfrac{1}{n}\sum_{t=1}^{n}(R_{jt} - \bar{R}_j)^2$

$$\sigma_A^2 = \frac{1}{10}(316.40) = 31.64$$

$$\sigma_B^2 = \frac{1}{10}(400.50) = 40.05$$

3. Standard Deviation, $\sigma = \sqrt{\sigma^2}$

$$\sigma_A = \sqrt{31.64} = 5.62\%$$
$$\sigma_B = \sqrt{40.05} = 6.33\%$$

4. Covariance, $Cov_{AB} = \dfrac{1}{n}\sum_{t=1}^{n}(R_{At} - \bar{R}_A)(R_{Bt} - \bar{R}_B)$

$$Cov_{AB} = \frac{1}{10}(47.00) = 4.70$$

5. Correlation Coefficient, $\rho_{AB} = \dfrac{Cov_{AB}}{\sigma_A \sigma_B}$

$$\rho_{AB} = \frac{4.70}{(5.62)(6.33)} = .1321$$

return, R, variance, σ^2, standard deviation, σ, the covariance of assets A and B, Cov_{AB}, and the correlation coefficient, ρ_{AB}, between the returns of assets A and B. Historical returns are used because it is assumed that the *ex-post* return volatility of assets A and B are good estimates of *ex-ante* return volatility.

The value of the correlation coefficient in Table 6.2 is .1321, reasonably close to 0. This would indicate that there is not a very strong linear relationship between the returns of assets A and B. The importance of this relatively low correlation between assets A and B will become evident when the risk of the portfolio containing these two assets is estimated.

Suppose that assets A and B are combined in equal proportions to form a portfolio. That is, 50 percent of the portfolio's value is invested in asset A and 50 percent in asset B. Given this assumption, the weights of asset A, X_A, and asset B, X_B, are both equal to 50 percent. With this additional information, it is possible to calculate the total risk of the portfolio.

Recall from Equation 6.10 that the risk of a portfolio can be estimated as

$$\sigma_p = \sqrt{\sum_{i=1}^{n} \sum_{j=1}^{n} X_i X_j \rho_{ij} \sigma_i \sigma_j}$$

For a two-asset portfolio composed of assets A and B, Equation 6.10 can be rewritten as

$$\sigma_p = \sqrt{X_A^2 \sigma_A^2 + X_B^2 \sigma_B^2 + 2 X_A X_B \rho_{AB} \sigma_A \sigma_B} \tag{6.11}$$

Given the equal weights assigned to assets A and B and the information from Table 6.2, we can calculate the risk, σ_p, of the portfolio as follows:

$$\sigma_p = \sqrt{(.5)^2 (5.62)^2 + (.5)^2 (6.33)^2 + 2(.5)(.5)(.1321)(5.62)(6.33)}$$
$$= \sqrt{7.90 + 10.02 + 2.35}$$
$$= \sqrt{20.27}$$
$$= 4.50\%$$

It is important to note that the expected risk of the portfolio, ($\sigma_p = 4.50\%$) is *less* than the expected risk of either asset A (5.62%) or asset B (6.33%). This reduction in risk illustrates the portfolio effect of combining assets that are less than perfectly correlated (i.e., the correlation between the returns of the two assets is less than +1.0). As will be shown below, the higher the correlation between two assets, the lower the impact on expected portfolio risk of combining them in a portfolio.

Breaking the right side of Equation 6.11 into its parts illustrates the portfolio effect. The first two terms ($X_A^2 \sigma_A^2 + X_B^2 \sigma_B^2$) are very similar to a portfolio's expected return (Equation 6.2) calculation. Rather than using the weighted average of the assets' expected returns, the weighted average of the assets' variances are used. The last term in Equation 6.11 considers the degree to which the two assets move together. The lower the correlation coefficient, the lower the risk of the portfolio. Thus, it is clear from the equation that combining two assets with negative correlation ($\rho_{AB} < 0$) will significantly reduce the risk of the portfolio.

2. THE THREE-ASSET CASE Suppose a third asset, C, is included in the portfolio, and asset C has the following expected characteristics:

$$\bar{R}_C = 16\% \qquad \rho_{BC} = .2000$$
$$\sigma_C = 7.50\% \qquad X_A = .33$$
$$\rho_{AC} = .1500 \qquad X_B = .33$$
$$X_C = .34$$

Note that the addition of asset C requires the calculation of three correlation coefficients (ρ_{AB}, ρ_{AC}, and ρ_{BC}) as opposed to one in the two-asset case. The addition of assets under consideration for a portfolio adds to the complexity of the calculations. This problem is addressed in the discussion of capital market theory in the next section of the chapter.

Using Equation 6.10 where $n = 3$, the variance of the portfolio can be estimated as follows[5]:

$$\sigma_p^2 = (X_A^2)(\sigma_A^2) + (X_B^2)(\sigma_B^2) + (X_C^2)(\sigma_C^2) + 2X_A X_B \rho_{AB}\sigma_A\sigma_B$$
$$+ 2X_B X_C \rho_{BC}\sigma_B\sigma_C + 2X_A X_C \rho_{AC}\sigma_A\sigma_C$$
$$= (.33)^2(5.62)^2 + (.33)^2(6.33)^2 + (.34)^2(7.50)^2$$
$$+ 2(.33)(.33)(.1321)(5.62)(6.33) + 2(.33)(.34)(.2000)(6.33)(7.50)$$
$$+ 2(.33)(.34)(.1500)(5.62)(7.50)$$
$$= 3.44 + 4.36 + 6.50 + 1.02 + 2.13 + 1.42$$
$$= 18.87$$

The standard deviation can be estimated as

$$\sigma_p = \sqrt{\sigma_p^2} = \sqrt{18.87}$$
$$= 4.34\%$$

The risk of this three-asset portfolio, 4.34 percent, is less than the risk of any of the three individual assets in the portfolio. This is because in this case the correlation between assets A and B, B and C, and A and C are all substantially less than $+1$. Also, the fact that the risk of the three-asset portfolio, 4.34 percent, is less than the risk of the two-asset portfolio, 4.50 percent, illustrates the impact of portfolio diversification. This reduction in risk occurred even though the expected return of 9.76 percent for the three-asset portfolio [i.e., $(.33)(4.60\%) + (.33)(8.50\%) + (.34)(16.00\%)$] is greater than the 6.55 percent return estimated for the portfolio containing only assets A and B [i.e., $(.5)(4.60\%) + (.5)(8.50\%)$].

3. CORRELATION COEFFICIENT AND PORTFOLIO RISK In order to assess the impact of the correlation coefficient on portfolio risk, assume that the calculated correlation coefficients for assets A and B in Table 6.2 have the following values rather than the calculated value of .1321:

Case 1: $\rho_{AB} =$ 1.00

Case 2: $\rho_{AB} =$ 0.00

Case 3: $\rho_{AB} = -1.00$

Also, assume the weights, X_j, of assets A and B in the portfolio are allowed to have values ranging between 0 and 100 percent. Table 6.3 shows the portfolio's expected return and risk for varying weights, for each of the three correlation coefficients.

---

[5] Equation 6.10 reduces to the three-asset case shown by recalling that $\sigma_A \times \sigma_A = \sigma_A^2$, $X_A \times X_A = X_A^2$, $\rho_{AA} = 1$, and $\rho_{AB} = \rho_{BA}$.

TABLE 6.3 CORRELATION COEFFICIENT AND PORTFOLIO RISK

Case 1: $\rho_{AB} = 1.00$, $\bar{R}_A = 4.60\%$, $\bar{R}_B = 8.50\%$, $\sigma_A = 5.62\%$, $\sigma_B = 6.33\%$

X_A	X_B	σ_p	$E(R_p)$
100%	0%	5.62%	4.60%
75	25	5.80	5.58
50	50	5.98	6.55
25	75	6.15	7.52
0	100	6.33	8.50

Case 2: $\rho_{AB} = 0.00$, $\bar{R}_A = 4.60\%$, $\bar{R}_B = 8.50\%$, $\sigma_A = 5.62\%$, $\sigma_B = 6.33\%$

X_A	X_B	σ_p	$E(R_p)$
100%	0%	5.62%	4.60%
75	25	4.50	5.58
50	50	4.24	6.55
25	75	4.95	7.52
0	100	6.33	8.50

Case 3: $\rho_{AB} = -1.00$, $\bar{R}_A = 4.60\%$, $\bar{R}_B = 8.50\%$, $\sigma_A = 5.62\%$, $\sigma_B = 6.33\%$

X_A	X_B	σ_p	$E(R_p)$
100%	0%	5.62%	4.60%
75	25	2.63	5.58
50	50	0.46	6.55
25	75	3.34	7.52
0	100	6.33	8.50

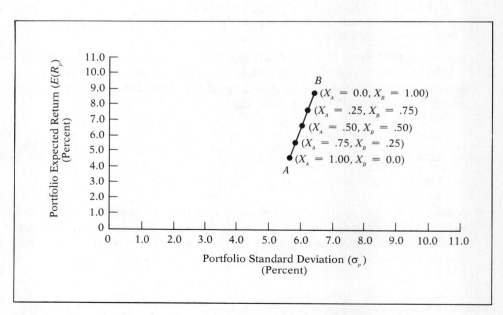

FIGURE 6.4 Plot of risk and return for perfectly positively correlated assets ($\rho = 1.00$)

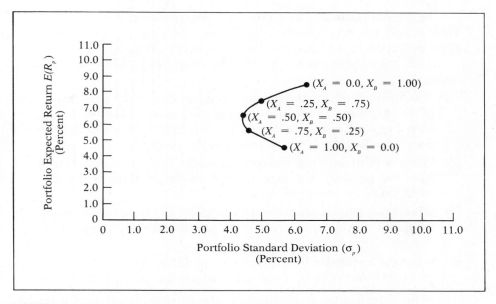

FIGURE 6.5 Plot of risk and return for zero-correlated assets ($\rho = 0.00$)

Figures 6.4, 6.5, and 6.6 are plots of the information from Table 6.3. The points in the figures are connected on the assumption that the proportion invested in each asset, X_j, can vary in much smaller increments than shown in Table 6.3.

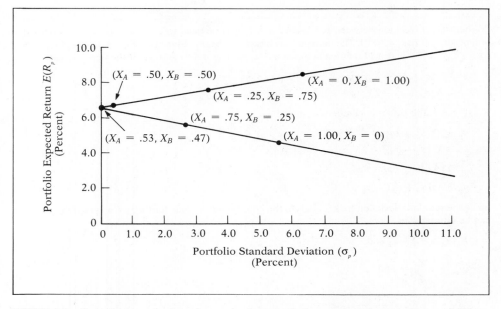

FIGURE 6.6 Plot of risk and return for perfectly negatively correlated assets ($\rho = -1.00$)

Figure 6.6 contains one more point estimate than that provided from Table 6.3. This portfolio (with $X_A = .53$, $X_B = .47$, and $\rho_{AB} = -1.00$) has an expected return of 6.43 percent and an expected risk of $0.$[6]

Table 6.3 and Figures 6.4, 6.5, and 6.6 allow us to make several observations:

(1) The expected return of a portfolio is a function of the expected returns of the assets in the portfolio and the proportion of the portfolio represented by each asset. The correlation between the assets in the portfolio does not affect the expected return of the portfolio.

(2) When a portfolio contains only one asset (i.e., $X_A = 100$ percent, or $X_B = 100$ percent), the expected risk of the portfolio is the standard deviation of the return of the asset.

(3) When asset weights are not equal to 0, the lower the correlation between the assets, the lower the risk of the portfolio for any given set of asset weights.

(4) When the correlation between assets is perfectly positive (i.e., $\rho_{AB} = +1$), the risk of the portfolio is the weighted average of the risk of the assets in the portfolio ($\sigma_p = \sum_{j=1}^{n} X_j\sigma_j$) and the portfolios plot along a straight line.

(5) When the correlation between assets is perfectly negative (i.e., $\rho_{AB} = -1$), it is possible to create a portfolio with 0 risk.

(6) Some portfolios dominate other portfolios (e.g., for a given level of risk, the expected return of one portfolio is greater than the expected return of another portfolio), and the dominant portfolio would be preferred by the investor. For example, in the case where the correlation coefficient

---

[6] When the correlation between two assets is -1, it is possible to calculate the asset weights that will produce 0 risk ($\sigma_p = 0$). The derivation is based on algebra. Since the sum of the weights is equal to 1, ($X_B = 1 - X_A$) from Equation 6.10 for $n = 2$, we know the variance of the portfolio is

$$\sigma_p^2 = X_A^2\sigma_A^2 + (1 - X_A)^2\sigma_B^2 + 2X_A(1 - X_A)\rho_{AB}\sigma_A\sigma_B$$
$$= X_A^2\sigma_A^2 + \sigma_B^2 - 2X_A\sigma_B^2 + X_A^2\sigma_B^2 + 2X_A\rho_{AB}\sigma_A\sigma_B - 2X_A^2\rho_{AB}\sigma_A\sigma_B$$

If $\rho_{AB} = -1$, the equation can be rearranged as

$$\sigma_p^2 = X_A^2[\sigma_A^2 + 2\sigma_A\sigma_B + \sigma_B^2] - 2X_A[\sigma_B^2 + \sigma_A\sigma_B] + \sigma_B^2$$
$$= X_A^2[\sigma_A + \sigma_B]^2 - 2X_A\sigma_B[\sigma_A + \sigma_B] + \sigma_B^2$$
$$= (X_A[\sigma_A + \sigma_B] - \sigma_B)^2$$

$$\sigma_p = X_A[\sigma_A + \sigma_B] - \sigma_B$$

Since the standard deviation (risk) equals 0, the appropriate weights for the two assets in the portfolio can be estimated as

$$X_A[\sigma_A + \sigma_B] - \sigma_B = 0$$

$$X_A = \frac{\sigma_B}{\sigma_A + \sigma_B}, \text{ and}$$

$$X_B = 1 - X_A = \frac{\sigma_A}{\sigma_A + \sigma_B}$$

equals 0, a portfolio with asset A representing 36 percent of the portfolio and asset B the remaining 64 percent, the risk of this portfolio is approximately 4.5 percent ($[(.36)^2(5.62)^2 + (.64)^2(6.33)^2]^{1/2}$). This is the same risk level as a portfolio consisting of 75 percent asset A and 25 percent asset B (Table 6.3). However, the portfolio with $X_A = 36$ percent and $X_B = 64$ percent has an expected return of 7.1 percent [$(.36)(4.60) + (.64)(8.50)$], whereas the portfolio with $X_A = 75$ percent and $X_B = 25$ percent has an expected return of only 5.58 percent. Thus, portfolio $X_A = 36$ percent and $X_B = 64$ percent dominates the portfolio with $X_A = 75$ percent and $X_B = 25$ percent.

The Efficient Frontier

To this point we have dealt with portfolios containing only one, two, or three assets. Figures 6.4, 6.5, and 6.6 demonstrated that with only two assets being considered for inclusion in the portfolio, a large number of potential portfolios can be generated by simply varying the proportion invested in each asset.

If n assets are considered (where n can take on values of 100, 500, 1000, etc.) the number of potential portfolios is even larger. If potential portfolios are plotted in risk-return space, as shown by the dots in Figure 6.7, it is apparent that certain portfolios are preferred over others.

You will recall that we defined a rational investor as one who attempts to maximize expected return for any given level of expected risk or minimize expected risk for any given level of expected return. In Figure 6.7, portfolio R is preferred by rational investors to portfolio T, since at the given level of expected

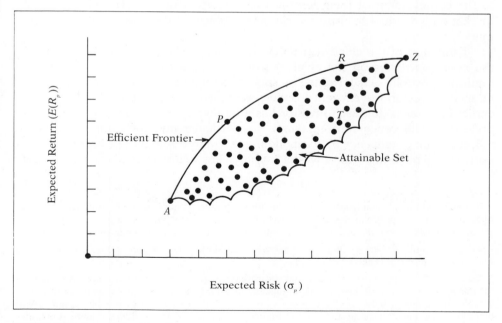

FIGURE 6.7 The efficient frontier

risk, the expected return for portfolio R is greater than the expected return for portfolio T. Portfolio P is also preferred to portfolio T by rational investors, since portfolios P and T have the same level of expected return but portfolio P has a lower level of expected risk.

All possible portfolios, including one-asset portfolios, comprise what is called the *attainable set* of investment opportunities. However, at any given level of expected risk (return) there is one portfolio that provides the highest (lowest) level of expected return (risk). This set of portfolios dominates all other portfolios in the attainable set and lies on what is referred to as the *efficient frontier*. With the possible exception of portfolios A and Z, portfolios on the efficient frontier will contain more than one asset, because of the portfolio effect of combining assets with returns that are less than perfectly correlated ($\rho < +1.0$).

Construction of the "true" efficient frontier requires that we consider the risk and return statistics for *all* assets. Even if it were possible to get return and risk data for all assets, the information and computation costs would be formidable.[7] Even if the assets to be considered for inclusion in the estimation of the efficient frontier were limited just to common stocks traded in the United States, the information and computation costs for these thousands of issues would be prohibitive.

Research has shown that when considering only common stocks as components of portfolios on the efficient frontier, a sample size of several hundred randomly selected securities will provide an estimate of the efficient frontier not significantly different from the one using the entire universe of common stocks.[8] In other words, increasing the number of securities beyond several hundred in estimating the efficient frontier only marginally improves the expected return at any given level of risk.[9] This reduction in the necessary number of securities is related to the fact that a certain portion of the returns on common stocks is due to the comovement of their returns with "market forces." The impact of the market on individual security returns is the subject of the next section on capital market theory.

Estimaton of the efficient frontier still requires the investor to select one of the many portfolios on the efficient frontier. The selection of the appropriate (optimal) portfolio is determined by superimposing the investor's family of indifference curves on the efficient frontier, as shown in Figure 6.8. Recall from the earlier discussion that each investor has a family of indifference curves, and the preferred indifference curve maximizes a particular investor's utility. In Figure 6.8, the point of tangency between indifference curve I_B and the efficient frontier, portfolio S, maximizes the investor's utility. Portfolios on indifference curve I_C

---

[7] Estimation of the efficient frontier requires quadratic programming which will simultaneously estimate the minimum portfolio risk at each level of expected return. When a large number of assets are under consideration, the computational requirement, even with a computer, is quite demanding.

[8] See, for example, Robert A. Olsen, "Sample Size and Markowitz Diversification," *The Journal of Portfolio Management* (Fall 1983): pp. 18—22.

[9] The advent of the personal computer and software developed to perform portfolio analysis allows for this analysis to be undertaken by the individual investor. The software accompanying this book contains a Markowitz-based portfolio analysis program. Software for portfolio analysis, along with other investment analysis programs, is sold commercially by a number of vendors. Chapter 4 provides information on software and hardware costs.

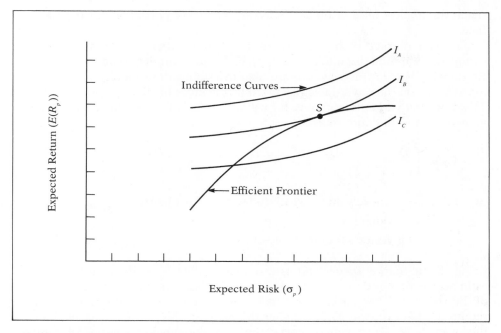

FIGURE 6.8 Optimum portfolio selection

would not be selected because investor utility is higher for portfolios on indifference curve I_B than for those on I_C. Portfolios to reach indifference curve I_A with even higher utility, are not attainable. Thus, portfolio S is optimal for an investor with the family of indifference curves shown in Figure 6.8.

Unless investors have identical families of indifference curves, investors will select different portfolios on the efficient frontier. An investor more risk averse than that shown in Figure 6.8 will have an indifference curve with a tangency point to the left of portfolio S on the efficient frontier (i.e., the investor will select a portfolio with lower expected return and risk). An investor with a very high tolerance for risk will have a family of indifference curves that indicate the selection of a portfolio on the efficient frontier to the right of portfolio S. In sum, the selection of the optimal portfolio will depend on the individual investor's utility preference.

CAPITAL MARKET THEORY

Overview

To this point in the chapter we have examined portfolio risk and return, and established that investors should be interested in investing only in diversified portfolios that lie on the efficient frontier. In Figure 6.7, it is apparent that there are many assets and portfolios that do not lie on the efficient frontier. If these assets are purchased, the investor will not be fully compensated (i.e., will not reach the highest level of utility), relative to efficient portfolios, for the total risk faced.

Capital market theory allows us to examine these inefficient assets and subdivide their total risk into its "rewardable" and "nonrewardable" components. By dividing risk in this way, we are able to establish the required return on an asset, based on the rewardable risk faced by the investor. For example, in Chapter 11 we present various techniques for valuing common stock. One basic technique is the dividend discount model:

$$V_0 = \frac{D_1}{(1 + K)^1} + \frac{D_2}{(1 + K)^2} + \frac{D_3}{(1 + K)^3} + \cdots + \frac{D_\infty}{(1 + K)^\infty} \qquad (6.12)$$

where V_0 = intrinsic value of stock today or at time period 0

D_t = dividends per share in period t

K = investor's required rate of return

Using capital market theory and assessing rewardable risk, the investor is able to estimate the required rate of return, K, for the stock. The estimated intrinsic value of the stock, V_0, has an inverse relationship with the investor's estimate of the required rate of return, K. The higher the K, other things remaining unchanged, the lower the V_0. Thus, capital market theory has pricing implications for common stocks and helps explain why its derivative security returns model is called the capital asset pricing model, CAPM.

Whereas portfolio theory deals with the selection of optimal portfolios, capital market theory deals with a general equilibrium model of asset prices, assuming that investors behave in the optimal manner specified by portfolio theory. Specifically, capital market theory postulates the *ex-ante* risk-return relationship of individual assets as well as portfolios under equilibrium conditions.

Capital Market Theory Assumptions

Capital market theory, CMT, uses portfolio theory as its starting point; thus, the assumptions underlying portfolio theory also pertain to CMT. The additional assumptions underlying CMT appear less realistic than the portfolio theory assumptions. The relaxation of assumptions and the impact of relaxing these assumptions on CMT will be discussed in Chapter 7. The assumptions of CMT are as follows:

1. All investors maximize mean/variance utility functions and are risk averse. Thus, all investors seek to be on the efficient frontier.

2. There are no constraints on the amount of money that can be borrowed or lent. Borrowing and lending occur at the identical risk-free rate, R_f.

3. All investors have identical expectations about the returns and risks of assets and portfolios; that is, all investors have homogeneous expectations.

4. All investors have a common investment horizon, whether it be one month, three months, one year, etc.

5. All investments are infinitely divisible and marketable; that is, it is possible to buy or sell any portion of an asset or portfolio.

6. Taxes and costs of buying and selling securities do not exist. That is, there are no tax effects, costs of acquiring information, or transaction costs associated with buying or selling securities. These are often referred to as perfect market characteristics. Markets are assumed to be competitive: the same investment opportunities are available to all investors.

7. There are no unanticipated changes in inflation or interest rates.

8. The capital markets are in a state of equilibrium or striving toward equilibrium.

The Capital Market Line

1. RISK-FREE ASSET CMT assumes that a "riskless" asset exists and that all investors can borrow or lend in unlimited amounts at the risk-free rate, R_f (assumption 2, above). In order for an asset to be classified as riskless, its expected rate of return must be known with certainty. In other words, there is no deviation around the expected return. The yield on U.S. Treasury bills is often used as a proxy for the risk-free asset. Because of the short maturity and backing by the U.S. government, Treasury bills have relatively stable returns, and the risk of default is nil.

2. THE TWO-ASSET CASE REVISITED Adding a risk-free asset means that investors can allocate a portion of their investment wealth to the risk-free asset and the remaining portion to a portfolio on the efficient frontier. The expected return on this portfolio will be the weighted average of the expected returns on the risk-free asset and the portfolio. The weights are the proportions of the investor's wealth invested in each asset. Since we know that the sum of the weights, X_j, must equal 1, the expected return of the portfolio can be expressed as

$$E(R_p) = \sum_{j=1}^{n} X_j R_j \qquad (6.13)$$
$$= X_f R_f + (1 - X_f)E(R_j)$$

where X_f is the proportion invested in the risk-free asset, R_f is the rate of return on the risk-free asset, and $E(R_j)$ is the expected return of the portfolio on the efficient frontier. The equation for the risk of this two-asset portfolio can be derived starting with Equation 6.11 as follows:

$$\sigma_p = \sqrt{X_A^2 \sigma_A^2 + X_B^2 \sigma_B^2 + 2X_A X_B \rho_{AB} \sigma_A \sigma_B}$$
$$= \sqrt{X_f^2 \sigma_f^2 + (1 - X_f)^2 \sigma_j^2 + 2X_f(1 - X_f)\rho_{fj}\sigma_f \sigma_j}$$

Since the variance of the risk-free asset, σ_f^2, is, by definition, 0 and the correlation (and covariance) of returns between the risk-free asset and the portfolio on the efficient frontier, ρ_{fj}, is also 0,

$$\sigma_p = \sqrt{0 + (1 - X_f)^2 \sigma_j^2 + 2X_f(1 - X_f)(0)(0)(\sigma_j)} \qquad (6.14)$$
$$= \sqrt{(1 - X_f)^2 \sigma_j^2}$$
$$= (1 - X_f)\sigma_j$$

where σ_j is the standard deviation of the portfolio on the efficient frontier.

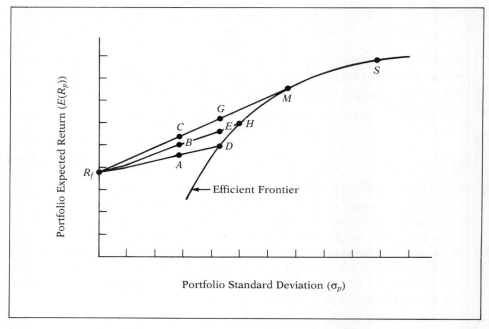

FIGURE 6.9   Portfolios formed by combining portfolios on the efficient frontier with the risk-free asset

Figure 6.9 shows several possible portfolios—*A*, *B*, *C*, *E*, and *G*—that can be constructed by combining the risk-free asset with a portfolio on the efficient frontier. For example, portfolios *B* and *E* are formed by combining the risk-free asset with portfolio *H* on the efficient frontier. Portfolio *B* contains a higher proportion of the risk-free asset than does portfolio *E*.

Equations 6.13 and 6.14 indicate that the portfolio expected return and risk are linear functions of the proportion invested in the risk-free asset, X_f. Thus, as plotted in Figure 6.9, portfolios composed of the risk-free asset and a single portfolio on the efficient frontier will plot as a straight line, with the intercept equal to the return on the risk-free asset. The portfolio's expected return and risk will vary directly with the proportion invested in the risk-free asset.

Assuming that investors are rational (i.e., for any given level of risk, a higher expected return is preferred to a lower expected return), then from Figure 6.9, portfolio *C* is preferred to portfolio *B*, and portfolio *B* is preferred to portfolio *A*. In other words, portfolio *C* dominates portfolios *A* and *B*. Using the same logic, portfolio *G* dominates portfolios *E* and *D*.

The number of lines emanating from R_f to the efficient frontier is limited only by the number of portfolios on the efficient frontier.[10] The risk-return

---

[10] Many additional portfolios could be constructed by combining the risk-free asset with portfolios in the attainable set. However, since it has been shown that portfolios on the efficient frontier dominate all other portfolios in the attainable set, a rational investor would not consider these alternative portfolios.

characteristics of these alternative portfolios is a function of the proportion of the portfolio invested in the risk-free asset.

A line emanating from R_f to the efficient frontier with the greatest slope will contain portfolios that have the highest expected return for any given level of risk. Alternatively, a line emanating from R_f to the efficient frontier with the greatest slope will contain the lowest risk for any given level of expected return. The line with the greatest slope will have a tangency point with the efficient frontier. In Figure 6.9, it is line R_fM. Every portfolio alternative on line R_fM dominates all other portfolios, including those on the efficient frontier below portfolio M.

3. BORROWING AND LENDING PORTFOLIOS Recall from assumption 2 of CMT that there are no constraints on the amount of money that investors can borrow or lend and that borrowing and lending occurs at the risk-free rate R_f. This assumption allows us to extend the R_fM line as shown in Figure 6.10.

The extended R_fM line is known as the *capital market line*, CML. Investors wishing to face less risk will combine an investment in portfolio M with an investment in the risk-free asset. In other words, they will lend a portion of their investable funds at the risk-free rate R_f. These portfolios are designated as lending portfolios in Figure 6.10.

Investors willing to face higher levels of risk in order to achieve expected returns higher than that offered by portfolio M will borrow at the risk-free rate and will buy portfolio M with their investable funds as well as funds borrowed at the risk-free rate. These leveraged portfolios are designated as borrowing portfolios in Figure 6.10.

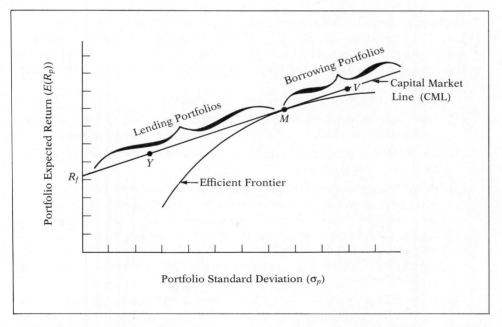

FIGURE 6.10 The capital market line with unlimited borrowing and lending at the risk-free rate

Using Equations 6.13 and 6.14, the impact of borrowing and lending on expected return and risk can be demonstrated. Assume that portfolio M has an expected return, $E(R_M)$, of 16 percent and expected risk, σ_M, of 5 percent and that the risk-free rate, R_f, is 7 percent. Also assume that portfolio Y in Figure 6.10 has 60 percent of investable funds in portfolio M and that portfolio V has 130 percent of investable funds in portfolio M (i.e., X_f for portfolio Y is .40, and X_f for portfolio V is $-.30$). The expected returns for portfolios Y and V, using Equation 6.13, can be calculated as

$$E(R_Y) = (.40)(.07) + (1 - .40)(.16)$$
$$= .028 + .096$$
$$= 12.4\%$$

$$E(R_V) = (-.30)(.07) + [(1 - (-.30)](.16)$$
$$= -.021 + .208$$
$$= 18.7\%$$

Using Equation 6.14, the expected risks of portfolios Y and V can be calculated as

$$\sigma_Y = (1 - .40)(.05)$$
$$= 3\%$$

$$\sigma_V = [(1 - (-.30)](.05)$$
$$= 6.5\%$$

Comparing the expected returns and risks of the lending and borrowing portfolios with portfolio M ($E(R_M) = 16\%$, and $\sigma_p = 5\%$) shows the impact of borrowing and lending. The lending portfolio Y has less expected return and risk than portfolio M, and the borrowing portfolio has a higher expected return and risk.

Figure 6.10 allows us to make several observations about the CML:

(1) Portfolios on the CML dominate all other portfolios and are thus preferred to all portfolios on the efficient frontier except portfolio M.

(2) The CML is a straight line consisting of various combinations of portfolio M and the risk-free asset.

(3) Recall from Figure 6.4 that two assets that are perfectly positively correlated plot as a straight line in risk-return space as the weights of the assets in the portfolios vary. The portfolios on the CML consisting of a combination of portfolio M and the risk-free asset are thus perfectly positively correlated. This is a logical conclusion since from Equation 6.14, the standard deviation of a portfolio on the CML is a function of volatility of only one portfolio, portfolio M.

(4) If all investors vary their portfolio composition between portfolio M and the risk-free asset, then the selection of a risk level is separated from the problem of choosing risky assets to be included in the portfolio. In other words, all investors will choose the same portfolio of risky assets, port-

folio M, regardless of their individual utility preferences (indifference curves). This important distinction, known as the *separation theorem*, was first suggested by James Tobin.[11]

(5) The CML expresses the relationship between expected return and *total* portfolio risk. Since portfolio M is assumed to be perfectly diversified, portfolios on the CML are also perfectly diversified and contain only "rewardable" risk. This means that only portfolios and not individual assets will lie on the CML.

This last observation will become more meaningful when portfolio M is defined in the next section and the distinction between "rewardable" and "nonrewardable" risk is explained.

4. THE MARKET PORTFOLIO If the investment holdings of all investors willing to face some level of risk should contain portfolio M, then this portfolio must be a very large portfolio, consisting of all risky assets. Given that the capital markets are in equilibrium (assumption 8), portfolio M is constructed in such a way that each risky asset is represented in the portfolio in proportion to its value relative to the total value of all risky assets:

$$X_j = \frac{\text{total value of risky asset } j}{\text{total value of all risky assets}} \qquad (6.15)$$

This hypothetical portfolio, M, is called the *market portfolio*.[12] Since it contains all risky assets, in proportion to their market value, it is a perfectly diversified portfolio. That is, the market portfolio (or any of the portfolios on the CML) is subject only to *systematic risk* or "nondiversifiable" risk. The volatility of the market portfolio is due to macroeconomic factors that affect all risky assets (e.g., change in expected rates of inflation, interest rates, etc.) and not company-or industry-specific factors (i.e., change in sales expectations for a particular product, pollution laws, etc.). Volatility in returns created by unique company-or industry-specific factors is called *unsystematic* or "diversifiable" risk, and this risk can be diversified away by adding risky assets to the portfolio.[13]

A portfolio's (or a single asset's) total risk is equal to the sum of its systematic risk and unsystematic risk. In the case of the market portfolio there is no unsystematic or diversifiable risk, and total risk equals systematic risk. Since it is possible to eliminate all unsystematic risk through perfect diversification, the capital markets do not reward investors for facing unsystematic risk. (This is why total risk for inefficient assets was referred to earlier as being separated into its "rewardable" and "non-rewardable" components.) Thus, the CML shown in Figure 6.10 holds only for perfectly diversified portfolios and not for portfolios that have diversifiable or unsystematic risk.

---

[11] James Tobin, "Liquidity Preference as Behavior towards Risk," *Review of Economic Studies* (February 1958): pp. 65–86.

[12] Eugene Fama, "Risk, Return and Equilibrium: Some Clarifying Comments," *Journal of Finance* (March 1968): pp. 32–33.

[13] In the discussion of the security market line, below, the measures of systematic and unsystematic risk will be developed.

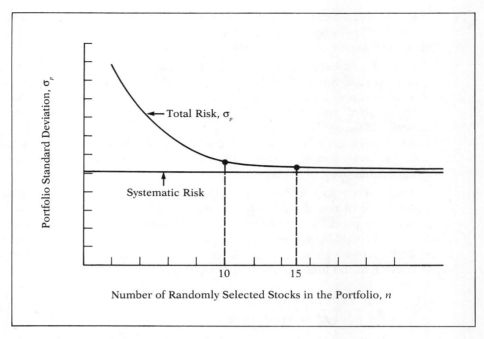

FIGURE 6.11 Naive diversification and portfolio unsystematic risk

We have been very careful to this point in defining the market portfolio as consisting of all risky assets, combined in proportion to their market value. Realistic measures of the market portfolio defined in this way are impractical to estimate. Therefore, proxies for the market portfolio, such as the Dow Jones Industrial Average or the Standard & Poor's Composite 500 Stock Index, are often used.[14] When using these proxies, the market portfolio can be thought of as a composite of common stocks.

A number of studies have been conducted to determine how many stocks must be included in a portfolio in order to eliminate diversifiable risk.[15] That is, using random selection or naive diversification, how many stocks, on average, must be included in a portfolio for total risk to equal systematic risk? The answer is that between ten to fifteen stocks will remove a large proportion of the unsystematic or diversifiable risk of the portfolio and that adding additional stocks beyond this number only marginally reduces the unsystematic risk of the portfolio. Figure 6.11 illustrates the impact of naively diver-

---

[14] The problem associated with using proxies for the "true" market portfolio will be discussed in Chapter 7.

[15] These studies include Lawrence Fisher and James H. Lorie, "Some Studies of Variability of Returns on Investment in Common Stock," *Journal of Business* (April 1970): pp. 99–134; John L. Evans and Stephen H. Archer, "Diversification and the Reduction of Dispersion: An Empirical Analysis," *Journal of Finance* (December 1968): pp. 761–67; and Wayne H. Wagner and S. C. Lau, "The Effect of Diversification on Risk," *Financial Analysts Journal* (November-December 1971): pp. 48–53.

sifying a portfolio by adding randomly selected securities to the portfolio. As Figure 6.11 illustrates, after about ten stocks, the impact of additional stocks in reducing total risk to the systematic level of risk is quite small.

5. THE PRINCIPLE OF RISK COMPENSATION In Figure 6.10, the CML goes through the point of the market portfolio's expected return, $E(R_M)$, and risk, σ_M, and the intercept of the CML is the risk-free rate, R_f. The equation for the CML can thus be expressed as

$$E(R_p) = R_f + \left[\frac{E(R_M) - R_f}{\sigma_M}\right]\sigma_p \tag{6.16}$$

where $E(R_p)$ and σ_p are the expected return and standard deviation of a portfolio on the CML.

Equation 6.16 expresses the principle of risk compensation.[16] For a portfolio on the CML, the expected return is equal to the risk-free rate plus a return proportional to the total risk of the portfolio. The slope of the CML

$$\frac{E(R_M) - R_f}{\sigma_M}$$

is the same for all portfolios on the CML and is called the *market price of risk*. Since each of the portfolios on the CML is perfectly diversified, these portfolios have an expected return above the risk-free rate proportional to their own total risk.

The Security Market Line

The CML defines the relationship between total risk and expected return for portfolios consisting of the risk-free asset and the market portfolio. How is the risk-return relationship for *individual* assets defined in a capital market that is in equilibrium? Earlier it was indicated that investors are rewarded only for assuming systematic or nondiversifiable risk. In this section, the relationship between an asset's systematic risk and the expected rate of return will be developed.

1. SYSTEMATIC AND UNSYSTEMATIC RISK Recall from Equation 6.9 that the risk of a portfolio is a function of the covariance of the individual assets in the portfolio. The higher the covariance between the assets, the higher the risk. From CMT we know that the investment holdings of all investors willing to face some level of risk will contain some proportion of the market portfolio. Individual assets or portfolios that have a high covariance of returns with the market portfolio will not significantly reduce the risk of the portfolio; thus, their prices will reflect this lack of popularity. Since the income-generating ability of these assets is unaffected by their covariance with the market portfolio, the lower their prices, the higher their expected returns. The opposite

---

[16] For an excellent discussion of this principle, see Oldrich A. Vasicek and John A. McQuown, "The Efficient Market Model," *Financial Analysts Journal* (September-October 1972): pp. 71–84.

relationship will exist for assets with low covariances of returns with the market portfolio. They will be actively sought by investors, with resultant price increases and lower expected returns.

Following this line of reasoning, the relationship between the expected rate of return for *any* asset or portfolio, $E(R_j)$, and its covariance with the market portfolio can be expressed as

$$E(R_j) = R_f + (P)Cov_{jM} \tag{6.17}$$

where Cov_{jM} is the covariance of the asset or portfolio j with the market portfolio, and P is a constant of proportionality.

Since Equation 6.17 holds for any asset or portfolio of assets, the expected return of the market portfolio, $E(R_M)$, is

$$E(R_M) = R_f + (P)Cov_{MM}$$

Since the covariance of any asset's return with itself is the the variance of the asset's return, the expected return of the market portfolio is

$$E(R_M) = R_f + (P)\sigma_M^2 \tag{6.18}$$

Solving for P in Equation 6.18 ($P = [E(R_M) - R_f]/\sigma_M^2$) and substituting this expression for P in Equation 6.17 allows us to express the expected return for any asset or portfolio as

$$E(R_j) = R_f + \left[\frac{E(R_M) - R_f}{\sigma_M^2}\right] Cov_{jM} \tag{6.19}$$

$$= R_f + \left[\frac{E(R_M) - R_f}{\sigma_M}\right]\left[\frac{Cov_{jM}}{\sigma_M}\right] \tag{6.20}$$

Comparing Equation 6.20, which holds for any asset or portfolio, with Equation 6.16, which holds for perfectly diversified portfolios on the CML, illustrates that investors are compensated only for the covariance of the return of an asset with the return of the market portfolio. In order for an asset to lie on the CML, the total risk of the asset, σ_j, must equal its systematic risk, or risk due to its covariance with the market portfolio.

Systematic risk is defined as Cov_{jM}/σ_M. Those assets with systematic risk less than total risk will fall below the CML, and only a portion of their risk is "rewarded." The unrewarded portion of risk is unsystematic or diversifiable risk. This risk is eliminated in perfectly diversified portfolios (i.e., when $\sigma_j = Cov_{jM}/\sigma_M$).

Since the total risk of the asset or portfolio equals the sum of systematic and unsystematic risk,

$$\sigma_j = \frac{Cov_{jM}}{\sigma_M} + \text{Unsystematic Risk} \tag{6.21}$$

and recalling from Equation 6.8 that $Cov_{jM} = \rho_{jM}\sigma_j\sigma_M$, then rearranging Equation 6.21 results in unsystematic risk being defined as

$$\text{Unsystematic Risk} = \sigma_j - \frac{Cov_{jM}}{\sigma_M} \tag{6.22}$$

$$= \sigma_j - \frac{\rho_{jM}\sigma_j\sigma_M}{\sigma_M}$$

$$= \sigma_j - \rho_{jM}\sigma_j$$

$$= \sigma_j(1 - \rho_{jM})$$

Thus, total asset or portfolio risk can be defined as

Total Risk = Systematic Risk + Unsystematic Risk

$$\sigma_j = \frac{Cov_{jM}}{\sigma_M} + \sigma_j(1 - \rho_{jM}) \tag{6.23}$$

Equation 6.23 makes it clear that the risk of an asset or portfolio consists of two parts: the systematic risk, which is due to the correlation (covariance) of the asset or portfolio with the market, and the unsystematic risk, which is caused by unique company-or industry-specific factors and is not related to market movements. The lower the asset's correlation with the market (e.g., $\rho_{jM} < 0$), the higher the proportion of unsystematic risk to total risk, and vice versa.

2. SYSTEMATIC RISK AND EXPECTED RETURN Equation 6.19 can be rearranged as

$$E(R_j) = R_f + [E(R_M) - R_f]\frac{Cov_{jM}}{\sigma_M^2} \tag{6.24}$$

The term Cov_{jM}/σ_M^2 is called the beta of asset j and it is denoted as β_j. Note that the beta of an asset is its systematic risk, Cov_{jM}/σ_M, expressed in units of market risk, σ_M. Using β_j, Equation 6.24 can be rewritten as

$$E(R_j) = R_f + [E(R_M) - R_f]\beta_j \tag{6.25}$$

Equation 6.25 is the equation for the *security market line*, SML, and is illustrated in Figure 6.12. Figure. 6.12 shows the relationship between the measure of systematic risk, β_j, and the expected return of an asset. In Figure 6.12, $\beta_M = 1$. This is true by definition since $Cov_{MM} = \sigma_M^2$, and thus $\beta_M = \sigma_M^2/\sigma_M^2 = 1$.

From Equation 6.25 for the SML, the expected return of an asset is a function of the return on the risk-free asset, the risk premium in the market $[(E(R_M) - R_f]$, and the asset's β_j. Only the last measure, β_j, is asset-specific, and thus an asset's expected return will be higher or lower than other assets' expected returns, based upon its relative level of covariance with the market.

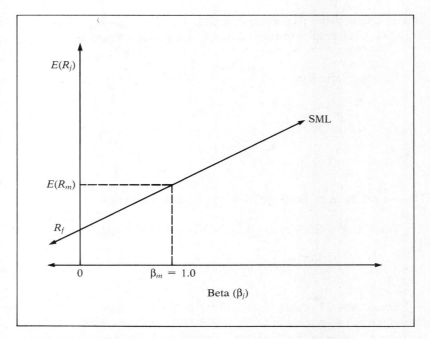

FIGURE 6.12 The security market line

For example, if the risk-free rate is 8 percent, the expected return on the market portfolio is 16 percent, the beta of asset A is 1.2, and the beta of asset B is 0.6, then the expected return from Equation 6.25 for these two assets would be

$$E(R_A) = .08 + (.16 - .08)(1.2)$$
$$= 17.6\%$$
$$E(R_B) = .08 + (.16 - .08)(.6)$$
$$= 12.8\%$$

3. ESTIMATING BETA Since beta reflects the relationship between an asset's return and those of the market portfolio, it is possible to estimate this relationship, using a simple a linear regression model:

$$R_{jt} = \hat{a}_j + \hat{b}_{jt} R_{Mt} + e_{jt} \tag{6.26}$$

where $\hat{a}_j$ = the intercept estimate of the regression

$\hat{b}_j$ = the slope estimate for the regression line, which is the estimate of beta, Cov_{jM}/σ_M^2

R_{Mt} = the return of the market in time period t

R_{jt} = the return of asset j in time period t

e_{jt} = the random error term for asset j around the regression line in time period t

The linear regression model shown in Equation 6.26 is the line of best fit and is called the *characteristic line* for the security. Figure 6.13 shows a scatter diagram, from the information in Table 6.4, of the returns of the market as reflected by the Standard & Poor's 500, the quarterly returns over ten years for the common stock of Martin Marietta, and the characteristic line for Martin Marietta. The statistics from the return data are as follows:[17]

	MARTIN MARIETTA	S&P 500
Variance of returns, σ^2	148.80	75.69
Standard deviation of returns, σ	12.2%	8.7%
Mean return, $\bar{R}$	7.0%	2.4%

The correlation coefficient, ρ_{jM}, derived from the regression is .556. With this information, the slope of the characteristic line, b_j, and the intercept, a_j, can be calculated.

$$b_j = \frac{Cov_{jM}}{\sigma_M^2} = \frac{\rho_{jM}\sigma_j\sigma_M}{\sigma_M^2}$$
$$= [(.556)(12.2)(8.7)]/75.69$$
$$= .780$$

$$a_j = \bar{R}_j - b_j\bar{R}_M \qquad\qquad (6.27)$$
$$= .07 - (.780)(.024)$$
$$= .07 - .0187$$
$$= 5.13\%$$

This method of calculating beta coefficients can also be applied to a portfolio. Rather than regressing an individual asset's returns against the returns of the market portfolio, the returns of the portfolio are regressed against the market returns. If the individual betas of the stocks in a portfolio are available,

---

[17] For Martin Marietta, the dispersion of the quarterly returns around the mean return (7 percent) is the variance of returns (148.80). The square root of the variance, standard deviation, is 12.2%. This total risk can be divided into its systematic and unsystematic components. In Equation 6.23. it was shown that total risk can be defined as the sum of systematic risk plus unsystematic risk:

$$\sigma_j = \frac{Cov_{jM}}{\sigma_M} + \sigma_j(1 - \rho_{jM})$$

Recalling that $Cov_{jM} = \rho_{jM}\sigma_j\sigma_M$, then Martin Marietta's total risk can be separated into the components as: systematic and unsystematic risk

$$\sigma_j = \frac{(.556)(12.2)(8.7)}{8.7} + (12.2)(1 - .556)$$
$$= 6.78 + 5.42$$
$$= 12.20\%$$

For Martin Marietta over this 10-year period, systematic risk accounted for approximately 56 percent of total risk (6.78/12.20), unsystematic risk for 44 percent (5.42/12.20).

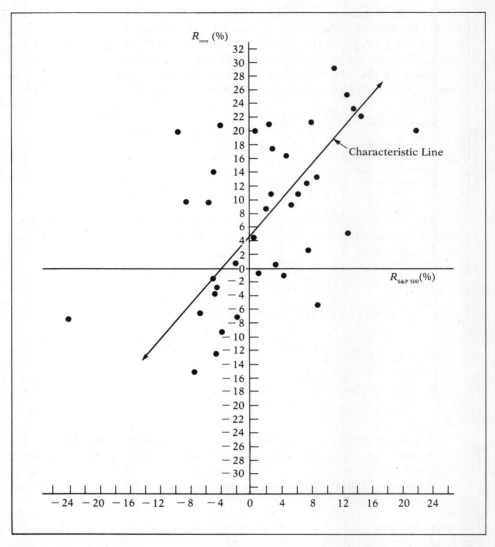

FIGURE 6.13 Plot of Martin Marietta and Standard & Poor's 500 returns and characteristic line

the portfolio's beta, b_p, can be calculated as the weighted average of the individual betas:

$$b_p = \sum_{j=1}^{n} X_j b_j \qquad (6.28)$$

Some observations about the slope coefficient, or beta, are in order. These observations hold whether the beta is calculated as shown above or is obtained from sources such as Value Line or Merrill Lynch. Beta values are rarely negative. They generally range between +.5 and 2.0. Stocks or port-

TABLE 6.4 QUARTERLY RETURNS FOR MARTIN MARIETTA
AND THE STANDARD & POOR'S 500

YEAR	QUARTER	MARTIN MARIETTA HPR	S&P500 HPR
1	1	21.727%	9.699%
	2	4.311	0.165
	3	−2.209	−0.589
	4	−1.687	4.594
2	1	9.441	5.758
	2	−7.931	0.651
	3	0.759	3.901
	4	−2.994	7.497
3	1	−1.800	−4.859
	2	−12.897	−5.788
	3	15.565	4.784
	4	−17.447	−9.255
4	1	21.404	−2.778
	2	−7.059	−7.560
	3	−6.935	−25.072
	4	−4.779	9.317
5	1	21.524	22.926
	2	22.080	15.305
	3	20.260	−10.917
	4	13.333	8.632
6	1	25.846	12.874
	2	20.994	2.384
	3	−0.625	1.844
	4	11.064	3.072
7	1	−6.893	−7.438
	2	17.989	3.201
	3	−10.000	−2.812
	4	0.615	−0.271
8	1	14.093	−4.932
	2	9.862	8.461
	3	9.106	8.652
	4	−3.715	−5.034
9	1	10.250	7.054
	2	8.812	2.613
	3	12.500	7.568
	4	20.013	0.030
10	1	−3.458	−4.076
	2	5.864	13.384
	3	29.793	11.150
	4	23.899	12.952

folios with betas above 1.0 are classified as "aggressive" since they are expected to have more volatile returns than the market. Stocks or portfolios with betas less than 1.0 are classified as "defensive" since their volatility of return is less than that of the market.

Beta estimates are based on historical information, and it is assumed that this historical relationship with the market will remain constant. Many articles have examined the stationarity of beta.[18] These studies consider factors such as the time intervals (daily, weekly, monthly, quarterly, and annually) used to calculate *HPR*s, the method of portfolio construction, and the impact of the number of securities in a portfolio on the stationarity of portfolio beta. The general conclusions: betas for individual securities are not stationary over time; the method of portfolio construction does affect beta stationary; and as the number of securities in a portfolio is increased, the stationarity of the portfolio's beta improves significantly. These findings have serious implications for security selection, portfolio construction, and portfolio evaluation techniques. These and other aspects of CMT will be examined in Chapter 7.

SUMMARY

This chapter presented portfolio and capital market theory, CMT. It was shown that rational investors should desire the highest level of expected return for any given level of expected risk or the lowest level of expected risk for any given level of expected return.

In examining Markowitz diversification, the efficient frontier was developed. Portfolios on the efficient frontier were seen to dominate all other assets or portfolios in the attainable set. Thus, rational investors will prefer the portfolios on the efficient frontier to all other investment opportunities.

Introducing borrowing and lending at the risk-free rate and establishing the existence of the market portfolio created a second efficient frontier called the capital market line, CML. The CML was seen to consist of some combination of the market portfolio and the risk-free asset. Given this composition of portfolios on the CML, it was shown that all the portfolios on the CML were perfectly positively correlated.

The CML consists of perfectly diversified portfolios: these portfolios contain no diversifiable or unsystematic risk. Therefore, for portfolios on the CML, total risk is equal to systematic risk. In order to estimate the expected return for less than perfectly diversified portfolios or individual assets, the relationship between systematic risk and expected return was introduced. This relationship was expressed by the security market line, SML, and the appropriate index of systematic risk, the beta coefficient was defined.

The most important concepts developed in this chapter were the impact of diversification on risk and the fact that the market will reward investors only for nondiversifiable or systematic risk. This latter concept has pricing implications for assets. The development of CMT has applications not only for portfolio construction but also for common stock valuation (Chapter 11) and analysis of portfolio performance (Chapter 8).

In the next chapter we will examine the impact of relaxing the relatively restrictive assumptions of CMT. We will also examine the numerous tests of asset pricing theories and an alternative pricing theory called the *arbitrage pricing theory*.

---

[18] References related to beta stationarity and other tests of capital market theory are provided in Chapter 7.

1. From an investment perspective, define what is meant by the term *risk aversion*. What is the relationship between risk aversion and asset prices?

2. In Figure 6.1, four indifference curves are illustrated. For the individuals with the characteristics described below, match the individual with the appropriate indifference curve, and explain your selection.

   a. Retired college professor, sixty-five years old, living on Social Security and income from the college's retirement plan.

   b. Young professional, unmarried and living in an apartment.

   c. Middle-aged executive with a spouse and two high-school-age children.

   d. Young executive with a working spouse and no children.

3. Define what is meant by the "dominance principle," and explain the role of this principle in portfolio theory.

4. Explain how a portfolio's return is calculated. How are the weights assigned to the assets in the portfolio?

5. Why is it inappropriate to use price changes of an asset to measure its risk?

6. What are the dangers associated with using historical return variability to make estimates of future risk?

7. Describe what is meant by the "portfolio effect." Why is this concept important in measuring portfolio risk?

8. Interpret a correlation coefficient of $+1$, of 0, and of -1.

9. Explain how it is possible for the risk of a portfolio, as measured by its standard deviation, to be less than the standard deviation of any of the assets in the portfolio.

10. What are the characteristics of assets that lie on the efficient frontier? What is the difference between the efficient frontier and the attainable set of investment opportunities? What role does the dominance principle play in this difference?

11. What role does the individual's family of indifference curves play in the selection of the optimal portfolio?

12. In this chapter, the terms *rewardable, systematic,* and *nondiversifiable risk* were used. Are these terms interchangeable? Explain.

13. In this chapter, the terms *nonrewardable, unsystematic,* and *diversifiable risk* were used. Are these terms interchangeable? Explain.

14. What is meant by a "risk-free" asset? What are its characteristics?

15. Explain the role of the risk-free asset in the construction of the capital market line (CML)?

16. How are borrowing and lending portfolios created in capital market theory? Explain why a borrowing portfolio will be more risky than a lending portfolio.

17. Define what is meant by the market portfolio, and describe how it is constructed.

18. A portfolio's total risk can be divided into systematic risk and unsystematic risk. For which part of total risk can the investor expect to receive a return? Why?

19. Define what is meant by the "market price of risk."

20. Compare and contrast the capital market line with the security market line. Include in your discussion the type of assets that will be on both lines and how risk is measured.

21. What does a beta coefficient measure? How is it calculated for an individual asset? For a portfolio of assets?

22. In terms of a beta coefficient, define what is meant by an "aggressive" and "defensive" security or portfolio.

23. Explain how the security market line can be used in estimating the cost of equity capital for a firm.

24. Are betas for individual securities stationary over time? If they are not stationary, what factors might contribute to this lack of stationarity?

25. Using the latest issue of the *Value Line Investment Survey* in your library, find the beta coefficient for General Motors, American Telephone and Telegraph, Chrysler Corportation, Homestake Mining, and Anheuser-Busch, Inc. What explanations can you offer for the differences in the beta coefficients?

PROBLEMS

1. An investor purchased a share of common stock for $45 one year ago. During the year the stock paid a cash dividend of $2.25. The stock is currently selling for $51.25. What is the investor's holding period return?

2. You are anticipating investing equally in three common stocks with 60 percent of your investable funds. The remaining 40 percent of your funds will remain in a savings account earning 6 percent interest. If the expected returns on the three stocks are 12 percent, 10 percent, and 15 percent, respectively, what is the expected return for your portfolio?

For problems 3 through 12, use the following information:

	QUARTERLY HOLDING PERIOD RETURNS			
	STOCK 1	STOCK 2	STOCK 3	MARKET INDEX
1984				
1	7.2%	0.6%	16.2%	19.6%
2	12.9	6.0	−12.7	−15.1
3	7.4	0.6	16.4	3.1
4	−2.1	9.7	−11.5	4.6
1985				
1	4.0	−18.0	−10.7	−12.0
2	6.9	6.1	−0.6	−2.6
3	−8.4	−1.8	3.4	4.7
4	1.3	6.5	−3.4	−6.3
1986				
1	−5.6	−10.3	−8.8	−18.6
2	0.1	12.0	26.9	4.6
3	20.2	0.8	6.8	−1.0
4	−3.7	−0.3	9.2	−11.5
1987				
1	9.2	−14.6	−7.4	7.9
2	3.8	1.2	2.8	−6.8
3	1.2	3.2	−8.7	3.6
4	5.1	−0.7	−8.8	−6.6
1988				
1	7.2	−8.2	0.4	−7.8
2	16.7	23.0	8.2	6.7
3	7.4	1.7	13.6	−1.5
4	17.2	−0.9	0.1	−6.9

3. Calculate the mean return and standard deviation for the three stocks and the market index.

4. Calculate the correlation coefficient between stocks 1 and 2.

5. Assume that you invested 60 percent of your investable funds in stock 1 and 40 percent in stock 2. Using the historical information, what is the expected quarterly return and risk (standard deviation) of your portfolio? How does the risk of your portfolio compare with the individual risks of stocks 1 and 2?

6. Calculate the correlation coefficient between stock 1 and the market index.

7. Calculate the beta coefficient for stock 1. Interpret your answer.

8. Assuming an equal dollar investment in each stock, how many different combinations of portfolios can be formed with the three stocks. Without an equal dollar investment in each stock, how many portfolios can be formed? Explain.

9. Assuming that the quarterly risk-free rate is 2 percent, graph the capital market line using the historical mean quarterly market return. Would you expect any of the stocks or portfolios formed with these stocks to be on the capital market line? Why, or why not?

10. What is the systematic and unsystematic risk for stock 1?

11. Assuming a quarterly risk-free rate of 2 percent and using the equation for the security market line, what is the expected quarterly return for stock 1?

12. Use the program on the floppy disk to determine the efficient frontier for the three stocks.

COMPUTER APPLICATIONS

The floppy disk includes programs that can be used to calculate the following:

1. Mean return and standard deviation of individual stocks and portfolios;

2. Alpha, beta, and coefficient of determination from the characteristic line;

3. Correlation and covariance; and

4. Efficient frontier.

These programs can be used to solve some of the problems in this chapter and to analyze other common stocks and portfolios. Instructions and illustrations are provided on the disk.

REFERENCES

Arnott, Robert D. "Modeling Portfolios with Options: Risks and Returns." *Journal of Portfolio Management* (Fall 1980): pp. 66–73.

———. "What Hath MPT Wrought: Which Risks Reap Rewards?" *Journal of Portfolio Management* (Fall 1983): pp. 5–11.

Babcock, Guilford C. "The Roots of Risk and Return." *Financial Analysts Journal* (January-February 1980) pp. 56–63.

Ben-Horim, Moshe, and Haim Levy. "Total Risk, Diversifiable Risk and Nondiversifiable Risk: A Pedagogic Note." *Journal of Financial and Quantitative Analysis* (June 1980): pp. 289–98.

Bernstein, Peter L. "Markowitz Marked to Market." *Financial Analysts Journal* (January-February 1983): pp. 18–22.

Blume, Marshall. "On the Assessment of Risk." *Journal of Finance* (March 1971): pp. 1–10.

Carman, Peter. "The Trouble with Asset Allocation." *Journal of Portfolio Management* (Fall 1981): pp. 17–22.

Chen, Son-Nan, and William T. Moore. "Uncertain Inflation and Optimal Portfolio Selection: A Simplified Approach." *Financial Review* (November 1985): pp. 343–56.

Elton, Edwin J., Martin J. Gruber, and Manfred W. Padberg. "Simple Criteria for Optimal Portfolio Selection: Tracing Out the Efficient Frontier." *Journal of Finance* (March 1978): pp. 296–302.

Evans, John L., and Stephen H. Archer. "Diversification and the Reduction of Dispersion: An Empirical Analysis." *Journal of Finance* (December 1968): pp. 761–67.

Fama, Eugene. "Risk, Return and Equilibrium: Some Clarifying Comments." *Journal of Finance* (March 1968): pp. 32–33.

Findlay, M. Chapman III, and Edward E. Williams. "Better Betas Didn't Help the Boat People." *Journal of Portfolio Management* (Fall 1986): pp. 4–9.

Fisher, Lawrence, and James H. Lorie. "Some Studies of Variability of Returns on Investments in Common Stocks." *Journal of Business* (April 1970): pp. 99–134.

Frost, Peter A., and James E. Savarino. "Portfolio Size and Estimation Risk." *Journal of Portfolio Management* (Summer 1986): pp. 60–64.

Hill, Joanne M. "Is Optimal Portfolio Management Worth the Candle?" *Journal of Portfolio Management* (Summer 1981): pp. 59–69.

Hill, Ned C., and Bernell K. Stone. "Accounting Betas, Systematic Operating Risk, and Financial Leverage: A Risk-Composition Approach to the Determinants of Systematic Risk." *Journal of Financial and Quantitative Analysis* (September 1980): pp. 595–637.

Jeffrey, Robert H. "A New Paradigm for Portfolio Risk." *Journal of Portfolio Management* (Fall 1984): pp. 33–40.

Lee, Chi-Wen Jevons. "Market Model Stationarity and Timing of Structural Change." *Financial Review* (November 1985): pp. 329–42.

Levy, Haim, and Harry M. Markowitz. "Approximating Expected Utility by a Function of Mean and Variance." *American Economic Review* (June 1979): pp. 308–17.

Lintner, John. "Security Prices, Risk and Maximal Gains from Diversification." *Journal of Finance* (December 1965): pp. 587–615.

Lloyd, William P., John H. Hand, and Naval K. Modani. "The Effect of Portfolio Construction Rules on the Relationship between Portfolio Size and Effective Diversification." *Journal of Financial Research* (Fall 1981): pp. 183–93.

Lloyd, William P., and Steven J. Goldstein. "Simulation of Portfolio Returns: Varying Numbers of Securities and Holding Periods." *Journal of Financial Research* (Spring 1982): pp. 27–30.

Lloyd, William P., and Naval K. Modani. "Stock, Bonds, Bills, and Time Diversification." *Journal of Portfolio Management* (Spring 1983): pp. 7–11.

Markowitz, Harry M., "Portfolio Selection." *Journal of Finance* (March 1952): pp. 77–91.

_____. *Portfolio Selection*. New York: Wiley, 1959.

_____. "The 'Two Beta' Trap." *Journal of Portfolio Management* (Fall 1984): pp. 12–19.

Olsen, Robert. "Sample Size and Markowitz Diversification. *Journal of Portfolio Management* (Fall 1983): pp. 18–22.

Pari, Robert A., and Son-Nan Chen. "Estimation Risk and Optimal Portfolios." *Journal of Portfolio Management* (Fall 1985): pp. 40–43.

Rubinstein, Mark. "A Mean-Variance Synthesis of Corporate Finance Theory." *Journal of Finance* (March 1973): pp. 167–81.

Schnabel, J. A. "A Note on Inflation, The Capital Asset Pricing Model, and Beta Estimations with Nominal Data." *Journal of Financial Research* (Fall 1980): pp. 261–67.

Spiceland, J. David, and Jerry E. Trapnell. "The Effect of Market Conditions and Risk Classifications on Market Model Parameters." *Journal of Financial Research* (Fall 1983): pp. 217–22.

Statman, Meir. "Betas Compared: Merrill Lynch vs. Value Line." *Journal of Portfolio Management* (Winter 1981): pp. 41–44.

Subrahmanyam, Marti G., and Stavros B. Thomadakis. "Systematic Risk and the Theory of the Firm." *Quarterly Journal of Economics* (May 1980): pp. 437–51.

Tobin, James. "Liquidity Preference as Behavior towards Risk." *Review of Economic Studies* (February 1958): 65–86.

Tole, Thomas M. "You Can't Diversify Without Diversifying." *Journal of Portfolio Management* (Winter 1982): pp. 5–11.

Treynor, Jack L. "How to Rate Management of Investment Funds." *Harvard Business Review* (January-February 1965): pp. 63–75.

Umstead, David A. "Volatility, Growth, and Investment Policy." *Journal of Portfolio Management* (Winter 1981): pp. 55–59.

Vasicek, Oldrich A., and John A. McQuown. "The Efficient Market Model." *Financial Analysts Journal* (September-October 1972): pp. 71–84.

Wagner, Wayne H., and S. C. Lau. "The Effect of Diversification on Risk." *Financial Analysts Jorunal* (November-December 1971): pp. 48–53.

CHAPTER 7

ASSET PRICING THEORIES: ASSUMPTIONS, TESTS, AND OTHER MODELS

INTRODUCTION

Capital Market Theory, CMT, is just that—theory. Its construction is based on assumptions that are not totally realistic in the real world. Empirical tests have shown that CMT does not precisely reflect the *ex-post* risk-return relationships predicted by the theory. These results may be due to (1) imprecise specification of the market portfolio, (2) the constraints of the model associated with its assumptions, (3) the inability to forecast accurately asset sensitivity to market movements (beta) based on historical data, (4) the lack of an identifiable risk-free asset, or (5) many other reasons.

In an *Institutional Investor* article, Anise Wallace asked the question "Is Beta Dead?"[1] In response to this question, Peter Bernstein, in an editorial in *The Journal of Portfolio Management*, offered the following answer:[2]

The question is ridiculous. As long as individual securities continue to move up and down in sympathy with—or as part of—broad market movements, portfolio managers must be concerned about the sensitivity of their portfolios to the general market, the stability of that relationship, and the accuracy of the measurement tools that they employ.

Is the capital asset pricing model dead? This question is also ridiculous. As long as we have free markets in which investors are risk averse rather than risk-seekers, they will tend to price securities so that the riskier asset classes will have higher expected returns than the less risky classes.

Is modern portfolio theory dead? How ridiculous can you get? As long as the interaction of individual securities within a portfolio produces results that are different from the performance of a single security, the art of composing a portfolio will remain a different art from the skills employed in security selection as such.

Are the tools that we use to measure the sensitivity of individual securities to the general market, their sensitivity to one another, or the degree of rationality in investor expectations alive and well? Ah, there's the rub!

While the special series of articles in this issue provides strong evidence that beta, the CAPM, and modern portfolio theory are robust descriptions of how free markets work under conditions of uncertainty and how investors can expect their portfolios to perform under those conditions, the authors do raise a whole set of important questions about the quantitative concepts that we use to put theory into practice. Nevertheless, the thrust of the entire discussion is that these quantitative concepts readily lend themselves to improvement and revision.

There is nothing here to justify doubts about the ability of valid measurement techniques to enhance the value of the theoretical structure for the active portfolio manager. On the contrary, active management can be far more effective with than without the use of these tools.

---

[1] Anise Wallace, "Is Beta Dead?" *Institutional Investor* (July 1980): pp. 23–30.

[2] Peter L. Bernstein, "Dead—or Alive and Well?" *The Journal of Portfolio Management* (Winter 1981): p. 4.

Dead or alive, there is no question that CMT has provided us with a vocabulary and perspective that are valuable and insightful. The concepts of the market portfolio, systematic (rewardable) risk, and unsystematic (nonrewardable) risk are important and useful constructs of modern portfolio theory. Additionally, no one questions the important insights provided by Markowitz's portfolio theory, in which the expected return of an individual security is related to its contribution to portfolio risk rather than to the variability of its own expected return.

In this chapter, the consequences of relaxing the assumptions of CMT are examined. Empirical tests of CMT are reviewed, including a discussion of whether or not CMT is even testable. Finally, factor models and the extension of CMT, *arbitrage pricing theory*, are introduced and analyzed.

RELAXING THE ASSUMPTIONS: THE IMPACT ON CAPITAL MARKET THEORY

As indicated in Chapter 6, the assumptions underlying CMT are less realistic than portfolio theory assumptions. If the CMT assumptions reflected the "real world," each investor would hold only the market portfolio, since any other portfolio would contain some diversifiable risk. Further, investors would price each asset with respect to its covariance with the market portfolio, as indicated in the equation for the security market line. Relaxing the assumptions of CMT changes this "idealized" world.

The Efficient Frontier, Homogeneous Expectations, and Common Investment Horizon

Assumptions 1, 3, and 4 of CMT (see Chapter 6) assume that all investors have homogeneous expectations about the risk and return of assets and common investment horizons, and seek to be on the efficient frontier. If these assumptions were true in an absolute sense, there would be no need for active portfolio management. With homogeneous expectations and the ability to identify, *ex-ante*, the efficient frontier, all investors would hold some combination of the market portfolio and the risk-free asset.

Investors have different investment horizons and diverse expectations about the risk and return of individual assets. Thus, a unique, *ex-ante* market portfolio, identifiable by all investors, cannot exist. Rather, each investor creates a portfolio that is efficient in terms of the individual investor's expectations and investment horizon. These portfolios are not necessarily efficient as defined in a CMT framework.

Does the existence of these "inefficient" portfolios held by investors make CMT an invalid concept? The answer is no, if one is willing to accept Lintner's argument that the market clearing process does not reflect homogeneous expectations of market participants but rather a "consensus expectation" of market participants.[3] The impact of these heterogeneous expectations is such that rather than

---

[3] John Lintner, "The Aggregation of Investor's Diverse Judgments and Preferences in Purely Competitive Security Markets," *Journal of Financial and Quantitative Analysis* (December 1969): pp. 347–400, and Joseph T. Williams, "Capital Asset Prices with Heterogeneous Beliefs," *Journal of Financial Economics* (November 1977): pp. 219–239.

only one portfolio, the market portfolio, being on the capital market line, CML, a number of portfolios would be on the CML.

Defining equilibrium in the capital market in terms of consensus expectations does not invalidate the concepts of rewardable (systematic) and nonrewardable (unsystematic) risk. It simply means that rather than one security market line, SML, defining the risk-return trade-off, there may be multiple SMLs, reflecting differing expectations and investment horizons.

Unlimited Borrowing and Lending at the Risk-Free Rate and Certainty of Interest Rates and Inflation

Relaxing assumption 2 of CMT (see Chapter 6) means that all borrowing and lending may not occur at the risk-free rate, R_f. This has important implications for the shape of the CML. Recall from Chapter 6, Figure 6.10, that the CML was constructed assuming lending and borrowing at the risk-free rate, R_f. A more reasonable assumption is that investors can lend at a risk-free rate (e.g., buying Treasury bills), but they cannot borrow at a rate this low. In other words, the borrowing rate, R_B, is expected to be higher than R_f.

Differentiating between lending and borrowing rates creates two tangency portfolios, as shown in Figure 7.1, compared to the one tangency portfolio in Fig-

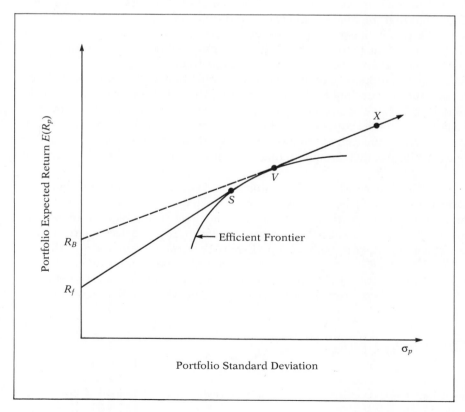

FIGURE 7.1 The capital market line with different borrowing and lending rates

ure 6.10. Lending portfolios will be located along the line segment R_fS, depending on the investor's risk-return preference. Borrowing portfolios will be located on line segment VX, again depending on the investor's risk-return preference.

The dash portion of the R_BX line in Figure 7.1, not a part of the "new" efficient frontier when different borrowing and lending rates exist, is shown to illustrate that the slope of the R_BX line is less than the slope of the R_fS line. Recall from Chapter 6 that the market price of risk is the slope of the CML. Under assumption 2 of CMT, the borrowing and lending rate is R_f and the slope of the CML is

$$\text{Slope} = \frac{E(R_M) - R_f}{\sigma_M} \tag{7.1}$$

Since R_B is assumed to be greater than R_f, compensation per unit of total risk will be less with borrowing portfolios as opposed to lending portfolios:

$$\frac{E(R_M) - R_B}{\sigma_M} < \frac{E(R_M) - R_f}{\sigma_M} \tag{7.2}$$

As will be seen in the next section on the empirical tests of CMT, studies have indicated that the relationship between the expected return and the measure of systematic risk is linear, with a positive intercept. However, the slope of the SML is less than that predicted by CMT; this may well be due to the unrealistic assumption that investors can borrow at the risk-free rate.

Relaxing assumption 7, with respect to no unanticipated changes in inflation or interest rates, raises doubts about whether a "true" risk-free rate exists. Yields on Treasury bills have been suggested as a proxy for the risk-free rate; however, although Treasury bills contain no default risk, their yields will vary with unanticipated changes in the rate of inflation. Thus, there is some variance in the return on Treasury bills, related directly to macroeconomic variables; thus Treasury bills are not "risk-free."

Fischer Black derived a market equilibrium model, assuming that there was no risk-free asset.[4] In Black's model, every portfolio contains a combination of the market portfolio and a portfolio with no systematic risk. Thus, Black's substitution for the risk-free asset is called a *zero-beta portfolio* and is constructed by combining risky assets (taking both long and short positions) in such a way that the beta of the portfolio is 0. A zero-beta portfolio contains risk, but no systematic risk.

Figure 7.2 illustrates the SML when the expected return for a zero-beta portfolio, $E(R_Z)$, replaces the return for the risk-free asset. The equation for a zero-beta SML is

$$E(R_j) = E(R_Z) + [E(R_M) - E(R_Z)]\beta_j \tag{7.3}$$

---

[4] Fischer Black, "Capital Market Equilibrium with Restricted Borrowing," *Journal of Business* (July 1972): pp. 444–55.

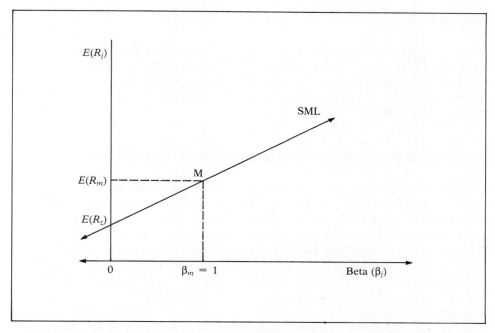

FIGURE 7.2 The security market line with zero-beta portfolio replacing the risk-free asset

Investors wishing to face relatively low levels of risk will combine an investment in portfolio M with an investment in a zero-beta portfolio. Investors willing to face higher levels of risk, in order to achieve higher expected returns than that offered by portfolio M, will sell short a zero-beta portfolio and and invest the proceeds in portfolio M. In this latter case, the proportion of the investor's wealth invested in the zero-beta portfolio will be negative.

Since we know that the beta of a portfolio, β_p, is the weighted average of the betas of the individual assets in the portfolio, with the weights, X_j, being the proportion of the investor's wealth invested in each asset, then β_p can be expressed as

$$\beta_p = \sum_{j=1}^{n} X_j \beta_j \tag{7.4}$$

In the case of the investor wishing to face less risk than portfolio M, X_Z (the proportion invested in a zero-beta portfolio) will be positive, and since β_Z is 0 by definition, β_p will be less than β_M. In the case of the investor willing to face higher risk than portfolio M in order to achieve higher expected returns, X_Z will be negative, and X_M will be greater than 1.0.[5] Thus, β_p will be greater than β_M, and the expected return of the portfolio will be greater than $E(R_M)$.

---

[5] Recall from Chapter 6 that the sum of the weights must equal 1 $\left(\text{i.e., } \sum_{j=1}^{n} X_j = 1 \right).$

Investment Divisibility

The impact of relaxing assumption 5 of CMT, that it is possible to buy or sell any portion of a share of an asset or portfolio, is rather minor. Rather than a continuous or solid line segment representing the SML, there would be discrete or discontinuous segments. Thus, portfolios with all possible combinations of risk-return would not be available.

Taxes, Transaction and Information Costs, and Market Equilibrium

The Tax Reform Act of 1986 eliminated the favorable treatment given long-term capital gains; the tax rates on capital gains and ordinary income are equal. However, there is still a difference in the investor's ability to control the timing of taxes. Ordinary income—for example, cash dividends—is generally not controlled by the investor. On the other hand, the investor can control when capital gains are taken and thus the timing of the taxes associated with capital gains. In addition, there is a tax effect which manifests itself not only in the differential rates of taxation among individual investors but also in the applicability of the tax law to types of investors and investment instruments. For example, municipal bonds, which are tax-exempt, are held by taxable investors, not by investors that are tax-exempt. Further, the vast majority of preferred stock shares are held by corporations because of the dividend exclusion features of preferred and common stock held as investments by corporations.

Clearly, investors will hold the types of investments that provide the largest tax advantage. Thus, on an after-tax basis, investors will have different perspectives on what comprises an efficient portfolio, resulting in more individualized security market lines.

A number of researchers have incorporated taxes into the CAPM.[6] The after-tax CAPM assumes that tax rates differ for capital gains and dividend/interest income and that rates also may differ among investors. Essentially, the model assumes that investors would base decisions on after-tax expected returns, and consequently, there would be differences in the before-tax and after-tax SMLs and efficient frontiers. Also, the after-tax SML would be three-dimensional rather than two-dimensional because of different tax treatments for cash dividends and capital gains.

As previously discussed, the Tax Reform Act of 1986 requires that capital gains be taxed at the same rate as dividends. Therefore, there is presently no need to consider a three-dimensional SML. The after-tax SML, however, will lie below the before-tax SML because of the tax liability. The after-tax SML will be linear, however, and will have the same tangency point on the efficient frontier as the before-tax SML.

---

[6] M. J. Brennan, "Taxes, Market Valuation and Corporate Finance Policy," *National Tax Journal* (December 1970): pp. 417–27, and Robert H. Litzenberger and Krishna Ramaswamy, "The Effect of Personal Taxes and Dividends on Capital Asset Prices: Theory and Empirical Evidence," *Journal of Financial Economics* (June 1979) pp. 163–95.

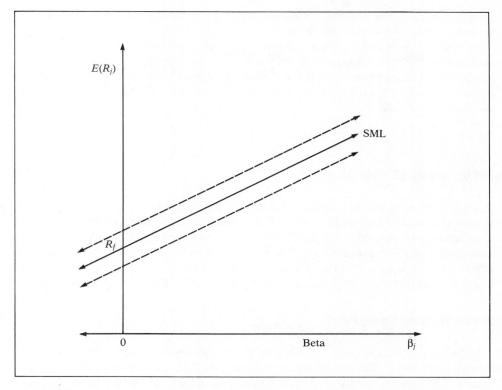

FIGURE 7.3 Impact of transaction and information costs on the security market line

Removing the assumption of no transaction and information costs creates a range of possible SMLs, as shown in Figure 7.3. Because of the existence of transaction costs, a certain degree of disequilibrium in the capital markets will be allowed. That is, the increase in expected return from discovering an undervalued security may not be large enough to compensate for the transaction costs associated with taking advantage of the undervalued situation. The width of the band around the SML will therefore be a function of the size of the transaction costs. Given that (1) a large proportion of all security transactions are undertaken by institutions that have very low transaction costs, (2) commissions on transactions have been negotiable since May 1, 1975, and (3) the number of discount brokerage houses has increased, the size of the band around the SML is relatively narrow.

The same logic that created a range of SMLs for transaction costs also applies to information costs.[7] The costs of acquiring information and research must be

---

[7] For a rigorous analysis of the impact of information costs on CMT, see John Lintner, "The Aggregation of Investor's Diverse Judgments and Preferences in Purely Competitive Security Markets," *Journal of Financial and Quantitative Analysis* (December 1969): pp. 347–400, and Sanford J. Grossman and Joseph E. Stiglitz, "On the Impossibility of Informational Efficient Markets," *American Economic Review* (June 1980): pp. 393–408.

weighed against the possible increased returns from using this information. For example, discount brokerage firms have lower commission costs but do not provide research services for their clients. To acquire this information, the investor would be expected to trade with the source of the information, the nondiscount broker, at a higher transaction cost. There is a point where increased expected return is offset by increased transaction costs, and thus a disequilibrium situation would be allowed.[8]

TESTS OF CAPITAL MARKET THEORY

With the relaxing of CMT assumptions to reflect the real world more clearly, the question naturally arises whether CMT accurately reflects the relationship between the measure of risk and expected return. The appeal of CMT is its rather simple expression of the relationship between risk and expected return. However, if it does not accurately reflect this relationship, its usefulness in assessing security risk, portfolio construction, and portfolio performance evaluation is questionable.

Is Capital Market Theory Testable?

In addressing this question, it is important to distinguish Markowitz's portfolio theory from CMT. Markowitz suggested a *normative* approach to portfolio management in which the return of an individual security is a function of its contribution to a portfolio's risk. This analysis required the estimation of the expected return, variance of returns, and the correlation of return between each pair of securities being considered for the portfolio. For a portfolio manager considering a significant number of securities, the calculation of all possible correlation coefficients is a large task. Recognizing this difficulty, Markowitz suggested that an *index model* be developed that could explain the correlations among the returns of the securities under consideration.[9] The index model is also referred to as the *single-index model* and the *market model*.

---

[8] Studies of the effect of firm size on return illustrate the impact of transaction and information costs. Leaving aside the question of whether CMT properly specifies expected return, these studies found that smaller firms, in terms of total market value, provided higher returns than larger firms with similar levels of systematic risk. When the costs of transactions, information costs, and premiums for liquidity are considered, the superiority of the net returns for the small firms is not as clear. See the discussion in Chapter 13 and R. W. Banz, "The Relationship Between Return and Market Value of Common Stocks," *Journal of Financial Economics* (March 1981): pp. 3–18; Marc R. Reinganum, "Abnormal Returns in Small Firm Portfolios," *Financial Analysts Journal* (March-April 1981): pp. 52–57; Hans R. Stoll and Robert E. Whaley, "Transaction Costs and the Small Firm Effect," *Journal of Financial Economics* (June 1983): pp. 57–80; and Avner Arbel and Paul Strebel, "Pay Attention to Neglected Firms!" *The Journal of Portfolio Management* (Winter 1983): pp. 37–42.

[9] For a discussion of the distinction between Markowitz's theory and the index model, see Harry M. Markowitz, "The 'Two Beta' Trap," *The Journal of Portfolio Management* (Fall 1984): pp. 12–20, and Barr Rosenberg, "The Capital Asset Pricing Model and the Market Model," *The Journal of Portfolio Management* (Winter 1981): pp. 5–16.

This normative theory did not identity the market portfolio as such. Nor did it have the restrictive assumptions associated with CMT. The *positive* CMT was developed later, and as Markowitz suggests,

> *Tobin, Sharpe, and Lintner knew, as well as you and I do, that investors have different beliefs, that borrowing rates are typically higher than lending rates, and that there are credit restrictions on the amount that one can borrow. They chose these assumptions to have a theory with neat, quantitative implications. They left it to empirical research to see whether the conclusions deduced from these idealized assumptions fit aggregate economic data.*[10]

Empirical research on CMT has been considerable. Concern has been expressed by researchers about the ability of the single-index or market model to (1) capture total systematic risk, (2) capture the stationarity of the measure of systematic risk, and (3) explain differences in observed and expected returns. These issues and empirical tests will be examined later in this chapter.

The empirical tests of CMT have relied on proxies for the market portfolio. Recall from Chapter 6 that the market portfolio is defined as a portfolio consisting of all risky assets combined in proportion to their market values. There is no quantifiable measure of the market portfolio, and researchers have generally substituted a capitalization-weighted index, such as the S&P 500 or the NYSE index, for the market index. The assumption is that the proxy index is a "good" substitute for the market portfolio.

Richard Roll contends that proxies for the market portfolio may not be efficient, in the sense that they would not lie on the efficient frontier.[11] The implications of this assertion are serious for empirical tests of CMT and of portfolio evaluation techniques using CMT (see Chapter 8).

The implications of Roll's analysis can be illustrated for both the capital market line, CML, and the security market line, SML. Recall from Chapter 6 that total asset or portfolio risk can be defined as

Total Risk = Systematic Risk + Unsystematic Risk

$$\sigma_j = \frac{Cov_{jM}}{\sigma_M} + \sigma_j(1 - \rho_{jM}) \tag{7.5}$$

If the proxy for the market portfolio is not efficient in a Markowitz sense, then its unsystematic risk measure will not equal 0, and the proxy market portfolio will not be on the efficient frontier. Figure 7.4 illustrates the impact of using an inefficient proxy market portfolio on the slope of the CML. The slope of the proxy CML will be less than that of the true CML.

---

[10] Harry M. Markowitz, "The 'Two Beta' Trap," *The Journal of Portfolio Management* (Fall 1984): p. 13.

[11] Richard Roll, "A Critique of the Asset Pricing Theory's Tests," *Journal of Financial Economics* (March 1977): pp. 129–176, and "Ambiguity When Performance Is Measured by the Security Market Line," *Journal of Finance* (September 1978): pp. 1051–69.

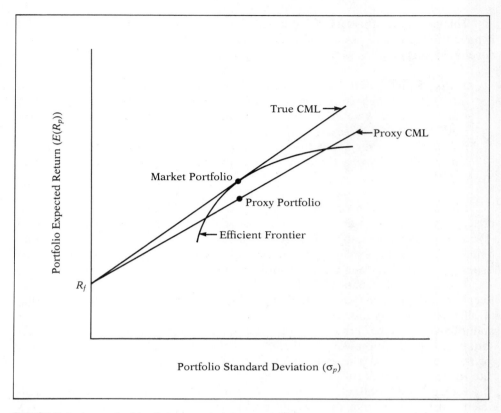

FIGURE 7.4   Impact of inefficient market proxy on CML

One effect on the SML of substituting a proxy portfolio that is not mean-variance efficient for the true market portfolio is illustrated in Figure 7.5. Since the beta of the proxy portfolio is assumed by definition to equal 1 and the expected return of the proxy portfolio is less than the market portfolio, expected returns from assets and portfolios based on the estimated SML will be understated.[12] In an *ex-post* sense asset and portfolio returns will not be linearly related to beta and will not lie on the estimated SML.

Tests of Capital Market Theory[13]

According to Roll, misspecification of the market portfolio raises serious doubts about empirical tests of CMT. Nevertheless, numerous studies, both prior and subsequent to Roll's articles, have tested the stationarity of beta values and the

---

[12] Empirical tests of CMT suggest that the slope of the SML is less than that suggested by CMT, using a proxy for the market portfolio. This apparent contradiction may be consistent with Roll's claim that the proxy portfolio for the market is not Markowitz efficient.

[13] This section draws heavily on the presentation of earlier studies in Franco Modigliani and Gerald A. Pogue, "An Introduction to Risk and Return (Part II)," *Financial Analysts Journal* (May-June 1974): pp. 69–85.

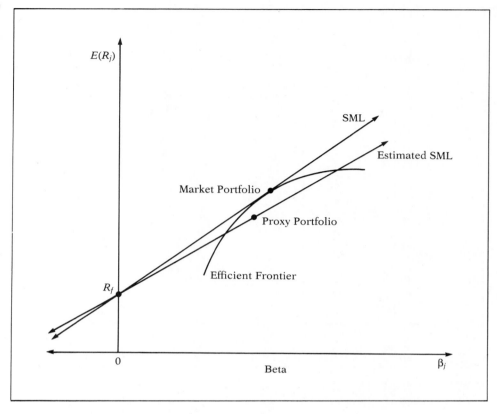

FIGURE 7.5 Impact of inefficient market proxy on SML

theory itself.[14] In this section, we will examine several studies representing the general findings of tests of CMT and beta stationarity.

1. TESTS OF CMT—INDIVIDUAL SECURITIES CMT is stated in terms of investor expectations, yet tests of CMT are stated in terms of realized or *ex-post HPR*s. The difference between realized and expected *HPR*s is the residual term which, if the model is correctly specified, should be 0 on average.

Figure 7.6 illustrates the test for CMT based on individual securities. Each point represents a security's actual return versus its estimated beta. If CMT is correct, the regression of returns against beta should result in a positive slope equal to the average market risk premium $(R_M - R_f)$ and should have an intercept on the vertical axis at the average risk-free rate, R_f.

The results of empirical tests based on individual securities are mixed in support of the theory. Some tests showed that, on average, securities with larger betas had higher rates of return, and the relationship between beta and

---

[14] It should be noted that academicians appear to be taking seriously the problems with using a market proxy pointed out by Roll. At the April 1988 annual meeting of the Eastern Finance Association, relatively few papers dealing with empirical tests of CMT were delivered. This is in sharp contrast to previous meetings of the association.

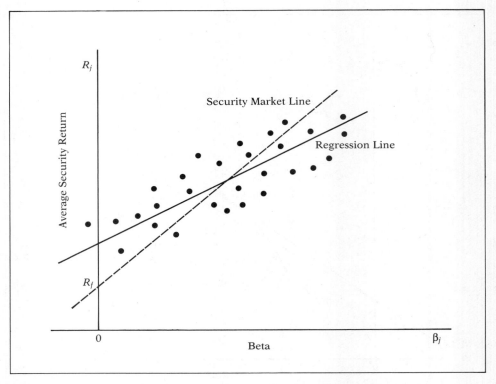

FIGURE 7.6 Relationship between average security return and security beta

returns was linear.[15] However, other studies found that the slope of the regression line between beta and returns was somewhat lower than predicted, and the intercept was somewhat higher than the average risk-free rate.[16] This empirical relationship between beta and returns and the SML is shown in Figure 7.6.

Finally, one study found that returns on individual securities were significantly and positively related to the variance of returns but not to covariances with the market index.[17] Lintner also found that the variance of residuals

---

[15] See, for example, Nancy Jacob, "The Measurement of Systematic Risk for Securities and Portfolios: Some Empirical Results," *Journal of Financial and Quantitative Analysis* (March 1971): pp. 815–34; Merton H. Miller and Myron Scholes, "Rates of Return in Relation to Risk: A Reexamination of Some Recent Findings," in *Studies in the Theory of Capital Markets*, ed. Michael Jensen (New York: Praeger, 1972): pp. 47–78.

[16] For example, see Irwin Friend and Marshall E. Blume, "Measurement of Portfolio Performance under Uncertainty," *American Economic Review* (September 1970): pp. 561–75, and Fischer Black, Michael C. Jensen, and Myron Scholes, "The Capital Asset Pricing Model: Some Empirical Tests," in *Studies in The Theory of Capital Markets*, ed. Michael C. Jensen (New York: Praeger, 1972), pp. 79–121.

[17] G. W. Douglas, "Risk in the Equity Markets: An Empirical Appraisal of Market Efficiency," *Yale Economic Essays* (Spring 1969): pp. 3–48.

from the characteristic line estimate had significant explanatory power for security returns.[18]

2. TESTS OF CMT—PORTFOLIOS Tests of CMT based on individual securities, while somewhat supportive, have several problems. First, the estimated beta contains some measurement errors. These errors are random; some estimates for individual securities are too high, and others are too low. Therefore, using estimated betas in tests of CMT weaken the results. This type of measurement error can be greatly reduced by grouping securities into portfolios.

    A second problem relates to the fact that the proxies used for the market (e.g., S&P 500) explain on average only about 30 percent of the variation in the *HPR*s of individual stocks. Therefore, approximately 70 percent of the variation in the *HPR*s is residual variation, or diversifiable or unsystematic risk. By combining securities into portfolios, much of this unsystematic risk can be diversified away.

    Tests of CMT conducted on portfolios generally take the same form as tests based on individual securities.[19] The results of the tests generally indicated that the slope of the relationship between beta and returns was positive, but that the slope was lower than that indicated by CMT. The intercept was also less than the average risk-free rate. The empirical tests also confirmed a relationship between systematic risk and return. There was some evidence that both systematic and unsystematic risk are positively related to security returns.

    In summary, these results are generally more supportive of CMT than tests using individual securities but do not prove the empirical CMT. However, the results do confirm that beta is a useful, though perhaps not a complete, measure of risk.

3. BETA STATIONARITY The calculation of beta values for securities and portfolios is a relatively straightforward procedure. These calculated betas based on historical *HPR*s are useful for investment decisions, however, only if they provide information about the future relationships between security or portfolio returns and market returns. The empirical results indicate that the stationarity of the beta estimates is directly related to (1) the number of securities in the portfolio, (2) the length of the period used to estimate beta, (3) the length of the period for estimating returns or the holding period (e.g., returns may be estimated over daily, weekly, monthly or annual intervals), (4) the level of the beta estimate, (5) structural variations in the market, and (6) changes in certain company-specific attributes.

---

[18] John Lintner, "Security Prices, Risk and Maximal Gain from Diversification," *Journal of Finance* (December 1965): pp. 587–615.

[19] This is true, for example, of the tests conducted by Marshall E. Blume and Irwin Friend, "A New Look at the Capital Asset Pricing Model," *Journal of Finance* (March 1973): pp. 19–33, and Fischer Black, Michael C. Jensen, and Myron S. Scholes, "The Capital Asset Pricing Model: Some Empirical Tests," in *Studies in the Theory of Capital Markets*, ed. Michael Jensen (New York: Praeger, 1972), pp. 79–121. Eugene F. Fama and James D. MacBeth, "Risk Return and Equilibrium: Empirical Tests," *Journal of Political Economy* (May-June 1973): pp. 607–636, extended the tests of Black, Jensen, and Scholes to test for nonlinearities in the relationship between beta and realized return and for the relationship between returns and residual variations.

Robert Levy addressed a number of these issues in a 1971 study.[20] Levy used the *weekly* returns of 500 stocks over the period December 30, 1960, through December 18, 1970, a 520-week period. His proxy for the market portfolio was the S&P 500. He developed betas for all non-overlapping 51-week periods (500 betas), 26-week periods (1,000 betas), and 13-week periods (2,000 betas) by regressing the weekly *HPR*s of the securities upon the appropriate *HPR*s for the S&P 500.

The distribution of the 52-week beta coefficients over each of the ten periods is shown in Table 7.1. As Levy points out,

> *Over the entire 10-year period the average beta was 1.043, the median was .976 and the first and ninth decile points respectively were 0.400 and 1.756. For investors searching for high beta stocks, it is worth noting that in no 52-week period were there as many as 10 percent of the stocks with betas of 2.00 or greater. Conversely for those investors seeking stocks which have moved counter to the market only 1.7 percent of the companies qualify.*[21]

In order to test for beta stationarity, Levy correlated each period's 52-week betas with the next period's 52-week betas. Thus, over the 10-year period he performed nine correlation studies of 52-week betas.

After arranging the betas for individual securities in ascending order, Levy constructed equally weighted portfolios of n securities (where n varied over the range 1 to 500). For example, when constructing portfolios of five securities ($n = 5$), the first portfolio would contain the five securities with the five lowest historical betas, the second portfolio would contain the five securities with the sixth through tenth lowest historical betas, etc. He repeated this process of portfolio formation for historical betas calculated over 26-week and 13-week periods.

In order to test for beta stationarity, Levy performed two tests of statistical association. One test involved the estimation of the correlation coefficient between historical betas of portfolios of n securities and the betas of portfolios of n securities in the subsequent period. Because of possible errors of estimation, Levy also estimated rank-order correlation coefficients.[22]

Correlations for 52-weeks and 13-weeks are presented in Tables 7.2 and 7.3.[23] The average of explained variation between the forecast beta and the "actual" beta in the subsequent period can be estimated by squaring the quadratic mean of the product-moment correlation coefficient. For example, in Table 7.2 for the one-security portfolio, the average percentage of explained variation is 23.6 percent ($.486^2$), while the average percentage of explained variation for the fifty-

---

[20] Robert A. Levy, "On the Short-Term Stationarity of Beta Coefficients," *Financial Analysts Journal* (November-December 1971): pp. 55–62.

[21] Ibid, pp. 56–57.

[22] In calculating rank-order coefficients, each set of observations is ranked, and the closeness of the fit of the ranks, rather than the observations, is estimated. Thus, rank-order coefficients address the issue of the predictability of relative portfolio risk levels, while the correlation coefficients indicate the predictability of absolute levels of risk.

[23] The results of the 26-week forecasting period are not shown. However, they displayed the same pattern of predictability as that between the 52-week and 13-week forecasting periods.

TABLE 7.1 DISTRIBUTION OF 52-WEEK BETA COEFFICIENTS—500 NYSE COMMON STOCKS (1961 THROUGH 1970)

52 WEEKS ENDED	MEAN	STD. DEV.	NO. BELOW ZERO	LOW	DECILES									HIGH
					.10	.20	.30	.40	.50	.60	.70	.80	.90	
12/29/61	.924	.520	15	− .541	.278	.507	.633	.749	.892	1.029	1.200	1.325	1.551	3.375
12/28/62	1.074	.408	4	− .405	.592	.739	.833	.943	1.029	1.145	1.242	1.410	1.614	2.289
12/27/63	1.060	.682	2	− .094	.355	.496	.635	.774	.901	1.083	1.286	1.568	1.933	4.034
12/25/64	.998	.679	24	− .638	.188	.425	.595	.780	.942	1.114	1.283	1.534	1.899	3.268
12/24/65	1.085	.586	7	−1.259	.354	.592	.766	.899	1.051	1.247	1.402	1.572	1.793	3.024
12/23/66	1.052	.517	0	.095	.429	.630	.731	.844	.944	1.112	1.279	1.491	1.824	2.812
12/22/67	1.026	.551	14	− .966	.362	.586	.751	.890	1.007	1.154	1.273	1.484	1.726	3.017
12/20/68	1.032	.603	8	−1.194	.355	.539	.687	.821	.961	1.120	1.301	1.479	1.767	3.155
12/19/69	1.113	.496	5	− .697	.567	.732	.849	.947	1.046	1.172	1.319	1.479	1.763	2.875
12/18/70	1.065	.475	4	− .705	.520	.674	.797	.884	.990	1.135	1.293	1.485	1.687	2.474
Average	1.043	.558	8	− .640	.400	.592	.728	.853	.976	1.131	1.288	1.483	1.756	3.032

SOURCE: Robert A. Levy, "On the Short-Term Stationarity of Beta Coefficients," *Financial Analysts Journal* (November-December 1971): p. 56. Reprinted by permission.

TABLE 7.2 52-WEEK FORECASTS—PRODUCT-MOMENT AND RANK-ORDER CORRELATION COEFFICIENTS OF BETAS FOR PORTFOLIOS OF *N* SECURITIES (1962 THROUGH 1970)

FORECAST FOR 52 WEEKS ENDED	PRODUCT-MOMENT CORRELATIONS: *N* =					RANK-ORDER CORRELATIONS: *N* =				
	1	5	10	25	50	1	5	10	25	50
12/28/62	.385	.711	.803	.933	.988	.349	.647	.784	.907	1.000
12/27/63	.492	.806	.866	.931	.963	.499	.820	.877	.944	.988
12/25/64	.430	.715	.825	.945	.970	.448	.749	.878	.956	1.000
12/24/65	.451	.730	.809	.936	.977	.457	.726	.828	.950	.964
12/23/66	.548	.803	.869	.952	.974	.544	.782	.846	.953	.927
12/22/67	.474	.759	.830	.900	.940	.425	.725	.831	.902	.988
12/20/68	.455	.732	.857	.945	.977	.428	.701	.842	.956	.988
12/19/69	.556	.844	.922	.965	.973	.501	.792	.887	.944	.976
12/18/70	.551	.804	.888	.943	.985	.509	.764	.863	.899	.988
Quadratic Mean	.486	.769	.853	.939	.972	.466	.747	.849	.935	.980

SOURCE: Robert A. Levy, "On the Short-Term Stationarity of Beta Coefficients," *Financial Analysts Journal* (November-December 1971): p. 57. Reprinted by permission.

TABLE 7.3   13-WEEK FORECASTS—PRODUCT-MOMENT AND RANK-ORDER CORRELATION COEFFICIENTS OF BETAS FOR PORTFOLIOS OF N SECURITIES (1962 THROUGH 1970)

FORECAST FOR 13 WEEKS ENDED	PRODUCT-MOMENT CORRELATIONS: $N =$					RANK-ORDER CORRELATIONS: $N =$				
	1	5	10	25	50	1	5	10	25	50
3/30/62	.133	.250	.356	.608	.692	.144	.277	.389	.565	.636
6/29/62	.329	.628	.738	.850	.887	.317	.577	.700	.836	.855
9/28/62	.522	.814	.892	.943	.953	.479	.761	.835	.890	.927
12/28/62	.498	.778	.887	.976	.985	.497	.758	.859	.976	.988
3/29/63	.216	.462	.567	.836	.875	.257	.496	.576	.814	.939
6/28/63	.256	.495	.598	.731	.820	.230	.460	.594	.779	.855
9/27/63	.407	.659	.760	.930	.948	.399	.649	.746	.902	.952
12/27/63	.506	.794	.882	.931	.961	.495	.780	.886	.950	.976
3/27/64	.105	.247	.355	.445	.629	.107	.241	.375	.513	.830
6/26/64	.371	.634	.730	.889	.949	.375	.647	.720	.896	.939
9/25/64	.272	.567	.691	.822	.925	.285	.525	.641	.761	.842
12/25/64	.177	.366	.447	.687	.843	.207	.433	.521	.759	.891
3/26/65	.205	.428	.541	.739	.866	.201	.476	.561	.791	.867
6/25/65	.276	.536	.659	.862	.966	.279	.526	.674	.910	.976
9/24/65	.362	.657	.735	.855	.943	.359	.684	.770	.916	.976
12/24/65	.091	.197	.238	.382	.430	.156	.212	.370	.411	.721
3/25/66	.114	.246	.366	.574	.786	.171	.314	.422	.617	.770
6/24/66	.537	.865	.931	.980	.989	.551	.836	.908	.971	.988
9/23/66	.489	.772	.854	.963	.992	.463	.745	.822	.931	.988
12/23/66	.583	.815	.892	.957	.979	.581	.812	.901	.950	.988
3/24/67	.236	.462	.583	.694	.809	.195	.343	.499	.508	.721
6/23/67	.391	.669	.830	.934	.952	.406	.670	.850	.940	.964
9/22/67	.246	.478	.583	.738	.796	.267	.465	.593	.728	.745
12/22/67	.221	.417	.523	.671	.849	.220	.379	.464	.638	.964
3/22/68	.348	.616	.723	.913	.953	.297	.568	.665	.920	.976
6/21/68	.388	.659	.747	.904	.919	.379	.601	.687	.875	.879
9/20/68	.377	.634	.777	.879	.932	.358	.553	.717	.854	.952
12/20/68	.258	.510	.653	.787	.941	.222	.408	.611	.759	.927
3/21/69	.372	.674	.796	.909	.940	.291	.561	.734	.854	.903
6/20/69	.295	.596	.719	.807	.840	.296	.579	.694	.798	.915
9/19/69	.409	.705	.848	.923	.955	.422	.676	.823	.913	.964
12/19/69	.350	.672	.772	.886	.921	.304	.575	.677	.883	.903
3/20/70	.331	.639	.788	.900	.944	.295	.537	.690	.862	.891
6/19/70	.444	.756	.868	.958	.972	.408	.702	.821	.946	.927
9/18/70	.468	.772	.866	.926	.952	.489	.787	.918	.958	.976
12/18/70	.423	.685	.776	.916	.956	.396	.668	.757	.937	.964
Quadratic Mean	.357	.613	.715	.838	.897	.349	.587	.697	.832	.906

SOURCE: Robert A. Levy, "On the Short-Term Stationarity of Beta Coefficients," *Financial Analysts Journal* (November-December 1971): p. 59. Reprinted by permission.

security portfolios is 94.5 percent ($.972^2$). The conclusions from Tables 7.2 and 7.3, as expressed by Levy, are as follows:[24]

1. Average betas are reasonably predictable for large portfolios, less predictable for smaller portfolios, and quite unpredictable for individual securities.

---

[24] Robert A. Levy, "On the Short-Term Stationarity of Beta Coefficients," *Financial Analysts Journal* (November-December 1971): p. 60.

2.   Forecasts are clearly better over longer periods.

3.   Although predictability improves as the forecast period lengthens, the relative improvement tends to be less for larger portfolios.[25]

4.   Product-moment and rank-order coefficients display similar patterns and are of similar magnitude.

5.   Reversals in the market occurring near the forecast date do not diminish the degree of predictability.[26]

Levy also addressed the question whether the level of the beta estimate affected forecast accuracy. To test this hypothesis, Levy held the number of securities in the portfolio at fifty. His analysis found that the forecast betas of the portfolios with the lowest betas tended to be underestimated, and the forecast betas of the portfolios with the higher betas tended to be overestimated.[27] These results occurred for both the 13- and 52-week forecasts, but the use of a 13-week period produced some very large forecasting errors.

Levy's study allows us to conclude that the stationarity of the beta estimates is (1) positively related to the number of secuities in the portfolio, (2) more predictable for the beta, the longer the estimating period, (3) less predictable for the beta, the further the estimated beta is from 1, and (4) not affected regarding beta predictability when the market reverses itself after the forecast period.

Fundamental economic and financial variables influence betas for individual securities. For example, Beaver, Kettler, and Scholes found that betas are related to the firm's dividend payout ratio, growth rate in assets, and variability in earnings.[28] Essentially, firms with high levels of business and financial risk should have larger betas than firms with lower levels of business and financial risk. It also follows that firms experiencing significant changes in business and financial risk would have unstable betas. For example, if the firm experienced an improved bond rating, the beta for its common stock might decline, reflecting the lower level of default risk.[29]

A recent article by McDonald suggests that nonstationarity in individual stock betas may be due to structural variations in the market resulting from major political and economic shocks such as the Arab oil embargo, peace negotiations in

---

[25] Levy did find, however, that "there is a much greater deterioration in forecasting accuracy when moving from 26-week to 13-week projections than when moving from 52-week to 26-week projections." Ibid. This deterioration in predictability held even for large portfolios.

[26] Levy was able to draw this last conclusion since over the nine correlation studies (52-week forecasting periods) and the eighteen correlation studies (26-week forecasting periods), reverses occurred in the market during the preceding period approximately half the time.

[27] This finding is consistent with Blume's results, which indicated a regression tendency for betas to move toward 1. See Marshall E. Blume, "On the Assessment of Risk," *Journal of Finance* (March 1971): pp. 1–10; "Betas and Their Regression Tendencies," *Journal of Finance* (June 1975): pp. 785–795; and "Betas and Their Regression Tendencies: Some Further Evidence," *Journal of Finance* (March 1979): pp. 265–67.

[28] William Beaver, Paul Kettler, and Myron Scholes, "The Association between Market Determined and Accounting Determined Risk Measures," *Accounting Review* (October 1970): pp. 654–82.

[29] See, for example, Naval K. Modani and William P. Lloyd, "Bond Rating Changes and Behavior of Risk Proxies," *Akron Business and Economic Review* (Spring 1984): pp. 46–49.

the Middle East, financial stability of Mexico, etc.[30] McDonald found that the 1958–1972 interval (the period of Levy's study) was relatively stable, but the 1974–1975 period should be avoided because of evidence of structural shifts in the economy. McDonald was careful to point out that large fluctuations in the market index (e.g., October 19, 1987) do not necessarily reflect structural shifts.

Robert Levy's study was based on weekly *HPR*s. Haim Levy contends that in estimating a security's beta, the estimate of beta is a function of the length of the period used for estimating the security and market returns.[31] Haim Levy shows that for aggressive stocks (beta greater than 1), systematic risk increases with the lengthening of the return estimating period (investment horizon) and that with defensive stocks (beta less than 1), systematic risk decreases as the estimating period increases. These results indicate that the selection of different estimating intervals will result in different beta estimates for securities and that in evaluating performance using CMT or conducting empirical research on the validity of CMT, the selection of the investment horizon is crucial. Levy's conclusions are directly related to the relaxation of assumption (4) of CMT, that all investors have a common investment horizon.

If betas calculated on the relationship between the *HPR*s on individual securities and the market are unstable over time, are there ways to produce more predictable future betas? A number of approaches to improving beta predictability have been suggested. For example, Steven Carvell and Paul Strebel suggest that beta estimates for small firms, not regularly followed by a large number of analysts, can be improved by combining the traditional beta estimation procedure with a second "beta" based on the standard deviation of the analysts' forecast.[32]

Barr Rosenberg has combined industry and company-fundamental factors with historical stock price movements to improve beta predictability. According to Rosenberg, his "BARRA E1" predictive beta improves the predictive power of beta by more than a factor of 1.6.[33]

George M. Frankfurter and Herbert E. Phillips describe a technique of employing traditional beta calculation techniques, factor and statistical cluster analysis, and fundamental security analysis to improve risk-adjusted portfolio returns.[34] A final example is provided by Dan French, John Groth, and James Kolari who claim to have produced superior estimates of future betas by estimating betas using variances estimated from the Black-Scholes option pricing model (see Chapter 19) and combining it with betas estimated from historical data.[35]

---

[30] Bill McDonald, "Making Sense Out of Unstable Alphas and Betas," *The Journal of Portfolio Management* (Winter 1985): pp.19–22.

[31] Haim Levy, "The CAPM and the Investment Horizon," *The Journal of Portfolio Management* (Winter 1981): pp. 32–40.

[32] Steven Carvell and Paul Strebel, "A New Beta Incorporating Analysts' Forecasts," *The Journal of Portfolio Management* (Fall 1984): pp. 81–85.

[33] Barr Rosenberg, "Prediction of Common Stock Betas," *The Journal of Portfolio Management* (Winter 1985): pp. 5–14.

[34] George M. Frankfurter and Herbert E. Phillips, "MPT plus Security Analysis for Better Performance," *The Journal of Portfolio Management* (Summer 1982): pp. 29–36.

[35] Dan W. French, John C. Groth, and James W. Kolari, "Current Investor Expectations and Better Betas," *The Journal of Portfolio Management* (Fall 1983) pp. 12–17.

ARBITRAGE PRICING THEORY

The *arbitrage pricing theory*, APT, suggested by Stephen Ross is, like capital market theory, an equilibrium theory of expected return.[36] The central thesis of APT is that more than one systematic factor affects the long-term average returns on financial assets. Unlike CMT, APT requires a *factor model*. While APT has less restrictive assumptions than CMT (e.g., assumptions related to investment horizon, existence of market portfolio, and riskless borrowing and lending rates), APT does share with CMT assumptions related to perfect capital markets and common investment horizons. Additionally, APT assumes that the arbitrage portfolio can be achieved with no money invested, a rather unrealistic assumption for the majority of investors. However, it is important to consider that it takes only a few investors (arbitrageurs) to bring expected return and risk for assets into proper proportion.

Factor Models

Factors models have been used in finance for a long time. Initially they were known as *index models*. The change in terminology has come about as the result of using *factor analysis* to identify the major forces that influence the returns on a large number of securities. As Sharpe points out,

> *As a practical matter one must employ a factor model, either explicitly or implicitly. It is impossible to think separately about the interrelationship of every security with every other. Abstraction is essential. Good investment managers identify important factors in the economy and marketplace and assess the extent to which different securities will respond to changes in these factors. Passive managers attempt to assess the market's predictions about the risks and returns associated with the factors and security-specific returns. Active managers also attempt to outguess the market on likely outcomes for factors and/or stocks.*
>
> *There is no reason to assume or believe that a good factor model for one period will be a good one for the next period; key factors change–remember OPEC! So do the risks and returns associated with various factors and the sensitivities of securities to factors. Causes of changes include mergers, new lines of business, changes in leverage, etc.[37]*

A factor model can take the following general form:

$$\tilde{R}_i = a_i + b_{i1}\tilde{F}_1 + b_{i2}\tilde{F}_2 + \ldots + b_{im}\tilde{F}_m + \tilde{e}_i \tag{7.6}$$

where the tildes are placed over variables not known in advance. R_i is the return on security i; F_1 is the value of the first factor; F_2 is the value of the second factor,

---

[36] Stephen A. Ross. "The Arbitrage Theory of Capital Asset Pricing," *Journal of Economic Theory* (December 1976): pp.341–60.

[37] William F. Sharpe, "Factor Models, CAPMs, and the APT," *The Journal of Portfolio Management* (Fall 1984): pp. 21–25.

etc.; b_{ij} is the sensitivity of security i's returns to movements in the factor (factor loadings); and e_i is the variation in return unexplained by the factors. The e_i term is called the *security-specific return* or more commonly, security i's *idiosyncratic return*. The e_i values for securities are assumed to be uncorrelated.

As indicated earlier in the discussion of portfolio theory, the use of a factor model is a practical necessity for portfolio managers considering a large number of securities for a portfolio. It is virtually impossible for the portfolio manager to identify the interrelationships among many pairs of securities. Markowitz suggested an index model; Sharpe is credited with being among the first to develop the single-index model, using the market as the factor; and Kalman Cohen and Gerald Pogue were among the first researchers to employ multifactor models.[38]

The Elements of APT

APT is an *ex-ante* and an *ex-post* model in its specification of returns, R_i, as shown in the following equation:

$$R_i = E_i + b_{i1}\delta_1 + b_{i2}\delta_2 + \ldots + b_{iK}\delta_K + e_i \qquad (7.7)$$

where E_i = the *ex-ante* expected return of asset i

   δ_i = an *ex-post* sample factor, systematic in that it influences the return of all assets and is uncorrelated with other factors

   b_{ij} = sensitivity of the returns of asset i to the movements of factor j

   e_i = the idiosyncratic return (residual) of asset i's return, e_i having an expected value of 0 and no correlation with idiosyncratic returns of other assets

According to APT, asset returns covary with the movement of the factors and are thus the sources of systematic risk. It would logically follow then that these factors and an asset's sensitivity to these factors would determine the *expected* and *actual* returns. Given this relationship, expected return (E_i from Equation 7.7) can be expressed as

$$E_i = \lambda_0 + \lambda_1 b_{i1} + \lambda_2 b_{i2} + \ldots + \lambda_K b_{iK} \qquad (7.8)$$

where λ_0 is the return on a risk-free asset, and λ_j is the market price of risk related to the jth factor. If there was only one factor, the market, then λ_1 would equal

---

[38] Harry M. Markowitz, *Portfolio Selection: Efficient Diversification of Investments* (New York: John Wiley, 1959); William F. Sharpe, "A Simplified Model for Portfolio Analysis," *Management Science* (January 1963): pp. 277–93; and Kalman J. Cohen and Gerald A. Pogue, "An Empirical Evaluation of Alternative Portfolio Selection Models," *Journal of Business* (April 1967): pp. 166–93. A number of researchers have identified relevant factors: Benjamin F. King, "Market and Industry Factors in Stock Price Behavior," *Journal of Business* (January 1966): pp. 139–90; Edwin Elton and Martin Gruber, "Estimating the Dependence Stucture of Share Prices—Implications for Portfolio Selection," *Journal of Finance* (December 1973): pp. 1203–32; Eugene Fama and James MacBeth, "Risk, Return and Equilibrium: Empirical Tests," *Journal of Political Economy* (May-June 1973): pp. 607–36.

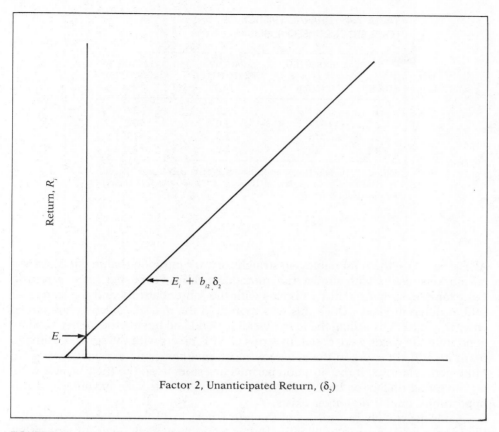

FIGURE 7.7 Factor and asset return

$R_f - E(R_m)$, and Equation 7.8 would be similar to the equation for the security market line. Thus, CMT can be seen as a special case of the APT.

The λ's in Equation 7.8 represent anticipated changes, while the δ's in Equation 7.7 represent unanticipated changes. Thus, if unanticipated changes for all factors are 0, the asset will simply achieve its expected return, E_i.

An example may help to explain the difference between anticipated and unanticipated changes in the factors. Assume that there are four factors that affect securities' returns and that the unanticipated change in factors 1, 3, and 4 is 0. The return, R_i, on the asset can be shown in Figure 7.7 which shows the straight-line relationship between the actual returns for asset i and the return (movement) in factor 2. The slope of the line is a function of the sensitivity of asset i's return to factor 2, b_i. If the b_i value is larger (smaller) than shown, the slope of the line will be higher (lower). The value for b_i can be negative, indicating that an unanticipated increase in the factor would cause a decrease in the asset's return. Note that if the unanticipated return of factor 2 was 0, the return on asset i would not be 0, but its expected return, E_i.

TABLE 7.4 CHARACTERISTICS OF
FOUR STOCKS: DISEQUILIBRIUM

STOCK	EXPECTED RETURN $(E(R_i))$	FACTOR 1 SENSITIVITY (b_{i1})	FACTOR 2 SENSITIVITY (b_{i2})
#1	13%	0.2	2.0
#2	27	3.0	0.2
#3	16	1.0	1.0
#4	20	2.0	2.0

SOURCE: Dorothy H. Bower, Richard S. Bower, and Dennis E. Logue, "A Primer on Arbitrage Pricing Theory," *Midland Corporate Finance Journal* (Fall 1984): pp. 31–40.

Arbitrage

APT is based on the reasonable and straightforward intuition that in efficient capital markets, assets with similar risk must have similar expected rates of return. For example, suppose that two bonds with the same maturity and the same risk sold at different yields. Once this was spotted in the market, arbitrageurs would enter the market by selling the lower-yielding bond and buying the higher-yielding bond until the yields were equal. In terms of APT, assets with the same sensitivity, b_i, to identified factors in the economy must have the same expected return. In more general terms, if the situation permits investors to add to their wealth without investing dollars or facing risk, they will continue to take advantage of this opportunity until it no longer exists.

Consider the characteristics of the four stocks in Table 7.4, and assume that the idiosyncratic return (residual risk) has been diversified away through other investments.[39] For purposes of this example, only two factors are considered to be statistically significant.[40] Could this situation exist in an efficient capital market? The answer is no, because an opportunity is present for positive risk-free returns. Arbitrageurs would enter the market and create an arbitrage portfolio like the one shown in Table 7.5.

The investment weights (X_i in Table 7.5) are determined as a result of an arbitrage portfolio having 0 investment (some stocks are sold short) and 0 factor risk. In this example, these requirements can be expressed as

$$X_1 + X_2 + X_3 + X_4 = 0 \quad \text{(0 investment risk)}$$
$$X_1 b_{11} + X_2 b_{21} + X_3 b_{31} + X_4 b_{41} = 0 \quad \text{(0 factor 1 risk)}$$
$$X_1 b_{12} + X_2 b_{22} + X_3 b_{32} + X_4 b_{42} = 0 \quad \text{(0 factor 2 risk)}$$

In order to solve for the amount of investment in each of the four stocks, X_i, as shown in Table 7.5 a fourth equation can be created by setting the investment

---

[39] This example is from Dorothy H. Bower, Richard S. Bower, and Dennis E. Logue, "A Primer on Arbitrage Pricing Theory," *Midland Corporate Finance Journal* (Fall 1984): pp. 31–40.

[40] Clearly, additional factors could be used, but this would only complicate the exposition.

TABLE 7.5 ARBITRAGE PORTFOLIO

STOCK	INVESTMENT PROPORTION (X_i)	EXPECTED RETURN $(X_i \times E(R_i))$	FACTOR 1 WEIGHTED SENSITIVITY $(X_i \times b_{i1})$	FACTOR 2 WEIGHTED SENSITIVITY $(X_i \times b_{i2})$
#1	+1.000	+13.000%	+0.200	+2.000
#2	+0.643	+17.361	+1.929	+0.129
#3	−1.157	−18.512	−1.157	−1.157
#4	−0.486	− 9.720	−0.972	−0.972
Portfolio	0.000	+ 2.129%	0.000	0.000

SOURCE: Dorothy H. Bower, Richard S. Bower, and Dennis E. Logue, "A Primer on Arbitrage Pricing Theory," *Midland Corporate Finance Journal* (Fall 1984) pp.: 31–40.

in one of the stocks equal to 1 and then solving for the remaining proportions in the other stocks. For example, if the investment in the first stock is set at, $X_1 = 1$, then from Table 7.4

$$X_2 + X_3 + X_4 = -1 \tag{7.9}$$

$$X_2(3.0) + X_3(1.0) + X_4(2.0) = -.2 \tag{7.10}$$

$$X_2(.2) + X_3(1.0) + X_4(2.0) = -2 \tag{7.11}$$

Subtracting Equation 7.11 from Equation 7.10 solves for the proportional investment in Stock 2, X_2 of .643 ($2.8X_2 = 1.8$; $X_2 = .643$). Subtracting Equation 7.10 from Equation 7.9 and substituting .643 for X_2, results in X_4 equal to −.486 ($-2X_2 - X_4 = -.8$; $-2(.643) - X_4 = -.8$; $X_4 = -.486$). Substituting the solved values for X_2 and X_4 in Equation 7.9 gives the proportional investment in stock 3 of −1.157 ($.643 + X_3 - .486 = -1$; $X_3 = -1.157$).

As Table 7.5 illustrates, when the investment weights are as shown, the total investment in the arbitrage portfolio is 0, and a positive, risk-free return is available. As a result of this action by arbitrageurs, the expected returns of stocks 1 and 2 will be lower than those of stocks 3 and 4. This relative change is the result of stocks 1 and 2 being bought (their prices rise and expected returns decrease) and stocks 3 and 4 being sold (their prices decline and expected returns increase.)

Empirical Tests of APT and Factors

In an initial empirical test of APT, Stephen Ross and Richard Roll used factor analysis to analyze 1,260 NYSE stocks over the period 1962 through 1972.[41] The stocks were divided into groups of 30 stocks each. The first step estimated the factor coefficients and expected returns from the daily returns of each stock. The sensitivity of the security's returns to movements in the factor, b_{ij} was used as the independent variable in the second step: cross-sectional regression analysis to estimate the factor's risk premium, λ_j. The hypothesis tested was that one or more

---

[41] Richard Roll and Stephen A. Ross, "An Empirical Investigation of the Arbitrage Pricing Theory," *Journal of Finance* (December 1980): pp. 1073–1103.

of the coefficients, λ_j should be non-0 constants. The authors found, in several different tests, that between two and four factors were significantly different from 0. That is, these factors are "priced," in the sense that they affect the returns of the stocks.

Additional research has indicated that more than four factors are priced.[42] Others contend that the number of securities in the portfolios determines the number of factors that are priced.[43] A recent article, however, concludes that

> *APT provides a powerful and appealing framework to consider security returns. Its acceptance, in both the academic and business community, is contingent upon supportive empirical tests of the theory. The standard empirical methodology is inadequate because inappropriate tests for the sufficient number of factors are being employed and because the standard tests fail to determine if the estimated model satisfies equilibrium conditions.*[44]

The lack of agreement about the exact number of factors that are appropriate is not as important as that empirical research indicates that more than one factor has been found to be statistically significant in pricing assets. This raises serious questions about traditional CMT, which depends on one factor, the market portfolio.

Another issue concerning APT: Even if statistically significant factors can be identified from security return data, what are these factors? In other words, what are the economic variables that these factors represent? Progress is being made in this area. Roll and Ross, based on their research with Nai-Fu Chen, suggest that the following four economic factors are related to unanticipated returns on large portfolios:[45]

1. Unanticipated changes in inflation;
2. Unanticipated changes in industrial production;
3. Unanticipated changes in risk premiums (as measured by the spread between low-grade and high-grade bonds); and
4. Unanticipated changes in the slope of the term structure of interest rates.

Presently there is considerable debate in the literature about the correctness and relevancy of the CAPM versus APT. One issue is the "testability" of APT.[46]

---

[42] D. C. Cho, Edwin J. Elton, and Martin J. Gruber, "On the Robustness of the Roll and Ross Arbitrage Pricing Theory," *Journal of Financial and Quantitative Analysis* (March 1984): pp. 1–10.

[43] Phoebus J. Dhrymes, Irwin Friend, and N. Bulent Gultekin, "A Critical Reexamination of the Empirical Evidence on the Arbitrage Pricing Theory," *Journal of Finance* (June 1984): pp. 323–46.

[44] Michael C. Ehrhardt, "Arbitrage Pricing Models: The Sufficient Number of Factors and Equilibrium Conditions," *The Journal of Financial Research* (Summer 1987): pp. 111–20.

[45] N. F. Chen, "Some Empirical Tests of The Theory of Arbitrage Pricing," *Journal of Finance* (December 1983): pp, 1394–1414, and Richard Roll and Stephen A. Ross, "The Arbitrage Pricing Theory Approach to Strategic Portfolio Planning," *Financial Analysts Journal* (May-June 1984): pp. 14–26.

[46] For example, see Jay Shanken, "The Arbitrage Pricing Theory: Is It Testable?" *Journal of Finance* (December 1982): pp. 1129–40; Philip H. Dybvig and Stephen A. Ross, "Yes, the APT Is Testable," *Journal of Finance* (September 1985): pp. 1173–88, and Jay Shanken, "Multi-Beta CAPM or Equilibrium APT? A Reply," *Journal of Finance* (September 1985): pp. 1189–96.

Essentially, questions similar to those raised about the empirical tests of CAPM have been extended to the tests of APT. A second issue is whether APT is a more robust and appropriate asset pricing model than the CAPM.[47] A possible solution is to recognize that both models have strengths and weaknesses, but the combined models may provide more guidance for investment decision making than either model alone.[48]

APT does not overcome all the shortcomings of CMT. Both theories of asset pricing will continue to undergo empirical tests. The multifactor model of APT is quite appealing, but its application in risk analysis awaits further empirical testing.

SUMMARY

This chapter began by tracing the impact of relaxing the rather restrictive assumptions of CMT and reporting the general results of empirical tests of CMT. It was shown that relaxing the assumptions of CMT presented in Chapter 6 results in a modification of the theory but does not necessarily invalidate its underlying constructs. That is, the theory, with its original assumptions in place, allows for an explanation of the expected relationship between risk and return. As the assumptions are removed to reflect more readily the "real world," the relationships between risk and return remain, but the exactness of this expected relationship is lessened.

While the assumptions of CMT are restrictive, the test of the theory is related to its ability to fit economic data. Numerous empirical tests of beta stationarity and CMT indicate that betas for individual stocks are not stationary but that betas for large portfolios of securities remain relatively stable from period to period. Tests of CMT using individual securities and portfolios of securities were found to be somewhat supportive of the theory. However, differences from the expected relationship between risk and return were observed.

The question of whether CMT is even testable was also examined. Richard Roll contends that proxies for the market portfolio used in the tests of CMT are not Markowitz efficient and thus cannot be used in the empirical testing of CMT.

The one-factor or market model of CMT has been challenged by Richard Roll and Stephen Ross. Ross developed a multifactor model, arbitrage pricing theory, in which CMT, using one factor, is a special case. APT is shown to be a serious challenge to CMT's preeminence in explaining the expected relationship between risk and return. While much developmental work and empirical investigation of APT has been undertaken, much remains to be done. This is particularly true of the problem of identifying the actual economic factors that relate to unanticipated returns on large portfolios.

---

[47] See, for example, Phoebus Dhrymes, "Arbitrage Pricing Theory," *Journal of Portfolio Management* (Summer 1984): pp. 35–44, and Stephen A. Ross, "A Reply to Dhrymes: APT Is Empirically Relevant," *Journal of Portfolio Management* (Fall 1984): pp. 21–25.

[48] William F. Sharpe, "Factor Models, CAPMs, and The APT," *Journal of Portfolio Management* (Fall 1987): pp. 21–25.

QUESTIONS

1. Capital Market Theory, CMT, assumes that investors have homogeneous expectations. Explain this assumption. Discuss the impact of heterogeneous expectations on CMT.

2. In the real world, individual investors do not actually hold efficient portfolios consisting of various combinations of the market portfolio and a risk-free asset. Does this observation invalidate CMT? Discuss.

3. Explain how different borrowing and lending risk-free rates modify the CML. Is the relationship between expected return and risk still linear?

4. Actual and unanticipated inflation causes changes in Treasury bill yields. Explain how inflation and its impact on Treasury bill yields affect CMT.

5. Compare and contrast a risk-free asset with a zero-beta portfolio.

6. Because of differences in transaction costs, investors generally trade in round lots of 100 shares. Explain how this behavior and the inability to buy fractional shares of common stock influence CMT.

7. Explain the impact of taxes on the CAPM and SML. How did the Tax Reform Act of 1986 modify the effect of taxes on the CAPM and SML?

8. Individual investors generally incur costs in acquiring investment information. Explain how costly information may influence the SML.

9. Briefly summarize the empirical conclusions of Robert Levy's study of beta stationarity. What are the practical implications of these conclusions to investors who use ex-post betas to make investment decisions?

10. Explain how the use of a proxy market portfolio can influence the empirical tests of CMT.

11. Compare and contrast the CAPM and APT.

12. Based on the current theoretical and empirical development of APT, do you think that this approach offers a practical alternative to the CAPM for individual investors?

13. Compare the "market" factor with "economic" factors that have been identified by APT. Are all APT factors aggregate economic factors? Do you think it would be appropriate to consider industry factors as part of an APT model for an individual security?

14. Briefly discuss some of the empirical problems that have been encountered in empirically testing APT.

PROBLEMS

1. Consider an asset with a beta of 1.3:
   a. If the expected return on the market is 15 percent and the risk-free return 10 percent, calculate the expected return on the asset, using the CAPM.
   b. Assume that the return on the zero-beta portfolio is 11 percent and the expected return on the market portfolio is 15 percent. Calculate the expected return on the asset, using the zero-beta form of the CAPM.
   c. Explain why the return on the zero-beta portfolio may be above the risk-free return.

2. Assume that the expected return on the market is 18 percent and the standard deviation of the market is 6 percent.

a. If the risk-free return is 10 percent, calculate the slope of the CML. Calculate the slope of the SML.

b. Suppose investors can lend at a risk-free rate of 10 percent, but the borrowing rate is 12 percent.

    (1) Calculate the slope of the lending segment of the CML.

    (2) Calculate the slope of the borrowing segment of the CML.

    (3) Explain why the "market price for risk" for lending portfolios is more than that for borrowing portfolios.

3. Assume two common stocks have the following betas:

$$\beta_1 = 1.2; \qquad \beta_2 = 0.9$$

a. Calculate the beta for a portfolio consisting of equal dollar investments in each stock.

b. If an investor thought that a portfolio beta of 1.4 was appropriate, indicate the proportion of funds that could be invested in *both* stocks to form this portfolio.

4. Suppose your stock broker indicates that Growth, Inc. is likely to have an *HPR* for the next year of 18 percent. Based on the CAPM, you think the appropriate expected return for this common stock is likely to be 15 percent. Assume that your broker is correct.

a. Is it feasible for you to purchase the stock if brokerage costs are estimated to be 1 percent of the initial investment?

b. Is it feasible for you to purchase the stock if brokerage costs are estimated to be 3 percent of the initial investment?

5. Consider the following information on three common stocks:

STOCK	BETA	CORRELATION OF *HPR*s WITH MARKET PORTFOLIO *HPR*s
Alpha	1.2	1.0
Delta	−0.8	−0.8
Gamma	1.6	0.3

a. Indicate the stock(s) with no unsystematic risk.

b. Based on the CAPM, which stock would have the highest expected return? The lowest expected return?

6. Consider the following information on the market and a proxy market portfolio:

	MARKET PORTFOLIO	PROXY MARKET PORTFOLIO
Expected return	18%	16%
Standard deviation	6%	8%

a. If the risk-free return is 8 percent, calculate the slope for the "true" CML and "proxy" CML.

b. Is the proxy market portfolio efficient in the Markowitz sense? Explain.

c. Suppose a specific common stock portfolio has an expected return of 20 percent and standard deviation of 7 percent. How does this portfolio compare to both the market and proxy portfolios?

7. Suppose you are attempting to estimate an appropriate expected return for a particular common stock. Assume the risk-free return is 8 percent.

   a. If the expected return on the market is 15 percent and the stock's beta is 1.2, use the CAPM to calculate the expected return.

   b. Using an APT approach, the following factors and sensitivity indexes have been identified:

FACTOR	MARKET PRICE OF RISK	SENSITIVITY INDEX
Unanticipated changes in inflation	6.0%	1.1
Unanticipated changes in industrial production	2.0%	0.8
Unanticipated changes in risk premiums	3.0%	1.0
Unanticipated changes in term structure	4.0%	−0.9

   Use an appropriate APT model to calculate the expected return.

   c. What explanations can you offer to explain the difference in the two estimates of expected return?

REFERENCES

Arbel, Avner, and Paul Strebel. "Pay Attention to Neglected Firms!" *Jounal of Protfolio Management* (Winter 1983): pp. 37–42.

Banz, R. W. "The Relationship between Return and Market Value of Common Stocks." *Journal of financial Economics* (March 1981): pp. 3–18.

Beaver, William, Paul Kettler, and Myron Scholes. "The Association Between Market Determined and Accounting Determined Risk Measures." *Accounting Review* (October 1970): pp. 654–82.

Bernstein, Peter L. "Dead–or Alive and Well?" *Journal of Portfolio Management* (Winter 1981): p. 4.

Black, Fischer, Michael C. Jensen, and Myron S. Scholes. "The Capital Asset Pricing Model: Some Empirical Tests." In *Studies in the Theory of Capital Markets*, edited by Micheal Jensen, pp. 79–121. New York: Praeger, 1972.

Blume, Marshall E. "On the Assessment of Risk," *Journal of Finance* (March 1971): pp. 1–10.

———. "Betas and Their Regression Tendencies." *Journal of Finance* (June 1975): pp. 785–95.

———. "Betas and Their Regression Tendencies: Some Further Evidence." *Journal of Finance* (March 1979): pp. 265–67.

Blume, Marshall E., and Irwin Friend. "A New Look at the Capital Asset Pricing Model." *Journal of Finance* (March 1973): pp. 19–33.

Bodie, Zvi. "Inflation Risk and Capital Market Equilibrium." *Financial Review* (May 1982): pp. 1–25.

Bower, Dorothy H., Richard S. Bower, and Dennis E. Logue, "A Primer on Arbitrage Pricing Theory." *Midland Corporate Financial Journal* (Fall 1984): pp. 31–40.

Brennan, M. J. "Taxes, Market Valuation and Corporate Finance Policy." *National Tax Journal* (December 1970): pp. 417–27.

Brenner, Menachem. "The Effect of Model Misspecification on Tests of the Efficient Market Hypothesis." *Journal of Finance* (March 1977): pp. 57–66.

———. "The Sensitivity of the Efficient Market Hypothesis to Alternative Specifications of the Market Model." *Journal of Finance* (September 1979): pp. 915–29.

Carvell, Steven, and Paul Strebel. "A New Beta Incorporating Analysts' Forecasts," *Journal of Portfolio Management* (Fall 1984): pp. 81–85.

Chance, Don M. "Empirical Estimates of Equivalent risk Classes and the Effect of Financial Leverage on Systematic Risk." *Financial Review* (Fall 1981): pp. 12–29.

Chen, N. F. "Some Empirical Tests of the Theory of Arbitrage Pricing." *Journal of Finance* (December 1983): pp. 1394–1414.

Cho, D. C., Edwin J. Elton, and Martin J. Gruber. "On the Robustness of the Roll and Ross Arbitrage Pricing Theory." *Journal of Financial and Quantitative Analysis* (March 1984): pp. 1–10.

Coggin, T. Daniel, and John E. Hunter. "A Meta-Analysis of Pricing 'Risk' Factors in APT." *Journal of Portfolio Management* (Fall 1987): pp. 35–38.

Cohen, Kalman J., and Gerald A. Pogue. "An Empirical Evaluation of Alternative Portfolio Selection Models." *Journal of Business* (April 1967): pp. 166–93.

Dhrymes, Phoebus, J., Irwin Friend, and N. Bulent Gultekin. "A Critical Reexamination of the Empirical Evidence on the Arbitrage Pricing Theory," *Journal of Finance* (June 1984): pp. 323–46.

———. "Arbitrage Pricing Theory." *Journal of Portfolio Management* (Summer 1984): pp. 35–44.

Douglas, G. W. "Risk in the Equity Markets: An Empirical Appraisal of Market Efficiency." *Yale Economic Essays* (Spring 1969): pp. 3–48.

Dybvig, Philip H., and Stephen A. Ross. "Yes, the APT is Testable." *Journal of Finance* (September 1985): pp. 1173–88.

Ehrhardt, Michael C. "Arbitrage Pricing Models: The Sufficient Number of Factors and Equilibrium Conditions." *Journal of Financial Research* (Summer 1987): pp. 111–20.

Elton, Edwin, and Martin Gruber. "Estimating the Dependence Structure of Share Prices—Implications for Portfolio Selection." *Journal of Finance* (December 1973): pp. 1203–32.

Fama, Eugene F., and James D. MacBeth. "Risk Return and Equilibrium: Empirical Tests." *Journal of Political Economy* (May/June 1973): pp. 607–36.

Fogler, H. Russell. "Common Sense on CAPM, APT, and Correlated Residuals." *Journal of Portfolio Management* (Summer 1982): pp. 20–28.

Frankfurter, George M., and Herbert E. Phillips. "MPT plus Security Analysis for Better Performance." *Journal of Portfolio Management* (Summer 1982): pp. 29–36.

French, Dan W., John C. Groth, and James W. Kolari. "Current Investor Expectations and Better Betas." *Journal of Portfolio Management* (Fall 1983): pp. 12–17.

Grossman, Sanford J., and Joseph E. Stiglitz. "On the Impossibility of Informational Efficient Markets." *American Economic Review* (June 1980): pp. 393–408.

Jacob, Nancy. "The Measurement of Systematic Risk for Securities and Portfolios: Some Empirical Results." *Journal of Financial and Quantitative Analysis* (March 1971): pp. 815–34.

Kaufman, George G. "Duration, Planning Period, and Tests of the Capital Asset Pricing Model." *Jounal of Financial Research* (Spring 1980): pp. 1–9.

King, Benjamin F. "Market and Industry Factors in Stock Price Behavior." *Journal of Business* (January 1966): pp. 139–90.

Levy, Robert A. "On the Short-Term Stationarity of Beta Coefficients." *Financial Analysts Journal* (November-December 1971): pp. 55–62.

Levy, Haim. "The CAPM and the Investment Horizon." *Journal of Portfolio Management* (Winter 1981): pp. 32–40.

Lintner, John. "Security Prices, Risk, and Maximal Gain from Diversification." *Journal of Finance* (December 1965): pp. 587–615.

———. "The Aggregation of Investor's Diverse Judgements and Preferences in Purely Competitive Security Markets." *Journal of Financial and Quantitative Analysis* (December 1969): pp. 347–400.

Litzenberger, Robert H., and Krishna Ramaswamy. "The Effect of Personal Taxes and Dividends on Capital Asset Prices: Theory and Empirical Evidence." *Journal of Financial Economics* (June 1979): pp. 163–95.

Markowitz, Harry M. *Portfolio Selection: Efficient Diversification of Investments*. New York: Wiley, 1959.

———. "The 'Two Beta' Trap." *Journal of Portfolio Management* (Fall 1984): pp. 12–20.

McDonald, Bill. "Making Sense Out of Unstable Alphas and Betas." *Journal of Portfolio Management* (Winter 1985): pp. 19–22.

Miller, Merton H., and Myron Scholes. "Rates of Return in Relation to Risk: A Reexamination of Some Recent Findings." In *Studies in the Theory of Capital Markets*, edited by Michael Jensen, pp. 47–48. New York: Praeger, 1972.

Modani, Naval K., William P. Lloyd, and John H. Hand. "Behavior of Risk Proxies and Merger Activity." *Review of Business and Economic Research* (Spring 1984): pp. 81–89.

———. "Bond Rating Changes and Behavior of Risk Proxies." *Akron Business and Economic Review* (Spring 1984): pp. 46–49.

Modigliani, Franco, and Gerald A. Pogue. "An Introduction to Risk and Return (Part II)." *Financial Analysts Journal* (May-June 1974): pp. 69–86.

Ohlson, James, and Barr Rosenberg. "Systematic Risk of the CRSP Equal-Weighted Common Stock Index: A History Estimated by Stochastic-Parameter Regression." *Journal of Business* (January 1982): pp. 121–45.

Pari, Robert A., and Son-Nan Chen. "An Empirical Test of the Arbitrage Pricing Theory." *Journal of Financial Research* (Summer 1984): pp. 121–30.

Reinganum, Marc R. "Abnormal Returns in Small Firm Portfolios." *Financial Analysts Journal* (March-April 1981): pp. 52–57.

Roll, Richard. "A Critique of the Asset Pricing Theory's Tests." *Journal of Financial Economics* (March 1977): pp. 129–76.

———. "Ambiguity When Performance Is Measured by the Security Market Line." *Journal of Finance* (September 1978): pp. 1051–69.

Roll, Richard, and Stephen A. Ross. "An Empirical Investigation of the Arbitrage Pricing Theory." *Journal of Finance* (December 1980): pp. 1073–1103.

———. "The Arbitrage Pricing Theory Approach to Strategic Portfolio Planning." *Financial Analysts Journal* (May-June 1984): pp. 14–26.

Rosenberg, Barr. "Prediction of Common Stock Betas." *Journal of Portfolio Management* (Winter 1985): pp. 5–14.

Ross, Stephen A. "The Arbitrage Theory of Capital Asset Pricing." *Journal of Economic Theory* (December 1976): pp. 341–60.

————. "A Reply to Dyrymes: APT Is Empirically Relevant." *Journal of Portfolio Management* (Fall 1984): pp. 54–56.

Sharpe, William F. "A Simplified Model for Portfolio Analysis." *Management Science* (January 1963): pp. 277–93.

————. "Factor Models, CAPMs, and the APT." *Journal of Portfolio Management* (Fall 1984): pp. 21–25.

Shanken, Jay. "The Arbitrage Pricing Theory: Is It Testable?" *Journal of Finance* (December 1982): pp. 1129–40.

————. "Multi-Beta CAPM or Equilibrium APT: A Reply." *Journal of Finance* (September 1985): pp. 1189–96.

Stoll, Hans R., and Robert E. Whaley. "Transaction Costs and the Small Firm Effect." *Journal of Financial Economics* (June 1983): pp. 57–80.

Sweeney, Richard J., and Arthur D. Warga. "Interest-Sensitive Stocks: An APT Application." *Financial Review* (November 1983): pp. 257–69.

Tole, Thomas M. "How to Maximize Stationarity of Beta." *Journal of Portfolio Management* (Winter 1981): pp. 45–49.

Wallace, Anise. "Is Beta Dead?" *Institutional Investor* (July 1980): pp. 23–30.

Williams, Joseph T. "Capital Asset Prices with Heterogeneous Beliefs." *Journal of Financial Economics* (November 1977): pp. 219–39.

CHAPTER 8

ANALYSIS OF PORTFOLIO PERFORMANCE

INTRODUCTION

One important aspect of investment decision making is the historical or ex-post analysis of a portfolio's performance. The analysis of historical performance is an indication of the success of the portfolio's investment strategy and the skill of the portfolio's manager. The results of the performance analysis may suggest the need for portfolio revisions, modification of the investment strategy, or even a change in the portfolio manager.

As a simple illustration, assume that two highly diversified common stock portfolios earned the following holding period returns, *HPR*s, for 1988:

PORTFOLIO	HPR
A	15%
B	20%

Would it be correct to conclude that the performance of portfolio B was superior to portfolio A's? The correct answer, of course, is no, since a valid performance analysis should consider both return and *risk*. Further, the return should be computed as net of transactions costs and expenses incurred by the portfolio. It is quite possible that the risk of portfolio B is substantially above that of portfolio A, even though both portfolios contain only common stocks. If the risk of both portfolios is equal, however, then portfolio B has outperformed portfolio A.

Calculating Ex-Post Returns for Performance Analysis

1. SINGLE HOLDING PERIOD In analyzing a portfolio's performance, the *HPR* of the portfolio needs to be correctly calculated over the period of the evaluation. For a single holding period, the ex-post *HPR* of the portfolio can be calculated as

$$HPR_{p,t} = \frac{V_{t+1} - V_t + I_t}{V_t} \qquad (8.1)$$

where V_{t+1} = the market value of the portfolio at the end of the holding period

V_t = the market value of the portfolio at the beginning of the holding period

I_t = income that was *distributed* by the portfolio during the period of evaluation

As an illustration, assume that on January 1, 1988, the market value of the portfolio was $8,100. By December 31, 1988, the market value increased to $11,000 *after* a distribution of income (dividends and interest) of $1,000 to the portfolio's owner. The *HPR* for 1988 would be

$$HPR_{p,1988} = \frac{\$11,000 - \$8,100 + \$1,000}{8,100} \qquad (8.2)$$

$$= 48.15\%$$

2. MULTIPLE HOLDING PERIODS The length of the holding period must always be specified for the *HPR*. If the holding period is not specified, it is assumed to be one year. Suppose, however, that you have the following data on a portfolio's performance:

	MARKET VALUE	INCOME DISTRIBUTION
January 1, 1987	$ 8,000	—
December 31, 1987	8,100	$ 500
December 31, 1988	11,000	1,000

The *HPR* for 1987 is 7.50 percent and as previously calculated, 48.15 percent for 1988. How can a *two*-year *HPR* be calculated? The correct calculation would consider the timing of the income distributions as well as the appreciation in the market value of the portfolio.

There are, however, two assumptions that can be made about the income distribution of $500 paid on December 31, 1987. One assumption would treat the $500 distribution as income that was *not* reinvested, indicating a two-year *HPR* of

$$HPR_{p,2t} = \frac{\$11{,}000 - \$8{,}000 + \$500 + \$1{,}000}{\$8{,}000} \qquad (8.3)$$

$$= 56.25\%$$

The second, more accurate assumption assumes that the $500 is reinvested and that it was received on December 31, 1987. It is reinvested for one year at the *HPR* of 48.15 percent for 1988:

$$HPR_{p,2t} = \frac{\$11{,}000 - \$8{,}000 + \$500(1.4815) + \$1{,}000}{\$8{,}000} \qquad (8.4)$$

$$= 59.26\%$$

Notice, however, that the calculations in Equations 8.3 and 8.4 ignore the portfolio's value on December 31, 1987. This suggests that the *annual* HPRs may be more appropriate since they consider each of the end-of-year portfolio values.

3. ANNUALIZED HOLDING PERIOD RETURNS The above example assumed a two-year holding period and calculated a two-year *HPR*. Typically, however, *HPRs* are based on a holding period of one year or less. How should the annualized *HPR* be calculated for this example? One possibility is to take a simple average of the one-year *HPRs*:

$$\frac{.0750 + .4815}{2} = 27.825\% \qquad (8.5)$$

This simple average, however, ignores the compounding effect that results if the $500 received on December 31, 1987, is reinvested. The compounding effect can be considered by taking the geometric average (see Chapter 2) of the annual *HPR*s:

$$\overline{HPR}_g = \left[\prod_{t=1}^{n} (1 + HPR_t)^{1/n} \right] - 1.0 \tag{8.6}$$
$$= [(1.075)(1.4815)]^{1/2} - 1.0 = 26.2\%$$

Thus, assuming annual compounding and reinvestment of income, the two-year *HPR* would be

$$HPR_{p,2t} = (1.2620)^2 - 1 = 59.26\% \tag{8.7}$$

The geometric average *HPR* is, therefore, consistent with the assumption of reinvesting income when it is received. This point is illustrated by comparing the results from Equations 8.4 and 8.7.

In summary, all income distributions and portfolio values over the holding period should be considered. In most cases when dealing with portfolio performance evaluation, income distributions are assumed to be reinvested at the *HPR*s for the following periods. These assumptions can be correctly incorporated into the calculations by reinvesting the cash flows, as in Equation 8.4, or by calculating the annual *HPR*s, using Equation 8.1, and then calculating the geometric average *HPR*, using Equation 8.6.

Table 8.1 provides annual *HPR*s over the 1976–1985 period for a sample of three mutual funds, the S&P 500, and one-year Treasury bills. The *HPR*s were calculated using Equation 8.1.[1] The income distributions, *I*, used in calculating the *HPR*s include both capital gains and dividend distributions made by the funds. The second column under each fund ("End-of-Year Value") is calculated by assuming that an initial investment of $10,000 was made on January 1, 1976. It is also assumed that the distributions (capital gains and dividends) were reinvested.

For example, a $10,000 investment in the Fidelity Magellan Fund on January 1, 1976, would have grown to $181,172 by December 31, 1985, assuming all distributions were reinvested. The geometric average annual *HPR* for the Fidelity Magellan Fund can be calculated using Equation 8.6:

$$\overline{HPR}_g = [(1.336)(1.145) \ldots (1.431)]^{1/10} - 1 = 33.60\% \tag{8.8}$$

Alternatively, the geometric average annual *HPR* could be calculated, using the initial investment of $10,000 and the 1985 ending portfolio value:

$$\$181,172 = \$10,000(1 + \overline{HPR}_g)^{10}$$
$$\overline{HPR}_g = 33.60\%$$

---

[1] The *HPR*s do not reflect the initial investment fee or "load" charge. The Fidelity Magellan Fund charges a fee of 3 percent, while the other two funds do not charge a fee. The importance of fees for mutual fund investing is discussed in Chapter 24.

TABLE 8.1 MEASURE OF RISK AND RETURN FOR SELECTED MUTUAL FUNDS, S&P 500, AND ONE-YEAR TREASURY BILLS (1976–1985)

	FIDELITY MAGELLAN FUND		THE 44 WALL STREET FUND		T. ROWE PRICE NEW HORIZONS FUND		S&P 500		ONE-YEAR TREASURY BILL	
	HPR	END-OF-YEAR VALUE	HPR	END-OF-YEAR VALUE	HPR	END-OF-YEAR VALUE	HPR	END-OF-YEAR VALUE	HPR	END-OF-YEAR VALUE
1976	33.6%	$ 13,360	46.5%	$14,650	11.1%	$11,110	17.1%	$11,710	5.77%	$10,577
1977	14.5	15,297	16.5	17,067	12.7	12,521	14.5	13,408	5.29	11,137
1978	31.7	20,146	32.9	22,682	20.9	15,138	8.5	14,548	7.28	11,947
1979	51.7	30,562	73.6	39,377	35.5	20,512	15.6	16,817	10.41	13,191
1980	76.5	53,942	36.4	53,710	57.6	32,327	34.1	22,552	12.06	14,782
1981	12.1	60,469	−22.8	41,464	−7.8	29,805	−4.8	21,469	14.08	16,863
1982	48.1	89,555	8.5	44,988	22.8	36,601	22.2	26,235	14.32	19,278
1983	38.6	124,123	6.8	48,048	19.5	43,738	21.3	31,823	8.62	20,940
1984	2.0	126,605	−59.6	19,411	−9.6	39,539	4.1	33,128	9.90	23,013
1985	43.1	181,172	−20.1	15,510	24.3	49,147	29.9	43,033	9.33	25,160
Average Annual HPR	35.19%		11.87%		18.70%		16.25%		9.71%	
Geometric Average Annual HPR	33.60%		4.50%		17.26%		15.71%		9.67%	
Standard Deviation	21.85%		38.65%		19.57%		11.65%		3.14%	
Correlation with S&P 500	0.82		0.34		0.82		1.00		—	
Beta	1.54		1.13		1.38		1.00		—	

SOURCE: Data to calculate the *HPR*s was obtained from Wiesenberger Financial Services, *Investment Companies*, 1986; *Federal Reserve Bulletin*, various issues; and Standard & Poor's Statistical Service. Reprinted by permission.

The simple arithmetic average and the geometric average of the annual *HPR*s are provided in Table 8.1 for each fund. For the 44 Wall Street Fund, the difference in the two averages is large because of the extreme variability of the yearly *HPR*s. This is a good example of why the geometric mean should be used as an indication of "average" return performance.

Analysis of Risk in Performance Analysis

The sample of three mutual funds in Table 8.1 represents common stock funds with an investment objective of "growth," with an emphasis on "maximum capital gains." Since the three funds have the same investment objectives and invest almost exclusively in common stocks, is the risk of each fund equal? The correlation coefficients and betas provided in Table 8.1 suggest otherwise. As would be expected, because of the investment objective, all three betas are greater than 1. There are, however, large differences in the standard deviations, correlation coefficients with the S&P 500, and betas of the three funds. These differences suggest that any performance analysis of the three funds should consider *both HPRs* and risk.

As an illustration, for the period 1976–1985 the geometric average *HPR* for the New Horizons Fund is 17.26 percent versus 15.71 percent for the S&P 500. Therefore, did this fund outperform the market during this period? The 19.57 percent standard deviation of the fund's returns, versus the market's 11.65 percent, suggests otherwise. The beta, or measure of systematic risk of the fund, at 1.38 is also considerably higher than the beta of the market. These initial observations suggest that a more detailed analysis is needed.

As suggested above, one approach to performance analysis is to compare a portfolio to a benchmark or market portfolio. Another approach is to rank portfolios by performance. Using this latter ranking procedure, how should the three mutual funds in Table 8.1 be ranked? Based on returns, it appears that the Magellan Fund clearly had the best performance. The beta of 1.54, however, suggests that the fund incurred more systematic risk than the other two funds.

The above discussion reinforces the assertion that risk needs to be considered in any analysis of portfolio performance. There are, however, different measures of risk, such as beta and standard deviation. The correlation coefficient may also need to be considered since it provides an indication of diversification relative to some benchmark portfolio. The next section presents a number of techniques that can be used in a risk-adjusted performance analysis. These techniques can be used both to rank portfolios and to compare their performances to a benchmark portfolio.

TECHNIQUES TO MEASURE PORTFOLIO PERFORMANCE

The development of portfolio theory—and specifically capital market theory, CMT, and the capital asset pricing model, CAPM, —provided the foundation for risk-adjusted performance analysis. These developments provided empirical risk measures that could be used in conjunction with return measures.

The Treynor Portfolio Performance Technique

Jack L. Treynor, in an article in the *Harvard Business Review* in 1965[2], presented the first formal technique to combine both risk and returns in a single performance measure. His technique used the systematic or nondiversifiable risk of the portfolio as the appropriate measure of risk. Treynor argued that the *HPR*s of the portfolio that deviate from the characteristic line of the portfolio represent unsystematic or diversifiable risk. The portfolio manager, through adequate diversification, should be able to reduce these deviations so that they are relatively unimportant in the analysis. The appropriate measure of risk then becomes beta or the systematic risk of the portfolio.

Treynor's technique used the ratio of the *risk premium* of the portfolio, divided by the beta:

$$T_p = \frac{\overline{HPR}_p - \bar{R}_f}{\beta_p} \tag{8.9}$$

where T_p = Treynor's portfolio performance measure

    $\overline{HPR}_p$ = the average holding period return on the portfolio over the evaluation period

    $\bar{R}_f$ = the average risk-free return over the evaluation period

    β_p = the beta of the portfolio over the evaluation period

Since T_p is a ratio of excess return, or the risk premium divided by a measure of the portfolio's systematic risk, larger ratios indicate superior performance. T_p can be viewed essentially as excess return per unit of systematic risk. Portfolios can consequently be ranked by T_p.

Using Treynor's technique, a similar measure for the benchmark or market portfolio can be calculated:

$$T_m = \frac{\overline{HPR}_m - \bar{R}_f}{\beta_m} \tag{8.10}$$

where T_m = Treynor's performance measures for the market

    $\overline{HPR}_m$ = the average holding period return on the market portfolio over the evaluation period

    $\bar{R}_f$ = the average risk-free return over the evaluation period

    β_m = the beta of the market portfolio

Since, by definition, the beta of the market portfolio, β_m, is 1, T_m reduces to $\overline{HPR}_m - \bar{R}_f$. If $T_p > T_m$, then according to Treynor's technique, the portfolio outperformed the market. If $T_p \leq T_m$, then the market did as well as or better than the portfolio.

---

[2] Jack L. Treynor, "How to Rate Management of Investment Funds," *Harvard Business Review,* (January–February 1965): pp. 63–75.

The data on the mutual funds provided in Table 8.1 can be used to illustrate the use of the Treynor technique:

Magellan Fund:

$$T_p = \frac{33.60\% - 9.67\%}{1.54} = 15.54\%$$

44 Wall Street Fund:

$$T_p = \frac{4.50\% - 9.67\%}{1.13} = -4.58\%$$

New Horizons Fund:

$$T_p = \frac{17.26\% - 9.67\%}{1.38} = 5.50\%$$

S&P 500:

$$T_m = 15.71\% - 9.67\% = 6.04\%$$

Notice that the geometric average *HPR*s are used rather than the simple average. The Magellan Fund clearly had the best performance, followed by New Horizons and 44 Wall Street. Magellan also outperformed the market over the period, while 44 Wall Street and New Horizons underperformed the market.

Figure 8.1 provides a security market line, SML, using the data in Table 8.1. It also shows the three mutual funds relative to the SML. The graph illustrates

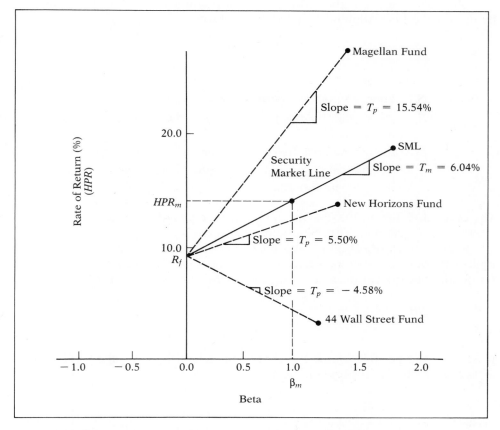

FIGURE 8.1   *SML and Treynor's performance measure: 1976–1985*

that T_m is simply the slope of the SML (6.04 percent in this case). The T_p measure may be viewed as the slope of a risk-return line drawn from R_f through the average *HPR* of the portfolio. These risk-return lines are represented by dashes in Figure 8.1. The slope of these risk-return lines are simply the Treynor performance measure for each fund. If the slope or T_p is less than the slope of the SML or T_m, then the market's performance is superior to the portfolio's performance. In summary, Treynor's technique indicates the performance of a portfolio relative to other portfolios or to a benchmark portfolio.

The Sharpe Portfolio Performance Technique

Shortly after Treynor's technique was published in 1965, William F. Sharpe introduced an alternative technique for performance evaluation and illustrated the technique in evaluating the performance of a large number of mutual funds.[3] Sharpe's technique used total risk, as indicated by the standard deviation of the *HPR*s over the evaluation period, as the appropriate risk measure. This was surprising because Sharpe was recognized for his contribution in developing the CAPM, which suggested the importance and usefulness of beta as a risk measure. Sharpe's measure, however, used the capital market line, CML, rather than the SML as the foundation of its performance measure.

Sharpe's measure is the ratio of the risk premium of the portfolio, divided, by the standard deviation of the portfolio's return:

$$S_p = \frac{\overline{HPR}_p - \bar{R}_f}{\sigma_p} \tag{8.11}$$

where
S_p = Sharpe's portfolio performance measure

$\overline{HPR}_p$ = the average holding period return of the portfolio over the evaluation period

$\bar{R}_f$ = the average risk-free return over the evaluation period

σ_p = the standard deviation of the portfolio's *HPR*s calculated over the evaluation period

The only difference in the Treynor and Sharpe techniques is the risk measure: Treynor uses systematic risk; Sharpe uses total risk.

Sharpe's measure also indicates relative performance, since it can be used to rank portfolios and to compare their performance to the benchmark or market portfolio. Sharpe's performance measure for the market is calculated as

$$S_m = \frac{\overline{HPR}_m - \bar{R}_f}{\sigma_m} \tag{8.12}$$

If $S_p > S_m$, the portfolio outperformed the market. If $S_p \leq S_m$, the portfolio did as well as the market or underperformed the market.

---

[3] William F. Sharpe, "Mutual Fund Performance," *Journal of Business* (January 1966): pp. 119–38.

Again using the data for the three mutual funds presented in Table 8.1, Sharpe's measure can be illustrated:

Magellan Fund:	$S_p = \dfrac{33.60\% - 9.67\%}{21.85\%} =$	1.10
44 Wall Street Fund:	$S_p = \dfrac{4.50\% - 9.67\%}{38.65\%} =$	-0.13
New Horizons Fund:	$S_p = \dfrac{17.26\% - 9.67\%}{19.57\%} =$	0.39
S&P 500:	$S_m = \dfrac{15.71\% - 9.67\%}{11.65\%} =$	0.52

Notice that as a ratio of the risk-premium, expressed as a percentage return divided by the standard deviation in percentage units, S_p is an index number that is not

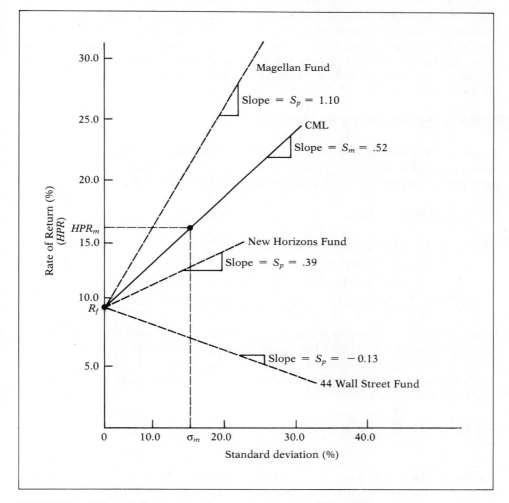

FIGURE 8.2 CML and Sharpe's performance measure: 1976–1985

expressed in percentage units. It is simply the ratio of the portfolio's excess return per unit of portfolio total risk. Magellan again shows superior performance compared to the other two funds and to the market. The remaining two funds underperformed the market, with 44 Wall Street demonstrating particularly poor performance.

Figure 8.2 provides the CML using the data in Table 8.1 and illustrates the ex-post performance analysis of the three mutual funds. Like the Treynor measure, Sharpe's measure can also be thought of as the slope of a risk-return line drawn between the risk-free rate and the average *HPR* of the portfolio. These risk-return lines are shown as dashes in Figure 8.2.

If a portfolio plots above the CML, Sharpe's measure indicates superior performance. For the Treynor technique, if the fund plots above the SML, its performance is better than the market on a risk-adjusted basis.

The importance of considering both risk and return in the performance evaluation is vividly illustrated by New Horizons. Its geometric average *HPR* of 17.26 percent is above the S&P 500 average of 15.71 percent; thus, strictly on a return basis, the fund outperformed the market. When risk is considered, however, the fund underperformed the market. This is true whether systematic or total risk is used as the risk measure. Both the Treynor and Sharpe measures indicate that while the fund did earn a risk premium greater than the risk premium offered by the market, this additional return was not sufficient to compensate for the additional risk.

The Jensen Portfolio Performance Technique

Following Treynor and Sharpe, Michael C. Jensen developed a third measurement technique.[4] Like Treynor's technique, Jensen's measure is based on the capital asset pricing model, CAPM. The basic equation for the CAPM is

$$E(R_j) = R_f + \beta_j[E(R_m) - R_f] \tag{8.13}$$

where $E(R_j)$ = the expected return on security j
   R_f = the risk-free rate of return
   β_j = the systematic risk of security j
   $E(R_m)$ = the expected return on the market portfolio

While the CAPM represents a theory describing how risk and expected returns are related, empirical tests of the model typically use ex-post or historical data. The ex-post *HPR*s are calculated for an individual security, R_{jt}, the risk-free rate, R_{ft}, and for a proxy of the market portfolio, R_{mt}. These time series variables can then be used in a regression:

$$R_{jt} - R_{ft} = \hat{\alpha}_j + \hat{\beta}_j(R_{mt} - R_{ft}) + e_{jt} \tag{8.14}$$

---

[4] Michael C. Jensen, "The Performance of Mutual Funds in the Period 1945–1964," *Journal of Finance* (May 1968): pp. 389–416.

The dependent and independent variables are the risk premium on the security or portfolio and the risk premium on the market proxy, respectively. Notice that the risk-free rate, R_f, is not a constant but has a different value for each time period. Treasury bill yields are usually used to represent R_f. Also, the maturity of the bill should match the holding period used to calculate returns. For example, if annual *HPRs* are calculated for a fund, then the yield on a Treasury bill with a one-year maturity should be used. The y intercept of the regression, $\hat{\alpha}_j$, is the estimate of alpha for the security or portfolio, and the slope of the regression, β_j, is an estimate of the beta. The deviations or errors around the regression line are represented by e_{jt}.

Jensen argued that an indication of a portfolio's performance is $\hat{\alpha}_j$ or the risk-adjusted excess return. It can be measured as the regression intercept, estimated using Equation 8.14. Essentially, if $\hat{\alpha}_j > 0$ and is significantly different from 0 in a statistical test, then the portfolio had superior performance. If $\hat{\alpha}_j < 0$ and is statistically significant, then the portfolio demonstrated poor performance. Finally, if $\hat{\alpha}_j$ is not statistically different from 0, the portfolio did not provide a risk-adjusted excess return. Jensen's alpha can be interpreted simply as the additional return (or loss) earned by the portfolio after adjusting for systematic risk.

Another way to view Jensen's alpha is to rearrange Equation 8.14 by solving for $\hat{\alpha}_j$:

$$\hat{\alpha}_j = \overline{RP}_j - \beta_j(\overline{RP}_m) = J_j \tag{8.15}$$

where $\overline{RP}_j$ = the average risk premium on the security or portfolio

$\overline{RP}_m$ = the average risk premium on the market portfolio

Since the average error term, $\bar{e}_j$, is 0, Jensen's alpha, J_j, is therefore simply the vertical distance between the SML and the security or portfolio's average return.

As an illustration, assume that a portfolio's $\hat{\alpha}_p = 5.0\%$ and that it is statistically significant. On average over the evaluation period, the portfolio earned 5.0 percent additional return after accounting for the risk of the portfolio as indicated by β_p. On the other hand, if $\hat{\alpha}_p = -8.0\%$ and it is statistically significant, the risk-adjusted returns on the portfolio are judged to be inadequate, based on its level of systematic risk.

Jensen's technique is applied to Magellan in Table 8.2 and Figure 8.3. The *HPRs* from Table 8.1 were used to calculate the risk premium for each year 1976–1985. A regression equation was estimated, using the formulation provided in Equation 8.14. The regression or characteristic line parameters are given in Table 8.2. Magellan's beta based on risk premiums is 1.42, versus 1.54 based on *HPRs* (see Table 8.1). The reasons for this difference in betas is discussed later in this chapter. The correlation coefficient between the fund and the S&P 500 using risk premiums is 0.81. Thus, 65.6 percent of the variability of the fund's risk premiums is explained by the variability in the market's risk premiums.

The alpha of 16.04 percent indicates the excess returns the fund earned after allowing for the systematic risk of the portfolio. Figure 8.3 provides a scatter diagram and characteristic line for the fund. The y intercept of 16.04 percent is Jensen's alpha, and it is statistically significant.

TABLE 8.2 JENSEN'S PORTFOLIO PERFORMANCE MEASURE:
FIDELITY MAGELLAN FUND (1976–1985)

	HOLDING PERIOD RETURNS			RISK PREMIUMS	
	FIDELITY MAGELLAN	S&P 500	RISK-FREE	FIDELITY MAGELLAN	S&P 500
1976	33.6%	17.1%	5.8%	27.8%	11.3%
1977	14.5	14.5	5.3	9.2	9.2
1978	31.7	8.5	7.3	24.4	1.2
1979	51.7	15.6	10.4	41.3	5.2
1980	76.5	34.1	12.1	64.4	22.0
1981	12.1	−4.8	14.1	−2.0	−18.9
1982	48.1	22.2	14.3	33.8	7.9
1983	38.6	21.3	8.6	30.0	12.7
1984	2.0	4.1	9.9	−7.9	−5.8
1985	43.1	29.9	9.3	33.8	20.6

Geometric mean of risk premiums:

Fidelity Magellan = 23.82%

S&P 500 = 5.48%

Standard deviation of risk premiums:

Fidelity Magellan = 21.25%

S&P 500 = 12.15%

Characteristic line parameters based on risk premiums:

alpha = 16.04%

beta = 1.42

correlation = 0.81

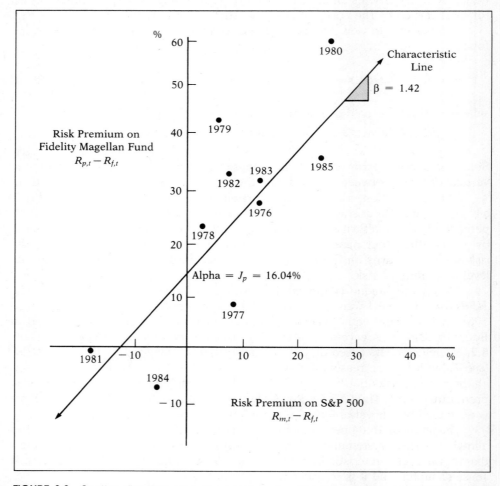

FIGURE 8.3 Scatter diagram and characteristic line: Fidelity Magellan Fund (1976–1985)

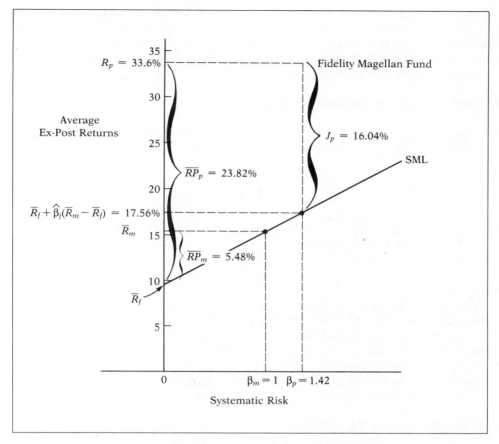

FIGURE 8.4 SML and Jensen's performance technique: Fidelity Magellan Fund (1976–1985)

The data in Tables 8.1 and 8.2 are used to construct the SML given in Figure 8.4 which can be used to provide additional insights into Jensen's technique. Figure 8.4 shows that the geometric average annual return on Magellan was 33.6 percent. The fund's beta of 1.42 and the mean risk-free and mean S&P 500 returns, however, indicate that the expected return of the fund was 17.56 percent. Thus, on a risk-adjusted basis, the fund earned an additional return of 16.04 percent because of success at security selection and/or market timing. This additional return represents Jensen's performance measure for the fund; using Equation 8.16 in risk premium form, the alpha can be calculated as

$$\overline{RP}_j - \hat{\beta}_j(\overline{RP}_m) = \alpha_j = J_p \qquad (8.16)$$

$$23.82\% - 1.42(5.48\%) = 16.04\%.$$

Jensen's technique was also applied to 44 Wall Street and New Horizons:

44 Wall Street Fund: $J_p = -13.69\%$

New Horizons Fund: $J_p = +0.18\%$

The J_p, alpha, for 44 Wall Street is statistically significant and indicates poor performance. J_p for New Horizons, while positive, is not statistically different from 0. This fund's performance, therefore, is about the same as the S&P 500's on a risk-adjusted basis. In summary, Jensen's technique provides an indication of the relative and absolute performance of a portfolio.

Summary of Results from Performance Examples

Three different evaluation techniques have been used to analyze the performance of three mutual funds over the period 1976–1985. In summary, the results are

	TREYNOR T_p	SHARPE S_p	JENSEN J_p
Fidelity Magellan Fund	15.54%	1.10	16.04%
T. Rowe Price New Horizons Fund	5.50	0.39	0.18
44 Wall Street Fund	−4.58	−0.13	−13.69
S&P 500	6.04	0.52	0.00

The rankings indicated by the three performance measures are identical, with Magellan ranked as the best performer and 44 Wall Street the worst. All three techniques also indicate that Magellan outperformed the market, while the other two funds according to the T_p and S_p measures underperformed the market. Jensen's technique, however, indicates that the New Horizons Fund's excess return is not statistically significant, while the alpha for 44 Wall Street is negative and is statistically significant.

Comparison of Performance Techniques

Based on the identical rankings and performances indicated by the three techniques for the three mutual funds, it is logical to assume that the techniques are very similar. Major similarities include:

1. The techniques are based on CMT or the CAPM;
2. The techniques provide a way to combine risk and returns into a single performance measure;
3. The techniques measure aggregate or overall performance, without being able to explain why the performance was good or bad;
4. The techniques have been criticized because they are "crude" or not sensitive enough to measure slight differences in performance;[5] and
5. Mathematically, it can be shown that all three measures are approximately linear transformations of each other under typical market conditions.

The last point, concerning the linear transformation relationship between the three techniques, can easily be demonstrated. First, it can be shown that the

---

[5] For example, see Dan W. French and Glenn V. Henderson, Jr., "How Well Does Performance Evaluation Perform?" *Journal of Portfolio Management* (Winter 1985): pp. 15–18.

Jensen and Treynor techniques are identical *if* the risk-free rate of return is constant over the evaluation period. If the risk-free rate is constant, then its variance, $\sigma^2_{R_f}$, would be 0, and the betas using risk premium (Equation 8.14) and the market model are identical. Given this assumption, the following equations show the equivalency of Jensen's and Treynor's techniques:

$$\text{Jensen:} \quad \bar{R}_p - \bar{R}_f = \alpha_p + \beta_p(\bar{R}_m - \bar{R}_f) \tag{8.17}$$

$$\alpha_p = (\bar{R}_p - \bar{R}_f) - \beta_p(\bar{R}_m - \bar{R}_f)$$

Dividing both sides of Equation 8.17 by β_p gives

$$\frac{\alpha_p}{\beta_p} = \frac{\bar{R}_p - \bar{R}_f}{\beta_p} - (\bar{R}_m - \bar{R}_f) \tag{8.18}$$

Notice that the first term on the right side of Equation 8.18 is Treynor's performance measure and that $(\bar{R}_m - \bar{R}_f)$ is a constant for all portfolios. Thus, Jensen's measure is a linear transformation of Treynor's measure.

The previous example, using three mutual funds, calculated the Jensen and Treynor performance measures for Magellan as

Jensen measure = J_p = 16.04%

Treynor measure = T_p = 15.54%

The two performance values are different, as Equation 8.18 indicates they should be. This occurs because the risk-free rate used in the analysis was not constant. As Table 8.1 indicates, the risk-free rate was very volatile during 1976–1985, ranging from 5.29 percent in 1977 to 14.32 percent in 1982. The standard deviation was 3.14 percent. This variability in the yield to maturity on one-year Treasury bills (used as the risk-free rate) caused the difference in the betas. The two estimates of beta for Magellan are slightly different:

beta calculated from risk premiums (Equation 8.14) = 1.42

beta calculated using market model (Equation 8.13) = 1.54

The variability in the risk-free rate and its impact on the beta estimate caused the difference in the performance values for the Treynor and Jensen measures.

A similar analysis for the Treynor and Sharpe techniques shows that they are also essentially linear transformations. Repeating Equation 8.9, the Treynor measure is

$$T_p = \frac{\overline{HPR} - \bar{R}_f}{\beta_p} \tag{8.19}$$

where $\quad \beta_p = \dfrac{Cov\,(R_p,\,R_m)}{\sigma^2_m}$

Since the covariance is the product of the correlation coefficient $(\rho_{p,m})$ and the standard deviations of the market and portfolio returns, beta can be defined as

$$\beta_p = \frac{\rho_{p,m}\sigma_p\sigma_m}{\sigma_m^2} \tag{8.20}$$

If the portfolio manager has perfect diversification in terms of the market portfolio, then $\rho_{p,m} = 1$, and the beta of the portfolio would be

$$\beta_p = \frac{\sigma_p\sigma_m}{\sigma_m^2} \tag{8.21}$$

Substituting Equation 8.21 into the Treynor measure given in Equation 8.19 results in

$$T_p = \frac{\overline{HPR}_p - \bar{R}_f}{\dfrac{\sigma_p\sigma_m}{\sigma_m^2}} = \frac{\overline{HPR}_p - \bar{R}_f}{\dfrac{\sigma_p}{\sigma_m}} \tag{8.22}$$

The Sharpe performance measure is

$$S_p = \frac{\overline{HPR}_p - \bar{R}_f}{\sigma_p} \tag{8.23}$$

It can be seen that Equations 8.22 and 8.23 differ only in their denominators and that σ_m is a constant for all portfolios. In summary, if the right side of Equation 8.22 is divided by σ_m, the resulting value is the Sharpe measure:

$$\frac{T_p}{\sigma_m} = S_p \tag{8.24}$$

In other words, if a portfolio is perfectly diversified, T_p and S_p are linear transformations of each other.

To illustrate the case when less than perfect diversification exists, the correlation coefficient for Magellan with the S&P 500 is 0.82, and Magellan has a beta of 1.54 (see Table 8.1). Since the correlation coefficient is not perfect ($\sigma_p/\sigma_m > \beta_p$ or $21.85/11.65 = 1.88 > \beta_p$), there is a resulting difference in the Sharpe and Treynor performance measures:

$$T_p = 15.54\%$$

$$S_p = 1.10$$

$$S_p = \frac{T_p}{\sigma_m} = \frac{15.54\%}{11.65\%} = 1.33 \neq 1.10$$

If the unsystematic risk in the Magellan returns is not important, T_p is the appropriate measure. If both systematic and unsystematic risk need to be considered in the performance evaluation, then S_p is the appropriate measure.

TABLE 8.3 RANK CORRELATION COEFFICIENTS USING MUTUAL FUND DATA FOR JENSEN, SHARPE, AND TREYNOR PERFORMANCE MEASURES (Level of Significance)

	SHAWKY STUDY			MOSES, CHENEY, AND VEIT STUDY		
	JENSEN	SHARPE	TREYNOR	JENSEN	SHARPE	TREYNOR
Jensen	1.000 (.001)	.932 (.001)	.916 (.001)	1.000 (.001)	.967 (.001)	.837 (.001)
Sharpe		1.000 (.001)	.967 (.001)		1.000 (.001)	.985 (.001)
Treynor			1.000 (.001)			1.000 (.001)
Sample Size:	255 funds			53 funds		
Time Period:	January 1973–December 1977			1957–1978		
Holding Period Used to Calculate Returns:	Month			Year		
Market Index Used:	NYSE Composite Index			S&P 500		

The similarities in the three performance measures can be further illustrated by looking at the results from mutual fund performance studies. A 1982 study by Hany A. Shawky of 255 mutual funds found very high rank correlation coefficients using the three measures.[6] A 1987 study of 53 funds produced similar results.[7] Table 8.3 summarizes the results from these two studies. The correlation coefficients in Table 8.3 confirm that the three performance measures can be expected to rank portfolios in almost identical order. The lowest rank correlation coefficient is 0.837. Also, it appears that neither the market index nor the length of the holding period used to calculate returns has much influence on the rank correlation coefficients. The relative lack of importance of the market index has been confirmed in other studies.[8]

There may, however, be greater differences in ranking when the classification of the mutual funds is considered. The rankings of "income" funds show more disagreement between the performance measures than the rankings for "growth" and "balanced" funds. This may occur because income funds typically have fixed-income and equity securities in their portfolios.

Up to this point, the discussion has concentrated on the similarities in the three performance evaluation techniques. There are some important differences. The major difference is the appropriate measure of risk. The Jensen and Treynor techniques use systematic risk, or beta. As previously discussed, however, the two betas may be different, depending on the behavior of the risk-free return. Sharpe's measure uses total risk, or standard deviation. A second major difference is that Jensen's measure provides for a statistical test of significance for the performance

---

[6] Hany A. Shawky, "An Update on Mutual Funds: Better Grades," *Journal of Portfolio Management* (Winter 1982): pp. 29–34.

[7] Edward A. Moses, John M. Cheney, and E. Theodore Veit, "A New and More Complete Performance Measure," *Journal of Portfolio Management* (Summer 1987): pp. 24–33.

[8] For example, see David Peterson and Michael L. Rice, "A Note on Ambiguity in Portfolio Performance Measures," *Journal of Finance* (December 1980): pp. 1251–56.

measure, while the Treynor and Sharpe techniques do not allow for a test of significance.

In summary, none of the techniques should be rejected, nor should one be selected as a superior performance measure. If unsystematic risk must be considered in the analysis, the Sharpe technique is recommended. Before any conclusions concerning good or bad performance is reached, however, the Jensen measure should be calculated and tested for statistical significance.

Issues and Problems in the Measurement of Portfolio Performance

A number of criticisms and objections have been made concerning the traditional techniques used to measure the risk-adjusted return performance of portfolios. These criticisms and objections can be categorized as those made primarily by practitioners or portfolio managers and those made by the academic community.

Practitioners take exception to published studies that show that few portfolios are able to outperform the benchmark or market portfolio on a consistent basis. Their criticism often centers on problems with CMT and the CAPM and with the identification of an appropriate benchmark portfolio. Some of these criticisms are presented in two articles by Robert Ferguson and in an article by Walter Good.[9]

A number of academic articles focus on problems with the existing performance evaluation techniques. Most of these articles deal with *measurement* problems. For example, how can a portfolio's "true" beta or standard deviation be measured? Empirical techniques provide only estimates of the actual risk measures.

The following discussion briefly outlines some of the major criticisms.

1. IDENTIFICATION OF THE BENCHMARK PORTFOLIO Richard Roll, in a series of articles, has criticized empirical tests of the CAPM and the application of CMT and the CAPM to performance evaluation (see Chapter 7). These tests and applications use a proxy for the true market portfolio, and any estimates based on an inappropriate proxy are biased. These inappropriate proxies, typically the NYSE Composite Index or S&P 500, do not provide an accurate estimate of the CML or SML. Roll's criticisms are strengthened and extended in articles by Dybvig and Ross, and Green.[10] Recently, Brown and Brown published a study of mutual funds which found that the composition of the market proxy does influence the performance results.[11] This finding conflicts with some other studies cited earlier.

---

[9] Robert Ferguson, "Performance Measurement Doesn't Make Sense," *Financial Analysts Journal* (May-June 1980): pp. 59–69, and "The Trouble with Performance Measurement," *Journal of Portfolio Management* (Spring 1986): pp. 4–9. Walter R. Good, "Measuring Performance," *Financial Analysts Journal* (May-June 1983): pp. 19–23.

[10] Philip H. Dybvig and Stephen A. Ross, "The Analytics of Performance Measurement Using a Security Market Line," *Journal of Finance* (June 1985): pp. 401–16; Richard C. Green, "Benchmark Portfolio Inefficiency and Deviations from the Security Market Line," *Journal of Finance* (June 1986): pp. 295–312.

[11] Keith C. Brown and Gregory D. Brown, "Does the Composition of the Market Portfolio Really Matter?" *The Journal of Portfolio Management* (Winter 1987): pp. 26–32.

   It has also been shown that even in the absence of measurement problems, a portfolio with superior performance may plot above, on, or below the SML.[12] Problems with the CAPM and SML suggest that new performance measures, possibly based on Arbitrage Pricing Theory (see Chapter 7), are needed.

2. INTERVAL OF TIME USED TO CALCULATE RETURNS Haim Levy has shown that beta values depend on the length of the horizon over which they are calculated.[13] His results show that a longer interval (horizon) causes betas less than 1 to decline significantly, while betas greater than 1 increase significantly. The beta estimate obviously will influence the performance measures of Jensen and Treynor. This raises the issue that the portfolio rankings can change depending on the interval used to calculate the *HPR*s.

3. CORRELATION OF PERFORMANCE MEASURES WITH RISK Since the performance measures are risk adjusted, their values should not be correlated with portfolio risk measures. However, studies have shown that the measures are significantly correlated with risk, suggesting a bias in the measures.[14] One interesting aspect of these studies is that the correlation coefficient is not stable; it can be positive during some periods and negative during others. Thus, a portfolio with "good" performance may also have "high" risk for one period of evaluation (positive correlation between performance measure and risk) and "low" risk over another (negative correlation between performance measure and risk). An article by Wilson and Jones addresses this apparent conflict. Their study indicates that market conditions producing the slope and position (intercept) of the CML and SML over the evaluation period explain this apparent conflict.[15]

4. STABILITY OF RISK MEASURES The three traditional portfolio evaluation techniques calculate a single measure of risk for the evaluation period. Is it appropriate to assume that the risk is constant over the evaluation period? In a study of mutual funds, Francis and Fabozzi found that some funds exhibit a beta best described as a "random" coefficient.[16] An evaluation technique applied to these funds should not assume that the beta is constant over the evaluation period.

5. ACCURACY OF PERFORMANCE MEASURES The traditional techniques have also been criticized because they do not measure slight but important differences

---

[12] Philip H. Dybvig and Stephen A. Ross, "Performance Measurement using Differential Information and a Security Market Line," *Journal of Finance* (June 1985): pp. 383–99.

[13] Haim Levy, "Measuring Risk and Performance over Alternative Investment Horizons," *Financial Analysts Journal* (March-April 1984): pp. 61–68.

[14] For example, see Irwin Friend and Marshall Blume, "Measurement of Portfolio Performance under Uncertainty," *American Economic Review* (September 1970): pp. 561–75, and James S. Ang and Jess H. Chua, "Composite Measures for the Evaluation of Investment Performance," *Journal of Financial and Quantitative Analysis* (June 1979): pp. 361–84.

[15] Jack W. Wilson and Charles P. Jones, "The Relationship between Performance and Risk: Whence the Bias?" *Journal of Financial Research* (Summer 1981): pp. 103–108.

[16] Jack Clark Francis and Frank J. Fabozzi, "Stability of Mutual Fund Systematic Risk Statistics," *Journal of Business Research* (April 1980): pp. 263–75.

in performance.[17] For example, the French and Henderson study found that a portfolio manager would need to earn approximately 1 percent of excess returns per month, or about 12 percent per year, to produce a statistically significant Jensen measure.[18] Given the efficiency of the market, this would be an exceptional performance. However, if the excess returns were only 10 percent (also an exceptional performance), Jensen's alpha would not be statistically significant.

In summary, a number of problems have been identified in the three traditional techniques. These include a misspecified benchmark, problems with using the CAPM and SML, differences in intervals used in calculating *HPR*s, significant but unstable correlations of performance measures with risk measures, unstable risk measures, and measures that are too "crude" to measure performance accurately. The next section of this chapter will discuss some recent developments in the measurement of portfolio performance which attempt to address some of the problems identified.

RECENT DEVELOPMENTS IN THE MEASUREMENT OF PORTFOLIO PERFORMANCE

Since the three traditional measures were developed in the late 1960s, research has continued to attempt to improve techniques of measuring performance. This research addresses some of the problems with portfolio performance measures discussed in the previous section. The following discussion focuses on two aspects: benchmark portfolios and the decomposition of performance.

Benchmark Portfolios

Any attempt to measure risk-adjusted performance must be based on a reference or benchmark portfolio. As previously discussed, CMT indicates that a market portfolio is the appropriate benchmark. This market portfolio should theoretically include all financial assets, real assets, and other assets, weighted according to their market values. The complexity and difficulty in calculating a true market portfolio has precluded its development. Without having a true market portfolio, empirical studies of performance have used proxies like the S&P 500 or the NYSE Composite Index.

One problem with such proxies is that the investment objectives of many portfolios have a broader or narrower universe of investment alternatives than the index represents. For example, a portfolio with an objective of "income" may

---

[17] See, for example, J. Michael Murphy, "Why No One Call Tell Who's Winning," *Financial Analysts Journal* (May-June 1980): pp. 49–57; Dan W. French and Glenn V. Henderson, Jr., "How Well Does Performance Evaluation Perform?" *Journal of Portfolio Management* (Winter 1985): pp. 15–18.

[18] French and Henderson, p. 17.

include both fixed-income securities and common stocks. Is an all-equity index like the S&P 500 an appropriate benchmark to use in evaluating this portfolio's performance?

Table 8.4 illustrates this problem, using the three mutual funds previously analyzed, and provides the asset composition of the funds in terms of cash (and equivalents), bonds and preferred stocks, and common stocks. It should also be remembered that each fund is a growth fund, with an emphasis on maximizing capital gains. This investment objective indicates a common stock strategy. Table 8.4, however, shows that cash may represent up to 15 percent of a portfolio's composition during some years. Also, 44 Wall Street has a policy of having a negative cash position (borrowing) that results in the use of financial leverage. The stated investment objectives of these funds permit investments in ''securities of foreign companies,'' ''securities convertible into common stock,'' ''new issues,'' and ''small growth companies.'' These investment objectives, as well as the cash holdings, suggest that the S&P 500 or the NYSE Composite Index may not be an appropriate benchmark.

As previously discussed, an article by Walter Good suggests the advantages of using a unique benchmark, specifically calculated to measure the performance of the portfolio. Other articles have also suggested a unique benchmark.[19]

An article by Moses, Cheney, and Veit applies the concept of a unique, asset-weighted benchmark portfolio (UABP) to performance evaluation.[20] The UABP can be constructed from indices representing the different types of securities actually held by the portfolio. For example, a UABP for a ''balanced'' portfolio could use three indices: cash and equivalents, bonds, and common stocks. The values of the UABP for each time period would be calculated by a weighted average of the *HPR* on each index for the period, where the weights are the actual percentage asset composition of the portfolio. If a portfolio had 10 percent cash and equivalents, 40 percent bonds, and 50 percent common stocks for a period, these proportions would be used to calculate the *HPR* of the UABP.

The use of a UABP has the advantage of providing a more realistic benchmark. A disadvantage, however, is that the percentage asset composition of the portfolio may not be appropriate for a particular market environment. Using the UABP would therefore be based on an inefficient benchmark portfolio. A test of this possibility is provided in Figure 8.5, taken from the Moses-Cheney-Veit study. The efficient frontier was determined using the Markowitz procedure from indices representing cash and equivalents, bonds, and common stocks. It represents the optimal risk-return combinations for these classes over the 1957–1978 period. The points to the right of the efficient frontier represent UABPs calculated for a sample of fifty-three mutual funds.

[19] See, for example, Robert S. Carlson, ''Aggregate Performance of Mutual Funds,'' *Journal of Financial and Quantititive Analysis* (March 1970): pp. 1–31; Tye Kim, ''An Assessment of the Performance of Mutual Funds Management: 1969–1975,'' *Journal of Financial and Quantitative Analysis* (September 1978): pp. 385–406; and Barr Rosenberg, ''The Capital Asset Pricing Model and the Market model,'' *Journal of Portfolio Management* (Winter 1981): pp. 5–16.

[20] Edward A. Moses, John M. Cheney, and E. Theodore Veit, ''A New and More Complete Performance Measure,'' *Journal of Portfolio Management* (Summer 1987); pp. 24–33.

TABLE 8.4 PERCENTAGE ASSET COMPOSITION OF SELECTED MUTUAL FUNDS (1975–1985)

	FIDELITY MAGELLAN FUND			44 WALL STREET FUND			T. ROWE PRICE NEW HORIZONS FUND		
	CASH AND EQUIVALENTS	BONDS AND PREFERRED STOCKS	COMMON STOCKS	CASH AND EQUIVALENTS	BONDS AND PREFERRED STOCKS	COMMON STOCKS	CASH AND EQUIVALENTS	BONDS AND PREFERRED STOCKS	COMMON STOCKS
1975	3%	–	97%	–6%	–	106%	9%	–	91%
1976	2	–	98	–14	–	114	7	–	93
1977	2	–	98	–29	–	129	10	–	90
1978	5	1%	94	–7	–	107	12	–	88
1979	2	2	96	4	–	96	15	–	85
1980	1	–	99	–3	–	103	11	–	89
1981	–	3	97	–15	–	115	15	–	85
1982	2	2	96	–22	–	122	9	–	91
1983	2	6	92	–29	–	129	8	–	92
1984	1	2	97	–31	–	131	13	–	87
1985	1	5	94	–47	–	147	6	1%	93

SOURCE: *Investment Companies*, Wiesenberger Financial Services, 1986. Reprinted courtesy of Wiesenberger Investment Companies Service, division of Warren, Gorham & Lamont, Inc.

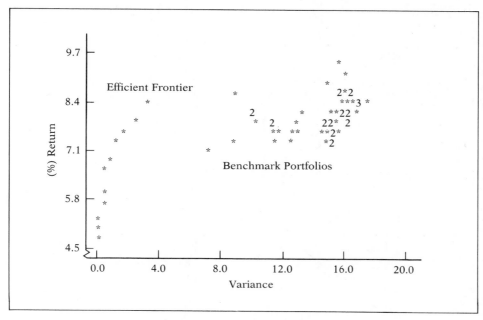

FIGURE 8.5   Benchmark portfolios versus efficient frontier
Source: Edward A. Moses, John M. Cheney, and E. Theodore Veit, "A New and More Complete Performance Measure," *Journal of Portfolio Management*, (Summer 1987): pp. 24–33.

Figure 8.5 shows that all of the UABPs are inefficient when compared to the efficient frontier because of their large variances, which indicate the presence of unsystematic or diversifiable risk. This shows that the asset allocation decisions made by this sample of fifty-three managers resulted in considerably more risk than was necessary had the optimal allocations been made. At the same time, several of the UABPs provided significantly higher returns than the maximum return portfolio (100 percent common stock) on the efficient frontier. This suggests some success at market timing by the managers in determining the asset allocations.

Decomposition of Performance

Eugene Fama, in an important article published in 1972, was one of the first researchers to realize that the traditional techniques of Sharpe, Treynor, and Jensen do not indicate the reasons for a certain level of performance.[21] He argued that the techniques evaluate only performance resulting from the selection of under- or overvalued securities, which may come at the unmeasured expense of less diversification. Fama's article presented a technique that could be used to "decompose" or divide overall performance into two components: security selection and diversification.

---

[21] Eugene F. Fama, "Components of Investment Performance," *Journal of Finance* (June 1972): pp. 551–67.

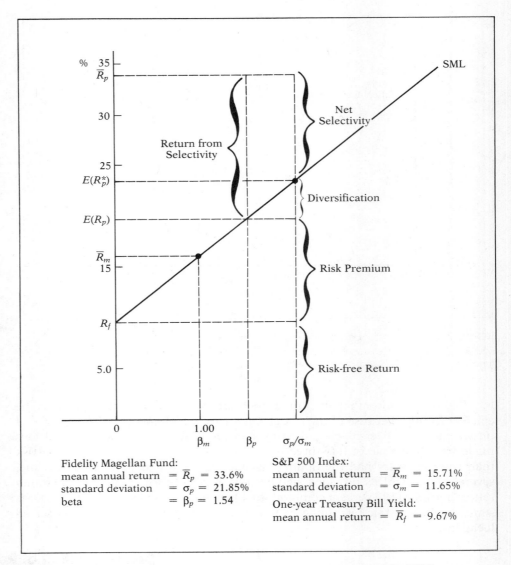

FIGURE 8.6 Fama's technique applied to Fidelity Magellan Fund: (1976–1985)

1. FAMA'S TECHNIQUE This section presents Fama's technique and applies the technique to the Magellan Fund. Magellan was selected because of its comparatively high level of investment in common stocks and its lack of financial leverage. The Sharpe, Treynor, and Jensen analyses of Magellan indicated superior performance. Why did Magellan "beat the market" during 1976–1985? Fama's technique provides insights that can be used to answer this question.

Figure 8.6 provides summary data previously computed for Magellan and illustrates Fama's analysis. The ex-post SML was constructed using the mean risk-free rate of 9.67 percent and the mean return on the S&P 500 of

15.71 percent. Magellan's geometric mean return was 33.6 percent. The CAPM, as given in Equation 8.13, indicates that the expected return for Magellan was

$$E(R_p) = R_f + \beta_j[E(R_m) - R_f]$$
$$= 9.67 + 1.54(15.71 - 9.67)$$
$$= 18.97\%$$

The difference in the actual and expected returns was defined by Fama as the "return from selectivity", R_s:

$$R_s = \bar{R}_p - E(R_p)$$
$$= 33.6\% - 18.97\%$$
$$= 14.63\%$$

Did the fund incur additional risk to earn R_s? The beta of the portfolio can be expressed as

$$\beta_p = (\rho_{p,m}\sigma_p\sigma_m)/\sigma_m^2 \qquad (8.25)$$

where $\rho_{p,m}$ denotes the correlation coefficient of the portfolio's HPRs with the market's HPRs, and σ_p and σ_m represent the standard deviation of HPRs for the portfolio and the market, respectively. For a complete or perfectly diversified portfolio, $\rho_{p,m} = 1$, and as shown earlier, Equation 8.25 reduces to

$$\beta_p = \frac{\sigma_p\sigma_m}{\sigma_m^2} = \frac{\sigma_p}{\sigma_m} \qquad (8.26)$$

Equation 8.26 indicates that β_p for a perfectly diversified portfolio should be equal to σ_p/σ_m. This ratio of the standard deviations is called the *index of total portfolio risk*. For Magellan, the index of total portfolio risk is greater than its beta:

$$\frac{21.85\%}{11.65\%} > 1.54$$

$$1.88 > 1.54.$$

Thus, Magellan was not perfectly diversified since its HPRs were not perfectly correlated with the S&P 500 benchmark. This indicates the presence of unsystematic or diversifiable risk.

Fama argues that this additional risk should be considered, so that the expected HPR on the portfolio becomes

$$E(R_p^*) = R_f + \sigma_p/\sigma_m[E(R_m) - R_f] \qquad (8.27)$$
$$= 9.67 + 1.88(15.71 - 9.67)$$
$$= 21.03\%.$$

The return on Magellan can now be decomposed or divided into the following components:

$$\bar{R}_p = R_f + [E(R_p) - R_f] + [E(R_p^*)] - E(R_p)] + [\bar{R}_p - E(R_p^*)]$$

$$
\begin{array}{lll}
& & \text{additional} \\
& & \text{return for} \\
= \text{risk-free return} + \text{risk premium} + \text{lack of} & + \text{net selectivity} \\
& & \text{diversification} \quad \text{return}
\end{array}
$$

$$= 9.67\% + (18.97\% - 9.67\%) + (21.03\% - 18.97\%) + (33.6\% - 21.03\%)$$

$$= 33.6\%$$

This analysis shows that the performance of Magellan was quite good. Of the total 14.63% return from selectivity, however, only 12.57% (33.60% − 21.03%) was due to net selectivity. The remaining 2.06% was due to imperfect diversification. Therefore, the fund did incur additional risk in attempting to beat the market. The net selectivity return was positive, however, so that the fund shareholders were more than adequately compensated for the additional risk.

2. MARKET TIMING Fama's analysis did not attempt to evaluate performance due to market timing.[22] For example, was the superior performance of Magellan due in part to predicting bull and bear markets correctly and making the appropriate portfolio revisions? The correct timing strategy would be to lower β_p in anticipation of bear markets and increase β_p prior to bull markets. This strategy could be implemented in anticipation of a bull market by selling stocks with "high" betas and replacing them with "low" beta stocks. The portfolio could also lower β_p by selling stocks and buying bonds or money market securities, or simply holding cash.

Table 8.4 provides some insights into possible timing activities of the portfolio managers of Magellan. Notice that in 1978, 1983, and 1985, the fund slightly reduced the percentage of funds invested in common stocks by increasing cash and/or increasing the investment in bonds and preferred stocks. Table 8.1 can be used to determine if these three years were "bear" market years. Since the *HPR* on the S&P 500 for each year was positive, these years do not represent true bear markets. This simple analysis indicates that Magellan did not appear to engage in successful timing activities by changing the asset composition of the portfolio. Another test for timing would be to estimate the fund's beta for both bull and bear markets. Due to the use of annual data and the resulting limited number of observations, this procedure will not be attempted for Magellan.

An alternative test of timing success could be conducted by developing a long-term or target beta for a portfolio. The beta for the period of the evaluation could then be compared to the target beta. If the betas were different, then any return attributed to the difference in betas could be attributed to timing activities.

---

[22] Techniques that can simultaneously analyze security selection and market timing are given in Anat R. Admati, Sudipto Bhattacharya, Paul Pfleiderer, and Stephen A. Ross, "On Timing and Selectivity," *Journal of Finance* (July 1986): pp. 715–30.

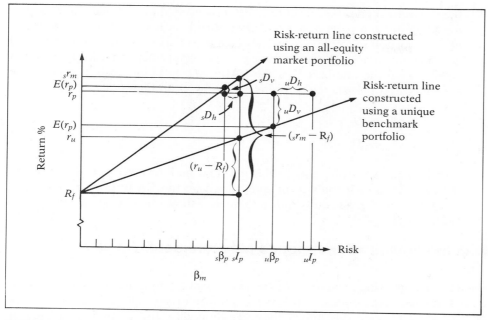

FIGURE 8.7 Example illustrating performance evaluation

Source: Edward A. Moses, John M. Cheney, and E. Theodore Veit, "A New and More Complete Performance Measure," *Journal of Portfolio Management*, (Summer 1987): pp. 24–33.

The idea of using a unique benchmark portfolio can also provide insights into timing activities by managers. For example, the previously discussed article by Moses, Cheney, and Veit constructed unique, asset-weighted benchmark portfolios, UABPs, for each mutual fund in the study. Since the UABPs use the actual asset composition of the fund, this aspect of timing (switching to and from different classes of securities) is removed from the performance analysis. The portfolio is then evaluated in terms of security selection, diversification, and one aspect of timing (switching within security classes). Figure 8.7 presents an example of the evaluation of one mutual fund in this study.

The variables and notation in Figure 8.7 require a brief explanation. Two risk-return lines are illustrated because two benchmark portfolios are considered. One benchmark portfolio, the S&P 500, represents an all-equity portfolio, and the other benchmark is the UABP. The mean *HPR* on the stock benchmark portfolio is $_sr_m$, and the mean *HPR* on the UABP is denoted as r_u. The actual *HPR* for the mutual fund is denoted as r_p. The various risk and return measures for the mutual fund are assigned s (stock) and u (unique) subscripts to indicate the appropriate benchmark.

Notice that the conclusions about the fund's performance depend entirely on the benchmark portfolio. Using an all-equity benchmark (S&P 500), the fund's performance is judged to be unfavorable because the fund plots *below* the risk-return line. Based on a UABP, however, the fund had superior performance since it plots *above* the risk-return line. Notice also that the index of total portfolio risk, $I_p = \sigma_p/\sigma_m$, also changes depending on the proxy used for the benchmark. The index based on the equity benchmark, $_sI_p$, is much smaller than the one based on the UABP, $_uI_p$. In either case, however, the fund incurred unsystematic risk as shown by D_h in Figure 8.7 since

$$_sI_p - {_s\beta_p} = {_sD_h} > 0$$
$$_uI_p - {_u\beta_p} = {_uD_h} > 0$$

Finally, Figure 8.7 also shows that the fund had net selectivity success (see the discussion of Fama's technique) based on the UABP since $r_p - E(r_p) = {_uD_v} > 0$. Using an all-equity index, however, shows no net selectivity success since $r_p - E(r_p) = {_sD_v} < 0$.

Developments in the Portfolio Performance Measurement Industry

Because of a growing awareness in the investment community of the importance of risk-adjusted performance analysis, a number of specialized businesses have developed to provide this information. Traditionally, this analysis consisted of presenting the ex-post *HPR*s for each portfolio, and the portfolios were grouped into homogeneous categories, based on investment objectives, in an attempt to control for risk. For example, the performance of an "income" mutual fund would be compared to the performance of other funds in this category.

Many of the larger companies in the performance measurement industry—such as A. G. Becker, Frank Russell Company, Callan Associates, and Merrill Lynch—essentially follow the traditional practices. They collect data on a large number of certain portfolios, such as bank trust department portfolios, and use this base as a benchmark to analyze the performance of a specific portfolio. These companies, however, do not publish the Treynor, Sharpe, or Jensen performance measures for specific portfolios.

Recently some progress has been made in calculating empirical risk measures and including these measures in the evaluation data. For example, Wiesenberger Financial Services, in *Investment Companies*, provides the price volatility of individual mutual funds during both bull and bear markets. The price volatility measure is *not* beta, but is calculated for each bull and bear market as

$$V_p = \frac{\text{Percentage change in price of mutual fund over the bull or bear market, adjusted for capital gain distributions}}{\text{Percentage change in NYSE Index over the bull or bear market}} \tag{8.28}$$

If $V_p > 1$, the mutual fund has greater price volatility than the NYSE Index during the measurement period. Also, if V_p increases during bull markets and decreases during bear markets, the fund could be successfully using market timing strategies. Unfortunately, Wiesenberger does not attempt to relate these risk measures to the *HPR*s of the funds.

At present there appears to be limited application of the techniques presented in this chapter by the performance industry. As the general acceptance of empirical risk measures derived from CMT increases, there appears to be an opportunity to apply these procedures by the industry.

STUDIES OF THE PERFORMANCE OF PROFESSIONALLY MANAGED PORTFOLIOS

There have been numerous studies of the ex-post, risk-adjusted return performance of professionally managed portfolios. The most commonly studied group is mutual funds since they are publicly traded and data is readily available. However, there are some studies of other professionally managed portfolios, such as those of pension funds, commercial banks, and life insurance companies. This section provides a brief summary of the conclusions reached by these studies.

Mutual Funds

1. OVERALL PERFORMANCE Beginning with the classical studies of Treynor, Sharpe, and Jensen in the mid to late 1960s, the performance of mutual funds has been a popular research topic. The general conclusion reached by these studies is that when expenses are considered, mutual funds do not consistently beat the market and typically underperform the market. For example, Jensen concluded that his sample of funds earned "about 1.1 percent less per year (compounded continuously) than they should have earned given their level of systematic risk."[23]

    In a more recent study, Shawky analyzed the performance of all mutual funds (255) from January 1973 through December 1977.[24] His analysis included the traditional Treynor, Sharpe, and Jensen measures. In addition, he also provided an analysis of diversification and performance during bull and bear markets. Shawky concluded that "the performance of the mutual fund industry in the 1970s seems to be better than what has been reported earlier for the 1950s and 1960s. Specifically, funds seem to earn a return that is generally commensurate with their systematic risk."[25] He also concluded that the diversification efforts improved over early years, with a 75 percent coefficient of determination, R^2, for all funds.

2. ANALYSIS OF SECURITY SELECTION A number of studies have specifically analyzed the security selection success of mutual funds. The initial study in this area was by Jensen in 1968. A recent study of forty-three mutual funds by Chen and Stokum provided some interesting results that conflict, to a certain

---

[23] Michael C. Jensen, "The Performance of Mutual Funds in the Period 1945–1964," *Journal of Finance* (May 1968): p. 405.

[24] Hany A. Shawky, "An Update on Mutual Funds: Better Grades," *Journal of Portfolio Management* (Winter 1982): pp. 29–34.

[25] Ibid, pp. 33–34.

degree, with the earlier studies.[26] Using an improved methodology, they concluded that 30 percent of the funds (thirteen of the forty-three funds) demonstrated statistically significant security selection performance. The results of the empirical tests led the authors to conclude that some mutual funds had the ability to select under-valued securities. Earlier studies had generally concluded that, on average, funds showed little if any ability in security selection.

3. ANALYSIS OF MARKET TIMING One of the classic articles on mutual fund timing activity is that by Fabozzi and Francis.[27] Their methodology consisted of testing for a nonlinear relationship in the characteristic lines estimated for a sample of eighty-five mutual funds. Specifically, a quadratic term was added to the simple linear regression equation usually used to estimate the characteristic line. If the quadratic term was statistically significant, this would be evidence that mutual funds increased their betas in bull markets and reduced them in bear markets. Their study found that there was no evidence of curvilinear characteristic lines for the sample of funds.

In addition to testing for changes in the fund's beta, another methodology analyzes the asset composition of the mutual fund's portfolio. A study by Cheney and Veit analyzed the balance sheet proportions of funds in terms of cash, fixed-income securities, and stocks.[28] If funds increased the proportion of stocks during bull markets and increased cash during bear markets, this would be evidence of successful timing activity. Their analysis detected statistically significant but relatively small shifts in the asset compositions. The significant shifts, however, were almost always incorrect. Funds tended to shift into cash prior to bull markets and into stock prior to bear markets— evidence of *incorrect* timing decisions.

Regardless of the methodology, time period, or sample, there appears to be no evidence that mutual funds can successfully time the market; the evidence suggests that some funds do attempt timing but that they are usually unsuccessful.

4. ADVANTAGES OF MUTUAL FUND INVESTING The previous discussion is generally unfavorable in terms of mutual funds outperforming the market on a risk-adjusted basis. Some funds appear to be able to select securities successfully, but few, if any, demonstrate expertise in market timing. However, studies do find that mutual funds provide adequate diversification, follow their stated investment objectives, and generally maintain relatively low expenses. These positive factors indicate that mutual funds serve an important function for many investors. On the other hand, the evidence suggests that investors in mutual funds should *not* expect to beat the market consistently on a risk-adjusted basis. Chapter 24 provides a detailed discussion of mutual fund investing.

---

[26] Carl R. Chen and Steve Stockum, "Selectivity, Market Timing, and Random Beta Behavior of Mutual Funds: A Generalized Model," *Journal of Financial Research* (Spring 1986): pp. 87–96.

[27] Frank Fabozzi and Jack Francis, "Mutual Fund Systematic Risk for Bull and Bear Markets," *Journal of Finance* (December 1979): pp. 1243–50.

[28] John M. Cheney and E. Theodore Veit, "Evidence of Shifts in Portfolio Asset Composition as a Market Timing Tool," *The Financial Review* (February 1983): pp. 56–78.

Performance of Other Professionally Managed Portfolios

A limited number of studies have analyzed the risk-adjusted return performance of commercial banks, insurance companies, and pension fund portfolios. A study by Bogle and Twardowski compared the performances of mutual funds, commercial banks, insurance companies, and investment counselors.[29] Their study covered the ten-year period ending December 31, 1977, and included *HPR*s on approximately 1,738 portfolios. They concluded that mutual funds had the best performance, followed (in order) by investment counselors, insurance companies, and commercial banks. The results of this study, when combined with the results from the mutual fund studies previously discussed, suggest that *no* group of professional managed portfolios can consistently beat the market on a risk-adjusted basis.

A study by Dunn and Theisen, providing additional evidence of the difficulty facing professional portfolio managers, consisted of data for 1973–1982 on 201 "institutional portfolios," supplied by the Frank Russell Company.[30] The purpose of the study was to analyze the performance consistency by looking at what proportion of managers successful in one period were also successful in the following period. They concluded that, at best, picking a portfolio for the future by using past performance measures has a 50 percent chance of success. This suggests that historical performance should play a minor role in selecting a portfolio or a portfolio manager. The inconsistency of annual mutual fund performance was illustrated in a classic 1965 study by Fama.[31]

These studies suggest that it is extremely difficult and uncommon for a portfolio to outperform the market on a risk-adjusted basis. If this difficult feat is accomplished in one period, it is unlikely that the success can be continued in the following period.

SUMMARY

The major purpose of this chapter has been to present techniques that can be used to analyze the ex-post performance of portfolios on a risk-adjusted basis.

As a prerequisite to a performance analysis, it is necessary to calculate *HPR*s for the portfolio correctly. The calculation should consider all income distributions from the portfolio and the timing of the distributions. It is also common to assume that distributions are reinvested in the portfolio and earn the *HPR*s following the reinvestment dates. Performance measurement also requires an analysis of risk. Traditionally, this was ignored or was handled by grouping portfolios into homogeneous risk categories.

---

[29] John C. Bogle and Jan M. Twardowski, "Institutional Investment Performance Compared: Banks, Investment Counselors, Insurance Companies, and Mutual Funds," *Financial Analysts Journal* (January-February 1980): pp. 33–41.

[30] Patricia C. Dunn and Rolf D. Theisen, "How Consistently Do Active Managers Win?" *Journal of Portfolio Management* (Summer 1983): pp. 47–50.

[31] Eugene Fama, "The Behavior of Stock Prices," *Journal of Busines* (January 1965): pp. 34–105.

Based on the development of CMT and specifically the CAPM, formal techniques were developed that combined return and risk into a single performance measure. The techniques of Treynor, Sharpe, and Jensen were presented, compared, and illustrated. A number of weaknesses in these techniques were also discussed, along with an indication of the impact of these weaknesses on conclusions concerning portfolio performance.

Given the weaknesses in the traditional techniques, recent developments improving on the earlier methods were discussed. These developments concentrate on the identification of an appropriate benchmark portfolio and on analyzing the individual components of performance: selection, timing, and diversification.

Finally, a few of the numerous studies dealing with the performance of professionally managed portfolios were reviewed. Due to the availability of data, the majority of those studies covered mutual funds. Earlier studies conducted in the late 1960s generally concluded that, on average, mutual funds do not beat the market on a risk-adjusted basis. More recent studies suggest that their performance has improved, but only a small percentage of funds seem to be able to beat the market.

Recent studies on individual aspects of performance indicate that some funds are successful in selecting securities for the portfolio. Few if any funds are able to demonstrate success at market timing. However, mutual funds do generally provide adequate diversification, as measured by their correlation with the market or a benchmark portfolio.

Mutual fund managers are not the only ones that have difficulty in beating the market on a consistent basis. Studies of the peformances of commercial banks, insurance companies, and pension fund portfolios also indicate an overall failure to beat the market. In defense of mutual funds, one study concluded that their performance was better than that of other types of professionally managed portfolios.

QUESTIONS

1. Explain why an analysis of portfolio performance should consider both returns and risk.

2. Discuss how portfolio ex-post returns should be calculated for a performance analysis. Explain how the length of the holding period influences the return calculations.

3. Compare and contrast the arithmetic mean return with the geometric mean return. Which mean is more appropriate for a performance analysis?

4. The three mutual funds analyzed in the chapter (Fidelity Magellan Fund, The 44 Wall Street Fund, and T. Rowe Price New Horizons Fund) are all common stock funds with an investment objective of "growth." What are some problems that might occur if a fund with a different investment objective was included in the analysis?

5. Briefly define Treynor's portfolio performance technique. Do larger or smaller values for the Treynor technique indicate better performance? Explain how a portfolio can be compared to the market portfolio using the Treynor technique.

6. Assume that a portfolio had a low correlation with the S&P 500 over the last 10 years. Does the Treynor technique consider the level of unsystematic risk implied by the correlation coefficient?

7. Can the Treynor performance measure be a negative number? Under what conditions could this occur?

8. Briefly define Sharpe's portfolio performance technique. Explain how a portfolio can be compared to the market portfolio using the Sharpe technique.

9. Discuss the implications of using the CML in Sharpe's performance technique rather than the SML.

10. Explain how the CAPM provides the foundation for Jensen's portfolio performance technique.

11. Consider the following performance information on three portfolios:

	TREYNOR T_p	SHARPE S_p	JENSEN J_p
Portfolio A	−4.0%	−.5	−5.0%
Portfolio B	8.0	1.2	3.0
Portfolio C	4.0	.3	0
S&P 500	5.0	.6	0

a. Rank each of the portfolios, using each of the performance measures. Are the rankings consistent for the three techniques?

b. Compare each portfolio's performance to the market's performance. Are the comparisons consistent for the three techniques?

12. Explain how the selection of a benchmark portfolio might have important implications for the performance evaluation.

13. The performance techniques of Treynor, Sharpe, and Jensen assume that the risk of the portfolio remained constant over the evaluation period. Discuss the implications of this assumption for the performance evaluation.

14. Explain how the security selection success of a portfolio might be evaluated.

15. Explain how the market timing success of a portfolio might be evaluated.

16. Explain how the diversification success of a portfolio might be evaluated.

17. Empirical studies of mutual funds' performances generally conclude that, on average, funds do not outperform the market on a risk-adjusted basis. Despite this evidence, explain why mutual funds are popular and viable investments for many individuals.

PROBLEMS

1. A portfolio's market value increased from $10 to $11 million during the year. In addition, the portfolio distributed $500,000 to its investors at the end of the year. Calculate the holding period return, *HPR*.

2. Consider the following data on a portfolio's performance:

	MARKET VALUE	INCOME DISTRIBUTION
January 1, 1987	$10,000	—
December 31, 1987	8,000	$1,000
December 31, 1988	11,000	1,500

   a.   Calculate the *HPR*s for 1987 and for 1988.

   b.   Calculate the simple or arithmetic mean *HPR* over the two-year period.

   c.   Calculate the geometric mean *HPR* over the two-year period.

   d.   Explain any difference in the arithmetic and geometric means.

3.   The ex-post return and risk measures for two mutual funds and a benchmark portfolio over the period 1979–1988 are

	FUND A	FUND B	BENCHMARK
Geometric mean annual *HPR*	18.0%	12.0%	15.0%
Standard deviation	9.0%	6.0%	7.0%
Beta	1.2	0.8	1.0
Geometric mean of annual risk premiums	10.0%	4.0%	7.0%

The geometric mean risk-free return over the period was 8 percent.

   a.   Calculate the Treynor, Sharpe, and Jensen performance measures for both funds and the benchmark portfolio.

   b.   Rank the funds, using each performance measure.

   c.   Compare each fund's performance to the benchmark portfolio, using the three performance measures.

   d.   Calculate the index of total portfolio risk for each fund. Was each fund perfectly diversified?

4.   Use the information in problem 3 to calculate Fama's

   a.   "Net selectivity return" for each fund.

   b.   "Additional return for lack of diversification" for each fund.

   c.   Use this information to analyze the selection and diversification success of each fund.

5.   Consider the following annual *HPR*s for two portfolios, a benchmark portfolio, and one-year Treasury bills:

	PORTFOLIO X	PORTFOLIO Y	BENCHMARK	TREASURY BILLS
19 × 1	20.0%	15.0%	12.0%	8.0%
19 × 2	25.0	5.0	2.0	6.0
19 × 3	18.0	12.0	10.0	7.0
19 × 4	4.0	3.0	5.0	6.0
19 × 5	30.0	20.0	15.0	8.0

   a.   Calculate the arithmetic and geometric means for portfolios X and Y, the benchmark portfolio, and Treasury bills.

   b.   Calculate the standard deviations for portfolios X and Y, the benchmark portfolio, and Treasury bills.

   c.   Calculate the correlation coefficient for each portfolio with the benchmark portfolio.

   d.   Calculate the betas for each portfolio.

   e.   Calculate the Treynor, Sharpe, and Jensen performance measures for portfolio X and Y and the benchmark portfolio.

COMPUTER APPLICATIONS

The floppy disk includes programs that can be used to calculate the following:

1. Treynor's, Sharpe's, and Jensen's performance measures;
2. Arithmetic and geometric means; and
3. Portfolio betas, variances, and standard deviations.

These programs can be used to solve some of the problems in this chapter and to analyze the performance of portfolios. Instructions and illustrations are provided on the disk.

REFERENCES

Admati, Anat R., Sudipto Bhattacharya, Paul Pfleiderer, and Stephen A. Ross. "On Timing and Selectivity." *Journal of Finance* (July 1986): pp. 715–30.

Ambachtsheer, Keith P., and James L. Farrell, Jr.. "Can Active Management Add Value?" *Financial Analysts Journal* (November-December 1979): pp. 39–47.

Bierman, Harold. "How Much Diversification Is Desirable?" *The Journal of Portfolio Management* (Fall 1980): pp. 42–44.

Bogle, John C., and Jan M. Twardowski. "Institutional Investment Performances Compared: Banks, Investment Counselors, Insurance Companies and Mutual Funds." *Financial Analysts Journal* (January-February 1980): pp. 33–41.

Brown, Keith C., and Gregory D. Brown. "Does the Market Portfolio's Composition Matter?" *The Journal of Portfolio Management* (Winter 1987): pp. 26–32.

Chen, Carl R., and Steve Stockum. "Selectivity, Market Timing, and Random Beta Behavior of Mutual Funds: A Generalized Model." *The Journal of Financial Research* (Spring 1986): pp. 87–96.

Cheney, John M., and E. Theodore Veit. "How Do Mutual Fund Managers Make Investment Decisions?" *Pension World* (February 1985): pp. 24–27.

Dunn, Patricia C., and Rolf D. Theisen. "How Consistently Do Active Managers Win?" *The Journal of Portfolio Management* (Summer 1983): pp. 47–50.

Dybvig, Philip H., and Stephen A. Ross, "Performance Measurement Using Differential Information and a Security Market Line." *Journal of Finance* (June 1985): pp. 383–99.

———. "The Analytics of Performance Measurement Using a Security Market Line." *Journal of Finance* (June 1985): pp. 401–16.

Fama, Eugene. "The Behavior of Stock Prices," *Journal of Business* (January 1965): pp. 34–105.

———. "Components of Investment Performance." *Journal of Finance* (June 1972): pp. 551–67.

Ferguson, Robert. "Performance Measurement Doesn't Make Sense." *Financial Analysts Journal* (May-June 1980): pp. 59–69.

———. "The Trouble with Performance Measurement." *The Journal of Portfolio Management* (Spring 1986): pp. 4–9.

Ferri, Michael G., and H. Dennis Oberhelman. "How Well Do Money Market Funds Perform?" *The Journal of Portfolio Management* (Spring 1981): pp. 18–26.

Francis, Jack Clark, and Frank J. Fabozzi. "Stability of Mutual Fund Systematic Risk Statistics." *Journal of Business Research* (Spring 1980): pp. 263–75.

French, Dan W., and Glenn V. Henderson, Jr.. "How Well Does Performance Evaluation Perform?" *The Journal of Portfolio Management* (Winter 1985): pp. 15–22.

Good, Walter R. "Measuring Performance." *Financial Analysts Journal* (May-June 1983): pp. 19–23.

Granatelli, Andy, and John D. Martin. "Management Quality and Investment Performance." *Financial Analysts Journal* (November-December 1984): pp. 72–74.

Green, Richard C. "Benchmark Portfolio Inefficiency and Deviations from the Security Market Line." *Journal of Finance* (June 1986): pp. 295–312.

Gressis, Nicholas, George C. Philippatos, and George Vlahos. "Net Selectivity as a Component Measure of Investment Performance." *The Financial Review* (February 1986): pp. 103–10.

Horowitz, I. "The 'Reward-to-Variability' Ratio and Mutual Fund Performance." *Journal of Business* (October 1966): pp. 485–88.

Jensen, Michael C. "The Performance of Mutual Funds in the Period 1945–1964." *Journal of Finance* (May 1968): pp. 389–416.

Kane, Edward J., and Stephen A. Buser. "Portfolio Diversification at Commercial Banks." *Journal of Finance* (March 1979): pp. 19–34.

Korkie, Bob. "External vs. Internal Performance Evaluation." *The Journal of Portfolio Management* (Spring 1983): pp. 36–42.

Kritzman, Mark. "How to Detect Skill in Management Performance." *The Journal of Portfolio Management* (Winter 1986): pp. 16–20.

Levitz, Gerald D. "Market Risk and the Management of Institutional Equity Portfolios." *Financial Analysts Journal* (January-February 1974): pp. 53–55, 59–60, 91.

Levy, Haim. "Measuring Risk and Performance over Alternate Investment Horizons." *Financial Analysts Journal* (March-April 1984): pp. 61–68.

Moses, Edward A., John M. Cheney, and E. Theodore Veit. "A New and More Complete Performance Measure." *The Journal of Portfolio Management* (Summer 1987): pp. 24–33.

Murphy, J. Michael. "Why No One Can Tell Who's Winning." *Financial Analysts Journal* (May-June 1980): pp. 49–57.

Peterson, David, and Michael L. Rice. "A Note on Ambiguity in Portfolio Performance Measures." *Journal of Finance* (December 1980): pp. 1251–56.

Pohlman, Randolph A., James S. Ang, and Robert D. Hollinger. "Performance and Timing: A Test of Hedge Funds." *The Journal of Portfolio Management* (Spring 1978): pp. 69–72.

Roll, Richard. "A Critique of the Asset Pricing Theory's Tests; Part I on Past and Potential Testability of the Theory." *Journal of Financial Economics* (March 1977): pp. 129–76.

———. "Performance Evaluation and Benchmark Errors (I)." *The Journal of Portfolio Management* (Summer 1980): pp. 5–11.

———. "Performance Evaluation and Benchmark Errors (II)." *The Journal of Portfolio Management* (Winter 1984): pp. 17–22.

Rosenberg, Barr. "The Capital Asset Pricing Model and the Market Model." *Journal of Portfolio Management* (Winter 1981): pp. 5–16.

Sharpe, William F. "Mutual Fund Performance." *Journal of Business* (January 1966): pp. 119–38.

———. "Likely Gains from Market Timing." *Financial Analysts Journal* (March-April 1975): pp. 60–69.

Shawky, Hany A. "An Update on Mutual Funds: Better Grades." *The Journal of Portfolio Management* (Winter 1982): pp. 29–34.

Treynor, Jack L. "How to Rate Management of Investment Funds." *Harvard Business Review* (January-February 1965): pp. 63–75.

Treynor, Jack L., and Kay K. Mazuy. "Can Mutual Funds Outguess the Market?" *Harvard Business Review* (July-August 1966): pp. 131–36.

Veit, E. Theodore, and John M. Cheney. "Managing Investment Portfolios: A Survey of Mutual Funds." *The Financial Review* (November 1984): pp. 321–38.

Wilson, Jack W., and Charles P. Jones. "The Relationship between Performance and Risk: Whence the Bias?" *Journal of Financial Research* (Summer 1981): pp. 103–8.

PART 3

ANALYSIS OF COMMON STOCKS

CHAPTER 9

COMMON STOCK BASICS AND ECONOMIC ANALYSIS

INTRODUCTION

Overview of Common Stock Analysis

Part 3 deals with the analysis of common stocks. Chapters 9 through 11 present the fundamental approach to the analysis of common stock, and Chapter 12 presents the technical view of common stock analysis. Part 3 concludes with Chapter 13, which discusses the efficient market viewpoint and its possible implications for fundamental and technical analysis.

As previously discussed in Chapter 5, *fundamental analysis* comprises analyses of the economy, the industry, and the company. Essentially, this is a "top-down" approach that starts with a macro analysis of the economy and the industry before undertaking the company, or micro, analysis. This method centers on an identification and estimate of the "fundamental" factors that will determine a stock's price in the future. The historical financial statements of the company are an important element in the fundamental analysis of the company.

Benjamin Graham is recognized as the father of fundamental analysis because of his work in the 1930s.[1] In a broader sense, however, the principles of fundamental analysis have their origins in the natural sciences. This view is reflected in the following:

> *Fundamental analysis is a method of systematically modeling facts—economic and industry statistics, financial rates, et al.—in order to derive in a logically coherent manner an explanation, hence an understanding, of observed phenomena. We employ this understanding to pass judgment and ultimately influence behavior. This is procedurally congruent to the method articulated by Darwin with respect to the natural sciences; both his method and explanations provide the theoretical foundation for modern scientific, economic, and social thought and, yes, even fundamental analysis.[2]*

The analogy with the work of Darwin to explain the three steps of fundamental analysis is apparent in the following relationships:[3]

DARWIN	FUNDAMENTAL ANALYSIS
Environment	Economy
Species	Industries
Organisms	Firms

This analogy supports the view that fundamental analysts are applied business scientists.

---

[1] Benjamin Graham and David Dodd, *Security Analysis* (New York: McGraw-Hill, 1934).

[2] Malvin C. Spooner, "Origin of Fundamental Analysis," *Financial Analysts Journal* (July-August 1984): pp, 79–80.

[3] Ibid, p. 79.

Introduction to Common Stock Valuation

Investment theory and the fundamental approach define *value* by using estimates of future income that are discounted to present value terms, assuming a required rate of return. The value of a financial asset is simply the present value of its future income stream. For example, a widely used valuation model is the *dividend discount model*, DDM. The *constant growth* version of this model is

$$V_o = \frac{D_o(1 + g)}{k - g} \tag{9.1}$$

where V_o = intrinsic value of stock today

D_o = current dividends per share

g = constant annual expected growth rate in dividends

k = investor's required rate of return

To use this model, the analyst must estimate the average long-term growth rate in dividends and an appropriate required rate of return. Despite the apparent simplicity of this model, the difficulty in estimating g and k should not be underestimated. The usual approach to solving these estimation problems is to use an economy-industry-company procedure.

The economic analysis, with its forecast, provides a possible justification for an investment in common stocks. It also provides a foundation for estimating a particular industry's and company's revenue growth prospects and for forecasting interest rates, which are then incorporated into the estimate of the required rate of return. The company analysis provides the foundation needed to estimate future earnings and dividends, and indicates the appropriate *risk premium* that should be included in the required rate of return.

The above discussion is obviously an oversimplification of common stock valuation. The purpose of the discussion, however, is to provide an overview of the three-step procedure of fundamental analysis, consisting of economic, industry, and company analyses. The details of this approach are presented in the chapters that follow.

Common Stock Characteristics

Prior to discussing the fundamental approach to stock analysis, it is necessary to have a clear understanding of the characteristics of common stock. Common stock represents an ownership interest in a corporation. As owners, common stockholders are entitled to certain rights and privileges that are discussed below.

1. CONTROL Common stock has voting rights that can be used to elect corporate directors who, in turn, appoint the corporate officers. The extent of control depends on the number of shares held relative to the total shares outstanding, the method of voting, and the stock ownership of the officers and their representation on the board of directors.

    There are two methods of voting common stock: *straight* and *cumulative*. Straight voting is essentially one vote per share for each director. If the shares allow cumulative voting, however, the investor can use all his votes for a *single* candidate. For example, if a stockholder has 100 shares and five directors are to be elected, a total of 500 votes can be cast for one or more of the directors. The majority of states now require or permit cumulative voting, with the intent of increasing voting control for minority stockholders.

Rather than actually attending the annual stockholders' meeting to vote, stockholders may use a *proxy* that temporarily transfers their voting rights to another individual, such as a corporate officer, a member of the board of directors, or an individual trying to gain control of the corporation. It is not unusual to see proxy battles occur where two or more individuals are trying to obtain proxies. Due to the economic significance of voting control, the SEC regulates and supervises proxy procedures.

In some cases, a corporation may have more than one category or class of common stock because of differences in voting rights. For example, Class A may be nonvoting, while Class B has voting rights. The Toronto Stock Exchange, the AMEX, and the OTC market allow trading in shares with restricted voting rights. The NYSE, for over sixty years, did not allow listings for firms that issued multiple classes of shares with different voting rights; this prohibition was lifted in 1986.

A study of voting and nonvoting common stock traded on the Toronto Stock Exchange provides evidence of the importance that some investors place on voting rights.[4] The study analyzed companies that issued both voting and nonvoting shares to existing stockholders in exchange for the original voting stock. (This procedure is similar to a stock split, except that the new shares differ in their voting rights.) The restricted-voting shares declined in price, and the superior voting shares increased in price, providing a "positive premium of roughly 7 percent." The evidence also suggests that investors "vote with their feet" by selling the restricted-voting shares in favor of alternative investments.

2. PREEMPTIVE RIGHT The preemptive right allows existing stockholders the first option to purchase a proportionate interest in a new issue of a corporation. The purpose of this provision is to protect stockholders against a loss of voting control and a dilution in the value of their shares. The preemptive right is usually satisfied by the use of a *rights offering* (discussed in Chapter 19).

3. LIQUIDATION RIGHTS As owners rather than creditors, common stockholders receive no priority in the distribution of assets resulting from a liquidation of the corporation. Typically, after assets are sold and liabilities and preferred stockholders are satisfied, little if any cash will be available for common stockholders.

4. RIGHT TO INCOME Common stockholders have no legal right to receive income distributions from the corporation. As a practical matter, however, the board of directors may declare cash dividends to stockholders, provided the financial

---

[4] Vijay M. Jog and Allan L. Riding, "Price Effects of Dual-Class Shares," *Financial Analysts Journal* (January-February 1986): pp. 58–67.

resources are available, even for periods when the corporation experienced a loss.

5. STOCK DIVIDEND In lieu of or in conjunction with a cash dividend, the board of directors may declare a *stock dividend*. In an efficient market, the economic significance of a stock dividend should be negligible because the price of the stock would decline to reflect the additional shares. For example, a 4 percent stock dividend declared on a stock selling for $26 should result in a new price of $25 ($26/1.04). Assuming an investor previously held 100 shares, the new price of $25 would keep the total value of the investment at $2,600 ($25 × 104). Thus, the investor neither gains nor loses as a result of the stock dividend.

6. STOCK SPLIT A *stock split* is similar to but usually larger than a stock dividend, and the two transactions are handled differently on the balance sheet. A *stock split* results in a reduction in the par value of the stock and a corresponding increase in the number of shares. In a stock dividend the corporation adjusts the balance sheet by transferring an amount equal to the market value of the stock dividend from the retained earnings account to the paid-in capital and common stock accounts.

    Generally, a stock dividend of 25 percent or greater is essentially a stock split. For NYSE-listed stocks, the exchange uses the 25 percent level to classify the distribution as a dividend or split. Esssentially, a 25 percent stock dividend is equivalent to a five-for-four stock split.

    Corporations that declare stock dividends and splits often justify their actions, using a variety of reasons that include

    a. Investor psychology—investors prefer stocks that are not too expensive and trading in a "desirable" price range;

    b. Trading volume—the increased number of shares causes greater trading activity and improves liquidity;

    c. Signaling to investors—a decision to split or declare a stock dividend indicates that management and the directors are bullish about the stock; and

    d. Naive investors—the feeling that some stockholders equate cash and stock dividends and do not realize that stock dividends and splits have little economic significance.[5]

    Numerous empirical studies have examined the possible economic significance of stock dividends and stock splits.[6] Surprisingly, some of these studies indicate that stockholder wealth does increase prior to the announcement

---

[5] For a typical discussion, see Lawrence Ingrassia, "Recent Increase in Share Prices Has Led to Flurry of Stock Splits, Stock Dividends," *Wall Street Journal*, 27 Jan. 1983. p. 56. For an understanding of management's reasons for paying stock dividends, see Peter C. Eisemann and Edward A. Moses, "Stock Dividends: Management's View," *Financial Analysts Journal* (July-August 1978): p. 77–80.

[6] For example, see E. Fama et al., "The Adjustment of Stock Prices to New Information," *International Economic Review* (February 1969): pp. 1–21; M. Grinblatt, R. Masulis, and S. Titman, "The Valuation Effects of Stock Splits and Stock Dividends," *Journal of Financial Economics* (December 1984):p. 461–90; and R. Spudeck and R. Moyer, "Reverse Splits and Shareholder Wealth: The Impact of Commissions," *Financial Management* (Winter 1985): pp. 52-56.

of the stock dividend or split. The reason for this, however, appears to be that stockholders view a stock dividend or split as a favorable message or *signal* from management that it is optimistic about the prospects of the company. The increase in stockholder wealth occurs, therefore, because of the signal and not because of the increase in number of shares. This issue and other issues of market efficiency are discussed in Chapter 13.

7.   COMMON STOCK VALUES Terms that are frequently used to refer to common stock values include *par value*, *book value*, and *market value*. These terms are quite different, and in most cases, the dollar amount of each is not related for an individual stock.

Par value represents the face value of the stock, established at the time the stock is initially issued. Without a stock split or other action by the board of directors, the par value of the stock does not change. For new issues, popular par values are $1 or $.01 per share, but the directors are free to select any value that seems appropriate. Stock is often issued without a par value. Low- or no-par values are usually selected because they eliminate any contingent liability that stockholders may incur by purchasing stock for a price below par value.

Book value per share is calculated by dividing the total common equity on the balance sheet (book) by the number of common shares outstanding. This figure represents the asset value per share after deducting liabilities and preferred stock. Typically, common stock in a profitable corporation will be valued based on *earning power* and will sell at prices significantly greater than book value. Likewise, common stock in unprofitable companies and companies experiencing financial distress will be valued based on *liquidation* or book value and will sell at prices close to or below book value. Traditionally, fundamental analysts often compare market and book values because stock's selling below book value may be one indication that the stock is undervalued.

Market value is determined by supply-and-demand factors and reflects the consensus opinion of investors and traders concerning the "value" of the stock. As the following chapters indicate, factors that influence market value include economic and industry conditions, expected earnings and dividends, and market and company risk considerations.

8.   QUOTATIONS Table 9.1 provides examples of stock quotations for the NYSE, AMEX, and OTC markets. As the table illustrates, the formats of the quotations for the AMEX, NYSE, and "National Market Issues" on the OTC are identical. However, the quotes for secondary or regional stocks provided by the NASDAQ for the OTC market consist of only "bid" and "asked" prices. Prices for stocks are quoted in dollars and eighths of dollars. For example, the closing quote on Aetna Life, $42\frac{5}{8}$ in the table, indicates a price of $42.625.

The dividend yield, "Yld. Div %", is calculated by dividing the *annual* cash dividends, based on the last quarter or semiannual declaration, by the closing price. The price/earnings ratio, "P/E Ratio", is calculated by dividing the closing price by the most recent four-quarter earnings per share, EPS. EPS excludes extraordinary items and is generally defined as "primary" earnings. The 52-week high and low prices are adjusted to reflect stock dividends or splits of more than 10 percent. The trading volume, "sales 100s",

TABLE 9.1 EXAMPLES OF PRICE QUOTATION FOR COMMON STOCKS TRADED ON THE NYSE, AMEX, AND OTC MARKETS

NYSE

52 Weeks High	Low	Stock	Div.	Yld %	P-E Ratio	Sales 100s	High	Low	Close	Net Chg.
		−A−A−A−								
25⅝	14	AAR s	.36	1.5	19	66	24	23⅜	23⅜	...
12⅛	8¾	ACM GI n	.88e	7.7	...	341	11⅝	11½	11½	...
12⅛	10¾	ACM GS n	1.26	11.1	...	612	11½	11¼	11⅜	...
27	10½	AGS s		...	13	232	17¾	17¼	17½	+ ⅜
10½	4⅜	AMCA		...	...	35	5⅛	4¾	5⅛	+ ½
8⅝	3¼	AM Intl		...	...	6282	3¾	3½	3¾	...
29⅜	17	AM Int pf	2.00	10.6	...	x92	19	18¾	18⅞	− ⅛
65½	26¾	AMR		....	11	3847	44⅛	42⅞	43⅝	+ ¼
12¼	6⅜	ARX		...	9	43	8⅞	8⅝	8¾	+ ⅛
72⅞	40⅛	ASA	3.00	6.7	...	143	45¼	44½	44⅞	+ ⅛
22⅜	9½	AVX		...	13	234	17¼	17	17¼	− ¼
66⅜	40	AbtLab	1.20	2.5	16	3536	47⅜	46½	47⅜	+ 1⅛
28	15⅜	Abitibi g	1.00	...	...	28	18	17⅞	18	...
16¾	8½	AcmeC	.40	3.4	...	x74	12	11¾	11¾	− ¼
10½	6¾	AcmeE	.32b	4.7	18	140	7	6¾	6¾	− ⅛
20	14⅛	AdaEx	3.05e	19.7	...	162	15⅝	15½	15½	...
19	6⅞	AdamMI	.24	1.3	15	391	18¾	18¼	18⅝	+ ⅛
24⅞	7½	AMD		...	...	5994	13⅝	13⅛	13½	+ ⅜
56¾	29¼	AMD pf	3.00	7.9	...	100	38	38	38	+ ¼
11⅞	4⅝	Adobe		...	12	63	7¾	7⅝	7¾	+ ⅛
20¼	16¼	Adob pf	1.84	10.2	...	7	18	17⅞	18	+ ⅛
15	6⅛	Advest	.12a	1.7	7	49	7¼	7⅛	7⅛	...
64¼	42⅜	AetnLf	2.76	6.5	6	x2520	42⅞	42⅜	42⅝	+ ⅝
83½	41	AflIPub	.40	.7	33	377	58⅜	58	58	− ⅛
23¾	13	Ahmans	.88	6.3	7	3214	14⅛	13¾	14	+ ⅛
4⅞	1¾	Aileen		...	...	149	3⅝	3½	3½	...
53⅞	29	AirPrd	1.00	2.2	13	1621	47¼	46⅛	46½	+ ⅛
36	11⅛	AirbFrt	.60	3.7	18	304	16⅝	16	16⅜	...
16½	6¾	Airgas		...	17	31	12⅞	12¾	12⅞	...
19¾	13½	Airlease	2.30	12.4	10	22	18¾	18½	18½	...
27¾	25½	AlaP pf	2.04e	7.8	...	1304	26⅛	26⅛	26⅛	...
10⅜	7⅝	AlaP dpf	.87	9.3	...	29	9⅜	9⅛	9⅜	+ ⅛
99½	81½	AlaP pf	9.00	9.9	...	z10	91	91	91	− ¾

AMEX

52 Weeks High	Low	Stock	Div.	Yld %	P-E Ratio	Sales 100s	High	Low	Close	Net Chg.
		−A−A−A−								
13½	6⅛	ABI		...	12	5	9	9	9	...
10⅞	4⅜	ABM G n		...	54	73	5	4⅞	4⅞	...
15⅞	5⅞	AL Lab s	.12	.8	20	169	14⅝	14	14½	+ ⅝
10⅝	3½	AMC s	.10	1.7	...	67	6	5¾	6	...
1⅝	1	AM Int wt		...	...	301	1¼	1¼	1¼	...
6¼	1 11/16	ARC g		...	...	53	2 13/16	2 11/16	2 11/16	− 1/16
31⅞	5⅞	AT&E		...	...	69	9⅜	9	9⅜	+ ¼
44½	30¼	ATT Fd	2.04e	5.4	...	151	38¼	37⅜	38⅛	+ ½
15¼	4¾	Abimd n		...	...	21	10½	10½	10½	− ⅛
6	1⅝	AcmePr		...	...	10	2	2	2	− ⅛
8¾	5⅛	AcmeU	.08e	1.1	44	20	7	7	7	...
7¾	3	Action		...	10	44	5	4⅞	5	...
26½	11⅝	Acton s		...	3	234	15⅝	14¾	15	− ⅝
4⅛	1¼	AdmRs		...	7	65	1⅞	1⅞	1⅞	+ ⅛
18⅜	6⅛	AdRslEl		...	...	6	8⅜	8¼	8¼	+ ⅛
21¾	8½	AirExp		...	13	48	19½	19⅛	19½	+ ¼
18⅝	10	Aircoa	2.40	19.4	...	10	12½	12⅜	12⅜	...
10⅜	5½	AlbaW		...	...	1	7¾	7¾	7¾	− ⅛
7½	2¾	Alfin s		...	...	247	3⅝	3¼	3⅝	+ ⅜
8½	5	AlliBc n		...	...	1	5¾	5¾	5¾	− ⅛
11½	4½	Allstr n	1.38	19.7	100	29	7	6¾	7	...
11⅛	3	Alphaln		...	...	133	3⅞	3⅞	3⅞	...
21¼	4⅝	AlpinGr		...	...	2	6⅜	6⅜	6⅜	− ⅛
9/16	⅛	Altex n		...	...	162	3/16	3/16	3/16	...
46	36½	Alcoa pf	3.75	8.9	...	z50	42¼	42¼	42¼	+ ¼
42⅝	16	Alza		...	55	614	23½	23	23¼	+ ⅜
5⅝	3⅝	AmBrit	.08	1.8	...	1	4⅜	4⅜	4⅜	− ⅛
50⅛	19⅛	Amdahl	.20	.5	13	2799	38⅝	38	38½	+ ¾
17¼	7	AmBilt	.15	1.1	10	2	13¾	13¾	13¾	+ ¼
21½	12½	ABkCT	1.00	5.4	8	2	18½	18½	18½	+ ⅛
27	20	ACap pf	3.75	16.5	...	10	23	22¾	22¾	...
5	2⅛	AExpl		...	8	31	2¾	2⅝	2¾	...
15/16	½	AExpl wt		...	...	10	13/16	13/16	13/16	...
4⅛	⅜	AExFF wt		...	...	746	7/16	⅜	7/16	...

NATIONAL OTC

365-day High	Low	Stock	Div.	Yld	P-E	Sales (hds)	High	Low	Last	Net Chg.
		−−A A−−								
16⅝	6¼	A&W Brands		..	42	50	15	15	15	+ ½
T4¾	6½	AaronRent	.10	.9	11	1	10¾	10¾	10¾	+ ¼
19¾	8	Abington Bcp		..	..	25	10	9¾	9¾	− ¼
15	8¾	Abraham Linc		..	..	1	11	11	11	...
21¼	10¾	ABQ Corp		..	6	2	13½	13½	13½	+ 1
3⅜	1 11-16	Acadmy Ins		..	69	1571	2 3-16	2 1-16	2 1-16	− 1-16
3⅜	1⅛	ACC Corp		..	13	119	3	2⅞	2⅞	− 3-16
11⅞	4¼	AccelIntl	10i	..	8	x1	8⅛	8⅛	8⅛	+ ½
15¾	7⅛	Acceptnc Ins		..	5	85	11½	11	11½	+ ½
18	10½	Aceto Cp	1.32f	9.3	12	85	14½	14	14¼	− ¼
17¼	6	ACMAT A		..	..	2	8¾	8¾	8¾	+ ¾
23¼	9⅛	AcmeSteel Cp		..	18	355	22½	22	22	...
18½	7½	ActAutRn	5i	..	30	x3	16½	16	16	+ ⅜
9½	3¾	ActnAuto St		..	..	146	7⅝	7⅜	7⅝	+ ¼
3	¾	Activision Inc		..	..	148	1½	1 7-16	1½	+ 1-16
28	10¼	Actmedia		..	23	120	13	12¾	12¾	...
24¾	10¼	Acuson Corp		..	34	290	24½	23½	24½	+ ½
3 1-16	1⅛	Adac Labs		..	37	366	3	2⅞	2 15-16	− 1-16
1 1-16	⅝	Adage Inc		..	..	576	15-16	13-16	⅞	+ 1-16
16¼	4½	Adaptec Inc		..	10	126	6¼	6	6¼	...
24	11⅝	ADC Telecom		..	16	593	21¾	21	21¾	+ ¾
24½	18¼	Addington Rs		..	10	62	23	22	22	− ½
32¼	12½	ADIA Sv	.10	.4	23	81	25¼	24¼	25¼	+ ¼
2½	½	Admac Inc		..	..	32	1	¾	1	+ ⅛
56	13	Adobe Systm		..	33	1942	34⅜	33½	34¼	+ ¼
13½	3¼	Adtec Inc		..	..	23	4¼	4⅛	4⅛	− ⅛
6¾	2¼	Advnc Circuit		..	..	16	3⅞	3¾	3⅞	+ ⅛
12	5⅛	Advance Ross		..	17	35	10	9¾	10	+ ¼
6⅜	1	AdvCptr Tech		..	..	10	1½	1½	1½	...
8⅝	2¼	AdvGenetc Sci		..	..	75	3	2⅝	2⅞	+ ⅛
.10¾	4¼	Adv Magnetc		..	23	1	6½	6½	6½	...
16¼	5	Advnc MktgSv		..	19	171	14¼	13¾	14	− ¼

SOURCE: *Wall Street Journal*, 26 Apr. 1988.

represents the number of shares traded for the day. "Net Chg." represents the change in price from the previous day's close.

The quotations also include other letters or symbols, explained in a footnote that accompanies the quotations. These include "pf," a preferred stock; "wt," a warrant; "rt," rights; and "vj," a company in bankruptcy or receivership.

For the supplemental or regional OTC quotes, the *bid* represents the price the dealer is willing to pay to buy the security, and the *asked* is the price at which the dealer is willing to sell. The difference between the bid and asked represents the *spread* and indicates the dealer's markup. Widely traded secondary issues tend to have smaller spreads than thinly traded issues. The size of the spread is one indication of a security's marketablility. Other factors that influence the spread include beta, price level, and market characteristics.[7]

Classifications of Common Stock

As opposed to fixed-income securities, common stock is often viewed as a homogeneous type of security. The majority of common stocks have similar voting, income, and liquidation rights. Despite the homogeneous nature of common stock,

[7] Frank J. Fabozzi, "Bid-Ask Spreads for Over-The-Counter Stocks," *Journal of Economics and Business* (Fall 1979): pp. 56–65.

it is important to realize that stocks can differ widely in their risk-return characteristics. These differences are often recognized by classifying stocks into categories, as discussed below.

1. BLUE-CHIP STOCKS Stocks of very large, established corporations, such as General Motors, IBM, and Xerox, are often referred to as *blue chips*. Many of these are included in the thirty stocks that compose the DJIA. Because of a dominant industry position, strong balance sheet, and size, these stocks are often viewed as conservative investments. After the market crash on October 19, 1987, the interest in blue-chip stocks increased because of their perceived stability.

2. GROWTH STOCKS Investors often try to identify stocks that are likely to experience above-average price appreciation. This may be a more difficult task to accomplish than it first appears to be. First, the business may be successful in increasing revenues by increasing its market share or developing new markets. This revenue growth, however, may not necessarily increase EPS and the stock price. Thus, the company may be a *growth company*, but its stock is not a *growth stock*. Second, other more-skilled investors may already have recognized the growth prospects, and these expectations are currently reflected in the stock's price. Unusual growth will not, therefore, result in a further increase in the stock's price. Finally, it may be very difficult to distinguish between ''superficial'' or ''transitory'' growth as opposed to ''sustainable'' growth.[8] Only sustainable growth should cause an increase in the stock's price. For example, an observed significant increase in EPS that results because of an increase in financial leverage would not be a reason to expect sustainable growth.

3. INCOME STOCKS Stocks that have a long-term record of stable cash dividends are often referred to as *income stocks*. For example, utilities are noted for their stable cash dividends. Their stock prices, however, can be quite volatile, depending on economic and market cycles. Other companies, because of perceived growth opportunities and/or lack of profitable operations, do not pay cash dividends on a regular basis. Investors with a preference for income would be attracted to companies that stress cash dividends rather than companies primarily motivated by the desire to increase their stock's price. There are numerous cases where investors did not match their expectations of income, as opposed to capital gains, when selecting individual stocks or investment advisors.[9]

Financial research has also identified a dividend *clientele effect*.[10] Essentially, investors who stress income are attracted to dividend-paying stocks, and they expect the established dividend policy to continue. The board of directors, therefore, should cater to its clientele of stockholders.

---

[8] Meir Statman, ''Growth Opportunities vs. Growth Stocks,'' *Journal of Portfolio Management* (Spring 1984): pp. 70–74.

[9] For example, see R. Foster Winans, ''Investors Sue an Advisory Firm in Boston, Charging Loss of Millions on AZL Stock,'' *Wall Street Journal*, 18 May 1983, p. 60.

[10] For example, see Edwin Elton and Martin Gruber, ''Marginal Stockholder Tax Rates and the Clientele Effect,'' *Review of Economics and Statistics* (February 1970): pp. 68–74.

4. CYCLICAL AND DEFENSIVE STOCKS Most stocks are influenced by economic and industry cycles. For example, companies in the home-building and machine-tool-manufacturing industries are affected by recessions and periods of economic growth. Other types of industries and companies, however, are viewed as *defensive*. These industries and companies appear to be less susceptible to economic cycles. For example, stocks in gold-mining companies are commonly viewed as defensive or even counter-cyclical in periods of adverse economic developments.

5. SPECULATIVE STOCKS The distinction between *speculative* and *investment-quality* stocks is difficult to quantify. Clearly, an initial public offering, IPO, of a relatively new company without a successful track record would be viewed by most investors as a highly risky and consequently a speculative issue. However, established companies that are experiencing financial difficulties may also be speculative investments. Essentially, the classification of a stock as speculative or investment quality depends on the risk attitude of the investor. A stock that is classified as speculative by one investor may be viewed as less speculative by another investor.

6. QUALITY RATINGS Investment organizations such as Standard & Poor's Corporation assign *quality ratings* to common stocks to reflect the classifications discussed above. The ratings are similar to bond ratings and are designated as A+, A, A−, B+, etc. The stock ratings are designed to indicate likely long-term risk-return performance. Empirical studies have shown that the ratings are closely related to risk measures, such as beta and earnings variability, and to fundamentals, such as firm size and financial leverage.[11] These studies suggest that the ratings are excellent proxies for risk measures and are useful in common stock analysis.

ECONOMIC ANALYSIS

The first step in the traditional fundamental approach is an economic analysis-and-forecast. This section discusses how stock prices are related to economic activity and how an economic forecast can be used in a valuation of common stock.

Stock Prices and the Economy

Stock prices and economic activity are closely related. For the eight business cycles between 1948 and 1988, the stock market declined significantly before the peak of the business cycle and rose significantly before the trough of the cycle. Stock market changes, therefore, lead economic activity. Figure 9.1 illustrates how the S&P 500 behaves relative to economic activity, as shown by four recessionary periods (shaded areas) between 1961 and 1988.

Figure 9.1 also shows one of the problems in relating stock prices and business cycles. Stocks may experience a significant decline that is not followed by a

---

[11] For example, see Frederick L. Muller and Bruce D. Fielitz, "Standard & Poor's Quality Rankings Revisited," *Journal of Portfolio Management* (Spring 1987): pp. 64–68.

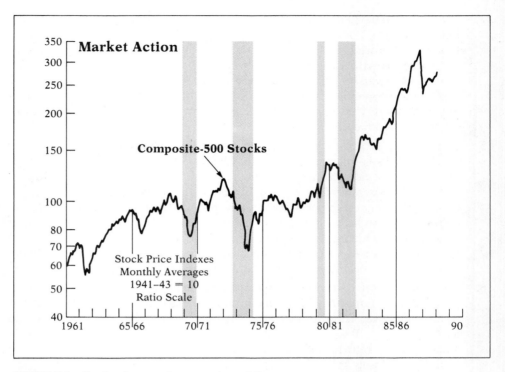

FIGURE 9.1   Stock prices and economic activity
Source: *Analysts Handbook, 1987* (Standard & Poor's) p. 180 (updated through March 1988).

recession. The Wall Street adage that "the stock market has correctly forecast fifteen of the last eight recessions" refers to this problem. The market crash during October 1987 illustrates that factors other than economic events can greatly influence stock prices. Computerized program trading and speculation in stock-index futures are commonly cited reasons for "Black Monday." However, the strength of the economy in late 1987 and early 1988 was a hotly debated topic. Did the dramatic decline in stock prices occur in a reasonably strong economic environment, or was the market correctly forecasting a major recession for 1988?

Despite the possibility that a significant bear market in stocks may not be followed by a recession, the stock market has never failed to forecast a postwar recession in the United States. For this reason, most fundamental analysts use an economic forecast in making investment decisions. The economic forecast is typically for a year or more, however, because the market *leads* economic activity.

Using the period 1900–1979, the United States economy experienced thirteen peacetime expansions. An analysis of this period indicates the following:

1. The average duration of a recession (contraction) in the economy is eighteen months, and the average expansion is twenty-seven months.
2. The ideal time to sell stocks is one to three months before a recession begins. However, because stocks usually do not continue to increase in price in the

TABLE 9.2 PERCENTAGE CHANGES IN THE DJIA DURING AND AFTER A RECESSION

	PERCENTAGE CHANGES IN DJIA	
RECESSIONARY PERIOD	DURING RECESSION	TWELVE MONTHS AFTER ECONOMIC TROUGH
1929–33	52.7%	61.7%
1937–38	40.3	− 3.8
1945	22.8	−12.7
1948–49	17.7	18.2
1953–54	37.1	33.6
1957–58	8.5	32.2
1960–61	16.9	6.1
1969–70	25.8	4.6
1973–75	36.2	23.9
1980	18.6	5.8
Average	27.8%	17.0%

SOURCE: Alfred L. Malabre, Jr., "Perverse Stocks: Just As the Economy May be Recovering, Share Prices Wobble," *Wall Street Journal*, (February 2, 1983): p. 1. Reprinted by permission.

latter phase of the expansion, stocks could be sold up to eight months prior to the peak in economic activity.

3. Stocks should be purchased approximately six months into a recession.[12]

The importance of purchasing stocks prior to the trough in the business cycle is illustrated in Table 9.2. This table shows that the largest gains in stock prices occur *during* the recession, with smaller gains occurring in the twelve-month period following the economic trough. This occurs because stock prices increase prior to the trough in the economic cycle.

The Business Cycle

The National Bureau of Economic Research identifies the specific months of the peaks and troughs in a business cycle. Officially, a decline in economic activity is classified as a recession when there have been two consecutive monthly declines in *real* GNP. The economy, like the stock market, fluctuates from month to month, but minor fluctuations are not classified as a recession.

The economy of the United States, and those of other industrialized nations, has periods of recession and periods of real economic growth. No agreement exists, however, about the causes of these cycles. Debate continues concerning the importance of such factors as monetary, fiscal, and trade policies. Often these arguments are supported by various economic theories, such as Keynesian, monetarism, neo-Keynesian, supply-side, and rational expectations. No one theory or viewpoint appears to be able to explain consistently the level and direction of economic activity.

---

[12] Raymond Piccini, "Stock Market Behavior around Business Cycle Peaks," *Financial Analysts Journal* (July-August 1980): pp. 55–57.

Most investors and financial analysts do not attempt to be experts in economic theories or in economic forecasting. The importance of the economic environment on stock prices, however, requires that knowledgeable investors have a basic understanding of what causes the business cycle. A sound and logical analysis of the causes of a business cycle is provided by Fischer Black.[13] His analysis indicates that cycles are caused by shifting supply-and-demand curves. These shifts occur because of changing technology and tastes of consumers. These changes cause wage differentials between different sectors of the economy and lead to layoffs and unemployment. The peak of the cycle occurs when there is a good match between the availability and demand of physical capital. Troughs in the cycle occur when there is a poor match between wants and physical capital.

Black's analysis also suggests that the desire for rapid economic growth contributes to the severity of the cycle. If investments are limited to potentially high-growth alternatives, the severity of the recession will be increased. Investing in both "high"- and "low"-growth sectors results in a more diversified economy, less subject to severe cycles. Investment in sectors that do not move together would also improve economic diversification. Economic cycles occur, therefore, because of the trade-offs that exist between (1) economic growth, (2) fluctuation in the level of economic output, and (3) unemployment.

Key Economic Variables

This section discusses key economic variables that are usually analyzed in an economic forecast oriented toward an analysis of common stocks.

1. LEADING, COINCIDENT, AND LAGGING COMPOSITE INDEXES Perhaps the most widely followed and reported economic indicators are the leading, coincident, and lagging composite indexes, published on a monthly basis by the U.S. Department of Commerce in *Business Conditions Digest*. Table 9.3 indicates the individual time series that are used to construct each of the three composite indexes. The standardization factors in the table are calculated by dividing the monthly percentage change for the series by the long-run average percentage change in the series. This process prevents a relatively volatile series from dominating changes in the entire composite index. The last column in the table represents the weight each series is given in calculating the composite index. The weight is based on the performance of the series relative to other series in the index. Weights above one indicate above-average performance. It is interesting to note that the series with the best performance in the leading index is the stock price series.

   The economic analysts at the Department of Commerce are constantly evaluating individual economic time series that might be used in one of the composite indexes. A desirable series should

   a. represent and accurately measure important economic variables or processes;

   b. bear a consistent relationship over time with business-cycle movements and turns;

---

[13] Fischer Black, "The ABCs of Business Cycles," *Financial Analysts Journal* (November-December 1981): pp. 75–80.

TABLE 9.3 COMPONENTS AND WEIGHTS OF THE LEADING, COINCIDENT AND LAGGING COMPOSITE INDEXES

	STANDARDIZATION FACTOR[1]	WEIGHT[2]
I. Leading Index Components:		
1. Average weekly hours of production of nonsupervisory workers, manufacturing	0.467	1.014
2. Average weekly initial claims for unemployment insurance, State programs	5.374	1.041
3. Manufacturers' new order, in 1972 dollars; consumer goods and materials industries	2.818	.973
4. Vendor performance, percent of companies receiving slower deliveries	3.840	1.081
5. Index of net business formation	.996	.973
6. Contracts and orders for plant and equipment, in 1972 dollars	6.194	.946
7. Index of new private housing units authorized by local building permits	5.064	1.054
8. Changes in manufacturing and trade inventories on hand and on order, in 1972 dollars; smoothed	2.530	.986
9. Change in sensitive materials prices, smoothed	.324	.892
10. Index of stock prices, 500 common stocks	2.633	1.149
11. Money supply (M2), in 1972 dollars	.417	.932
12. Change in business and consumers' credit outstanding	2.627	.959
II. Coincident Index Components:		
1. Employees on nonagricultural payrolls	.321	1.064
2. Personal income less transfer payments, in 1972 dollars	.502	1.003
3. Index of industrial production	.924	1.028
4. Manufacturing and trade sales, in 1972 dollars	1.021	.905
III. Lagging Index Components:		
1. Average duration of unemployment in weeks	3.587	1.098
2. Ratio, manufacturing and trade inventories to sales, in 1972 dollars	0.016	.894
3. Index of labor cost per unit of output, manufacturing—actual data as a percent of trend	.557	.868
4. Average prime rate charged by banks	.376	1.123
5. Commercial and industrial loans outstanding, in 1972 dollars	.901	1.009
6. Ratio, consumer installment credit outstanding to personal income	.062	1.009

[1] Standardization factors are computed over the period 1948–81.

[2] The weight for a given series is the ratio of its performance score to the average score of all series in that index.

Source: Ronald A. Ratti, "A Descriptive Analysis of Economic Indicators," *Review: Federal Reserve Bank of St. Louis* (January 1985): pp. 14–24. Reprinted by permission.

    c.   not be dominated by irregular and non-cyclical movements; and

    d.   be promptly and frequently reported.[14]

---

[14] Ronald A. Ratti, "A Descriptive Analysis of Economic Indicators," *Review: Federal Reserve Bank of St. Louis* (January 1985): p. 14.

The twenty-two individual series that have been chosen for the three composite indexes satisfy the above characteristics. The individual series also represent a broad array of sectors and activities in the economy.

Figure 9.2 shows the movement of the three composite indexes from 1952 to early 1988. The dark vertical bars on the graph represent recessionary

CYCLICAL INDICATORS

COMPOSITE INDEXES AND THEIR COMPONENTS

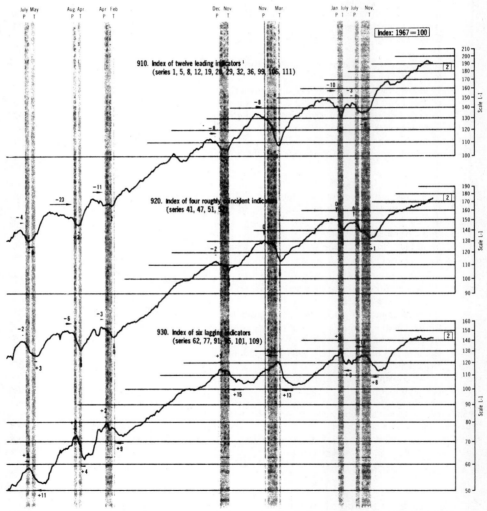

FIGURE 9.2 Composite indexes and the business cycle

Source: *Business Conditions Digest* (March 1988).

periods. A straightforward test of an economic indicator is to look at past successes in forecasting recessions. A casual analysis of Figure 9.2 shows that all seven recessions over the period were preceded by a significant decline in the Index of Leading Indicators. The Index of Coincident Indicators usually peaks at the beginning of a recession, and the Index of Lagging Indicators reaches a trough after the recession. The small numbers above and below the series during the recessionary periods indicate the leads and lags in months of the series with the peaks and troughs in the business cycle. As the figure indicates, however, the leads and lags vary considerably from recession to recession. The Indexes may also indicate false signals—where an index declines without being followed by a recession. Examples of this for the Leading Index are significant declines in 1966 and 1984. It appears that the Leading Index needs to indicate two to three months of consecutive declines to clearly signal an upcoming recession.

2.   MONEY SUPPLY Milton Friedman is generally recognized for his contribution toward understanding how the money supply and changes in the rate of growth in the money supply influence economic activity.[15] Beryl W. Sprinkel is also recognized for his studies relating the money supply to stock-price movements.[16] Sprinkel's analysis indicates that a decline in the rate of monetary growth leads bear markets by an average of nine months, and an increase in the monetary growth rate leads bull markets by an average of two months.

Many fundamental analysts consider the money supply in developing an economic forecast used in a stock market analysis. There is strong evidence that the money supply influences economic activity, but there is debate about its influence on stock prices. In an efficient market stock prices would lead changes in the money supply since the market would anticipate money-supply changes. Monetarists usually recommend that the money supply should be managed to avoid radical changes. A gradual, steady increase in the money supply would discourage inflationary expectations and promote long-term economic growth. To the extent this policy recommendation is implemented, the use of changes in the money supply to forecast stock movements would be limited.

3.   INTEREST RATES The level of interest rates influences economic activity through the capital investment process because low rates encourage capital expenditures by individuals and businesses. These expenditures provide additional employment, increased output of goods and services, and overall increases in GNP.

Historically, interest rates are closely correlated with economic activity since they usually move with the business cycle. Figure 9.3 illustrates this relationship for both long-term and short-term interest rates or yields on a variety of securities, including U.S. Treasury bills and bonds, corporate and

---

[15] Milton Friedman and Anna J. Schwartz, "Money and the Business Cycle," *Review of Economics and Statistics* (February 1963): pp. 32–78.

[16] Beryl W. Sprinkel, *Money and Markets: A Monetarist View* (Homewood, Ill.: Richard D. Irwin, 1971).

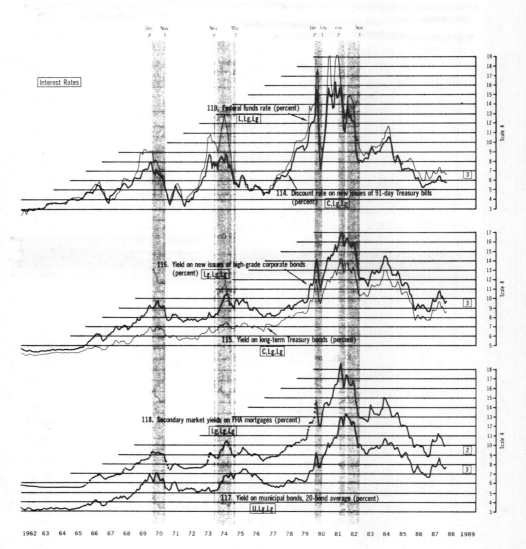

FIGURE 9.3 Interest rates and economic activity
Source: *Business Conditions Digest* (March 1988): p. 34.

municipal bonds, and secondary mortgage yields. If this relationship continues in the future, interest rate and GNP forecasts may be quite similar in terms of their implications for stock prices.

One alternative to an actual forecast of interest rates is to use the observed yield differential between two types of securities. For example, the ratio of EPS to price or *earnings yield* on the S&P 500 could be compared to the yield on high-grade corporate bonds. An increasing or "large" difference between the yields is traditionally interpreted as a bullish signal for stocks. A second popular relationship is the ratio of the highest- to medium-grade bond yields to maturity. This relationship is known as the *confidence index* and is reported weekly in *Barron's*. When the ratio is "high" or is increasing, it indicates that investors are confident in the economy and are willing to invest in lower-grade bonds. "Low" and decreasing values of the ratio indicate a preference for high-quality bonds and a lack of confidence in the economy.

One study used the total return on the S&P Utility Index, less the yield on Treasury bills, to calculate a yield differential or risk premium.[17] Using the period 1964–1984, this study found five years (1968, 1969, 1972, 1975, and 1980) where the year-end risk premium was less than three percentage points. In four of the following five years, the *HPR* on the S&P 500 was negative (1970 was the exception). "Low" values of the risk premium, therefore, suggest a bearish stock forecast.

4. BUDGET SURPLUSES AND DEFICITS The state of the federal budget is often cited as a key economic variable. During the 1980s, attention focused on the historically large budget deficit and the inability of the President or Congress to agree on ways to reduce the deficit. Generally, the debate concerns the desirability of spending cuts versus tax increases as the primary methods to reduce the deficit. Typically, either method would be bearish for stocks since corporate tax increases would lower earnings and spending cuts may reduce the overall level of economic activity. The size of the present deficit and concern over the inability to reduce it have caused a reversal in thinking about the likely influence on stocks. Political announcements concerning possible agreements on spending cuts and tax increases are often accompanied by increases in stock prices.

In the 1880s, the country faced a different problem—a *surplus* of such a magnitude that the entire national debt could have been retired.[18] There was considerable political debate concerning how the problem of the surplus could be solved. Increases in spending failed to eliminate the surplus, so Congress resorted to eliminating outstanding debt by buying United States government debt. Unfortunately, this resulted in a contraction of currency in circulation which, in turn, caused an economic contraction. The problem of the surplus was finally solved by increasing expenditures rather than by cutting taxes.

Unfortunately, the United States currently has few periods of budget surpluses and more commonly has budget deficits. Attempts to deal with surpluses, deficits, and fiscal policy in general can have a significant impact on the economy. Determining the impact of these activities on stock prices is difficult, given the economic environment of the 1980s.

---

[17] Edward F. Renshaw, "A Risk Premium Model for Market Timing," *Journal of Portfolio Management* (Summer 1985): pp. 33–35.

[18] Alexander Dana Noyes, "God Help the Surplus!" *Journal of Portfolio Management* (Winter 1982): pp. 88–90.

5. TRADE DEFICITS The large trade deficits incurred by the United States in the 1980s has been a significant economic and political problem. Rising imports have reduced domestic employment in many sectors of the economy, such as textiles, electronics, and automobiles. The impact of the deficit on the stock market has often been significant. For example, the announcement in February 1988 that the trade deficit was $13.83 billion, well above the consensus estimate of $11.2 billion, caused large declines in the value of the dollar and a significant drop in stock prices.

6. POLITICAL FACTORS The influence of politics on the economy, through fiscal and monetary policies, should not be underestimated. A realistic economic analysis and forecast should therefore include an assessment of the political environment.

     Domestic *political risk* takes the form of changes in governmental regulations, subsidies, and tax policy.[19] An increase in political risk can damage financial markets by reducing the expected cash flows from investments and/or raising the required rate of return, resulting in a decline in the value of securities. A more serious reaction would occur if investors liquidated their securities portfolios in favor of cash or real assets, such as gold or real estate.

     The importance of political risk for financial markets can be demonstrated by studies that relate market cycles to political cycles. In an efficient market, the stock market should closely follow or lead political cycles that cause major changes in monetary and fiscal policies. Using the period 1926–1977, a study found evidence that supports a strong relationship between economic and political cycles.[20] This study found that there are market cycles closely associated with presidential election years. The evidence suggests a four-year cycle where stock prices peak in November of presidential election years. There also appears to be a two-year cycle where stock prices peak, on average, nine months following the election. The evidence supporting the two-year cycle, however, is not as strong as that for the four-year cycle. The implications of this study are that the period before the election is generally bullish and that the period after the election tends to be bearish.

Professional Economic Forecasts

Numerous economic forecasts are routinely published in business publications such as *Barron's*, *Wall Street Journal*, *Fortune*, and *Business Week*. The beginning of the year is a popular time for these publications to provide an economic forecast for the coming year. Often these forecasts are based on the economic analysis performed by economists at large banks such as Manufacturers Hanover, Citicorp, and Bank of America. Brokerage firms, insurance companies, universities, and mutual funds also provide economic forecasts that are often reported in business publications.

---

[19] Tamir Agmon and M. Chapman Findlay, ''Domestic Political Risk and Stock Valuation,'' *Financial Analysts Journal* (November-December 1982): pp. 74–77.

[20] Anthony F. Herbst and Craig W. Slinkman, ''Political-Economic Cycles in the U.S. Stock Market,'' *Financial Analysts Journal* (March-April 1984): pp. 38–44.

It is usually not feasible for individual investors to perform an economic analysis that can provide a forecast. A more practical approach is to rely on published forecasts provided by professional economic forecasters. A major problem with this approach, however, is that economists are notorious for disagreeing about the outlook for the economy. One popular solution is to use a consensus forecast.

1. CONSENSUS ECONOMIC FORECAST A *consensus forecast* is simply an average of published forecasts. It does not represent an economic theory but simply uses forecasts that are made by monetarists, Keynesians, and supply-siders. Table 9.4 provides forecasts for 1985 from a large number of economists and econometric services, along with the average forecast and the actual results for 1985.

    The accuracy of each forecast and of the consensus forecast is measured as the absolute percentage deviation from the actual value. For example, a forecast of 2.6 percent for real GNP growth versus an actual growth rate of 2.9 percent is a 10.3 percent error $[|(2.6 - 2.9)/2.9|]$. Using absolute values treats under- and over-estimation errors the same. In terms of the accuracy of the GNP forecast, notice that fourteen of the twenty-seven forecasts by individuals, and six of the twelve econometric forecasts, have errors equal to or smaller than the errors for the averages or consensus. On the other hand, some of the individual forecasts are very accurate, and some have very large forecasting errors. In terms of the inflation rate, only six of twenty-seven forecasts by individuals, and one of twelve econometric forecasts, have errors equal to or smaller than the consensus forecast. Finally, notice that the consensus forecast by individuals for the unemployment rate was equal to the actual rate, resulting in no forecasting error.

    One of the most widely recognized consensus forecasts is provided by Blue Chip Economic Indicators. This organization publishes a newsletter based on a poll of an anonymous, fixed sample of economists. The average of their forecasts is published as a consensus economic forecast. The logic of this approach is that it is difficult for an individual economist consistently to produce a more accurate forecast than the average forecast.

    Studies of the accuracy of consensus forecasts generally conclude that it is likely that the consensus will be "less wrong" than the forecast of a single economist. Using data over the period 1980–1983, one study found an average error of only 1.1 percent between the actual real GNP and the forecast.[21] The consensus forecast usually correctly forecasts the direction of the economy but has occasionally missed predicting an economic turning point, such as the recession in 1981. The evidence seems to indicate that the consensus forecasting approach is not as accurate as one might hope, but it does minimize the risk of using a single bad forecast.

2. PRESIDENT'S ECONOMIC REPORT In addition to the economic forecasts provided by private organizations, the United States government also provides a comprehensive economic forecast. The most widely known forecast is provided

---

[21] Peter L. Bernstein and Theodore H. Silbert, "Are Economic Forecasters Worth Listening To?" *Harvard Business Review* (September-October 1984): p. 38.

TABLE 9.4 ACCURACY OF CONSENSUS ECONOMIC FORECAST FOR 1985

| I. FORECASTER | PERCENT CHANGE IN REAL GNP ANNUAL RATE | | | | IVQ '84-IVQ '85 PERCENT CHANGE | | IVQ '85 UNEMPLOYMENT RATE | ERROR OF FORECAST (%)* | | |
	I	II	III	IV	GNP	PRICES		ANNUAL GNP	ANNUAL INFLATION	UNEMPLOYMENT
Robert J. Barbera E. F. Hutton	1.9%	4.9%	1.8%	1.8%	2.6%	3.8%	7.6%	10.3%	0.0%	8.6%
Jason Benderly Kidder Peabody	6.0	5.5	4.5	3.5	4.9	4.3	6.3	69.0	13.2	10.0
Robert G. Dederick Northern Trust	4.0	5.5	4.0	4.0	4.4	4.1	6.8	51.7	7.9	2.9
Heather Dillenbeck U.S. Trust	4.0	3.0	2.0	4.0	3.3	4.5	6.9	13.8	18.4	1.4
A. Nicholas Filippetto Monsanta	4.0	4.4	2.6	2.2	3.3	4.7	7.0	13.8	23.7	0.0
William E. Gibson Republic National Bank	4.0	4.3	5.0	4.8	4.5	4.1	6.8	55.2	7.9	2.9
Edward Guay Cigna Capital Advisers	3.4	6.0	6.4	6.3	5.5	4.0	6.8	89.7	5.3	2.9
A. Gilbert Heebner CoreStates Financial	4.4	4.7	3.3	1.7	3.5	4.2	7.3	20.7	10.5	4.3
Lacy H. Hunt CM&M Group	6.3	5.5	4.5	3.6	5.0	4.4	6.3	72.4	15.8	10.0
Edward S. Hyman, Jr. Cyrus J. Lawrence	5.0	5.0	2.0	2.0	3.5	3.0	7.3	20.7	21.1	4.3
Irwin L. Kellner Manufacturers Hanover	1.1	3.9	4.8	5.7	3.9	3.5	7.0	34.5	7.9	0.0
Ben E. Laden T. Rowe Price	4.5	3.8	3.6	2.7	3.6	4.4	6.7	24.1	15.8	4.3
S. Jay and David A. Levy Levy Economic Forecasts	-1.0	-2.5	-3.5	-3.5	-2.6	2.5	9.5	89.7	34.2	35.7
Tor Meloe Texaco	4.5	4.0	4.0	3.5	4.0	4.5	7.0	37.9	18.4	0.0
Lloyd T. O'Carrol Reynolds Metals	3.0	2.4	2.8	2.6	2.7	3.4	7.3	6.9	10.5	4.3
Robert H. Parks R. H. Parks Associates	6.0	6.0	4.0	3.0	4.8	5.0	6.6	65.5	31.6	5.7
Richard W. Rahn	5.1	5.3	5.1	5.4	5.2	3.3	6.6	79.3	13.2	5.7

Forecaster										
U.S. Chamber of Commerce										
Richard D. Rippe — Dean Witter Reynolds	3.6	5.0	3.3	1.6	3.4	4.7	7.1	17.2	23.7	1.4
Francis H. Schott — Equitable Life Assurance	3.0	3.0	3.5	4.0	3.0	5.0	7.0	3.4	31.6	0.0
Howard Sharpe — Bishop, Camp & Dewey	6.0	6.0	6.0	6.0	6.0	3.0	6.0	106.9	21.1	14.3
A. Gary Shilling — A. Gary Shilling & Co.	0.9	1.2	1.9	1.7	1.4	2.5	8.2	51.7	34.2	17.1
Allen Sinai — Shearson Lehman/Amex	4.3	4.2	3.5	1.9	3.5	3.8	6.8	20.7	0.0	2.9
James R. Solloway, Jr. — Argus Research	2.3	4.0	5.0	2.5	3.4	5.0	6.9	17.2	31.6	1.4
Albert T. Sommers — Conference Board	4.7	5.1	3.2	2.2	3.6	3.8	7.4	24.1	0.0	5.7
Martin B. Tolep — F. W. Woolworth	3.0	4.0	3.0	3.0	3.2	4.5	7.0	10.3	18.4	0.0
Robert P. Ulin — Bank of New York	4.4	4.2	3.9	3.3	4.0	3.9	6.9	37.9	2.6	1.4
John O. Wilson	4.5	4.0	2.7	2.2	3.4	3.6	7.0	17.2	5.3	0.0
Average	3.8	4.2	3.4	3.0	3.6	4.0	7.0	24.1	5.3	0.0
ECONOMETRIC SERVICES										
Chase Econometrics	4.1	3.2	3.6	1.0	3.0	4.3	7.2	3.4	13.2	2.9
Citicorp Info. Services	4.1	4.9	4.1	3.4	4.1	4.8	7.0	41.4	26.3	0.0
Data Resources	3.3	3.5	3.3	2.8	3.2	3.3	7.2	10.3	13.2	2.9
Evans Economics	4.1	4.0	4.3	3.7	4.1	3.6	6.8	41.4	5.3	2.9
FairModel	5.1	4.8	4.6	3.9	4.6	4.8	6.7	58.6	26.3	4.3
Georgia State University	5.4	4.4	2.9	1.7	3.6	3.7	6.9	24.1	2.6	1.4
Merrill Lynch Economics	4.3	3.6	3.0	4.1	3.8	4.1	7.0	31.0	7.9	0.0
Laurence H. Meyer & Assoc.	4.9	3.6	3.2	3.1	3.7	2.9	6.7	27.6	23.7	4.3
RSQE, Univ. of Michigan	4.7	5.6	4.8	3.3	4.6	3.4	6.8	58.6	10.5	2.9
Townsend-Greenspan	4.3	4.0	4.5	3.4	4.1	4.2	6.9	41.4	10.5	1.4
UCLA	5.0	4.2	3.8	3.2	4.0	3.5	6.9	37.9	7.9	1.4
Wharton Econometrics	4.9	2.9	1.7	1.7	2.8	4.1	7.2	3.4	7.9	2.9
Average	4.5	4.1	3.6	2.9	3.8	3.9	6.9	31.0	2.6	1.4
II. ACTUAL	3.8	2.1	4.1	3.1	2.9	3.8	7.0	—	—	—

* Calculated as absolute value of (Forecast-Actual)/Actual, expressed as a percentage.

SOURCES: Reprinted from March 22, 1985 issue of *Business Week* by special permission, copyright (c) 1985 by McGraw-Hill, Inc. Actual data from various issues of *Business Conditions Digest*.

in the President's Economic Report, prepared by the Council of Economic Advisors. This annual report is often accused of making an overly optimistic forecast because of political considerations. An objective analysis of the President's Economic Report is presented in the summer issue of the *Journal of Portfolio Management*. These annual critiques have been appearing in this journal since 1975 and are prepared by Raymond J. Saulnier, a former chairman of the Council of Economic Advisors.[22]

3. EXAMPLE OF A PROFESSIONAL FORECAST Excellent examples of a professional economic forecast, directed specifically toward the stock market, are two articles written by William S. Gray.[23] These articles provide an economic analysis and forecast based on key variables such as the growth rate in real GNP, inflation rates, and corporate profits. These variables are then used to analyze and forecast key stock market variables such as returns on equity, dividend payout ratios, and corporate bond yields. These estimates are then used to provide specific forecasts for the stock market (using the S&P 400) and for rates of return on stocks. The forecast made in the 1979 article concerning stock prices was surprisingly accurate.

   The update forecast published in 1984 predicted that the S&P 400 would reach 299 on October 15, 1988, from a level of 192 on October 15, 1983. In mid-September 1988, the S&P 400 was 306.95. It ranged from 255 to 393 during 1987 because of the October crash.

Relating an Economic Forecast to the Stock Market

Despite the use of an economic forecast in a traditional fundamental analysis, debate continues about the usefulness and correctness of this "top-down" decision-making process. As previously discussed, there is a strong relationship between earnings and the stock market. For example, a recent study, based on the period 1964–1983, found that changes in the yield to maturity on government bonds and changes in aggregate after-tax corporate profits explain over 50 percent of the changes in the S&P 500.[24] The changes in government bond yields and after-tax corporate profits were found to be almost equally important in explaining stock market cycles. Table 9.5 summarizes the empirical results of this study. Results such as those found by this study indicate the inter-relationships between two key economic variables and stock prices. On the other hand, approximately 50 percent of the changes in the S&P 500 are not explained by the model, suggesting that other variables are also important.

   In an efficient stock market, investors analyze available information and form expectations concerning future developments. Stock price changes therefore reflect these expectations, so that the stock market is a reliable indicator of business

---

[22] For a recent critique, see Raymond J. Saulnier, "The President's Economic Report: A Critique," *Journal of Portfolio Management* (Summer 1987): pp. 83–84.

[23] William S. Gray, "Developing a Long-term Outlook for the U.S. Economy and Stock Market," *Financial Analysts Journal* (July-August 1979): pp. 29–39; and "The Stock Market and the Economy in 1988," *Journal of Portfolio Management* (Summer 1984): pp. 73–80.

[24] Steven E. Bolten and Susan W. Long, "A Note on Cyclical and Dynamic Aspects of Stock Market Price Cycles," *Financial Review* (February 1986): pp. 145–49.

TABLE 9.5 ECONOMIC VARIABLES AND STOCK PRICES

Regression Model:

$$\% \Delta \text{ S\&P 500} = \alpha + \beta_1(\% \Delta \text{ LTINT}) + \beta_2(\% \Delta \text{ PFT}) + e$$

where $\% \Delta$ LTINT = percentage change in long-term yield-to-maturity on government-bond index, at half-cycle points in S&P 500

$\% \Delta$ PFT = percentage change in aggregate after-tax corporate profits, at half-cycle points in S&P 500

Results:

constant = α = 26.4285

VARIABLE	COEFFICIENT	BETA	F-RATIO	STANDARD ERROR
$\% \Delta$ LTINT	−1.5162	−0.4144	4.153	0.7440
$\% \Delta$ PFT	1.6411	0.7306	12.907	0.4568

coefficient of multiple determination = .5684 (adjusted .5055)

coefficient of multiple correlation = .7539 (adjusted .7110)

standard error of multiple estimate = 38.2919 (adjusted 42.2984)

SOURCE: Steven E. Bolten and Susan W. Long, "A Note on Cyclical and Dynamic Aspects of Stock Market Price Cycles," *Financial Review* (February 1986): pp. 146–47. Reprinted by permission.

activity. A different view argues that stock prices move because investors react to changing economic conditions such as liquidity, real income, and consumption-savings choices.[25] This demand-side viewpoint suggests that an analysis of current conditions affecting investors may be more appropriate in explaining stock market movements than a forecast of the future economic environment.

1. PRICE/EARNINGS RATIO Most fundamentalists would argue that the most important variable affecting stock prices is earnings. A key variable in an aggregate stock market forecast is therefore the price/earnings, P/E, ratio of the market. A study, using the period 1973–1980,[26] found that of the nine variables tested, the following five variables were the most important in explaining the market's P/E ratio:

a.   growth rate in EPS;

b.   dividend payout ratio;

c.   yield on high-grade corporate bonds, adjusted for inflation;

d.   rate of inflation as indicated by the CPI; and

e.   business failure rate.

The validity of this approach was confirmed by using the model to forecast the market's P/E ratio and making market-timing decisions based on the forecast. This strategy produced absolute and risk-adjusted returns superior to those of a buy-and-hold strategy.

[25] Robert J. Shiller, "Theories of Aggregate Stock Price Movements," *Journal of Portfolio Management* (Winter 1984): pp. 28–37.

[26] Frank K. Reilly, Frank T. Griggs, and Wenchi Wong, "Determinants of the Aggregate Stock Market Earnings Multiple," *Journal of Portfolio Management* (Fall 1983): pp. 36–45.

2. DIVIDEND DISCOUNT MODEL A traditional and popular model to value the aggregate market or individual stocks is the dividend discount model, DDM. Despite the popularity of the DDM, it has been criticized because of the difficulty of incorporating economic forecasts into the analysis.[27] Fundamentalists traditionally follow a "top-down" approach, and the DDM has been criticized because it tends to force a "bottom-up" approach that starts with a stock market or a company analysis rather than an economic analysis. A modification of the traditional DDM model may therefore be needed to adequately incorporate an economic forecast and to correct for the biases that exist in the model.

3. OTHER VALUATION MODELS In addition to the popular P/E and DDM models, many other models are used to analyze the aggregate stock market. Important questions about the desirability of a particular model deal with its ability to incorporate an economic forecast and to provide an accurate forecast. Studies have shown that a particular model may perform well in one economic environment but perform poorly in another.[28] Some models appear to perform better during periods of high inflation; others perform better during a weak economic climate with low rates of inflation.

These observations suggest that the ability to incorporate an economic forecast into a market forecast correctly depends on the model used for common stocks. One approach may be to select the common stock valuation model after completing the economic forecast. If the forecast indicates high inflation and economic growth, a model that stresses "growth," such as the DDM, may be appropriate. On the other hand, if the forecast predicts a weak economy, a "value-oriented" model may be more appropriate. A value-oriented model may be built around asset value and stability of earnings rather than earnings growth. These issues are discussed in more detail in Chapter 11.

SUMMARY

Two major topics were presented in this chapter: an introduction to common stocks and economic analysis. This chapter provides a foundation for Chapters 10 and 11 that deal with a fundamental approach to industry and company analysis.

An understanding of the characteristics of common stock and of the rights of stockholders regarding control, dividends, and liquidation provides a foundation for understanding the risk-return characteristics of common stocks. Common stocks are fairly homogeneous in their characteristics. However, individual common stocks can differ significantly in their risk-return characteristics. Traditionally, these differences were recognized by classifying stocks into categories

---

[27] Richard O. Michaud, "A Scenario-Dependent Dividend Discount Model: Bridging the Gap Between Top-Down Investment Information and Bottom-Up Forecasts," *Financial Analysts Journal* (November-December 1985): pp. 49–59.

[28] Robert D. Arnott and William A. Copeland, "The Business Cycle and Security Selection," *Financial Analysts Journal* (March-April 1985): pp. 26–32.

such as blue chip, growth, income, cyclical, etc. The development of modern portfolio theory resulted in empirical risk estimates, such as beta, that can be used to classify stocks.

A tradtionally fundamental analysis of common stocks is a "top-down" approach that begins with an economic analysis, used in the industry and company analyses. Historically, the stock market has been closely correlated with economic activity. Stocks, however, lead economic turning points by varying lead times.

As a practical matter, individual investors typically rely on widely published professional economic forecasts. Disagreements between economists concerning forecasts have encouraged the use of consensus forecasts. An economic forecast may be incorporated into a stock market forecast, using a price/earnings forecast, dividend discount model, or other common stock valuation models.

QUESTIONS

1. Briefly explain the top-down or three-step procedure that fundamental analysts use to analyze common stocks. What are the strengths and weaknesses of this approach?

2. Explain how economic and industry analyses and forecasts can be incorporated into the estimate of a common stock's value.

3. Common stock price movements are widely recognized as a reliable leading indicator of economic activity. If stocks lead economic activity, why do most analysts use an economic forecast to estimate common stock values?

4. Common stocks often experience a significant price decline that is not followed by a recession in the economy. What are some possible reasons for this false recessionary signal?

5. Explain the justification for using a consensus economic forecast. What are the advantages and disadvantages of this approach?

6. What is meant by the leading, coincident, and lagging composite indexes, and indicate how they can be used in an economic analysis.

7. Some studies have suggested that the results from the economic forecast should be used to select an appropriate model to value common stock. Explain the justification for this recommendation.

8. Explain how a stock dividend or split may influence a fundamental analysis of the common stock. Is the possibility of a stock dividend or split an advantage or disadvantage in holding a particular stock?

9. Compare and contrast the book and market value for a share of common stock. In your opinion, is the book value of the stock a major determinent of its market value?

10. Provide a clear distinction between a blue-chip and speculative stock. Do you think that betas for blue-chip stocks are generally below those of speculative stocks?

11. Would you expect that a company that has a high dividend payout ratio price would be a growth company? Would its stock be likely to be a growth stock?

12. Can a company be a growth company without its stock price experiencing growth? Explain.

13. How would the betas for cyclical stocks compare to those of defensive stocks? How would you classify a stock with a negative beta?

14. 1988 was a presidential election year. Did the stock market follow its usual pattern during the election year?

PROBLEMS

1. Assume that an economic analysis-forecast indicates the following for next year:

   Increase in corporate profits = 20 percent

   Dividend payout ratio expected to remain constant

   Long-term interest rates are expected to increase from 10 to 12 percent because of inflationary expectations

   a. Using the framework of the constant-growth dividend discount model, explain the likely impact of this economic forecast on common stock prices.

   b. Using the framework of the price/earnings ratio model, explain the likely impact of the forecast on common stock prices.

2. Suppose you discover that the common stock of JAM , Inc. is selling for a price that is 1.2 times its book value per share and it has historically sold for 1.7 times book value. Do you think that the stock is currently undervalued? Explain.

3. A fundamental analyst notices the following behavior of bond yields over the last six months:

	YIELD TO MATURITY	
MONTH	Aaa	Baa
1	8.2%	9.1%
2	8.3	9.4
3	8.2	9.5
4	8.1	9.5
5	8.3	9.8
6	8.4	10.1

   a. Calculate the confidence index for each month, using the yields.

   b. What economic and stock-market forecast is suggested by the trend in the confidence indexes? Explain.

4. Assume that an individual investor collects the following information about the economic forecasts of five professional economists:

	REAL RATE OF GNP GROWTH	
ECONOMISTS	FORECAST FOR NEXT YEAR	LAST YEAR'S FORECAST
1	2.0%	3.5%
2	−1.0	−2.0
3	2.5	4.0
4	3.5	2.0
5	6.0	5.5

   a. Calculate the consensus forecast for both years.

   b. Suppose last year's *actual* real GNP growth was 2.75 percent. Calculate the accuracy of each economist's forecast for last year and the consensus forecast as the absolute percentage deviation from the actual value. Compare and contrast the accuracy of each forecast with the consensus forecast.

5. A reliable economic forecast indicates that the long-term yield to maturity on U.S. Treasury bonds is likely to increase from 8 to 9.5 percent next year and that corporate profits are expected to increase 20 percent. Use the regression model illustrated in Table 9.5 to estimate the change in the S&P 500 based on the economic forecast. Does the S&P 500 forecast indicate a bullish or bearish stock market?

REFERENCES

Agmon, Tamir, and M. Chapman Findlay. "Domestic Political Risk and Stock Valuation." *Financial Analysts Journal* (November-December 1982): pp. 74–77.

Arnott, Robert D., and William A. Copeland. "The Business Cycle and Security Selection." *Financial Analysts Journal* (March-April 1985): pp. 26–32.

Black, Fischer. "The ABCs of Business Cycles." *Financial Analysts Journal* (November-December 1981): pp. 75–80.

———. "The Trouble with Econometric Models." *Financial Analysts Journal* (March-April 1982): pp. 29–37.

Bolten, Steven E., and Susan W. Long. "A Note on Cyclical and Dynamic Aspects of Stock Market Price Cycles." *Financial Review* (February 1986): pp. 145–49.

Castanias, Richard P. "Macroinformation and the Variability of Stock Market Prices." *Journal of Finance* (May 1979): pp. 439–65.

Dean, James W. "The Rise and Fall of Neomonetarism." *Financial Analysts Journal* (September-October 1985): pp.72–77.

Elton, Edwin, and Martin Gruber. "Marginal Stockholder Tax Rates and the Clientele Effect." *Review of Economics and Statistics* (February 1970): pp. 68–74.

Eisemann, Peter C., and Edward A. Moses. "Stock Dividends: Management's View." *Financial Analysts Journal* (July-August 1978): pp. 77–80.

Fabozzi, Frank J. "Bid-Ask Spreads for Over-the-Counter Stocks." *Journal of Economics and Business* (Fall 1979): pp. 56–65.

Fama, Eugene, Lawrence Fisher, Michael Jensen, and Richard Roll. "The Adjustment of Stock Prices to New Information." *International Economics Review* (February 1969): pp. 1–21.

Graham, Benjamin, and David Dodd. *Security Analysis*. New York: McGraw-Hill, 1934.

Gray, William S. "Developing a Long-term Outlook for the U.S. Economy and Stock Market," *Financial Analysts Journal*, (July-August 1979,): pp. 29–39.

———. "The Stock Market and the Economy in 1988." *Journal of Portfolio Management* (Summer 1984): pp. 73–80.

Grinblatt, M., R. Masulis, and S. Titman. "The Valuation Effects of Stock Splits and Stock Dividends." *Journal of Financial Economics* (December 1984) pp. 461–90.

Herbst, Anthony F., and Craig W. Slinkman. "Political-Economic Cycles in the U.S. Stock Market." *Financial Analysts Journal* (March-April 1984): pp. 38–44.

Ingrassia, Lawrence. "Recent Increase in Share Prices Has Led to Flurry of Stock Splits, Stock Dividends." *Wall Street Journal*, 27 Jan. 1983.

Jog, Vijay M., and Allan L. Riding. "Price Effects of Dual-Class Shares." *Financial Analysts Journal* (January-February 1986): pp. 58–67.

Malabre, Alfred L. "Perverse Stocks: Just As the Economy May Be Recovering, Share Prices Wobble." *Wall Street Journal*, 2 Feb 1983, pp. 1, 22.

McWilliams, James D. "Watchman, Tell Us of the Night!" *Journal of Portfolio Management* (Spring 1984): pp. 75–80.

Michaud, Richard O. "A Scenario-Dependent Dividend Discount Model: Bridging the Gap Between Top-Down Investment Information and Bottom-Up Forecast." *Financial Analysts Journal* (November-December 1985): pp. 49–59.

Muller, Frederick L., and Bruce D. Fielitz. "Standard & Poor's Quality Rankings Revisited." *Journal of Portfolio Management* (Spring 1987): pp. 64–68.

Noyes, Alexander Dana. "God Help the Surplus!" *Journal of Portfolio Management* (Winter 1982): pp. 88–90.

Piccini, Raymond. "Stock Market Behavior around Business Cycle Peaks." *Financial Analysts Journal* (July-August 1980): pp. 55–57.

Putka, Gary. "Raging Bulls: In Binge of Optimism, Stock Market Surges by Record 38.81 Points." *Wall Street Journal*, August 18, 1982, pp. 1, 19.

Ratti, Ronald A. "A Descriptive Analysis of Economic Indicators." *Review: Federal Reserve Bank of St. Louis* (January 1985): pp. 14–24.

Reilly, Frank K., Frank T. Griggs, and Wenchi Wong. "Determinants of the Aggregate Stock Market Earnings Multiple." *Journal of Portfolio Management* (Fall 1983): pp. 36–45.

Renshaw, Edward F. "A Risk Premium Model for Market Timing." *Journal of Portfolio Management* (Summer 1985): pp. 33–35.

Saulnier, Raymond J. "The President's Economic Report: A Critique." *Journal of Portfolio Management* (Summer 1987): pp. 83–84.

Shiller, Robert J. "Theories of Aggregate Stock Price Movements." *Journal of Portfolio Management* (Winter 1984): pp. 28–37.

Spooner, Malvin C. "Origin of Fundamental Analysis." *Financial Analysts Journal* (July-August 1984): pp. 79–80.

Spudeck, R., and R. Moyer. "Reverse Splits and Shareholder Wealth: The Impact of Commissions." *Financial Management* (Winter 1985) pp. 52–56.

Statman, Meir. "Growth Opportunities vs. Growth Stocks." *Journal of Portfolio Management* (Spring 1984): pp. 70–74.

Winans, R. Foster. "Investors Sue an Advisory Firm in Boston, Charging Loss of Millions on AZL Stock." *Wall Street Journal*, 18 May, 1983, p. 60.

CHAPTER 10

INDUSTRY AND COMPANY ANALYSIS

INTRODUCTION

After completing an economic forecast and relating the forecast to common stocks in general, the next step in a traditional fundamental approach is the *industry analysis*. The purpose of the industry analysis is to identify industries that can be expected to have the best relative performance over a particular investment horizon. For example, a pessimistic economic forecast suggests an investigation of "defensive" industries; an optimistic forecast suggests "growth" industries.

This chapter discusses the importance of industry analysis and suggests key variables that should be included in the analysis. It also discusses sources of information that can be used to obtain industry data needed for the analysis. The first half of the chapter concludes with four techniques to identify industries with the potential for above-average performance. Appendix 10A presents a brief illustration of an industry analysis, using the automobile industry.

The second half of the chapter introduces *company analysis*. Essentially, after appropriate industries are identified, companies within these industries must be analyzed. This approach suggests that the performances of companies within the same industry may be quite different. The company analysis attempts to identify companies with the best prospects within a particular industry. Appendix 10B illustrates a brief company analysis, using Chrysler Corporation.

INDUSTRY ANALYSIS

Definition of an Industry

In the broadest sense, an *industry* is a group of companies with common products and services. A classification of companies into industry groups is an attempt to identify similar companies that can be analyzed without regard to differing industry factors. For example, the classification would eliminate the problem of comparing a manufacturing firm with a financial services firm. The rationale of this approach suggests that industry factors have a significant effect on an individual company's performance.

Industry classification schemes vary considerably in the criteria used to represent each classification. A very broad industry classification is used by Dow Jones & Company to provide price indices from three categories: (1) industrials, (2) transportation, and (3) utilities. Figure 10.1 illustrates the price behavior of these three "industries" over the period November 1987–April 1988. A comparison of these indices reveals very similar patterns of price movements. There are, however, some notable differences that suggest the importance of an industry factor.

1. VALUE LINE INDUSTRY CLASSIFICATIONS The *Value Line Investment Survey* uses ninety-four industry classifications for the approximately 1,650 stocks that they analyze. A two- to three-page industry analysis and forecast precedes the individual company analysis for each company in the industry. Value Line also compiles price indices for each of these ninety-four industries

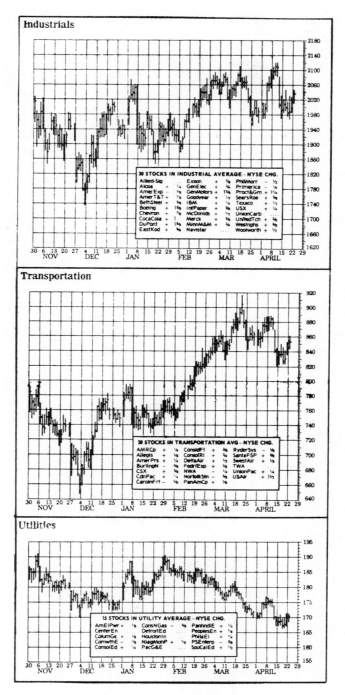

FIGURE 10.1 Dow Jones Industrials, Transportation, and Utilities Averages

Source: *Wall Street Journal*, 26 April 1988, p. 70. Reprinted by permission.

TABLE 10.1 VALUE LINE INDUSTRY PRICE PERFORMANCE AND INDUSTRY RANK

INDUSTRY	COMPOSITE PRICE CHANGE			IND. RANK NOW	IND. RANK 6 MOS. AGO	NO. OF STKS. IN IND.
	LAST 3 MOS.	LAST 6 MOS.	LAST 12 MOS.			
Japanese Diversified	15.8%	5.8%	89.6%	1	64	9
Investment Co. (Income)	8.3	5.1	−3.8	2	59	5
Cement	42.1	3.9	16.5	20	42	8
Home Appliance	52.8	3.0	4.7	47	25	6
R.E.I.T.	14.5	−0.1	−9.3	57	93	12
Tire & Rubber	36.0	−0.6	16.1	15	6	8
Steel (General)	21.0	−2.1	30.9	3	18	10
Steel (Integrated)	18.2	−3.9	29.4	24	5	8
Electric Util. (Central)	6.0	−4.7	−13.0	61	89	48
Textile	32.6	−4.9	3.0	68	73	9
Electric Utility (West)	6.3	−5.3	−8.9	45	91	18
Electric Utility (East)	5.1	−5.7	−13.3	72	88	34
Natural Gas (Distrib.)	7.8	−7.0	−13.3	55	87	31
Drugstore	22.1	−7.2	−3.7	4	53	7
Telecom. Services	13.5	−9.0	3.3	42	80	22
Petroleum (Integrated)	15.1	−9.5	−6.5	56	74	24
Machine Tool	22.0	−9.9	3.4	35	47	11
Telecom. Equipment	23.2	−10.3	2.3	37	38	12
Canadian Energy	16.3	−10.4	−0.3	39	23	14
Building Supplies	13.4	−10.7	−12.8	25	29	6
Metal Fabricating	23.1	−10.8	5.6	26	32	18
Toiletries/Cosmetics	18.0	−10.9	−2.6	12	11	11
Medical Supplies	26.9	−11.0	−2.1	5	16	31
Chemical (Diversified)	14.9	−11.1	9.4	7	24	13
Bank (Midwest)	11.0	−11.2	−5.9	76	85	17
Broadcasting/Cable TV	15.1	−11.7	8.6	77	43	9
Petroleum (Producing)	25.4	−11.7	−6.7	69	34	12
Chemical (Specialty)	15.8	−11.8	0.4	8	12	33
Auto Parts (Repl.)	21.2	−12.4	−10.4	63	69	12
Beverage	10.1	−12.8	−9.8	30	15	8
Food Processing	15.1	−12.8	−5.9	27	45	43
Furn./Home Furnishings	23.5	−13.3	−6.6	17	20	12
Publishing	25.4	−13.7	−3.5	70	31	21
Metals & Mining (Ind'l)	10.0	−13.7	16.7	6	17	8
Office Equip. & Supplies	17.5	−13.8	−6.3	11	56	17
Chemical (Basic)	6.5	−14.3	−9.6	60	51	7
Insurance (Life)	19.0	−14.9	−8.3	40	48	12
Building	23.0	−15.1	−14.8	43	39	35
Machinery	17.8	−15.3	−1.1	28	27	37
Tobacco	6.7	−15.4	−7.0	31	33	8
Coal/Alternate Energy	16.1	−15.5	−23.5	16	82	10
Grocery	13.7	−15.8	3.3	32	21	19
Packaging & Container	14.1	−16.1	−11.6	44	52	16
European Diversified	6.8	−16.2	−5.8	21	10	12
Bank	14.2	−16.6	−18.2	75	86	47
Food Wholesalers	20.4	−16.6	−18.4	33	65	10
Restaurant	16.0	−16.7	−21.8	59	71	20

TABLE 10.1 (*Continued*)

INDUSTRY	COMPOSITE PRICE CHANGE			IND. RANK NOW	IND. RANK 6 MOS. AGO	NO. OF STKS. IN IND.
	LAST 3 MOS.	LAST 6 MOS.	LAST 12 MOS.			
Advertising	12.5%	−17.1%	−15.6%	29	14	4
Industrial Services	15.3	−17.1	−6.3	9	9	22
Household Products	6.3	−17.3	−5.1	18	22	11
Paper & Forest Products	8.5	−17.4	−14.8	13	35	27
Shoe	27.2	−17.6	−10.7	50	57	11
Auto & Truck	21.3	−17.7	−7.1	58	50	10
Insurance (Diversified)	12.9	−17.9	−19.2	54	62	17
Machinery (Const. & Mining)	12.1	−18.0	7.7	22	37	12
Precision Instrument	22.1	−18.4	−16.6	65	61	25
Electrical Equipment	13.6	−18.5	−3.9	38	41	24
Retail Store	29.0	−18.6	−20.4	84	49	31
Steel (Specialty)	2.1	−18.6	−7.1	79	77	2
Maritime	28.9	−19.2	−4.5	62	55	6
Insurance (Prop./Casualty)	5.2	−19.4	−20.9	19	26	14
Newspaper	7.4	−19.6	−3.1	23	3	10
Hotel/Gaming	28.4	−20.2	−13.6	48	46	12
Railroad	16.5	−20.2	−6.6	71	67	8
Aerospace/Defense	18.0	−20.3	−16.7	52	63	29
Recreation	22.2	−21.0	−15.0	34	28	18
Computer Software/Services	7.8	−21.0	−8.2	14	8	15
Apparel	26.5	−21.2	−28.0	90	76	17
Real Estate	13.4	−21.3	−19.0	82	81	13
Multiform	21.0	−22.1	−16.2	51	68	46
Trucking/Transp. Leasing	11.4	−22.7	−25.3	80	84	14
Air Transport	23.3	−23.1	−16.5	87	70	17
Financial Services	13.7	−23.3	−21.7	46	36	20
Auto Parts (OEM)	23.4	−24.1	−17.0	85	66	9
Drug	7.9	−24.5	−19.9	41	19	21
Computer & Peripherals	8.3	−24.6	−16.3	36	13	39
Medical Services	9.6	−25.5	−28.1	74	79	12
Electronics	15.7	−25.5	−19.2	53	60	33
Savings & Loan	14.2	−25.9	−36.2	83	83	16
Retail (Special Lines)	19.6	−25.9	−26.9	66	72	34
Investment Co. (Domestic)	6.1	−26.2	−23.9	49	54	8
Natural Gas (Diversified)	10.1	−27.1	−27.5	88	75	18
Copper	−3.6	−27.3	0.1	10	4	4
Mfd. Housing/Rec. Vehicles	14.8	−27.4	−27.9	86	44	9
Metals & Mining (General)	4.8	−28.8	−24.0	64	7	5
Oilfield Services/Equip.	26.6	−29.9	−8.4	78	30	20
Aluminum	−1.7	−30.3	4.4	67	2	4
Precious Metals	−4.7	−33.6	−12.4	73	—	7
Securities Brokerage	10.0	−33.8	−41.8	89	90	11
Semiconductor	10.2	−35.2	−20.2	81	40	14
Toys & School Supplies	7.1	−36.9	−32.8	91	78	6
Bank (Texas)	4.9	−68.7	−84.8	92	92	3

SOURCE: *Value Line Selection and Opinion*, 8, April 1988, pp. 978–79. © 1988 by Value Line, Inc.; used by permission of Value Line, Inc.

and ranks industries by their probable price performance (timeliness rank) over the next six months. Table 10.1 provides data on industry price changes for ninety-two of the ninety-four industries over the last three-, six-, and twelve-month periods, along with the current Value Line industry ranks and their ranks six months earlier. The last column in Table 10.1 indicates the number of companies in each industry that are analyzed by Value Line. The industries in Table 10.1 are listed according to their relative price performance over the last six months. (Table 10.1 is on pp. 262–263.)

It is interesting to note that eighty-eight of the ninety-two industries experienced price declines over the last six months (October 1987–March 1988) primarily because of the market collapse in October. Over the last three months (January–March 1988), only three of the ninety-two industries posted negative price changes. A comparison of the current industry ranks with the ranks six months prior reveals some significant changes. For example, the Japanese Diversified Industry was ranked first (top timeliness rank) in March 1988 and sixty-fourth in October 1987. Other industries, like Medical Supplies, maintained or improved their relatively high industry rank.

2. STANDARD & POOR'S INDUSTRY CLASSIFICATIONS Standard & Poor's Corporation uses twenty-two major industry classifications and subgroups to compile and report industry data. Detailed industry data, analyses, and forecasts are given in Standard & Poor's *Industry Surveys*. This publication provides a "Current Analysis" for each industry, followed by a detailed "Basic Analysis" that can be ten to twenty pages in length, depending on the industry. In addition, the "Earnings Supplement" section of the *Surveys* lists each company in the industry and provides recent data on its revenues, income, and profitability. Each company is ranked on its performance in each of these three criteria relative to other companies in the industry. These rankings are designed to indicate companies with superior performance within the industry.

The Outlook, also published by Standard & Poor's, provides economic, industry, and company analyses and forecasts. The industry analysis usually takes the form of a discussion of the "best and worst" industries based on past performance and makes recommendations for the following year. Individual stocks in each of the recommended industries are also discussed. Table 10.2 provides information concerning nine industries recommended for 1988. This group of nine industries was selected by S&P 500 analysts as "the best situated, based on earnings prospects and current market valuations." Table 10.2 also gives the companies that are recommended in each industry group.

3. STANDARD INDUSTRIAL CLASSIFICATIONS The most comprehensive and detailed system of industry classification is the Standard Industrial Classification, SIC, codes. This system was developed by the federal government through the Office of Management and Budget. Definitions of each "industry" or classification, and types of business that meet these definitions, are given in the *Standard Industrial Classification Manual* that was published in 1972.

This system uses a four-digit numerical code to represent each industry. The first two digits of the code represent the "major" industry group. The ten codes that are used to represent the major industries are:

01 to 09	Agriculture, forestry, and fishing
10 to 14	Mining
15 to 27	Construction
20 to 39	Manufacturing
40 to 49	Transportation, communication, electric, gas, and sanitary services
50 to 59	Wholesale and retail trade
60 to 67	Finance, insurance, and real estate
70 to 89	Services
91 to 97	Government
99	Nonclassifiable

For example, a code 17-- represents one segment of the construction industry. The last two digits of the code provide more details concerning the industry. The entire code 1711 represents air conditioning, plumbing, and heating contractors. Based on this system, there are literally thousands of four-digit codes that can be used to classify accurately any type of business or organization.

There are several ways the SIC codes can be used in an industry analysis. First, if an analyst has an interest in a particular industry, the four-digit SIC code can be determined by using an alphabetical listing of the codes.[1] The code can then be used to obtain specific industry data from sources such as the *U.S. Industrial Outlook* published by the U.S. Department of Commerce.

Second, the codes can be used to identify all companies in a particular code. Publications such as Standard & Poor's *Corporate Records* and Moody's *Industrial Manual* indicate SIC codes for companies included in their manuals. Lists are then compiled that indicate all the companies in each four-digit SIC code.[2]

One problem with using the SIC codes is that many large publicly traded companies have a large number of codes because many companies are diversified both vertically and horizontally, even into areas not related to their principal business. The detailed criteria used by the SIC system, therefore requires that a single company be assigned multiple SIC codes. The analysis of the company would therefore require an identification of its principal industry or an analysis of each of the primary industries in which the company operates.

In addition to their usefulness in analyzing publicly traded companies, the SIC codes are also used to classify privately held business. Publications such as the *Million Dollar Directory*, by Dun's Marketing Service, use the SIC system to classify both private and publicly traded companies by geographic region. This information can be useful to an analyst if the economic forecast indicates that one area of the country has better prospects than other areas.

---

[1] For example. see Volume T–Z of Standard & Poor's *Corporate Records*.

[2] For example, see the "blue section" of Volume T–Z of Standard & Poor's *Corporate Records*.

TABLE 10.2 STANDARD & POOR'S INDUSTRY AND COMPANY RECOMMENDATIONS: Favored stocks in favored groups

	EARNINGS $ PER SHARE			INDIC. DIVD.	†PAYOUT RATIO	YIELD %	1987–88 PRICE RANGE	CURRENT PRICE	% BELOW 1987–88 HIGH	†P/E RATIO
	5-YEAR GROWTH RATE	1987	EST. 1988							
Chemicals										
Dow Chemical	20%	6.50	7.50	$2.40	32	2.9	$199\frac{5}{8}-58\frac{3}{4}$	84	23	11.2
Ethyl Corp.	23	1.57	1.75	0.44	25	2.1	$32\frac{1}{4}-15$	21	35	12.0
Goodrich (B.F.)	d	3.17	4.00	1.56	39	3.5	$65-27\frac{3}{4}$	44	32	11.0
Monsanto	d	5.63	7.00	2.80	40	3.3	$100\frac{1}{4}-57$	86	14	12.3
Quantum Chemical	22	4.38	6.00	2.20	37	2.9	$88-42\frac{1}{2}$	77	13	12.8
Drugs										
*Abbott Laboratories	18	2.78	3.20	1.00	31	2.1	$67-40$	48	28	15.0
*Bristol-Myers	13	2.47	2.85	1.68	59	3.8	$55\frac{7}{8}-28\frac{1}{4}$	44	21	15.4
§Genentech Inc.	d	0.50	1.50	None	...	Nil	$65\frac{1}{4}-26$	40	39	26.7
Lilly (Eli)	10	2.83	5.00	2.30	46	3.0	$107\frac{1}{4}-57\frac{3}{4}$	77	29	15.4
*Merck & Co.	17	6.68	8.50	3.20	38	2.0	$223-122$	160	28	18.8
Schering-Plough	8	2.73	3.25	1.20	37	2.2	$57\frac{3}{4}-31\frac{1}{4}$	55	5	16.9
Warner-Lambert	d	4.15	4.90	2.16	44	2.8	$87\frac{1}{2}-48\frac{1}{4}$	77	12	15.4
Electric Utilities										
*Consolidated Edison	4	4.42	4.55	3.20	70	7.1	$52-37\frac{1}{2}$	45	13	9.9
Northern States Power	5	3.01	3.15	2.02	64	6.5	$39\frac{3}{4}-26\frac{1}{4}$	31	22	9.8
PacifiCorp.	1	3.60	3.50	2.52	72	7.4	$39-26\frac{3}{4}$	34	13	9.7
*Potomac Electric	14	2.11	2.30	1.38	60	6.0	$27\frac{3}{8}-18$	23	16	10.0
TECO Energy	7	1.95	2.15	1.34	62	5.6	$27\frac{7}{8}-20\frac{1}{8}$	24	14	11.2
*Wisconsin Energy	7	2.55	2.65	1.44	54	5.8	$28\frac{1}{16}-21$	25	14	9.4
Food										
*CPC Int'l	12	⁵2.81	3.30	1.44	44	3.2	$58\frac{1}{2}-26$	45	23	13.6
General Mills	d	²E3.30	²³3.75	1.60	43	3.2	$62\frac{1}{8}-40\frac{3}{4}$	50	20	13.3
*Kellogg Co.	17	3.20	3.80	1.52	40	2.9	$68\frac{1}{4}-37\frac{7}{8}$	52	24	13.7
Sara Lee	12	2.35	2.75	1.20	44	3.0	$49\frac{1}{8}-26\frac{1}{2}$	40	19	14.5
Pollution Control										
*Browning-Ferris	18	³1.15	³1.50	0.48	32	1.8	$35\frac{3}{4}-17\frac{1}{2}$	26	27	17.3
Rollins Environmental	58	³⁰0.60	³⁰0.95	0.08	8	0.4	$25\frac{7}{8}-11\frac{1}{2}$	21	19	22.1
Waste Management	31	1.46	1.90	0.36	19	1.1	$48\frac{1}{4}-27\frac{3}{4}$	34	30	17.9
*Zurn Industries	2	¹E1.55	¹1.75	0.68	39	3.1	$30\frac{1}{4}-15$	22	28	12.6

Railroads

Consolidated Rail	N.A.	3.62	3.90	$1.00	26	3.1	$40\frac{7}{8}$–20	32	22	8.2
CSX Corp.	d	2.78	3.25	1.24	38	4.1	$41\frac{3}{4}$–$22\frac{1}{8}$	30	28	9.2
*Norfolk & Southern	–11%	0.91	2.80	1.20	43	4.4	$38\frac{1}{4}$–21	27	29	9.6
Union Pacific	11	4.90	5.50	2.00	36	3.5	$86\frac{5}{8}$–$45\frac{1}{8}$	57	34	10.4

Regional Banks

§Citizens & Southern	9	2.52	3.25	1.12	34	4.5	29–$19\frac{3}{4}$	25	14	7.7
First Wachovia	13	3.24	4.15	1.36	33	3.6	$46\frac{3}{8}$–$30\frac{1}{2}$	38	18	9.2
Fleet/Norstar	11	1.85	3.15	1.00	32	4.0	$30\frac{5}{8}$–17	25	18	7.9
NBD Bancorp	12	3.47	4.45	1.32	30	3.9	$40\frac{1}{8}$–$25\frac{3}{4}$	34	15	7.6
PNC Financial	10	2.96	4.90	1.68	34	4.0	51–$33\frac{1}{4}$	42	18	8.6
*Security Pacific	– 3	[4]0.01	5.60	1.80	32	5.8	$43\frac{7}{8}$–$20\frac{1}{2}$	31	29	5.5
SunTrust Banks	12	2.17	2.40	0.68	28	3.0	$27\frac{3}{4}$–17	23	17	9.6

Telephone Utilities

ALLTEL	0	3.07	2.95	1.52	52	5.1	$34\frac{1}{8}$–23	30	12	10.2
*Ameritech	N.A.	8.47	8.75	5.40	62	5.9	$99\frac{7}{8}$–74	92	8	10.5
BellSouth	N.A.	3.46	3.70	2.20	59	5.5	$44\frac{1}{4}$–$28\frac{7}{8}$	40	10	10.8
Cincinnati Bell	12	2.01	2.15	0.96	45	4.2	$26\frac{7}{8}$–$19\frac{3}{8}$	23	14	10.7
NYNEX	N.A.	6.26	6.65	3.80	57	5.6	$78\frac{3}{8}$–58	68	13	10.2
*Pacific Telesis	N.A.	2.21	2.70	1.64	61	5.7	$34\frac{1}{2}$–$22\frac{1}{2}$	29	16	10.7
Rochester Telephone	2	3.20	3.90	2.27	70	6.0	$49\frac{3}{4}$–37	45	10	11.5
*Southwestern Bell	N.A.	3.48	3.70	2.32	63	6.3	$45\frac{1}{2}$–$27\frac{1}{2}$	37	19	10.0

Tobacco

American Brands	3	4.42	5.20	2.20	42	4.9	60–$36\frac{1}{2}$	45	25	8.6
Philip Morris	20	7.75	10.00	3.60	36	4.0	$124\frac{1}{2}$–$72\frac{5}{8}$	89	29	8.9
RJR Nabisco	8	5.02	5.75	1.92	33	3.9	$71\frac{1}{8}$–$34\frac{1}{2}$	49	31	8.5
UST Inc.	14	2.25	2.80	1.48	53	5.1	$32\frac{1}{4}$–$19\frac{1}{2}$	29	10	10.4

* Master List issue. § Over the counter. E-Estimated. d-Deficit in last five years. N.A.-Not available. ² Year ending May of following year. † Based on estimated 1988 earnings. ‡ Current indicated dividend rate as a percentage of estimated 1988 earnings. ¹ Year ending March of following year. ³ Year ending September. ⁴ After substantial increase in loan loss reserve. ⁵ Before one-time gain of $1.53.

SOURCE: Standard & Poor's *Outlook*, 24 February 1988, pp. 904–05. Reprinted by permission.

Importance of Industry Analysis

The previous discussion and the traditionalist's viewpoint suggest that industry factors have a significant influence on the performance of an individual company. This section reviews some of the empirical studies that have analyzed the *industry effect*.

One of the first major empirical studies of the industry effect was by Benjamin F. King.[3] This study analyzed the monthly returns over the period 1927–1960 of a sample of sixty-three common stocks traded on the NYSE. The stocks represented six industries (tobacco, petroleum, metals, railroads, utilities, and retail). The definition of the industries was broad, and the study used a limited number of stocks and, consequently, industries. King's analysis revealed the following observations:

1. The industry effect is significant but accounts, on average, for approximately 10 percent of the variance of returns for individual common stocks;
2. The importance of the industry effect varies significantly from industry to industry;
3. The importance of the industry effect within a single industry varies over time;
4. On average, the market effect explains approximately 50 percent of the variance of returns for individual stocks.

The observations from the King study suggest that, on average, the combined industry and market (economic) effects explain 60 percent of the variance of monthly returns, with the remaining variance due to company effects or other factors. The magnitude of these percentages suggests that the economic and company analyses may be more important than the industry analysis.

A study by Meyers updated and expanded the sample size used in the King study.[4] The data used in the Meyers' study consisted of monthly returns on sixty stocks from twelve industries over the period 1927–1967. Using the same time period but a different methodology, Meyers concluded that "King's results overstate the role of industry factors. . . ."[5] His analysis suggested that the industry effect was less important in the six new industries studied compared to the six industries used in the King study. Also, the industry effect seemed to be less important after 1960 than for the earlier period.

The results obtained by Meyers confirm the importance of the industry effect but indicate that the results cannot be extrapolated to industries and stocks in general. The importance of the effect appears to vary from industry to industry

---

[3] Benjamin F. King, "Market and Industry Factors in Stock Price Behavior," *Journal of Business* (January 1966): pp. 139–90.

[4] Stephen L. Meyers, "A Reexamination of Market and Industry Factors in Stock Price Behavior," *Journal of Finance* (June 1973): pp. 695–705.

[5] Ibid., p. 695.

and over time within industries. Because of the discrepancies between the King and Meyers' studies, a third major study was undertaken by Livingston.[6]

Livingston's paper demonstrates that different statistical procedures may reach different conclusions concerning the importance of the industry effect. Based on monthly returns, over the period January 1966–June 1970, of 50 companies representing ten industries, Livingston obtained results indicating that the industry effect is more important than indicated by the King and Meyers' studies. Based on these preliminary findings, Livingston constructed a much larger sample consisting of 734 companies in over one hundred industries. Monthly returns were calculated over the period January 1966 through June 1970.

Table 10.3 indicates the importance of the industry and market effects for eighty-eight of the industries in the Livingston study. The first column of the table indicates the level of significance for tests of the industry effect. Notice that approximately 66 percent (fifty-eight of eighty-eight) of the industries demonstrate significant industry effects at the .05 or lower level of significance. On the other hand, approximately 34 percent (thirty of eighty-eight) of the industries demonstrate no significant industry effects. The second column in the table indicates the residuals from the regression as a percentage of the total variance of returns. A statistical procedure was used to indicate the importance of the industry effect. Based on this procedure, Livingston concluded that "approximately 18 percent of total variance was explained by the residual industry effects."[7] This percentage is significantly higher than that indicated by the King and Meyers' studies.

The final column in Table 10.2 indicates the importance of the market effect in explaining monthly return variability. The market was defined as the S&P 500. The R^2s reported in the table represent the coefficient of determination or the proportion of variability in the dependent variable (stock's return) explained by the independent variable (market's return). The R^2s vary from almost 0 (.01 for meat packers and vegetable oil industries) to .43 for the hotel industry. The mean R^2 is 23%. On average, therefore, the industry effect explains 18% of the variability, and the market effect explains 23%. The remaining 58% is unexplained but essentially represents the company effect.

Livingston suggested that his empirical results have the following implications:

1. The importance of the industry effect for many industries confirms the logic of an industry analysis as part of a security analysis;

2. The significance of the industry effect suggests that portfolios should be diversified by industry;

3. Industry price indexes should help in explaining the returns for individual securities.

---

[6] Miles Livingston, "Industry Movements of Common Stocks," *Journal of Finance* (June 1977): pp. 861–74.

[7] Ibid., p. 873.

TABLE 10.3 IMPORTANCE OF INDUSTRY AND MARKET EFFECTS: Residual Industry Effects Estimated by Regression

INDUSTRY	LEVEL OF SIGNIF. OF X^2	RESIDUAL IND. FACTOR % OF TOTAL VAR.	R^2 WITH S&P INDEX	INDUSTRY	LEVEL OF SIGNIF. OF X^2	RESIDUAL IND. FACTOR % OF TOTAL VAR.	R^2 WITH S&P INDEX
Aerospace	.01**	.23	.21	Mach. Constr.	.02*	.26	.17
Aircraft	.01**	.52	.05	Mach. G. Ind.	.02*	.34	.22
Air Transport	.01**	.39	.26	Mach. Indus.	.01**	.24	.21
Aluminum	.01**	.30	.40	Mach. Metal Fab.	.01**	.22	.23
Auto Parts	.01**	.18	.25	Mach. Oil Well	.01**	.29	.19
Auto Trucks	.85	.27	.31	Mach. Spec.	.01**	.18	.22
Auto Temp Cntrl.	.56	.25	.31	Mach. Tools	.01**	.29	.32
Automobile	.01**	.30	.40	Manu Ind.	.33	.24	.23
Brewers	.40	.19	.14	Meat Packers	.01**	.41	.01
Building Mat.	.01**	.26	.32	Metal Work	.08	.28	.14
Business Forms	.84	.31	.21	Metal Mis.	.01**	.20	.31
Cement	.01**	.32	.34	Motion Pict.	.77	.24	.22
Chemicals	.01**	.16	.35	Newspapers	.17	.37	.22
Chem Prep.	.98	.15	.27	Off & Bus Equip	.01**	.27	.26
Cigarette	.01**	.52	.21	Oil Crude	.08	.28	.16
Coal	.02*	.41	.24	Oil Intgrt Dom.	.01**	.21	.25
Confectioners	.26	.30	.16	Oil Intgrt Int.	.01**	.36	.33
Containers	.01**	.22	.35	Paint	.07	.39	.11
Copper	.01**	.44	.30	Paper	.01**	.25	.30
Cosmetics	.01**	.23	.31	Paper Contain.	.03*	.22	.22
Dept. Stores	.20	.38	.04	Photographic	.01**	.40	.23
Distillers	.77	.21	.12	Publishing	.01**	.22	.31
Drugs	.01**	.20	.30	Publ. Books	.06	.43	.13
Eating + Hotel	.01**	.26	.23	Radio TV Brdc.	.01**	.23	.42
El Equip.	.50	.19	.21	Radio TV Manu.	.01**	.42	.28
El Hshld App.	.62	.21	.39	Rlrd Equip	.02*	.22	.29
El + Electronic	.01**	.21	.33	Real Estate	.44	.30	.31
Electronics	.01**	.25	.22	Shipbuilding	.49	.33	.12
Electron Comp.	.01**	.32	.17	Shoes	.03*	.40	.06
El Ind Cntrl.	.13	.24	.40	Small Loan	.01**	.25	.24
Eng Lab Equip.	.10	.30	.26	Soaps	.66	.30	.10
Finance	.08	.28	.33	Soft Drinks	.07	.26	.30
Food Bakers	.05*	.29	.23	Steam Gen. Mach.	.02*	.39	.29
Food Biscuit	.48	.30	.28	Steel	.01**	.30	.27
Food Canned	.05*	.42	.18	Sugarcane Rf.	.64	.34	.04
Food Chains	.01**	.31	.08	Telephone	.01**	.27	.34
Food Dairy	.21	.31	.32	Textile Appor.	.03*	.22	.18
Food Packed	.45	.33	.15	Textile Prod.	.01**	.22	.14
Forest Prod.	.01**	.28	.34	Tire Rubber	.01**	.21	.27
Gold Mining	.01**	.75	.02	Trucking	.01**	.22	.28
Home Furnish.	.01**	.21	.34	Variety	.82	.25	.20
Hotels	.01**	.37	.43	Veg. Oil	.74	.40	.01
Lead Zinc	.20	.32	.16	Vending Mach.	.02*	.30	.15
Mach. Agric.	.01**	.46	.05	Wholesale	.04*	.28	.15

* Significant at 5% level
** Significant at 1% level

SOURCE: Miles Livingston, "Industry Movement of Common Stocks," *Journal of Finance* (June 1977): p. 872. Reprinted by permission.

Key Industry Fundamentals

This section briefly discusses the key fundamentals that are usually included in an industry analysis. It should be recognized that the importance of each variable may vary from industry to industry. Also, unique variables may need to be considered for certain industries.

1. HISTORICAL FINANCIAL PERFORMANCE Historical industry financial information is available from a number of sources that include *U.S. Industrial Outlook,* Standard & Poor's *Analysts Handbook, Value Line Investment Survey,* and Standard & Poor's *Industry Surveys.* Table 10.4 provides an example of industry data provided by Standard & Poor's.

   The historical financial data can be analyzed using ratio analysis that assesses the industry's liquidity, financial leverage, profitability, and asset utilization characteristics. The ratios and analysis of the actual data can be used to identify significant trends or developments in the industry. Analyst often use the historical data to calculate growth rates in key variables such as sales and earnings.

2. RELATIONSHIP OF INDUSTRY TO ECONOMY The historical relationship between the industry and economy can be useful in applying the economic forecast to a specific industry. A comparison of the industry's sales and profits during recessionary periods would indicate the impact of the business cycle on the industry.

TABLE 10.4 EXAMPLE OF INDUSTRY FINANCIAL DATA

				AUTOMOBILES THE COMPANIES USED FOR THIS SERIES OF PER SHARE DATA ARE: AMERICAN MOTORS; CHRYSLER; FORD MOTOR; AND GENERAL MOTORS.					
		1979	1980	1981	1982	1983	1984	1985	1986
Sales		401.51	331.87	350.53	329.55	385.64	457.99	524.03	586.95
Operating Income		32.20	5.73	17.99	22.71	45.41	52.64	54.30	57.46
Profit Margins %		8.02	1.73	5.13	6.89	11.78	11.49	10.36	9.79
Depreciation		16.89	21.21	21.71	21.52	22.64	22.73	27.34	31.46
Taxes		8.12	cr2.48	cr0.54	0.03	8.26	11.67	10.56	7.20
Earnings		9.58	d13.12	d4.27	0.06	15.90	25.39	24.35	22.94
Dividends		6.42	3.70	2.64	2.20	2.27	5.69	6.40	7.46
Earns. as a % of Sales		2.39	def.	NM	0.02	4.12	5.54	4.65	3.91
Divds. as a % of Earnings		67.01	def.	NM	36.67	17.42	22.41	26.28	32.52
Price (1941–43) = 10	—High	78.62	67.29	63.55	78.24	107.21	109.01	116.97	151.15
	—Low	60.74	47.33	39.87	40.53	72.02	83.04	94.46	110.95
P-E Ratios	—High	8.21	def.	def.	. . .	6.74	4.29	4.80	6.59
	—Low	6.34	def.	def.	. . .	4.53	3.27	3.88	4.84
Divd. Yield %	—High	10.57	7.82	6.62	5.43	3.85	6.85	6.78	6.72
	—Low	8.17	5.50	4.15	2.80	2.58	5.22	5.47	4.94
Book Value		99.76	82.44	74.92	71.02	83.27	106.91	119.60	137.77
Return on Book Value %		9.60	def.	def.	0.08	19.09	23.75	20.36	16.65
Working Capital		29.25	11.27	5.34	1.02	16.25	21.46	11.43	21.43
Capital Expenditures		30.94	35.92	38.37	29.99	20.66	31.56	44.21	54.05

SOURCE: Standard & Poor's *Industry Surveys,* 19 November 1987, p. A93. Reprinted by permission.

FIGURE 10.2 Automobile industry and industrial stocks.
Source: *Standard & Poor's Analyst's Handbook*, 1987 ed., p.6.

Regression analysis of key economic and industry variables may also reveal interesting and useful relationships. For example, it may help explain how industry sales relate to GNP, aggregate consumer spending, or industrial output.

3. RELATIONSHIP OF INDUSTRY TO STOCK MARKET Industry stock prices may exhibit different patterns than do stocks in general because of unique industry factors. Figure 10.2 illustrates how a common stock price index for the automobile industry behaves relative to the S&P 400 Industrials. As expected, the two indices are closely correlated, but the automobile index is much more volatile. Notice the declines in the automobile index are typically much more severe than those for industrials in general. Figure 10.2 also illustrates how prices for industrial stocks in general and automobile stocks behave during recessions (shaded areas) and during periods of economic growth. The price behavior suggests that the systematic (beta) and total risk (variance) of the automobile stocks are greater than the market's.[8]

---

[8] For a discussion of industry betas, see Barr Rosenberg and James Guy, "Predictions of Beta from Investment Fundamentals," *Financial Analysts Journal* (July-August 1976): pp. 62–70, and Frank Reilly and Eugene Drzycimski, "Alternate Industry Performance and Risk," *Journal of Financial and Quantitative Analysis* (June 1974): pp. 423–46.

4. IMPORTS AND EXPORTS A key variable for many industries is their ability to compete in international markets. Often this involves competition against imports in the domestic market and the ability to penetrate foreign markets. For industries that depend on international trade, factors such as currency rates, trade policies, and economic conditions in other countries would be important variables. The automobile industry is significantly affected by imports from Japan and Germany.

5. REGULATORY ENVIRONMENT Many industries are subject to regulations imposed by local, state, and federal agencies. The regulations may deal with areas such as the environment, job safety, and restraint of trade. Many industries such as mining, chemicals, and energy are significantly affected by these regulations.

6. LABOR ENVIRONMENT Manufacturing industries have historically had unionized workers; the status of wage contracts and bargaining positions of labor and management can be significant factors in the industry analysis. An assessment of these factors may reveal the likelihood of a strike or of major wage concessions that can have a significant impact on the profitability of the industry.

7. INDUSTRY STRUCTURE Some industries have a few large dominant firms, while other consists of numerous small firms. An analysis of the structure of the industry provides a basis for an analysis of the competition between firms in the industry and their relative market share. The structure may also indicate the life cycle of the products or services provided by the industry. This analysis may indicate the likelihood that new firms will enter the industry to exploit the early stages of a product's life cycle.

8. TECHNOLOGY AND INNOVATION Many new industries are highly dependent on technological developments in engineering, computer science, or health sciences. These "high tech" industries require careful analysis because of the rapid changes in technology and innovation.

Forecasting Earnings

The importance of economic and industry effects on common stock returns was discussed earlier in this chapter. This section reviews research that analyzes the stability of an industry's returns over time and the impact of industry earnings on individual firms. Analysts generally agree that the most significant variable determining stock prices is earnings. Fundamental economic and industry analyses therefore ultimately lead to an earnings forecast for the firm. The stability of an industry's returns and the possible influence on individual companies are important parts of an earnings forecast.

1. STABILITY OF INDUSTRY PERFORMANCE Forecasting industry earnings would be relatively simple if the industry had a stable earnings pattern. A forecast could be made based on an extrapolation of historical earnings. Unfortunately, research has shown that industries generally do not have stable returns, which suggests that earnings are not stable over time.

   A study by Tysseland over the period 1949–1966, using approximately 470 firms in a variety of industries, analyzed stock returns by industry and the stability of industry returns over time.[9] Dividing the total period of the study into subperiods of various lengths, Tysseland found "little consistency" in industry returns. This was especially true when relating returns over longer subperiods such as successive six- and nine-year periods. The returns were more consistent when shorter subperiods were used, such as successive one-year and three-year periods. Tysseland concluded: "The lack of homogeneity within industries is great and industry consistence in performance over time is unimpressive.[10]

Tysseland's and other studies suggest that forecasting future industry returns or earnings based on past performance is not likely to succeed. Extrapolating past results may be somewhat justified for short-term forecasts such as one year but not for long-term forecasts. Essentially, past industry performance should not be ignored, but it should not be the sole factor used to predict future earnings.

2. RELATIONSHIP BETWEEN MARKET, INDUSTRY, AND FIRM EARNINGS Several studies in the 1960s and 1970s looked at the importance of market and industry earnings to the earnings of individual firms. A study by Brown and Ball found that industry earnings explained 10 to 15 percent of the variability of an individual firm's earnings, and the overall earnings of the market explained 35 to 40 percent of the variability.[11] This conclusion suggests the importance of economic and industry analyses in attempting to forecast an individual firm's earnings.

A study by Magee also found that market and industry earnings influence firm earnings.[12] His results, however, differed from those of Brown and Ball in that the importance of market earnings was less, and market and industry earnings were approximately of equal importance. Recognizing the need to use an industry definition that would identify homogeneous firms, Magee used the SIC codes to select 165 firms from thirty-nine industries. The data for his study covered the period 1953–1966.

Magee used the following regression equation:

$$\Delta E_j = \alpha_0 + \alpha_1 \Delta E_M + \alpha_2 \Delta E_I + V_j \tag{10.1}$$

where ΔE_j = change in firm j's earnings from period $t - 1$ to t

ΔE_M = change in an economy-wide index of earnings from period $t - 1$ to t

ΔE_I = change in earnings index for firm j's industry from period $t - 1$ to t

V_j = random disturbance term

---

[9] Milford S. Tysseland, "Further Tests of the Validity of the Industry Approach to Investment Analysis," *Journal of Financial and Quantitative Analysis* (March 1971): pp. 835–45.

[10] Ibid., p. 844.

[11] Philip Brown and Ray Ball, "Some Preliminary Findings on the Association Between the Earnings of a Firm, Its Industry, and the Economy," *Empirical Research in Accounting: Selected Studies 1967, Journal of Accounting Research* (Supplement 1967): pp. 55–77.

[12] Robert H. Magee, "Industry-wide Commonalities in Earnings," *Journal of Accounting Research* (Autumn 1974): pp. 270–287.

The results of Magee's regression indicated that changes in economy-wide earnings explain 18.5% of the earning changes for individual firms and that changes in industry earnings explain 16.2%. Economic and industry earnings were therefore of approximately equal importance in explaining changes in a firm's earnings.

Based on the above results, Magee tested Equation 10.1 by using an investment strategy that bought stock in firms with reported earnings changes above those forecast and sold short shares of companies with earnings changes below the forecast. This strategy, tested using ex-post data, resulted in significant risk-adjusted excess returns.

3. REGRESSION MODEL A 1982 article by Eckel provides an empirical test of the usefulness of using a regression analysis of economic and industry variables in forecasting firm earnings.[13] This study also used the SIC codes to identify thirty-one firms; data over the period 1963–1975 were used. Eckel hypothesized that the earnings relationship would be interactive or have a nonlinear relationship. The regression equation was therefore stated in natural log form:

$$ln(E_{t+1}) = ln\ \alpha_0 + \alpha_1\ ln(E_t) + \alpha_2\ ln(\Delta GNP_{t+1})$$
$$+ \alpha_3\ ln(1 + \Delta I_{t+1}) + ln(e_t) \tag{10.2}$$

where
E_{t+1} = predicted EPS for firm for next time period

E_t = reported EPS for firm in period t

ΔGNP_{t+1} = predicted GNP for next time period

$1 + \Delta I_{t+1}$ = one plus the predicted percentage change in value of shipments for industry for next time period

e_t = the error term for time period t

One interesting aspect of Eckel's model is that he used published economic and industry forecasts as independent variables. The GNP forecast was based on the "composite diffusion index" for the leading economic indicators, as published in *Business Conditions Digest*. The industry forecast was the value of shipment estimates published in the *U.S. Industrial Outlook*. The *Million Dollar Directory* was used to determine the SIC code for each company in the sample.

The usefulness of Eckel's model was demonstrated by comparing earnings forecasts, using Equation 10.2, against "naive" forecasts based on an extrapolation of the firm's historical earnings. Using a six-month forecasting horizon, Eckel found that the model's forecasts were significantly more accurate than the naive forecasts over the four periods tested. The model forecasts, however, were not as accurate as management forecasts of earnings that are provided by some companies.

4. PRO FORMA INCOME STATEMENT A popular technique used by fundamental analysts to forecast both industry and company earnings is to construct a pro

---

[13] Norm Eckel, "An EPS Forecasting Model Using Macroeconomic Performance Expectations," *Financial Analysts Journal* (May-June 1982): pp. 68–77.

TABLE 10.5   INDUSTRY EARNINGS FORECAST USING PRO FORMA STATEMENT FORMAT

						CONSOLIDATED FINANCIAL REPORT & FORECAST OF 69 AUTO & TRUCK COMPANIES	
1983	1984	1985	1986	1987	1988	© VALUE LINE, INC.	90–92E
139.1	165.1	176.3	188.1	*200*	*200*	**Sales ($bill)**	*240*
8.8%	9.2%	7.6%	6.7%	*8.0%*	*7.6%*	**Operating Margin**	*8.0%*
4.2	4.4	4.5	5.4	*6.5*	*6.5*	**Depreciation ($bill)**	*6.0*
5.9	9.1	8.1	7.6	*9.5*	*7.1*	**Net Profit ($bill)**	*9.0*
330.0%	31.5%	30.2%	31.0%	*38.0%*	*37.0%*	**Income Tax Rate**	*35.0%*
4.3%	5.5%	4.6%	4.1%	*4.8%*	*3.6%*	**Net Profit Margin**	*3.8%*
6.2	8.1	4.1	7.0	*16.0*	*17.0*	**Working Cap'l ($bill)**	*13.0*
8.5	6.7	8.2	14.3	*20.5*	*22.0*	**Long-Term Debt ($bill)**	*17.0*
30.9	38.8	46.8	50.7	*55.0*	*57.0*	**Net Worth ($bill)**	*70.0*
16.2%	20.9%	15.5%	12.7%	*13.5%*	*10.0%*	**% Earned Total Cap'l**	*11.5%*
19.1%	23.5%	17.3%	15.1%	*17.5%*	*12.5%*	**% Earned Net Worth**	*13.0%*
15.8%	18.4%	12.7%	10.3%	*12.5%*	*8.0%*	**% Retained to Comm Eq**	*9.0%*
19%	23%	27%	32%	*27%*	*38%*	**% All Div'ds to Net Prof**	*31%*
5.7	3.9	4.5	5.7	Bold figures are		**Avg Ann'l P/E Ratio**	*8.7*
.48	.36	.36	.39	Value Line		**Relative P/E Ratio**	*.70*
3.0%	5.8%	6.1%	5.6%	estimates		**Avg Ann'l Div'd Yield**	*3.5%*

SOURCE: Value Line Investment Survey, 25 March 1988, p. 101. © 1988 by Value Line, Inc.; used by permission of Value Line, Inc.

forma income statement. Typically, four to five years of historical income statements will be provided, along with the estimates for the next one or two years. An example of this approach is given in Table 10.5. The advantage of this approach is that it bases the earnings estimate on individual estimates of key variables including sales, operating costs, taxes, etc. These key variables are often estimated using their historical relationships to revenues. This approach is the *percentage of sales method* discussed in most introductory corporate finance texts. Regression analysis can also be used to generate forecasts of individual expense categories and revenues.

Industry Selection

Selecting industries that are expected to achieve above- or below-average performance is the ultimate objective of an industry analysis. This section briefly discusses techniques and procedures that might be used.

1. RELATIVE STRENGTH   Relative strength measures have been traditionally used to select industries and individual companies. One measure of relative strength for an industry is the ratio of industry stock prices to the prices of stocks in general. If the relative strength ratios are increasing, the industry stock prices are increasing at a faster rate than that for stocks in general. If the analysts thought the overall market was bullish, industries with the highest relative strength would be attractive. A bearish forecast would indicate low relative strength industries. Figure 10.3 provides two illustrations of relative

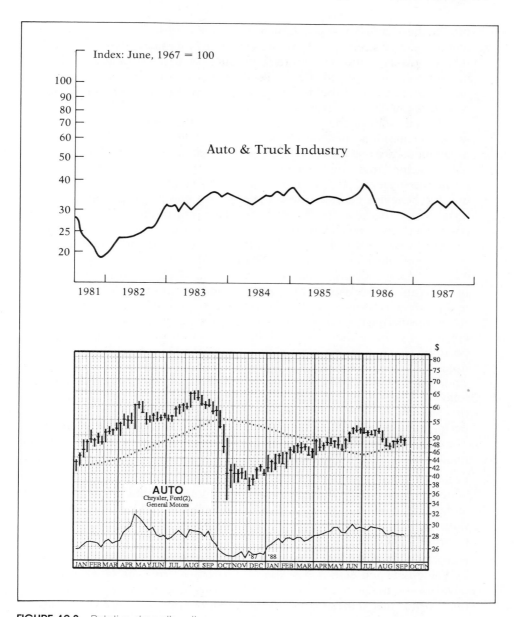

FIGURE 10.3 Relative strength ratio

Sources: *Value Line Investment Survey*, 25 December 1987, p. 1, © 1987 by Value Line, Inc; used by permission of Value Line, Inc. *The SRC Red Book*, (May 1988): p. 4.

strength ratios for the automobile industry. Values of the index for January–April 1988 show that increases in automobile industry stock prices have increased more than those of stocks in general.

Several empirical studies have tested the relative strength industry selection technique. A study of seventy-three industries by Akemann and Keller from 1967 through October 1975 used a strategy of selecting industries with the "highest" relative strength measured over a thirteen-week period.[14] The highest relative strength industry was identified by calculating each industry's relative strength ratio. The strategy of "purchasing the strongest stock group in a thirteen-week period showed itself capable of selecting investments that, on average, exceeded the performance of the market index by more than 10 percent annually, after transaction costs."[15]

The authors of the study suggested that the relative strength strategy works because it is applied to industries rather than to individual stocks. The use of industries and the thirteen-week observation period caused a "substantial averaging" that eliminated small price changes. The second reason offered is that the strategy identified industries exhibiting unusual price behavior and that the behavior persisted over a period long enough to provide excess returns. While this strategy did produce excess returns above the S&P 500, no risk adjustments were made to the excess returns.

A second empirical study of relative strength used one hundred industry groups identified by Standard & Poor's and data from the period 1969–1980.[16] "Each industry's stock price change for each year was calculated and used to rank the industries. The ranked industries were divided into quintiles, and portfolio returns were calculated for each quintile for the following year. After considering transaction costs, the highest quintile portfolio returns were consistently above the lower quintile portfolio returns. The highest quintile portfolio also had higher returns than the S&P 500 in ten of the eleven years used in the study. A comparison of the highest quintile portfolio's beta and standard deviation with the market risk measures indicated that the portfolio's risk was approximately equal to the risk of the market. In summary, this study concluded that there was a strong correlation between industry performance in the following year and the first and fifth quintile portfolios. The industries in the first quintile generally demonstrated superior performance, while industries in the fifth quintile generally had poor performance.

2. INDUSTRY BETA A number of studies have shown that portfolio and industry betas are more stable than betas for individual securities.[17] If the economic and overall market forecasts indicate a favorable environment for stocks, industries with betas greater than 1 may be appropriate. On the other hand, a pessimistic forecast suggests industries with low betas.

3. PUBLISHED FORECASTS As previously discussed, industry ranks are published by Value Line and Standard & Poor's. Brokerage firms and other investment advisors also make industry recommendations. Depending on the confidence the investor has in these forecasts, they can be used directly to make investment decisions or as a starting place for additional analysis.

---

[14] Charles A. Akemann and Werner E. Keller, "Relative Strength Does Persist!" *Journal of Portfolio Management* (Fall 1977): pp. 38–45.

[15] Ibid., p. 39.

[16] James Bohan, "Relative Strength: Further Positive Evidence," *Journal of Portfolio Management* (Fall 1981): pp. 36–39.

[17] For example, see Frank Reilly and Eugene Drzycimski, "Alternative Industry Performance and Risk," *Journal of Financial and Quantitative Analysis* (June 1974): pp. 423–46.

4. INDUSTRY DIVERSIFICATION The empirical research reviewed in this chapter strongly supports the observation that there are significant industry commonalities. The magnitude of these commonalities, however, varies among industries and over time. One implication of this observation is that portfolios should have industry diversification. The number of industries needed to eliminate diversifiable risk attributed to industry effects depends on the industries in the portfolio.

Illustration of Industry Analysis

Appendix 10A provides an illustration of a basic industry analysis, using the automobile industry. The procedures and techniques discussed in this chapter are utilized in the illustration. The illustration is also incorporated into a company analysis of Chrysler Corporation, presented in Appendix 10B. The next section of the chapter discusses the procedures used by fundamental analysts to analyze an individual company.

COMPANY ANALYSIS

Overview

The purpose of this section is to discuss the analysis of individual companies, using a fundamental approach. As the name indicates, the analysis deals with the key fundamentals of the company. The financial statements of the company are at the center of the analysis; typically, a five-year financial history of the company is analyzed, using balance sheets, income statements, and supporting notes prepared by accountants. The statements are analyzed using financial ratios with comparisons to industry norms and constructing *common size* or percentage statements. Historical growth rates for key variables such as sales and earnings are also analyzed.

Financial analysts often do not accept the financial statements as reported by the company. As discussed later in this section, the statements are often adjusted or "normalized" to make them more comparable over time and to eliminate any unusual or nonrecurring events that are unlikely to recur. This normalization procedure is designed to indicate the "normal" operating earnings of the firm which may be different from the reported or accounting earnings.

In addition to an analysis of the financial statements, a fundamental analysis of a company considers other factors. These include quality of management, employees and labor relations, and the overall business and financial plans of the company.

Analysis of Financial Statements

An essential source of information for a company analysis is the financial statements of the firm over the most recent five-year period. Five years is often cited as a rule of thumb, but many analysts use a longer period such as ten years. The appropriate period depends on the particular company and industry. Ideally, the period should cover periods of economic growth and of recession, so that the performance of the company in both types of environment can be analyzed. Also, the industry may be subject to growth cycles that require a longer period. Essentially, the length of the period should include both "good" and "bad" years for the company and the industry.

1. FINANCIAL RATIOS There are literally hundreds of financial ratios that can be constructed from data on the balance sheet and income statement. All of these ratios, however, can be categorized into four groups: liquidity, leverage, activity, and profitability ratios. Table 10.6 illustrates fourteen of the more commonly used ratios. Other ratios are often calculated, such as the P/E ratio, earning yields, and growth rates. These are discussed later in this section.

Liquidity ratios indicate the company's ability to pay its short-term obligations. Typically, these ratios relate current assets and current liabilities. It is usually advisable to analyze individual current assets and liabilities in addition to the totals. For example, cash and near-cash items represent the most liquid asset of the firm. "Low" cash may indicate a significant liquidity problem, even though the relationship between total current assets and current liabilities is acceptable. Inventory is usually viewed as a firm's least-liquid asset. The quick or acid ratio is a more conservative measure of liquidity since it subtracts inventory from total current assets.

Leverage ratios measure the extent to which a company is using debt financing and its ability to pay interest expense and other obligations associated with debt or "debt-like" financing from operating earnings. The importance of debt in the capital structure can be measured by comparing debt

TABLE 10.6 FINANCIAL RATIOS

I. LIQUIDITY RATIOS	
1. Current	= current assets/current liabilities
2. Quick or Acid	= (current assets − inventory)/current liabilities
II. LEVERAGE RATIOS	
1. Debt	= total liabilities/total assets
2. Debt/equity	= long-term liabilities/stockholders' equity
3. Times interest earned	= earnings before interest and taxes/interest expense
4. Fixed charge coverage	= (earnings before interest and taxes + lease expense)/(interest expense + lease expense)
III. ACTIVITY RATIOS	
1. Inventory turnover	= cost of goods sold/inventory
2. Asset turnover	= sales/total assets
3. Fixed asset turnover	= sales/fixed assets
4. Working capital turnover	= sales/net working capital
5. Average collection period	= accounts receivable/average daily credit sales
IV. PROFITABILITY RATIOS	
1. Profit margin	= net income/sales
2. Return on investment	= net income/total assets
3. Return on equity	= net income/stockholders' equity

to total assets or to stockholders' equity. The firm's ability to meet its interest expense is reflected in the times-interest-earned ratio. Many firms lease assets rather than borrow funds to finance their purchase. The fixed-charge-coverage ratio indicates the firm's ability to meet interest and lease expenses from current operating earnings.

Activity ratios relate assets to revenues and are sometimes referred to as *turnover* ratios. This category of ratios indicates how well a firm is using its assets. Another interpretation is the level of sales generated by the level of assets. Since these ratios essentially measure the efficiency of asset utilization, higher ratios are generally more desirable.

Profitability ratios indicate the relationship between profits, assets, and sales. The profit margin ratio relates the amount of profits after taxes to sales. The return on investment, ROI, and return on equity, ROE, ratios relate profit after taxes to total assets and to stockholders' equity, respectively.

Prior to calculating ratios, it is advisable to obtain industry norms. As discussed in the industry analysis section, there are a number of sources of industry financial norms. Unfortunately, the number of ratios provided and the formulas used to calculate the ratios vary from source to source. For example, the inventory turnover ratio may be calculated using sales or cost of goods in the numerator. The source of the norms should be consulted to determine the exact formula for each ratio.

Once norms are obtained, it is useful to compare the firm's ratios to the norms. It is usually not very helpful, however, to limit the analysis to observing which company ratios are above or below the norm. Typically, most companies will have ratios both above and below the norms. If a particular ratio appears to be significantly different from the norm, the analyst should attempt to determine *why*. For example, is the asset turnover ratio low because of an unusually high level of current or fixed assets or because of declining sales relative to the level of assets? A skilled analyst can often answer these questions by using several ratios.

The analysis of the financial ratios should also detect any trends in the ratios. Using a five-year financial history provides the data that can be used to observe any significant changes. It is also important to distinguish between trends and cyclical or irregular changes in ratios. For example, a decline in liquidity for a single year may not indicate a trend or cycle.

2. PERCENTAGE STATEMENTS It is common to convert balance sheets and income statements to percentages with the income statement items expressed as a percentage of total sales and the balance sheet items as a percentage of total assets. These statements are often referred to as *common size statements* since they remove the influence of size, and changes in the size, of the firm.

3. ANALYSIS OF GROWTH RATES Financial analysts typically calculate annual growth rates for key variables such as revenues, earnings, and dividends. The growth rates may be used in forecasting or in comparing the firm with the industry or other firms. As the next chapter indicates, earnings growth is recognized as one of the most important variables in a fundamental analysis.

Growth rates should assume compounding. For example, annual growth rates should be calculated assuming annual compounding, quarterly rates assuming quarterly compounding. Suppose a firm's EPS increased from $2 in 1983 to $5 in 1988. Equation 10.3 illustrates a procedure for calculating the annual compounded rate of growth:

$$g = \sqrt[n]{\frac{EPS_n}{EPS_0}} - 1 \tag{10.3}$$

$$g = \sqrt[5]{\$5/\$2} - 1$$

$$g = (2.5)^{.2} - 1$$

$$= 20.11\%$$

Notice that there are six years in the period 1983–1988 but only five periods of growth. Therefore, n in Equation 10.3 represents the periods of growth.[18]

The use of the beginning and ending period to calculate the annual growth rate essentially ignores the growth rate for the individual years during the period. However, it is important to look at the *stability* of growth. The attractiveness of a high annualized five-year growth rate may be significantly reduced if rates for individual years are volatile. One measure that has been suggested for the stability of growth:[19]

$$Stab_{EPS} = \frac{\sigma_{EPS}\sqrt{1 - R^2}}{\overline{EPS}} \tag{10.4}$$

where $Stab_{EPS}$ = measure of EPS stability

σ_{EPS} = standard deviation of EPS over the time series

R^2 = coefficient of determination from the linear trend line of EPS

$\overline{EPS}$ = arithmetic mean of the EPS time series

If all the annual *EPS*s fall exactly on the trend line, then $R^2 = 1$, and $Stab_{EPS} = 0$. Lower values of $Stab_{EPS}$, therefore, imply stability of earnings. This approach suggests that historical earnings growth rates should be used only as an estimate of future growth if $Stab_{EPS}$ is relatively "low."

4. QUALITY OF FINANCIAL STATEMENTS Financial analysts are aware that the "quality" of statements may vary from firm to firm.[20] This occurs because generally accepted accounting principles, GAAP, allow for considerable flexibility in the treatment of certain transactions and reporting (or not reporting) certain items. Financial analysts generally feel that GAAP need to be tightened so that there is more *consistency* in statements, over time and between firms.

---

[18] Many calculators do not have root functions above the square root but do have y^x functions. Remember that $\sqrt[y]{X} = X^{1/y}$, so that the y^x function can be used to find higher-order roots.

[19] T. Daniel Coggin and John E. Hunter, "Measuring Stability and Growth in Annual EPS," *Journal of Portfolio Management* (Winter 1983): pp. 75–78.

[20] Financial publications often publish articles dealing with the quality of financial statements. For example, see Lee Berton, "Loose Ledgers, Many Firms Hide Debt to Give Them an Aura of Financial Strength," *Wall Street Journal*, 13 Dec. 1983, pp. 1, 12, and Gregory Stricharchuk, "More Ailing Concerns are Firing Auditors in Hopes of Keeping Bad News from Public," *Wall Street Journal*, 12 May 1983, p. 35.

Accountants argue, however, that *flexibility* is more important than consistency.

Opinions and research differ on the importance of an analyst's "adjusting" or *normalizing* statements to improve their quality. One study used a sample of ninety-six firms to test the significance of normalization to the financial ratios.[21] Adjustments included converting all firms to FIFO inventory accounting, using tax-reported depreciation expense and net asset values, eliminating the effects of deferred tax accounting, recognizing pension obligations as liabilities, and consolidating wholly owned subsidiaries. Net income and financial ratios based on the reported and normalized statements were then compared. With few exceptions, the correlations between the net income and financial ratios from both sets of statements were very high. The magnitude of the correlations, however, depended on the particular adjustment. For example, based only on the FIFO adjustment, the correlation was 99 percent. The adjustment for the consolidation of wholly owned subsidiaries had the largest impact; based on this adjustment, the correlation of the accounts receivable turnover ratios was only 43 percent. The importance of normalization on net income and financial ratios, therefore, depends on the type of adjustment made.

Determining the quality of a financial statement is somewhat subjective. A study using a survey of accountants, security analysts, and financial managers discovered a number of factors that can be used to assess the quality of a statement.[22] This study identified thirty-six "situations" dealing with a company's financial position that influence the quality of earnings. Examples of situations that *reduce* the quality of earnings included

(1) an unwarranted change in pension accounting, such as actuarial assumptions dealing with interest rates and mortality;

(2) reporting lower depreciation expense as a percentage of fixed assets, coupled with a reduction in repairs and maintenance expense;

(3) reporting disappointing earnings for the year and significant reductions in "discretionary" costs such as advertising;

(4) substantial changes in deferred charges, such as start-up and moving expense; and

(5) reporting a significant increase in intangible assets as a percentage of total assets.

These situations and others may serve as "red flags" since the occurrence of one or more of these factors may indicate the need for normalization.

Finally, there is evidence that the quality of a firm's statements may vary over different reporting periods. For example, there is evidence that quarterly statements are of a lower quality than annual statements.[23] This occurs be-

---

[21] James P. Dawson, Peter M. Neupert, and Clyde P. Stickney, "Restating Financial Statements for Alternative GAAPs: Is it Worth the Effort?" *Financial Analysts Journal* (November-December 1980): pp. 38–46.

[22] Joel G. Siegel, "The 'Quality of Earnings' Concept: A Survey," *Financial Analysts Journal* (March-April 1982): pp. 60–68.

[23] Frank J. Fabozzi and Robert Fonfeder, "Have You Seen Any Good Quarterly Statements Lately?" *Journal of Portfolio Management* (Winter 1983): pp. 71–74.

cause auditors do not usually have an important role in preparing the quarterly statements.

Other Key Fundamentals

In addition to an analysis of financial statements, a traditional fundamental analysis includes a consideration of other company attributes. An assessment of these factors often requires subjective judgment.

1. ANALYSIS OF MANAGEMENT The strengths and weaknesses of management are often reflected in the financial statements and can be revealed in a ratio analysis. However, there are intangible factors that can have an important impact on the performance of the company. The commitment of management toward the goal of maximizing shareholder wealth is important. Recently there has been considerable financial research directed at the *agency problem*. Essentially, this research looks at problems that arise because corporate managers are actually agents for stockholders. Do the managers or agents always make decisions that are in the best interest of stockholders? One solution to the problem is to equate better the interests of managers and stockholders. This may take the form of tying management compensation to the performance of the company through profit sharing, bonuses, or stock options.

    Changes in key management personnel may have a significant impact on a company. For example, the past success of a company may be due to the skill of a key executive, as is the case with Cray Research, Inc. Because of their skills, other firms may hire them away. On the other hand, a weak management team may be replaced, providing a justification for optimism concerning new management. Major changes in top management at Chrysler Corporation are often cited for the dramatic improvement in its performance.

    Professional financial analysts often visit a company and confer with key management. This allows the analysts to form opinions about the quality of the management team. These opinions can also be influenced by a discussion of company policies dealing with areas such as product development, research and development, and financial planning.

2. ANALYSIS OF EMPLOYEES The real strength of many companies lies in their employees. Some companies, such as IBM, have historically stressed the importance of hiring and retaining excellent employees. Good employees are retained by competitive compensation packages and other benefits such as continued training and education, rapid advancement, and participation in management decisions that leads to the development of a team spirit.

    Unfortunately, other companies have a reputation for poor employee relations. This often results in rapid employee turnover and lack of commitment to the overall goals of the organization. Without dedicated employees who have a long-term interest in the firm, it is unlikely the firm will be highly successful.

3. ANALYSIS OF OTHER FACTORS Other factors, such as customer relations, advertising, philosophy, corporate ethics, awareness of environmental concerns, and willingness to be a good corporate citizen, are intangible factors that may significantly influence the long-term success of a company.

Illustration of Company Analysis

Appendix 10B uses Chrysler Corporation to illustrate a basic company analysis. This appendix provides historical balance sheets and income statements, and calculates a number of financial ratios, using the statements. Key growth rates are calculated, and stock prices and P/E ratios over the period 1982–1987 are provided. Other factors that fundamentalists might consider are briefly discussed. The company analysis concludes with a basic investment recommendation. The valuation models that will be discussed in Chapter 11 can be used to provide a more specific investment recommendation for a company.

SUMMARY

This chapter discussed the industry and the company analysis from the viewpoint of a traditional fundamental analysis. An industry analysis is important because performances of industries vary over time. The fact that an industry performed well in the past, however, is not sufficient reason to expect it to perform well in the future. The economic environment is likely to have an important influence on many industries. An economic forecast is a logical first step in identifying industries that may offer viable investments.

Once an industry is identified, individual companies in the industry must be analyzed. The cornerstone of the company analysis is an analysis of the financial statements. Frequently used tools of analysis include financial ratios that are analyzed for possible trends and compared to industry norms.

Financial analysts also recognize that reported financial statements may not reflect an accurate picture of the firm. This occurs because GAAP allows for considerable flexibility in reporting financial performance. Analysts usually attempt to determine the "quality" of the statements by looking for factors such as changes in pension fund accounting from one period to the next. The discovery of these factors suggests that the statements may be of low "quality" and thus require adjustments or normalization so that the firm's results can be analyzed over time or compared to other firms in the industry.

The chapter concluded with other factors that should be considered in the company analysis. This discussion suggested that a company analysis is more than a "number crunching" analysis of the financials. Intangibles such as the abilities and commitment of management and employees are also important.

QUESTIONS

1. Briefly define an *industry*. Explain how industry classification procedures are used in a fundamental analysis of common stocks.

2. Briefly explain the SIC industry classification system. What problems are encountered when this system is applied to large diversified corporations?

3. Use the empirical studies summarized in the chapter to discuss the importance of industry factors in explaining company earnings and returns.

4. Should historical industry earnings be extrapolated to estimate future earnings? What are the advantages and disadvantages of this approach?

5. Suppose a company you are analyzing has three SIC codes. What problems do these multiple classifications cause in the industry analysis? How would you solve these problems?

6. How can industry rankings such as those prepared by Value Line and Standard & Poor's be used as part of a fundamental approach to common stock valuation?

7. Briefly identify and discuss the "key industry fundamentals" that are commonly used in an industry analysis. Are these fundamentals equally important to all industries?

8. Discuss the two empirical models presented in the chapter that can be used to forecast an individual company's earnings based on industry and economic factors.

9. Explain how a pro forma income statement can be used to forecast industry earnings.

10. Explain the concept of "relative strength" as applied to industries. Based on the empirical studies reviewed in this chapter, do you think industry selection strategies based on relative strength can be used to earn risk-adjusted excess returns?

11. Explain the similarities and differences in an industry's relative strength measure and its beta. Do you feel that industries with high relative strength measures have more systematic risk than the average industry?

12. Would a portfolio of ten to fifteen common stocks, all from the same industry, offer the same degree of diversification as a portfolio of ten to fifteen stocks from several different industries? Explain.

13. Explain the concept of "normalization" as it applies to the financial statements of an individual firm.

14. Identify at least four factors or events that could be identified from an analysis of financial statements that reduce the "quality" of the statements. Indicate how the "quality" of a firm's financial statements relates to the concept of normalization.

15. In addition to the analysis of financial statements, what other company attributes are usually considered in a fundamental analysis? Briefly discuss these attributes.

PROBLEMS

1. Assume that the yield on one-year Treasury bills is presently 9.3 percent and you estimate that the *HPR* on the S&P 500 will be 15 percent for next year. Use the CAPM to estimate the expected return on the following industries:

INDUSTRY	INDUSTRY BETA
1	1.3
2	0.8
3	1.1

2. Consider the following composite industry earnings over the last five years:

YEAR	INDUSTRY COMPOSITE EPS
1	$12.00
2	8.00
3	−2.00
4	10.00
5	15.00

a. Calculate the annual compounded growth rate, using the first and last year's earnings.

b. Calculate the growth rate in earnings for each year.

c. Calculate the earnings stability measure, $Stab_{EPS}$, suggested by Coggin and Hunter.

d. Does your analysis suggest that estimates of earnings for this industry can be based on historical growth rates? Discuss.

3. In analyzing a particular industry and company, assume that you collect the following industry and market index values and common stock prices for the company:

MONTH	INDUSTRY	S&P 500	COMPANY
1	110	260	$69
2	112	283	72
3	111	271	66
4	115	282	73
5	126	285	74
6	138	289	72

a. Calculate the monthly relative strength ratios for the industry and company using the S&P 500.

b. Based on the relative strength ratios, explain what is happening to the prices of the company and industry stocks versus stocks in general.

c. If the trend in the relative strength ratios continues, would this industry be attractive in a bull market? Would the company be attractive?

4. Consider the following composite per share data on the entertainment industry compiled by Standard & Poor's:

	1981	1982	1983	1984	1985
Sales	$282.13	$339.97	$341.47	$274.81	$319.03
Operating income	$ 36.81	$ 50.00	$ 15.05	$ 60.76	$ 74.31
Profit margin	13.05%	14.71%	4.79%	22.11%	23.29%
Depreciation	$ 4.83	$ 6.68	$ 9.73	$ 33.24	$ 39.12
Taxes	$ 11.53	$ 13.70	$ 1.33	$ 3.67	$ 16.97
Earnings	$ 21.75	$ 25.74	$ (6.13)	$ 7.22	$ 18.22
Dividends	$ 5.49	$ 6.89	$ 6.35	$ 5.69	$ 4.36
Earnings/sales	7.71%	7.57%	def.	2.63%	5.71%
Dividends/earnings	25.24%	26.77%	def.	78.81%	23.93%
Price:					
High	331.63	373.45	328.19	299.86	494.53
Low	250.34	263.81	253.83	250.37	260.73
P/E ratios:					
High	15.25	14.51	def.	41.53	27.13
Low	11.51	10.25	def.	34.68	14.31
Dividend yield:					
High	2.19%	2.61%	2.50%	2.27%	1.67%
Low	1.66%	1.84%	1.94%	1.90%	0.88%
Book value	$132.15	$164.48	$158.63	$118.31	$131.46
Return on book value	16.46%	15.65%	def.	6.10%	13.86%
Working capital	$ 55.80	$ 63.25	$ 63.47	N/A	N/A
Capital expenditures	$ 23.87	$ 39.39	$ 24.28	$ 55.69	$ 57.71

Discuss the strengths and weaknesses of this industry's performance over the period 1981–1985.

5. Consider the following condensed balance sheets and income statements for Walt Disney Company:

	BALANCE SHEETS (000's)				
	1982	1983	1984	1985	1986
Current assets	$ 262,339	$ 333,102	$ 454,037	$ 364,300	$ 481,300
Fixed and other assets	1,840,477	2,048,093	2,285,406	2,533,000	2,639,700
Total	$2,102,816	$2,381,195	$2,739,443	$2,897,300	$3,121,000
Current liabilities	$ 237,313	$ 238,198	$ 264,137	$ 329,000	$ 436,400
Long-term debt and other liabilities	590,719	742,469	1,319,821	1,383,400	1,265,900
Common stock	588,250	661,934	359,988	255,700	283,200
Retained earnings	686,534	738,594	795,497	929,200	1,135,500
Total	$2,102,816	$2,381,195	$2,739,443	$2,897,300	$3,121,000
	INCOME STATEMENTS (000's)				
Revenues	$1,030,250	$1,307,357	$1,656,000	$2,015,400	$2,470,900
Operating costs	830,134	1,086,982	1,372,000	1,604,000	1,901,400
Operating income	200,116	220,375	284,000	411,400	569,500
General and admin. expense	30,957	35,554	59,600	49,900	66,000
Other expenses	5,147	7,295	89,900	–	–
Interest expense	14,781CR	14,066	41,700	51,600	41,300
Earnings before taxes	178,793	163,460	92,800	309,900	462,200
Taxes	78,700	70,300	5,000CR	136,400	214,900
Net Income	$100,093	$ 93,160	$ 97,800	$173,500	$247,300

a. Analyze the strengths and weaknesses of the company in terms of liquidity, leverage, activity, and profitability.

b. Compare the performance of the company to the industry using the data given in Problem 4.

COMPUTER APPLICATIONS

The floppy disk includes programs that perform basic industry and company financial analyses by calculating ratios and common size statements. The disk also has a regression program that can be used to perform a trend analysis or to develop other forecasting models. Instructions and illustrations are provided on the disk.

REFERENCES

Akemann, Charles A., and Werner E. Keller. "Relative Strength Does Persist!" *Journal of Portfolio Management* (Fall 1977): pp. 38–45.

Bar-Yosef, Sassin, and Baruch Lev. "Historical Cost Earnings versus Inflation-adjusted Earnings in Dividend Decisions." *Financial Analysts Journal* (March-April 1983): pp. 41–50.

Beaver, William H., and Stephen G. Ryan. "How Well Do Statement No. 33 Earnings Explain Stock Returns?" *Financial Analysts Journal* (September-October 1985): pp. 66–71.

Berliner, Robert W. "Do Analysts Use Inflation-adjusted Information? Results of a Survey." *Financial Analysts Journal* (March-April 1983): pp. 65–72.

Bierman, Harold. "Toward a Constant Price-Earnings Ratio." *Financial Analysts Journal* (September-October 1982): pp. 62–65.

Black, Fischer. "The Magic in Earnings: Economic Earnings versus Accounting Earnings." *Financial Analysts Journal* (November-December 1980): pp. 19–24.

Bohan, James. "Relative Strength: Further Positive Evidence." *Journal of Portfolio Management* (Fall 1981): pp. 36–39.

Brown, Philip, and Ray Ball. "Some Preliminary Findings on the Association between the Earnings of a Firm, Its Industry, and the Economy," *Journal of Accounting Research: Empirical Research in Accounting: Selected Studies* (1967): pp. 55–77.

Callard, Charles G., and David C. Kleinman. "Inflation-adjusted Accounting: Does It Matter? *Financial Analysts Journal* (May-June 1985): pp. 51–59.

Clancy, Donald K., and John A. Yeakel. "On Reporting Dilutionary Exchanges." *Financial Analysts Journal* (September-October 1981): pp. 70–73.

Coggin, T. Daniel, and John E. Hunter. "Measuring Stability and Growth in Annual EPS." *Journal of Portfolio Management* (Winter 1983): pp. 75–78.

Dawson, James P., Peter M. Neupert, and Clyde P. Stickney. "Restating Financial Statements for Alternative GAAPs: Is It Worth the Effort?" *Financial Analysts Journal* (November-December 1980): pp. 38–46.

Eckel, Norm. "An EPS Forecasting Model Utilizing Macroeconomic Performance Expectations." *Financial Analysts Journal* (May-June 1982): pp. 68–77.

Fabozzi, Frank J., and Robert Fonfeder. "Have You Seen Any Good Quarterly Statements Lately?" *Journal of Portfolio Management* (Winter 1983): pp. 71–74.

Hertzberg, Daniel. "Bank Profit Reports Are Distorted by New SEC Rules, Other Changes." *Wall Street Journal*, 19 January 1984, p. 33.

King, Benjamin F. "Market and Industry Factors in Stock Price Behavior." *Journal of Business* (January 1966): pp. 139–90.

Livingston, Miles. "Industry Movements of Common Stocks." *Journal of Finance* (June 1977): pp. 861-74.

Magee, Robert H. "Industry-wide Commonalities in Earnings." *Journal of Accounting Research* (Autumn 1974): pp. 270–87.

Meyers, Stephen L. "A Reexamination of Market and Industry Factors in Stock Price Behavior." *Journal of Finance* (June 1973): pp. 695–705.

Nichols, Donald R. "A Study of the Market Valuation of Extraordinary Items Reported in Financial Statements." *Financial Review* (Fall 1977): pp. 1–17.

Norby, William C. "Applications of Inflation-Adjusted Accounting Data." *Financial Analysts Journal* (March-April 1983): pp. 33–39.

Peavy, John W., and David A. Goodman. "How Inflation, Risk and Corporate Profitability Affect Common Stock Returns." *Financial Analysts Journal* (September-October 1985): pp. 59–65.

Rappaport, Alfred. "Inflation Accounting and Corporate Dividends." *Financial Executive* (February 1981): pp. 20–22.

Reilly, Frank, and Eugene Drzycimski. "Alternative Industry Performance and Risk." *Journal of Financial and Quantitative Analysis* (June 1974): pp.423–46.

Rosenberg, Barr, and James Guy. "Predictions of Beta from Investment Fundamentals." *Financial Analysts Journal* (July-August 1976): pp. 62–70.

Siegel, Joel G. "The 'Quality of Earnings' Concept: A Survey." *Financial Analysts Journal* (March-April 1982): pp. 60–68.

Stricharchuk, Gregory. "More Ailing Concerns Are Firing Auditors in Hopes of Keeping Bad News from Public." *Wall Street Journal*, 12 May 1983, p. 35.

Tysseland, Milford S. "Further Tests of the Validity of the Industry Approach to Investment Analysis." *Journal of Financial and Quantitative Analysis* (March 1971): pp. 835–45.

ILLUSTRATION OF BASIC INDUSTRY ANALYSIS: AUTOMOBILES

I. Historical Performance:

	PER SHARE DATA				
	1982	1983	1984	1985	1986
Sales	$329.55	$385.64	$457.99	$524.03	$586.95
Operating income	22.71	45.41	52.64	54.30	57.46
Depreciation	21.52	22.64	22.73	27.34	31.46
Taxes	0.03	8.26	11.67	10.56	7.20
Earnings	0.06	15.90	25.39	24.35	22.94
Dividends	2.20	2.27	5.69	6.40	7.46
Stock prices:					
High	$ 78.24	$107.21	$109.01	$116.97	$151.15
Low	40.53	72.02	83.04	94.46	110.95
P/E ratios:					
High	NMF	6.74	4.29	4.80	6.59
Low	NMF	4.53	3.27	3.88	4.84

II. Financial Ratios:

Operating profit margin	6.89%	11.78%	11.49%	10.36%	9.79%
Return on investment	0.08%	19.09%	23.75%	20.36%	16.65%
Return on equity	1.80%	37.93%	39.70%	27.10%	21.13%
Current ratio	1.00 ×	1.07 ×	1.17 ×	1.10 ×	1.13 ×
Long-term debt to net working capital	569.80%	299.45%	99.55%	241.93%	426.33%
Long-term debt to assets	37.47%	27.37%	14.83%	18.70%	20.73%

* This appendix is designed to illustrate the basic financial data impacting the industry. A comprehensive analysis would include other factors and estimates that influence industry performance.

III. Annual Growth Rates:

	1983	1984	1985	1986	1982–86
Sales	17.02%	18.76%	14.42%	12.01%	15.52%
Earnings	NMF	59.69	(4.10)	(5.79)	NMF

IV. Other Industry Fundamentals:

	1984	1985	1986
Value of shipments in 1982 $ (millions)	$112,404	$114,151	$123,025
Ratio of value of imports to shipments	0.171	0.206	0.255
Total automobiles sold (thousands)	7,621.2	8,002.3	7,516.2
U.S. auto registrations (thousands)	126,869	131,067	134,587
Annual increases in new car prices	7.5%	5.2%	8.4%
Average age of cars in use (years)	7.5	7.6	7.6
Auto installment credit to disposable personal income	6.46%	7.29%	8.11%
Average maturity of new car loans (months)	48.3	51.5	50.0

V. Industry Recommendations:

Based on an economic forecast of slow to moderate growth, automobile sales and profits will likely decline, despite continued efforts to reduce operating costs. Forecasts of an increase in the import share of the market, higher interest rates, and high levels of consumer installment debt are negative factors for the industry. Since the average industry beta is 1.23, stocks in this industry are more volatile than stocks in general. Value Line indicates that industry sales in 1990–92 are unlikely to exceed the 1986 level. A slight improvement in the industry P/E ratio, however, may provide modest intermediate price appreciation for stocks in this industry.

ILLUSTRATION OF BASIC COMPANY ANALYSIS: CHRYSLER CORPORATION

I. Historical Performance:

	BALANCE SHEETS (millions $)				
	1982	1983	1984	1985	1986
Current assets	$ 2,369.1	$ 2,753.8	$ 3,979.9	$ 5,313.5	$ 5,364.0
Fixed and other assets	3,894.4	4,018.5	5,082.8	7,291.8	9,099.2
Total	$ 6,263.5	$ 6,772.3	$ 9,062.7	$12,605.3	$14,463.2
Current liabilities	$ 2,112.6	$ 3,453.9	$ 4,115.7	$ 4,729.2	$ 5,121.0
Long-term debt and other liabilities	3,159.8	1,953.1	1,641.1	3,660.8	3,997.4
Common and preferred stock	2,514.8	2,620.4	2,384.7	2,062.0	1,777.3
Retained earnings	(1,523.7)	(1,255.1)	921.2	2,153.3	3,567.5
Total	$ 6,263.5	$ 6,772.3	$ 9,062.7	$12,605.3	$14,463.2
	INCOME STATEMENTS (millions $)				
Revenues	$10,070.3	$13,387.5	$19,717.2	$21,553.1	$23,005.6
Cost of sales	8,606.2	10,861.2	15,528.2	17,467.7	18,635.2
Operating profits	1,464.1	2,526.3	4,189.0	4,085.4	4,370.4
General and admin. expense	669.8	804.9	987.7	1,144.4	1,376.6
Other expenses	465.3	536.8	(62.2)	696.1	635.8
Interest expense	158.0	82.1	(50.7)	(124.9)	32.7
Earnings before taxes	171.0	1,102.5	3,314.2	2,369.8	2,325.3
Taxes	0.9	401.6	934.2	734.6	921.7
Net Income	$170.1	$ 700.9	$2,380.0	$1,635.2	$1,403.6
EPS	$ 2.11	$ 4.80	$ 19.22	$ 10.76	$ 6.48

* This appendix is designed to illustrate the basic financial data impacting the company. A comprehensive analysis would include other factors and estimates that influence company performance.

II. Financial Ratios:

	1982	1983	1984	1985	1986
Operating profit margin	14.54%	18.87%	21.25%	18.96%	19.00%
Return on investment	2.72%	10.35%	26.26%	12.97%	9.70%
Return on equity	17.16%	51.34%	71.99%	38.79%	26.26%
Current ratio	1.12	0.80	0.97	1.12	1.05
Long-term debt to net					
working capital	12.32	(2.79)	(12.08)	6.27	16.45
Long-term debt to assets	50.45%	28.84%	18.11%	29.04%	27.64%
Asset turnover	1.61	1.98	2.18	1.71	1.59
Fixed asset turnover	2.59	3.33	3.88	2.96	2.53
Net working capital turnover	39.26	(19.12)	(145.19)	36.89	94.67
[sales/(current assets-					
current liabilities)]					

III. Annual Growth Rates:

	1983	1984	1985	1986	1982–86
Revenues	32.9%	47.3%	9.3%	6.7%	22.9%
Net income	312.1	239.6	(31.3)	(14.2)	69.5
Assets	8.1	33.8	39.1	14.7	23.3
EPS	127.5	300.4	(44.0)	(39.8)	32.4

IV. Stock Prices and P/E Ratios:

	1982	1983	1984	1985	1986	1987
Stock prices:						
High	$18\frac{5}{8}$	$35\frac{5}{8}$	$33\frac{1}{4}$	47	$47\frac{1}{8}$	48
Low	$3\frac{1}{2}$	14	$20\frac{7}{8}$	$29\frac{7}{8}$	$27\frac{1}{8}$	$19\frac{5}{8}$
P/E ratios:						
High	8.83	7.42	1.73	4.37	7.27	8.14
Low	1.66	2.92	1.09	2.78	4.19	3.33

V. Other Company Fundamentals:

Since Congress passed a loan guarantee program for Chrysler in late December 1979, the company has significantly improved its financial position. Chrysler has been increasing its share of the domestic market relative to General Motors and Ford. The acquisition of American Motors Corp. in August 1987 and the acquisition of Gulfstream Aerospace Corp. broaden their product line. Continued modernization and cost-cutting efforts are expected to improve long-term profitability. Chrysler's top management is considered a strength of the company.

VI. Company Recommendations:

Based on the economic and industry analyses and forecasts for 1988, the automobile industry is not expected to perform well relative to other industries. Consequently, an investment in Chrysler for 1988 is not recommended. The performance of Chrysler, however, is expected to compare favorably with other companies in the industry. For investors with an investment horizon of 3–5 years, Chrysler could offer attractive returns.

CHAPTER 11

COMMON STOCK VALUATION

INTRODUCTION

Overview

This chapter discusses common stock valuation models that are typically used in fundamental analysis. This is the final step in the three-step fundamental approach: economic, industry, and company analyses. The results of the economic, industry, and company analyses are used to estimate a stock's value. The estimated value represents the *intrinsic* value of the stock or the value that is suggested by the fundamentals. A comparison of the intrinsic value with the current market price of the stock provides a basis for the investment decision. The analyst attempts to answer the question, Does the existing stock price provide the opportunity to earn excess returns, based on the estimates of risk and intrinsic value over the investment horizon?

Since one of the key variables that determines a stock's value is earnings, this chapter begins with a discussion of forecasting earnings. The earnings forecast provides an indication of the future income stream that the stock may provide the investor.

The next section of the chapter presents the *dividend discount model* and the numerous variations of this model. As the name implies, this model uses estimates of future dividends to estimate the stock's intrinsic value. The *price/earnings model*, another widely used valuation model, is closely related to the dividend discount model but uses earning estimates rather than dividends. Once the two models are illustrated, their strengths and weaknesses are discussed.

Since the early 1980s, a number of "new" valuation models have been developed. Some are simply variations of the two traditional models. Other new models represent different approaches to and viewpoints of common stock valuation. The newer models are discussed in this chapter.

The chapter concludes with a discussion of the investment decision suggested by the fundamental approach. The basic decision possibilities are

1. purchase the stock by taking a long position;
2. sell the stock by taking a short position; and
3. do not take a long or short position in the stock.

These possibilities assume that there is no position in the stock at the present time. The analysis may also be used to recommend strategies using options, financial futures, or options on futures. These strategies are discussed in Chapters 19–21. The basic decision possibilities also assume that the final decision will use portfolio considerations that deal with the risk-return relationships between the stocks under consideration. If a portfolio of common stocks already exists, the decision should consider how the stock under consideration will change the risk-return characteristics of the portfolio.

Common Stock Valuation Models

A common stock valuation model is an attempt to develop a mathematical formulation of the variables (and their relationships) that determine value. It is important to recognize that the models are a gross oversimplification of the valuation process. In reality, many factors determine the market price of a stock. These factors may change, and the relationships between factors may change. No model can consider all the complexities of the "real world" process. The models, however, can provide a useful framework for the analysis.

Mathematical models imply preciseness and accuracy, and the valuation models in this chapter give the impression that valuation is essentially a quantitative procedure. In reality, however, common stock valuation is an *art*. Models are useful to the analyst but are not substitutes for judgment and common sense. A skilled analyst might be able to use a model successfully to help make accurate forecasts, but the model may not improve the forecasts of an unskilled analyst. Models should therefore be viewed as tools for decision making and not as the decision maker.

Finance theory indicates that the value of a financial asset is essentially a function of the future income the asset can provide and the riskiness of the income stream. Valuation models, therefore, generally take the form

$$V_n = f(\text{income, risk}) \tag{11.1}$$

where V_n represents the intrinsic value of the asset in period n. For example, if the analyst has a one-year investment horizon, the value of the stock one year from now, V_1, would be estimated. In other words the estimate of V_n would indicate the likely selling price one year from today.

Given an estimate of the cash dividends that the stock might pay the next year, D_1, the expected one-year holding period return could be calculated as

$$E(HPR_1) = \frac{V_1 - P_0 + D_1}{P_0} \tag{11.2}$$

The analyst would also estimate the risk of the stock over the investment horizon. The risk estimate may simply be a historical or ex-post risk measure such as the stock's beta or variance. This approach assumes that risk will remain constant over the investment horizon. An alternative ex-ante risk estimate may be made. This may be an adjustment of the ex-post beta or the variance of the estimated probability distribution associated with $E(HPR)$.

Once estimates of $E(HPR)$ and risk are made, the analyst can compare the stock to other stocks or to the estimated risk-return relationship for stocks in general. This procedure is discussed at the end of this chapter. Portfolio considerations should also be included in the final recommendation.

FORECASTING EARNINGS

Importance of Earnings Forecasts

Corporate earnings are a key variable in determining stock prices. The ability to forecast earnings and earnings changes accurately can be used to earn risk-adjusted excess returns. The above observations are supported by numerous research studies. A 1981 study by Morse analyzed the price and trading volume reactions to annual and quarterly earnings announcements that appeared in the *Wall Street Journal.*[1] This study used a sample of fifty common stocks traded on the NYSE, AMEX, and the OTC market for the period 1973–1976. The empirical results indicated that significant price changes and increased trading volume occurred on the day prior to and on the day of the announcement. The price adjustment before the announcement suggested that the earnings information was already public knowledge prior to its publication in the *Wall Street Journal.* Also, there appeared to be no evidence of market reaction two days before the announcement, but there were adjustments that occurred "several" days after the announcement.

The evidence dealing with *unexpected earning announcements* strongly supports the importance of earnings. One recent study found that "'approximately' 15 to 20 percent of the variation in individual security returns is explained by either actual or unexpected earnings changes."[2]

For empirical research purposes, *unexpected earnings* are usually defined as the difference between actual (reported) earnings and expected earnings. Studies use both quarterly and annual reported earnings in analyzing unexpected earnings. Several different procedures have been used in previous research to measure *expected* earnings. One approach is to estimate expected earnings using a regression trend line of historical earnings:[3]

$$EPS_t = \hat{a}_0 + \hat{a}_1(Time)_t + e_t \tag{11.3}$$

where EPS_t = reported earnings per share for period t

$Time_t$ = index variable representing time

For example, assume that the data consisted of reported EPS for the period 1982–1987. The index variable for time could be 1 for 1982, 2 for 1983, etc. Given the regression constants $\hat{a}_0$ and $\hat{a}_1$, the expected EPS for 1988 (the seventh time period) could be calculated as

$$E(EPS_{1988}) = \hat{a}_0 + \hat{a}_1(7) \tag{11.4}$$

The estimate of *standardized unexpected earnings* is typically calculated as

$$SUE_t = \frac{EPS_t - E(EPS_t)}{\sigma_{EPS}\sqrt{1 - R^2}} \tag{11.5}$$

[1] Dale Morse, "Price and Trading Volume Reaction Surrounding Earnings Announcements: A Closer Examination," *Journal of Accounting Research* (Autumn 1981): pp. 375–83.

[2] Gary A. Benesh and Pamela P. Peterson, "On the Relationship between Earnings, Changes, Analysts' Forecast and Stock Price Fluctuations," *Financial Analysts Journal* (November-December 1986): p. 35.

[3] This approach is used in Henry A. Latane and Charles P. Jones, "Standardized Unexpected Earnings—1971–77," *Journal of Finance* (June 1979): pp. 717–24, and Charles P. Jones, Richard J. Rendleman, Jr., and Henry A. Latane, "Earnings Announcements: Pre-and-Post Responses," *Journal of Portfolio Management* (Spring 1985): pp. 28–32.

where SUE_t = standardized unexpected earnings for period t

EPS_t = reported EPS for period t

$E(EPS_t)$ = expected EPS estimated using a model like Equation 11.4

σ_{EPS} = standard deviation of historical EPS

R^2 = coefficient of determination from time series regression, using a model like Equation 11.3

The denominator in Equation 11.5 is simply the standard error of the estimate from the time series regression and adjusts for the degree of forecasting error in estimating earnings.

Figure 11.1 illustrates expected and unexpected EPS and the standardization procedure. Notice that the EPS are very unpredictable from year to year, resulting in considerable scatter around the regression line. The coefficient of determination is therefore low for the trend line. The estimate of EPS for year 7 of $1.97 is below the actual earnings of $2.25, resulting in unexpected earnings of $.28. Because of the variability of historical earnings, the standardized unexpected earnings are $.58. Since the unexpected earnings of $.28 are less than the standardized unexpected earnings of $.58, the stock price may not have a significant price adjustment. To the extent that the actual earnings were significantly underestimated by the market, the stock price would increase because of the announced higher earnings.

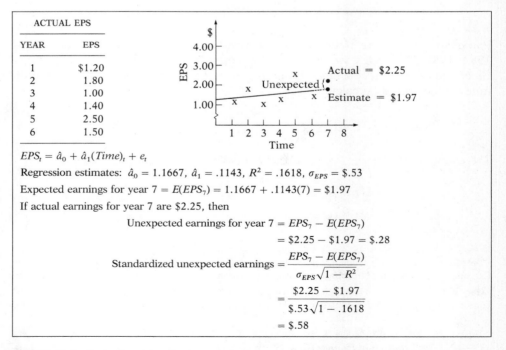

ACTUAL EPS	
YEAR	EPS
1	$1.20
2	1.80
3	1.00
4	1.40
5	2.50
6	1.50

$EPS_t = \hat{a}_0 + \hat{a}_1(Time)_t + e_t$

Regression estimates: $\hat{a}_0 = 1.1667$, $\hat{a}_1 = .1143$, $R^2 = .1618$, $\sigma_{EPS} = \$.53$

Expected earnings for year 7 = $E(EPS_7)$ = $1.1667 + .1143(7) = \$1.97$

If actual earnings for year 7 are $2.25, then

$$\text{Unexpected earnings for year 7} = EPS_7 - E(EPS_7)$$
$$= \$2.25 - \$1.97 = \$.28$$

$$\text{Standardized unexpected earnings} = \frac{EPS_7 - E(EPS_7)}{\sigma_{EPS}\sqrt{1 - R^2}}$$
$$= \frac{\$2.25 - \$1.97}{\$.53\sqrt{1 - .1618}}$$
$$= \$.58$$

FIGURE 11.1 Illustration of actual, expected, unexpected, and standardized unexpected earnings.

A second methodology that can be used to obtain estimates of *expected* earnings uses published forecasts of EPS made by security analysts.[4] A number of private firms publish earnings forecasts. For example, the Institution Brokers Estimate System, IBES, monitors earnings estimates for over three thousand companies that are produced by more than eighteen hundred brokerage firm analysts. A second source of earnings forecasts is *Earnings Forecasts*, published monthly by Standard & Poor's. Using this methodology, unexpected earnings are calculated as the difference between reported earnings and the consensus earnings forecast made by analysts.

Most of the unexpected earnings announcement studies (including the studies previously cited) conclude that significant stock price adjustments occur for firms that report earnings significantly different from expected earnings. Portfolios formed from stocks reporting the largest positive unexpected earnings also appear to offer risk-adjusted excess returns for the months immediately following the period of unexpected earnings. However, there is also evidence that stock prices adjust prior to the announcement of unexpected earnings. This suggests that additional risk-adjusted excess returns are possible if unexpected earnings can be forecast prior to the earnings announcement date. The results from these studies indicate the "reward" that the market offers—excess returns for investors who can accurately forecast earnings.

Difficulty of Forecasting Earnings

Despite the significant risk-adjusted excess returns that are possible with superior earnings forecasting skills, the difficulty of making an accurate forecast should not be underestimated. A number of studies of historical earnings suggest that the year-to-year changes are random. To the extent that this is true for a particular company, a simple extrapolation of historical earnings would not provide an accurate forecast.

Table 11.1 presents the reported earnings for a sample of companies over the period 1978–1987. These companies were selected to illustrate the potential variability of earnings from year to year. The amount of variability, however, is different from company to company. Because of economic, industry, and company factors, some companies have more stable patterns of earnings than others. This implies that historical earnings may be more useful in predicting earnings for some companies than for others.

Analysts and investors may be tempted to select companies that appear to have more stable earnings since earnings forecasts may be easier than for companies with volatile earnings. However, research has shown that risk-adjusted excess returns are proportionate to the magnitude of the difference between forecast and reported earnings.[5] The rewards for accurate forecasts are therefore much greater for companies with significant variability in reported earnings.

---

[4] This methodology is used in Leonard Zacks, "EPS Forecasts—Accuracy Is Not Enough," *Financial Analysts Journal* (March-April 1979): pp. 53–55, and Robert C. Kleinkosky and William P. Miller, "When Forecasting, It Pays to Be Right!" *Journal of Portfolio Management* (Summer 1984): pp. 13–18.

[5] For example, see Benesh and Peterson.

TABLE 11.1 SAMPLE OF REPORTED EPS: 1978–1987

YEAR	AMERICAN EXPRESS	AMERICAN HOME PROD.	BANK AMERICA	BOSTON EDISON	CHRYSLER	LIZ CLAIBORNE	TECO ENERGY	ZAYRE
1978	$1.08	$2.21	$3.53	$1.48	$(1.57)	–	$1.27	$0.37
1979	1.21	2.51	4.10	1.76	(7.64)	$0.05	1.06	0.44
1980	1.32	2.84	4.39	1.88	(11.56)	0.08	1.56	0.45
1981	1.40	3.18	3.02	2.08	(3.19)	0.13	1.50	0.55
1982	1.51	3.59	2.60	1.59	(0.57)	0.17	1.25	0.77
1983	1.27	4.00	2.18	1.80	1.91	0.27	1.57	1.20
1984	1.40	4.26	1.77	2.43	5.22	0.50	1.86	1.50
1985	1.78	4.70	(4.26)	2.52	6.25	0.71	1.79	1.62
1986	2.27	5.08	(3.74)	2.58	6.31	1.00	1.73	1.55
1987	0.87	5.73	(6.43)	1.97	5.90	1.32	1.95	0.40
Beta	1.40	0.90	1.00	0.70	1.50	1.55	0.60	1.45
Market Traded	NYSE	NYSE	NYSE	NYSE	NYSE	OTC	NYSE	NYSE

SOURCE: *Value Line Investment Survey.* © 1988 by Value Line, Inc.; used by permission of Value Line, Inc.

Professional Earnings Forecasts

Investors always have the option of using earnings forecasts made by professional security analysts and by company management. These forecasts are discussed below.

1. SECURITY ANALYSTS Thousands of professional security analysts are employed by brokerage firms, financial institutions, and mutual funds. Often the analysts specialize in a single industry, even a specific company. Essentially, their job is to be aware of all publicly available information that will have an impact on the industry and companies.

    Security analysts' reports that include earnings estimates are available from the large brokerage firms and from other organizations that employ analysts. As previously discussed, forecasts and recommendations from many analysts are available in publications such as the Institution Brokers Estimate System, IBES.

2. MANAGEMENT FORECASTS Under SEC regulations, many companies publish earnings estimates by top management. Companies, however, are not required to publish forecasts, and the SEC does not regulate how the forecasts are made or the "quality" of the forecasts. These forecasts are made available in a number of ways, including stockholder reports, stockholder meetings, press releases, and management interviews.[6]

3. INVESTMENT PUBLICATIONS Many investment publications provide both short- and long-term earnings forecasts. Some of the better known publications are *Value Line Investment Survey* and Standard & Poor's *Earnings Forecaster*.

4. CONSENSUS FORECAST As discussed in the economic forecasting section of Chapter 9, the use of a consensus forecast is growing in popularity. This information is reported in IBES. Individual investors could apply the concept by obtaining earnings estimates from several sources and using the average as the consensus forecast.

5. COMPARISON OF ACCURACY A limited number of studies have compared the accuracy of earnings forecasts made by different groups using different forecasting methods.[7] For example, the study might compare the accuracy of forecasts made by security analysts, management, and statistical estimates.

    Different conclusions are reached by the studies concerning accuracy of forecasts. A 1982 study by Imhoff and Parr compared the accuracy of security

---

[6] For a discussion of the history and empirical tests of management forecasts, see Donald R. Nichols and Jeffrey J. Tsay, "Security Price Reaction to Long-Range Executive Earnings Forecast," *Journal of Accounting Research* (Spring 1979): pp. 140–55, and William Ryland, "Management Forecasts, Stock Prices, and Public Policy," *Review of Business and Economic Research* (Winter 1979): pp. 16–29.

[7] For example, see Lawrence D. Brown and Michael S. Rozeff, "The Superiority of Analyst Forecasts as Measures of Expectations: Evidence from Earnings," *Journal of Finance* (March 1978): pp. 1–16; Eugene A. Imhoff and Paul V. Pare, "Analysis and Comparison of Earnings Forecast Agents," *Journal of Accounting Research* (Autumn 1982): pp. 429–39; and Dan Givoly and Josef Lakonishok, "The Quality of Analysts' Forecasts of Earnings," *Financial Analysts Journal* (September-October 1983): pp. 40–47.

analysts, of management, and of statistical forecasts.[8] Four earnings estimates were made, using various statistical procedures and historical data. The study, therefore, compared six (security analyst, management, and four statistical) earnings estimates. The empirical evidence in the study indicated that the estimates were not statistically independent, and "no difference exists between the six forecast agents."[9]

A 1984 study concluded that earnings forecasts made by financial analysts are "significantly more accurate" than statistical model predictions that extrapolate past earnings trends.[10] This study also found that analysts' forecasts incorporate historical trends and are reasonable proxies of consensus earnings. However, a large difference between forecasts appears to be useful information since it represents a risk proxy. A measure of the dispersion of analysts' forecasts is a measure of the uncertainty associated with predicting the earnings of a company and therefore represents a risk measure.

A third study is less complimentary toward security analysts' earnings forecasts.[11] This study found that the forecasts of different analysts were closely related; "strong trends prevail among analysts' forecasts." This study used the consensus forecast of earnings to select stocks that were expected to have the largest changes in forecast earnings. The consensus forecast over a three-month period was used to forecast earning revisions over the following nine-month period. Portfolios formed from the 20 percent of the sample of 240 firms with the largest revised earnings during a three-month period produced risk-adjusted excess returns over the following nine-month period. This study suggested that revisions of earnings forecast by analysts are predictable and can be used to forecast the direction of the change in their forecasts, thus generating forecasts that are more accurate than the consensus.

Methods of Forecasting Earnings

This section discusses some of the more widely used techniques and procedures used to forecast earnings. In many cases, analysts do not rely on a single technique, so that several independent estimates can be made.

1. STATISTICAL METHODS Historical earnings can be used to develop a regression model that can be used to forecast earnings. Equations 11.3 and 11.4 in the previous section illustrated a simple linear regression model. It should also be noted that the historical earnings may suggest a nonlinear trend. For example, earnings may be increasing or decreasing at an exponential rate rather than a constant rate. One solution to this problem is to convert the historical data to log form so that a linear regression model can be used. Re-

---

[8] Eugene A. Imhoff and Paul V. Pare, "Analysis and Comparison of Earnings Forecast Agents," *Journal of Accounting Research* (Autumn 1982): pp. 429–39.

[9] Ibid., p. 436.

[10] Dan Givoly and Josef Lakonishok, "The Quality of Analysts' Forecast of Earnings," *Financial Analysts Journal* (September-October 1984): pp. 40–47.

[11] Thomas J. Kerrigan, "When Forecasting Earnings, It Pays to Watch Forecasts," *Journal of Portfolio Management* (Summer 1984): pp. 19–26.

member that an exponential relationship approaches a linear relationship in log form.

Table 11.2 illustrates this procedure by showing the regression equation based on raw data and on logs. In this example, the equation based on logs appears to provide a better fit since the coefficient of determination, R^2, for the linear regression is .8257 versus .9467 for the regression in log form. Notice that the estimates of earnings for year 11 are significantly different, since the estimate based on the linear regression is $2.14 versus $2.46 based on the log form of the equation.

In addition to simple linear regression, there are many other statistical methods that can be used as forecasting tools. As illustrated in the industry analysis section of the previous chapter, multiple regression models allow the analyst to use other explanatory variables in the equation. For example, a model may be developed that uses both economic and industry variables as independent variables.

There is an extensive body of research on advanced statistical forecasting models. A popular model is the Box-Jenkins or ARIMA models. Tests of the accuracy of these models in predicting earnings generally conclude that they provide superior forecasts compared to naive models.

2.   PRO FORMA INCOME STATEMENT A popular procedure for estimating earnings is to construct a pro forma income statement over the investment horizon.

TABLE 11.2   REGRESSION ESTIMATES OF EARNINGS

YEAR	EPS
1	$ .50
2	.45
3	.56
4	.80
5	.75
6	.90
7	1.10
8	1.30
9	1.80
10	2.50

I. Linear regression:

$$EPS_t = \hat{a}_0 + \hat{a}_1(Time)_t + e_t$$

$$\hat{a}_0 = -.0073, \ \hat{a}_1 = .1952, \ R^2 = .8257$$

Estimate of year 11 earnings $= -.0073 + .1952(11) = \$2.14$

II. Linear regression based on natural log (base e) transformations of EPS.

For example: $ln(\$.50) = -.6931$

$$ln(EPS)_t = \hat{a}_0 + \hat{a}_1(Time)_t + e_t$$

$$\hat{a}_0 = -1.0671, \ \hat{a}_1 = .1790, \ R^2 = .9467$$

Estimate of year 11 earnings is antilog of

$$-1.0671 + .1790(11) = .9019$$

$$e^{.9019} = \$2.46$$

This approach, actually more a procedure than a model, lets the analyst develop individual forecasts of the key variables that determine earnings, such as sales, cost of goods, operating expenses, interest expense, taxes, and the number of shares of common stock. Considerable effort may go into estimating each of these key variables. For example, a regression model may be developed to estimate sales. Many corporate finance texts devote at least one chapter to financial forecasting. These texts develop in detail methods that can be used to forecast earnings, including the percent of sales method, simulation, leverage analysis, and break-even analysis. These texts can be consulted for details concerning these methods.[12] Chapter 10 presented an illustration of the pro forma statement approach for an industry analysis. Essentially, this same procedure can be used for the company analysis.

3. ADJUSTMENTS FOR INFLATION The double-digit inflation rates of the late 1970s and early 1980s generated considerable discussion and research on the implications of inflation for accounting statements, earnings estimates, and stock prices.[13] In general, it appears that stock prices did not provide an adequate inflation hedge during periods of high inflation. This suggests that investors realized that the inflated earnings of many companies did not reflect real earnings growth. Stock prices, therefore, did not increase because of the inflated earnings. The implication of this research indicates that earning estimates should be inflation adjusted or stated in real rather than nominal dollars.

Since inflation may have a different impact on the revenues and costs of a particular firm, a pro forma statement is one procedure that can be used to allow for these possible differences. Essentially, both revenues and costs can be forecast in nominal dollars and then adjusted, using the appropriate rates of inflation. This procedure results in an estimate of EPS in real or constant dollars.

4. GROWTH RATES Analysts often estimate the growth rate for earnings rather than estimating dollar earnings directly. This approach is useful because many valuation models require an estimate of earnings or dividend growth. As with estimates of earnings, growth estimates should be adjusted for inflation or factors that may overstate the true growth rate. Various techniques to estimate growth have been suggested in the investment literature.[14]

---

[12] For example, see Chapter 7 of Jeff Madura and E. Theodore Veit, *Introduction to Financial Management* (New York: West Publishing Company, 1988).

[13] For example, see Suleman A. Moosa, "Inflation and Common Stock Prices," *Journal of Financial Research* (Fall 1980): pp. 115–28; G. William Schwert, "The Adjustment of Stock Prices to Information about Inflation," *Journal of Finance* (March 1981): pp. 15–29; Russell J. Fuller and Glenn H. Petry, "Inflation, Return on Equity, and Stock Prices," *Journal of Portfolio Management* (Summer 1981): pp. 19–25; Ahmet Tezel, "The Effect of Inflation on Common Stock Values," *Journal of Financial Research* (Spring 1982): pp. 17–25; and David C. Leonard and Michael E. Solt, "Stock Market Signals of Changes in Expected Inflation," *Journal of Financial Research* (Spring 1987): pp. 57–63.

[14] For example, see A. J. Merrett and Gerald D. Newbould, "CEPS: The Illusion of Corporate Growth," *Journal of Portfolio Management* (Fall 1982): pp. 5–10, and Lewis D. Johnson, "Growth Prospects and Share Prices: A Systematic View," *Journal of Portfolio Management* (Winter 1987): pp. 58–60.

Summary

Despite the numerous earnings forecasting techniques, the success and accuracy of the forecast depends essentially on the experience and skill of the analyst. All forecasts depend on the same set of publicly available information. The ability to use this information in unique ways, to discover information that is not generally known, or to draw conclusions based on many factors may result in more accurate estimates. Making or using an average or consensus forecast of earnings is therefore unlikely to result in risk-adjusted excess returns.

DIVIDEND DISCOUNT MODEL

Overview

One of the most widely used common stock valuation models is the *dividend discount model*, DDM. In its simplest form, the DDM defines the intrinsic value of a share as the present value of future dividends. Despite its simplicity, the DDM is a useful tool in fundamental analysis. This section illustrates basic and more complex DDMs.

Controversy over Dividends

The importance of dividends to common stock values is one of the most controversial subjects in investment theory. The controversy began with an article published in 1961 by Merton Miller and Franco Modigliani.[15] Miller and Modigliani (MM) developed a model illustrating that dividends are irrelevant in determining value. The model, developed under the assumption of perfect capital markets and no risk, showed that the decision to pay dividends requires the firm to issue new shares of stock to obtain additional financing. The firm's financing needs may vary, depending on its investment opportunities through capital expenditures. Thus, the dividend decision and the investment decision are related. The value of the firm, and therefore its stock, depends on the profitability of the assets and the opportunities for additional capital investment. How these opportunities are financed is not important in determining value.

Since MM's 1961 article, many additional studies have been published, but the importance of dividends in determining value is still an unresolved issue. The evidence indicates that dividends do have some importance:

1. Informational content—dividends are signals by management to stockholders and have value because they convey information.
2. Bird-in-hand-investors may view dividends as a less risky return than future capital gains.

---

[15] Merton Miller and Franco Modigliani, "Dividend Policy, Growth, and the Valuation of Shares," *Journal of Business* (October 1961): pp. 411–33.

3. Clientele effect—if some investors prefer certain dividend policies over others, a company should establish a policy and maintain it for the benefit of its stockholders or "clients."

4. Other factors—taxes, flotation costs on new issues of stock, and transaction costs for investors also make dividend policy important.

In addition to theoretical questions about the importance of dividends, there are other difficulties with the DDM:[16]

1. Forecasting—estimating the stream of dividends over the investment horizon.

2. Model assumptions—how risk is incorporated into the model through the discount rate used to calculate present values; adjusting the model's assumption of an infinite investment horizon to the investor's investment horizon that might be finite.

3. Interpretation of model results—the model overly simplifies stock valuation and gives the user a false impression of the accuracy of the estimate.

Basic Models

There are several variations of the basic DDM because of different assumptions about the growth rate of dividends and its relationship to the discount rate used to calculate present values.

1. ZERO GROWTH DDM The most basic of all the DDMs is the zero growth model. This model assumes that dividends will be constant over time, so that growth is 0, and that the investor's required rate of return is constant. This model is

$$V_0 = \frac{D_1}{(1 + K)^1} + \frac{D_2}{(1 + K)^2} + \frac{D_3}{(1 + K)^3} + \cdots + \frac{D_\infty}{(1 + K)^\infty} \qquad (11.6)$$

where V_0 = intrinsic value of stock today or at time period 0

   D_t = dividends per share in period t

   K = investor's required rate of return.

Since $D_1 = D_2 = D_3 = \ldots = D_\infty$ by assumption, the time subscript can be dropped. The dividend income stream is essentially a perpetuity, and the value can be calculated simply as

$$V_0 = \frac{D}{K} \qquad (11.7)$$

For example, assume that the dividends per share are estimated to be $2 per year indefinitely, and the investor requires a 16 percent rate of return. The intrinsic value of the stock is $2/.16 = $12.50.

---

[16] For a discussion, see John J. Nagorniak, "Thoughts on Using Dividend Discount Models," *Financial Analysts Journal* (November-December 1985): pp. 13–15.

This model is more appropriate for an analysis of preferred stock because of the constant dividend assumption. The use and illustration of this model for preferred stock analysis is discussed in Chapter 17.

2. CONSTANT GROWTH DDM It is unlikely that many common stocks pay a constant dividend. A more realistic assumption is that dividends will change. The simplest assumption assumes a *constant* rate of change. If an analyst forecasts that dividends will grow by g percent per year, then

$$D_1 = D_0(1 + g)$$
$$D_2 = D_0(1 + g)^2$$
$$\vdots \qquad \vdots$$
$$D_n = D_0(1 + g)^n$$

For example, assume $D_0 = \$2$, and $g = 5\%$, or .05:

$$D_1 = \$2(1 + .05) \quad = \$2.1000$$
$$D_2 = \$2(1 + .05)^2 \quad = \$2.2050$$
$$\vdots \qquad \vdots \qquad \vdots$$
$$D_{10} = \$2(1 + .05)^{10} = \$3.2578$$

Notice that this procedure assumes that dividends are growing at a rate of 5 percent per year *compounded* annually. Assuming a constant required rate of return, the intrinsic value of the stock can be calculated as

$$V_0 = \frac{D_0(1 + g)}{(1 + K)^1} + \frac{D_0(1 + g)^2}{(1 + K)^2} + \ldots + \frac{D_0(1 + g)^\infty}{(1 + K)^\infty} \qquad (11.8)$$

If the assumption is made that the growth rate is less than the investor's required rate of return, $g < k$, Equation 11.8 simplifies to

$$V_0 = \frac{D_0(1 + g)}{K - g} = \frac{D_1}{K - g} \qquad (11.9)$$

Equation 11.9 is a widely used DDM. Sometimes it is referred to as the *Gordon Model* or the *Constant Growth Model*.[17]
To illustrate, assume that $g = .05$, $k = .16$, and $D_0 = \$2$:

$$V_0 = \frac{\$2(1 + .05)^1}{(1 + .16)^1} + \frac{\$2(1 + .05)^2}{(1 + .16)^2} + \ldots + \frac{\$2(1 + .05)^\infty}{(1 + .16)^\infty}$$

$$= \frac{\$2.10}{.16 - .05} = \$19.09$$

Additional insights concerning a stock's intrinsic value, as indicated by the constant growth model, can be made by relating dividends to earnings,

---

[17] Myron Gordon, *The Investment, Financing and Valuation of the Corporation* (Homewood, Ill.: Irwin, 1962).

growth to dividend policy and the rate of return the firm earns on its equity capital. If E_t represents EPS in period t and b is the *earnings retention rate* for the firm,

$$D_0 = E_0(1 - b)$$

For example, assume that the firm has EPS of $5 and that the directors decide to retain 60 percent of earnings for reinvestment in the firm. Dividends per share, DPS, are

$$D_0 = \$5(1 - .6) = \$2.00$$

Next, assume that the firm's retention rate, b, is constant and that the after-tax rate of return the firm earns on its equity capital, r, is constant. Under these very restrictive assumptions, it can be shown that the firm's growth rate in earnings and dividends will be constant:

$$g = br \qquad (11.10)$$

For example, if the firm retains 60 percent of its profits and earns 10 percent after taxes on its equity:

$$g = (.6)(.1) = 6\%$$

These relationships can be incorporated into the constant growth model:

$$V_0 = \frac{E_0(1 - b)(1 + br)}{(1 + K)^1} + \frac{E_0(1 - b)(1 + br)^2}{(1 + K)^2} + \cdots + \frac{E_0(1 - b)(1 + br)^\infty}{(1 + K)^\infty}$$

$$= \frac{E_0(1 - b)(1 + br)}{K - br} \qquad (11.11)$$

Equation 11.11 indicates that the intrinsic value of the stock depends on earnings, dividend policy, profitability of the firm's asset investments, and the investor's required rate of return.

To illustrate Equation 11.11, assume $E_0 = \$5$, $b = .6$, $r = .1$, and $K = .16$:

$$V_0 = \frac{\$5(1 - .6)[1 + (.6)(.1)]}{.16 - (.6)(.1)} = \frac{\$2.12}{.1} = \$21.20$$

3. SENSITIVITY OF THE MODEL TO ESTIMATES Table 11.3 provides five cases that illustrate the sensitivity of the basic DDMs to estimates of K and g. In comparing Cases 1 and 2, an increase in K from 16 percent to 20 percent results in a 20 percent reduction in V_0. Cases 3 and 4 illustrate that increasing the growth rate assumption from a "normal" rate of 6 percent to a "rapid" rate of 12 percent increases V_0 from $21.20 to $56.00, or 164 percent. Finally, Case 5 considers the impact of a negative or declining growth rate. V_0 for Case 5 is $8.55 using a negative 6 percent growth rate, compared to $V_0 = \$21.20$ for a positive 6 percent growth rate in Case 3. The purpose of this illustration is to indicate that an analyst should be extremely careful in estimating the variables needed in the DDM.

TABLE 11.3   ILLUSTRATION OF BASIC DIVIDEND DISCOUNT MODELS

CASE 1 = NO GROWTH	CASE 2 = NO GROWTH	CASE 3 = NORMAL GROWTH
$D_0 = \$2$	$D_0 = \$2$	$D_0 = \$2$
$K = 16\%$	$K = 20\%$	$K = 16\%$
$g = 0$	$g = 0$	$g = 6\%$
$V_0 = \dfrac{D}{K}$	$V_0 = \dfrac{D}{K}$	$V_0 = \dfrac{D_1}{K - g}$
$V_0 = \dfrac{\$2}{.16} = \$12.50$	$V_0 = \dfrac{\$2}{.20} = \$10.00$	$V_0 = \dfrac{\$2(1 + .06)}{.16 - .06} = \$21.20$

CASE 4 = RAPID GROWTH	CASE 5 = DECLINING GROWTH
$D_0 = \$2$	$D_0 = \$2$
$K = 16\%$	$K = 6\%$
$g = 12\%$	$g = -6\%$
$V_0 = \dfrac{D_1}{K - g}$	$V_0 = \dfrac{D_1}{K - g}$
$V_0 = \dfrac{\$2(1 + .12)}{.16 - .12} = \$56.00$	$V_0 = \dfrac{\$2(1 - .06)}{.16 - (.06)} = \$8.55$

4. FINITE HOLDING PERIOD The basic DDMs can be modified to reflect a specific investment horizon. For example, assume that the investment horizon is one year:

$$V_0 = \frac{D_0(1 + g)}{(1 + K)} + \frac{P_1}{(1 + K)} \tag{11.12}$$

In this case, the analyst must estimate the dividend for the next year and the likely price of the stock at the end of one year, P_1. A two-year horizon model would be

$$V_0 = \frac{D_0(1 + g)}{(1 + K)} + \frac{D_0(1 + g)^2}{(1 + K)^2} + \frac{P_2}{(1 + K)^2} \tag{11.13}$$

In this particular case, the analyst assumes that dividends will increase by rate g for the next two years. The appropriate models for P_2 is either Equations 11.7 or 11.9 depending on the dividend growth assumption starting in year 3.

More Complex Models

One of the obvious problems with the basic DDMs is the restrictive assumptions that the models require, such as constant growth rate, constant required rate of return, and that $g < K$. Removing these restrictive assumptions, and thereby providing a more flexible model, results in more complex DDMs. There is evidence, however, that more complex DDMs improve the accuracy of the forecast and therefore their usefulness in selecting stocks.

A 1985 article tested four valuation models using a sample of 150 stocks.[18] The four models tested were

1. no growth (Equation 11.7)
2. constant growth (Equation 11.9)
3. finite holding period—two years (variation of Equation 11.13)
4. finite holding period—three years (variation of Equation 11.13)

Earnings for each stock were estimated using IBES data, and growth rates were calculated using historical earnings and earnings forecasts. The CAPM was used to adjust for risk. Each model was used to rank the 150 stocks into five portfolios of 30 stocks each. For each of the four models, the top-ranked portfolios outperformed lower-ranked portfolios, and the S&P 400. Portfolio returns also improved "considerably" as the complexity of the ranking model increased. This study indicates that there may be some tangible benefits associated with using more complex models.

1. TWO-PHASE MODEL The two-phase model allows the analyst to use two growth rate estimates. Typically, a "high" growth rate is used in phase one, and a "normal" rate in phase two, resulting in a high-growth, two-phase model. This model could be used for a company that was expected to have super growth for a period of years, declining to a normal rate of growth for phase two.

    Let g_1 represent the growth rate for phase one, which lasts from period $t = 1$ to $t = A$, and g_2 represent the growth rate for phase two:

$$V_0 = \frac{D_0(1 + g_1)}{(1 + K)} + \frac{D_0(1 + g_1)^2}{(1 + K)^2} + \cdots + \frac{D_0(1 + g_1)^A}{(1 + K)^A} \qquad (11.14)$$

$$+ \frac{D_0(1 + g_1)^A(1 + g_2)}{(1 + K)^{A+1}} + \frac{D_0(1 + g_1)^A(1 + g_2)^2}{(1 + K)^{A+2}} + \cdots$$

$$+ \frac{D_0(1 + g_1)^A(1 + g_2)^\infty}{(1 + K)^\infty}$$

Notice that g_1 can be greater than K since phase one lasts for a finite number of years. Usually it is assumed that $g_2 < K$ to simplify the calculations for phase two.

By using present-value-of-annuity relationships and assuming $g_2 < K$, Equation 11.14 can be simplified for calculation purposes:

$$V_0 = D_0(1 + g_1)\left(\frac{1 + g_1}{1 + K}\right)\left(\frac{(1 + K)^{A-1} - 1}{K}\right) \qquad (11.15)$$

$$+ \frac{\dfrac{D_0(1 + g_1)^A(1 + g_2)}{K - g_2}}{(1 + K)^A}$$

---

[18] Eric H. Sorensen and David A. Williamson, "Some Evidence on the Value of Dividend Discount Models," *Financial Analysts Journal* (November–December 1985): pp. 60–69.

TABLE 11.4 ILLUSTRATION OF TWO-PHASE MODEL

Assumptions: $D_0 = \$2$; $K = 16\%$; $g_1 = 20\%$; $g_2 = 10\%$; $A = 4$ years

PERIOD	D	PRESENT VALUE FACTOR	PRESENT VALUE
1	$2.40	.8621	$2.07
2	2.88	.7432	2.14
3	3.46	.6407	2.22
4	4.15	.5524	2.29
		Total present value of phase one dividends	$8.72

Using Equation 11.15:

$$V_0 = \$2(1 + .2)\left(\frac{1 + .20}{1 + .16}\right)\left(\frac{(1 + .16)^3 - 1}{.16}\right) + \frac{\dfrac{\$2(1 + .2)^4(1 + .1)}{16 - .1}}{(1 + .16)}$$

$$= \$2.40(1.0345)(3.5056) + \frac{\$76.03}{1.8106}$$

$$= \$8.70 + \$41.99$$

$$= \$50.69$$

Value of stock at $t = 4$, using Equation 11.9:

$$V_4 = \frac{D_4(1 + g_2)}{k - g_2}$$

$$= \frac{\$4.15(1 + .1)}{.16 - .1}$$

$$= \$76.08$$

Present value of $V_4 = \dfrac{\$76.08}{(1 + .16)^4} = \$42.02$

Intrinsic value of stock:

$$V_0 = \$8.72 + \$42.02 = \$50.74$$

Table 11.4 uses a table format as well as Equation 11.15 to illustrate the two-phase model. The estimates of V_0 differ because of rounding.

2. THREE-PHASE MODEL A number of modifications can be made to the two-phase model. Notice that in Equation 11.14 the change in the growth rate from g_1 to g_2 occurred instantaneously. In the example in Table 11.4, g_1 was 20 percent for years 1–4 and immediately dropped to 10 percent for year 5 and the following years. One commonly used modification is to allow for a transition period during which earnings change from g_1 to g_2. This essentially results in three phases: phase one, with rapid growth; phase two, with a transition in growth; and phase three, with steady-state growth. Figure 11.2 illustrates these phases.

Without the help of a computer, calculations for the three-phase model can be tedious if phase two represents a relatively long period. An article by Fuller and Hsia, however, develops a simplified model that provides estimates closely approximating the results from the more tedious calculation.[19] The

[19] Russell J. Fuller and Chi-Cheng Hsia, "A Simplified Common Stock Valuation Model," *Financial Analysts Journal* (September-October 1984): pp. 49–56.

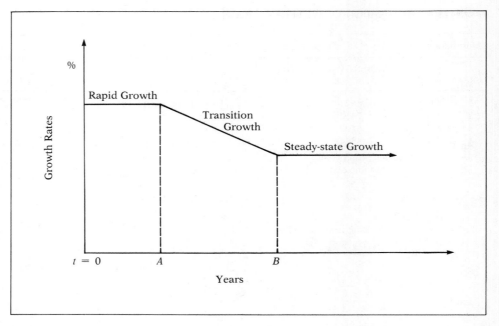

FIGURE 11.2 Three-phase model growth rates

model is called the *H-model* since it uses the "halfway" point of phase two. The H-model:

$$P_0 = \frac{D_0}{K - g_2}\left[(1 + g_2) + \frac{A + B}{2}(g_1 - g_2)\right] \tag{11.16}$$

where A is the number of years to phase two, and B is the number of years until phase three. These points are labeled in Figure 11.2. The term $(A + B)/2$ is therefore the midpoint or halfway point of phase two. Table 11.5 provides an illustration of the three-phase model and of the H-model. Notice that the two estimates are very close ($58.42 versus $58.33). The H-model, however, greatly simplifies the calculations.

PRICE/EARNINGS MODEL

Overview

Many analysts use a price/earnings model as part of a fundamental analysis. Essentially, the model requires only an estimate of the P/E ratio and earnings at the end of the investment horizon. For example, assume that the analyst has a one-

TABLE 11.5 ILLUSTRATION OF THREE-PHASE AND H-MODEL

Assumptions: $D_0 = \$2$, $K = 16\%$, $g_1 = 20\%$, $g_2 = 10\%$, $A = 4$ years

Phase two assumes that the growth rate declines in a linear fashion from 20% to 10% over a 4-year period or by 2% per year. In other words, the growth rate for years 1–4 = 20%, year 5 = 18%, year 6 = 16%, year 7 = 14%, year 8 = 12%, years 9-∞ = 10%.

Three-phase model calculations:

PERIOD	GROWTH RATE	D	PRESENT VALUE FACTOR	PRESENT VALUE
1	20%	$2.40	.8621	$ 2.07
2	20	2.88	.7432	2.14
3	20	3.46	.6407	2.22
4	20	4.15	.5524	2.29
5	18	4.90	.4761	2.33
6	16	5.68	.4104	2.33
7	14	6.48	.3538	2.29
8	12	7.25	.3050	2.21
			Total	$17.88

Phase-three value: $V_8 = \dfrac{D_8(1 + g_2)}{K - g_2} = \dfrac{\$7.25(1 + .1)}{.16 - .1} = \$132.92$

Present value of phase-three value: $\dfrac{\$132.92}{(1 + .16)^8} = \$40.54$

Total value of stock: $V_0 = \$17.88 + \$40.54 = \$58.42$

H-model calculations:

$$V_0 = \frac{\$2}{.16 - .10}\left[(1 + .1) + \frac{4 + 9}{2}(.2 - .1)\right] = \$33.33(1.75) = \$58.33$$

year investment horizon. The model would be

$$V_1 = (M_1)(E_1) \tag{11.17}$$

where V_1 = intrinsic value at end of year 1

M_1 = estimate of P/E ratio at end of year 1

E_1 = estimate of earnings at end of year 1

As illustrated below, this model is closely related to the dividend discount models. Its simplicity and use of earnings rather than dividends make it popular with analysts. Despite its apparent simplicity, however, the difficulty in estimating P/E ratios should not be underestimated; the major factors determining P/E ratios are dividend payout, earnings growth, and earnings volatility. These factors appear in models for estimating P/E ratios. Earnings multiples can be very volatile for stocks in general and especially for individual stocks. Table 11.6 illustrates this point by providing a sample of P/E ratios for a number of companies and the S&P 500 over the period 1978–1987. Estimating a future P/E ratio by an extrapolation of historical ratios does not appear to be advisable.

TABLE 11.6 SAMPLE OF P/E RATIOS OF INDIVIDUAL COMMON STOCKS AND S&P 500

YEAR	AMERICAN EXPRESS	AMERICAN HOME PROD.	BANK AMERICA	BOSTON EDISON	CHRYSLER	LIZ CLAIBORNE	TECO ENERGY	ZAYRE	S&P 500
1978	8.0	13.1	7.0	8.1	d	–	7.2	4.8	7.9
1979	6.6	10.9	6.4	6.3	d	NMF	8.3	3.8	7.0
1980	6.4	9.6	5.7	5.7	d	NMF	5.4	5.0	8.1
1981	8.0	10.3	8.2	5.2	d	8.3	6.4	6.9	8.2
1982	8.0	10.9	7.3	7.1	d	15.4	7.9	9.1	9.7
1983	15.5	11.8	9.8	7.6	5.8	13.1	7.4	12.1	11.1
1984	11.3	12.1	10.5	5.9	2.4	10.0	7.1	10.1	9.6
1985	12.5	12.7	d	7.8	2.6	14.2	8.9	16.0	12.9
1986	13.3	15.4	d	9.8	4.0	19.7	12.8	20.2	15.8
1987	37.8	14.4	d	11.4	5.8	21.2	11.6	NMF	16.4
Beta	1.40	0.90	1.00	0.70	1.50	1.55	0.60	1.45	1.00

d = negative EPS

NMF = not meaningful figure because EPS are close to zero.

SOURCE: *Value Line Investment Survey*, various issues; © 1988 by Value Line Inc.; used by permission of Value Line, Inc. Standard & Poor's *Analysts' Handbook*, 1987; and Standard & Poor's *Stock Guide*, January 1988.

Basic Models

This section describes some of the more popular models used to estimate a future P/E ratio. Most of these models define the P/E ratio using the same variables used in the DDMs.

1. NO GROWTH A P/E ratio, where all earnings are distributed as dividends and has no earnings growth, is

$$M = \frac{1}{K} \qquad (11.18)$$

For example, assume that the investor's required rate of return is 16 percent, indicating a P/E ratio of 6.25. If K is constant, then the multiplier will also be a constant.

If the company retains earnings by reducing dividends, however, so that $b > 0$, and these retained earnings do not produce earnings growth, the multiplier should decline. If the dividend payout rate is defined as D/E, and $D/E < 1$, the multiplier becomes

$$M = \frac{D/E}{K} \qquad (11.19)$$

For example, if $K = 16\%$ and $D/E = .5$, then $M = .5/.16 = 3.125$. If the company distributes all earnings as dividends, M would be 6.25. Earnings should be retained only if they can be used to produce earnings growth.

The no-growth P/E model and DDM provide identical valuation estimates using the above multiplier models. Assume $K = .16$, $E = \$4$, and all earnings are distributed as dividends. Both models indicate the same value:

DDM: $V_0 = D/K = \$4/.16 = \$25.00$

P/E Model: $V_0 = ME = (1/K)E = (1/.16)(\$4) = \$25.00$

Suppose the company retains 50% of earnings with zero earnings growth

DDM: $V_0 = \dfrac{E(1 - b)}{K} = \dfrac{\$4(1 - .5)}{.16} = \$12.50$

P/E Model: $V_0 = [(D/E)/K]E = (.5/.16)\$4 = \$12.50$

2. CONSTANT GROWTH If the company retains earnings, the multiplier can be calculated as

$$M = \frac{(D/E)(1 + g)}{K - g} \qquad (11.20)$$

For example, assume that $g = 10\%$, $K = 16\%$ and the firm retains 50% of the earnings. The multiplier would be

$$M = \frac{(.5)(1 + .1)}{.16 - .1} = 9.17$$

The similarity of the constant-growth DDM and the P/E model can be shown using the same example of $E = \$4$, $K = 16\%$, and $D/E = .5$, $g = .1$:

$$\text{DDM:} \quad V_0 = \frac{E(1 - b)(1 + g)}{K - g} = \frac{\$4(1 - .5)(1 + .1)}{.16 - .1} = \$36.67$$

$$\text{P/E Model:} \quad V_0 = \left[\frac{(D/E)(1 + g)}{K - g}\right] E = \left[\frac{(.5)(1 + .1)}{.16 - .1}\right]\$4 = \$36.67$$

Whitbeck-Kisor Model

One of the first and best-known attempts at developing an econometric model of theoretical P/E ratios was by Whitbeck and Kisor.[20] This study used a sample of 135 NYSE stocks to estimate the following regression model:

$$(P/E)_j = \hat{a}_0 + \hat{a}_1 g_j + \hat{a}_2 (D/E)_j + \hat{a}_3 \sigma_j + e_j \tag{11.21}$$

where $(P/E)_j$ = price earnings ratio for firm j

$\hat{a}_0 - \hat{a}_3$ = regression constants

g_j = historical earnings growth for firm j

$(D/E)_j$ = historical dividend payout ratio for firm j

σ_j = standard deviation of the past earnings growth rate around the earnings trend line for firm j

e_j = random disturbance term

The results of their regression:

$$P/E = 8.2 + 1.5g + 6.7(D/E) - .2\sigma \tag{11.22}$$

While this model was reasonably accurate in estimating the theoretical P/E ratios for stocks in the early 1960s, its validity for the late 1980s is questionable. The regression equation would need to be reestimated, using more recent data and possibly new or different independent variables. This model does illustrate, however, that econometric models of P/E ratios may provide valuable insights into the analysis of common stocks.

RECENT DEVELOPMENTS IN COMMON STOCK VALUATION MODELS

The discussion of the basic DDM and P/E models presented previously illustrates that the same estimates needed for the DDMs are also needed for the P/E models. The key variables are dividend policy, growth prospects, and the investor's required rate of return.

---

[20] V. S. Whitbeck and M. Kisor, "A New Tool in Investment Decision-making," *Financial Analysts Journal* (May-June 1963): pp. 55–62.

In reality, however, the relationships between these key variables and their importance in determining value are complex. A number of recently published articles provide some practical guidelines that can be used to incorporate these key variables and their relationships into the basic models.

Two articles by Merrett and Newbould address the relationship between dividend policy and the valuation models.[21] Their analysis suggests a procedure that can be used to estimate the impact of dividend policy on future earnings. The major insight provided by their model involves replacing the traditional estimate of earnings with an estimate of *corrected earnings per share*, CEPS. Their model is the *CEPS model*, and the name is protected by trademark registration. The DDM form of their model is:

$$V_0 = \frac{CEPS(1 + g_{CEPS})}{K - g_{CEPS}} \tag{11.23}$$

Notice that the traditional measure of dividends is replaced by *CEPS* and that g is replaced by a growth estimate based on *CEPS*.

This model recognizes the fact that corporations can achieve higher EPS simply by the retention of earnings. Part of this apparent growth, however, is "illusory" if the retained earnings are reinvested by the company at a rate of return equal to or below the stockholders' required rate of return. The top panel in Table 11.7 is adopted from the 1982 Merrett and Newbould article and demonstrates this illusory growth. Notice that the EPS, DPS, and the stock's value are growing at 9 percent per year because the company is retaining 50 percent of its earnings and reinvesting the earnings at the stockholders' 18 percent required rate of return. If the company elected to distribute all earnings, the growth rate would be zero, but the stockholders would be just as well off. The CEPS model indicates that the illusory portion of growth should be removed in an analysis of the stock.

The lower panel of Table 11.7 calculates CEPS by removing the portion of earnings due to reinvestment of earnings at a rate of return of 18 percent. Notice that the annual returns on the retentions must consider the fact that returns on retained earnings are cumulative. The CEPS and corrected DPS, CDPS, are constant, indicating $g_{CEPS} = 0$, and consequently, the stock's intrinsic value is constant.

In summary, the CEPS for a company will always be less than reported EPS if the company retains part of its earnings. It is also possible that CEPS will increase, representing growth that occurs because the company is able to reinvest earnings at a rate greater than the stockholders' required rate of return. Essentially, the analyst should calculate the marginal after-tax rate of return on additions to retained earnings and compare this rate to the stockholders' required rate of return. If the comparison is favorable, then the company can have real growth that would benefit the stockholders by increasing the value of the stock.

[21] A. J. Merrett and Gerald D. Newbould, "CEPS: The Illusion of Corporate Growth," *Journal of Portfolio Management* (Fall 1982): pp. 5–10; "Integrating Financial Performance and Stock Valuation," *Journal of Portfolio Management* (Fall 1983) pp. 27–32.

TABLE 11.7   ILLUSTRATION OF CEPS MODEL

I. ILLUSORY GROWTH

Assumptions: Annual EPS growth of 9% resulting from retaining 50% of earnings. The firm's cost of equity capital and stockholders' required rate of return is 18%.

	YEAR				
	1	2	3	4	5
EPS	$ 2.00	$ 2.18	$ 2.38	$ 2.59	$ 2.82
DPS	1.00	1.09	1.19	1.29	1.41
Retention	1.00	1.09	1.19	1.30	1.41
Stock Value*	12.11	13.22	14.33	15.67	17.08

* Calculated using the constant growth DDM (Equation 11.9)

II. CEPS MODEL

	YEAR				
	1	2	3	4	5
Reported EPS	$ 2.00	$ 2.18	$ 2.38	$ 2.59	$ 2.82
Retention	1.00	1.09	1.19	1.30	1.41
Returns on Retention*	–	.18	.38	.59	.82
CEPS**	$ 2.00	$ 2.00	$ 2.00	$ 2.00	$ 2.00
CDPS	1.00	1.00	1.00	1.00	1.00
Stock Value***	11.11	11.11	11.11	11.11	11.11

* Calculated as the cumulative retentions per share times the shareholders' required rate of return.
** Calculated as reported EPS minus returns on retention.
*** Calculated using Equation 11.23, where $g_{CEPS} = 0$.

Two articles deal with the relationship between the investor's required rate of return, K, and the P/E ratio or its reciprocal, the E/P ratio.[22] The articles illustrated that investors consider variability in K as a source of risk and that this risk is not reflected in the stock's beta. The volatility of K reflects economic factors such as inflation, and these should be incorporated into the estimates of K.

Additional insights into the influence of growth on valuations are presented in a 1987 article.[23] This article explains the relationship between growth, P/E ratios, and required rates of return. Models are developed that incorporate additional variables into the basic valuation models.

The article extends the analysis offered by Estep, Hanson, and Johnson by considering additional risk factors that influence K or E/P. The following *inflation adjustment model* is suggested by Johnson:

$$V_o = \frac{D(1 + g)(1 + fI)}{(K - g) + (h - f)I} \tag{11.24}$$

---

[22] Tony Estep, Nick Hanson, and Cal Johnson, "Sources of Value and Risk in Common Stocks," *Journal of Portfolio Management* (Summer 1983): pp. 5–13, and Lewis D. Johnson, "Sources of Risk and Value in Common Stocks: Comment," *Journal of Portfolio Management* (Spring 1984): pp. 84–85.

[23] Lewis D. Johnson, "Growth Prospects and Share Prices: A Systematic View," *Journal of Portfolio Management* (Winter 1987): pp. 58–60.

where $g = real$ rate of dividend growth
$I =$ the anticipated rate of inflation
$f =$ an inflation flow through constant
$h =$ a risk aversion parameter greater than unity

This model shows that the impact of inflation on dividends and on the discount rate should be explicitly incorporated into the model. Additional details concerning these models are presented in the articles.

INVESTMENT DECISION

Overview

After a traditional fundamental analysis is completed, the final step involves an investment decision concerning the stock under consideration. This section provides a procedure that can be used to determine what recommendation should be made relative to other stocks under consideration or to stocks in general.

Estimate of Expected Holding Period Return

The expected HPR over a one-year holding period can be calculated as

$$E(HPR_1) = \frac{V_1 - P_0 + D_1}{P_0}$$ (11.25)

For example, assume that the fundamental analysis indicates that the stock should be selling for $22 in one year, V_1, and is currently selling for $20. Dividends for the next year are estimated to be $3.

$$E(HPR_1) = \frac{\$22 - \$20 + \$3}{\$20} = 25\%$$

This indicates that the stock will provide a 25 percent return over the next year. Is this return adequate to justify a long position? The $E(HPR)$ can be compared to the return suggested by the CAPM:

$$R_j = R_f + \beta_j[E(R_m) - R_f]$$ (11.26)

Based on the economic analysis, assume that the expected market return for the next year, $E(R_m)$, is 15 percent and that the yield to maturity on one-year Treasury bills is presently 9 percent. If the beta for the stock is 1.3, the CAPM suggests the stock should provide a return of

$$R_j = 9\% + 1.3[15\% - 9\%] = 16.8\%$$

The analyst can now compare $E(HPR)$ and R_j, and conclude that the stock appears to be undervalued. The present price of $20 suggests that the stock may appreciate over the next year and provide a *HPR* of 25 percent. Stocks with the same degree of systematic risk are expected to provide a return of only 16.8 percent. Figure 11.3 illustrates this relationship.

Stocks that plot above the SML offer higher returns than their systematic risk suggests. Thus, they are *undervalued*, and a long position is appropriate. Stocks that plot below the SML are *overvalued*, and a short position may be justified. Stocks that plot on the SML are correctly valued.

A variation of this approach, called the *market plane approach*, was developed by Wells Fargo Bank. This approach requires that $E(HPR)$ be available for a number of stocks. These expected returns are then plotted against the betas for each stock. A regression or best-fit line is then estimated using these points. Stocks that plot above the regression line offer high expected returns relative to their

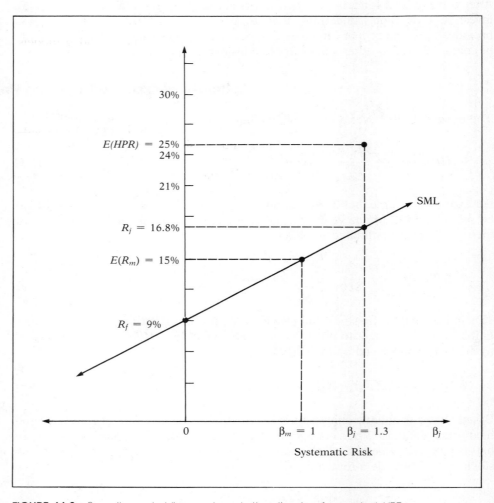

FIGURE 11.3 Security market line and analyst's estimate of expected *HPR*

betas and may therefore be undervalued. Stocks plotting below the regression line offer small expected returns relative to their systematic risk and may be overvalued. The market plane approach eliminates the need to estimate the expected return for the market.[24]

SUMMARY

This chapter presented a traditional fundamental analysis approach to common stock valuation. The key variable in valuation is the estimate of future earnings and dividends. Numerous research articles have demonstrated the importance of earnings and changes in earnings to stock value. Individual investors can formulate their own estimates of earnings, using techniques discussed in the chapter. An alternative is to rely on estimates published by professional analysts or by company managements.

Dividend discount models, DDM, and Price Earnings models, P/E, are the traditional common stock valuation models. They are quite similar in terms of the variables that are used in the models. Recent research has provided models that incorporate additional variables and relationships into the traditional models. There appears to be evidence that more complex models can produce more accurate value estimates and therefore increase the likelihood of risk-adjusted excess returns.

Despite the availability of numerous models, common stock valuation is essentially an art, not a science. The success of the valuation depends on the skills of the analyst in making accurate forecasts and using an appropriate model.

The final investment decision should be made by comparing the expected *HPR* to the expected return on other stocks with the same degree of risk. This procedure attempts to identify over- and undervalued stocks.

QUESTIONS

1. Explain how an estimate of a stock's intrinsic value is used by fundamental analysts to make an investment recommendation.

2. Discuss the pros and cons of viewing common stock valuation as an art rather than a scientific procedure.

3. Clearly distinguish between expected and unexpected earnings. How can unexpected earnings be measured? In terms of an active investment strategy, would expected or unexpected earnings be more valuable in attempting to beat the market? Explain.

4. Using the sample of companies in Table 11.1, comment on the apparent difficulty or ease of forecasting future earnings based on historical earnings. Which of these companies would likely report unexpected earnings? Explain.

---

[24] For more details, see Robert Ferguson and Richard Lynn, ''A Security Market Plane Approach to Stock Selection,'' *Financial Analysts Journal* (September-October 1984): pp. 75–80, and James L. Farrell, Jr. ''The Dividend Discount Model: A Primer,'' *Financial Analysts Journal* (November-December 1985); pp. 16–25.

5. Discuss the advantages and disadvantages of using a consensus approach to forecasting a company's earnings.

6. Discuss the empirical evidence dealing with the accuracy of earnings estimates made by analysts, management, and statistical procedures. Based on this evidence, what technique or method of forecasting is suggested?

7. Explain how a pro forma income statement can be used as an earnings forecasting procedure.

8. Suppose you estimate that the EPS of a company will increase by 10 percent next year, primarily because of an increase in the inflation rate in the economy. Based on this forecast, do you think the company's common stock will increase in price? Explain.

9. Compare and contrast the constant-growth dividend discount model with the equivalent P/E model. Discuss the advantages and disadvantages of both models.

10. If investment theory indicates that dividend policy is irrelevant to common stock value, why do many analysts use dividends in valuing common stock?

11. Explain the two-phase dividend discount model. What advantages does it have over the constant-growth dividend discount model?

12. Suppose your analysis indicates that a particular company may experience several years of declining dividends, followed by constant dividends for a number of years, with a later period of increasing dividends. Explain how this anticipated dividend pattern can be incorporated into a common stock valuation model.

13. Explain the concept of cash equivalents or corrected earnings per share. How does this approach measure earnings growth compared to the growth rate in reported earnings?

14. In your opinion, is it appropriate to assume that the required rate of return on a particular stock will be constant over time? What factors may cause the required rate of return to change? How would a change in the required rate of return influence the risk of a particular stock?

15. Explain how inflation can be incorporated into the common stock valuation models. Would you expect inflation to affect all stocks equally?

16. Indicate how the CAPM and SML can be used to make an investment recommendation concerning a particular stock.

PROBLEMS

1. Consider the folllowing information on a share of common stock:

Current dividend per share	$2.50
Investor's required rate of return	16%

a. Calculate the intrinsic value of the stock assuming that the dividend will remain at $2.50 indefinitely.

b. Calculate the intrinsic value assuming that dividends will increase by 8% per year indefinitely.

c. Calculate the intrinsic value assuming that dividends will remain at $2.50 for the next three years and then increase at a rate of 5% per year indefinitely.

2. Boston Edison reported the following EPS:

1981	$2.08
1982	1.59
1983	1.80
1984	2.42
1985	2.51
1986	2.58

a. Estimate the EPS for 1987 using a regression trend line. Also calculate the coefficient of determination for the regression.

b. Given that Boston Edison reported EPS of $2.27 for 1987, calculate the standardized unexpected earnings for 1987 using your estimates from part a.

c. Based on your analysis, do you think that the stock likely had a significant price adjustment because of the announced earnings of $2.27? Explain.

3. A fundamental analysis of DSK, Inc. resulted in the following:

Current stock price	$18.00
Estimate of stock's price in one year	$20.00
Estimate of dividends for next year	$2.50
Present yield on one-year Treasury bill	8.62%
Beta	1.50
Estimate of HPR on S&P 500 for next year	14.00%

a. Calculate the stock's expected one-year *HPR*.

b. Use the CAPM to calculate the required rate of return for the stock.

c. Does the stock appear to be priced to offer a risk-adjusted excess return for next year? Explain.

d. Based on this analysis, would you recommend a long, short, or no position in the stock?

4. Suppose the DPS for a particular stock increased from $1.00 in 1980 to $2.25 in 1988. The required rate of return on the stock is 15%. Calculate the intrinsic value of the stock on January 1, 1989, assuming that dividends will continue to grow at the same rate as they did over the period 1980–1988.

5. PIL, Inc. distributes 40% of earnings to stockholders. Based on a fundamental analysis, you estimate next year's earnings at $3.29 and expect earnings to increase by 8% per year. Given a required rate of return of 15%, calculate the intrinsic value of the stock.

6. EAM, Inc. retains 70% of earnings to finance the rapid sales growth it has been experiencing. An analysis of the company indicates that, on average, it earns a 14% rate of return on incremental equity capital. Based on the business and financial risk of the company, you conclude that a required rate of return on the common stock is 16%.

a. Calculate the likely growth rate in earnings and dividends.

b. If current earnings are $3.86 per share, use your answer to part a to calculate the stock's value.

    c.   Suppose the company changes its dividend policy, so that 40% of earnings are retained. Calculate the stock's value.

    d.   What dividend policy would you recommend to maximize the value of the stock?

7.   Kevin O'Hare, a local stockbroker, indicates that Holiday, Inc. is presently under-valued and recommends that you buy 100 shares of the stock. His opinion is based on a projected 20% increase in EPS for next year, combined with an optimistic market forecast that indicates an increase of 5% in the P/E ratio for stocks in general.

    a.   Assume that the stock of Holiday, Inc. is currently priced at $8\frac{1}{4}$ with EPS of $1.37. Calculate the P/E ratio.

    b.   Suppose that the EPS and P/E ratio increase at the rates suggested by Kevin. Calculate the value of the stock one year from now.

    c.   Assuming the company will not pay any dividend, calculate the expected *HPR* based on your answer to part b.

    d.   If you think a required rate of return of 18% is appropriate, should you follow Kevin's recommendation?

8.   A company you are analyzing presently has EPS of $2.29 and distributes 60% of earnings to stockholders. Assume that the required rate of return is 14% and that this is also the rate the firm earns on its equity capital.

    a.   Calculate an appropriate theoretical multiplier for this stock.

    b.   If the stock is currently selling for $19\frac{1}{2}$ per share, would you recommend a long position? Would you recommend a short position?

    c.   Assume a short position is taken at the current price. Calculate the expected *HPR* if the stock is purchased at the end of the year to cover the short position. Base your calculations on the assumption that the P/E ratio will decline to its theoretical value by the end of the year. Also remember that dividends represent a cash *outflow* to a shortseller. Does this analysis indicate that a short position is desir-able?

9.   Hanna, Inc. presently has EPS of $3.69. An analysis indicates that it earns approxi-mately 15% on equity capital. Its beta and current market condition indicate that a 14% required rate of return on the stock is appropriate.

    a.   Calculate the theoretical multiplier for the company assuming it distributes all earnings to stockholders.

    b.   Calculate the theoretical multiplier assuming it distributes 60% of its earnings to stockholders.

    c.   Suppose Hanna, Inc. distributes 60% of its earnings and uses the retained profits to acquire a small company that produces no additional earnings for Hanna, Inc. Calculate its theoretical multiplier.

10.   Growth, Inc. is currently being recommended by several investment advisory services. The stock is presently priced at $118 per share with current dividends of $3.00 per share. Analysts are optimistic about the stock's prospects because earnings are ex-pected to grow at 25% per year for the next five years and then at 10% per year indefinitely. Calculate the value of the stock if the required rate of return is 15%. Do you think a long position is appropriate?

11.   Use the information in problem 10 about Growth, Inc., but assume that the dividend growth rate will decline from 25% to 10% over a three-year transition period. Thus, the growth rates will be 25% for years 1–5 and 10% starting in year 9. Years 6–8 represent the transition period for the growth rate. Calculate the value of the stock using the H-model and indicate whether a long position is appropriate.

12. Suppose an economic analysis indicates a long-term inflation forecast of 4%. HHL, Inc. is expected to have a long-term real dividend growth rate of 5% and will *also* increase dividends by the rate of inflation. Its inflation-flow through constant is therefore unity. If your risk aversion inflation parameter is 1.3 and required rate of return is 16%, calculate the intrinsic value of the stock using the inflation adjustment model. Assume that the current dividend is $3 per share.

13. Oviedo Manufacturing is a small struggling firm that is unable to increase dividends from the present level of $1.20. In addition, revenues and consequently dividends are expected to remain constant despite a long-term rate of inflation of 3%. The CAPM indicates an appropriate required rate of return of 16.8%. For an investor with a risk aversion inflation parameter of 1.2, what is the value of the stock? Calculate the value of the stock assuming there will be no long-term inflation.

14. Suppose Illusory, Inc. has current earnings of $3.00 per share and distributes 40% of earnings as dividends. The appropriate required rate of return on the stock is 18%. Assume the firm reinvests retained earnings at a rate of return of 18%.

    a. Calculate the intrinsic value of the stock using the constant growth DDM.

    b. Calculate the growth rate based on corrected earnings per share, CEPS.

    c. Calculate the intrinsic value of the stock using the CEPS model developed by Merrett and Newbould.

    d. Suppose the company is able to reinvest retained profits at a rate of return of 20% but maintains the same dividend policy. What impact will this have on CEPS and the CEPS growth rate? Would the intrinsic value of the stock increase? Explain.

COMPUTER APPLICATIONS

The floppy disk includes the following programs:

1. Simple or bi-variate regression
2. Multiple regression
3. Spread sheet for estimating earnings
4. Zero and constant-growth DDMs
5. Two-phase DDM
6. Three-phase DDM
7. CEPS model
8. Inflation adjustment model

These programs can be used to solve most of the problems in this chapter and to analyze other common stocks. Instructions and illustrations are provided on the disk.

REFERENCES

Aharony, Joseph, and Itzhak Swary. "Quarterly Dividend and Earnings Announcements and Stockholders' Returns: An Empirical Analysis." *Journal of Finance* (March 1980): pp. 1–12.

Benesh, Gary A., and Pamela P. Peterson. "On the Relationship between Earnings, Changes, Analysts' Forecast and Stock Price Fluctuation." *Financial Analysts Journal* (November-December 1986): pp. 29–39.

Bethke, William M., and Susan E. Boyd. "Should Dividend Discount Models Be Yield-tilted?" *Journal of Portfolio Management* (Spring 1983): pp. 23–27.

Bidwell, Clinton M., III. "SUE/PE Revista." *Journal of Portfolio Management* (Winter 1981): pp. 85–87.

Blume, Marshall E. "Stock Returns and Dividend Yields: Some More Evidence." *Review of Economics and Statistics* (November 1980): pp. 567–77.

Chu, Chen-Chin, and David T. Whitford. "Stock Market Returns and Inflationary Expectations: Additional Evidence for 1975–1979." *Journal of Financial Research* (Fall 1982) pp. 261–71.

Cole, John A. "Are Dividend Surprises Independently Important?" *Journal of Portfolio Management* (Summer 1984): pp. 45–50.

Darlin, Damon. "Picking a Loser: Young Analyst Defied 'Expert' and Foresaw Baldwin-United's Ills." *Wall Street Journal*, 28 September, 1983, pp. 1, 14.

Dennis, Debra K., and Dan W. French. "The CEPS Model for Common Stock Valuation: Comment." *Journal of Portfolio Management* (Summer 1984): pp. 83–85.

Einhorn, Steven G., and Patricia Shangquan. "Using the Dividend Discount Model for Asset Allocation." *Financial Analysts Journal* (May-June 1984): pp. 30–32.

Ellis, Charles D. "Ben Graham: Ideas as Mementos." *Financial Analysts Journal* (July-August 1982): pp. 41–48.

Estep, Preston W. "A New Method for Valuing Common Stocks." *Financial Analysts Journal* (November-December 1985): pp. 26–33.

Estep, Tony, Nick Hanson, and Cal Johnson. "Sources of Value and Risk in Common Stocks." *Journal of Portfolio Management* (Summer 1983): pp. 5–13.

Farell, James L., Jr. "The Dividend Discount Model: A Primer." *Financial Analysts Journal* (November-December 1985): pp. 16–25.

Ferguson, Robert, and Richard Lynn. "A Security Market Plane Approach to Stock Selection." *Financial Analysts Journal* (September-October 1984): pp. 75–80.

Fielitz, Bruce D., and Frederick L. Muller. "A Simplified Approach to Common Stock Valuation." *Financial Analysts Journal* (November-December 1985): pp. 35–41.

Fraser, Donald R. "Do Analysts' Forecasts Matter?" *University of Michigan Business Review* (Spring 1979): pp. 15–19.

Friend, Irwin, and Joel Hasbrouck. "Inflation and the Stock Market: Comment." *American Economic Review* (March 1982): pp. 237–46.

Fuller, Russel J., and Chi-Cheng Hsia. "A Simplified Common Stock Valutation Model." *Financial Analysts Journal* (September-October 1984): pp. 49–56.

Fuller, Russel J., and Glenn H. Petry. "Inflation, Returns on Equity, and Stock Prices." *Journal of Portfolio Management* (Summer 1981): pp. 20–25.

Gentry, James A., Paul Newbold, and David T. Whitford. "Predicting Bankruptcy: If Cash Flow's Not the Bottom Line, What Is?" *Financial Analysts Journal* (September-October 1985): pp. 47–56.

Givoly, Dan, and Josef Lakonishok. "The Quality of Analysts' Forecast of Earnings." *Financial Analysts Journal* (September-October 1984): pp. 40–47.

Groth, John C., Wilbur G. Lewellen, Gary G. Schlarbaum, and Ronald C. Lease. "An Analysis of Brokerage House Securities Recommendations." *Financial Analysts Journal* (January-February 1979): pp. 32–40.

Harris, Robert S. "Using Analysts' Growth Forecasts to Estimate Shareholder Required Rates of Return." *Financial Management* (Spring 1986): pp. 58–67.

Hawkins, Eugene H., Stanley C. Chamberlin, and Wayne E. Daniel. "Earnings Expectations and Security Prices." *Financial Analysts Journal* (September-October 1984): pp. 24–38, 74.

Hayes, Linda Snyder. "Fresh Evidence That Dividends Don't Matter." *Fortune*, 4 May, 1981, pp. 351–54.

Illingworth, Montieth M. "The Ruckus over Rating Analysts' Stock Picks." *Institutional Investor* (April 1982): pp. 73–76.

Imhoff, Eugene A., and Paul V. Pare. "Analysis and Comparison of Earnings Forecast Agents." *Journal of Accounting Research* (Autumn 1982): pp. 429–39.

Jahnke, Gregg, Stephen J. Klaffke, and Henry R. Oppenheimer. "Price-Earnings Ratios and Security Performance." *Journal of Portfolio Management* (Fall 1987): pp. 39–46.

Johnson, Lewis D. "Sources of Risk and Value in Common Stocks: Comment." *Journal of Portfolio Management* (Spring 1984): pp. 84–85.

———. "Dividends and Share Value: Graham and Dodd Revisited, Again." *Financial Analysts Journal* (September-October 1985): pp. 79–80.

———. "Growth Propsects and Share Prices: A Systematic View." *Journal of Portfolio Management* (Winter 1987): pp. 58–60.

Jones, Charles P., Richard J. Rendleman, Jr. and Henry A. Latane. "Stock Returns and SUEs during the 1970s." *Journal of Portfolio Management* (Winter 1984): pp. 18–22.

———. "Earning Announcements: Pre-and-Post Responses." *Journal of Portfolio Management* (Spring 1985): pp. 28–32.

Jones, Charles P., and Jack W. Wilson. "Stocks, Bonds, Paper, and Inflation: 1870–1985." *Journal of Portfolio Management* (Fall 1987): pp. 20–24.

Kerrigan, Thomas J. "When Forecasting Earnings, It Pays to Watch Forecast." *Journal of Portfolio Management* (Summer 1984): pp. 19–26.

Klemkosky, Robert C., and William P. Miller. "When Forecasting Earnings, It Pays to Be Right!" *Journal of Portfolio Management* (Summer 1984): pp. 13–18.

Kolluri, Bharat R. "Anticipated Price Changes, Inflation Uncertainty, and Capital Stock Returns." *Journal of Financial Research* (Summer 1982): pp. 135–49.

Latane, Henry A., and Charles P. Jones. "Standardized Unexpected Earnings—1971–77." *Journal of Finance* (June 1979): pp. 717–24.

Leonard, David C., and Michael E. Solt. "Recent Evidence on the Accuracy and Rationality of Popular Inflation Forecasts." *Journal of Financial Research* (Winter 1986): pp. 182–90.

———."Stock Market Signals of Changes in Expected Inflation." *Journal of Financial Research* (Spring 1987): pp. 57–63.

Livnat, Joshua. "A Generalization of the APT Methodology as a Way of Measuring the Association between Income and Stock Prices." *Journal of Accounting Research* (Autumn 1981): pp. 350–59.

Malkiel, Burton G., "Common Stocks—The Best Inflation Hedge for the 1980s." *Forbes*, 18 February, 1980, pp. 118–22.

McClay, Marvin. "Is the Equity Market Becoming More Volatile?" *Journal of Portfolio Management* (Spring 1981): pp. 51–54.

McWilliams, James D., and James Wei. "Some Like To-matoes and Some Like To-matoes." *Journal of Portfolio Management* (Summer 1981): pp. 43–47.

Merrett, A. J., and Gerald D. Newbould. "CEPS: The Illusion of Corporate Growth." *Journal of Portfolio Management* (Fall 1982): pp. 5–10.

————. "Integrating Financial Performance and Stock Valuation." *Journal of Portfolio Management* (Fall 1982): pp. 27–32.

Michaud, Richard O. "Should Dividend Discount Models Be Yield-tilted? Comment." *Journal of Portfolio Management* (Summer 1984): pp. 85–86.

Moosa, Suleman A. "Inflation and Common Stock Prices." *Journal of Financial Research* (Fall 1980): pp. 115–28.

Morse, Dale. "Price and Trading Volume Reaction Surrounding Earnings Announcements: A Closer Examination." *Journal of Accounting Research* (Autumn 1981): pp. 374–83.

Murray, Roger F. "Graham and Dodd: A Durable Discipline." *Financial Analysts Journal* (September-October 1983): pp. 18–23.

Nagorniak, John J. "Thoughts on Using Dividend Discount Models." *Financial Analysts Journal* (November-December 1985): pp. 13–15.

Nichols, Donald R., and Jeffrey J. Tsay. "Security Price Reaction to Long-range Executive Earnings Forecast." *Journal of Accounting Research* (Spring 1979): pp. 140–55.

Officer, Dennis T., and William J. Boyes. "The Behavior of Brokerage Firm Shares." *Financial Analysts Journal* (May-June 1983): pp. 41–46.

Oppenheimer, Henry R. "A Test of Ben Graham's Stock Selection Criteria." *Financial Analysts Journal* (September-October 1984): pp. 68–74.

————. "Ben Graham's Net Current Asset Values: A Performance Update." *Financial Analysts Journal* (November-December 1986): pp. 40–47.

Patell, James M., and Mark A. Wolfson, "The Ex-Ante and Ex-Post Price Effects of Quarterly Earnings Annoucements Reflected in Optimal Stock Prices." *Journal of Accounting Research* (Autumn 1981): pp. 434–58.

Rie, Daniel. "How Trustowrthy Is Your Valuation Model?" *Financial Analysts Journal* (November-December 1985): pp. 42–48.

Rozeff, Michael S. "Growth, Beta and Agency Costs as Determinants of Dividend Payout Ratios," *Journal of Financial Research* (Fall 1982): pp. 249–59.

Ruland, William. "Management Forecasts, Stock Prices, and Public Policy." *Review of Business & Economic Research* (Winter 1979): pp. 16–29.

Schwert, G. William. "The Adjustment of Stock Prices to Information about Inflation." *Journal of Finance* (March 1981): pp. 15–29.

Severn, Alan K., James C. Mills, and Basil L. Copeland, Jr. "Capital Gains Taxes After Tax Reform." *Journal of Portfolio Management* (Spring 1987): pp. 69–75.

Shiller, Robert J. "Do Stock Prices Move Too Much to be Justified by Subsequent Changes in Dividends?" *American Economic Review* (June 1981): pp. 421–36.

Smith, Gary. "A Simple Model for Estimating Intrinsic Value." *Journal of Portfolio Management* (Summer 1982): pp. 46–49.

Sorensen, Eric H., and David A. Williamson. "Some Evidence on the Value of Dividend Discount Models." *Financial Analysts Journal* (November-December 1985): pp. 60–69.

Soter, Dennis S. "The Dividend Controversy—What It Means for Corporate Policy." *Financial Executive* (May 1979): pp. 38–43.

Stanley, Kenneth L., Wilbur G. Lewellen, and Gary C. Schlarbaum. "Investor Response to Investment Research." *Journal of Portfolio Management* (Summer 1980): pp. 20–26.

Tezel, Ahmet. "The Effect of Inflation on Common Stock Values." *Journal of Financial Research* (Spring 1982): pp. 17–25.

Tobin, James. "A Mean-Variance Approach to Fundamental Valuation." *Journal of Portfolio Management* (Fall 1984): pp. 26–32.

Vandell, Robert F., and Mark T. Finn. ''Portfolio Objective: Win Big, Lose Little.'' *Journal of Portfolio Management* (Summer 1982): pp. 37–45.

Vandell, Robert F., and Marcia L. Pontius. ''The Impact of Tax Status on Stock Selection.'' *Journal of Portfolio Management* (Summer 1981): pp. 35–42.

Wilcox, Jarrod W. ''The P/B-ROE Valuation Model.'' *Financial Analysts Journal* (January-February 1984): pp. 58–66.

Wong, Shee Q. ''The Contribution of Inflation Uncertainty to the Variable Impacts of Money on Stock Prices.'' *Journal of Financial Research* (Spring 1986): pp. 97–101.

Zacks, Leonard. ''EPS Forecasts—Accuracy Is Not Enough.'' *Financial Analysts Journal* (March-April 1979): pp. 53–55.

CHAPTER 12

TECHNICAL ANALYSIS

INTRODUCTION

It is probably safe to say that attempts to discover methods of interpreting current price trends and forecasting future price trends of securities and financial markets have consumed as much human time and effort as any act intended to enhance the pecuniary desires of mankind! Numerous avenues or approaches have been tested, and with the advent of the general availability of microcomputers, still another generation of searching has appeared.

There is very little in human experience that cannot be subjected to some sort of mechanical data analysis. This analysis attempts to assist in the discovery of changes in a multitude of trends, such as general economic time series, fiscal and monetary developments, social behavior, voter preferences, and consumer buying intentions. Technical analysis of common stocks is an attempt to identify likely future prices through an analysis of demand and supply factors.

Overview of Technical Analysis

Technical analysis attempts to resolve the *investment timing* issue by gaining insight into market behavior through a variety of studies. These studies have included the analysis of market prices, "breadth" of the market, general investor sentiment, attractive industries for investment, and the price behavior of individual securities.

Many technical methods that periodically achieve public prominence or attention in the media are in fact extensions or reorderings of basic concepts from earlier days.

In volatile financial markets, timing is the central issue. Modern research has clearly shown that most securities are highly correlated with the general securities markets. As one old finance professor used to say, "To make your pile, you have to be in style." Of course, everyone can't agree upon the correct time to buy or sell, or there would be no one to buy from when buy signals were perceived and no one to sell to when sell signals were perceived. There are two parties to every transaction; the buyer is motivated by an expected increase in price, and the seller is motivated by an expected decrease in price.

Today it is widely recognized that many traders and/or investors act upon their own technical interpretations of price trends and/or those of a virtual army of technical advisory services. Most market advisories issued by the best-known and most-reputable brokerage firms provide *both* a "fundamental" opinion and a "technical" opinion on individual securities and on the overall status of the markets. Cable TV systems furnish day-long programming of financial news whose commentaries are much influenced by technical developments in the markets.

It is therefore appropriate that some familiarity with technical analysis be part of any attempt to grasp an overall picture of investment strategies and the behavior of financial markets. Some of the most widely followed investment advisory services that purport to base their recommendations on "fundamentals" do extensive computer screening of technical relationships for thousands of securities. This, in a broad sense, could be considered a form of technical analysis to support their forecasts of security prices.

History of Technical Analysis

In the late 1800s and early 1900s, most securities trading and most market participants were located in the New York City area. In addition, the number of securities actively traded was much smaller than the thousands of issues traded today. Furthermore, the stocks of many major companies were directly associated with individuals who were known to have significant holdings in those companies. It was commonly believed then (and probably now with some validity) that "financial barons" were not above manipulating the shares of those companies.

As a result, lesser market participants began to attempt seriously to discover the trading intentions of the major players by carefully following certain price changes. Were the "big" players accumulating or distributing shares, and what were the short, intermediate, and long-term price trends that they were trying to cause? Hence, the study of stock prices and volume (especially for relatively short periods of time, by both graphical and numerical means) became popular. Some market traders began to believe that market transactions were more important than economic developments or fundamental company factors (and that it was better to be on the side of the powers moving prices than to act upon widely accepted and rationally considered economic factors). Of particular interest to these traders were the patterns of prices and volume that were exhibited prior to and during significant changes in prices. Their interpretations of these patterns (primarily price patterns) were often based upon a method of charting price movements still referred to as the *point-and-figure* method.

Prior to the Securities Act of 1933, which required full financial disclosure, companies did not provide investors with income statements and balance sheets. Therefore, there was no information for fundamental analysis. The only available data were transactions data on volume and prices.

The technical interpretation of market and stock price movements has been heavily influenced by the writings of Charles H. Dow, which appeared in a series of articles in the *Wall Street Journal* between 1900 and 1902. His original narrow "theory" was that stock prices forecast business conditions.

Dow was followed at the *Journal* by William Peter Hamilton, who continued to write on the implications and interpretations of Dow's observations. Hamilton extended the theory to explain how it could be used as a barometer to forecast the stock market itself. In 1922 he published *The Stock Market Barometer: A Study of Its Forecast Value Based on Charles H. Dow's Theory of the Price Movement.*

Robert Rhea, an avid follower of Dow and Hamilton, applied the theory to his personal stock investing in the 1920s. Rhea used the Dow theory when he began to buy stocks in 1921 and was completely out of stocks in the final stages of the 1929 stock debacle. In addition, he claimed to have held small short positions during the two years after the 1929 crash. As a result of his seeming success from closely applying the *Dow Theory* and with the encouragement of friends who were also serious students of the stock market, he produced charts for their use. The eventual popularity of the charts with other market traders led him to a more careful study of the 252 editorials written by Dow and Hamilton. Based upon his personal experience and study, in 1932 he published his classic *The Dow Theory (An Explanation of Its Development and an Attempt to Define Its Usefulness as an Aid in Speculation).*

Today there seems to be an unending list of exotic technical analyses readily available from various sources. Some of these approaches result from applying the highest order of modern mathematical and statistical methods and theory. There is a virtual industry of "technical" advisory services and publications, covering every conceivable financial product and market sector. In more recent years we have seen sophisticated electronic data processing brought to bear on discovering what are essentially technical behavioral characteristics of securities and markets.

The growth of program or computerized trading illustrates the impact of technology on investment strategies and consequently on financial markets. It is generally believed, however, that the basic identifications of the early technical writers continue to provide much of the basis for current technical interpretation. A review of many investment advisory letters employing technical analysis makes it apparent that much current technical market advice is consistent with the Dow Theory.

REVIEW OF DOW THEORY

The essential underpinning of the theory, which purports to interpret the market through an index such as the Dow Jones Industrial Average DJIA, is that closing prices of the DJIA reflect all known and anticipated information available to market participants. In this respect the theory is not unlike the Efficient Market Hypothesis (and its several forms) that is widely accepted by many scholars in the academic investment community.

Price Trends

A general statement of the Dow Theory departs from the efficiency and randomness purportedly found by academic studies of the market. Dow Theory states that there are three types of market movements (trends) that can be used to forecast future market trends: (1) *primary trend*, which may last several years; (2) *secondary reactions*, which may last from several weeks to several months; and (3) *minor movements* of several hours, days, or as long as three weeks. These movements are present in both advancing and declining markets.

Students of the theory believe that at times the market may move sideways for some time, with perhaps a 4 to 5 percent deviation on either side of an average price (referred to as a *Dow line*). When this phenomenon is observed, stocks are *under accumulation* or *distribution*. This does not mean that the primary trend is changing, but that the possibility of some secondary market adjustment (either above or below the longer-term price line) exists. The longer the "line" remains relatively flat, the greater the expected eventual adjustment in market prices.

Volume Analysis

Volume analysis has been incorporated into technical theory. It is generally believed by modern Dow theorists that volume and price are typically positively correlated. It follows, therefore, that in an upward moving market advances (rallies) should typically see high volume, and declines (reactions) should be accompanied by low volume. The opposite tends to be true in a *bear* market. The original theory, however, would maintain that in the final analysis, it is *only* price that should be the ultimate test of market direction.

Bull and Bear Markets

Bullish (up) or bearish (down) price behavior is identified by the relationship between the DJIA highs on successive rallies and the DJIA lows on successive secondary reactions. If the DJIA is higher than the previous high that was followed by a secondary decline, and any secondary decline is higher than the preceding secondary decline, the market is said to be in a bullish trend. In a primary *bull* trend, when short rallies are followed by secondary declines, these declines would not be expected to retrace more than about 60 percent of the rally. The most common secondary decline is approximately 50 percent. However, if volume and price repeatedly appear to be uncorrelated, a change in the prevailing market trend could be starting.

The theory further holds that a *change* in the primary trend of the DJIA must be confirmed by a similar change in the Dow Jones Transportation Average, DJTA, previously known as the "Rail Average." In order to validate a change in the primary trend of the DJIA, such as a change from a bull trend to a bear trend, resulting from lower highs or lower lows and correlated volume, the DJTA must exhibit similar behavior in a fairly short period of time—the closer the better.

Some critics complain, however, that it is not uncommon for a significant reversal from a peak in the DJIA to occur before confirmation takes place in the DJTA. As a result, most technicians have a number of other tests they apply in an attempt to anticipate correctly the DJTA confirmation. One such test is the *dividend yield*. Since the early 1930s, whenever the dividend yield on the DJIA falls below 3 percent and remains there, the bull market is reflecting full valuation of equities: stock prices have increased much more than dividends. In such a circumstance, unforeseen events have tended to precipitate a change in bullish primary trends. Thus, the dividend yield decline "confirmed" the primary trend change from bullish to bearish. (As of the middle of August 1987, or approximately two months before the market collapse in October, the dividend yield on the DJIA was 2.8 percent.)

It has been observed that there are often five identifiable secondary "moves" or price patterns found in primary bull markets: (1) rally, (2) reaction, (3) rally, (4) reaction, and (5) rally. In primary bear markets, many maintain, three secondary moves are typical (reaction, rally, reaction). Dow theorists contend that these secondary moves can be identified. Unfortunately, however, the theory gives little guidance with respect to the length of time of a primary trend, and other technical tools must be relied upon by technicians to provide those insights. It has been generally observed that bull markets have a life of three to five years; bear markets, one to two years.

CHARTING METHODS

Point-and-Figure Charts

The *point-and-figure* charting method is based solely on "recordable" price changes. Time and volume are deemed of little or no importance; the price of a stock, and only the price, reflects the total and appropriate current and/or possible trend of a security's price or a market index. An ''appropriate'' price change is defined prior to constructing the chart. The price change could be a fraction of one point, or as much as 25 points or more if charting a market index. A decision is also made as to how many price changes constitute a reversal in a trend. When the defined price change is reached, an entry is made on the chart. The chart entry is either a continuation of an upward column of entries or a continuation of a downward column of entries. On a given market day, if no appropriate price change occurs, no entry is made on the chart.

A computer-generated *weekly* point-and-figure chart of the DJIA is reproduced in Figure 12.1. This chart has a price (point) change of 20 points and requires three value point changes (60-point reversal) to indicate a reversal in the price trend.

If an index or security is advancing in price, chart entries are in an upmoving column. If three downward value point changes are observed, then a new column is started, to the right and down from the just-reversed high. A second rule that could be used to confirm buy/sell decisions would be that a reversal high or low would have to be confirmed by a *consecutive* higher high or a lower low, depending upon whether the market was heading up or down. This is illustrated in Figure 12.1, where there is a confirmed ''buy'' (B) for the market in November 1986 at 1730, and the ''buy'' position is maintained to August 1987. The sell signal given in Figure 12.1 in May 1987 was unconfirmed and is indicated by ''unconfirmed S'' (sell).

As a security or market index advances and declines and the chart develops, a technical analyst would attempt to discover buy or sell signals. The DJIA point-

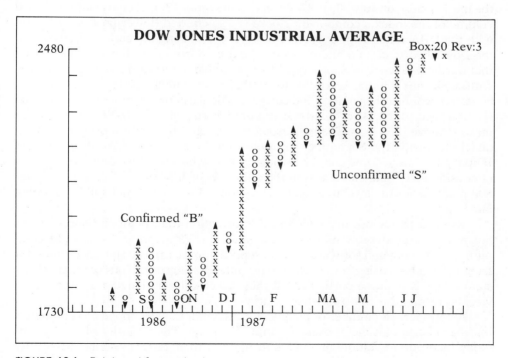

FIGURE 12.1 Point and figure chart

and-figure chart in Figure 12.1, with a 20-point value interval and a three-interval reversal requirement, would seem appropriate for an intermediate or long-term trader/investor. A short-term trader would probably prefer a daily price chart with a much smaller value interval and perhaps a reversal requirement of only two intervals.

Some technicians, depending on how a point-and-figure chart is constructed, maintain that it can also be used to set price objectives. These price objectives are set when confirmed buy or sell signals have been developed following a major market reversal pattern and movement. In Figure 12.1, for instance, the column containing the buy signal is identified (''confirmed B'') and the number of value intervals in that column is counted. In this case, there are eight value intervals of 20 points, or 160 total points. Since this is a three-point reversal chart, 160 is multiplied by 3 and then added to the base of the formation where the buy column originated—1730. The result provides a price objective of 2210. It can be seen that this was obtained on a strong price advance in March 1987, and then a reaction took place, bringing the index back to approximately 2100.

Bar Charts

Bar charts attempt to capture the total range of price movements during each market session as well as the closing price for the session. The closing price is noted by a cross hatch on the session's price range. These charts can be used to track individual securities or other financial instruments as well as market indices such as the DJIA.

Figure 12.2 presents a weekly bar chart of the DJIA from August 1986 through the market close on July 20, 1987. As shown in Figure 12.2, each week's combined volume of the index's component stocks is also charted (lower portion of figure) with the DJIA values (upper portion of figure). Recalling the earlier discussion of the Dow Theory, certain inferences can be drawn from this chart. It can be seen that during one week in September 1986, a sizable downward reaction occurred, with significant volume. According to the theory, the validity of this reversal should be tested against other market indicators, particularly the Dow Jones Transportation Average, DJTA. After that time and until April 1987, the DJTA was in a clear upward move. If a Dow Theory devotee interpreted the price movement immediately following the September reaction until the obvious breakout of prices in January 1987 as a ''Dow line,'' he would probably have suggested that a price rise of considerable significance was in the offing. As of July 1987, after a rise of over 800 points from the level in September/October 1986, he would still be claiming fame.

Bar charts disclose more technical information than point-and-figure charts but require considerably more time to maintain (although with the right computing equipment and software, this presents no problem). It is not uncommon for technical analysts using bar charts to have different interpretations of the market's status. This is the case particularly if they select different lengths of time (daily, weekly, or monthly data) for their charts.

A considerable number of technical studies can now be applied to computerized bar charts that incorporate volume of trading. The majority of technicians today incorporate volume analysis into most of their interpretations of security

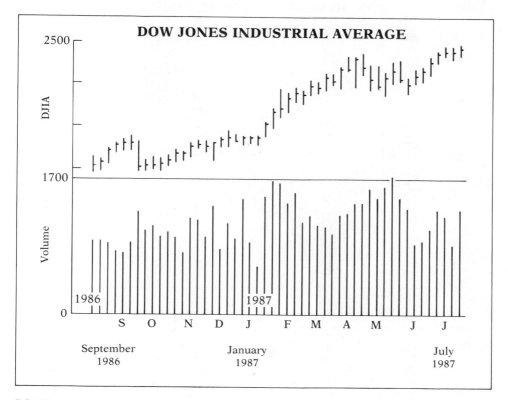

FIGURE 12.2 Bar chart

and of market price behavior. With the substantial volatility in the volume of today's markets, volume analyses cannot be overlooked if any credence is given to the gains that would result from improved market timing and price forecasting.

Equivolume Charts

Richard W. Arms, Jr., in his *Volume Cycles in the Stock Market: Market Timing through Equivolume Charting*, maintains that the relationship between price and volume is much more significant than that normally depicted by traditional charting methods. If this is true, price should be plotted in direct relationship to volume.

Instead of plotting prices by a single bar for each trading day, a rectangle is constructed for each day's trading in a stock or an index. The vertical dimension of the rectangle represents the price range for the trading session, and the volume determines the width of each rectangle. If volume is twice as high on day 2 as it was on day 1, the rectangle for day 2 should be twice as wide as the rectangle for day 1.

An "equivolume" chart is shown in Figure 12.3. It is possible, according to Arms, to obtain special insights into the meaning of price and volume for purposes of market forecasting. His book can be consulted for these interpretations.

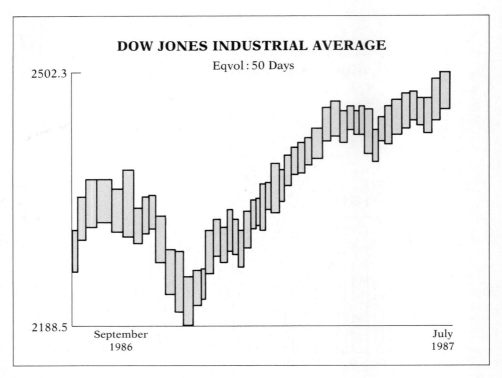

FIGURE 12.3 Equivolume chart

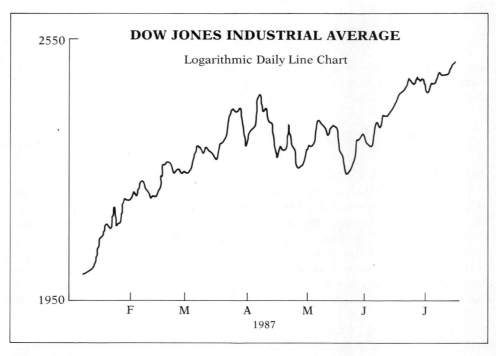

FIGURE 12.4 Log chart

Log Charts

It is sometimes helpful to compare percentage changes from dissimilar chart data. Because various time series will have different absolute scales, direct comparison is less than optimum. To overcome this, data can be plotted on logarithmic charts. This makes it possible to visualize quickly relative rates of change or the slope of price functions during different periods or market environments for individual securities and for market indicators. A log chart of DJIA daily closing prices for January through July 15, 1987, is illustrated in Figure 12.4. Some very good chart services provide log-scaled charts on a large number of market indicators and actively traded securities.

ELEMENTS OF TECHNICAL ANALYSIS

After charts are constructed, many additional measures are studied by technical analysts. These efforts attempt to judge the overall strength or "health" of the market in conjunction with any selected market indices. These measures may include the number of securities with advancing, declining, and unchanged prices; number of issues making new yearly highs or lows; the cash or liquidity position of major investing institutions; the extent of the "short interest" of the "public" and that of exchange specialists and members, along with the short interest ratio; put and call options; types of stocks participating in the market trend (companies with large capitalizations, secondary and smaller sized companies, speculative companies); historical relationships of price/earnings ratios, earnings yields, and dividend yields; and correlations of general market levels and certain industry indices with a multitude of aggregate economic variables that are readily available.

To discover the relationships between certain technical developments and market behavior, it is usually necessary to study a large amount of historical data. Once a relationship or pattern is perceived, there is a great temptation to begin acting upon that one relationship in formulating trading rules or making investing decisions. Because of the tremendous number of variables that can affect securities markets at a given time, however, it is very unlikely that one relationship between two variables would ever be duplicated in the future. Relationships between variables can change in dynamic fashion, and there is no guarantee that past relationships will be sustained in the future.

As the preceding paragraphs indicate, there are many areas for potential investigation that may provide improved understanding of market behavior at a particular time or over some period of time. A detailed discussion of all of these techniques is beyond the scope of this book. It is recommended that interested readers examine some of the references listed at the end of this chapter. A word of warning: claims of superior technical relationships should be accepted with caution.

Nevertheless, for introductory purposes, some common technical studies and techniques will be briefly reviewed in the following sections. In addition, several brief descriptions and illustrations of computer-generated analyses of relatively recent origin will be given. Although the DJIA will be used in most illustrations, individual securities can be analyzed in exactly the same way.

Breadth of the Market

The *breadth of the market* involves the relationship between the number of stocks with advancing and with declining prices. This information is published in *Barron's*. The basic theory is that in a bona fide bull market, the majority of securities will be advancing in price; in a bear market, most securities will be declining. Technicians look carefully at the ratio of advancing to declining issues and attempt to determine if the ratio is behaving in a consistent fashion with the market. Should a major market index trend up for some length of time while the ratio of advancing/declining issues is declining, this inconsistency may suggest the possibility of a change in market direction.

One of the ways to analyze the ratio of advancing to declining, A/D, issues is to maintain a running net cumulative sum $(X = A - D)$ of issues changing price on a daily basis. If the cumulative sum increases and the market is rising, the sum is confirming the bull market. If the cumulative sum declines in a rising market, then "nonconformance" is present, and concern about the continuation of a rising market may be justified. This measure is illustrated in Figure 12.5. The analysis of this A/D line is similar for individual securities or a market index.

There is not always agreement about the time over which A/D values should be summed, but for intermediate trading fifty weeks is considered sufficient. In

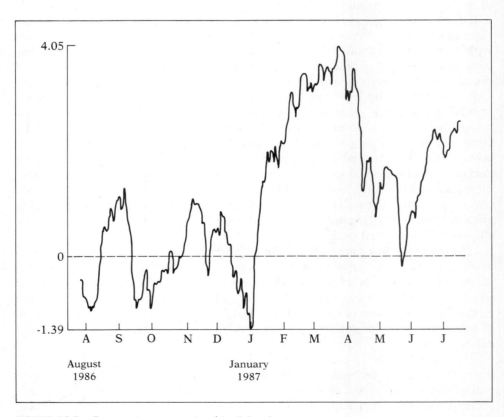

FIGURE 12.5 Cumulative advancing/declining issues

Figure 12.5 (when used in connection with a market index) sharp reversals of trend can be easily noted. In the period covered by the chart (August 1986–July 1987), the A/D sum sharply reversed in late 1986 and then rapidly moved toward positive values where it remained except for a negative value in May 1987. Important new market trends are sometimes associated with sharp trend reversals in a number of technical indicators. During mid-1987, the A/D was lagging the DJIA, which had been reaching new highs. This can be seen by comparing Figures 12.2 and 12.5. If the market is in the latter stages of a long bull period, it can be expected that fewer and fewer stocks will be advancing on a relative basis. This may mean that there is a growing susceptibility to a secondary downward reaction in the market.

Two additional approaches to identifying the breadth of the market are the Haurlan Index and the Arms Index. These are illustrated on Figure 12.6.

1. HAURLAN INTERMEDIATE INDEX This index was developed by Dave Holt (publisher of the *Trade Levels* advisory letter). It is a twenty-day moving average of the difference between the number of advancing and declining issues over a selected time period. The index can be interpreted in the same way as a security or market price chart. The index gives further indication of market breadth as it moves from positive to negative values.

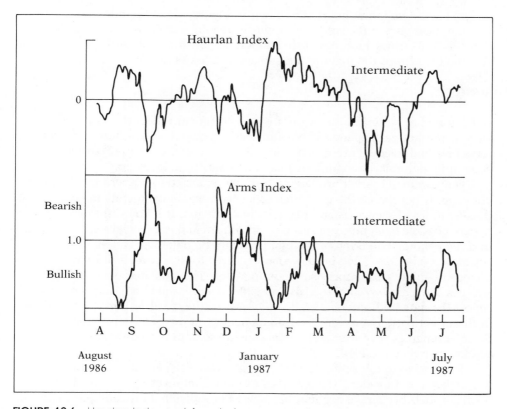

FIGURE 12.6 Haurlan Index and Arms Index

2. ARMS INDEX The Arms Index, which can be calculated for varying lengths of time and integrates volume, attempts to measure trading volume associated with the number of advancing issues compared to volume associated with the number of declining issues. The theory is that in advancing market environments, the trading volume associated with advancing issues should be greater than the trading volume associated with declining issues. This index, sometimes referred to as the "TRIN," is continuously calculated and accessible through brokerage office computer screens throughout the trading day and is reported weekly in *Barron's*. The last calculation of the index after the close of the market is identified as the index for a given day (Arms Index = (Number of Advancing Issues/Number of Declining Issues) ÷ (Volume of Advancing Issues/Volume of Declining Issues)). If the index is below 1.00, it is considered "bullish," and if it is above 1.00, it is considered "bearish." Technicians would be alert to extreme readings as an indication that the breadth of the market is on the verge of changing, with a commensurate change in the general market trend.

The Arms Index shown in the lower half of Figure 12.6 is an intermediate index which is simply a ten-day moving average of the daily index. It can be seen that the index reached values substantially below 1 in August and September of 1986 and was reversed particularly sharply in November 1986. After a pattern of improved readings in December 1986, the market exploded on the upside in January 1987 (see Figure 12.2). As of July 1987 the DJIA was still setting all-time highs. As shown in Figure 12.6, the index remained for the most part in the range of "bullish" readings after December 1986. As of July 1987 (three months before the October crash), the Arms Index confirmed the breadth of the market and suggested a long position in stocks.

Market Sentiment

Indicators that attempt to measure market sentiment reflect the "moods" of the various market participants. The commonly expressed theory is that market professionals and insiders are much more likely to anticipate important changes in economic and market conditions than small part-time investors.

One group of market professionals that is expected to outperform the market consistently comprises the exchange specialists, exchange members, and market makers in listed securities and financial instruments. It follows, therefore, that if it were possible to identify optimism or pessimism in these specialists, some insight into the pending condition of the market might be obtained. Much of the trading (including short sales) and position data required for this analysis is reported to exchange regulators and supervisory commissions. The data are published in various sources, such as *Barron's*. It is also possible to subscribe to advisory services that report the data and provide detailed analyses of the trend of "insider" activity—both market participants and the trading activity of top officers of publicly owned listed companies. Unfortunately, however, these data are not available until two weeks after they are filed.

In addition to the activities of exchange specialists, exchange members, market makers, and insiders, the activities of individual investors can be analyzed in terms of their brokerage account balances. For individual investors, any extreme short selling or idle cash balances may hold some predictive value in terms of potential market moves. A rather cynical view holds that the average individual is always wrong at key market turning points. This information can be obtained from various sources, such as *Barron's*.

Still another group that has an impact on the securities markets consists of the many investment advisory services. There are services that track the consensus of investment advisors, and interpretations can be made about the level and trend of the bullish or bearish consensus being stated by the investment advisors. For example, *Hulbert's Financial Digest* analyzes the recommendations from approximately one hundred investment newsletters.

Monetary and Economic Indicators

Many technicians (and fundamentalists) consider most of the same monetary policy and aggregate economic time series used by policy makers in the public and private sectors. These include monetary indicators such as bank ''free'' reserves, federal funds rate, discount rate, T-bill rates, bond rates, savings rate, borrowed bank reserves, level of consumer loans, business borrowing, etc. Additionally, a good technician will understand and attempt to include in his analysis the economic indicator times series reported regularly by the U.S. Department of Commerce (e.g., industrial production, manufacturing capacity utilization rate, business inventory changes, inflation rate, and trade import/export balances). By keeping up to date on these variables, technicians gain further insight into market adjustments. The way the market reacts to unexpected economic news may also provide some insight into the general market trend and its strength or weakness. For example, if announced inflation indices differ markedly from expectations, there may be rapid changes in security prices.

Trend Analysis

Many technicians construct charts that attempt to indicate the trend of an index or individual security. For example, they would counsel that as long as a particular security or market index remains above some moving average of its closing price, the security is in a bullish posture, and a long position should be maintained. As the security crosses from above or below the ''average'' on significant volume, they would position themselves consistent with this perceived new trend. A 39-week moving average is widely considered to be a good working average with which to follow a charted security or market index.

Figure 12.7 shows a 39-week average (curved line below price bars) superimposed on a DJIA weekly bar chart. For the period covered, the DJIA never closed below the moving average. In September 1986, a significant reversal took place that took the DJIA down through the moving average line, but the DJIA closed above the line for the week on very heavy volume. This could be construed as a test that was ''passed,'' and the market began to rally strongly thereafter.

Also shown in Figure 12.7 are two ''resistance-support'', R-S, lines drawn at 30-degree and 60-degree angles, respectively, from an important reaction low in January 1986. Except for the six weeks when the DJIA was falling toward the 39-week moving average, the index has remained above the top R-S line and never

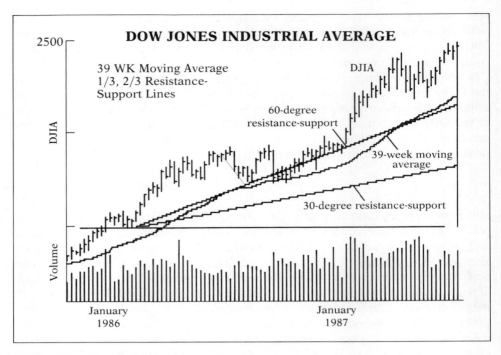

FIGURE 12.7 39-week moving average

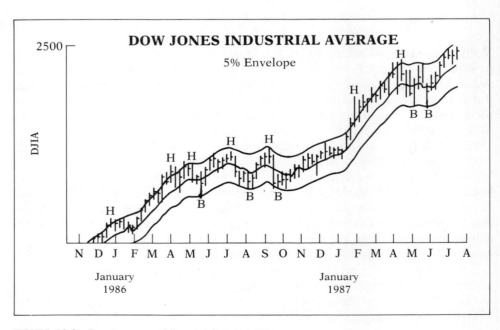

FIGURE 12.8 Envelopes and the moving average

approached the lower R-S line. According to trend analysis, if the index had proceeded down to the first R-S line, it would typically have rallied back to the top R-S line but would not have penetrated it. Some technicians would trade accordingly.

Another method of following a primary trend is with parallel lines drawn in conjunction with the moving average, as illustrated in Figure 12.8. These parallel lines are sometimes referred to by technicians as *envelopes* and are used to determine opportune entry or exit points in a primary market trend. The lines are constructed to remain within 5 percent of a nine-week moving average of the closing prices of the DJIA. In Figure 12.8 several buy, B, opportunities were indicated over the 1986–87 period. A buy is indicated when the DJIA declines to the level of the lower envelope. Opportunities were available in May, August, and September 1986, and in May and June 1987. This type of chart is designed to assist an intermediate- to long-term investor identify entry points. H indicates where a short-term reversal could take place, but it also indicates that existing positions be *held*, H.

Recent Computer Trend Studies

The lower portion of Figure 12.9 illustrates two computer-generated price studies that have received considerable interest from technicians in recent years. The first study, called *convergence/divergence*, is usually considered a short-term trading

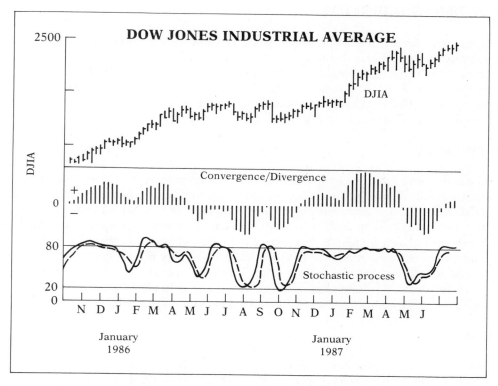

FIGURE 12.9 Convergence/divergence and the stochastic process

guide. An oscillator can be constructed by plotting the difference between two moving price averages against a third longer-term moving average. This oscillator series is plotted as the middle chart in Figure 12.9. As the oscillator changes, buy or sell signals are generated. This would, of course, be only one of a number of signals routinely calculated. On the basis of this study, however, a sell signal might have been acted upon in May 1986 after the oscillator indicated a negative value. A trader might have remained invested in a "safe" T-bills position until late October 1986 when the oscillator turned positive. Following this trend would have brought attractive market returns.

At the bottom of Figure 12.9, a second technique, called a *stochastic process*, incorporates the observation that as prices decrease, the closing prices for the sessions tend to bunch closer and closer to the extreme lows of the session trading ranges. Inversely, as prices increase, the session closing prices tend to bunch closer to the extreme highs in the session ranges. The difference between the closing and opening price divided by the range for the trading session can be calculated and plotted against a moving average of these values. When price "crossovers" occur for the stochastic line, certain interpretations of the pattern would provide buy or sell signals. For example, an excellent buy signal was indicated during October 1986. Other signals are sometimes given when the trend of the stochastic lines diverges from that exhibited by the charted index or security.

OTHER MARKET TIMING INDICATORS

If one is uncertain about the future price movements suggested by one or more indicators, still other indicators may be consulted. This is particularly true with respect to the general "health" of the market and would be essential for an intermediate- or long-term investor who is interested mainly in the primary trend of the market. The indicators discussed below have been widely used and may be found helpful in making timing decisions.

The Confidence Index

The *confidence index* is a technical indicator that originated in 1932 and is reported each week in *Barron's*. The index compares the yield on high-grade bonds to the yield on medium-grade bonds. The underlying logic of this indicator is that when investors are confident in the economy, they are willing to move funds from high- to medium-quality bonds. As this takes place, the yield on the lower-quality bonds tends to increase more slowly than the yield on quality bonds, causing the yield spread to narrow and the ratio to rise, implying market confidence. In recent years, however, this index has not been as reliable as in earlier years. One reason for this may be more aggressive monetary policy management.

The Yield Curve

Because of the magnitude of federal debt issues in financial markets today, in combination with monetary policy shifts, the *yield curve* (see Chapter 16) on government securities is usually watched carefully by both technicians and fun-

damentalists. Since credit costs play a central role in consumer and business decisions, any apparent shifts in the level of interest rates will have a direct impact on
economic conditions and, in turn, on financial markets. A plot of the yields on
different maturities will usually produce an upward-sloping function and reflects
the fact that yields on shorter maturities are normally lower than those of longer
maturities. The reasons for this are discussed in Chapter 16. When the yield curve
is downward sloping (atypical), this is viewed as bearish for financial markets.
Upward-sloping yield curves have often been associated with primary bull markets,
downward-sloping yield curves with primary bear markets.

Interest Rate Spread

The difference in the yields of a representative group of high-quality long-term
debt instruments and high-quality short-term debt instruments is termed the *interest rate spread*. This can be calculated by taking the difference between the
yields on high-grade corporate bonds and on commercial paper or short-term
Treasuries, or the yield difference between long-term Treasuries and short-term
Treasuries. A large positive difference is an indication that general financial liquidity
is present at reasonable costs for consumers, businesses, and governments. Yield
spreads should be studied not only for the absolute size of the spread but for the
rate of change per unit of time of the spread. If there is a rapid and significant
change, a major reevaluation of credit conditions may be underway.

Mutual Funds' Cash Position

High liquidity in mutual funds signifies a large amount of investable funds. If
conditions are perceived by mutual fund managers to be positive, this money may
quickly be invested in the market, with an attendant positive impact on security
prices. On the other hand, if portfolio managers are generally optimistic, they
tend to be fully invested, and their cash position is negligible; hence, little or no
buying power could be expected from mutual funds to propel the market higher.

Because of changes in financial regulation, tax legislation, pension alternatives,
etc., it may be increasingly difficult to establish the extremes of cash positions;
thus, care should be taken in interpreting this indicator. Mutual funds' cash positions in conjunction with other financial flow information, however, may improve
some forecasts. Most recently there has been a marked increase in the total size
of mutual fund assets. It may be that extreme levels of cash positions could now
be even more important in understanding the "technical position" of the market
and the existence or lack of potential "buying power." Monthly data on the cash
position of mutual funds is published in the "Market Laboratory" section of
Barron's.

Put-Call Ratio

With the advent of equity and index options, it is possible for speculators (small
and large) to speculate or limit losses by buying or "writing" (selling) contracts
to buy or sell individual securities or indices (see Chapters 19 and 21 for a discussion of options). For an investor attempting to limit losses, a *put* (the right to
sell) would be purchased if prices are expected to fall. A *call* (right to buy) would

be purchased by a speculator if prices are expected to increase. Therefore, the relationship (ratio) of the number of puts to calls would give an indication of the degree of bullish or bearish sentiment on the part of option market participants. Typically, the ratio of puts to calls would be "low" during optimistic periods and "high" during pessimistic periods. Extreme readings of this ratio have been found to be present in close proximity to major market reversals. Information that can be used to construct this ratio is available in *Barron's* and other publications.

Advisors' Sentiment

The majority of investment advisors are believed to be trend followers, and many have very good records of staying with major market trends. It has been observed, however, that a preponderance of advisory opinion in the same camp can signal important reversal points. To the extent that investment advisors have a large following, their clients may be completely invested (no more buying power) or completely liquid (substantial buying power). When price direction significantly reverses, these advisors quickly change their advice. By following the trend of sentiment among investment advisors (and the rapidity with which they change their recommendations), major market tops and bottoms may receive confirmation. Market letters providing consensus opinions frequently advertise in *Barron's* and other financial publications.

Secondary Stock Offerings

Barron's reports the *secondary offerings* (large sales of listed shares that are not made on the stock exchanges) of major individual company stockholders. If large numbers of secondary offerings appear, and selling continues for some time, this is considered to be bearish, for two reasons: (1) the supply of stock available in the market increases and (2) such stockholders are believed to have somewhat superior knowledge of their company's outlook. Conversely, if there are virtually no secondary offerings for some time, the "big players" may have decided that their company is undervalued or that the outlook is improving. This would suggest a market bottom. The number of secondary offerings is probably more significant than the dollars or magnitude of shares offered.

Bellwether Issues

Bellwether issues are securities that are traditionally believed to mirror correctly the condition of the overall securities market. These may be individual stocks or stock groups such as utilities. One of the most closely followed bellwether stocks is General Motors. Sometimes analysts talk about the "group of generals." These would include General Motors, General Electric, General Mills, and General Dynamics.

The record of individual bellwether issues has been spotty in recent times. One bellwether with a reasonably good record as an indicator has been the Dow Jones Utility Average. This no doubt reflects investors' perceptions that utility stocks, because of their heavy use of debt, are directly affected by changes in the general level of interest rates, and utilities therefore tend to reflect quickly and correctly the supply and cost of long-term capital. Utilities, however, may not be as good a leading indicator now as in recent years because their expansion and changing technology are much less pronounced than in earlier decades.

Negative Volume Indications

In theory, strategic positions are established by savvy market participants in market sessions of relative calm—low-volume days. The theory would suggest that the direction of the market on days when volume declines from the preceding day may signal accumulation or distribution by participants who "know what they are doing." After establishing a base value for the indicator, percentage points can be added or deducted, consistent with the percentage move in some broad market index such as the DJIA. The direction of such an indicator would then move in a direction similar to the market moves on decreased-volume sessions. The indicator (index) can be analyzed through the use of moving averages, in much the same way as a market index or an individual security might be analyzed.

Conclusions

The indicators presented in this section by no means represent the entire list of timing indicators, but rather some of the more common ones. All indicators of market timing should be used with caution, and then only with the benefit of the perspective one might develop by examining their respective behavior over a number of market cycles and many years. For the reader interested in pursuing this topic further, the references at the end of this chapter provide a representative sample of additional information.

SUMMARY

This chapter introduced the reader to technical analysis but did not attempt to provide a set of technical tools that can immediately be applied in making investment decisions. A substantial number of techniques and tools employed by technical analysts are not reviewed in this chapter. Further study and observation by the reader is required. This chapter does, however, provide the reader with an introduction to the logic underlying technical analysis and to a number of the more popular techniques used in market timing strategies.

No attempt has been made to discuss the continuing heated debate about whether technical analysis will indeed result in risk-adjusted excess returns relative to a buy-and-hold investment strategy. This issue, however, is discussed in Chapter 13 and in the references at the end of this chapter and Chapter 13.

With the advent of microcomputers, on-line computer data bases, and readily available technical analysis software, it is possible to perform technical studies in substantially less time than in the past. This technology encourages further development of technical analysis and provides opportunities to test the success and reliability of various technical strategies.

QUESTIONS

1. Explain the difference between a "fundamental" approach to investment or trading decisions and the "technical" approach.

2. Technical analysis is believed to have its modern genesis around the turn of the twentieth century in New York. What were some of the main characteristics of that time period and how did this encourage the technical approach to securities trading?

3. Who was Charles H. Dow and what were his contributions to the development of technical analysis?

4. What was the basic interpretation that Charles H. Dow initially made concerning the behavior of the stock market?

5. What does the Dow Theory attempt to explain and what are its major elements as used by technical analysts today?

6. As the Dow Theory has evolved and as it is currently interpreted, how is the volume of shares traded related to price movements?

7. What would you expect to be taking place in many issues if a technician makes the statement that the "breadth of the market is very good"?

8. What is a "Dow line"?

9. If you were attempting to gauge the current position of the market within a primary trend, what are some technical signs that you would attempt to identify?

10. What are the differences between point-and-figure, bar line, and equivolume charts?

11. Would an individual who is a proponent of the so-called "Efficient Market Hypothesis" employ Dow Theory? Why, or why not?

12. How might security or market price objectives be set using a point-and-figure chart?

13. How should the cumulative volume of trading be related to prices in an advancing market?

14. Once a trend has been identified in the price behavior of the market or of an individual security, what method(s) might you use to identify when the trend is changing?

15. What is the theory behind the construction of the Arms Index and how is this index interpreted?

16. What phenomenon does the "stochastic process" recognize, and how could it be used to make market entry and exit decisions?

COMPUTER APPLICATIONS

The floppy disk includes programs that perform a basic technical analysis including point-and-figure charts, bar charts, and other trend analysis programs. Instructions and illustrations are provided on the disk.

REFERENCES

Arms, Richard W., Jr. *Volume Cycles in the Stock Market: Market Timing through Equivolume Charting.* Homewood, Ill.: Dow Jones-Irwin, 1983.

Arnold, Curtis M., and Dan Rahfeldt. *Timing the Market.* Chicago: Probus Publishing, 1986.

Business Conditions Digest (monthly). U.S. Government Printing Office, Washington, DC 20402.

Cootner, Paul H., ed. *The Random Character of Stock Market Prices.* Cambridge: The M.I.T. Press, 1964.

Drew, Garfield A. *New Methods for Profit in the Stock Market.* Wells, Vt: Fraser Publishing, 1966.

Drinka, Thomas P., and Steven L. Kille. "Profitability of Selected Technical Indicators: U.S. Treasury Bonds." *Technical Analysis of Stocks and Commodities* 5, no. 2 (February 1987): pp. 19–21.

Edwards, Robert D., and John Magee. *Technical Analysis of Stock Trends.* Springfield, Mass.: John Magee, 1966.

Ehlers, John F. "A Complete Computer Trading Program." *Technical Analysis of Stocks and Commodities* 5, no. 3 (March 1987): pp. 37–39.

Five-Trend Security Charts (monthly). Securities Research Company, 208 Newbury Street, Boston, MA 02116.

Fosback, Norman G. *Stock Market Logic.* Fort Lauderdale, Fla.: Institute for Econometric Research, 1976.

Frost, A., and Robert Prechter. *Elliot Wave Principle.* Chappaqua, N.Y.: New Classics Library, 1981.

Granville, Joseph E. *A Strategy of Daily Stock Market Timing for Maximum Profit.* Englewood Cliffs, N.J.: Prentice-Hall, 1960.

Growth Fund Guide (monthly). Growth Fund Research Bldg., Box 6600, Rapid City, SD 57709.

Hamilton, William Peter. *The Stock Market Barometer.* New York: John Wiley and Sons, 1976.

Jiler, William L. *How Charts Can Help You in the Stock Market.* New York: Trendline, Standard and Poor's, 1962.

Kaufman, P. J. *Commodity Trading Systems and Methods.* New York: John Wiley and Sons, 1976.

Kuhn, Bill, and James Alphier. "A Helping Hand from the Arms Index." *Technical Analysis of Stocks and Commodities* 5, no. 4 (April 1987): p. 44.

Lerro, A. J., and C. B. Swayne, Jr. *Selection of Securities.* Morristown, N.J.: General Learning, 1970.

Levy, Robert A. "Random Walks: Reality or Myth." *Financial Analysts Journal* (November-December, 1967); p. 76.

Livermore, Jesse L. *How to Trade in Stocks.* New York: Duell, Sloan and Pearce, 1940.

Neill, Humphrey B. *The Art of Contrary Thinking.* Caldwell, Idaho: Claxton Printers, 1967.

Point and Figure Stock Market Trading. Larchmont, N.Y.: Chartcraft 1980.

Pratt, Shannon P., and Charles W. DeVere, "Insider Trading and Market Returns." Unpublished manuscript, Portland State University, September 1968.

Pring, Martin J. *International Investing Made Easy.* New York: McGraw-Hill, 1981.

————. *Technical Analysis Explained.* New York: McGraw-Hill, 1985.

Trendline's Current Market Perspectives (monthly). Trendline, Standard and Poor's Corporation, 25 Broadway, New York, NY 10004.

CHAPTER 13

MARKET EFFICIENCY

INTRODUCTION

Overview

Chapters 9 through 12 presented the two traditional views of common stock analysis: fundamental analysis and technical analysis. This chapter discusses one of the most profound but controversial theories of stock market behavior and its implications for investment decision making. This theory deals with the *degree* of capital market efficiency. Efficiency in this context refers to the market's ability to price securities correctly and instantaneously change prices to reflect new information. In other words, does the market price of a security reflect its investment value, or are market prices poor indicators of investment value? In an efficient market, security prices would correctly reflect the important variables for a security and represent an unbiased estimate of its investment value. Market efficiency also implies that as new information becomes available, it is quickly analyzed by the market, and any necessary price adjustments occur rapidly.

The degree of market efficiency has important implications for the economy and for investment decision makers. In an economic sense it is important that security prices provide accurate signals that can be used to allocate capital resources correctly. Mispriced securities would result in incorrect allocations of capital. The importance and desirability of efficient markets in an economic sense, however, present a dilemma to investors in terms of an appropriate investment strategy.

Efficient markets imply that securities are unlikely to be under- or overvalued and therefore do not offer risk-adjusted excess returns. That is, in an efficient market, an investor's expected return is directly proportionate to the risk level of the security; the expected return provides appropriate compensation for risk. For example, traditional technical and fundamental analyses are designed to identify securities that are not correctly priced. Once these securities are identified, an appropriate investment strategy can be formulated that will earn excess returns and "beat the market" on a risk-adjusted basis. However, if the market is highly efficient, it cannot be beaten. Therefore, efficient markets suggest a passive investment strategy that does not attempt to earn excess returns. If the market is somewhat efficient, it might be possible to earn risk-adjusted excess returns, but it would be difficult to achieve any degree of consistency. Finally, if the market is not efficient, it would be relatively easy to develop investment strategies to earn risk-adjusted excess returns. The real question for investors is, How efficient are capital markets?

History

Prior to the 1950s, it was generally believed that the traditional technical and fundamental approaches could be used to beat the market. During the 1950s, however, two important empirical studies of security prices provided the initial evidence against the traditional view.[1] These early studies analyzed the price

---

[1] Maurice G. Kendall, "The Analysis of Economic Time-Series, Part I: Prices," *Journal of the Royal Statistical Society* (Part 1, 1953): pp. 11–25; Harry V. Roberts, "Stock Market 'Patterns' and Financial Analysis: Methodological Suggestions," *Journal of Finance* (March 1959): pp. 1–10.

changes of both British and U.S. stock prices and concluded that the patterns of changes were indistinguishable from patterns generated by a series of random numbers.

These two early studies provided the basis for a number of additional studies during the 1960s that also analyzed patterns of stock price changes but, more importantly, began to develop a theory to explain the apparent random behavior. Thus, the early empirical work was used to develop a theory—rather than the normal procedure of developing and then empirically testing a theory. These studies provided the basis for the *random walk* or *fair game* theory of market efficiency. The fair game theory suggests that there is a 50 percent chance of earning a return above or below the expected return. It also suggests that the next price change in a security has an equal probability of increasing or decreasing, regardless of the previous price change. The price changes are therefore random and do not reflect any distinguishable pattern.

Other studies analyzed the pattern and speed of stock price adjustments to specific types of new information that reaches the market. Two of the more important early studies considered how stock prices react to stock splits and annual earnings announcements.[2] Surprisingly, the stock split study found that generally the stock price correctly adjusted to the split *prior* to the actual announcement date, and little adjustment occurred after the announcement date. The earnings announcement study also found that the market generally anticipated the increased or decreased earnings, with little price adjustment at or before the announcement date.

These types of studies are generally called *event studies* and provide the empirical evidence of the *semistrong form* theory of market efficiency. Essentially, this theory states that security prices reflect all publicly available information.

A third type of study analyzes the actual investment behavior of different groups of investors that might be expected to beat the market. Two of the more important studies published in 1968 deal with the investment performance of mutual funds and corporate insiders.[3] The mutual fund study found evidence that after considering risk and expenses, mutual funds, on average, did not outperform the market. The study of corporate insiders (defined as an officer, director, an owner of 10 percent or more of the stock or some combination of these criteria) found mixed results. Generally, "insider buyers" outperformed "insider sellers," and knowledge of buyer actions may be useful in making investment decisions.

The results for these types of studies are used to support the *strong form* of market efficiency. This hypothesis suggests that all available information (public or private) is fully reflected in the security's price. The empirical evidence supporting this hypothesis is mixed. It appears that mutual funds, with the benefit of professional analysts and portfolio managers, are unable consistently to out-

---

[2] Eugene F. Fama, Lawrence Fisher, Michael Jensen, and Richard Roll, "The Adjustment of Stock Prices to New Information," *International Economic Review* (February 1969): pp. 1–21; Ray Ball and Philip Brown, "An Empirical Evaluation of Accounting Income Numbers," *Journal of Accounting Research* (Autumn 1968): pp. 159–78.

[3] Michael C. Jensen, "The Performance of Mutual Funds in the Period 1945–64," *Journal of Finance* (May 1968): pp. 389–416; Shannon P. Pratt and Charles W. DeVere, "Relationship between Insider Trading and Rates of Return for NYSE Common Stocks, 1960–66," in *Modern Developments in Investment Management*, James Lorie and Richard Brealey (New York: Praeger Publishers, 1972).

perform the market. The theory suggests that their skills and access to information are not in themselves advantages that can produce superior investment performance. In the case of corporate insiders and specialists on the NYSE, the evidence suggests that the nonpublic information available to them can be used to outperform the market.[4]

In summary, empirical studies that began in the 1950s provided the foundation for a theory of stock market behavior that has become known as the *Efficient Market Hypothesis*, EMH. Based on the early studies and numerous more-recent studies, there appears to be little doubt that capital markets are efficient. The controversial and unresolved issue, however, is the *degree* of market efficiency. The debate about the degree of efficiency generally follows the three degrees of efficiency suggested by Fama in 1970: weak, semistrong, and strong form efficiency.[5] The remaining material in this chapter is organized according to these three degrees of efficiency. In each case, the theory is explained in more detail, empirical tests are discussed, and implications for investment decision making are suggested.

The last section of the chapter discusses the degree of market efficiency for other types of securities, such as bonds and options, and in other markets, such as the regional stock exchanges and foreign markets. The idea of market efficiency was first developed for common stocks primarily traded on the NYSE, AMEX, and OTC market. Studies and tests have also been conducted for other types of securities traded in different markets.

WEAK FORM MARKET EFFICIENCY

Overview

The initial efforts in developing the EMH concerned the historical behavior of common stock price changes observed over relatively short periods, such as a day or week. As discussed in Chapter 12, traditional technical analysis deals with the behavior of prices and volume. The basic assumption of technical analysis is that there are recurring and therefore predictable patterns of price behavior. An analysis of historical prices can consequently be used to forecast the direction and the level of prices. Presently, many technical analysts concentrate on identifying changes in price trends rather than attempting to forecast prices.

The weak form hypothesis indicates that past prices do not provide information that can be used to outperform the market. Essentially, if short-run price changes follow a "random walk," then an analysis of a historical time series cannot provide any useful information about future price changes.

---

[4] An early study of NYSE specialists is Victor Niederhoffer and M. F. M. Osborne, "Market Making and Reversal in the Stock Exchange," *Journal of the American Statistical Association* (December 1966): pp. 897–916.

[5] Eugene F. Fama, "Efficient Capital Markets: A Review of Theory and Empirical Work," *Journal of Finance* (May 1970): pp. 383–417.

Random Walk

As previously discussed, one of the first American researchers to offer evidence of the *random walk* hypothesis was Harry V. Roberts. Figure 13.1 reproduces graphs that were published in his 1959 paper. Using a published table of random numbers, Roberts constructed a simulated time series, then calculated the weekly point changes in this random series. The resulting values are depicted in Figure 13.1, along with actual weekly values and point changes in the DJIA. By comparing these four figures, Roberts argued that the simulated time series was "hauntingly realistic" to typical stock price behavior and that the simulated series had an "unmistakable" resemblance to the DJIA series.

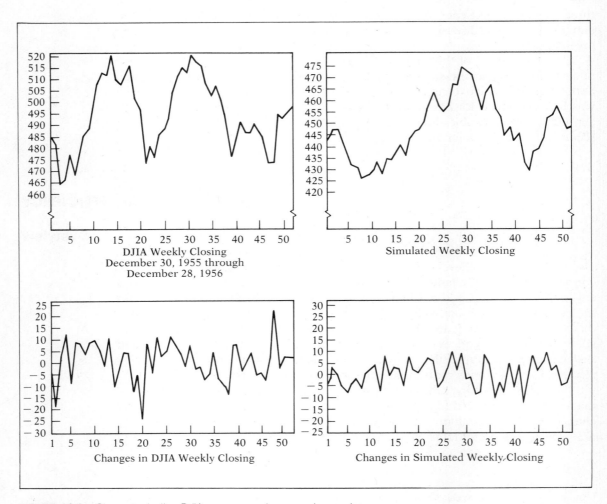

FIGURE 13.1 Changes in the DJIA versus random number series

Source: Harry V Roberts, "Stock Market 'Patterns' and Financial Analysis: Methodological Suggestions," *Journal of Finance* (March 1959): pp. 4–6: Reprinted by permission.

Fama's 1970 article formally defined the random walk model[6]:

$$f(\Delta P_{j,t+1}|\Phi_t) = f(\Delta P_{j,t+1}) \tag{13.1}$$

where
f = probability density function of price changes
$\Delta P_{j,t+1}$ = change in security j's price from period t to $t+1$
Φ_t = information set used in period t by investors to price security j

This equation indicates that

1. security price changes fully reflect the available information set which includes all public information;
2. successive price changes are independent; and
3. the probability density function is constant for all t's, which implies that the rates of return (price changes) are independent and identically distributed.

Empirical Tests of Random Walk

Many of the statistical tests of the random walk model analyzed the independence of successive price changes. The methodology consisted of *serial correlations*, *runs tests*, *filter rules*, and *relative strength*. These are discussed below.

1. SERIAL CORRELATIONS The correlation coefficient, defined and illustrated in Chapter 2, is essentially a measure of how two variables are related. A serial correlation coefficient indicates how a variable is related to lagged values. For example, in calculating a serial correlation for stock j's price, the two variables would be

WEEK	OBSERVED PRICE	LAGGED PRICE
1	$10	$11
2	11	9
3	9	12
4	12	⋮
⋮	⋮	⋮

If the serial correlation coefficient is significantly different from 0, then successive weekly price changes for stock j are related. This finding would contradict the random walk hypothesis. On the other hand, if the serial correlation coefficient is essentially 0, the random walk hypothesis is supported.

Table 13.1 presents serial correlation coefficients for the thirty stocks in the DJIA over the period January 1956 to April 1958. The coefficients are computed using the log of daily price changes with lags from one to ten days.

---

[6] Fama, ''Efficient Capital Markets,'' pp. 386–87.

TABLE 13.1 SERIAL CORRELATION COEFFICIENTS FOR STOCKS IN DJIA

STOCK	1	2	3	4	5	6	7	8	9	10
Allied Chemical	.017	−.042	.007	−.001	.027	.004	−.017	−.026	−.017	−.007
Alcoa	.118*	.038	−.014	.022	−.022	.009	.017	.007	−.001	−.033
American Can	−.087*	−.024	.034	−.065*	−.017	−.006	.015	.025	−.047	−.040
A.T.&T.	−.039	−.097*	.000	.026	.005	−.005	.002	.027	−.014	.007
American Tobacco	.111*	−.109*	−.060*	−.065*	.007	−.010	.011	.046	.039	.041
Anaconda	.067*	−.061*	−.047	−.002	.000	−.010	.009	.016	−.014	−.056
Bethlehem Steel	.013	−.065*	.009	.021	−.053	−.038	−.010	.004	−.002	−.021
Chrysler	.012	−.066*	−.016	−.007	−.015	−.098*	.037	.056*	−.044	.021
Du Pont	.013	−.033	.060*	.027	−.002	.009	.020	.011	−.034	.001
Eastman Kodak	.025	.014	−.031	.005	−.022	.012	.007	.006	.008	.002
General Electric	.011	−.038	−.021	.031	−.001	.000	−.008	.014	−.002	.010
General Foods	.061*	−.003	.045	.002	−.015	−.052	−.006	−.014	−.024	−.017
General Motors	−.004	−.056*	−.037	−.008	−.038	−.006	.019	.006	−.016	.009
Goodyear	−.123*	.017	−.044	.043	−.002	−.003	.035	.014	−.015	.007
International Harvester	−.017	−.029	−.031	.037	−.052	−.021	−.001	.003	−.046	−.016
International Nickel	.096*	−.033	−.019	.020	.027	.059*	−.038	−.008	−.016	.034
International Paper	.046	−.011	−.058*	.053*	.049	−.003	−.025	−.019	−.003	−.021
Johns Manville	.006	−.038	−.027	−.023	−.029	−.080*	.040	.018	−.037	.029
Owens Illinois	−.021	−.084*	−.047	.068*	.086*	−.040	.011	−.040	.067*	−.043
Procter & Gamble	.099*	−.009	−.008	.009	−.015	.022	.012	−.012	−.022	−.021
Sears	−.097*	.026	.028	.025	.005	−.054	−.006	−.010	−.008	−.009
Standard Oil (Calif.)	.025	−.030	−.051*	−.025	−.047	−.034	−.010	.072*	−.049*	−.035
Standard Oil (N.J.)	.008	−.116*	.016	.014	−.047	−.018	−.022	−.026	−.073*	.081*
Swift & Co.	−.004	−.015	−.010	.012	.057*	.012	−.043	.014	.012	.001
Texaco	.094*	−.049	−.024	−.018	−.017	−.009	.031	.032	−.013	.008
Union Carbide	.107*	−.012	.040	.046	−.036	−.034	.003	−.008	−.054	−.037
United Aircraft	.014	−.033	−.022	−.047	−.067*	−.053	.046	.037	.015	−.019
U.S. Steel	.040	−.074*	.014	.011	−.012	−.021	.041	.037	−.021	−.044
Westinghouse	−.027	−.022	−.036	−.003	.000	−.054*	−.020	.013	−.014	.008
Woolworth	.028	−.016	.015	.014	.007	−.039	−.013	.003	−.088*	−.008

* Coefficient is twice its computed standard error.

SOURCE: Eugene F. Fama, "The Behavior of Stock-Market Prices," *Journal of Finance* (January 1965): p. 71. Reprinted by permission.

Notice that most of the coefficients are close to 0 and that the largest value is .123. Only 42 of the 300 correlations are statistically significant. The correlations are also slightly larger for shorter lags than for longer lags. Fama concluded that, "'dependence' of such a small order of magnitude is, from a practical point of view, probably unimportant for both the statistician and the investor."[7]

Other researchers have analyzed serial correlation coefficients, using a different sample of common stocks and stock indices. There is some evidence that smaller, less actively traded, stocks do tend to have slightly larger coefficients, but their magnitude does not offer much hope in forecasting price changes using historical price changes. The results of the serial correlation tests generally support the random walk hypothesis.

2. RUNS TESTS A runs tests is a nonparametric statistical test that can be used to test for dependence in successive price changes. Instead of the actual numerical values for the price changes, the sign (positive or negative) of the price change is used. A run is simply a sequence of price changes with the same sign. If price changes were dependent, then there would be "long" runs of positive or negative signs. Tables are available to test for the statistical significance of runs of a certain length. Based on runs tests for the DJIA, Roberts did not find any evidence of dependence in weekly changes.[8] Fama, using daily prices of the thirty stocks in DJIA, found little evidence of statistically significant runs.[9]

The results of the runs tests support the random walk hypothesis. These tests indicate that successive price changes are generally independent.

3. FILTER RULES A third test of the dependence in successive price changes, this test involves developing mechanical trading rules, based on price changes that can be used to simulate buying and selling individual securities. Filter rule's producing risk-adjusted returns greater than returns from a buy-and-hold strategy would be evidence against the random walk hypothesis. For example, a simple filter rule would be to buy the stock the day after the price increased by x percent and to sell (or short) the stock the day after the price declined by y percent. Filter rules are a more direct test of price-change dependency since they test actual investment strategies that depend on the existence of dependent prices.

Early tests of various filter rules were conducted by Alexander, by Mandelbrot, and by Fama.[10] These early tests used filters ranging from .5 percent to 50 percent applied to the DJIA and to individual common stocks. "There is no evidence at all, however, that there is any dependence in the

[7] Eugene F. Fama," The Behavior of Stock-Market Prices," *Journal of Finance* (January 1965): p. 70.

[8] Roberts, p. 9.

[9] Fama, "Behavior," p. 80.

[10] S. S. Alexander, "Price Movements in Speculative Markets: Trends or Random Walks," *Industrial Management Review* (May 1961): pp. 7–26; Benoit Mandelbrot, "The Variation of Certain Speculative Prices," *Journal of Business* (October 1961): pp. 394–419; Fama, "Behavior," pp. 81–87.

stock-price series that would be regarded as important for investment purposes."[11] Essentially, the studies found that after taking into account transaction costs, no filter rule could be found that outperformed a naive buy-and-hold strategy.

A 1986 study of United Kingdom stocks came to the same conclusion as the studies on U.S. stocks.[12] One interesting aspect of this study, however, deals with potential changes in the behavior of stock prices over a long period. Using an index of UK stocks over the period 1919 to 1970, approximately 2,000 statistically significant filter strategies were identified. Using these same filter strategies over the period 1971–1984, however, resulted in no successful filters being identified. The important implication of this finding is that possible dependency in stock price changes had declined over time.

4. RELATIVE STRENGTH The fourth methodology used to test the random walk hypothesis deals with trading rules based on relative strength measures. Rather than analyzing price changes on an individual security or index, relative strength relates price changes to previous (lagged) price changes for the security under study or to some other variable. For example, a relative strength ratio may be calculated by dividing the price change of a stock by the price change for an index of stocks in the same industry. This ratio represents price changes (returns) for the security relative to similar securities.

In a 1967 study, Levy investigated the relative strength trading approach by testing the ability of one relative strength measure to outperform a buy-and-hold strategy.[13] Levy's relative strength measure is

$$PR_{jt} = P_{jt} / \bar{P}_{jt} \tag{13.2}$$

where PR_{jt} = relative strength measures for security j in period t

P_{jt} = price of security j in period t

$\bar{P}_{jt}$ = average price of security j calculated over the last 27 weeks.

Essentially, Levy calculated PR_{jt} for a sample of stocks and took a long position in the stocks with the largest PR_{jt} values. He tested several rules in an attempt to identify what percentage of the two hundred stocks in the sample with the highest relative strength measures should be purchased. In other words, should the top 5, 10, 15, . . . percent of the stocks in the sample with the highest values of PR_{jt} be used as the cutoff point? He concluded that either the top 5 or 10 percent, in equal dollar amounts, represented the optimal percentages. He reported that the returns from these rules were 20.0 percent and 26.1 percent, respectively, versus 13.4 percent for a simple buy-and-hold strategy. His findings appear to reject the random walk hypothesis.

---

[11] Fama, "Behavior," p. 87.

[12] John O'Hanlon and Charles W. R. Ward, "How to Lose at Winning Strategies," *Journal of Portfolio Management* (Spring 1986): pp. 20–23.

[13] Robert A. Levy, "Random Walks: Reality or Myth," *Financial Analysts Journal* (November–December 1967): pp. 69–76.

A 1970 study discovered several errors in Levy's methodology.[14] Using the same sample and trading rules used by Levy, this study found that "after explicit adjustment for the level of risk, it was shown that net of transaction costs of the two trading rules we tested earned an average $-.31\%$ and -2.36% less than an equivalent risk B & H policy."[15]

Implications for Technical Analysis

The empirical tests discussed above provide very strong support for the random walk hypothesis. Short-term stock price changes are essentially independent, and trading rules based on historical changes should not be successful in outperforming a buy-and-hold strategy. The small degree of observed dependency is not significant enough to offset the transaction costs involved in applying the trading rules.

Chapter 12 presented an overview of technical analysis and considered several traditional and recent techniques used by technicians. A major question deals with the implications of the random walk hypothesis for technical analysis. If technical analysis is defined simply as a mechanical analysis of past price changes or relative strength measures, then the random walk hypothesis indicates that these approaches are doomed to failure. If, on the other hand, technical analysis is more broadly defined, as indicated in Chapter 12, then the implications are not as clear.

A recent paper discusses the implications of the weak form of the EMH for technical analysis.[16] This paper argues that tests of the random walk hypothesis are often incorrectly equated to tests of technical analysis by scholarly researchers. This leads to the false conclusion that acceptance of the random walk hypothesis also requires a rejection of technical analysis. This study argues that technical analysis has not been throughly tested and that

1. "There is not a one-to-one mapping between weak form analysis and technical analysis."

2. "Many weak form tests are not direct tests of specific forms of technical analysis."[17]

Based on these observations, it is apparent that modern technical analysis is much more complex than a simple analysis of past price changes. The methology of technical analysis continues to be developed for a dynamic and changing market environment in the same fashion as changes in the techniques of fundamental analysis. It should also be noted that many analysts and investors believe in the validity of technical analysis. Are all of these individuals incorrect? It appears that additional empirical research needs to be undertaken to test correctly the validity of specific techniques of technical analysis.

---

[14] Michael C. Jensen and George A. Bennington, "Random Walks and Technical Theories: Some Additional Evidence," *Journal of Finance* (May 1970): pp. 469–82.

[15] Ibid., p. 482.

[16] O. Maurice Joy and Charles P. Jones, "Should We Believe the Tests of Market Efficiency?" *Journal of Portfolio Management* (Summer 1986): pp. 49–54.

[17] Ibid., p. 51.

SEMISTRONG FORM MARKET EFFICIENCY

Overview

Based on the results of empirical tests of the weak form of the EMH conducted during the 1950s and 1960s, research turned toward other aspects of market efficiency. These tests measured the speed with which stock prices adjusted to new publicly available information. For example, what price adjustment patterns could be observed for companies announcing stock splits, significant changes in dividend policies, or unusually large or small earnings per share? The weak form of the EMH postulates that past prices do not reflect future prices of the security. The *semistrong* form indicates that prices reflect all publicly available information. Thus, any significant new public information should immediately be reflected in the stock price. Further, there would be no lag between the time the information is available and the adjustment of the stock price.

Figure 13.2 illustrates the price adjustment patterns that might occur in inefficient and efficient markets. The left panel shows a stock price that appears to be following a random walk prior to period $t = 0$. At period $t = 0$, however, significant new information relative to the stock is made available to the market. Investors, reacting to the new information, cause the stock price to increase for a number of periods until it finally reaches a new price equilibrium at time period $t = n$ and resumes a random walk. This price adjustment pattern would not occur in a semistrong efficient market becausse of the period of time ($t = 0$ to $t = n$) needed before the price fully reflects the new information.

The right panel of Figure 13.2 illustrates the pattern of price adjustment suggested by the semistrong form of the EMH. Notice that the stock price instantaneously reflects the new information at time period $t = 0$. Essentially, no time elapses between the date the new information is available and the date the new equilibrium price is established. The market immediately obtains the new information, correctly analyzes its significance for the price, and incorporates the new information into the price.

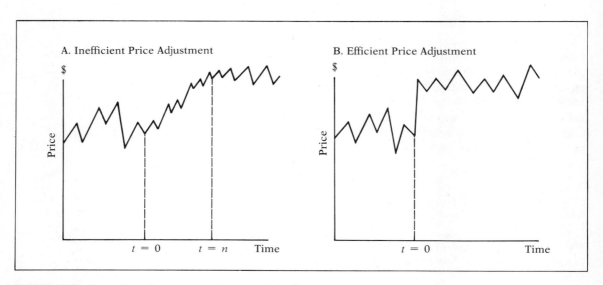

FIGURE 13.2 Illustration of semistrong form market efficiency

The market crash in October 1987 raises some interesting questions about market efficiency in terms of the magnitude and speed of price adjustments.[18] An EMH viewpoint suggests that the very large and rapid drop in common stock, option, and futures prices supports the semistrong form of hypothesis. Proponents, however, may argue that the reaction was due to panic selling that resulted largely from irrational market behavior. This initial debate will likely be followed by a number of empirical studies that attempt to explain the very unusual events that occurred in October 1987.

Event Study Methodology

Numerous *event* studies provide insights concerning the degree of market efficiency. As the name implies, this type of study identifies a specific development or event that is expected to influence stock prices, and a sample of companies is identified where the "event" has occurred. Previously studied events include stock splits, earnings announcements, acquisitions and divestitures, and financial distress. Once the event and sample of firms is identified, *HPR*s are calculated, usually on a daily or weekly basis, for periods both before and after the event.

The *HPR*s are analyzed using some form of the CAPM. For example, assume that 60 weeks of *HPR*s are calculated for each stock in the sample involved in the event study. The 30 earliest observations before the event could be used to estimate the regression parameters of the characteristic line, CL, for the stock:

$$r_{j,t} = \hat{\alpha}_j + \hat{\beta}_j r_{m,t} + e_t \tag{13.2}$$

where $r_{j,t}$ = *HPR* for stock j in period t
$\qquad \hat{\alpha}_j$ = estimate of alpha or intercept for stock j
$\qquad \hat{\beta}_j$ = estimate of stock j's beta
$\qquad r_{m,t}$ = *HPR* for market index for period t
$\qquad e_t$ = residual error in period t

If the event under study is defined to occur in week 0 ($t = 0$), then $\hat{\alpha}_j$ and $\hat{\beta}_j$, calculated using Equation 13.2, could be used to estimate the *HPR*s for 20 weeks immediately prior to the event ($t = -20$ to -1) and the 10 weeks ($t = 0$ to 9) after the event, including the week the event occurred. The *HPR* for each of these 30 weeks would be *estimated* as

$$\hat{r}_{j,t} = \hat{\alpha}_j + \hat{\beta}_j r_{m,t} \tag{13.3}$$

where $\hat{r}_{j,t}$ = *estimate* of *HPR* for stock j in period t
$\qquad \hat{\alpha}_j$ = estimate of stock j's alpha from Equation 13.2
$\qquad \hat{\beta}_j$ = estimate of stock j's beta from Equation 13.2
$\qquad r_{m,t}$ = *actual HPR* for market index for period t

---

[18] For recent studies that do not include October 1987 data, see Keith C. Brown and C. V. Harlow, "Market Overreaction: Magnitude and Intensity," *Journal of Portfolio Managment* (Winter 1988): pp. 6–13, and Hans R. Stoll and Robert E. Whaley, "Volatility and Futures: Message versus Messenger," *Journal of Portfolio Management* (Winter 1988): pp. 20–22.

The error or residual term can be calculated for each period as

$$e_{j,t} = r_{j,t} - \hat{r}_{j,t} \qquad (13.4)$$

If $e_{j,t} > 0$, then the actual *HPR* is greater than the estimated return. This implies that after removing the influence of the market, stock j's price increased more than expected.

The next step in this procedure involves calculating an average residual for each week, using all of the stocks in the sample. For example, assume that n stocks are included in the event study so that the average residual for week $t = -20$ can be calculated as

$$\bar{e}_{t=-20} = \left[\sum_{j=1}^{n} e_{j,t=-20} \right] \Big/ n \qquad (13.5)$$

Equation 13.5 would be used to calculate an average residual for each of the 30 weeks ($t = -20$ to 9). Finally, the average weekly residuals would be added together to produce a time series of *cumulative average residuals, CARs*.

$$CAR_t = \sum_{t=-20}^{t=9} \bar{e}_t \qquad (13.6)$$

An analysis of the *CARs* for the weeks prior to and after the event could then be used to analyze the pattern and speed of the price adjustments to the event.

Empirical Results from Event Studies

1. STOCK SPLITS The event study methodology that was summarized in the previous section was developed and illustrated using stock splits in a 1969 study.[19] The empirical analysis was based on a sample of all 940 stock splits that occurred on the NYSE from 1927–1959. The purpose of the study was to see if there is any unusual price behavior before or after the split date. The split itself is an event that should not affect the wealth of the stockholder. For example, if a company has a two-for-one split, the price of the stock should decrease by 50 percent, and the stockholder will have double the number of original shares. It is possible, however, that the change in cash dividends may not match the terms of the split. The company may use the split to increase or decrease dividends. Prior to the two-for-one split, the company may be paying $1 per share. Effective with the date of the split, the dividend may be $.60 per share, which represents a 20 percent increase in dividends. In an efficient market, the stock price should increase before or on the split date to reflect the increase in dividends.

   Figure 13.3 provides graphs of the *CARs* from the Fama-Fisher-Jensen-Roll study for the period $t = -29$ to $t = 30$ for all splits and for splits

---

[19] Eugene F. Fama, Lawrence Fisher, Michael C. Jensen, and Richard Roll, "The Adjustment of Stock Prices to New Information," *International Economic Review* (February 1969): pp. 1–21.

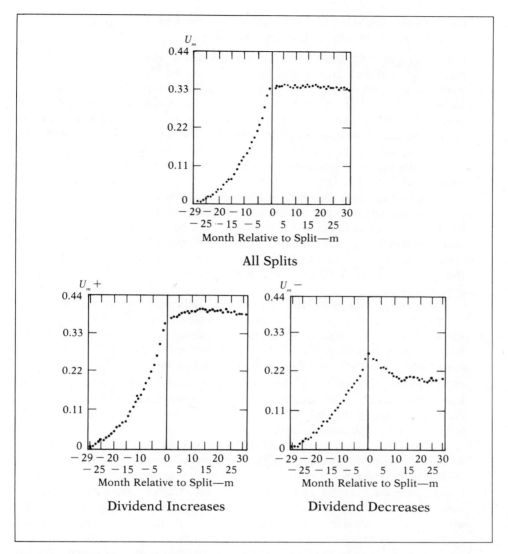

FIGURE 13.3   Analysis of residuals for stock splits

Source: Eugene F. Fama, Lawrence Fisher, Michael C. Jensen, and Richard Roll, "The Adjustment of Stock Prices to New Information" *International Economic Review*, (February 1969) pp. 13–14

accompanied by dividend increases and decreases. The *CAR*s (labeled as U_m) increase in the 29 months prior to the split, which indicates an increasing stock price with a higher than expected return for the stocks in the sample. After the month of the split ($t = 0$) there are few significant changes in the *CAR*s. The authors argued that the market appeared to anticipate correctly the split and the likely impact of dividend changes. Notice that the *CAR*s calculated for splits with dividend increases reached a higher level than those associated with dividend decreases. Also, the *CAR*s quickly declined after the split month for the stocks with dividend decreases. Based on these results, the authors concluded that the market was efficient in terms of its ability to adjust to dividend information implied in a split.

2. EARNINGS ANNOUNCEMENTS Two other important event studies were conducted by Ball and Brown and Latane and Jones.[20] Using the event study methodology and a sample of 261 firms over the period 1946–1966, Ball and Brown tested for the market reactions to "increased" or "decreased" announced earnings. The announced earnings were classified as increased or decreased based on a comparison with an earnings trend line estimated for each company. If the announced earnings were below the trend line, they were classified as "decreased," with earnings above the line classified as "increased."

The results from this study supported the semistrong form of the EMH, since the market correctly anticipated the earnings announcements. In other words, stock prices declined before the announcement of decreased earnings and increased before the announcement of increased earnings. Ball and Brown concluded that only about 10 to 15 percent of the information contained in the earnings announcement had not been anticipated by the month of the announcement.

The Latane and Jones study also analyzed *unexpected* earnings announcements, defined as the difference in the consensus earnings forecast of professional security analysts and the actual announced earnings. These results were not as supportive of the EMH since there were delayed price adjustments associated with stocks not as closely followed by analysts.

3. OTHER EVENT STUDIES Since the initial event studies were published in the late 1960s, many additional studies have been conducted. This section briefly mentions some of the different "events" that have been analyzed but is by no means a complete summary.

Many investors rely on the *Wall Street Journal* and similar publications to follow economic and financial developments in general as well as specific company information. Do stock prices change significantly before or after important public announcements such as information about new products, new contracts, or acquisitions? A 1982 study found that significant price changes occurred, along with unusual trading volume, *prior* to the announcement of the new information appearing in the *Wall Street Journal*.[21] This finding supports market efficiency and argues against an investment strategy based on trading securities on days when new information appears in the *Wall Street Journal*.

A number of studies have analyzed the investment success of corporate insiders. Some of these studies will be reviewed later in the chapter. A related issue, however, is how the market reacts to *announcements* about insider trading. By law, corporate insiders must report their transactions to the SEC by the tenth of the month following the trade. Once this information is pub-

---

[20] Ray Ball and Philip Brown, "An Empirical Evaluation of Accounting Income Numbers," *Journal of Accounting Research* (Autumn 1968): pp. 159–78; Henry A. Latane and Charles P. Jones, "Standardized Unexpected Earnings—1971–77," *Journal of Finance* (June 1979): pp. 717–24.

[21] Dale Morse, "Wall Street Journal Announcements and the Securities Markets," *Financial Analysts Journal* (March-April 1982): pp. 69–76.

lished by the SEC or by an investment advisory letter, can the information be used to outperform the market? A recent study found that price adjustments occurred up to four months *prior* to publication of the information and that "moderate" excess returns occurred in the twelve months after the published information appeared.[22]

Individual stocks often have "extreme" daily price changes. This is to be expected in an efficient market since no time lag should occur between the arrival of new information and the appropriate stock price adjustment. Would it be possible, however, either to buy or to sell (short) stocks on the day after an "extreme" price change, with the expectation that additional price adjustments would occur? A 1982 study concluded that the market was efficient in making rapid and complete price adjustments, since no effective investment strategy could be found based on extreme price changes.[23]

The majority of event studies report results that support the semistrong form of the EMH. There are, however, a limited number of studies that report events contrary to the hypothesis; two examples are analysts' recommendations and financial distress.[24]

4. SUMMARY OF EVENT STUDIES Based on the evidence from many event studies, it appears that the market is efficient in the sense suggested by the semistrong form of the EMH. It should not be concluded from these studies, however, that the market is efficient in reacting to every possible event. Not all events have been studied, and not all possible investment strategies based on events have been analyzed.

There is also evidence that the results from some event studies may be biased in the case where the beta is nonstationary around the event date.[25] As previously discussed, the event study methodology calculates the beta based on dates prior to the event and then uses the beta to estimate returns. This implies beta stationarity.

Other Empirical Tests

In addition to event studies, other types of research have tested the semistrong form of the EMH. These studies test whether various investment strategies based on publicly available information outperform the market. If no strategy can be found, it is likely that the market is efficient. Successful strategies, however, indicate that the market may be inefficient in using certain types of information.

---

[22] Gary A. Benesh and Robert A. Pari, "Performance of Stocks Recommended on the Basis of Insider Trading Activity," *Financial Review* (February 1987): pp. 145–58.

[23] Avner Arbel and Bikki Jaggi, "Market Information Assimilation Related to Extreme Daily Price Jumps," *Financial Analysts Journal* (November-December 1982): pp. 60–66.

[24] For examples of these two types of studies, see James H. Bjerring, Josef Lakonishok, and Theo Vermaelen, "Stock Prices and Financial Analysts Recommendations," *Journal of Finance* (March 1983): pp. 187–204; Donald R. Fraser and R. Malcolm Richards, "The Penn Square Failure and the Inefficient Market," *Journal of Portfolio Management* (Spring 1985): pp. 34–36; and Steven Katz, Steven Lilien, and Bert Nelson, "Stock Market Behavior around Bankruptcy Model Distress and Recovery Predictions," *Financial Analysts Journal* (January-February 1985): pp. 70–74.

[25] Bill McDonald and William D. Nichols, "Nonstationarity of Beta and Tests of Market Efficiency," *Journal of Financial Research* (Winter 1984): pp. 315–22.

Beginning in the late 1970s, a number of studies reported evidence that suggested market inefficiencies. This section reports the results of some of these studies based on strategies dealing with firm size, the level of P/E ratios, recurring daily or weekly price patterns, neglected firms, and other strategies.

1. SIZE EFFECT Beginning in the early 1980s, a number of studies noted that, after adjusting for risk, small firms appeared to offer significantly larger returns than large firms. Size is usually measured by the market value of the firm's outstanding stock. Typically, these studies rank stocks by size and form a portfolio of the smallest stocks. The actual returns on the portfolio are then compared to the returns estimated by the CAPM. In a 1981 study, Reinganum found that the excess return (actual returns less the CAPM estimated return) was approximately 18 percent per year for the decile consisting of the smallest firms.[26] Clearly, this level of excess return is significant.

Debate followed about whether the findings indicated market inefficiency or the CAPM methodology was flawed. Essentially, do small firms have greater risk than large firms, and is this difference not reflected in their betas? Reinganum concluded that the CAPM was not appropriate in analyzing the risk of small firms. A study by Roll also indicated that beta did not adequately measure the risk of small firms and that infrequent trading in these stocks may have influenced the results.[27]

One study argues that small firms are actually "neglected" firms that do not receive the degree of investment research and analysis that large firms do.[28] Thus, the observed excess returns are due partly to the "neglect effect" rather than to the size effect. This finding suggests that excess returns may be available on small firms that receive limited investor attention.

Additional studies have noted that the stocks of small firms have more *unsystematic* risk than large firms.[29] Investors who purchase stocks of small companies should therefore adequately diversify the number of small stocks in the portfolio. With adequate diversification, the unsystematic risk of the portfolio can essentially be eliminated.

Another factor that has been offered in an attempt to explain the small firm effect is the influence of industry classification.[30] Since some industries include many small firms while others consist of a few large firms, the observed small firm effect may actually be an industry effect. Thus, buying small firms may result in concentrating investments in certain industries that outperform industries dominated by large firms. The conclusion reached by this

---

[26] Marc R. Reinganum, "Misspecification of Capital Asset Pricing: Empirical Anomalies Based on Earnings' Yield and Market Values," *Journal of Financial Economics* (March 1981): pp. 19–46.

[27] Richard Roll, "A Possible Explanation of the Small Firm Effect," *Journal of Finance* (September 1981): pp. 879–88.

[28] Avner Arbel and Paul Strebel, "The Neglected and Small Firm Effects," *Financial Review* (November 1982): pp. 201–18.

[29] Marc R. Reinganum, "Portfolio Strategies for Small CAPS versus Large," *Journal of Portfolio Management* (Winter 1983): pp. 29–36; K. C. Chen and R. Stephen Sears, "How Many Small Firms Are Enough?" *Journal of Financial Research* (Winter 1984): pp. 341–49.

[30] Willard T. Carleton and Josef Lakonishok, "The Size Anomaly: Does Industry Group Matter?" *Journal of Portfolio Management* (Spring 1986): pp. 36–40.

1986 study, however, indicated that the small firm effect still existed after removing the possible industry effect.

As the above discussion indicates, the small firm effect and its implications on the EMH remain controversial. Despite the extensive research, "these efforts have yet to provide a full explanation of the anomaly."[31] The small firm effect cannot be fully explained by problems with the CAPM, neglect effect, industry influence, or unsystematic risk.

2. JANUARY EFFECT A second possible market anomaly deals with apparent recurring patterns in stock returns. This evidence has implications for both the weak and semistrong forms of the EMH. The January effect essentially finds that stock returns appear to be higher in January than in other months of the year. The January effect may also be related to the size effect since stocks of small companies outperform stocks of large companies in the month of January.[32]

There is also evidence that there may be daily patterns in stock returns.[33] Based on daily stock prices over the period 1963–1985 for a large sample of NYSE and AMEX issues, it appears that daily returns are higher on Fridays and weaker on Mondays. This pattern also exists in January and is related to the size effect since stocks of small firms demonstrate higher returns on Friday.

3. P/E EFFECT Traditionally, fundamentalists like Benjamin Graham recommended using the P/E ratio in selecting stocks. Basically, this strategy suggests that stocks should be purchased when their P/E ratios are "low" and sold (shorted) when they are "high." Using a CAPM methodology to adjust for risk, a number of empirical studies have reported that portfolios of stocks with low P/E ratios outperformed portfolios with high P/E stocks.[34] Other studies suggest that this apparent market inefficiency is due to problems with the CAPM and a failure adequately to consider transaction costs.[35]

It should also be noted that the P/E effect and size effect are probably related. The P/E ratio is highly correlated with the stock price usually used to calculate the size variable. Buying stocks with low P/E ratios may be essentially equivalent to buying stocks of small companies.

4. OTHER MARKET ANOMALIES Many additional studies appear to suggest market inefficiencies. Briefly, some of these studies indicate that using variables such

---

[31] James R. Booth and Richard L. Smith, "An Examination of the Small-Firm Effect on the Basis of Skewness Preference," *Journal of Financial Research* (Spring 1987): p. 77.

[32] Richard J. Rogalski and Seha M. Tinic, "The January Size Effect: Anomaly or Risk Measurement?" *Financial Analysts Journal* (November-December 1986): pp. 63–70.

[33] Donald B. Keim, "Daily Returns and Size-Related Premiums: One More Time," *Journal of Portfolio Management* (Winter 1987): pp. 41–47.

[34] For example, see Clinton M. Bidwell III, "SUE/PE Revista," *Journal of Portfolio Management (Winter 1981):* pp. 85–88; John W. Peavy III and David A. Goodman, "The Significance of P/Es for Portfolio Returns," *Journal of Portfolio Management* (Winter 1983): pp. 43–47; and Richard J. Dowen and W. Scott Bauman, "The Relative Importance of Size, P/E, and Neglect," *Journal of Portfolio Management* (Spring 1986): pp. 30–34.

[35] For example, see Haim Levy and Zvi Lerman, "Testing P/E Ratio Filters with Stochastic Dominance," *Journal of Portfolio Management* (Winter 1985): pp. 31–40.

as book value,[36] presidential elections,[37] and investing in special offerings or new issues,[38] may help in developing an investment strategy that generates risk-adjusted excess returns.

Implications for Fundamental Analysis

Fundamental analysis assumes that public information can be used to develop superior investment strategies. Event studies, however, have shown that the market quickly reacts to new information and that appropriate changes in stock prices occur rapidly. In many cases it can be shown that the market actually anticipates the information. Recently, a number of studies have reported on what appear to be market anomalies. Portfolios formed with stocks of small companies, stocks with "low" P/E ratios, or stocks of firms experiencing financial distress are examples of strategies that provide excess returns. Based on the empirical research to date, what conclusions are appropriate in terms of the usefulness of fundamental analysis? The following quote effectively summarizes the key issue:[39]

> There can be little dispute that the accumulated empirical evidence is inconsistent with any view other than that the market is a highly efficient information processor. What is in dispute is the degree of efficiency—whether there is sufficient deviant price behavior to make it worthwhile for the ordinary investor to seek out opportunities for abnormal gain, or whether the reasonable policy for most investors is simply to buy and hold an internationally diversified portfolio.

Fundamentalists and investors in general should recognize that the markets are efficient to the extent that naive strategies can probably not beat the market consistently. On the other hand, there is evidence that market inefficiencies exist. One view that seems reasonable is that some investment strategies are superior to others and "that anomaly-based strategies dominate random selection strategies."[40]

Another interesting aspect about the debate concerning the degree of market efficiency is that many analysts do not believe in market efficiency. This belief justifies their active investment strategies that attempt to beat the market. Their efforts, however, increase market efficiency, since they are always seeking and analyzing information in making investment decisions. If most investors think that the market is inefficient, it is likely to be efficient because of these activities directed at obtaining and analyzing new information.

---

[36] Barr Rosenberg, Kenneth Reid, and Ronald Lanstein, "Persuasive Evidence of Market Market Inefficiency," *Journal of Portfolio Management* (Spring 1985): pp. 9–16.

[37] Gerald R. Hobbs and William B. Riley, "Profiting from a Presidential Election," *Financial Analysts Journal* (March-April 1984): pp. 46–47; Roger D. Huang, "Common Stock Returns and Presidential Elections," *Financial Analysts Journal* (March-April 1985): pp. 58–61.

[38] Ben Branch, "Special Offerings and Market Efficiency," *Financial Review* (March 1984): pp. 26–35.

[39] Simon M. Keane, "The Efficient Market Hypothesis on Trial," *Financial Analysts Journal* (March-April 1986): p. 63.

[40] Joy and Jones, p. 52.

STRONG FORM MARKET EFFICIENCY

Overview

The *strong* form of the EMH hypothesizes that *all* information is reflected in stock prices. "Information" includes both public and private information. Private information implies that certain individuals or organizations, such as corporate insiders or trading specialists, may have monopolistic access to information. According to the strong form of market efficiency, however, the availability of private information is limited and is not a significant factor in security prices.

Fama, in suggesting the strong form of market efficiency, recognized that it is an "extreme null hypothesis" and that "we do not expect it to be literally true."[41] It seems obvious that if an investor has significant monopolistic information, it can be used profitably. The theory does not dispute this possibility. Rather, the theory argues that it is unlikely that monopolistic information is available to any significant extent. The information that may initially be private or secret will quickly be discovered by the market and reflected in the stock's price.

The strong form of the EMH is equivalent to perfect markets in that the market correctly prices securities at all times. Prices adjust quickly to new information, public or private.

Empirical Tests of Strong Form Efficiency

Two studies published in the late 1960s, dealing with specialists on the stock exchanges and corporate insiders, are recognized as important initial tests of strong form efficiency.[42] Both studies found evidence that private information available to these two groups could be used to earn risk-adjusted excess returns. The empirical results showed that specialists had monopolistic access to information concerning unexecuted limit orders. This information allowed the specialists to earn trading profits.

1. CORPORATE INSIDERS A number of studies have analyzed the investment success of corporate insiders. These studies dealt with legal trading activities rather than illegal insider trading. Generally, a coporate insider can make legal trades as long as privately available information is not used and the trade is reported to the SEC. The distinction between legal and illegal insider trading is defined by laws and regulations. However, there is often a very fine line separating the two activities. It has also been argued that the SEC too broadly defines illegal activities which results in reducing market efficiency.[43]

---

[41] Fama, "Efficient Capital Markets," p. 388.

[42] Victor Niederhoffer and M. F. M. Osborne, "Market Making and Reversal of the Stock Exchange," *Journal of the American Statistical Association* (December 1966): pp. 897–916, and Myron Scholes "A Test of the Competitive Hypothesis: The Market for New Issues and Secondary Offerings.. (Ph.D. diss, Graduate School of Business, University of Chicago, 1969).

[43] Homer Kripke, "Inside Information and Efficient Markets," *Financial Analysts Journal* (March-April 1980): pp. 20–24.

Some studies on the performance of corporate insider trading find evidence of risk-adjusted excess returns.[44] There is also evidence that some corporate insiders are more successful than others. For example, a 1983 study found that CEOs and directors had better performances than vice presidents and beneficial owners.[45] Somewhat surprising, however, is the finding that aggregate trading by corporate insiders was not an effective overall market timing indicator. The empirical evidence indicated that there was a tendency for a rise in the stock after "intensive" insider buying *and* selling.[46]

2.   PERFORMANCES OF PROFESSIONALLY MANAGED PORTFOLIOS A somewhat indirect test of strong form efficiency deals with the performances of mutual funds and other professionally managed portfolios. Since these portfolios employ skilled analysts and forecasters, it can be argued that these individuals should be able to discover information that may not be reflected in stock prices. For example, an analyst may be able to make a personal visit to a company and discover information that is not publicly known. Given this information and the expertise of the analyst, superior performance of the portfolio would be an indication of market inefficiency.

As Chapter 8 indicated, however, mutual funds and other professionally managed portfolios, on average, do not earn risk-adjusted excess returns. This finding supports the strong form of the EMH.

Implications for Investors

The evidence supporting the strong form of market efficiency is not as convincing as the evidence supporting the weak and semistrong forms. There appear to be groups of investors, such as corporate insiders and specialists, who have information that can be used to beat the market. In a broader sense, however, there is evidence that professional investors like mutual funds have difficulty in discovering information that can be used to outperform the market consistently. This suggests that the availability of monopolistic information is limited.

A logical conclusion seems to be that if significant private information can be discovered, it can be profitably used. This provides an incentive for investors to discover information that is not generally known. It also indicates, however, that access to monopolistic information should be closely regulated and controlled. Investors should support the SEC and other regulatory agencies in assuring that the markets remain compeitive and that no individuals or groups be allowed to profit by using illegally acquired information.

---

[44] For example, see Jeffrey F. Jaffe, "Special Information and Insider Trading," *Journal of Business* (July 1974): pp. 410–28, and Gary A. Benesh and Robert A. Pari, "Performance of Stocks Recommended on the Basis of Insider Trading Activity," *Financial Review* (February 1987): pp. 145–58.

[45] Kenneth P. Nunn. Jr., Gerald P. Madden, and Michael J. Gombola, "Are Some Insiders More 'Inside' than Others?" *Journal of Portfolio Management* (Spring 1983): pp. 18–22.

[46] Wayne Y. Lee and Michael E. Solt, "Insider Trading: A Poor Guide to Market Timing," *Journal of Portfolio Management* (Summer 1986): pp. 65–71.

OTHER ASPECTS OF MARKET EFFICIENCY

Common Stocks versus Other Types of Securities

The initial theory of efficient markets and the supporting empirical work were directed at common stocks traded on the major exchanges. The theory and empirical investigations have been expanded to include other types of securities such as preferred stock (Chapter 17), convertible securities (Chapter 18), bonds (Chapter 16), commodities and financial futures (Chapters 20 and 21), and options (Chapter 19). These studies generally confirm the conclusions about market efficiency that were discussed for common stocks. Studies dealing with market efficiency for these other types of securities are presented in the applicable chapters. The references listed at the end of this chapter also provide a representative sample of these studies.

Regional and Foreign Markets

The majority of empirical studies of market efficiency are based on common stocks traded in the United States on the NYSE, AMEX, or OTC market. As previously discussed, the empirical evidence suggests that these markets are generally efficient. There are also a limited number of studies that test for market efficiency in regional or foreign markets.

In the United States there are a number of small regional markets located in Denver, Boston, Philadelphia, Chicago, Los Angeles, San Francisco, and some other major cities. These markets trade securities of smaller companies that have regional interest to investors. They may also trade some of the stocks listed on the NYSE and AMEX.

Because fewer investors trade on the regional exchanges and information about the small companies may not be as extensive as that for large companies, are the regional exchanges inefficient? A study of the Rocky Mountain market located in Denver provides some insights into this question.[47] The study was based on a sample of "penny stocks" over the period from late 1977 to mid-1980. The sample represented stocks of small regional companies that were attempting to "go public" with an initial offering of stock. These securities are frequently called penny stocks since the offering prices typically range from $.05 to $2 per share, with an average of approximately $.10. Because of the speculative nature of many of the offerings and the local trading, the authors expected to find evidence of market imperfections and inefficiencies. The empirical results indicated some initial inefficiencies, since excess returns accrued from the initial offering to the first trade on the local exchange. The excess returns disappeared, however, after listing and subsequent trading. The evidence suggested that the stocks may have been initially underpriced but that the market quickly recognized and eliminated this opportunity.

---

[47] Robert J. Angell and Jerry G. Hunt, "Is the Denver Market Efficient?" *Journal of Portfolio Management* (Spring 1982): pp. 10–16.

Chapter 23 deals with investing internationally. One preliminary consideration, however, is the degree of market efficiency for markets outside the United States. The results from empirical tests of this question are mixed. A 1982 study of the Japanese bond market found evidence supporting the efficiency of the market.[48] A study of the Hong Kong stock market found evidence of market inefficiencies.[49] This study found risk-adjusted excess returns for a strategy based on purchasing stocks recommended by the largest securities firm in Hong Kong. This evidence suggests that the Hong Kong market is not efficient in either the strong or semistrong form.

Based on the limited studies, it appears that some of the regional and foreign markets may be more efficient than is generally believed. The degree of efficiency relative to the major U.S. equity markets is a question that deserves additional research.

Market Mechanisms versus Pricing Efficiency

This chapter deals with the market's efficiency in correctly pricing securities and in instantaneously changing prices to reflect new information. A second aspect of efficiency deals with *institutional* or *trading procedure efficiency*. Clearly, the U.S. financial markets are highly efficient in the speed and costs associated with transactions. This efficiency is due to information processing and communications technology. The markets therefore provide an environment that promotes pricing efficiency.

Also, trading procedures insure that prices can fluctuate and that pricing information is provided to market participants on a timely basis. Competition and the regulatory environment also increase pricing efficiency. Because of the influence of regulations on market efficiency, many investors and industry leaders are recommending that trading procedures and regulations be carefully reviewed in light of the October 1987 crash.

Implications for Investors

The degree of market efficiency remains a hotly debated issue. There is no debate, however, about the significance of the issue for an appropriate investment strategy. In light of the debate, is it rational for individual investors to pursue strategies that attempt to beat the market? Unfortunately, there is no simple answer to this question. Each investor must reach his or her own conclusion.

For investors who conclude that it is worthwhile to pursue a course of active management, the following strategies appear to be reasonable and logical.

1. ANOMALY-BASED STRATEGIES Empirical evidence suggests that portfolios consisting of small firms, firms with low P/E ratios, or initial public offerings may offer risk-adjusted excess returns. The January effect may also be significant.

---

[48] Akio Kuroda, ''Is the Japanese Bond Market Rational and Efficient?'' *Journal of Portfolio Management* (Fall 1982): pp. 46–51.

[49] Steve M. Dawson, ''Is the Hong Kong Market Efficient?'' *Journal of Portfolio Management* (Spring 1982): pp. 17–20.

2. FUNDAMENTAL ANALYSIS There is evidence that some investment firms have developed techniques or models using fundamental analysis that can beat the market.[50] While these firms do not usually reveal the details of their techniques, investors may benefit by relying on their recommendations. The apparent success of some fundamental approaches indicates the possibility of discovering techniques that can earn risk-adjusted excess returns.

3. UNIQUE AND INNOVATIVE USES OF FUNDAMENTAL AND TECHNICAL ANALYSIS A number of research articles report on the success of investment strategies based on unique or innovative uses of traditional fundamental and technical analysis.

    Bidwell reported that portfolios using both P/E and "unexpected" earnings announcement criteria provided risk-adjusted excess returns.[51] Using data for the period November 1976 to February 1979, this study found that stocks reporting "unexpected" good earnings and a "low" P/E ratio outperformed other stocks in the sample. The use of the "dual screening" procedure, a somewhat unique approach, appears to offer excess returns.

    The combined use of the familiar relative strength measure employed by technicians and the CAPM has also been suggested as a viable strategy.[52] Using data on over 300 stocks over an 18-year period, this study reported that the strategy resulted in an annual compounded rate of return after transaction costs of 15.2 percent, versus 5.9 percent for the S&P 500. Essentially, the strategy ranked stocks on a beta-adjusted recent price momentum basis and formed a portfolio of the stocks in the top decile.

    A third example of a possible successful strategy used the ratio of book value per share to price.[53] The strategy involved buying stocks with a high ratio since they may be undervalued relative to their asset value. This study also reported that a strategy based on stocks that exhibit a "specific-return-reversal" can earn excess returns.

    A final example is a study that reported excess returns based on a model that contains "nothing particularly novel" and "no special insights."[54] The authors argued that the strategy was successful because it provided a *highly disciplined approach* that avoided decisions based on market emotions. The model, described in detail in the article, utilized P/E and book value ratios as screening variables.

---

[50] For example, see Richard S. Bower and Dorothy H. Bower, "The Salomon Brothers Electric Utility Model: Another Challenge to Market Efficiency," *Financial Analysts Journal* (September-October 1984): pp. 57–67; C. Holloway, "A Note on Testing the Aggressive Investment Strategy Using Value Line Ranks," *Journal of Finance* (June 1981): pp. 711–19; and Ronald C. Rogers and James E. Owers, "The Impact of Value Line Special Situation Recommendations on Stock Prices," *Financial Review* (May 1984): pp. 195–207.

[51] Clinton M. Bidwell, III. "SUE/PE Revista," *Journal of Portfolio Management* (Winter 1981): pp. 85–88.

[52] John S. Brush and Keith E. Boles, "The Predictive Power in Relative Strength & CAPM," *Journal of Portfolio Management* (Summer 1983): pp. 20–23.

[53] Barr Rosenberg, Kenneth Reid, and Ronald Lanstein, "Persuasive Evidence of Market Inefficiency," *Journal of Portfolio Management* (Spring 1985): pp. 9–16.

[54] Robert F. Vandell and Robert Parrino, "A Purposeful Stride down Wall Street," *Journal of Portfolio Management* (Winter 1986): pp. 31–39.

SUMMARY

This chapter traced the development of the EMH from its beginning in the late 1950s through the many empirical tests that continue to the present. The key question for investors is the *degree* of market efficiency. In terms of theory, the three degrees of efficiency are represented by the weak, semistrong, and strong form hypotheses of the EMH.

The empirical studies reviewed in this chapter lead to the conclusion that it is highly unlikely that investment strategies based on a naive use of technical or fundamental analysis can beat the market. Security prices reflect publicly available information and react quickly to new information. Advances in communication and data processing technology improve market efficiency.

There are, however, a growing number of studies that appear to indicate market anomalies which constitute evidence against the EMH. Studies have also demonstrated that investment strategies based on the anomalies, or on unique and innovative approaches, may provide risk-adjusted excess returns.

Individual investors should carefully consider the arguments and evidence both for and against the EMH. The decision to be a passive or an active investor depends on a conclusion concerning the degree of market efficiency.

QUESTIONS

1. Briefly define the three forms of the Efficient Market Hypothesis. Why is the *degree* of market efficiency an important issue for investors who might pursue an active strategy?
2. Describe the empirical tests of the random walk hypothesis.
3. Briefly outline the research methodology that is usually used in event studies.
4. Compare and contrast the "size" and "January" effects. Do studies of these possible anomalies indicate that risk-adjusted excess returns are available to investors?
5. Generally, how do studies of market efficiency for other types of securities such as bonds and preferred stock compare to common stock market efficiency studies?
6. Do U.S. financial markets appear to be more efficient than foreign markets?
7. Can knowledge concerning the trading activity of insiders be used to earn risk-adjusted excess returns?
8. One form of market efficiency suggests that the speed of price adjustments to new information is an indication of efficiency. Do you think that the 508-point drop in the DJIA on October 19, 1987, indicates market efficiency or inefficiency?
9. Explain how studies of the investment performances of professionally managed portfolios can be used as tests of market efficiency.
10. Distinguish between a correlation coefficient and a serial correlation coefficient. Which type of statistic is usually used in efficiency studies?
11. Discuss the implications of market efficiency for technical analysis.
12. Discuss the implications of market efficiency for fundamental analysis.
13. Based on the discussion and review of efficient market studies in this chapter, do you think that a passive or active investment strategy is appropriate for individual investors?

14. Many financial researchers and some practitioners think that the market is efficient because many investors are convinced it is not and therefore attempt to beat the market. If everyone was convinced that the market was highly efficient, what would be the likely impact of this view on the degree of market efficiency? If everyone was convinced the market was highly inefficient, what would be the likely impact of this view on the degree of market efficiency?

15. Suppose you are convinced that your skills as an analyst are superior to those of the average analyst. Would you feel confident to pursue an active investment strategy? On an ex-post basis, how could you test your hypothesis that your skills are superior to those of the average analyst?

PROBLEMS

1. Assume that an analyst was interested in the reaction of a particular stock's price to a significant event. The following weekly *HPR*s were calculated for the stock and the S&P 500:

WEEK RELATIVE TO THE EVENT WEEK	HPR	
	STOCK	S&P 500
−5	.010	.005
−4	.015	.006
−3	.015	.004
−2	.020	.020
−1	.032	.025
0	.016	.015
1	−.020	−.018
2	−.026	−.022
3	−.030	−.028
4	−.011	−.006

a. If the stock's beta is 1.2 and alpha is .01, *estimate* the *HPR*s for each of the ten weeks.

b. Calculate the error or residual term for each week using your answers to part a.

c. Calculate the cumulative average residuals for the 10-week period.

d. Briefly describe the price adjustment pattern that this analysis indicates. Do you think the market was efficient in adjusting to the significance of the event?

2. Assume that you observe the following weekly stock prices:

WEEK	PRICE
1	$18.00
2	17.00
3	19.00
4	20.00
5	21.00
6	24.00
7	23.00
8	20.00
9	21.00

a. Calculate the weekly *HPR*s for weeks 2–9, assuming that no dividends were received over this time period.

b. Calculate the serial correlation coefficient for a 1-week lag using the *HPR*s.

c. Does the serial correlation coefficient indicate that the weekly *HPR*s are related?

d. Use your answers to part a to calculate a time series that can be used in a runs test. What is the longest run observed in this time series? Intuitively, does it appear that the weekly *HPR*s are related?

COMPUTER APPLICATIONS

The floppy disk includes programs that can be used to apply the event study methodology and calculate correlation and serial correlation coefficients. Instructions and illustrations are provided on the disk.

REFERENCES

Angell, Robert J., and Jerry G. Hunt. "Is the Denver Market Efficient?" *Journal of Portfolio Management* (Spring 1982): pp. 10–16.

Arbel, Avner, and Bikki Jaggi, "Market Information Assimilation Related to Extreme Daily Price Jumps." *Financial Analysts Journal* (November-December 1982): pp. 60–66.

Arbel, Avner, and Paul Strebel. "The Neglected and Small Firm Effects." *Financial Review* (November 1982): pp. 201–19.

Arbel, Avner. "Generic Stocks: An Old Product in a New Package." *Journal of Portfolio Management* (Summer 1985): pp. 4–13.

Barrett, W. Brian, Andrea J. Heuson, Robert W. Kolb, and Gabriele H. Schropp, "The Adjustment of Stock Prices to Completely Unanticipated Events." *Financial Review* (November 1987): pp. 345–54.

Benesh, Gary A., and Robert A. Pari, "Performance of Stocks Recommended on the Basis of Insider Trading Activity." *Financial Review* (February 1987): pp. 145–58.

Bey, Roger P., Richard C. Burgess, and Richard B. Kearns. "Moving Stochastic Dominance: An Alternative Method of Testing Market Efficiency." *Journal of Financial Research* (Fall 1984): pp. 185–96.

Bidwell, Clinton M, III. "SUE/PE Revista." *Journal of Portfolio Management* (Winter 1981): pp. 85–88.

Bjerring, James H., Josef Lakonishok, and Theo Vermaelen. "Stock Prices and Financial Analysts' Recommendations." *Journal of Finance* (March 1983): pp. 187–204.

Bloch, Howard, and Roger Pupp, "The January Barometer Revisited and Rejected." *Journal of Portfolio Management* (Winter 1983): pp. 48–50.

Booth, James R., and Richard L. Smith, "An Examination of the Small-Firm Effect on the Basis of Skewness Preference." *Journal of Financial Research* (Spring 1987): pp. 77–86.

Bower, Richard S., and Dorothy H. Bower. "The Salomon Brothers Electric Utility Model: Another Challenge to Market Efficiency." *Financial Analysts Journal* (September-October 1984): pp. 57–67.

Branch, Ben. "Special Offerings and Market Efficiency." *Financial Review* (March 1984): pp. 26–35.

Brennan, Micheal J., and Edwards S. Schwartz. "Bond Pricing and Market Efficiency." *Financial Analysts Journal* (September-October 1982): pp. 49–56.

Brown, Stephen J., and Christopher B. Barry. "Anomalies in Security Returns and the Speculation of the Market Model." *Journal of Finance* (July 1984): pp. 807–15.

Brown, Keith C., and C. V. Harlow, "Market Overreaction: Magnitude and Intensity." *Journal of Portfolio Management* (Winter 1988): pp. 6–13.

Brush, John S., and Keith E. Boles. "The Predictive Power in Relative Strength & CAPM." *Journal of Portfolio Management* (Summer 1983): pp. 20–23.

Cabanilla, Nathaniel B. "Directly-Placed Bonds: A Test of Market Efficiency." *Journal of Portfolio Management* (Winter 1984): pp. 72–74.

Carleton, Willard T., and Josef Lakonishok. "The Size Anomaly: Does Industry Group Matter?" *Journal of Portfolio Management* (Spring 1986): pp. 36–40.

Chen K. C. and R. Stephen Sears. "How Many Small Firms Are Enough?" *Journal of Financial Research* (Winter 1984): pp. 341–49.

Conroy, Robert M., and Richard J. Rendleman, Jr. "A Test of Market Efficiency in Government Bonds." *Journal of Portfolio Management* (Summer 1987): pp. 57–64.

Dawson, M. Steve. "Is The Hong Kong Market Efficient?" *Journal of Portfolio Management* (Spring 1982): pp. 17–20.

Dowen, Richard J., and W. Scott Bauman. "The Relative Importance of Size, P/E, and Neglect." *Journal of Portfolio Management* (Spring 1986): pp. 30–34.

Edmister, Robert O., and James B. Greene. "Performance of Super-Low-Price Stocks." *Journal of Portfolio Management* (Fall 1980): pp. 36–41.

Edmister, Robert O., and Christopher James. "Is Illiquidity a Bar to Buying Small Cap Stocks?" *Journal of Portfolio Management* (Summer 1983): pp. 14–19.

Fama, Eugene, Lawrence Fisher, Michael C. Jensen, and Richard Roll. "The Adjustment of Stock Prices to New Information." *International Economic Review* (February 1969): pp. 1–21.

Fama, Eugene F. "Efficient Capital Markets: A Review of Theory and Empirical Work." *Journal of Finance* (May 1970): pp. 383–423.

Ferguson, Robert. "An Efficient Stock Market? Ridiculous!" *Journal of Portfolio Management* (Summer 1983): pp. 31–38.

Fraser, Donald R., and R. Malcolm Richards. "The Penn Square Bank Failure and the Inefficient Market." *Journal of Portfolio Management* (Spring 1985): pp. 34–36.

Goodman, David A., and John W. Peavy. "The Risk Universal Nature of the P/E Effect." *Journal of Portfolio Management* (Summer 1985): pp. 14–16.

Hobbs, Gerald R., and William B. Riley. "Profiting from a Presidential Election." *Financial Analysts Journal* (March-April 1984): pp. 46–52.

Hoffer, George E., Stephen W. Pruitt, and Robert J. Reilly. "Automotive Recalls and Informational Efficiency." *Financial Review* (November 1987): pp. 433–42.

Huang, Roger D. "Common Stock Returns and Presidential Elections." *Financial Analysts Journal* (March-April 1985): pp. 58–61.

Jensen, Michael C., and George A. Bennington. "Random Walks and Technical Theories: Some Additional Evidence." *Journal of Finance* (May 1970): pp. 469–82.

Joy, O. Maurice, and Charles P. Jones. "Should We Believe the Tests of Market Efficiency?" *Journal of Portfolio Management* (Summer 1986): pp. 49–54.

Katz, Steven, Steven Lilien, and Bert Nelson. "Stock Market Behavior around Bankruptcy Model Distress and Recovery Predictions." *Financial Analysts Journal* (January-February 1985): pp. 70–74.

Keane, Simon M. "The Efficient Market Hypothesis on Trial." *Financial Analysts Journal* (March-April 1986): pp. 58–63.

Keim, Donald B. "Dividend Yields and the January Effect." *Journal of Portfolio Management* (Winter 1986): pp. 54–59.

———. "The CAPM and Equity Return Regularities." *Financial Analysts Journal* (May-June 1986): pp. 19–34.

———. "Daily Returns and Size-Related Premiums: One More Time." *Journal of Portfolio Management* (Winter 1987): pp. 41–47.

Kosmicke, Ralph. "The Contradiction between Keynes and the EMH." *Journal of Portfolio Management* (Fall 1984): pp. 41–43.

Kripke, Homer. "Inside Information and Efficient Markets." *Financial Analysts Journal* (March-April 1980): pp. 20–24.

Kuroda, Akio. "Is the Japanese Bond Market Rational and Efficient?" *Journal of Portfolio Management* (Fall 1982): pp. 46–51.

Lakonishok, Josef, and Seymour Smidt. "Trading Bargains in Small Firms at Year-end." *Journal of Portfolio Management* (Spring 1986): pp. 24–29.

Lee, Wayne Y., and Michael E. Solt. "Insider Trading: A Poor Guide to Market Timing." *Journal of Portfolio Management* (Summer 1986): pp. 65–71.

Levy, Haim, and Zvi Lerman. "Testing P/E Ratios Filters with Stochastic Dominance." *Journal of Portfolio Management* (Winter 1985): pp. 31–40.

Levy, Robert A. "Random Walks: Reality or Myth?" *Financial Analysts Journal* (November-December 1967): pp. 69–76.

Malkiel, Burton G. *A Random Walk Down Wall Street*. 4th ed New York: W. W. Norton 1985.

McConnell, John J., and Gary G. Schlarbaum. "Another Foray into the Backwaters of the Market." *Journal of Portfolio Management* (Fall 1980): pp. 61–65.

McDonald, Bill, and William D. Nichols. "Nonstationarity of Beta and Tests of Market Efficiency." *Journal of Financial Research* (Winter 1984): pp. 315–22.

Miller, Edward M. "Bounded Efficient Markets: A New Wrinkle to the EMH." *Journal of Portfolio Management* (Summer 1987): pp. 4–13.

Morse, Dale. "Wall Street Journal Announcements and Securities Markets." *Financial Analysts Journal* (March-April 1982): pp. 69–76.

Nunn, Kenneth P. Jr., Gerald P. Madden, and Michael J. Gombola. "Are Some Insiders More 'Inside' than Others?" *Journal of Portfolio Management* (Spring 1983): pp. 18–22.

O'Hanlon, John, and Charles W. R. Ward. "How to Lose at Winning Strategies." *Journal of Portfolio Management* (Spring 1986): pp. 20–23.

Peavy, John W. III., and David A. Goodman. "The Significance of P/Es for Portfolio Returns." *Journal of Portfolio Management* (Winter 1983): pp. 43–47.

Reinganum, Marc R. "Abnormal Returns in Small Firm Portfolios." *Financial Analysts Journal* (March-April 1981): pp. 52–56.

———. "Portfolio Strategies Based on Market Capitalization." *Journal of Portfolio Management* (Winter 1983): pp. 29–36.

Renshaw, Edward F. "Stock Market Panics: A Test of the Efficient Market Hypothesis." *Financial Analysts Journal* (May-June 1984): p. 48–51.

Roberts, Harry V. "Stock Market 'Patterns' and Financial Analysis: Methodological Suggestions." *Journal of Finance* (March 1959): pp. 1–10.

Rogalski, Richard J., and Seha M. Tinic. "The January Size Effect: Anomaly or Risk Mismeasurement?" *Financial Analysts Journal* (November-December 1986): pp. 63–70.

Rogers, Ronald C., and James E. Owers. "The Impact of Value Line Special Situation Recommendation on Stock Prices." *Financial Review* (May 1984): pp 195–207.

Roll, Richard. "A Possible Explanation of the Small Firm Effect." *Journal of Finance* (September 1981): pp. 879–88.

———. "Vas Ist Das?" *Journal of Portfolio Management* (Winter 1983): pp. 18–28.

Rosenberg, Barr. "The Current State and Future of Investment Research." *Financial Analysts Journal* (January-February 1982): pp. 43–50.

Rosenberg, Barr, Kenneth Reid, and Ronald Lanstein. "Persuasive Evidence of Market Inefficiency." *Journal of Portfolio Management* (Spring 1985): pp. 9–16.

Scholes, Myron S. "The Market for Securities: Substitution versus Price Pressure and the Effects of Information on Share Price." *Journal of Business* (April 1972): pp. 179–211.

Sorensen, Roy A. "An 'Essential Reservation' about the EMH." *Journal of Portfolio Management* (Summer 1983): pp 29–30.

Stoll, Hans S., and Robert E. Whaley. "Volatility and Futures: Message versus Messenger." *Journal of Portfolio Management* (Winter 1988): pp. 20–22.

Strebel, Paul J., and Avner Arbel. "Pay Attention to Neglected Firms!" *Journal of Portfolio Management* (Winter 1983): pp. 37–42.

Treynor, Jack L. "Market Efficiency and the Bean Jar Experiment." *Financial Analysts Journal* (May-June 1987): pp. 50–53.

Vandell, Robert F., and Robert Parrino. "A Purposeful Stride down Wall Street." *Journal of Porfolio Management* (Winter 1986): pp. 31–39.

Whitford, David T., and Frank K. Reilly. "What Makes Stock Prices Move?" *Journal of Portfolio Management* (Winter 1985): pp. 23–30.

PART 4

ANALYSIS
OF
BONDS

CHAPTER 14

BOND FUNDAMENTALS

BOND CHARACTERISTICS

Definition

The term *bond* is a general description of one type of fixed-income security issued by a borrowing entity in which the amount of income to the investor is specified in the investment contract or indenture. This is a major distinguishing characteristic of a bond. In contrast, income from common stock, cash dividends, is determined periodically by the board of directors. A *trustee* (usually a large commercial bank) is appointed when the bond is issued to represent the collective interests of the investors.

The other major type of fixed-income security issued by corporations, preferred stock, will be covered in Chapter 17. Convertible bonds and convertible preferred stock are covered in Chapter 18. As this chapter will demonstrate, there are many types of bonds.

It is important to remember that a bond represents a debt of the issuer. Essentially, the issuer has borrowed funds and agreed to specified payments to the bondholders that represent periodic interest payments and the ultimate repayment of principal. Since a bond is a liability of the issuer, the bondholders receive priority over common stockholders in two important ways. First, they have priority in receiving interest income each period; the issuer has a contractual obligation to make these distributions, even if the issuer's income is not adequate for the period. Second, the bondholders have priority in the event of liquidation of the issuer's assets; since bonds are liabilities, funds from a liquidation must first be used to pay these claims before any distribution can be made to preferred or common stock investors.

Risk and Return—Comparison with Common Stock

These two priorities (income and liquidation) mean that bonds, as a general class of security, have less risk than common stocks. "Risk" in this sense refers to the greater likelihood of receiving income (interest or dividends) and repayment of principal. It should be noted, however, that some individual bonds have greater risk than some stocks. This could be the case when comparing bonds and stocks of different corporations. For example, most investors would view the bonds of a corporation with a significant bankruptcy probability as considerably more risky than the common stock of a large successful firm like IBM. When considering the risks of the bonds and common stock of the same corporation, however, bonds always have less risk.

COMPARING BONDS WITH OTHER TYPES OF INVESTMENTS

Return Comparison—*HPRs*

One of the best ways to compare bonds with other types of securities is to look at an example of ex-post return performance. Table 14.1 provides the annual holding period returns of four classes of securities. The returns for the bonds and

TABLE 14.1 ANNUAL EX-POST HOLDING PERIOD RETURNS

YEAR	TREASURY BILLS	LONG-TERM U.S. TREASURY BONDS	LONG-TERM CORPORATE BONDS	COMMON STOCKS
1975	5.8%	9.2%	14.6%	37.2%
1976	5.1	16.8	18.6	23.8
1977	5.1	−0.7	1.7	−7.2
1978	7.2	−1.2	−0.1	6.6
1979	10.4	−1.2	−4.2	18.4
1980	11.2	−4.0	−2.6	32.4
1981	14.7	1.8	−1.0	−4.9
1982	10.5	40.3	43.8	21.4
1983	8.8	0.7	4.7	22.5
1984	9.8	15.4	16.4	6.3
1985	7.7	31.0	30.9	32.2
1986	6.2	24.4	19.8	18.5
Arithmetic Mean	8.5	11.0	11.9	17.3
Standard Deviation	2.91	14.60	14.92	14.34
Coefficient of Variation*	0.34	1.33	1.25	0.83

* Calculated as standard deviation/mean.

SOURCE: Ibbotson, Roger G., and Rex A. Sinquefield, Stocks, Bonds, Bills, and Inflation (*SBBI*), 1982, updated in SBBI 1987 Yearbook, Ibbotson Associates, Chicago.

common stocks are calculated as

$$HPR_t = \frac{P_{t+1} - P_t + I_t \text{ or } D_t}{P_t} \qquad (14.1)$$

where P represents the index value or price, I represents the annual interest, and D represents the annual dividend. The return for the one-year Treasury bill is calculated using the annualized return on 30-day bills.[1]

As would be expected, there is considerable variability in returns from year to year. In addition, notice that for a number of years the returns on Treasury and corporate bonds are higher than those on common stocks. These periods are generally characterized by falling interest rates that produce large capital gains for bonds. The year 1982 is also quite unique. It has been called a "once-in-a-lifetime" opportunity for bond investors because of the extraordinarily high capital gains that were realized.

Risk Comparison

The summary statistics at the bottom of Table 14.1 illustrate that, on average for the period 1975–1986, the total risk of Treasury and corporate bonds, as measured by the standard deviation, is more than that for common stocks. The coefficients of variation for both categories of bonds are also greater than that for stocks over this period of time. However, a study by Sharpe for longer periods of time,

---

[1] Annualized returns are fully explained in Chapter 8, and details for calculating bond returns are provided in Chapter 15.

1938–1971 and 1946–1971, showed that bonds offered less return and less risk.[2] Sharpe's study has been updated and expanded in a 1987 study.[3] This study, based on the period 1926–1985, found that the risk-adjusted returns from the common stocks were superior to those from bonds during the post-war period, while bonds had higher risk-adjusted returns for the twenty-year period prior to the war.

Chapter 15 will present considerable detail on specific risk measures for bonds and a discussion of the systematic and unsystematic components of bond risk. In addition, several measures of bond return will be presented. Now, however, it should be noted that the unique features of bonds provide bonds' risk-return characteristics and make them quite different from common stocks. As Table 14.1 illustrates, bond prices and returns have been very volatile relative to stocks over the period 1975–1986. These characteristics provide both advantages and disadvantages that will be apparent from the material that follows.

CHANGING INVESTOR ATTITUDES TOWARD BONDS

The economic environment of the late 1970s and early 1980s has resulted in some dramatic changes in the bond market and, consequently, investors' attitudes toward bonds. Historically, investing in bonds has been characterized as simply "buy and hold" or "clipping coupons"—a passive investment strategy (see Chapter 5) that lacks the glamour of investing in other types of securities. Since the early 1980s, double-digit inflation, monetary and fiscal policies, and international events have produced not only extremely high nominal interest rates but also considerable volatility in interest rates, which resulted in fluctuating bond prices.

A casual glance at Figure 14.1 confirms these observations. Notice the inverted scale on the yield axis. With the exceptions of the postdepression period and a small but persistent overall upward trend in yields, bond yields were reasonably stable until the 1970s and 1980s. During this period, yields reached all-time highs, and the distances between yield peaks and troughs increased. The implications of these developments for the risk-return characteristics of bonds are quite apparent.

Edward H. Ladd, in an address to a seminar for Chartered Financial Analysts in 1983, provided an interesting observation that illustrates the impact of volatile yields.[4] He noted that when he started his bond career in the early 1960s, using technical analysis was a popular device for following and forecasting yields. He began charting the yield on long-term Treasury bonds. After a $2\frac{1}{2}$-year period, the yield had fluctuated only from 4.22 percent to 4.25 percent, or 3 "basis" points. By contrast, the yield on long-term Treasury bonds declined from 14.16 percent

---

[2] W. F. Sharpe, "Bonds versus Stocks, Some Lessons from Capital Market Theory," *Financial Analysts Journal* (November-December 1973): pp. 74–79.

[3] Meir Statman and Neal L. Ushman, "Bonds versus Stocks: Another Look," *Journal of Portfolio Management* (Winter 1987): pp. 33–38.

[4] Edward H. Ladd, "The Changing Structures of the American Capital Market: The Past, the Present, and the Future," *The Revolution in Techniques for Managing Bond Portfolios*, The Institute of Chartered Financial Analysts, 1983.

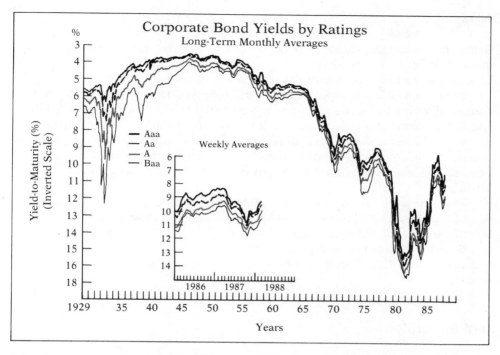

FIGURE 14.1 Moody's corporate yields-to-maturity by ratings 1929–FEBRUARY 1988
Source: *Bond Record*, Moody's, March 1988, p. 412. Reprinted by permission.

in January 1982 to 10.46 percent in November 1982—a decline of 370 basis points in less than a year.[5]

Investors in today's bond market are well aware of the changing bond environment. As a consequence, the emphasis has shifted from "passive" to "active" bond portfolio management. In addition, bond issuers have responded to this new environment by offering bonds with features that are compatible with this market. Bonds without coupon payments (commonly called zeros), bonds with indexed interest rates, and bonds with options attached (such as warrants and "put" options) are attempts by issuers to modify the risk-return characteristics of bonds.

Predictably, there is considerable debate about the future bond environment. On one extreme, the 1970s and 1980s are viewed simply as another page in history that will be remembered as unusual but not predictive, with a resulting return to more passive bond portfolio management.[6] On the other hand, the period is seen as a good indication that financial markets will be more volatile with resulting implications for more-active bond portfolio management strategies. Volatile markets encourage active management and question the advisability of buy-and-hold strategies. Both viewpoints have some validity, and bond investing and portfolio management will be discussed under both types of investment environments.

---

[5] Based on yield-to-maturity of Moody's long-term "Government Bond Yield Averages" in *Moody's Municipal & Government Manual*, vol. 1, Moody's, 1984, p. a7.

[6] Ladd.

TYPES OF BONDS

Before discussing the topics of bond valuation, analysis, and portfolio management, it is necessary to cover some descriptive material to ensure an adequate background and provide a complete discussion of bond investing.

Bonds can be categorized using several schemes. One possibility is to group bonds according to the issuer—U.S. government, U.S. agencies, municipalities, and corporations. Another possibility is by term-to-maturity—"short" (less than one year), "intermediate" (one to ten years), "long" (over ten years). Another approach is to categorize bonds by using the various levels of default risk, ranging from almost absolute security (U.S. government issues) to subordinated debentures.

The approach we have selected categorizes bonds according to their risk-return features. This approach has the advantage of relating basic bond characteristics to overall risk-return considerations. We will begin by discussing the bonds with the least risk and (in an efficient market) the lowest expected return and conclude with a discussion of bonds with the greatest risk and the highest return.

U.S. Government Securities

1. TREASURY BILLS T-bills are viewed as the safest of all fixed income securities because of the lack of default risk and because the term-to-maturity is one year or less. The bills lack default risk because they are issued by the U.S. Treasury and backed by the full credit of the U.S. government. Their short term-to-maturity also results in reasonably stable prices, even though short-term interest rates may fluctuate. There is also an active secondary market for T-bills which provides the investor with considerable liquidity.

    T-bills have an interesting feature that sets them apart from other Treasury obligations: the investor does not receive interest payments. Rather, T-bills are sold at a discount from their maturity value, with the desired yield determining the size of the discount. This point is discussed in more detail in the next section.

2. TREASURY NOTES AND BONDS Treasury notes have maturities of ten years or less, while Treasury bonds have maturities over ten years. The longer term-to-maturity results in both having more interest rate risk than T-bills. These securities also differ from T-bills in that interest is paid semiannually by the Treasury, and the investor does not depend entirely on the discount from par to achieve the appropriate yield.

    Table 14.2 provides an example of the daily quotes on Treasury bills, bonds, and notes as they appear in the *Wall Street Journal*. The quotes are conveniently arranged by the term-to-maturity of the securities. Notice that the "bid" and "ask" columns for T-bills are actually discounts rather than prices. The size of the discount determines the yield that is given in the last column. Bond and note prices are quoted for both the "bid" and "ask" and are in terms of "points" and thirty-seconds of a point. For example, if the bid is given as 80.10, the price is $803.125 (i.e., $[(80 + \frac{10}{32}) \times 10]$). These

TABLE 14.2 TREASURY ISSUES: BONDS, NOTES, AND BILLS

Thursday, April 7, 1988

Representative Over-the-Counter quotations based on transactions of $1 million or more as of 4 p.m. Eastern time.

Decimals in bid-and-asked and bid changes represent 32nds; 101.1 means 101 1/32. a-Plus 1/64. b-Yield to call date. d-Minus 1/64. k-Nonresident aliens exempt from withholding taxes. n-Treasury notes. p-Treasury note; nonresident aliens exempt from withholding taxes.

Source: Bloomberg Financial Markets

U.S. Treas. Bills

Mat. date	Bid (Discount)	Asked (Discount)	Yield	Mat. date	Bid (Discount)	Asked (Discount)	Yield
-1988-				7-28	5.95	5.88	6.07
4-14	6.01	5.89	5.98	8- 4	6.11	6.04	6.25
4-21	6.52	6.40	6.50	8-11	6.03	5.96	6.17
4-28	5.31	5.19	5.28	8-18	6.07	6.00	6.22
5- 5	5.77	5.70	5.80	8-25	6.07	6.00	6.23
5-12	6.06	5.99	6.11	9- 1	6.12	6.05	6.29
5-19	5.93	5.86	5.98	9- 8	6.17	6.10	6.35
5-26	5.89	5.82	5.95	9-15	6.18	6.11	6.37
6- 2	5.99	5.92	6.06	9-22	6.25	6.18	6.45
6- 9	5.99	5.92	6.06	9-29	6.27	6.20	6.48
6-16	5.90	5.83	5.98	10- 6	6.19	6.13	6.41
6-23	5.90	5.83	5.98	10-27	6.28	6.21	6.50
6-30	5.96	5.89	6.05	11-25	6.40	6.33	6.64
7- 7	6.05	6.01	6.19	12-22	6.48	6.41	6.75
7-14	6.01	5.94	6.12	-1989-			
7-21	5.98	5.91	6.10	1-19	6.55	6.48	6.84
				2-16	6.60	6.53	6.92
				3-16	6.59	6.55	6.97

Treasury Bonds and Notes

Rate	Mat. Date		Bid	Asked	Bid Chg.	Yld.
13¼	1988	Apr n	100.2	100.6	.....	3.23
6⅝	1988	Apr p	99.30	100.1	+ .1	5.93
8¼	1988	May n	100.3	100.6	.....	6.19
7⅛	1988	May p	100.1	100.4	.....	6.10
9⅞	1988	May n	100.9	100.12	+ .1	5.93
10	1988	May p	100.9	100.12	.....	6.05
7	1988	Jun p	100.2	100.5	− .1	6.19
13⅝	1988	Jun n	101.17	101.20	.....	6.17
6⅝	1988	Jul p	99.30	100.1	.....	6.44
14	1988	Jul n	101.31	102.2	.....	6.10
6⅛	1988	Aug p	99.24	99.27	.....	6.49
9½	1988	Aug p	100.30	101.1	.....	6.43
10½	1988	Aug n	101.9	101.12	.....	6.43
6⅜	1988	Sep p	99.25	99.28	− .1	6.64
11⅜	1988	Sep p	102.4	102.7	.....	6.57
15⅜	1988	Oct n	104.12	104.16	.....	6.46
6⅜	1988	Oct p	99.22	99.26	.....	6.71
6¼	1988	Nov p	99.16	99.20	.....	6.84
8¾	1988	Nov n	101	101.4	.....	6.79
8⅝	1988	Nov p	100.30	101.2	+ .1	6.77
11¾	1988	Nov n	102.26	102.30	+ .2	6.66
10⅝	1988	Dec p	102.13	102.17	.....	6.97
6¼	1988	Dec p	99.13	99.17	.....	6.90
6⅛	1989	Jan n	99.8	99.12	+ .1	6.91
14⅝	1989	Jan n	105.27	105.31	.....	6.53
8	1989	Feb p	100.21	100.25	.....	7.02
6¼	1989	Feb p	99.7	99.11	.....	7.01
11⅜	1989	Feb n	103.13	103.17	.....	7.02
11¼	1989	Mar p	103.24	103.28	− .1	7.08
6⅜	1989	Mar p	99.7	99.11	.....	7.08
7⅛	1989	Apr p	99.28	100	+ .1	7.12
14⅜	1989	Apr n	106.30	107.2	.....	7.08
6⅞	1989	May p	99.19	99.23	+ .1	7.14
9¼	1989	May n	102.8	102.14	− .1	6.90
8	1989	May n	100.25	100.29	− .1	7.15
11¾	1989	May n	104.20	104.24	− .3	7.17
7⅜	1989	Jun p	100.3	100.7	− .1	7.17
9⅝	1989	Jun p	102.20	102.24	.....	7.23
7⅝	1989	Jul p	100.11	100.15	.....	7.23
14½	1989	Jul n	108.19	108.23	.....	7.18
7¾	1989	Aug p	100.16	100.20	.....	7.26
6⅝	1989	Aug p	99.3	99.7	.....	7.23
13⅞	1989	Aug n	108.8	108.12	.....	7.25
8½	1989	Sep k	101.16	101.20	+ .1	7.32
9⅜	1989	Sep p	102.22	102.26	− .1	7.33
11⅞	1989	Oct n	106.9	106.13	.....	7.34
7⅞	1989	Oct p	100.20	100.24	− .1	7.35
6⅜	1989	Nov p	98.13	98.17	.....	7.36
10¾	1989	Nov n	104.31	105.3	+ .1	7.31
12¾	1989	Nov p	107.27	107.31	− .4	7.37
7¾	1989	Nov p	100.14	100.18	.....	7.37
7⅞	1989	Dec p	100.17	100.21	.....	7.45
8⅜	1989	Dec p	101.10	101.14	+ .1	7.46
7⅜	1990	Jan k	99.23	99.27	− .1	7.46
10½	1990	Jan n	104.26	104.30	+ .1	7.45
3½	1990	Feb	92.31	93.17	+ .1	7.29
6½	1990	Feb k	98.8	98.12	.....	7.45
7⅛	1990	Feb k	99.9	99.13	+ .1	7.46
11	1990	Feb p	105.28	106	.....	7.46
7¼	1990	Mar p	99.13	99.17	− .1	7.51
7⅜	1990	Mar p	99.22	99.26	+ .1	7.48
10½	1990	Apr n	105.12	105.16	+ .1	7.51
7⅞	1990	May k	100.16	100.20	+ .1	7.54
8¼	1990	May	102.9	102.19	+ .2	6.90
11⅜	1990	May p	107.4	107.8	.....	7.57
7¼	1990	Jun p	99.8	99.12	+ .1	7.55
10¾	1990	Jul n	106.12	106.16	.....	7.57
7⅞	1990	Aug k	100.15	100.19	+ .2	7.59
9⅞	1990	Aug p	104.20	104.24	− .1	7.62
10¾	1990	Aug n	106.16	106.20	− .1	7.61
6¾	1990	Sep p	97.30	98.2	− .1	7.62
11½	1990	Oct n	108.19	108.23	+ .2	7.63
8	1990	Nov p	100.20	100.24	− .1	7.67
9⅝	1990	Nov k	104.12	104.16	+ .1	7.68
13	1990	Nov n	112.5	112.9	.....	7.69
6⅝	1990	Dec p	97.10	97.14	.....	7.68
11¾	1991	Jan n	109.26	109.30	+ .2	7.69
7⅜	1991	Feb p	99.2	99.6	+ .1	7.69
9⅛	1991	Feb k	103.11	103.15	+ .1	7.74
6¾	1991	Mar p	97.8	97.12	.....	7.75
12⅜	1991	Apr n	112	112.4	+ .1	7.79
8⅛	1991	May p	100.26	100.30	+ .1	7.77
14½	1991	May n	118.4	118.8	.....	7.76
7⅞	1991	Jun n	100.1	100.5	− .1	7.81
13¾	1991	Jul n	116.20	116.24	− .1	7.83
7½	1991	Aug p	98.29	99.1	.....	7.83
14⅞	1991	Aug n	120.17	120.21	.....	7.76
9⅛	1991	Sep k	103.19	103.23	− .1	7.88
12¼	1991	Oct p	113	113.4	.....	7.90
6½	1991	Nov p	95.20	95.24	− .1	7.87
14¼	1991	Nov n	119.19	119.23	.....	7.85
8¼	1991	Dec k	100.29	101.1	.....	7.92
11⅝	1992	Jan p	111.17	111.21	− .1	7.97
6⅝	1992	Feb p	95.20	95.24	+ .1	7.92
14⅝	1992	Feb n	121.27	121.31	.....	7.90
11¾	1992	Apr	112.16	112.20	+ .2	8.01
6⅝	1992	May k	95.7	95.11	+ .2	7.98
13¾	1992	May n	119.16	119.20	− .1	8.03
10⅜	1992	Jul p	108.5	108.9	+ .1	8.04
4¼	1987-92	Aug	93.1	93.19	+ .1	5.94
7¼	1992	Aug	98.28	99.2	.....	7.50
8¼	1992	Aug p	100.21	100.25	.....	8.03
9¾	1992	Oct p	106.3	106.7	+ .1	8.08
8⅜	1992	Nov p	101	101.4	+ .2	8.07
10½	1992	Nov n	109.1	109.5	.....	8.07
8¾	1993	Jan p	102.8	102.12	− .1	8.13
4	1988-93	Feb	93.1	93.19	+ .1	5.57
6¾	1993	Feb	95.9	95.27	.....	7.79
7⅞	1993	Feb	99.13	99.17	.....	7.99
8¼	1993	Feb p	100.10	100.14	.....	8.12
10⅞	1993	Feb n	110.19	110.23	− .1	8.15
7⅜	1993	Apr p	96.23	96.27	.....	8.15
7⅝	1993	May	97.28	98	+ .1	8.10
10⅛	1993	May n	107.27	107.31	+ .3	8.18
7¼	1993	Jul p	95.29	96.1	.....	8.19
7½	1988-93	Aug	96.25	96.31	.....	8.21
8⅝	1993	Aug	101.24	102	.....	8.15
11⅞	1993	Aug n	115.9	115.13	+ .1	8.23
7⅛	1993	Oct p	95	95.4	− .1	8.24
8⅝	1993	Nov	101.26	102	.....	8.17
11¾	1993	Nov	115.6	115.10	+ .1	8.27
7	1994	Jan	94.5	94.9	+ .1	8.26
9	1994	Feb	103.1	103.5	+ .1	8.30
7	1994	Apr p	93.27	93.31	− .1	8.22
4⅛	1989-94	May	93.1	93.19	.....	5.37
13⅛	1994	May p	122.13	122.17	− .2	8.33
8	1994	Jul n	98.12	98.16	+ .3	8.31
8¾	1994	Aug	102.4	102.8	+ .3	8.28
12⅝	1994	Aug p	120.16	120.20	− .3	8.37
9½	1994	Oct k	105.14	105.18	+ .1	8.37
10⅛	1994	Nov	108.15	108.19	+ .2	8.40
11⅝	1994	Nov	115.30	116.2	− .1	8.40
8⅝	1995	Jan p	101	101.4	.....	8.40
3	1995	Feb	93.1	93.19	+ .1	4.08
10½	1995	Feb	110.17	110.21	− .1	8.42
11¼	1995	Feb p	114.8	114.12	+ .1	8.44
10⅜	1995	May	110.3	110.7	.....	8.43
11¼	1995	May p	114.16	114.20	+ .3	8.46
12⅝	1995	May	122.12	122.16	+ .1	8.36
10½	1995	Aug p	110.22	110.26	− .2	8.49
9½	1995	Nov p	105.10	105.14	− .1	8.51
11½	1995	Nov	116.29	117.1	+ .1	8.42
8⅞	1996	Feb p	101.25	101.29	.....	8.53
7⅜	1996	May p	93.2	93.6	+ .1	8.56
7¼	1996	Nov p	91.29	92.1	+ .2	8.58
8⅝	1997	Aug k	99.29	100.1	+ .3	8.62
8½	1997	May k	99.7	99.11	+ .3	8.60
8⅞	1997	Nov	101.12	101.16	+ .1	8.64
8⅛	1998	Feb p	96.29	97.1	+ .1	8.57
7	1993-98	May	89	89.4	.....	8.63
3½	1998	Nov	93.4	93.22	+ .4	4.25
8½	1994-99	May	98.24	98.28	+ .3	8.66
7⅞	1995-00	Feb	93.24	93.28	+ .1	8.71
8⅜	1995-00	Aug	97.9	97.13	+ .7	8.72
11¾	2001	Feb	122.30	123.4	− .1	8.72
13⅛	2001	May	133.3	133.9	− .9	8.79
8	1996-01	Aug	94.26	95	+ .3	8.64
13⅜	2001	Aug	135.22	135.28	+ .4	8.76
15¾	2001	Nov	155.19	155.25	.....	8.68
14¼	2002	Feb	143.16	143.22	.....	8.75
11⅝	2002	Nov	122.9	122.15	+ .5	8.85
10¾	2003	Feb	115.3	115.9	.....	8.88
10¾	2003	May	115.7	115.13	+ .1	8.88
11⅛	2003	Aug	118.8	118.14	+ .1	8.90
11⅞	2003	Nov	124.21	124.27	+ .5	8.90
12⅜	2004	May	129.3	129.9	+ .5	8.91
13¾	2004	Aug	141.11	141.17	+ .4	8.88
11⅝	2004	Nov k	123.2	123.8	+ .6	8.91
8¼	2000-05	May	94.24	94.30	+ .2	8.83
12	2005	May k	126.17	126.23	+ .4	8.92
10¾	2005	Aug k	115.25	115.31	+ .1	8.92
9⅜	2006	Feb k	104.22	104.28	− .1	8.83
7⅝	2002-07	Feb	88.27	89.1	− .2	8.83
7⅞	2002-07	Nov	90.26	91	− .5	8.85
8⅜	2003-08	Aug	94.31	95.5	+ .1	8.89
8¾	2003-08	Nov	98.8	98.14	.....	8.92
9⅛	2004-09	May	101.14	101.20	− .7	8.93
10⅜	2004-09	Nov	111.23	111.29	.....	8.98
11¾	2005-10	Feb	123.20	123.26	− .1	8.98
10	2005-10	May	108.22	108.28	− .4	8.97
12¾	2005-10	Nov	133.1	133.7	+ .3	8.96
13⅞	2006-11	May	143.13	143.19	+ .4	8.96
14	2006-11	Nov	144.31	145.5	.....	8.96
10⅜	2007-12	Nov	112.20	112.26	− .1	8.97
12	2008-13	Aug	128.1	128.7	+ .1	8.96
13¼	2009-14	May	140.2	140.8	+ .4	8.97
12½	2009-14	Aug k	133.14	133.20	+ .3	8.94
11¾	2009-14	Nov k	126.20	126.26	− .1	8.93
11¼	2015	Feb k	124.15	124.21	− .1	8.83
10⅝	2015	Aug k	118.12	118.18	− .3	8.82
9⅞	2015	Nov	110.17	110.23	.....	8.83
9¼	2016	Feb k	104.8	104.14	+ .2	8.82
7¼	2016	May k	83.18	83.24	.....	8.82
7½	2016	Nov k	86.6	86.12	.....	8.81
8¾	2017	May k	99.9	99.15	+ .2	8.80
8⅞	2017	Aug k	100.29	101.3	+ .1	8.77

SOURCE: *Wall Street Journal*, 8 April 1988. Reprinted by permission.

"point" values can be viewed as a percentage of face value; for a bond or note with a face value of $1,000, each point is equivalent to $10. The bond and note prices are also net of interest that has accrued since the last coupon payment. The accrued interest must be paid to the seller by the purchaser.

It can also be seen from Table 14.2 that the coupon rate, maturity date, bid change, and yield-to-maturity are given for each bond and note. The influence of these factors on the risk-return characteristics of the securities will be discussed in Chapter 15. Treasury bill and bond pricing are discussed in more detail in Chapter 21.

Information about the exact dates of interest payments and maturity, along with other features, can be found in publications such as Moody's *Municipal and Government Manual*.

U.S. Savings Bonds

U.S. savings bonds are similar to other U.S. government securities but also have some significant differences. First, they are not negotiable since no secondary market exists. They can be redeemed, however, at any bank without any fees or commission. Second, they do not pay interest directly to the investor but rather compound the interest semiannually.[7] This feature is similar to that of T-bills; the yield is determined by the discount from face value. The investor receives the accumulated interest as a lump sum when the bond is redeemed. Third, the new Series EE bonds, introduced on November 1, 1982, have a market-based interest rate that is 85 percent of the market average for five-year Treasury securities.[8] The Series EE bonds must be held at least five years to qualify for market-based rates. The current minimum yield on these bonds (held five years or longer) is 6 percent. Fourth, the initial price of the bond can be as little as $50 or as much as $10,000. The face value is always twice the purchase price, but the investor may receive more or less than the face value, depending on the length of time the security is held. Another difference between these and other U.S. government securities is that savings bonds cannot be redeemed within six months after the initial purchase, unless there is an emergency. Finally, savings bonds offer less liquidity since interest is credited only semiannually, which would cause a loss of interest if the security was redeemed prior to an interest payment date.[9]

U.S. savings bonds are similar to other government securities in that both are free of credit (default) risk. Income from both types of securities is exempt from state and local taxes but is subject to federal taxes. Savings bonds have an added tax advantage; investors can defer the federal tax on the accrued interest until the bond is redeemed. This may be an especially attractive feature to investors approaching retirement, since their tax bracket may be considerably lower after retirement. Series EE bonds can be exchanged for Series HH bonds that pay semiannual interest. The Series HH bonds are designed to appeal to retired individuals.

Federal Agencies and Miscellaneous Securities

These securities differ from Treasury securities in that they are not issued by the federal government. In one case (Government National Mortgage Association), however, the securities are backed by the full credit of the U.S. government. With the exception of the guaranteed securities, these bonds have slightly more default risk and as a consequence offer slightly higher yields.

---

[7] Series HH bonds do pay interest semiannually. These bonds, however, are only available in exchange for Series E and EE bonds.

[8] Older Series E and EE bonds issued before November 1982 earn market-based interest rates, beginning with their first interest date on or after November 1, 1987.

[9] Additional facts are available in a brochure, ''U.S. Savings Bonds: The Great American Investment,'' published by the Treasury. Current interest rates are available by calling 1-800-US-BONDS.

One of the largest and fastest-growing groups of this type of security is *mortgage-backed* securities. These are securities that are collateralized by pools of mortgages. The major agencies that issue mortgage-backed securities are Federal National Mortgage Association (FNMA or "Fannie Mae"), Government National Mortgage Association (GNMA or "Ginnie Mae"), and Federal Home Loan Mortgage Corporation (FHLMC or "Freddie Mac"). All three of these agencies were created by the federal government to increase available funds for mortgages.

Ginnie Mae is the largest of the three and is a government-owned corporation. Its mortgage-backed securities are known as Ginnie Maes and are backed by the full faith and credit of the U.S. government. The mortgages behind the Ginnie Maes are FHA- or VA-insured loans. The minimum denomination of these securities is $25,000, and they pay interest and principal payments on a monthly basis.

Freddie Mac is a federally chartered agency and guarantees the conventional mortgage pool through *participation certificates*. These securities, unlike those issued by Ginnie Mae, are not officially backed by the federal government. This fact gives them slightly more credit risk, but they are still considered extremely safe.

Fannie Mae, while a federally-chartered institution, is a privately-owned corporation; its common stock is traded on the New York Stock Exchange. While the corporation guarantees the conventional mortgage pool behind each bond, its securities are not backed by the U.S. government.

All of these securities are highly liquid and considered quite safe, with Ginnie Maes having essentially no credit risk. All of them provide yields in excess of those on U.S. Treasury securities.[10] One potential problem with these securities is the *pass-through* feature that allows the interest and principal from the mortgages to be paid to the bond investors. A mortgage may be paid off early, or if the property is sold or damaged, it is likely that the mortgage will be paid, resulting in *prepayment risk* to the investor. The investor is usually unable to anticipate these prepayments and as a consequence would have uncertain cash flows. This is because the pass-through payments include a partial repayment of principal that can vary considerably from period to period. This in turn causes the interest portion or coupon receipt to decline.[11]

Other federal agency securities include Federal Farm Credit, Student Loan Marketing, World Bank, Federal Land Bank, and Federal Home Loan Bank. Daily quotes on these securities are given in the *Wall Street Journal* on the same page as the Treasury issues, and the format is the same.

Municipal Securities

States, counties, cities, and other governmental units also issue bonds to finance public needs. These types of securities are classified under the general category of *municipals*. These securities have a greater risk of default than Treasury or agency securities and therefore offer higher after-tax yields.

---

[10] For a discussion and empirical evidence, see Terrence M. Clauretie, "Why Do GNMAs Yield More Than Treasuries?" *Journal of Portfolio Management* (Spring 1982): pp. 72–74, and Kenneth B. Dunn and John J. McConnell, "Rate of Return Indices for GNMA Securities," *Journal of Portfolio Management* (Winter 1981): pp. 65–74.

[11] For a discussion and analysis of the pass-through feature, see Hugh R. Lamle, "Ginnie Mae: Age Equals Beauty," *Journal of Portfolio Management* (Winter 1981): pp. 75–79.

One very attractive aspect of municipals is their interest is exempt from federal income taxes. Any short-term or long-term capital gain (loss) realized on the security is subject to federal income taxes. The interest is also exempt from state and local taxes if the bond is issued by the investor's state of domicile.

Many investors have great confidence in the creditworthiness of municipal issuers. It should be pointed out, however, that there are infrequent but very significant defaults and near-defaults on municipal securities. Two of the most dramatic defaults were by New York City and the Washington Public Power Supply System (frequently referred to as WHOOPS rather than WPPSS).[12]

Because of the defaults and near-defaults of the 1970s and 1980s, a number of private companies insure municipal bonds. The insurance, obtained by the issuer, guarantees the payment of interest and principal to the investor. The insurance essentially eliminates the risk of default and causes a low-quality bond to be viewed as high-quality.

Due to the favorable tax treatment and relatively low probability of default, many investors (primarily those in high tax brackets) devote part of their portfolios to municipals. Historically, most municipals were not registered and therefore required the investor to clip coupons semiannually to receive the interest. Banks and other financial institutions usually accepted the coupons much as they would accept a check for deposit. Since 1981, however, new issues of municipals must be registered to receive the tax-exempt status.

One potential problem for investors in municipals who follow a very passive or buy-and-hold strategy concerns the possibility of a *call* by the issuer. The call feature essentially allows the issuer to force the investor to sell the bond back at a predetermined price specified when the bond is initially sold. As some consolation to the investor, the price paid by the issuer is usually greater than the face value of the bond. This difference is referred to as the *call premium*. During the high interest rate period of 1981–1985, the vast majority of municipals issued allowed the issuer to call the bond before maturity.[13] During periods of falling interest rates, many states and municipalities may elect to exercise the call feature. Since the call premium declines over time, however, call risk exists even during periods of increasing interest rates.[14]

Since most of the bonds issued before 1981 are unregistered, there is no way for an issuer directly to notify the investors if a call feature is exercised. Thus, most issuers resort to using some form of advertisement to advise investors of the redemptions. The advertisements often use the serial numbers of the affected bonds. Without close attention to the financial news, many investors are often unaware that their bonds have been called.[15] This can be costly to the investor, since the

---

[12] For a discussion of the factors that determine the creditworthiness of municipals, see Jack L. Treynor, "On the Quality of Municipal Bonds," *Financial Analysts Journal* (May-June 1982): pp. 25–30. For an analysis of the WPPSS crisis, see John W. Peavy III and George H. Hensel, "The Effect of the WPPSS Crisis on the Tax-exempt Bond Market," *Journal of Financial Research* (Fall 1987): pp. 239–47.

[13] One recent study found that 90 percent of a random sample of 160 municipals had a call feature.

[14] James C. Van Horne, "Call Risk and Municipal Bonds," *Journal of Portfolio Management* (Winter 1987): pp. 53–57.

[15] "Some Municipal Investors Get Nasty Surprises When the Bonds Are Called in Early by Issuers," *Wall Street Journal*, 16 May 1983, p. 58.

issuer stops paying interest on the called bonds. The call also denies the individual the opportunity to follow a buy-and-hold investment strategy since the proceeds from the call must be reinvested at rates that are often lower than the coupon rate on the called bonds.

There are two major types of municipal bonds: *general obligation* and *revenue*. These are discussed below:

1. GENERAL OBLIGATION MUNICIPALS This type of municipal bond is backed by the general or total taxing power of the municipality. They are also referred to as *full-faith-and-credit* bonds because all the taxing authority and tax revenues of the issuer can be used to satisfy the interest and principal payments.

2. REVENUE BONDS The funds needed to pay principal and interest are derived from specific municipality-owned projects such as hospitals, waterworks, or sewerage systems. Only revenue from the specified project can be used to service the bonds.

Corporate Bonds

Bonds issued by corporations are often grouped under the general category of *corporates*. Corporates, as a general class of bonds, have more default risk than government agency or municipal bonds and therefore offer higher returns.

Most corporate bonds are traded in the Over-the-Counter market, unless the issuing firm has its stock listed on the New York Stock Exchange, NYSE, or American Stock Exchange, AMEX. In these instances, the bonds are traded on the bond annex of the NYSE or the AMEX. An example of quotations from the *Wall Street Journal* is given in Table 14.3. In contrast to Treasury notes and bonds that are quoted in points and thirty-seconds of a point, the prices for corporates are quoted in points and eighths of a point. For example, consider the first Alabama Power, AlaP, bond in Table 14.3, with a quote of $92\frac{1}{2}$ which indicates a price of $925.00 (i.e., $[(92 + \frac{1}{2}) \times 10]$) since each point is $10 for a bond with a face value of $1,000.

Notice that the information in Table 14.3 gives the coupon rate and year of maturity directly after the abbreviated corporate name. Exact interest payment and maturity dates can be found in publications such as Moody's *Corporate Bond Manual*. The "Cur Yld," or current yield, is calculated by dividing the annual interest by the closing price. This represents only a "partial" rate of return, since any price change occurring after the bond's purchase is ignored. For the first Alabama Power bond, the current yield is 9.6 percent. The "vol," or volume, indicates the number of bonds that were traded on the particular day, or a total of 10 for the Alabama Power bonds. Finally, the "net chg" represents the change in the "close" from the previous day. For the Alabama Power bond the change from the previous day's close was $\frac{3}{8}$ or $3.75.

Summary

Because of differences in risk and tax treatment of income, different categories of bonds should be priced to provide appropriate returns. Figure 14.2 illustrates

TABLE 14.3 QUOTATIONS FOR NEW YORK STOCK EXCHANGE BONDS

CORPORATION BONDS
Volume, $30,430,000

Bonds	Cur Yld	Vol	Close	Net Chg.
AVX 8¼12	cv	5	97	+ ½
AlaBn 6¾99t	6.8	10	99⅝	+ 1
AlaP 8⅞s03	9.6	10	92½	+ ⅜
AlaP 8¼s03	9.2	9	89⅞	− ⅛
AlaP 9¼07	9.8	46	94½	...
AlaP 9⅝08	9.8	12	98	+ 1
AlaP 12⅝10	11.8	10	107	...
AlskH 16¼99	14.8	26	109¾	...
viAlgl 10.4s02f	...	29	42½	− ½
viAlgl 9s89f	...	75	54	+ 1¾
AlldC zr92	...	7	69	+ ½
AlldC zr96	...	10	50½	+ ½
AlldC zr98	...	24	39	+ ¼
AlldC zr2000	...	32	33	+ ⅝
AldC dc6s88	6.1	23	99	− 3/32
AldC dc6s90	6.4	29	93⅞	+ ⅛
AlldC zr97	...	25	44	+ 1¾
AlldC zr09	...	55	13¾	...
Alcoa 6s92	6.4	3	93⅜	− ⅛
Alcoa 9s95	9.0	4	99¾	...
AMAX 8½96	9.3	5	91	+ 2¾
AMAX 14½94	12.4	4	116½	+ 1¼
AForP 5s30	9.6	3	52	− ⅛
AAir dc6¼96	7.4	100	84¾	+ ½
ABrnd 8⅝90	8.5	5	101⅜	+ ⅞
ACeM 6¾91	cv	34	50	...
AHoist 5½93	cv	5	81	...
AmMed 9½01	cv	20	95½	...
AmMed 8¼08	cv	11	77½	− ¼
ATT 3⅞90r	4.1	25	94¼	...
ATT 5⅛01	7.5	3	68½	+ ⅜
ATT 8¾00	9.0	313	96⅞	− ⅛
ATT 7s01	8.4	38	83	− ¼
ATT 7⅛03	8.7	21	82¼	+ ⅛
ATT 8.80s05	9.3	232	95	+ ⅜
ATT 8⅝s07	9.3	79	92⅝	+ ⅞
ATT 8⅝26	9.7	55	89⅜	+ ⅝
Amfac 5¼94	cv	10	97	...
Amoco 9.2s04	9.2	10	99½	...
Amoco 14s91	13.8	126	101½	...
Ancp 13⅞02f	cv	25	105¾	...
Anhr 11⅞12	10.7	10	111	...
Anhr 8s96	8.6	23	93	− 2¾
Apch 7½12	cv	13	84¾	+ ⅞
ArkBst 7s11	8.4	37	83	+ 3
Arml 13½94	12.6	30	107	− ¾

Bonds	Cur Yld	Vol	Close	Net Chg.
Atchn 4s95st r	5.5	30	72⅜	...
Atchsn 4s95	5.6	11	71½	− 1⅛
Atchn 4s95r	5.5	10	72¼	...
ARch dc7s91	7.3	30	95⅞	+ ½
ARch 10⅜95	9.7	65	107	+ ⅜
ARch 9½96	9.3	10	102	+ ¾
AutDt 6½11	cv	31	118	+ 1
Avnet 8s13	cv	10	91¾	− ¼
Avnet 6s12	cv	27	86	+ 1
BakrHgh 9½06	cv	26	97½	...
Bally 10s06	cv	28	90	...
BalGE 8⅜06	9.2	16	90⅞	+ ½
BalGE 8¼07	9.5	15	87	...
BkNY 8¼10	cv	135	106	+ 2¼
Banka 8¾01	10.6	10	82½	...
Bkam 8.35s07	10.8	13	77⅝	...
Bkam zr90s	...	8	81	− ⅜
Bkam zr92s	...	39	64	− ⅞
Bkam zr91s	...	20	76½	+ ½
Bkam zr93s	...	112	60⅜	+ ½
viBASIX 8¾05	cv	6	35½	+ ½
viBeker 15⅞03f	...	1	37½	...
BellPa 7½13	9.4	1	80	− ½
BellPa 8⅛17	9.5	3	85⅜	+ ⅜
BellPa 9¼19	9.7	17	95⅝	− ¼
BenCp 8.3s03	9.4	20	88	+ 1¼
BenCp 8.4s08	8.4	5	100¼	+ ½
BestPrd 9s94	9.0	10	99¾	+ 9¾
BestPr 12⅝96	12.6	88	100	+ ½
BethSt 4½90	5.0	146	90⅜	+ ¼
BethSt 5.4s92	6.4	2	84⅛	− ⅝
BethSt 6⅞99	9.8	5	70	+ ⅞
BethSt 9s00	11.0	161	81½	...
BethSt 8.45s05	11.2	229	75½	+ ½
BethSt 8⅜01	11.1	290	75¼	− ¼
Bevrly 7⅝03	cv	159	59	− ½
Beverly zr03	...	130	26⅞	...
Boeing 8⅜96	8.6	50	97⅞	− ⅛
BoltBer 6s12	cv	1	76	+ ¼
BorW 5½s92	6.6	10	83	+ 3
BrkUn 9⅝96	9.7	4	99⅝	− ⅜
BwnSh 9¼05	cv	10	96⅛	...
BwnFer 6¼12	cv	224	92¾	+ ¾
BusInd 8s06	cv	1	98	+ 2
BusInd 5½07	cv	4	67	...

Bonds	Cur Yld	Vol	Close	Net Chg.
CBS 10⅞95	10.2	61	106⅞	− ⅜
CIT 9½95	9.5	25	100	...
CIT 8.8s93	8.9	20	99¼	− ⅝
CPc4s perp	9.5	4	42	− ½
CPC 4sr	9.6	16	41¾	...
CaroFrt 6¼11	cv	10	76	− ¾
CarPL 7¾02	9.0	18	86	+ 1⅝
CaroT 9⅛00	9.4	17	97½	...
CaroT 9s08	9.8	5	92¼	+ ¼
CartHaw 12¼96	12.6	10	97	+ 1
CartHaw 12½02	13.4	30	93⅝	+ ⅝
CatTr 5.3s92	5.8	5	91¼	+ 3¼
Centel 8.1s96	8.7	4	92¾	− 1¾
CATS zr11-01	...	20	29⅜	+ ⅛
ChartC 12s99	12.8	7	94	...
viChmtrn 9s94f	...	22	66	+ ⅝
ChNY 8.4s99	9.5	10	88½	...
CPoM 7¼12	9.2	10	78½	+ 1⅜
CPoV 8⅝09	9.5	10	91⅛	− ⅜
CPoV 9½19	9.7	10	98	...
ChvrnC 11s90	10.8	35	102	− 1
ChvrnC 10¾95	10.0	5	107¼	+ ⅜
Chvrn 5¾92	6.3	8	91⅛	...
Chvrn 7s96	7.9	25	88¾	− ½
Chvrn 8¾05	9.2	32	95	+ ¼
Chvrn 8½95	8.7	25	97½	− 1⅜
Chvrn 8¾96	8.9	5	98⅜	+ ⅜
ChiPac 6½12	cv	15	87	− 1
Chrysl 8⅞95	9.1	11	97	− 1⅛
Chryslr 13s97	11.2	65	116½	+ 10¼
Chryslr 12s15	11.2	20	107	...
Chryslr 9.6s94	9.5	17	100¾	− 1¼
ChryF 11¾90	11.3	25	103¾	− ¾
ChryF 12⅛90	11.4	10	106⅛	− ¼
ChryF 10.6s90	10.2	261	104¼	+ ¼
ChryF 9⅜91	9.2	49	102	+ ⅜
ChryF 9¼91	9.1	20	101¾	...
ChryF 7⅞91	8.2	1	96	...
CirclK 8¼05	cv	40	108⅛	+ 1⅛
CirclK 7¼06	cv	35	96	− 1
CirclK 13s97	12.8	5	101⅜	+ 1⅜
Citicp 8.45s07	9.5	55	88⅞	+ ⅛
Citicp 8.6s04t	9.3	57	92¼	− 1¾
Citicp 12¼93	12.0	10	101⅞	− ¼
Claytn 7¾01	cv	6	101	+ 1

EXPLANATORY NOTES
(For New York and American Bonds)
Yield is current yield.
cv-Convertible bond. cf-Certificates. dc-Deep discount. ec-European currency units. f-Dealt in flat. kd-Danish kroner. m-Matured bonds, negotiability impaired by maturity. na-No accrual. r-Registered. rp-Reduced principal. st Stamped. t-Floating rate. wd-When distributed. ww-With warrants. x-Ex interest. xw-Without warrants. zr-Zero coupon.
vi-In bankruptcy or receivership or being reorganized under the Bankruptcy Act, or securities assumed by such companies.

SOURCE: *Wall Street Journal*, 8 April 1988. Reprinted by permission.

this point by providing the yields over the period 1946–1987 for municipals, Treasuries, and corporate bonds. Notice the inverted scale on the yield axis. As expected, the yield on Treasuries is below the municipal yields, with corporates providing the highest yields. The yield spreads between the three categories are not constant. The long-term upward trend in yields and the large cyclical swings in yields since the 1970s are clearly evident.

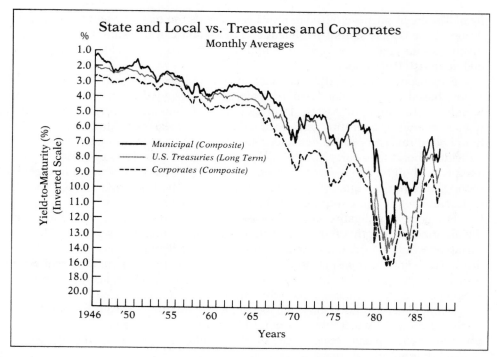

FIGURE 14.2 Yields-to-maturity on municipal, long-term Treasury, and corporate bonds 1946–FEBRUARY 1988

Source: *Bond Record,* Moody's, March 1988, p. 416. Reprinted by permission.

BASIC FEATURES OF BOND ISSUERS AND INDIVIDUAL BONDS

All bond investors need a general understanding of the basic features and characteristics of individual securities and issuers. For new bond issues, the most comprehensive source of information would be the prospectus, which can be obtained from the investment banker underwriting the issue or directly from the issuer. The SEC requires the issuer to provide very detailed information concerning the issuer's financial condition and the characteristics of the particular security being offered. Essentially, any information that may be of interest to a potential investor can be found in the lengthy prospectus.

For bonds issued previously and traded in the secondary market, an investor would need to obtain detailed information from sources cited earlier such as the *Wall Street Journal,* Moody's *Bond Record,* or Standard and Poor's *Bond Guide.* In addition, current financial information on the issuer can be found in sources such as Moody's *Industrial Manuals* or similar publications, depending on the classification of the issuer.

Issuer Characteristics

A knowledgeable bond investor should be familiar with characteristics of the bond issuer. For corporate and municipal issuers, this requires an analysis comparable to one performed by an investor interested in purchasing the stock of the firm. The main purpose of the analysis is to assess the business and financial condition of the issuer, so that the likelihood of default can be estimated. This might involve some analysis of economic and industry prospects, along with a financial analysis of the issuer.

For corporate issues, the financial analysis could begin by calculating financial ratios, based on historical financial statements, designed to measure the firm's liquidity, utilization of assets, leverage, and profitability. Particular attention would be paid to operating and financial leverage measures. Many large institutional bond investors spend considerable time performing this analysis. For small individual bond investors, however, the judgment of a professional analyst, who assigns the bond a *rating*, is often used. The rating, which is discussed in the next section, attempts to quantify the risk of default of the bond and is based on the characteristics of the issuer and of the individual bond.

For general obligation municipal issues, the analysis would concentrate on the financial strength of the governmental unit issuing the security. The key variables would be the tax base and the amount of debt that has been issued on this base.[16] For example, a ratio of total debt to the assessed value of real estate or net debt per capita could be used for this purpose. It would also be important to analyze local and regional economic factors.

Municipal revenue bonds can be analyzed much as corporate bonds are, since the project financed by the bond has specific revenues and expenses. This analysis would typically concentrate on the stability of revenues and the coverage of fixed operating and financial charges.

Bond Characteristics

Bonds, unlike common stocks, can have many unique and important characteristics. Corporations typically have only one type of common stock; where more than one type does exist, it is usually because of differences in voting rights. An example is General Motors, which has three classes of common stock with differences in voting rights. Corporations, municipalities, and governmental units, however, issue many different types of debt instruments, each with special characteristics. A discussion of some of the more important characteristics follows.

1. DENOMINATION The face value, or *denomination*, of a bond can be as low as $250 or as high as millions of dollars. Typically, this value is $1,000.

2. MATURITY DATE All bonds, with the exception of *consols* or *perpetuities*, have a maturity date.[17] This provides the essential information that is necessary to calculate the term-to-maturity at the date of issue or at any time during the life of the bond. For example, if the bond has a maturity date of June 15, 2010, the term-to-maturity would be the time from the date of analysis

---

[16] For a discussion, see Jack L. Treynor, "On the Quality of Municipal Bonds," *Financial Analysts Journal* (May-June 1982); pp. 25–30.

[17] Consols or perpetuities are issued without a maturity date. There are a small number of these bonds traded in the United States. The most actively traded issue is the Canadian Pacific Consols that were issued in 1921. These bonds are discussed in Chapter 15.

to June 15, 2010. Term-to-maturity would be expressed in time units such as nineteen years and six months, 19.5, or twenty years and nine months, 20.75. In some bond offerings, the maturities are staggered over a period of years, resulting in what is called a *serial issue.*

3.   COUPON The *coupon* is established at the time the bond is issued and represents the nominal interest rate that will be paid. It is stated as an annual percentage rate, such as $7\frac{3}{8}$, which can be applied to the denomination or face value of the bond to calculate the dollar interest. Since interest is generally paid semiannually, the issuer pays only one-half of the interest each semiannual period.

Traditionally, the coupon is constant over the life of the bond. Recently, however, some bonds "index" coupons to inflation or to market interest rates. These are much like an adjustable-rate mortgage, ARM, on real estate, since the interest rate on the mortgage or the coupon on the bond is adjusted for the rate of inflation. If the inflation rate is above a predetermined level, then the rates (coupons) are adjusted upward.

At the other extreme, a number of corporate bonds offered in the early 1980s pay no coupon and are appropriately referred to as *zeros.* These bonds are sold at discounts from face value, much like Treasury bills. Zero corporate bonds are subject to federal income taxes on the "implied" interest income, while zeros issued by municipalities maintain their tax-exempt status. Examples of corporations that have issued zeros are American Medical International, Archer-Daniel-Midland, Barclays-American, and CIT Financial.

4.   REGISTRATION Bonds can be *registered or bearer* bonds, for interest and/or principal payments. The issuer maintains records on ownership of registered bonds, but the holder is assumed to be the owner of bearer bonds. Municipal bonds issued after 1981 must now be registered to be exempt from federal income taxes.

5.   CALL FEATURE It is quite common for corporate, municipal, and some Treasury securities to be *callable* by the issuer. The earliest call date and call price are specified when the bonds are issued. It should always be remembered that the call feature is an advantage to the issuer and can be exercised at the issuer's discretion.

6.   CONVERTIBILITY This feature can be added to a bond as a "sweetener" to the investor. The *convertible* feature may also be advantageous to the issuer; the marketability of the bond is improved, and the feature provides flexibility in the capital structure of the issuer. At the option of the investor, the bond can be exchanged for common stock, using a specified fixed conversion ratio or conversion price. For example, if the conversion ratio is 50, then one bond can be exchanged for 50 shares of stock. The conversion price would be $20 since this would be the conversion value per share for a bond with a denomination of $1,000. Typically, only the more speculative bonds are offered with a convertible feature. This feature may provide considerable help in marketing the bond if there are prospects that the value of the firm's stock may increase above the conversion price. It is also common for the issuer to offer a lower coupon rate than would be the case for a "straight" (nonconvertible) bond with similar characteristics. A detailed discussion and analysis of convertible bonds is provided in Chapter 18.

TABLE 14.4 TYPES AND CHARACTERISTICS OF BONDS

	MARKET TRADED	DENOMINATION OR FACE VALUE	FREQUENCY OF COUPON PAYMENTS	MATURITY	SECURITY OR COLLATERAL	TAX STATUS
I. U.S. GOVERNMENT SECURITIES						
A. Treasury Bills	Treasury Auction/OTC	$10,000–$100,000 with increments of $5,000	No coupon (Discounted)	13, 26, 52 weeks	Full backing of U.S. Government	Subject to federal taxes; exempt from state and local taxes
B. Treasury Notes	Treasury Auction/OTC	$5,000 minimum with increments of $1,000	Semiannual	1–10 years	Full backing of U.S. Government	Subject to federal taxes; exempt from state and local taxes
C. Treasury Bonds	Treasury Auction/OTC	$5,000 minimum with increments of $1,000	Semiannual	10–30 years	Full backing of U.S. Government	Subject to federal taxes; exempt from state and local taxes
II. U.S. SAVINGS BONDS						
A. Series EE	Not marketable	$50–$10,000	No coupon (Discounted)	Minimum of 5 years	Full backing of U.S. Government	Federal taxes deferred until cashed or matures; exempt from state and local taxes.
B. Series HH	Not marketable	Multiples of $500	Semiannual	Minimum of 5 years	Full backing of U.S. Government	Interest received subject to federal taxes; exempt from state and local taxes
III. FEDERAL AGENCY BONDS						
A. FHLMC	OTC	Minimum of $25,000	Monthly	1–20 years	Not guaranteed by U.S. Government	Subject to federal, state, and local taxes
B. FNMA	OTC	Minimum of $25,000	Monthly	1–20 years	Not guaranteed by U.S. Government	Subject to federal, state, and local taxes
C. GNMA	OTC	Minimum of $25,000	Monthly	1–20 years	Full backing of U.S. Government	Subject to federal, state, and local taxes
IV. MUNICIPAL BONDS						
A. General Obligation	OTC	$1,000 or more	Semiannual	5–30 years	Depends on issuer/insurance	Interest exempt from federal taxes but capital gains taxable; exempt from state and local taxes if issued by state of domicile
B. Revenue Bonds	OTC	$1,000 or more	Semiannual	5–30 years	Depends on issuer/insurance	Interest exempt from federal taxes but capital gains taxable; exempt from state and local taxes if issued by state of domicile
V. CORPORATE BONDS	NYSE, AMEX, OTC	$250 or more $1,000 standard	Semiannual	5–30 years	Depends on issuer/provisions of bond	Subject to federal, state, and local taxes

7. COLLATERAL This feature is important for bonds that have some probability of default. Obviously the investor should be concerned about the assets pledged as collateral in the event of default on interest or principal payments.

   a. SECURED Bonds that have specific assets pledged as collateral are *secured* bonds. The collateral may be real assets such as real estate, in which case the bonds would be *mortgage* bonds. If stocks or bonds are given as collateral, the bonds are *collateral trust* bonds. For mortgage bonds, the bond contract or indenture can specify either a *closed-* or *open-ended* mortgage. A closed-end feature offers more security, since additional bonds cannot be issued using the same collateral.

   b. UNSECURED Bonds without specific collateral are *unsecured* except for the general creditworthiness of the issuer. Debentures or subordinated debentures are examples of this type of security.

   c. SINKING FUND When investigating the provisions of a bond, it is advisable to know details concerning any sinking fund requirements. A *sinking fund* is an advantage to the investor, since it either forces the issuer periodically to allocate funds to repay the principal or requires that funds be used to purchase the bonds in the market and effectively retire them before maturity.

Table 14.4 provides a summary of the different types of bonds and their characteristics. As previously discussed, the majority of bonds are traded in the Over-the-Counter, OTC, market by dealers and market makers. U.S. government securities, however, can also be purchased by individuals directly in the Treasury auction, through a *noncompetitive tender*. Many corporate bonds are traded on the NYSE and AMEX. Bond markets are discussed in more detail in the last section of this chapter.

In addition to an indication of where each type of bond is traded, Table 14.4 indicates the denomination, frequency of coupon payments, maturity, security or collateral, and tax status for each type of bond.

Bond Ratings

All of the above factors for both the issuer and the individual bond are used by firms such as Standard and Poor's and Moody's to assign a *rating* to a bond. The rating reflects the likelihood that the issuer will default on the payments of interest and/or principal. These firms employ professional analysts to evaluate the bond, using fairly standard financial analysis techniques. It should also be pointed out that the issuer must pay to have a rating assigned to a bond. Since many investors consider the rating essential information, it is uncommon for bonds not to be rated. It should be realized, however, that a bond's lack of a rating does not necessarily imply poor investment quality.[18]

---

[18] For details on these procedures, see Hugh C. Sherwood, *How Corporate and Municipal Debt Is Rated* (New York: John Wiley and Sons, 1976) and *Credit Overview: Corporate and International Ratings* (Standard and Poor's).

TABLE 14.5 RATING CHANGES , MARKET PRICES AND YIELD-TO-MATURITY ON BRANIFF AIRWAYS SINKING FUND DEBENTURE DUE IN 1997 WITH A 9.125 PERCENT COUPON

| | | | YIELD-TO-MATURITY | |
DATE	MOODY'S RATING	PRICE	BRANIFF BOND	STANDARD & POOR'S INDEX OF BONDS RATED BBB
December 1980	Ba	$600.00	16.17%	14.36%
January 1981	Ba	580.00	16.73	13.92
February 1981	Ba	530.00	18.28	14.40
March 1981	Ba	558.75	17.38	14.55
April 1981	B	550.00	17.67	15.04
May 1981	B	510.00	19.01	15.99
August 1981	B	520.00	18.71	15.97
September 1981	B	440.00	21.93	16.95
October 1981	B	440.00	21.95	16.94
December 1981	B	480.00	20.27	15.72
January 1982	Caa	461.25	21.06	16.53
February 1982	Caa	450.00	21.85	16.67
March 1, 1982	Caa	400.00	23.95	16.29
March 8, 1982	Caa	258.75	35.93	16.03
March 15, 1982	Caa	330.00	28.63	16.14
March 22, 1982	Caa	333.75	28.33	16.08
March 29, 1982	Caa	355.00	26.76	16.35
April 5, 1982	Caa	347.50	27.29	16.26
April 12, 1982	Caa	348.75	27.20	16.27
April 19, 1982	Caa	352.50	26.94	16.02
April 26, 1982	Caa	360.00	26.41	16.02
May 3, 1982	Caa	355.00	26.76	16.06
May 10, 1982	Caa	358.75	26.50	15.74
May 17, 1982	Ca	328.75	flat*	15.72
May 24, 1982	Ca	352.50	flat*	15.85

*Bond is traded without interest.

SOURCE: Moody's *Bond Record;* Moody's *Bond Survey,* Standard & Poor's *Statistical Service:* all reprinted by permission. Material from *Barron's* reprinted courtesy of *Barron's Weekly.*

Assigning a rating to a particular bond is an art rather than a science. In fact, the rating firms have always indicated that a mathematical model designed to assign a rating cannot duplicate the success of a team of skilled bond analysts. It is also common for Standard and Poor's and Moody's to disagree about the rating of a particular bond, resulting in a *split rating.* One study based on a sample of 218 bonds, found that Moody's and Standard and Poor's disagreed 58 percent of the time, and Moody's tends to rate bonds significantly lower than Standard and Poor's.[19]

There are numerous instances of a corporation or municipality experiencing serious financial difficulties well in advance of a rating change. This leads many

[19] Larry G. Perry, "The Effect of Bond Rating Agencies on Bond Rating Models," *Journal of Financial Research* (Winter 1985): pp. 307–15. For a study of the impact of split ratings on yields, see Pu Liu and William T. Moore, "The Impact of Split Bond Ratings on Risk Premia," *Financial Review* (February 1987): pp. 71–85.

investors to conclude that ratings are "sticky" and are not changed as frequently or accurately as they should be.

An interesting example of how ratings are changed in response to a company's experiencing financial difficulty is provided by Braniff Airways. Table 14.5 provides information on a sinking fund debenture issued by Braniff in 1976 and on an index of yields for corporate bonds. The initial issue was for $50 million, with a coupon of 9.125 percent and a maturity date of January 1, 1997. Moody's assigned the bond a rating of Baa in 1979. Based on developments in the airline industry and particularly at Braniff, the rating was reduced one grade, to Ba, in 1980. As Table 14.5 illustrates, the price of the bond began a significant decline in early 1981 which partly reflected an increase in the overall yield-to-maturity on corporate bonds in general and the conditions in the industry and the company. Moody's changed the rating to B in April 1981. Due to the declines in the yield-to-maturity for bonds in general in the latter part of 1981, the price of the bond increased in December. However, Moody's lower rating of Caa in January 1982 was followed by dramatic price declines. The price reached $258.75 in early March 1982, several months before Moody's reduced the rating to Ca in May.

On May 13, 1982, Braniff filed for reorganization under Chapter 11 of the bankruptcy laws after suspending all service on May 12. Moody's recognized this development in its weekly *Bond Survey* of May 17 by announcing a rating change to Ca, effective May 13. The prices and ratings in Table 14.5 illustrate that the bond market recognized the deteriorating condition of Braniff prior to and during the period of rating change announcements. Small price changes occured after the rating change announcements. This implies that the market, in general, analyzes the credit condition of companies independently of the rating agencies.

Table 14.6 provides a brief summary of the definition of each rating category used by Moody's. Most investors view bonds rated Aaa–Baa as "investment" quality, with ratings of Ba–B designating "speculative," "high yield," or "junk" bonds. A rating of Caa–C warns of an extremely risky bond that may have already defaulted and be moving toward bankruptcy.

Chapters 15 and 16 provide additional information concerning ratings. This information includes techniques that can be used independently to evaluate the safety of the bond and to employ ratings in implementing bond portfolio strategies.

BOND MARKETS

Primary Market

Bonds, like stocks, are initially traded in the *primary market* that entirely comprises new issues. This is the market where the underwriter or investment banker sells the bonds to initial investors—financial institutions or individuals. These transactions are between the underwriting syndicate or marketing group for the underwriter and the investor. Recall from Chapter 3 that the underwriter purchases the securities from the issuer and then resells them to investors. U.S. government securities are initially sold mainly to institutions and some individuals through auctions conducted by the Treasury.

TABLE 14.6 DEFINITIONS OF MOODY'S BOND RATINGS

Aaa

Bonds which are rated **Aaa** are judged to be of the best quality. They carry the smallest degree of investment risk and are generally referred to as "gilt edge." Interest payments are protected by a large or by an exceptionally stable margin and principal is secure. While the various protective elements are likely to change, such changes as can be visualized are most unlikely to impair the fundamentally strong position of such issues.

Aa

Bonds which are rated **Aa** are judged to be of high quality by all standards. Together with the **Aaa** group they comprise what are generally known as high grade bonds. They are rated lower than the best bonds because margins of protection may not be as large as in **Aaa** securities or fluctuation of protective elements may be of greater amplitude or there may be other elements present which make the long term risks appear somewhat larger then in **Aaa** securities.

A

Bonds which are rated **A** possess many favourable investment attributes and are to be considered as upper medium grade obligations. Factors giving security to principal and interest are considered adequate but elements may be present which suggest a susceptibility to impairment sometime in the future.

Baa

Bonds which are rated **Baa** are considered as medium grade obligations, i.e., they are neither highly protected nor poorly secured. Interest payments and principal security appear adequate for the present but certain protective elements may be lacking or may be characteristically unrealiable over any great length of time. Such bonds lack outstanding investment characteristics and in fact have speculative characteristics as well.

Ba

Bonds which are rated **Ba** are judged to have speculative elements; their future cannot be considered as well assured. Often the protection of interest and principal payments may be very moderate and thereby not well safeguarded during other good and bad times over the future. Uncertainly of position characterizes bonds in this class.

B

Bonds which are rated **B** generally lack characteristics of the desirable investment. Assurance of interest and principal payments or of maintenance of other terms of the contract over any long period of time may be small.

Caa

Bonds which are rated **Caa** are of poor standing. Such issues may be in default or there may be present elements of danger with respect to principal or interest.

Ca

Bonds which are rated **Ca** represent obligations which are speculative in a high degree. Such issues are often in default or have other marked shortcomings.

C

Bonds which are rated **C** are the lowest rated class of bonds and issues so rated can be regarded as having extremely poor prospects of ever attaining any real investment standing.

Note: Moody applies numerical modifiers, **1, 2,** and **3** in each generic rating classification from **Aa** through **B** in its corporate bond rating system. The modifier 1 indicates that the security ranks in the higher end of its generic rating category; the modifier **2** indicates a mid-range ranking; and the modifier **3** indicates that the issue ranks in the lower end of its generic rating category

SOURCE: *Bond Records,* Moody's, March 1988. Reprinted by permission.

Potential investors learn of the new issue through the financial news and watch for offering announcements that appear in the *Wall Street Journal* and other publications. *Barron's* also has a weekly feature in the statistical section entitled, "Coming Financing." This feature provides information on new issues of bonds, preferred stock, and common stock for the coming week and on new offerings filed with the SEC. Account executives at brokerage firms often call potential investors about new offerings. Upon learning of the new offering, the investor should request a copy of the prospectus giving the details of the offering. It is also quite common to see announcements that "appear as a matter of record only." These usually indicate that a "direct placement" of the securities has been made and that they are therefore not offered to other investors.[20] These announcements simply provide advertising for the underwriting firm.

Secondary Market

Once bonds have been placed through the primary market, they can be traded in the secondary market. For the majority of corporate bonds, this is the Over-the-Counter market. For large firms, the bonds will be traded on the NYSE or AMEX if the company's stock is traded there.

Quotes

Bond quotations are not as readily available as stock quotes, because of the large number of outstanding bonds and the infrequent trading in many of the smaller issues. Quotes can be obtained from brokerage houses or publications that specialize in bonds, such as Moody's *Bond Record*.

Transaction Costs

Transaction costs, or brokerage fees, are quite nominal for bonds. There is no standard fee since brokerage fees can be negotiated, but it is not uncommon to pay as little as $3.50 to $4.50 per bond traded. There are no brokerage fees for new issues. Many small bond issues, however, do not have the market liquidity that the stocks of large firms offer. In addition, many bonds are often sold in "blocks," so that the purchase or sale of a denomination of $1,000 to $10,000 may be more difficult. Institutional investors dominate the secondary bond market and typically trade in very large blocks.

Indices

Bond investors can follow general price and yield movements by watching numerous bond indices. This is similar to following stock prices using the DJIA or

---

[20] For a study of direct placements of corporate bonds, including how prices are determined, see Nathaniel B. Cabanilla, "Directly-placed Bonds: A Test of Market Efficiency," *Journal of Portfolio Management* (Winter 1984): pp. 72–74. For a study of municipals, see David S. Kidwell and Eric H. Sorensen, "Pricing of Municipal Bond Underwritings: It May Pay to Invest When Underwriters Don't," *Financial Analysts Journal* (March-April 1983): pp. 58–64.

TABLE 14.7 EXAMPLE OF BOND YIELD AVERAGES

Moody's Corporate Bond Yield Averages

	Av.	Corporate by Ratings				Corporate by Groups				Public Utility Bonds					Industrial Bonds					Railroad Bonds			
	Corp.	Aaa	Aa	A	Baa	P.U.	Ind.	R.R.		Aaa	Aa	A	Baa		Aaa	Aa	A	Baa		Aaa	Aa	A	Baa
1982																							
Mar.	15.68	14.58	15.21	16.12	16.82	16.07	15.29	14.00	Mar.	15.05	15.57	16.50	17.16	Mar.	14.09	14.85	15.73	16.47	Mar.	---	13.22	14.17	14.62
Apr.	15.53	14.46	14.90	15.95	16.78	15.82	15.22	14.03	Apr.	14.86	15.12	16.31	17.00	Apr.	14.07	14.68	15.58	16.55	Apr.	---	13.27	14.11	14.72
May	15.34	14.26	14.77	15.70	16.64	15.60	15.08	13.93	May	14.68	15.01	16.04	16.68	May	13.83	14.53	15.35	16.60	May	---	13.17	13.96	14.66
June	15.77	14.81	15.26	16.07	16.92	16.18	15.35	13.99	June	15.32	15.78	16.42	17.21	June	14.30	14.73	15.72	16.63	June	---	13.27	14.06	14.64
July	15.70	14.61	15.21	16.20	16.80	16.04	15.37	14.05	July	14.96	15.67	16.42	17.09	July	14.24	14.74	15.98	16.50	July	---	13.41	14.03	14.71
Aug.	15.06	13.71	14.48	15.70	16.32	15.22	14.88	13.90	Aug.	13.98	14.71	15.83	16.37	Aug.	13.43	14.25	15.56	16.28	Aug.	---	13.27	13.61	14.81
Sept.	14.34	12.94	13.72	15.07	15.63	14.56	14.11	13.69	Sept.	13.24	13.92	15.40	15.68	Sept.	12.64	13.51	14.73	15.57	Sept.	---	13.07	13.41	14.61
Oct.	13.54	12.12	12.97	14.34	14.73	13.88	13.19	13.08	Oct.	12.42	13.21	14.79	15.10	Oct.	11.81	12.73	13.88	14.35	Oct.	---	12.28	12.75	14.21
Nov.	13.08	11.68	12.51	13.81	14.30	13.58	12.57	12.74	Nov.	12.11	12.92	14.46	14.81	Nov.	11.24	12.10	13.15	13.79	Nov.	---	11.74	12.48	14.01
Dec.	13.02	11.83	12.44	13.66	14.14	13.55	12.48	12.60	Dec.	12.32	12.76	14.43	14.69	Dec.	11.34	12.12	12.88	13.58	Dec.	---	11.42	12.63	13.75
1983																							
Jan.	12.90	11.79	12.35	13.53	13.94	13.46	12.34	12.27	Jan.	12.29	12.74	14.24	14.56	Jan.	11.28	11.94	12.81	13.33	Jan.	---	11.24	12.55	13.02
Feb.	13.02	12.01	12.58	13.52	13.95	13.60	12.43	12.13	Feb.	12.48	13.02	14.26	14.61	Feb.	11.54	12.14	12.77	13.27	Feb.	---	11.12	12.34	12.93
Mar.	12.71	11.73	12.32	13.15	13.61	13.28	12.12	12.11	Mar.	12.19	12.67	13.94	14.33	Mar.	11.27	11.97	12.36	12.89	Mar.	---	11.14	12.27	12.92
Apr.	12.44	11.51	12.06	12.86	13.29	13.03	11.84	11.90	Apr.	12.00	12.43	13.61	14.07	Apr.	11.03	11.69	12.11	12.52	Apr.	---	11.11	12.00	12.58
May	12.30	11.46	11.95	12.68	13.09	13.00	11.59	11.62	May	12.01	12.44	13.50	14.05	May	10.91	11.46	11.86	12.12	May	---	10.91	11.68	12.28
June	12.54	11.74	12.15	12.88	13.37	13.17	11.90	11.78	June	12.23	12.64	13.64	14.16	June	11.25	11.66	12.12	12.57	June	---	11.26	11.89	12.19
July	12.73	12.15	12.39	12.99	13.39	13.28	12.18	12.07	July	12.69	12.86	13.58	14.01	July	11.61	11.93	12.41	12.76	July	---	11.69	12.04	12.48
Aug.	13.01	12.51	12.72	13.17	13.64	13.50	12.52	12.13	Aug.	13.04	13.18	13.57	14.21	Aug.	11.99	12.26	12.77	13.07	Aug.	---	11.90	12.15	12.34
Sept.	12.91	12.37	12.62	13.11	13.55	13.35	12.46	12.04	Sept.	12.85	13.04	13.42	14.10	Sept.	11.87	12.19	12.80	12.99	Sept.	---	11.86	12.06	12.22
Oct.	12.79	12.25	12.49	12.97	13.46	13.19	12.39	12.08	Oct.	12.66	12.88	13.25	13.95	Oct.	11.83	12.09	12.68	12.95	Oct.	---	11.84	12.13	12.27
Nov.	12.93	12.41	12.61	13.09	13.61	13.33	12.54	12.35	Nov.	12.82	12.97	13.38	14.12	Nov.	12.00	12.25	12.79	13.10	Nov.	---	12.14	12.36	12.54
Dec.	13.07	12.57	12.76	13.21	13.75	13.48	12.66	12.46	Dec.	13.00	13.14	13.52	14.23	Dec.	12.14	12.36	12.88	13.27	Dec.	---	12.27	12.46	12.66
1984																							
Jan.	12.92	12.20	12.71	13.13	13.65	13.40	12.63	12.41	Jan.	---	13.02	13.39	14.05	Jan.	12.08	12.39	12.85	13.24	Jan.	---	12.22	12.42	12.59
Feb.	12.88	12.08	12.70	13.11	13.59	13.50	12.60	12.28	Feb.	---	13.04	13.41	14.05	Feb.	12.08	12.37	12.81	13.13	Feb.	---	12.05	12.30	12.50
Mar.	13.33	12.57	13.22	13.54	13.99	14.03	13.00	12.54	Mar.	---	13.66	13.87	14.56	Mar.	12.57	12.78	13.21	13.42	Mar.	---	12.30	12.55	12.75
Apr.	13.59	12.81	13.48	13.77	14.31	14.30	13.25	12.81	Apr.	---	13.93	14.16	14.82	Apr.	12.81	13.02	13.38	13.78	Apr.	---	12.56	12.78	13.09
May	14.13	13.28	14.10	14.37	14.74	14.95	13.72	13.25	May	---	14.66	14.90	15.28	May	13.28	13.54	13.84	14.21	May	---	12.75	13.34	13.65
June	14.40	13.55	14.33	14.66	15.05	15.16	14.03	13.31	June	---	14.90	15.09	15.50	June	13.55	13.76	14.22	14.60	June	---	13.04	13.35	13.55
July	14.32	13.44	14.12	14.57	15.15	14.92	14.09	13.60	July	---	14.42	14.82	15.50	July	13.44	13.80	14.30	14.79	July	---	13.39	13.62	13.79
Aug.	13.78	12.87	13.47	14.13	14.63	14.29	13.61	13.82	Aug.	---	13.67	14.43	14.79	Aug.	12.87	13.26	13.82	14.48	Aug.	---	13.54	13.87	14.05
Sept.	13.56	12.66	13.27	13.94	14.35	14.04	13.42	13.68	Sept.	---	13.43	14.17	14.51	Sept.	12.66	13.12	13.70	14.19	Sept.	---	13.31	13.77	13.97
Oct.	13.33	12.63	13.11	13.61	13.94	13.68	13.10	13.44	Oct.	13.00	13.38	13.80	14.17	Oct.	12.42	12.85	13.42	13.71	Oct.	---	12.94	13.56	13.83
Nov.	12.88	12.29	12.66	13.09	13.48	13.15	12.61	13.02	Nov.	12.66	13.00	13.23	13.72	Nov.	11.92	12.32	12.94	13.24	Nov.	---	12.53	13.15	13.37
Dec.	12.74	12.13	12.50	12.92	13.40	12.96	12.51	12.69	Dec.	12.49	12.76	13.11	13.46	Dec.	11.76	12.23	12.72	13.34	Dec.	---	12.22	12.77	13.09
1985																							
Jan.	12.64	12.08	12.43	12.80	13.26	12.88	12.41	12.62	Jan.	12.47	12.68	12.99	13.36	Jan.	11.67	12.18	12.61	13.15	Jan.	---	12.15	12.72	12.98
Feb.	12.66	12.13	12.49	12.80	13.23	13.00	12.32	12.38	Feb.	12.61	12.87	13.08	13.44	Feb.	11.64	12.10	12.51	13.00	Feb.	---	12.10	12.38	12.66
Mar.	13.13	12.56	12.91	13.36	13.69	13.66	12.60	12.57	Mar.	13.08	13.50	13.87	14.19	Mar.	12.04	12.32	12.84	13.18	Mar.	---	12.17	12.56	12.97
Apr.	12.89	12.23	12.69	13.14	13.51	13.42	12.37	12.60	Apr.	12.77	13.17	13.61	14.11	Apr.	11.67	12.22	12.71	12.90	Apr.	---	12.08	12.55	13.17
May	12.47	11.72	12.30	12.70	13.15	12.89	12.04	12.39	May	12.18	12.65	13.12	13.62	May	11.26	11.95	12.28	12.68	May	---	11.94	12.32	12.92
June	11.70	10.94	11.46	11.98	12.40	11.91	11.48	11.81	June	11.17	11.68	12.13	12.66	June	10.71	11.24	11.83	12.14	June	---	11.26	11.95	12.21
July	11.69	10.97	11.42	11.92	12.43	11.88	11.49	11.63	July	11.18	11.55	12.07	12.70	July	10.74	11.29	11.77	12.17	July	---	11.05	11.81	12.03
Aug.	11.76	11.05	11.47	12.00	12.50	11.93	11.57	11.56	Aug.	11.23	11.65	12.13	12.73	Aug.	10.87	11.29	11.87	12.27	Aug.	---	11.22	11.62	11.85
Sept.	11.75	11.07	11.46	11.99	12.48	11.95	11.55	11.63	Sept.	11.27	11.68	12.13	12.72	Sept.	10.86	11.24	11.85	12.24	Sept.	---	11.23	11.61	12.05
Oct.	11.69	11.02	11.45	11.94	12.36	11.84	11.53	11.54	Oct.	11.23	11.61	12.01	12.52	Oct.	10.80	11.29	11.85	12.20	Oct.	---	11.17	11.58	11.86
Nov.	11.29	10.55	11.07	11.54	11.99	11.33	11.23	11.35	Nov.	10.71	11.10	11.49	12.04	Nov.	10.38	11.03	11.58	11.93	Nov.	---	10.95	11.39	11.70
Dec.	10.89	10.16	10.63	11.19	11.58	10.82	10.96	11.18	Dec.	10.24	10.57	10.97	11.48	Dec.	10.08	10.69	11.39	11.67	Dec.	---	10.75	11.25	11.53
1986																							
Jan.	10.75	10.05	10.46	11.04	11.44	10.66	10.83	10.86	Jan.	10.14	10.44	10.79	11.24	Jan.	9.95	10.47	11.27	11.63	Jan.	---	10.45	10.88	11.24
Feb.	10.40	9.67	10.13	10.67	11.11	10.16	10.63	10.58	Feb.	9.65	9.98	10.26	10.74	Feb.	9.68	10.27	11.07	11.48	Feb.	---	10.18	10.62	10.93
Mar.	9.79	9.00	9.49	10.15	10.49	9.33	10.24	10.05	Mar.	8.75	9.16	9.48	9.91	Mar.	9.23	9.82	10.81	11.07	Mar.	---	9.74	9.98	10.42
Apr.	9.51	8.79	9.21	9.83	10.19	9.02	9.98	9.78	Apr.	8.45	8.87	9.14	9.63	Apr.	9.13	9.55	10.51	10.74	Apr.	---	9.39	9.71	10.24
May	9.69	9.09	9.43	9.94	10.29	9.52	9.85	9.58	May	9.07	9.38	9.59	10.02	May	9.11	9.47	10.28	10.55	May	---	9.13	9.38	10.24
June	9.73	9.13	9.49	9.96	10.34	9.51	9.95	9.72	June	9.02	9.36	9.62	10.03	June	9.24	9.61	10.29	10.65	June	---	9.30	9.68	10.19
July	9.52	8.88	9.28	9.76	10.16	9.19	9.85	9.73	July	8.66	9.05	9.37	9.69	July	9.09	9.51	10.14	10.64	July	---	9.27	9.66	10.26
Aug.	9.44	8.72	9.22	9.64	10.18	9.15	9.73	9.69	Aug.	8.59	9.03	9.29	9.70	Aug.	8.85	9.41	9.97	10.66	Aug.	---	9.24	9.70	10.13
Sept.	9.55	8.89	9.36	9.73	10.20	9.42	9.68	9.57	Sept.	8.91	9.28	9.52	9.96	Sept.	8.87	9.45	9.95	10.44	Sept.	---	9.10	9.65	9.97
Oct.	9.54	8.86	9.33	9.72	10.24	9.39	9.68	9.65	Oct.	8.84	9.24	9.52	9.52	Oct.	8.88	9.24	9.52	9.95	Oct.	---	9.26	9.67	10.01
Nov.	9.37	8.68	9.20	9.51	10.07	9.15	9.58	9.56	Nov.	8.59	9.01	9.28	9.69	Nov.	8.77	9.38	9.73	10.44	Nov.	---	8.98	9.50	10.19
Dec.	9.23	8.49	9.02	9.41	9.97	8.96	9.49	9.37	Dec.	8.41	8.81	9.12	9.49	Dec.	8.57	9.23	9.70	10.45	Dec.	---	8.74	9.26	10.09
1987																							
Jan.	9.04	8.36	8.86	9.23	9.72	8.77	9.31	9.19	Jan.	8.23	8.62	8.95	9.27	Jan.	8.48	9.09	9.51	10.17	Jan.	---	8.64	9.09	9.82
Feb.	9.03	8.38	8.88	9.20	9.65	8.81	9.25	9.22	Feb.	8.29	8.69	9.00	9.24	Feb.	8.47	9.06	9.39	10.06	Feb.	---	8.63	9.08	9.95
Mar.	8.99	8.36	8.84	9.13	9.61	8.75	9.23	9.13	Mar.	8.21	8.64	8.93	9.19	Mar.	8.51	9.04	9.33	10.02	Mar.	---	8.57	9.02	9.80
Apr.	9.35	8.85	9.15	9.36	10.04	9.30	9.40	9.30	Apr.	8.83	9.15	9.38	9.85	Apr.	8.87	9.15	9.34	10.24	Apr.	---	8.76	9.07	10.06
May	9.82	9.33	9.59	9.83	10.51	9.82	9.81	9.53	May	9.34	9.63	9.91	10.40	May	9.31	9.56	9.73	10.62	May	---	8.95	9.46	10.17
June	9.87	9.32	9.65	9.98	10.52	9.87	9.87	9.56	June	9.37	9.61	10.02	10.46	June	9.26	9.69	9.93	10.58	June	---	8.75	9.74	10.19
July	9.92	9.42	9.64	10.00	10.61	10.01	9.82	9.52	July	9.56	9.70	10.15	10.62	July	9.26	9.58	9.86	10.59	July	---	8.71	9.68	10.18
Aug.	10.14	9.67	9.86	10.20	10.80	10.33	9.94	9.69	Aug.	9.92	10.05	10.45	10.90	Aug.	9.42	9.68	9.95	10.70	Aug.	---	9.04	9.80	10.23
Sept.	10.64	10.18	10.35	10.72	11.31	11.00	10.28	9.96	Sept.	10.53	10.66	11.22	11.58	Sept.	9.83	10.03	10.22	11.04	Sept.	---	9.37	10.10	10.42
Oct.	10.97	10.52	10.74	10.98	11.62	11.32	10.60	10.07	Oct.	10.92	11.11	11.34	11.91	Oct.	10.11	10.36	10.62	11.33	Oct.	---	9.64	10.03	10.55
Nov.	10.54	10.01	10.27	10.63	11.23	10.82	10.25	10.30	Nov.	10.43	10.62	10.82	11.40	Nov.	9.59	9.91	10.43	11.05	Nov.	---	10.00	10.18	10.71
Dec.	10.59	10.11	10.33	10.62	11.29	10.99	10.18	10.08	Dec.	10.64	10.78	10.98	11.55	Dec.	9.58	9.87	10.25	11.02	Dec.	---	9.58	9.94	10.71
1988																							
Jan.	10.37	9.68	10.09	10.43	11.07	10.75	9.98	10.04	Jan.	10.39	10.52	10.76	11.34	Jan.	9.37	9.65	10.09	10.79	Jan.	---	9.62	9.91	10.59
Feb.	9.89	9.40	9.60	9.94	10.62	10.11	9.67	9.85	Feb.	9.77	9.91	10.10	10.65	Feb.	9.02	9.29	9.79	10.59	Feb.	---	9.58	9.72	10.24

Notes: See Moody's Bond Survey for a brief description and the latest published list of bonds included in the averages. Because of the dearth of **Aaa**-rated railroad term bond issues, Moody's **Aaa** railroad bond yield average was discontinued as of December 18, 1967. Moody's **Aaa** public utility average suspended from Jan. 1984 thru Sept. 1984. Oct. 1984 figure for last 14 business days only.

SOURCE: *Bond Record*, Moody's, March 1988. Reprinted by permission.

the S&P 500. There are many bond indices, however, because of the many issuers and characteristics of bonds. Each index is constructed using a specific type
of bond and can be based on yield-to-maturity, prices, or *HPR*s.

1.   YIELD INDICES Some of the more common indices based on yield-to-maturity
     are Moody's Corporate Bond Yield Averages, Moody's Government Bond
     Yield Averages, and Moody's Municipal Bond Yield Averages. Different
     indices within each of these classifications are constructed to recognize
     differences in term-to-maturity and ratings. For example, Moody's has
     yield-to-maturity indices for utilities, industrials, and railroads, for rating
     classifications Baa–Aaa. Similar indices are provided by Standard & Poor's
     Corporation. Table 14.7 provides an example of Moody's indices.

2.   PRICE INDICES Several firms calculate and publish bond price indices. These
     indices are for a homogeneous sample of bonds with respect to classification,
     rating, and term-to-maturity. Examples include the Dow Jones Industrial and
     Utility Bond Averages.

3.   NEWER INDICES The indices discussed above have been criticized because of
     the sample size and accuracy of price data for individual bonds.[21] Several
     newer indices developed by Salomon Brothers and BEA Associates are gen-
     erally considered superior because of the larger sample, requirements con-
     cerning minimum dollar value, and the type of price data used for individual
     bonds. Since many bonds trade infrequently and in large blocks, it is difficult
     to construct a time series of yields or prices. These newer indices use prices
     that are often estimated by bond traders based on their knowledge of the
     market rather than actual transaction prices. These newer measures of bond
     prices and yields should aid bond investors and should be useful in financial
     research.

Annual and monthly holding period returns, *HPR*s, for long-term U.S.
government and corporate bonds and for Treasury bills are available for the
period 1926–1986.[22] These returns are widely used in financial research and
investment performance evaluations.

SUMMARY

This chapter provided the basic fundamentals of bond terminology, types of
bonds, and characteristics important to investors. A comparison of the risk-return
characteristics of bonds with stocks was also made.
    Bonds can be classified using various procedures. This chapter used risk as
the classification factor and therefore started with U.S. Treasury bills and ended

---

[21] For example, see Richard Norgaard, "Bond Indices and Optimal Portfolios," *The Financial Review*
(Fall 1978): pp. 12–21, and Richard W. McEnally and Calvin M. Boardman, "Aspects of Corporate
Bond Portfolio Diversification," *Journal of Financial Research* (Spring 1979): pp. 27–36.

[22] *Stock, Bonds, Bills and Inflation 1987 Yearbook*, (Chicago: Ibbotson Associates, 1987).

with corporate bonds. The primary differences in risk are due to higher default probabilities and term-to-maturity.

The major types of bonds discussed in the chapter are U.S. government issues, U.S. savings bonds, federal agency securities, municipals, and corporate bonds. This listing order corresponds to the risk-return trade-offs between these securities. One obvious fact is that there are hundreds of different types of fixed-income securities when differences in issuers and security characteristics are considered.

One very important feature of municipal and corporate securities is default risk and its impact on the bond's return. Traditionally, many investors have used bond ratings provided by Moody's or Standard & Poor's. Recently, more attention has been given to independent analysis of the credit risk of bonds by investors. One justification is that ratings seem to be "sticky"; bond prices often indicate major developments in a company that are not recognized until later by a rating change.

Bond markets were also discussed, including a comparison of the primary and secondary markets, along with sources of information for current prices and typical transaction costs for trading in bonds. The chapter also provided a brief discussion of bond indices and their use in following historical and current prices and yields.

This chapter provides the foundations for the following two chapters, dealing with bond valuations, portfolio considerations, and investment strategies. The three chapters should provide a clear understanding of the advantages and disadvantages of bond investing, along with the tools needed to analyze bonds and make intelligent bond investment decisions.

QUESTIONS

1. Compare and contrast the risk-return characteristics of bonds versus stocks.

2. The years 1974, 1980 and 1981–82 represent periods of recession in the United States. Using these dates along with Table 14.1, which of the four types of securities in the table seem to offer the best returns during both recessions and periods of economic growth?

3. Figure 14.1 indicates that the yield-to-maturity on corporate bonds is influenced by agency ratings. Explain what the rating indicates about the bond and how the yield-to-maturity is affected by those ratings.

4. Based on this chapter and on your general knowledge, explain what recent developments in the economy and bond markets have caused a number of bond investors to reexamine bond trading strategies. Do you think bonds are now more attractive to "speculators"? Why?

5. All stocks involve more risk than bonds. Is this a true statement? Explain.

6. Assume you are interested in analyzing a particular corporate bond as a possible investment. What information would you like to have concerning both the issuer and the particular bond? Indicate sources where this information can be found.

7. There are major differences in the federal tax laws concerning income receipts from U.S. government, municipal, and corporate bonds. Explain these differences.

8. Explain why there may be significant differences in liquidity between corporate bonds and stocks from the investor's viewpoint.

9. Would you expect corporations with very strong financial positions to offer secured bonds? Explain

10. Compare and contrast the primary and secondary bond markets.

11. Bond indices are much more numerous than stock indices. Why?

REFERENCES

Ahearn, Daniel S. "The Strategic Role of Fixed Income Securities." *The Journal of Portfolio Management*, (Spring 1975): pp. 12–16.

Asinof, Lynn. "Some Municipals Investors Get Nasty Surprises When the Bonds Are Called In Early by Issuers." *Wall Street Journal*, 16 May 1983, p. 58.

Cabanilla, Nathaniel B. "Directly-placed Bonds: A Test of Market Efficency." *Journal of Portfolio Management* (Winter 1984): pp. 72–74.

Cheney, John M. "Rating Classification and Bond Yield Volatility." *The Journal of Portfolio Management* (Spring 1983): pp. 51–57.

Clauretie, Terrence M. "Why Do GNMAs Yield More Than Treasuries?" *Journal of Portfolio Management* (Spring 1982): pp. 72–74.

"Deep Discount Bonds: Ripe for the Picking." *Financial World* (August 1979): p. 37.

Dunn, Kenneth B., and John J. McConnell. "Rate of Return Indexes for GNMA Securities." *Journal of Portfolio Mangement* (Winter 1981): pp. 65–74.

Fitzpatrick, John D., and Jacobus T. Severiens. "Hickman Revisited: The Case for Junk Bonds." *The Journal of Portfolio Management* (Summer 1978): pp. 53–57.

Fong, Gifford, Charles Pearson, and Oldrich Vasicek. "Bond Performance: Analyzing Sources of Return." *Journal of Portfolio Management* (Spring 1983): pp. 46–50.

Forsyth, Randall W. "Nuclear Meltdown, The Whoops Default and Fallout." *Barron's* 1 August, 1983, pp.11, 32.

———. "Supporting Uncle, How to Buy Treasuries in One Easy Lesson." *Barron's*, 25 June, 1984, p. 27.

Groth, John C., and Brian I. Neysmith. "Bond Ratings—A Needed Reappraisal." *Financial Executive* (Sepember 1979): pp. 20–25.

Hertzberg, Daniel. "Some Gimmicks Used to Sell Bonds Sour as Rates Fall, Inflation Slows." *Wall Street Journal*, 14 December, 1982, pp. 32, 39.

Joehnk, Michael D., and James F. Nielsen. "Return and Risk Characteristics of Speculative Grade Bonds." *Quarterly Review of Economics and Business* (Spring 1975): pp. 27–46.

Kidwell, David S., and Eric H. Sorensen. "Pricing of Municipal Bond Underwritings: It May Pay to Invest When Underwriters Don't." *Financial Analysts Journal* (March-April 1983): pp. 58–64.

Lamle, Hugh R. "Ginnie Mae: Age Equals Beauty." *Journal of Portfolio Management* (Winter 1981): pp. 75–79.

Liu, Pu, and William T. Moore. "The Impact of Split Bond Ratings on Risk Premia." *Financial Review* (February 1987): pp. 71–85.

Norgaard, Richard. "Bond Indices and Optimal Portfolios." *The Financial Review* (Fall 1978): pp. 12–21.

Peavy, John W, III. "Bond Ratings as Risk Surrogates—How Reliable Are they?" *Best's Review* (April 1980): p. 24

Peavy, John W, III. and George H. Hempel. ''The Effect of the WPPSS Crisis on the Tax-exempt Bond Market,'' *Journal of Financial Research* (Fall 1987): pp. 239–47.

Perry, Larry G. ''The Effect of Bond Rating Agencies on Bond Rating Models.'' *Journal of Financial Research* (Winter 1985): pp. 307–15.

Sharpe, W. F. ''Bonds versus Stocks—Some Lessons from Capital Market Theory.'' *Financial Analysts Journal* (November-December 1973): pp. 74–79.

Sherwood, Hugh C. *How Corporate and Municipal Debt Is Rated.* New York: John Wiley and Sons, 1976.

Slater, Karen. ''Before Selecting Municipal Bonds, Buyers Should Judge Issues' Future Marketability.'' *Wall Street Journal*, 30 January, 1984.

Smith, Randall. ''Zero-Coupon Bonds' Price Swings Jolt Investors Looking for Security.'' *Wall Street Journal*, 1 June, 1984.

Soldofsky, Robert M. ''Risk and Return for Long-term Securities: 1971–1982.'' *Journal of Portfolio Management* (Fall 1984): pp. 57–64.

Standard & Poor's Corporation. *Credit Overview: Corporate and International Ratings.*

Statman, Meir, and Neal L. Ushman. ''Bonds versus Stocks: Another Look,'' *Journal of Portfolio Management* (Winter 1987): pp. 33–38.

Treynor, Jack L. ''On the Quality of Municipal Bonds.'' *Financial Analysts Journal* (May-June 1982): pp. 25–30.

Tuttle, Donald L., ed. *The Revolution in Techniques for Managing Bond Portfolios.* Charlottesville, Va.: The Institute of Chartered Financial Analysts, 1983.

Uginas, Luis. ''Small Bond Rating Firms Are Competing Aggressively for a Bigger Share of Market.'' *Wall Street Journal*, 7 September, 1984, p. 28.

Van Horne, James C. ''Call Risk in Municipal Bonds.'' *Journal of Portfolio Management* (Winter 1987): pp. 53–57.

White, Shelby. ''Reaping the Rewards of 'Junk' Bonds.'' *Institutional Investor* (March 1976): pp. 51–52.

Yawitz, Jess B., and William J. Marshall. ''Risk and Return in the Government Bond Market.'' *The Journal of Portfolio Management* (Summer 1977): pp. 48–52.

CHAPTER 15

BOND VALUATION: RETURNS AND RISK

BOND VALUATION

Overview

Bonds, like any other financial asset, can be valued by estimating future cash flows and computing the total present value of these flows, using an appropriate discount rate. This approach is generally much easier to apply to fixed-income securities than to common stocks or other types of securities, since the bond indenture provides cash-flow information that can only be estimated by the analyst of common stocks. The indenture indicates the interest or coupon rate and the frequency of payment, along with the maturity value and maturity date, key factors in determining value. This, of course, assumes that the issuer will be able to honor all of the contractual obligations in the indenture. If the issuer defaulted on interest or principal payments, in either amount or timing, the value of the bond would be fundamentally changed.

The other variable that is needed to value a bond is the appropriate discount rate. This rate should represent the investor's required rate of return and include the risk-free rate of return plus a risk premium (see Chapter 2). The market consensus estimate of this rate can be observed at any time by examining the yield-to-maturity on a particular bond or by observing the yield-to-maturity on an appropriate bond index. This is in sharp contrast to a common stock; the investor is unable to determine the required rate of return because future cash flows are unknown and comparative required return estimates are not as readily available.

Bond valuation may initially appear to be fairly routine or mechanical, since the analyst is not forced to estimate many of the key variables that determine the value of the bond. As we will see, however, when factors such as default risk, changing market interest rates, and unexpected inflation are considered, bond analysis becomes much more challenging. In addition, if the analyst hopes to discover bonds that are currently over- or undervalued, estimates of future cash flows and the appropriate discount rate must be determined. This analysis must include a complete assessment of risk for the economy, the bond market, and the company over the analyst's investment horizon.

Basic Equation

This section presents a basic valuation equation commonly used in the analysis of bonds. For bonds with a stated coupon rate and maturity date the equation is

$$V_0 = \frac{C_1}{(1+i)^1} + \frac{C_2}{(1+i)^2} + \ldots + \frac{C_N + M_N}{(1+i)^N}$$

$$= \sum_{t=1}^{N} \frac{C_t}{(1+i)^t} + \frac{M_N}{(1+i)^N} \tag{15.1}$$

where V_0 = present value of the bond

C_t = annual dollar coupon in period t

i = rate of discount or required rate of return

N = number of time periods remaining until the bond matures

M_N = maturity value of the bond.

For purposes of calculating V_0, the analyst can use the present value of an annuity, PVIFA, and the present value of a future sum, PVIF, tables given in Appendix A1, use bond valuation tables or a financial calculator.

Equation 15.1 can be restated to facilitate computations with a calculator:

$$V_0 = C \left[\frac{1 - \frac{1}{(1 + i)^n}}{i} \right] + \frac{M_N}{(1 + i)^N} \tag{15.2}$$

Notice that the subscript t is not necessary for C, since the equation assumes that the annual coupons are constant and therefore relies on the present value of annuity procedures. For example, assume that a bond has a stated annual coupon rate of 12 percent, a term-to-maturity of 20 years, a face value of $1,000, and the discount rate is 15 percent. Using Equation 15.2, the value of the bond is

$$V_0 = .12(\$1,000) \left[\frac{1 - \frac{1}{(1.15)^{20}}}{.15} \right] + \frac{\$1,000}{(1.15)^{20}}$$

$$= \$120[6.259] + \frac{\$1,000}{16.366}$$

$$= \$751.08 + \$61.10$$

$$V_0 = \$812.18$$

Since the typical bond pays interest semiannually, Equation 15.2 can be modified to

$$V_0 = \frac{C}{2} \left[\frac{1 - \frac{1}{(1 + i/2)^{2n}}}{i/2} \right] + \frac{M_N}{(1 + i/2)^{2n}} \tag{15.3}$$

Using the example above, but assuming that the bond has a 12 percent coupon that is paid semiannually, the value is

$$V = \$120/2 \left[\frac{1 - \frac{1}{(1 + .15/2)^{40}}}{.15/2} \right] + \frac{\$1,000}{(1 + .15/2)^{40}}$$

$$= \$60[12.594] + \frac{\$1,000}{18.044}$$

$$= \$755.66 + \$55.42$$

$$V_0 = \$811.08$$

Two factors cause the values of V_0 ($812.18 versus $811.08) to differ. First, a bond paying interest semiannually is more valuable than one paying interest annually because cash flows are received earlier. Second, Equation 15.3 calculates a semiannual rate of discount as $i/2$, which in this case is $.15/2 = .075$. This semiannual rate results in an annual rate greater than .15, since $(1 + .075)^2 - 1 = .1556$. These two factors offset each other. Semiannual payment of interest increases V_0; converting the annual discount rate to a semiannual rate by dividing by two lowers V_0.[1] (You might like to convince yourself by recomputing V_0, using a semiannual rate that is equivalent to an effective annual rate of .15. This rate would be $\sqrt{1.15} - 1 = .0724$. Using this rate with Equation 15.3, the bond's value would be $839.15, which is greater than the value assuming annual coupons.)

Another factor that must often be considered when computing V_0 is that bonds are often bought or sold on dates other than the interest payment dates. The same problem for cash dividends on common stocks is handled by using ex-dividend dates, so that the dividend does not need to be divided between the seller and buyer. This practice is not used for bonds, since bonds are sold at prices that include interest accrued daily. For example, if a bond that has interest payment dates of January 1 and July 1 is sold on April 1, the seller is due the interest that has accrued on the bond over the period January through March. The buyer must pay the seller this amount since the *issuer* of the bond will pay the entire semiannual interest amount to the new owner on July 1. This problem also causes some difficulties in computing V_0.[2]

Consols, Zeros, OIDs, and LYONs

While most bonds have finite maturity periods and fixed coupon payments, some bonds have infinite lives (theoretically), and some do not pay interest. A *consol* is a bond with an infinite term-to-maturity, while a bond that does not pay interest is commonly called a *zero*. The value of a consol can be computed as:[3]

$$V_0 = \frac{C}{(1 + i)^1} + \frac{C}{(1 + i)^2} + \ldots + \frac{C}{(1 + i)^\infty} = \frac{C}{i} \qquad (15.4)$$

For example, assume annual interest of 12 percent and a face value of $1,000; the desired rate of return is 15 percent. The value is simply $(.12 \times \$1,000)/.15 = \$800$. This $800 value is the present value of an infinite stream of annual cash flows of $120, discounted at 15 percent. If the consol pays interest semiannually, appropriate adjustments must be made in the values of C and i.

For a zero, V_0 can be computed as

$$V_0 = \frac{0}{(1 + i)^1} + \frac{0}{(1 + i)^2} + \ldots + \frac{M_N}{(1 + i)^N} = \frac{M_N}{(1 + i)^N} \qquad (15.5)$$

---

[1] For a discussion and derivation of the correct procedure, see Keong Chew and Ronnie J. Clayton, "Bond Valuation: A Clarification," *Financial Review* (May 1983): pp. 234–36.

[2] These aspects are discussed in more detail in the appendix of this chapter, and an example of the appropriate calculations is given.

[3] Equation 15.4 can be derived as follows: multiplying the original Equation 15.4 by $(1 + i)$ gives $V_0(1 + i) = C + C/(1 + i) + \ldots + C/(1 + i)^{\infty - 1}$, and subtracting this equation from the original Equation 15.4 gives $V_0 (1 - i - 1) = -C + C/(1 + i)^\infty$. Since $C/(1 + i)^\infty$ is 0, $V_0 = C/i$.

where M_N is the maturity value of the bond, and N is the number of time periods remaining until maturity. For example, assume that a zero has a maturity value of \$1,000 and a term-to-maturity of 25 years. If an investor requires a 15 percent annual rate of return, then $V_0 = \$1,000/(1 + .15)^{25} = \$1,000/32.919 = \$30.38$. This value may appear to be low but, with "high" values for N and i, the present value of M_N is smaller than might be expected. This aspect has resulted in zeros often being referred to as *multipliers*, since a \$30.38 investment would "multiply" to \$1,000 in 25 years at a 15 percent return.

Another type of bond, similar to a zero, is an *original issue discount* bond or *OID*. The first OID was issued by Martin Marietta in March 1981 and was essentially a bond with a "low" coupon initially sold at a sizable discount. Traditionally, corporate bonds are issued at or near par, or face value, since the coupon rate was set at the yield-to-maturity for similar quality bonds. OIDs, however, are issued with coupons below prevailing market yields, thus requiring that they be sold at a discount. A zero is actually a special case of an OID.[4] The Tax Equity and Fiscal Responsibility Act, TEFRA, of 1982 eliminated the favorable tax treatment of zeros and OIDs, for bonds issued after July 1, 1982.

Another unique type of zero is a *liquid yield option note*, or *LYON*, first issued in 1985. This bond has a zero coupon, but is also convertible, callable, and puttable. The *put* feature allows the investor to sell the bond to the issuer at a predetermined price. The convertible and puttable features increase the value of the bond, but the callable feature lowers its value. The combined influence of these factors makes valuation of LYONs difficult.[5]

Table 15.1 provides a sample of zeros, OIDs, and LYONs, and a consol. With the exception of the consol, all of the bonds were issued after 1981. Table 15.2 gives the characteristics of the LYON issued by Merrill Lynch. Notice that the prices specified for the put feature increase each year until 2005, when the put price is approximately equal to the maturity value of \$1,000.

Investment Decision Making

The basic concepts and valuation equations discussed earlier in the chapter provide the foundation for investment decisions concerning bonds. For a passive or buy-and-hold investor, the decision is straightforward. The investor may be quite willing to assume that the current market price of a bond, P_0, is a good indication of the investment value of the bond, which is essentially V_0, so that $P_0 = V_0$. This type of investor is not concerned with finding over- or undervalued bonds and essentially is willing to accept the general market consensus of the bond's value as indicated by P_0. If the issuer pays interest and principal according to the indenture provisions and the bond is held to maturity, the annual rate of return to the investor would be i, the yield-to-maturity prevailing on the date the bond is purchased.

---

[4] For a discussion and analysis of OIDs, see Andrew J. Kalotay, "An Analysis of Original Issue Discount Bonds," *Financial Management* (Autumn 1984): pp. 29–38, and Marcelle Arak, "Profit Opportunities with Old OIDs," *Journal of Portfolio Management* (Spring 1985): pp. 63–66.

[5] For the development of the valuation methodology and examples, see John J. McConnell and Eduardo S. Schwartz, "LYON Taming," *Journal of Finance* (July 1986): pp. 561–77.

TABLE 15.1 EXAMPLES OF ZEROS, OIDS, LYONS, AND A CONSOL

	DATE ISSUED	COUPON RATE	MATURITY DATE	INITIAL PRICE*	INITIAL YIELD	AMOUNT OUTSTANDING (MILLION $)	PRICE	CALL PRICE	YIELD-TO-MATURITY
1. ZEROS:									
a. McDonald's	08/20/82	–	1994	25.00%	12.60%	$ 31.30	$61\frac{3}{8}$	100.0	8.65%
b. Chase Man. Bank	04/29/82	–	1992	22.29	14.25	83.70	$69\frac{1}{2}$	100.0	9.12
c. Citicorp	01/06/84	–	1990	50.00	11.50	50.00	–	N/C	–
d. Ford Motor Credit	08/17/82	–	1992	25.00	15.00	59.60	$71\frac{5}{8}$	100.0	8.49
e. J. C. Penney	03/30/82	–	1992	25.00	13.50	150.00	$66\frac{3}{8}$	100.0	8.99
2. OIDS:									
a. Martin Marietta	03/10/81	7.00%	2011	53.83	13.25	96.15	$67\frac{3}{4}$	100.0	10.81
b. Orion Pictures	01/27/84	10.00	1994	77.67	14.25	39.40	$87\frac{1}{2}$	100.0	13.13
c. Owens-Illinois	05/21/87	15.00	2003	42.58	14.75	400.00	50	114.8	–
d. Philip Morris	11/17/81	6.00	1999	47.39	14.13	47.40	$76\frac{3}{8}$	100.0	9.38
e. Transamerica	03/19/81	6.50	2011	48.07	13.80	98.40	$71\frac{3}{4}$	100.0	9.55
3. LYONS:									
a. Merrill Lynch	08/15/85	–	2006	20.00	–	222.80	24	107.2	–
b. Nat'l Medical E.	01/31/86	–	2004	25.00	–	800.00	$29\frac{1}{2}$	106.0	–
c. Seagram (Jos. E.)	08/23/85	–	2006	20.00	–	500.00	$26\frac{7}{8}$	106.4	–
d. Staley Continental	05/01/85	–	2001	24.12	–	110.00	37	106.3	–
e. Waste Management	04/22/85	–	2001	25.00	–	200.00	61	107.2	–
4. CONSOL:									
a. Canadian Pacific	12/01/21	4.00	–	–	–	185.00	–	–	–

* Price is expressed as a percentage of par value.
SOURCE: *Bond Record*, Moody's, April 1988, and *Bond Guide*, Standard & Poor's, April 1988. Reprinted by permissions.

TABLE 15.2 CHARACTERISTICS OF LIQUID YIELD OPTION NOTE (LYON) ISSUED BY MERRILL LYNCH & CO., INC.

Denominations:	$1,000 and $5,000				
Callable Feature:	Callable on or after August 15, 1987, at the following prices:				
	1987	108.00%	1992	104.00%	
	1988	107.20	1993	102.40	
	1989	106.40	1994	101.60	
	1990	105.60	1995	100.80	
	1991	104.80	1996 and after	100.00	
Put Feature:	The investor (holder) can sell the LYON to Merrill Lynch on August 15, 1988, and each August thereafter, at the following prices:				
	1988	$238.81	1994	$405.16	2000	$648.68
	1989	259.32	1995	438.22	2001	701.61
	1990	286.24	1996	473.98	2002	758.86
	1991	320.21	1997	512.66	2003	820.79
	1992	346.34	1998	554.49	2004	887.76
	1993	374.60	1999	599.74	2005	960.20
Convertible Feature:	Convertible at any time into 5.31 shares of common stock.				

SOURCE: *Bank and Finance Manual*, vol. 2, Moody's, 1986. Reprinted by permission.

For individuals attempting to pursue a more active strategy, the possibility exists that $P_0 \lessgtr V_0$. In these instances, the bond would be overvalued, $P_0 > V_0$, or undervalued, $P_0 < V_0$, providing the investor with an opportunity to earn risk-adjusted excess returns. To pursue this strategy, the investor must compute V_0 using estimates of an appropriate discount rate, i, and, for a risky bond with default probabilities, estimate the amount and timing of future cash flows. By using these individual estimates of the key variables that determine V_0, the investor may discover that the current value of the bond is different from the market's assessment, so that $V_0 \neq P_0$. Of course, if the investor is correct and the market is incorrect, and the price changes in the direction anticipated by the investor, excess returns will result.

BOND RETURN MEASURES

Overview

This section discusses various rate of return measures for fixed-income securities and is closely related to the previous section on bond valuation. The previous section essentially assumed that the desired rate of return is given and used this rate to compute value. This section assumes that the price or investment value of the bond is given and uses this value to compute a rate of return.

The final part of this section provides an illustration of each return measure for an actual corporate bond and illustrates how each measure may be interpreted and used by an analyst.

Current Yield

A bond return measure that is popular with investors and is provided on a daily basis in the *Wall Street Journal* is the *current* or *coupon* yield. As its name implies, this yield is based entirely on the relationship between the coupon rate and the current price:

$$i_c = \frac{C}{P_0} \tag{15.6}$$

where: i_c = current or coupon yield
C = annual dollar coupon
P_0 = current market price

This return measure is only a partial indication of the return. First, the price of the bond will move toward face value as the bond approaches maturity, so that the actual return, i, would be more or less than i_c, depending on whether the bond is purchased at a discount or premium price. Second, the price is likely to change over the holding period because of changes in market conditions. For investors who do not plan to hold the bond to maturity, the capital gains and losses resulting from price changes are ignored in calculating i_c. It is also easy to show that a bond currently selling at its face value will have a yield-to-maturity equal to the coupon rate, so that i_c is equal to the yield-to-maturity i. At any other price, however, $i_c \lessgtr i$.

The popularity of the current yield as a return measure can be explained by its ease of calculation and interpretation. Also, it can be useful to individuals most concerned about evaluating bonds in terms of the current returns they are providing. It should be stressed, however, that i_c is an indication of only one part of the return a bond is likely to provide. For this reason, it should be used sparingly and for the specific reason noted above.

Yield-to-Maturity

The yield-to-maturity of a bond represents the annual rate of return that will occur if certain conditions are satisfied. In computing the yield-to-maturity, several important assumptions are made:

1. The bond will be held to maturity.
2. All cash flows (interest and principal) will occur as indicated in the indenture (i.e., the issuer will not default on its contractual obligation).
3. The bond will not be called or redeemed by the issuer before the specified maturity date.
4. Coupon receipts will be reinvested at a rate of return equal to the yield-to-maturity.

Yield-to-maturity can be computed using Equations 15.2, 15.3, 15.4, or 15.5, depending on the characteristics of the bond. These equations all require that V_0

be equated with the current market price of the bond, P_0. By letting $V_0 = P_0$, the investor is able to determine what yield-to-maturity is implied by the current market price.

Unfortunately, the calculation for finding the yield-to-maturity can be quite time-consuming for bonds with a finite life and annual or semiannual coupon payments. This results because Equations 15.2 and 15.3, when solved for the yield-to-maturity, are higher-order polynomials. Second-degree polynomials can be solved with the quadratic equation or a factoring procedure. The equation for bonds with a 20-year maturity is a 20- or 40-degree polynomial, depending on the frequency of interest payments. Assuming the availability of a calculator, the best solution procedure is trial-and-error.

To illustrate, using the simplified case of a zero, assume the current price is $100, term-to-maturity is 25 years, and maturity value is $1,000. Using Equation 15.5, the calculations are

$$V_0 = \frac{M_N}{(1 + i)^n}$$

$$\$100 = \frac{\$1,000}{(1 + i)^{25}}$$

$$(1 + i)^{25} = \frac{1,000}{100}$$

$$1 + i = \sqrt[25]{10}$$

$$1 + i = 1.0965$$

$$i = 9.65\%$$

Thus, if this zero is purchased for $100 and held to maturity, and the issuer pays $1,000 at maturity, the yield-to-maturity is 9.65 percent, compounded annually.

An example of a more difficult calculation, which cannot be solved explicitly using algebra, is provided by a bond with a finite life and semiannual coupon payments. A trial-and-error procedure (with, possibly, the need for linear interpolation) is required. Consider a corporate bond with a face value of $1,000, a term-to-maturity of 25 years, a coupon rate of 12 percent paid semiannually, and a current market price of $750 on an interest payment date. Also assume that the first "trial" in the solution procedure uses $i = .15/2 = .075$. Using Equation 15.3, the equation becomes

$$\$750 = \$60 \left[\frac{1 - \dfrac{1}{(1.075)^{50}}}{.075} \right] + \frac{\$1,000}{(1 + .075)^{50}}$$

$$\$750 = \$60(12.975) + \$1,000/37.190$$

$$\$750 = \$778.50 + \$26.89$$

$$\$750 \neq \$805.39$$

The above calculation indicates that 15 percent is *not* the yield-to-maturity and also indicates that the yield-to-maturity is greater than 15 percent. This results because the calculation shows that a price of $805.39 would provide a yield-to-maturity of exactly 15 percent, and since the bond is priced at $750, the yield-to-maturity is greater than 15 percent. For the next trial, try $i = .16/2 = .08$, which results in the following relationship:

$$\$750 = \$734.01 + \$21.32$$

$$\$750 \neq \$755.33.$$

This relationship indicates that the yield-to-maturity is slightly greater than 16 percent, so the third trial could assume $i = .162/2 = .081$. Performing the necessary calculation results in

$$\$750 = \$725.66 + \$20.36$$

$$\$750 \neq \$746.02.$$

The results of the second and third trials indicate that $.16 < i < .162$. The trial-and-error procedure has "bracketed" the correct i. Using linear interpolation, the following relationship can be specified:

$$.16 = \$755.33$$

$$i = \$750.00$$

$$.162 = 746.02.$$

Creating appropriate proportions results in a single equation that can be solved for i:

$$\frac{.16 - i}{.162 - .16} = \frac{\$755.33 - \$750.00}{\$746.02 - \$755.33}$$

$$-1.490 + 9.31i = .011$$

$$i = 16.12\%$$

This bond is therefore currently priced to provide a yield-to-maturity of 16.12 percent.

Due to the time required to solve for i using trial-and-error procedures, many financial calculators are preprogrammed to compute these values. Also, bond tables are available that indicate i for various combinations of price, coupon, and maturity. Due to the many possible combinations, bond tables are quite bulky and often resemble a large dictionary.

Approximate Yield-to-Maturity

Since calculating the yield-to-maturity can be time-consuming, an approximation technique can be useful. The *approximate yield-to-maturity*, i_A, provides an estimate of the yield-to-maturity. Also, the approximate yield can be used as the value for i in the first trial for finding the true yield-to-maturity.

The approximate yield-to-maturity can be calculated as

$$i_A = \frac{C + \dfrac{M_N - P_0}{N}}{\dfrac{P_0 + M_N}{2}} \tag{15.7}$$

where
$\quad i_A$ = approximate yield-to-maturity
$\quad\ C$ = annual dollar coupon
$\quad M_N$ = maturity value of the bond
$\quad\ P_0$ = current market price of the bond
$\quad\ N$ = number of time periods remaining until the bond matures

An examination of Equation 15.7 indicates that i_A is simply the average annual cash flow consisting of the coupon plus the amortization of discount or premium, divided by the "average" investment in the bond. It is, therefore, an average return that ignores the implications of present-value calculations.

Using the same bond information from the above yield-to-maturity calculation, the approximate yield-to-maturity can be calculated as

$$i_A = \frac{\$120 + \dfrac{\$1000 - \$750}{25}}{\dfrac{\$750 + \$1000}{2}} = \frac{\$120 + \$10}{\$875} = \frac{\$130}{\$875} = 14.86\%$$

Notice that there is a considerable difference in i and i_A (16.12% versus 14.86%).

Yield-To-Maturity for Callable Bonds

Most bonds issued recently have a call feature that allows the issuer to redeem the bonds prior to maturity. Thus, the issuer can take advantage of lower yields by calling outstanding bonds and refinancing at lower rates. This possibility presents a problem in calculating the yield-to-maturity, since yield-to-maturity is based on the full term of the bond.

To reflect the impact of a possible call on the yield, the "yield-to-first-call" should be calculated in addition to the yield-to-maturity. Equation 15.3 can simply be modified as

$$V_0 = \frac{C}{2}\left[\frac{1 - \dfrac{1}{(1 + i_{call}/2)^{2T}}}{i_{call}/2}\right] + \frac{\text{call price}}{(1 + i_{call}/2)^{2T}} \tag{15.8}$$

Where the previous definitions given for Equation 15.3 apply and

$\quad i_{call}$ = yield-to-first-call

$\quad\ T$ = length of time to first call date, in years

$\quad$ call price = price that issuer will pay at first call date

TABLE 15.3 EXAMPLE OF CALCULATING YIELD-TO-FIRST-CALL

Characteristics of bond and current market information:

Face value	$1,000
Coupon rate (paid semiannually)	12%
Term-to-maturity	5 years
Term-to-first-call-date	3 years
Current price	$900
Yield-to-maturity	14.91% (calculated using 15.3)
First call price	$1,100

Yield-to-first-call:

$$\$900 = \$60 \left[\frac{1 - \dfrac{1}{(1 + i_{call}/2)^6}}{i_{call}/2} \right] + \frac{\$1100}{(1 + i_{call}/2)^6}$$

Solve by trial and error, with the first iteration using $i_{call} = .19$ or $i_{call}/2 = .095$, gives

$$\$900 \neq \$903.33$$

Therefore, $i_{call} > .19$, so the second iteration should use a slightly higher value for i_{call}. Using .192 gives

$$\$900 \neq \$899.05$$

By interpolation, $i_{call} = 19.15\%$.

As with the yield-to-maturity, the equation must be solved using trial-and-error procedures. Table 15.3 provides an illustraton of this calculation. In addition, the approximate yield-to-maturity calculation given in Equation 15.7 can be modified by replacing the maturity value with the call price and by replacing N with the time until the first call.

The importance of yield-to-call versus yield-to-maturity depends on the probability that the bond will be called. The probability of a call increases during periods of declining yields, especially when the yield-to-maturity declines below the coupon yield. The relationship between the market and call prices is also considered by the issuer in analyzing the feasibility of a call. An approach to analyzing the implications of a call for returns is presented later in the chapter.

Holding Period Return

Investors are often concerned about bond returns over a particular holding period. If the holding period was in the past, the return is a historical, or ex-post, measure. The investor concerned with a future holding period calculates the return that is expected, or ex-ante. One of the major problems with yield-to-maturity is that it requires an assumption about the length of the holding period. The yield-to-maturity assumes that the bond will be held until maturity, and the current yield ignores the term of the bond.

Recently, attention has moved from the traditional measures of bond returns to the *holding period return*, or *HPR*. This is consistent with the idea that more-active bond investment strategies may be desirable. These strategies may be for relatively short periods of time, as opposed to a long-term, buy-and-hold strategy.

For example, a bond may be purchased and sold in a one-month period. The *HPR* represents an appropriate measure of the return for this type of strategy.

For bonds with coupons, the *HPR* can be calculated as

$$P_{t+1} + I_{t+1} = P_t(1 + HPR_t)$$

$$\frac{P_{t+1} + I_{t+1}}{P_t} = 1 + HPR_t$$

$$HPR_t = \frac{P_{t+1} - P_t + I_{t+1}}{P_t} \tag{15.9}$$

where HPR_t = holding period return for period t

P_t = the beginning or purchase price of the bond

P_{t+1} = the ending or selling price of the bond

I_{t+1} = the coupon or interest received for period t

Notice that this equation assumes that interest will be received at the end of holding period t. This assumption is likely to be correct for bonds, since they are sold with accrued interest due to the seller. This point is discussed in more detail in the appendix to this chapter.

To illustrate Equation 15.9, assume that a bond is purchased on January 1 for $800 and sold on July 1 for $850. The bond pays a 12 percent coupon semiannually on January 1 and July 1. The ex-post *HPR* is

$$\begin{aligned}
HPR_t &= \frac{\$850 - \$800 + \dfrac{.12(\$1,000)}{2}}{800} \\[2ex]
&= \frac{\$50}{\$800} + \frac{\$60}{\$800} \\[1ex]
&= .0625 + .075 \\
&= 13.75\%
\end{aligned}$$

Notice that the price appreciation represents a return of 6.25 percent, while the interest income represents a 7.50 percent return. It should also be recognized that the length of the holding period is 6 months, so the *HPR* is a semiannual return. Since it is common to state returns on an annual basis, the semiannual return can be *annualized* as $(1 + .1375)^2 - 1 = .2939$, or 29.39 percent. This approach assumes semiannual *compounding* and therefore produces a higher annualized return than would result if compounding is ignored [or $(2)(.1375) = .275 = 27.5$ percent]. If the holding period for the above example was 5 months, the annualized *HPR* would be $(1 + .1375)^{12/5} - 1 = .3623$, or 36.23 percent.

Variations in Equation 15.9 may be needed if the holding period is longer and/or the pattern of cash flows is different. For example, assume that the above bond is bought on January 1 for $800 and sold on January 1 of the following year for $850. The length of the holding period is now 1 year; but, since the bond pays interest semiannually, the *HPR* calculation must be modified:

$$P_{t+1} + I_{t+1/2} + I_{t+1} = P_t(1 + HPR)$$

$$P_t = \frac{I_{t+1/2}}{(1 + HPR)^{1/2}} + \frac{I_{t+1}}{(1 + HPR)^t} + \frac{P_{t+1}}{(1 + HPR)^t}$$

$$\$800 = \frac{\$60}{(1 + HPR)^{1/2}} + \frac{\$60}{(1 + HPR)^1} + \frac{\$850}{(1 + HPR)^1}$$

It should be recognized that this problem can be solved like a yield-to-maturity problem, using trial-and-error procedures. Using trial-and-error and interpolation, one must find the value of *HPR* that will make the right-hand side equal to $800. Since time is defined as 1 year, the *HPR* will be an annual rate and does not need to be annualized. Following this procedure, you should be able to show that annual *HPR* = .2204, or 22.04 percent. This *HPR* can also be converted to a *HPR* assuming semiannual compounding: $(1 + .2204/2)^2 - 1 = .2325$, or 23.25 percent.

As was pointed out earlier, the *HPR* can be used to compute ex-ante or expected returns. This would require the analyst to estimate future interest income and selling price. The following section develops the idea of an expected rate of return for a bond.

Expected Rate of Return

In analyzing bonds for investment, the analyst must consider the *expected rate of return* that each bond can provide. For default-free bonds like U.S. Treasury securities that are held to maturity, the analyst might feel comfortable in equating the yield-to-maturity of the bond to the expected rate of return. If a bond has default probabilities and will not be held to maturity, and yields in general may change over the holding period, a more detailed analysis is needed.

Table 15.4 provides an outline and example of an approach that can be used to analyze the influence of default risk on the expected rate of return. The purpose of the analysis is to calculate the expected *HPR*, or *E(HPR)*. The top section shows the basic characteristics of the bond, along with the current price and the resulting current yield and yield-to-maturity. The analyst also assumes that the bond will be held for one year and, as a result, estimates the economic environment for the coming year. For each of these states of nature, a probability, coupon, and end-of-year price for the bond must be estimated. If a recession occurs, the company will experience severe financial problems and will be unable to pay the coupon. As a result, the bond will be traded "flat," or without interest, so that the price is expected to take a dramatic drop.

A *HPR* can be computed for each state of nature, using Equation 15.9, and the *E(HPR)* can be calculated as illustrated at the bottom of Table 15.4. The *E(HPR)* of 7.86% should be compared to the yield-to-maturity of 14.99% and the current yield of 14.67%. This comparison is useful in illustrating why the yield-to-maturity or current yield should not be used as an indicator of the expected return for a bond with default probabilities that will not be held to maturity. For investment decision making, it is much more appropriate to think in terms of *E(HPR)* than in terms of the yield-to-maturity or current yield. Finally, it should be pointed out that the approach outlined in Table 15.4 can be expanded or devel-

TABLE 15.4 CALCULATING THE EXPECTED RATE OF RETURN ON A RISKY
CORPORATE BOND

Characteristics of bond and current market information:

Face value:	$1,000
Coupon rate (paid annually):	11%
Term-to-maturity:	20 years
Rating by Moody's:	B
Current price:	$750

Current yield: $\dfrac{(.11)(1,000)}{750} = 14.67\%$

Yield-to-maturity: 14.99% (calculated using 15.3)

Estimate by analyst for coming year:

STATE OF NATURE	PROBABILITY	COUPON	PRICE END-OF-YEAR
1. Recession	.1	$ 0	$400
2. No-growth economy	.5	$110	$700
3. Moderate-growth economy	.4	$110	$800

Calculations:

STATE OF NATURE	HOLDING PERIOD RETURN
1. Recession	$\dfrac{400 - 750 + 0}{750} = -.4667$
2. No growth	$\dfrac{700 - 750 + 110}{750} = .0800$
3. Moderate growth	$\dfrac{800 - 750 + 110}{750} = .2133$

$$\text{Expected } HPR = E(HPR) = \sum_{i=1}^{n} (\text{Probability})_i \times (HPR)_i$$

$$= .1(-.4667) + .5(.08) + .4(.2133)$$

$$= -.0467 + .04 + .0853$$

$$= 7.86\%$$

oped in much greater detail. Additional states of nature—holding periods longer than one year and other factors, such as the probability of a call—can be incorporated into this approach.

An Illustration and Comparison of Return Measures

Table 15.5 provides the characteristics, prices, coupon yields, yields-to-maturity, and *HPR*s for a debenture issued by AT&T. Notice that the coupon rate is below the yields-to-maturity because the bond is selling at a discount. The monthly *HPR*s are calculated using Equation 15.9 and recognizing that the monthly interest is $5.83. ($70/12). The variability and magnitude of the *HPR*s indicate that the realized or ex-post returns may be quite different from the coupon or yield-to-maturity for short holding periods. The volatility in the monthly prices also indicates that forecasting the ex-ante, or *E*(*HPR*), is a challenging problem. This example is further analyzed after bond risk analysis is presented below.

TABLE 15.5 RATE OF RETURN MEASURES FOR DEBENTURE ISSUED BY AMERICAN TELEPHONE AND TELEGRAPH

I. Characteristics of Debenture

Coupon rate:	7.00%
Maturity value:	$1,000
Maturity date:	February 15, 2001
Interest payment dates:	February and August 15th
Amount outstanding:	$500 million
Traded on NYSE	

Call Prices (percent of maturity value):	1988	102.25%	1991	101.50%	1994	100.75%
	1989	102.00	1992	101.25	1995	100.50
	1990	101.75	1993	101.00	1996	100.25

II. Prices and Return Measures

	END-OF-MONTH PRICE	COUPON YIELD	YIELD-TO-MATURITY	MONTHLY HPR
1987 March	90	7.78%	8.21%	–
April	$88\frac{1}{4}$	7.93	8.45	−1.30%
May	$82\frac{3}{8}$	8.50	9.29	−6.00
June	$81\frac{1}{8}$	8.63	9.48	−0.81
July	$82\frac{5}{8}$	8.47	9.27	2.56
August	$80\frac{1}{4}$	8.72	9.64	−2.17
September	79	8.86	9.84	−0.83
October	75	9.33	10.52	−4.33
November	$78\frac{1}{2}$	8.92	9.95	5.44
December	$79\frac{5}{8}$	8.79	9.78	2.17
1988 January	$81\frac{1}{8}$	8.63	9.55	2.61
February	$84\frac{3}{4}$	8.26	9.00	5.18
March	$87\frac{1}{4}$	8.02	8.65	3.63
April	$83\frac{7}{8}$	8.35	9.15	−3.20

SOURCE of prices and yields-to-maturity: *Bond Record*, Moody's. Reprinted by permission.
SOURCE of characteristics: *Public Utility Manual*, vol. 1, Moody's, 1987. Reprinted by permission.

In this example, the bond is unlikely to be called in the immediate future because the coupon rate is below the yield-to-maturity. The call price of $102.25 for 1988 is also substantially above the April 1988 price of $83\frac{7}{8}$. If the analyst anticipates a longer holding period, however, the yield-to-call should be calculated.

BOND RISK ANALYSIS

Overview

Bond valuation depends on the expected return and risk associated with the bond. The previous two sections presented some basic concepts of bond valuation and return measures. This section discusses some of the unique risk factors associated with bonds. It also looks at both traditional and at more-recent approaches to bond risk analysis that attempt to measure bond risk empirically. The section concludes with an illustration and comparison of risk measures.

Systematic Sources of Bond Risk

One basic source of bond risk is interest rate changes that occur after a bond is purchased and the resulting impact on bond prices and reinvestment rates of return. Unanticipated inflation and its impact on fixed-income securities through loss in purchasing power is another important source of risk. These factors basically represent systematic or nondiversifiable risk for bonds, since they generally have an impact on all bonds. Each of the three types of systematic risk (yield changes, reinvestment risk, and purchasing power risk) are discussed below.

1. PRICE CHANGES RESULTING FROM CHANGES IN YIELDS Since the majority of bonds have fixed coupon and maturity values, any change in market interest rates will result in changes in bond prices. This results because coupon income will not increase if market interest rates increase, nor will the maturity value change. Therefore, for investors to receive the higher market rates on bonds currently outstanding, bond prices must decline. Conversely, if market interest rates decline, bond prices will increase.

    Changes in market interest rates or yields cause all bond prices to change. The amount of change, however, depends on the characteristics of the bond. These relationships were formally specified by B. G. Malkiel in 1961[6] and are referred to as theorems about bond price changes:

    1. Prices and yields move inversely.

    2. For a given change in yield, bonds with longer terms-to-maturity have greater percentage price changes, but these changes diminish as the term increases. For example, if bonds with terms of five, ten, and fifteen years are considered, the relative price changes of the ten-year bond and the five-year bond will be greater than those between the ten- and fifteen-year bonds.

    3. For a given change in yield, bonds with lower coupons have greater (percentage) price changes.

    4. For a given price and equal increases or decreases in yields, the percentage increase in price resulting from a yield decline will be larger than the percentage decrease in price from an increase in yield.

    As shown in Table 15.6 these theorems can be illustrated using the basic bond valuation Equations 15.1 and 15.2.

2. REINVESTMENT RATE RISK Since the majority of bonds provide periodic income to the investor through coupon payments, a potential reinvestment problem can arise. This results because of uncertainty about the rates of return that will be available when the coupons and principal are to be reinvested. As previously discussed, the yield-to-maturity implicitly assumes that coupons are reinvested at the yield-to-maturity that existed at the time the bond was purchased. Investors using other return measures such as the expected holding period return, $E(HPR)$, and attempting to determine an appropriate holding period also must deal with reinvestment risk. For example,

---

[6] Burton G. Malkiel, "Expectations, Bond Prices, and the Term Structures of Interest Rates," *Quarterly Journal of Economics* (May 1961): pp. 197–218.

TABLE 15.6 ILLUSTRATIONS OF BOND PRICE THEOREMS

1. Theorem 1: Face value = $1,000, coupon = $90 paid annually, term = 10 years, current price = $900, yield-to-maturity = 10.67 percent. Assume that the general market yields on similar bonds increased to 12 percent from the current rate of 10.67 percent. The bond's price would decline to

$$V_0 = \$90 \left[\frac{1 - \dfrac{1}{(1.12)^{10}}}{.12} \right] + \frac{\$1,000}{(1.12)^{10}} = \$508.52 + \$321.97 = \$830.49$$

2. Theorem 2: Consider the following three bonds:

	A	B	C
Annual coupon:	$90	$90	$90
Face value:	$1,000	$1,000	$1,000
Moody's rating:	Aa	Aa	Aa
Term-to-maturity:	5 years	10 years	15 years
Yield-to-maturity:	9%	10%	11%
Current price:	$1,000	$938.55	$856.18

Suppose yields decrease by 10 percent for each bond to

Yield-to-maturity:	8.1%	9%	9.9%

The new prices and resulting percentage price changes are

New price:	$1,035.84	$1,000.00	$931.15
Price change:	3.58%	6.55%	8.76%

Therefore, bonds with longer terms-to-maturity have greater price changes. In addition, the differences in the price changes are 2.97 percent (6.55% − 3.58%) between the ten- and five-year bonds and 2.21 percent (8.76% − 6.55%) between the fifteen- and ten-year bonds. Therefore, the rate of price change decreases as the term increases.

3. Theorems 3 and 4: Consider the following two bonds:

	A	B
Annual coupon:	$60	$100
Face value:	$1,000	$1,000
Moody's rating:	Aa	Aa
Term-to-maturity:	10 years	10 years
Yield-to-maturity:	12%	12%
Current price:	$660.98	$886.99

Suppose yields *increase* to 13 percent. The new prices and resulting percentage price changes are

New price:	$620.16	$837.21
Price change:	−6.18%	−5.61%

Therefore, bonds with lower coupons have greater percentage price changes. Suppose that yields *decrease* from the original level of 12 percent to 11 percent. The new prices and resulting percentage price changes are

New price:	$705.52	$941.95
Price change:	6.74%	6.20%

For an increase and decrease of 1 percentage point from an original yield of 12 percent, the percentage increase in price is greater than the percentage decrease for both bonds, illustrating theorem 4.

should a "low" or "high" coupon bond be purchased, and should the hold-ing period be "long" or "short"? If yields are expected to increase, and thereby provide higher reinvestment rates, the higher coupon bond may be preferred (Theorem 3). In addition, a shorter maturity may be better since the principal can be received earlier and reinvested at a higher rate.

To illustrate the reinvestment rate problem and the impact of the coupon and term, consider an investor who is deciding between an 8 percent coupon bond with a two-year term (Bond A) and a 12 percent coupon bond with a four-year term (Bond B). Both bonds are rated Aa by Moody's and pay in-terest annually. First, assume a constant yield-to-maturity over the two-year holding period. As Part I of Table 15.7 illustrates, if the investor purchases Bond A, the total value of the cash flows will be $1,168.80 at the end of year 2. This value is calculated by assuming the first coupon is received after one year and reinvested for one year at 11 percent, resulting in a terminal value at the end of year 2 of $88.80. The second coupon is received at the end of the second year, and since the holding period is assumed to be two years, the terminal value is simply $80. The last cash flow for Bond A is the maturity value of $1,000 which will be received at the end of year 2. The annualized *HPR* of 11 percent is identical to the original yield-to-maturity. For Bond B, the calculations assume that the bond is sold for its market va-lue at the end of year 2. Since the yield-to-maturity is equal to the coupon rate and both are constant, the bond's price will not change. Its annualized *HPR* is also equal to the yield-to-maturity, or 12 percent. Comparing the re-sults and assuming that yields do in fact remain constant, the investor would undoubtedly select Bond B based on its higher *HPR*.

Part II or Table 15.7 assumes that cash flows must be reinvested at the rate of 8 percent, which lowers the annualized *HPR* on Bond A to 10.89 percent. It should also be pointed out that the investor would not benefit from an increase in the price of Bond A due to the decline in yield, since it is held to maturity. For Bond B, the decline in reinvestment income is more than offset by the price appreciation that results because the yield-to-maturity declined to 8 percent. The annualized *HPR* of 14.93 percent for Bond B is considerably higher than the yield-to-maturity of 12 percent. Again the results favor Bond B.

Reconstructing the example by assuming that cash flows are reinvested at *higher* rates, however, would make Bond A more attractive; Bond B would experience a price decline that would offset the higher reinvestment income. This is illustrated in Part III of Table 15.7.

If the assumed holding period of two years is increased, and again as-suming that reinvestment rates increase, Bond A would be more attractive since the maturity value of $1,000 could be reinvested after two years. If re-investment rates *decrease*, however, Bond B would provide a higher *HPR*.

This example illustrates why bond investors should be concerned about reinvestment rate risk for both coupons and maturity values. The general conclusions that can be drawn from the discussion and examples in Table 15.7:

a.   If reinvestment rates of return are not equal to the yield-to-maturity, then the *HPR* will not equal the yield-to-maturity.

TABLE 15.7   ILLUSTRATIONS OF REINVESTMENT RATE RISK

I. *HPRs* if coupons are reinvested at the yield-to-maturity (yield-to-maturity remains constant):

	BOND A	BOND B
Current yield-to-maturity:	11%	12%
Current price:	$948.62	$1,000
Assume a two-year holding period:		
Values of cash flows at end of year 2:		
Coupon for year 1:	80(1.11) = $88.80	120(1.12) = $134.40
Coupon for year 2:	80(1.0) = $80.00	120(1.0) = $120.00
Maturity value:	$1,000.00	–
Price at end of year 2:	–	$1,000.00
Total value at end of year 2:	$1,168.80	$1,254.40

Annualized *HPR*:

Bond A: $1,168.80 = $948.62(1 + r)^2$

$\qquad$ $1.2321 = (1 + r)^2$

$\qquad$ $1 + r = \sqrt{1.2321}$

$\qquad$ $r = 11\%$

Bond B: $1,254.40 = $1,000(1 + r)^2$

$\qquad$ $1.2544 = (1 + r)^2$

$\qquad$ $1 + r = \sqrt{1.2544}$

$\qquad$ $r = 12\%$

II. *HPRs* if coupons are reinvested at a rate *lower* than the current yield-to-maturity:

	BOND A	BOND B
Assumed reinvestment rate:	8%	8%
Total value of cash flows		
end of year 2:	$1,166.40	$1,320.93
Annualized *HPR*:	10.89%	14.93%

III. *HPRs* if coupons are reinvested at a rate *higher* than the current yield-to-maturity:

	BOND A	BOND B
Assumed reinvestment rate:	14%	14%
Total value of cash flows at		
end of year 2:	$1,171.20	$1,223.86
Annualized *HPR*:	11.11%	10.63%

---

b.   If the term and the desired holding period of a bond are equal (Bond A), the HPR and yield-to-maturity will still not be equal if yields change.

c.   Anticipated higher reinvestment rates make high-coupon and short-term bonds more attractive.

d.   If yields decline, resulting in lower reinvestment rates, lower-coupon and long-term bonds will experience larger price increases, which may offset the lower reinvestment income.

One of the major reasons why newer bonds such as zeros were readily accepted by investors is their ability to eliminate reinvestment rate risk. Since no coupons are received, the investor can simply purchase a zero with a term equal to the desired holding period. The disadvantage, however, is that rates may increase over the holding period, and the investor will not benefit from higher reinvestment income. Other factors that should be considered in the decision to purchase a zero or a coupon bond include tax considerations, call features, default risk, and the risk attitude of the investor.[7]

3.   PURCHASING POWER RISK   Investors should always be concerned about after-tax returns rather than before-tax returns. This should also be true for *real* versus *nominal* rates of return. Real rates of return are adjusted for the impact of inflation and the resulting decline in purchasing power. Fixed-income securities are especially susceptible to purchasing power risk when inflation is unanticipated. For example, suppose bonds of a certain classification are priced to provide a nominal rate of return of r_n, which includes a real return, r_r, and inflation premium, I_p.[8]

$$r_n = r_r + I_p \tag{15.10}$$

If r_n is observed to be 12 percent and the desired real return is 5 percent, then the inflation premium would be 7 percent. If inflation is actually 7 percent, then the realized or ex-post value of r_r will be 5 percent. If, however, the rate of inflation is more or less than 7 percent, the real return will not be 5 percent.

A long-running debate, dating back to a 1930 study by Irving Fisher, concerns the ability of the market to correctly anticipate inflation and price financial assets to provide an inflation hedge. If the market can collectively anticipate inflation and incorporate this estimate into prices, then financial assets should provide an adequate inflation hedge, so that $r_r \geq 0$. If $r_r < 0$, individuals would not have an incentive to reduce their level of current consumption and save part of their income. Recent evidence for both fixed-income securities and common stocks, however, suggests that neither provides an effective inflation hedge during periods of "high" inflation.[9] This has naturally led to the suggestion that bonds are poor investments during inflationary periods.[10]

Before discussing this point further, the procedures for adjusting nominal returns for inflation, or calculating real rates of return, should be considered. Assume that inflation will be measured by the Consumer Price Index, CPI, and, for convenience, that the value of this index is now 100. Also assume that you would like to earn a real rate of return of 8 percent on a $1,000 investment for one year and that you anticipate inflation will be 7 percent

---

[7] A framework for this analysis is provided in James M. Johnson, "When Are Zero Coupon Bonds the Better Buy?" *Journal of Portfolio Management* (Spring 1984): pp. 36–41.

[8] This general relationship, often referred to as the Fisher effect, is discussed in some detail in Irving Fisher, *The Theory of Interest*, (New York: Macmillan, 1930).

[9] See, for example, Russell J. Fuller and Glenn H. Petry, "Inflation, Return on Equity and Stock Prices," *The Journal of Portfolio Management* (Summer 1981): pp. 19–25.

[10] J. Parker Hall III, "Shouldn't You Own Fewer Long-term Bonds?" *Financial Analysts Journal* (May-June 1981): pp. 45–48.

for the year (i.e., the CPI will increase to 107). What nominal rate of return must an investment provide? At first glance, you may think that the correct rate is 15 percent, as indicated by Equation 15.10. This rate, however, would *not* protect both your principal and income from the impact of inflation.

To illustrate, assume that you invest $1,000 today at 15 percent and receive $1,000(1.15) = $1,150 at the end of the year. Adjusting this value for the decline in purchasing power results in $1,150/1.07 = $1,074.77, providing a real rate of return of only ($1,074.77 − $1,000)/$1,000 = 7.48%.

This 7.48 percent is less than the desired real rate of return, 8 percent. The problem, of course, is that both income and principal are not protected against inflation. The correct procedure:

$$P_{t+1} = P_t(1 + r_r)(1 + I_p) \qquad (15.11)$$
$$= P_t(1 + r_r + I_p + r_r I_p)$$
$$= \$1,000[1 + .08 + .07 + (.08)(.07)]$$
$$= \$1,000[1 + .1556]$$
$$= \$1,155.60$$

Thus, you must receive $1,155.60 at the end of the year, which would be a nominal holding period return of 15.56 percent. This would provide a real rate of return of

$$r_r = \frac{\dfrac{P_{t+1} + I_{t+1}}{(1 + I_p)} - P_t}{P_t} \qquad (15.12)$$
$$= [\$1,155.60/1.07 - \$1,000]/\$1,000$$
$$= \frac{\$1,080 - \$1,000}{\$1,000}$$
$$r_r = 8.0\%$$

Notice that both principal and income ($1,000 and $155.60) are protected against the loss in purchasing power. Equation 15.12 provides a procedure for calculating the real rate of return. It can be compared with Equation 15.9, which computes the nominal holding period return, *HPR*.

As mentioned earlier, there is debate about the market's ability to provide inflation hedges. One of the most comprehensive studies of nominal and real rates of return on various types of financial assets over a long period is by Ibbotson and Sinquefield.[11] Table 15.8 is prepared from data in their studies; this information suggests that bonds, as well as stocks, often provide very low and even negative real rates of return.[12]

---

[11] Their studies are presented in articles and books, and deal not only with ex-post returns but also future or ex-ante returns. Their first two articles are cited as references at the end of this chapter.

[12] For an empirical study of Treasury bills, see W. Bradford Cornell, "Inflation Measurement, Inflation Risk, and the Pricing of Treasury Bills," *Journal of Financial Research* (Fall 1986): pp. 193–202. For a study of bonds, see Albert Eddy and Bruce Seifert, "Inflation, the Fisher Hypothesis, and Long-term Bonds," *Financial Review* (February 1985): pp. 21–35.

TABLE 15.8   REAL RATES OF RETURN ON FINANCIAL ASSETS* AND RATE OF INFLATION

YEAR	TREASURY BILLS	LONG-TERM U.S. TREASURY BONDS	LONG-TERM CORPORATE BONDS	COMMON STOCKS	RATE OF INFLATION (CPI)
1975	−1.1%	2.1%	7.1%	28.2%	7.0%
1976	0.3	11.5	13.2	18.1	4.8
1977	−1.6	−7.0	−4.8	−13.1	6.8
1978	−1.7	−9.4	−8.4	−2.2	9.0
1979	−2.6	−12.8	−15.5	4.5	13.3
1980	−1.1	−14.6	−13.5	17.8	12.4
1981	5.3	−6.5	−9.1	−12.7	8.9
1982	6.4	35.0	38.4	16.8	3.9
1983	4.8	−3.0	0.9	18.0	3.8
1984	5.6	11.0	11.9	2.2	4.0
1985	3.8	26.2	26.1	27.4	3.8
1986	5.0	23.1	18.5	17.2	1.1
Arithmetic Mean:	1.93%	4.63%	5.40%	10.18%	6.57%
Geometric Mean:	1.87%	3.48%	4.21%	9.30%	6.50%
Standard Deviation:	3.48%	16.54%	16.82%	14.18%	3.73%
Coeff. of Var.:**	1.80	3.57	3.11	1.39	0.57

* Calculated using nominal holding period returns, *HPR*, and rate of inflation, *I*, as real rate of return = $[(1 + HPR)/(1 + I)] - 1$.

** Calculated as standard deviation/arithmetic mean.

SOURCE: (nominal returns and rate of inflation):   Ibbotson, Roger G., and Rex A. Sinquefield, *Stocks, Bonds, Bills, and Inflation (SBBI)*, 1982, updated in *SBBI 1987 Yearbook*, Ibbotson Associates, Chicago.

Unsystematic Sources of Bond Risk

Interest rate changes and unanticipated inflation are major sources of systematic risk to bondholders. General economic conditions and specific developments in money and capital markets are responsible for these sources of risk. In addition, however, company and possibly industry developments must be considered when analyzing total risk. These factors can generally be classified as unsystematic or diversifiable risk because they do not influence the bond markets in general. The major source of unsystematic or diversifiable risk for bonds is the *risk of default*.

Unique company factors are important to a bond investor only if they are expected to have a major impact on the company meeting the obligations detailed in the indenture. Essentially, the investor must assess the probability that the company will default on the indenture contract. For bonds that are generally viewed as default-free, such as U.S. Treasury securities, the probability of default is nil. Uninsured municipal and corporate debt always have the danger of default, so the probability of default is greater than zero.

Historically, many investors have been willing to leave this risk assessment to Moody's and Standard & Poor's, and have used their bond ratings as a proxy for default risk. Recently, however, other firms have entered the rating business and provide investors with additional ratings.[13]

The basic validity of bond ratings can be illustrated by noting that yield-to-maturity is closely correlated with rating. High-rated bonds always have a lower yield-to-maturity than lower-rated bonds with similar indenture characteristics.

A number of studies have been somewhat critical of bond ratings.[14] This criticism generally points to a lack of flexibility: an issuer may develop serious financial problems that are recognized by the market before the rating is changed, and ratings in general are not rapidly adjusted for changing conditions. These criticisms have led to suggestions that in-house analyses should be performed, especially by large institutional investors, as supplements to or replacements for the assigned ratings.

The market's general dependence on ratings can be demonstrated by studies showing that bond yields and prices adjust to rating changes.[15] The question of which comes first remains: Do prices and yields adjust prior to the rating change, or do the analysts who assign ratings recognize the change in the firm's condition and change the rating before the market discovers the change? Some evidence suggests that the price changes occur from seven to eighteen months *prior* to the rating change, and little if any price change occurs six months prior to, and after, the announced rating change.[16] This, of course, indicates that the market is performing its own credit analysis and does not rely heavily on the assigned rating. Thus, there may be some fundamental flaws in a bond strategy that relies entirely on agency ratings rather than performing an independent analysis. There is also evidence, however, that rating changes can be predicted using a statistical model. To the extent that the model could forecast rating changes prior to the market reaction, a successful investment strategy could be developed.[17]

The bond ratings assigned by the rating agencies are based on a financial analysis of the issuer and depend on the skills and judgment of the analysts. Studies have developed statistical models that are quite successful in predicting a bond's rating, based on a fairly small number of financial variables.[18] Generally, these models correctly predicted two-thirds or more of the ratings. The models, of course, did not use any subjective, or judgmental, factors. These models have identified the following variables as determinants of bond ratings:

1. leverage as measured by the balance sheet;
2. interest and fixed charge coverage;

---

[13] Luis Uginas, "Small Bond Rating Firms are Competing Aggressively for a Bigger Share of Market," *Wall Street Journal*, 7 Sep. 1984, p. 28.

[14] For example, see John C. Groth and Brian I. Neysmith, "Bond Ratings: A Needed Reappraisal," *Financial Executive* (September 1979): pp. 20–25, and John W. Peavy III, "Bond Ratings as Risk Surrogates: How Reliable Are They?" *Best's Review* (April 1980): p. 24.

[15] As an example, see Steven Katz, "The Price Adjustment Process of Bonds to Rating Reclassification: A Test of Bond Market Efficiency," *Journal of Finance* (May 1974): pp. 551–59.

[16] Mark I. Weinstein, "The Effect of a Rating Change Announcement on Bond Price," *Journal of Financial Economics* (December 1977): pp. 329–50.

[17] Lloyd McAdams, "How to Anticipate Utility Bond Rating Changes," *Journal of Portfolio Management* (Fall 1980): pp. 56–60.

[18] For a discussion and comparison of the models, see Louis H. Ederington, "Classification Models and Bond Ratings," *The Financial Review* (November 1985): pp. 237–62.

3. profitability;
4. ratio of cash flow to long-term debt;
5. firm size; and
6. subordination status.

In summary, bond ratings are important as measures of default risk. Ratings do contain additional information above and beyond the information available in accounting variables.[19] Studies also indicate, however, that investors should depend on their own evaluations of creditworthiness.

Empirical Measures of Bond Risk

Traditional bond risk measures include rating, coupon, and term. As discussed previously, rating indicates default risk, while coupon and term indicate price volatility and reinvestment rate risk. Since risk is often equated with the variability of price and the resulting *HPR*s, low-coupon and long-term bonds will have larger price changes than high-coupon and short-term bonds.

1. TOTAL RISK A measure of the total risk of a bond is the variance or standard deviation of the various return measures such as coupon yield, yield-to-maturity, or *HPR*. The variance can be ex-post or ex-ante depending on whether historical or forecast returns are used. This measure of risk includes all variability in returns and as a consequence, includes both systematic and unsystematic risk.

   As an illustration, consider the analysis presented earlier in Table 15.4, showing an *E(HPR)* of 7.86 percent. The ex-ante variance and standard deviation associated with this estimate can be calculated as

$$\sigma^2_{HPR} = \sum_{i=1}^{n} (\text{probability})_i [(HPR)_i - E(HPR)]^2 \tag{15.13}$$

where σ^2_{HPR} = variance of holding period return

i = states of nature, $i = 1 \ldots n$

HPR_i = estimated holding period return for state of nature i

$E(HPR)$ = expected holding period return.

The calculation is

$$\sigma^2_{HPR} = .1(-.4667 - .0786)^2 + .5(.08 - .0786)^2 + .4(.2133 - .0786)^2$$
$$= .1(.2974) + .5(.000002) + .4(.0181)$$
$$= .0297 + .000001 + .0072$$
$$= .0369$$
$$\sigma_{HPR} = 19.21\%$$

---

[19] Louis H. Ederington, Jess B. Yawitz, and Brian E. Roberts, "The Informational Content of Bond Ratings," *Journal of Financial Research* (Fall 1987): pp. 211–26.

This value indicates that considerable total risk exists for this bond, primarily because of a possible recession and the resulting low *HPR* for this state of nature.

Recent bond research has focused on other empirical risk measures that indicate the systematic risk of an individual bond or portfolio of bonds. *Duration*, a concept which was developed in the 1930s, has received considerable recent attention as a risk measurement and management tool to *immunize* a bond portfolio against interest rate risk.[20] It has been shown that duration is a superior measure of price or systematic risk for bonds.[21] Capital market theory and the concept of beta have also been extended to fixed-income securities. Each of these two "new" systematic risk measures, duration and beta, are discussed below.

2. DURATION Duration was originally viewed as a measure of the "life" or "average" term of a bond that would be more useful to the analyst than the term of the bond. Since most bonds pay coupons, the investor receives income prior to the maturity date. This presents problems when bonds with different terms and coupons are compared since their income streams will be quite different. *Duration* is defined as the weighted average number of years that cash flows occur. Cash flows include both coupon and principal payments. The weights are the present value of each cash flow as a percentage of the total present value of all cash flows. These weights are applied to the time period of the cash flow so that a weighted average time period or duration is computed. The resulting measure of duration, like the term of the bond, is expressed in units of time (e.g., 5.2 years). Duration can be defined and calculated as

$$D = \frac{\sum_{t=1}^{N} \dfrac{tC_t}{(1 + i)^t} + \dfrac{NM_N}{(1 + i)^N}}{\sum_{t=1}^{N} \dfrac{C_t}{(1 + i)^t} + \dfrac{M_N}{(1 + i)^N}} \tag{15.14}$$

where D = duration in time units

   t = time period when cash flow is received, $t = 1 \ldots N$

   N = term of the bond or number of time periods remaining until maturity

   C_t = dollar coupon in period t

   i = yield-to-maturity

   M_N = maturity value of the bond.

An examination of Equation 15.14 reveals that the denominator is simply the present value or price of the bond, as previously defined in Equation 15.1. The numerator appears to be very similar to the denominator,

---

[20] Frederick R. Macaulay, *The Movement of Interest Rates, Bonds, Yields, and Stock Prices in the United States Since 1865* (New York: Columbia University Press, 1938).

[21] Michael H. Hopewell and George G. Kaufman, "Bond Price Volatility and Term to Maturity: A Generalized Respecification," *American Economic Review* (September 1973): pp. 749–53.

but notice that t is multiplied by C_t for $t = 1 \ldots N$ and that M_N is multiplied by N. Table 15.9 illustrates how duration can be calculated using this equation and a table format.

Notice that the fourth column in Table 15.9 provides the present value of each cash flow and the sum of these present values. This value of $828.39 is the denominator in Equation 15.14 and represents the current price of the bond. The fifth column indicates the proportion of each cash flow, in present value terms, to the total present value. The first coupon represents 9.53 percent of the total present value of the cash flows, while the last flow of $1,090 represents 68.35 percent. Also, notice that the duration of 4.16 years is less than the term of 5 years. The duration for coupon-paying bonds will always be less than the term. For zeros, or bonds that do not pay a coupon, the duration and term are equal.

Equation 15.14, as illustrated in Table 15.9, vividly shows how tedious duration calculations can be. This problem is magnified for bonds with long terms because the present value of each coupon must be calculated. Because

TABLE 15.9 EXAMPLE OF DURATION CALCULATION

Assume that a bond provides a yield-to-maturity of 14 percent, has a face value of $1,000, pays a 9 percent coupon annually, and has five years remaining until maturity.

I. Table Format for Calculating Duration:

TIME IN YEARS (1)	CASH FLOW (2)	PRESENT VALUE FACTOR USING YIELD-TO-MATURITY OF 14% (3)	PRESENT VALUE OF CASH FLOW (4)	PERCENTAGE OF PRESENT VALUE OF EACH CASH FLOW TO TOTAL (5)
1	90	.8772	$78.95	.0953
2	90	.7695	69.25	.0836
3	90	.6750	60.75	.0733
4	90	.5921	53.29	.0643
5	1090	.5194	566.15	.6835
			$828.39	1.0000

"WEIGHTS" OR PRESENT VALUES
MULTIPLIED BY TIME PERIOD [(1) × (5)]

.0953
.1672
.2199
.2572
3.4175

Duration = 4.1571 years

II. Using Equation 15.14 directly, the calculation would be

$$D = \frac{\dfrac{1(\$90)}{(1+.14)^1} + \dfrac{2(\$90)}{(1+.14)^2} + \dfrac{3(\$90)}{(1+.14)^3} + \dfrac{4(\$90)}{(1+.14)^4} + \dfrac{5(\$1090)}{(1+.14)^5}}{\dfrac{\$90}{(1+.14)^1} + \dfrac{\$90}{(1+.14)^2} + \dfrac{\$90}{(1+.14)^3} + \dfrac{\$90}{(1+.14)^4} + \dfrac{\$1090}{(1+.14)^5}}$$

$$D = \frac{\$3,443.60}{\$828.39} = 4.157 \text{ years}$$

of the tedious calculations, duration tables have been developed, and simplified equations have been derived.[22]

The following equation presents an efficient method to calculate durations, provided that a calculator with an exponential key, Y^x, is available or that compound-value tables are available, FVIF:

$$D = \frac{C\left[\dfrac{(1 + i)^{N+1} - (1 + i) - iN}{i^2(1 + i)^N}\right] + \dfrac{M_N N}{(1 + i)^N}}{C\left[\dfrac{1 - \dfrac{1}{(1 + i)^N}}{i}\right] + \left[\dfrac{M_N}{(1 + i)^N}\right]} \tag{15.15}$$

The terms in the equation are the same as those defined for Equation 15.14. The example in Table 15.9 can be used to illustrate Equation 15.15:

$$D = \frac{90\left[\dfrac{(1 + .14)^6 - (1 + .14) - (.14)(5)}{(.14)^2(1 + .14)^5}\right] + \dfrac{(1000)(5)}{(1 + .14)^5}}{90\left[\dfrac{1 - \dfrac{1}{(1 + .14)^5}}{.14}\right] + \dfrac{1000}{(1 + .14)^5}}$$

$$D = \frac{90\left[\dfrac{2.1950 - 1.14 - .70}{(.0196)(1.9254)}\right] + \dfrac{5000}{1.9254}}{90\left[\dfrac{1 - \dfrac{1}{(1.9254)}}{.14}\right] + \dfrac{1000}{1.9254}}$$

$$D = \frac{90\,[9.4164] + 2596.86}{90\,[3.4331] + 519.37}$$

$$= \frac{847.48 + 2596.86}{828.39}$$

$$= 4.158 \text{ years}$$

Another very important observation about duration is that it is a function of term, coupon, maturity value, and yield-to-maturity. Duration is directly related to term and inversely related to coupon and yield-to-maturity. Bonds with "low" coupons and "long" terms will have durations greater than bonds with "high" coupons and "short" terms. Also, as yield-to-maturity increases, duration will decrease. Based on this information and the bond theorems presented earlier, it is important to realize that duration is *directly* related to price volatility, since bonds with a longer duration will have more price volatility as interest rates change.[23] Therefore, bond investors would find it very helpful

---

[22] For example, see Jess H. Chua, "A Closed-form Formula for Calcuating Bond Duration," *Financial Analysts Journal* (May-June 1984): pp. 76–78, and Gary A. Benesh and Stephen E. Celec, "A Simplified Approach for Calculating Bond Duration," *Financial Review* (November 1984): pp. 394–96.

[23] For a discussion and analysis, see Russell J. Fuller and John W. Settle, "Determinants of Duration and Bond Volatility," *Journal of Portfolio Management* (Summer 1984): pp. 66–72.

to know the duration of bonds. For example, if interest rates are expected to decline and the investor is interested in capital gains, bonds with longer durations should be purchased.

The approximate relationship between duration and bond price changes is

$$\Delta P_j = \frac{-D_j}{(1 + i_j)} \left(\frac{\Delta \text{ basis points}}{100} \right) \tag{15.16}$$

where
$$\Delta P_j = \text{percentage change in price of bond } j$$
$$D_j = \text{duration of bond } j$$
$$i_j = \text{yield-to-maturity of bond } j$$
$$\Delta \text{ basis points} = \text{change in yield-to-maturity of bond } j \text{ expressed in basis points, where } 1\% = 100 \text{ basis points}$$

Equation 15.16 indicates that duration and price volatility are directly related. Thus, bonds with long duration have more price risk than short-duration bonds. Equation 15.16 can be illustrated using the previous example of a bond with a duration of 4.16 years that is currently priced at $828.39. Suppose the yield-to-maturity declines from 14.0 percent to 12.0 percent, a decrease of 200 basis points. The price of the bond would increase 7.30 percent to $888.86:

$$\Delta P_j = \frac{-4.16}{1.14} \left(\frac{-200}{100} \right) = 7.30\%$$

$$\$828.39 \ (1 + .0730) = \$888.86$$

As mentioned earlier, duration is an indication of systematic risk for bonds. It is also useful in analyzing and managing the risk of bond portfolios. These points are discussed in detail in Chapter 16.

3. BOND BETA A second measure of the systematic risk of a bond is beta. As is the case for common stocks, beta is defined as

$$\beta_j = \frac{Cov(r_j, \ r_m)}{\sigma_m^2} = \frac{\sigma_j \sigma_m \rho_{j,m}}{\sigma_m^2} \tag{15.17}$$

where
$$\beta_j = \text{beta for bond } j$$
$$Cov(r_j, \ r_m) = \text{covariance between returns of bond } j \text{ and the market}$$
$$\sigma_m^2 = \text{variance of market returns}$$
$$\sigma_j = \text{standard deviation of bond } j \text{ returns}$$
$$\sigma_m = \text{standard deviation of market returns}$$
$$\rho_{j,m} = \text{correlation coefficient between returns of bond } j \text{ and market returns}$$

Several problems have been encountered in trying to apply the concept of beta to fixed-income securities. The most important of these are

a. What is an appropriate market index?

TABLE 15.10   COMPARISON OF BOND RISK MEASURES

NUMBER OF BONDS IN SAMPLE	MOODY's RATING	AVERAGE COUPON	AVERAGE TERM (YEARS)	AVERAGE DURATION (YEARS)	AVERAGE YIELD-TO-MATURITY	AVERAGE σ OF YIELD-TO-MATURITY	AVERAGE BETAS BASED ON	
							HPR	YIELD-TO-MATURITY
12	Aaa	5.38%	18.17	13.0	7.97%	.61%	.807	.744
32	Aa	5.36	17.38	12.9	8.14	.70	.805	.793
74	A	5.67	16.32	12.2	8.63	.84	.795	.896
32	Baa	5.97	17.00	11.8	9.23	.97	.782	.953
12	Ba	6.24	14.50	10.4	10.47	1.23	.905	1.140
10	B	6.68	17.50	10.1	12.51	1.85	1.460	2.133
172		5.75%	16.71	12.1	8.68%	.91%	.926	.890

SOURCE: Richard M. Duvall and John M. Cheney, "Bond Beta and Default Risk," *Journal of Financial Research* (Fall 1984): pp. 243–54.

b.   How should returns be measured for individual bonds and for the index?

c.   The term of the bond declines each period, so it is a "wasting asset." Thus, there is a potential problem of instability in betas over time that is not present with stocks with a theoretically infinite life. This causes the covariance between the bond and market to be unstable.

In terms of an appropriate index, some researchers have used an all-equity index such as the S&P 500, an all-bond index, or some combination of the two. Generally, however, the best empirical results have been obtained through the use of a bond index. Some researchers have suggested the use of *HPR* as the appropriate measure of return, since this is commonly done for equities. Another possibility, however, is to use yield-to-maturity. Finally, no adequate solution can be found dealing with the declining term other than to point out that this is a potential disadvantage of bond betas. The same problem exists with duration, however, since duration declines as the bond approaches maturity. Thus, neither systematic risk measure for an individual bond is stable.

A study by Duvall and Cheney provided comparisons of traditional risk measures (rating, coupon, and term) with the newer risk measures of standard deviation, duration, and beta.[24] A summary of these risk measures is presented in Table 15.10. The study was based on a random sample of 172 corporate bonds over the 1973–1976 period. All of the bonds are long-term and are rated Aaa to B. Notice the pattern of duration relative to yield-to-maturity, coupon, and term. In terms of the total variability of yield-to-maturity, as measured by σ, the lower-rated bonds are considerably more volatile. The last two columns provide betas estimated by using an all-debt index constructed from the entire sample of 172 bonds. The first column of betas is calculated based on *HPR*s as the return measure, while the second column uses yield-to-maturity. The beta values are similar for rating categories Aaa–A, but major differences occur for categories Baa–B.

The Duvall and Cheney study concluded that bond betas calculated using *HPR*s were closely related to duration as a measure of systematic risk. As

---

[24] Richard M. Duvall and John M. Cheney, "Bond Beta and Default Risk," *Journal of Financial Research* (Fall 1984): pp. 243–54.

TABLE 15.11   RISK MEASURES FOR DEBENTURE ISSUED BY AMERICAN TELEPHONE & TELEGRAPH*

I. Price Ranges:

	1982	1983	1984	1985	1986	1987	1988
High	$71\frac{3}{8}$	$72\frac{1}{2}$	$65\frac{5}{8}$	$77\frac{7}{8}$	90	$91\frac{3}{4}$	$87\frac{1}{4}$
Low	$51\frac{1}{8}$	$61\frac{1}{8}$	$53\frac{3}{4}$	$61\frac{7}{8}$	$74\frac{1}{4}$	$71\frac{1}{2}$	$80\frac{1}{2}$

II. Total Risk or Standard Deviation:

Standard deviation of monthly prices = 4.12%

Standard deviation of yield-to-maturity = .62%

Standard deviation of monthly *HPR*s = 3.66%

III. Systematic Risk:

Duration in April 1988   = 8.24 years

Beta based on yield-to-maturity = 1.11

IV. Unsystematic Risk:

Moody's Rating = A1

---

* Risk measures calculated using data in Table 15.5.

SOURCE, price ranges: *Bond Record* and *Public Utility Manual*, Vol. 1, Moody's, 1987. Reprinted by permission.

expected, both duration and beta were a function of coupon, term, and yield-to-maturity. Betas based on yield-to-maturity also provided an indication of reinvestment risk. This study also concluded that there was a weak inverse relationship between ratings and both duration and beta since lower-quality bonds have shorter durations and smaller betas than higher-quality bonds. This suggests that measures of systematic and unsystematic risk must be considered when analyzing individual bonds.

4.   COMPARISON OF DURATION AND BETA Both duration and beta are measures of systematic risk for bonds. There are some other similarities between the two risk measures. First, both beta and duration are inherently nonstationary and decrease over time as the bond approaches maturity. Second, bonds with shorter durations also have lower betas. Third, bond returns are not linear with respect to duration or beta. This nonlinear relationship argues against using a CAPM framework for relating risk and return. Finally, there is evidence that duration cannot explain bond returns any better than a traditional risk measure such as term-to-maturity.[25]

An Illustration and Comparison of Risk Measures

Table 15.11 provides risk measures for the AT&T debenture that was used to illustrate return measures earlier in this chapter. Table 15.11 provides price ranges for the years 1982–1987 and for the first three months of 1988. Over the entire period,

---

[25] These issues are discussed in Ali Jahankhani and George Pinches, "Duration and the Non-stationarity of Systematic Risk for Bonds," *Journal of Financial Research* (Summer 1982): pp. 151–60, and G. O. Bierwag, George G. Kaufman, Cynthia M. Latta, and Gordon S. Roberts, "The Usefulness of Duration: Response to Critics," *Journal of Portfolio Management* (Winter 1987): pp. 48–52.

the debenture sold for a minimum price of $51\frac{1}{8}$ and a maximum price of $91\frac{3}{4}$. This overall range provides another indication of the volatility of bond prices in the 1980s.

Measures of total risk given in Table 15.11 include the standard deviation of monthly prices, yields-to-maturity, and *HPR*s using data in Table 15.5. As expected, the standard deviation of yield-to-maturity is relatively small compared to the variability in prices and *HPR*s.

Systematic risk measures for the debenture include duration and beta. The debenture has a term of approximately 12.8 years from April 1988 and a duration of 8.24 years. Thus, using Equation 15.16, a decline in yield-to-maturity of 1 percentage point (i.e., 9.15 percent to 8.15 percent) will result in a 7.55 percent increase in the price of the debenture. This debenture, therefore, because of its relatively long duration, has considerable price risk.

The beta is calculated using Moody's yield-to-maturity index for corporate bonds and represents a measure of the reinvestment rate risk. The beta of 1.11 indicates that the AT&T debenture has above-average reinvestment rate risk because its yield-to-maturity relative to other corporate bonds is more volatile.

Finally, the unsystematic risk of the debentures is indicated by Moody's rating of A1. This relatively high rating indicates that the debenture does not have significant default risk.

Which risk measure is best? The answer depends on how the risk measure will be used but generally speaking, one measure is not adequate. It appears that duration is a superior measure of price volatility, while a beta based on yield-to-maturity volatility indicates the reinvestment rate risk of the bond. Since neither of these two measures seems to measure default risk adequately, the investor should also consider the agency rating or some independently determined measure of the issuer's creditworthiness.

Portfolio considerations are also important in an analysis of risk measures for individual bonds. Chapter 16 addresses these issues and indicates how risk measures developed in this chapter can be used to manage a bond portfolio.

SUMMARY AND CONCLUSIONS

The primary purpose of this chapter has been to provide an overview of bond valuation and to present several bond return and risk measures. As is the case with most traditional security valuation techniques, bond valuation depends on the length, timing, and appropriately discounted future cash flows.

Bond return measures include both ex-post, or historical, measures and ex-ante, or expected, returns. These measures allow a bond investor to compute realized rates of return from previous investments and also attempt to forecast the returns on investments that are being considered.

The simplest return measure to calculate is the current or coupon yield, since it is defined as the coupon divided by the bond's current price. The most widely used return measure is the yield-to-maturity. This return measure considers both coupon income and the movement of the price to maturity value over the term of the bond. The yield-to-maturity has drawbacks, however, since the calculation implicitly assumes that the bond will be held to maturity and that coupon income will be reinvested at a rate equal to the yield-to-maturity. Also, the yield-to-maturity does not consider the riskiness of the coupon and principal payments if the bond has default risk. If the bond has a call feature and the investor expects that yields in general may fall during the holding period, the yield-to-call should be used instead of the yield-to-maturity.

Another important return measure is the holding period return, *HPR*, which can be defined as either an ex-post or an ex-ante measure. The *HPR* defines the return on the bond over the actual or anticipated holding period. This return measure is better suited for active bond investors who may not hold a bond to maturity and who may also be interested in an analysis that attempts to discover under- or overvalued bonds.

Risk analysis is also important for bond investors. Risk can be divided into two parts: unsystematic and systematic. Unsystematic risk is dependent on unique factors that may influence the bond issuer. Severe financial problems that may lead to default and bankruptcy are a major source of unsystematic risk. Price changes for bonds, due to changes in the general level of yields, unanticipated inflation, and fluctuating yields over the holding period are major sources of systematic risk.

The analysis and measurement of bond risk has undergone significant changes. The most significant of these changes deals with empirical measures of risk like variance, duration, and beta. Duration was developed in the 1930s but received only minor attention until the early 1970s. Since that time, numerous articles have considered the value of duration in bond analysis and portfolio management. More recently, articles have developed and discussed the concept of beta for fixed-income securities. Thus, investors now have several new tools of risk analysis that can be more useful than the traditional measures of coupon and term.

The following chapter, building on the foundations of this chapter, discusses bond strategies that consider various return and risk measures. For example: Can duration be used to select an appropriate bond portfolio and to manage its performance? Bond portfolio risk management is also discussed.

QUESTIONS

1. Compare and contrast bond and stock valuation methods.
2. Bond valuation is mechanical. Discuss.
3. Explain how two bonds can have different coupon rates and yet provide identical yields-to-maturity.
4. Explain how bond valuation is influenced by the frequency of coupon payments.
5. Briefly compare and contrast a "zero," "OID," "LYON," and "consol." Under what circumstances would these types of bonds be desirable investments?
6. Should the yield-to-maturity on a corporate bond be interpreted as the return an investor expects to receive, even if the bond is held to maturity? Explain.
7. Discuss the implicit assumptions of the yield-to-maturity calculation.
8. Will the yield-to-call always be greater than the yield-to-maturity if the bond is called? How, generally, will these two return measures be related for a single bond?
9. Discuss the advantages and disadvantages of using the current or coupon yield on a bond as a return measure.

10. Is the holding period return an ex-post or an ex-ante return measure? Explain.

11. Explain what conditions are necessary to show that the annualized *HPR* of a bond is equal to its yield-to-maturity.

12. Discuss the relationships between coupon, term, and duration. Can two bonds with different coupons and terms have the same duration? Explain.

13. What are the advantages and disadvantages of using an agency rating as a measure of default risk?

14. Do bonds with "low" coupons have "high" interest rate risk and "low" reinvestment rate risk? Explain.

15. In general terms, how would you expect duration to be related to bond beta? Why may it be a good idea to use both risk measures?

16. Assume that a bond has the following risk values:

Beta based on HPR:	1.3
Beta based on yield-to-maturity:	2.1
Duration:	11.4 years
Rating:	Baa

Explain what each measure indicates about the riskiness of the bond. Also, indicate how an investor can use each measure in an analysis of the bond.

PROBLEMS

1. Find the value of a bond if its yield-to-maturity is 14 percent, coupon is 10 percent, face value is $1,000, and interest is paid annually. Assume the bond is purchased on an interest payment data and matures in 12 years.

2. Calculate V_0 for the bond described in question 1, but assume that interest is paid semiannually. Use a semiannual yield-to-maturity of 7 percent. Also calculate V_0 using the *effective* semiannual yield.

3. Find the yield-to-maturity on a zero that is currently priced at $400 and matures at $1,000 in eight years.

4. Calculate the value of a $1,000 face value consol that pays an annual coupon of 10 percent if the desired rate of return is 14 percent.

5. Find the yield-to-maturity of a $1,000-face-value bond that pays interest semiannually based on a 12 percent coupon. Its current price is $900, and it matures in eight years.

6. Calculate the yield-to-call on the bond described in question 5 if the bond is callable in three years at 110 percent of face value.

7. Assume that you bought a bond for $800 and sold it for $900. Calculate the annual *HPR* under each of the following assumptions:

    a. The bond is held for one year, but no interest is paid by the corporation.

    b. The bond is held for one year, and $80 of interest is received the day the bond is sold.

    c. The bond is held for one year; $40 of interest is received after six months, $40 the day the bond is sold.

    d. The bond is held for *two* years, and interest is received at the end of each year.

8. Consider the following corporate bond characteristics and analysts' estimates. Calculate $E(HPR)$ and σ^2_{HPR}.

Face value:	$1,000
Coupon rate (paid annually):	12%
Term-to-maturity:	15 years
Current price:	$400
Rating by Moody's:	Caa

STATE OF NATURE	PROBABILITY	COUPON	PRICE END-OF-YEAR
1. recession	.2	0	$100
2. no economic growth	.6	0	$300
3. moderate economic growth	.2	$120	$600

9. Consider the following information:

		END-OF-YEAR	
YEAR	CPI BEGINNING OF YEAR	COUPONS	CAPITAL GAIN
1	100	$100	$500
2	110	$150	$300
3	114	$125	$800
4	122	–	–

Assume that you had invested $4,000 at the beginning of each of these years and earned the indicated coupon and capital gain income.

a. Calculate the inflation rate for each of the first three years.

b. Calculate each year's nominal HPR.

c. Calculate each year's real HPR.

10. Assume that you purchase a bond for $900 that has a face value of $1,000 and matures in five years. The coupon rate is 10 percent paid annually, and the yield-to-maturity is 12.83 percent.

a. Calculate the terminal value of your investment, assuming the coupons are reinvested at 12.83 percent. Use this terminal value and initial investment to show that the annualized HPR is 12.83 percent

b. Calculate the terminal value assuming you reinvest coupons at 6 percent. Also calculate the annualized HPR for this assumption.

11. Consider the following information on a corporate bond:

Face value:	$1,000
Annual coupon rate:	12%
Term:	5 years
Yield-to-maturity:	15%

a. Calculate duration assuming interest is paid annually.

b. Calculate duration assuming interest is paid semiannually.

12. Using the bond described in question 11 and a second bond that has the same face value and yield-to-maturity but an annual coupon rate of 14 percent and term of ten years, compute the duration of this second bond, assuming that interest is paid annually. Explain the difference in the durations of the two bonds, using the differences in coupons and terms.

COMPUTER APPLICATIONS

The floppy disk includes programs that can be used to calculate the following:
1. Value of a bond
2. Yield-to-maturity
3. Yield-to-call
4. Holding period return
5. Duration
6. Beta
7. Variance and standard deviation

These programs can be used to solve most of the problems in this chapter and to analyze other bonds. Instructions and illustrations are provided on the disk.

REFERENCES

Alexander, Gordon J. "Applying the Market Model to Long-term Corporate Bonds." *Journal of Financial and Quantitative Analysis* (December 1980): pp. 1063–80.

Arak, Marcelle. "Profit Opportunities with Old OIDs." *Journal of Portfolio Management* (Spring 1985): pp. 63–66.

Benesh, Gary A., and Stephen E. Celec. "A Simplified Approach for Calculating Bond Duration." *Financial Review* (November 1984): pp. 394–96.

Bierwag, G. O., George G. Kaufman, and Alden L. Toevs. "Duration: Its Development and Use in Bond Portfolio Management." *Financial Analysts Journal* (July-August 1983): pp. 15–35.

Bierwag, G. O., George G. Kaufman, Cynthia M. Latta, and Gordon S. Roberts. "Duration: Response to Critics." *Journal of Portfolio Management* (Winter 1987): pp. 48–52.

Boardman, Calvin M., and Richard W. McEnally. "Factors Affecting Seasoned Corporate Bond Prices." *Journal of Financial and Quantitative Analysis* (June 1981): pp. 207–26.

Boquist, John A., George A. Racette, and Gary G. Schlarbaum. "Duration and Risk Assessment for Bonds and Common Stocks." *Journal of Finance* (December 1975): pp. 1360–65.

Caks, John, William R. Lane, Robert W. Greenleaf, and Reginald G. Joules. "A Simple Formula for Duration." *Journal of Financial Research* (Fall 1985): pp. 245–49.

Chew, I. Keong, and Ronnie J. Clayton. "Bond Valuation: A Clarification." *Financial Review* (May 1983): pp. 234–36.

Chua, Jess H. "A Closed-form Formula for Calculating Bond Duration." *Financial Analysts Journal* (May-June 1984): pp. 76–78.

Cornell, W. Bradford. "Inflation Measurement, Inflation Risk, and the Pricing of Treasury Bills." *Journal of Financial Research* (Fall 1986): pp. 193–202.

Duvall, Richard M. "The Association of Default Risk Factors with the Systematic Risk of Corporate Bonds." Paper presented at Eastern Finance Association Meeting, Jacksonville, Florida, 1982.

Duvall, Richard M., and John M. Cheney. "Bond Beta and Default Risk." *Journal of Financial Research* (Fall 1984): pp. 243–54.

Dyl, Edward A., and Michael D. Joehnk. "Riding the Yield Curve: Does It Work?" *Journal of Portfolio Management* (Spring 1981): pp. 13–17.

Eddy, Albert, and Bruce Seifert. "Inflation, the Fisher Hypothesis, and Long-term Bonds." *Financial Review* (February 1985): pp. 21–35.

Ederington, Louis H. "Classification Models and Bond Ratings." *Financial Review* (November 1985): pp. 237–62.

Ederington, Louis H., Jess B. Yawitz, and Brian E. Roberts. "The Information Context of Bond Ratings." *Journal of Financial Research* (Fall 1987): pp. 211–26.

Einhorn, Madeline W. "Breaking Tradition in Bond Portfolio Investment." *Journal of Portfolio Management* (Spring 1975): pp. 38–43.

Ferri, Michael G. "An Empirical Examination of the Determinants of Bond Yield Spreads." *Financial Management* (Autumn 1978): pp. 40–46.

Fisher, Irving. *The Theory of Interest.* New York: Macmillan, 1930.

Fogler, H. Russell, and William A. Groves. "How Much Can Active Bond Management Raise Returns?" *Journal of Portfolio Management* (Fall 1976): pp. 35–40.

Fuller, Russell J., and Glenn H. Petry. "Inflation, Return on Equity and Stock Prices." *Journal of Portfolio Management* (Summer 1981): pp. 19–25.

Fuller, Russell J., and John W. Settle. "Determinants of Duration and Bond Volatility." *Journal of Portfolio Management* (Summer 1984): pp. 66–72.

Groth, John C., and Brian I. Neysmith. "Bond Ratings—A Needed Reappraisal." *Financial Executive* (September 1979): pp. 20–25.

Hall, J. Parker III. "Shouldn't You Own Fewer Long-term Bonds?" *Financial Analysts Journal* (May-June 1981): pp. 45–48.

Homer, Sidney, and Martin L. Leibowitz. *Inside the Yield Book.* Englewood Cliffs, N.J.: Prentice-Hall, 1972.

Ibbotson, Roger G., and Rex A. Sinquefield. "Stocks, Bonds, Bills, and Inflation: Year-by-Year Historical Returns (1926–1974)." *Journal of Business* (January 1976): pp. 11–47.

———. "Stocks, Bonds, Bills, and Inflation: Simulation of the Future (1976–2000)." *Journal of Business* (July 1976): pp. 313–37.

Jahankhani, Ali, and George E. Pinches. "Duration and the Nonstationarity of Systematic Risk for Bonds." *Journal of Financial Research* (Summer 1982): pp. 151–60.

Joehnk, Michael D., H. Russell Fogler, and Charles E. Bradley. "The Price Elasticity of Discounted Bonds: Some Empirical Evidence." *Journal of Financial and Quantitative Analysis* (September 1978): pp. 559–56.

Johnson, James M. "When Are Zero Coupon Bonds the Better Buy?" *Journal of Portfolio Management* (Spring 1984): pp. 36–41.

Kalotay, Andrew J. "An Analysis of Original Issue Discount Bonds." *Financial Management* (Autumn 1984): pp. 29–38.

Katz, Steven. "The Price Adjustment Process of Bonds to Rating Reclassification: A Test of Bond Market Efficiency." *Journal of Finance* (May 1974): pp. 551–59.

Malkiel, Burton G. "Expectations, Bond Prices, and the Term Structure of Interest Rates." *Quarterly Journal of Economics* (May 1962): pp. 197–218.

Martin, John D., and R. Malcolm Richards. "The Seasoning Process for Corporate Bonds." *Financial Management* (Summer 1981): pp. 41–47.

McAdams, Lloyd. "How to Anticipate Utility Bond Rating Changes." *Journal of Portfolio Management* (Fall 1980): pp. 56–60.

McConnell, John J., and Eduardo S. Schwartz. "LYON Taming." *Journal of Finance* (July 1986): pp. 561–77.

McEnally, Richard W. "Duration as a Practical Tool for Bond Management." *Journal of Portfolio Management* (Summer 1977): pp. 53–57.

_____. "What Causes Bond Prices to Change?" *Journal of Portfolio Management* (Spring 1981): pp. 5–11.

McEnally, Richard W., and Michael G. Ferri. "Determinants of Systematic Bond Price Volatility." Paper presented at Eastern Finance Association Annual Meeting, Washington, D.C., 1979.

Meyer, Kenneth R. "Forecasting Interest Rates: Key to Active Bond Management." *Financial Analysts Journal* (November-December 1978): pp. 58–63.

Peavy, John W. III. "Bond Ratings as Risk Surrogates—How Reliable Are They?" *Best's Review* (April 1980): pp. 24, 26, 72, 74, 76.

Percival, John. "Corporate Bonds in a Market Model Context." *Journal of Business Research* (October 1974): pp. 461–68.

Perry, Larry G., Glenn V. Henderson, Jr., and Timothy P. Cronan. "Multivariate Analysis of Corporate Bond Ratings and Industry Classifications." *Journal of Financial Research* (Spring 1984): pp. 27–36.

Rao, Ramesk K. S. "The Impact of Yield Changes on the Systematic Risk of Bonds." *Journal of Financial and Quantitative Analysis* (March 1982): pp. 115–27.

Reilly, Frank K., and Rupinder S. Sidhu. "The Many Uses of Bond Duration." *Financial Analysts Journal* (July-August 1980): pp. 58–72.

Reilly, Frank K., and Michael D. Joehnk. "The Association between Market-Determined Risk Measures for Bonds and Bond Ratings." *Journal of Finance* (December 1976): pp. 1387–1403.

Roberts, Gordon S. "On the Stability of Beta for Fixed-Income Securities." Paper presented at the Eastern Finance Association Meeting, Newport, RI, 1981.

Sherwood, Hugh C. *How Corporate and Municipal Debt Is Rated.* New York: John Wiley and Sons, 1976.

Uginas, Luis. "Small Bond Rating Firms Are Competing Aggressively for a Bigger Share of Market." *Wall Street Journal*, 7 September, 1984. p. 28.

Weinstein, Mark I. "The Effect of a Rating Change Announcement on Bond Price." *Journal of Financial Economics* (December 1977): pp. 329–50.

_____. "The Systematic Risk of Corporate Bonds." *Journal of Financial and Quantitative Analysis* (September 1981): pp. 257–78.

Yawitz, Jess B., and William J. Marshall. "The Shortcomings of Duration as a Risk Measure for Bonds." *Journal of Financial Research* (Summer 1981): pp. 91–101.

ACCRUED INTEREST AND BOND VALUATION ON DATES OTHER THAN COUPON PAYMENT DATES

This appendix illustrates how the value of a bond can be calculated at a time other than an interest payment date. Since most bonds pay interest semiannually, it is very likely that a bond will be bought or sold on a non–interest payment date. This procedure considers the calculation of accrued interest and also deals with more complex present value calculations.

Assume that a corporate bond pays interest on January 1 and July 1, has a $1000 face value, and matures on January 1, 2000. Also assume that the coupon rate is 12 percent, the discount rate 15 percent. The value of the bond will be calculated on September 1, 1989. Since September 1 is not an interest payment date, accrued interest will be due to the seller and must be paid immediately by the buyer. This accrued interest is for July and August, since the corporation paid the seller interest on July 1, 1989. Assuming a 360-day year, or that each month has 30 days, the accrued interest is $(2/12)(.12 \times \$1,000) = \$20$.[26]

The following diagram illustrates the other problem that must be considered in this example:

First, it should be recognized that a semiannual "annuity" of $60 will be paid to the buyer by the issuer. However, as of September 1, 1989, the next interest payment (on January 1, 1990) is only four months away, and the interest payment

---

[26] U. S. Treasury securities are priced using the actual number of days in each month rather than assuming a 360-day year with each month having 30 days.

of July 1, 1990, is ten months away, etc. This timing of interest payments must be considered in the present value calculations. One approach is to compute V_0 on January 1, 1990, the next interest payment date, and, recognizing that there are 20 interest payment dates, starting with July 1, 1990, and ending with January 1, 2000. Using present value annuity factor and present value factor.

$$V_{1/1/90} = \$60\ (10.1945) + \frac{\$1,000}{4.2479}$$

$$= \$611.67 + \$235.41$$

$$= \$847.08$$

The next step is to find the present value of $847.08 on September 1, 1989. The length of time between September 1, 1989 and January 1, 1990 is four months or four/sixth of a half-year.

$$\text{Present value on } 9/1/89 = \frac{\$847.08}{(1 + .15/2)^{4/6}} = \frac{\$847.08}{1.0494} = \$807.20$$

Finally, the interest payment on 1/1/90 must be considered, along with the accrued interest due to the seller, with the following calculation:

$$\text{Present value on } 9/1/89 \text{ including } 1/1/90 \text{ coupon} = \$807.20 + \frac{\$60}{(1 + .15/2)^{4/6}}$$

$$= \$807.20 + \$57.18$$

$$= \$864.38$$

The value of $864.38 represents the total present value of future cash flows, assuming that the buyer is entitled to the entire coupon payment on January 1, 1990.

Since the accrued interest is $20 and must be paid on the purchase date by the buyer, the value of the bond on September 1, 1989, is

$$V_{9/1/89} = \$864.38 - \$20 = \$844.38$$

The value of $844.38 represents the total present value of future cash flows the bond will provide to the purchaser.

CHAPTER 16

BOND INVESTMENT STRATEGIES AND PORTFOLIO CONSIDERATIONS

BOND INVESTMENT STRATEGIES

Overview

There are many bond investment strategies. Very passive strategies involve assembling a diversified bond portfolio to be held for a relatively long period, while very active strategies may involve same-day trading. This chapter discusses passive, active, and combination strategies that are appropriate for bonds.

This chapter also looks at the important aspect of diversification in fixed-income security portfolios. What are the benefits of diversification in a bond portfolio, and how do these compare to the diversification benefits for common stock portfolios? Recently, there has been an increased interest in this aspect of research as it relates to fixed-income securities. These studies provide the foundation for the discussion of this topic.

This chapter builds on the foundations of bond fundamentals developed in Chapter 14 and the material on bond valuation, returns, and risk presented in Chapter 15. This chapter integrates this material and develops concepts and ideas that can lead to successful investment decisions for fixed-income securities.

Before specific investment strategies and portfolio considerations are discussed, however, the investment and portfolio *objectives* should be clearly established. As discussed in Chapter 5, the objectives provide guidelines for identifying appropriate strategies. For fixed-income investing, important factors include annual income (cash flow) requirements, taxes, investment horizon, and risk-return preferences dealing with reinvestment rate, default, purchasing power, and interest rate risk. The strategies discussed in this chapter differ greatly in their risk-return characteristics, and the specific objectives of the portfolio should be considered in evaluating the appropriateness of individual strategies.

Passive Investment Strategies

Traditionally, bond investments were viewed as conservative investments that typically involved a relatively long investment horizon. This strategy was appropriately labeled a buy-and-hold strategy. To implement such a strategy, the investor would simply select the type of bond that seemed most appropriate and form a portfolio with bonds of this type. For individuals in high marginal tax brackets, municipal securities were often appropriate. If the investor was conservative, often only the highest-quality municipals would be considered. The investor who felt that additional default risk would be tolerable would consider lower-quality securities with their higher coupon yields and yields-to-maturity.

This passive strategy could also involve corporate, U.S. Treasury, or agency issues. Typically, the investor would be interested in securities with long terms-to-maturity, since selling the securities before maturity would be unlikely. This strategy required that the investor accept the market rate of return since no attempt was made to outperform the market.

Figure 16.1 provides a comparison of the performance of Treasury bills and bonds, "small" common stocks (stocks with the smallest capitalization, on the NYSE), and common stocks with the inflation rate. The vertical scale is logarithmic and reflects the value of $1 invested at the end of 1925. For example, an

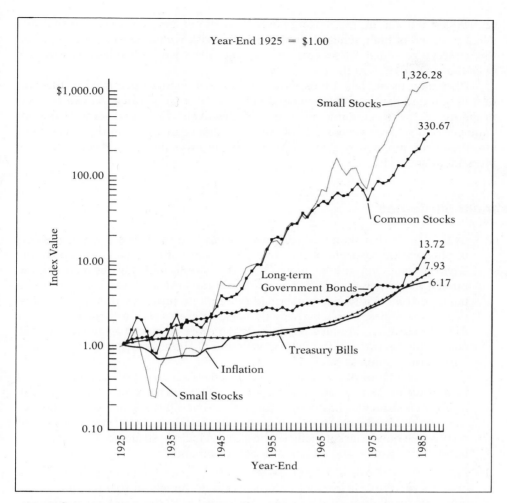

FIGURE 16.1   Wealth indices and inflation for Treasury bills and bonds and common stocks: 1925–1986

Source: Ibbotson, Roger G, and Rex A Sinquefield. *Stocks, Bonds, Bills, and inflation* (SBBI) 1982, updated in SBBI 1987 Yearbook. Ibbotson Associates, Chicago

investment of $1 in long-term Treasury bonds at the beginning of 1926 would have increased to $13.72 by 1986. Notice that the return on Treasury bills closely follows the rate of inflation over the entire period. From 1925 to the mid-1960s, the return on long-term Treasury bonds was reasonably stable. Starting in the late 1960s and continuing through the mid-1980s, however, the return on Treasury bonds exhibited much more volatility. A passive strategy using Treasury bonds over the period 1925–1965 would have been reasonably successful. With increasing inflation rates and the resulting variability of Treasury bond yields since the late 1960s, however, a passive strategy appears less attractive.

A passive strategy is most advantageous when interest rate risk is low; intervening price changes can be ignored and reinvestment risk minimized since yields are stable. In addition, purchasing power risk should be low. Given a well-diversified portfolio of high-quality securities, default risk would also be minor.[1] Thus, this strategy provided an acceptable real rate of return with relatively low risk over the period 1925 to the mid-1960s.

Beginning in the late 1960s, however, radical changes occurred in the rate of inflation and the resulting level and volatility of interest rates. As can be seen in Figure 16.1, the economic environment effectively eliminated some of the advantages of a passive strategy. Consequently, passive investors in this type of environment might elect to abandon fixed-income investments or to change their investment strategies.

Active Investment Strategies

1. OVERVIEW Rather than following a strict buy-and-hold strategy, it is possible to alter various aspects of the strategy to deal with an uncertain economic environment. One strategy would be to hold bonds with various maturities to pursue a stratgey based on *structuring* maturities; for example, forming a bond portfolio with a combination of different maturities. Other more-sophisticated strategies, involving hedging using interest rate futures (see Chapter 21) and duration, are also possible. These more-advanced strategies are discussed later in this and the following chapters. These strategies do not require a forecast of interest rates.

    A second type of active strategy is based on a forecast of the direction and magnitude of interest rate changes. These strategies are similar to active common stock strategies based on a forecast of overall stock price movements.

    The final category of active strategies includes specific strategies based on possible bond market inefficiencies. These include strategies based on *junk* bonds, new issues, and seasonal price movements.

2. STRATEGIES BASED ON STRUCTURING MATURITIES Uncertainty about interest rate changes requires the investor to forecast these changes or to attempt to eliminate part or all of the unfavorable consequences of these unknown changes. For example, a forecast of decreasing interest rates may suggest investing in bonds with long durations. An unwillingness or inability to make a specific forecast requires a strategy that allows for the possibility of both increases and decreases in rates.

    a. MATCHING STRATEGY An alternative to forecasting rates is to pursue a *matching* strategy. This strategy essentially ignores possible interest rate changes; two steps are involved: (1) identify an appropriate holding period or investment horizon and (2) form a bond portfolio with a duration equal to the holding period. Thus, if the holding period is two years, a portfolio with a duration of two years is appropriate for a matching strategy. The details and the advantages and disadvantages of the strategy are discussed in more detail later in this chapter.

---

[1] The exception would be during the Depression, where Hickman (see references) showed that the number of bond defaults increased significantly.

b. LADDERED STRATEGY A *laddered* strategy forms a portfolio of bonds with various maturities. A ladder of N-years length would be formed by using $1/N$ proportion of the available funds for each maturity, 1 to N. For example, a five-year laddered portfolio would include 20 percent of the funds in bonds with a one-year maturity, 20 percent in bonds with a two-year maturity, etc. Essentially, this strategy invests equal dollar amounts in bonds with maturities staggered by one year.

c. BARBELL STRATEGY A *barbell* strategy is a modification of the laddered strategy. Rather than buying equal amounts of all maturities within the length of the ladder, the barbell strategy uses only short-term and long-term bonds. No intermediate-term bonds are included in the portfolio. This strategy is also referred to as the *dumbbell* strategy: a graph of portfolio values by maturity would show "bulges" or "bells" at either end of the maturity spectrum. This strategy is based on the assumption that intermediate-term bonds are not necessary in a portfolio because they have less liquidity than short-term bonds and lower yields than long-term bonds. The barbell portfolio obtains liquidity from the short-term maturities and return (yield) from the long-term maturities.

d. TESTS OF STRATEGIES By staggering the maturities of bonds in the portfolio, by a laddered or a barbell approach, the investor attempts to earn the average market return over the holding period and to eliminate some of the effects of interest rate movements on portfolio value and income. There have been a number of studies of the risk-return characteristics of these strategies.

A 1984 study used a sample of eighty-seven corportate bonds over the period 1969–1981 to test six different strategies: equal dollar allocation, barbell, laddered, duration or matching, buy-and-hold, and low-rated.[2] The study reached the following conclusions:

(1) On a return basis, no one strategy dominated any other strategy since the mean returns between strategies were not significantly different at the .05 level of significance;

(2) On a risk-adjusted performance basis, none of the strategies outperformed an investment in ninety-day Treasury bills over the period 1969–1981. This result occurred because of the dramatic increase in interest rates between 1979 and 1981;

(3) During the subperiods of increasing interest rates, all strategies had negative returns except the "short" (greater proportion of short-term bonds), barbell, and duration strategies;

(4) During the subperiods of decreasing interest rates, all strategies had positive returns, with the "long" (greater proportion of long-term bonds) barbell strategy providing the highest return and "short" barbell the lowest return. All strategies had returns above ninety-day Treasury bills;

---

[2] Tom Barnes, Keith Johnson, and Don Shannon, "A Test of Fixed-Income Strategies," *Journal of Portfolio Management* (Winter 1984): pp. 60–65.

TABLE 16.1 AVERAGE ANNUAL RETURNS BY DURATION: U.S. TREASURY BONDS: LADDERED VERSUS BARBELL STRATEGIES

I. Returns Considering Tax Swaps

	ANNUAL AFTER-TAX RATE OF RETURN		
DURATION	LADDERED	BARBELL	RETURN DIFFERENCE
6 Years	.01768	.01737	.00031
7	.01672	.01616	.00056
8	.01576	.01494	.00082
9	.01480	.01373	.00107
10	.01384	.01251	.00133
11	.01288	.01129	.00159

II. Returns Without Tax Swaps

	ANNUAL AFTER-TAX RATE OF RETURN		
DURATION	LADDERED	BARBELL	RETURN DIFFERENCE
6 Years	.01707	.01694	.00013
7	.01556	.01564	−.00008
8	.01406	.01435	−.00029
9	.01255	.01305	−.00050
10	.01105	.01176	−.00071
11	.00955	.01047	−.00092

SOURCE: Edward A. Dyl and Stanley A. Martin, Jr., "Another Look at Barbells versus Ladders," *Journal of Portfolio Management* (Spring, 1986): pp. 57–58. Reprinted by permission.

(5) The returns from all strategies compared favorably with the returns on six bond mutual funds. In general, these strategies outperformed the six actively managed funds over the period 1969–1981.

A 1986 study compared the performance of barbell versus laddered portfolios for U.S. Treasury bonds over the period 1954–1976.[3] A total of twenty-one laddered portfolios with maturities of ten to thirty years were analyzed. Barbell portfolios were created by varying the proportion of short-term bonds from 30 to 70 percent of the portfolio. The study also considered the tax savings that can result from maintaining the barbell structure and the additional trading commissions involved in these periodic *tax swaps*. The tax swap involves selling bonds at a capital loss and reinvesting the proceeds plus the tax savings resulting from capital loss.

The study also examined differences in risk between the strategies by comparing returns for portfolios of equal duration (risk). Table 16.1

---

[3] Edward A. Dyl and Stanley A. Martin, Jr., "Another Look at Barbells versus Ladders," *Journal of Portfolio Management* (Spring 1986): pp. 54–59.

provides a comparison of the returns from the laddered and barbell strategies. The annual returns in the table may appear to be small, but it should be remembered that the annual compounded rate of return on Treasury bonds for the period 1954–1976 was 3.1 percent.[4]

Based on the empirical results, using Treasury bonds, the authors concluded that "laddered portfolios do slightly better than barbell portfolios,"[5] primarily because of the higher transaction costs associated with barbell strategies. Overall, the authors thought that barbell strategies are "not a particularly useful bond portfolio management technique."[6]

3. STRATEGY BASED ON FORECASTING INTEREST RATE MOVEMENTS

a. TRENDS AND CYCLES A successful active strategy based on interest rate movements depends on an accurate interest rate forecast. The difficulty of this task should not be underestimated.[7] Many economic analyses have been directed at simplifying interest rate forecasts, without much success. There is no one technique or procedure that correctly forecasts the level, or perhaps even the direction, of interest rate changes. In fact, there is considerable debate about what variables actually determine interest rates; current attention focuses on budget and trade deficits, inflation and inflationary expectations, money supply, and the real rate of interest.

Despite this somewhat pessimistic beginning, however, it is possible to develop a general framework that will allow the analyst to attempt to forecast interest rates. Historically, there has been a very close association between economic turning points and peaks and troughs in interest rates. Interest rates and economic activity traditionally peak and trough at approximately the same time. As Figure 16.2 illustrates, recessionary periods are associated with lower interest rates, with a resulting rise in bond prices. Thus, an accurate economic forecast can be used as a basis for forecasting interest rates. The economic analysis material in Chapter 9 also applies to bond analysis. If the economic forecast can be used to forecast interest rate turning points accurately, then an active strategy of "buy low" (at the peak of the interest rate cycle) and "sell high" (at the trough of the interest rate cycle) can be implemented.

The impacts of inflation and expected inflation are critical factors in forecasting interest rates. In addition to the importance of the Fisher effect, discussed in Chapter 15, studies indicate that both short- and long-term interest rates increase above their average levels during periods of inflation and of deflation. During periods of high inflation, however, interest rates lag behind the rate of inflation. For example, over the 189-year period 1791–1979, only 14 of the 189 years had inflation rates greater than 9 percent, and the average yield on long-term bonds for

---

[4] *Stocks, Bonds, Bills, and Inflation, 1987 Yearbook*, p. 109.

[5] Dyl and Martin, p. 58.

[6] Ibid, p. 58.

[7] For example, see Kenneth R. Meyer, "Forecasting Interest Rates: Key to Active Bond Management," *Financial Analysts Journal* (November-December 1978): pp. 58–63.

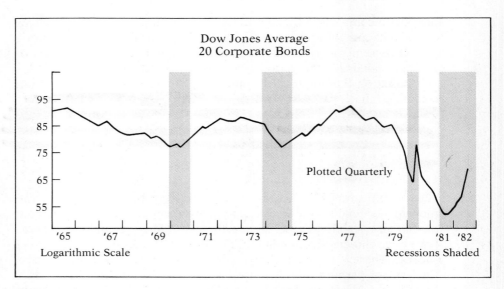

FIGURE 16.2   Bond prices and economic activity
Source: Alfred L. Malabre, Jr., "Bond Prices, Rising Briskly of Late, Excel as Leading Indicator of Economy's Ups, Downs," *Wall Street Journal*, 28 September 1982, p. 56. Reprinted by permission.

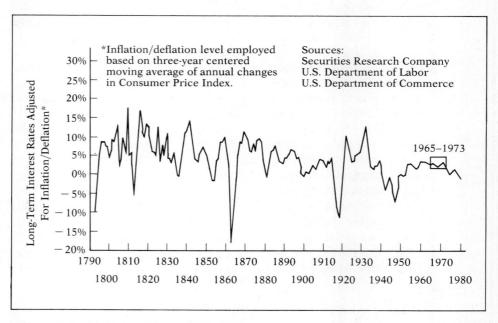

FIGURE 16.3   Real interest rates: 1791–1979
Source: Steven C. Leuthold, "Interest Rates, Inflation and Deflation," *Financial Analysts Journal*, (January-February 1981): p. 35.

these 14 years was approximately 6 percent.[8] Figure 16.3 provides a historical record of *real* interest rates over the period 1791–1979. As the chart shows, many periods are characterized by negative real rates of interest; the Fisher effect does not appear to explain these periods. However, for the more recent period 1950–1978, the real rate of interest is positive. These observations suggest that the relationship between inflation and interest rates is complex and perhaps unstable over time. Despite these problems, an inflation forecast is an important element in forecasting interest rates.

b. STRUCTURE OF INTEREST RATES Another tool considers how rates differ between short-term and long-term bonds and between bonds with different ratings. The most common analysis deals with the *term structure* of interest rates, relating term-to-maturity to yield-to-maturity. This analysis requires a homogeneous sample of bonds, so that all other factors that influence yield (except term) are held constant. The most commonly used sample is U.S. government securities; thus, differences in default risk, major tax implications, or industry factors would not be a problem. Also, the term structure is analyzed at one point in time, which may be the present or a point in the future.

Figure 16.4 illustrates the term structure of Treasury securities at three different points in time. These dates were selected to show the three major types of yield curves: increasing, decreasing, and flat. Thus, there is not necessarily a stable relationship between term and yield-to-maturity. Most commonly, short-term securities have lower yields than long-term securities. At other times, however, the reverse is true. Also, short-term yields are more volatile than long-term yields. Thus, most of the shifts in the yield curve occur for short-term securities. It should also be pointed out, however, that short-term bond prices are more stable than long-term bond prices. (See Theorem 2 in Chapter 15.)

Considerable research has been directed toward an explanation of why yield curves have the shapes and moves indicated by the data. Construction of yield curves is very easy, but explaining their shapes and movements has proved to be challenging and controversial. There are three main theories about the yield curve:

(1) EXPECTATIONS THEORY This theory maintains that long-term yields are a function of the anticipated short-term rates that will prevail during the term of the long-term security. For example, assume that you have a five-year investment horizon and can invest in a bond with a five-year term or, sequentially, in five bonds, each with a one-year term. Thus, you could earn the yield-to-maturity on the five-year bond—or perhaps a higher yield on five one-year bonds if one-year yields increase over the five-year period. You could buy a one-year bond and then "roll over" into a second one-year bond at a higher rate. This implies that an upward-sloping yield curve is

---

[8] Steven C. Leuthold, "Interest Rates, Inflation and Deflation," *Financial Analysts Journal* (January-February 1981): p. 28.

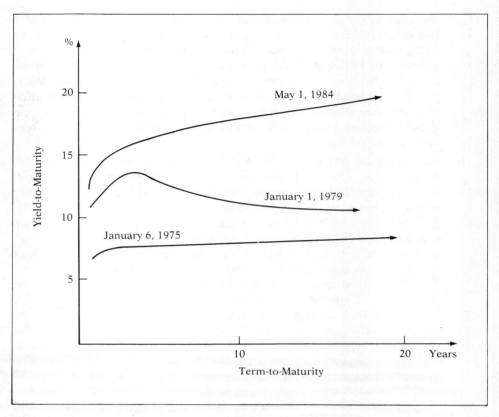

FIGURE 16.4 Term structure of U.S. Treasury securities
Source: Figure constructed from data obtained from *Wall Street Journal*.

explained by expectations of increasing yields. Thus, investors are purchasing short-term rather than long-term, with the hopes of favorably "rolling over." Conversely, a downward-sloping yield curve suggests expectations of declining yields.

The expectations theory can be used to calculate the *forward* or expected yields implied by the yield curve. As a simple example, assume that the yield today on a bond with a two-year maturity, $_2Y_0$, is 7 percent and that the yield on a one-year bond, $_1Y_0$, is 6 percent. If an investor has a two-year holding period, should the two-year bond be purchased, or should the one-year bond be purchased and rolled over into a second one-year bond at the end of the first year? According to the expectation theory, the *HPR*s from each strategy will be equal because the forward yield on a one-year bond one year from now, $_1f_1$, will be higher than $_1Y_0$ (6 percent). The forward yield that will equate the *HPR*s can be calculated as

$$(1 + {_1Y_0})(1 + {_1f_1}) = (1 + {_2Y_0})^2$$
$$_1f_1 = [(1 + {_2Y_0})^2/(1 + {_1Y_0})] - 1 \tag{16.1}$$

Using the previous example gives

$$_1f_1 = [(1 + .07)^2/(1 + .06) - 1$$
$$= 8\%$$

Thus, an investment in a one-year bond at 6 percent, followed by a second one-year bond with a yield of 8 percent, will have an annualized yield of 7 percent, or the yield on the two-year bond today.

In general, the yield today on a bond with maturity n is equal to the geometric average of the forward rates over its life:

$$_nY_0 = [(1 + {}_1Y_0)(1 + {}_1f_1)(1 + {}_1f_2) \ldots (1 + {}_1f_n)]^{1/n} - 1 \quad (16.2)$$

Continuing with the previous example gives

$$_2Y_0 = [(1 + {}_1Y_0)(1 + {}_1f_1)]^{1/2} - 1$$
$$= [(1 + .06)(1 + .08)]^{1/2} - 1$$
$$= 7\%$$

This example illustrates that when the yield curve is upward-sloping, investors expect yields to increase, so that forward rates are greater than the respective spot rates. Conversely, a downward-sloping yield curve indicates that investors expect rates to decline.

(2) LIQUIDITY PREMIUM THEORY This theory agrees with the expectations theory but also argues that short-term bond prices are more stable and their liquidity is better than long-term bonds. This advantage (less risk) indicates that their yields should be lower than those of long-term bonds. This theory suggests that the yield curve should be upward-sloping. The shape of the yield curve is therefore determined by expectations concerning future rates and by liquidity preferences.

(3) SEGMENTED MARKET THEORY Many investors, especially financial institutions, often view bonds with different terms as imperfect substitutes. That is, a commercial bank may invest only in short-term securities because of the nature of its liabilities, but an insurance company may be quite willing to invest in long-term securities. This theory suggests, for example, that an analysis of credit conditions in the banking industry would be useful in explaining the shape of the short-term segment of the yield curve, and knowledge of the situation in the insurance industry would be helpful in explaining the long-term segment. Supply and demand in each segment of the market determine the slope of the yield curve. Thus, increasing, decreasing, "humped," or flat yield curves could be explained by factors in each segment of the market.

(4) STRATEGIES BASED ON AN ANALYSIS OF THE YIELD CURVE Understanding yield curves and their anticipated movements can provide a foundation for an active bond investment strategy. For example, given a particular yield curve on the date an investment decision is made and

a forecasted yield curve at the end of the investment horizon, an appropriate strategy would be indicated. For the simplest case, assume that the yield curve is currently upward-sloping and is expected to remain stable, both in shape and level of yields. This suggests that the higher yields of long-term bonds are attractive since interest rate risk is not anticipated to be a factor. This strategy is referred to as *riding the yield curve.*

Table 16.2 provides a simple illustration of riding the yield curve. The figure at the top of the table shows that the yield curve is presently upward-sloping, with a one-year bond offering a 6 percent yield and a two-year bond a 7 percent yield. Given a one-year holding period, an investor might buy a one-year bond and hold it to maturity. A second strategy, however, would be to buy a two-year bond and sell it after one year. If the yield curve remains constant, the yield on a one-year

TABLE 16.2   ILLUSTRATION OF RIDING THE YIELD CURVE

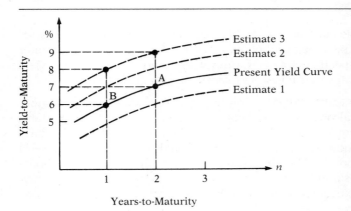

Assumptions: Holding period is one year
Pure discount bonds (no coupons)
Three estimates of yield curve one year from now

Strategy 1:   Buy a bond priced at $943.40 with a one-year maturity and yield of 6%

Strategy 2:   Buy a bond priced at $873.44 with a two-year maturity and initial yield of 7%, and sell at the prevailing yield after one year.

YIELD CURVE AFTER ONE YEAR	HPRs		ADDITIONAL RETURN FROM RIDING THE YIELD CURVE
	STRATEGY 1	STRATEGY 2	
No shift—remains stationary	6.00%	8.01%	2.01%
Shifts to Estimate 1	6.00	9.04	3.04
Shifts to Estimate 2	6.00	7.00	1.00
Shifts to Estimate 3	6.00	6.01	0.01

bond one year from now would be 6 percent. The second strategy, therefore, "rides the curve" from point A to B.

The *HPR*s at the bottom of Table 16.2 show that riding the yield curve (strategy 2) provides significantly higher returns when the yield curve is constant or declines. If the yield curve shifts upward, strategy 2 still provides higher returns until the curve reaches the position shown by estimate 3. At this point, a one-year bond would be priced to yield 8 percent, resulting in a *HPR* for strategy 2 of 6.01 percent. If the yield curve shifts above the estimate 3 level, strategy 1 (buy-and-hold) would produce a higher *HPR*.

An investor (speculator) attempting to ride the yield curve would concentrate on the probability that the yield curve would shift upward to the extent that excess returns would be eliminated. In this example, the key estimate would be the probability that the yield on a one-year bond one year from now, $_1Y_1$, will be greater than or equal to 8 percent, or $P(_1Y_1 \geq 8\%)$.

The success of riding the yield curve depends on inefficiencies in the market; the expectations hypothesis indicates that an upward-sloping curve implies that yields will increase. This theory indicates that the forward rate $(_1f_1)$ would be 8 percent, which would eliminate the extra returns for this strategy. Empirical studies using Treasury bills have generally found that riding the yield curve involved additional risk and provided only small incremental returns over a buy-and-hold strategy.[9]

A second strategy dealing with the structure of interest rates uses the yield spread between bonds with different ratings. For example, higher-rated bonds will always provide lower yields-to-maturity than lower-rated bonds with the same maturity. This *default risk spread*, however, is not constant over the business cycle; it typically narrows at the peak of the interest rate cycle (peak of economic activity) and increases at the trough (recession or no-growth periods of economic activity). This implies that higher-quality bonds are better correlated with the business cycle and that their price appreciation will be larger during periods of falling rates than that of the lower-quality bonds. This suggests a strategy of buying lower-quality bonds during the growth phase of the economic cycle, to take advantage of their higher yields, and shifting to the highest quality at the peak of yields, in anticipation of declining economic activity.

c. MODELS FOR FORECASTING INTEREST RATES This section briefly discusses three models that have been suggested in the investment literature for forecasting and analyzing interest rates.

(1) STRUCTURAL MODELS Traditionally, the two most widely used aggregate forecasting models are econometric and flow-of-funds models.

---

[9] For example, see Edward A. Dyl and Michael D. Joehnk, "Riding the Yield Curve: Does It Work?" *Journal of Portfolio Management* (Spring 1981): pp. 13–17, and Stanley Diller, "Analyzing the Yield Curve: A New Approach," *Financial Analysts Journal* (March-April 1981): pp. 23–41.

Econometric models are constructed as a series of equations that describe the relationships between key economic variables. Historical relationships and estimates of key variables allow for a simultaneous solution of the model. Elaborate models that include hundreds of equations have been developed by firms such as Chase Econometrics, Merrill Lynch Economics, and Wharton Econometric. These firms often publish their economic forecasts. These models forecast many key economic variables, including interest rates.

A *flow-of-funds* approach analyzes the supply of and demand for funds in different segments of the economy such as households, businesses, financial institutions, governmental units, and foreigners. By analyzing each segment, the analysts attempt to measure aggregate demand and supply, and detect any imbalances that may lead to higher or lower interest rates.

Table 16.3 provides an example of the flow-of-funds data available from the Federal Reserve. This table shows the recipients of funds by sectors and the sources of funds over the period 1982 to mid-1987. Notice that total sources (supply) equal total uses (demand).This historical data can be used to forecast any imbalances or trends that might provide an indication of future interest rates.

A modification of the traditional flow-of-funds model is a *disaggregated* structural model.[10] This model forecasts yields for U.S. Treasury securities, corporate bonds, and equities by analyzing the demand for and supply of securities using portfolio considerations and shifts in financial structure. The model considers the investor's risk aversion and the risk-return characteristics of individual securities for eleven categories of investors. The model allows investors to reallocate assets in their portfolios and considers transaction costs associated with these portfolio revisions. As Roley concluded. "As a whole, the empirical results suggest that a properly specified structural model can be a valuable forecasting tool."[11]

(2) CAPITAL ASSET PRICING MODEL APPROACH Many analysts were surprised by the behavior of interest rates in the early 1980s. After historically high rates in the late 1970s, many analysts expected nominal rates to decline because of the reduction in the actual and expected rate of inflation. Rates, however, remained high.

One empirical study demonstrated that the variance (total risk) of long-term bonds increased appreciably during 1977–1979 and 1980–1981 and that the correlations of their returns with common stocks also increased.[12] According to the CAPM, the increase in the systematic risk of bonds would result in an increase in their expected

---

[10] V. Vance Roley, "Forecasting Interest Rates with a Structural Model," *Journal of Portfolio Management* (Spring 1982): pp. 53–63.

[11] Roley p. 62.

[12] Zvi Bodie, Alex Kane, and Robert McDonald, "Why Haven't Nominal Rates Declined?" *Financial Analysts Journal* (March-April 1984): pp. 16–27.

TABLE 16.3 FLOW-OF-FUNDS IN U.S. CREDIT MARKETS

1.57 FUNDS RAISED IN U.S. CREDIT MARKETS

Billions of dollars; half-yearly data are at seasonally adjusted annual rates.

Transaction category, sector	1982	1983	1984	1985	1986	1984 H1	1984 H2	1985 H1	1985 H2	1986 H1	1986 H2	1987 H1
						Nonfinancial sectors						
1 Total net borrowing by domestic nonfinancial sectors......	388.9	550.2	753.9	854.8	833.4	717.3	790.4	722.7	986.8	676.9	989.9	568.3
By sector and instrument												
2 U.S. government	161.3	186.6	198.8	223.6	214.3	190.4	207.2	204.8	242.5	207.2	221.5	151.1
3 Treasury securities.......................	162.1	186.7	199.0	223.7	214.7	190.7	207.3	204.9	242.5	207.4	222.0	151.7
4 Agency issues and mortgages	-.9	-.1	-.2	-.1	-.3	-.2	-.1	-.1	-.1	-.1	-.5	-.4
5 Private domestic nonfinancial sectors	227.6	363.6	555.1	631.1	619.0	526.9	583.3	518.0	744.3	469.6	768.4	417.0
6 Debt capital instruments	148.3	253.4	313.6	447.8	445.0	284.7	342.5	350.4	545.2	363.4	546.7	407.1
7 Tax-exempt obligations	44.2	53.7	50.4	136.4	35.4	33.8	67.0	67.0	205.8	-16.9	87.7	20.0
8 Corporate bonds.....................	18.7	16.0	46.1	73.8	121.7	22.5	69.8	62.2	85.3	135.3	108.1	89.0
9 Mortgages...........................	85.4	183.6	217.1	237.7	298.0	228.5	205.7	221.2	254.2	245.0	350.9	298.1
10 Home mortgages.................	50.5	117.5	129.7	151.9	199.4	139.5	119.9	139.2	164.7	163.8	234.9	217.5
11 Multifamily residential...........	5.4	14.2	25.1	29.2	33.0	27.8	22.4	25.0	33.4	31.2	34.8	27.7
12 Commercial	25.2	49.3	63.2	62.5	73.9	62.6	63.8	59.5	65.5	58.9	88.9	62.5
13 Farm	4.2	2.6	-.9	-6.0	-8.3	-1.4	-.4	-2.5	-9.5	-8.9	-7.7	-9.6
14 Other debt instruments	79.3	110.2	241.5	183.3	164.0	242.2	240.8	167.5	199.1	106.2	221.8	9.9
15 Consumer credit	19.3	56.6	90.4	94.6	65.8	94.7	86.2	95.3	93.9	71.0	60.6	15.7
16 Bank loans n.e.c.	50.4	23.2	67.1	38.6	66.5	71.2	63.0	21.0	56.2	12.2	120.8	-40.2
17 Open market paper.................	-6.1	-.8	21.7	14.6	-9.3	26.6	16.8	14.4	14.8	-13.1	-5.5	4.5
18 Other...........................	15.8	31.3	62.2	35.5	41.0	49.7	74.7	36.8	34.2	36.2	45.9	29.9
19 By borrowing sector	227.6	363.6	555.1	631.1	619.0	526.9	583.3	518.0	744.3	469.6	768.4	417.0
20 State and local governments	21.5	34.0	71.7	91.8	46.4	16.2	38.6	56.3	127.2	3.1	89.7	28.6
21 Households	90.0	188.2	234.6	293.4	279.9	235.0	234.2	259.8	327.1	232.8	326.9	224.0
22 Farm	6.8	4.1	-.1	-13.9	-15.1	-.5	-.4	-7.0	-20.8	-16.8	-13.3	-19.5
23 Nonfarm noncorporate	40.2	77.0	97.0	93.1	115.9	101.8	92.2	85.7	100.5	96.2	135.5	92.8
24 Corporate	69.0	60.3	196.0	166.7	192.0	174.3	217.8	123.2	210.3	154.3	229.7	91.2
25 Foreign net borrowing in United States......	16.0	17.3	8.3	1.2	9.0	36.1	-19.4	-5.8	8.2	21.5	-3.5	-12.6
26 Bonds	6.6	3.1	3.8	3.8	2.6	1.3	6.3	5.5	2.1	6.2	-1.1	-1.1
27 Bank loans n.e.c.	-5.5	3.6	-6.6	-2.8	-1.0	-1.3	-11.9	-5.8	.1	1.5	-3.5	-3.5
28 Open market paper.....................	1.9	6.5	6.2	6.2	11.5	16.6	-4.3	2.8	9.6	19.1	9.9	-5.3
29 U.S. government loans	13.0	4.1	5.0	-6.0	-4.0	19.5	-9.6	-8.2	-3.7	-5.3	-2.7	-2.8
30 Total domestic plus foreign	404.8	567.5	762.2	856.0	842.4	753.4	771.0	716.9	995.0	698.3	986.4	555.7
						Financial sectors						
31 Total net borrowing by financial sectors	90.3	99.3	151.9	199.0	291.1	153.0	150.7	175.1	222.8	238.8	343.4	317.5
By instrument												
32 U.S. government related................	64.9	67.8	74.9	101.5	174.3	72.5	77.3	96.8	106.3	133.8	214.8	180.2
33 Sponsored credit agency securities........	14.9	1.4	30.4	20.6	13.2	29.4	31.5	26.6	14.6	6.4	20.0	7.8
34 Mortgage pool securities..............	49.5	66.4	44.4	79.9	161.4	43.1	45.8	70.3	89.5	126.6	196.3	171.8
35 Loans from U.S. government	.4			1.1	-.4				2.2	.8	-1.5	.5
36 Private financial sectors	25.4	31.5	77.0	97.4	116.8	80.5	73.5	78.3	116.5	105.0	128.6	137.4
37 Corporate bonds	12.7	17.4	36.2	48.6	68.7	30.8	41.5	48.9	48.3	70.9	66.5	92.5
38 Mortgages...........................	.1	*	.4	.1	.1	.4	.4	*	.1	.6	-.5	.2
39 Bank loans n.e.c.	1.9	-.1	.7	2.6	4.0	.6	.7	2.3	2.9	4.0	4.0	-7.4
40 Open market paper....................	9.9	21.3	24.1	32.0	24.2	32.1	16.0	14.6	49.4	15.1	34.4	38.3
41 Loans from Federal Home Loan Banks	.8	-7.0	15.7	14.2	19.8	16.5	14.9	12.5	15.9	14.4	25.2	13.6
By sector												
42 Sponsored credit agencies	15.3	1.4	30.4	21.7	12.9	29.4	31.5	26.6	16.8	7.2	18.5	8.3
43 Mortgage pools	49.5	66.4	44.4	79.9	161.4	43.1	45.8	70.3	89.5	126.6	196.3	171.8
44 Private financial sectors	25.4	31.5	77.0	97.4	116.8	80.5	73.5	78.3	116.5	105.0	128.6	137.4
45 Commercial banks	11.7	5.0	7.3	-4.9	-3.6	19.8	-5.3	-4.7	-5.0	-2.7	-4.6	4.4
46 Bank affiliates	6.8	12.1	15.6	14.5	4.6	20.4	10.8	10.2	18.9	-1.7	10.9	21.6
47 Savings and loan associations	2.5	-2.1	22.7	22.3	29.3	22.0	23.3	14.2	30.4	25.5	33.1	30.7
48 Finance companies	4.5	12.9	18.9	53.9	50.2	8.2	29.6	49.7	58.1	53.1	47.2	27.2
49 REITs	-.2	-.1	.1	-.7	-.3	.2	.1	-.6	-.8	.6	-1.3	-.2
50 CMO Issuers	.2	3.7	12.4	12.2	36.7	9.8	15.0	9.5	14.9	30.2	43.3	53.7
						All sectors						
51 Total net borrowing	495.1	666.8	914.1	1,054.9	1,133.5	906.4	921.8	892.1	1,217.8	937.1	1,329.8	873.2
52 U.S. government securities	225.9	254.4	273.8	324.2	389.0	263.1	284.5	301.7	346.6	340.2	437.8	331.0
53 State and local obligations	44.2	53.7	50.4	136.4	35.4	33.8	67.0	67.0	205.8	-16.9	87.7	20.0
54 Corporate and foreign bonds	38.0	36.5	86.1	126.1	192.9	54.6	117.6	116.6	135.7	212.4	173.5	180.5
55 Mortgages.............................	85.4	183.6	217.4	237.7	298.0	228.8	206.0	221.2	254.2	245.6	350.4	298.3
56 Consumer credit	19.3	56.6	90.4	94.6	65.8	94.7	86.2	95.3	93.9	71.0	60.6	15.7
57 Bank loans n.e.c.	46.7	26.7	61.1	38.3	69.5	70.4	51.8	17.5	59.2	17.7	121.3	-51.0
58 Open market paper.....................	5.7	26.9	52.0	52.8	26.4	75.4	28.6	31.8	73.7	21.0	31.7	37.5
59 Other loans	30.0	28.4	82.9	44.8	56.5	85.7	80.0	41.1	48.6	46.1	66.9	41.1
						External corporate equity funds raised in United States						
60 Total new share issues	25.8	61.8	-36.4	19.9	91.6	-47.9	-24.9	3.0	36.7	100.8	82.3	61.8
61 Mutual funds...........................	8.8	27.2	29.3	85.7	163.3	26.5	32.2	64.2	107.1	155.5	171.1	123.3
62 All other...............................	17.0	34.6	-65.7	-65.8	-71.7	-74.4	-57.1	-61.2	-70.4	-54.7	-88.7	-61.5
63 Nonfinancial corporations...............	11.4	28.3	-74.5	-81.5	-80.8	-79.5	-69.4	-75.5	-87.5	-68.7	-92.7	-70.0
64 Financial corporations..................	4.2	2.6	7.8	12.0	8.3	6.8	8.8	11.2	12.8	7.5	9.1	6.7
65 Foreign shares purchased in United States..........	1.4	3.7	.9	3.7	.7	-1.6	3.5	3.1	4.3	6.6	-5.1	1.9

SOURCE: Board of Governors of the Federal Reserve, *Federal Reserve Bulletin*, April 1988, pp. A42–A43.

(continued)

TABLE 16.3 (*Continued*)

1.58 DIRECT AND INDIRECT SOURCES OF FUNDS TO CREDIT MARKETS

Billions of dollars, except as noted; half-yearly data are at seasonally adjusted annual rates.

Transaction category, or sector	1982	1983	1984	1985	1986	1984 H1	1984 H2	1985 H1	1985 H2	1986 H1	1986 H2	1987 H1
1 Total funds advanced in credit markets to domestic nonfinancial sectors	**388.9**	**550.2**	**753.9**	**854.8**	**833.4**	**717.3**	**790.4**	**722.7**	**986.8**	**676.9**	**989.9**	**568.3**
By public agencies and foreign												
2 Total net advances	114.9	114.0	157.6	202.3	317.3	132.7	182.5	195.8	208.7	264.1	370.6	241.3
3 U.S. government securities	22.3	26.3	39.3	47.1	84.8	27.6	51.0	50.3	43.9	74.0	95.6	46.3
4 Residential mortgages	61.0	76.1	56.5	94.6	158.5	55.5	57.4	88.6	100.7	123.8	193.2	164.9
5 FHLB advances to savings and loans	.8	−7.0	15.7	14.2	19.8	16.5	14.9	12.5	15.9	14.4	25.2	13.6
6 Other loans and securities	30.8	18.6	46.2	46.3	54.2	33.2	59.2	44.4	48.2	52.0	56.5	16.5
Total advanced, by sector												
7 U.S. government	15.9	9.7	17.1	16.8	9.5	7.5	26.6	25.1	8.4	10.8	8.2	−4.1
8 Sponsored credit agencies	65.5	69.8	74.3	101.5	175.5	73.3	75.2	96.4	106.7	128.2	222.8	167.7
9 Monetary authorities	9.8	10.9	8.4	21.6	30.2	12.0	4.8	27.5	15.8	13.2	47.2	10.8
10 Foreign	23.7	23.7	57.9	62.3	102.1	39.8	75.9	46.8	77.8	111.9	92.3	66.9
Agency and foreign borrowing not in line 1												
11 Sponsored credit agencies and mortgage pools	64.9	67.8	74.9	101.5	174.3	72.5	77.3	96.8	106.3	133.8	214.8	180.2
12 Foreign	16.0	17.3	8.3	1.2	9.0	36.1	−19.4	−5.8	8.2	21.5	−3.5	−12.6
Private domestic funds advanced												
13 Total net advances	354.8	521.3	679.5	755.2	699.3	693.2	665.7	618.0	892.5	568.0	830.6	494.6
14 U.S. government securities	203.6	228.1	234.5	277.0	304.2	235.5	233.5	251.3	302.7	266.3	342.2	284.7
15 State and local obligations	44.2	53.7	50.4	136.4	35.4	33.8	67.0	67.0	205.8	−16.9	87.7	20.0
16 Corporate and foreign bonds	14.7	14.5	35.1	40.8	84.3	17.3	53.0	39.7	42.0	100.8	67.8	61.6
17 Residential mortgages	−5.3	55.0	98.2	86.4	73.8	111.7	84.8	75.5	97.4	71.3	76.4	80.3
18 Other mortgages and loans	98.3	162.4	276.9	228.8	221.4	311.5	242.3	197.0	260.6	161.0	281.8	61.6
19 LESS: Federal Home Loan Bank advances	.8	−7.0	15.7	14.2	19.8	16.5	14.9	12.5	15.9	14.4	25.2	13.6
Private financial intermediation												
20 Credit market funds advanced by private financial institutions	274.2	395.8	559.8	579.5	726.1	587.5	532.1	483.8	675.2	638.9	813.2	485.1
21 Commercial banking	110.2	144.3	168.9	186.3	194.7	192.2	145.5	143.3	229.4	117.2	272.3	49.9
22 Savings institutions	22.9	135.6	150.2	83.0	105.8	167.0	133.5	54.5	111.4	94.5	117.2	85.7
23 Insurance and pension funds	96.6	100.1	121.8	156.0	175.9	148.3	95.3	139.4	172.5	170.6	181.2	213.3
24 Other finance	44.5	15.8	118.9	154.2	249.6	80.0	157.8	146.5	161.9	256.7	242.4	136.2
25 Sources of funds	274.2	395.8	559.8	579.5	726.1	587.5	532.1	483.8	675.2	638.9	813.2	485.1
26 Private domestic deposits and RPs	196.2	215.4	316.9	213.2	272.8	280.2	353.5	191.4	235.0	252.2	293.4	15.1
27 Credit market borrowing	25.4	31.5	77.0	97.4	116.8	80.5	73.5	78.3	116.5	105.0	128.6	137.4
28 Other sources	52.6	148.9	165.9	268.9	336.4	226.8	105.1	214.1	323.6	281.7	391.1	332.6
29 Foreign funds	−31.4	16.3	5.4	17.7	12.4	10.9	−.1	21.3	14.2	12.3	12.5	41.8
30 Treasury balances	6.1	−5.3	4.0	10.3	1.7	−2.8	10.8	13.9	6.6	−4.2	7.6	−4.4
31 Insurance and pension reserves	106.0	109.7	118.6	141.0	152.5	162.5	74.6	118.6	163.4	138.6	166.4	234.4
32 Other, net	−28.1	28.2	37.9	99.9	169.8	56.1	19.7	60.3	139.4	134.9	204.6	60.8
Private domestic nonfinancial investors												
33 Direct lending in credit markets	106.0	157.0	196.7	273.2	90.1	186.2	207.1	212.5	333.9	34.1	146.1	146.9
34 U.S. government securities	68.5	99.3	123.6	145.3	43.4	162.8	84.3	156.2	134.5	37.4	49.4	69.9
35 State and local obligations	25.0	40.3	30.4	47.6	−.8	10.4	50.4	14.8	80.4	−68.7	67.2	21.7
36 Corporate and foreign bonds	*	−11.6	5.2	11.8	34.4	−26.4	36.9	15.4	8.2	68.1	.8	39.0
37 Open market paper	−5.7	12.0	9.3	43.9	−4.8	15.6	3.0	3.5	84.2	−16.3	6.7	7.7
38 Other	18.2	17.0	28.1	24.6	17.9	23.8	32.5	22.6	26.6	13.6	22.1	8.5
39 Deposits and currency	205.5	232.8	320.4	223.5	293.2	286.8	354.0	198.3	248.7	262.0	324.4	10.2
40 Currency	9.7	14.3	8.6	12.4	14.4	13.7	3.6	15.9	8.8	10.7	18.2	10.0
41 Checkable deposits	18.0	28.6	27.9	41.4	97.7	26.0	29.8	14.6	68.2	79.9	115.5	−28.5
42 Small time and savings accounts	136.0	215.7	150.1	139.1	122.5	129.0	171.2	161.5	116.7	115.4	129.5	33.9
43 Money market fund shares	33.5	−39.0	49.0	8.9	43.8	24.5	73.4	10.6	7.1	46.9	40.6	−4.6
44 Large time deposits	−2.4	−8.4	84.9	7.2	−9.3	92.0	77.9	−7.6	21.9	*	−18.7	1.5
45 Security RPs	11.1	18.5	5.0	16.6	18.3	8.7	1.2	12.2	21.1	10.0	26.5	12.7
46 Deposits in foreign countries	−.4	3.1	−5.1	−2.1	5.9	−7.1	−3.1	−9.0	4.9	−.9	12.8	−14.9
47 Total of credit market instruments, deposits, and currency	311.5	389.9	517.1	496.7	383.3	473.0	561.1	410.7	582.6	296.0	470.5	157.1
48 Public holdings as percent of total	28.4	20.1	20.7	23.6	37.7	17.6	23.7	27.3	21.0	37.8	37.6	43.4
49 Private financial intermediation (in percent)	77.3	75.9	82.4	76.7	103.8	84.7	79.9	78.3	75.6	112.5	97.9	98.1
50 Total foreign funds	−7.7	40.0	63.3	80.1	114.5	50.7	75.8	68.1	92.0	124.2	104.9	108.7
MEMO: Corporate equities not included above												
51 Total net issues	25.8	61.8	−36.4	19.9	91.6	−47.9	−24.9	3.0	36.7	100.8	82.3	61.8
52 Mutual fund shares	8.8	27.2	29.3	85.7	163.5	26.5	32.2	64.2	107.1	155.5	171.1	123.3
53 Other equities	17.0	34.6	−65.7	−65.8	−71.7	−74.4	−57.1	−61.2	−70.4	−54.7	−88.7	−61.5
54 Acquisitions by financial institutions	25.9	51.1	19.7	42.8	48.2	−.2	39.7	58.8	26.8	56.6	39.7	65.5
55 Other net purchases	−.1	10.7	−56.1	−22.9	43.4	−47.7	−64.6	−55.8	10.0	44.2	42.6	−3.6

NOTES BY LINE NUMBER.
1. Line 1 of table 1.57.
2. Sum of lines 3–6 or 7–10.
6. Includes farm and commercial mortgages.
11. Credit market funds raised by federally sponsored credit agencies, and net issues of federally related mortgage pool securities.
13. Line 1 less line 2 plus line 11 and 12. Also line 20 less line 27 plus line 33. Also sum of lines 28 and 47 less lines 40 and 46.
18. Includes farm and commercial mortgages.
26. Line 39 less lines 40 and 46.
27. Excludes equity issues and investment company shares. Includes line 19.
29. Foreign deposits at commercial banks, bank borrowings from foreign branches, and liabilities of foreign banking agencies to foreign affiliates, less claims on foreign affiliates and deposits by banking in foreign banks.
30. Demand deposits and note balances at commercial banks.

31. Excludes net investment of these reserves in corporate equities.
32. Mainly retained earnings and net miscellaneous liabilities.
33. Line 13 less line 20 plus line 27.
34–38. Lines 14–18 less amounts acquired by private finance plus amounts borrowed by private finance. Line 38 includes mortgages.
40. Mainly an offset to line 9.
47. Lines 33 plus 39, or line 13 less line 28 plus 40 and 46.
48. Line 2/line 1.
49. Line 20/line 13.
50. Sum of lines 10 and 29.
51, 53. Includes issues by financial institutions.
NOTE. Full statements for sectors and transaction types in flows and in amounts outstanding may be obtained from Flow of Funds Section, Division of Research and Statistics, Board of Governors of the Federal Reserve System, Washington, D.C. 20551.

returns. This increase in systematic risk may have more than offset the decline in the actual and expected inflation rates.

(3) VARIANCE OF INTEREST RATES   A recent study showed that the standard deviations of yield changes are "surprisingly regular" and that a model can be developed to forecast a range of interest rates for a specified confidence interval.[13] Yield data for corporate bonds over the period 1900–1965 were used to determine the historical standard deviation over various holding periods from one to eight years. This analysis showed that the standard deviations were larger for bonds with longer maturities and for longer holding periods. A model was developed that used the present yield-to-maturity on a specific bond to estimate a range of possible yields at a specified future date. This approach recognized the difficulty of attempting to establish a point estimate of a bond's yield in the future.

4. ACTIVE STRATEGIES BASED ON INTEREST RATE FORECASTS AND MARKET INEFFICIENCIES The previous discussion concerned forecasting interest rate movements within the framework of economic trends and cycles, and the structure of yields relative to term and to other characteristics. This section discusses some general bond investment strategies, given specific interest rate forecasts, as well as strategies based on perceived bond market inefficiencies.

A forecast of declining yields suggests attractive opportunities for fixed-income investing. To maximize the *HPR* by earning capital gains requires investing in securities that are expected to have the greatest increase in prices. This suggests long-term, low-coupon, and high-quality bonds, or essentially long durations combined with high agency ratings. The investor should also be aware, however, that the probability of a call increases during periods of declining yields.

A forecast of increasing yields suggests a poor environment for fixed-income securities due to anticipated falling prices. If bonds are still desirable for other reasons, as opposed to holding cash or other types of securities, then very short-term securities are appropriate. This would minimize interest rate risk and also provide an opportunity to reduce the reinvestment rate risk since cash flows can be reinvested at the increasing short term rates.

For an existing bond portfolio during a period of increasing yields, one appropriate strategy involves quarterly trading that sells bonds presently in the portfolio and uses the proceeds and interest income to acquire bonds selling at par with the same maturity as the bond that was sold.[14] This strategy would be superior to a buy-and-hold strategy for an existing port-folio.

One study has also shown that strategies using "naive" interest rate fore-casts may be able to outperform a buy-and-hold strategy.[15] The interest rate

---

[13] J. E. Murphy and M. F. M. Osborne, "Predicting the Volatility of Interest Rates," *Journal of Portfolio Management* (Winter 1985): pp. 66–69.

[14] Carol J. Billingham, "Strategies for Enhancing Bond Portfolio Returns," *Financial Analysts Journal* (May-June 1983): pp. 50–56.

[15] H. Gifford Fong and Frank J. Fabozzi, "How to Enhance Bond Returns with Naive Strategies," *Journal of Portfolio Management* (Summer 1985): pp. 57–60.

forecasts were considered naive since they used only current and historical data—and in one case a simple analysis of the yield curve or term structure. Using a six-year historical simulation of the strategies for the period 1978–1984, the study concluded that one (yield curve analysis) of the two strategies tested outperformed an index of Treasury securities by a "comfortable margin."

In addition to strategies based on forecast of interest rate movements there are numerous strategies based on perceived inefficiencies in the bond market and for individual bonds. For example, two identical bonds may temporarily have unequal prices. This offers an active bond investor the opportunity to purchase an undervalued bond for anticipated short-term capital gains when the market realizes that the bond is undervalued. These types of strategies are often referred to as *bond swaps*, implying that an existing bond portfolio is actively managed for maximum return. The above swap is typically referred to as a *substitution swap*. Other commonly used strategies are *yield pickup swaps*, *tax swaps*, *spread swaps*, and *rate anticipation swaps*. Examples of many types of swaps and procedures that can be used to evaluate their desirability can be found in an excellent text by Homer and Leibowitz.[16] Bond swaps will be discussed in greater detail later in this chapter.

Another market inefficiency that may offer excess returns deals with *high-yield* or *junk* bonds. These bonds do not have an "investment grade" rating (Baa or higher for Moody's, BBB or higher for Standard & Poor's).

One study found that nonconvertible publicly traded junk bonds grew from under $10 billion in 1978 to almost $42 billion by mid-1984.[17] This study also found that over the period 1974–1984, 1.52 percent of the outstanding junk bonds defaulted each year. The average defaulted bond traded at 41 percent of par shortly after default. The analysis also found that the incidence of default varied substantially from year to year and among industries. The returns on junk bonds also averaged 490 to 580 basis points above the long-term government bond index.

The debate in the investment literature concerns the market's efficiency at pricing these bonds. One viewpoint suggests that they tend to be underpriced and offer excess returns, while an alternative states that they are correctly priced or even overpriced. A number of recent studies have been directed at resolving this issue.

Two recent studies concluded that junk bonds, on average, appear to be undervalued.[18] These studies found that a well-diverisified portfolio of junk bonds provided returns that more than compensated for losses due to default.

---

[16] Sidney Homer and Martin Leibowitz, *Inside the Yield Book* (Englewood Cliffs, N. J.: Prentice-Hall, 1972).

[17] Edward I. Altman and Scott A. Nammacher, "The Default Rate Experience on High-yield Corporate Debt," *Financial Analysts Journal* (July-August 1985): pp. 25–41.

[18] Christopher K. Ma and Garry M. Weed," Fact and Fancy of Takeover Junk Bonds," *Journal of Portfolio Management* (Fall 1986): pp. 34–37, and Jerome S. Fons, "The Default Premium and Corporate Bond Experience," *Journal of Finance* (March 1987): pp. 81–97.

This implies that the bonds provide a yield above that necessary to compensate for default risk.

A different conclusion was reached by Weinstein.[19] Using data over the period June 1962 through July 1974, his study concluded that junk bonds have been "fairly priced." He argued that it is also unlikely that the entire junk bond sector is mispriced. This observation suggests that each junk bond needs to be individually analyzed and that a diversified portfolio is appropriate for bonds that appear to be undervalued.

Numerous additional studies of possible bond market efficiencies have examined U.S. Treasury securities,[20] corporate bonds,[21] and municipal bonds.[22] Some of these studies report evidence of inefficiencies; others find evidence of efficient pricing. As Chapter 13 concluded, the debate about the degree of market efficiency is not resolved. For the bond markets, the evidence is inconclusive because of the possible influences of risk differences, transaction costs, and tax implications. Additional research is needed to resolve these issues.

The discussion of bond investment strategies up to this point has essentially been concerned with individual bonds or categories of bonds and the returns that active management strategies can offer. Extremely important considerations are portfolio effects and the impact of diversification on the risk and return of the bond portfolio. The following section deals with bond portfolio considerations.

BOND PORTFOLIO STRATEGIES

Overview

Investors should appreciate the benefits of diversification in every investment portfolio. This appreciation may be based on the simple realization that there are real advantages to "not putting all your eggs in one basket." It may also be based on the knowledge that an adequately diversified portfolio offers the opportunity to reduce total risk by minimizing unsystematic risk, often without a significant reduction in portfolio returns. The next section of this chapter discusses a number of diversification techniques that can be used for bond portfolios.

---

[19] Mark I. Weinstein, "A Curmudgeon's View of Junk Bonds," *Journal of Portfolio Management* (Spring 1987): pp. 76–80

[20] Michael J. Brennan and Eduardo S. Schwartz, "Bond Pricing and Market Efficiency," *Financial Analysts Journal* (September-October 1982): pp. 49–56, and Robert M. Conroy and Richard J. Rendleman, Jr., "A Test of Market Efficiency in Government Bonds," *Journal of Portfolio Management* (Summer 1987): pp. 57–64.

[21] Michael Smirlock, "Seasonality and Bond Market Returns," *Journal of Portfolio Management* (Spring 1985): pp. 42–44.

[22] Duane Stock, "Does Active Management of Municipal Bond Portfolios Pay?" *Journal of Portfolio Management* (Winter 1982): pp. 51–55.

Diversification by Number of Bonds in the Portfolio

Previous studies on diversification for common stock portfolios indicate that a portfolio of ten to fifteen randomly selected stocks essentially eliminates most unsystematic or diversifiable risk. Is this also true for fixed-income security portfolios? This question was addressed in two studies that investigated this and other issues concerning bond diversification.[23]

Historically, many investors and analysts have thought that bonds, unlike common stocks, have a total risk which is essentially systematic rather than unsystematic. When interest rates and yields change, all bond prices and yields respond in essentially the same fashion. This implies that there are very few independent price or yield movements from one bond to the next and thus a limited degree of unsystematic risk. Diversification by numbers, therefore, would offer a limited benefit.

Figure 16.5, from the McEnally and Boardman study, contradicts this point by showing the dramatic reduction in total portfolio risk (variance) that occurs as bonds are added to the portfolio. As with common stocks, the variances of returns of the bond portfolio decrease rapidly as bonds are added to the portfolio. As the lower limit of risk is approached, adding a bond to the portfolio has a minimal impact on portfolio risk. This optimal number occurs in the range of eight to sixteen bonds, depending on the agency rating. It appears that diverisification by numbers is much more effective for bonds with lower ratings than for those judged to be higher-quality bonds.

Similar results were found in the Hill and Schneeweis study, but they concluded that "for the bonds analyzed in this study a smaller number of securities are required to reduce portfolio risk to a level approximating that of a market portfolio of similar securities than has been found to be the case for common stock."[24] For public utility and industrial bonds, a portfolio size of ten to twelve bonds provides the lower limit of risk.

The clear message from both of these studies is to diversify bond portfolios, using even naive strategies (random selection). Portfolios consisting of eight to sixteen bonds will result in considerably less portfolio return variability than portfolios of one or two bonds. Portfolios containing more than this number offer few added benefits, with the possible exception of lower-rated corporate bonds.

Techniques of Bond Portfolio Diversification

1. MARKOWITZ AND SHARPE Bond portfolios can be constructed using either a Markowitz or a Sharpe procedure, as discussed earlier for common stocks. This approach is somewhat mathematical and is designed to identify bond portfolios offering the highest expected return for a given level of risk.

---

[23] Richard W. McEnally and Calvin M. Boardman, "Aspects of Corporate Bond Portfolio Diversification," *Journal of Financial Research* (Spring 1979): pp. 27–36, and Joanne Hill and Thomas Schneeweis, "Diversification and Portfolio Size for Fixed-Income Securities," *Journal of Economics and Business* (Winter 1981): pp. 115–21.

[24] Hill and Schneeweis, p. 120.

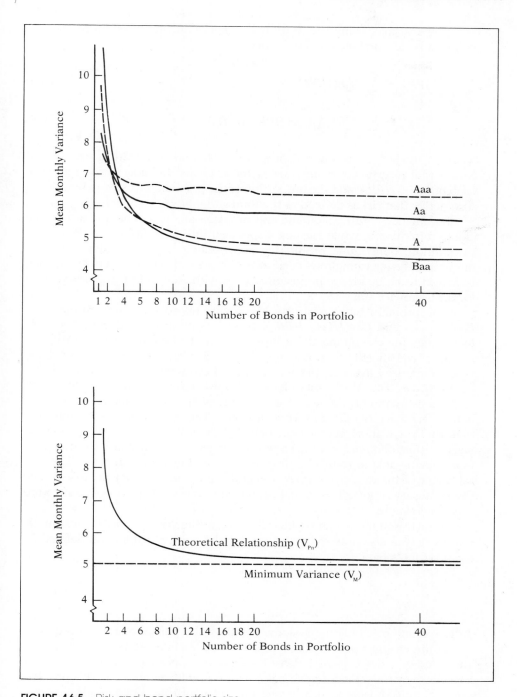

FIGURE 16.5 Risk and bond portfolio size

Source: Richard W. McEnally and Calvin M. Boardman, "Aspects of Corporate Bond Portfolio Diversification," *Journal of Financial Research*, (Spring 1979): pp. 33 and 35. Reprinted by permission.

For example, using the Markowitz approach, the expected return and risk of a bond portfolio can be defined as

$$E(HPR_p) = \sum_{j=1}^{n} X_j E(HPR_j) \tag{16.3}$$

$$\sigma_p^2 = \sum_{i=1}^{n} \sum_{j=1}^{n} X_i X_j Cov(HPR_j, HPR_m) \tag{16.4}$$

where X_i and X_j represent the proportion of funds invested in each bond. Notice that returns are defined using the expected holding period return of each bond, $E(HPR_j)$, and the proportion of the portfolio invested in bond j, X_j. Also notice that risk is defined as the total variability of the portfolio's return, σ_p^2, that includes both systematic and unsystematic risk. The investor would like to minimize σ_p^2 while earning a specified rate of return on the portfolio. In addition, constraints prohibiting short-selling, $X_j \geq 0$, and requiring a minimum agency rating may need to be considered. The problem could then be solved using quadratic programming, as with computer programs written for a Markowitz analysis.

One problem with using the Markowitz approach is the estimates of $E(HPR)$, σ_j^2, and $Cov(HPR_j, HPR_m)$. A 1985 study investigated five possible techniques for estimating these inputs.[25] The techniques are (1) historical averages over most recent sixteen quarters, (2) Sharpe's diagonal model, (3) yield-to-maturity average, (4) duration bond estimates, and (5) lagged historical returns. The Markowitz efficient frontiers were estimated using each of these estimating techniques for a sample of U.S. and Canadian corporate bonds, Treasury bonds, and Treasury bills. The empirical results indicated that the correlation coefficients between bonds were sufficiently low to warrant portfolio analysis. These results suggest that a properly formed portfolio may be able to reduce both systematic and unsystematic risk. The performance of the model, however, depends on the technique used to estimate the necessary inputs. The model performed poorly when ex-post data were used to estimate the inputs.

Similar equations can be identified for a Sharpe analysis. For example, Equation 16.3 also applies to a Sharpe model, with portfolio risk defined by the portfolio's beta:

$$\beta_p = \sum_{j=1}^{n} X_j \beta_j \tag{16.5}$$

In Equation 16.5, only the systematic risk of the portfolio and of each bond is considered since beta is the measure of risk. As indicated earlier, however, the value of n needs to be at least 8–16 bonds to be reasonably sure that diversifiable or unsystematic risk has been essentially eliminated. This problem could be solved using a linear programming algorithm, since quadratic equations are not involved.

---

[25] Tom Barnes, "Markowitz Allocation—Fixed-Income Securities," *Journal of Financial Research* (Fall 1985): pp. 181–90.

2. CLASSICAL IMMUNIZATION Another diversification technique that has received considerable recent attention is *classical immunization*. This techique is designed to "immunize" a bond portfolio from interest rate risk, including both price risk and reinvestment rate risk. Immunization deals with the formation of a bond portfolio, including bonds of various coupons and terms-to-maturity, that will provide a specified *HPR*.

This technique requires that the investor specify the desired length of the holding period. Once this is done, the key to the immunization strategy is to *match* the duration of the portfolio to the desired holding period. If the desired holding period or investment horizon is five years, a bond portfolio with a duration of five years would be constructed.

To illustrate this concept for a single bond, assume that the desired holding period is three years. Thus, a bond with a duration equal to three years must be purchased. Assume that a corporate bond is currently selling for $900, has a 12 percent coupon paid annually, and a term-to-maturity of four years. You should be able to verify that the yield-to-maturity for this bond is 15.54 percent and that the duration is approximately three years (see Chapter 15). This bond could therefore immunize the investor against interest rate risk, so that even if yields and (therefore) prices change over the three-year horizon, the *HPR* will be equal to the yield-to-maturity. Table 16.4 illustrates this technique.

Notice from Part I of Table 16.4 that the terminal value of the three coupons is calculated using an assumed yield-to-maturity of 13 percent. The yield-to-maturity dropped one year after the bond was purchased, from 15.54 percent to 13 percent. Also, since the bond has a term-to-maturity of four years, its price will not be the face value after three years, since the coupon rate is 12 percent and the yield-to-maturity is 13 percent. Thus the value of the bond, or selling price, must be calculated. This calculation indicates that the bond will be selling at $991.15 at the end of the investor's desired holding period. Combining the terminal value of the coupons with the selling price indicates that the investor will have a total terminal value of $1,399.98, based on a $900 investment three years earlier. The annualized *HPR* of 15.86 percent is approximately equal to the initial yield-to-maturity of 15.54 percent. This slight difference is due to the fact that the duration of the bond is not exactly three years; its actual duration is 3.37 years.

Part II of Table 16.4 calculates the annualized *HPR*, assuming that yields do not change after the bond is purchased. As the calculations indicate, the annualized *HPR* is 15.54 percent, or the yield-to-maturity when the bond was purchased. The *HPR* from the immunized strategy is larger, however, 15.86 percent, because of the decline in yields.

The major purpose of this example is to show how duration can be used to immunize a bond portfolio. Classical immunization works because price risk and reinvestment rate risk are exactly offset when the holding period equals duration. Notice in the example that income from reinvesting the coupons was less than anticipated because the yield-to-maturity declined from 15.54 to 13 percent. This was offset by the price appreciation resulting from the decline in yield. To illustrate, if the yield-to-maturity had remained at 15.54 percent, the bond's price would have been $P_0 = \$1120/(1 + .1554) = \$969.36$, rather than $991.15. If yields had increased, then the higher income

TABLE 16.4 ILLUSTRATION OF THE CLASSICAL IMMUNIZATION TECHNIQUE FOR A CORPORATE BOND

I. IMMUNIZATION

Desired Holding Period:	3 years
Characteristics of an Available Corporate Bond:	
Duration:	3 years
Term-to-maturity:	4 years
Coupon (paid annually):	12%
Current price:	$900
Yield-to-maturity when bond was purchased:	15.54%

Assume that the bond is purchased, and *one* year later the yield-to-maturity declines to 13%. Thus, coupons must be reinvested at lower rates, but the price of the bond will increase.

Calculation of the Annualized *HPR*:

Termination value of first coupon:	$120(1 + .13)^2 = $153.23
Termination value of second coupon:	$120(1 + .13)^1 = 135.60
Termination value of third coupon:	$120(1 + .13)^0 = 120.00
Total Terminal Value of Coupons:	$408.83

Value of bond at end of 3 years with yield-to-maturity of 13%:

$$P_0 = \frac{\$120}{(1 + .13)} + \frac{\$1000}{(1 + .13)} = \$991.15$$

Therefore, the total terminal value is $408.83 + $991.15 = $1,399.98, and the annualized *HPR* is

$$\$1,399.98 = \$900(1 + r)^3$$
$$1.5555 = (1 + r)^3$$
$$\sqrt[3]{1.5555} = 1 + r$$
$$1.1586 = 1 + r$$
$$r = 15.86\%$$

II. CALCULATION OF ANNUALIZED *HPR*, ASSUMING YIELDS DO NOT CHANGE

Terminal value of first coupon:	$120(1 + .1554)^2 = $160.19
Terminal value of second coupon:	$120(1 + .1554)^1 = 138.65
Terminal value of third coupon:	$120(1 + .1554)^0 = 120.00
Total Terminal Value of Coupons:	$418.84

Value of bond at end of three years with yield-to-maturity of 15.54%:

$$P_0 = \frac{\$120}{(1 + .1554)} + \frac{\$1000}{(1 + .1554)} = \$969.36$$

Annualized HPR is

$$\$418.84 + \$969.36 = \$900(1 + r)^3$$
$$1.5424 = (1 + r)^3$$
$$r = 15.54\%$$

---

from reinvestment returns would also have offset the price decline exactly. It should also be pointed out that if more than one yield change occurred, the portfolio would no longer be immunized. It would be necessary to *rebalance* the portfolio by equating duration to the remaining length of the holding period.

Since it is important that more than one bond is included in a portfolio, the concept of immunization should be viewed in a portfolio context. This is quite easy to do since duration, like beta, is additive; the duration of a portfolio D_p can be defined as

$$D_p = \sum_{j=1}^{n} X_j D_j \qquad (16.6)$$

where X_j is the proportion of funds invested in bond j, and D_j is the duration of bond j. The portfolio can be immunized if its duration is equal to the investor's desired holding period.

The duration measure that we have been discussing is called the classical or the single-factor model. When used to immunize a bond porfolio, this model assumes that the term structure is flat and subject only to parallel shifts.[26] These assumptions can present problems for investors attempting to immunize; the portfolio must be rebalanced to reflect changes in yields, price, and term-to-maturity. That is, the duration of the portfolio must always be equal to the investment horizon. If an investor started with a five-year horizon, the initial portfolio's duration must also be five years. After one year, however, the remaining horizon is only four years, and the portfolio must be rebalanced or revised so that its duration is also four years. It should also be recognized that the change in term of the portfolio is unlikely to equal the change in duration. For example, if the term declines from five to four years, the duration of the portfolio will not necessarily be four years. This suggests that transaction costs may be significant, and gains or losses may occur during the process of rebalancing.

3. CONTINGENT IMMUNIZATION Attempts have been made to develop other measures of duration that do not require an assumption of a flat yield curve limited to parallel shifts. Efforts have also been directed at improving the classical immunization strategy, so that the portfolio will provide a minimum return but will also have an opportunity to provide a higher return.

This approach, *contingent immunization*, involves active management of the bond portfolio in an attempt to earn at least a specified minimum rate of return, with the possibility that the return can be higher. The portfolio is therefore immunized against downside risk but allows for upside potential. The strategy requires that the specified minimum rate be set below the prevailing market yield and that the investment horizon may need to be shortened or lengthened, depending on yield movements.

To provide a simple example of contigent immunization, assume that an investor is considering a long-term bond portfolio. The investor is unsure about future yield movements but thinks that both increases and decreases are possible. Rather than initially forming a portfolio with a duration equal to the holding period, the investor may simply purchase bonds with maturities longer than the anticipated investment horizon. If yields decline, the portfolio will increase in value, providing a *HPR* above the minimum. If yields increase to a certain level, however, the investor will immediately rebalance

---

[26] Kevin J. Maloney and Jess B. Yawitz, "Interest Rate Risk, Immunization, and Duration," *Journal of Portfolio Management* (Spring 1986): pp. 41–48.

the portfolio so that duration equals the desired holding period. The rebalancing will require selling existing bonds and purchasing new bonds to achieve the desired portfolio duration.

Contingent immunization allows active management prior to the time that the portfolio needs to be immunized. For example, the investor may trade in bonds that are perceived to be over or undervalued. If losses occur to the extent that the specified minimum *HPR* is threatened, then active trading will cease, and the portfolio will be immunized to guarantee the desired minimum *HPR*.

There are a number of excellent papers on the historical development of duration and immunization, and the assessment of the strengths and weaknesses of these techniques.[27] As you might expect, much research is currently being conducted concerning bond risk management; it is likely that significant progress will be made in this area. It should be emphasized, however, that research has already shown the advantages of duration as a risk measure and as a tool to manage risk. In addition, duration has been shown to be a superior measure of risk when compared to a traditional risk measure such as term-to-maturity.

There are other important bond portfolio strategies and diversification techniques, used primarily by institutional investors such as pension funds. For example, many pension funds use a technique, *portfolio insurance*, to protect against downside risk using financial futures. This and other techniques used primarily by institutional investors are discussed in Chapter 25.

Bond Portfolio Revisions

1. BOND SWAPS An active bond portfolio management strategy may often involve frequent transactions that replace current bonds with new bonds. This strategy is commonly referred to as *bond swaps*. The motivation is to earn short-term gains by exploiting perceived inefficiencies in the bond markets. The most frequently used swaps are *substitution*, *yield pickup*, and *tax swaps*.

    a. SUBSTITUTION SWAP This swap is designed to take advantage of a perceived temporary yield differential between bonds that are similar with respect to coupons, ratings, maturities, and industry. To illustrate this type of swap, Table 16.5 provides data on two similar utility bonds that have a yield-to-maturity spread of sixty basis points. The price of the Duke Power Company bond is $83\frac{7}{8}$ ($838.75), and the Commonwealth Edison bond's price is $79\frac{7}{8}$ ($798.75). If the bond portfolio currently contains the Duke Power bonds, then a substitution swap may be feasible; a similar bond can be purchased for $40.00 below the bond that is cur-

---

[27] G. O. Bierwag, George G. Kaufman, and Alden L. Toevs, "Duration: Its Development and Use in Bond Portfolio Management," *Financial Analysts Journal* (July-August 1983): pp. 15–35; Martin L. Leibowitz and Alfred Weinberger, "The Uses of Contingent Immunization," *Journal of Portfolio Management* (Fall 1981): pp. 51–55; Martin Leibowitz and Alfred Weinberger, "Contingent Immunization—Part I," *Financial Analysts Journal* (November-December 1982):pp. 17–31, and ". . . Part II," (January-February 1983): pp. 35–50; G. O. Bierwag, George G. Kaufman, and Cynthia M. Latta, "Bond Portfolio Immunization: Test of Maturity, One- and Two-factor Duration Matching Strategies," *Financial Review* (May 1987): pp. 203–19.

TABLE 16.5 BOND SUBSTITUTION SWAP

	DUKE POWER COMPANY	COMMONWEALTH EDISON
Moody's rating (December 1987):	Aa2	Baa1
Standard & Poor's rating (December 1987):	AA−	BBB+
Coupon rate:	$8\frac{1}{8}\%$	$8\frac{1}{8}\%$
Maturity date:	7/1/2007	1/15/2007
Interest payment dates:	1/1 and 7/1	1/15 and 7/15
Current call price:	104.78	105.26
Amount outstanding (millions):	$119.5	$180
Price at end of December 1987:	$83\frac{7}{8}$	$79\frac{7}{8}$
Yield-to-maturity at end of December 1987:	10.00%	10.60%

SOURCES: *Bond Record*, Moody's, December 1987. *Bond Guide*, Standard & Poor's, December 1987. Reprinted by permission.

rently in the portfolio. This would be a simple transaction that sells an overvalued bond and replaces it with an undervalued bond. The underlying assumption is that one or both of the bonds are incorrectly priced, based on the fairly sizable difference in their prices.

The feasibility of this potential substitution swap would need to be determined by an analysis of the anticipated return and risk associated with the swap. The following factors should be considered in this analysis:

(1) The *workout period*, or the period before the market recognizes that the bonds are incorrectly valued.

(2) The equilibrium bond price at the end of the workout period.

(3) The reinvestment rate that will apply to the additional funds realized from selling the higher priced Duke Power bonds and buying the Commonwealth Edison bonds.

(4) Taxes resulting from a gain or loss on the sale of the Duke Power bonds.

(5) Commissions and other transaction costs resulting from the swap.

(6) A careful analysis of any potential risk differences between the two bonds.

These factors would be used to calculate an $E(HPR)$ of the proposed swap. This $E(HPR)$ can then be compared to the $E(HPR)$ resulting from continuing to hold the Duke Power bonds, or to other possible swaps or investment alternatives.

b. YIELD PICKUP SWAP A second type of swap is the *yield pickup swap*. This swap is designed to change the cash flow of the portfolio by exchanging similar bonds that have different coupon rates. For example, if additional cash flow was desired, an existing "low" coupon bond in the portfolio could be swapped for a similar "high" coupon bond. Table 16.6 illustrates two likely candidates for a yield pickup swap. Notice that the two bonds are similar except for their coupon rates. If a bond portfolio currently contained the Philadelphia Electric bond, it might be feasible to swap for the Consumer Power bond, with a resulting increase in coupon

TABLE 16.6   BOND YIELD PICKUP SWAP

	PHILADELPHIA ELECTRIC	CONSUMER POWER COMPANY
Moody's rating (December 1987):	Baa3	Baa3
Standard & Poor's rating (December 1987):	BBB−	BBB−
Coupon rate:	$7\frac{3}{4}$%	$11\frac{1}{2}$%
Maturity date:	12/15/2000	7/1/2000
Interest payment dates:	6/15 and 12/15	1/1 and 7/1
Current call price:	103.30	105.75
Amount outstanding (millions):	$71.4	$45.0
Price at end of December 1987:	$83\frac{7}{8}$	104
Yield-to-maturity at end of December 1987:	9.98%	10.90%
Current or coupon yield at end of December 1987:	9.24%	11.06%

SOURCES: *Bond Record*, Moody's, December 1987. *Bond Guide*, Standard & Poor's, December 1987. Reprinted by permission.

income. Notice that the yields-to-maturity are similar, but the Philadelphia Electric bond is selling at a discount because of its relatively low coupon. Thus a large portion of the yield-to-maturity is based on the assumed increase in price to the maturity value of $1,000 over the life of the bond. On the other hand, a large portion of the yield-to-maturity of the Consumer Power bond is based on its high coupon, since the bond is selling for $40 over its face value.

The proposed swap would therefore result in an exchange of potential returns: capital gains for coupon income. Thus, the portfolio would have higher coupon income and a small increase in the overall yield-to-maturity of the portfolio.

The feasibility of the swap would need to be analyzed using the same factors that were presented for the substitution swap. Particular attention should be given to tax implications: coupon income is taxed for the period received, while taxes on capital gains do not occur until the bond is sold or matures.

The yield pickup swap can also be based on a desire to change the yield-to-maturity of the portfolio rather than the coupon yield. In this case, a portfolio with the Philadelphia Electric bond may consider a *yield-to-maturity pickup* swap, swapping for the Consumer Power bond with its slightly higher yield-to-maturity.

c.   TAX SWAP Another important type of bond swap is the *tax swap*.[28] As its name implies, the swap is made for tax purposes. There are many types of swaps that can have a favorable impact on taxes. One very effective swap involves selling a bond at a loss so that a book loss can be converted to an actual loss, offsetting capital gains from other transactions. The proceeds from the sale can be used to acquire a similar bond, so that the overall characteristics of the portfolio are not changed. One restriction imposed by the Internal Revenue Code is that the bond that

---

[28] For an analysis, see Edward A. Dyl and Stanley A. Martin, Jr. ''Rules of Thumb for the Analysis of Tax Swaps,'' *Journal of Portfolio Management* (Fall 1983): pp. 71–74.

was sold cannot be repurchased. This transaction would be classified as a *wash sale* and could not be recognized as a taxable loss.

A second type of tax swap involves the exchange of bonds that receive different tax treatments. For example, corporate bonds may be exchanged for municipals if the marginal tax rate of the investor and the market yield spread between the two will provide a higher after-tax return. Again, any risk difference must be carefully considered.

d. OTHER TYPES OF SWAPS Other swap strategies are based on forecasts of general interest rate changes and are referred to as *rate anticipation* swaps. For example, a forecast of increasing yields may motivate a swap of long-term for short-term securities, so that price declines are minimized. In this case, the securities may have significant differences in coupons, ratings, durations, or other important characteristics.

There are a number of other strategies. The *intermarket-spread* swap is based on an analysis of yield spreads between different bond market segments. For example, a spread may exist between similar bonds in different industries, between similar bonds in the same industry but with different ratings, or between corporate or government bond markets. The assumption is that these spreads change as economic conditions change, and the correct forecast of the change in spreads can be used to formulate successful swap strategies.

2. REBALANCING A concept that is closely related to bond swaps is portfolio *rebalancing*. Swaps are motivated by the investor's perceptions of potentially successful strategies based on forecasts of market changes; rebalancing, however, occurs because of developments in the market. Rebalancing is undertaken in order to maintain the desired characteristics of the portfolio. For example, the duration of a bond portfolio is calculated as a weighted average of the durations of the bonds in the portfolio, with the weights based on the market value of each bond relative to the total market value of the portfolio. If the market prices of one or more of the bonds change, then the weights and durations of these bonds have changed, and the duration of the portfolio has also changed. If the investor desires to maintain the previous duration of the portfolio, a rebalancing or portfolio revision must be undertaken. This action is dictated by market developments rather than a desire to change the characteristics of the portfolio. The benefits from rebalancing, however, should be greater than the transaction and other costs associated with the rebalancing.

Other market developments, such as rating changes, yield changes (price changes), and spreads, may force the investor to rebalance or revise the portfolio. This requires that market conditions be closely monitored and their impact on the portfolio's characteristics evaluated.

Other Considerations

It should be understood that the bond portfolio management strategies discussed in this chapter are techniques that can assist in the risk-return management of a bond portfolio. There should also be an appreciation of the complexity and difficulties that a bond investor faces in the real world. For example, a duration-immunization strategy provides a technique for management of interest rate risk.

If this strategy is followed, however, the investor must still deal with the risk of default and purchasing power risk.

These problems might be handled simply by making sure that the bond portfolio is adequately diversified. For default risk purposes, this may mean holding only the highest-quality bonds or, if lower-quality bonds look attractive, adequately diversifying the *number* of bonds in the portfolio. For management of purchasing power risk, bonds with both short and long maturities may be desirable. Diversifying into other types of securities, such as common stocks, convertible bonds, or real assets, might also be considered. These issues are discussed in Chapter 26, on personal investment management.

Another problem that individual bond investors may face is the lack of sufficient funds to ensure adequate diversification. A frequently cited rule-of-thumb is that a minimum of $50,000 is needed for fixed-income security investing. Since bonds typically have face values of $1,000 and are usually sold in blocks of five or more bonds, a fairly large sum is needed to ensure adequate diversification. This problem may be solved for the small investor through the use of mutual funds that specialize in bond portfolios. Most of the major "families" of mutual funds, such as the Fidelity Group, T. Rowe Price Funds, and Vanguard, offer one or more bond funds. Mutual funds are discussed in detail in Chapter 24. This approach, however, eliminates the possibility of actively managing the bond portfolio, since it is managed by the fund's portfolio manager.

SUMMARY

This chapter integrated the previous material on bonds and provided an extension of that material by discussing bond investment strategies and portfolio considerations. Strategies can range from buy-and-hold to a very active strategy directed at "beating the market." A key ingredient to a successful active strategy is accurate interest rate forecasting. Forecasting interest rates was discussed in the context of trend and cyclical movements, yield curve analysis, and specific forecasting models.

Bond portfolio management strategies can range from a naive diversification by number of securities to the mathematical approaches of Markowitz and Sharpe. Empirical studies have shown that sizable benefits may be derived even from naive diversification, especially for lower-quality corporate bonds. This research indicates that eight to sixteen bonds are needed to eliminate unsystematic or diversifiable risk. Portfolios with bonds beyond this number provide only nominal additional reduction in unsystematic risk.

Strategies involving management of interest rate risk were also discussed. By matching the portfolio's duration to the desired holding period, the portfolio can be immunized against changes in yields. This provides an ex-post portfolio return that essentially equals the ex-ante or expected return indicated by the yield-to-maturity that existed when the portfolio was formed.

Factors such as managing purchasing power risk and default risk need to be considered. To date, no one strategy has been developed to deal with all of the major types of risk for fixed-income portfolios. Bond portfolio management in the real world can be quite challenging in the current economic environment. Bond portfolio management is probably more an art than a science.

1. Compare and contrast active and passive bond investment strategies.
2. What bond investment strategy is suggested by a period of stable yields? By a period of volatile yields?
3. Describe the *dumbbell* and *laddered* strategies. What type of risk are they designed to manage?
4. Discuss the advantages and disadvantages of a bond strategy that equates the term of the bond to the desired holding period.
5. Is an economic forecast useful in forecasting interest rate movements? Discuss.
6. Assume that the yield curve is currently upward-sloping. According to the expectations theory, what interest rate forecast does this imply?
7. There is some evidence that diversification by the number of bonds in the portfolio is more attractive for low- rather than high-quality bonds. What are some explanations of this evidence?
8. What type of risk is reduced as the number of bonds in the portfolio increases? What type of risk is not reduced? Why?
9. Do you think that a Markowitz or Sharpe bond portfolio analysis would be superior to a random selection of bonds? Explain.
10. Explain the theory underlying the concept of immunization.
11. It is often stated that an immunization strategy requires an assumption of a flat yield curve. Explain this statement and its implication for an immunization strategy.
12. For each of the following forecasts, outline an appropriate bond investment strategy for an investor with a five-year investment horizon.
    a. Rapid increase in interest rates.
    b. Rapid decrease in interest rates.
    c. No clear interest rate forecast. Rates may increase or decrease.

1. Assume that the following yields will be available on three short-term bonds selling at par and on an intermediate-term bond. Calculate the annualized *HPR* of a roll over strategy using the three short-term bonds versus a buy-and-hold strategy using the intermediate term bond. Assume that all income is reinvested at the available yield and your investment horizon is three years. Discuss the risk and return characteristics of the two strategies.

ONE YEAR BONDS			INTERMEDIATE-TERM BOND
YEAR	YIELD	MATURITY	(TERM = 3 YEARS)
1	12%	1 year	current price = $1,000
2	14%	1 year	face value = $1000
3	11%	1 year	coupon rate = 13%

2. Consider the following yields and terms-to-maturity on U.S. government securities:

SECURITY	TERM (YEARS)	YIELD
1	1	10.4%
2	2	11.6
3	4	12.4
4	8	14.2
5	16	14.0

    a. Use the above data to construct a yield curve.

    b. Does the yield curve indicate any inefficiencies in the market? Explain.

    c. Does it appear that there are any pricing inefficiencies that might provide profit opportunities? Explain.

3. Consider the following two bonds:

	BOND A	BOND B
Current price:	$900	$950
Term:	4 years	6 years
Coupon:	10%	12%
Face value:	$1000	$1000

    a. Calculate the yield-to-maturity for both bonds.

    b. Calculate the duration for both bonds.

    c. What investment horizons would be necessary so that each bond individually could be used in an immunization strategy?

    d. Assume that your investment horizon is four years. Explain how both bonds could be used to form an immunized portfolio. Calculate the proportion each bond must represent in the portfolio for this strategy.

4. Assume that you would like to have $30,000 in three years to buy your "dream" car. Suppose you have the following two investment options available today:

	OPTION 1	OPTION 2
Security:	U.S. Treasury Note	Corporate bond
Term:	3 years	4 years
Yield-to-maturity:	12%	15%
Coupon:	10%	10%

    a. Calculate the amount you must invest in each option today to have $30,000 in three years. Assume a rate of return equal to the yield-to-maturity on each security.

    b. Discuss which strategy you would follow, and the advantages and disadvantages of each, in your quest for a "dream" car.

5.   A friend asks you to evaluate her bond portfolio and supplies the following information:

SECURITY	FACE VALUE	CURRENT MARKET VALUE	TERM (YEARS)	COUPON	YIELD-TO-MATURITY	DURATION (YEARS)
U.S. Treasury bill:	$10,000	$ 9,091	1	0%	10.00%	1
U.S. Treasury note:	20,000	19,500	5	10	10.67	4.16
Corporate bond, Ba rated:	15,000	12,000	10	12	16.16	5.90
Corporate bond, Aa rated:	10,000	11,000	5	15	12.21	3.91

a.   Calculate the term-to-maturity of the portfolio.

b.   Calculate the duration of the portfolio.

c.   Calculate the annual cash flow for the next year. What is the coupon yield of the portfolio?

d.   Suppose your friend has an investment horizon of three years, and the portfolio will be liquidated at that time. Would you make any recommendations for a portfolio revision? Specifically, what are your recommendations?

e.   Is default risk a major concern for this portfolio?

f.   Does the portfolio provide liquidity in case your friend needs cash? Explain.

g.   Do you think that the portfolio has adequate diversification in terms of the number and types of bonds? Explain.

h.   Suppose your friend thinks that interest rates are likely to *increase* dramatically during the coming year. What recommendation would you make?

i.   Answer part h assuming she expects rates to decline.

6.   Consider the following information on a corporate bond:

Face value:	$1,000
Coupon:	11% (paid annually)
Current market value:	$850
Moody's rating:	A
Term:	6 years

a.   Calculate the yield-to-maturity of this bond.

b.   Calculate the duration of the bond.

c.   Assume that your investment horizon is equal to the duration calculated in part b.

   (1)   Calculate the annualized *HPR* for the investment horizon, assuming that the yield-to-maturity remains constant. What does this calculation illustrate?

   (2)   Assume that the yield-to-maturity is 14 percent after two years and 13 percent after three years. Calculate the annualized *HPR* over the investment horizon. Is the investment immunized? Explain.

d.   What other risk should you consider in attempting to use this bond for immunization purposes?

COMPUTER APPLICATIONS

The floppy disk includes programs that can be used to calculate the following:

1. Duration
2. Markowitz portfolio analysis
3. Sharpe portfolio analysis
4. Immunization

These programs can be used to solve most of the problems in this chapter and to analyze bonds in general. Instructions and illustrations are provided on the disk.

REFERENCES

Altman, Edward I., and Scott A. Nammacher. "The Default Rate Experience on High-yield Corporate Debt." *Financial Analysts Journal* (July-August 1985): pp. 25–41.

Asinof, Lynn. "Bond Swaps Can Reduce Taxes While You Keep Your Portfolio Intact, but You Should Act Soon." *Wall Street Journal*, 17 October 1983, p. 60.

Atkinson, Thomas R. *Trends in Corporation Bond Quality.* New York: Columbia University Press, 1967.

Barnes, Tom. "Markowitz Allocation—Fixed-income Securities." *Journal of Financial Research* (Fall 1985): pp. 181–91.

Barnes, Tom, Keith Johnson, and Don Shannon. "A Test of Fixed-income Strategies," *Journal of Portfolio Management* (Winter 1984): pp. 60–65.

Bierwag, G. O., George C. Kaufman, and Cynthia M. Latta. "Bond Portfolio Immunization: Tests of Maturity, One- and Two-factor Duration Matching Strategies," *Financial Review* (May 1987): pp. 203–19.

Bierwag, G. O., and Chulsoon Khang. "An Immunization Strategy is a Minimax Strategy." *Journal of Finance* (May 1979): pp. 339–414.

Billingham, Carol J. "Strategies for Enhancing Bond Portfolio Returns." *Financial Analysts Journal* (May-June 1983): pp. 50–56.

Boardman, Calvin M., and Stephen E. Celec. "Bond Swaps and the Application of Duration." *Business Economics* (September 1980): pp. 49–54.

Bodie, Zvi, Alex Kane, and Robert McDonald. "Why Haven't Nominal Rates Declined?" *Financial Analysts Journal* (March-April 1984): pp. 16–27.

Bradley, Stephen P., and Dwight B. Crane. "A Dynamic Model for Bond Portfolio Management." *Management Science* (October 1972): pp. 139–51.

Brennan, Michael J., and Eduardo S. Schwartz. "Bond Pricing and Market Efficiency." *Financial Analysts Journal* (September-October 1982): pp. 49–56.

Conroy, Robert M., and Richard J. Rendleman, Jr. "A Test of Market Efficiency in Government Bonds." *Journal of Portfolio Management* (Summer 1987): pp. 57–64.

Diller, Stanley. "Analyzing the Yield Curve: A New Approach." *Financial Analysts Journal* (March-April 1981): pp. 23–41.

Dyl, Edward A., and Michael D. Joehnk. "Riding the Yield Curve: Does It Work?" *Journal of Portfolio Management* (Spring 1981): pp. 13–17.

Dyl, Edward A., and Stanley A. Martin, Jr. "Rules of Thumb for the Analysis of Tax Swaps." *Journal of Portfolio Management* (Fall 1983): pp. 71–74.

————. "Another Look at Barbells versus Ladders." *Journal of Portfolio Management* (Spring 1986): pp. 54–59.

Evans, Daniel Lon. "An Asset Management Concept: Immunization with Bond Duration." *Florida Banker* (April 1983): pp. 14–15.

Fogler, H. Russell, William A. Groves, and James G. Richardson. "Managing Bonds: Are 'Dumbbells' Smart? *Journal of Portfolio Management* (Winter 1975): pp. 54–60.

Fong, H. Gifford. "Portfolio Construction: Fixed Income." Chap. 9 in *Managing Investment Portfolios*. Chartered Financial Analysts, 1983.

Fong, H. Gifford and Frank J. Fabozzi. "How to Enhance Bond Returns with Naive Strategies." *Journal of Portfolio Management* (Summer 1985): pp. 57–60.

Fons, Jerome S. "The Default Premium and Corporate Bond Experience." *Journal of Finance* (March 1987): pp. 81–97.

Forsyth, Randall W. "Bond Swap Season Returns to Wall Street." *Barron's*, 31 October 1983, p. 66.

Goulet, Peter G. "How Sophisticated Are Bond Portfolio Managers?" *Journal of Portfolio Management* (Winter 1978): pp. 23–26.

Gushee, Charles H. "How to Hedge a Bond Investment." *Financial Analysts Journal* (March-April): pp. 44–51.

Hickman, W. Braddock. *Corporate Bond Quality and Investor Experience*. Princeton, N. J.: Princton University Press, 1958.

Hill, Joanne, and Thomas Schneeweis, "Diversification and Portfolio Size for Fixed-income Securities." *Journal of Economics and Business* (Winter 1981): pp. 115–21.

Jenkins, James W. "Taxes, Margining and Bond Selection." *Financial Analysts Journal* (May-June 1980): pp. 41–42.

Kaufman, George G. "Duration, Planning Period, and Tests of the Capital Asset Pricing Model." *Journal of Financial Research* (Spring 1980): pp. 1–9.

Leibowitz, Martin L. "Horizon Annuity, Linking the Growth and Payout Phases of Long-term Bond Portfolios." *Financial Analysts Journal* (May-June 1979): pp. 68–74.

Leibowitz, Martin L., and Alfred Weinberger. "The Uses of Contingent Immunization." *Journal of Portfolio Management* (Fall 1981): pp. 51–55.

————. "Contingent Immunization—Part I: Risk Control Procedures," *Financial Analysts Journal*. (November-December 1982): pp. 17–31.

————. "Contingent Immunization—Part II: Problem Areas." *Financial Analysts Journal* (January-February 1983): pp. 35–50.

Liss, Herman. "A Backward Glance O'er Travelled Roads." *Financial Analysts Journal* (March-April): pp. 55–59.

Ma, Christopher K., and Garry M. Weed. "Fact and Fancy of Takeover Junk Bonds." *Journal of Portfolio Management* (Fall 1986): pp. 34–47.

Magee, H. Robert, and Gordon S. Roberts. "On Portfolio Theory, Holding Period Assumptions, and Bond Maturity Diversification." *Financial Management* (Winter 1979): pp. 68–71.

Malabre, Alfred L. Jr. "Bond Prices, Rising Briskly of Late, Excel as Leading Indicator of Economy's Ups, Downs." *Wall Street Journal*, 28 September 1982, p. 56.

Maloney, Kevin J., and Jess B. Yawitz. "Interest Rate Risk, Immunization, and Duration." *Journal of Portfolio Management* (Spring 1986): pp. 48–48.

Marshall, William J., and Jess B. Yawitz. "Lower Bounds on Portfolio Performance: An Extension of the Immunization Strategy." *Journal of Financial and Quantitative Analysis* (March 1982): pp. 101–13.

McEnally, Richard W. "Rethinking Our Thinking about Interest Rates." *Financial Analysts Journal* (March-April): pp. 62–67.

McEnally, Richard W., and Calvin M. Boardman. "Aspects of Corporate Bond Portfolio Diversification." *Journal of Financial Research* (Spring 1979): pp. 27–36.

Murphy, J. E., and M. F. M. Osborne. "Predicting the Volatility of Interest Rates." *Journal of Portfolio Management* (Winter 1985): pp. 66–69.

Rao, Ramesh K. S. "The Impact of Yield Changes on the Systematic Risk of Bonds." *Journal of Financial and Quantitative Analysis* (March 1982): pp. 115–27.

Roley, V. Vance. "Forecasting Interest Rates with a Structural Model," *Journal of Portfolio Management* (Spring 1982): pp. 53–63.

Roll, Richard. "After-tax Investment Results from Long-term vs. Short-term Discount Coupon Bonds." *Financial Analysts Journal* (January-February 1984): pp. 43–54.

Sanger, Elizabeth. "Best of Both Worlds, That's the Promise of Closed-end Bond Funds." *Barron's*, 31 October 1983, pp. 23, 30.

Schneeweis, Thomas, and Ben Branch. "Capital Market Efficiency in Fixed Income Securities." *Review of Business and Economic Research* (Winter 1980–81): pp. 34–42.

Smirlock, Michael. "Seasonality and Bond Market Returns." *Journal of Portfolio Management* (Spring 1983): pp. 42–44.

Stock, Duane. "Does Active Management of Municipal Bond Portfolios Pay?" *Journal of Portfolio Management* (Winter 1982): pp. 51–55.

Thomas, Ted. "Improving Yields with Arbitrage Trading." *Mortgage Banking* (July 1982): p. 8.

Weinstein, Mark I. "A Curmudgeon's View of Junk Bonds." *Journal of Portfolio Management* (Spring 1987): pp. 76–80.

PART 5

ANALYSIS OF ALTERNATIVE INVESTMENTS

PREFERRED STOCK

INTRODUCTION

Preferred stock, while not as popular with investors as bonds and common stock, offers unique features that make it attractive under certain circumstances. First, it represents a *hybrid* security because it has characteristics of two types of securities: debt and common stock. Second, it is essentially a fixed-income security since preferred stock typically receives a fixed dollar dividend.

The dollar amount of new issues of corporate bonds, preferred stock, and common stock over the period 1984–October 1987 are listed in Table 17.1. The amounts of new issues of convertible bonds and convertible preferred stock are included in the figures. Notice that the percentage of new issues of preferred stock ranges from approximately 1 to 6 percent. The value of new issues of convertible preferred stock exceeds the value of new issues of "straight" (nonconvertible) preferred.

INVESTMENT CHARACTERISTICS OF PREFERRED STOCK

Debt or Equity?

As a hybrid security, preferred stock has characteristics of both debt and equity. Legally, however, preferred stockholders are considered owners rather than creditors. Corporate balance sheets, therefore, show preferred stock in the equity section. The legal classification as equity has important implications for voting rights, the right to receive income, and rights in liquidation.

While preferred stock represents equity and therefore suggests control, it is uncommon for the preferred stock of publicly traded firms to have significant voting rights. Typically, if voting rights exist, they allow preferred stockholders to vote only in the election of corporate directors and only if preferred dividends have not been paid over a designated number of periods. If dividends are in arrears, the preferred stockholders may be allowed to vote for a minority of the directors to be elected. Unlike preferred stockholders, common stockholders usually have voting control.

Preferred stockholders receive dividend income declared by the board of directors. Since dividends represent income distributions to owners rather than to creditors, preferred stockholders have no legal right to receive dividends. Bondholders, as creditors, do have legal rights to force interest payments or to force the corporation into bankruptcy, reorganization, or liquidation. Legally, however, preferred stockholders are entitled to receive dividends before any distribution can be made to common stockholders.

In a corporate liquidation, preferred shareholders' claims are subordinated to those of bondholders and other creditors. They are entitled to receive distributions prior to common stockholders. Liquidation procedures require that proceeds be paid first to creditors and that all liabilities must be satisfied before any distributions can be made to preferred stockholders.

In summary, preferred stockholders have a "preferred" claim relative to common stockholders in terms of receiving income and in the event of liquidation.

TABLE 17.1 NEW ISSUES OF BONDS, PREFERRED STOCK, AND COMMON STOCK: 1984–1987 (millions of dollars)

	CORPORATE BONDS[1]		PREFERRED STOCK[2]		COMMON STOCK	
	$	% OF TOTAL	$	% OF TOTAL	$	% OF TOTAL
1984	133,113	85.47	4,118	2.64	18,510	11.89
1985	203,500	85.14	6,505	2.72	29,010	12.14
1986	355,293	85.18	11,514	2.76	50,316	12.06
1987						
January	21,253	87.94	429	1.78	2,486	10.28
February	23,281	86.07	905	3.35	2,862	10.58
March	28,154	74.16	2,257	5.95	7,553	19.89
April	19,518	82.23	526	2.22	3,691	15.55
May	13,431	67.26	1,170	5.86	5,368	26.88
June	22,094	77.67	1,202	4.23	5,150	18.10
July	22,071	80.52	1,157	4.22	4,183	15.26
August	17,685	80.80	906	4.14	3,297	15.06
September	23,635	80.68	1,112	3.80	4,546	15.52
October	17,341	85.17	236	1.16	2,783	13.67

[1] Includes convertible bonds
[2] Includes convertible preferred stock

SOURCE: *Board of Governors of the Federal Reserve, Federal Reserve Bulletin,* various issues.

Unlike common stockholders, however, they can exercise little if any control through their voting rights. In comparison to bondholders, preferred stockholders have a secondary claim in receiving income and liquidation proceeds. Thus, for a single corporation, preferred stock has less risk than common stock but more risk than bonds.

Dividends

Dividends on preferred stock are generally fixed. The dividend will be stated as a dollar amount or as a percentage of par value; for example, $2 paid quarterly ($8 per year), or 8 percent per year, based on $100 par value. Since 1982, a number of preferred stocks have been issued with adjustable dividend rates. This feature is discussed later in the chapter.

Historically, some corporations issued *participating* preferred stock that allowed the holders to participate with the common stockholders in receiving income above a certain level of earnings. Presently, there are very few participating preferred stocks outstanding and publicly traded.

In the vast majority of new issues, preferred stock has a *cumulative* dividend feature rather than a participating feature. The cumulative feature provides that any omitted dividends accrue to the preferred stockholders and must be paid in full before any dividends can be paid on the common stock. The cumulative feature also allows the corporation to pay the accrued dividends to the current stockholder rather than to the stockholder who owned the stock when the dividend was skipped. Cumulative preferred stock is therefore traded with the right to receive accrued dividends when and if they are paid.

Taxes

There are advantages and disadvantages in the tax treatment of preferred stock dividends. For the issuing corporation, the preferred dividend must be paid from after-tax income. This unfavorable tax treatment is one reason for corporations that have a tax liability to consider preferred stock an unattractive financing alternative. Consequently, most new issues of preferred stock are from regulated utilities or are issued in connection with corporate takeovers or buyouts.

The major tax advantage is that corporations that *receive* common or preferred dividends from a nonaffiliated corporation are allowed to exclude a portion of the dividends from taxable income. Prior to January 1, 1987, corporations were allowed to exclude 85 percent of these dividends. If a corporation was subject to the maximum marginal tax rate of 46 percent, the effective tax rate on dividended income was 6.9 percent $[(1 - .85)(.46)]$. The Tax Reform Act of 1986 reduced the exclusion to 80 percent. The Act, however, also reduced the maximum marginal corporate tax rate to 34 percent. The net effect of these two changes is slightly positive; the maximum effective rate on preferred stock dividend income is reduced to 6.8 percent $[(1 - .80)(.34)]$.

The tax code creates an unusual yield relationship between bonds and preferred stock. As previously noted, bonds have less risk than preferred stock and therefore should offer lower yields. However, the *before-tax* yield, BTY, on bonds is almost always above the BTY on preferred stock. This occurs because for corporate investors, the favorable tax treatment of preferred dividends causes the *after-tax* yield, ATY, on preferred stock to exceed that of bonds. Corporations that are seeking income therefore have a tax incentive to invest in preferred stock, while non-corporate investors do not enjoy this tax advantage. This is discussed in more detail later in the chapter.

Call Feature

Traditionally, most preferred stock was not callable and was issued without a maturity date. Now, the vast majority of new preferred stock issues are redeemable and have a *sinking fund*. The sinking fund can be used to buy the stock directly in the market. More commonly, the stock has a *call feature* that allows the issuer to redeem the shares at predetermined prices. The sinking fund is then used to pay the investors for the called shares. The call price places an upper limit on the market price of the preferred stock.

Convertibility

Preferred stock may be issued with a convertible feature, to be exercised at the option of the investor. If the preferred is both convertible and callable, the investor still has the option of converting the stock between the call announcement date and the call date. For example, Masco Industries announced that its preferred stock would be redeemed on September 28, 1987, for $27.03 plus accrued dividends of $.28. A share of preferred stock was convertible into 2.0 shares of common stock through September 25, 1987. Since the common stock was trading between $16 and $17 per share during mid-September and thus, the conversion value of the preferred stock was $32 to $34 per share, investors should have converted prior to September 25 rather than have the shares called.

Adjustable Dividend Rates

Traditionally, preferred stock was issued with a fixed dividend and was therefore subject to a considerable degree of *interest rate risk*. That is, as market yields increased because of inflation pressures or other factors, the prices of preferred stock fell.

The volatility of market interest rates and yields in the 1970s and 1980s, however, provided an incentive to offer *adjustable rate preferred stock*, which adjusts the dividend to provide market yields. Adjustable rate preferred stock, ARPS, was first issued in 1982 by Chase Manhattan Corporation and Manufacturer's Hanover Trust Company.[1] These issues provided a fixed yield spread between the preferred yield and the highest of the yields on short-, intermediate-, and long-term U.S. Treasury bonds. The quarterly preferred dividend adjustments were designed to keep the preferred price relatively constant, thereby eliminating interest rate risk.

Most of the initial ARPS issues were by banks or bank holding companies. Problems in the banking industry in the 1983–1984 period, such as losses on loans to less-developed countries, reduced the creditworthiness of many of the multinational banks and therefore reduced the popularity of ARPS. For example, approximately $8–$10 billion of ARPS was issued over the period 1982–1984, but less than $1 billion was issued in 1985.[2]

To deal with both interest and credit risk problems, *Dutch auction rate preferred stock*, DARPS, was first issued in 1984; approximately $10 billion has been issued through 1986.[3] The yield on DARPS is adjusted by auction every seven weeks instead of quarterly. The rate is set by a Dutch auction procedure where bidding occurs between both current and potential investors. The bids naturally incorporate market yield changes and an assessment of the creditworthiness of the issuer. Since the price of DARPS is fixed at par by the auction procedure, both interest rate and credit risks are eliminated. DARPS yields, therefore, are close to those on money market securities.

Marketability

While preferred stock is usually marketable, it should be recognized that the market may be "thin," even though the company's common stock is actively traded. This occurs because preferred issues are often small relative to the size of the common stock issues. Also, investor interest and trading frequency for the typical preferred stock are much lower than those for common stock.

A "thin" market for a specific issue of preferred stock may limit its marketability and increase the "spread" or difference between the bid and ask prices.

---

[1] For a discussion of the history, see Michael J. Alderson, Keith C. Brown, and Scott L. Lummer, "Dutch Auction Rate Preferred Stock," *Financial Management* (Summer 1987): pp. 68–73.

[2] Alderson, Brown, and Lummer, p. 69.

[3] Ibid., p. 70

TABLE 17.2   TRADING VOLUME OF SELECTED ISSUES OF PREFERRED AND COMMON STOCK

	SHARES OUTSTANDING DECEMBER 1987 (000's)	SHARES TRADED IN DECEMBER (000's)						
		1981	1982	1983	1984	1985	1986	1987
1. Commonwealth Edison								
Common Stock	31,660	3,471	7,487	7,213	16,511	20,921	28,771	23,790
Preferred Stock								
($1.90 Cumulative)	4,250	143	80	60	127	116	180	130
2. General Motors								
Common Stock	314,685	8,980	13,943	10,200	11,334	16,259	25,046	18,180
Preferred Stock								
($5.00 Cumulative)	1,530	42	42	102	75	42	122	32
3. Goodrich (B. F.)								
Common Stock	25,078	580	802	1,027	711	990	1,264	5,529
Preferred Stock								
($7.85 Cumulative)	150	–	15	1	1	–	17	–
4. McDermott International								
Common Stock	37,249	2,077	5,080	2,830	2,008	3,733	4,616	21,974
Preferred Stock								
($2.60 Cumulative B)	3,725	723	157	77	174	82	196	320
5. Tenneco								
Common Stock	147,036	3,526	4,086	2,960	5,312	5,256	8,737	11,589
Preferred Stock								
($7.40 Cumulative)	1,814	16	3	13	52	30	19	26

SOURCE: Standard & Poor's *Stock Guide.* Reprinted by permission.

Table 17.2 provides a selected sample of trading activity for the common and preferred stock of five corporations traded on the NYSE. Notice the differences in the volume of trading, relative to the shares outstanding, for preferred and common stock.

INVESTMENT ANALYSIS OF PREFERRED STOCK

Valuation of Preferred Stock

Traditional preferred stock with a fixed dividend can be valued like a perpetuity (see Chapter 15):

$$V_0 = \frac{D}{R} \tag{17.1}$$

where V_0 = current intrinsic value of preferred stock
   D = annual cash dividend
   R = investor's required rate of return

The market's required rate of return can be found by equating V_0 with the market price of the preferred stock, P_0, and rearranging Equation 17.1:

$$R = \frac{D}{P_0} \qquad (17.2)$$

The valuation of newer types of preferred, such as ARPS and DARPS, must consider the fact that dividends are adjusted periodically to reflect market yields. The dividend adjustments and auction procedures, however, result in very stable if not constant prices for these types of preferred stock.

Calculating Returns for Preferred Stock

There are two measures of return that can be used in an investment analysis of preferred stock: (1) dividend or current yield and (2) holding period return.

As with common stock, the *dividend yield* is calculated as

$$Y_{PS} = \frac{D_t}{P_0} \qquad (17.3)$$

where Y_{PS} = dividend yield on preferred stock

   D_t = annual cash dividend

   P_0 = current price of the preferred stock

The dividend yield for preferred stock is provided in the *Wall Street Journal* and other sources of market quotations.

The dividend yield represents only a partial indication of the return, since it ignores capital gains or losses. The holding period return, *HPR*, considers dividends and price changes:

$$HPR_{PS,t} = \frac{P_{t+1} - P_t + D_{t+1}}{P_t} \qquad (17.4)$$

where $HPR_{PS,t}$ = holding period return on a share of preferred stock for period t

   P_{t+1} = price of the preferred stock at the end of the holding period

   P_t = price at the beginning of the holding period

   D_{t+1} = cash dividend received during the holding period

Since dividends are paid quarterly, the *HPR* for a month may not include a dividend; preferred stock is traded with ex-dividend dates. Equation 17.4 should be used in an investment analysis of preferred stock. The equation can be used to calculate the historical or ex-post *HPR* but can also be used to calculate the expected or ex-ante *HPR*, *E(HPR)*. Calculation of the expected *HPR* requires the analyst to estimate the future price, $E(P_{t+1})$, and dividend, $E(D_t)$. These estimates are then used as

$$E(HPR_{PS,t}) = \frac{E(P_{t+1}) - P_t + E(D_{t+1})}{P_t} \qquad (17.5)$$

Traditional Risk Analysis for Preferred Stock

A traditional risk analysis for preferred stock would consider two sources of risk: interest rate risk and credit risk. With regard to interest rate risk, the lack of a maturity date can cause the duration (see Chapter 15) of a preferred stock to be longer than the duration of bonds with finite lives. A longer duration indicates that the price of the preferred stock will be more volatile than the bond price, given equal percentage changes in yields.

Table 17.3 demonstrates the greater interest rate risk for a preferred stock. A hypothetical preferred stock and a bond are compared. The required rates of return under present market conditions are 8 percent for the preferred stock and 9 percent for the bond. (Recall that the tax treatment of preferred dividends received by corporations results in before-tax yields below those of bonds.) The illustration assumes that market conditions change so that the required rates of return increase by 20 percent. The new required rates of return would be 9.60 percent on the preferred stock and 10.80 percent on the bond. The value of the preferred stock is calculated using Equation 17.1, and the value of the bond is calculated using Equation 15.2 from Chapter 15.

Table 17.3 shows that an increase of 20 percent in the required rate of return caused the value of the preferred stock to *decline* from $62.50 to $52.08, or by

TABLE 17.3   ILLUSTRATION OF INTEREST RATE RISK FOR A PREFERRED STOCK VERSUS A BOND

	PREFERRED STOCK	BOND
Term-to-maturity:	∞	10 years
Annual dividend (interest):	$5	$100
Required rate of return:	8%	9%
Current value*	$62.50	$1064.17
New required rate of return:	8%(1.2) = 9.60%	9%(1.2) = 10.80%
New value:**	$52.08	$952.48
Percentage change in value:	($52.08 − $62.50)/$62.50 = −16.67%	($952.48 − $1064.17)/$1064.17 = −10.50%

* Current value calculations:

$$\text{preferred stock value} = \frac{D}{R} = \frac{\$5}{.08} = \$62.50$$

$$\text{bond value} = \$100 \left[\frac{1 - \dfrac{1}{(1.09)^{10}}}{.09} \right] + \frac{\$1000}{(1 + .09)^{10}}$$

$$= \$100 \, [6.4177] + 1000/2.3674 = \$1064.17$$

** New value calculations:

$$\text{preferred stock value} = \frac{\$5}{.0960} = \$52.08$$

$$\text{bond value} = \$100 \left[\frac{1 - \dfrac{1}{(1.108)^{10}}}{.108} \right] + \frac{\$1000}{(1 + .108)^{16}}$$

$$= \$100 \, [5.9389] + 1000/2.7887 = \$952.48$$

TABLE 17.4 PREFERRED STOCK RATINGS

MOODY'S PREFERRED STOCK RATINGS*

Moody's Rating Policy Review Board extended its rating services to include quality designations on preferred stock on October 1, 1973. The decision to rate preferred stock, which Moody's had done prior to 1935, was prompted by evidence of investor interest. Moody's believes that its rating of preferred stock is especially appropriate in view of the ever-increasing amount of these securities outstanding, and the fact that continuing inflation and its ramifications have resulted generally in the dilution of some of the protection afforded them as well as other fixed-income securities.

Because of the fundamental differences between preferred stocks and bonds, a variation of our familiar bond rating symbols, is being used in the quality ranking of preferred stock. The symbols, presented below, are designed to avoid comparison with bond quality in absolute terms. It should always be borne in mind that preferred stock occupies a junior position to bonds within a particular capital structure and that these securities are rated within the universe of preferred stocks.

Note: Moody's applies numerical modifiers **1**, **2** and **3** in each rating classification: the modifier **1** indicates that the security ranks in the higher end of its generic rating category; the modifier **2** indicates a mid-range ranking and the modifier **3** indicates that the issue ranks in the lower end of its generic rating category.

Preferred stock rating symbols and their definitions are as follows:

''**aaa**''

An issue which is rated ''**aaa**'' is considered to be a top-quality preferred stock. This rating indicates good asset protection and the least risk of dividend impairment within the universe of preferred stocks.

''**aa**''

An issue which is rated ''**aa**'' is considered a high-grade preferred stock. This rating indicates that there is a reasonable assurance that earnings and asset protection will remain relatively well maintained in the foreseeable future.

''**a**''

An issue which is rated ''**a**'' is considered to be an upper-medium grade preferred stock. While risks are judged to be somewhat greater than in the ''**aaa**'' and ''**aa**'' classification, earnings and asset protection are, nevertheless, expected to be maintained at adequate levels.

''**baa**''

An issue which is rated ''**baa**'' is considered to be a medium-grade preferred stock, neither highly protected nor poorly secured. Earnings and asset protection appear adequate at present but may be questionable over any great length of time.

''**ba**''

An issue which is rated ''**ba**'' is considered to have speculative elements and its future cannot be considered well assured. Earnings and asset protection may be very moderate and not well safeguarded during adverse periods. Uncertainty of position characterizes preferred stocks in this class.

''**b**''

An issue which is rated ''**b**'' generally lacks the characteristics of a desirable investment. Assurance of dividend payments and maintenance of other terms of the issue over any long period of time may be small.

''**caa**''

An issue which is rated ''**caa**'' is likely to be in arrears on dividend payments. This rating designation does not purport to indicate the future status of payments.

''**ca**''

An issue which is rated ''**ca**'' is speculative in a high degree and is likely to be in arrears on dividends with little likelihood of eventual payments.

''**c**''

This is the lowest rated class of preferred or preference stock. Issues so rated can be regarded as having extremely poor prospects of ever attaining any real investment standing.

---

* SOURCE: Moody's *Bond Record*, February 1988, p. 138. Reprinted by permission.

TABLE 17.4 (continued)

STANDARD & POOR'S PREFERRED STOCK RATINGS**

A Standard & Poor's preferred stock rating is an assessment of the capacity and willingness of an issuer to pay preferred stock dividends and any applicable sinking fund obligations. A preferred stock rating differs from a bond rating inasmuch as it is assigned to an equity issue, which issue is intrinsically different from, and subordinated to, a debt issue. Therefore, to reflect this difference, the preferred stock rating symbol will normally not be higher than the bond rating symbol assigned to, or that would be assigned to, the senior debt of the same issuer.

The preferred stock ratings are based on the following considerations:

I. Likelihood of payment—capacity and willingness of the issuer to meet the timely payment of preferred stock dividends and any applicable sinking fund requirements in accordance with the terms of the obligation.

II. Nature of, and provisions of, the issue.

III. Relative position of the issue in the event of bankruptcy, reorganization, or other arrangements affecting creditors' rights.

"AAA" This is the highest rating that may be assigned by Standard & Poor's to a preferred stock issue and indicates an extremely strong capacity to pay the preferred stock obligations.

"AA" A preferred stock issue rated "AA" also qualifies as a high-quality fixed income security. The capacity to pay preferred stock obligations is very strong, although not as overwhelming as for issues rated "AAA."

"A" An issued rated "A" is backed by a sound capacity to pay the preferred stock obligations, although it is somewhat more susceptible to the adverse effects of changes in circumstances and economic conditions.

"BBB" An issue rated "BBB" is regarded as backed by an adequate capacity to pay the preferred stock obligations. Whereas it normally exhibits adequate protection parameters, adverse economic conditions or changing circumstances are more likely to lead to a weakened capacity to make payments for a preferred stock in this category than for issues in the "A" category.

"BB," "B," "CCC" Preferred stock rated "BB," "B," and "CCC" are regarded, on balance, as predominately speculative with respect to the issuer's capacity to pay preferred stock obligations. "BB" indicates the lowest degree of speculation and "CCC" the highest degree of speculation. While such issues will likely have some quality and protective characteristics, these are outweighed by large uncertainties or major risk exposures to adverse conditions.

"CC" The rating "CC" is reserved for a preferred stock issue in arrears on dividends or sinking fund payments but that is currently paying.

"C" A preferred stock rated "C" is a non-paying issue.

"D" A preferred stock rated "D" is a non-paying issue with the issuer in default on debt instruments.

NR indicates that no rating has been requested, that there is insufficient information on which to base a rating, or that S&P does not rate a particular type of obligation as a matter of policy.

Plus (+) or Minus (−) To provide more detailed indications of preferred stock quality, the ratings from "AA" to "CCC" may be modified by the addition of a plus or minus sign to show relative standing within the major rating categories.

** SOURCE: Standard & Poor's *Stock Guide*, January 1988, p. 6. Reprinted by permission.

16.67 percent. The value of the bond declined from $1,064.17 to $952.48, or by 10.50 percent. The preferred stock has more potential price volatility than the bond because of its longer duration.

A second type of risk exhibited by preferred stock is *credit risk*, which essentially represents the business and financial risk of the issuer. Credit analysis measures the company's ability to make the preferred dividend payment. A traditional credit analysis would use financial ratios that measure the liquidity, financial leverage, and profitability of the issuer. The procedures presented in Chapter 10 for common stocks can also be used for preferred stocks.

As with bonds, independent agencies like Moody's and Standard & Poor's provide preferred stock ratings, which reflect the security of the preferred dividend and provide an indication of credit risk. Table 17.4 provides Moody's and Standard & Poor's rating categories and definitions of each category.

Systematic and Nonsystematic Risk for Preferred Stock

The market model, or CAPM, has been applied to the analysis of preferred stock.[4] One question raised by this research is, What is the appropriate benchmark or market portfolio to use in estimating the beta of a preferred stock? Preferred stock has characteristics of both common stocks and bonds. Therefore, should a stock, bond, or some combination index be used as a proxy for the market portfolio? Capital market theory, as discussed in Chapter 6, indicates that the market portfolio should be defined to include all assets, weighted according to their aggregate market values.

The top portion of Table 17.5 provides insights into the ex-post *HPR*s on preferred stocks compared to the S&P 500, U.S. government bonds, and high-quality corporate bonds. The lower portion of Table 17.5 provides estimates of betas using two market proxies. There is a relationship between the ratings and beta. Lower-quality preferred stocks have more systematic risk than higher-quality preferred stocks. When the S&P 500 is used as the market index, it is interesting to note that all three preferred stock betas are greater than or approximately equal to the betas for U.S. government bonds and high-quality (Aaa rated) corporate bonds. When the "market composite" is used as the index, however, the beta for corporate bonds is higher than the preferred stock betas.

Table 17.6 provides additional insight into preferred stock betas and the impact of the index on the calculated beta value. This table is constructed using data from a study by Bildersee, which was based on a sample of seventy-two preferred stocks listed on the New York Stock Exchange.[5] The sample included both "high"- and "low"-quality preferreds issued by industrial, utility, transportation, and financial corporations.

The results for both the Soldofsky (Table 17.5) and Bildersee (Table 17.6) studies were consistent in showing that the market index did have an important influence on the beta estimates. Bildersee found that each of the seventy-two preferred stock betas was less than the beta for the common stock of the *same* company when using a common stock index to represent the market. Also, when

---

[4] For example, see John S. Bildersee, "Some Aspects of the Performance of Nonconvertible Preferred Stocks," *Journal of Finance* (December 1973): pp. 1187–1201 and Robert M. Soldofsky, "Risk and Return for Long-term Securities: 1971–1982," *Journal of Portfolio Management* (Fall 1984): pp. 57–64.

[5] Bildersee.

TABLE 17.5 COMPARISON OF PREFERRED STOCK RETURNS AND RISK

	1971	1972	1973	1974	1975	1976	1977	1978	1979	1980	1981	1982
ANNUAL HOLDING PERIOD RETURNS (%)												
"High" Quality Preferred Stock	9.5	6.7	0.3	−7.2	14.3	16.3	4.8	−2.1	−6.5	−2.0	5.2	31.1
"Medium" Quality Preferred Stock	9.8	8.6	−1.5	−10.2	22.8	25.2	8.0	−1.7	−0.4	−1.0	4.9	26.4
"Speculative" Quality Preferred Stock	9.3	20.8	1.2	−5.0	35.3	23.0	7.2	−0.9	−6.2	0.7	6.6	31.1
S&P 500	13.2	21.3	−16.2	−26.7	36.9	22.4	−6.5	6.8	18.1	32.3	−5.8	20.4
U.S. Government Bonds	16.2	5.3	−0.4	4.9	9.6	14.2	−0.9	−0.4	−1.1	−3.3	−0.8	42.7
Corporate Bonds (Aaa rated)	13.9	7.9	2.0	−3.3	12.1	18.7	−1.5	−1.6	−3.5	−5.1	−0.8	42.3

	MARKET INDEX	
	S&P 500	MARKET COMPOSITE*
BETA ESTIMATES:		
"High" Quality Preferred Stock	.25	.50
"Medium" Quality Preferred Stock	.37	.56
"Speculative" Quality Preferred Stock	.40	.61
U.S. Government Bonds	.19	.56
Corporate Bonds (Aaa rated)	.26	.63

* Market composite index was constructed as a market value weighted index of common stocks, U.S. government bonds, corporate bonds, and 1–4 family nonfarm mortgages.

SOURCE: Robert M. Soldofsky, "Risk and Returns for Long-term Securities: 1971–1982," *Journal of Portfolio Management* (Fall 1984): pp. 58, 62. Reprinted by permission.

TABLE 17.6 PREFERRED AND COMMON STOCK BETAS CALCULATED FOR THREE INDICES

	MEAN BETA	MEAN COEFFICIENT OF DETERMINATION
1. Common Stock Index:		
Preferred stock	.198	6.1%
Common stock (same company)	.999	28.4
2. Government Bond Index:		
Preferred stock	.820	8.9%
Common stock (same company)	−1.228	2.2
3. Composite Index:*		
Preferred stock	.325	6.9%
Common stock (same company)	1.516	28.2

* Composite index was constructed as weighted average of the returns on common stocks (65%), preferred stocks (5%), and government bonds (30%).

SOURCE: John S. Bildersee, "Some Aspects of the Performance of Nonconvertible Preferred Stocks," *Journal of Finance* (December 1973): pp. 1191, 1196, 1197. Reprinted by permission.

the common stock index was used, the coefficients of determination, R^2, were much lower for the preferred stocks relative to common stocks.

In conclusion, preferred stock betas can be estimated using the market model, and the betas are measures of systematic risk. Preferred stock betas are significantly smaller than common stock betas when calculated using an equity index. The betas are positively correlated with ratings, which indicates that they also reflect credit, or unsystematic, risk. The betas for medium- and speculative-grade preferreds are also greater than U.S. government and corporate bond betas (see Table 17.5). This suggests that betas also indicate interest rate risk. Bildersee concluded that "it appears that preferreds with low betas relative to the common stock index perform primarily like bonds in the market while preferreds with higher betas perform primarily like common stocks in the market."[6] Thus, low-beta preferreds with low credit risk are very similar to bonds; High-beta preferreds, however, with high credit risk, are similar to common stocks.

It should also be pointed out, however, that preferred stocks have *more* unsystematic risk than common stocks, based on their relationship to a common stock index. Notice that in Table 17.6 only 6.1 percent of the return variability for preferred stocks is explained by the common stock index, while 28.4 percent is explained for common stocks.

INVESTMENT STRATEGIES FOR PREFERRED STOCK

Passive Strategies

Table 17.7 provides yields on market indices of preferred stocks and bonds. The key point of this table is that before-tax preferred yields are *lower* than before-tax yields on bonds. Thus, an investor who held a preferred stock strictly for the

---

[6] Bildersee, p. 1201.

TABLE 17.7   YIELDS ON PREFERRED STOCKS AND CORPORATE BONDS

	YIELDS		
	NEW ISSUES OF INVESTMENT-GRADE BONDS	"MEDIUM-GRADE" INDUSTRIAL PREFERRED STOCK	YIELD SPREAD
1965	4.71%	4.38%	0.33%
1966	5.59	4.95	0.64
1967	5.91	5.39	0.52
1968	6.91	5.83	1.08
1969	7.97	6.38	1.59
1970	8.85	7.25	1.60
1971	7.74	6.84	0.90
1972	7.47	6.85	0.62
1973	7.88	7.01	0.87
1974	9.08	8.14	0.94
1975	9.42	8.18	1.24
1976	8.72	7.81	0.91
1977	8.32	7.44	0.88
1978	9.17	8.12	1.05
1979	10.30	9.16	1.14
1980	12.60	10.63	1.97
1981	15.26	13.07	2.19
1982	14.23	14.04	0.19
1983	12.20	11.71	0.49
1984	13.05	12.14	0.91
1985	11.71	11.04	0.67
1986	9.42	9.23	0.19

SOURCE: Moody's *Industrial Manual*, vol. 1, 1987. Reprinted by permission.

dividend income would earn a lower return but incur *more* risk. The before-tax yields on preferred stock are below those of bonds because of the favorable tax treatment given corporate investors. For the individual investor, the importance of this point is well taken in the following statement: " . . . Where comparable preferred stocks and bonds are available, the non-corporate investor should keep one phrase in mind: Ladies and gentlemen prefer bonds." [7]

Table 17.8 illustrates the difference in after-tax yields, ATY, for preferred stocks and bonds from the standpoints of a corporate and an individual investor. Notice that the before-tax yield, BTY, on the bond is greater than that on the preferred stock (9.50% versus 9.11%). For a corporate investor, however, the ATY on the preferred stock is greater than that on the bond (8.49% versus 6.27%); the reverse is true for the individual investor. Assuming equal risk and ignoring possible price changes (passive strategy), the corporate investor should purchase the preferred stock, the individual investor the bond.

In addition to the tax treatment, a second reason why preferred stocks are generally not good passive investments for individuals is high transaction costs. Brokerage fees are higher for preferred stocks than for bonds.

---

[7] Jeffrey R. Scharf, "Question of Preference; How Preferred Stocks Stack Up vs. Bonds," *Barron's*, 8 Sep. 1986, p. 71.

TABLE 17.8 AFTER-TAX YIELDS FOR PREFERRED STOCKS VERSUS BONDS

I. Investment Alternatives:
  A. Duke Power preferred stock:
    Dividend: $8.70
    Price: $95\frac{1}{2}$

  B. Duke Power bond:
    Coupon: 9.75%
    Maturity date: 2004
    Price: $102\frac{5}{8}$

BEFORE-TAX YIELD	AFTER-TAX YIELD

II. Corporate Investor:

  Assume: Maximum marginal tax rate = 34%
          80% dividend income exclusion

  Preferred stock: BTY = $8.70/$95.50 = 9.11%

  $ATY = BTY(1 - MTR)$
       $= 9.11\%[1 - (1 - .8)(.34)]$
       $= 8.49\%$

  Bond: BTY = $97.50/$1026.25 = 9.50%

  $ATY = 9.50\%(1 - .34)$
       $= 6.27\%$

III. Individual Investor:

  Assume: Maximum marginal tax rate = 28%

  Preferred stock: BTY = 9.11% $ATY = 9.11\%(1 - .28) = 6.56\%$

  Bond: BTY = 9.50% $ATY = 9.50\%(1 - .28) = 6.84\%$

SOURCE of data: *Wall Street Journal*, 26 Feb., 1988. Reprinted by permission.

Active Strategies

Nonconvertible preferred stock may provide some favorable investment characteristics for individuals using an active investment strategy. Since preferred stock has considerable interest rate risk, it may be an attractive investment prior to a general decline in interest rates and yields. For example, Table 17.5 shows that the *HPR* on high-quality preferred stocks was 31.1 percent in 1982 because of declining yields during 1982 (see Table 17.7). It is important to remember, however, that this strategy can backfire if market yields increase.

A limited number of studies have analyzed the market's efficiency at pricing preferred stock. If market inefficiencies were discovered, they might indicate active strategies that could be used to "beat the market."

A study by Stevenson and Rozeff examined returns and risk from a strategy that involved buying preferred stock with dividends in arrears.[8] A company that has not been paying preferred dividends is likely to be having severe financial problems, and the preferred stock price should reflect this credit risk. Is it possible to buy the stock while the price is depressed, with the hope that the company will recover and eventually pay the skipped dividends? The study concluded that after adjusting for risk, the market was efficient in pricing these preferred shares. There was no evidence that this strategy could be used to "beat the market."

---

[8] Richard A. Stevenson and Michael S. Rozeff, "Are the Backwaters of the Market Efficient?" *Journal of Portfolio Management* (Spring 1979): pp. 31–34.

A recent efficiency study by Hetherington assessed the strategy of buying preferred stock after a call announcement and detected market inefficiencies.[9] One of his examples concerned Nevada Power Preferred C shares that were called at $21.48 (including accrued dividends). For several weeks after the call announcement, Hetherington noted, the preferred stock traded as low as $21.00 and as high as $22.75. His strategy would be to buy at any price less than $21.48, and sell when the price exceeds $21.48. The annualized *HPR* on this transaction would obviously be very high. Hetherington argued that these small dollar trading opportunities could be profitably exploited by using a discount broker (lower commission) and, possibly, a favorable margin transaction. Buying the stock on margin would increase the *HPR* if the rate of interest charged on the margin account was less than the *HPR* on the investment. He concluded: "Trading in called preferred presents attractive opportunities for investors and furnishes a simple and decisive example for academics of a less than efficient market."[10]

SUMMARY

Preferred stocks represent an important but relatively minor source of equity financing for utilities and other industries. The attractiveness of preferred stock as a passive investment alternative is generally limited to corporate investors. Beginning on January 1, 1987, corporations can exclude 80 percent of the dividends received on preferred and common stock. This favorable tax treatment results in before-tax yields on preferred stocks below the yields on bonds. Since individuals cannot exclude any portion of dividends from taxable income, bonds are more attractive than preferred stock on an after-tax basis.

Preferred stocks, because of their long duration and susceptibility to credit risk, can be quite volatile in price. This price volatility may appeal to investors who pursue active strategies such as market timing. There is also some evidence that market inefficiencies for preferred stocks may exist, offering excess returns. Additional research is needed, however, on the market's efficiency in pricing preferred stock.

QUESTIONS

1. Does preferred stock represent debt or equity to the issuing corporation?
2. Does an adjustable rate preferred stock have less interest rate risk than a fixed dividend preferred stock with the same degree of credit risk?
3. Explain why preferred stocks are less actively traded than common stocks.
4. Explain why preferred stocks are generally not attractive to individuals pursuing a *passive* investment strategy.

---

[9] Norriss Hetherington, "High Returns and Low Risk in Called Preferreds," *Journal of Portfolio Management* (Spring 1987): pp. 81–82.

[10] Hetherington, p. 82.

5. Explain why preferred stocks may be attractive to individuals pursuing an *active* investment strategy.

6. Explain the similarities and differences in adjustable rate preferred stock and Dutch auction rate preferred stock.

7. Compare and contrast systematic risk for preferred stock versus common stock.

8. Compare and contrast unsystematic risk for preferred stock versus common stock.

9. Explain why the credit risk for preferred stock is less than for common stock but greater than for bonds, for securities issued by the same corporation.

10. Table 17.7 illustrates that the yield spread between investment-grade bonds and medium-grade industrial preferred stocks varies from .19% to 1.97% over the period 1965–1986.

    a. Explain why the yield spread exists.

    b. Why would the yield spread vary over time?

11. In general terms, discuss the risk-return characteristics of an active strategy that buys preferred stock with dividends in arrears.

PROBLEMS

1. Consider the following data on a straight preferred stock:

Face value:	$100
Price on January 1, 1990:	$ 80
Price on January 1, 1989:	$ 70
Dividend rate:	7%

   a. Calculate the dividend yield on January 1, 1989, and on January 1, 1990.

   b. Calculate the holding period return for 1989.

2. Assume that a straight preferred stock is currently priced to provide a 9% required rate of return and pays a $6 dividend.

   a. Calculate the value of the stock.

   b. Assume that the required rate of return declines to 8%. Calculate the new value for the stock.

   c. Calculate the holding period return, assuming that you purchased the preferred stock when it was priced to provide a 9% required rate of return and sold when required rate of return reached 8%. Also assume that you held the stock long enough to receive an annual dividend.

3. Assume that a preferred stock is currently priced to provide a yield of 10% and a bond provides a 11% yield.

   a. Calculate the after-tax yields for a corporate investor with a marginal tax rate of 34%.

   b. Calculate the after-tax yields for an individual investor with a marginal tax rate of 28%.

   c. Ignoring risk considerations, indicate which of the two securities is most desirable for corporate and individual investors pursuing a passive investment strategy.

4. The beta for the preferred stock of ETV Corporation is .5, and the beta for their debentures is .3. The beta estimates were made using the S&P 500 as the market index. Assume that the risk-free return is 8% and the expected return on the market is 15%.

   a. Use the CAPM to calculate the expected rate of return for the preferred stock and debenture.

   b. For an individual pursuing an active investment strategy, which security is more desirable from a return standpoint?

   c. Assume that the coefficient of determination from the beta regression equation is .1 for the preferred stock and .2 for the debenture. Explain how this information might influence the risk analysis of the two investment alternatives.

5. Consider the following two investment alternatives:

	PREFERRED STOCK	BOND
Term-to-maturity:	∞	5 years
Annual dividend (interest):	$6	$80
Required rate of return:	9%	10%

   a. Calculate the intrinsic values for the preferred stock and the bond.

   b. Assume that the required rate of return on the preferred stock declines to 7% and the bond's return declines to 8%. Calculate the intrinsic values for both securities.

   c. Calculate the percentage changes in the intrinsic values for the preferred stock and bond.

   d. Calculate the *HPRs*, assuming that the securities were purchased for their intrinsic values when the yields were high and were sold when the yields declined. Assume that the holding period includes an annual dividend and interest payment.

   e. For an individual pursuing an active investment strategy, which security appears more attractive on a return basis?

6. On January 1, 1989, the $5 cumulative preferred stock of GM is priced to provide a required rate of return of 10%. Its 8 5/8% debenture that matures in 2005 is priced to provide an 11% coupon yield.

   a. Calculate the after-tax yield on the preferred stock and the debenture for a corporate investor with a marginal tax rate of 34%.

   b. Calculate the after-tax yields for an individual investor with a marginal tax rate of 28%.

   c. Assuming a passive investment strategy for both the corporate and individual investors, which security appears to be more attractive to each investor?

   d. Assuming an active investment strategy and a forecast of declining interest rates and yields, which security might be more attractive to each investor? Explain your answer.

REFERENCES

Alderson, Michael J., Keith C. Brown, and Scott L. Lummer, "Dutch Action Rate Preferred Stock." *Financial Management* (Summer 1987): pp. 68–73.

Bildersee, John S. "Some Aspects of the Performance of Nonconvertible Preferred Stocks." *Journal of Finance* (December 1973): pp. 1187–1201.

Curran, Ward S. "Preferred Stock in Public Utility Finance—A Reconsideration." *Financial Analysts Journal* (March-April 1972): pp. 71–76.

Fischer, Donald E., and Glenn A. Wilt, Jr. "Nonconvertible Preferred Stock as a Financing Instrument, 1950–1965." *Journal of Finance* (September 1968): pp. 611–24.

Hetherington, Norriss. "High Return and Low Risk in Called Preferreds." *Journal of Portfolio Management* (Spring 1987): pp. 81–82.

Scharf, Jeffrey R. "Questions of Preference: How Preferred Stocks Stack Up vs. Bonds." *Barron's*, 8 September 1986, p. 71.

Soldofsky, Robert M. "Risk and Return for Long-term Securities: 1971–1982." *Journal of Portfolio Management* (Fall 1984): pp. 57–64.

———. "The Risk-Return Performance of Convertible Securities: Reply." *Journal of Portfolio Management* (Winter 1984): pp. 79–80.

CHAPTER 18

CONVERTIBLE SECURITIES

INTRODUCTION

This chapter covers the two types of convertible securities: bonds and preferred stocks. *Convertible securities* are fixed-income securities that can be exchanged for the issuing company's common stock. Convertibles are often described as *hybrid* securities since they resemble fixed-income and common stock securities. The convertible feature creates unique investment characteristics; the securities must be analyzed as fixed-income and as equity securities.

Convertible securities are considered an alternative investment. They are not as popular as traditional investments in straight (nonconvertible) bonds and common stocks; their unique features, however, may make them attractive alternatives in an active investment strategy. The volatility of the bond and stock markets during the 1980s and especially in 1987 has increased investor interest in convertibles: new issues of convertibles increased from $5.6 billion in 1980 to $18.3 billion in 1986.

The stock market collapse on October 19, 1987, also affected convertibles. Their price decline, however, was considerably smaller than the decline in common stocks. For example, the NASDAQ composite index fell 11.6 percent from January through November 1987, while the Value Line Convertible Index declined 7.9 percent. Convertible prices did not decline as much as common stocks because their value, in part, is determined by their straight or nonconvertible value. Their relatively high yields after the crash and their more stable prices have increased investor interest.[1]

As with all securities, convertibles exist because they offer advantages to both the issuer and investor. This chapter examines specific characteristics of convertibles and provides three approaches for investment analysis. Finally, a number of investment strategies are presented.

Another important aspect of this chapter is the foundation it provides for the analysis of options and futures in Chapters 19–21. A convertible is essentially a *derivative* security since it derives part of its value from an underlying common stock. This insight into convertibles was developed in the literature in the 1960s and 1970s and provides the foundation for option and future valuation.

CHARACTERISTICS OF CONVERTIBLES

Conversion Ratio

The *conversion ratio* indicates the number of shares of common stock that will be received at conversion. For example, a conversion ratio of 25 to 1 indicates that 25 shares of common stock would be received for each bond (or preferred stock). The conversion ratio is specified at the time the security is initially issued and is protected from dilution caused by stock splits and large stock dividends. If the conversion ratio is 25 to 1 and the stock has a 2 for 1 stock split, the conversion ratio would automatically become 50 to 1.

---

[1] For an analysis and discussion, see "How Convertibles Fared during the Crash," *Value Line Convertibles*, 2 Nov. 1987, pp. 57, 60.

Conversion Price

A *conversion price* rather than a conversion ratio may be specified in the indenture. The conversion price represents the price per share at which the convertible can be exchanged for common stock. For example, if a convertible debenture with a face value of $1,000 and conversion price of $40 was converted, the investor would receive 25 shares of stock with a value of $1,000. A conversion price of $40 is therefore equivalent to a conversion ratio of 25 to 1.

Conversion Value

The *conversion value* represent the *market* value of the common stock received at conversion and can be calculated as

$$CV = (P_s)(CR) \tag{18.1}$$

where CV = conversion value

       P_s = market price of common stock

      CR = conversion ratio

For example, if the conversion price was $40 but the stock was actually selling for $50, the conversion value for the 25 shares would be ($50)(25) = $1,250.

Straight Value

The analysis of a convertible requires a determination of the value of a *straight* or nonconvertible bond or preferred stock that is identical to the convertible in all other characteristics. For example, assume that you are analyzing a convertible debenture with an 8 percent coupon and 20 years to maturity. Because of the bond's characteristics and convertible features, the bond is selling for $1,200. What would be the price of an "identical" nonconvertible bond? Assume that these nonconvertible bonds are selling for $900. The $1,200 price of the convertible can therefore be divided into two parts: value due to bond characteristics or the straight value ($900) and the value of the convertible feature ($300). The value of the convertible feature essentially represents the value of the implied call option on the common stock.

Minimum Value

A convertible security will not sell for a price below the higher of the conversion value or straight value:

$$MV = \max (CV, P_b) \tag{18.2}$$

where MV = minimum value

       CV = conversion value

       P_b = price of a straight bond or preferred stock

The *minimum* value therefore represents a *floor* or lower limit for the market value. If the conversion price is substantially above the market price of the stock, the convertible security will be priced ignoring the convertible feature. For example, if the conversion price is $40 and the market price of the common stock is $20, the minimum value will be the straight value. In Wall Street terminology, this security would be called a *busted* bond or preferred stock. If the conversion price is below the market value of the common stock, the convertible's price will reflect the conversion feature. For example, this would occur if the conversion price was $40 and the market price of the common stock was $60. The minimum value then becomes the conversion value. These securities would be referred to as *in-the-money* convertibles.

Premium

The *premium* on a convertible represents the difference between market value and the conversion value (or straight value for a busted convertible). The premium is usually expressed as a percentage of conversion value:

$$\text{Premium} = \frac{P_c - CV}{CV} \qquad (18.3)$$

where P_c = market price of the convertible
         CV = conversion value of the convertible

For example, assume that a convertible debenture is selling for $1,200 and has a conversion ratio of 20. If the stock price is $50, the conversion value is $1,000, and the premium is $200, or 20 percent. An analysis of the premium is an important part of an investment analysis of convertibles.

Call Feature

Almost all debentures, including convertibles, are issued with a call feature and are therefore subject to *call risk*. Typically, the bonds cannot be called until several years after they are issued, and initial call prices are set above the original offering price. For example, a convertible debenture issued on January 1, 1989, might have a call provision permitting a first call on January 1, 1992. The call price might be 110 ($1,100) in 1992 and decline to 100 ($1,000) by 1995. The issuer can use the call provision to force conversion since the investor has the option of accepting the call price or converting the security. The call features limits the premium since normally only a short period is allowed to make the conversion once the issue has been called.

Rating

Convertibles are rated by Moody's and Standard & Poor's, using the same rating categories used for straight debt and preferred stock. An explanation and definition of Moody's bond ratings is given in Table 14.5; preferred stock ratings are defined in Table 17.4. A large number of outstanding convertibles have low ratings because of two factors. First, many issuers of convertibles have weak balance sheets that do not justify an investment-grade rating for the bonds. Second, many convertible debentures are subordinate to straight debentures and would have a

TABLE 18.1   SAMPLE OF STRAIGHT AND CONVERTIBLE BONDS

ISSUER	SECURITY	MATURITY DATE	COUPON	RATING	AMOUNT OUTSTANDING (MILLIONS)	PRICE
1. AFG Industries	Senior subordinated notes	1992	13.625%	Ba1	$ 70.0	$103\frac{1}{2}$
	Convertible subordinated debenture	2006	6.500	Ba2	100.0	—
2. Ashland Oil	Sinking fund debenture	1992	6.150	A3	19.9	$90\frac{3}{4}$
	Convertible subordinated debenture	1993	4.750	Baa1	2.0	$181\frac{1}{2}$
3. CBS	Debenture	2001	7.850	A3	37.5	$93\frac{7}{8}$
	Eurodollar convertible sub. debenture	2002	5.000	Baa1	400.0	$88\frac{1}{8}$
4. W. R. Grace	Sinking fund debenture	2008	11.750	Baa3	100.0	$105\frac{5}{8}$
	Convertible subordinated debenture	1996	6.500	Ba2	2.6	$205\frac{5}{8}$
5. IBM	Debenture	2004	9.375	Aaa	404.0	102
	Convertible subordinated debenture	2004	7.875	Aaa	1.3	$102\frac{7}{8}$
6. Pan American World	Senior debenture	2003	13.500	B3	87.0	$63\frac{3}{4}$
	Convertible senior sub. debenture	2010	9.000	B3	165.0	$45\frac{1}{4}$
	Convertible subordinated debenture	1989	5.250	Caa	37.0	$84\frac{3}{4}$
7. USX Corporation	Sinking fund debenture	2001	7.750	Ba1	83.0	$85\frac{1}{2}$
	Convertible subordinated debenture	2001	5.750	Ba3	254.0	$75\frac{1}{2}$
8. Western Union	Subordinated debenture	1997	10.750	Ca	25.1	62
	Convertible subordinated debenture	1997	5.250	Ca	62.5	$39\frac{1}{4}$

SOURCE: Moody's *Bond Record*, February 1988. Reprinted by permission.

lower priority in a corporate bankruptcy. *Credit risk*, therefore, can be an important part of an investment analysis of convertibles. The techniques of credit analysis for common stocks (Chapter 10) and bonds (Chapters 14 and 15) can be used for convertibles.

Table 18.1 provides a sample of eight corporations showing that different bond issues of a corporation may be assigned different ratings. A good example of this is the three bonds issued by Pan American World. Notice that the ratings for the two convertibles are different because of a subordination provision. For financially strong corporations like IBM however, the subordination provision does not reduce the rating for the convertible bond.

Taxes

Prior to the Tax Reform Act of 1986, investors were able to use favorable capital gain tax rates for long-term profits from converting or from selling the convertible for a price above cost. Tax reform, however, eliminates the capital gain exclusion for individuals and corporations and taxes capital gains as ordinary income. Some analysts think that tax reform will benefit convertibles since it favors investments that pay dividends and interest and reduces the incentive to buy common stocks to obtain long-term capital gains.[2]

Put Feature

Some convertibles (and nonconvertibles) are now issued with a *put feature* that allows the investor to sell the security back to the issuer at a specified price. For example, in 1984 Ohio Edison issued a convertible preferred stock with a put feature; the put allows investors to exchange the convertible for cash or common stock for a fixed value and therefore establishes a floor or minimum value.

INVESTMENT ANALYSIS OF CONVERTIBLES

Graphic Approach

Two classic articles published in 1966 provide the foundation for an analysis of convertibles.[3] Brigham's *graphic model* provides a basis for understanding the determinants of a convertible's value. Despite its age, this model is still used extensively by practitioners and appears in investment publications such as *Value Line Options and Convertibles*.

Figure 18.1 illustrates the various factors that influence the value of a hypothetical convertible bond over its life. The figure assumes that the convertible was sold at face value with a delayed call date. The convertible feature allows the

---

[2] See, for example, "A Connoisseur of Convertibles," *Fortune*, 29 Sep. 1987, p. 157.

[3] Eugene F. Brigham, "An Analysis of Convertible Debentures: Theory and Some Empirical Evidence," *Journal of Finance* (March 1966): pp. 35–54, and William J. Baumol, Burton G. Malkiel, and Richard E. Quandt, "The Valuation of Convertible Securities," *Quarterly Journal of Economics* (February 1966): pp. 48–59.

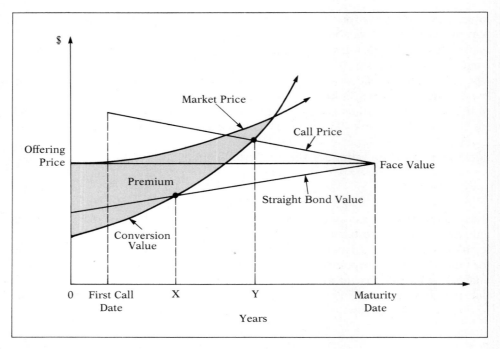

FIGURE 18.1 Graphic analysis of a convertible bond.

corporation to offer a coupon yield below that required for a similar straight bond. This is illustrated by showing that a straight bond with the same coupon yield would be initially valued at a discount relative to the convertible. The value of the straight bond will move toward face value as it matures. It is important to realize that the indicated behavior of the straight bond's value *assumes* that market yields are constant over the life of the bond.

Notice that the convertible is initially offered at a price substantially above its conversion value. For recent new issues of convertibles, the initial offering premium is usually 20 to 30 percent.

Figure 18.1 assumes that the common stock price begins to increase at a constant rate shortly after the convertible bond is issued. This is illustrated by the exponential upward-sloping conversion value function. Initially the *floor* or *minimum value* of the convertible is the value of the straight bond. After *X* years, however, the conversion value equals the straight bond value. Additional increases in the common stock price cause the conversion value to exceed the straight bond value. The floor then becomes the conversion value.

The function indicating the market price of the convertible is drawn so that a sizable initial premium exists. Why would a premium exist and behave in the fashion indicated in the figure? Brigham argued that the premium exists because of the following factors:

1. Expectations that the stock price will increase causing an increase in the convertible's price.
2. Downside risk is reduced because if the stock price declines substantially, the convertible will sell at a price reflecting its straight bond value.

Brigham argued that these factors make the convertible less risky than the common stock because of the floor but do not substantially reduce the upside price potential. The convertible investor benefits from increases in the stock price in approximately the same fashion as a stockholder but is protected from declines in the stock price.

Brigham also argued that the size of the premium will decline, even though the stock price continues to increase. He cited three factors:

1. The bond is callable. At time period *Y*, the conversion value and call price are equal. Further increases in the stock price would allow the issuer to force conversion by calling the bond. Since the probability of a call increases, investors will be unwilling to pay a large premium because the premium would disappear when the call was announced (or before, if the market anticipates the call).
2. The amount of "loss protection" offered by the straight value decreases as the conversion value increases. This causes investors to reduce the premium to maintain the same degree of protection.
3. The yield spread between the convertible bond and the common stock is likely to decline as the stock price increases. If the issuer increases dividends because of the increased profitability of the company as reflected in the stock price, the stock becomes relatively more attractive than the bond, resulting in a smaller premium.

Brigham's explanations of why the premium exists and why it behaves in the manner suggested by his analysis have been debated in the literature. A 1968 article concluded that the loss protection provided by the floor was relatively unimportant in explaining the premium.[4] The floor itself changes because of general interest rate changes. If interest rates increase, the value of the straight bond will decline, and the downside protection or the value of the floor is reduced. This conclusion was confirmed in a 1973 study by Walter and Que.[5] This study concluded that in the case where the conversion values equal or exceed straight bond values, the bond floor contributes less to the worth of the convertible bond than is normally believed."[6] In summary, it appears that the downside risk protection, or "insurance," provided by the floor has a limited influence in determining the premium if interest rates increase. If interest rates are stable or decline, as during the market crash of 1987, the floor can provide downside protection.

Table 18.2 provides a numerical illustration of a convertible bond analysis based on Brigham's graphic analysis. The analysis uses common stock prices both below and above the current price of $26. At the time of the analysis, the convertible bond has a market price of $102\frac{3}{4}$, which reflects the conversion value and a 12.37% premium. The size of the premium is limited, however, because the

---

[4] Roman L. Weil, Jr., Joel E. Segall, and David Green, Jr., "Premiums on Convertible Bonds," *Journal of Finance* (June 1968): pp. 445–63.

[5] James E. Walter and Agustin V. Que, "The Valuation of Convertible Bonds," *Journal of Finance* (June 1973): pp. 713–31.

[6] Walter and Que, p. 729.

TABLE 18.2 NUMERICAL ILLUSTRATION OF CONVERTIBLE BOND ANALYSIS

I. DATA:

	MARKET PRICE	COUPON	MATURITY DATE	CONVERSION PRICE	CONVERSION RATIO	CALL PRICE
W. R. Grace Company						
Common Stock	$26	–	–	–	–	–
Convertible subordinated debenture	$102\frac{3}{4}$	$4\frac{1}{4}\%$	1990	$28.43	35.17	$1001.30

II. CONVERTIBLE ANALYSIS:

STOCK PRICE	CONVERSION VALUE[1]	ESTIMATES OF STRAIGHT VALUE[2]	MINIMUM VALUE[3]	ESTIMATES OF PREMIUM[4]	ESTIMATES OF MARKET VALUE[5]
22	$ 773.74	$883.75	$ 883.75	0%	$ 883.75
23	$ 808.91	883.75	883.75	3.00	910.26
24	844.08	883.75	883.75	7.00	945.61
25	879.25	883.75	883.75	10.00	972.13
26	914.42	883.75	914.42	12.37	1027.53
27	949.59	883.75	949.59	14.00	1082.53
28	984.76	883.75	984.76	15.00	1132.47
29	1019.93	883.75	1019.93	14.00	1162.72
30	1055.10	883.75	1055.10	13.00	1192.26

[1] Calculated as (stock price) × (conversion ratio).

[2] Estimate based on a sample of prices for six straight debentures with similar coupon rates, maturity dates, and ratings. Assumes market yield will not change even if stock price changes.

[3] Defined as the higher of the conversion value or straight value.

[4] Premium is defined as the difference in market value and conversion value expressed as percentage of conversion value. At the current price of $26 for the common stock and $1027.50 for the bond, the actual premium is 12.37%. The premiums for the other stock prices are estimates based on Brigham's analysis.

[5] For stock prices other than the actual price of $26, the market values are estimated by increasing the minimum value by the premium percentage.

SOURCE: Moody's *Bond Record*, February 1988, and *Barron's*, 8 Feb. 1988. Reprinted by permission of Moody's and courtesy of *Barron's Weekly*.

convertible is callable at $1,001.30 and and matures in 1990. The behavior of the premium for different stock prices is consistent with Brigham's hypothesis. Obviously, the estimates of likely premiums are a key factor in the analysis.

Option Pricing Model

The *option pricing* approach to analyzing the premium on a convertible was initially developed by Ingersoll and by Brennan and Schwartz.[7] These studies applied the framework of the Black-Scholes call option pricing model to analyze the premium. Chapter 19 presents an analysis of call options, including a discussion of the Black-Scholes model. At this point, however, it is important to realize that the convertible feature is essentially a call option issued by the corporation. The convertible feature does not expire like a call option, but unlike a call option, it can be effectively canceled if the corporation calls the bonds.

The following conclusions result from an analysis of the convertible premium, using an option pricing model:

1. Higher common stock prices generally increase the premium because the market price of the convertible increases relative to the conversion value.
2. The lack of a call provision or a long period before the first call date increases the premium.
3. Premiums on convertible bonds and preferred stocks are larger if the underlying common stock has significant price volatility, indicated by a high beta.
4. Cash dividends paid on the common stock *reduce* the premium because of their influence on the stock price and dividend yield.
5. Higher risk-free rates of return *increase* the premium.

A recent paper by King used the option pricing model to analyze convertible bonds.[8] Using a sample of 103 convertible bonds, the model was tested by determining the theoretical prices for the bonds and comparing them to actual market prices. King concluded that "90 percent of the model predictions are within 10 percent of market values."[9] The option pricing approach appears to model accurately the market's analysis of the premiums.

Capital Asset Pricing Model

Convertibles have also been analyzed using the market model or CAPM. The previously cited study by Walter and Que calculated the betas for a sample of convertible bonds and common stocks issued by the same corporation. The S&P 500 was used as the proxy for the market; as previously discussed, the selection of the market proxy significantly influences the results. As expected, the common stock

---

[7] Jonathan Ingersoll, "An Examination of Corporate Call Policies on Convertible Securities," *Journal of Finance* (May 1977): pp. 463–78, and M. J. Brennan and E. S. Schwartz, "Convertible Bonds: Valuation and Optimal Strategies for Call and Conversion," *Journal of Finance* (December 1977): pp. 1699–1715.

[8] Raymond King, "Convertible Bond Valuation: An Empirical Test," *Journal of Financial Research* (Spring 1986): pp. 53–69.

[9] King, p. 53.

betas were larger than the convertible betas when compared on a company-by-company basis. There was also evidence of considerable nonstationarity in the convertible betas. This would be expected since the convertible would behave like the common stock when the conversion value was high and like a bond when the conversion value was low. The results from the Walter and Que and other studies suggested that there are major problems in using the CAPM as a foundation for a convertible analysis.[10] Essentially, a convertible beta will be useful only when the convertible is in-the-money or when it is selling to reflect the conversion feature. During these time periods, the convertible price can be expected to behave like that of the underlying common stock. The use of the beta for the underlying common stock may therefore be more appropriate during these periods than trying to estimate a beta directly for the convertible.

INVESTMENT STRATEGIES FOR CONVERTIBLES

As a general rule, convertible securities should not be used in a buy-and-hold or passive investment strategy (see Chapter 5). Convertibles, because of their hybrid nature, require careful analysis. The potential rapid change in the premium also requires that investment developments be followed closely, indicating that convertibles should not be bought and "forgotten."

However, there are a number of active investment approaches that can be used for convertibles. These approaches deal with market timing (when to buy convertibles) and selection (which convertibles should be bought).

Traditional Premium Analysis

A successful active strategy depends essentially on the correct analysis of the premium. A basic and traditional strategy is to invest in convertibles when the premium is below 20 percent, provided the security offers a reasonable yield.[11] The 20 percent cutoff is commonly cited in the popular literature, but there is little evidence to support the idea that this is the optimal cutoff value.

Payback Analysis

Another strategy frequently cited in the popular literature uses a *payback analysis* of the premium.[12] The payback period for a convertible can be calculated as

$$PP = \frac{\dfrac{P_c - CV}{CV}}{Y_c - Y_s} = \frac{\text{Premium}}{\text{Yield Spread}} \tag{18.4}$$

---

[10] Also see A. W. Frankle and C. A. Hawkins, "Beta Coefficients for Convertible Bonds," *Journal of Finance* (March 1975): pp. 207–10.

[11] For example, see "Convertible Bonds Are Looking Good," *Fortune*, 17 Sept. 1984, pp. 182–84.

[12] For example, see Randall W. Forsyth, "Flashy Convertibles: Why They're an Attractive Investment Vehicle," *Barron's*, 20 Aug. 1984, pp. 28, 31.

where PP = payback period in years

P_c = market price of the convertible

CV = conversion value of the convertible

Y_c = coupon yield on the convertible

Y_s = dividend yield on the underlying common stock

To illustrate Equation 18.4, assume that the common stock dividend yield is 4 percent; the convertible bond coupon yield is 12 percent, and the premium on the convertible is 24 percent. The premium would be recovered in 3 years, or 24%/(12% − 4%). According to this strategy, convertibles with shorter payback periods are more attractive investments than long-payback-period convertibles.

There are some basic problems with this strategy. First, the payback calculation ignores the time value of money. This is important because the premium is paid immediately when the convertible is purchased, but the interest income is received in the future. Second, what is the appropriate critical value for the payback? Is a convertible with a payback of 3 years a "good" investment, or should the payback be no more than 2.5 years? Finally, how can the possibility of a call be incorporated into the analysis?

Net Present Value Analysis

An article by Bierman modified the traditional payback analysis by developing a net present value, NPV, approach.[13] Rather than comparing the yields on the common stock and the convertible, Bierman looked at the yield differential between the convertible and a straight bond. Bierman's model considered the lower yield of the convertible and assumed that the convertible bond would be called when the conversion value equals the call price.

Assuming that the convertible and straight bonds are selling for their face values, NPV can be calculated as

$$\text{NPV} = \frac{\text{call} - \text{face}}{(1 + K_{nc})^n} - \sum_{t=1}^{n} \frac{\text{face}(K_{nc} - K_c)}{(1 + K_{nc})^t} \qquad (18.5)$$

where call = call price of the convertible bond

face = face value of the convertible and straight bonds

K_{nc} = coupon yield on the straight bond

K_c = coupon yield on the convertible bond

n = number of years before the convertible bond is called.

For example, assume that the yields on a straight and convertible bond are 10 percent and 8 percent, respectively, and that both are selling for their face value

---

[13] Harold Bierman, Jr., "Convertible Bonds as Investments," *Financial Analysts Journal* (March-April 1980): pp. 59–61.

of $1,000. The convertible bond is callable at 110 and the analyst feels that it will be called at the earliest date, which will occur in 3 years.

$$\text{NPV} = \frac{\$1100 - \$1000}{(1 + .1)^3} - \sum_{t=1}^{3} \frac{\$1000(.1 - .08)}{(1 + .1)^t}$$

$$= \$75.13 - \frac{\$20}{(1 + .1)} - \frac{\$20}{(1 + .1)^2} - \frac{\$20}{(1 + .1)^3}$$

$$= \$25.39$$

Since the NPV is positive, the convertible bond is more attractive than the straight bond. This occurs because the present value of the call premium of $100 is greater than the present value of the "lost" coupon income that results from purchasing the convertible.

Bierman extended this basic model to consider the case where the convertible and straight bonds are not selling for their face values. An analysis of his models indicated that if convertibles are called when their conversion values reach the call values, the NPVs are positive for only relatively short periods of time. The NPV also depends, however, on the call premium, length of time before call, time value of money, purchase prices, and conversion price relative to the stock price.

Hedging

Traditionally, convertibles are often recommended when there is considerable uncertainty about the outlook for bonds and common stock.[14] Since a convertible is a hybrid, it may offer a strategy that deals with the inability to make a selection between bonds or common stocks. The danger of this strategy, however, is that the convertible will not provide a hedge if interest rates increase and stock prices decline. The increase in interest rates reduces the value of bonds and decreases the floor for the convertible. The premium on the convertible is also likely to decline because of the declining stock price. The hedge will work if the stock price increases and interest rates remain constant or decline.

Busted Convertibles

As discussed above, if the conversion price is substantially above the market price of the common stock, the convertible is referred to as a busted bond (or preferred stock). The convertible's price will not reflect the conversion feature but will be based on the straight bond's value. Several studies have analyzed an investment strategy that buys busted convertible bonds.[15] The studies used various definitions of "busted" or "deep discount" to identify a sample of convertibles for analysis. One screen would classify a convertible as busted if its coupon yield exceeded the yield on the Moody's AAA utility bond index by X percent. Another screen would require the bond to be selling for a price below $700 or some other price substantially below face value.

---

[14] For example, see Ben Weberman, "Fence-Sitter Bonds," *Forbes*, 9 Feb. 1987, p. 143.

[15] W. Bradford Cornell, "Are Deep-Discount Convertibles Underpriced?" *Journal of Portfolio Management* (Spring 1977): pp. 55–57, and Richard A. Stevenson, "Deep-Discount Convertible Bonds: An Analysis," *Journal of Portfolio Management* (Summer 1982): pp. 57–64.

Generally, these studies concluded that busted or deep discount convertibles appeared to be underpriced and offer excess returns, even after adjusting for risk. Typically, a CAPM methodology was used to adjust for risk, and the results applied to portfolios of convertible bonds, not to individual bonds in the sample. Because of the previously discussed problems encountered in applying the CAPM to convertibles, the risk-adjustment methodology is questionable. Do the busted convertibles offer risk-adjusted excess returns because the market is not efficient? An alternative interpretation would be that the market correctly prices the bonds and that the risk-adjustment methology is incorrect. The observed risk-adjusted excess return is simply additional return to compensate for the additional risk not detected by the CAPM methodology.

New Issue Convertibles

A study by Alexander and Stover found that new issues of convertibles tended to be underpriced.[16] The initial offering price is determined by the investment banker, with the concurrence of the issuing company's management. Based on a study of 142 convertible debentures, Alexander and Stover concluded that "the empirical results illustrate positive excess returns immediately after the offering, followed by price behavior typical of an efficient capital market."[17] The tendency for new convertible offerings to be underpriced suggests a strategy of buying new convertibles for a short holding period rather than buying seasoned issues.

Mutual Funds

Business Week reported that as of mid-1987, there were twenty-five mutual funds that specialized in convertible securities.[18] At the end of 1986, there were eleven funds that invested primarily in convertibles. Some of the better-known convertible funds are Value Line Convertible Fund, Putnam Convertible Income-Growth Trusts, and Fidelity Convertible Securities Fund. The growth in the number of specialized convertible funds provides additional opportunities for a convertible investment strategy.

SUMMARY

Convertibles may be bonds or preferred stock. Investment analysis of convertibles is complicated by the fact that as hybrid securities, they must be analyzed both as fixed-income and equity securities. Approaches that can be used to analyze convertibles include a graphic approach, an option pricing framework, and a CAPM framework. Studies indicate that the use of an option pricing model, such as the Black-Scholes model, provides the best framework for an analysis of the premium on a convertible. This approach is discussed in detail in Chapter 19.

---

[16] Gordon J. Alexander and Roger D. Stover, "Pricing in the New Issue Convertible Debt Market," *Financial Management* (Fall 1977): pp. 35–39.

[17] Alexander and Stover, p. 39.

[18] "A Note of Caution on the Rush to Convertibles," *Business Week*, 18 May 1987, p. 158.

Traditional strategies for convertible investors include simple screens to determine if the premium is too low (underpriced) or too high (overpriced). The simple payback analysis from capital budgeting can also be used. Other strategies suggest using convertibles as hedges, buying deep discount or busted convertibles, and investing in new issues of convertible debentures. There are a number of mutual funds that specialize in convertibles.

QUESTIONS

1. Explain why many convertible securities are issued with a call feature.
2. Discuss the characteristics of convertibles that cause them to be classified as hybrid securities.
3. Define the conversion value and straight value of a convertible security, and indicate how these values determine the floor or minimum value.
4. Explain how the call price limits the premium on a convertible.
5. Explain the likely behavior of the premium on a convertible bond as the bond approaches maturity.
6. Explain why the premium is likely to be larger on convertibles where the underlying common stock has a high beta.
7. Define a busted convertible, and discuss the risk-return characteristics of an investment strategy using busted convertibles.
8. Explain why the conversion feature is similar to a call option for common stock. Also explain the differences.
9. Investing in convertibles is often referred to as a hedging strategy. Explain how convertibles may (or may not) provide a portfolio hedge under the following conditions:
   a. Interest rates and common stock prices are expected to *decline*.
   b. Interest rates are expected to remain stable, common stock prices to increase.
   c. Interest rates and common stock prices are expected to *increase*.
   d. The investor is not sure about the future directions of interest rates and common stock prices.
10. Explain how payback analysis is used to identify under- and overvalued convertibles. Discuss the weaknesses of this approach.
11. Discuss the potential problems that have been identified in applying the CAPM to convertibles. Does this research indicate that a convertible's beta would be useful in an investment analysis?
12. Discuss the advantages and disadvantages of investing in a mutual fund that specializes in convertibles rather than investing directly in convertibles.

PROBLEMS

1. The common stock of IBM is selling for $108, and its 7.85% coupon convertible subordinated debenture is priced at 102. The conversion ratio is 6.51, and the debenture matures in 2004. The current call price is $104\frac{3}{4}$.

a. Calculate the conversion price.

b. Calculate the conversion value.

c. Calculate the premium.

d. Assuming that similar straight bonds are selling at 89, calculate the minimum value for the convertible.

e. Briefly discuss the factors that explain the size of the premium for the IBM convertible debenture.

2. Assume that the dividend yield on the common stock of IBM is 4.1%. Use the information and your answers to problem 1 to calculate the payback period for the premium on the convertible debenture. In your opinion, does the payback period indicate the convertible is correctly valued, overvalued, or undervalued?

3. Chock Full O'Nuts Corporation has a convertible subordinated debenture with a coupon yield of 8.0%, a Moody's rating of B2, and matures in 2006. The convertible is priced at 80, and the common stock is currently trading at a price of $3\frac{3}{4}$. The conversion ratio is 98.04; the convertible is callable at $107\frac{1}{4}$.

a. Calculate the conversion price.

b. Calculate the conversion value.

c. Calculate the premium.

d. Is the convertible priced to reflect its conversion value or its straight value?

e. Does this bond appear to be suitable for a "busted convertible" strategy? Explain.

4. Crazy Eddie, Inc. has a convertible subordinated debenture with a coupon yield of 6.0%, Moody's rating of B3, and matures in 2011. The convertible is priced at 32, the common stock at $1\frac{3}{8}$. The conversion price is $46.25; the convertible is callable at $105\frac{3}{8}$.

a. Calculate the percentage price increase in the common stock that will be necessary for the conversion value to equal the current market price of the convertible.

b. Does this bond appear to be suitable for a "busted convertible" strategy? Explain.

5. Use Moody's *Bond Record*, Standard & Poor's *Bond Guide*, or other appropriate sources to obtain the necessary data to analyze the 8.50% convertible subordinated debentures issued by Humana, Inc.

REFERENCES

Alexander, Gordon J., and Roger D. Stover. "Pricing in the New Issue Convertible Debt Market." *Financial Managment* (Fall 1977): pp. 35–39.

Baumol, Willaim J., Burton G. Malkiel, and Richard E. Quandt. "The Valuation of Convertible Securities." *Quarterly Journal of Economics* (February 1966): pp. 48–59.

Bierman, Harold, Jr." Convertible Bonds as Investments." *Financial Analysts Journal* (March-April 1980): pp. 59–61.

Brennan, M. J., and E. S. Schwartz. "Convertible Bonds: Valuation and Optimal Strategies for Call and Conversion." *Journal of Finance* (December 1977): pp. 1699–1715.

Brigham, Eugene F. "An Analysis of Convertible Debentures: Theory and Some Empirical Evidence." *Journal of Finance* (March 1966): pp. 35–54.

Brooks, LeRoy D., Charles E. Edwards, and Eurico J. Ferreira. "Risk-Return Characteristics of Convertible Preferred Stock: Comment." *Journal of Portfolio Management* (Winter 1984): pp. 76–78.

"A Connoisseur of Convertibles." *Fortune*, 29 September, 1986, p. 157.

"Convertible Bonds are Looking Good." *Fortune*, 17 September 1984, pp. 182, 184.

Cornell, W. Bradford. "Are Deep-Discount Convertibles Underpriced?" *Journal of Portfolio Management* (Spring 1977): pp. 55–57.

Dannen, Frederick. "Cashing in on Converts." *Institutional Investor* (December 1984): pp. 141–43, 148.

Dawson, Steven M. "Timing Interest Payments for Convertible Bonds." *Financial Management* (Summer 1974): pp. 14–16.

"Fence-straddling with Convertible Bond Funds." *Fortune*, 4 August, 1986, p. 220.

Fisher, Kenneth L. "15% with Little Risk." *Forbes*, 18 May 1987, p. 256.

Forsyth, Randall W. "Flashy Convertibles, Why They're an Attractive Investment Vehicle." *Barron's*, 20 August 1984, pp. 28, 31.

Frankle, A. W., and C. A. Hawkins. "Beta Coefficients for Convertible Bonds." *Journal of Finance* (March 1975): pp. 207–10.

Hitchings, Bradley. "Bonds That Can Bring You the Best of Two Worlds." *Business Week*, 22 September 1986, pp. 98-99.

Ingersoll, Jonathan. "An Examination of Corporate Call Policies on Convertible Securities." *Journal of Finance* (May 1977): pp. 463–78.

Janus, Richard, and Tim Ringler. "Five Questions to Ask When Choosing a Convertibles Manager." *Pension World* (June 1986): pp. 47–48.

Jennings, Edward H. "An Estimate of Convertible Bond Premiums." *Journal of Financial and Quantitative Analysis* (January 1974): pp. 33–56.

King, Raymond, "Convertible Bond Valuation: An Empirical Test." *Journal of Financial Research* (Spring 1986): pp. 53–69.

Kuntz, Mary. "Old Money in New Bottles." *Forbes*, 6 October 1986, p. 194.

McGough, Robert. "Convertibles without a Top." *Forbes*, 22 October 1984, pp. 139, 141.

Morrison, Tex. "A Note of Caution on the Rush to Convertibles." *Business Week*, 18 May 1987, p. 158.

Parker, Marcia. "Convertible Investors Fight Losses." *Pensions & Investments Age*, 27 July 1987, pp. 1, 51.

Soldofsky, Robert M. "The Risk-Return Performance of Convertibles." *Journal of Portfolio Management* (Winter 1981): pp. 80–84.

Stevenson, Richard A. "Deep-Discount Convertible Bonds: An Analysis." *Journal of Portfolio Management* (Summer 1982): pp. 57–64.

Vinson, Charles E. "Rates of Return on Convertibles: Recent Investor Experience." *Financial Analysts Journal* (July-August 1970): pp. 110–14.

Walter, James E., and Agustin V. Que. "The Valuation of Convertible Bonds." *Journal of Finance* (June 1973): pp. 713–31.

Weberman, Ben. "Fence-Sitter Bonds." *Forbes*, 9 February 1987, p. 143.

Weil, Roman L., Jr. Joel E. Segall, and David Green, Jr.. "Premiums on Convertible Bonds." *Journal of Finance* (June 1968): pp. 445–63.

CHAPTER 19

OPTIONS, WARRANTS, AND RIGHTS

INTRODUCTION

This chapter deals with three alternative investments termed *derivative securities* because their value depends on an underlying security such as common stock. Rights and warrants are issued by a company in connection with a new issue of bonds, preferred or common stock. Options are issued by investors or speculators. All three of these alternative investments provide the investor with the opportunity to buy or sell the underlying security, for a specified price, within a designated period of time.

Rights allow existing common stockholders to acquire a proportionate share of a new issue of common stock. If stockholders are protected with a *preemptive right*, a rights offering satisfies this requirement. The use of rights may also benefit the corporation because of the ease of distribution of the new stock issue and lower flotation costs. Rights are usually transferable or marketable; the stockholder who receives the rights can either exercise them or sell them. Rights are therefore traded along with the common stock on the stock exchanges and the OTC market.

Warrants allow the holder to acquire the common stock of the issuing corporation. They are usually used as "sweeteners" to enhance a new issue of debt or preferred stock. The investor in the new offering receives the bond or preferred stock along with the attached warrants. Generally, the warrants are transferable and therefore can be traded separately on the exchanges or the OTC market. One major difference between warrants and rights and options is that warrants have longer lives. Typically, a warrant's life is from three to five years and may be longer. Rights typically have a life of ninety days or less, while the life of an option is usually nine months or less.

An *option* is a legal contract that gives the holder the right to buy or sell a specifed amount of the underlying asset at a fixed price within a specifed period of time. The underlying asset may be an individual common stock, a stock index, U.S. government debt, a commodity, or foreign currency. Due to the large number of underlying assets that options can be issued against, the number of options is far greater than the number of rights or warrants. To illustrate, Value Line typically monitors approximately one hundred warrants and over ten thousand options.

Traditionally, options were traded in the OTC market through individual brokerage firms. Because of this somewhat informal market structure, options were not widely traded. In 1973, however, the Chicago Board Options Exchange, CBOE, was established; as a result, investor interest and trading activity increased dramatically. In addition to the CBOE, options are now traded on the NYSE, AMEX, Philadelphia and Pacific exchanges, and a number of foreign exchanges.

In addition to a formalization of the markets, the volatility of the financial and commodity markets during the 1970s and 1980s increased investor interest in options. Volatile markets make options more attractive since they can be used to reduce the volatility of a portfolio or to speculate on future price movements of the underlying asset. These uses of options are discussed in detail. Trading volume in options declined significantly, however, immediately after the October 19, 1987, stock market decline.

TABLE 19.1 TYPES OF OPTIONS AND TRADING EXCHANGES

1. Equity Options on Individual Stocks	NYSE
	CBOE
	AMEX
	PHLX
	PSE
2. Equity Index Options	
a. S&P 100	CBOE
b. S&P 500	CBOE
c. NYSE Composite Index	NYSE
d. Major Market Index	AMEX
e. Oil Stock Index	AMEX
f. Institutional Index	AMEX
g. Value Line Index	PHLX
h. Financial News Composite Index	PSE
3. Foreign Currency Options	PHLX
4. Gold/Silver Index Options	PHLX
5. Interest Rate Options:	
a. U.S. Treasury Notes	CBOE
	AMEX
b. U.S. Treasury Bonds	CBOE
6. Options on Futures:	
a. Crude Oil	New York Mercantile Exchange
b. Gold	New York Commodity Exchange
c. Silver	New York Commodity Exchange
d. NYSE Composite Index	New York Futures Exchange
e. Russell 2000 Index	New York Futures Exchange
f. Russell 3000 Index	New York Futures Exchange
g. S&P 500	Chicago Mercantile Exchange
h. Foreign Currencies	International Monetary Market
i. Treasury Bonds	Chicago Board of Trade
j. Agricultural	Chicago Board of Trade
k. Livestock	Chicago Mercantile Exchange

PUT AND CALL STOCK OPTIONS

Overview of Options

This section discusses traditional call and put options, where the underlying asset is a specific common stock. These options are the most actively traded and are referred to as *equity* options. Table 19.1 provides a summary of the six different types of options that are actively traded and indicates the exchanges and markets where they are traded. Newer types of options are discussed later in this chapter.

Development of the Options Clearing Corporations, OCC, facilitated and improved option trading.[1] The OCC guarantees the provisions specified in the option

---

[1] Details about the OCC and the options markets are provided in a booklet entitled *Characteristics and Risks of Standardized Options*, published by the OCC in September 1987.

contract since it acts as an intermediary between the buyer and writer. The OCC actually issues *standardized options*, so that the buyer relies on the OCC rather than the individual writer to fulfill the obligations of the option . Likewise, the option writer has an obligation to the OCC rather than to any particular buyer. However, no physical certificate is created when options are written. All transactions are simply bookkeeping entries maintained by the OCC. The OCC is owned by the stock exchanges and the National Association of Securities Dealers (OTC market) that trade options and is regulated by the SEC. The obligation of the individual writers and buyers are guaranteed to the OCC by *clearing members*, the brokerage firms representing the individuals. The clearing members provide the OCC with the margin required of option traders and also contribute funds to ensure that the OCC can fulfill its obligations.

Characteristics of Stock Options

A *call* contract (or simply a call) grants the holder the right to buy, while a *put* contract (a put) grants the right to sell. For example, an investor who *purchases* a put or call is buying the right to sell or purchase 100 shares of the underlying stock, at a specified price, within a specified period of time. The *seller*, or *writer*, of the put or call has the opposite legal obligation. The writer of the call promises to sell the stock; the writer of a put promises to buy the stock. The option buyer has the right to exercise the option, sell it in the secondary market, or let it expire. The option writer, however, cannot force the option holder to exercise the option.

Standardized options have specified exercise prices and expiration dates. For options on individual stocks, the maximum life is nine months. The *expiration date* falls on the Saturday following the third Friday of the expiration month. There are three life cycles that may be used for options, and one of these cycles is assigned to each stock by the exchange:

- January, April, July, and October
- February, May, August, and November
- March, June, September, and December

However, at any point in time, the exchange may allow options to be traded with expiration dates for successive months. For example, in September, options with expiration months of September, October, and November could be available, depending on investor interest.

Standardized options also have uniform *exercise* or *striking prices*, in increments of $2.50, $5, or $10, depending on the price of the underlying common stock. For example, options on a particular stock might have striking prices of $65, $70, $75, or $80. The striking price is the price at which the stock may be acquired or sold if the investor exercises the option. The striking prices are established by the markets on which the options are traded. Striking price intervals of $2.50 are used for lower-priced stocks, while intervals of $10 are used for higher-priced stocks. Generally, striking prices will be both above and below the market price of the underlying common stock; as the price of the common stock moves up or down, additional options can be issued with striking prices that reflect these price changes.

A comparison of the striking price and actual market price of the underlying stock categorizes options as *out-of-the-money, at-the-money,* or *in-the-money.* For example, assume that the following three call options are available on XYZ common stock:

OPTION	STRIKING PRICE	COMMON STOCK PRICE	CLASSIFICATION
1	$55	$60	in-the-money
2	$60	$60	at-the-money
3	$65	$60	out-of-the-money

The first option is in-the-money since the striking price is below the common stock price; the second option is at-the-money since the common stock price and striking price are equal; and the third option is out-of-the-money since the striking price is above the common stock price. For *put* options, the classifications are simply reversed.

Option 1, from the example above, has value because it allows the holder to acquire a stock selling at $60 for the striking price of $55. This $5 difference is called the *intrinsic value* of the option. Except for the case of mispricing, the actual price of the call option is always equal to or greater than the intrinsic value. If the price of the option is above the intrinsic value, this additional amount is the *time value* of the option. For example, if the option price is $8 and the intrinsic value is $5, the time value is $3. The time value depends on expectations of future stock price increases before the expiration date. Options 2 and 3 do not have intrinsic value since they are at- or out-of-the-money. Since their prices cannot be negative or zero, however, they will be priced to reflect time value.

Although the holder of an option has the right to exercise before expiration, the vast majority of investors do not exercise options because they do not want a position in the underlying stock. Rather, most investors make a *closing transaction,* which effectively cancels the position; for example, the buyer of an option would write (sell) an identical option as a closing transaction, while the option writer would cancel by purchasing an identical option. Closing transactions generally have lower transaction costs compared to the cost of exercising the option.

Where an option holder elects to exercise the option, the OCC randomly assigns the *exercise notice* to option writers. Typically, the writer is listed as the brokerage firm that represents the individual investor. The brokerage firm then receives the exercise notice and must randomly assign it to one or more of its customers who wrote the specific option. Once the exercise has been assigned to a particular writer, the position cannot be cancelled by using a closing transaction. Thus, one of the risks of writing options is that the investor may be randomly assigned an exercise notice at any time during the life of the option. Since less than 5 percent of the options are exercised, however, the likelihood of being assigned an exercise notice is small.

Options can be either *American-style* or *European-style.* The difference is related to the terms of exercising the option. An American option may be exercised by the holder at any time after it is purchased, until it expires. A European option may be exercised only during a specified period, which may end on the expiration date or for a designated period prior to the expiration date. Historically, options traded in the United States are American-style, but since 1985, some European-style options are traded, and it is likely that others may be introduced in the future. American-style options provide the holder more flexibility in designing strategies to deal with factors such as cash dividends. For the typical investor, however, the distinction between an American- and European-style option is immaterial because an option with some time remaining before expiration is likely to have time value. A rational investor would, therefore, not exercise an American-style option and lose the time value. Rather, the option would be sold, or it would be exercised at the expiration date if the stock price was above the exercise price.

Option writers must meet applicable *margin requirements*. There is, however, a major difference in margin requirements on stocks or bonds and those on options. A margin requirement on a stock or bond purchase is a required down payment, and the remaining funds are borrowed from the broker. Options cannot be bought on credit; when options are purchased, the full purchase price must be paid at the time of purchase. When an option is written without an existing position in the underlying stocks, the *issuer* must deposit cash or U.S. Treasury bills with the broker as collateral—usually called a margin but actually a type of performance bond. The option writer may also have to meet margin calls if the underlying stock moves in an unfavorable direction. If an option is written against an existing position in the common stock, the common stock must be on deposit with the broker and serves as the margin.

Margin requirements for option writers without a position in the underlying stock vary, depending on the brokerage firm, the price of the underlying stock, the price of the option, and whether the option is a put or a call. As a general rule, initial margins are at least 30 percent of the stock price when the option is written, plus the intrinsic value of the option. The amount of the margin influences the degree of *financial leverage* the investor has and consequently the returns and risk on the position.[2]

Tax Considerations

The tax treatment of gains and losses on option transactions can be quite complicated. The tax rules are different for the four major types of options: equity, index, debt, and foreign currency. The tax liability also depends on whether the option was exercised or was closed and whether the option was covered or uncovered. (A *covered* option indicates that the writer has a position in the underlying common stock, while the writer of an *uncovered* or *naked* option has no position in the underlying stock.) Most of the options markets and brokerage firms that deal in options have publications that deal with specific tax aspects on options.

In very general terms, the Tax Reform Act of 1986 effectively eliminated the favorable tax treatment for long-term capital gains. As of January 1, 1987, all profits on options transactions are taxed at the maximum rate of 28 percent, regardless of the length of the holding period. The actual tax rate depends on the

---

[2] For example, see Michael R. Asay, ''Implied Margin Requirements on Options and Stocks,'' *Journal of Portfolio Management* (Spring 1981): pp. 55–59.

investor's marginal rate. If an option is exercised and therefore used to acquire or sell a stock, the price of the option is included in the tax basis for the stock and influences the ultimate capital gain or loss on the stock. If an individual writes an option, the proceeds are not recognized as income until the position is terminated, by expiration, delivery of the underlying stock, or a closing transaction.

Quotations on Put and Call Stock Options

As previously discussed, standardized options are traded on the NYSE, AMEX, Philadelphia and Pacific Exchanges, and the CBOE. Table 19.2 provides a sample of quotations for put and call options on individual common stocks. Notice that put contracts are indicated by a "P" immediately following the striking price. The quoted price represents the price for the right to buy or sell one share of the underlying stock. Since an option contract is for 100 shares, the indicated price must be multiplied by 100 to determine the price of the contract.

Notice that both "sales" and "open int." are given for each contract in Table 19.2. The sales figure represents the number of options traded during the week; the open interest represents the total number of contracts outstanding.

Some basic pricing relationships are evident in Table 19.2. A more distant expiration date and a lower striking price increase the price of call options. For put options, however, a lower striking price reduces the price of the option. It is also interesting that many options that are out-of-the-money have significant value because of the time value of the option. These relationships are explained in detail later in the chapter.

TABLE 19.2 QUOTATIONS ON PUT AND CALL STOCK OPTIONS

[Table 19.2: Quotations on put and call stock options, reprinted from Barron's, containing option listings for Chicago Board, Pacific Exchange, New York Stock Exchange (Equity Options), American Stock Exchange, and Philadelphia Exchange. Column headers: Expire date / Strike price, Sales, Open Int., Week's High, Low, Price, Net Chg., N.Y. Close.]

SOURCE: *Barron's*, 8, February 1988. Reprinted courtesy of *Barron's Weekly*.

Risk and Return on Equity Options

This section discusses the risks and returns associated with writing or buying call and put options on individual common stocks. To simplify the examples, several assumptions are made. First, as previously discussed, the options will not be exercised before the expiration date. Second, the option positions are uncovered or naked since hedging (strategies dealing with covered options) is discussed later in the chapter. Finally, brokerage commissions and taxes are ignored in calculating gains and losses. Brokerage fees in options can be negotiated but generally involve a minimum charge of $20–$50 for small trades under $1,000 or 2–3 percent of the value for larger trades. Brokerage fees are assessed on the initial trade and when the option is sold or a reversing transaction is made. Consideration of brokerage fees and taxes would obviously reduce the gains and increase the losses in the examples.

1. CALL OPTIONS Table 19.3 provides an illustration of possible profits and losses on an at-the-money call option on IBM's common stock. Investor A writes the call, while investor B takes a long position. Investor A earns a profit of $5,000 if the stock price remains constant or declines, because the option will not be exercised. This profit is the proceeds or *premium* received from writing the options. If the stock price increases above $150, Investor A's profit declines until it reaches zero when the stock price is at $160. At stock prices above $160, the option writer loses money, because the option will be exercised or more commonly the writer will need to make a reversing transaction. Theoretically, there is no limit for A's losses if the stock price continues to increase and the writer does not use a closing transaction by purchasing an identical call.

Investor B has exactly the opposite situation. Losses occur until the stock price reaches $160 because the option cannot be profitably exercised. For stock prices between $150 and $160, losses can be reduced by selling the option for its intrinsic value or exercising the option. Profits occur only when the stock price is above $160. There is no upper limit on the profits if the stock price continues to increase. The maximum loss, however, is $5,000.

This illustration indicates that an investor who thinks that IBM's common stock will be above $160 at expiration should go long or buy a call option. An investor who thinks that the stock price will remain constant or decline should go short or write a call option. The risk of the two positions is quite different, however, since the short position is subject to unlimited losses while the long-position loss is limited to $5,000.

The *leverage effect* also influences the returns and risks. Essentially, the price or premium on an option is a fraction of the cost of a position in the underlying common stock. If an option is traded at its intrinsic value, however, the dollar losses and gains on options approximately match the losses and gains on the underlying stock. Thus, a "small" dollar investment in options can result in extremely large positive or negative *HPRs*. For example, the *HPR* over the 3.5 months for the option purchaser (Investor B) if IBM's price at expiration was $180 would be 200 percent ($10,000/5,000). If the actual stock was purchased in January for $150 and sold for $180, the *HPR*

TABLE 19.3 ILLUSTRATION OF PROFITS AND LOSSES ON CALL OPTIONS

Contract: Call on IBM common stock
Expiration month: March 1988
Striking price: $150
Price of option: $10 on January 1, 1988
Price of common stock: $150 on January 1, 1988
Investor A: Writes 5 contracts and receives $5,000 ($10 × 100 × 5)
Investor B: Buys 5 contracts for $5,000

PRICE OF IBM ON LAST TRADING DATE BEFORE EXPIRATION (3/18/88)	INVESTOR A (WRITER)		INVESTOR B (PURCHASER)	
	PROFIT (LOSS)	HPR*	PROFIT (LOSS)	HPR*
$140	$5,000	100.0%	$(5.000)	(100.0)%
150	5,000	100.0	(5,000)	(100.0)
160	0	0.0	0	0.0
170	(5,000)	(100.0)	5,000	100.0
180	(10,000)	(200.0)	10,000	200.0

Investor A

Investor B

* The HPRs are calculated as the profit or loss/initial investment. The initial investment for both the call writer and buyer is assumed to be the value of the contracts or $5,000. Because of the margin, however, the actual initial investment may be smaller and could differ between the writer and buyer. This simplifying assumption facilitates comparing the HPRs between the two investors.

would be 20 percent ($30/150). As illustrated in the table, the leverage effect can increase HPRs, but it also increases the risk when the stock price declines. The relationship between the striking price and the price of the stock when the option position is taken influences the option's price and consequently the leverage effect.

2. PUT OPTIONS Table 19.4 illustrates a long and a short position in an IBM put. Investor A writes puts; Investor B buys puts. The writer earns a profit if the stock price is above $140 at the expiration date. Losses occur at prices below $140 and can theoretically reach $70,000 [($150 × 100 × 5) − $5,000] if the stock price declines to zero.

The maximum loss to the put purchaser is $5,000, the price of the options. The maximum loss occurs if the stock price at expiration is $150 or greater. Profits occur if the stock price is below $140 and can reach $70,000 if the stock price declines to zero.

TABLE 19.4   ILLUSTRATION OF PROFITS AND LOSSES ON PUT OPTIONS

Contract: Put on IBM common stock
            Expiration month: March 1988
            Striking price: $150
            Price of option: $10 on January 1, 1988
            Price of common stock: $150 on January 1, 1988
Investor A: Writes 5 contracts and receives $5,000 ($10 × 100 × 5)
Investor B: Buys 5 contracts for $5,000

PRICE OF IBM ON LAST TRADING DATE BEFORE EXPIRATION (3/18/88)	INVESTOR A (WRITER)		INVESTOR B (PURCHASER)	
	PROFIT (LOSS)	HPR*	PROFIT (LOSS)	HPR*
$120	$(10,000)	(200.0)%	$10,000	200.0%
130	(5,000)	(100.0)	5,000	100.0
140	0	0.0	0	0.0
150	5,000	100.0	(5,000)	(100.0)
160	5,000	100.0	(5,000)	(100.0)

Investor A   Investor B

* The *HPRs* are calculated as the profit or loss/initial investment. For the put writer and buyer, the initial investment is assumed to be the price of the contracts or $5,000. Because of the margin, however, the actual initial investment may be smaller and could differ between the writer and buyer. This simplifying assumption facilitates comparing the *HPRs* between the two investors.

This example illustrates that an investor will write puts if the stock price is expected to remain constant or increase. Puts will be purchased if the investor anticipates that the stock price will decline.

Hedging Using Call and Put Options

Hedging is a common strategy designed to limit losses in one position by simultaneously taking an offsetting second position in the same or a different security. In most cases, hedges are not perfect; they cannot eliminate all losses. Typically, a hedge strategy attempts to eliminate large losses without significantly reducing gains.

Equity options are often used to hedge a long or short position in the underlying common stock and represent covered option positions. When options are used to hedge an investment in individual stocks or a portfolio of stocks, they reduce risk. A correctly hedged portfolio of common stocks and options, therefore, has less risk than a portfolio without options.

1. HEDGING A SHORT POSITION IN STOCK A short-seller of stock anticipates that the stock will decline in price. By selling or shorting the stock now and buying it at a lower price in the future, the short-seller earns a profit. The losses from this strategy can be large if the price increases since the short-seller has an obligation to purchase the stock in the future. A hedge would be designed to minimize this risk. One hedge would be to short the stock and simultaneously *buy* a call with a striking price equal to or close to the selling price of the stock. The call option could be used to acquire the stock in the event the stock increased in price. If the stock price declined as expected, however, the option would be worthless, and this loss would reduce the gain on the short position.

   The top portion of Table 19.5 illustrates the short hedge. Notice that losses occur in the hedged position until the stock price falls below $95. However, the maximum loss on the hedged position is $500. Therefore, the hedge is not perfect in the sense that all possible losses are eliminated. The ''cost'' of forming the hedge is the price for the call, which will be lost if the stock price declines.

2. HEDGING A LONG POSITION IN STOCK An investor who buys common stock anticipates that the stock will increase in value. The risk, of course, is that the stock's price will decline. One hedge could be formed by buying the stock and simultaneously *buying* a put. The lower portion of Table 19.5 illustrates the possible gains and losses from this strategy. Notice that the losses on the hedged position are limited to $500, while the gains are reduced by the cost of the put option when the stock price increases.

Writing Covered Calls and Puts

The hedging strategies discussed above were designed to limit the *risk* of an underlying position in common stocks. Puts and calls can also be used to increase the *returns* from a position in stocks. This strategy may be particularly appropriate if the common stocks in the portfolio are not expected to have significant short-term price changes. For example, an investor may think that the stocks are good long-term investments (short position in an expected down market or a long position in an expected rising market), but short-term price changes are expected to be small. By *writing* options, the investor can increase the short-term returns of the portfolio. The investor will not benefit if large stock price changes occur because the option would be exercised or the writer will need to make a reversing transaction. Writing covered options is a very conservative strategy for both individual and institutional investors. Table 19.6 illustrates the possible gains and losses from a strategy of writing a call against a long position in the stock.

TABLE 19.5 ILLUSTRATIONS OF HEDGING USING CALL AND PUT OPTIONS

1. Short the stock and buy a call:
   Stock: $100 per share, 100 shares
   Call Option: $500 per contract (100 shares), striking price $100

STOCK PRICE AT EXPIRATION	STOCK POSITION		OPTION POSITION		HEDGED POSITION	
	GAIN (LOSS)	HPR	GAIN (LOSS)	HPR	GAIN (LOSS)	HPR
$ 80	$2,000	20.0%	$(500)	(100.0)%	$1,500	14.29%
90	1,000	10.0	(500)	(100.0)	500	4.76
100	0	0.0	(500)	(100.0)	(500)	(4.76)
110	(1,000)	(10.0)	500	100.0	(500)	(4.76)
120	(2,000)	(20.0)	1,500	300.0	(500)	(4.76)

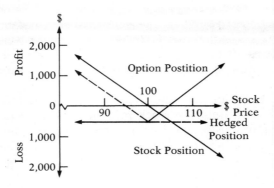

2. Buy the stock and a put:
   Stock: $100 per share, 100 shares
   Put Option: $500 per contract (100 shares), striking price $100

STOCK PRICE AT EXPIRATION	STOCK POSITION		OPTION POSITION		HEDGED POSITION	
	GAIN (LOSS)	HPR	GAIN (LOSS)	HPR	GAIN (LOSS)	HPR
$ 80	$(2,000)	(20.0)%	$1,500	300.0%	$ (500)	(4.76)%
90	(1,000)	(10.0)	500	100.0	(500)	(4.76)
100	0	0.0	(500)	(100.0)	(500)	(4.76)
110	1,000	10.0	(500)	(100.0)	500	4.76
120	2,000	20.0	(500)	(100.0)	1,500	14.29

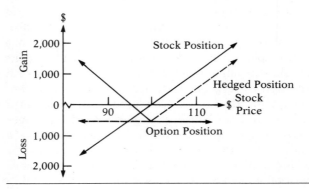

TABLE 19.6   ILLUSTRATION OF WRITING COVERED CALLS

Long Position: 100 shares of stock purchased for $50, for long-term price appreciation.
Short Position: Write one call contract with striking price of $50, for $400.

STOCK PRICE AT EXPIRATION	STOCK POSITION		OPTION POSITION		COMBINED POSITION	
	GAIN (LOSS)	HPR	GAIN (LOSS)	HPR	GAIN (LOSS)	HPR
$45	$(500)	(10.0)%	$400	100.0%	$(100)	(2.17)%
46	(400)	(8.0)	400	100.0	0	0.00
47	(300)	(6.0)	400	100.0	100	2.17
48	(200)	(4.0)	400	100.0	200	4.35
49	(100)	(2.0)	400	100.0	300	6.52
50	0	0.0	400	100.0	400	8.70
51	100	2.0	300	75.0	400	8.70
52	200	4.0	200	50.0	400	8.70
53	300	6.0	100	25.0	400	8.70

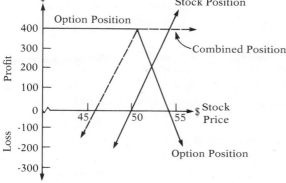

* HPRs are based on an initial investment of $4,600 or $5,000 less a $400 premium received for the options.

As the secondary market for options developed during the 1970s, institutional investors frequently wrote call options against long positions in stocks. A 1980 article by Yates and Kopprasch, using data over the period 1973 to mid-1980, reported that writing covered call options was an effective strategy since risk-adjusted excess returns were discovered.[3] This finding suggests that call options may have been overpriced during this period.

Other Option Strategies Using Puts and Calls

There are hundreds of option strategies when *combinations* are considered. For example, an investor may simultaneously take a put and a call position on the same common stock or take several call positions at different striking prices and/or expiration dates. The most common of these combination strategies are straddles, spreads, strips, and straps.

---

[3] James W. Yates, Jr. and Robert W. Kopprasch, Jr., "Writing Covered Call Options: Profits and Risks," *Journal of Portfolio Management* (Fall 1980): pp. 74–79.

1. STRADDLES This strategy consists of simultaneously taking a position in a put and a call on the same underlying security, with the same striking price and expiration date. The put and call will be *purchased* (long position) if the investor thinks that the underlying stock is likely to have a *large* price movement but is uncertain of the direction of the price change. For example, if a company was a likely takeover candidate, the stock price might be bid up, and the call would increase in value. If the speculation was incorrect and no takeover attempt occurred, however, the stock would decrease, and the put would increase in value. Table 19.7 illustrates a long straddle strategy. Notice that the stock price must fall below $20 or increase above $30 before the strategy results in profits.

   A *short straddle* position is appropriate if the investor thinks that the underlying stock price is *unlikely* to have a significant change, up or down. As long as the stock price remains relatively constant, the writer benefits from the premiums received from writing the put and call. In writing both a put and call, however, large losses can occur if the stock price changes significantly in either direction. Table 19.8 illustrates a short straddle strategy. Notice that the profit/loss function is simply the inverted function of the long straddle function in Table 19.7.

2. SPREADS A spread is a more general type of straddle; the put and call may have different striking prices and/or expiration dates. An investor who creates a *long spread* is motivated by the expectation that the underlying stock will have a *large* price change. The purchase prices for the call and put options

TABLE 19.7 ILLUSTRATION OF LONG STRADDLE STRATEGY

Long Positions: Purchase a put and a call contract, with same expiration date and a striking price of $25. The put is bought for $200 and the call for $300. The common stock is currently selling for $26.

STOCK PRICE AT EXPIRATION	PUT POSITION GAIN (LOSS)	PUT POSITION HPR	CALL POSITION GAIN (LOSS)	CALL POSITION HPR	STRADDLE POSITION GAIN (LOSS)	STRADDLE POSITION HPR
$20	$300	150.0%	$(300)	(100.0)%	$ 0	0.0%
25	(200)	(100.0)	(300)	(100.0)	(500)	(100.0)
30	(200)	(100.0)	200	66.7	0	0.0
35	(200)	(100.0)	700	233.3	500	100.0

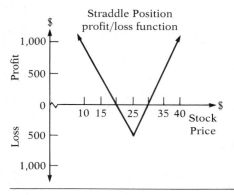

Straddle Position profit/loss function

TABLE 19.8   ILLUSTRATION OF SHORT STRADDLE STRATEGY

Short Positions: Write a put and a call contract, with the same expiration date and a striking price of $25. The put is sold for $200 and the call for $300. The common stock is currently selling for $26.

STOCK PRICE AT EXPIRATION	PUT POSITION		CALL POSITION		STRADDLE POSITION	
	GAIN (LOSS)	HPR	GAIN (LOSS)	HPR	GAIN (LOSS)	HPR
$20	$(300)	(150.0)%	$300	100.0%	$ 0	0.0%
25	200	100.0	300	100.0	500	100.0
30	200	100.0	(200)	(66.7)	0	0.0
35	200	100.0	(700)	(233.3)	(500)	(100.0)

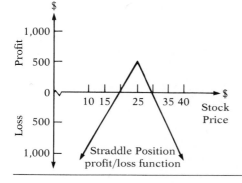

are likely to be lower for a spread than for a straddle. To form a long spread, "cheap" puts and calls that are out-of-the-money and have only time value are purchased. The price change of the stock must be larger for the spread than for the straddle before profits occur. Table 19.9 illustrates the possible gains and losses from a long spread strategy. Table 19.9 should be compared with Table 19.7.

A *short spread* strategy involves writing both puts and calls under the assumption that the underlying stock will *not* have a large price change. Writing a put with a striking price below that of the call increases the range of the stock price where profits occur. The premium income will also be lower, however, than with a straddle strategy. As with the long and short straddle strategies, the profit/loss function for the short spread is the inverted function for the long spread, as shown in Table 19.9.

There are many more spread than straddle strategies—for example, bullish, bearish, and neutral spread strategies, in addition to calendar (different expiration dates), vertical (different striking prices), or combination (different expiration dates and striking prices) strategies. A number of studies have discussed the various spread strategies and developed techniques to analyze the risk-return characteristics of each strategy.[4]

---

[4] For example, see Ronald T. Slivka, "Call Option Spreading," *Journal of Portfolio Management* (Spring 1981): pp. 71–76, and Peter H. Ritchken and Harvey M. Salkin, "Safety First Selection Techniques for Option Spreads," *Journal of Portfolio Management* (Spring 1983): pp. 61–67.

TABLE 19.9   ILLUSTRATION OF A LONG SPREAD STRATEGY

Long Positions: Purchase a put contract for $100, with a striking price of $20 and expiration date in 3 months. Purchase a call contract for $200 with a striking price of $30 and expiration date in 3 months. The common stock is currently selling for $27, so that both options are priced out-of-the-money.

STOCK PRICE AT EXPIRATION	PUT POSITION GAIN (LOSS)	HPR	CALL POSITION GAIN (LOSS)	HPR	SPREAD POSITION GAIN (LOSS)	HPR
$15	$400	400.0%	$(200)	(100.0)	$200	66.7%
20	(100)	(100.0)	(200)	(100.0)	(300)	(100.0)
25	(100)	(100.0)	(200)	(100.0)	(300)	(100.0)
30	(100)	(100.0)	(200)	(100.0)	(300)	(100.0)
35	(100)	(100.0)	300	150.0	200	66.7

3. STRIPS AND STRAPS The strip and the strap strategies are special cases of a straddle. In a straddle, the striking price and expiration date are the same for the put and the call. This is also the case for the strip and strap strategies. A *strip*, however, involves two puts and one call, while a *strap* involves two calls and one put. In both cases, an investor can take a short (write) or long (buy) position.

In a strip strategy, a long position is appropriate if a *large* stock price change is anticipated. In buying two puts and one call, however, the profit will occur sooner and be larger if the stock price *declines* rather than increases. The buyer is uncertain about the direction of the stock price movement but is more confident of a decline than an increase. This strategy is illustrated in Table 19.10 which shows that significant profits occur when the stock price declines below $19.50. Profits also occur when the stock price increases above $36. If the investor thinks that a large price *increase* is more likely, the appropriate strategy will be a long strap, involving two calls and one put. A graph of this strategy would illustrate a greater slope of the profit function for stock price increases than that shown in Table 19.10.

A short strip or strap strategy is appropriate if the stock price is *not* expected to change significantly. In writing two puts and one call (strip), the profit potential in the case of a stock price increase is greater. The reverse

TABLE 19.10   ILLUSTRATION OF A LONG STRIP STRATEGY.

Long Positions: Purchase two put contracts for $400 each and one call contract for $300. The striking price on both the puts and the call is $25, and they expire in 3 months. The common stock is currently selling for $24.

STOCK PRICE AT EXPIRATION	PUT POSITION		CALL POSITION		STRIP POSITION	
	GAIN (LOSS)	HPR	GAIN (LOSS)	HPR	GAIN (LOSS)	HPR
$15	$1200	150.0%	$(300)	(100.0)%	$ 900	81.8%
20	200	25.0	(300)	(100.0)	(100)	(9.1)
25	(800)	(100.0)	(300)	(100.0)	(1100)	(100.0)
30	(800)	(100.0)	200	66.7	(600)	(54.5)
35	(800)	(100.0)	700	233.3	(100)	(9.1)
36	(800)	(100.0)	800	266.7	0	0.0
37	(800)	(100.0)	900	300.0	100	9.1

is true for a short strap strategy. Graphs of the strategy would be similar to the one in Table 19.8, except that the slopes of the profit/loss functions would change.

Option Pricing

This section deals with techniques and models to determine the value of options: first, a generalized graphic model is presented that establishes upper and lower limits to an option's value and identifies the key variables that influence value; second, the Black-Scholes call option model is presented and illustrated; finally, the put-call parity principal is presented that can be used to value puts.

1.   GRAPHIC ANALYSIS OF CALL AND PUT VALUES Figure 19.1 provides a graphic analysis of call and put values on individual common stocks. The major variable that determines an option's value is the price of the underlying asset. This price is shown on the horizontal axis. The upper panel of Figure 19.1 illustrates a call option. The call cannot have a value above the value of the stock because of the striking price, or $V_c \leq V_s$. The *maximum value* line is therefore drawn as a 45-degree line from the origin. The call option cannot have a value less than its value if exercised, or $V_c \geq V_s - S$, where S is the striking

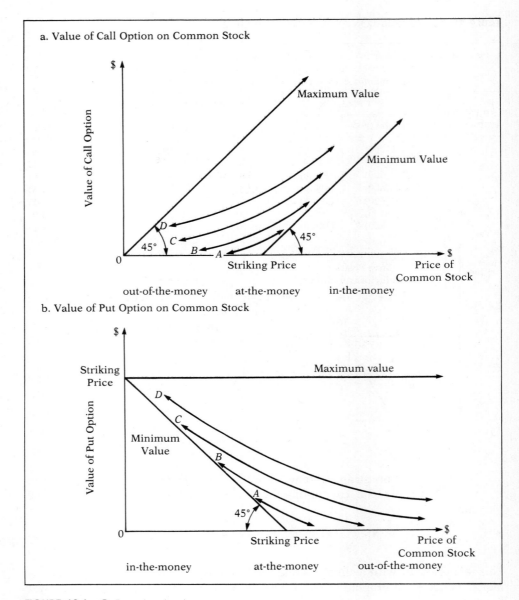

a. Value of Call Option on Common Stock

b. Value of Put Option on Common Stock

FIGURE 19.1 Call and put values.

price. This relationship defines the *minimum value* line, drawn at a 45-degree angle from the exercise price. The call option, therefore, must have a value on or above the minimum value function and on or below the maximum value function. For example, assume that a call option has a striking price of $25 and that the common stock is currently selling for $28. Since the option is in-the-money, its price cannot be less than $3, its intrinsic value. If the stock price increases to $29, the minimum value of the option will increase to $4. Thus, the slope of the minimum value function is 1 and is therefore drawn with a 45-degree angle from the striking price on the horizontal axis.

The functions labeled *A*, *B*, *C*, and *D* represent hypothetical values for identical call options with different times before expiration. Function *A* represents the possible values for the option with the shortest time before expiration. These functions indicate that options with longer lives will have higher values than options with short lives. The curvature of the function indicates that in-the-money call options will have greater values than out-of-the-money options, but the relationship is not linear. The out-of-the-money call options have *time* value because of expectations about future increases in the stock price. The in-the-money options' value contains both intrinsic and time values. The key to option valuation is the correct estimate of the time value.

The lower portion of Figure 19.1 deals with a put option. The minimum value function for puts is drawn from the striking price on the horizontal axis to an equal value point on the vertical axis. For example, assume that the stock price was $0 and that the striking price was $30. The put option would have a minimum value equal to its intrinsic value, or the striking price of $30, as shown on the vertical axis. If the stock price increased to $15, the minimum value of the option would decrease to $15. When the stock price and striking price were equal, the minimum value of the put would be $0.

The put cannot have a value greater than the striking price since the stock price cannot be negative. The maximum value function is therefore drawn as a horizontal line originating from a point equal to the striking price on the vertical axis. A put's value must be on or above the minimum value function and on or below the maximum value function.

In-the-money puts have value because of their intrinsic value and time value. Thus, in-the-money puts will have higher values than out-of-the-money puts, but the relationship is not linear. Functions labeled *A–D* in the lower panel of Figure 19.1 represent hypothetical values for puts. They differ only in lengths of time before expiration. As with calls, puts with longer lives have greater value.

Based on the above discussion and Figure 19.1, the key variables that influence an option's value are

(1) value of underlying common stock;

(2) striking price; and

(3) length of time before expiration.

Other variables that have been identified and, in some cases, incorporated into option pricing models are

(1) price volatility of the underlying common stock;

(2) risk-free rate of return over the same period as the option's life;

(3) cash dividends on the common stock; and

(4) market imperfections.

The discussion that follows will explain how these variables influence option values.

2. THE BLACK-SCHOLES OPTION PRICING MODEL In 1973 a paper was published that represented the first rigorous effort toward developing a mathematical model

for valuing European-style calls on stocks that do not pay cash dividends.[5] The model also assumes that the call is used to form a perfect hedge for a stock portfolio; thus, the return on the hedged portfolio should be the risk-free rate of return. The *Black-Scholes* model:

$$V_c = P_s N(d_1) - Se^{-rt}N(d_2) \tag{19.1}$$

where V_c = value of the call option

          P_s = current stock price

          S = striking price

          t = length of time before expiration, expressed as a fraction of one year

          e = base e antilog = 2.7183 . . .

          r = risk-free rate of return for one year

$N(d_1)$ and $N(d_2)$ are probabilities from a standard normal cumulative probability table evaluated at d_1 and d_2.

$$d_1 = \frac{ln(P_s/S) + (r + .5\sigma^2)t}{\sigma t^{.5}}$$

$$d_2 = d_1 - \sigma t^{.5}$$

where $ln(P_s/S)$ = natural logarithm (base e logs) of P_s/S

          σ^2 = variance of stock's continuously compounded rate of return

          σ = standard deviation of stock's continuously compounded rate of return

An inspection of Equation 19.1 indicates that the value of a call option is a function of the current stock price, striking price, length of time before expiration, risk-free rate of return, and variance of the stock return. These variables and their influence on call option values are discussed below.

a.   CURRENT STOCK PRICE The most important variable influencing an option's value is the price of the underlying stock. Other things equal, higher stock prices result in higher option prices because higher-priced stocks can have larger dollar price changes which are magnified in terms of their influence on the option's value.

b.   STRIKING PRICE Other things equal, a higher striking price reduces the value of the option because the higher the striking price, the lower the probability the call will be exercised..

c.   LENGTH OF TIME BEFORE EXPIRATION Other things equal, options with longer lives have higher values because of the higher probability that a

---

[5] Fischer Black and Myron Scholes, "The Pricing of Options and Corporate Liabilities," *Journal of Political Economy* (May-June 1973): pp. 637–54.

TABLE 19.11   ILLUSTRATION OF BLACK-SCHOLES MODEL

Stock price $= P_s = \$50$
Striking price $= S = \$45$
Length of time before expiration $= t = 3$ months $= .25$
Risk-free rate of return $= r = 10\%$ per year
Variance of stock's return $= \sigma^2 = .16$
Standard deviation of stock's return $= \sigma = .4$

$$d_1 = \frac{ln(50/45) + [.1 + .5(.16)].25}{(.4)(.25)^{.5}}$$

$$= (.1054 + .0450)/.2 = .7520$$

$$d_2 = .7520 - .4(.25)^{.5} = .5520$$

$N(d_1) \sim .7740$ (interpolation estimate from the cumulative normal distribution table in Appendix A2)

$N(d_2) \sim .7095$ (interpolation estimate from the cumulative normal distribution table in Appendix A2)

$$V_c = \$50(.7740) - \$45e^{-(.1)(.25)}(.7095)$$

$$= \$38.70 - (\$43.89)(.7095)$$

$$= \$38.70 - \$31.14$$

$$V_c = \$7.56$$

---

significant change will occur in the stock's price. Thus, the time value of the option is directly related to the option's life.

d.   RISK-FREE RATE OF RETURN The risk-free rate of return is used to calculate the present value of the striking price. Therefore, higher values for the risk-free rate reduce the present value of the striking price and *increase* the option's value. Since the Black-Scholes model assumes that call options are written to create a riskless hedge, the value of the options must increase to provide a higher risk-free return on the hedged portfolio.

e.   VARIANCE OF THE STOCK'S RETURN Other things equal, options on stocks with volatile prices (returns) will be more valuable than options on stocks with stable prices (returns). The higher volatility increases the probability that a significant change will occur in the stock's price.

Table 19.11 provides an illustration of the Black-Scholes model. Using this model, the calculated value for the option can be compared to its actual market price. If the value is higher than the market price, the option is considered to be undervalued. The opposite assessment is made if the market price is higher than the value.

The major problem encountered in using the Black-Scholes model is determining the variance of the stock's return. As Equation 19.1 indicates, the other variables can easily be determined. Typically, historical stock prices are used to calculate an estimate of the stock's return variance. There is considerable debate, however, over the correct length of the historical period and the interval of time between the observed stock prices used to calculate the variance.[6]

Table 19.12 demonstrates the sensitivity of a call option's value to variables used in the Black-Scholes model. The top portion of the table provides

---

[6] For a discussion and suggested procedure, see J. S. Butler and Barry Schachter, "Unbiased Estimation of the Black-Scholes Formula," *Journal of Financial Economics* (March 1986): pp. 341–57.

TABLE 19.12 SENSITIVITY OF CALL OPTION
VALUES TO KEY VARIABLES

I. Sensitivity to stock price and striking price
   Length of time before expiration = t = 3 months = .25

   Risk-free rate of return = r = 10% per year

   Variance of stock's return = σ^2 = .16

Option Values for Combinations of Stock and Striking Prices

STOCK PRICE	STRIKING PRICE			
	$35	$40	$45	$50
$35	$ 3.18	$ 1.34	$0.49	$0.12
40	6.74	3.64	1.72	0.73
45	11.14	7.13	4.09	2.12
50	15.94	11.42	7.56	4.55

II. Sensitivity to risk-free return and variance
    Length of time before expiration = t = 3 months = .25

    Stock price = P_s = $50

    Striking price = S = $45

Option Values for Combinations of Risk-free Rate and
Variance

ANNUAL RISK-FREE RETURN	VARIANCE OF RETURNS			
	.08	.16	.24	.32
.06	$6.38	$7.22	$7.94	$8.57
.08	6.55	7.37	8.08	8.70
.10	6.73	7.53	8.22	8.84
.12	6.90	7.68	8.37	8.98

option values for various stock prices and striking prices. Notice that changes in the stock's price have a significant impact on the option's value, but the relationship is not linear or one-for-one. The lower portion of the table illustrates the influence of the risk-free return and the variance on option values. Notice that changes in the variance cause larger changes in the values than those caused by changes in the risk-free return.

An interesting aspect of the Black-Scholes model is that $N(d_1)$ is the *hedge ratio*, or the number of shares of stock relative to one option contract needed to form a risk-free hedged position. From Table 19.11, the value of $N(d_1)$ is given as .774. Thus, 77.4 shares of stock along with one call option are needed to form a riskless hedge. Essentially, $N(d_1)$ represents how the option's price will change relative to a change in the stock price. For *small* changes in the stock's price, the change in the option's value would be

$$\Delta V_c = (\Delta P_s)N(d_1) \tag{19.2}$$

For example, if the stock's price increased from its current level of $50, to $51, the value of the option would increase by $.774. Thus, the portfolio would not be completely hedged if one option was held for each 100 shares of stocks. The perfect or riskless hedge would require 1.2920 (1/.774) options for each

100 shares of stock. Since $N(d_1)$ is calculated using the current stock price, however, the hedge ratio changes as the price of the stock changes.

One problem with the Black-Scholes model is the influence of cash dividends on the value of the option; cash dividends influence the stock's price and variance of the stock's return and thus influence the option's value. This occurs because the price of the stock will decline by the approximate value of the dividend on the ex-dividend date. The decline in the stock's value would cause a decline in the value of the call. The Black-Scholes model was developed for European-style calls that can be exercised only at expiration and are written against stocks that do not pay dividends. Applying this model to American-style calls, however, is not appropriate for stocks that are likely to pay a cash dividend during the life of the option. Option traders would try to estimate the impact of the dividend on the value of the option. If the present value of the anticipated dividend was greater than the estimated change in the option's value, the option could be exercised to *capture* the dividends.

In order to analyze options on dividend-paying stocks, the present value of the estimated future dividends must be subtracted from the value of the stock. Using the example in Table 19.11, the indicated option value of $7.56 is correct, assuming no cash dividends. If the analyst expects a $1 dividend to be paid in three months, then $.98 [$1/(1 + .025)] should be subtracted from the current stock price of $50 and the value of the option recalculated. This results in $6.82 as the dividend-adjusted option value.[7]

There have been many empirical tests of the Black-Scholes model (see the references at the end of this chapter for many of these studies). Essentially, these tests concluded that the model provided reasonably accurate estimates of an option's value. Problems occur, however, in valuing options on dividend-paying stocks, options that are out-of-the-money, and options on stocks with "high" or "low" variances. A large research effort continues, directed at improving and expanding the Black-Scholes model.[8] One important development deals with the influence of the early exercise available on American-style option.[9]

3. PUT-CALL PARITY The Black-Scholes model can be used to value put options based on the principal of *put-call parity*.[10] This approach can be demon-

---

[7] For details and other more accurate techniques for making dividend adjustments, see Richard Roll, "An Analytic Valuation Formula for Unprotected American Call Options with Known Dividends," *Journal of Financial Economics* (Novemeber 1977): pp. 251–58, and William Sterk, "Tests of Two models for Valuing Call Options on Stocks with Dividends," *Journal of Finance* (December 1982): pp. 1229–37.

[8] For a review of the history of option pricing models, see Thomas J. O'Brien and Michael J. P. Selby, "Option Pricing Theory and Asset Expectation: A Review and Discussion in Tribute to James Boness," *Financial Review* (November 1986): pp. 399–418.

[9] For example, see Fischer Black, "Fact and Fantasy in the Use of Options," *Financial Analysts Journal* (July-August 1975): pp. 36–41, 61–72, and Robert Geske and Richard Roll, "On Valuing American Call Options with the Black-Scholes European Formula," *Journal of Finance* (June 1984): pp. 443–55.

[10] For a review and discussion of put valuation techniques, see Walter L. Eckardt, Jr., "The American Put: Computational Issues and Value Comparisons," *Financial Management* (Autumn 1982): pp. 42–52, and Robert Geske and H. E. Johnson, "The American Put Option Valued Analytically," *Journal of Finance* (December 1984): pp. 1511–24.

strated forming a portfolio by (1) writing one call option, (2) buying one put with the same striking price and time to expiration as the call option, and (3) purchasing one share of the underlying stock. Thus, price changes in the stock will be exactly offset by changes in the option values. This portfolio should provide a risk-free return so that

$$V_p - V_c + P_s = P_t e^{-rt} \tag{19.3}$$

where V_p = value of the put option

V_c = value of the call option

P_s = current stock price

P_t = value of the portfolio at the expiration date of the options

e = base e antilog = 2.7183 . . .

t = length of time before expiration, expressed as a fraction of one year

r = continuously-compounded risk-free rate of return over the life of the options

Equation 19.3 can be solved for the put's value:

$$V_p = P_t e^{-rt} + V_c - P_s \tag{19.4}$$

Using the example in Table 19.11, the value of the put is

$$V_p = \$45 e^{-(.1)(.25)} + \$7.56 - \$50$$

$$= \frac{\$45}{1.0253} + \$7.56 - \$50$$

$$= \$1.45$$

INDEX, DEBT, CURRENCY, AND COMMODITY OPTIONS

Overview

Beginning in 1982, the number of underlying assets that options are written against increased dramatically. This section briefly discusses these newer types of options.

Index Options

1.   HISTORY The first options contract against an index of common stocks began trading on March 11, 1983, on the CBOE. The underlying index for this contract is the S&P 100. The AMEX and NYSE quickly started trading index options. The AMEX introduced the Major Markets Index, MMI, in April 1983. This index is designed to be very similar to the DJIA. In September 1983, the NYSE began trading options on the NYSE Composite Index. These first con-

tracts were issued on *broad-based* indices. Stock index options are also now written against *narrow-based* indices like the Oil Stock Index and the Institutional Index, and are traded on the AMEX. Table 19.1 provides a list of the actively traded equity index options and the exchanges or markets where the options are traded.

2. CHARACTERISTICS OF INDEX OPTIONS As the name implies, index options are written against an underlying index of common stocks. Since the value of the option depends on the value and changes in value of the underlying index, it is important to understand how the index is calculated (see Chapter 3). Each index is designed to represent a different segment of the stock market and can be calculated in a number of different ways. For example, the index may be a simple equal-weighted index, MMI, or it may be a value-weighted index like the S&P 100 or S&P 500.

Unlike options on individual stocks, index options are not written against a particular number of shares. The size of the contract is determined by the *multiplier*. The quoted price for the option is multiplied by the multiplier to determine the total value of the contract. For example, the multiplier for the S&P 100 and MMI is 100. If the quoted option price is $18\frac{1}{4}$, the total contract value is $1,825.

The procedures for exercising index options are essentially the same as those for equity options. Index options, however, must be *settled by cash* since there is actually no underlying deliverable asset. The cash settlement amount is calculated as the difference between the index value and the striking price, times the applicable multiplier. Because of the cash settlement requirement, call writers cannot completely hedge by taking a position in the underlying asset. The hedge would be formed by taking a position (either long or short) in an actual portfolio of stocks that was identical to the stocks included in the index. This would not be practical for most investors.

An index options risk that does not exist for equity options is *timing risk*, which occurs for option writers because of the delay in receiving a notice of exercise and the exercise date. The writer may not be informed of the exercise until a minimum of one day after the exercise. In the meantime, the value of the index may change substantially. This is not a problem for an equity option if the writer has a position in the underlying stock since the exercise can be covered by delivery; for an index option, however, there must be a cash settlement. Even if the writer attempted to hedge by holding a position in a stock portfolio similar to the index, timing risk could not be eliminated; the stocks would also change in value without the writer realizing that the option had been exercised.

Another risk factor for index options is the influence of dividends. As discussed for equity options, cash dividends cause problems in analyzing American options using the Black-Scholes model. This problem is more complex for index options because the stocks in the index will have different dividend rates and payment dates. Also, it is likely that many of the companies composing the index may change their dividends, thus increasing the uncertainty of the dividend stream. The dividend problem therefore complicates the valuation of index options and influences trading strategies.

Table 19.13 provides an example of quotations on the most actively traded index options. Notice that options are available with expiration dates

TABLE 19.13   QUOTATIONS ON INDEX OPTIONS

Expire date Strike price	Open Int.	Week's High	Low	Price	Net Chg.	N.Y. Close

INDEX OPTIONS

Chicago Board

S&P 100 INDEX

SP100	Sep260..	404 1679	54	50	54	− 7	317.16
SP100	Sep260 p	180 16948	1-16	1-16	1-16..		317.16
SP100	Sep275 p	2033 18759	⅛	1-16	1-16..		317.16
SP100	Sep280..	658 460	37⅝	29⅝	37⅝−	1¾	317.16
SP100	Sep280 p	6340 27469	¼	1-16	1-16..		317.16
SP100	Sep285..	323 793	32	25	32	+ 2	317.16
SP100	Sep285 p	19384 45160	7-16	1-16	1-16 − 1-16		317.16
SP100	Sep290..	625 2457	27½	16½	27½+	4	317.16
SP100	Sep290 p	22657 58697	⅞	1-16	1-16 − 3-16		317.16
SP100	Sep295..	751 2833	23	12½	22¾+	1¾	317.16
SP100	Sep295 p	52102 51855	1⅝	1-16	1-16 − ½		317.16
SP100	Sep300..	8873 10399	17⅞	8¼	17½+	3½	317.16
SP100	Sep300 p	126075 74219	2⅞	1-16	1-16 − 15-16		317.16
SP100	Sep305..	37152 16951	13⅛	4⅞	12⅞+	2⅞	317.16
SP100	Sep305 p	151869 56485	5	¼	5-16 − 1¾		317.16
SP100	Sep310..	132050 34334	8½	2 15-16	8	+ 1¾	317.16
SP100	Sep310 p	178215 56857	8	11-16	⅞ − 3		317.16
SP100	Sep315..	177054 56045	4¾	1½	4¼+	⅝	317.16
SP100	Sep315 p	96903 39452	12	1⅞	2 − 4½		317.16
SP100	Sep320..	165080 74418	2⅛	11-16	1¾ − 5-16		317.16
SP100	Sep320 p	41138 29183	16½	4⅜	4⅞ − 4⅞		317.16
SP100	Sep325..	10939 78367	1⅛	5-16	⅝ − 9-16		317.16
SP100	Sep325 p	16196 28579	17	8¼	8½ − 5		317.16
SP100	Sep330..	62277 90292	⅝	⅛	3-16 − 7-16		317.16
SP100	Sep330 p	10105 14557	26	13¼	13¼ − 5-16		317.16
SP100	Sep335..	38024 105355	5-16	1-16	⅛ − 3-16		317.16
SP100	Sep335 p	1671 3705	30	18¼	18¼ − ½		317.16
SP100	Sep340..	16886 71814	3-16	1-16	1-16 − 1-16		317.16
SP100	Sep340 p	213 351	36	25¼	25½−	1	317.16
SP100	Sep345..	2757 62265	1-16	1-16	1-16..		317.16
SP100	Sep350..	1668 50785	1-16	1-16	1-16..		317.16
SP100	Oct285..	140 1097	30	27	29	− 3	317.16
SP100	Oct285 p	14895 16621	1 9-16	⅜	7-16 − 5-16		317.16
SP100	Oct290..	135 238	29½	29¼	29¼−	1	317.16
SP100	Oct290 p	13455 13613	2½	9-16	⅝ − ¾		317.16
SP100	Oct295..	110 215	24¾	16	24¾+	2½	317.16
SP100	Oct295 p	18455 14663	4	1	1 − 3¼		317.16
SP100	Oct300..	1098 2382	21	13	20½+	1¾	317.16
SP100	Oct300 p	19813 16354	4¼	1 11-16	1¾ − 2¼		317.16
SP100	Oct305..	2264 1912	16½	10	16	+ 1½	317.16
SP100	Oct305 p	39427 26981	8	2¾	2¾ − 1⅞		317.16
SP100	Oct310..	15917 9343	12½	7½	12¾+	1½	317.16
SP100	Oct310 p	18363 23495	8¼	4½	4⅛ − 2⅞		317.16
SP100	Oct315..	22972 11589	10	5¾	9½+	1	317.16
SP100	Oct315 p	21229 15472	13½	5⅝	6⅛ − 3¼		317.16
SP100	Oct320..	20451 20330	7¼	4½	6¾+	¾	317.16
SP100	Oct320 p	9576 16107	16½	8⅜	8½ − 2½		317.16
SP100	Oct325..	27167 20507	5½ 2 5-16		4¾+	⅜	317.16
SP100	Oct325 p	4439 6729	21¼	11½	11½−	4	317.16
SP100	Oct330..	33537 29728	3½	1⅞	3¼..		317.16
SP100	Oct330 p	1767 4427	26	14½	14½−	5-16	317.16
SP100	Oct335..	19772 20691	2 5-16	1⅞	2 − 3-16		317.16
SP100	Oct335 p	443 2173	30	19¼	19¼ − 2¾		317.16
SP100	Oct340..	18600 27055	1½	¾ 1 3-16 −	¼		317.16

S&P 500 INDEX

SP500	Sep225..	4852 37063	196⅞	86	196⅞+ 102⅞		321.98
SP500	Sep225 p	550 35191	1-16	1-16	1-16..		321.98
SP500	Sep245..	4807 4324	77¼	69	77¼+ 4¼		321.98
SP500	Sep245 p	50 3087	1-16	1-16	1-16..		321.98
SP500	Sep250..	64 1306	71½	66¼	71½− 10		321.98
SP500	Sep250 p	70 2254	1-16	1-16	1-16..		321.98
SP500	Sep260..	775 1520	61⅝	55	61⅛− ⅜		321.98
SP500	Sep260 p	625 4671	1-16	1-16	1-16..		321.98
SP500	Sep270..	1620 2616	45	44	44 − 5		321.98
SP500	Sep2/0 p	125 5238	1-16	1-16	1-16..		321.98
SP500	Sep285..	185 2940	35	29¼	35 − 16		321.98
SP500	Sep285 p	457 4106	⅛	1-16	1-16..		321.98
SP500	Sep290..	261 5812	24¾	18¾	22½− 3¼		321.98
SP500	Sep290 p	918 8524	5-16	1-16	1-16..		321.98
SP500	Sep295..	295 3734	27¼	26¾	27 + 6		321.98
SP500	Sep295 p	2737 6897	¾	1-16	1-16 − 3-16		321.98
SP500	Sep300..	2568 9331	22⅝	10¼	22⅝+ 4⅝		321.98
SP500	Sep300 p	5852 8731	1 13-16	1-16	1-16 − 9-16		321.98
SP500	Sep305..	1268 2824	17⅝	8½	17 + 1½		321.98
SP500	Sep305 p	5585 4244	3¼	1-16	1-16 − 1 1-16		321.98
SP500	Sep310..	3900 7510	12½	4½	12¼+ 1½		321.98
SP500	Sep310 p	5036 7347	5¾	5-16	5-16 − 2 3-16		321.98
SP500	Sep315..	9722 9950	8	2 5-16	7⅝+ 2¾		321.98
SP500	Sep315 p	9010 11463	8½	¾	¾ − 3½		321.98
SP500	Sep320..	7775 8039	4½	1⅛	4⅛+ 1¾		321.98
SP500	Sep320 p	5072 6000	12¼	2	2 1-16 − 4 15-16		321.98
SP500	Sep325..	11056 32960	2	⅜	1⅞− ⅛		321.98
SP500	Sep325 p	1396 30923	16½	4½	4⅝− 6		321.98
SP500	Sep330..	2983 5581	13-16	¼	½− ⅜		321.98
SP500	Sep330 p	655 2638	21½	8⅜	8¾− 6¾		321.98
SP500	Sep335..	1851 6487	7-16	1-16	1-16 − 3-16		321.98
SP500	Sep335 p	259 4961	26½	12¾	12¾− 5⅝		321.98
SP500	Sep340..	1072 3364	3-16	1-16	1-16 − 3-16		321.98
SP500	Sep340 p	242 1377	31⅝	18⅞	18⅞− 2¼		321.98
SP500	Sep345..	199 869	1-16	1-16	1-16 − 1-16		321.98
SP500	Sep345 p	302 1584	35½	23	23 − 2		321.98
SP500	Sep350 p	70 421	33¼	29	29 − 4¾		321.98
SP500	Oct295 p	227 12	2	¾	¾..		321.98
SP500	Oct305 p	749 358	6¼	2	2 − 1¾		321.98
SP500	Oct310..	798 725	16¼	9¼	16⅝+ 2¾		321.98
SP500	Oct310 p	878 518	9½	3⅛	3½ − 1⅞		321.98
SP500	Oct315..	238 454	12½	7	12¼+ 2½		321.98
SP500	Oct315 p	736 671	11½	4¾	4½ − 2¾		321.98
SP500	Oct320..	554 500	9¾	4⅞	9½+ 2½		321.98
SP500	Oct320 p	776 1128	14	6¼	6¼ − 3¾		321.98
SP500	Oct325..	1808 1048	7¼	3½	7 + 1¼		321.98
SP500	Oct325 p	82 345	18¾	9⅞	9⅞− 2⅞		321.98
SP500	Oct330..	1096 1278	5½	2½	4⅞+ ⅝		321.98
SP500	Oct335..	168 396	3⅝	1⅞	3⅝+ ⅝		321.98
SP500	Oct335 p	102 747	20¼	17½	17½− ½		321.98
SP500	Oct340..	1327 785	2¾	1	2 5-16+ ⅛		321.98
SP500	Oct340 p	106 104	23¾	21¼	21¼+ 3¾		321.98
SP500	Oct345..	52 372	1½	13-16	1 7-16 + 1-16		321.98
SP500	Oct350..	144 187	15-16	½	⅞− ⅛		321.98
SP500	Dec250..	81 55	33	27¼	27¼..		321.98
SP500	Dec250 p	503 824	9-16	⅜	½− ⅛		321.98
SP500	Dec250 p	6744 3400	73	65	73 − 9¾		321.98
SP500	Dec255..	2390 4505	3-16	1-16	1-16− ⅛		321.98
SP500	Dec255..	5060 5	68½	67½	68½− 9¾		321.98
SP500	Dec255 p	335 931	½	½	⅜− 3-16		321.98
SP500	Dec260 p	572 1721	11-16	½	½− 3-16		321.98
SP500	Dec265 p	226 2663	⅞	7-16	7-16..		321.98
SP500	Dec270 p	83 5195	1½	11-16	11-16 − 5-16		321.98
SP500	Dec275 p	97 1788	1⅞	⅞	⅞− 3-16		321.98
SP500	Dec280 p	87 1895	2⅜	1⅛	1⅛− 3-16		321.98
SP500	Dec285 p	70 2251	3⅛	2¼	2¼+ 1-16		321.98
SP500	Dec290 p	96 3231	4½	2¼	2¼− ¾		321.98
SP500	Dec295 p	166 1937	6	3⅜	3⅜− ¾		321.98
SP500	Dec300..	455 836	24½	22⅛	24½..		321.98

New York Stock Exchange

COMPOSITE INDEX

NY Idx	Sep165..	100 44	11¼	8⅝	11¼+ 1¼		180.02
NY Idx	Sep165 p	541 1698	5-16	1-16	1-16..		180.02
NY Idx	Sep170..	236 306	7¼	4½	7⅛− 2½		180.02
NY Idx	Sep170 p	4010 3810	1⅜	1-16	1-16− ⅜		180.02
NY Idx	Sep175..	1296 1009	5¾	2	5¼+ ½		180.02
NY Idx	Sep175 p	4524 2100	3⅝	3-16	¼− 1½		180.02
NY Idx	Sep180..	3858 3503	1 11-16	½	1⅝+ ⅜		180.02
NY Idx	Sep180 p	2850 2222	7½	1½	½− 2⅞		180.02
NY Idx	Sep185..	2158 4075	5-16	⅛	3-16 − 3-16		180.02
NY Idx	Sep185 p	927 999	11¾	5¾	5¾− 2⅞		180.02
NY Idx	Sep190..	337 2970	1-16	1-16	1-16..		180.02
NY Idx	Sep190 p	64 122	15¾	14½	15¾+ 1⅜		180.02
NY Idx	Sep172½	50 33	4 9-16	3¾	4 9-16− 2 7-16		180.02
NY Idx	Sep172½ p	2080 1133	2¾	1-16	1-16− ⅞		180.02
NY Idx	Sep177½	2447 1505	3½	1	3 1-16+ 9-16		180.02
NY Idx	Sep177½ p	1345 602	5¼	⅝	⅝− 1¾		180.02
NY Idx	Sep182½	2831 2504	11-16	3-16	½..		180.02
NY Idx	Sep182½ p	158 1611	9	3½	3½− 2¾		180.02
NY Idx	Oct160 p	1785 2345	3-16	1-16	1-16− ⅛		180.02
NY Idx	Oct165 p	902 1091	⅝	3-16	3-16− ⅜		180.02
NY Idx	Oct165 p	619 1142	1⅝	¼	¼− ⅝		180.02
NY Idx	Oct170 p	652 546	3 1-16	15-16	15-16− ⅝		180.02

American Stock Exchange

MAJOR MARKET INDEX

MMIdx	Sep455..	75 1185	1-16	1-16	1-16 − 1		516.19
MMIdx	Sep460..	785 2429	1	1-16	1-16− 1		516.19
MMIdx	Sep465..	869 1983	5-16	1-16	1-16− ⅛		516.19
MMIdx	Sep470..	2100 3234	13-16	1-16	1-16 − 3-16		516.19
MMIdx	Sep475..	2376 2283	1½	1-16	1-16 − 1		516.19
MMIdx	Sep480..	90 243	37	20	37 + 1		516.19
MMIdx	Sep480 p	7540 3870	2½	1-16	1-16 − 1		516.19
MMIdx	Sep485 p	5963 3946	3⅝	1-16	⅛− ⅞		516.19
MMIdx	Sep490..	126 450	25	13¾	25 + 1		516.19
MMIdx	Sep490 p	10218 5170	4¾	1-16	3-16− 1¾		516.19
MMIdx	Sep495..	335 554	22½	9½	21¼+19		516.19
MMIdx	Sep495 p	11413 5592	8¾	½	⅝− 2¾		516.19
MMIdx	Sep500..	2948 1450	17¼	7	16¾+ 3¾		516.19
MMIdx	Sep500 p	14848 6612	9	11-16	¾− 3¾		516.19
MMIdx	Sep505..	11119 2603	14½	4⅝	13 + 1		516.19
MMIdx	Sep505 p	19958 5576	12¾	2½	3− 4¾		516.19
MMIdx	Sep510..	20639 4525	10	3½	9 + 1¾		516.19
MMIdx	Sep510 p	12711 5073	16	2½ 2 13-16 − 5 15-16			516.19

OIL INDEX

Oil Idx	Sep195 p	97 50	2½	11-16	¾+ ⅛		201.38
Oil Idx	Sep205..	106 87	1 11-16	1	1⅛− 3½		201.38
Oil Idx	Sep205 p	300 171	7⅞	4¾	4¾+ ¾		201.38
Oil Idx	Sep210..	91 391	1	⅜	⅜− 11-16		201.38
Oil Idx	Sep210 p	142 269	11½	7⅞	10¼+ 2½		201.38
Oil Idx	Oct190 p	103 2	1⅝	1⅝	1⅝+ ½		201.38
Oil Idx	Oct195 p	108 3	3¾	2¾	3½+ 1 15-16		201.38
Oil Idx	Oct200 p	67 110	6⅝	4⅞	4⅞+ 1⅜		201.38
Oil Idx	Oct205 p	71 97	10	7¼	7¼− ¼		201.38

INSTITUTIONAL INDEX

Instldx	Sep250..	1511 19034	73⅞	67	73⅞− ⅝		328.09
Instldx	Sep250 p	1461 20134	1½	½	½+ 1-16		328.09
Instldx	Sep290 p	100 450	1-16	1-16	1-16 − 1-16		328.09

SOURCE: *Barron's*, 8 February 1988. Reprinted courtesy of *Barron's Weekly*.

every month rather than on a three-month cycle like equity options. Also notice the volume of trading (sales) that many of these contracts enjoy; index option contracts are heavily traded. For example, the weekly volume of put and call index options on the S&P 100 contract for the week of September 11, 1987, was 2.13 million contracts, compared to a total volume of 3.18 million for puts and calls on individual stocks.[11]

3. INVESTMENT STRATEGIES USING INDEX OPTIONS Like stock options, index options may be used to speculate or hedge. The major difference is that the speculating or hedging is on stocks in general or a major segment of the market rather than on an individual stock. The investor with a long or short position in an option on an individual stock is subject to *company-related risk*. Index options do not have company-related risk since the underlying asset

is an index representing many different stocks. Narrow-based index options do, however, involve *industry* or *specific sector* risk.

Since index options are new products in the financial markets, a limited number of published articles deal with tests of various investment strategies. A 1985 study of the S&P 100 and MMI contracts over the period June 26, 1984, through August 30, 1984, provided some interesting observations.[12] The empirical evidence over this period suggested "violation of the arbitrage condition" and that the "market is inefficient to some degree."[13]

A more recent paper developed a trading strategy using index options designed to *capture dividends*.[14] A very simple dividend capture hedge strategy would involve taking a long position in stocks in the index and writing call index options. Using data for 1984, this study found that the hedged dividend capture strategy provided after-tax returns "substantially greater" than the returns on Treasury bills and the market portfolio. These results also suggested possible market inefficiencies in pricing index options.

The rather limited number of studies to date suggests the possibility that there may have been some inefficiencies in the index option markets in the early 1980s. Additional research, however, is needed to understand fully these new option products and the degree of market efficiency in pricing these contracts.

Debt Options

In November 1982, the CBOE began trading in options on Treasury bonds. The exercise prices are set two basis points above and below the price established after the Treasury auction. Different exercise or striking prices are allowed as the bond price changes. Options are now available on Treasury bills, notes, and bonds, and are written against a specific security rather than an index. Exercise is also handled by the delivery of the underlying security rather than by cash. Contract sizes for Treasury notes and bonds is $100,000, while the contract for bills is $1 million.

The prices for puts and calls on debt securities depend on movements in the underlying security. The price of debt securities declines when interest rates increase and increases when rates fall. Therefore, when interest rates fall, prices for call options increase, and prices for put options decrease. Speculating in interest rate decreases could be accomplished by writing puts or buying calls. If a speculator thought that interest rates were going to rise, a short position in calls or a long position in puts would be appropriate, to take advantage of the expected decline in the price of debt securities.

Trading activity in debt options has been relatively minor since their introduction in 1982. Activity is much greater for options on futures, where the futures contract represents a position in Treasury securities. Options on financial futures are discussed in Chapter 21.

---

[12] Jeremy Evnine and Andrew Rudd, "Index Options: The Early Evidence," *Journal of Finance* (July 1985): pp. 743–56.

[13] Evnine and Rudd, p. 755.

[14] Terry L. Zivney and Michael J. Alderson, "Hedged Dividend Capture with Stock Index Options," *Financial Management* (Summer 1986): pp. 5–12.

Because of the lack of trading activity and the resulting paucity of price history, there are no comprehensive empirical studies of the debt option markets. Models have been developed, however, to value these types of options.[15] The exchanges have also proposed introducing yield-based European options that can be settled with cash. These newer options may generate more trading activity.

Currency Options

Foreign currency options were first traded on the Philadelphia Stock Exchange, PHLX, in December 1982. The first currency traded was the British pound, but beginning in 1983, trading included other currencies—the Canadian dollar, Japanese yen, Swiss franc, Australian dollar, and West German mark. The majority of the traded options are American-style, but European options are also traded.

All of the options traded on the PHLX are options to purchase or sell foreign currencies for U.S. dollars. The exercise price and quoted prices are therefore stated in terms of U.S. dollars and cents. For example, a December call on Canadian dollars with a striking price of $.75 allows the holder the right to buy a Canadian dollar for $.75. The contract size is different for each currency and may range from 12,500 British pounds to 6.25 million Japanese yen. The total price of the contract is, therefore determined by multiplying the per-unit option price by the size of the contract.

A valuation of a particular currency option depends on an analysis of the U.S. dollar and the specific foreign currency. Together, these two values determine the *exchange rate* (see Chapter 23) for the currency. This complicates the analysis, since most other option types are written against a single underlying asset. For currency options, however, changes in the value of the U.S. dollar and changes in the foreign currency both influence the value of the option.

Under a floating exchange rate system, each currency's value is determined by supply and demand factors. It is common, however, for foreign governments to use market intervention and/or changes in regulatory controls to increase or decrease the value of their currency relative to another currency; these efforts are a unique type of risk for currency options.

If a foreign currency decreases in value relative to the U.S. dollar (exchange rate decline), call prices will decrease, and put prices will increase. On the other hand, if a foreign currency increases relative to the U.S. dollar, call prices will increase, and put prices will decrease. For example, if an investor expected the yen to increase in value relative to the dollar, an appropriate strategy would be to purchase calls and/or write puts.

A number of studies have shown that currency options can be valued using variations of the Black-Scholes model.[16] Empirical tests of these models have shown mixed results. Model prices were generally biased estimates of out-of-the-

---

[15] For example, see Michael Parkinson, "The Valuation of GNMA Options," *Financial Analysts Journal* (September-October 1982): pp. 66–76; Laurie S. Goodman, "Put-Call Parity with Coupon Instruments," *Journal of Portfolio Management* (Winter 1985): pp. 59–60; and Mark Pitts, "The Pricing of Options on Debt Securities," *Journal of Portfolio Management* (Winter 1985): pp. 41–50.

[16] For example, see Nahum Biger and John Hull, "The Valuation of Currency Options," *Financial Management* (Spring 1983): pp. 24–28, and J. Grabbe, "The Pricing of Call and Put Options on Foreign Exchange," *Journal of International Money and Finance* (December 1983): pp. 239–53.

money options and options with a relatively long period before expiration.[17] A limited number of studies have also tested the efficiency of the currency options market. Generally, these studies concluded that the market was efficient in that riskless arbitrage profits were not available.[18]

Commodity Options

Contracts are also available for a gold/silver index through the PHLX. In addition, one of the fastest-growing segments of the option market is options written against commodity and financial futures contracts. Chapter 20 deals with commodity futures, and Chapter 21 covers financial futures. A discussion of options on futures appears at the end of Chapter 21.

Option Trading Strategies

Throughout the section on options, basic strategies that can be used to speculate or to hedge with options have been identified. A number of studies that deal with option market efficienty were also briefly mentioned. Some of these studies suggest that it is possible to find mispriced options when model or estimated values are compared to market-determined prices. These findings suggest market inefficiencies and/or problems with the available option pricing models. Generally, it is believed that after correctly considering transaction costs and risk, the option market is efficient. Thus, it would be very difficult, if not impossible, to develop simple trading rules to beat the options market.

In addition to problems with option pricing models and the lack of a long price history to test option market efficiency, risk analysis of portfolios that include options is difficult. As Chapter 8 indicated, portfolio performance analysis should be on a risk-adjusted basis. Efforts are incomplete, however, in developing performance evaluation methods for portfolios that include long or short positions in options.[19] The lack of performance models is a major problem for additional tests of option market efficiency.

SUMMARY

This chapter discussed a number of different options. Warrants and rights are discussed in more detail in the appendices to this chapter. All of these securities derive their value from the value of the underlying asset; in this sense, they are

---

[17] James N. Bodurtha and Georges R. Courtadon, "Tests of an American Option Pricing Model on the Foreign Currency Options Model," *Journal of Financial and Quantitative Analysis* (June 1987): pp. 153–67.

[18] For example, see Alan L. Tucker, "Empirical Tests of the Efficiency of the Currency Options Market," *Journal of Financial Research* (Winter 1985): pp. 275–85, and Larry J. Johnson, "Foreign Currency Options, Ex-ante Exchange-rate Volatility, and Market Efficiency: An Empirical Test," *Financial Review* (November 1986): pp. 433–51.

[19] For a discussion of the problems and procedures, see Dan Galai and Robert Geske, "Option Performance Measurement," *Journal of Portfolio Management* (Spring 1984): pp. 42–46, and Richard Bookstaber and Roger Clarke, "Problems in Evaluating the Performance of Portfolios with Options," *Financial Analysts Journal* (January-February 1985): pp. 48–62.

similar types of securities that exhibit common risk-return characteristics. Each can be used to speculate in price changes of the underlying asset or to hedge or reduce the risk of a portfolio. Because of the increased volatility in the financial and commodity markets during the 1980s, speculator and investor interest has increased in options types of securities. Because of the increased interest, these markets are likely to continue to grow in trading volume. In the future a number of new financial products will probably be developed, and some existing products may no longer exist. For this reason, interested investors should closely follow market developments, especially in the area of options.

QUESTIONS

1. Options, rights, and warrants can be described as derivative securities. Explain this terminology.
2. Compare and contrast put and call stock options.
3. Briefly define the following as they apply to options:
    a. Standardized options
    b. Options Clearing Corporation
    c. Expiration date
    d. Striking price
    e. Clearing members
4. Striking prices on options are often compared to the price of the underlying stock using the following terminology: out-of-the-money, at-the-money, and in-the-money. Briefly define each of these terms.
5. Compare and contrast the intrinsic value and time value of an option. Can an option that is out-of-the-money have intrinsic value? Can an out-of-the-money option have time value?
6. Explain the differences between a European-style call option and an American-style call option.
7. An investor who purchases calls that are not covered by the underlying stock has limited risk exposure, while an investor who writes uncovered calls has unlimited risk exposure. Explain this statement.
8. Explain the leverage effect in options investing.
9. Explain why the potential losses from writing uncovered puts are much larger than the possible losses from buying uncovered puts.
10. Explain the justification for a hedge that consists of a long position in a call and a short position in the underlying stock. Does this hedge eliminate the possibilities of both large losses and large gains?
11. Explain the justification for a hedge that consists of a long position in a put and in the underlying stock. Does this hedge eliminate the possibilities of both large losses and large gains?
12. Discuss the risk-return characteristics of a strategy of writing covered calls.
13. Compare and contrast straddle and spread strategies using options.
14. Compare and contrast strip and strap strategies using options.
15. Discuss the key variables that determine an option's value. Also indicate if the variable has a positive or negative influence on the option's value.

16. How do index options differ from options on individual common stocks?
17. Explain the put-call parity principal, and indicate how it can be used to value a put.

PROBLEMS

1. Consider the following three call options:

OPTION	STRIKING PRICE	COMMON STOCK PRICE	OPTION PRICE
1	$60	$50	$ 2
2	50	50	6
3	40	50	15

a. Indicate which option is in-the-money and which is out-of-the-money.
b. Calculate the intrinsic value of each option.
c. Calculate the time value of each option.

2. Consider the following three put options:

OPTION	STRIKING PRICE	COMMON STOCK PRICE	OPTION PRICE
1	$40	$50	$ 2
2	50	50	6
3	60	50	15

a. Indicate which option is in-the-money and which is out-of-the money.
b. Calculate the intrinsic value of each option.
c. Calculate the time value of each option.

3. Assume that an investor *purchases* five call options for $5,000. The options have a striking price of $100 per share. Calculate the profits and losses on the options for each of the following stock prices:

STOCK PRICE
$ 80
90
100
110
120

4. Assume that an investor purchases five put options for $5,000. Use the striking price and stock prices in problem 3 to calculate the profits and losses for each of the stock prices.

5. Answer problem 3, assuming that the investor writes five call options,

6. Answer problem 4, assuming that the investor writes five put options.

7. Consider an investor who purchases 100 shares of XYZ common stock at $50 per share and buys a put on the stock for $300 with a striking price of $45.

   a. Calculate the *HPR* if both positions are liquidated when the stock price is $60.

   b. Calculate the *HPR* if both positions are liquidated when the stock price is $40.

   c. Calculate the maximum dollar loss and minimum *HPR* that can occur for this strategy.

   d. Is there a maximum dollar gain for this strategy?

8. Consider an investor who shorts 100 shares of XYZ common stock at $50 per share and buys a call on the stock for $300 with a striking price of $45.

   a. Calculate the *HPR* if both positions are liquidated when the stock price is $60.

   b. Calculate the *HPR* if both positions are liquidated when the stock price is $40.

   c. Calculate the maximum dollar *loss* and minimum *HPR* that can occur for this strategy.

   d. Calculate the maximum dollar *gain* and maximum *HPR* that can occur for this strategy.

9. Assume that an investor with a long position of 100 shares of common stock purchased for $50 per share writes a call option with a striking price of $48, for $600.

   a. Calculate the maximum possible dollar *gain* for this strategy.

   b. Calculate the minimum possible dollar *loss* for this strategy.

   c. Compare your answers to parts a and b with the maximum and minimum possible gains from the stock position only.

10. Consider the following data on a common stock and call option on the stock:

    Stock price: $50
    Striking price: $48
    Time to expiration: 3 months
    Risk-free rate of return: 8% per year
    Variance of stock's return: .25
    ---

    a. Calculate the value of the option, using the Black-Scholes model.

    b. If the option is priced at $6, what investment strategy is suggested?

    c. Use your answer to part a to calculate the value of a put with the same time to expiration and striking price.

COMPUTER APPLICATIONS

The floppy disk includes programs that can be used to calculate the following:

1. Black-Scholes call option value

2. Black-Scholes put option value

3. Hedge ratio

These programs can be used to solve some of the problems in this chapter and to analyze other options. Instructions and Illustrations are provided on the disk.

REFERENCES

Arnott, Robert D. "Modeling Portfolios with Options: Risk and Returns." *Journal of Portfolio Management* (Fall 1980): pp. 66–73.

Asay, Michael R. "Implied Margin Requirements on Options and Stocks." *Journal of Portfolio Management* (Spring 1981): pp. 55–59.

Barone-Adesi, Giovanni, and Robert E. Whaley. "The Valuation of American Call Options and the Expected Ex-Dividend Stock Price Decline." *Journal of Financial Economics* (September 1986): pp. 91–111.

Bick, Avi. "On the Consistency of the Black-Scholes Model with a General Equilibrium Framework." *Journal of Financial and Quantitative Analysis* (September 1987): pp. 259–75.

Biger, Nahum, and John Hull. "The Valuation of Currency Options." *Financial Management* (Spring 1983): pp. 24–58.

Billingsley, Randall S., and Don M. Chance. "Options Market Efficiency and the Box Spread Strategy." *Financial Review* (November 1985): pp. 287–301.

Bodurtha, James N., and Georges R. Courtadon. "Tests of an American Option Pricing Model on the Foreign Currency Options Market." *Journal of Financial and Quantitative Analysis* (June 1987): pp. 153–67.

Bookstaber, Richard, and Roger Clarke. "Options Can Alter Portfolio Returns Distribution." *Journal of Portfolio Management* (Spring 1981): pp. 63–70.

————. "Problems in Evaluating the Performance of Portfolios with Options." *Financial Analysts Journal* (January-February 1985): pp. 48–62.

Borch, Karl. "A Note on Option Prices." *Financial Review* (March 1984): pp. 124–127.

Brenner, Menachem, and Dan Galai. "On Measuring the Risk of Common Stocks Implied by Options Prices: A Note." *Journal of Financial and Quantitative Analysis* (December 1984): pp. 403–12.

Brill, Susan L., and Susan Jayson. "Pricing American Options: Managing Risk with Early Exercise." *Financial Analysts Journal* (November-December 1986): pp. 48–55.

Butler, J. S., and Barry Schachter. "Unbiased Estimates of the Black/Scholes Formula." *Journal of Financial Economics* (March 1986): pp. 341–57.

Camerer, Colin. "The Pricing and Social Value of Commodity Options." *Financial Analysts Journal* (January-February 1982): pp. 62–66.

Chance, Don M., and Stephen P. Ferris. "The CBOE Call Option Index: A Historical Record." *Journal of Portfolio Management* (Fall 1985): pp. 75–83.

Chang, Jack S. K., and Latha Shanker. "Option Pricing and the Arbitrage Pricing Theory." *Journal of Financial Research* (Spring 1987): pp. 1–16.

"Characteristics and Risks of Standardized Options." Options Clearing Corporation, September 1987.

Chen, Nai-Fu, and Herb Johnson. "Hedging Options." *Journal of Financial Economics* (June 1985): pp. 317–21.

Cinar, E. Mine, and Joseph Vu. "Evidence on the Effect of Option Expirations on Stock Prices." *Financial Analysts Journal* (January-February 1987): pp. 55–57.

Eckardt, Walter L. Jr. "The American Put: Computational Issues and Value Comparisons." *Financial Management* (Autumn 1982): pp. 42–52.

Eckardt, Walter L. Jr., and Stephen L. Williams. "The Complete Options Index." *Financial Analysts Journal* (July-August 1984): pp. 48–57.

Evnine, Jeremy, and Andrew Rudd. "Index Options: The Early Evidence." *Journal of Finance* (July 1985): pp. 743–56.

Galai, Dan, and Robert Geske. "Option Performance Measurement." *Journal of Portfolio Management* (Spring 1984): pp. 42–46.

Garman, Mark B. "The Duration of Option Portfolios." *Journal of Financial Economics* (July 1985): pp. 309–15.

Garven, James R. "A Pedagogic Note on the Derivation of the Black-Scholes Option Pricing Formula." *Financial Review* (May 1986): pp. 337–44.

Gastineau, Gary L. and Albert Madansky. "Some Comments on the CBOE Call Option Index." *Financial Analysts Journal*, July-August 1984, pp. 58–67.

Geske, Robert, and Richard Roll. "On Valuing American Call Options with the Black-Scholes European Formula." *Journal of Finance* (June 1984): pp. 443–55.

Geske, Robert, and H. E. Johnson. "The American Put Option Valued Analytically." *Journal of Finance* (December 1984): pp. 1511–24.

Geske, Robert, and Kuldeep Shastri. "Valuation by Approximation: A Comparison of Alternative Options Valuation Techniques." *Journal of Financial and Quantitative Analysis* (March 1985): pp. 45–71.

Gombola, Michael J., Rodney L. Roenfeldt, and Philip L. Cooley. "Some Additional Evidence on Pricing Efficiency of CBOE Options." *Financial Review* (Winter 1980): pp. 9–19.

Goodman, Laurie S. "Put-Call Parity with Coupon Instruments." *Journal of Portfolio Management* (Winter 1985): pp. 59–60.

Heaton, Hal. "Volatilities Implied by Options Premia: A Test of Market Efficiency." *Financial Review* February 1986): pp. 37–49.

Hsia, Chi-Cheng. "On Binomial Option Pricing." *Journal of Financial Research* (Spring 1983): pp. 41–46.

Johnson, Herb, and David Shanno. "Option Pricing When the Variance is Changing." *Journal of Financial and Quantitative Analysis* (June 1987): pp. 143–51.

Johnson, Larry J. "Foreign-Currency Options, Ex-ante Exchange-rate Volatility and Market Efficiency: An Empirical Test." *Financial Review* (November 1986): pp. 433–50.

Kim, Moon K., and Allan Young. "Rewards and Risks from Warrant Hedging." *Journal of Portfolio Management* (Summer 1980): pp. 65–68.

Luft, Carl F., and Bruce D. Fielitz. "An Empirical Test of the Commodity Option Pricing Model Using Ginnie Mae Call Options." *Journal of Financial Research* (Summer 1986): pp. 137–51.

MacBeth, James D., and Larry J. Merville. "Tests of the Black-Scholes and Cox Call Option Valuation Models." *Journal of Finance* (May 1980): pp. 285–303.

Merton, Robert C. "Theory of Rational Option Pricing." *Bell Journal of Economics and Management* (August 1973): pp. 141–83.

O'Brien, Thomas J., and William F. Kennedy. "Simultaneous Options and Stock Prices: Another Look at the Black-Scholes Model." *Financial Review* (November 1982): pp. 219–27.

O'Brien, Thomas J., and Michael J. P. Selby. "Options Pricing Theory and Asset Expectation: A Review and Discussion in Tribute to James Boness." *Financial Review* (November 1986): pp. 399–418.

Parkinson, Michael. "The Valuation of GNMA Options." *Financial Analysts Journal* (September-October 1982): pp. 66–76.

Pettit, R. Richardson, and Ronald F. Singer. "Instant Options Betas." *Financial Analysts Journal* (September-October 1986): pp. 51–62.

Pitts, Mark. "The Valuation of Currency Options: Comment." *Financial Management* (Summer 1984): pp. 51–52.

Pitts, Mark. "The Pricing of Options on Debt Securities." *Journal of Portfolio Management* (Winter 1985): pp. 41–50.

Reilly, Frank K., and Sandra G. Gustavson. "Investing in Options on Stocks Announcing Splits." *Financial Review* (May 1985): pp. 121–43.

Rendleman, Richard J. Jr. "Optional Long-run Option Investment Strategies." *Financial Management* (Spring 1981): pp. 62–76.

Ritchken, Peter H., and Harvey M. Salkin. "Safety First Selection Techniques for Option Spreads." *Journal of Portfolio Management* (Spring 1983): pp. 61–67.

Ritchken, Peter H. "Enhancing Mean-Variance Analysis with Options." *Journal of Portfolio Management* (Spring 1985): pp. 67–71.

Rubinstein, Mark, and Hayne E. Leland. "Replicating Options with Positions in Stock and Cash." *Financial Analysts Journal* (July-August 1981): pp. 63–72.

Rubinstein, Mark. "A Simple Formula for the Expected Rate of Return of an Option over a Finite Holding Period." *Journal of Finance* (December 1984): pp. 1503–09.

———. "Nonparametric Tests of Alternative Option Pricing Models Using All Reported Trades and Quotes on the 30 Most Active CBOE Option Classes from August 23, 1976, through August 31, 1978." *Journal of Finance* (June 1985): pp. 455–80.

Sears, R. Stephen, and Gary L. Trennepohl. "Diversification and Skewness in Option Portfolios." *Journal of Financial Research* (Fall 1983): pp. 199–212.

Slivka, Ronald T. "Call Options Spreading." *Journal of Portfolio Management* (Spring 1981): pp. 71–76.

Stanton, Thomas C., and Philip H. Maxwell. "Warrants: A Cost of Capital Perspective." *Financial Executive* (September 1980): pp. 27–31.

Sterk, William. "Tests of Two Models for Valuing Call Options on Stocks with Dividends." *Journal of Finance* (December 1982): pp. 1229–37.

———. "Option Pricing: Dividends and the In- and Out-of-the-Money Bids." *Financial Management* (Winter 1983): pp. 47–53.

Tilley, James A., and Gary D. Latainer. "A Synthetic Option Framework for Asset Allocation." *Financial Analysts Journal* (May-June 1985): pp. 32–43.

Tucker, Alan L. "Empirical Tests of the Efficiency of the Currency Option Market." *Journal of Financial Research* (Winter 1985): pp. 275–85.

Whaley, Robert E. "On Valuing American Futures Options." *Financial Analysts Journal* (May-June 1986): pp. 49–59.

Yates, James W. Jr., and Robert W. Kopprasch Jr. "Writing Covered Call Options: Profits and Risks." *Journal of Portfolio Management* (Fall 1980): pp. 74–79.

Zivney, Terry L., and Michael J. Alderson. "Hedged Dividend Capture with Stock Index Options." *Financial Management* (Summer 1986): pp. 5–12.

APPENDIX 19A

WARRANTS

Characteristics of Warrants

Warrants are essentially a call option and can be defined as a contract issued by a corporation that grants the holder the option to purchase that corporation's stock, at a stated price, within a stated time. Warrants are most often used as a *sweetener* in a new bond issue (or, less often, a preferred stock) to enhance its marketability and/or lower the interest or dividend rate. Warrants are also issued in corporate reorganizations or mergers. Warrants are traded on the organized exchanges and the OTC market.

Warrants have historically been used mainly by small, growing corporations. When initially issued, the exercise price is usually 15 to 20 percent above the current market price of the common stock, so that as a firm prospers and its stock price rises above the exercise price, the warrant can be exercised. When the warrants are exercised, the firm benefits by receiving the exercise price in cash.

Warrants may also be *callable* by the issuing corporation. The call feature may allow the corporation to force the holder to exercise the warrant. For example, Genesco Corporation (OTC) has a warrant outstanding with an expiration date of February 15, 1993; the exercise price is $8 per share, and one warrant is needed to acquire one share. The warrant is callable at $2 if the price of the common stock is at least $12 for 20 out of 30 consecutive trading days. In early October 1987, the common stock was trading at $6\frac{3}{8}$, the warrant at $2\frac{1}{8}$.

The exercise price on warrants is stated when the warrants are issued. It is fairly common, however, to issue a warrant with an increasing exercise price over its life. The exercise price is adjusted downward for stock dividends or splits that reduce the price of the common stock. This *dilution clause* protects the warrant holder. Warrants are usually issued with an expiration date. In some cases, however, the warrant is issued without an expiration date; for example, Atlas Corporation's warrant, traded on the AMEX, does not have an expiration date and is a *perpetual warrant*.

Another interesting characteristic of warrants is that in many cases the exercise "price" can be paid by surrendering a bond or preferred stock, usually at par, rather than cash. Since the market price of the bond or preferred stock is likely to change over the life of the warrant, the effective exercise price also changes.

These characteristics suggest that warrants have less risk than call options but more risk than the underlying common stock. The longer lives of warrants relative to call options reduce their risk. Thus, in an efficient market, the *HPR*s on warrants should be greater than the *HPR*s on the underlying common stock, but below the *HPR*s on call options.

Valuation of Warrants

The valuation of warrants is somewhat more complicated than the valuation of options. One complicating factor is that the issuing corporation is likely to receive cash when the warrants are exercised. This may well change the value of the underlying common stock and therefore the value of the warrant. A second factor is the potential *dilution* of EPS when the warrants are exercised. The problems with valuing warrants are therefore due to the warrants' influence on the price of the common stock. This is not a problem with options valuation because options do not directly influence the underlying common stock.

Ignoring the possible influence on the value of the underlying common stock, determining the value of a warrant is a simple matter. Since the warrant is essentially a call option, it can be valued using a variation of the Black-Scholes model. A number of studies have attempted to develop a specific warrant pricing model.[1] These studies suggest that the most important variables are

$$V_w = f(EP, T_n, P_0, D_1, P_c) \tag{19A.1}$$

where V_w = value of the warrant

       EP = exercise price

       T_n = time remaining before the warrant's expiration date

       P_0 = current price of the common stock

       D_1 = potential dilution

       P_c = expected future common stock price

In addition to the variables in Equation 19A.1, other factors determine the warrant's price. Studies have found that these other factors include (1) dividend

---

[1] For example, see John P. Shelton, "The Relation of the Price of a Warrant to the Price of Its Associated Stock—Part I," *Financial Analysts Journal* (May-June 1967): pp. 149–51, and Part II, (July-August 1967): pp. 88–89; Andrew N. Y. Chen, "A Model of Warrant Pricing in a Dynamic Market," *Journal of Finance* (December 1970): pp. 1041–59; and David F. Rush and Ronald W. Melicher, "An Empirical Examination of Factors Which Influence Warrant Prices," *Journal of Finance* (December 1974): pp. 1449–66.

yield on the common stock, (2) exchange listing, (3) number of warrants outstanding for a particular issue, and (4) the "effective" cost of exercising the warrant.[2] The identified variables not only are determinants in themselves but they also have combined effects. The current price of the common stock, P_0, is a function of the possible dilution of earnings, D_1. Also, the expected future common stock price P_c is a function not only of D_1 but also the remaining life of the warrant, T_n. The reasons for a price or premium above the theoretical value will be discussed below.

Investors need an estimate of the value of a warrant that can be compared to the market value of the warrant. The market value is determined by supply and demand factors. The value of a warrant consists of two parts: *intrinsic* value and *time* value. The intrinsic or *minimum value* of a warrant is determined as

$$V_w = (P_0 - EP)N \qquad (19A.2)$$

where
V_w = minimum or intrinsic value of warrant
P_0 = current market price of the common stock
EP = exercise price
N = number of warrants needed to purchase one share of common stock (usually a one-to-one relationship)

If the actual price of the warrant was less than V_w, then arbitrage activities would be possible—buying the warrant and using it to acquire the common stock at a cost below its market value. It can also be seen that if P_0 is greater than EP and P_0 increases, the value of the warrant will increase. If the value of $P_0 < EP$, the intrinsic value will not be negative, even though the equation value is less than 0, because the market value cannot be negative. It is common for warrants to sell above their minimum value, primarily because of the call option characteristics of the warrant and the expectation that the price of the common stock will increase before the warrant expires. This additional value represents the *time* value of the warrant.

Other Factors That Influence a Warrant's Price

The difference between market value and minimum value is defined as the *time value*, which depends on several factors that are interrelated: (1) time remaining before expiration, (2) volatility of the stock price, and (3) leverage of the warrant contract.

1. TIME The time value declines as the time remaining until expiration decreases. Based on equation 19A.2, it is easy to see that as the underlying stock price rises, the warrant will also increase in value. Time value will likely

---

[2] For example, see Rush and Melicher, and Chen.

exist if the stock price has a significant probability of increasing above the exercise price before expiration.

2.   PRICE VOLATILITY OF UNDERLYING STOCK As with any option type of contract, the volatility of the underlying stock is a major consideration. The more volatile the stock, the higher the value of the warrant; this occurs because of the increased probability that the price of the stock will move to a higher level. For example, if a $10 stock has a 25 percent chance of falling to $8, a 50 percent chance of staying the same, and a 25 percent chance of moving to $12, then the expected stock price, $E(P_s)$, is

PROBABILITY	PRICE	PROBABILITY × PRICE
.25	$ 8	$ 2
.50	10	5
.25	12	3
Expected Stock Price = $E(P_s)$ =		$10

If the expected stock price is $10 and the exercise price is also $10, Equation 19A.2 indicates that the value of the warrant will be $0. This would be the case only if the stock price was $8 or $10. If the stock price is $12, the value of the warrant will be ($12 − $10), or $2. The expected value of the warrant can be calculated as

$$E(V_w) = .25(0) + .50(0) + .25(\$2) = \$.50.$$

Since the value of the warrant will increase with increases in the stock price, a warrant on a more volatile stock will have a greater value than a warrant on a less volatile stock. This can easily be shown by increasing the maximum possible stock price in the previous example.

3.   LEVERAGE The third reason that a warrant might sell for more than its intrinsic value is due to the speculative appeal of warrants. They give an investor the possibility of very large *HPR*s because their market prices are low relative to the underlying common stock.

For example, suppose XYZ, Inc. warrants are priced above their intrinsic value and you are considering purchasing the common stock or the warrant. The common stock is currently selling for $25, the warrant for $3. The exercise price on the warrant is also $25, indicating that its intrinsic value is 0. If you buy the stock and it goes to $50, your *HPR* is 100 percent. However, if you had bought the warrant instead, at $3, your *HPR* would be 733 percent [(25 − 3)/3]. Your potential dollar loss with the warrant is limited to $3 (*HPR* = −100%). The dollar loss on the stock, however, could be greater than $3.

The large capital appreciation possibility, combined with the loss limitation, clearly have value to some investors. The exact determination of their worth, however, is a function of supply and demand forces in the market.

Market Efficiency

Despite the difficulty in developing a comprehensive warrant pricing model, several studies have analyzed warrant prices in tests of the EMH. A 1975 study by Leabo and Rogalski tested warrant prices against the random walk hypothesis.[3] Their test was based on all warrants traded on the NYSE and AMEX over the period January 1, 1967, to March 31, 1973. The empirical test suggested that warrant prices did not follow a random walk because of the price limits imposed by the exercise price and the price of the underlying stock. Serial correlation coefficients and runs test also suggested a relationship between prices over time. These results indicated that some type of technical analysis (see Chapter 12) and/ or time series analysis may be valuable in developing a warrant trading strategy.

A 1980 study also provided evidence that the market for warrants may not be efficient.[4] This study was based on a sample of eighteen warrants traded on the NYSE and AMEX over the period January 1965 through December 1976. The methodology used in the study involved forming a hedged portfolio consisting of a long position in the underlying common stock and a short position in the related warrant. The *HPR*s on the hedged portfolios were compared to the *HPR*s from a simple buy-and-hold, SBH, strategy based on the S&P 500. Since the risk of the hedged portfolio was less than that of the SBH strategy, the *HPR*s for the hedged portfolios should have been less if the market for warrants was efficient. The empirical results, however, indicated that "the returns from the warrant-hedging strategy studied in the paper appear favorable when compared with the returns achieved by a SBH rule and the returns realized by looking at appropriate holding periods for the S&P 500."[5]

Based on the evidence from the limited number of empirical studies, the warrant market may not be efficient. This suggests that technical and fundamental analyses—and perhaps hedging strategies using warrants—may offer risk-adjusted excess returns.

---

[3] Dick A. Leabo and Richard J. Rogalski, "Warrant Price Movements and the Efficient Market Model," *Journal of Finance* (March 1975): pp. 163–77.

[4] Moon K. Kim and Allan Young, "Rewards and Risks for Warrant Hedging," *Journal of Portfolio Management* (Summer 1980): pp. 65–68.

[5] Kim and Young, p. 68.

STOCK RIGHTS

For common stocks with a preemptive right, it is normal for a stockholder to receive one right for each share of common stock when the company issues additional shares of common stock. In order to determine how many rights are needed to keep proportionate control, the following calculations can be made:

$$\text{Number of Rights Needed} = \frac{\text{Number of Shares Outstanding}}{\text{Number of New Shares to Be Issued}} \qquad (19B.1)$$

For example, if the company is offering 1 million new shares of common stock and you now own 10 percent of the total of 9 million shares outstanding, or 900,000 shares, you would need to purchase 10 percent of the new shares, or 100,000 shares, to maintain proportionate control. Thus, the company would specify that nine rights are needed to acquire one additional share of stock:

$$\frac{9,000,000}{1,000,000} = 9 \qquad (19B.2)$$

These nine rights, plus a *subscription price* per share, would be needed to purchase each new share of stock. The subscription price is generally set lower than the current market price to persuade the existing stockholders to purchase the new shares.

Value of Stock Rights

The exercise period or life of a right can be divided into two periods: rights-on period and rights-off period. This can be seen in the following illustration:

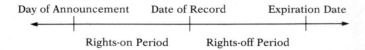

On the day that the board of directors announces the rights offering until approximately four days prior to the date of record, the rights are traded with the shares of stock, or *rights-on*.

1. VALUE WITH RIGHTS ON During the rights-on period, rights are included when the stock is traded, so that their value is reflected in the market price of the stock. The value of the right can be calculated as

$$V_{on} = \frac{M_1 - S}{N + 1} \qquad (19B.3)$$

   where V_{on} = Value of right, rights-on

   M_1 = Market price of the stock with rights

   S = Subscription price per share for new shares of stock

   N = Number of rights needed to purchase one new share of stock

2. VALUE WITH RIGHTS OFF When the stock begins trading rights-off, the owner has a two-part investment: (1) one share of stock and (2) the rights. The rights are traded in the same market as the common stock. Unless other factors change the market price of the stock, the two should theoretically add to the value of the stock rights-on. The new price of the *stock* can be calculated as:

$$M_{off} = \frac{M_1 N + S}{N + 1} \qquad (19B.4)$$

   or

$$M_{off} = M_1 - V_{on}$$

The theoretical value of the right in the rights-off period can be calculated as

$$V_{off} = \frac{M_{off} - S}{N} \qquad (19B.5)$$

Continuing with the example where $N = 9$, $S = \$30$, and $M_1 = \$40$, the value of the right can be calculated as

$$V_{on} = \frac{\$40 - \$30}{9 + 1} = \$1$$

The value of the stock rights-off can be calculated as

$$M_{off} = \frac{\$40(9) + \$30}{9 + 1} = \frac{\$390}{10} = \$39$$

or as

$$\begin{aligned} M_{off} &= M_1 - V_{on} \\ &= \$40 - \$1 \\ &= \$39 \end{aligned}$$

The value of M_{off} can then be used to calculate V_{off}:

$$V_{off} = \frac{\$39 - \$30}{\$9} = \$1$$

Notice that the value of the right did not change in this example between rights-on and rights-off: $V_{on} = V_{off}$. The value of the right and share of stock, V_t, is

$$\begin{aligned} V_t &= M_{off} + V_{off} \\ &= \$39 + \$1 = \$40 \end{aligned} \tag{19B.6}$$

When the right is separated from the stock, the value of the stock should always decrease by the value of right.

3.   VALUING A RIGHT AS A CALL OPTION The traditional way to determine the theoretical or intrinsic value of a right is presented above. However, rights, can be valued as a call option, using a variation of the Black-Scholes option pricing model.[1] This approach is superior to the traditional approach since it recognizes the right's additional value due to possible increases in the common stock price. An estimate of the future common stock price is not needed to value the right using the call option approach.

Basic Investment Strategies

Subsequent to the effective data of record (when the books are closed as to ownership of the stock), an investor has three possible courses of action with respect to rights:

(1)   Exercise the rights:

(2)   Sell the rights; or

(3)   Do nothing—let the rights expire.

---

[1] Dan Galai and M. Schneller, "The Pricing of Warrants and the Value of the Firm," *Journal of Finance* (December 1978): pp. 1333–42.

Continuing with the example used above, assume that you own 9 shares of stock on the date of record and that the subscription price is set at $30 per share. The 9 shares entitle you to receive 9 rights that can be used to purchase 1 additional share. Also assume that you have an initial cash balance of $30. As previously indicated, the stock value was $40 prior to the day of announcement ($M_1 = \$40$), and the value of the right is $1, or $V_{on} = V_{off} = \$1$. The three possible courses of action and the ending portfolio values:

Beginning Portfolio Value:		
9 shares @ $39/share:	$351	
9 rights @ $1/right:	9	
Cash	30	
	$390	
1. *Exercise:*	Ending Portfolio Value:	
	10 shares @ $39/share:	$390
2. *Sell Rights:*	Ending Portfolio Value:	
	9 shares @ $39/share:	$351
	Cash ($30 + $9):	39
		$390
3. *Do Nothing:*	Ending Portfolio Value:	
	9 shares @ $39:	$351
	Cash:	30
		$381

As can be seen from the "do nothing" option, the value of the portfolio declines by the value of the rights that were allowed to expire. Obviously, this third alternative is not a good course of action.

Stock price volatility and its impact on the return from owning rights can be easily demonstrated. Continuing with the previous example, suppose you could buy a share of the stock for $39 or a right for $1. What is the better strategy if the stock price increases to $45 per share?

Holding period return on stock strategy (assuming no cash dividends):

$$HPR_s = \frac{\$45 - \$39}{\$39} = 15.38\%$$

Holding period return on rights strategy:

$$V_{off} = \frac{\$45 - \$30}{9} = \$1.67$$

$$HPR_r = \frac{\$1.67 - \$1.00}{\$1.00} = 67.0\%$$

The *HPR* calculations above illustrate the *leverage* effect of trading (speculating) in stock rights. Also, in terms of dollar profits, assume that you buy 39 rights, since this is the amount of the investment one share of stock would require. Your profit on the stock investment is $6, but your profit on the rights investment is $26.13 ($.67 × 39). Given a volatile stock price, the dollar return and *HPR* resulting from an increase in the value of the rights could far exceed that of the stock. A decline in the stock price, however, has the opposite effect: the dollar and *HPR* losses will be significantly larger than the losses associated with owning the stock.

An additional risk factor is that the right has an expiration date. At expiration, the right has no value, but it is unlikely that the stock's price would decline to zero. If the right is purchased in anticipation of stock price increases, the *HPR* on the right might be -100 percent if the right cannot be exercised profitably before expiration.

CHAPTER 20

COMMODITY FUTURES

INTRODUCTION

Overview

A *forward contract* is a formal agreement between a buyer and seller in which the buyer agrees to accept delivery of a specified quantity of the commodity, on a specific date, at a fixed price. The seller agrees to make delivery according to the specified terms. Forward contracts have existed for centuries and were typically made by farmers or producers of some commodity. One problem with forward contracts, however, is that they depend on the performance of the buyer and seller to fulfill the contract obligations. If one party to the contract defaults, the other party suffers the loss or sues for damages.

To overcome this and other problems with forward contracts, the Chicago Board of Trade, CBOT, began trading *future contracts* in the 1860s. The CBOT established a *clearing corporation* that acts as an intermediary for each contract; the clearing corporation actually guarantees the performance of all participants in the market.

Both the buyer and writer of future contracts are free to transfer their interest in the contract to another party, so that the contracts are essentially marketable financial instruments. Either party can also liquidate his or her position by initiating a *reversing* trade. For example, the original buyer can sell (write) an identical contract at a later date, so that the original contract is effectively cancelled.

The prices for commodity contracts, like other securities, are determined by supply and demand factors. Brokers at commodity exchanges negotiate the highest price for the seller and the lowest price for the buyer. Future contracts are traded on organized exchanges that are similar to a stock exchange. The contracts are also *standardized* by the exchanges; the quantity and quality of the particular commodity is specified.

In actual trading of commodities, few contracts are held to the delivery or maturity date. Typically, less than five percent of commodity contracts will be settled by the delivery of the specified commodity. However, if a buyer holds the contract on the maturity date, it is settled by having the title or ownership interest in the specified commodity transferred from the seller to the buyer.

The initial purpose of commodity markets was to provide a mechanism for a farmer or commodity producer to hedge against a future decline in the commodity's price. A manufacturer or user of a particular commodity could also buy a contract to hedge against future price increases. Traders or speculators are also attracted to the market because of their desire to assume the price risk in anticipation of trading profits. A traditional view of a commodity market is one in which hedgers (actual producers and users of commodities) attempt to reduce or eliminate price risk, and speculators seek trading profits by eliminating imbalances in trading between the hedgers. Because very few contracts are actually settled by delivery, speculators play a very important role as both writers and buyers of contracts. A basic speculative strategy would be to write a contract if the commodity's price was expected to decline and buy a contract if the price was expected to increase. The traditional role of hedgers has also expanded, since some investors attempt to use commodity contracts to hedge against inflation, changes in stock prices, and changes in interest rates.

There are basically two categories of commodity contracts: (1) contracts on real assets such as agricultural products, metals, and petroleum products; and (2) financial futures on currencies, U.S. Treasury securities, municipal bonds, and stock indices such as the S&P 500 and NYSE Composite. This chapter discusses commodity futures, and Chapter 21 discusses financial futures and options on both commodity and financial futures.

Commodity Markets

Commodity futures are traded on organized markets that must be licensed by the federal government through the Commodity Futures Trading Commission, CFTC. Presently there are twelve licensed exchanges. The larger and better-known exchanges are the Chicago Board of Trade, Chicago Mercantile Exchange, New York Mercantile Exchange, and New York Commodity Exchange. Table 20.1 indicates the ten commodity exchanges and the contracts that each exchange trades; in addition, the New York Futures Exchange and the New York COMEX trade financial futures and options on futures.

Commodity markets operate in much the same fashion as stock markets. Trading is accomplished by *floor brokers*, using an auction procedure where buy and sell orders are executed in the *trading pit*. Unlike the stock markets, however, there are no specialists in the commodity markets. Copies of the actual commodity contract are not delivered to the buyer and seller since transactions result only in bookkeeping entries. Sample contracts, however, are available from each exchange and provide prospective traders with the specific details of trading for each commodity.

The clearing corporation uses the fees it collects on transactions to provide the necessary funds to guarantee each contract. Buyers and sellers are also required to deposit an *initial margin* on the contract—typically, 5 to 10 percent of the contract's value. The exact amount of the margin is set by the exchange and the clearing corporation. The margin is actually a *performance* bond rather than a down payment on the contract; it thus differs from the margin required

TABLE 20.1 COMMODITY EXCHANGES AND MAJOR CONTRACTS TRADED

1. Chicago Board of Trade:	Wheat, corn, oats, soybeans, soybean oil, soybean meal, silver
2. Kansas City Board of Trade:	Wheat
3. Chicago Mercantile Exchange:	Cattle, feeder cattle, hogs, pork bellies, lumber, gold
4. New York Cotton Exchange:	Cotton, orange juice
5. New York Commodity Exchange:	Gold, silver, copper, aluminum
6. New York Mercantile Exchange:	Crude oil, heating oil, unleaded gasoline, platinum, palladium
7. NewYork Coffee, Sugar, Cocoa Exchange:	Sugar-World 11, sugar 14, coffee C, cocoa
8. Minneapolis Grain Exchange:	Wheat
9. New Orleans Cotton Exchange:	Cotton, milled rice, rough rice, soybeans
10. Mid-America Commodity Exchange (Chicago):	Cattle, corn, gold, hogs, oats, silver, soybeans, sugar, wheat

to purchase stocks. A low margin encourages active trading and increases the leverage effect on returns. The margin requirement serves to reduce the loss to the clearing corporation from a possible default by the buyer or seller. Additional factors that are used to determine the margin are the underlying commodity's price volatility, the daily price moves (*limits*) permitted for the contract, and the time required to collect position losses from customers.[1]

After the initial margin is deposited, either in cash or U.S. Treasury bills, a change in the price of the contract causes a change in the percentage relationship between the margin and the contract value. The customer is therefore required to ensure a *maintenance* or *variation* margin on a day-by-day basis. Typically, the maintenance margin is 75 percent of the initial margin. At the close of each day's trading, the clearing house credits each customer's account with the gains or losses due to price changes. Losses and gains are netted against the initial margin. This process is called *marking to market*. If the net gains and losses cause the initial margin to decline below the required maintenance margin, the account receives a *margin call* that requires additional cash or U.S. Treasury bills to be deposited. If the customer cannot meet the margin call, the contract position is liquidated, and any remaining margin is distributed to the customer. Daily marking to market is one reason the initial margin is low on commodity contracts relative to common stocks. The initial margin needs to be only large enough to cover one day's price change.

To illustrate, assume that a December-delivery wheat contract is purchased, for 5,000 bushels, at $2.50 per bushel, with a 10 percent initial margin. The contract value is $12,500, indicating a $1,250 initial margin. If the maintenance margin is 75 percent of the initial margin, a minimum of $937.50 must be maintained. Therefore, if the price declines by more than 6.25 cents per bushel [($1,250 − $937.50)/5,000], an additional deposit to the margin account is required. If the price increases by 6.25 cents per bushel, however, $312.50 ($.0625 × 5,000) can be withdrawn from the margin account.

The daily marking-to-market practice of the clearing corporation results in daily debits and credits to each customer's account, based on the change in the contract price. For a customer who purchases a contract, price increases in the contract will result in additional cash being credited to the account. The contract writer, however, will have cash deducted from his or her account. Since daily cash flows occur, many traders provide their brokers with additional funds above the required minimum. This eliminates the need to make frequent margin calls. Since the gains and losses are recognized on a daily basis, the required cash settlement when the contract is traded will be small relative to the possible overall price change over the holding period. The clearing corporation also benefits, because on a day-by-day basis, it can maintain a net zero position since each credit to a margin account is offset by a debit to another trader's margin account.

The use of initial and maintenance margins also means that investors are required to pay for only a small portion of the cost of the contract at the time of purchase. For example, on Septemeber 11, 1987, a 10 percent initial margin on a New York Commodity Exchange gold contract would be $4,643. The contract

---

[1] Susan M. Phillips and Paula A. Tosini, "A Comparison of Margin Requirements for Options and Futures," *Financial Analysts Journal* (November-December 1982): p. 55.

represents 100 troy ounces of gold for December 1987 delivery at $464.30 per ounce. The margin essentially represents a small "down payment" toward the contract value. This provides considerable leverage to an investor/speculator: a 1 percent increase (decrease) in the price of gold results in a 10 percent increase (decrease) in the wealth of the investor.

Another difference between the margin requirements for commodities and those for stocks and bonds is that the initial margin on commodities can be paid with U.S. Treasury bills rather than cash. The investor is entitled to any interest income received on the Treasury bills. Therefore, if an investor already has a portfolio of Treasury bills of sufficient size, the initial investment in a commodity contract can be essentially zero.

Commodity Contracts and Quotations

Contracts are available on many types of assets, such as wheat, soybeans, cotton, sugar, coffee, unleaded gasoline, foreign currencies, gold, silver, and U.S. Treasury securities. Each contract specifies both the quality and quantity of the asset (e.g., 5,000 bushels of winter wheat, grade 2).

Obviously, not all commodities are traded on exchanges. Generally, in order for a commodity to be traded, it must be storable and in high demand. It should also be capable of being classified into clearly identifiable grades or categories. Each commodity must be approved for trading by the exchange and the Commodity Futures Trading Commission, CFTC. The CFTC is a federal regulatory agency that also controls contract provisions and trading procedures. The authority of the CFTC is much weaker than that of the SEC. Regulatory reform, initiated in part because of the market collapse on October 19, 1987, may result in abolishment of the CFTC.

Typically, commodity contracts for agricultural products are not issued with a delivery or maturity date of over one year. Due to the seasonal nature of some agricultural commodities, contracts with delivery dates in some months are not available. For precious metals, there may be contracts that mature every month for the next two years.

Based on the value of the contract, commissions on trading commodity contracts are lower than commissions on common stock trades. For example, Dean, Witter, Reynolds, Inc., as of September 1, 1987, charged a $90 flat fee to write (buy) and close the position with a reversing trade (a round-trip transaction). For a contract such as gold, this fee represented approximately 0.2 percent of the contract's value as of September 1987. For a wheat contract on the Chicago Board of Trade, however, the $90 fee represented 0.6 percent of the contract's value. In either case, however, the brokerage fee is lower than that for a common stock transaction of equal dollar value.

Table 20.2 provides a sample of quotations for various commodities on several of the commodity exchanges. Notice that the "prices" are for different units of measurement, such as dollars per bushel or cents per pound, depending on the commodity. The amount or volume of the commodity for each contract is given directly below the contract's name. Also, notice that there is not always a clear relationship between the price and the length of the contract. For example, the "price" of the corn contracts increases as the delivery period lengthens, but prices for feeder cattle decrease as the delivery period increases. The reasons for

TABLE 20.2 QUOTATIONS ON COMMODITY FUTURES

Chicago Board of Trade

Season's High	Season's Low		Week's High	Week's Low	Close	Net Chg	Open Int.
WHEAT							
5,000 bu minimum; dollars per bushel							
3.39	2.53	Mar	3.39	3.25	3.32¾	+.06¾	21,038
3.38½	2.63	May	3.38½	3.25	3.33¼	+.06¼	7,498
3.27½	2.53½	Jul	3.27½	3.13½	3.24	+.11½	9,671
3.30½	2.72	Sep	3.30½	3.17	3.27½	+.12	875
3.40½	2.89	Dec	3.40½	3.28½	3.38	+.12	683
3.43	3.30	Mar	3.43	3.43	3.41	+.12	8
Fri. to Thurs. sales 37,657.							
Total open interest 41,041.							
CORN							
5,000 bu minimum; dollars per bushel							
2.22¾	1.71	Mar	2.03¾	1.95½	2.01¼	+.04½	58,613
2.25½	1.74	May	2.09¼	2.01	2.07	+.04½	36,904
2.26½	1.80	Jul	2.12½	2.04	2.10½	+.05	28,179
2.23	1.80¾	Sep	2.14	2.05½	2.12	+.06½	5,242
2.16½	1.85¼	Dec	2.16½	2.07	2.14¼	+.06¾	16,566
2.23½	1.93½	Mar	2.23½	2.14	2.21	+.06½	948
2.27½	2.07½	May	2.27½	2.18¾	2.26	+.07½	85
Fri. to Thurs. sales 130,819.							
Total open interest 147,670.							
OATS							
5,000 bu minimum; dollars per bushel							
2.05½	1.29½	Mar	1.95½	1.88	1.93½	−.01½	4,300
1.94½	1.50¾	May	1.84¼	1.79	1.82¼	−.02¾	2,071
1.77	1.44	Jul	1.77	1.71	1.75¾	+.01¼	992
1.73	1.43	Sep	1.73	1.67½	1.71½	+.02	753
1.80	1.62	Dec	1.80	1.76	1.78½	+.02½	187
Fri. to Thurs. sales 7,405.							
Total open interest 8,429.							
SOYBEANS							
5,000 bu minimum; dollars per bushel							
6.42½	4.74	Mar	6.14	5.94½	6.08½	−.01	41,906
6.51	4.76	May	6.23	6.03½	6.17¾	+.01¼	26,732
6.57	4.88½	Jul	6.31	6.12	6.25½	......	23,525
6.56	5.12	Aug	6.32	6.13½	6.25½	−.01	3,338
6.53	5.03	Sep	6.31½	6.13	6.26½	+.02½	2,454
6.56	4.99¼	Nov	6.39½	6.20½	6.33¼	+.02¾	20,403
6.62	5.53	Jan	6.46½	6.29	6.40½	+.02½	605
6.67	5.79	Mar	6.52	6.42	6.48½	+.02½	81
6.64	6.59	May	.....	.....	6.53	+.02	6
Fri. to Thurs. sales 203,650.							
Total open interest 119,645.							
SOYBEAN OIL							
60,000 lbs; dollars per 100 lbs.							
23.55	16.29	Mar	21.15	20.35	20.79	−.25	34,368
23.70	16.50	May	21.46	20.66	21.15	−.18	20,227
23.90	16.65	Jul	21.68	20.90	21.40	−.15	17,981
23.90	16.71	Aug	21.75	21.01	21.50	−.15	3,592
23.77	16.55	Sep	21.80	21.10	21.52	−.13	3,209
23.65	17.25	Oct	21.75	21.10	21.62	−.01	1,664
23.75	18.30	Dec	21.85	21.20	21.70	−.05	3,909
23.30	21.30	Jan	21.90	21.30	21.75	......	106
Fri. to Thurs. sales 84,178.							
Total open interest 85,050.							
SOYBEAN MEAL							
100 tons; dollars per ton							
205.00	135.00	Mar	181.70	174.30	179.70	+1.50	18,725
199.00	148.00	May	180.50	174.50	178.70	+.60	17,187
198.00	148.10	Jul	181.60	175.60	179.90	+1.60	11,647
198.00	148.00	Aug	182.20	177.10	181.00	+2.00	4,904
189.00	153.00	Sep	183.00	178.50	182.00	+1.30	3,571
186.00	159.00	Oct	185.00	180.00	183.20	+2.50	2,134
187.00	159.00	Dec	186.50	180.50	184.50	+2.80	4,933
188.00	176.00	Jan	186.00	183.00	186.70	+4.20	88
Fri. to Thurs. sales 85,427.							
Total open interest 63,868.							
SILVER(1000)							
1,000 oz.; cents per oz.							
1003.0	569.5	Feb	663.0	625.0	629.0	−21.0	51
715.0	630.0	Mar	667.0	630.0	631.5	−23.5	29
1015.0	576.0	Apr	674.0	632.0	636.0	−24.0	6,276
1030.0	600.0	Jun	683.0	642.0	644.5	−24.5	3,544
1040.0	650.0	Aug	693.0	650.0	653.0	−25.0	224
937.0	661.5	Oct	690.0	661.5	661.5	−25.5	86
945.0	670.0	Dec	708.0	670.0	670.0	−26.0	1,099
775.0	680.0	Feb	715.0	680.0	678.5	−26.5	62
Fri. to Thurs. sales 6,129.							
Total open interest 11,293.							

Chicago Mercantile Exchange

Season's High	Season's Low		Week's High	Week's Low	Close	Net Chg	Open Int.
CATTLE							
40,000 lbs.; cents per lb.							
70.70	55.10	Feb	70.70	67.37	70.62	+2.97	11,717
71.60	57.70	Apr	71.60	67.55	71.45	+3.65	37,621
69.87	60.60	Jun	69.87	66.70	69.80	+2.95	18,684
68.00	59.17	Aug	67.12	64.15	67.05	+2.73	11,305
67.15	58.65	Oct	66.20	63.32	66.05	+2.73	5,919
66.70	60.25	Dec	66.70	64.25	66.47	+2.37	1,522
66.50	66.15	Feb	66.50	66.15	66.60	......	......
Fri. to Thurs. sales 117,912.							
Total open interest 86,768.							
FEEDER CATTLE							
44,000 lbs.; cents per lb.							
81.30	66.20	Mar	81.30	78.30	81.02	+2.57	7,503
80.15	67.20	Apr	80.15	76.95	79.90	+2.73	4,989
79.00	67.20	May	79.00	75.75	78.97	+3.07	4,322
77.77	68.30	Aug	77.77	74.90	77.65	+2.70	1,703
77.15	69.40	Sep	77.15	74.90	77.15	+2.65	581
76.75	69.70	Oct	76.75	74.85	76.72	+2.62	635
77.50	70.25	Nov	77.50	75.00	77.50	+2.60	98
Fri. to Thurs. sales 15,262.							
Total open interest 19,831.							
HOGS							
30,000 lbs.; cents per lb.							
49.00	37.55	Feb	49.00	47.10	48.70	+1.43	2,967
46.30	35.90	Apr	46.10	43.95	45.82	+1.67	12,596
49.25	37.50	Jun	49.25	46.90	48.75	+1.80	5,334
49.50	39.60	Jul	48.70	46.92	48.60	+1.40	1,864
48.60	39.60	Aug	47.60	45.60	47.27	+1.72	6,236
43.30	37.52	Oct	42.95	41.75	42.95	+1.05	787
43.45	38.30	Dec	43.30	42.40	43.40	+1.00	377
43.00	41.80	Feb	42.90	42.20	42.90	+1.03	8
Fri. to Thurs. sales 35,259.							
Total open interest 30,169.							
PORK BELLIES							
40,000 lbs.; cents per lb.							
69.00	49.00	Feb	55.70	52.95	54.97	+1.02	652
68.60	49.60	Mar	56.50	53.55	55.45	+1.05	3,155
67.40	51.00	May	57.97	54.50	56.95	+1.20	3,487
74.50	51.00	Jul	58.15	55.00	57.15	+1.05	1,679
62.80	50.10	Aug	56.65	54.00	55.87	+.87	1,131
58.40	52.10	Feb	58.40	57.00	58.95	+1.45	27
58.80	52.10	Mar	58.80	57.55	58.75	+1.25	1
Fri. to Thurs. sales 20,922.							
Total open interest 10,132.							
LUMBER							
130,000 bd. ft.; $ per 1,000 bd. ft.							
196.80	156.00	Mar	196.80	189.80	191.90	+.30	3,082
193.60	164.50	May	193.60	187.60	189.80	+.70	2,186
190.00	165.20	Jul	190.00	185.90	187.50	+.30	1,024
187.80	164.80	Sep	187.80	183.90	184.80	+.50	548
182.30	161.00	Nov	182.30	180.00	181.00	+.80	93
180.00	160.00	Jan	180.00	176.30	178.30	+1.30	19
182.00	174.50	Mar	179.00	179.00	181.00	−1.00	1
Fri. to Thurs. sales 8,640.							
Total open interest 6,953.							
GOLD							
100 troy oz.; dollars per troy oz.							
509.00	440.00	Mar	457.50	440.00	440.40	−15.70	102
514.70	447.00	Jul	463.00	447.00	448.60	−17.10	2
Fri. to Thurs. sales 8.							
Total open interest 104.							
N.Y. GOLD							
100 troy oz.; dollars per troy oz.							
No open contracts.							

N.Y. Commodity Exchange

Season's High	Season's Low		Week's High	Week's Low	Close	Net Chg	Open Int.
GOLD							
100 troy oz.; dollars per troy oz.							
510.50	371.50	Feb	457.50	436.50	439.40	−14.80	2,602
488.80	440.00	Mar	458.20	440.00	440.40	−15.30	4
514.00	378.00	Apr	461.90	439.80	443.20	−15.30	81,203
523.00	399.00	Jun	466.70	444.00	447.70	−15.50	16,701
527.00	425.00	Aug	471.00	451.00	452.30	−15.80	8,237
533.50	429.00	Oct	476.50	455.00	457.10	−16.20	9,289
546.00	430.80	Dec	482.00	457.80	462.00	−16.50	11,443
549.50	469.50	Feb	487.50	469.50	467.20	−16.80	5,071
550.00	470.00	Apr	489.00	470.00	472.60	−17.20	6,390
570.00	476.00	Jun	498.50	476.00	478.10	−17.60	6,968
575.00	483.00	Aug	504.60	483.00	483.90	−18.00	1,735
575.50	488.00	Oct	507.60	488.00	489.90	−18.40	2,686
504.00	498.50	Dec	504.00	498.50	496.10	−18.60	901
Fri. to Thurs. sales 261,803.							
Total open interest 153,230.							
SILVER							
5,000 troy oz.; cents per troy oz.							
700.0	649.0	Feb	659.0	652.0	629.5	−21.0	3
1030.1	535.0	Mar	667.9	628.0	632.5	−22.0	37,569
662.0	640.5	Apr	662.0	640.5	636.2	−22.2	8
1041.4	567.0	May	676.0	637.0	640.6	−22.3	16,872
1053.0	580.0	Jul	685.0	645.0	648.4	−22.5	11,729
1064.7	588.0	Sep	685.0	655.0	656.0	−23.0	6,664
1082.9	606.0	Dec	707.0	666.7	668.4	−23.8	6,115
1088.9	711.0	Jan	.....	.....	672.1	−24.0	5
1073.0	658.0	Mar	717.0	684.0	681.3	−24.4	1,309
965.0	714.0	May	718.0	714.0	690.3	−24.9	473
985.0	701.0	Jul	726.0	701.0	700.0	−25.4	359
820.0	749.0	Sep	.....	.....	701.8	−33.9	48
.....	.....	Dec	.....	.....	725.1	−26.4	......
Fri. to Thurs. sales 72,568.							
Total open interest 81,154.							
COPPER							
25,000 lbs.; cents per lb.							
127.00	90.20	Feb	103.00	90.20	101.40	−2.35	40
127.80	60.70	Mar	98.90	87.50	95.40	−.35	19,153
.....	.....	Apr	.....	.....	90.65	−.10	......
109.00	60.90	May	89.50	79.10	85.90	+.05	13,058
99.70	62.30	Jul	83.50	74.00	79.40	−.10	7,964
96.00	64.85	Sep	80.00	73.50	76.40	−1.10	2,112
96.50	64.70	Dec	78.00	72.00	74.60	−1.90	3,043
85.50	66.70	Jan	77.00	77.00	74.50	−1.90	18
93.00	66.50	Mar	77.40	74.00	74.20	−2.00	603
89.00	73.15	May	.....	.....	74.20	−2.00	67
89.00	73.70	Jul	.....	.....	74.20	−2.00	26
.....	.....	Sep	.....	.....	74.20	−2.00	2
.....	.....	Dec	.....	.....	74.20	−2.00	......
Fri. to Thurs. sales 52,732.							
Total open interest 46,086.							
ALUMINUM							
40,000 lbs.; cents per lb.							
.....	.....	Feb	.....	.....	89.20	+2.20	......
90.25	59.70	Mar	90.25	87.00	89.20	+2.20	75
87.00	87.00	Apr	87.00	87.00	88.00	+2.80	1
85.00	71.00	May	84.60	83.25	84.00	+.50	115
81.50	67.00	Jul	80.00	79.00	79.50	+1.50	45
82.00	79.50	Sep	.....	.....	77.00	+1.50	3
82.00	73.75	Dec	75.00	75.00	74.50	+.75	61
.....	.....	Jan	.....	.....	74.25	−2.25	......
.....	.....	Mar	.....	.....	74.25	+.50	......
.....	.....	May	.....	.....	74.25	+.50	......
.....	.....	Jul	.....	.....	74.25	+.50	......
.....	.....	Sep	.....	.....	74.25	+.50	......
.....	.....	Dec	.....	.....	74.25	+.50	......
Fri. to Thurs. sales ·78.							
Total open interest 300.							

SOURCE: *Barron's*, 8 February 1988. Reprinted courtesy of *Barron's Weekly*.

these differences are discussed later in the chapter. This is in contrast to put and call options on common stocks, where the price increases with the term to expiration.

Another important item of information is the *open interest*, the total number of contracts outstanding at a given point in time. The quotations indicate the total number of contracts for each delivery month and the total number of contracts for all delivery months. The open-interest figures should not be confused with the volume or number of contracts traded during the day or week. When an investor/speculator writes a contract that is purchased by a buyer, the open interest increases by one. When trading is initially started on a contract, the open interest is typically low but increases over the life of the contract, depending on investor interest. Since over 95 percent of contracts are cancelled by reversing trades prior to delivery, there may be many more contracts outstanding than the actual supply of the commodity. As the delivery date approaches, however, the open interest declines to a level indicating the number of contracts that will be settled by delivery.

INVESTMENT CHARACTERISTICS OF COMMODITY FUTURES

Introduction

This section discusses the investment characteristics of commodity contracts. The discussion covers the behavior of futures prices relative to cash or spot prices. Ex-post *HPR*s and risk measures for commodity contracts are also discussed.

Commodity Prices

The vast majority of commodities are actually bought and sold in the *cash* or *spot* market at price P_S, rather than in the futures market. The *futures price*, P_F, represents the price of the commodity at some future point in time. The difference in the futures price and spot price is called the *basis, B*, as illustrated by the following equation:

$$B = P_F - P_S \qquad\qquad (20.1)$$

Ignoring market pricing inefficiencies, the basis on most agricultural commodities will be positive, indicating that the futures price, P_F, is greater than the spot price, P_S. The basis will be positive because of the *carrying cost* associated with a particular commodity: storage costs, insurance, financing expense, and other costs incurred to keep the commodity in inventory until its delivery date. Typically, the longer the time before delivery, the greater the carrying cost. As the delivery month approaches, the basis will decline until the spot and future prices are approximately equal. This price behavior is referred to as *convergence*.

Figure 20.1 illustrates the behavior of the basis for a Kansas City Hard Red Wheat contract. Notice that the basis is initially positive but narrows considerably as the contract approaches the delivery data. The wheat harvest season is late May through July; thus, prices are low during and following the harvest and prices tend to increase as the inventory of wheat declines during the year. Thus, there are significant seasonal price patterns for wheat. In addition to the seasonal pattern noted in the chart, both cash and futures prices exhibit significant volatility, and the two prices are highly correlated.

Commodity contracts can also have a negative basis. This may occur because the particular commodity is currently in short supply in the cash market, causing upward pressure on prices. If the future supply is expected to increase (because of a good harvest), future prices are likely to be below spot prices, creating a negative basis.

In addition to carrying cost, however, there may be other factors that influence the basis. For example, how accurately do futures prices reflect *expected*

FIGURE 20.1 Cash versus futures price of Kansas City hard red wheat

Contract Description: Hard red wheat traded on KCBT
Delivery date: March 22, 1988
Contract size: 5,000 bushels
Prices are cents per bushel

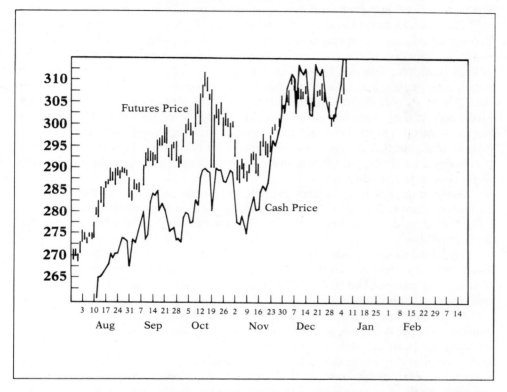

Source: *Futures Charts,* Commodity Trend Service, North Palm Beach, FL (1-800-331-1069). Reprinted by permission.

spot prices? If the market was completely accurate (efficient), the observable futures price today would equal the unobservable but expected spot price in the future. In a market without carrying costs and other inefficiencies (i.e., a perfect market), the expected basis, $E(B)$, would be zero.

There are three theories or hypotheses and some empirical evidence that attempt to explain $E(B)$. The *normal backwardation* hypothesis suggests that the "future price tends to be a downward biased estimate of its spot price in the cash market at the contract's maturity date,"[2] or $B < 0$ and $P_F < E(P_S)$, so $E(B) < 0$. This hypothesis was first suggested by J.M. Keynes in 1924. Keynes

---

[2] Zvi Bodie and Victor I. Rosansky, "Risk and Return in Commodity Futures," *Financial Analysts Journal* (May-June 1980): pp. 27–39.

essentially argued that the futures market is dominated by hedgers attempting to avoid the risk associated with a decrease in a commodity's price. The hedgers depend on speculators who are willing to assume this risk by taking a long position in the contract. The hedgers must therefore write contracts at prices below the expected spot price to compensate the speculator for assuming the risk. The expected basis is therefore negative. This theory assumes that hedgers usually write (net short) contracts and that speculators usually buy (net long) contracts.

The second hypothesis is that $B > 0$ and $P_F > E(P_S)$, so $E(B) > 0$.[3] This hypothesis suggests that speculators are more than willing to assume the price risk in anticipation of earning profits, because of market inefficiencies or because of their particular skill and knowledge about the futures market. Because of these anticipated profits, speculators will bid up the prices of commodity contracts, so that $B > 0$, $P_F > E(P_S)$, and $E(B) > 0$. Speculators would earn their anticipated profit only if they were net short and the futures price declined. This price behavior—with the initial price of the futures contract above the spot price and the futures price declining over time—is known as *contango*. This theory assumes that hedgers generally purchase contracts (net long) and that speculators generally write contracts (net short).

Early empirical tests did not provide conclusive evidence of the validity of either hypothesis. A more recent study, using data on a commodity futures portfolio, found evidence of positive excess mean returns.[4] This finding supported the normal backwardation hypothesis, since $P_F < E(P_S)$.

The third theory is that $E(B) = 0$, as would be the case in an efficient market. Essentially, this view argues that futures prices are unbiased estimates of expected futures spot prices. The market, therefore, does not provide excess returns to hedgers or to speculators.

In summary, the observed basis, B, may be positive or negative for futures contracts. There is debate, however, about the expected basis, $E(B)$, and whether it should be positive, negative, or 0. If $E(B) < 0$, the market offers *speculators* excess returns for taking long positions and assuming the price risk. If $E(B) > 0$, speculators earn excess returns by being net short while hedgers are generally net long. Both of these theories (normal backwardation and contango) assume that the net positions of hedgers and speculators do not change over the life of the contract. This eliminates the possibility that $B > 0$ and $E(B) < 0$, or that $B < 0$ and $E(B) > 0$. Finally, if $E(B) = 0$, the market is efficient and does not offer excess returns on short or long positions. An important but unanswered question: If $E(B) \neq 0$, are there opportunities for hedgers and speculators to earn *excess* or abnormal returns? In other words, the value of $E(B)$ must be significantly larger or smaller than 0 to provide an opportunity for excess returns. Small values (either positive or negative) for $E(B)$ would not provide excess returns above those necessary to compensate for transaction costs and for assuming the price risk. Excess returns would occur only if profits were above the level necessary to compensate for the risk and cost associated with the contract. Empirical studies of the risk-return characteristics of commodities are discussed later in the chapter.

---

[3] C. O. Hardy and L. S. Lyon, "The Theory of Hedging," *Journal of Political Economy* (April 1923): pp. 276–87.

[4] Bodie and Rosansky, p. 33.

Price Limits

In 1987, the CBOT reported a record volume of over 127 million contracts. In a completely free or unregulated market, prices are determined by supply and demand, and fluctuate as market conditions change. For example, assume that a severe and unexpected freeze damages the orange crop in Florida. Because of the freeze, the future supply of fresh and frozen orange juice concentrate is likely to be significantly reduced if there is no significant inventory of frozen concentrate. This event is likely to be immediately reflected in spot market prices. However, there are maximum *price limit* changes imposed by the commodity exchange. Orange juice futures are traded on the New York Cotton Exchange, a contract representing 15,000 pounds of frozen concentrate. The exchange limits the daily price change to 5 cents per pound (either up or down) or $750 (15,000 × $.05) per contract. The price *range* during the day is limited to 10 cents per pound. Bid and ask prices outside these limits are not allowed. The necessary adjustment to the futures prices due to a freeze may not take place within a single trading day because of the price limit.

These restrictions obviously reduce the potential price volatility of option contracts in the short run. Over a longer period, however, prices would reflect the underlying supply and demand conditions. The justification for the price limits is to ensure a viable and orderly market. This, however, may favor the hedger, at the expense of speculators who hope for large excess returns in a short time. In comparison, there are no price limits imposed by the stock markets. Prices are free to fluctuate to the extent that buyers and sellers, often through the help of specialists, are able to execute transactions. On rare occasions, trading may be temporarily suspended in a particular stock because of a potentially large price change. The CBOT was able to maintain trading in all contracts during the October 1987 market collapse.

Calculating Holding Period Returns on Commodity Contracts

An investor with a long (or short) position in a commodity contract will not receive any interest or dividend income on the investment. Gains or losses are determined solely by price changes in the contract over the holding period.

One complication in calculating a holding period return, *HPR*, for a commodity contract is that a position (short or long) requires the investor to provide an initial margin, cash or Treasury bills. Should the *HPR* be calculated using only the initial margin (equity) as the initial investment? Typically, *HPR*s for stocks are calculated as unlevered returns, even if margin trading is used. If the *HPR*s on commodities and stock are to be compared, the influence of leverage should be removed. One approach is to calculate the *HPR* on the commodity as

$$HPR_t = \frac{P_1 - P_0}{P_0} \tag{20.2}$$

where P_0 is the beginning price of the contract rather than the amount of the initial margin required of the investor, and P_1 is the ending price of the contract. This procedure ignores the leverage effect.

TABLE 20.3 CALCULATING *HPRs* ON COMMODITY CONTRACTS

1. Data:

   Contract: Gold, traded on New York Commodity Exchange
   One contract represents 100 troy ounces of gold
   Delivery month is December, 1987
   Initial margin requirement is 10 percent of contract value

DATE	CLOSING PRICE OF COMMODITY CONTRACT (DOLLARS PER TROY OZ.)	INITIAL MARGIN ON CONTRACT 10%	QUARTERLY YIELDS-TO-MATURITY ON 90-DAY U.S. TREASURY BILLS
October 1, 1986	$454.30	$4543	1.30%
January 1, 1987	421.70	4217	1.39
April 1, 1987	440.50	4405	1.42
July 1, 1987	459.20	4592	1.38
October 1, 1987	466.60	4666	1.61
December 21, 1987	479.80	4798	–

2. Holding Period Returns:

	HPRs		
PERIOD	CALCULATED FROM PRICE CHANGES (EQ. 20.2)	CALCULATED CONSIDERING LEVERAGE (EQ. 20.3)	CALCULATED CONSIDERING INTEREST INCOME (EQ. 20.4)
1986 Fourth Quarter,	−7.18%	−71.76%	−5.88%
1987 First Quarter,	4.46	44.58	5.85
1987 Second Quarter,	4.25	42.45	5.67
1987 Third Quarter,	1.61	16.11	2.99
1987 Fourth Quarter,	2.83	28.29	4.44

SOURCE: Prices and Treasury bill yields from *Barron's*, various issues. Reprinted courtesy of *Barron's Weekly*

The impact of leverage on returns can be measured by defining the *HPR* as

$$HPR_t = \frac{P_1 - P_0}{mP_0} \tag{20.3}$$

where m is the margin requirement in decimal form. Since m is usually 10 percent or less, the *HPR* will be magnified or levered, given price changes over the holding period of the contract.

An alternative calculation reflects the fact that the initial margin may be in Treasury bills where the investor is entitled to any interest income from the bills. This interest income can be considered in calculating the *HPR*.[5] Because of the practice of marking to market every day, the investor may be required to post additional margin or be able to remove funds for other purposes. These daily cash inflows and outflows change the margin and therefore influence the *HPR*.

---

[5] For example, see the appendix in Bodie and Rosansky, pp. 38–39.

If Treasury bills are used for the initial margin, the *HPR* is

$$HPR_t = \frac{P_1 - P_0}{P_0} + R_{F,0} \qquad\qquad (20.4)$$

where $R_{F,0}$ is the yield-to-maturity or *HPR* on a U.S. Treasury bill of the same maturity as the holding period on the commodity contract.[6] Equation 20.4 ignores the leverage effect and the daily inflows and outflows of cash that may occur because of marking to market. Table 20.3 presents a simple illustration of alternative *HPR* calculations for commodities. Notice the large difference that leverage causes in the *HPRs*.

Ex-Post Returns and Risk on Commodity Contracts

Table 20.4 provides the *real HPRs* (*HPR* less the rate of inflation) on Treasury bills and bonds, common stocks, and commodity futures. The returns are adjusted for the rate of inflation, using the CPI. The commodity returns for the years 1953–1963 are based on a portfolio composed of 13 commodities. As new commodity contracts were introduced for trading over the 1964–1981 period, they were added to the portfolio. In the more recent years (1964–1981), the number of commodities in the portfolio varied from 18 to 22. The real *HPRs* for commodities, based on price changes, do *not* reflect the impact of leverage (Equation 20.3) or of using U.S. Treasury bills for the margin (Equation 20.4). The returns on bonds and stocks, however, reflect price changes and interest and dividend income.

Several interesting observations can be made from the data in Table 20.4. First, the real *HPRs* from the commodities portfolio ranged from −33.08 percent in 1981 to 72.69 percent in 1973, while the real *HPRs* on common stocks ranged from −34.47 percent in 1974 to 53.39 percent in 1954. Despite the larger *HPR* range for commodities, the standard deviation for the stock returns (19.48 percent) is larger than the standard deviation for commodities (17.36 percent). The arithmetic mean return for stocks is also larger than the mean for the commodities portfolio (6.68 percent versus 5.69 percent). The coefficient of variation (see Chapter 2) for stocks is 2.92, 3.05 for commodities. The coefficient of variation indicates that the relative risk of stocks is less than that of commodities. Second, notice that for the years with relatively high rates of inflation (1969, 1973–1975, and 1979–1981), the real *HPRs* for commodities were usually quite favorable, compared to generally negative real *HPRs* for common stocks and U.S. Treasury bills and bonds.

Table 20.5 provides the correlation coefficients between the real *HPRs* for U.S. Treasury bills and bonds, common stocks, commodity futures, and the rate of inflation. The real returns on commodity futures are positively correlated with inflation (+.247); bills (−.673), bonds (−.579), and common stock (−.467) are negatively correlated. This suggests that commodity returns may provide an inflation hedge. The negative correlation between commodity real returns and the

---

[6] Bodie and Rosansky, p. 39.

TABLE 20.4 HISTORICAL REAL RATES OF RETURNS AND STANDARD DEVIATIONS ON COMMODITIES, U.S. TREASURY BILLS AND BONDS, STOCKS, AND THE RATE OF INFLATION: 1953–1981

YEAR	U.S. TREASURY BILLS	U.S. TREASURY BONDS	S&P 500	COMMODITY FUTURES	RATE OF INFLATION (CPI)
1953	1.19%	2.99%	−1.60%	−3.46%	0.62%
1954	1.37	7.73	53.39	13.23	−0.50
1955	1.20	−1.66	31.08	−7.63	0.37
1956	−0.39	−8.22	3.60	12.38	2.86
1957	0.12	4.30	−13.40	−5.04	3.02
1958	0.22	−7.72	40.88	−3.47	1.76
1959	1.43	−3.70	10.30	−2.84	1.50
1960	1.16	12.12	−1.00	−3.93	1.48
1961	1.45	0.30	26.05	0.02	0.67
1962	1.50	5.60	−9.83	−2.40	1.22
1963	1.45	−0.43	20.81	16.32	1.65
1964	2.32	2.29	15.11	4.54	1.19
1965	1.97	−1.18	10.33	5.13	1.92
1966	1.36	−0.29	−12.98	9.70	3.35
1967	1.34	−11.87	20.32	−0.06	3.04
1968	0.47	−4.76	6.05	−3.18	4.72
1969	0.44	−10.55	−13.77	12.20	6.11
1970	0.99	6.27	−1.40	−1.62	5.49
1971	1.00	9.55	10.59	−1.65	3.36
1972	0.42	2.20	15.06	29.35	3.41
1973	−1.72	−9.11	−21.56	72.69	8.80
1974	−3.74	−7.00	−34.47	17.97	12.20
1975	−1.13	2.04	28.21	−10.03	7.01
1976	0.26	11.39	18.16	5.30	4.81
1977	−1.55	−6.92	−13.07	−4.90	6.77
1978	−1.83	−7.34	−2.42	18.60	9.03
1979	−2.59	−12.82	4.53	15.91	13.31
1980	−1.79	−15.80	17.44	5.24	12.41
1981	4.35	−6.47	−12.68	−33.08	8.90
Mean	0.37	−1.65	6.68	5.69	4.50
Standard Deviation	1.68	7.43	19.48	17.36	3.86

SOURCE: Zvi Bodie, "Commodity Futures as a Hedge against Inflation," *Journal of Portfolio Management* (Spring 1983): p. 13. Reprinted by permission.

TABLE 20.5 CORRELATION COEFFICIENTS BETWEEN REAL RATES OF RETURN ON COMMODITIES, U.S. TREASURY BILLS AND BONDS, STOCKS, AND INFLATION: 1953–1981

	TREASURY BILLS	TREASURY BONDS	COMMODITIES	COMMON STOCKS	INFLATION RATE (CPI)
Treasury Bills	1.000				
Treasury Bonds	0.430	1.000			
Commodities	−0.512	−0.230	1.000		
Common Stocks	0.252	0.187	−0.210	1.000	
Inflation Rate (CPI)	−0.673	−0.579	0.247	−0.467	1.000

SOURCE: Zvi Bodie, "Commodity Futures as a Hedge against Inflation," *Journal of Portfolio Management* (Spring 1983): p. 13. Reprinted by permission.

returns on financial assets suggests that diversification benefits may result from including commodities in an investment portfolio. This possibility is discussed in Chapter 26.

INVESTMENT ANALYSIS OF COMMODITY CONTRACTS

This section discusses different approaches that may used in an investment analysis of commodity contracts. It also considers empirical studies that have attempted to model commodity returns, using the CAPM or other models of risk and return.

Overview

It is unlikely that most individuals trade in commodities to hedge. This is because individuals are typically not commodity producers (excluding farmers), nor do they have a large inventory of a commodity. Their motivation, therefore, is likely to be speculation. Individuals may be attracted to commodity trading because of its large and rapid price changes and their ability to use small initial margins to take trading positions. It is quite possible that the *HPR* on a commodity contract will be over 100 percent, given a 10 percent change in the spot price of the commodity. On the other hand, it is quite likely that the loss will be more than 100 percent if the initial margin is totally lost and additional margin is used to maintain the position.

A number of studies have shown that hedgers in commodity markets have been able to purchase their "insurance" very cheaply since, as a general rule, futures prices contain a very small risk premium. This suggests that, on average, a speculator should expect a loss or very low returns on the majority of trades. There is, however, the possibility that the current futures price does not accurately reflect the commodity's price in the future. This possibility provides the speculator's motivation. As a word of warning, however, it should be noted that "analyses of the returns to speculators have shown that speculation should be regarded as a skilled occupation, not merely as risk-bearing; returns vary greatly with the ability and knowledge of the speculators."[7]

Demand-and-Supply Analysis

A fundamental approach to speculation in commodity futures requires a demand-and-supply analysis of the underlying commodity. For agricultural commodities, demand is somewhat stable and predictable since many of these commodities represent food staples. The supply of agricultural commodities can be very volatile, however, because of uncertain harvests due to unpredictable weather conditions, diseases affecting crops, and other factors. The drought during the summer of 1988 and its impact on commodity prices is a recent example of the affects of weather on commodity prices.

---

[7] Avraham Kamara, "The Behavior of Futures Prices: A Review of Theory and Evidence," *Financial Analysts Journal* (July-August 1984): p. 70.

Much of the information needed for a demand-and-supply analysis is developed and reported by the U.S. Department of Agriculture, USDA. Data is collected by the USDA, using regional field offices that monitor local growing conditions and take crop samples to forecast the harvest. The individual speculator can obtain information directly from the USDA or through commodity research organizations and brokerage firms.

Systematic and Unsystematic Risk

A number of studies have attempted to apply the CAPM to commodity contracts.[8] Generally, these studies (using the S&P 500 as the market proxy) concluded that the CAPM did *not* adequately model the risk-return relationship in commodity markets. On average, the betas were not statistically significant and tended to be negative. There was also a negative relationship between the mean excess returns and betas, which contradicted the positive slope of the SML when the CAPM was applied to stocks. The validity of the results from these studies, however, depends on the correctness of using the S&P 500 as the market portfolio and assuming that the commodity's beta is constant.

Recognizing these problems, a 1985 study used a consumption-based, intertemporal CAPM approach.[9] This model does not require return estimates for a benchmark portfolio like the S&P 500 and also allows systematic stochastic variations in betas over time. After empirical tests of the model, using three agricultural commodity contracts over the 1960–1978 period, the author rejected the use of the model for commodities.

Based on the empirical results from these studies, it appears that systematic risk estimates (beta) for commodity futures contracts are neither valid nor useful in an investment analysis. As Table 20.4 indicates, however, there is considerable risk in commodity contracts. The majority of the risk therefore appears to be nonsystematic or nonmarket-related. Thus, factors unique to each commodity appear to be primarily responsible for price changes and the resulting returns on the commodity contracts.

INVESTMENT STRATEGIES FOR COMMODITY CONTRACTS

In addition to speculative short-term trading in commodity contracts, a number of other reasons for trading in commodity contracts can be cited.

Inflation Hedge

Can commodity contracts be used to provide an inflation hedge? Surprisingly, the answer to this question is not clear, because of contradictory empirical results in

---

[8] See, for example, Katherine Dusak, "Futures Trading and Investor Return: An Investigation of Commodity Market Risk Premiums," *Journal of Political Economy* (December 1973): pp. 1387–1406, and Z. Bodie and V. Rosansky, "Risk and Return in Commodity Futures," *Financial Analysts Journal* (May-June 1980): pp. 27–39.

[9] Ravi Jagannathan, "An Investigation of Commodity Futures Prices Using the Consumption-based Intertemporal Capital Asset Pricing Model," *Journal of Finance* (March 1985): pp. 175–91.

the literature. For example, as shown in Table 20.4, the study by Bodie over the 1953–1981 period concluded that commodity futures correlated relatively well with the rate of inflation (CPI) and consequently provided an effective hedge.[10] A recent study, using data for fourteen agricultural and two metals contracts over the 1967–1982 period, reached a different conclusion.[11] The study tested whether portfolios of common stocks and commodity futures contracts provided an inflation hedge against *unexpected* inflation in the cost of consumer goods, shelter, and transportation. The empirical results suggested that hedging was possible but that "commodity futures contracts contributed nothing to hedging effectiveness."[12] Essentially, the hedging strategy worked because of the performance of common stocks in the portfolio.

One reason for the contradictory results from the two studies may be related to the measures of inflation employed. Bodie used the CPI to calculate annual price changes and *assumed* that this rate was entirely *unexpected* inflation. Bernard and Frecka, on the other hand, actually estimated unexpected inflation as opposed to expected inflation. A second possible reason for the contradictory result is that Bodie simply observed that inflation-adjusted returns on the commodities contract portfolio were positive during most inflationary years, while inflation-adjusted common stock returns were often negative. The Bernard and Frecka paper compared the portfolio returns to unexpected price increases for specific consumer cost items.

In summary, the empirical tests indicate that returns on a portfolio of commodity contracts are usually above the observed rate of inflation and consequently provide a positive real return. It is also generally recognized that common stocks, and particularly long-term bonds, do not provide adequate real rates of return during periods of high inflation. In terms of unexpected inflation, common stocks rather than commodities appear to provide a hedge against cost increases in specific items such as food, shelter, and transportation.

Market Inefficiencies

Numerous studies have tested for nonrandom price movements and other types of market inefficiencies in commodity prices. If nonrandom patterns of sufficient magnitude could be discovered, then trading rules or strategies could be developed to earn excess returns. Despite some evidence of seasonality and serial correlation in futures prices, the evidence is not very compelling. This suggests that "the mere existence of some nonrandom components is not sufficient evidence against the random walk hypotheses; they must present unexploited opportunities for above-average profits."[13] This conclusion tends to discount the usefulness of technical analysis (see Chapter 12) in identifying speculative trading opportunities in commodity futures.

---

[10] Zvi Bodie.

[11] Victor L. Bernard and Thomas J. Frecka, "Commodity Contracts and Common Stocks as Hedges against Relative Consumer Price Risk," *Journal of Financial and Quantitative Analysis* (June 1987): pp. 169–88.

[12] Bernard and Frecka, pp. 185–86.

[13] Avraham Kamara, p. 71.

TABLE 20.6 PERFORMANCE OF PUBLICLY TRADED COMMODITY FUNDS

I. Return and Risk Data for Commodity Funds

YEAR	NUMBER OF FUNDS	GEOMETRIC AVERAGE OF MONTHLY *HPR*s	AVERAGE STANDARD DEVIATION
1979–80	12	0.27%	15.77%
1980–81	16	0.90	12.11
1981–82	34	1.12	8.24
1982–83	49	−2.67	11.67
1983–84	70	−0.54	7.93
1984–85	85	0.48	9.43
		Average −0.07%	Average 11.30%

II. Comparison of Commodity Funds to Other Financial Assets

	GEOMETRIC AVERAGE OF MONTHLY *HPR*s JULY 1979–JUNE 1985	AVERAGE STANDARD DEVIATION
S&P 500	1.31%	3.99%
"Small" NYSE Stocks	1.68	4.65
Long-term Corporate Bonds	0.79	4.28
Long-term Government Bonds	0.75	4.35
Shearson Index of Corporate and Government Bonds	0.97	2.93
Treasury Bills	0.85	0.15
Commodity Funds	−0.07	11.30

SOURCE: Edwin J. Elton, Martin J. Gruber, and Joel C. Rentzler, "Professional Managed Publicly Traded Commodity Funds," *Journal of Business* (April 1987): pp. 178–79. Reprinted by permission.

Publicly Traded Commodity Funds

As of mid-1987, there were over one hundred publicly traded funds that specialized in gold, silver, and other types of commodities. A number of funds and other professionally managed portfolios use futures contracts and options to hedge their stock or bond portfolios. An individual investor therefore has the ability to invest both directly and indirectly in futures, through professionally managed portfolios.

A 1987 study analyzed the investment performance of publicly traded commodity funds over the period July 1979 to June 1985.[14] Table 20.6 summarizes the return and risk measures for the funds and for other categories of financial assets. The top panel of the table provides average monthly *HPR*s and standard deviations. Notice that the average *HPR* for the funds was negative for two of the six years, and negative overall. The average standard deviations were also very large. The bottom panel of the table shows that the performance of the funds was very poor relative to stocks, bonds, and bills. Notice that the funds had the lowest average monthly *HPR* but the largest standard deviation.

---

[14] Edwin J. Elton, Martin J. Gruber, and Joel C. Rentzler, "Professionally Managed, Publicly Traded Commodity Funds," *Journal of Business* (April 1987): pp. 175–99.

Because of the transaction costs incurred by the funds and inconsistent return performances between the funds, the study concluded that a randomly selected fund did not offer an attractive alternative to stocks, bonds, or bills. The funds were also not attractive as additions to a portfolio of stocks and bonds. Finally, the study was unable to develop a procedure using past performance that could be used to select a fund that might have superior investment performance in the future.

Portfolio Considerations

Commodity speculators, because of their investment philosophy and motivation, are not interested in reducing risk at the expense of returns. A typical small individual speculator actively trades in only one or a few specific types of futures contracts, because of the difficulty in obtaining and analyzing demand and supply factors for each commodity. Since it has been shown that most of the risk of commodity contracts is unsystematic, an overall economic or market analysis is not generally useful. Unique supply and demand factors must be individually analyzed for each commodity.

Investment advisors and brokerage houses often recommend that individuals segregate funds for commodity speculation from other investment funds. In this sense, commodity speculation is not viewed in a portfolio context. This practice is designed to limit the risk exposure from commodity speculation because if the entire amount is lost, it will represent only a small portion of the individual's total wealth. As this chapter indicates, commodity investing is *very risky*. In a portfolio context, however, there is some evidence that commodity futures returns are negatively correlated with bond and stock returns (see Table 20.5). This suggests that the risk of a securities portfolio may be reduced by adding commodity futures.

SUMMARY

This chapter discussed commodity futures—contracts on physical commodities like agricultural crops, precious metals, and livestock. The introduction discussed commodity markets, contracts provision, and pricing or quotations. Investment characteristics of commodity futures were also discussed.

Given this introduction and background, the remaining sections discussed investment analysis and investment strategies for commodity futures. A traditional investment analysis was presented, along with an analysis using a CAPM approach. Investors should realize that investing in commodity futures is *very risky* relative to traditional investments in stocks and bonds. However, commodity futures may offer an inflation hedge and may reduce the risk of a securities portfolio. These portfolio hedging strategies are discussed in more detail in Chapter 21.

QUESTIONS

1. Define the following terms dealing with commodity futures:
   a. Commodity contract
   b. Commodity contract price

   c.   Commodity futures market

   d.   Clearing corporation

   e.   Initial margin

   f.   Open interest

2.   Compare and contrast the cash and futures markets.

3.   Explain the concept of basis. Why is the analysis of the basis an important aspect of investing in commodity futures?

4.   Assume that the spot price for feeder cattle is $.7765 per pound and that the futures price for a contract with three months until delivery is $.7820 per pound.

   a.   Explain why the basis for this commodity is positive.

   b.   Does the value of the basis support the normal backwardation hypothesis? Explain.

   c.   Suppose the spot price was $.7820 and the futures price was $.7765. What explanation could be offered to explain this relationship between the two prices?

5.   Discuss the empirical evidence dealing with the ability of an investment in commodity futures to provide an inflation hedge.

6.   Discuss the pros and cons of adding commodity futures to a portfolio of stocks and bonds.

7.   The correlation coefficients in Table 20.5 indicate that the real *HPR*s on commodities are negatively correlated with the real *HPR*s on common stocks and Treasury bonds. Discuss the investment implications of these "low" but negative correlation coefficients.

8.   Discuss the appropriateness of using the CAPM to analyze commodity futures.

9.   Should only speculators or commodity producers and users trade in commodity futures? What role, if any, should commodity futures have for an individual investor?

PROBLEMS

1.   Assume that the price of gold based on a commodity contract increased from $450 per ounce on January 1, 1988, to $470 on April 1, 1988. The quarterly yield on Treasury bills was 2.0% on January 1, 1988.

   a.   Suppose an investor took a *long* position on January 1 with a 10% initial margin and closed the position on April 1:

      (1) Calculate the *HPR*, based only on the commodity price change.

      (2) Calculate the *HPR*, based on the price change and leverage.

      (3) Calculate the *HPR*, assuming that Treasury bills were used for the margin. Ignore the influence of leverage.

   b.   Suppose an investor took a *short* position on January 1 with a 10% initial margin and closed the position on April 1. Calculate the three *HPR*s that are described in part a of this problem.

2.   A long position in a silver contract was taken at a price of $6.50 per troy ounce; three months later the position was closed at $6.75 per troy ounce.

   a.   Ignoring leverage and transactions cost, calculate the quarterly *HPR*.

   b.   Use the quarterly *HPR* calculated in part a to calculate the annualized *HPR*. Assume quarterly compounding.

c. Assume that the CPI increased from 300 to 325 during the year. Did the silver commodity investment provide an inflation hedge?

REFERENCES

Bernard, Victor L., and Thomas J. Frecka. "Commodity Contracts and Common Stocks as Hedges against Relative Consumer Price Risk." *Journal of Financial and Quantitative Analysis* (June 1987): pp. 169–88.

Bodie, Zvi, and Victor I. Rosansky. "Risk and Return in Commodity Futures." *Financial Analysts Journal* (May-June 1980): pp. 27–39.

Bodie, Zvi. "Commodity Futures as a Hedge against Inflation." *Journal of Portfolio Management* (Spring 1983): pp. 12–17.

Chiang, Thomas C. "Empirical Analysis on the Predictors of Future Spot Rates." *Journal of Financial Research* (Summer 1986): pp. 153–62.

Ederington, Louis H. "New Futures and Options Markets." *Financial Analysts Journal* (January-February 1980): pp. 42–48.

Elton, Edwin J., Martin J. Gruber and Joel C. Rentzler. "Professionally Managed, Publicly Traded Commodity Funds." *Journal of Business* (April 1987): pp. 175–99.

Fama, Eugene F., and Kenneth R. French. "Commodity Futures Prices: Some Evidence on Forecast Power, Premiums, and the Theory of Storage." *Journal of Business* (January 1987): pp. 55–73.

Jagannathan, Ravi. "An Investigation of Commodity Futures Prices Using the Consumption-based Intertemporal Capital Asset Pricing Model." *Journal of Finance* (March 1985): pp. 175–91.

Kamara, Avraham. "The Behavior of Futures Prices: A Review of Theory and Evidence." *Financial Analysts Journal* (July-August 1984): pp. 68–75.

Livingston, Miles. "The Delivery Option on Forward Contracts." *Journal of Financial and Quantitative Analysis* (March 1987): pp. 79–87.

Moriarty, Eugene, Susan M. Phillips, and Paula A. Tosini. "A Comparison of Options and Futures in the Management of Portfolio Risk." *Financial Analysts Journal* (January-February 1981): pp. 61–67.

Phillips, Susan M., and Paula A. Tosini. "A Comparison of Margin Requirements for Options and Futures." *Financial Analysts Journal* (November-December 1982): pp. 54–58.

CHAPTER 21

FINANCIAL FUTURES

INTRODUCTION

Overview

This chapter discusses several new types of securities: interest rate futures, stock index futures, foreign currency futures, and options on financial futures. The mechanics of trading, contract characteristics, and institutional arrangements for financial and currency futures are essentially the same as those for commodity futures, covered in Chapter 20. Much of the previous discussion of these details for commodity futures applies to financial and currency futures.

There are, however, several differences between commodity, currency, and financial futures. First, there is no underlying real asset for financial futures. For example, a futures contract on the S&P 500 represents a hypothetical common stock portfolio. Second, stock index futures are settled on the delivery date for *cash*, while interest rate futures can be settled by delivery of the securities. Third, contract maturity dates are standardized for financial futures; contracts are available with maturities in March, June, September, and December. Maturity months for commodity contracts vary from commodity to commodity, depending on the characteristics of the commodity. Fourth, financial futures are available with longer lives than commodity futures; for example, contracts on U.S. Treasury bonds are traded with settlement dates over two years away.

Table 21.1 provides a list of the five U.S. markets where financial and currency futures and options on futures are traded. As the table indicates, there are seven futures contracts on money-market and fixed-income securities, six contracts on stock indices, eleven contracts on U.S. dollars and foreign currencies, and three options on futures. In addition, markets such as the Toronto Stock Exchange, Winnipeg Commodity Exchange, and London Exchange trade financial and currency futures.

History

Many individual and institutional investors that traditionally concentrated investments in stocks and bonds have readily accepted the introduction of financial and currency futures. As previously discussed, investing in commodity futures requires an analysis of the underlying asset, which may be an agricultural commodity or a precious metal. Typically, few stock and bond investors have the necessary understanding of the supply and demand factors for commodities. Their expertise is analysis of financial assets, such as stocks and bonds.

The first financial future came into existence in the United States in 1972 with the introduction of currency futures by the Chicago Mercantile Exchange. Contracts on Treasury securities were introduced by the International Monetary Market and Chicago Mercantile Exchange in 1975. Stock index futures were first offered in 1982 by the Kansas City Board of Trade. Because of the enthusiastic acceptance by investors, other exchanges began to offer financial futures.

Exchanges are also constantly seeking to add new types of contracts. Before a new type of contract can be introduced, however, it must be approved by the Commodity Futures Trading Commission, CFTC. There has been some concern in the investment community that the financial futures markets are growing too rapidly. For example, in 1983 the Securities Industry Association called for a moratorium on new products. This trade association thought that the rapid growth taxed the operational and sales capacities of the securities industry and caused confusion for investors.

Based on the rapid developments during the 1970s and 1980s, it appears that investors have recognized the advantages of these new products and markets. Today, financial futures and options are an important part of the investment portfolios of many institutions and individuals. The market collapse in October 1987, however, has raised some serious issues about the role and regulation of the

TABLE 21.1 TYPES OF FINANCIAL AND CURRENCY FUTURES AND OPTIONS ON FUTURES AND U.S. TRADING MARKETS

FINANCIAL AND CURRENCY FUTURES

A. **Chicago Board of Trade**
1. Ten-year Treasury Bonds
2. Government National Mortgage Association (GNMA)
3. U.S. Treasury Bonds
4. Municipal Bonds
5. Major Market Maxi Index

B. **Chicago Mercantile Exchange**
1. U.S. Treasury Bills
2. S&P 500
3. Certificates of Deposit
4. Eurodollars
5. European Currency Units
6. British Pound
7. Canadian Dollar
8. French Franc
9. German Mark
10. Japanese Yen
11. Mexican Peso
12. Swiss Franc
13. Australian Dollar

C. **New York Cotton Exchange**
1. European Currency Units
2. U.S. Dollar
3. Five-year Treasury Notes

D. **New York Futures Exchange**
1. NYSE Composite
2. Commodity Research Bureau Index
3. Russell 2000
4. Russell 3000

E. **Kansas City Board of Trade**
1. Value Line Stock Index

OPTIONS ON FINANCIAL AND CURRENCY FUTURES

A. **Chicago Board of Trade**
1. Treasury Bonds

B. **Chicago Mercantile Exchange**
1. S&P 500
2. German Mark

TABLE 21.2 QUOTATIONS ON INTEREST RATE FUTURES

Season's		Week's			Net	Open
High	Low	High	Low	Close	Chg	Int.

CERT. DEPOSIT
$1 million; pts of 100 pct
No open contracts.

US T. BILLS
$1 million; pts of 100 pct.

Season's High	Low		Week's High	Low	Close	Net Chg	Open Int.
94.63	91.45	Mar	94.53	94.25	94.50	+.13	15,961
94.40	91.28	Jun	94.36	94.08	94.33	+.15	4,995
94.21	91.15	Sep	94.08	93.85	94.06	+.14	873
94.09	91.17	Dec	93.82	93.54	93.75	+.11	161
93.49	91.26	Mar	93.49	93.31	93.49	+.08	118
93.30	92.12	Jun	93.30	93.09	93.29	+.08	31

Fri. to Thurs. sales 31,887.
Total open interest 22,139.

5-Year Treasury Notes

$100,000 prin; pts & 32nds of 100 pct

Season's High	Low		Week's High	Low	Close	Net Chg	Open Int.
101.100	90.200	Mar	101.100	100.075	101.030	+.905	6,687
100.225	94.000	Jun	100.225	99.210	100.175	+.920	2,496
.....	.....	Sep	.....	.....	100.010	+.930	.....
.....	.....	Dec	.....	.....	99.160	......	......

Fri. to Thurs. sales 16,596.
Total open interest 9,183.

10 YR. TREASURY
$100,000 prin; pts & 32nds of 100 pct

Season's High	Low		Week's High	Low	Close	Net Chg	Open Int.
98-29	84-10	Mar	98-29	97-18	98-20	+ 24	66,207
98-4	83-30	Jun	98-4	96-24	97-28	+ 25	13,102
97-12	89-13	Sep	97-12	96-10	97-3	+ 24	306
.....	.....	Dec	.....	.....	96-12	......	2

Fri. to Thurs. sales 116,489.
Total open interest 77,722.

GNMA
$100,000 prin; pts & 32nds of 100 pct
No open contracts.

US TREASURY BONDS
(8 pct-$100,000;pts & 32nds of 100 pct)

Season's High	Low		Week's High	Low	Close	Net Chg	Open Int.
100-26	67	Mar	95-18	93-15	94-30	+1-1	262,976
99-23	66-25	Jun	94-17	92-14	93-28	+ 30	51,434
99-12	74-20	Sep	93-18	91-23	92-30	+ 28	9,393
99-2	74-1	Dec	92-21	90-29	92-2	+ 26	2,868
95-10	73-20	Mar	91-27	90-6	91-8	+ 24	3,221
94-4	73-11	Jun	91-3	89-24	90-16	+ 22	2,088
93-16	72-26	Sep	90-10	89-21	89-26	+ 20	372
92-22	72-18	Dec	89-17	88-15	89-5	+ 18	134
88-31	72-1	Mar	88-31	87-31	88-17	+ 16	47
88-13	75	Jun	88-13	87-30	87-30	+ 15	26
87-30	81-1	Sep	87-30	87-12	87-12	+ 14	4

Fri. to Thurs. sales 1,540,666.
Total open interest 328,744.

MUNICIPAL BONDS
$1000x index;pts & 32nds of 100 pct

Season's High	Low		Week's High	Low	Close	Net Chg	Open Int.
91-15	71-12	Mar	91-15	89-17	90-31	+ 21	13,492
89-25	70-3	Jun	89-25	87-29	89-10	+ 21	2,078
88-8	81-2	Sep	88-8	86-21	87-28	+ 21	320
86-29	83-8	Dec	86-29	85-10	86-17	+ 21	104
85-3	84-17	Mar	85-3	84-17	85-8	......	5

Last index 92-1 , up 17.
Fri. to Thurs. sales 34,127.
Total open interest 16,370.

SOURCE: *Barron's*, 8 February 1988. Courtesy of *Barron's Weekly.*

options and futures markets. Congressional investigations and studies by the SEC, the exchanges, and a presidential study commission have made numerous recommendations: (1) increasing the required margins on options and futures; (2) reducing the daily price limits on futures contracts; (3) regulating arbitrage trading involving index options, futures, and common stocks; and (4) making regulatory reforms, involving the SEC, Federal Reserve, and CFTC. The proposed reforms suggest abolishing the CFTC and giving overall regulatory control to the Federal Reserve.

INTEREST RATE FUTURES

Interest rate futures are available on U.S. Treasury bills, notes, and bonds; GNMAs; certificates of deposit; and municipal bonds. These contracts represent a promise to buy or sell a specified amount of the fixed-income security at some future time. For example, a contract on Treasury bills represents $1 million. The contract writer (short position) promises to deliver, and the buyer (long position) promises to accept delivery. The motivation of both the buyer and seller is to hedge or to speculate on interest rate changes over the life of the contract. For example, the contract writer may be trying to hedge against the impact of increases in interest rates to protect a long position in Treasury bills.

Rather than hedging, the writer may be speculating that Treasury bills will be less valuable in the future because of increases in interest rates. In this instance, the seller will not actually have a long position in Treasury bills. In general, a trader who expects interest rates to *increase* will write a contract (short position), while a trader who expects rates to *decrease* will buy a contract (long position).

Table 21.2 provides an example of the quotations on five interest rate futures. For the Treasury bill futures traded on the Chicago Mercantile Exchange, the quotations are a percentage. For example, the December 1988 contract is quoted at 93.75, or 93.75 percent. Since Treasury bills are quoted on an annualized discounted-yield basis rather than as a dollar price, the future's price is determined as the Treasury bill futures yield subtracted from 100 percent:

$$\text{Quoted Futures Price} = 100.0\% - \text{Treasury Bill Futures Yield} \qquad (21.1)$$

Thus, the future's closing price on the December 1988 contract of 93.75 indicates a yield of 6.25 percent; therefore, as yields increase, the price of the futures contract will decline.

Treasury bill yields are based on a one-year bill with a year of 360 days (30 days for each month). Their quoted yields are therefore *annualized* and do not reflect the actual price of the bill. Using the futures contract for December 1988 90-day bills, a one basis-point (.01 percent) change in its price represents a $25 increase in the value of the contract:

$$\binom{\text{basis-point}}{\text{change}} \binom{\text{days to maturity}}{360 \text{ Days}} \binom{\text{delivery value}}{\text{of contract}} = \text{change in value} \qquad (21.2)$$

$$(.0001)(90/360)(\$1,000,000) = \$25.$$

The actual value of the 90-day bills represented in the December 1988 futures contract can be calculated as

$$\begin{aligned}
\text{Actual Value} \atop \text{of Bills} &= \left[1.0 - \frac{\left(\text{days to} \atop \text{maturity} \right) \times \left(1 - \text{quoted} \atop \text{contract price} \right)}{360} \right] \text{delivery value} \atop \text{of contract} \\
&= \left[1.0 - \frac{(90) \times (1.0 - .9375)}{360} \right] \$1,000,000 \qquad (21.3) \\
&= \$984,375.
\end{aligned}$$

Therefore, the reported futures prices for Treasury bill contracts do not represent the dollar value of the Treasury bills represented by the contract.

Assume that a speculator buys the December contract at the quoted price of 93.75 and that market yields do in fact immediately decline. Because of the yield decline, the future's price will increase. The profit to the speculator from a 10-basis-point yield decline can be calculated as

$$(\text{basis-point change})(\$25) = \text{profit} \qquad (21.4)$$

$$(10)(\$25) = \$250.$$

Another way to illustrate the profit to the speculator is to calculate the new value of the Treasury bills using Equation 21.3 (note the quoted contract price of .9385 reflects the 10-basis-point yield decline):

$$\left[1.0 - \frac{90 \times (1.0 - .9385)}{360} \right] \$1,000,000 = \$984,625. \qquad (21.5)$$

The profit represents the $250 increase in the value of bills ($984,625 − $984,375). The easiest way to calculate profit and loss for a Treasury bill future is to use the relationship that a 1-basis-point change in the contract's price equals $25 of gain or loss to the trader.

It may also be useful to calculate the discount yield on the Treasury bills. This procedure is used by practitioners to calculate the annualized yield and is reported in quotations of Treasury bills.

$$\text{discount yield} = \frac{[(\text{face value} - \text{price})(360)]/\text{days to maturity}}{\text{face value}} \qquad (21.6)$$

For a quote of 93.75 for the December contract, with an actual price of $984,375 (Equation 21.3), the discount yield is

$$\frac{[(\$1,000,000 - \$984,375)(360)]/90}{\$1,000,000} = 6.25\%$$

Notice that this procedure uses a 360-day year and ignores compounding. The *effective annualized yield*, considering quarterly compounding, a 365-day year, and the time value of money, would be

$$\text{effective annualized yield} = \left(\frac{\text{face value}}{\text{price}}\right)^{(365/\text{days to maturity})} - 1 \qquad (21.7)$$

$$= \left(\frac{\$1,000,000}{984,375}\right)^{(365/90)} - 1$$

$$= (1.0159)^{4.0556} - 1 = 6.60\%$$

The effective annualized yield is higher than the discount yield because of the effects of compounding over a 365-day year.

Hedging Using Treasury Bill Futures

There are two basic hedging strategies using Treasury bills—a short hedge and a long hedge.

1. SHORT HEDGES A short hedge, used by the investor with a long position in Treasury bills, is designed to protect the long position from increases in yields that might occur before the bills mature or are sold. Ideally, the hedger *writes* (shorts) a futures contract with a face value equal to the value of the long position. If interest rates increase, the values of the long position and the futures contract will decline. Since the hedger is short in the futures contract, however, the position can be closed by buying an identical contract, at a price below the issue price. The difference will be a gain that offsets at least a portion of the loss on the long position. A short hedge strategy is illustrated in Table 21.3.

TABLE 21.3 ILLUSTRATION OF SHORT HEDGE FOR TREASURY BILLS

I. Data:
   Long position: Portfolio of 90-day Treasury bills with face value of $1,000,000 purchased for $984,349 with an *effective annualized yield* of 6.60%
   Short position: *Issue* one Treasury bill futures contract at 94.33
   Assume that the effective annualized yield on Treasury bills increases 15 basis points after the long and short positions are taken.

II. Loss on Long Position in Treasury Bills:
   Calculate the price of the Treasury bills after the yield increase, using Equation 21.7:

$$[1,000,000/\text{Price}]^{365/90} = 1 + \text{effective annualized yield}$$

$$[1,000,000/\text{Price}]^{4.0556} = 1.0675$$

$$1,000,000/\text{Price} = 1.0675^{.2466}$$

$$\text{Price} = \$984,058$$

$$\text{Loss} = \$984,058 - \$984,349 = \$291$$

III. Gain on Short Position in Futures Contract:
   Calculate the gain on futures contract after the yield increase, using Equation 21.4:

$$\text{Gain} = (15)(\$25) = \$375$$

TABLE 21.4 ILLUSTRATION OF LONG HEDGE FOR TREASURY BILLS

I. Data:

Long position: No current position in Treasury bills. However, will invest $984,349 in Treasury bills in 30 days.

Long position: Immediately *purchase* one Treasury bill futures contract for 94.33

Assume that the investor expects Treasury bill yields to *decline* before funds are available to purchase bills.

II. Gain on long position in futures contract:

BASIS-POINT CHANGE IN EFFECTIVE ANNUALIZED YIELD ON TREASURY BILLS	GAIN ON LONG POSITION IN FUTURES CONTRACT (EQUATION 21.4)
−5 basis points	$125
−10	250
−15	375
−20	500

III. The gain on the long position in the futures contract will partly offset the lower yield that will be earned on the Treasury bills because of the delay in their purchase.

There has been considerable research directed toward determining the optimal *hedge ratio*: the number of futures contracts needed to hedge a long position in the underlying asset.[1] Usually it is not possible to form a perfect hedge where all risk is eliminated; futures contracts are not available for all maturities of Treasury bills, and futures contracts are available only for a fixed amount of $1 million. For example, suppose a trader had a long position in 90-day Treasury bills with a $1.5 million maturity value. Should one or two futures contracts be issued?

2. LONG HEDGES A long hedge is used if the investor does not currently have a position in Treasury bills but anticipates going long at some time in the immediate future. This may occur if the hedger expects a large cash inflow within a short period of time. The hedger expects yields to decline prior to buying Treasury bills. How can the hedger "lock in" the higher yields today? The correct strategy is to buy a futures contract immediately. If yields do decline, the value of the long position in the futures contract will increase. This profit will then offset the lower yield that will be earned when the Treasury bills are actually purchased in the future. An example of a long hedge is given in Table 21.4.

---

[1] See, for example, Robert W. Kolb and Raymond Chiang, "Duration, Immunization, and Hedging with Interest Rate Futures," *Journal of Financial Research* (Summer 1982): pp. 161–70; Francis H. Trainer, Jr., "The Uses of Treasury Bond Futures in Fixed-Income Portfolio Management," *Financial Analysts Journal* (January-February 1983): pp. 27–34; Jimmy E. Hilliard, "Hedging Interest Rate Risk with Futures Portfolios under Term Structure Effects," *Journal of Finance* (December 1984): pp. 1547–69; and Alden L. Toevs and David P. Jacob, "Futures and Alternative Hedge Ratio Methodologies," *Journal of Portfolio Management* (Spring 1986): pp. 60–70.

TABLE 21.5 ILLUSTRATIONS OF SPECULATIVE STRATEGIES FOR TREASURY BILL FUTURES

A. Gain on Short Position Strategy:

Sell a Treasury bill futures contract at 93.75 with an initial margin of $2,500. Assume that the yield on Treasury bills *increases* by 20 basis points in one month.

Gain on contract (Equation 21.4): $(20)(\$25) = \$500$

HPR considering leverage: $\$500/\$2500 = 20\%$

Annualized *HPR*: $(1 + .2)^{12} - 1 = 791.61\%$

B. Gain on Long Position Strategy:

Purchase a Treasury bill futures contract at 93.75 with an initial margin of $2,500. Assume that the yield on Treasury bills *decreases* by 20 basis points in one month.

Gain on contract (Equation 21.4): $(20)(\$25) = \$500$
HPR considering leverage: $\$500/\$2500 = 20\%$

Annualized *HPR*: $(1 + .2)^{12} - 1 = 791.61\%$

C. Loss on Long Position Strategy:

Purchase a Treasury bill futures contract at 93.75 with an initial margin of $2,500. Assume that the investor thought that yields would decrease, but they actually *increased* by 20 basis points in one month. The investor closed the position when the minimum maintenance margin was reached ($2,000). Thus, no additional margin was required.

Loss on contract (Equation 21.4): $(20)(\$25) = (\$500)$

HPR considering leverage: $(\$500)/\$2500 = -20\%$

Annualized *HPR*: $(1 - .2)^{12} - 1 = -93.13\%$

Speculating with Treasury Bill Futures

Speculators can also take a short or a long position in Treasury bill futures in anticipation of yield changes. These strategies are illustrated in Table 21.5.

1. SHORT POSITIONS A short position should be taken if the speculator anticipates that yields will increase during the life of the contract. Because of low commission cost (approximately $45 per trade) and the relatively low initial margins (0.25 percent, or .0025 times the face value of the contract), large gains can result from small increases in yields. The speculator will essentially be (a) selling the contract at a "high" price and (b) buying an identical contract at a "low" price (to cancel the short position).

2. LONG POSITIONS A long position is appropriate for speculators in anticipation of yield decreases. The speculator buys a contract (long position) and profits from the increase in the contract's price because of yield declines.

Futures on Notes and Bonds

Contracts are also available on ten-year and long-term Treasury bonds, Government National Mortgage Association mortgage pools, GNMAs, and municipal bonds. The exchanges where these contracts are traded are shown in Table 21.1, and examples of price quotations are presented in Table 21.2. The "price" quotes for the note and bond futures in Table 21.2 are in "points" and thirty-seconds of a point. For example, a quote of 94-30 for a Treasury bond future is equivalent to 94.9375 percent ($\frac{30}{32} = .9375$) of the face value of $100,000. The contract also specifies that the coupon on the underlying Treasury bond is 8 percent.

Another interesting aspect of Treasury bond futures is that the contract writer (short position) can settle the contract by actual delivery of the bonds. This presents something of a problem since only 8 percent coupon bonds with a maturity of 15 years or longer can be delivered. However, many of these long-term bonds may not have an 8 percent coupon. To resolve this problem, there is a complex adjustment procedure to allow the delivery of bonds with different coupons and maturity dates.[2]

Treasury bill futures, as well as note and bond futures have some characteristics that are important to both hedgers and speculators.

1. PRICE VOLATILITY The price of a futures contract is closely correlated with the price of the underlying security or index. Long-term bond prices are more volatile than short-term bond prices. Therefore, prices for futures on long-term bonds are *more* volatile than Treasury bill futures prices. Essentially, the price risk or duration of a bond future is directly related to the duration of the underlying bond.[3]

   A recent empirical study found that both term-to-maturity and quarterly refunding activities by the U.S. Treasury had significant effects on the price variance of bond futures.[4] This study also found that the future's price variance increased as the delivery date approached and that a "distant" contract may have a variance over 350 basis points greater than a "nearby" contract.

2. BASIS RISK Bond futures are also subject to basis risk. As previously discussed in Chapter 20, the basis is the difference between the future's price and the cash or spot price. The basis can increase or decrease during the life of the contract but approaches zero on the delivery date. A change in the basis during the life of the contract represents gains or losses to the trader.

3. LEVERAGE Positions in note and bond futures can be obtained by making the initial margin deposit (less than 5 percent) and maintaining the margin. The low margin requirement and the resulting high degree of leverage cause *HPRs* on futures contracts to be much more sensitive to changes in market yields. In this sense, a long position in a bond future is much riskier than a long position in Treasury bills or notes.

4. LIQUIDITY Because the clearing corporation performs marking to market on a daily basis, traders must maintain adequate liquidity to cover margin calls. Kolb, Gay, and Hunter developed a model to estimate the quantity of cash a trader should maintain.[5] Their model showed that the liquidity pool de-

---

[2] For a discussion of this adjustment procedure, see Francis H. Trainer, Jr., "The Uses of Treasury Bond Futures in Fixed-Income Portfolio Management," *Financial Analysts Journal* (January-February 1983): pp. 31–32.

[3] For the development of the concept of duration for a futures contract, see Gerald D. Gay and Robert W. Kolb, "Interest Rate Futures as a Tool for Immunization," *Journal of Portfolio Management* (Fall 1983): pp. 65–70.

[4] Theodore M. Barnhill, James V. Jordan, and William E. Seale, "Maturity and Refunding Effects on Treasury-Bond Futures Price Variance," *Journal of Financial Research* (Summer 1987): pp. 121–31.

[5] Robert W. Kolb, Gerald D. Gay, and William C. Hunter, "Liquidity Requirements for Financial Futures Investments," *Financial Analysts Journal* (May-June 1985): pp. 60–68.

pended on four factors: (1) the length of time the futures position is to be held; (2) the number of contracts in the position; (3) the investor's acceptable "probability of ruin"; and (4) the volatility of the futures contract. This last factor indicates that greater liquidity is required for trading in Treasury note and bond futures than in Treasury bill futures.

Market Efficiency of Interest Rate Futures

Numerous studies have anlayzed the efficiency of the interest rate futures market, especially that for Treasury bills.[6] Generally, these studies examined the relationship between the spot or cash price and the futures price. Surprisingly, the issue of the extent of market efficiency remains somewhat unresolved, based on the conflicting results from the empirical tests. Some studies concluded that the market was efficient, while other studies found arbitrage opportunities that suggested inefficiencies. A recent paper suggested that the reason the implied rate on Treasury bill futures is below the implied forward rate is *carrying costs* rather than market inefficiencies.[7]

The evidence indicates that some speculators may earn excess returns in the Treasury bill market. The magnitude of these excess returns, however, is likely to be very small. In fact, annualized excess returns may be less than 30 basis points, which, while statistically significant, will not represent large dollar profits unless large sums are invested.

Because of the market collapse in 1987, additional studies are needed on market efficiency. For example, after the stock market collapse, many investors sought safety in Treasury securities. How efficient was the interest rate futures market in reacting to the rapid and unexpected increases in the prices of Treasury notes and bonds?

STOCK INDEX FUTURES

Futures are available on four major stock market indices: (1) S&P 500, (2) NYSE Composite, (3) Value Line Composite Average, and (4) Major Market Maxi Index. The first three are relatively well known. The fourth, however, was developed by the Chicago Board of Trade by creating a portfolio of twenty of the largest companies traded on the NYSE. This contract was developed because Dow Jones & Company refused to allow a contract on the DJIA.

Table 21.6 provides quotations for the four major stock index futures. The "prices" in Table 21.6 are in terms of "points" that represent the level of the index. For example, the close for the December 1988 S&P 500 contract is $255.00. The dollar value of this contract is determined by multiplying the quoted "price" by $500, or $255.00 × $500 = $127,500. A 1-point change in the "price" of the

---

[6] For a review of these studies, see "Robert W. Kolb and Gerald D. Gay, "A Pricing Anomaly in Treasury Bill Futures," *Journal of Financial Research* (Summer 1985): pp. 157–67.

[7] Brian C. Gendreau, "Carrying Costs and Treasury Bill Futures," *Journal of Portfolio Management* (Fall 1985): pp. 58–64.

TABLE 21.6 QUOTATIONS ON STOCK INDEX FUTURES

	Season's			Week's			Net	Open
	High	Low		High	Low	Close	Chg	Int.

Chicago Mercantile Exchange

S&P 500

343.75	181.00	Mar	259.10	250.20	250.70	6.35	113,971
345.90	190.00	Jun	260.60	251.40	252.00	6.55	5,201
341.60	193.00	Sep	261.00	253.00	253.45	6.65	137
260.00	254.30	Dec	260.00	254.30	255.00	6.60	2

Last index 250.96, off 6.11.
Fri. to Thurs. sales 231,785.
Total open interest 119,311.

Kansas City Board of Trade

Value Line

5286.40	170.00	Mar	212.85	206.60	210.70	−.20	1,551
285.80	.20	Jun	212.25	200.90	209.00	+.20	31

Last index 210.92, up .19.
Fri. to Thurs. sales 1,414.
Total open interest 1,582.

Chicago Board of Trade

Major Market Maxi Index

mmi + 250 x index

418.25	368.50	Feb	393.25	378.75	379.10	−9.65	2,118
509.00	330.00	Mar	394.00	379.25	379.50	−9.85	349
397.00	371.00	Apr	394.00	380.75	380.75	−10.00	33
411.25	373.50	Jun	395.25	382.00	382.00	−5.30	18

Last index 379.75, off 10.94.
Fri. to Thurs. sales 24,416.
Total open interest 2,817.

N.Y. Futures Exchange

NYSE Composite

193.00	104.00	Mar	145.45	140.60	140.75	−3.80	3,647
194.60	110.00	Jun	146.20	141.70	141.60	−3.85	1,100
191.40	112.50	Sep	147.05	142.50	142.45	−3.80	433
190.25	117.00	Dec	146.20	145.85	143.30	−3.75	30

Last index 141.35, off 2.78.
Fri. to Thurs. sales 37,410.
Total open interest 5,210.

SOURCE: *Barron's*, 8 February 1988. Courtesy of *Barron's Weekly*.

contract, therefore, represents $500. The $500 constant is also used for the NYSE Composite and Value Line contracts. The Major Market Maxi Index uses a constant of $250.

Stock index futures are similar in many respects to other financial futures. There are some important differences. First, there is no delivery option for a stock index future since there is no deliverable instrument; all delivery settlements are made in cash. Second, stock prices are generally more volatile than bond prices; since futures prices closely follow the prices of the underlying asset, stock index future prices are more volatile than prices on interest rate futures. Third, the prices of stock index futures are more volatile than the underlying indices. To illustrate, a 1986 empirical study of ten contracts on the S&P 500 found that the average standard deviation of daily future price changes was 1.57 versus 1.33 for the index.[8] Fourth, the basis risk on stock index futures is greater than that on interest rate futures.[9] Finally, there are differences in risk between the four major stock index futures. One reason for this is that stocks are not as homogeneous as

[8] Bruce D. Fielitz and Gerald D. Gay, "Managing Cash Flow Risk in Stock Index Futures," *Journal of Portfolio Management* (Winter 1986): pp.74–78.

[9] For a discussion of basis risk on stock index futures, see Stephen Figlewski, "Hedging Performance and Basis Risk in Stock Index Futures," *Journal of Finance* (July 1984): pp. 657–69, and Stephen Figlewski, "Explaining the Early Discounts on Stock Index Futures: The Case for Disequilibrium," *Financial Analysts Journal* (July-August 1984): pp. 43–47.

TABLE 21.7 CORRELATION COEFFICIENTS BETWEEN STOCK INDICES: January 1, 1977
to August 1, 1982

1. Correlation coefficients between *monthly* changes in the indices:

	NYSE	S&P 500	VALUE LINE	DJIA
NYSE	1.000			
S&P 500	0.993	1.000		
Value Line	0.922	0.986	1.000	
DJIA	0.905	0.921	0.857	1.000

2. Correlation coefficients between *weekly* changes in the indices:

	NYSE	S&P 500	VALUE LINE	DJIA
NYSE	1.000			
S&P 500	0.992	1.000		
Value Line	0.844	0.819	1.000	
DJIA	0.869	0.885	0.758	1.000

SOURCE: Richard Zeckhauser and Victor Niederhoffer, "The Performance of Market Index Futures Contracts,"
Financial Analysts Journal (January-February 1983): p.60. Reprinted by permission.

bonds. Thus, stock indices constructed from different types of stocks do not have
equal risk. For example, the S&P 500 includes stocks from the NYSE, AMEX,
and OTC markets; the NYSE Composite includes only stocks traded on that exchange. Table 21.7 provides the correlation coefficients between the four major
indices. Notice that the correlations are all close to 1, but the indices are not
perfectly correlated. The correlations are also sensitive to the period used to
calculate changes in the index values. The correlations calculated from monthly
price changes are slightly higher than the correlations based on weekly price
changes. Since a 1-"point" change in the index represents a $500 change in the
futures value, small differences between price changes in the stock indices can
be significant.

Speculating in Stock Index Futures

Speculating, as opposed to hedging, primarily deals with an anticipated short-term
market movement without an underlying position in common stocks. If a speculator is bullish about stocks in general, the speculator buys (long position) a stock
index future. The advantages of the futures position over a long position in stocks
include lower transaction costs and a lower initial margin. A third advantage is
that the speculator is not concerned about selecting individual stocks. The problem of being correct on the market's direction but incorrect on individual stocks
is eliminated.

A speculator who is bearish on stocks can take a short position. Rather than
shorting individual stocks, however, the speculator can *short the market* by writing
a stock index future.

Hedging Using Stock Index Futures

Many institutional and individual investors use stock index futures to hedge positions in common stocks. The rapid growth in stock index futures trading is primarily a result of this hedging process. This growth suggests that investors are aware of the advantages of using stock index futures in portfolio management decisions.

Before the introduction of index futures in 1982, portfolio management techniques were limited in dealing with nondiversifiable or systematic risk. Diversifiable or nonsystematic risk could essentially be eliminated by adding enough stocks to the portfolio. The beta of the portfolio, however, could be managed only by changing the mix of the portfolio between cash, bonds, or stocks and by adding "low" or "high" beta stocks to the portfolio. The introduction of index futures, however, has increased the ways to manage systematic risk.

To illustrate, assume that a common stock portfolio manager is bearish about stocks in the short run. This suggests that the beta of the portfolio should be reduced. Traditionally, this could be accomplished by selling stocks and investing the proceeds in near-cash or bonds and by selling stocks with high betas. Because of transaction costs and possible institutional restrictions, the portfolio manager had limited flexibility in attempting to hedge against a short-run decline in stock prices. Today, however, a hedge can be constructed by writing index futures. If stocks do in fact decline, the profit on the futures position will offset some or all of the losses on the long stock position. Essentially, by writing the index future, a *negative beta security* has been added to the existing portfolio. The overall beta of the portfolio is therefore reduced. The success of the strategy in reducing losses depends on the ability of the portfolio manager in structuring the hedge. However, it is unlikely that a perfect hedge can be constructed.

Empirical studies have demonstrated the effectiveness of index futures in reducing portfolio risk. For example, a 1984 study found that hedging with index futures could eliminate over 40 percent of the variability in all four stock indices.[10] Hedging with index futures, however, was not as effective as hedging bond portfolios with interest rate futures. The market collapse in October 1987 raises questions about these hedging techniques.

1. PROGRAM TRADING Stock index futures are used in *program trading* strategies employed by pension funds, mutual funds, brokerage firms, and other institutional investors. Program trading is actually *index arbitrage*, involving the simultaneous trading of large blocks of common stocks and opposing positions in stock index futures and/or index options to earn a riskless profit. For example, if index futures or options are priced "high" relative to the underlying stocks, arbitrageurs will write index futures or options and simultaneously buy the common stocks in the underlying index.

   Program trading is also referred to as *computerized trading* since actual trades can be executed with computers. The NYSE's Designated Order Turnaround, DOT, system executes orders for trades of 2,000 shares or less within

---

[10] Joanne M. Hill and Thomas Schneeweis, "Reducing Volatility with Financial Futures," *Financial Analysts Journal* (November-December 1984): pp. 34–40.

three minutes. Larger orders are not guaranteed such quick execution but are generally executed very rapidly. A program trader, therefore, can enter the desired trades in his computer in advance and then transmit the entire order at the appropriate time.

Program trading helps to coordinate or link the futures and stock markets by eliminating any price discrepancies. In this sense, it improves the pricing efficiency in the markets. Because of the October 19, 1987, market crash, however, program trading is under attack. Many critics are blaming program trading for starting the panic that caused the crash. For example, the SEC estimates that 30–68 percent of the trading volume on the NYSE during critical hours on October 19 was due to twelve to fifteen program traders.

Ironically, program trading and other forms of arbitrage did not eliminate pricing discrepancies during the market crash. Figure 21.1 shows the "prices" of the S&P 500 and a S&P 500 index future over the period October 19–23, 1987. Notice the dramatic increase in the basis (futures value − index value) that occurred on October 20 and 22. Normally, the basis is only 2–3 points, with the futures "price" above the S&P 500 index. As the chart indicates, however, the basis became negative and reached a level of over 40 points, which, prior to that time, was considered impossible. This occurred

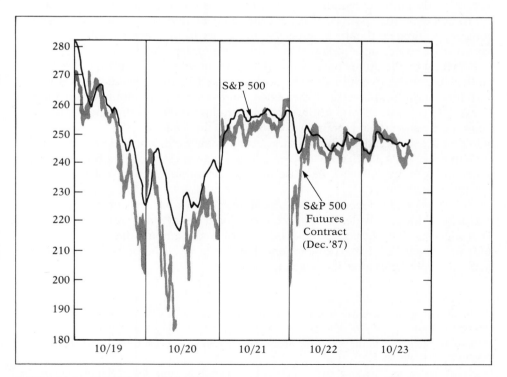

FIGURE 21.1   S&P 500 and S&P 500 futures contracts: October 19–23, 1987
Source: *Barron's* ,26 October 1987, p. 7. Reprinted courtesy of *Barron's Weekly.*

partly because futures traders could not get timely price information on the underlying common stocks and therefore could not correctly price the futures contracts.

2.   PORTFOLIO INSURANCE A second hedging strategy that is being blamed for contributing to the market collapse is *dynamic hedging* or *portfolio insurance*. This technique is designed to protect or insure an underlying stock or bond portfolio against price declines. For example, if common stocks are expected to decline in price, the insurer writes stock index futures. The profit on the futures from the decline in common stocks offsets part or all of the loss on the underlying long position in stocks. During the October crash, portfolio insurers were forced to continue writing futures contracts in an attempt to offset losses on their stock portfolios. Because the Chicago Mercantile Exchange was forced to suspend trading in the S&P 500 futures contracts, the portfolio insurance strategy did not work as expected, and many insurers resorted to selling the stocks in their portfolios, which intensified the market collapse.

Market Efficiency of Stock Index Futures

Studies of the efficiency of the stock index futures market have been limited because of the lack of a price history, since trading only began on February 24, 1982. Several early empirical studies noted that it was common for the futures price, P_F, to be below the spot price, P_S, causing a negative basis.[11] This relationship is contrary to finance theory; it suggests that index futures are biased estimates of future stock prices and implies that futures are undervalued.

Several explanations have been offered about why the basis on index futures tended to be negative initially; reasons suggested include transaction costs, uncertainty and "lumpiness" of dividends, and uncertainty about future interest rates.[12] Also, as investors' knowledge and trading interest continue to increase, market efficiency is likely to improve. "Overall, the evidence points to the conclusion that the stock index futures market is now fairly efficient and becoming more so with time."[13] A 1985 study also concluded that the stock index futures market is becoming more efficient, because of more accurate estimates of the dividend stream of each index.[14]

One major difference between a position in index futures and a long position in stocks is that no dividends are received or paid on an index futures investment. This suggests that because of ex-dividend price adjustments that $P_F < P_S$ and results in a negative basis. To the extent that this is true, the basis can be negative without implying market inefficiencies.

---

[11] For example, see Richard Zeckhauser and Victor Niederhoffer, "The Performance of Market Index Futures Contracts," *Financial Analysts Journal* (January-February 1983): pp. 59–65.

[12] David M. Modest, "On the Pricing of Stock Index Futures," *Journal of Portfolio Management* (Summer 1984): pp. 51–57.

[13] Stephen Figlewski, "Hedging Performance and Basis Risk in Stock Index Futures," *Journal of Finance* (July 1984):p. 669.

[14] Ed Peters, "The Growing Efficiency of Index-Futures Markets," *Journal of Portfolio Management* (Summer 1985): pp. 52–56.

Another approach to explaining the basis uses the idea that index futures offer riskless arbitrage opportunities. In an efficient market, the return on this strategy should be the risk-free rate.[15] Using the riskless arbitrage strategy, it can be shown that the theoretical value of the futures price, P_F, is a function of the spot price, P_S, the risk-free return, R_F, and the dividend yield, D, on the index:

$$P_F = P_S + (R_F - D) \tag{21.8}$$

Generally, the risk-free return is larger than the dividend yield on stocks, so that $R_F - D > 0$. In this case, $P_F > P_S$, and the theoretical basis is positive.

The behavior of the basis during and after the October 1987 market crash has raised questions about the efficiency of the stock index futures market. One obvious issue is the importance of trading mechanisms and regulatory controls in causing apparent pricing inefficiencies. Clearly, additional research is needed on institutional (trading) efficiency and pricing efficiency.

FOREIGN CURRENCY FUTURES

Foreign currency futures were the first financial commodity to be actively traded through a futures market. The Chicago Mercantile Exchange is now the largest currency futures market. Table 21.8 provides an example of quotations for the most actively traded currency futures. The prices for the Canadian dollar contract in Table 21.8 represent the number of U.S. dollars relative to one Canadian dollar. For example, the December 1988 close shows a price of $.7781; the reciprocal, $1.2852, is the number of Canadian dollars per U.S. dollar.

Currency futures, in addition to the forward markets, provide a way to eliminate *currency exchange risk* in international trade and investing (see Chapter 23). For example, a U.S. investor who wants to invest in Japanese stocks must convert dollars to yen to purchase the stocks, then yen to dollars after the stocks are sold. Since the exchange rate between the two currencies is likely to change, the investor is faced with currency exchange risk. If the investor expects the dollar to fall relative to the yen after the stocks are purchased, no hedging strategy is needed since the investor will benefit. However, if the dollar is expected to increase in value relative to the yen, then a currency future can be used to hedge against this risk.

Large international businesses also use currency futures to hedge against exchange risk. For example, a survey of Fortune 500 companies indicated that approximately 20 percent of the responding companies used futures and options to hedge and that the most widely used instruments are Treasury bill and Eurodollar futures.[16] This topic is discussed in more detail in Chapter 23 on international investing.

---

[15] For a more detailed explanation, see Gary Gastineau and Albert Madansky, "S&P 500 Stocks Index Futures Evaluation Tables," *Financial Analysts Journal* (November-December 1983): pp. 68–76.

[16] Stanley B. Block and Timothy J. Gallagher, "The Use of Interest Rate Futures and Options by Corporate Financial Managers," *Financial Management* (Autumn 1986): pp. 73–78.

TABLE 21.8 QUOTATIONS ON CURRENCY FUTURES

Season's		Week's			Net	Open
High	Low	High	Low	Close	Chg	Int.
CANADIAN DOLLAR						
$ per dlr; 1 point equals $0.0001						
.7885	.7052 Mar	.7885	.7806	.7871	+46	21,391
.7852	.7325 Jun	.7852	.7772	.7841	+46	3,616
.7820	.7307 Sep	.7820	.7750	.7811	+46	367
.7807	.7390 Dec	.7807	.7720	.7781	+46	192
.7785	.7570 Mar	.7785	.7705	.7751	+46	48
.7695	.7670 Jun	.7695	.7695	.7721	+46	6
Last spot .7886, up 45.						
Fri. to Thurs. sales 15,362.						
Total open interest 25,620.						
FRENCH FRANC						
$ per franc; 1 point equals $0.00001						
.18600	.16210 Mar	.17520	.17520	.17410	−270	68
.18470	.16260 Jun	.17450	.17340	.17340	−280	34
Last spot .17388, off 272.						
Total open interest 102.						
GERMAN MARK						
$ per mark; 1 point equals $0.0001						
.6426	.5350 Mar	.5973	.5886	.5896	−72	35,323
.6494	.5410 Jun	.6025	.5930	.5946	−74	5,549
.6555	.5609 Sep	.6075	.5995	.5999	−76	183
.6610	.5717 Dec	.6115	.6052	.6055	−77	85
Last spot .5869, off 79.						
Fri. to Thurs. sales 107,801.						
Total open interest 41,140.						
JAPANESE YEN						
$ per yen; 1 point equals $0.000001						
.008320	.006660 Mar	.007855	.007737	.007766	−72	49,922
.008390	.006735 Jun	.007905	.007792	.007817	−74	3,078
.008455	.007075 Sep	.007930	.007855	.007876	−76	147
.008530	.007115 Dec	.008000	.007920	.007934	−76	41
.008590	.007995 Mar	.008065	.007995	.007994	−71	43
Last spot .007730, off 86.						
Fri. to Thurs. sales 122,307.						
Total open interest 53,231.						
MEXICAN PESO						
$ per peso; 1 point equals $0.00001						
No open contracts.						
SWISS FRANC						
$ per franc; 1 point equals $0.0001						
.7955	.6450 Mar	.7335	.7196	.7210	−136	30,184
.8040	.6580 Jun	.7413	.7285	.7296	−130	2,002
.8115	.6950 Sep	.7482	.7370	.7381	−125	93
.8203	.7450 Dec	.7550	.7450	.7461	−130	23
Last spot .7165, off 136.						
Fri. to Thurs. sales 107,472.						
Total open interest 32,302.						
AUSTRAL. DOLLAR						
$ per dlr; 1 point equals $0.0001						
.7274	.6530 Mar	.7110	.7052	.7067	+42	593
.7055	.6660 Jun	.7007	.7007	.6987	+12	150
Last spot .7098, up 30.						
Fri. to Thurs. sales 588.						
Total open interest 743.						

SOURCE: Barron's, 8, February 1988. Reprinted courtesy of Barron's Weekly.

TABLE 21.9 QUOTATIONS FOR OPTIONS ON S&P 500 FUTURES

Season's		Week's			Net	Open
High	Low	High	Low	Close	Chg	Int.

Chicago Mercantile Exchange

S&P 500

CALLS

Mth.	Strike	Vol.	Open Int.	High	Low	Last	Net Change	Futures Close
Mar	88 260	635	1051	10.00	6.25	6.35	− 3.05	250.70
Mar	88 265	300	1033	7.65	4.40	4.35	− 2.85	250.70
Mar	88 270	1164	2900	5.60	3.05	2 80	− 2.55	250.70
Mar	88 280	494	1063	3.00	1.40	1.25	− 1.65	250.70
Mar	88 285	327	564	1.90	.90	.85	− 1.25	250.70
Mar	88 295	448	534	1.00	.40	.35	− .75	250.70
Mar	88 305	351	434	.70	.15	.20	− .50	250.70

PUTS

Mth.	Strike	Vol.	Open Int.	High	Low	Last	Net Change	Futures Close
Mar	88 200	362	1414	1.70	.75	1.45	+ .40	250.70
Mar	88 230	419	1050	5.20	3.40	4.95	+ 1.00	250.70
Mar	88 240	493	1002	8.00	5.00	7.25	+ 1.55	250.70
Mar	88 245	300	437	9.20	6.25	8.80	+ 2.10	250.70
Mar	88 250	505	680	10.50	7.50	10.65	+ 2.40	250.70
Mar	88 255	515	435	13.00	9.50	12.90	+ 2.65	250.70
Mar	88 260	300	287	15.20	11.40	15.60	+ 3.30	250.70
Sep	88 270	424	400	30.50	29.00	31.20	......	253 45

Calls Volume 5,403; Open Int 17,899
Puts Volume 5,230; Open Int 16,938
Volume figures reflect Friday through Thu.
Open Int figures as of close of business Thu.
High and Low Mon. thru Thu., close Fri
Strikes with less than 300 contracts not shown.

SOURCE: Barron's, 8, February 1988. Reprinted courtesy of Barron's Weekly.

Speculators also trade in currency futures. The recent rapid and large changes in the value of the U.S. dollar relative to other currencies have caused large changes in the prices of currency futures. Because of arbitrage activities, currency futures markets are expected to be efficient. A 1986 study, however, found that currency *forward* prices are biased estimates of future spot rates, indicating that the forward market (see Chapters 20 and 23) may not be efficient.[17] Additional studies of the forward and the futures currency markets are needed, especially after the market collapse in 1987.

---

[17] Thomas C. Chiang, "Empirical Analysis on the Predictors of Future Spot Rates," *Journal of Financial Research* (Summer 1986): pp. 153–62.

OPTIONS ON FINANCIAL FUTURES

This section discusses options on financial future contracts such as Treasury securities, currencies, and stock indices; options on indices, debt, currency, and commodities are covered in Chapter 19. Beginning in 1982, the Commodities Futures Trading Commission allowed the futures and stock exchanges to trade options on futures. A call option on the S&P 500 futures contract (or any other financial contract) allows the option holder to obtain a long position in the futures contract at a specified price. The holder of a put option in effect, acquires a short position in the futures contract. The holder of put and call options, however, is not required to exercise the option. If it cannot be favorably exercised, the holder can simply let the option expire. The expiration date of the option is always the delivery date of the underlying futures contract, but the option holder can exercise the option at any time prior to expiration.

Table 21.9 provides examples of quotations for options on the S&P 500 futures. There are seven March 1988 call options on the S&P 500 contract in Table 21.9. Notice that their striking prices range from 260 to 305. For example, consider the March call, with a striking price of 280, that closed at 1.25. If an investor purchases the call, he has the right to acquire one futures contract on the S&P 500 at any time before the March delivery date of the futures contract. The last column in Table 21.9 gives the closing price for the *futures* contract as 250.70. Since each "point" represents $500, the actual price for the call option is $625 (1.25 × $500). The actual value of the S&P 500 as of the date of these quotes is 250.96.

Options on futures can be analyzed using a variation of the Black-Scholes option pricing model presented in Chapter 19.[18] This model was recently tested, using data on options on NYSE and S&P 500 futures contracts.[19] The results of these tests indicated that the model prices were biased estimates of market prices. One factor apparently related to the bias was that the price variance of the underlying futures contract was not constant. The model, however, assumed a stable variance.

A more recent paper developed another model that considered the possibility that the option may be exercised before maturity.[20] Testing the model using data on options on the S&P 500 and German mark futures contracts, the authors found that the model-derived prices had "substantial deviations" from the actual market-determined prices. The size of the deviations and the speed at which they were eliminated by the market (within one trade after the observation), however, indicated that potential profits could not cover transaction costs.

---

[18] Fischer Black, "The Pricing of Commodity Contracts," *Journal of Financial Economics* (January-March 1976): pp. 169–79.

[19] Hun Y. Park and R. Stephen Sears, "Changing Volatility and the Pricing of Options on Stock Index Futures," *Journal of Financial Research* (Winter 1985): pp. 265–74.

[20] Kuldeep Shastri and Kishore Tandon, "An Empirical Test of a Valuation Model for American Options on Futures Contracts," *Journal of Financial and Quantitative Analysis* (December 1986): pp. 377–92.

Based on the models and empirical tests to date, it appears that the market for options on futures is efficient, in the sense that arbitrage profits are not available. An ability to forecast stock market movements accurately, however, could be used profitably, with an index futures strategy or with an option futures strategy.

SUMMARY

Financial futures were introduced to the United States in 1972 but were not readily accepted by investors until stock index futures appeared in 1982. There are also active markets for interest rate futures, currency futures, and options on financial futures. Financial futures are now actively traded on five U.S. markets.

Investors in financial futures may be motivated by speculative or hedging objectives. Speculators are attracted to futures because of low margins and volatile short-term price changes. Hedgers can use futures to reduce the risk of a long or short position in bonds or stocks. Speculating in futures is *extremely risky*; hedging with futures is viewed as a risk-reducing activity.

This chapter illustrated the risk-return characteristics of both hedging and speculating in financial futures, using a long or a short position. Essentially, speculators who anticipate an increase in the price of the financial asset underlying the futures contract will purchase a contract (long position). If the speculator anticipates a decline in price of the underlying asset, a contract will be written by the speculator (short position).

An investor who is attempting to hedge an actual long position in stocks or bonds will write (short) a contract. The securities portfolio will be hedged because the gain on the futures position will offset part or all of the loss on the long position in stocks or bonds.

QUESTIONS

1. Briefly discuss the history of financial futures in the United States.
2. Explain the function of the clearing corporation for the financial futures markets.
3. Discuss the logic and mechanics of long and short hedges for Treasury bills, using financial futures. Can all interest rate risk be eliminated by using a hedge?
4. Explain the concept of "leverage" as it applies to the *HPR*s for speculators in financial futures.
5. Explain the relationship between Treasury bill yields and prices, and a futures contract on Treasury bills. Do the prices of Treasury bills and futures on bills move in the same or opposite direction as yields change?
6. Discuss how stock index futures can be used to hedge a long position in stocks. Also explain how they can be used to hedge a short position in stocks.
7. Table 21.7 illustrates that the correlation coefficients between the four major stock indices are close to 1. Given these high correlations, why are stock index futures traded on all four of these indices?
8. Explain how currency futures can be used to hedge against currency exchange risk.

9. Speculators in currency futures must be aware of potential price changes in two underlying assets. Explain the logic of this statement.

10. Discuss the major characteristics of options on financial futures. Compare and contrast the risk-return characteristics of futures versus options on futures.

PROBLEMS

1. A futures contract for Treasury bills is quoted at 92.50.

   a. Calculate the change in price for the futures contract for each basis point change.

   b. Calculate the actual price of the bills represented by the futures contract.

   c. Calculate the simple annualized yield on the bills that is implied by the futures contract.

   d. Calculate the effective annualized yield on the bills that is implied by the futures contract.

2. Assume that an investor has a long position in 90-day Treasury bills with a face value of $1,000,000 that were purchased for $980,000. A Treasury bill futures contract is available for 93.50.

   a. Calculate the effective annualized yield on the Treasury bills, using the purchase price of $980,000.

   b. Assume that the investor takes a short position in the Treasury bill future:

      (1) Calculate the dollar gains (or losses) on the long and short positions if the effective annual yield *increases* 10 basis points.

      (2) Calculate the dollar gains (or losses) on the long and short positions if the effective annual yield *decreases* 10 basis points.

3. A futures contract on Treasury bills is available for 96.00

   a. Assume that a speculator takes a *short* position in the futures contract with an initial margin of $2,500. Calculate the *HPR*s for each of the following basis-point changes in yields:

BASIS-POINT CHANGE
−10
−5
0
+5
+10

   b. Assume that a speculator takes a long position in the futures contract with an initial margin of $2,500. Calculate the *HPR*s for each of the following basis-point changes in yields:

BASIS-POINT CHANGE
−10
−5
0
+5
+10

4. A futures contract on the S&P 500 is available for 250.00

   a. Assume that a speculator takes a *short* position in the futures contract with an initial margin of $6,000. Calculate the *HPR*s for each of the following point changes in the contract price:

POINT CHANGE
−10
−5
0
+5
+10

   b. Assume that a speculator takes a *long* position in the futures contract with an initial margin of $6,000. Calculate the *HPR*s for each of the following point changes in the contract price:

POINT CHANGE
−10
−5
0
+5
+10

5. A futures contract on Canadian dollars closed at .7882.
   a. Explain this price.
   b. How many Canadian dollars can be purchased by one U.S. dollar, based on the futures price?

REFERENCES

Barnhill, Theodore M., James V. Jordan, and William E. Seale. "Maturity and Refunding Effects on Treasury-Bond Futures Price Variance." *Journal of Financial Research* (Summer 1987): pp. 121–31.

Block, Stanley B., and Timothy J. Gallagher. "The Use of Interest Rate Futures and Options by Corporate Financial Managers." *Financial Management* (Autumn 1986): pp. 73–78.

Chiang, Thomas C. "Empirical Analysis on the Predictors of Futures Spot Rates." *Journal of Financial Research* (Summer 1986): pp. 153–62.

Fielitz, Bruce D., and Gerald D. Gay. "Managing Cash Flow Risks in Stock Index Futures." *Journal of Portfolio Management* (Winter 1986): pp. 74–78.

Figlewski, Stephen. "Explaining the Early Discounts on Stock Index Futures: The Case for Disequilibrium." *Financial Analysts Journal* (July-August 1984): pp. 43–47.

———. "Hedging Performance and Basis Risk in Stock Index Futures." *Journal of Finance* (July 1984): pp. 657–69.

Gastineau, Gary, and Albert Madansky. "S&P 500 Stock Index Futures Evaluation Tables." *Financial Analysts Journal* (November-December 1983): pp. 68–76.

Gay, Gerald D., and Robert W. Kolb. "Interest Rate Futures as a Tool for Immunization." *Journal of Portfolio Management* (Fall 1983): pp. 65–70.

Gendreau, Brian C. "Carrying Costs and Treasury Bill Futures." *Journal of Portfolio Management* (Fall 1985): pp. 58–64.

Grant, Dwight. "Market Index Futures Contracts: Some Thoughts on Delivery Dates." *Financial Analysts Journal* (May-June 1982): pp. 60–63.

———. "How to Optimize with Stock Index Futures." *Journal of Portfolio Management* (Spring 1982): pp. 32–36.

Hill, Joanne M., and Thomas Schneeweis. "Reducing Volatility with Financial Futures." *Financial Analysts Journal* (November-December 1984): pp. 34–40.

Hilliard, Jimmy E. "Hedging Interest Rate Risk with Futures Portfolios under Term Structure Effects." *Journal of Finance* (December 1984): pp. 1547–69.

Kolb, Robert W., and Gerald D. Gay. "Immunizing Bond Portfolios with Interest Rate Futures." *Financial Management* (Summer 1982): pp. 81–89.

———. "A Pricing Anomaly in Treasury Bill Futures." *Journal of Financial Research* (Summer 1985): pp. 157–67.

Kolb, Robert W., Gerald D. Gay, and William C. Hunter. "Liquidity Requirements for Financial Future Investments." *Financial Analysts Journal* (May-June 1985): pp. 60–68.

Kolb, Robert W., and Raymond Chiang. "Duration, Immunization, and Hedging with Interest Rate Futures." *Journal of Financial Research* (Summer 1982) pp. 161–70.

Leibowitz, Martin L. "A Yield Basis for Financial Futures." *Financial Analysts Journal* (January-February 1981): pp. 42–51.

Little, Patricia Knain. "Financial Futures and Immunization." *Journal of Financial Research* (Spring 1986): pp. 1–12.

Modest, David M. "On the Pricing of Stock Index Futures." *Journal of Portfolio Management* (Summer 1984): pp. 51–57.

Niederhoffer, Victor, and Richard Zeckhauser. "Market Index Futures Contracts." *Financial Analysts Journal* (January-February 1980): pp. 49–55.

Nordhauser, Fred. "Using Stock Index Futures to Reduce Market Risk." *Journal of Portfolio Management* (Spring 1984): pp. 56–62.

Park, Hun Y., and R. Stephen Sears. "Changing Volatility and the Pricing of Options on Stock Index Futures." *Journal of Financial Research* (Winter 1985): pp. 265–74.

Peters, Ed. "The Growing Efficiency of Index-Futures Markets." *Journal of Portfolio Management* (Summer 1985): pp. 52–56.

Shastri, Kuldeep, and Kishore Tandon. "An Empirical Test of a Valuation Model for American Options on Futures Contracts." *Journal of Financial and Quantitative Analysis* (December 1986): pp. 377–92.

Simpson, W. Gary, and Timothy C. Ireland. "The Impact of Financial Futures on the Cash Market for Treasury Bills." *Journal of Financial and Quantitative Analysis* (September 1985): pp. 371–79.

Toevs, Alden L., and David P. Jacob. "Futures and Alternative Hedge Ratio Methodologies." *Journal of Portfolio Management* (Spring 1986): pp. 60–70.

Trainer, Francis H. Jr. "The Uses of Treasury Bond Futures in Fixed-income Portfolio Management." *Financial Analysts Journal* (January–February 1983): pp. 27–34.

Zeckhauser, Richard, and Victor Niederhoffer "The Performance of Market Index Futures Contracts." *Financial Analysts Journal* (January-February 1983): pp. 59–65.

CHAPTER 22

PRECIOUS METALS, REAL ESTATE, AND COLLECTIBLES

INTRODUCTION

Traditionally, investment analysis and portfolio management dealt almost exclusively with financial assets. There are numerous valuation and portfolio management techniques for bonds, common stocks, options, futures, and other types of financial assets. Since the late 1970s, however, there has been growing interest in extending traditional investment analysis to include *real* or *tangible* assets such as real estate, diamonds, and gold.[1]

Several developments encourage the inclusion of real assets in the investment analysis process. First, the historically high inflation of the late 1970s and early 1980s increased interest in investments that might provide better hedges against inflation. Bond returns during much of this period were below the rate of inflation, resulting in a negative real rate of return. The return on common stocks was also low relative to the rate of inflation. During this period, however, gold, silver, real estate, and other real asset prices increased dramatically. Do real assets provide an effective hedge against inflation? If the average investor accepts this hypothesis and buys real assets prior to or during inflationary periods there will be a self-fulfilling prophecy: real asset prices would increase rapidly before and during an inflationary period.

The second development that has increased investor interest in real assets is the application of modern portfolio management techniques. In a portfolio analysis framework, potential investments are viewed in terms of their impact on the portfolio. There is a growing body of empirical evidence that real assets can have a very positive impact on a portfolio of financial assets.

Should real assets be included in an investment portfolio? Portfolio theory indicates that if the investments are not perfectly correlated, adding them to the portfolio reduces risk. In a practical sense, however, there are costs associated with adding assets to a portfolio. The real question is, Do the benefits from adding real assets to a portfolio exceed the cost? This question was analyzed in terms of financial assets in a 1980 article by Bierman and is discussed in detail in this chapter.[2]

An alternative viewpoint is that the interest in real assets is a passing fad.[3] Over the long term, bonds and stocks will provide adequate returns and a hedge against inflation; therefore, real assets are not needed.

The purpose of this chapter is to discuss the investment characteristics of three popular real assets: precious metals, real estate, and collectibles. Investment characteristics, investment strategies, and portfolio considerations will be presented for each.

---

[1] See, for example, Larry E. Wofford and Edward A. Moses, "The Relationship between Capital Markets and Real Estate Investment Yields: Theory and Application," *Real Estate Appraiser and Analyst* (November-December 1978): pp. 51–61, and Larry E. Wofford, Edward A. Moses, and John M. Cheney, "Using Capital Market Theory in Real Estate Appraisal: Evidence from Securities Markets," *Real Estate Appraiser and Analyst* (Fall 1982): pp. 34–39.

[2] Harold Bierman, Jr., "How Much Diversification is Desirable?" *Journal of Portfolio Management* (Fall 1980) pp. 42–44.

[3] Robert M. Lovell, Jr., "Alternative Investments, "*Financial Analysts Journal* (May-June 1980) pp. 19–21.

PRECIOUS METALS

Introduction

A widely discussed, and at times popular and glamorous, alternative investment is precious metals. The most popular metals for investment purposes are gold and silver. However, other metals—such as copper, aluminum, platinum, and palladium—attract some attention, primarily through trading in commodity futures. This section will primarily concentrate on gold with an occasional reference to silver. Most of the discussion of gold also applies to silver.

Gold has an interesting investment history. It has served as a medium of exchange and as a store of wealth since the early civilizations of Egypt and Rome. Beginning in the 1800s, industrialized nations used gold reserves to back their currencies and adopted the *gold standard*. The gold standard defined a fixed value for an ounce of gold relative to a currency. The gold standard was strengthened in 1944 when the United States agreed at the Bretton Woods Conference to a *gold exchange standard* that fixed the value of gold at $35 per ounce and redeemed dollars for gold at that price. In 1971, the official value of an ounce of gold in the United States was raised to $38, and to $42.22 in 1973. During this time, however, U.S. investors were not legally allowed to invest directly in gold. On January 1, 1975, restrictions on holding gold were abolished, and investor/speculator interest in gold since then has often been almost fanatical.

Another factor in gold's popularity was the high rate of inflation in the United States during the late 1970s and early 1980s. Historically, gold has always been viewed as an inflationary hedge. Fear of inflation and its impact on financial assets is often cited as the primary reason that the price of gold reached an all-time high of $850 an ounce on January 12, 1980. As inflation rates have declined, so has the price of gold. From 1982 to late 1987, the price of gold fluctuated between $300–$500 per ounce and finally broke $500 in November 1987.

Many gold "bugs" were surprised and possibly disappointed about gold's price behavior after the stock market collapse on October 19, 1987. On October 19, the price of gold increased by $10.10 to $481.75 per troy ounce but fell to $463.20 by the end of the next day. In October 1988, the price was approximately $395 per ounce.

Ways to Invest in Gold

1. NUMISMATIC COINS Prices are determined by rarity, condition, and beauty.

2. BULLION COINS The readily available and popular coins include the South African Krugerrand, Canadian Maple Leaf, Mexican Peso, Austrian Crown—and, beginning in 1986, the American Eagle. Because of the popularity and success of gold coins, other countries have introduced coins; these include Australia's Nugget, Britain's Britannia, Belgium's Ecu, and China's Panda. Coin prices are provided in *Barron's*, and Table 22.1 provides a sample of their quotations which include the dollar and percentage premiums of the coins.

3. BULLION Bullion represents a large quantity of gold that requires transport, storage, and possible insurance costs.

TABLE 22.1 PRICE QUOTATIONS AND PREMIUMS ON GOLD COINS

| COINS | PRICE | PREMIUM | |
		PER COIN	GOLD VALUE
Krugerrand	$477.00	$ 2.50	.53%
Maple Leaf	490.00	15.50	3.27
Mexican 1 oz.	476.60	2.50	.53
Mexican Peso	593.00	29.95	3.66
Austria Crown	465.25	.15	.03
U.S. Eagle '86	490.00	15.50	3.27
U.S. Eagle '87	490.00	15.50	3.27

Premium is the amount over the value of the gold content in the coin.

Mocatta spot gold price $474.50

SOURCE: Barron's, 1 January 1988, p. 154. Reprinted courtesy of *Barron's Weekly.*

4. GOLD CERTIFICATES   These are issued by financial institutions that have bullion as collateral for the certificates.

5. COMMON STOCK OF GOLD-MINING COMPANIES Table 22.2 provides a list of publicly traded gold-mining companies operating primarily in North America. In addition, a number of gold-mining stocks are traded on the Johannesburg Stock Exchange. As one would expect, common stock prices of gold-mining companies are closely correlated with the price of gold.

There is limited evidence that gold shares are superior investments to bullion for U.S. investors.[4] Gold-mining companies, however, typically have high degrees of operating and financial leverage. Also, as Table 22.2 illustrates, their P/E ratios often reach very high levels prior to and during periods when gold prices are increasing.

6. FUTURES AND OPTIONS Gold futures are actively traded on the New York Commodity Exchange and less actively on the Chicago Mercantile Exchange. A gold futures contract represents 100 troy ounces of gold. The issuer of the contract promises to deliver 100 troy ounces of gold, at a specified price, at some time in the future. The contract buyer agrees to a price today for delivery of the gold in the future. Call and put options on gold futures are traded on the New York Comex. (See Chapter 20 for a discussion of commodity futures, Chapter 21 for a discussion of options on futures.)

7. COMMODITY-BACKED BONDS A limited number of corporations recently issued bonds whose coupons and/or maturity values are indexed to the price of specific commodities such as gold or silver. For example, Sunshine Mining Company's bond has a maturity value of $1,000 *or* the market price of 50 troy ounces of silver, whichever is higher. An analysis of this bond, using the Black-Scholes option pricing methodology, concluded that the bond was

---

[4] Kevin J. Carter, John F. Affleck-Graves, and Arthur H. Money, ''Are Gold Shares Better than Gold for Diversification?'' *Journal of Portfolio Management* (Fall 1982): pp. 52–55.

TABLE 22.2 NORTH AMERICAN GOLD MINING STOCKS

	PRICE/EARNINGS RATIOS			
	DECEMBER 1984	DECEMBER 1985	DECEMBER 1986	DECEMBER 1987
1. New York Stock Exchange:				
a. Campbell Red Lake Mines	30.0	40.0	25.0	N/A
b. Dome Mines	d	46.0	31.0	N/A
c. Freeport-McMoRan Gold	N/A	164.3	47.0	8.0
d. Homestake Mining	29.0	58.0	63.0	12.0
e. LAC Minerals	N/A	32.0	21.0	29.0
f. Newmont Gold	25.0	d	62.0	54.0
2. American Stock Exchange:				
a. Dickenson Mines Limited	N/A	N/A	23.0	50.0
b. Echo Bay Mines	16.0	26.0	34.0	52.0
c. Giant Yellow Knife Mines	33.0	13.0	13.0	10.0
d. Placer Dome*	–	–	–	20.0
e. St. Joe Gold	N/A	N/A	42.0	41.0
3. Over-the-Counter Market:				
a. Agnico-Eagle Mines	30.0	35.0	90.0	24.0
b. Battle Mountain Gold	N/A	d	35.0	28.0
c. Lacana Mining	23.0	98.0	d	15.0
d. Silver State Mining	d	d	19.0	29.0
4. Toronto Stock Exchange:				
a. International Corona Resources	d	d	d	N/A

* Company formed by merger of Campbell Red Lake Mines and Dome Mines. d = deficit or negative earnings per share. N/A = Price or earnings not reported in Standard & Poor's *Stock Guide.*
SOURCE: Standard & Poor's *Stock Guide,* various issues. Reprinted by permission.

undervalued because of the "option" provided to investors from the indexed maturity value.[5] To the extent that the market underprices commodity-backed bonds, active investment strategies could be developed to "beat the market."

8. MUTUAL FUNDS By the end of the first quarter of 1987, Wiesenberger Investment Companies Service reported that there were fourteen mutual funds that specialized in gold and precious metals. There funds offer an alternative way to invest in gold and silver and can be used in a passive investment strategy.

Investment Characteristics of Gold

Since the commodity gold is not an income-producing investment, the holding period return, *HPR*, consists only of capital gains or losses. If, on the other hand, the investment takes the form of common stock of gold-mining companies that may pay a cash dividend, the *HPR* may include dividends as well as capital gains. Table 22.3 provides a comparison of the *HPR*s on gold, Treasury bills, and the S&P 500 from January 1, 1975, to May 1, 1987. The annualized *HPR*s over the 12.33 years for gold was 7.47 percent, compared to 8.42 and 17.70 percent

[5] Greggory A. Brauer and R. Ravichandran "How Sweet Is Silver?" *Journal of Portfolio Management* (Summer 1986) pp. 33–41.

TABLE 22.3 HOLDING PERIODS RETURNS ON GOLD, U.S.
TREASURY BILLS, AND S&P 500

	VALUE ON MAY 1, 1987 OF $1 INVESTED ON JANUARY 1, 1975	ANNUAL *HPR*
Gold	$2.43	7.47%
U.S. Treasury Bills	2.71	8.42
S&P 500	7.46	17.70

SOURCE OF VALUES: *Fortune*, 22 June 1987, p. 169. Reprinted by permission.

TABLE 22.4 RETURNS AND RISK FOR
GOLD AND SILVER

	HOLDING PERIOD RETURNS	
	GOLD	SILVER
1978	33.3%	27.0%
1979	126.5	361.3
1980	14.5	−44.1
1981	−31.6	−47.3
1982	13.9	32.1
1983	−16.5	−17.9
1984	−19.2	−28.9
1985	6.9	−8.3
1986	20.4	−7.9
1987	21.9	24.6
Arithmetic mean	17.01%	29.06%
Geometric mean	11.04%	3.43%
Standard deviation	43.72%	120.15%
Coefficient of variation	2.57	4.13

SOURCE: Return and risk measures calculated on per-troy-ounce base prices reported by Handy and Harman.

for Treasury bills and the S&P 500, respectively (the *HPR* on the S&P 500 does not include returns from dividends).

Table 22.4 provides the annual *HPR*s, arithmetic and geometric means, standard deviations, and coefficients of variation for gold and silver over the period 1978–1987. Notice that the *HPR*s for gold and silver are closely correlated. Also, notice the large differences in the arithmetic and geometric means, caused by the very volatile *HPR*s. For comparison purposes the arithmetic mean and standard deviation of the S&P 500 over the same period were 15.69 and 12.22 percent, respectively.

Herbst found that for the period 1952–1976, the *real* or inflation-adjusted annual *HPR*s for gold and common stocks were almost equal—2.28 and 2.58 percent, respectively.[6] The historical record indicates that the annualized *HPR* for gold, calculated over a relatively long period, is below the *HPR* for common stocks, in both nominal and real terms. However, for shorter periods, gold returns

---

[6] Anthony F. Herbst, "Gold versus U.S. Common Stocks: Some Evidence on Inflation Hedge Performance and Cyclical Behavior," *Financial Analysts Journal* (January-February 1983) pp. 66–74.

can be much higher or lower than stock returns. For example, during the inflationary period 1971–1976, the annualized *real HPR* on gold was 16.82 percent, compared to 10.46 percent for common stocks.[7]

As the ex-post *HPR*s imply, gold investments have some interesting risk characteristics. A study by Sherman of the five-year period ending December 31, 1981, reported the following results:[8]

1. Using the S&P 500 as the market proxy, the beta for gold is below 1 while the alpha is positive. The correlation with stocks is "very low." The beta indicates a low level of systematic risk, and the positive alpha indicates risk-adjusted excess returns.

2. Using the Salmon Brothers Index of high-grade corporate bonds as the market proxy, the gold beta is below 1, and the alpha is positive. The correlation with bonds is "nil."

Sherman summarized his empirical analysis by stating that "the price of gold is less volatile than are the prices for stocks and bonds and gives somewhat greater rewards for good market timing."[9] Despite the apparent low level of systematic risk, gold returns exhibited considerable unsystematic risk relative to stocks.

The study by Herbst, over a much longer period of time (1940 through 1976), found that the beta for gold was very unstable. The betas were calculated using *real HPR*s, with the Dow Jones Industrial Average representing the market proxy. Herbst found that for thirty-three five-year time spans from 1940 through 1976, the beta for gold was negative for six of the thirty-three periods. The betas ranged from −1.283 (1972–1976) to 1.097 (1966–1970).

The results from the Herbst and Sherman studies should be used cautiously, however, because of the market proxy problem, discussed in Chapters 6–8.

One historical disadvantage of investing in gold coins or bullion is the relatively high transactions costs. In early 1988, however, a number of discount brokers began offering precious metals through brokerage accounts. For example, Fidelity Brokerage Services, Inc, will handle minimum trades of $2,500 for a commission of 2.9 percent that declines to .99 percent for trades over $250,000. If precious metals are purchased through a brokerage account, the Securities Investor Protection Corporation, SIPC, does not insure the precious metals. Storage fees are charged if the investor leaves the metals with the brokerage firm. If an investor elects to take delivery of the metals, they are subject to delivery charges and (possibly) sales and use taxes. Precious metals are not marginable, and transactions must be settled in two business days.

Reasons for Investing in Gold

This section summarizes the reasons for including gold and silver in investment portfolios. Gold and silver have essentially the same investment characteristics;

---

[7] Herbst, p. 68.

[8] Eugene J. Sherman, "Gold: A Conservative, Prudent Diversifier," *Journal of Portfolio Management* (Spring 1982): pp. 21–27.

[9] Sherman, p. 23.

consequently, the same investment strategies can be applied to both. One major difference, however, is relative value; silver prices are much lower than gold prices. Traders often watch the ratio of gold to silver prices as a possible indication of over- or underpricing of one metal relative to the other.

1. INFLATION HEDGE Over short periods, gold provides an alternative to financial assets because it may increase in value faster than the rate of inflation. This was the case during the late 1970s and early 1980s. Over a longer time, however, "the historical evidence simply does not support the conclusion that, over the long run, gold is superior to common stocks as an inflation hedge."[10]

2. CONFIDENCE HEDGE Gold is often viewed as an "insurance" investment that would "pay off" if there was a collapse of the international monetary system. Fortunately, there has never been a test of this hypothesis in the United States. It is common for investment advisors to recommend that some percentage of a portfolio's assets be invested in gold, as "insurance."[11] The percentage may vary from 5 to 50 percent, depending on the confidence the advisor has in the health of the international economy and monetary system.

3. SPECULATION The extreme short-term price variability of gold relative to financial assets provides opportunities for market timing. To be successful, however, an investor would need to forecast correctly the rate of inflation, changes in the value of the U.S. dollar, and investor confidence in the world economy. These are the major factors most commonly cited as demand determinants for gold and silver, and consequently they have a major influence on prices. An analysis of supply factors is usually not as extensive, since the supply of gold is relatively constant. The supply is primarily controlled by five gold-producing nations: South Africa, USSR, Canada, United States, and Australia. These nations, however, time their sales of newly mined gold to exploit short-term price movements.

    In addition to a macroeconomic demand analysis, there is some evidence in the literature that some form of technical analysis (see Chapter 12) or time series analysis may be appropriate. For example, a study of daily prices of gold over the period February 5, 1969, through March 31, 1980, found "persistent dependence" in the time series that was both statistically and economically significant.[12] This suggests that a historical cyclical analysis may be helpful in developing timing strategies.

    Short-term market timing may be accomplished through the use of gold futures contracts, traded on the New York Commodity Exchange and Chicago Mercantile Exchange. Contracts are available with delivery dates up to two years. Despite their relatively short lives, gold contracts require a small margin relative to the value of the contract (100 troy ounces) and therefore offer considerable leverage. Call and put options on gold futures are available on the New York Comex.

---

[10] Herbst, p. 72

[11] For example, see John J. Curran. "How Good a Hedge Is Gold? *Fortune*, 22 June 1987, p. 70.

[12] G. Geoffrey Booth, Fred R. Kaen, and Peter E. Koveos, "Persistent Dependence in Gold Prices," *Journal of Financial Research* (Spring 1982): pp. 85–93.

4.   PORTFOLIO CONSIDERATIONS Any investment strategy should be considered in term of its impact on the overall portfolio. Using this viewpoint, gold is often recommended as a valuable addition to a portfolio of stocks and bonds. For example, the previously cited study by Sherman found that over the period 1977–1981, gold proved to be an "effective diversifier" and improved portfolio returns in almost all types of environments.[13] Its contribution to a portfolio of financial assets was extremely valuable since it improved returns and reduced risk. An alternative view, however, is that economic conditions during the late 1970s and early 1980s were unique and are not likely to be repeated.[14] Thus, without this unique environment, gold and silver are unlikely to provide significant benefits to a portfolio.

However, a number of factors reduce the attractiveness of gold. First, the liquidity of gold is less than that of other investments, such as stocks and bonds, since it is not traded on an organized exchange like the NYSE. Second, transaction costs for precious metals are generally higher than those for financial assets. Finally, delivery, storage, and safekeeping costs can be significant.

REAL ESTATE

Introduction

It has been estimated that the value of real estate represents 50 percent of the total value of the portfolio comprising U.S. assets and 33 percent of the portfolio comprising all assets.[15] As an investment, real estate has characteristics of both fixed-income and equity securities. Rental income provides a yield similar to the coupon yield on a bond, while changes in the value of the property provide capital gains or losses similar to those on common stock.

Traditionally, real estate has not been viewed as a viable investment by portfolio managers who deal primarily in financial assets such as stocks and bonds. One explanation for the exclusion of real estate is that "there seems to be a cultural gap between people who understand real estate and the stock and bond people."[16] Based on growing empirical evidence that real estate can be a valuable addition to a portfolio, this section of the chapter discusses the investment characteristics of real estate and suggests some strategies for individuals.

Real estate markets are becoming *institutionalized* because of the increased interest of mutual funds, real estate investment trusts, and other instutional investors. These institutions are becoming much more important in real estate markets in much the same way that financial institutions have greatly influenced

---

[13] Sherman, p. 25.

[14] Anthony and Edward Renshaw, "Does Gold Have a Role in Investment Portfolios?" *Journal of Portfolio Management* (Spring 1982): pp. 28–31.

[15] James R. Webb and Jack H. Rubens, "How Much in Real Estate? A Surprising Answer," *Journal of Portfolio Management* (Spring 1987): p.10.

[16] Quotation in Webb and Rubens, p. 14.

the bond and stock markets. "Institutionalization" should increase investment opportunities for individual investors.

Ways to Invest in Real Estate

Traditionally, individual investors made direct investments in real estate by buying specific properties. Of course, this avenue is still available, but because of institutional developments and the institutionalization of the real estate market, other ways to invest are available.

1. LIMITED PARTNERSHIPS Real estate syndications have traditionally taken the limited partnership form. This allows revenues and expenses to be "passed through" to individual investors for tax purposes. The investors, limited partners as opposed to the general partner, have limited liability. A limited partnership interest is typically sold in units of $5,000 to $10,000. Syndicators may be brokerage firms, specialized real estate companies operating on a national scale, or even individuals.

   Besides offering the small investor an opportunity to invest in real estate, limited partnerships were often marketed as excellent tax shelters. Because of accelerated depreciation, interest expense, and operating expense deductions, limited partners could be provided with tax-deductible losses of $2 to $4 for each $1 invested. The tax reforms of 1976, 1981, 1984, and 1986, however, have essentially eliminated these "abusive" shelters. Limited partnerships are now marketed for their potential returns rather than strictly as tax shelters. Many investment advisors recommend limited partnerships in real estate as appropriate IRA investments.[17] Since an IRA has a tax-free status for investment income, potential returns dominate the investment decision.

   Traditionally, one major disadvantage of a limited partnership interest was that it had little if any marketability since there was usually no secondary market for these investments. The investor is usually forced to hold the investment until the partnership is liquidated by a sale of the real estate. This may take seven to twelve years, or even longer. One reason for the lack of a secondary market is that the fair market value of the partnership interest is difficult to determine; The value of the partnership interest depends on the value of the underlying real estate, and the market value of the real estate cannot be easily determined by an individual investor until the property is actually sold. Recently, however, some larger partnerships are providing a secondary market.

   Another major disadvantage of a limited partnership is the fee of the syndicator and/or general partner. It is common for investors in limited partnerships to incur sales charges of 7 to 10 percent in addition to the syndicator's fee, with a total cost of 15–25 percent. These costs are much higher than transaction costs for stock and bond investments. Any publicly offered partnership must be registered with the SEC, and potential investors must be given a prospectus. A careful review of the prospectus should be made to

---

[17] For example, see Lynn Asinof, "Limited Partnerships Give IRA Investors Opportunity to Diversify Their Portfolios," *Wall Street Journal*, 17 Jan. 1984, p. 47.

determine the sales charges and other fees. These fees are often concealed in the prospectus and can be discovered only by careful analysis.

2. REAL ESTATE INVESTMENT TRUSTS (REITs) These companies had their beginning in legislation enacted in 1960 that provided a corporate income tax exemption for qualified REITs investing in real estate. Income is distributed to the stockholders with the trust incurring no tax liability. Thus, the dividend yields of REITs is higher than those of typical common stocks. REITS may invest in real estate in several ways, including lending funds for construction purposes, providing intermediate- and long-term mortgages on properties, buying equity positions in property, and combinations of these activities. They may also restrict investments to specific purposes, such as investing in run-down shopping malls or developing and managing mini-warehouses.

One major advantage of REITs is liquidity; their stocks are traded on the organized exchanges or the OTC market. This provides investors with liquidity that may not be available in a direct investment in real estate.

Despite the fact that REITs invest in real estate, their stocks can be quite risky because of high degrees of financial and operating leverage and major cycles in the overall real estate market. For example, during the recession of 1974–1975, many REITs experienced severe financial problems, and a number of REITs declared bankruptcy.

Despite these earlier problems and significant tax changes in 1984 and 1986, REITs are gaining in popularity with investors and provide a viable investment opportunity. Table 22.5 provides financial information on a sample

TABLE 22.5 SAMPLE OF REAL ESTATE INVESTMENT TRUSTS (REITs)

	1985			1986			1987		
	EPS	P/E	DIVIDEND YIELD	EPS	P/E	DIVIDEND YIELD	EPS	P/E	DIVIDEND YIELD
1. Americana	$(0.41)	d	11.9%	$(0.42)	d	–	$0.20	NMF	–
2. BRE Properties	2.29	12.8	8.0	4.12	7.1	8.2%	2.52	12.3	7.7%
3. Federal Realty	0.87	17.3	6.7	1.26	15.2	5.5	0.50	44.0	5.2
4. First Union	1.33	14.5	6.9	1.40	16.7	6.6	1.43	17.3	6.1
5. HRE Properties	2.01	12.6	8.9	1.94	11.0	9.1	1.52	15.7	8.1
6. L&N Housing	3.02	9.5	10.2	2.23	12.9	8.5	1.98	10.3	11.7
7. L&N Mortgage	2.49	8.8	11.0	2.62	10.8	10.1	2.49	11.3	8.3
8. MGI Properties	1.62	11.2	8.5	1.64	12.0	8.2	1.81	11.1	9.9
9. Mony Real Estate	0.92	9.0	9.9	0.79	11.6	9.6	0.69	14.0	8.7
10. Mtge. & Rlty. Trust	1.78	10.4	9.7	2.13	9.3	10.8	1.72	11.9	9.2
11. Property Capital	1.53	13.1	7.7	1.87	11.5	7.6	2.71	9.2	6.7
12. Santa Anita Rlty.	2.06	11.6	8.1	1.58	18.0	7.1	(0.65)	d	6.9
13. Wells Fargo Mtg.	2.45	10.5	10.9	2.42	10.6	11.0	1.52	16.1	9.8

d = deficit or negative earnings per share

NMF = no meaningful figure

SOURCE: *Value Line Investment Survey*, 12 February 1988, pp. 1171–83. © 1988 by Value Line, Inc.; used by permission of Value Line, Inc.

of REITs traded on the NYSE and AMEX. This sample represents some of the largest companies, but there are over 150 publicly traded REITs, many of these traded in the OTC market.

3. MUTUAL FUNDS National Securities' National Real Estates Stock Fund and Fidelity Real Estate Investment Portfolio are two mutual funds that invest in real estate through REITs. In buying shares in these mutual funds, an investor is actually buying an ownership interest in a diversified portfolio of REITs. Both of these open-ended funds charge a purchase or "load" fee (see Chapter 24). The open-ended feature provides liquidity.

Other larger mutual funds are beginning to offer real estate portfolios in their "family" of funds. In 1985, T. Rowe Price offered the Realty Income Fund I, organized as a limited partnership. This offering was unique; no sales fee was charged, and no leverage (borrowing) was used to purchase the real estate. These characteristics qualify the partnership as an IRA investment. As with most limited partnerships, however, there is a very limited secondary market for the partnership interest. Based on the success of the first two offerings, T. Rowe Price completed the sale of Realty Fund III in 1987.

Investment Analysis of Real Estate

Income-producing real estate can be analyzed with many of the tools and techniques previously discussed in this text. This section presents a brief discussion of two discounted cash-flow techniques and provides an illustration of this approach. In addition to these two techniques, real estate appraisers use a variety of other models and procedures that are beyond the scope of this text.

1. DISCOUNTED CASH FLOW MODEL The discounted cash-flow model, DCFM, calculates the present value of the annual after-tax cash flows and reversion value, using the investor's after-tax required rate of return. Typically, real estate is financed with both debt and equity capital, but the DCFM is usually defined to calculate the investment value of the equity.

The after-tax cash flow for period t, CF_t, is defined as:

$$CF_t = NOI_t - DS_t - T_t \tag{22.1}$$

where NOI_t = net operating income for period t

DS_t = debt service for period t including interest expense and amortization of principal

T_t = tax liability in period t

The estimate of NOI over the life of the investment includes all revenues and expenses for the property, such as rent income, maintenance, and management fees. NOI is calculated, however, before debt service and taxes. In calculating the income tax liability, the principal payments on debt are not tax deductible, but interest expense and depreciation changes are deductible.

The reversion value, RV, expected selling price at the end of the investment holding period, is estimated, since most investors do not anticipate holding the real estate indefinitely. RV is defined as

$$RV_n = SP_n - T_n - E_n - D_n \tag{22.2}$$

where RV_n = reversion value at period n

SP_n = selling price at period n

T_n = taxes incurred on the sale

E_n = expenses incurred such as brokerage fees when the property is sold

D_n = remaining mortgage or debt at time of sale

Combining the after-tax cash flow and reversion value, the investment value of the equity interest can be defined as

$$V_E = \sum_{t=1}^{n} \frac{CF_t}{(1 + K_e)^t} + \frac{RV_n}{(1 + K_e)^n} \tag{22.3}$$

where V_E = investment value of equity interest

K_e = investor's after-tax required rate of return on equity

CF_t = after-tax cash flow for period t

RV_n = after-tax reversion value at period n

Equation 22.3 is very similar to the bond valuation models presented in Chapter 15.

2. NET PRESENT VALUE MODEL The estimate of the equity value, V_e, as determined by Equation 22.3, can be used to compute the net present value, NPV, of the real estate investment:

$$NPV = V_E - PP_0 \tag{22.4}$$

where PP_0 = purchase price of the property

If $NPV > 0$, the property appears to be undervalued and may be an attractive investment. If $NPV \leq 0$, the property is correctly valued or overvalued, according to the analysis.

3. INTERNAL RATE OF RETURN MODEL An alternative or supplement to the NPV model is the internal rate of return, IRR, model. This model finds the discount rate that equates V_E with PP_0:

$$PP_0 = \sum_{t=1}^{n} \frac{CF_t}{(1 + IRR_e)^t} + \frac{RV_n}{(1 + IRR_e)^n} \tag{22.5}$$

Once Equation 22.5 is solved for IRR_e, an investment decision is made by comparing IRR_e and K_e. If $IRR_e > K_e$, the property is undervalued and may be a good investment alternative. If $IRR_e \leq K_e$, the property is correctly valued or overvalued.

4. ILLUSTRATION Table 22.6 presents a simple illustration of the NPV and IRR models applied to real estate. In this particular example, $NPV > 0$, and

TABLE 22.6 ILLUSTRATION OF REAL ESTATE INVESTMENT ANALYSIS

I. Data:

Property description:	small commercial office building
Purchase price:	$5,000,000
Holding period:	5 years
Estimate of annual net operating income:	$500,000
Annual debt service:	$100,000
Estimated annual tax liability:	$135,000
Estimate of after-tax reversion value:	$7,500,000
After-tax required rate of return on equity:	12%

II. Annual cash flow

$$CF_t = NOI_t - DS_t - T_t$$
$$= \$500,000 - \$100,000 - \$135,000 = \$265,000$$

III. Net present value:

$$NPV = \frac{\$265,000}{(1 + .12)} + \frac{\$265,000}{(1 + .12)^2} + \cdots + \frac{\$265,000}{(1 + .12)^5} + \frac{\$7,500,000}{(1 + .12)^5}$$
$$- \$5,000,000$$

$$= \$265,000 \left[\frac{1 - \frac{1}{(1 + .12)^5}}{.12} \right] + \frac{\$7,500,000}{(1 + .12)^5} - \$5,000,000$$

$$= \$265,000 \, [3.6048] + \frac{\$7,500,000}{1.7623} - \$5,000,000$$

$$= \$955,272 + \$4,255,802 - \$5,000,000$$

$$= \$211,074$$

IV. Internal rate of return:

$$\$5,000,000 = \$265,000 \left[\frac{1 - \frac{1}{(1 + IRR_e)^5}}{IRR_e} \right] + \frac{\$7,500,000}{(1 + IRR_e)^5}$$

by trial-and-error or calculator: $IRR_e = 13.01\%$.

$IRR_e > 12\%$, the after-tax required rate of return on equity, so that the commercial office building appears to be undervalued at $5 million.

Investment Characteristics of Real Estate

A number of studies have looked at the historical holding period returns on real estate. Webb and Rubens examined real estate returns over the period 1947–1984 for three categories of real estate: residential, farm, and business.[18] These studies compared real estate returns to the *HPR*s on NYSE common stocks, corporate

---

[18] James R. Webb and Jack H. Rubens, "How Much in Real Estate? A Surprising Answer," *Journal of Portfolio Management* (Spring 1987): pp. 10–14. Also see, H. Russell Fogler, "20% in Real Estate: Can Theory Justify It?" *Journal of Portfolio Management* (Winter 1984): pp. 6–13.

bonds, and common stocks of small companies. Almost all studies that have attempted to calculate and analyze *HPR*s for real estate recognize the difficulties that are encountered. A major problem is that there is no national real estate market that generates transaction prices on a continuous basis. Without prices at regular intervals, *HPR*s cannot be accurately calculated. Therefore, studies, often use proxies for prices or yield data from a specific geographical location. Because of these problems, the *HPR*s for real estate should be used with caution; they are typically not as reliable as *HPR*s for stocks and bonds.

Table 22.7 (p. 631) provides a comparison of real estate returns with the returns for three major categories of financial assets (common stocks, bonds, and "small" stocks). The coefficient of variation ratios for real estate are much lower than those for the three categories of financial assets. This data indicates that real estate has higher historical returns than common stocks and corporate bonds and *lower* risk than the three categories of financial assets used in the study.

The lower portion of Table 22.7 provides the correlation coefficient matrix for the six categories of investments. Notice that the correlations are low for the three categories of real estate; in one case, negative. Real estate returns also appear to be negatively correlated with corporate bond returns. The low and especially the negative correlations indicate that significant diversification benefits would result from combining these six categories of assets in a portfolio.

A number of studies have attempted to calculate betas for different categories of real estate. For example, Miles and McCue analyzed returns over the period September 30, 1973, through September 30, 1981, for 166 "properties."[19] The time series of returns for each property was regressed against a market portfolio formed from all 166 properties. The resulting betas indicated the systematic risk of individual properties relative to real estate returns in general. The authors concluded that "the non-market risk of real estate is in the range of 87 to 95 percent."[20] Their analysis suggested that systematic risk is a relatively small part of the total risk of real estate; the majority (87 to 95 percent) of the return variability was not related to the market and was therefore unsystematic. Since the risk is primarily unsystematic, it can be effectively reduced by holding a number of real estate investments in a portfolio.

Reasons for Investing in Real Estate

Real estate, because of its lack of liquidity and high transaction costs, has traditionally been viewed as a long-term investment. This viewpoint supports the idea that real estate investment strategies should be passive rather than active. The following discussion supports this view.

1. INFLATION HEDGE Considerable research has empirically tested the hypothesis that real estate provides an inflation hedge.[21] The results from these studies

---

[19] Mike Miles and Tom McCue, "Diversification in the Real Estate Portfolio," *Journal of Financial Research* (Spring 1984): pp. 57–68.

[20] Miles and McCue, p. 66.

[21] For example, see Richard W. Kopeke and Peter C. Aldrich, "A Real Estate Crisis: Averted or Just Postponed?" *Journal of Portfolio Management* (Spring 1984): pp. 21–29, and H. Russell Fogler, Michael R. Granito, and Laurence R. Smith, "A Theoretical Analysis of Real Estate Returns," *Journal of Finance* (July 1985): pp. 711–21.

are somewhat contradictory. Several studies conclude that some types of real estate are an effective hedge against expected inflation, but not unexpected inflation. Expected inflation is often measured by the observed yield on bonds; investor expectations of inflation are reflected in the inflation yield premium included in the overall yield. Unexpected inflation is not reflected in market yields on bonds. Other studies conclude that some types of real estate are an effective hedge against both expected and unexpected inflation.

One possible explanation for the contradictory results is differences in the time periods used for the studies. Studies that use data from the 1970s generally conclude that real estate is one of the few assets that provide an effective hedge against inflation. Fogler's study of the 1915–1978 period found that real estate was an effective hedge during the inflationary periods of the 1960s and 1970s, but not during earlier inflationary periods.[22]

Another possible explanation of the contradictory results is that studies generally use data from a specific geographic area. Real estate markets are highly segmented or regionalized. For example, there may be a real estate boom in one area of the country while prices are depressed or even declining in another area. If a study was based on data from Florida, with a booming real estate market during the 1980s, conclusions might be quite different from those of a study based on a "rust-belt" area. Real estate may be a better hedge during a certain period of time for a certain location, but not for all locations.

Real estate investments are not homogeneous. There are many different types of real estate, such as unimproved or "raw" land, farms, residential, and retail office buildings. Studies concerning real estate's record as an inflation hedge have found that the type of property influences the conclusions. For example, office properties may provide a better or worse hedge than retail properties in certain markets. After reviewing a number of studies, Sirmans and Sirmans concluded that "taken together, the studies seem to indicate that real estate served as a better inflation hedge over the time periods studied than common stocks and corporate or government bonds."[23]

Empirical evidence suggests that real estate should be included in an investment portfolio to protect against purchasing power loss during inflationary periods. Also, the evidence suggests that the proportion of the portfolio devoted to real estate should increase before or during periods of high inflation.

2. MARKET TIMING Is it possible to buy real estate "low" and sell it "high?" This would be similar to forecasting bull and bear stock markets and trading accordingly. Fogler argues that because real estate is illiquid, it is not possible to use short-term timing strategies.[24] For example, if an investor anticipates a decline in the real estate market and decides to sell a real estate investment, it may take many months to find a buyer. Likewise, it may be difficult to find and close on an appropriate property in a short time prior to a favorable market.

---

[22] Fogler.

[23] G. Stacy Sirmans and C. F. Sirmans, "The Historical Perspective of Real Estate Returns," *Journal of Portfolio Management* (Spring 1987): p. 31.

[24] Fogler, p. 12.

3. MARKET INEFFICIENCIES Is it possible to find real estate that is under- or overvalued? If so, the real estate market would be inefficient in correctly valuing some properties. A "weak form" test of market efficiency would be to evaluate whether past price information in real estate markets can be utilized to predict future prices. This would be an extension of the efficient market hypothesis, EMH, developed for the stock and bond markets. If the market is "weakly" efficient, then all information contained in past price movements is fully reflected in current prices. An analysis of the trends or cycles in historical prices in a "weakly" efficient market, therefore, cannot be successfully used to forecast future price movements.

A study using time series prices on real estate from a major Canadian metropolitan area concluded that the market was "weakly" efficient.[25] In other words, no model using sophisticated statistical techniques had any forecasting ability. This suggests that technical analysis (see Chapter 12), in general, cannot be used successfully to beat the real estate market. Other studies, however, are needed before conclusions can be reached about the efficiency of real estate markets.

4. PORTFOLIO CONSIDERATIONS There is growing empirical evidence that real estate can make a very valuable contribution to a portfolio.

    a. PORTFOLIOS OF STOCKS, BONDS AND REAL ESTATE As Table 22.7 illustrates, the returns on real estate may be higher than those on financial assets, and the total risk of real estate measured by the standard deviation may be lower. Also, real estate returns may be negatively correlated with bond returns. All of these characteristics suggest that adding real estate to a portfolio of stocks and bonds can improve the risk-return performance of the portfolio.

        Using historical returns, what proportion of a portfolio's funds should be invested in real estate? Fogler's 1984 study suggested that 15–20 percent of a portfolio's funds should be invested in real estate.[26] The 1987 study by Webb and Rubens reached the surprising conclusion that the majority of a portfolio's funds should be invested in real estate.[27] According to the authors, the return and risk characteristics of three types of real estate were much better than those of common stocks, corporate bonds, and small stocks. These favorable characteristics existed for three different time periods: 1947–1959, 1960–1972, and 1973–1984.

    b. DIVERSIFICATION BY NUMBER OF PROPERTIES IN A PORTFOLIO Another portfolio consideration is, How many properties should a real estate portfolio include to eliminate unsystematic or diversifiable risk? Studies of common stocks generally conclude that on average ten to fifteen randomly selected stocks essentially eliminate the unsystematic risk of the portfolio. Studies of real estate also show large potential gains from diversi-

---

[25] George W. Gau, "Weak Form Tests of the Efficiency of Real Estate Investment Markets," *Financial Review* (November 1984): pp. 301–20.

[26] Fogler.

[27] Webb and Rubens.

TABLE 22.7   RETURNS AND RISK ON REAL ESTATE AND FINANCIAL ASSETS: 1973–1984

	ARITHMETIC MEAN *HPR*	STANDARD DEVIATION OF *HPR*	COEFFICIENT OF VARIATION
Residential real estate	10.53%	4.44%	.42
Farmland	14.03	11.06	.79
Business real estate	10.78	2.77	.26
Common stocks	9.62	19.71	2.05
Corporate bonds	7.51	13.92	1.85
Small stocks	21.96	28.11	1.28

CORRELATION COEFFICIENT MATRIX

	RESIDENTIAL REAL ESTATE	FARMLAND	BUSINESS REAL ESTATE	COMMON STOCKS	CORPORATE BONDS	SMALL STOCKS
Residential real estate	1.00					
Farmland	0.15	1.00				
Business real estate	0.11	−0.56	1.00			
Common stocks	0.23	−0.31	0.31	1.00		
Corporate bonds	−0.25	−0.37	−0.24	0.39	1.00	
Small stocks	0.33	−0.39	0.35	0.85	0.21	1.00

SOURCE: James R. Webb and Jack H. Rubens, "How Much in Real Estate? A Surprising Answer," *Journal of Portfolio Management* (Spring 1987); pp. 10–13. Reprinted by permission.

fication by increasing the number of properties in the portfolio.[28] This occurs because much of the variability in real estate returns is unsystematic. These studies generally find that less than ten properties in a real estate portfolio essentially eliminate all of the unsystematic risk. For example, Miles and McCue found that ten properties removed 83 percent of the unsystematic risk of the portfolio.[29]

c.   DIVERSIFICATION BY PROPERTY TYPE AND LOCATION   Would it be equally effective to invest in a portfolio consisting of ten office buildings or a portfolio of ten different types of real estate in several geographic locations? Empirical evidence suggests that the correlation coefficients between the returns on different types of real estate are quite low and in some cases may be negative.[30] This suggests that real estate portfolios should be diversified by types of property, and as indicated earlier, by geographic location.

---

[28] For example, see Miles and McCue, and Terry V. Grissom, James L. Kuhle, and Carl H. Walther, "Diversification Works in Real Estate, Too," *Journal of Portfolio Management* (Winter 1987): pp. 66–71.

[29] Miles and McCue.

[30] For example, see Webb and Rubens or Table 22.7.

COLLECTIBLES

Introduction

A number of other tangible or real assets are sometimes viewed as investments; these include diamonds, paintings, prints, stamps, antiques, and rare coins. This view was strengthened by the high rates of inflation during the late 1970s and early 1980s. Many individuals thought that any type of real asset provided a better hedge against inflation than financial assets—and also provided intangible benefits and aesthetic value.

Because of the nature and characteristics of collectibles, it is difficult to apply traditional techniques of investment analysis to these assets. Consequently, there are few academic or rigorous investment studies of collectibles. The lack of time series price data and the unique characteristics of collectibles have hindered research efforts.

This section of the chapter provides a brief discussion of four types of collectibles: diamonds, modern prints, fine art, and numismatic coins.

Diamonds

The peak of the diamond craze occurred in 1980. The price of a "D flawless" one-carat diamond increased from approximately $1,500 in 1970 to a high of $65,000 in 1980.[31] This represents an annual compound *HPR* of 45.77 percent. Many "investors" were convinced that the rapid rate of inflation would continue and that diamonds would increase further in price. However, the peak occurred in 1980, with the price of the benchmark diamond (D flawless) declining by 75 percent within a few months. The spectacular price cycle has been attributed to speculation by investors attempting to identify and take advantage of inflation hedges. Since the price collapse in 1980, diamond prices have increased slowly because inflation rates have been nominal.

If an individual is inclined to view diamonds as investments, the following factors should be considered:

1. DIAMONDS LACK LIQUIDITY There is no national market where diamonds can easily be bought and sold.

2. DIAMONDS ARE NOT HOMOGENEOUS Diamonds are graded by color, clarity, weight, and proportion. No two diamonds are exactly alike, and prices of one-carat diamonds can vary considerably because of their grade. Grading is an art that requires considerable experience. Individuals without extensive training, therefore, will have difficulty in determining the quality of a stone.

3. TRANSACTION COSTS ARE HIGH Retail markups on diamonds can be as high as 100 percent, with wholesale markups of 15 percent on large quantities of quality stones. Investment returns on diamonds must be quite good to cover these very high transaction costs.

---

[31] Doron P. Levin, "A Diamond Is Forever; Its Value, However, Is Subject to the Vagaries of the Gem Market," *Wall Street Journal* 1 Aug. 1983.

4. CLOSELY CONTROLLED MARKET It has been estimated that the South African De Beers cartel controls 85 percent of the world's supply of uncut stones. This degree of control by a single supplier may not be advantageous to buyers.

Modern Prints

A 1980 investment study of modern prints concluded that they outperformed common stocks and commodities over the 1954–1978 period.[32] This study was based on a sample of fifteen original modern prints that were available in limited editions. The author argued that there was a reliable price history for these types of prints, so that *HPR*s and risk measures could be calculated. The annual volume of trading in modern prints, both in New York and London, was estimated at between $20 and $30 million. The author recognized the high level of transaction costs by using a commission rate of 25.3 percent for prints, compared to 2.0 percent for stocks and commodities.

The investment implications of the study suggest that the risk-return characteristics of modern prints compare favorably with those of stocks and commodities. Additional benefits occur when prints are included in a portfolio of stocks and commodities.

Fine Art

Fine art investments include paintings, sculptures, antiques, and many other items. The value of individual works of art are primarily determined by artist's reputation, rarity, condition, and popularity with other collectors and investors. Most experts advise collectors to value an item using aesthetics rather than potential profits. Investors and speculators are often advised to avoid buying items unless they are familiar with the particular type of art. Some dealers actually discourage considering fine art an investment.

Fine art must be appraised by an expert to determine its authenticity, condition, and value. Due to the uniqueness of most art objects, however, an auction is the only way to establish value firmly. There are many dealers and appraisers of fine art and professional associations such as the International Society of Appraisers and the International Society of Fine Art Appraisers. The better-known auction houses that also offer appraisal services are Christie's and Sotheby's both located in New York City.

Small investors/speculators may be attracted to the work of "up-and-coming young artists." Buying new works of art is very risky; most will never become collector items. Essentially, this is similar to buying the stock of a new, unproved corporation in its initial public offering.

Transaction costs are also a disadvantage of fine art investing. Auction houses typically charge a commission of 10 percent; dealers, who often sell items on a consignment basis, can charge a 10 to 25 percent commission, based on the selling price.

---

[32] Robert E. Penn, "The Economics of the Market in Modern Prints," *Journal of Portfolio Management* (Fall 1980): pp. 25–32.

Numismatic Coins

The American Numismatic Association estimates that approximately 500,000 Americans are serious coin collectors and that another 2.5 million are casual collectors, compared to approximately 9 million who trade in coins as investors or speculators. The growing interest of investors and speculators has occurred partly because of the *HPR*s that coins have provided. Salomon Brothers estimates that the annual *HPR* over the last fifteen years (1973–1987) is 18.8 percent. Recently, however, the *HPR*s have declined to 11.4 percent over the five-year period 1983–1987 and 10.7 percent for 1987.

One major disadvantage of investing in coins is that their value is greatly influenced by their condition and rarity. Consequently, it is usually necessary to have coins *graded* by a professional service like the Professional Coin Grading Service or the American Numismatic Association's Certification Service. The time and cost associated with grading reduce the liquidity and return of coin investments.

The value of numismatic coins does not depend on the value of the metal in the coin or bullion value. Thus, their prices do not respond to changes in the price of gold and silver. In addition to condition and rarity, the value of numismatic coins depends primarily on collector or speculator demand for a particular coin. Most investors or speculators, therefore, must use the services of a coin dealer to locate desired coins and to sell coins.

SUMMARY

This chapter presented empirical evidence suggesting that *HPR*s on real assets during some time periods are often much larger than *HPR*s on financial assets. There is also evidence that risk for some types of real assets may be below that of common stocks and in some cases, bonds. To the extent that these observations are correct, portfolios of rational investors should include real assets.

There is also evidence that the correlation coefficients between the returns on real assets and financial assets are low and in some cases, negative. This provides further evidence that real assets should be included in portfolios.

As with virtually all investment research, the above observations are based on historical or ex-post return data. If history repeats, then real assets should indeed be seriously considered for diversified portfolios. As is the case for all investments, however, investors must establish investment objectives and forecast the future economic environment.

QUESTIONS

1. Clearly define *real* and *financial* assets, and cite several examples of each.
2. Compare and contrast numismatic coins with bullion coins. In your opinion, which type of coin has greater investment risk? Justify your opinion.
3. Explain why a commodity-backed bond may provide a better inflationary hedge than a traditional bond.

4. Compare and contrast an inflation hedge with a confidence hedge.

5. Compare the P/E ratios for REITs in Table 22.5 with those for publicly traded gold-mining stocks in Table 22.2. Which type of company appears to have the more volatile earnings and common stock share prices?

6. Explain the three techniques that have been suggested to diversify a real estate portfolio.

7. Discuss the investment characteristics of gold.

8. Discuss the investment characteristics of real estate.

9. Compare and contrast the four major ways in which individuals can invest in real estate.

10. Discuss the pros and cons of considering diamonds, prints, fine art, numismatic coins, and other collectibles as investments.

PROBLEMS

1. Consider the following information on three investment alternatives:

	COST	SELLING PRICE	INCOME OVER HOLDING PERIOD	TRANSACTION COSTS	STORAGE COSTS
Blue-chip					
Common Stock	$ 20	$ 25	$1.00	5%	–
REIT Common stock	10	12	1.20	5	–
Gold coin	400	500	–	8	5%

   a. Calculate the gross *HPR*s for each investment alternative (i.e., ignore transaction costs and storage costs).

   b. Calculate the net *HPR*s for each investment alternative.

2. Assume that a gold coin increased in value from $100 to $160 over a six-year period and that the consumer price index increased from 100 to 140 over the same period.

   a. Calculate the annualized *HPR* for the gold coin and the annualized rate of inflation.

   b. Calculate the annualized *real HPR* for the gold coin.

   c. Did the gold coin provide an inflation hedge? Explain.

3. Consider the following potential real estate investments:

	COST	COMMISSION EXPENSE TO PURCHASE	ANNUAL INCOME	INITIAL SYNDICATION FEE	VALUE AFTER 1 YEAR
Limited partnership					
interest	$10,000	10%	$100	5%	$11,500
100 shares of REIT					
common stock	10,000	5	100	–	11,500

   a. Calculate the gross (before expenses and fees) *HPR*s for each investment alternative.

b.   Calculate the *net HPR* for each investment alternative.

c.   Can an investor actually realize these expected *HPR*s by selling the investments after one year? Explain.

4.   Consider the following potential real estate investment:

YEAR	AFTER-TAX CASH FLOW	AFTER-TAX REVERSION VALUE
0	$(100,000)	
1	15,000	
2	60,000	
3	30,000	$115,000

a.   Assume an after-tax required rate of return on equity of 12%. Calculate the net present value and indicate whether the real estate appears to be an acceptable investment.

b.   Calculate the internal rate of return and indicate whether the real estate appears to be an acceptable investment.

5.   Consider the following information on a small apartment complex that is being considered as an investment:

Purchase price:	$1,000,000
Holding period:	3 years
Estimate of annual net operating income:	$150,000
Annual debt service:	$50,000
Estimated annual tax liability:	$40,000
Estimate of after-tax reversion value:	$1,200,000
After-tax required rate of return on equity:	13%

a.   Calculate the annual after-tax cash flow.

b.   Calculate the net present value and indicate whether the property is an acceptable investment based on this analysis.

c.   Calculate the internal rate of return and indicate whether the property is an acceptable investment based on this analysis.

d.   Discuss other factors that would need to be analyzed before a final investment decision is made.

REFERENCES

Bierman, Harold. Jr. "How Much Diversification is Desirable?" *Journal of Portfolio Management* (Fall 1980): pp. 42–44.

Booth, G. Geoffrey, Fred R. Kaen, and Peter E. Koveos. "Persistent Dependence in Gold Prices." *Journal of Financial Research* (Spring 1982): pp. 85–93.

Brauer, Greggory A., and R. Ravichandran. "How Sweet Is Silver?" *Journal of Portfolio Management* (Summer 1986): pp. 33–42.

Burns, William L., and Donald R. Epley. "The Performance of Portfolios of REITs and Stocks." *Journal of Portfolio Management* (Spring 1982): pp. 37–41.

Carter, Kevin J., John F. Affleck-Graves, and Arthur H. Money. "Are Gold Shares Better than Gold for Diversification?" *Journal of Portfolio Management* (Fall 1982): pp. 52–55.

Corcoran, Patrick J. "Explaining the Commercial Real Estate Market." *Journal of Portfolio Management* (Spring 1987): pp. 15–21.

Coyne, Thomas J., Waldemar M. Goulet, and Mario J. Picconi. "Residential Real Estate versus Financial Assets." *Journal of Portfolio Management* (Fall 1980): pp. 20–24.

Curran, John J. "How Good a Hedge Is Gold?" *Fortune*, 22 June, 1987, pp. 169–70.

Fogler, H. Russell. "20% in Real Estate: Can Theory Justify It?" *Journal of Portfolio Management* (Winter 1984): pp. 6–13.

Fogler, Russell H., Michael R. Granito, and Laurence R. Smith. "A Theoretical Analysis of Real Estate Returns." *Journal of Finance* (July 1985): pp. 711–21.

Froland, Charles. "What Determines Cap Rates on Real Estate?" *Journal of Portfolio Management* (Summer 1987): pp. 77–82.

Gau, George W. "Weak Form Tests of the Efficiency of Real Estate Investment Markets." *Financial Review* (November 1984): pp. 301–20.

Grissom, Terry V., James L. Kuhle, and Carl H. Walther. "Diversification Works in Real Estate, Too." *Journal of Portfolio Management* (Winter 1987): pp. 66–71.

Herbst, Anthony F. "Gold versus U.S. Common Stocks: Some Evidence on Inflation Hedge Performance and Cyclical Behavior." *Financial Analysts Journal* (January-February 1983): pp. 66–74.

Kopcke, Richard W., and Peter C. Aldrich. "A Real Estate Crisis: Averted or Just Postponed?" *Journal of Portfolio Management* (Spring 1984): pp. 21–29.

Kuntz, Mary. "A Realty Fund Primer." *Forbes*, 9 March, 1987, pp. 162–63.

Lee, Susan. "Onward and Upward." *Forbes*, 1 June, 1987, p. 194.

Levin, Doron P. "A Diamond Is Forever; Its Value, However, Is Subject to the Vagaries of the Gem Market." *Wall Street Journal*, 1 August, 1983, p. 38.

Lovell, Robert M. Jr. "Alternative Investments." *Financial Analysts Journal* (May-June 1980): pp. 19–21.

Miles, Mike, and Arthur Esty. "How Well Do Commingled Real Estate Funds Perform?" *Journal of Portfolio Management* (Winter 1982): pp. 62–68.

Miles, Mike, and Tom McCue. "Diversification in the Real Estate Portfolio." *Journal of Financial Research* (Spring 1984): pp. 57–68.

Ozanian, Michael. "Risky Hedges." *Forbes*, 18 May, 1987, p. 248.

Penn, Robert E. "The Economics of the Market in Modern Prints." *Journal of Portfolio Management* (Fall 1980): pp. 25–32.

Renshaw, Anthony, and Edward F. Renshaw. "Does Gold Have a Role in Investment Portfolios?" *Journal of Portfolio Management* (Spring 1982): pp. 28–31.

Sherman, Eugene J. "Gold: A Conservative, Prudent Diversifier." *Journal of Portfolio Management* (Spring 1982): pp. 21–27.

Sirmans, G. Stacy, and C. F. Sirmans. "The Historical Perspective of Real Estate Returns." *Journal of Portfolio Management* (Spring 1987): pp. 22–31.

Slutsker, Gary. "All That Glitters . . . ." *Forbes*, 15 June, 1987, pp. 33–34.

Tauber, Ronald S. "Is Gold a Prudent Investment Under ERISA?" *Journal of Portfolio Management* (Fall 1981): pp. 28–31.

Webb, James R., and C. F. Sirmans. "Yields and Risk Measures for Real Estate, 1966–77." *Journal of Portfolio Management* (Fall 1980): pp. 14–19.

Webb, James R., and Jack H. Rubens. "How Much in Real Estate? A Surprising Answer." *Journal of Portfolio Management* (Spring 1987): pp. 10–14.

Wofford, Larry E., and Edward A. Moses. "The Relationship between Capital Markets and Real Estate Investment Yields: Theory and Application." *Real Estate Appraiser and Analyst* (November-December 1978): pp. 51–61.

Wofford, Larry E., Edward A. Moses, and John M. Cheney. "Using Capital Market Theory in Real Estate Appraisal: Evidence from the Securities Markets." *Real Estate Appraiser and Analyst* (Fall 1982): pp. 34–39.

Zerbst, Robert H., and Barbara R. Cambon. "Real Estate: Historical Returns and Risks." *Journal of Portfolio Management* (Spring 1984): pp. 5–20.

INVESTING INTERNATIONALLY

INTRODUCTION

Historically, many investors ignored international markets, for two reasons: (1) they didn't recognized the potential benefits from international diversification; (2) the information and transaction costs associated with international investing were high. In recent years, international investing has become increasingly popular, as its potential benefits are recognized. In addition, information and transaction costs have been substantially reduced. This chapter first provides a background on the international financial markets. It then examines evidence on the potential gains from international diversification. Finally, it explains how international investing can be accomplished.

Background on Financial Markets

Stock and bond markets exist in numerous countries. Portfolio managers are now becoming more familiar with foreign companies, on local exchanges and on foreign exchanges. Consequently, professionally managed portfolios now reflect a greater percentage of foreign companies.

As security portfolios become more internationalized, investment bankers are attempting to persuade corporations to list their stocks on foreign exchanges to facilitate international stock diversification. Investment companies such as Morgan Stanley, Merrill Lynch, and Goldman Sacks have been very active in this area.

It has been estimated that between 10 and 12 percent of all trading on the New York Stock Exchange is conducted by European and other overseas investors.[1] The breadth and depth of U.S. equity markets often encourage foreign companies to list their stocks on the U.S. exchanges. Browater Corporation, a British industrial products company, issued securities in the U.S. markets because it thought U.S. analysts understood its business better than others.[2]

Stock exchanges in Europe are creating a central market in stocks. Market information systems are being developed to cover some stocks listed on the London and Amsterdam exchanges, with plans to include the Brussels and Paris exchanges, and stocks from other foreign exchanges are expected to be included in the future.[3] Stocks of some very well known companies have become globally accessible to investors. For example, Toyota Motor Corporation of Japan is listed on at least nine different stock exchanges around the world.

Size of International Markets

Many individual investors may be surprised at the size of foreign markets and companies relative to those in the United States. For example, when Nippon Telegraph & Telephone went public in February 1987, its market value of $330 billion was above the combined values of IBM, AT&T, GE, and GM.[4] The market

---

[1] See Richard Karp, "Making an International Splash," *Institutional Investor* (April 1983): pp. 139–40.

[2] See "Why the Big Apple Shines for the World's Markets," *Business Week*, 23 July 1984, pp. 100–04.

[3] See Quek Peck Lim, "Trading Stocks across Frontiers," *Euromoney* (May 1984): pp. 110–12.

[4] Howard Rudnitsky, Allan Sloan, and Peter Fuhrman, "Land of Rising Stocks," *Forbes*, 18 May 1987, p. 139.

value of the 1,500 stocks listed on the Tokyo Stock Exchange is also greater than that of the 2,250 stocks traded on the NYSE. The Tokyo Stock Exchange is the largest exchange in the world. The exchanges of Canada, Japan, and the United Kingdom are the three largest markets outside the United States, together making up more than 50 percent of the market values of non-U.S. equities. The market value of Japan's largest brokerage house, Nomura Securities, is approximately $71 billion, larger than the combined values of all U.S. brokerage firms.

Table 23.1 provides a ranking by sales of the thirty largest international companies. The largest of these, Exxon had 1987 sales in excess of $83 billion. Notice that only seventeen of the thirty companies are U.S. firms. Ward's *Business Directory* provides information on the 15,000 leading world wide corporations as well as information on a total of 45,000 corporations. Therefore, U.S. investors who are willing to consider foreign investments dramatically increase their universe of alternative investments, in both the number and the size of corporations.

TABLE 23.1   THIRTY LARGEST INTERNATIONAL COMPANIES

RANK BY SALES	COMPANY NAME	CITY	STATE/COUNTRY
1	Exxon Corp.	New York	New York, U.S.
2	Royal Dutch Petroleum Company	The Hague	Netherlands
3	Shell Transport & Trading Company PLC	London	England
4	General Motors Corp.	Detroit	Michigan, U.S.
5	American Telephone & Telegraph Co.	New York	New York, U.S.
6	Mitsui & Co. Ltd.	Tokyo	Japan
7	Mitsubishi Corporation	Tokyo	Japan
8	Mobil Corp.	New York	New York, U.S.
9	Iton C & Co. Ltd.	Osaka	Japan
10	Mobil Oil Corp.	New York	New York, U.S.
11	Marubeni Corporation	Osaka	Japan
12	British Petroleum Co. PLC	London	England
13	Sumitomo Corporation	Osaka	Japan
14	Ford Motor Company	Dearborn	Michigan, U.S.
15	Texaco, Inc.	White Plains	New York, U.S.
16	IBM Corporation	Armonk	New York, U.S.
17	Sears Roebuck & Co.	Chicago	Illinois, U.S.
18	Du Point E I De Nemours	Wilmington	Delaware, U.S.
19	Nissho Iwai Corporation	Osaka	Japan
20	Cargill, Inc.-MM	Minneapolis	Minnesota, U.S.
21	Phibro-Salomon, Inc.	New York	New York, U.S.
22	Standard Oil Co. of Indiana	Chicago	Illinois, U.S.
23	Standard Oil Co. of California	San Francisco	California, U.S.
24	BP Oil International	London	England
25	Gulf Oil Corporation	Pittsburgh	Pennsylvania, U.S.
26	Atlantic Richfield Co.	Los Angeles	California, U.S.
27	General Electric Co.	Fairfield	Connecticut, U.S.
28	Eni-Ente Mazionale Indrocarburi Spa	Rome	Italy
29	Iri-Instituto Ricostruzione Industriale	Rome	Italy
30	Toyota Motor Corporation	Toyota	Japan

SOURCE: Ward's *Business Directory of Major International Companies,* 1987, p. 24. Ward's *Business Directory* is a product of Information Access Company, a division of Ziff–Davis Publishing.

BENEFITS OF INTERNATIONAL DIVERSIFICATION

Recent Developments in Foreign Markets

In October 1986, a computerized network was created in London which resembled the NASDAQ Over-the-Counter system in the United States. This event was referred to as the *Big Bang*. The system, called SEAQ (pronounced *see-yak*), allows international traders to conduct trading by telephones and computers. In addition, the London exchange now allows investment firms that trade in the United States and Japan to trade in London. Prior to the Big Bang, this was not allowed. As a result of this deregulatory provision, large investment firms that trade on the New York, London, and Tokyo exchanges are able to create a near-24-hour market. They can use the New York Stock Exchange from 9:30 A.M. to 4:00 P.M. Eastern time, the Tokyo Stock Exchange from 7:00 P.M. to 1:00 A.M. Eastern time, and the London Stock Exchange from 4:00 A.M. to 10:30 A.M. Eastern time. Those shares traded on all exchanges can be bought or sold at almost any time of the day. In the future, it is likely that shares of most companies will be available on these three major exchanges.

The fixed commission structure was eliminated in London as a result of the Big Bang. Consequently, the commissions paid on stock transactions in London are competitive (this form of deregulation occurred in the United States in 1975). The deregulated commission is likely to increase competition between brokerage firms and lower their profit margins.

Diversifying Internationally

As discussed in Chapter 6, a portfolio including securities which are not highly positively correlated with each other is beneficial to the investor. The lack of positive correlation between returns on different securities helps to reduce the risk of the portfolio.

Economic conditions will cause some securities in such a portfolio to provide higher-than-normal returns, while other securities will provide lower-than-normal returns. Under other economic conditions, the reverse would hold. This offsetting effect forces the overall portfolio returns to be less volatile over time. For those investors who use volatility as a measure of risk, portfolio risk is reduced when including securities which exhibit low or negative correlations with each other.

Unfortunately, there is a limit to the degree to which investors can reduce the risk of a purely domestic portfolio. Most corporations are affected by domestic economic conditions. Thus, the securities of these corporations will generate returns that are often highly correlated. Because the correlations between securities are never perfect (represented by a correlation of 1.0), portfolio risk can be reduced to a degree. However, the degree of risk reduction could be much greater if the portfolio contained securities whose returns were not highly correlated. To develop such a portfolio, many investment analysts and advisors suggest inclusion of foreign securities.

A portfolio containing foreign securities will be less volatile than a purely domestic portfolio if the returns of such securities are not highly correlated with the domestic securities. Because these foreign securities represent foreign corporations, their returns should not move in perfect tandem with those of domestic securities.

Much research has examined this issue. One of the first studies was conducted by Levy and Sarnat, who examined stock indices of various countries.[5] The use of indices rather than individual stocks simplified the analysis; yet, the results would not be expected to deviate substantially if individual stocks were examined instead. Levy and Sarnat found that stock indices of various countries were not as highly correlated as one would expect the individual securities in a given country to be. Such results imply potential gains from international diversification. In particular, the indices of the more-industrialized countries were found to exhibit higher correlations. Perhaps this can be explained by the high degree of interaction among more industrialized countries, which should cause the economic conditions in one country to influence conditions in others. In those countries where international transactions are more restricted, the degree of interaction (and therefore influence) is reduced. Thus, economic conditions in such countries are more insulated and should not be similar to economic conditions in other countries.

These findings suggest that securities of the less-industrialized countries should be included in a global portfolio in order to substantially reduce portfolio risk. To substantiate this implication, Levy and Sarnat applied a mean-variance model to their historical data to identify *efficient* portfolios. (Recall that a portfolio is "efficient" if it represents the highest mean return for a given level of risk (where risk is measured by the variance of returns).) Levy and Sarnat found that the less-industrialized stock indices represented a large portion of many efficient portfolios. A similar analysis was conducted by Grubel,[6] whose results were confirmed by the Levy and Sarnat study.

The benefits of international diversification were also analyzed by Solnik.[7] He first randomly selected U.S. securities and determined the average variance of those securities. He then randomly composed two-security portfolios (again using U.S. securities) and determined the average variance of these portfolios. This process was repeated for three-security portfolios, four-security portfolios, and so on. This procedure simply examined how diversification among U.S. securities can reduce risk. The results are shown in Figure 23.1. The variable on the vertical axis, $\bar{\sigma}_p^2/\bar{\sigma}_j^2$, is the ratio of the average portfolio variance, $\bar{\sigma}_p^2$, to the average variance of an individual security, $\bar{\sigma}_j^2$. From Figure 23.1, it can be seen that this ratio decreases as the number of securities within the portfolio is increased.

Solnik repeated the entire process to create international portfolios, using a sample of stocks from various countries. The lower portion of Figure 23.1 shows that the ratio $\bar{\sigma}_p^2/\bar{\sigma}_j^2$ also decreases as the number of securities in the portfolio is increased. However, the degree of reduction is significantly higher for the

[5] See Haim Levy and Marshall Sarnat, "International Diversification of Investment Portfolios," *American Economic Review* 60 (September 1970): pp. 668–75.

[6] Herbert G. Grubel, "Internationally Diversified Portfolios: Welfare Gains and Capital Flows," *American Economic Review* 58 (December 1968): pp. 1299–1314.

[7] See Bruno H. Solnik, "Why Not Diversify Internationally Rather than Domestically?" *Financial Analysts Journal* (July-August 1974): pp. 48–54.

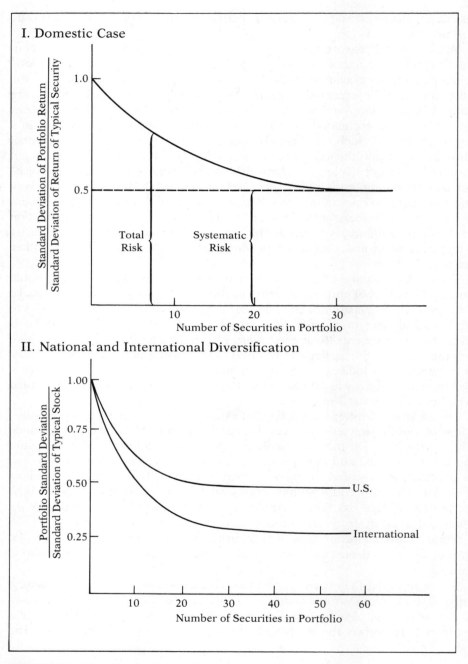

FIGURE 23.1 Diversification by number of securities in portfolio
Source: Bruno H. Solnik. "Why Not Diversify Internationally Rather than Domestically?" *Financial Analysts Journal* (July-August 1974) pp. 48–54. (Reprinted by permission.)

international portfolios. For a twenty-security portfolio, international diversification yields an average variance of about 50 percent of the average variance of a domestic portfolio. This suggests that international diversification can reduce risk far beyond what is possible domestically and that fewer stocks are needed to achieve this diversification.

Research by Levy and Sarnat, Grubel, and Solnik led to the conclusion that gains from international security diversification are possible from the perspective of the U.S. investor. They stimulated further research to examine many unanswered questions about international diversification. First, how do the implications from the research described above relate to securities of less-developed countries? Second, do the implications hold for investors residing in countries other than the United States? Third, are the correlations among stock indices stable over time? Fourth, are potential gains from international stock diversifications affected by the floating exchange rate system? Fifth, how can an individual investor capitalize on international stock diversification? Finally, can we apply the results described above for stocks to other financial assets that are internationally traded? These questions are examined in the following sections.

INCLUSION OF SECURITIES FROM LESS-DEVELOPED COUNTRIES

The results stated earlier suggest that the more restrictive a country's international transactions, the more insulated that country's economic conditions. Therefore, securities in that country should be less correlated with foreign securities and should therefore reduce portfolio risk.

Since the governments of less-developed countries, LDCs, often heavily restrict international transactions, stocks in these countries should serve as viable components of an internationally diversified portfolio. Errunza analyzed stock indices of LDCs and confirmed this hypothesis.[8] The problem with capitalizing on such a strategy is that the government restrictions that create the desirable characteristics (low correlations) of LDC stocks may also restrict investors' access to the stocks. Someday, restrictions on international transactions may be loosened, so that it will be easier for foreigners to purchase LDC stocks directly. Yet, once restrictions on international flows are lifted, interaction will increase. Consequently, the LDCs will be more highly influenced by economic conditions in other countries, and the correlations of LDC stocks with stocks of other countries will increase (thereby reducing the attractiveness of LDC stocks).

INTERNATIONAL DIVERSIFICATION BY NON-U.S. INVESTORS

Can non-U.S. investors also benefit from international portfolio diversification? This issue has been examined in several studies. Research by Solnik examined whether the potential gains from international diversification are achievable from

---

[8] See Vihang R. Errunza, ''Gains from Portfolio Diversification into Less Developed Countries' Securities,'' *Journal of International Business Studies* 8 (Fall-Winter 1977): pp. 83–99.

various perspectives.[9] His analysis from a U.S. investor's perspective (discussed earlier in this chapter) was replicated from the perspectives of investors in several countries. The same general results were found for investors in all countries, although the degree of risk reduction from international diversification differed with each perspective. However, his research was conducted over a period (1966–71) when exchange rates were relatively stable.

A more recent study by Biger analyzed the viability of international diversification from various perspectives, during a period of floating exchange rates.[10] Using a procedure similar to those used by Levy and Sarnat and Grubel, Biger examined returns of national stock indices over time. In general, he found that gains from international diversification were possible, regardless of the investor's home country. These results suggest that an international approach to stock portfolio management should not be unique to U.S. investors.

Consider an investor who is choosing among three hypothetical stocks—A, B, and C. Stocks A and B represent U.S. corporations; Stock C represents a corporation based in Great Britain, G.B. (Portfolio managers will normally evaluate more than three stocks for their portfolio, but a simplified example keeps the algebraic computations within a tolerable level while conveying the main point.) The risk of each stock has been measured by (1) its standard deviation and (2) its comovement with each of the other stocks. These characteristics are provided below.

| | | CORRELATION COEFFICIENT WITH OTHER STOCKS: | | |
STOCK	STANDARD DEVIATION OF RETURNS	STOCK $A_{U.S.}$	STOCK $B_{U.S.}$	STOCK $C_{G.B.}$
Stock $A_{U.S.}$	.10	1.00		
Stock $B_{U.S.}$	.09	.90	1.00	
Stock $C_{G.B.}$	.11	.30	.20	1.00

The portfolio manager is attempting to determine an appropriate combination of the stocks in order to reduce portfolio risk. The portfolio manager could include only two stocks in the portfolio, allocating an equal amount to each stock. The portfolio variability for each of these possible portfolios is provided in Table 23.2 as well as an equally weighted three-stock portfolio. Notice that the three stocks are designated A, B, and C and that the proportion of funds invested in each stock is indicated in the description of the portfolio. The risk of these portfolios can be compared to the risk of individual securities.

Using the standard deviation as a measure of risk, the risk of the three individual stocks varies between .09 and .11. Table 23.3 uses the data given above and the risk measures from Table 23.2 to provide a summary of the portfolio variability levels and the degree of risk reduction (relative to the mean risk level for any individual stock) achieved by that portfolio. The degree of risk reduction

---

[9] See Bruno H. Solnik, "Why Not Diversify Internationally Rather than Domestically?" *Financial Analysts Journal* (July-August 1974): pp. 48–54.

[10] See N. Biger, "Exchange Risk Implications of International Portfolio Diversification," *Journal of International Business Studies* (Fall 1979): pp. 64–74.

TABLE 23.2   COMPUTATION OF PORTFOLIO VARIABILITY FOR FOUR DIFFERENT PORTFOLIOS

DESCRIPTION OF PORTFOLIO	$\sigma^2 = \sum_{i=1}^{n} \sum_{j=1}^{n} X_i X_j \sigma_{ij}$
1. 50% of funds invested in Stock A and 50% of funds invested in Stock B	$\sigma^2 = .5^2(.10)^2 + .5^2(.09)^2 + 2(.5)(.5)(.10)(.09)(.90)$ $= .25(.01) + .25(.0081) + 2(.25)(.009)(.90)$ $= .0025 + .002025 + .00405$ $= .008575$ $\sigma = .0926$
2. 50% of funds invested in Stock A and 50% of funds invested in Stock C	$\sigma^2 = .5^2(.10)^2 + .5^2(.11)^2 + 2(.5)(.5)(.10)(.11)(.30)$ $= .25(.01) + .25(.0121) + 2(.25)(.011)(.30)$ $= .0025 + .003025 + .00165$ $= .007175$ $\sigma = .0847$
3. 50% of funds invested in Stock B and 50% of funds invested in Stock C	$\sigma^2 = .5^2(.09)^2 + .5^2(.11)^2 + 2(.5)(.5)(.09)(.11)(.20)$ $= .25(.0081) + .25(.0121) + 2(.25)(.0099)(.20)$ $= .002025 + .003025 + .00099$ $= .00604$ $\sigma = .0777$
4. Approximately 33% of funds invested in each security	$\sigma^2 = X_A^2\sigma_A^2 + X_B^2\sigma_B^2 + X_C^2\sigma_C^2 + 2X_AX_B\sigma_A\sigma_B\sigma_{AB} + 2X_AX_C\sigma_A\sigma_C\sigma_{AC} + 2X_BX_C\sigma_B\sigma_C\sigma_{BC}$ $= .33^2(.10)^2 + .33^2(.09)^2 + .33^2(.11)^2 + 2(.33)(.33)(.10)(.09)(.90) + 2(.33)(.33)(.10)(.11)(.30)$ $\quad + 2(.33)(.33)(.10)(.09)(.20)$ $= .1089(.01) + .1089(.0081) + .1089(.0121) + .2178(.009)(.90) + .2178(.011)(.30)$ $\quad + .2178(.0090)(.20)$ $= .006164$ $\sigma = .0785$

is computed as

$$\frac{\text{Portfolio Standard Deviation} - \text{Mean Standard Deviation of Individual Securities}}{\text{Mean Standard Deviation of Individual Securities}} \qquad (23.1)$$

For example, the equal-weighted portfolio of stocks A and B exhibits a standard deviation of .0926, so that its degree of risk reduction is

$$\frac{.0926 - (.10 + .09)/2}{(.10 + .09)/2} = -2.53\%$$

which reflects a 2.53 percent reduction in risk, relative to the mean risk of the individual stocks.

If variance, rather than standard deviation, is used as a measure of risk, then the reduction of risk will be

$$\frac{\text{Portfolio Variance} - \text{Mean Variance of Individual Securities}}{\text{Mean Variance of Individual Securities}} \qquad (23.2)$$

TABLE 23.3   RISK REDUCTION ACHIEVED BY VARIOUS PORTFOLIOS

PORTFOLIO DESCRIPTION	APPROXIMATE STANDARD DEVIATION	APPROXIMATE DEGREE OF RISK REDUCTION RELATIVE TO MEAN RISK LEVEL OF INDIVIDUAL STOCKS
1. Equal Allocation of Funds, Stocks A and B	.0926	2.53%
2. Equal Allocation of Funds, Stocks A and C	.0847	19.33
3. Equal Allocation of Funds, Stocks B and C	.0777	22.30
4. Equal Allocation of Funds, Stocks A, B, and C	.0785	21.50

The variances of stocks A and B, are .01, .0081, respectively. Thus, the mean variance of securities A and B is approximately .009. Using variance as a measure of risk, an equal-weighted portfolio of stocks A and B exhibits an approximate degree of risk reduction of

$$\frac{(.0926)^2 - .009}{.009} = -4.72\%$$

In Table 23.3, the three-security portfolio exhibits 21.50 percent less risk than the mean risk of the individual securities (using standard deviation as a proxy for risk). If variance is used as a measure of risk, the three-security portfolio will reduce risk by approximately 39 percent. (Verify this as an exercise.) Regardless of the risk proxy (standard deviation or variance) the degree of risk reduction is greatest when the portfolio includes the British stock. Risk reduction, therefore, is due to its low correlation with each of the U.S. stocks. The purpose of this example is to reinforce the concept of achieving gains by including stocks that exhibit low correlations with other stocks in the portfolio. Because foreign stocks often exhibit this characteristic, they serve as likely candidates for portfolio managers.

UNSTABLE CORRELATIONS OF STOCK INDICES

Most researchers who have attempted to determine whether gains from international diversification are possible have based their findings on the relatively low correlations between stock indices in the past. Yet the results from these studies do not guarantee gains from international diversification in the future. The correlations between stock indices could increase to the point that a portfolio manager would be able to achieve the same degree of risk reduction by focusing solely on domestic stocks. Correlations between stocks of different countries could increase if international transactions between countries increased. This would lessen the potential rewards of global diversification.

Since inter-country trading has become more common, some analysts think that the potential gains from international diversification are decreasing. To test this hypothesis, several studies have segmented a set of historical data into subperiods and analyzed whether correlations of stock index returns are increasing; again, the stock indices of countries have been used [11]. Each study has used a different time frame and/or holding period (monthly, quarterly, etc.). Thus, it is not surprising that results vary with each study. The majority of studies found that correlations between stock indices (as measured by their correlation coefficients) were not stable over time. Most studies concluded that correlations have been increasing, which implies that potential gains from international diversification may be decreasing. But if a portfolio manager can appropriately identify the stock indices with low correlations, there still appears to be room for substantial risk reduction by constructing a global portfolio.

The mean-variance procedure developed by Markowitz can utilize historical information (on returns, variances, and pairwise correlations of stock indices) to identify portfolios which would have been efficient over a particular period. Such portfolios are sometimes referred to as *ex-post efficient*. However, it was found that correlations were intertemporally unstable. Therefore, efficient international portfolios for the future (referred to as *ex-ante efficient* portfolios) will not necessarily be identical to the ex-post efficient portfolios. One may attempt to forecast future correlations based on past data. However, it is virtually impossible for a portfolio manager consistently to construct a global portfolio which is ex-ante efficient.

The above discussion is not intended to discourage international diversification. It is intended instead to stress that although gains from international diversification are possible, the performance of a global portfolio depends on its composition. Most studies that illustrate gains from international diversification have used an ex-post approach, where the ex-post efficient portfolios were found to outperform the domestic stock index. The input used in the mean-variance program assumes perfect foresight about the mean returns as well as variances and pairwise correlations of stock indices. The ex-post approach is sufficient for demonstrating that gains were "achievable" over a given period. But it would also be of interest to test whether international diversification is plausible with an ex-ante approach. To conduct such a study, a strategy for distributing funds among stock indices is needed. One possible strategy is the so-called naive method, where an equal distribution of funds is allocated to each investment. For example, if $X were to be invested in n number of indices, the amount X/n would be allocated to each index. Such a strategy does not require a model to allocate weights to each component within the portfolio.

INTERNATIONAL DIVERSIFICATION WITH FLOATING EXCHANGE RATES

The art of constructing a global portfolio becomes more complex when the impact of floating exchange rates is considered. This occurs because changes in the exchange rates affect the holding period return, *HPR*, on the security. The actual

---

[11] Several of these studies are cited in the Chapter references.

HPR, therefore, depends on two factors: (1) the performance of the security and (2) the exchange rates.

Consider a British investor who purchases 100 shares of a British stock on a British stock exchange. Assume that the stock was priced at 30 British pounds per share. Thus, the 100 shares would cost 3,000 pounds (assuming no transaction costs). Assume that three years later the investor sold the 100 shares for the current market price of 39 pounds per share. The *HPR*, assuming no cash dividends, is

$$HPR = \frac{\text{Proceeds From Stock Sale} - \text{Initial Investment}}{\text{Initial Investment}} \qquad (23.3)$$

$$= \frac{£3,900 - £3,000}{£3,000} = 30\%$$

The example reflects a British investor's perspective. The purchase of the British stock by a U.S. investor initially requires an exchange of U.S. dollars for the British pounds necessary to purchase the stock. Assume that the value of a British pound is $1.90 at the purchase date. If the U.S. investor sells the British stock three years after the purchase at a price of 39 pounds per share, the British pounds received from the sale will be exchanged for U.S. dollars. Assume that the value of the British pound declines and is $1.45 at the selling date. The return to the U.S. investor, adjusted for the exchange rates, HPR_E, is determined as follows (assuming no transaction costs):

Step 1: Determine how many U.S. dollars will be needed for the £3,000 necessary to purchase 100 shares of the British stock:

$£3,000 \times \$1.90$ per pound $= \$5,700$

Step 2: Determine the number of U.S. dollars to be received after selling the British stock and exchanging British pounds received from the sale for U.S. dollars:

$£39$ per share $\times$ 100 shares $= £3,900$

$£3,900 \times \$1.45$ per pound $= \$5,655$

Step 3: Determine the HPR_E as follows:

$$HPR_E = \frac{\begin{array}{c}\text{Total Number of}\\ \text{U.S. Dollars}\\ \text{Received After}\\ \text{Selling British}\\ \text{Stock}\end{array} - \begin{array}{c}\text{Initial}\\ \text{Investment of}\\ \text{U.S. Dollars}\end{array}}{\text{Initial Investment of U.S. Dollars}}$$

$$= \frac{\$5,655 - \$5,700}{\$5,700} = -.7895\%$$

Another method of computing the HPR_E would be first to compute the *HPR* on the stock without adjusting for the fluctuation in exchange rates. Using Equation 23.3, the *HPR* was 30 percent. Then, compute the percentage change in the

British pound's exchange rate over the holding period, E, as shown below:

$$E = \frac{\text{Exchange Rate at End of Period} - \text{Exchange Rate at Beginning of Period}}{\text{Exchange Rate at Beginning of Period}} \quad\quad (23.4)$$

$$= \frac{\$1.45 - \$1.90}{\$1.90}$$

$$E = -23.6842\%$$

Now that values for the stock's rate of return *unadjusted* for the exchange rate fluctuation, HPR, and the percentage change in the exchange rate over the holding period, E, have been computed, the stock's rate of return *adjusted* for the exchange rate fluctuation, HPR_E, is

$$HPR_E = (1 + HPR)(1 + E) - 1 \quad\quad (23.5)$$

$$= (1 + .30)[1 + (-.236842)] - 1$$

$$= -.7895\%$$

This computation for HPR_E coincides with the alternative computation provided earlier. The latter format is convenient in that it decomposes the HPR_E into the two factors (HPR and E) that influence it. The depreciation of the British pound against the U.S. dollar has more than offset the British stock's 30 percent appreciation. A British investor would not need to worry about the fluctuation of the pound's value against the dollar; however, the U.S. investor's return is affected, as demonstrated in the example.

The British pound's value actually depreciated more than 40 percent over the three-year period, 1981–84. The above example illustrates how an exchange rate fluctuation can hurt the international investor. Yet it is possible for the exchange-rate-adjusted stock return to be enhanced by the exchange rate fluctuation. The pound appreciated substantially against the U.S. dollar during the 1986–87 period, with the exchange rate at $1.77 in late February 1988. This appreciation of the pound relative to the dollar benefited U.S. investors.

To illustrate the potential benefits from a change in the foreign currency's value, assume that the pound was worth $1.45 at the beginning of the holding period and $1.90 at the end of the holding period. The percentage change in the pound's exchange rate over the holding period, E, assuming no transaction costs, would be

$$E = \frac{\$1.90 - \$1.45}{\$1.45}$$

$$= 31.03\%$$

Thus, the exchange-rate-adjusted return, HPR_E, on the British stock, from a U.S. investor's perspective, would be

$$HPR_E = (1 + HPR)(1 + E) - 1$$

$$= (1 + .30)(1 + .3103) - 1$$

$$= 70.34\%$$

The examples demonstrate the degree of influence that exchange rate fluctuations can have on an investment in a foreign stock. The expectation that a foreign currency will strengthen will make stocks denominated in that currency more attractive to U.S. investors. Unfortunately, it is extremely difficult to forecast exchange rates. With this limitation in mind, a portfolio manager should not make stock purchases based solely on exchange rate forecasts.

Because of the potentially large exposure of global portfolio performance to exchange rate fluctuations, some investors may think that international diversification is more risky than a purely domestic portfolio. However, one can reduce the exposure to the movements of any particular currency by diversifying among stocks denominated in different currencies. The degree to which such currency exposure can be reduced depends on the correlations among currency movements. For example, consider a U.S. investor who diversifies among stocks in France, the Netherlands, Switzerland, and West Germany. The currency exposure will be quite high, since all of these currencies move closely in tandem against the dollar. Thus, if any one of the currencies depreciates against the U.S. dollar, the other three currencies will probably depreciate as well and by about the same degree. Because movements in these currencies are highly correlated, diversifying among stocks denominated in each of these currencies is not much different from using stocks denominated in only one of these currencies. To reduce currency exposure substantially, an investor should assess the correlations of movements between currencies.

From the U.S. investor's perspective, there are some currencies that are not highly correlated with each other. The Canadian dollar, for example, normally exhibits a low correlation with other currencies. The same holds for the Japanese yen. International portfolio managers should not automatically purchase stocks of a particular country simply because the currency denominating those stocks exhibits desirable characteristics. They must also consider the potential increase in the stock's value.

Like stock index comovements, currency comovements are intertemporally unstable. Therefore, historical correlation coefficients of movements in currencies will not necessarily serve as accurate indicators of the future. However, the relative ranking of currency correlations have been somewhat stable; thus, it may be possible at least to determine which currency pairs will be less correlated on a relative basis.

Direct Foreign Investments

Individual investors generally do not invest in foreign securities directly. In addition to high transaction costs and problems of obtaining information on foreign firms and dealing with foreign currency transactions, investors may encounter vastly different trading rules and investment practices in foreign markets.

The Tokyo Stock Exchange, TSE, provides a good illustration of these problems. First, it is not uncommon for Japanese stocks to sell at 50 to 60 times earnings. U.S. analysts are usually not successful at explaining these high multiples, using Western analytical methods.[12] Second, the Japanese government and private firms do not publish detailed economic and trade statistics. This limits the

---

[12] Rudnitsky, Sloan, and Fuhrman, p. 140.

U.S. investor's ability to make the customary economic analysis and forecast. Third, security regulations in Japan do not require full financial disclosure by publicly traded firms. Fourth, the regulations allow margin trading but prohibit selling short. Finally, price manipulation by brokerage firms and large investors is fairly common on the TSE.

Because of these and other problems, it is probably not advisable for individuals to invest directly in foreign securities. The next section, however, discusses four avenues that can be used to invest internationally.

Operationalizing International Diversification

There are a number of methods that individuals can use to invest internationally: (1) listed foreign stocks on a local stock exchange, (2) international mutual funds, (3) American Depository Receipts, ADRs, and (4) multinational corporate stocks.

1. LISTED FOREIGN STOCKS ON A LOCAL EXCHANGE Some U.S. stock exchanges list foreign stocks. This allows a local investor easy access to such stocks and eliminates the necessity to exchange currencies. However, the number of foreign stocks listed on a local exchange is usually quite limited, providing investors only a small sample of foreign stocks. Four of the largest and most actively traded foreign issues on the NYSE are (1) British Petroleum Company P.L.C. (United Kingdom), (2) Schlumberger Limited (Netherlands), (3) Royal Dutch Petroleum Co. (Netherlands), and (4) Northern Telecom Limited (Canada).

2. INTERNATIONAL MUTUAL FUNDS International mutual funds, IMFs, are similar to domestic mutual funds in that they represent security portfolios constructed by an investment firm. The composition of an IMF is determined by mutual fund managers; therefore, investors in the fund rely on the management of the fund.

   The IMFs exhibit characteristics similar to those of domestic mutual funds, except that they include foreign securities (stocks, bonds, or both). An investor who purchases shares of an IMF is part owner of a portfolio of international securities. Because each share represents ownership in the entire portfolio, mutual funds offer diversification to the small investor. Because of the large volume of money in most funds, diversification may be achieved to a greater degree than possible for individual investors. This implies that even if individual foreign securities could be purchased and sold easily by investors, the IMFs might still retain their popularity.

   The shares of American IMFs are priced in U.S. dollars. Thus, there is no need for the investor to exchange dollars for other currencies. However, the dollar value of the shares is influenced by currency fluctuations. The market value of an IMF still reflects the foreign currency value of each stock, translated into U.S. dollar terms. An IMF's value is determined not only by the value of each foreign security but also by the exchange rate of the currency denominating that security with respect to the U.S. dollar. In other words, an IMF's value is equal to the weighted sum of the exchange-rate-adjusted values of the component securities.

   Most IMFs are diversified across several countries. However, each fund usually concentrates on a specific region or continent. Some funds purchase securities of mostly Far Eastern companies, while other funds purchase mostly European stocks. Because each fund is typically concentrated in a specific geographic region, the full benefits of international diversification may not be realized. To grasp this concept, consider a fund composed of securities of companies based in several different European countries. Because of the inter-country influence among European countries, the states of their economies may be somewhat similar. A portfolio that includes securities from several continents should be less exposed to any single economic event.

Even if individual IMFs are not as globally diversified as desired, one can invest in several different IMFs and create a portfolio of international security portfolios. To use such an approach, the investor may first identify the composition of each available IMF by country and then determine the appropriate mix of IMFs to achieve the desired global diversification. The composition of IMFs is identified in their prospectuses.

To illustrate how some IMFs have diversified their assets, Table 23.4 provides a breakdown of the assets of three specific funds by country. G.T. Europe Growth Fund concentrates on European stocks, G.T. Pacific Growth Fund concentrates primarily on Hong Kong and Japanese stocks, and the G.T. Japan Growth Fund focuses almost exclusively on Japanese stocks. The actual breakdown for any fund can change over time. Therefore, an investor who considers IMFs should not simply pick any fund but should obtain a prospectus for each fund and identify the countries where the fund makes its investments.

The number of IMFs increased from seventeen funds in 1983 to eighty-three funds at the end of 1987. Reasons for this rapid growth include the

TABLE 23.4 APPROXIMATE BREAKDOWNS OF THREE INTERNATIONAL MUTUAL FUNDS BY COUNTRY

	G.T. EUROPE GROWTH FUND	G.T. PACIFIC GROWTH FUND	G.T. JAPAN GROWTH FUND
Japanese stocks		46.9%	92.9%
Singapore/Malaysian stocks		18.1	
Hong Kong stocks		24.2	
Australian stocks		2.4	
United Kingdom stocks	13.8%		
German stocks	17.8		
French stocks	23.8		
Spanish stocks	3.8		
Italian stocks	8.0		
Norwegian stocks	4.2		
Swiss stocks	2.9		
Swedish stocks	4.4		
Dutch stocks	10.3		
Other Assets	11.0	8.4	7.1
	100.0%	100.0%	100.0%

SOURCE: 1986 Annual Report of G.T. Global Funds. Reprinted by permission.

recent performance of foreign stocks and the decline in the value of the U.S. dollar. Table 23.5 provides information on thirty-four of the largest IMFs. As the table indicates, the total market value of these funds was approximately $13 billion as of December 31, 1987. The average *HPR*s of these funds is also significantly higher than those of U.S. stocks in general. Notice that the average five-year *HPR* over the period 1983–1987 was 161.3 percent for IMFs, versus 128.2 percent and 113.5 percent for the DJIA and S&P 500, respectively. The return performance of IMFs over the ten-year period 1978–1987 was the best of any category of funds, except for gold and precious metal funds which had a ten-year *HPR* of 541.6 percent.

The performance of foreign markets relative to U.S. markets during the October 1987 crash is likely to increase investor awareness of international investing. For example, stock prices in Japan declined 5.9 percent on "Black Monday," compared to a 22.6 percent decline in the DJIA. However, in Hong Kong, stocks declined 45.0 percent; in Australia, 44.5 percent.

3. AMERICAN DEPOSITORY RECEIPTS An *American Depository Receipt*, ADR, is a certificate issued by a major bank that represents ownership of a foreign security. Because ADRs are traded on local stock exchanges, they give local investors easy access to foreign securities. Local trading eliminates the need to exchange currencies. The issuing bank collects dividends and pays these to the ADR investor.

Several hundred ADRs are now traded in the U.S. Table 23.6 provides an example of fifteen ADRs traded on the NYSE, regional exchanges, and the OTC. As this sample indicates, ADRs represent companies located in many different countries. U.S. investors may purchase ADRs to capitalize on the potential benefits of international diversification. However, information on the companies these ADRs represent is not as available as that on domestic companies. Also, foreign governments may impose taxes on ADRs. Consequently, investors may prefer that an investment firm construct an international portfolio for them. For this reason, international mutual funds may serve as a more appropriate alternative.

4. MULTINATIONAL CORPORATE STOCKS A final method of achieving the benefits of international diversification requires no ownership of any foreign securities. Instead, an investor simply buys common stocks of U.S. multinational corporations. The logic behind such an approach is that the multinational corporation represents an international portfolio, containing subsidiaries based in foreign countries. Its overall value will be influenced not only by the economy of its headquarters country but also by the economies of all countries where it does business.

Some research has been conducted to determine whether investment in multinational corporations can achieve the benefits available from other methods of international diversification. Jacquillat and Solnik found that the price movements of multinational stocks behaved much like movements of purely domestic stocks.[13] This implies that investments in multinational

---

[13] Bertrand Jacquillat and Bruno Solnik, "Multinationals are Poor Tools for Diversification," *Journal of Portfolio Management* (Winter 1978): pp. 8–12.

TABLE 23.5   INTERNATIONAL MUTUAL FUNDS

	TOTAL NET ASSETS 12/31/87 ($ MILLIONS)	HOLDING PERIOD RETURNS				CLASSIFICATION OF ASSETS 12/31/87			PERCENT YIELD LAST 12 MONTHS
		12 MONTHS 1987	4TH QUARTER 1987	5 YEARS 1983 TO 12/31/87	10 YEARS 1978 TO 12/31/87	CASH OR GOVT	BONDS OR PRFD	COMMON STOCK	
Alliance Global-Canadian Port	$ 22.9	11.7%	17.6%	60.1%	204.8%	(1)%	0%	101%	1.3%
Alliance International Fund	127.1	−5.4	−24.2	178.5		19	1	80	1.0
Dean Witter World Wide Inv.	377.0	5.5	−16.6			10	7	83	1.1
Europacific Growth Fund	184.7	7.4	−19.3			14	5	81	2.3
Fidelity Overseas Fund	1,363.4	18.4	−17.4			0	6	94	0.0
First Investors International	93.0	28.8	−18.9	133.5		7	4	89	0.2
Ft International	76.4	1.4	−21.4			10	0	90	1.3
G.T. Europe Growth Fund	10.4	9.1	−23.4			10	5	85	0.0
G.T. International Growth	17.1	5.9	−23.2			10	8	82	0.0
G.T. Japan Growth Fund	10.0	52.4	−3.5			10	0	90	0.0
G.T. Pacific Growth Fund	37.8	2.9	−23.0	154.6	303.5	2	22	76	0.0
Hancock (John) Global Trust	132.5	4.7	−20.5			2	0	98	0.3
IDS International Fund	257.8	0.0	−24.8			6	14	80	0.2
Kemper International	184.8	6.5	−16.1	178.5		4	4	92	0.6
Keystone International Fund	125.8	9.0	−18.2	137.4	322.8	22	0	78	1.0
Mass Fin Intl Bond Tr-Bd Port	159.9	24.5	17.7	118.7		30	70	0	16.7
Merrill Lynch Int'l Holdings	270.7	6.5	−15.1			15	12	73	2.3

TABLE 23.5 (*Continued*)

Merrill Lynch Pacific Fd.	283.9	13.4	−25.2	305.1	740.6	30	0	70	2.0
Paine Webber Atlas Fund	224.0	6.7	−24.5			26	0	74	1.1
Price (T. Rowe) Int'l Stock	642.5	8.0	−18.9	206.3		7	0	93	1.7
Putnam Int'l Equities Fund	524.2	7.2	−20.1	213.9	531.8	7	5	88	1.5
Scudder International Fund	471.7	0.9	−23.2	191.3	424.6	1	5	94	2.5
Shearson Lehman Global Opp	159.7	−9.5	−27.7			3	7	90	0.6
Templeton Foreign Fund	261.2	24.7	−16.8	174.9		18	2	80	2.9
Templeton Global I	236.4	−11.6	−26.4	91.5		9	0	91	3.3
Templeton Global II	423.5	−9.8	−24.9			20	0	80	3.2
Templeton Growth Fund	1,285.3	3.1	−22.2	116.9	356.4	17	8	75	3.2
Templeton World Fund, Inc.	3,479.1	3.4	−19.3	124.1		19	5	76	3.9
Transatlantic Growth Fund	53.9	9.3	−18.4	192.5	354.9	12	0	88	0.0
Trustees Commingled-Int'l	657.3	24.0	−11.9			12	0	88	1.6
United Int'l Growth Fund	275.1	17.1	−14.7	164.7	521.8	25	5	70	1.2
U.S. Boston Invest-Foreign Perf	7.0	21.5	−22.7			4	10	86	1.1
Vanguard World-Internat'l	472.2	11.0	−14.6			13	1	86	1.0
World Trends Fund	83.6	7.9	−12.5			6	24	70	2.7
TOTAL	$12,991.9								
AVERAGES		9.3%	−17.5%	161.3%	417.9%	11.7%	6.8%	81.5%	1.8%
Market Averages:									
DJIA		5.5%	−24.6%	128.2%	287.8%				
S&P 500		5.2	−22.5	113.5	312.2				

SOURCE: *Management Results*, Wiesenberger Investment Companies Service, pp. 10–11; data for period ending December 31, 1987. Wiesenberger Investment Companies Service Division of Warren, Gorham & Lamont, Inc.

TABLE 23.6 SAMPLE OF ACTIVELY TRADED AMERICAN DEPOSITORY RECEIPTS

	EXCHANGE OR MARKET	APRIL 1988 CLOSE
1. Aegon N.V.	OTC	$39\frac{3}{8}$
2. Anglo Am. Gold Inv.	OTC	$8\frac{1}{4}$
3. B.A.T. Indus. Ord	AMEX, Boston, Midwest, Pacific	$7\frac{7}{8}$
4. Beazer PLC	OTC	$13\frac{1}{2}$
5. Beecham Group	OTC	18
6. British Telecomm'n.	NYSE, Pacific	$46\frac{1}{2}$
7. Canon	OTC	$51\frac{1}{2}$
8. DeBeers Cons. Mns.	OTC	$10\frac{3}{4}$
9. Free St. Con. Gold Mines	OTC	$9\frac{1}{8}$
10. Honda Motor	NYSE, Boston, Midwest, Pacific, Philadelphia	$145\frac{1}{8}$
11. Matsushita El. Ind.	NYSE, Boston, Midwest, Pacific, Philadelphia	$222\frac{3}{8}$
12. Mitsui	OTC	$150\frac{3}{4}$
13. Oce-Van der Grinten	OTC	$23\frac{1}{4}$
14. Sony	NYSE, Boston, Cincinnati, Midwest, Pacific, Philadelphia, Toronto, Montreal	$44\frac{1}{4}$
15. Telefonos de Mexico	OTC	$\frac{1}{4}$

SOURCE: Standard & Poor's *Stock Guide*, May 1988. Reprinted by permission.

stocks would not provide as much diversification as a portfolio including foreign securities. Senchack and Beedles detected a slightly favorable performance from multinational stocks relative to domestic stocks.[14] However, the advantage was not sufficient to warrant the sole use of this strategy in attempting to benefit from international diversification. There has been additional research on this issue, but no consensus has been reached.

HEDGING CURRENCY RISK OF AN INTERNATIONAL PORTFOLIO

It was mentioned earlier that ownership of foreign securities will expose an investor to currency risk (risk that the currency will fluctuate against the the investor's home currency). Investors who desire to avoid this risk may be able to hedge their positions in the forward exchange market.[15] For the widely used currencies, forward rates are commonly available for maturities such as 30 days, 90 days,

---

[14] Andrew J. Senchack, Jr. and W. L. Beedles, "Is Indirect International Diversification Desirable?" *Journal of Portfolio Management* (Winter 1980): pp. 49–57.

[15] Forward and futures markets for foreign currencies and currency options are discussed in Chapters 19 and 21.

180 days, and one year. This means that an investor can buy or sell that currency forward for any of these maturities. Commercial banks offer this service; they are willing to deliver a currency or purchase a currency in the future and lock in the rate of exchange today. Regardless of how currency values move, the forward rate on the day the contract is established will serve as the rate of exchange on the settlement data. Because forward rates are offered only for large currency transactions, it is not practical for an individual to hedge using these contracts. They are more commonly used by international mutual funds to hedge foreign investments.

To illustrate how a hedge could work, assume that a U.S. investment firm has developed an international mutual fund which is partially composed of British stocks. If the British pound depreciates against the U.S. dollar, U.S. investors in the fund are adversely affected. A mutual fund can avoid this risk by ''selling British pounds forward'' for a particular date when it plans to liquidate British stocks. On that date, the firm will sell the stocks and exchange the pounds received from the sale for U.S. dollars, at the rate specified by the forward contract. If the firm decides not to sell the British stocks on this date, it can offset its ''short'' position in British pounds by purchasing pounds in the spot market at the spot exchange rate and selling those to fulfill its forward sale obligation. The gain (loss) from this strategy can offset most of the loss (gain) in the international mutual fund due to fluctuations in the British pound value. If the investment firm expects the British pound to appreciate (strengthen), it may prefer not to hedge; the pound's appreciation will enhance the performance of the fund from the U.S. investor's perspective.

The majority of foreign currency positions of international mutual funds are not hedged. Thus, the net asset values of most international mutual funds are highly susceptible to foreign currency movements against the U.S. dollar.

INTERNATIONAL MONEY MARKET DIVERSIFICATION

International investing is not confined to capital market instruments such as stocks and bonds. Large corporations often set up short-term (money market) deposits denominated in foreign currencies. In some cases, this approach is taken to offset a future payable in that currency, but sometimes a foreign currency deposit is set up to capitalize on higher foreign interest rates. The arena for international short-term investing is known as the *Eurocurrency market*. It is made up of large banks (called Eurobanks) which are willing to accept large short-term deposits in foreign currencies and lend these deposits to corporations and governments in need of short-term funds.

Assume that you are the treasurer of a large U.S. corporation. One of your jobs is to manage a short-term portfolio. You must decide how to invest the funds for, say, a three-month period and strive to meet specified goals related to high return and low risk. You may find that deposits denominated in French francs offer a higher quoted rate than U.S. dollar deposits. However, there is a risk that the French franc may depreciate during the life of the deposit. In this case, the deposit denominated in French francs may generate a return which is far lower than that of a U.S.-dollar-denominated deposit. This *currency risk* is similar to that which was discussed in the section on international stock investing. One way to avoid this risk is to hedge your currency positions by selling forward the currencies on the date the deposit matures, when you plan to convert the currency held back to U.S. dollars. Unfortunately, the forward rate will typically contain a discount for currencies whose interest rates exceed those in the United States. The size of the discount will be directly related to the interest rate differential. This relationship is known as *interest rate parity*. If interest rate parity exists, hedging a short-term deposit will force the rate of return on the foreign deposit to be no higher than the return on a U.S. deposit. This does not mean that you cannot earn a higher return on foreign currency deposits; instead, it implies that if you want to achieve higher gains than those possible domestically, you will have to remain unhedged (exposed to currency risk).

The first step in considering short-term deposits is to review all types of deposits and the rates offered on each. The next step is to forecast the percentage change in the exchange rate of the currency denominating each deposit over the life of the planned investment. Then, the exchange-rate-adjusted yield on each deposit can be forecast. This return accounts for not only the interest rate offered in the deposit but also the anticipated exchange rate fluctuation. Table 23.7 provides an example of an assessment of four possible deposits, each denominated in a different currency. The anticipated exchange-rate-adjusted yield shown in the final column of Table 23.7 is computed as follows:

$$\text{Exchange-Rate-Adjusted Yield on Deposit} = (1 + \text{quoted interest rate}) \times (1 + \Delta \text{ in exchange rate against U.S.\$}) - 1 \tag{23.6}$$

Table 23.7 illustrates the strong influence exchange rate fluctuations can have on the actual yield of foreign deposits. The French franc's quoted interest rate is the highest of all currencies. But the British deposit is expected to earn the highest yield after accounting for the expected exchange rate fluctuations, since the British pound is expected to appreciate relative to the U.S. dollar.

The appropriate selection of a foreign deposit depends on one's degree of risk aversion. An extremely risk-averse person would probably prefer the U.S. dollar investment, since the 6 percent earnings are assured. While the anticipated

TABLE 23.7 COMPUTATION OF EXCHANGE-RATE-ADJUSTED YIELD

CURRENCY DENOMINATING THE DEPOSIT	QUOTED INTEREST RATE OFFERED ON DEPOSIT	ANTICIPATED CHANGE IN THE EXCHANGE RATE AGAINST THE U.S. DOLLAR OVER THE LIFE OF THE DEPOSIT	ANTICIPATED RATE OF RETURN
British pound	9%	4%	$(1 + .09)(1 + .04) - 1 = 13.36\%$
Canadian dollar	8	−1	$(1 + .08)(1 - .01) - 1 = 6.92$
French franc	10	−2	$(1 + .10)(1 - .02) - 1 = 7.80$
U.S. dollar	6	0	$(1 + .06)(1 + 0) - 1 = 6.00$

yield is higher for the other three deposits, there is uncertainty about the actual yield to be generated by these deposits. This uncertainty comes from the forecast of each currency's fluctuation against the U.S. dollar. A poor forecast could result in an investment that generates a very low yield. To assess further the risk of each deposit denominated in a foreign currency, a probability distribution could be created for each currency's anticipated fluctuation. However, this risk assessment would be only as accurate as the probability distribution.

One way to reduce the currency risk on short-term deposits is to diversify the funds among several currencies (i.e., set up several different deposits, each deposit denominated in a different currency). The degree to which currency risk is reduced is dependent on the comovements of the currencies. If the currencies move in tandem against the U.S. dollar, such a portfolio will exhibit almost as much exposure as all funds being placed in a single deposit denominated in one of those foreign currencies. A more appropriate portfolio would contain currencies with low correlations.

SUMMARY

Over the last several years, major developments have encouraged international diversification. Local exchanges are offering more foreign stocks, and the numbers of ADRs and international mutual funds are increasing. This chapter summarized research that verified the potential benefits of international diversification. Yet, creating an efficient international portfolio for a future period is more difficult than identifying an efficient portfolio over a previous period because the returns, variability, and pairwise correlations of portfolio components change. However, investors can still benefit from international diversification, even if their portfolios are not ex-ante mean-variance efficient.

QUESTIONS

1. Why would correlations between stocks of different countries change over time?

2. Why is the use of the mean-variance portfolio model limited in its ability to identify appropriate global security portfolios in the future?

3. Define the "naive" method for international portfolio diversification.

4. Assume that you are a portfolio manager. If your local currency is expected generally to appreciate against foreign currencies, should this increase or decrease your potential benefits from international diversification? How could you insulate your portfolio from such exchange rate risk?

5. Explain how an investor can diversify internationally without having to purchase foreign stocks directly on foreign stock exchanges.

6. Explain why securities from an internationally diversified portfolio are expected to exhibit lower pairwise correlations than securities from a purely domestic portfolio.

7. Would you expect to achieve greater reduction in portfolio variability by including only securities from industrialized countries or by including securities from industrialized and less-developed countries? Why?

8. If the governments of less-developed countries loosened their restrictions on international transactions, how might this affect the correlations of their securities' returns with those of other countries? Does this have any effect on the desirability of such stocks for inclusion in an international security portfolio?

9. Consider an investor who purchases an international mutual fund which is composed of over twenty stocks in each of several European countries. Is there any reason for the investor to consider diversifying among international mutual funds, or is the one fund sufficient to achieve maximum reduction in portfolio variability? Explain your answer.

10. Discuss the possible disadvantages for a U.S. investor in investing internationally.

11. During early 1988, the U.S. dollar declined in value relative to many other currencies. Assuming that the dollar will continue to decline, discuss several appropriate international investment strategies.

12. Ignoring currency exchange risk, do you think that international investments for U.S. investors have more or less risk than similar domestic investments? Explain your answer.

13. Discuss the advantages and disadvantages of international money market diversification.

PROBLEMS

1. Assume that you are currently considering U.S. stocks X and Y and a Swiss stock Q. Assume the following risk characteristics for stocks X, Y, and Q.

STOCK	STANDARD DEVIATION OF RETURNS	CORRELATION COEFFICIENT WITH OTHER STOCKS		
		STOCK X	STOCK Y	STOCK Q
X	.08	1.00		
Y	.07	.80	1.00	
Q	.06	.10	.30	1.00

a. What would be the variance of a portfolio which has one third of its funds allocated to each of the three stocks?

b. What would be the standard deviation of a portfolio which has one third of its funds allocated to each of the three stocks?

c. What would be the standard deviation of a portfolio which has 50 percent of its funds allocated to stock Q, 25 percent allocated to stock X, and 25 percent allocated to stock Y?

d. Based on your answer to part b, what is the degree of risk reduction in this portfolio (using standard deviation as a proxy for risk) relative to the mean risk of the individual securities?

e. Based on your answer to part c, what is the degree of risk reduction in this portfolio (using standard deviation as a proxy for risk) relative to the mean risk of the individual securities?

f. A portfolio which assigns 50 percent of its funds to the foreign stock Q, while the remaining 50 percent is allocated equally to stocks X and Y, exhibits less risk than a portfolio which assigns an equal amount of its funds to each of the three securities. How do you explain this result?

2. Assume that a British and a U.S. investor each purchased 100 shares of a British stock one year ago. At that time, the stock was worth 4 pounds per share. The exchange rate of the pound was $2.00 at that time. Today, both investors sell their British stock for 5 pounds per share. The exchange rate of the pound today is $2.10 (Ignore all transaction costs and dividends).

   a. Calculate the *HPR* for the British investor.

   b. Calculate the *HPR* to the U.S. investor, considering the change in the exchange rate .

   c. Assume that the U.S. investor correctly forecast the number of pounds he would have at the end of one year and sold pounds one year forward to avoid the exchange rate risk. The forward rate at the time a contract was set up was $2.02. Given this information, what was the return to the investor? Is the return to this investor higher or lower than it would have been if the currency exposure had not been hedged?

3. Assume that the treasurer of a U.S. corporation plans to invest $1,000,000 in a three-month deposit denominated in French francs. The quoted interest rate over the three-month period is 5%. The franc is expected to appreciate by 2% over this period. What is the anticipated rate of return on this three-month investment? What is the anticipated rate of return if the franc is expected to depreciate by 4% over this period?

4. Assume that a U.S. investor purchased 100 shares of common stocks of the Hudson Bay Company, traded on the Toronto Stock Exchange, for $21 per share (Canadian). The investor exchanged U.S. dollars for Canadian dollars at an exchange rate of $.7918 U.S. dollars for each Canadian dollar. The stock appreciated to $22 per share (Canadian) and was sold. The Canadian dollars received from the sale were exchanged for U.S. dollars at an exchange rate of $.8123.

   a. Calculate the *HPR* on the stock investment, ignoring currency exchange rates.

   b. Calculate the *HPR*, considering changes in the stock price and in the currency exchange rate.

REFERENCES

Agmon, Tamir. ''The Relations among Equity Markets: A Study of Share Price Comovements in the United States, United Kingdom, Germany, and Japan.'' *Journal of Finance* 22 (September 1972): pp. 839–55.

Agmon, Tamir, and Donald R. Lessard. ''Investor Recognition of Corporate International Diversification.'' *Journal of Finance* 32 (September 1977): pp. 1049–58.

Bertoneche, Marc L. ''Spectral Analysis of Stock Market Prices.'' *Journal of Banking and Finance* 3 (July 1979): pp. 201–8.

Bicksler, James L. Discussion of Lessard's paper ''World, National, and Industry Factors in Equity Returns.'' *Journal of Finance* 29 (May 1974): pp. 395–98.

Biger, Nahum. ''Exchange Risk Implications of International Portfolio Diversification.'' *Journal of International Business Studies* 10 (Fall 1979): pp. 64–74.

Brewer, H. L. ''Investor Benefits from Corporation International Diversification.'' *Journal of Finance and Quantitative Analysis* 16 (March 1981): pp. 113–25.

Cohn, Richard A., and John J. Pringle. ''Imperfections in International Financial Markets: Implications for Risk Premia and the Cost of Capital to Firms.'' *Journal of Finance* (March 1973): pp. 59–66.

Errunza, Vihang R. ''Gains from Portfolio Diversification into Less Developed Countries' Securities.'' *Journal of International Business Studies* 8 (Fall/Winter 1977): pp. 83–99.

————. "Gains from Portfolio Diversification into Less Developed Countries' Securities: A Reply." *Journal of International Business Studies* 9 (Spring-Summer 1978): pp. 117–23.

Findlay, M. Chapman III, and William Smith. "Some Canadian Implications of International Portfolio Diversification." *Financial Review* (1976): pp. 36–48.

Fung, W. K. H. "Gains from International Portfolio Diversification: A Comment." *Journal of Business, Finance, and Accounting* 6 (Spring 1979): pp. 45–49.

Gray, H. Peter. "Gains from Diversification of Real Assets: An Extension." *Journal of Business Research* 6 (January 1978): pp. 81–83.

Grubel, Herbert G. "Internationally Diversified Portfolios: Welfare Gains and Capital Flows." *Journal of Finance* 26 (March 1971): pp. 89–94.

Guy, James R. F. "The Performance of the British Investment Trust Industry." *Journal of Finance* 33 (May 1978): pp. 443–45.

Haney, Richard L., Jr., and William P. Lloyd. "An Examination of the Stability of the Intertemporal Relationship among National Stock Market Indices." *Nebraska Journal of Economics and Business* 17 (Spring 1978): pp. 55–65.

Hill, Joanne, and Thomas Schneeweis. "International Diversification of Equities and Fixed Income Securities." *Journal of Financial Research* (Winter 1983): pp. 333–43.

Horn, Bernard. "International Investing Strategies." *American Association of Institutional Investors Journal* (November 1983): pp. 11–19.

Hughes, John S., Dennis E. Logue, and Richard James Sweeney. "Corporate International Diversification and Market Assigned Measures of Risk and Diversification." *Journal of Financial and Quantitative Analysis* 10 (November 1975): pp. 627–37.

Jacquillat, Bertrand, and Bruno Solnik. "Multinationals Are Poor Tools for Diversification." *Journal of Portfolio Management* (Winter 1978): pp. 8–12.

Joy, O. Maurice, Don B. Panton, Frank K. Reilly, and Stanley A. Martin. "Comovements of Major International Equity Markets," *Financial Review* (1976): pp. 1–20.

Karp, Richard. "Making an International Splash." *Institutional Investor* (April 1983): pp. 139–40.

Lessard, Donald R. "International Portfolio Diversification: A Multivariate Analysis for a Group of Latin American Countries." *Journal of Finance* 23 (June 1973): pp. 619–34.

————. "World, Country, and Industry Relationships in Equity Return." *Financial Analysts Journal* (January-February 1976): pp. 32–38.

Levy, Haim, and Marshall Sarnat. "International Diversification of Investment Portfolios." *American Economic Review* 60 (September 1970): pp. 668–75.

Lim, Quek Peck. "Trading Stocks across Frontiers." *Euromoney* (May 1984): pp. 110–12.

Lloyd, William P. "International Portfolio Diversification of Real Assets: An Inquiry." *Journal of Business Research* 3 (January 1975): pp. 113–20.

Lloyd, William P., Steven J. Goldstein, and Robert B. Rogow. "International Portfolio Diversification of Real Assets: An Update." *Journal of Business, Finance, and Accounting* 8 (Spring 1981): pp. 45–50.

Logue, Dennis E. "An Experiment in International Diversification." *Journal of Portfolio Management* (Fall 1982): pp. 22–27.

Logue, Dennis E., and Richard J. Rogalski. "Offshore Alphas: Should Diversification Begin at Home?: Reply." *Journal of Portfolio Management* (Winter 1979): pp. 76–78.

Makridakis, Spyros G., and Steven C. Wheelwright. "An Analysis of the Interrelationships among the Major World Stock Exchanges." *Journal of Business, Finance, and Accounting* 1 (Summer 1974): pp. 195–216.

McDonald, John G. " French Mutual Fund Performance: Evaluation of Internationally Diversified Portfolios." *Journal of Finance* 28 (December 1973): pp. 1161–80.

Mikhail, Azmi D., and Hany A. Shawky. "Investment Performance of U.S based Multinational Corporations." *Journal of International Business Studies* 10 (Spring-Summer 1979): pp. 53–66.

Osborn, Neil. "Why Europe Is Coming to New York." *Euromoney* (November 1983): pp. 77–83.

Panton, Don B., V. Parker Lessiq, and O. Maurice Joy. "Comovement of International Equity Markets: A Taxonomic Approach." *Journal of Financial and Quantitative Analysis* 11 (September 1976): pp. 415–32.

Rugman, Alan M. "Risk Reduction by International Diversification." *Journal of International Business Studies* 7 (Fall/Winter 1976): pp. 75–80.

Ripley, Duncan. "Systematic Elements in the Linkage of National Stock Market Indices." *The Review of Economics and Statistics* 15 (August 1973): pp. 356–61.

Rudnitsky, Howard, Allan Sloan, and Peter Fuhrman. "Land of the Rising Stocks." *Forbes*, 18 May 1987, pp. 139–43.

Saunders, Anthony, and Richard S. Woodward. "Gains from International Portfolio Diversification: U. K. Evidence 1971–75." *Journal of Business, Finance, and Accounting* 4 (Autumn 1977) pp. 299–309.

―――. "Gains from International Portfolio Diversification: A Reply." *Journal of Business, Finance, and Accounting* (Spring 1979): pp. 51–52.

Schneeweis, Thomas, and Joanne Hill. "The Benefits of Multinational Diversification: A New Look." Working paper, October 1981.

―――. "A Note on the Comovement of International Equity and Bond Markets." *Financial Review* (Winter 1980): pp. 30–37.

Senchack, Andrew J., Jr., and W. L. Beedles. "Is Indirect International Diversification Desirable?" *Journal of Portfolio Management* (Winter 1980): pp. 49–57.

Severn, Alan K. "Investor Evaluation of Foreign and Domestic Risk." *Journal of Finance* 29 (May 1974): pp. 545–50.

Shapiro, Alan C. "International Cash Management: The Determination of Multicurrency Cash Balances." *Journal of Financial and Quantitative Analysis* 11 (December 1976): pp. 893–900.

Shirreff, David. "Prepare for the Global Market." *Euromoney* (October 1983): pp. 124–27.

Shohet, Ruben. "Investing in Foreign Securities." *Financial Analysts Journal* (September-October 1974): pp. 55–72.

Solnik, Bruno H. "The International Pricing of Risk: An Empirical Examination of the World Market Structure." *Journal of Finance* 29 (May 1974): pp. 365–78.

―――. "Why Not Diversify Internationally Rather than Domestically?" *Financial Analysts Journal* (July–August 1974): pp. 48–54.

Stehle, Richard. "An Empirical Test of the Alternative Hypothesis of National and International Pricing of Risky Assets." *Journal of Finance* (May 1977): pp. 493–502.

Watson, J. "The Stationarity of Inter-Country Correlation Coefficients: A Note." *Journal of Business, Finance, and Accounting* (Spring 1980): pp. 297–303.

"Why the Big Apple Shines in the World's Markets." *Business Week*, 23 July 1984, pp. 100–104.

CHAPTER 24

MUTUAL FUNDS AND OTHER TYPES OF INVESTMENTS COMPANIES

INTRODUCTION

The purpose of this chapter is to provide an overview of investment companies. An *investment company* is simply a corporation that invests in marketable securities and other categories of investments such as real assets. There are two primary forms of investment companies: open-end and closed-end. *Mutual funds*, the largest and most popular, are *open-end* investment companies because they stand ready to issue new shares or redeem outstanding shares on a continuous basis. The number of shares, therefore, fluctuates as investors add or redeem shares. A *closed-end* investment company is more like a traditional, publicly traded corporation, with a fixed number of shares of common stock outstanding. An investment company is basically a corporation that provides "collective" investing opportunities to individuals, businesses, and other investors.

This chapter concentrates on mutual funds, or open-end companies. The chapter does, however, discuss the three types of closed-end companies: (1) funds, (2) unit trusts, and (3) dual funds. The remainder of the chapter discusses mutual funds: their characteristics, key investment decision variables, and strategies for investing in mutual funds.

CLOSED-END COMPANIES

Closed-end Funds

The share price of a closed-end investment company is determined by supply and demand factors; its shares are traded on a stock exchange or OTC market. There are approximately 150 publicly traded closed-end companies, but many of these are small in terms of assets. The shares of larger companies are traded on the New York Stock Exchange and American Stock Exchange; the smaller companies on the Over-the-Counter market.[1] Table 24.1 provides information on the more actively traded closed-end funds.

While the number of closed-end funds is small relative to mutual funds, they offer investors certain attractive characteristics. One interesting characteristic is the tendency for closed-end funds to sell at discounts from their *net asset value*, NAV. NAV is simply the total market value of the securities owned, less any liabilities, divided by the number of shares outstanding. If the price of the shares is less than NAV, the investor can buy $1 worth of assets for less than $1.

Numerous studies have attempted to explain why closed-end fund shares usually have prices below NAV.[2] Popular explanations include: (1) the shares must be bought through a broker that may prefer to sell more traditional investments such as common stocks; (2) the funds do not have an active marketing campaign;

---

[1] For information on the larger companies, see *Investment Companies* (New York: Wiesenberger Investment Companies Service, 1987), p. 19.

[2] See, for example, Burton Malkiel, "The Valuation of Closed-end Investment Company Shares," *Journal of Finance* (June 1977): pp. 847–51, and R. Malcolm Richards, Don R. Fraser, and John C. Groth, "Winning Strategies for Closed-end Funds," *Journal of Portfolio Management* (Fall 1980): pp. 50–55.

TABLE 24.1 CLOSED-END FUNDS

PUBLICLY TRADED FUNDS

Friday, May 13, 1988

Following is a weekly listing of unaudited net asset values of publicly traded investment fund shares, reported by the companies as of Friday's close. Also shown is the closing listed market price or a dealer-to-dealer asked price of each fund's shares, with the percentage of difference.

Fund Name	Stock Exch.	N.A. Value	Stock Price	% Diff.
Diversified Common Stock Funds				
Adams Express	NYSE	16.49	15½ −	6.00
Baker Fentress-n	OTC	49.29	38¾ −	21.38
Blue Chip Value	NYSE	6.98	5½ −	21.20
Clemente Global Gro	NYSE	gb8.42	6⅜ −	24.29
Equity Guard Stock	AMEX	b9.86	9⅜ −	4.92
Gemini II Capital	NYSE	f z	z	z
Gemini II Income	NYSE	z	z	z
General Amer Invest	NYSE	17.83	14⅛ −	20.80
Global Growth Capital	NYSE	8.40	8 −	4.76
Global Growth Income	NYSE	9.41	9⅜ −	0.37
Growth Stock Outlook	NYSE	9.59	9¼ −	3.50
Lehman Corp.	NYSE	13.67	12 −	12.20
Liberty All-Star Eqty	NYSE	8.14	6¼ −	23.20
Niagara Share Corp.	NYSE	15.47	12¾ −	17.58
Nicholas-Applegate	NYSE	8.15	6¾ −	17.18
Quest For Value Cap	NYSE	10.08	7⅞ −	21.87
Quest For Value Inco	NYSE	11.82	10⅛ −	14.34
Royce Value Trust	NYSE	9.18	8 −	12.85
Schafer Value Trust	NYSE	8.43	6⅞ −	18.45
Source Capital	NYSE	37.91	37½ −	1.08
Tri-Continental Corp.	NYSE	23.77	20⅞ −	12.20
Worldwide Value	NYSE	18.70	14¾ −	21.12
Zweig Fund	NYSE	9.98	10¼ +	2.71
Closed End Bond Funds				
CIM High Yield Secs	AMEX	9.68	10⅛ +	4.60
Specialized Equity and Convertible Funds				
American Capital Conv	NYSE	22.78	20¾ −	8.91
ASA Ltd	NYSE	bc49.96	43½ −	12.90
Asia Pacific	NYSE	7.98	6⅜ −	20.11
Bancroft Convertible	AMEX	22.66	20⅞ −	7.87
BGR Precious Metals	TOR	be13.84	10¼ −	25.94
Brazil	NYSE	11.59	9½ −	18.03
CNV Holdings Capital	NYSE	9.50	4¾ −	50.00
CNV Holdings Income	NYSE	9.49	11 +	15.91
Castle Convertible	AMEX	22.68	21¼ −	6.30
Central Fund Canada	AMEX	b6.32	5¾ −	9.00
Central Securities	AMEX	12.29	9⅞ −	19.65
Claremont Capital	AMEX	50.13	48¾ −	2.80
Couns Tandem Secs	NYSE	7.05	5¼ −	25.53
Cypress Fund	AMEX	9.19	6⅞ −	25.19
Duff&Phelps Sel Utils	NYSE	7.56	8¼ +	9.00
Ellsw Conv Gr&Inc	AMEX	8.45	7½ −	11.27
Engex	AMEX	12.36	9⅝ −	22.12
Financ'l News Compos	NYSE	15.35	12⅜ −	19.38
1stAustralia	AMEX	9.44	7⅞ −	16.57
First Financial Fund	NYSE	8.41	6¾ −	19.74
First Iberian	AMEX	9.15	8¼ −	9.84
France Fund	NYSE	b10.08	9 −	10.70
Gabelli Equity Trust	NYSE	10.71	8¾ −	18.30
Germany Fund	NYSE	7.21	6½ −	9.80
H&Q Healthcare Inv	NYSE	7.82	6⅝ −	15.28
Hampton Utils Tr Cap	AMEX	b8.99	7⅝ −	15.18
Hampton Utils Tr Pref	AMEX	b48.82	48⅝ −	0.40
Helvetia Fund	NYSE	11.09	10¼ −	7.57
Italy Fund	NYSE	b9.05	6⅞ −	24.03
Korea Fund	NYSE	39.61	71⅜ +	80.19
Malaysia Fund	NYSE	8.20	6¾ −	17.68
Mexico Fund	NYSE	b6.25	4¾ −	24.00
Morgan Grenf SmCap	NYSE	8.77	7⅝ −	13.10
Petrol & Resources	NYSE	26.36	25⅜ −	3.74
Pilgrim Reg Bk Shrs	NYSE	9.17	7 −	23.66
Progressive Inco Eqty	NYSE	8.71	8⅜ −	0.04
Regional Fin Shrs Inv	NYSE	7.47	5¾ −	23.02
Scandinavia Fund	AMEX	8.71	6¾ −	22.50
Scudder New Asia	NYSE	13.53	10⅞ −	19.62
Taiwan Fund	AMEX	b25.09	42⅛ +	67.90
TCW Convertible Secs	NYSE	b8.33	7⅛ −	14.50
Templeton Em Mkts	AMEX	b8.67	7 −	19.30
Thai Fund	NYSE	11.43	16 +	39.98
United Kingdom Fund	NYSE	11.52	9⅛ −	20.78
Z-Seven Fund	OTC	d14.20	14¾ +	3.90

a-Ex-dividend. b-As of Thursday's close. c-Translated at Commercial Rand exchange rate. d-NAV reflects $1.66 per share for taxes. e-In Canadian Dollars. f-5/6/88 NAV: $14.51; % Diff:−26.80. g-5/5/88 NAV: $8.61. z-Not avail-

SOURCE: *Wall Street Journal*, 16 May 1988, p. 41. Reprinted by permission.

(3) the market for the shares is "thin" because of the size of the companies and the lack of institutional investor interest; and (4) the market is inefficient in pricing the shares.

The idea that there may be some market inefficiencies in pricing the shares is of considerable interest to both financial researchers and investors. A recent study by Anderson confirmed the results of earlier studies concerning the existence of possible market inefficiency.[3] Based on a sample of seventeen closed-end equity funds over three different periods from January 1965 through August 1984, Anderson's findings supported conclusions by earlier researchers that market inefficiencies existed for closed-end shares. The inefficiencies were also of a magnitude and duration to allow investors to earn risk-adjusted excess returns from strategies based on the discounts and from buy-and-hold strategies. The study, however, did not address the issue of why the inefficiencies exist.

Active investor strategies based on the discounts involve identification of buy-and-sell points and filter rules. Under a buy-and-sell strategy, for example, an investor would purchase shares when the price was 15 percent below NAV and sell when the discount narrowed to 10 percent. An example of a filter rule strategy would be to buy when the price decreased by X percent or sell when the price increased by Y percent, where X and Y are the size of the filters.

A closed-end fund can operate as a diversified or nondiversified fund. A *diversified* fund holds a large number of securities from different industries and thus provides the investor with diversification. A *nondiversified* fund concentrates the portfolio in specific industry segments such as petroleum resources or gold-mining issues. Some nondiversified funds also concentrate in specific types of securities such as debenture bonds, real estate investment trusts, REITs, or preferred stock.

A study of one type of nondiversified or specialized closed-end fund—bond funds—confirmed the existence of market inefficiencies that provide trading opportunities for investors.[4] This study, using eighteen publicly traded bond funds from January 1975 through December 1979, found that the funds had average discounts from their NAV of 2.1 to 13.3 percent. An analysis of the monthly time series data led the authors to conclude that "an asymmetrical risk relationship has been shown to exist that provides the investor with down-side protection in the event of rising interest rates."[5] This conclusion essentially indicates that the pricing inefficiencies provided risk-adjusted excess returns. The data also suggest that the discount varies considerably over time, so that the funds can be purchased when the discount is the greatest and sold as the discount shrinks.

Closed-end funds fared poorly during the October 1987 market crash; their prices declined 30–35 percent, compared to 22.6 percent for the DJIA. This occurred because investors applied larger percentage discounts to the NAVs of the funds. However, in a bull market, it is likely that the size of discount from NAV will decline, causing the shares to appreciate more than stocks in general.

---

[3] Seth Copeland Anderson, "Closed-end Funds versus Market Efficiency," *Journal of Portfolio Management* (Fall 1986): pp. 63–65.

[4] R. Malcolm Richards, Donald R. Fraser, and John C. Groth, "The Attractions of Closed-end Bond Funds," *Journal of Portfolio Management* (Winter 1982): pp. 56–61.

[5] Ibid, p. 61.

The behavior of the discount over the market cycle, combined with the underlying volatility of the securities in the portfolio, cause the beta of many closed-end funds to exceed 1.

Other Types of Closed-end Companies

1. UNIT TRUST A special type of investment company is a *unit trust*. A "unit," or ownership interest, in this type of portfolio is typically sold for $1,000 and represents a claim to a *fixed* portfolio of securities. The securities in the portfolio are acquired before the units are offered to investors. The trust is then an unmanaged portfolio, since the composition of the portfolio is not changed. After the initial public offering, the units are traded in the Over-the-Counter market. The number of units of ownership is fixed as in the case of a closed-end fund.

    The portfolio of the unit trust normally consists of fixed-income securities that may be tax-exempt municipal bonds, corporate bonds, or government securities. All interest collected on the bonds is paid to the investor, usually on a monthly basis, by the trustee. When the bonds mature, the trustee distributes the principal, and the trust terminates. Information on unit trusts is available in Wiesenberger's *Investment Companies*.

2. DUAL FUNDS Another unique type of investment company is the closed-end *dual fund*. It is referred to as a dual fund because it has two types of shares, income and capital. The income shareholder receives all interest and dividends, while the capital shareholder receives all capital gain distributions. This type of fund was popular in the 1970s and early 1980s. However, the tax reforms of 1986 that eliminated preferential tax treatment for long-term capital gains may have unfavorable consequences for dual funds.

3. PRIMES AND SCORES Beginning in the early 1980s, a number of investment trusts were formed for the purpose of splitting blue-chip common stocks into conservative and speculative components.[6] A separate trust is created for each common stock, and the trust creates three different securities: trust units, primes, and scores. The *prime* (*p*rescribed *r*ight to *i*ncome and *m*aximum *e*quity) security is similar to preferred stock and is like an income share in a dual fund. The *score* (*s*pecial *c*laim *o*n *r*esidual *e*quity) security entitles the holder to all the stock's price appreciation above a specified price when the trust is liquidated. The score security is similar to a European warrant and is like a capital share of a dual fund. The trust units (both a prime and score), primes, and scores are traded on the AMEX. In early 1988, approximately eighteen trust securities were trading on the common stock of such well-known firms as AT&T, GE, GM, and Sears.

OVERVIEW OF MUTUAL FUNDS

Definition and Operations

Mutual funds hold cash, near-cash, stocks, bonds, other marketable securities, and in some cases, real assets. The exact composition of the portfolio depends on

---

[6] John Liscio, "Splitting Shares," *Barron's*, 14 Mar. 1988, pp. 13, 72–73.

the type of fund and the investment objective of the fund. A balance sheet and income statement for a typical mutual fund is provided in Table 24.2. Mutual funds have very few liabilities because of restrictions on the use of leverage imposed by the Investment Company Act of 1940.

Mutual funds operate like any other business, with a management staff, employees, and facilities. As corporations, they also have a board of directors. The key employees of a fund are the security analysts and portfolio managers, who develop investment strategies. For larger funds, such as T. Rowe Price and Fidelity Investments that offer a *family* or large number of individual funds, it is common to have an agreement with an *investment advisor*. The investment advisor provides services to all the funds in the family on a fee basis and is responsible for research, security analysis, execution of security transactions, portfolio management, and (possibly) administrative duties. The fund may also have an agreement with another firm to provide services dealing with record-keeping for transfers of cash and securities and maintaining shareholder records. A *custodian* may be employed for storage and safeguarding of the securities. As an example, Fidelity Investments Freedom Fund has agreements with an investment advisor, Fidelity Management & Research Company; a servicing agent, Fidelity Service Co.; and a custodian, Brown Brothers Harriman & Co. In addition, the fund conducts some of its security transactions through Fidelity Brokerage Services, Inc.

Historical Development of Mutual Funds

The concept of an open-end investment company (mutual fund) originated in England and found its way to the United States in 1924. Both open-end and closed-end funds were organized in Boston, New York, and Philadelphia. The purpose of these original funds was essentially the same as today's: to offer investors a way to obtain professional investment management, along with diversification in terms of the number of securities in the portfolio.

The stock market crash of 1929 halted the growth of the investment company industry, with many of the closed-end funds severely affected by the market collapse. After the market crash, the open-end company emerged as the dominant organizational form for investment companies.

In 1940 there were 68 mutual funds in existence, representing $448 million in assets and 296,000 shareholder accounts. At the end of 1987, there were more than 2,300 funds with $769 billion in assets.[7] One major development in the growth of the industry was the concept of a *money market* mutual fund, first offered in the early 1970s. These funds allowed small investors an opportunity to invest in money market securities rather than using only deposit accounts available at commercial banks or savings and loan associations.

Mutual fund assets have grown tremendously since their introduction in the United States in 1924. Figure 24.1 provides graphs representing the number of shareholder accounts and the assets of mutual funds over the 1940–87 period. Since about 1978, money market and short-term municipal bond funds have been the most rapidly growing segment of the industry.

---

[7] *Mutual Fund Fact Book* (Washington, D.C.: Investment Company Institute, 1988), pp. 10–11.

TABLE 24.2 T. ROWE PRICE NEW HORIZONS FUND

STATEMENT OF ASSETS AND LIABILITIES
T. Rowe Price New Horizons Fund / December 31, 1987

Amounts in Thousands

Assets

Investments in securities at value

Affiliated companies (Cost—$40,669)	$ 50,138	
Other companies (Cost—$794,024)	804,411	$854,549
Other assets		19,104
Total assets		873,653
Liabilities		18,192

Net Assets Consisting Of:

Undistributed net investment income	87	
Distributions in excess of accumulated net realized gains	(20,643)	
Unrealized appreciation of investments.................................	19,856	
Paid-in-capital applicable to 89,988,000 shares of $1.00 par value capital stock outstanding; 200,000,000 shares authorized	856,161	
Net Assets		$855,461
Net Asset Value per Share		$9.51

STATEMENT OF OPERATIONS
T. Rowe Price New Horizons Fund / Year Ended December 31, 1987

Amounts in Thousands

Investment Income

Income

Dividends

Affiliated companies	$ 99	
Other companies	5,747	$ 5,846
Interest...		5,739
Total income		11,585

Expenses

Investment management fee	6,519	
Shareholder servicing fees & expenses	1,765	
Custodian and accounting fees & expenses..........................	139	
Legal & auditing fees	58	
Prospectus & shareholder reports	201	
Registration fees & expenses	48	
Proxy & annual meeting..	78	
Directors' fees & expenses	49	
Miscellaneous..	59	
Total expenses...		8,916
Net investment income		2,669

Realized and Unrealized Gain (Loss) on Investments

Net realized gain on investments

Securities

Affiliated companies..	1,368	
Other companies	100,296	
Net gain on securities	101,664	
Futures..	6,488	
Net realized gain...	108,152	
Change in unrealized appreciation of investments	(161,202)	
Net loss on investments		(53,050)
Decrease in Net Assets from Operations...............................		$(50,381)

SOURCE: Annual Report provided to shareholders by T. Rowe Price. Reprinted by permission of T. Rowe Price Associates Inc.

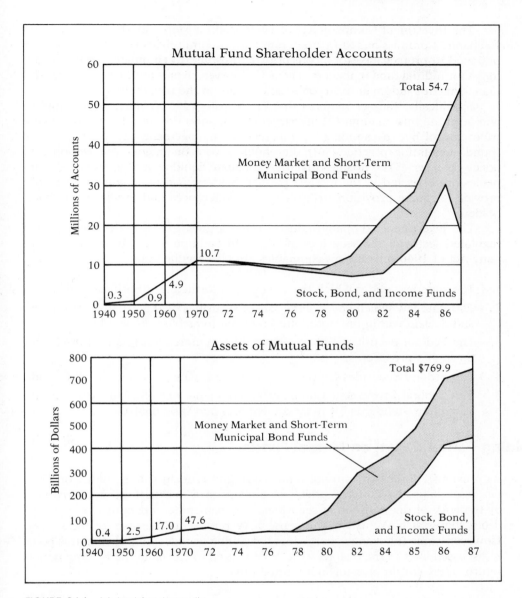

FIGURE 24.1 Mutual fund growth

Source Mutual Fund Fact Book, 1988, p. 14. Reprinted by permission of the Investment Company Institute, Washington, D.C.

Regulation of Mutual Funds

Mutual funds and other types of investments were essentially not regulated by the U.S. government prior to the market crash of 1929. In the aftermath of the crash, in 1936, Congress undertook a study of the investment company industry that resulted in the passage of the Investment Company Act of 1940.

The Investment Company Act of 1940 is administered by the Securities and Exchange Commission, SEC, and comprises a comprehensive set of provisions designed to protect investors from prior abuses and to eliminate conflicts of interest for mutual fund managers. The act, however, avoids any attempt to control management's judgment or to offer an opinion on the soundness of funds.

Specifically, the act requires that (1) investors be provided with complete and accurate information; (2) investment companies do not attempt to concentrate control by "pyramiding" companies or management; (3) companies use sound accounting practices; (4) shareholders vote on major organizational or policy changes; (5) companies maintain adequate liquidity and reserves; (6) companies are operated in the interest of shareholders; and (7) company securities provide adequate provisions to protect the preferences and privileges of shareholders.

The investment company industry often argues that it is the most closely regulated sector of the securities industry. In addition to the Investment Company Act of 1940, investment companies are also regulated by

1. The state law under which the company is formed as a business entity;
2. The state law which governs the sale of securities or the activities of brokers and dealers within the state, often referred to as blue sky legislation;
3. The Federal Securities Act of 1933, which requires full financial disclosure through a prospectus;
4. The Federal Securities Exchange Act of 1934, which created the SEC; and
5. The Federal Investment Company Amendments Act of 1970, which established new standards for management fees and sales charges.[8]

Ex-Post Holding Period Return on Mutual Funds

As previously discussed, mutual funds issue and redeem shares, based on their net asset value, NAV. The "price" of a share of a mutual fund is determined by the NAV of the portfolio of securities. An open-end company will issue or redeem shares at NAV, and in this sense NAV represents the price of the shares. However, some funds may charge fees for issuing or redeeming shares, this point is discussed later in the chapter. The NAV is used to calculate the holding period return, *HPR*, for an investor in a mutual fund

$$HPR_t = \frac{NAV_{t+1} - NAV_t + CG_{t+1} + Div_{t+1}}{NAV_t} \tag{24.1}$$

The calculation of *HPR* for mutual funds includes the two types of distributions to shareholders: (1) capital gains, CG, and (2) dividends, Div. In addition to these two sources of income, the NAV itself can change over the holding period, causing capital gains or losses. This formulation excludes sales or "load" fees that might be charged by the fund and is therefore a *gross HPR*.

---

[8] *Investment Companies*, p. 25.

To illustrate, assume that you purchased 100 shares of the International Stock Fund, offered by T. Rowe Price, for $18.13 per share on January 7, 1986. The fund paid $.22 per share in dividends and $.25 per share in capital gains during February 1986. In December 1986 the fund made another capital gains distribution of $2.50 per share. The NAV of the fund at the end of December 1986 was $24.63. The *HPR* is

$$HPR_{1986} = \frac{\$24.63 - \$18.13 + (\$.25 + \$2.50) + \$.22}{\$18.13} \tag{24.2}$$

$$= 52.2\%$$

The above calculation ignores the timing of the dividend and capital gain distributions, since the February and December distributions are treated equally. The unusually high return of 52.2 percent was caused by the decline in the value of the dollar during 1986 as well as price appreciation of foreign stocks held by the fund.

MUTUAL FUND CHARACTERISTICS

Size and Growth of Mutual Funds versus Closed-end Funds

Open-end companies (mutual funds) are by far the most popular type of investment company. *Investment Companies*, published by Wiesenberger Financial Services, is a principal source of information on investment companies. The 1987 edition provides data on 1,650 mutual funds and 39 closed-end investment companies. Table 24.3 provides data on growth of open- and closed-end funds, 1940–1986. In 1940 the assets of closed-end companies were larger than those of mutual funds. By the end of 1986, however, assets of mutual funds as reported by Weisenberger Investment Companies exceeded $699.0 billion, while closed-end fund assets had grown only to $10.7 billion.

Load versus No-Load Mutual Funds

A mutual fund can operate as a load or a no-load fund. A *load fund* charges sales commissions on the purchase, and sometimes on the sale, of shares; there are no sales charges on a *no-load fund*.

Historically, the sales charge or load has been 8.5 percent, charged as a *front-end* fee. For example, on a $10,000 investment, a fee of $850 would be deducted, leaving $9,150 for the actual purchase of shares. Load funds are marketed through a commissioned sales force; the fee is used to compensate salespersons. No-load funds are marketed directly, by mail or telephone, without a commissioned sales force. In 1987, of total sales of $190.8 billion of stock, bond, and income fund, 69 percent, or $132 billion, were by load funds, 28 percent, or $53.1 billion, by no-load funds. The remaining $5.7 billion in sales were from reinvested dividends and variable annuities.[9] The number of no-load funds is increasing, but load funds still outnumber the no-load funds.

---

[9] *Mutual Fund Fact Book, 1988*, p. 38.

TABLE 24.3 ASSETS OF CLOSED-END VERSUS OPEN-END INVESTMENT COMPANIES

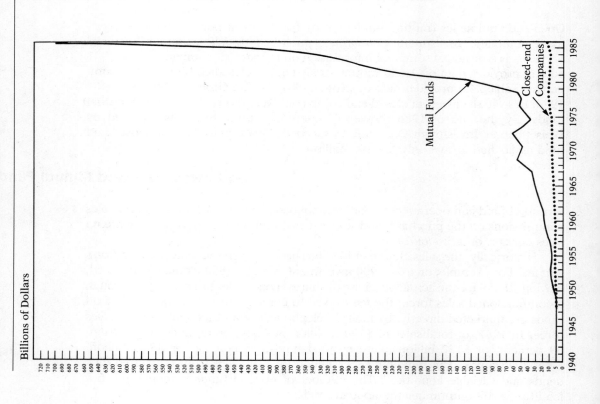

Billions of Dollars

TABLE 24.3 *(Continued)*

GROWTH OF INVESTMENT COMPANY ASSETS SINCE 1940

YEAR	MUTUAL FUNDS	CLOSED-END COMPANIES[†]	TOTAL	YEAR	MUTUAL FUNDS	CLOSED-END COMPANIES	TOTAL
1986	$699,461,000,000	$10,698,400,000	$710,159,400,000	1969	$52,621,400,000	$4,743,700,000	$57,365,100,000
1985	483,198,600,000	7,384,000,000	490,582,600,000	1968	56,953,600,000	5,170,800,000	62,124,400,000
1984	357,334,100,000	6,329,200,000	363,663,300,000	1967	44,701,302,000	3,777,100,000	48,478,402,000
1983	302,925,800,000	7,098,000,000	310,023,800,000	1966	36,294,600,000	3,162,900,000	39,457,500,000
1982	270,880,000,000	7,179,200,000	278,059,200,000	1964	30,370,300,000	3,523,413,000	33,893,713,000
1981	230,395,100,000	6,923,500,000	237,318,600,000	1962	22,408,900,000	2,783,219,000	25,192,119,000
1980	138,333,100,000	8,053,201,000	146,386,301,000	1960	17,383,300,000	2,083,898,000	19,467,198,000
1979	97,053,100,000	6,873,179,000	103,926,279,000	1958	13,242,388,000	1,931,402,000	15,173,790,000
1978	58,144,400,000	6,116,700,000	64,261,100,000	1956	9,046,431,000	1,525,748,000	10,572,179,000
1977	51,479,800,000	6,283,700,000	57,763,500,000	1954	6,109,390,000	1,246,351,000	7,355,741,000
1976	54,174,600,000	6,639,046,000	60,813,646,000	1952	3,931,407,000	1,011,089,000	4,942,496,000
1975	48,706,300,000	5,861,300,000	54,567,600,000	1950	2,530,563,000	871,962,000	3,402,525,000
1974	38,545,599,000	5,294,000,000	43,839,599,000	1948	1,505,762,000	767,028,000	2,272,790,000
1973	49,310,700,000	6,622,700,000	55,936,700,000	1946	1,311,108,000	851,409,000	2,162,517,000
1972	62,456,500,000	6,742,800,000	69,199,300,000	1944	882,191,000	739,021,000	1,621,212,000
1971	58,159,800,000	5,324,300,000	63,484,100,000	1942	486,850,000	557,264,000	1,044,114,000
1970	50,654,900,000	4,024,200,000	54,679,100,000	1940	447,959,000	613,589,000	1,061,548,000

[†] Includes funded debt and bank loans. Sources: Open-End—Wiesenberger Investment Company Service, 1960–1986. Investment Company Institute, 1940–1958 (data includes ICI member companies only). Closed End—Wiesenberger Investment Company Service, 1948–1986, Investment Company Institute, 1940–1946.

SOURCE: *Investment Companies, 1987*, p. 12. Reprinted by permission of Wiesenberger Investment Companies Service, Division of Warren, Gorham & Lamont, Inc.

If a load fund charges the full 8.5 percent front-end load, the charge is substantially above the brokerage commission incurred on the purchase of a closed-end fund. A brokerage commission, however, is also paid when the closed-end fund shares are sold, but no load fee is incurred on the sale of a front-end load fund.

Studies that test for possible differences in the investment performances of load versus no-load funds generally find that on average, investors realize higher *net* returns from no-load funds.[10] On the other hand, it appears that the operating expenses of load funds (excluding load fees) are somewhat lower than those of no-load funds. Therefore, if an investor has a "long" investment horizon, it might be advantageous to incur an initial load fee in exchange for lower annual operating expenses.

Recently a number of no-load funds have begun to charge a load of 2 to 3 percent, creating a third class—*low-load* funds. For example, the industry or sector funds offered by Fidelity Investments charge a 2 percent load. Its Select Electric Utility Portfolio had an offering price of $8.71, with a NAV of $8.54 according to the May 16, 1988, *Wall Street Journal*. The difference of $.17 represents a 2 percent load, added to the NAV.

According to a recent article in *Money*, it is becoming increasingly difficult to determine the actual cost of investing in some mutual funds.[11] This occurs because in addition to the traditional front-end loads, new funds may have *back-end* loads or exit fees, in addition to other expenses charged as annual operating expenses. An investor should check the prospectus of mutual funds to determine the buying and selling fees.

Other Types of Fees and Expenses

1. DIRECT CHARGES AGAINST NET ASSET VALUE Both load and no-load funds incur operating expenses, including management fees, salaries, costs of office space and facilities, investment advisor fees, accountant's fees, postage, printing, and other expenses. Brokerage commissions, however, are included directly in the calculation of NAV and are not reflected in operating expenses. It is now quite common for publications that provide data on mutual funds to provide expense ratios for mutual funds, calculated as

$$\text{Expense ratio} = \frac{\text{Operating expenses (excluding brokerage cost)}}{\text{NAV}} \quad (24.3)$$

On an annual basis, the expense ratio may be as low as .2 of 1 percent (.002) or as large as 7 percent. Many funds, by provisions in the prospectus, limit expenses to 1 to 2 percent of NAV.[12]

---

[10] For example, see E. Theodore Veit, John M. Cheney, Jeff Madura, and Mike Lucas, "The Combined Impact of Expense Ratios, Investment Horizon, and Transaction Costs on Mutual Fund Returns: An Empirical Examination;" paper presented at the 1985 Eastern Finance Association meeting.

[11] "At Last, a Way to Compare Loads and Fees," *Money*, May 1987, p. 37.

[12] *Investment Companies, 1987*, p. 16.

2. CHARGES FOR DISTRIBUTION SERVICES In 1980 the SEC (Rule 12b-1) allowed funds to establish a *Distribution Service Agreement*. This agreement permits funds to charge distribution and marketing expenses, directly or indirectly, to NAV. This allows both load and no-load funds to charge for commissions or other distribution expenses and provides an opportunity for low-load and no-load funds actually to have load fees above the stated no-load or low-load. Critics of the industry contend that some funds use the 12b-1 rule to hide fees and that brokers and fund managements do not explain these charges to investors.[13] Obviously it is important for investors to check the prospectus of a fund to determine the actual charges and expenses.

The following example shows the importance of fees and expenses in fund selection:[14]

MUTUAL FUND EXPENSES: A SAMPLE WORKSHEET

FUND	FRONT-END LOAD	MANAGEMENT FEE	EXPENSES TO NAV	12b-1 CHARGES	REDEMPTION FEE	TRANSACTION COSTS	TOTAL ANNUAL EXPENSES
Acorn	0.0%	0.6%	0.2%	0.00%	0.0%	1.3%	2.10%
Fidelity Magellan	3.1	0.8	0.3	0.00	1.0	5.0	10.20
Keystone S-3	0.0	0.7	0.3	1.25	4.0	5.5	11.75

The example was constructed assuming that the fund was held for one year and that the *portfolio turnover* rate was .4 times a year. The portfolio turnover rate indicates how much security trading takes place in the portfolio over a certain period of time. For mutual funds, it is usually calculated as the lesser of the value of security purchases or sales divided by average portfolio assets; higher ratios indicate more trading activity by the portfolio manager. This example shows that funds with no front-end load are not necessarily the cheapest to acquire. It should also be remembered that Rule 12b-1 charges, management fees, operating expenses, and transaction costs are incurred ever year, while a front-end or redemption fee is assessed only once.

3. TAXES Mutual funds, as regulated investment companies under Subchapter M of the Internal Revenue Code, do not pay federal income taxes on the dividends, interest, and capital gains they earn. To receive this tax-exempt status, funds must distribute 90 percent or more of their income to shareholders. After funds deduct their operating expenses and fees, most funds distribute the remaining income to their shareholders, who then incur the tax liability on both capital gains and income distributions. The shareholders have a tax liability whether the income is actually received or is reinvested in the fund (by the purchase of additional shares). Income distributions may also be subject to "backup withholding" of taxes, up to 20 percent of the distribution.

---

[13] Karen Slater, "Critics Say Brokerage Firms Hide Fees on Their New No-Load Mutual Funds," *Wall Street Journal*, 8 Aug. 1985.

[14] Gerald W. Perritt, "A Look Behind the Bottom Line," *Barron's*, 19 May 1986, p. 53. Reprinted courtesy of *Barrons Weekly*.

A 1976 change in the Tax Code allows mutual funds to invest in tax-free bonds (municipals). The interest received (or reinvested) by the shareholder is not subject to federal income tax. Capital gains on municipal bonds, however, represent taxable income to shareholders.

In summary, mutual fund investors should consider the impact of taxes when making investment decisions. For example, corporate bond funds or income stock funds are likely to distribute taxable income to their shareholders. An "aggressive growth" common stock fund, however, may receive a limited amount of taxable dividends from its investments. The returns from this fund would be in the form of capital gains over a long period of time so that the tax liability is postponed until the gains are realized.

Investment Objectives of Mutual Funds

1. CATEGORIES OF MUTUAL FUNDS Mutual funds can differ greatly in their stated investment objectives and the portfolio strategies designed to achieve these objectives. Traditionally, funds could be neatly categorized into common stock or balanced funds. *Balanced* funds were designed to provide a "complete investment program" to shareholders; the fund had common stocks, preferred stocks, and bonds in the portfolio. *Common stock* funds were not intended to offer a completely diversified portfolio since they consisted primarily of only one type of security—common stocks.

By 1975, there were seven major categories of funds according to their stated investment objective. By 1988, the categories had grown to twenty-two. The industry slogan seems to be "Today, there's a mutual fund to meet every investor's needs."

TABLE 24.4   TYPES OF MUTUAL FUNDS

Aggressive Growth Funds seek maximum capital gains as their investment objective. Current income is not a significant factor. Some may invest in stocks that are somewhat out of the mainstream, such as those in fledgling companies; new industries, companies fallen on hard times, or industries temporarily out of favor. They may also use specialized investment techniques such as option writing. The risks are obvious, but the potential for reward should also be greater.

Growth Funds invest in the common stock of more settled companies but, again, the primary aim is to produce an increase in the value of their investments through capital gains, rather than a steady flow of dividends.

Growth and Income Funds invest mainly in the common stock of companies with a longer track record—companies that have both the expectation of a higher share value and a solid record of paying dividends.

Precious Metals Funds invest in the stocks of gold mining companies and other companies in the precious metals business.

International Funds invest in the stocks of companies located outside the U.S.

Global Equity Funds invest in the stocks of both U.S. companies and foreign companies.

Income-Equity Funds invest primarily in stocks of companies with good dividend-paying records.

Option/Income Funds seek a high current return by investing primarily in dividend-paying common stocks on which call options are traded on national securities exchanges. Current return generally consists of dividends, premiums from writing call options, net short-term gains from sales of portfolio securities on exercises of options or otherwise, and any profits from closing purchase transactions.

(continued)

TABLE 24.4 (*Continued*)

Flexible Portfolio Funds invest in common stocks, bonds, money market securities, and other types of debt securities. The portfolio may hold up to 100 percent of any one of these types of securities or any combination thereof, and may easily change depending upon market conditions.

Global Bond Funds invest in bonds issued by companies or countries worldwide, including the U.S.

Balanced Funds generally have a three-part investment objective: 1) to conserve the investor's principal; 2) to pay current income; and 3) to increase both principal and income. They aim to achieve this by owning a mixture of bonds, preferred stocks, and common stocks.

Income-Mixed Funds seek a high level of current income for their shareholders. This may be achieved by investing in the common stock of companies which have good dividend-paying records. Often corporate and government bonds are also part of the portfolio.

Option/Income Funds seek a high current return by investing primarily in dividend-paying common stocks on which call options are traded on national securities exchanges. Current return generally consists of dividends, premiums from writing call options, net short-term gains from sales of portfolio securities on exercises of options or otherwise, and any profits from closing purchase transactions.

U.S. Government Income Funds invest in a variety of government securities. These include U.S. Treasury bonds, federally guaranteed mortgage-backed securities and other government issues.

GNMA or Ginnie Mae Funds (Government National Mortgage Association) invest in government-backed mortgage securities. To qualify for this category, the majority of the portfolio must always be invested in mortgage-backed securities.

Corporate Bond Funds, like income funds, seek a high level of income. They do so by buying bonds of corporations for the majority of the fund's portfolio. The rest of the portfolio may be in U.S. Treasury and other government entities' bonds.

High-Yield Bond Funds are corporate bond funds that predominantly invest in bonds rated below investment grade. In return for a generally higher yield, investors bear a greater degree of risk than for more highly rated bonds.

Long-Term Municipal Bond Funds invest in bonds issued by local governments—such as cities and states—which use the money to build schools, highways, libraries and the like. These funds predominantly invest at all times in municipal bonds that are exempt from federal income tax. Because the federal government does not tax the income earned on most of these securities, the fund can pass the tax-free income through to shareholders.

Long-Term State Municipal Bond Funds predominantly invest at all times in municipal bonds which are exempt from federal income tax as well as exempt from state taxes for residents of the state specified by the fund name.

Short-Term National Municipal Bond Funds invest in municipal securities with relatively short maturities. They are also known as tax-exempt money market funds.

Short-Term State Municipal Bond Funds invest in municipal securities with relatively short maturities. Because they contain the issues of only one state, they are exempt from state taxes for residents of the state specified by the fund name.

Money Market Mutual Funds invest in the short-term securities sold in the money market. (Large companies, banks, and other institutions invest their surplus cash in the money market for short periods of time.) In the entire investment spectrum, these are generally the safest, most stable securities available. They include Treasury Bills, certificates of deposit of large banks, and commercial paper (the short-term IOUs of large U.S. corporations).

SOURCE: *Mutual Fund Fact Book*, *1988*, pp. 8–9. Reprinted with permission from the Investment Company Institute, Washington, D.C.

Mutual fund reporting services, such as Wiesenberger Investment Companies Service, use the stated investment objective to categorize each fund. Table 24.4 provides a brief description of the twenty-two categories. As the table indicates, balanced funds are still in existence, but the traditional category of common stock funds has been expanded to four categories: aggressive growth, growth, growth and income, and income-equity. The traditional

TABLE 24.5 NUMBER OF MUTUAL FUNDS AND ASSETS, BY INVESTMENT OBJECTIVE

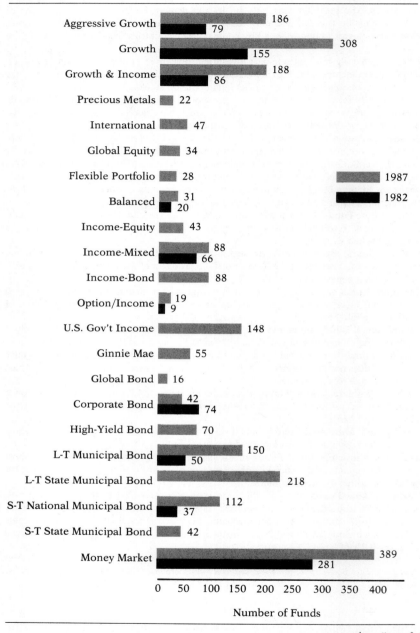

Investment Objective	1987	1982
Aggressive Growth	186	79
Growth	308	155
Growth & Income	188	86
Precious Metals	22	
International	47	
Global Equity	34	
Flexible Portfolio	28	
Balanced	31	20
Income-Equity	43	
Income-Mixed	88	66
Income-Bond	88	
Option/Income	19	9
U.S. Gov't Income	148	
Ginnie Mae	55	
Global Bond	16	
Corporate Bond	42	74
High-Yield Bond	70	
L-T Municipal Bond	150	50
L-T State Municipal Bond	218	
S-T National Municipal Bond	112	37
S-T State Municipal Bond	42	
Money Market	389	281

Number of Funds

(continued)

TABLE 24.5 (*Continued*)

INVESTMENT OBJECTIVE	ASSETS (BILLIONS OF DOLLARS)		
	1986	1987	PERCENT CHANGE
Aggressive Growth	$ 25.0	$ 27.3	+ 9.2%
Growth	43.6	48.0	+ 10.1
Growth and Income	55.9	64.0	+ 14.5
Precious Metals	2.0	4.1	+105.0
International	7.2	7.0	− 2.8
Global Equity	8.3	10.4	+ 25.3
Flexible Portfolio	1.5	4.3	+186.7
Balanced	7.5	9.0	+ 20.0
Income-Equity	12.6	14.7	+ 16.7
Income-Mixed	10.3	11.4	+ 10.7
Income Bond	11.4	12.6	+ 10.5
Option/Income	7.0	5.1	− 27.1
U.S. Government Income	82.4	88.9	+ 7.9
Ginnie Mae	39.6	34.2	− 13.6
Global Bond	0.5	2.1	+320.0
Corporate Bond	9.1	9.5	+ 4.4
High-Yield Bond	24.6	24.2	− 1.6
Long-Term Municipal Bond	49.9	49.9	− 1.4
Long Term State Municipal Bond	25.8	27.8	+ 7.8
Total Long-Term Funds	$424.2	$453.8	+ 7.0%

SOURCE: *Mutual Fund Fact Book, 1988.* Reprinted by permission from the Investment Company Institute, Washington, D.C.

categories have been supplemented by bond funds and by specialized categories such as global equity, global bond, option/income, and money market.

Table 24.5 provides a bar graph and table indicating the number of funds and level of assets in each of the twenty-two categories and the level of assets for the nineteen categories of the long-term funds. Taxable money market funds are the most common type of fund, and they had assets of $254.7 billion in 1987 representing an 11 percent increase from the 1986 year end total of $228.3 billion.

2. USEFULNESS OF INVESTMENT OBJECTIVES TO INVESTORS The stated objective obviously provides a means of classifying a mutual fund. Once classified, however, is this information useful for investment decision making?

Numerous academic studies, dating back to the 1960s and continuing into the 1980s, have analyzed the relationship between investment performance and fund classification.[15] Generally, these studies confirmed expectations that funds in a single category would display similar risk-return characteristics. For example, for the common stock categories ((1) aggessive

---

[15] For example, see Robert S. Carlson, "Aggregate Performance of Mutual Funds, 1948–1967," *Journal of Financial and Quantitative Analysis* (March 1970): pp. 1–30, and John G. McDonald, "Objective and Performance of Mutual Funds, 1960–69," *Journal of Financial and Quantitative Analysis (June 1974): pp. 311–33.*

TABLE 24.6 RISK AND RETURN BY MUTUAL FUND CLASSIFICATION: 1969–1983

CLASSIFICATION	SAMPLE SIZE	STANDARD DEVIATION OF RETURN	MEAN ANNUAL GROSS HOLDING PERIOD RETURN
Aggressive Growth	12	2.98%	10.48%
Growth	21	2.39	10.45
Growth and Income	20	2.31	10.95
Income	10	2.74	11.38

SOURCE: Risk and return measures computed from data available in *Investment Companies*. Reprinted by permission of Wiesenberger Investment Companies Service, Division of Warren, Gorham & Lamont, Inc.

growth, (2) growth, (3) growth and income, and (4) income), the standard deviation, σ, of returns and beta, β, should be larger for the aggressive growth category than for the income category. During a "bull" market, the holding period return, *HPR*, on the aggressive growth category should be greater than the *HPR* on the income category. By following their stated investment objective, funds determine their risk-return characteristics. A word of warning: the above statements are appropriate for mutual funds in general, but not for individual funds or a small random sample of funds. Table 24.6, a good illustration of this point, shows that the mean annual gross *HPR* of the income category over the period 1969-83, is higher than that of the agressive category. The standard deviation for the income classification is larger than might be expected, however, relative to the growth category and the growth and income category.

Wiesenberger's *Investment Companies* is a good source of information about the volatility of mutual funds in bull and bear markets. A section in the annual edition, entitled "Price Volatility of Mutual Fund Shares," provides the ratio of each mutual fund's percentage price change to the percentage change in the New York Stock Exchange Index, NYSEI. The ratios are provided for each bull and bear market over approximately the last ten years. For example, in the 1987 edition, Acorn Fund had a ratio of 1.41 for the bear market from September 11, 1978, to November 14, 1978, and a ratio of 0.91 for the bull market of March 8, 1982, to October 10, 1983.[16] Acorn Fund, with an objective of "maximum capital gains," declined 1.41 times as much as the NYSEI in the bear market but increased only .91 as much during the bull market. Acorn was therefore, not successful in adjusting to changing market conditions. These volatility ratios are provided for each mutual fund covered by Wiesenberger and are grouped by fund classifications. The ratios of volatility are useful to investors but should not be confused with the beta of a mutual fund.

The performance of mutual funds during the October 1987 crash was somewhat better than that of stocks in general. For example, the S&P 500 and DJIA declined 22.5 percent and 24.6 percent, respectively, during the fourth quarter of 1987, while mutual fund assets for Wiesenberger's fifteen categories declined 10.8 percent.[17] Some categories of common stock funds,

---

[16] *Investment Companies, 1987*, p. 650.

[17] *Management Results*, Wiesenberger Investment Companies Service, December 1987, p. 1.

however, such as maximum capital gains and specialized technology, declined as much as or more than the market indices.

INVESTING IN MUTUAL FUNDS

Sources of Information

As in the case when making any investment decision, it is important to obtain information about mutual funds to make informed investment decisions. Investment companies are required to furnish potential investors with a prospectus that provides detailed information about the fund. The prospectus provides the most complete and comprehensive source of information.

Wiesenberger Investment Companies Service provides detailed data about mutual funds and close-end investment companies in four publications:

1. INVESTMENT COMPANIES Published annually, is based on data compiled from reports of various investment companies that are issued to their respective stockholders. Table 24.7 provides an example of the information provided for each fund.

2. MUTUAL FUNDS PANORAMA "Includes virtually all mutual funds registered for sale in the United States, regardless of size." This publication provides summary data on each fund, including the fund's objective, year organized, total net assets and per-share net asset value, dividend and capital gain distributions over the last twelve months, sales charges, and expense ratio. A separate section provides the addresses of the listed funds.

3. MANAGEMENT RESULTS Reports the most current data on holding period returns, *HPR*, for individual funds. The most recent quarter's portfolio composition—in terms of cash and goverment securities, bonds and preferred stock, and common stock—is also provided.

4. CURRENT PERFORMANCE AND DIVIDEND RECORD A monthly publication that furnishes the most current data on "investment income and capital gains distributions declared, and asset value changes during the preceding six and twelve months."

Barron's and the *Wall Street Journal*, provide weekly and daily quotations on a large number of mutual funds. *Barron's* provides more-detailed information, including the most recent and last twelve-month dividend and capital gains distributions, along with the 52-week high and low quotations and the weekly high, low, close, and change in NAV. *Barron's* also provides a quarterly report on performance.

With the growing popularity of mutual funds, a number of other publications report quarterly or semiannual performance data on the larger funds. *Money*, *Forbes, Consumer Reports*, and *Business Week* are four of the better known of these magazines. *Business Week* also offers the "Mutual Fund Scoreboard," on diskette, which provides raw data and "over 25 key performance factors and data fields on each fund." The March 1988 diskettes provided data on over 700 equity funds and over 500 fixed-income funds.

TABLE 24.7   EXAMPLE OF MUTUAL FUND DATA

T. ROWE PRICE NEW HORIZONS FUND, INC.

The objective of the fund is long-term growth of capital through investment primarily in small growth companies which management believes have the potential to become major companies in the future. Investments are sought in such fields as science and technology, consumer and business services, retailing, entertainment and leisure, and energy, among others. The fund may also invest in larger companies which offer improved growth possibilities because of rejuvenated management, changes in product, or some other development that might stimulate earnings growth.

At the end of 1986, the fund had 93.9% of its assets in common stocks of which the substantial proportion was in five industry groups: Consumer products (9.8% of assets), specialty merchandisers (9.2%), insurance (8.3%), business services (7.9%), and electronic components (7.3%). The five largest individual common stock investments were Liz Claiborne (3% of assets), LIN Broadcasting (2.2%), Lorimar-Telepictures and Foremost Corp. of America (each 1.7%) and Molex (1.6%). The rate of portfolio turnover during the latest fiscal year was 34.8% of average assets. Unrealized appreciation in the portfolio at the year-end was 17.5% of total net assets.

Statistical History

			Net Asset		% of Assets in							
				AT YEAR-ENDS						ANNUAL DATA		
Year	Total Net Assets ($)	Number of Share-holders	Value Per Share ($)	Yield (%)	Cash & Equiv-alent	Bonds & Pre-ferreds	Com-mon Stocks	Income Div-idends ($)	Capital Gains Distribu-tion ($)	Expense Ratio (%)	Offering Price ($) High	Low
1986	1,034,082,754	80,815	12.38	0.6	5	1	94	0.09	2.64	0.73	17.35	12.32
1985	1,474,740,973	96,075	15.13	0.9	6	1	93	0.14	0.52	0.70	15.23	12.32
1984	1,273,033,157	99,044	12.78	1.0	13	—	87	0.16	3.72*	0.71	18.56	11.81
1983	1,355,433,903	99,027	17.90	1.1	8	—	92	0.20	0.758	0.61	21.35	15.31
1982	1,198,534,092	64,309	15.90	1.9	9	—	91	0.35	2.61*	0.56	16.08	10.11
1981	875,770,863	45,855	16.06	2.5	15	—	85	0.321	1.678*	0.53	19.60	14.07
1980	970,826,261	35,649	19.53	1.2	11	—	89	0.232	0.368	0.54	19.94	10.62
1979	604,843,958	29,596	13.01	1.2	15	—	85	0.157	—	0.60	13.01	9.65
1978	441,919,715	26,578	9.75	1.0	12	—	88	0.098	—	0.59	11.60	7.38
1977	393,447,413	27,268	8.17	0.9	10	—	90	0.071	—	0.60	8.17	6.68
1976	353,588,795	29,343	7.32	1.0	7	—	93	0.074	—	0.62	7.73	6.66

* Includes short-term capital gains of $0.17 in 1982; $0.13 in 1981; $0.29 in 1984.
Note: Figures adjusted for 3-for-1 split, effective 5/1/73.

An assumed investment of $10,000 in this fund, with capital gains accepted in shares and income dividends reinvested, is illustrated below. The explanation in the introduction to this section must be read in conjunction with this illustration.

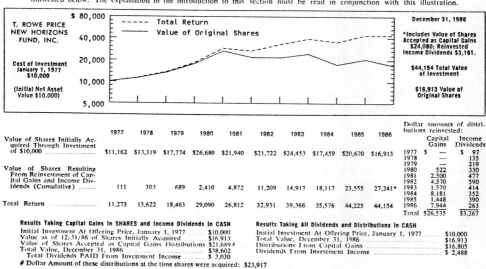

T. ROWE PRICE NEW HORIZONS FUND, INC.

Cost of Investment January 1, 1977 $10,000

(Initial Net Asset Value $10,000)

December 31, 1986

*Includes Value of Shares Accepted as Capital Gains $24,080; Reinvested Income Dividends $3,161.

$44,154 Total Value of Investment

$18,913 Value of Original Shares

	1977	1978	1979	1980	1981	1982	1983	1984	1985	1986		Capital Gains	Income Dividends
Value of Shares Initially Acquired Through Investment of $10,000	$11,162	$13,319	$17,774	$26,680	$21,940	$21,722	$24,453	$17,459	$20,670	$16,913	1977	$ —	$ 97
											1978	—	135
											1979	—	219
Value of Shares Resulting From Reinvestment of Capital Gains and Income Dividends (Cumulative)	111	303	689	2,410	4,872	11,209	14,913	18,117	23,555	27,241*	1980	522	330
											1981	2,500	477
											1982	4,370	590
											1983	1,570	414
											1984	8,181	352
Total Return	11,273	13,622	18,463	29,090	26,812	32,931	39,366	35,576	44,225	44,154	1985	1,448	390
											1986	7,944	263
											Total	$26,535	$3,267

Dollar amounts of distributions reinvested:

Results Taking Capital Gains in SHARES and Income Dividends in CASH

Initial Investment At Offering Price, January 1, 1977	$10,000
Value as of 12/31/86 of Shares Initially Acquired	$16,913
Value of Shares Accepted as Capital Gains Distributions	$21,689 #
Total Value, December 31, 1986	$38,602
Total Dividends PAID From Investment Income	$ 3,030

Dollar Amount of these distributions at the time shares were acquired: $23,917

Results Taking All Dividends and Distributions in CASH

Initial Investment At Offering Price, January 1, 1977	$10,000
Total Value, December 31, 1986	$16,913
Distributions From Capital Gains	$16,805
Dividends From Investment Income	$ 2,488

SOURCE: *Investment Companies, 1987*, p. 463. Reprinted by permission of Wiesenberger Investment Companies Service, Division of Warren, Gorham & Lamont, Inc.

There are also some specialized publications, such as *Mutual Fund Forecaster* published by the Institute for Econometric Research, that provide general information as well as specific buy and sell recommendations.

Determining an Investment Objective

As a prerequiste to any investment decision, careful consideration should be given to formulating specific objectives. This step may appear obvious, but its importance should not be overlooked. The objective might be focused in terms of the appropriate risk-return trade-offs but should also include consideration of taxes, investment horizon, liquidity, and the costs of investing.

Once an individual has clearly formulated his or her investment objective, it can be matched with the twenty-two categories of funds previously discussed. For example, does the objective suggest an equity fund, which stresses long-term capital gains, or a fixed income fund, which provides price stability and current income?

Services Provided by Mutual Funds

Most of the larger funds offer a number of services to their shareholders that may be important in achieving a specific investment objective. The more common services:

1. PERIODIC INVESTMENT PLANS After an account is opened, for a minimum amount that can be as small as $1,000, additional investments can be made, in amounts as small as $50. These additional investments can be on a *voluntary accumulation plan* or on a *fixed-amount–fixed-interval* using preauthorized checks drawn against the investor's checking account.

2. RECORD KEEPING Mutual funds often provide cumulative monthly statements that facilitate tracking investment performance and maintaining adequate tax records. Statements may also be issued after any transaction in the account.

3. DISTRIBUTIONS Funds typically offer several options dealing with dividend and capital gains income. A *share option* automatically reinvests all dividend and capital gain distributions in additional shares or fractions of a share. (Typically, the fund calculates fractional shares to three decimal places.) A second choice is an *income-earned option* that reinvests capital gains and pays dividend income to the investor in cash. A third choice is the *cash option* that pays both dividends and capital gains in cash.

4. EXCHANGE PRIVILEGES Funds offer telephone exchange privileges, using a toll-free number that is serviced by an account representative. These exchanges do not involve any fees in a no-load fund, but there may be restrictions on the number of exchanges allowed during a calender year. Some load or low-load funds charge fees for the exchanges.

5. COMPUTERIZED ACCOUNT INFORMATION AND TRANSACTIONS In addition to using an account representative, some larger funds now offer quotations and yields as well as specific account information by telephone, 24 hours a day, seven days a week. For example, "Tele*Access," offered by T. Rowe Price, provides a toll-free number; with a "touch-tone" phone and the appropriate codes,

specific information can be obtained. Price's "Transaction-line" allows shareholders to exchange shares among the "family" of funds or to move money between the fund and the investor's checking account.

6. CHECK-WRITING PRIVILEGES Many fixed-income and money market funds offer check-writing privileges, with certain limitations. Often there is a minimum check amount, such as $500, and a limit on the number of checks that can be written each month. Any check is considered a withdrawal from the fund, executed at the prevailing NAV at the time of the transaction.

7. WIRE TRANSFERS In addition to telephone, mail, and telegram exchange and transaction privileges, some funds offer electronic funds transfers. This service allows a very rapid transfer by an investor to or from a fund.

Key Decision Variables

In summary, the logical steps for investing in a mutual fund are

(1) develop an appropriate investment objective;

(2) match the investment objective to a specific fund category; and

(3) identify the types of services that may be useful or beneficial.

The final step is to obtain information on a number of specific funds, using the sources discussed previously, and to select one or more funds from this list. A major question that remains is what are the key variables that should be considered in selecting a specific fund?

The following factors are often cited in the investment literature as important in making a specific mutual fund investment decision.

1. CONSISTENCY OF PERFORMANCE The most popular variable used in mutual fund selection is ex-post returns, or *HPR*s. Wiesenberger's *Management Results* provides annual *HPR*s over the last ten years for most funds. Other previously discussed publications, such as *Forbes*, *Barron's*, and *Business Week*, also provide *HPR*s, which are used to rank funds. None of these rankings, however, are on a risk-adjusted return basis. Research has indicated that very few funds have consistently beaten the market on a risk-return basis (see Chapter 8). This suggests that investors should be very cautions in using historical returns to forecast ex-ante returns. It might be reasonable, however, to assume that superior ex-post return performances indicate that management has demonstrated the ability to perform successfully. A fund of this type would be a better selection than a fund that has never demonstrated superior return performance. However, many investment publications and advisors caution against using the most-recent short-term performance in selecting a fund.

2. EXPENSE RATIOS Other things being equal, investors benefit by investing in funds with low annual expense ratios. It is important to remember, however, that the type or classification of the fund and the size of the fund will influence this ratio. It is also critical to check for the existence of a 12b-1 plan that results in charges directly to NAV.

3. LOAD VERSUS NO-LOAD FUNDS If there are no differences in the risk and gross-return performances, no-load funds are generally a better choice for a "short"

holding period. A load fund might be better, however, for a "long" holding period if the annual expenses and fees were lower than those of a comparable no-load fund.

4. PORTFOLIO TURNOVER Actively managed mutual funds make numerous portfolio revisions that result in large portfolio turnover ratios. The brokerage commissions and other costs associated with these transactions reduce the *HPR*, since they are reflected in NAV. High turnover ratios are acceptable to shareholders only if the portfolio manager has demonstrated skill in security selection and/or market timing, which is reflected in superior risk-return performance.

5. ASSET SIZE Marketing literature provided by large mutual funds often stresses their size, as indicated by total assets, as a desirable investment characteristic. There is little in the academic literature, however, to suggest that size influences risk-adjusted performance. Large funds may enjoy economies of scale in expenses and management fees but may also find it more difficult to find an adequate number of undervalued securities when their assets reach the billion-dollar-plus level.

6. CORRECT MARKET TIMING Successful mutual fund investing, like any other type of investing, depends to a large extent on buying the right fund at the right time. Before buying an aggressive equity fund, it is advisable to develop a realistic stock market forecast. A "bearish" forecast does not suggest an aggressive equity fund. A realistic interest rate forecast is also necessary before investing in a fixed-income or bond fund. Once the market forecast is made, the beta of the fund would be useful.[18] Also, the historical performance during bull and bear markets indicates the ability of the fund's manager to take advantage of a bull market or to develop a defensive strategy for a bear market. Wiesenberger's "price volatility" ratios, previously discussed, provide useful insights for this analysis. Previous studies of mutual fund timing decision, however, have generally concluded that few if any funds have demonstrated consistent market timing activities.[19]

    Correct market timing, therefore, involves two aspects: (1) buying the right fund at the right time, and (2) finding a fund that may be expected to use market timing successfully in its portfolio management strategies. An additional discussion of using mutual funds for market timing appears later in the chapter.

7. FUND GROWTH Are mutual funds that have shown rapid growth in assets better investments than slow growth funds? Previous research has shown a very weak relationship between growth and performance. The level of marketing expenses is more important in explaining growth than risk-adjusted performance.

---

[18] See, for example, Robert Kinsman, "There Is a Beta Way—Measuring Risk in Your Mutual Fund," *Barron's*, 15 Oct. 1984, p. 15.

[19] See, for example, F. J. Fabozzi and J. C. Francis, "Mutual Fund Systematic Risk for Bull and Bear Markets," *Journal of Finance* (December 1979): pp. 1243–50, and E. Theodore. Veit and John. M. Cheney, "Are Mutual Funds Market Timers?" *Journal of Portfolio Management* (Winter 1982): pp. 35–42.

INVESTMENT STRATEGIES FOR MUTUAL FUNDS

Introduction

Investing in mutual funds has become more complicated because of the rapid growth in the number of funds and the resulting proliferation of investment objectives and strategies. With over 2,300 funds in 1987, there are now more mutual funds than common stocks listed on the NYSE. The following section of the chapter presents material that should help in developing a strategy that can be used to invest in mutual funds.

Passive Strategies

1. BUY AND HOLD   Traditionally, investment companies and specifically mutual funds were marketed as *passive* investments. Small investors, who typically lack the knowledge, time, or motivation for analysis, could depend on mutual funds for professional investment management, including security selection, market timing, and portfolio diversification. Mutual funds can still be used in this way, but there are several reasons why caution should be exercised in the selection of individual funds:

   a. Many new mutual funds are nondiversified; they restrict investments to a specific industry or place other limitations on the portfolio's composition. Therefore, passive investors generally do not receive the benefits of diversification. Small, passive investors generally do not have other investments in stocks and bonds to provide *personal* portfolio diversification.

   b. It is highly unlikely that an individual mutual fund can consistently beat the market on a risk-adjusted basis. To illustrate, "the average equity fund over the past five years has gained 112.40%, considerably behind the Dow's 150.26% gain and the S&P's 142.09% rise, assuming, in all three cases, that dividends and capital gain were reinvested."[20] The comprehensive review of studies dealing with mutual fund performance presented in Chapter 8 also supports this statement.

      Norman Fosback, a recognized authority on funds and the editor of *Mutual Fund Forecaster*, offered some practical observations:[21]

      In the aggregate, mutual funds cannot outperform the market because they are the market. Investors should formulate a realistic expectation of possible rewards or risks associated with any one fund. Then, to cope with the risks, buy several funds instead of just one.

   The suggestion that investors buy more than one fund has several advantages. First, it would improve the personal diversification of the investor. Second, the overall *HPR*s of the mutual fund portfolio would be more stable. This

---

[20] Jaye Scholl, "The Special Team Syndrome: A Boon and a Bane for Investors," *Barron's*, 10 Nov. 1986, p. 48.

[21] "What the Pros Say about Your Funds," *Money*, May 1987, pp. 44 and 46.

strategy would reduce the probability of large fluctuations in *HPR*s. The strategy could be implemented by buying shares of several funds within a single family of funds such as Fidelity or T. Rowe Price. Another recent innovative idea is the Star Fund, offered by the Vanguard Group, whose portfolio consists of shares in five other nondiversified Vanguard funds. This strategy is designed to create a balanced or diversified portfolio in a single package.[22]

2. INDEX MUTUAL FUNDS A second passive mutual fund investment strategy uses *index* or *market* funds. Index funds form a portfolio that duplicates the performance of a market indicator portfolio like the S&P 500. This type of fund arose because of the implications of the Efficient Market Hypothesis, EMH. A number of bank trust departments and insurance companies have also created index portfolios, and a growing number of pension funds use index portfolios (see Chapter 25). The largest index mutual fund is the Vanguard Index Trust, organized in 1976 as the First Index Investment Trust.

Advantages of an index fund include broad diversification (in a common stock portfolio), low operating expenses, and limited brokerage fees. Index funds, by their very nature, do not require active portfolio management or the services of security analysts.

An analysis of the Vanguard Index Trust provides an illustration of this type of investment strategy. Its investment objective, as presented in *Investment Companies*:

> *The fund seeks to provide investment results that correspond to the price and yield performance of publicly traded common stocks, as represented by the Standard & Poor's 500 Corporate Stock Price Index. It attempts to duplicate the investment performance of the S&P Index by owning all of the 500 stocks contained in the Index, appropriately weighted. The trust will seek to be fully invested in common stocks at all times, owning no fewer than the 200 stocks having the largest weightings in the index.[23]*

Table 24.8 provides key statistics for the fund for 1976–1986. In terms of net assets, the fund has grown rapidly—from $14.3 million in 1976 to $485.1 million in 1986. The annual *HPR*s of the fund are, as expected, closely correlated with the S&P 500. Notice also that the fund paid a constant dollar dividend of $.83 for 1980–1982, even though the dividend yield on the S&P 500 was not constant.

The lower portion of Table 24.8 provides Wiesenberger's price volatility ratios for eight bull and bear markets. The Vanguard Index Trust does not have a ratio of 1, as might be expected, but for seven of the eight periods had ratios below 1. This would be a desirable characteristic during bear markets but not during bull markets. Fund expenses, brokerage costs, and

---

[22] See the article by Elizabeth Sanger, "In the Time It Took to Write This Story, Another Fund Probably Was Launched," *Barron's*, 17 Feb. 1986, p. 59.

[23] Investment Companies, 1987, p. 566.

TABLE 24.8 VANGUARD INDEX TRUST

YEAR	TOTAL NET ASSETS (MILLIONS)	NAV	EXPENSE RATIO	DISTRIBUTION		HOLDING PERIOD RETURNS		PORTFOLIO COMPOSITION	
				DIVIDENDS	CAPITAL GAINS	FUND	S&P 500	CASH & EQUIVALENTS	COMMON STOCK
1986	$485.1	$24.27	0.28%	$0.89	$2.02	18.23%	18.60%	(1)%	101%
1985	394.3	22.99	0.28	0.91	1.61	30.69	29.88	(2)	102
1984	289.7	19.52	0.27	0.88	0.48	5.99	4.09	2	98
1983	233.6	19.70	0.28	0.87	0.71	21.18	21.25	(1)	101
1982	110.0	17.56	0.39	0.83	0.25	20.10	22.24	1	99
1981	91.2	15.52	0.42	0.83	0.56	(5.21)	(4.77)	–	100
1980	98.8	17.84	0.35	0.83	0.53	31.15	34.11	(1)	101
1979	78.9	14.64	0.30	0.75	0.06	17.85	15.60	–	100
1978	66.2	13.11	0.36	0.65	–	5.76	8.51	–	100
1977	21.0	13.01	0.46	0.57	–	(4.62)	14.54	–	100
1976	14.3	14.72	NM	0.17	–	–	17.06	–	100

WIESENBERGER'S "PRICE VOLATILITY" RATIOS

	DECLINING (BEAR) MARKETS				RISING (BULL) MARKETS			
	9/1/78 to 11/14/78	10/5/79 to 3/27/80	1/6/81 to 3/8/82	10/10/83 to 7/24/84	11/14/78 to 10/5/79	3/27/80 to 1/6/81	3/8/82 to 10/10/83	7/24/84 to 5/29/87
NYSE Common Stock Index	1.00	1.00	1.00	1.00	1.00	1.00	1.00	1.00
Vanguard Index Trust	0.90	0.87	0.97	1.01	0.84	0.89	0.97	0.98

SOURCE: Data from *Investment Companies, 1987*, with *HPR*s calculated using Equation 24.1. Reprinted by permission of Wiesenberger Investment Companies Service, Division of Warren, Gorham, & Lamont, Inc.

dividend distributions that don't match the dividend yield on the S&P 500 cause Vanguard's price volatility ratio to deviate from the expected value of 1. It is also interesting to note that the *HPR*s for the fund are both above and below those of the S&P 500.

The portfolio turnover rate for the Vanguard Index Trust was only 36 percent of average assets for 1986. Brokerage commissions were therefore small relative to other stock funds whose turnover ratios may be over 100 percent.

Annual expense ratios, while somewhat high when the fund started, are now quite low compared to those of other common stock funds. The fund is a no-load fund but does have a 12b-1 plan that charges all marketing and promotional expenses directly to NAV. The expense ratios are therefore understated by the amount of those marketing and promotional expenses.

Active Strategies

1. TRADITIONAL STRATEGIES Traditionally, because of the nature of mutual funds, investors did not attempt active strategies (market timing or switching between funds) seeking the best performance. Mutual fund managers selected individual securities for the fund and determined the appropriate diversification within the limitations of the stated investment objective. Also, most mutual fund managers attempted very limited switching between cash, bonds, or common stocks or trading in securities with high or low betas.[24] Funds were designed to be passive investments, were generally managed passively, and were viewed in this way by investors.

2. SWITCHING BETWEEN FUNDS Several developments in the mutual fund industry have facilitated and encouraged active investment strategies. The introduction of money market funds within a family of funds is a major factor. The proliferation of specialized sector or industry funds also offers more opportunities for active trading. The rapid growth of no-load funds provides the opportunity to eliminate brokerage costs when exchanges are made within a family of funds. Some funds, however, do charge fees for switching between family funds.

These developments now allow mutual fund investors to engage in the three major aspects of portfolio management: selection, market timing, and diversification. Investors do not participate in decisions regarding individual securities; they can, however, make selection decisions regarding specific industries. For example, as of July 1987, the Fidelity family of funds offered thirty-five select or industry-specific funds and twenty-two equity funds in addition to their money market and bond funds. A joke on Wall Street is "When will a fund offer the IBM common stock fund?" With the acceptance and rapid growth of the sector and specialized funds, it is not inconceivable that funds could be established to invest in a very limited number of securities. In fact, the AT&T Fund was started to "recreate" AT&T by holding only AT&T and its spin-off stocks.

---

[24] See, for example, John M. Cheney and E. Theodore Veit, "Are Mutual Funds Market Timers?" *The Journal of Portfolio Management* (Winter 1982): pp. 35–42.

Investors can pursue market timing by telephone exchanges and switching between money market, bond, common stock, and specialized funds within a single family of funds. Telephone exchanges have grown from $5.8 billion in 1979 to $46.0 billion in 1985.[25] On January 8, 1986, the DJIA lost 39 points— at that time a significant decline. One anonymous fund reported that its shareholders switched a net $27 million out of equity funds between January 8 and 10.[26] These statistics indicate that mutual fund investors are attracted to the potential benefits of market timing.

In terms of sector funds, telephone exchanges are common, with over $1 billion exchanged since the introduction of such funds in the early 1980s. Is this timing strategy successful? One study indicated that the majority of investors using this strategy were unsuccessful.[27] It suggested that investors often move into specific sector funds when they are "hot," move out when they are "cold," and essentially "buy high, sell low."

The developments in the mutual fund industry also offer investors the opportunity to engage in diversification activities. It is no longer necessary for investors to rely on balanced funds for diversification among classes of securities. Specialized funds such as international stock funds and precious metal funds offer the opportunity to add very specialized diversification to an individual's investment portfolio.

In summary, mutual funds are no longer seen as passive investments where a professional portfolio manager makes all the decisions. Individual investors who are so inclined can pursue many active strategies that include aspects of selection, market timing, and diversification.

SUMMARY

The purpose of this chapter has been to provide an overview of mutual funds and other types of investment companies. It also presented information about factors to consider in making investment decisions in mutual funds and discussed various investment strategies.

Major investment company characteristics include a distinction between open- and closed-end funds and between load and no-load mutual funds. Tax implications and fees and expenses incurred by mutual funds were also discussed. Mutual fund investors should be aware of the operating expenses of funds in the same way that an investor in a common stock should be aware of the company's operating expenses.

The possible decision variables, which vary in importance, in an investment decision include (1) consistency of performance, (2) expense ratios, (3) load fees, (4) turnover ratios, (5) asset size, (6) market timing, and (7) growth in assets.

Traditional strategies were essentially passive, since the portfolio manager made the decisions and investors often followed a buy-and-hold strategy. Index

[25] Kathleen Kerwin, "Dialing for Dollars: Switch Funds' Lure," *Barron's*, 17 Feb. 1986, p. 56.

[26] Ibid.

[27] Floyd Norris, "Sector Funds: A Lot More Fumbles than Touchdowns," *Barron's*, 10 Nov. 1986.

funds, however, offer investors an even more passive strategy. The traditional job of the portfolio manager is eliminated; the only task of the manager is to make portfolio revisions, so that the fund will mirror the performance of the index the fund is designed to match.

Recent developments in the mutual fund industry have greatly expanded the investment strategies available to individuals. Active strategies are now possible; investors may manage their investments in mutual funds using many of the same strategies used for individual securities. These developments, while increasing the flexibility of strategies available to investors, also create potential pitfalls for the uninformed. The data suggest that the average active mutual fund investor is finding that market timing, selection, and diversification are very difficult and challenging in efficient capital markets.

QUESTIONS

1. Distinguish between an open- and a closed-end fund.
2. Distinguished between a load and a no-load mutual fund.
3. Compare and contrast a mutual fund with a unit investment trust.
4. Discuss the different types of fees and charges that might be incurred by a mutual fund investor.
5. Define the "investment objective" of a mutual fund. How can the investment objective be used by investors to identify a fund for a possible investment?
6. Identify and briefly discuss the services that mutual funds may offer their shareholders.
7. Mutual funds and other investment companies were traditionally considered as appropriate investments for individuals pursuing a passive strategy. What recent developments have occurred that suggest mutual funds may be appropriate for active strategies?
8. Assume that an individual investor is attempting to identify one or more mutual funds for a potential investment. Discuss the key decision variables that should be considered in identifying appropriate funds.
9. Suppose an investor is attempting to select between the following two mutual funds:

	FUND A	FUND B
Front-end load fee	0	6.0%
Annual management fee	0.4%	0.2%
Annual 12b-1 charges	1.0%	0
Rear-end load fee	0	0
Annual transaction costs incurred by fund	2.0%	2.0%

If the investor thinks that there will be no difference in the gross *HPR*s (returns before expenses) and that the funds have equal risk:

a. Which fund would be better for a short holding period? Explain your answer.
b. Which fund would be better for a long holding period? Explain your answer.

10. Discuss the advantages and disadvantages of an index mutual fund versus an actively managed fund.

11. Explain how an open-end mutual fund calculates NAV. How is NAV used by the fund? What is the effect on NAV from income and capital gain distributions to shareholders?

PROBLEMS

1. Consider the following data on an open-end mutual fund:

	NAV ON JAN. 1	DISTRIBUTION AT END OF YEAR	
		DIVIDENDS	CAPITAL GAINS
1987	$10	$.75	$3.00
1988	15	.60	1.00
1989	12	–	–

   a. Calculate the *HPR* for 1987.

   b. Calculate the *HPR* for 1988.

2. Suppose that an individual invests $10,000 in an open-end mutual fund. The NAV is $48 and the offering price is $50. At the end of one year the investor receives $1.00 per share of dividends and sells the shares at a NAV of $51.

   a. Calculate the *HPR* considering the load fee.

   b. Assume that there is no load fee. Calculate the *HPR*.

3. Assume that an individual invested $10,000 in a closed-end fund. The shares were trading at $50 per share and the stock broker charged a 3 percent commission. At the end of one year, the investor received $1.00 per share of dividends and sold the shares at a price of $51 per share before the brokerage commission.

   a. Calculate the *HPR* considering the brokerage commission.

   b. Assume that there are no brokerage commissions. Calculate the *HPR*.

   c. Compare your answers to problems 2 and 3 in terms of the impact of load fees versus brokerage fees on *HPR*s.

4. Consider the following data on two mutual funds:

	FUND A	FUND B
Total net assets (assets less liabilities) beginning of year	$1,000,000	$1,000,000
Number of shares outstanding at beginning of year	100,000	100,000
Annual operating expenses	$ 10,000	$ 12,000
Value of securities sold during year	$ 500,000	$ 800,000
Value of securities purchased during year	$ 400,000	$ 900,000
Brokerage fees for the year	$ 9,000	$ 17,000
Number of shares outstanding at end of year	110,000	100,000
Total net assets end of year	$1,100,000	$1,200,000

For each fund, calculate

a. The net asset values per share at the beginning and end of the year. Assume that operating expenses and brokerage fees are reflected in the net asset values.

b. The expense ratios, using the beginning of the year net asset values.

c. The portfolio turnover ratios.

d. Do you think the higher operating expenses for Fund B are justified? Explain your answer.

e. Do you think the higher portfolio turnover ratio and brokerage fees are justified for Fund B? Explain your answer.

5. Assume that an investor is trying to decide between investing in a no-load fund with a 12b-1 plan or a fund with a front-end load:

	FUND X	FUND Y
Front-end load fee	0	4%
Annual 12b-1 charge	1%	0

The investor thinks that the risks and other characteristics of both funds are equal and that each fund will provide an annual *HPR* of 12% *before* considering the load fee and 12b-1 charge. Assume that the investor has $10,000 to invest in either fund.

a. Calculate the anticipated dollar values of each investment after a three-year holding period. Assume annual compounding. Which fund appears to be the better alternative?

b. Answer part a assuming a six-year holding period.

c. Calculate the length of the holding period that would make the investor indifferent between the two funds.

d. Explain why the length of the anticipated holding period should be considered in comparing load fees with annual expenses such as 12b-1 charges.

REFERENCES

Alexander, Gordon J., and Roger D. Stover. "Consistency of Mutual Fund Performance during Varying Market Conditions." *Journal of Economics and Business* (Spring 1980): pp. 219–25.

Anderson, Seth Copeland. "Closed-end Funds versus Market Efficiency." *Journal of Portfolio Management* (Fall 1986): pp. 64–65.

Ang, James S., and Jess H. Chua. "Mutual Funds: Different Strokes for Different Folks." *Journal of Portfolio Management* (Winter 1982): pp. 43–47.

Bergeron, Woodrow J. "How to Figure Taxes on Your Fund Shares." *Barron's*, 16 February 1987, p. 68.

Bogdanich, Walt. "Growth of No-Load Products Stirs Critics to Question True Savings." *Wall Street Journal*, 25 January 1985, p. 25.

Brealey, Richard A. "How to Combine Active Management with Index Funds." *Journal of Portfolio Management* (Winter 1986): pp. 4–10.

Brinson, Gary P., L. Randolph Hood, and Gilbert L. Beebower. ''Determinants of Portfolio Performance.'' *Financial Analysts Journal* (July-August 1986): pp. 39–44.

Carlson, Robert S. ''Aggregate Performance of Mutual Funds, 1948–1967.'' *Journal of Financial and Quantitative Analysis* (March 1970): pp. 1–31.

Ferguson, Robert. ''Active Portfolio Management—How to Beat the Index Funds.'' *Financial Analysts Journal* (May-June 1975): pp. 63–72.

Henriksson, Roy D., and Robert C. Merton. ''On Market Timing and Investment Performance: II. Statistical Procedures for Evaluating Forecasting Skills.'' *Journal of Business* (October 1981): pp. 513–33.

Horowitz, Ira. ''The 'Reward-to-Variability' Ratio and Mutual Fund Performance.'' *Journal of Business* (October 1966): pp. 485–88.

Investment Company Institute. *1988 Mutual Fund Fact Book.*

Kerwin, Kathleen. ''Dialing for Dollars: Switch Funds' Lure.'' *Barron's,* 17 February 1986, pp. 56–57.

Kinsman, Robert. ''There Is a Beta Way—Measuring the Risk in Your Mutual Fund.'' *Barron's,* 15 October 1984, p. 15.

Lakonishok, Josef. ''Performance of Mutual Funds versus Their Expenses.'' *Journal of Bank Research* (Summer 1981): pp. 110–13.

Liscio, John. ''Splitting Shares.'' *Barron's,* 14 March 1988, pp. 13, 72–73.

Madden, Gerald P., Kenneth P. Nunn, Jr. and Alan Wiemann. ''Mutual Fund Performance and the Size Effect.'' Paper presented at the 1984 Financial Management Association Meeting.

Mains, Norman E. ''Risk, the Pricing of Capital Assets, and the Evaluation of Investment Portfolios: Comment.'' *Journal of Business* (July 1977): pp. 371–84.

Martin, John D., Arthur J. Keown, and James L. Farrell., Jr. ''Do Fund Objectives Affect Diversification Policies?'' *Journal of Portfolio Management* (Winter 1982): pp. 19–28.

Merton, Robert C. ''On Market Timing and Investment Performance: I. An Equilibrium Theory of Value for Market Forecasts.'' *Journal of Business* (July 1981): pp. 363–406.

Moses, Edward A., John M. Cheney, and E. Theodore Veit. ''A New and More Complete Performance Measure.'' *Journal of Portfolio Management* (Summer 1987): pp. 24–33.

Murphy, J. Michael. ''Why No One Can Tell Who's Winning.'' *Financial Analysts Journal* (May-June 1980): pp. 49–55.

Norris, Floyd. ''Sector Funds: A Lot More Fumbles than Touchdowns.'' *Barron's,* 10 November 1986, pp. 55–56.

———. ''Tales of the New Tax Law: How It Will Affect Mutual Funds.'' *Barron's,* 10 November 1986, pp. 68–71.

———. ''Closed-end Funds: The Riddle of Net Asset Value.'' *Barron's,* 16 Febrary 1987, pp. 60–61.

Perritt, Gerald W. ''A Look behind the Bottom Line.'' *Barron's,* 19 May 1986, pp. 53–55.

Richards, R. Malcolm, Don R. Fraser, and John C. Groth. ''Winning Strategies for Closed-end Funds.'' *Journal of Portfolio Management* (Fall 1980): pp. 50–55.

———. ''The Attractions of Closed-end Bond Funds.'' *Journal of Portfolio Management* (Winter 1982): pp. 56–61.

Scholl, Jaye. ''The Special Team Syndrome: A Boon and a Bane for Investors.'' *Barron's,* 10 November 1986, p. 48.

Sharpe, William F. ''Mutual Fund Performance.'' *Journal of Business* (January 1966): pp. 119–38.

Slater, Karen. "Critics Say Brokerage Firms Hide Fees on Their New 'No-Load" Mutual Funds," *Wall Street Journal*, August 1985, p. 25.

Smith, Keith V. "Is Fund Growth Related to Fund Performance?" *Journal of Portfolio Management* (Spring 1978): pp. 49–54.

Smith, Randall. "S&P 500 Index Bests Many Managers in '83, Sharpening Debate on Investment Tactics." *Wall Street Journal*, 20 January 1984, p. 31.

———. "Some Mutual Funds' Hot Records May Hide Companies' Cool Moves." *Wall Street Journal*, 4 March 1985, p. 29.

Umstead, David A. "Volatility, Growth, and Investment Policy," *Journal of Portfolio Management* (Winter 1981): pp. 55–59.

Wiesenberger Financial Services. *Investment Companies, 1986*; *1987*.

Wong, Jan. "When It Comes to Mutual Funds, Bigger Might Be Better, After All." *Wall Street Journal*, 5 June 1986, p. 27.

CHAPTER 25

PENSION FUNDS AND INSURANCE PRODUCTS

INTRODUCTION

The purpose of this chapter is to provide an introduction to two important aspects of personal portfolio management: pension funds and insurance products. Individuals should be aware of the various investment alternatives, and they should analyze alternatives in terms of their entire portfolio of assets, which may include an investment portfolio, retirement (pension) benefits, and insurance products.

As employees, most individual investors do not have direct control of their pension funds. Control is exercised by their employer, who may be a small privately held business, a publicly traded corporation, or a governmental unit or agency. Employees cannot influence the investment policies of their pension funds. However, they should be aware of the various types of pension plans and the specific characteristics of the plans in which they have an interest. This information is essential in planning for retirement and in formulating strategies for the entire portfolio.

Insurance products have multiplied rapidly over the last decade. In many cases, these new products are a combination of products, providing death benefits and offering investment elements. Examples of these new products include universal life insurance, variable life insurance, guaranteed investment contracts, and many variations of "annuity" types of products.

This chapter provides an introduction to many of these newer types of insurance products. The chapter also compares the investment characteristics of these new products to traditional investments like common stocks and bonds. This approach is designed to aid individual investors in considering these new products as possible additions to their portfolios. The chapter, however, does not argue that these products are substitutes for traditional investments.

BACKGROUND ON PENSION FUNDS

History

Pension funds are essentially investment portfolios that provide future benefits to the employees of an organization. Pension plans may be sponsored by business (private plans) or by governmental units or agencies (public plans). There were approximately 850,000 pension plans in the United States at the end of 1987. Pension funds are by far the largest investors in common stocks and fixed-income securities. The investments and investment strategies of pension funds vary according to the type of plan and the risk-return attitudes of the fund's sponsor and manager.

Prior to the 1960s, pension funds received limited attention in financial research. Few regulations and laws governed pension funds. Beginning in the 1960s, however, more attention was focused on pension funds. In 1965, the Accounting Principles Board issued Opinion No. 8, dealing with accounting for the costs of pension plans and how this information should be disclosed on financial statements. The accounting profession, continuing to wrestle with pension accounting, issued Financial Accounting Standard Board Statement Number 35 (FASB No. 35) and

TABLE 25.1 ASSETS OF THE TWENTY LARGEST
PENSION FUNDS: (millions of dollars)

1.	TIAA-CREF	$66,171
2.	California Public Employees	44,036
3.	General Motors	40,000
4.	New York State/Local	38,747
5.	AT&T	37,577
6.	N.Y.C. Retirement Systems	33,633
7.	General Electric	27,300
8.	California State Teachers	23,714
9.	New York State Teachers	23,035
10.	IBM	22,457
11.	Ford Motor	19,800
12.	N.J. Division of Investment	19,785
13.	Texas Teachers	18,930
14.	E.I. duPont de Nemours	16,868
15.	Michigan State	16,680
16.	Wisconsin Investment Board	15,632
17.	Ohio Public Employees	14,985
18.	Ohio Teachers Retirement	14,821
19.	NYNEX Corp.	14,336
20.	Florida Board of Administration	13,700

SOURCE: *Pensions & Investment Age*, 25 January, 1988, p. 18.
Reprinted by permission.

36 (FASB No. 36) in 1980. These statements require uniform disclosure of the assets and liabilities of pension funds.

Another important development was the Employee Retirement Income Security Act of 1974, ERISA. This federal law provides stringent standards for private (corporate) pension plans, dealing with minimum funding by the sponsor and financial reporting. The law also imposes investment constraints on pension fund managers. Essentially, ERISA requires pension plans to be financed and managed in a manner that guarantees benefits to employees.

Because of the financial reporting and disclosure provisions mandated by ERISA, the average pension fund tends to be conservatively managed. The risk-return characteristics for individual funds, however, can vary significantly; this will be discussed in more detail later in the chapter.

Growth and Size of Pension Funds

The assets of pension funds increased dramatically over the period 1985–1987 because of the strong stock market up to October 19, 1987, and because of additional employer contributions to the plans. For the years ending September 30, assets of the one thousand largest funds increased from $1,073 billion in 1985 to $1,577.6 billion in 1987. The assets of the two hundreds largest funds increased from $812.4 billion in 1985 to $1,197.5 billion in 1987.[1]

Table 25.1 indicates the size of the twenty largest pension funds in the United States. Notice that both private and public funds are included in the sample. As-

---

[1] Chuck Panstian, "A $1 Trillion Milestone," *Pensions and Investment Age*, 25 Jan., 1988, pp. 1, 82.

sets, the market value of the funds' investments, typically include cash, common stocks, fixed-income securities, mortgages, and real estate investments.

CHARACTERISTICS OF PENSION FUNDS

How Pension Funds Operate

A pension fund is an organization separate from its sponsor. This arrangement protects the employees and permits the fund to receive funding from the sponsor for investment purposes. Contributions (funding) by the sponsor and investment income are used to provide income to retired employees or lump-sum benefits to employees who leave the organization.

Before an employee becomes eligible for pension benefits, certain requirements must be met. Historically, employees became *vested* or entitled to benefits after completing ten years of employment with the sponsoring organization. Under the Tax Reform Act of 1986, however, plans are required to reduce the vesting period. Beginning January 1, 1989, plans have two options: 100 percent vesting after five years of service; or 20 percent vesting after three years of service, rising in 20 percent increments to full vesting after seven years.

Once vested, an employee may leave the organization before retiring and retain his or her benefits. Typically, the pension fund maintains the accrued benefits in escrow until the former worker reaches retirement age; then benefits are paid monthly. A second option distributes accrued benefits as a lump sum upon the employee's leaving the organization. Because of possible tax consequences, the recipient of a lump-sum distribution should consider ''rolling over'' the distribution into another retirement fund.

Details about vesting and distribution options for employees are provided in the *Summary Plan Description* which pension funds are required to furnish to plan participants. The Summary Plan Description also provides other important characteristics of a plan, discussed below.

Defined Benefit Plan

The defined benefit plan, DBP, is the oldest type of pension plan and, as the name implies, specifies the benefits that will be received at retirement. The plan sponsor (employer) makes specified contributions to each employee's account; the employee's account is then used to provide the defined benefit at retirement.

The amount of the benefit, however, depends on a number of factors, including length of employment and level of income. Typically, DBP benefits are larger for employees with greater longevity and higher salaries: a typical benefit formula uses a percentage of the average of the last five years' salary, adjusted for length of employment to determine monthly retirement benefits. Benefits do not depend on the investment performance of the fund.

Defined Contribution Plan

The other major type of pension plan is the defined contribution plan, DCP. This plan specifies the contribution that the employer (and/or employees) will make to the plan, rather than stating pension benefits. There are a number of forms that a DCP may take, including profit-sharing plan, employee stock option plan, ESOP, 401(K) saving plan, and money-purchase pension plan. Some of these plans are discussed in more detail in Chapter 26.

One advantage of a DCP employee account is that after vesting it is considered the property of the employee and can easily be transferred. Another advantage is that this plan often allows employees to match the contributions of the employer; all contributions and earnings are tax-free until retirement distributions begin.

A disadvantage of a DCP is that the level of retirement benefits depends to a great extent on the investment performance of the plan; the employee does not know the value of his or her share in the plan until retirement. At that point, however, the funds may be used to purchase some type of annuity contract that will provide a defined benefit for a specified period of time.

RISK-RETURN ANALYSIS OF PENSION FUNDS

Default Risk

Because of the requirements of ERISA and a conservative investment management philosophy, the likelihood of default is small. Since 1974, however, approximately 1,400 defined benefit plans have failed, affecting over 400,000 participants. This section briefly discusses some of the factors that should be considered in an analysis of default risk.

1. PENSION BENEFIT GUARANTY CORPORATION The Pension Benefit Guaranty Corporation, PBGC, is a federal agency established by ERISA in 1974. This agency insures the majority of defined benefit pension plans.[2] However, the maximum guaranteed benefit is $1,858 per month, which may be less than the benefit that would have occurred if the plan had not defaulted.

    The default risk of a guaranteed DBP, therefore, is shifted from the beneficiary to the PBGC. The strength of this guarantee depends on the financial health of PBGC. This program was initially funded by a $1 annual per-person fee paid by each fund. In late 1987, the annual fee had risen to $8.50 per person, with legislation being considered that would raise the fee to $20 per person. It appears that the investment income from the initial fees has not been adequate to fund fully the commitments of the PBGC.

2. FUNDING PRACTICES OF INDIVIDUAL FUNDS Despite the requirements of ERISA and financial reporting standards, plan sponsors have considerable flexibility in determining the amount and timing of funding contributions. In theory, the funding decisions should be based on a comparison of the actuarial present value of vested benefits with the market value of the fund's assets. If the

---

[2] Plans not insured include those provided by professional association employers such as doctors and lawyers who have fewer than 26 employees and plans sponsored by religious organizations.

present value of vested benefits was less than or equal to the fund's asset value, the plan would be considered fully funded. If the present value of vested benefits exceeded asset value, the plan would be underfunded.

In practice, however, determining an appropriate level of funding is difficult. First, estimating future retirement benefits is complex because of factors such as future wage levels, life expectancies, and numbers of employees who will ultimately be vested. Second, pension fund assets are often invested in common stocks and other alternatives that provide an unknown stream of future cash flows; higher assumed rates of return on investments permit lower funding by the sponsor. Third, a discount rate must be assumed to calculate the present value of vested benefits.

Funds are required to disclose the rate of return they assume for their investment portfolio and to provide details on other actuarial assumptions. These assumptions and the current status of the fund in terms of under- or overfunding indicate the financial strength of a fund. There is considerable debate in the financial literature, however, about whether pension funds are "adequately" funded and how sponsors should deal with the funding issue.[3]

3. DEFAULT RISK EXAMPLE LTV Corp. was the second largest United States steel company before its bankruptcy. At the time of bankruptcy, LTV had approximately 60,000 retired employees entitled to $1.8 million in monthly benefits. As a DBP, the pension plan was involuntarily terminated by the PBGC because the plan was severely underfunded. The assets and liabilities of the plan were then assumed by the PBGC. Because of the success of LTV's reorganization under bankruptcy, however, the PBGC filed a motion on January 29, 1988, requesting that the court require LTV to resume its responsibility for the plan effective January 13, 1987.[4]

The LTV example, other corporate bankruptcies, and leveraged buy-outs have increased the awareness of many employees concerning the financial soundness of their pension plans. There is also concern that the PBGC's current assets may not be adequate to guarantee all of the DBPs that might default.

Systematic Risk

Pension fund portfolios include both unsystematic and systematic risk. The systematic risk of pension funds is generally below that of a market portfolio of common stocks. Consequently, changes in the values of pension fund assets are less volatile than those in common stocks in general. For example, a Congressional Research Service report issued in the wake of the October 19, 1987, crash found

---

[3] For example, see Fischer Black, "The Investment Policy Spectrum: Individuals, Endowment Funds, and Pension Funds," *Financial Analysts Journal* (January-February 1976): pp. 23–30; Zvi Bodie, Jay O. Light, Randall Morch, and Robert A. Taggart, Jr., "Corporate Pension Policy: An Empirical Investigation," *Financial Analysts Journal* (September-October 1985): pp. 10–16; and Patrick J. Regan and Steven D. Bleiberg, "Overfunded Pension Plans," *Financial Analysts Journal* (November-December 1985): pp. 10–12.

[4] Fred Williams, "Agency Renews Court Battle over LTV Termination," *Pension & Investments Age*, 8 Feb. 1988, p. 1.

TABLE 25.2   ASSET MIX OF 200 LARGEST CORPORATE PENSION FUNDS

	1986	1987
Common Stocks	50.1%	54.5%
Bonds	27.7	23.9
Cash	7.9	8.2
Real Estate Equity	4.5	4.2
Guaranteed Investment Contracts (GICs)	3.4	3.6
Annuities	1.3	1.7
Mortgages	0.5	0.6
Mortgage-backed Securities	1.0	0.9
Venture Capital, Oil and Gas and Miscellaneous Investments	3.6	2.4
	100.0%	100.0%

SOURCE: Reprinted with permission, *Pensions & Investment Age* (25 January 1988). Copyright, Crain Communications, Inc.

that the value of pension fund assets declined about 15 percent, compared to a plunge of over 30 percent for stocks during the period August 25–December 2, 1987.

Many pension fund managers also pursue active investment strategies, shifting funds between common stocks, bonds, and other investment alternatives.[5] Table 25.2 provides the asset mix of the two hundred largest corporate pension funds for 1986 and 1987. Notice that on average, these large funds invest in a variety of investments. This diversification is one factor that reduces the systematic risk of pension funds relative to a market portfolio of common stocks.

Investment Performance of Pension Funds

Numerous studies of actively managed mutual and pension funds indicate that they do not consistently outperform the market on a risk-adjusted basis. Many of these studies are reviewed in Chapter 8. Given this general conclusion, individuals should not expect their pension funds to provide above-average performance over a long period. Few if any fund managers have demonstrated an ability consistently to beat the market. On the other hand, a well-managed fund should provide long-run returns that are consistent with its degree of systematic risk.

Impact of Pension Funds on Corporate Sponsors

Studies relying on surveys of pension fund sponsors and managers reveal some interesting observations about pension fund management.[6] Tax considerations, the liquidity and financial condition of the sponsor, and actuarial recommendations are identified as important determinants of funding policies. Additionally, active investment strategies using common stocks are favored over passive strate-

---

[5] For example, see Joel Chernoff, "Equity Market Exodus," *Pension & Investment Age*, 8 Feb., 1988, pp. 1, 33.

[6] For example, see Susan L. Malley and Susan Jayson, "Why Do Financial Executives Manage Pension Funds the Way They Do?" *Financial Analysts Journal* (November-December 1986): pp. 56–62.

gies. Surprisingly, many executives also view the pension fund as an asset separate from the other assets of the sponsor. Technically, this viewpoint is correct, since fund assets are protected from creditors in the event of bankruptcy and are required to provide benefits to employees rather than stockholders. Recent evidence suggests, however, that pension funds should be managed from the viewpoint of the sponsor's overall portfolio.[7] The evidence indicates that pension policies are linked to overall corporate profitability and the assessment of corporate risk by potential investors. Thus, pension policies have an important impact on stockholder wealth.

Research studies using an ''event methodology'' (see Chapter 13) indicate that share prices respond to significant pension fund events such as announcing the discount rate used to compute the present value of vested benefits and announcing the voluntary termination of an overfunded pension plan. In the case of the discount rate announcement, firms reporting the use of a ''low'' discount rate outperformed firms announcing a ''high'' discount rate.[8] Shareholders therefore appear to recognize that using a ''low'' rate is conservative and overstates the liabilities of a fund, while using a ''high'' rate understates the liabilities. For firms announcing the termination of overfunded pension plans, the evidence suggests that positive abnormal returns occurred around the announcement period.[9] This evidence suggests that stockholders recognize the termination as a windfall— they will receive benefits from the termination of an overfunded pension plan.

INVESTMENT STRATEGIES OF PENSION FUNDS

Within the constraints imposed by ERISA, pension fund sponsors and managers are free to pursue a wide variety of investment strategies. These strategies may be passive, such as buying-and-holding and indexing, or they may be active, such as changing the asset mix. This section briefly discusses some of these strategies and the implications for the fund sponsor.

Passive Strategies

Accepting the view that common stockholders will ultimately incur the costs and benefits of the corporate pension plan, what investment strategies are appropriate for pension funds? Many fund managers are reaching the conclusion that passive strategies are appropriate. One of the most popular passive strategies is *indexing*. Index funds (see Chapter 24) are designed to match the performance of broad

---

[7] For example, see Zvi Bodie, Jay O. Light, Randall Morch, and Robert A. Taggart, Jr., ''Corporate Pension Policy: An Empirical Investigation,'' *Financial Analysts Journal* (September-October 1985): pp. 10–16; K. C. Chen and Stephen P. D'Arcy, ''Market Sensitivity to Interest Rate Assumption in Corporate Pension Plans,'' *Journal of Risk and Insurance* (June 1986): pp. 209–25; and Jack L. VanDerhei, ''The Effect of Voluntary Termination of Overfunded Pension Plans on Shareholder Wealth, *Journal of Risk and Insurance* (March 1987): pp. 130–56.

[8] Chen and D'Arcy.

[9] VanDerhei.

TABLE 25.3 TEN LARGEST INDEX PENSION FUND MANAGERS: (millions of dollars)

	DOMESTIC EQUITY	DOMESTIC FIXED	INTERNATIONAL	OTHER	TOTAL
1. Wells Fargo Investment Advisors	$35,000	$10,500	$ 761	$4,339	$50,600
2. Bankers Trust	20,250	2,750	250	50	23,300
3. Mellon Capital Management	14,745	2,780	148	370	18,043
4. State Street Bank & Trust	8,010	1,980	3,190	4,140	13,690
5. American National Bank	8,250	1,200	100	–	9,550
6. Manufacturers Hanover Investments	236	6,900	–	–	7,136
7. Mellon Bond Associates	–	5,900	–	–	5,900
8. Alliance Capital Management	3,707	50	250	–	4,007
9. Dimensional Fund Advisors	2,888	–	169	–	3,057
10. Chase Investors Management	1,225	1,400	350	–	2,975

SOURCE: Reprinted with permission, *Pensions & Investment Age* (11 January 1988). Copyright, Crain Communications, Inc.

market indices like the S&P 500. Index portfolios attempt to minimize investment expenses such as management fees and transaction costs.

In addition to indexing common stock portfolios, fixed-income and international portfolios may be indexed to appropriate market benchmarks. Table 25.3 provides data on the ten largest index pension fund managers in terms of assets under management. Notice that equity indexing is the most popular, but fixed-income and international index portfolios also exist.

Active Strategies

Many managers believe that active investment strategies are appropriate for pension funds. One of the most widely used strategies is varying the asset mix of the portfolio.[10] Essentially, this involves market timing. As the discussion in Chapter 13 on market efficiency indicated, however, active strategies are appropriate only if they generate risk-adjusted excess returns. The performance of an actively managed fund can be evaluated with techniques presented in Chapter 8.

Other Portfolio Strategies

Pension funds use many of the management tools discussed throughout this text. Strategies to hedge or modify risk include options and financial futures, duration and immunization (for fixed-income portfolios), and diversification by numbers and types of securities.

---

[10] For a detailed discussion, see Robert D. Arnott, "The Pension Sponsor's View of Asset Allocation," *Financial Analysts Journal* (September-October 1985): pp. 17–23, and Richard Bookstaber and Jeremy Gold, "In Search of the Liability Asset," *Financial Analysts Journal* (January-February 1988): pp. 62, 70–80.

Pension fund managers have developed some unique approaches, including *portfolio insurance*. This hedging technique (see Chapter 21) is designed to protect the portfolio from a significant decline in value. Traditionally, such an approach for equity portfolios was implemented by buying put contracts on individual stocks in the portfolio. However, for large equity portfolios such as pensions funds, this approach would not be practical. It is also possible to form a hedge by taking a short position in stock-index futures. Pension management firms such as Morgan Stanley and Salomon Brothers have developed strategies that use the portfolio insurance concept. Because of the controversy these techniques generated in light of the October market collapse, many institutional investors may elect to discontinue using these hedging strategies.

Another hedging or risk-reducing strategy used by pension funds is *dedicated portfolios*. Essentially, this strategy tries to manage both the liabilities and assets of the fund by matching or "locking up" a cash inflow stream from investments that equals the cash outflow stream needed for pension benefits.[11]

IMPORTANCE OF PENSION PLANS FOR RETIREMENT INCOME

Most individuals depend on a combination of benefits from Social Security, a pension plan, and individual savings to provide income for retirement. The importance of each source depends on the pre- and post-retirement income level of the individual.

Table 25.4 provides some interesting insights into these relationships. Traditionally, financial planners have recommended that individuals in the middle to upper pre-retirement income brackets receive approximately 50 percent of their pre-retirement income during retirement to maintain the same standard of living; a lower retirement income is sufficient because of reduced expenses during retirement. As Table 25.4 indicates, however, recent evidence indicates the need for a higher percentage; an individual with a pre-retirement income of $50,000 should plan on a replacement ratio of 66 percent, which indicates a retirement income of $33,000. Lower levels of pre-retirement income require much higher replacement ratios.

Another interesting observation from Table 25.4 is the relative importance of pension plans and personal savings in providing retirement income. For example, an individual with a pre-retirement income level of $50,000 (retirement income of .66 × $50,000 = $33,000) should expect to receive 38 percent, or $19,000 per year, from a combination of retirement plan and savings. Only 28 percent, or $14,000, would be received from Social Security. Proposed changes in Social Security benefits suggest that higher-income individuals should continue to anticipate the growing importance of private pension and individual savings and investment plans in providing retirement income. The last chapter in this text (Chapter 26) includes an illustration of personal financial planning which shows how the above information can be incorporated into a financial plan.

---

[11] For a discussion, see Bookstaber and Gold.

TABLE 25.4   U.S. RETIREMENT INCOME REPLACEMENT RATIOS

GROSS PRE-RETIREMENT INCOME	GROSS SALARY REPLACEMENT RATIO	RETIREMENT BENEFITS FROM	
		SOCIAL SECURITY	RETIREMENT PLAN AND INDIVIDUAL SAVINGS
$15,000	82%	61%	21%
20,000	75	55	20
25,000	71	50	21
31,250	68	42	26
40,000	68	34	34
50,000	66	28	38
60,000	66	23	43
80,000	68	17	51

SOURCE: Data from a study by the Center for Risk Management and Insurance Research at Georgia State University. Reproduced from the February 1, 1988 issue of the Property/Casualty ed. of the *National Underwriter*, page 9, with permission of the National Underwriter Co.

INSURANCE PRODUCTS

This section briefly defines a number of traditional and newer types of "products" offered by insurance companies. The discussion begins with traditional life insurance policies, followed by new products such as universal and variable life policies. The traditional and newer products are then compared.

Term Life

Term life insurance is priced to provide the insurance company with funds to cover the yearly cost of dying (i.e., mortality) for their policyholders, plus loading. The *cost of dying*, or *mortality*, represents the face value of the policy that the insurer must pay upon the death of the insured. *Loading* is an all-inclusive expression that includes all expenses associated with marketing and servicing the product, plus profits and contingency charges. The annual premium on a one-year term policy increases geometrically over time because the size of the insurance group is growing smaller and the rate of mortality increases dramatically for older individuals. The insured accumulates no cash value in a term policy.

Ordinary Whole Life

The insurer's cost of ordinary whole life contracts includes the yearly cost of mortality, plus loading, with an increasing annual mortality exposure. This type of contract also results in an annual *savings/reserve* increment, which accumulates over the life of the policy. Savings are accumulated by the policyholder because the premium is in excess of that needed to pay for mortality and loading expenses in the early years of the policy. This policy is designed to provide protection until death. A variation of this plan is the *single-premium whole life policy* which requires the payment of only an initial premium.

This savings/reserve concept is used in several different ways, one of the most important of which is to provide *nonforfeiture options;* the savings/reserve in the policy may at any time be used to purchase a life insurance policy that is "paid up" therefore nonforfeitable. The face value of the "paid up" policy, however, will be below the face value of the original policy. Policyholders can also borrow against their savings/reserve balances.

Endowment Life

Endowment life policies are priced to cover the mortality factor for the policy period, plus loading, in the same manner as whole life. Savings are accumulated at a much faster rate, since they must equal the face value of the policy in a specified number of years—such as ten, fifteen, or twenty—at which time the policy matures and requires no additional premium payments.

Universal Life

This product, introduced in 1979, has captured a major share (over one-third) of the life insurance market. The key word describing this product is *flexibility*. This interest-sensitive policy works much like a whole life policy but has numerous options for changing premiums and death benefits. Figure 25.1 shows how the

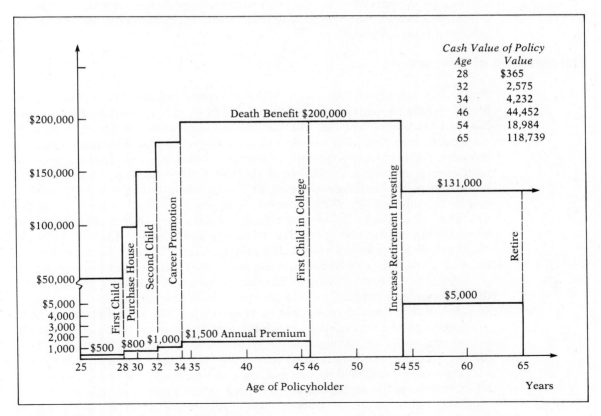

FIGURE 25.1   Illustration of a universal life policy

Source: Adapted from Robert Runde, "At Last an Almost Ideal Policy. *Money,* July 1981, p. 88. Reprinted by permission.

premium, death benefit, and cash value can fluctuate over the lifetime of a policyholder.

Variable Life

If the key word describing universal life is flexibility, the key phrase for a variable life policy is *separate account*. Because of the nature of this contract, it is regulated by federal and state securities laws, a unique feature of this product. The contract consists of two parts: (1) a whole life policy and (2) a separate *investment account*, which can be invested in common stocks, bonds, and other types of investments which are prohibited or greatly restricted under state regulations. The whole life part of the contract guarantees a minimum death benefit, and the investment account reflects the return on the underlying instruments, with their associated risks. The *unit values* for a number of variable life accounts are provided each week in *Barron's*.

These abbreviated descriptions are not intended to provide a detailed working knowledge of the five basic types of life insurance policies. They simply provide a background for a discussion about these policies relative to investment alternatives. The term life policy, however, should be considered a pure insurance product. There is no provision for an investment option within this product, and there is no cash value; no part of the premium is used to create an investment account for the policyholder. The other four products do involve a savings/reserve component in addition to the cost of pure insurance; in this sense, these products offer investment features.

Comparison of Policies

Figure 25.2 compares four types of life insurance policies: (1) ordinary whole life, (2) whole life with premium paid in twenty years, (3) single-premium whole life, and (4) endowment life. The vertical axis represents the savings/reserve of each policy over time. The savings/reserve value is calculated by subtracting the mortality and load factors from the premiums. The savings/reserve is also credited with interest income over the life of the policy. For example, for an ordinary whole life policy with face value of $1,000 purchased at age 35, the savings/reserve would be $300 at age 55 and reach the face value at age 100. If the individual died at age 55, the insurer would have a net outflow of cash of $700 after considering the savings/reserve balance of $300. Notice that the single-premium whole life policy has an *initial* savings/reserve balance because the premium is above the amount necessary to cover the mortality and loading costs.

By their very nature, ordinary life and endowment contracts are designed for the long run. Any product making promises about long-term interest rates (perhaps for thirty or more years) must be conservative. The policyholder is subject to limited risk since guarantees provide interest rate floors, such as 5 percent. Actual returns on the savings/reserve balances, however, may be higher. This, coupled with legislated restrictions concerning investment alternatives for insurance companies, results in modest but low-risk returns. When one examines the actual return on the savings/reserve element, a modest rate of return is indeed what is found. However, there are certain tax advantages accruing to these policies that are not available in other savings media. This feature tends to complicate

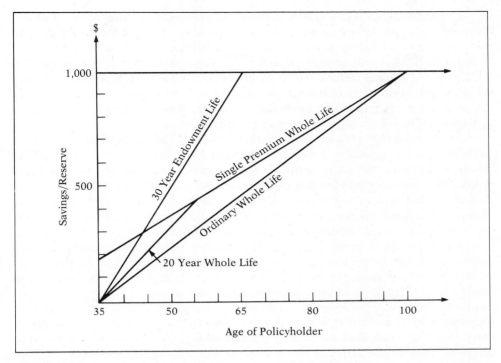

FIGURE 25.2 Savings/reserve on four types of life insurance policies

calculating the "return." The older, nonparticipating policies have experienced considerable *disintermediation* from policyholders canceling their policies and receiving the cash reserve. The disintermediation is attributed to the lack of investment competitiveness of older policies, compared with the new interest-sensitive products.[12]

The universal life policy has considerable flexibility in responding to the changing circumstances of the policyholder. Neither the premium nor the death benefit is fixed, as with ordinary whole life and endowment policies. Most companies, however, limit the timing and the number of changes permitted. The basic principle is that loading and mortality charges are deducted from the annual premium. The difference, the savings/reserve element, is then credited with a *current* market rate of interest. The older whole life and endowment policies do not credit interest at prevailing market rates. An option in universal life policies allows the policyholder to pay no premium in a given year as long as there is a savings/reserve sufficient to carry the mortality and loading charges. In addition, the policyholder may withdraw a portion of the savings/reserve. Later, premium payments may be voluntarily increased, with the goal of increasing retirement savings.

---

[12] Harold Skipper, Jr., "Replacement Vulnerability of Older Nonparticipating Ordinary Life Policies," *Journal of Risk & Insurance* (December 1980): p. 691–712.

Competition has also forced companies to use lower loading factors. Current mortality rates are below those used in older policies. Both of these factors have reduced the cost of these products to the policyholder. The policyholder is provided with a statement at least annually, showing the breakdown of premiums, mortality and loading factors, interest credited, and total savings/reserve. Because of these developments, universal life policies can offer policyholders low-cost life insurance coverage. The flexibility, however, does not provide the built-in discipline of policies with fixed annual premiums.

For variable life policies, key characteristics include a separate investment account and the necessity for SEC regulation. Most firms offer a variety of investment options, including common stocks, bonds, and money market securities. After mortality and loading expenses are paid, the balance of the premiums is invested at the direction of the policyholder, who then assumes the risk of the investments. Since no guarantees are made on the savings/reserve portion, however, its value could fall to zero if investment results were very unfavorable.

Another critical factor for these new policies is how much one-year term insurance should be provided to provide the desired face value, or death benefit, at any given time. Better investment results cause the savings/reserve to increase more rapidly, resulting in smaller annual mortality charges. There is one major problem, however. Suppose a policyholder pursuing a high-risk investment program should suddenly, at age fifty-five, find that equity values in the policy have fallen by one-half or more. Will the annual savings increment be enough to keep the plan at the targeted death benefit? Considering the high cost of pure mortality protection (one-year term policy) during the remaining years of life, the plan could fail by a considerable margin to provide the desired death benefit.

ANALYZING INSURANCE POLICIES

Return versus Risk

The answer to the question Is life insurance an acceptable investment alternative? depends on what alternative it is compared with. Given an investment of $2,000 per year for the past 10 years for a male age thirty-five, which alternative could show the largest accumulated estate: (1) the whole life, level-premium policy, based on the average performance of the industry's two largest life insurers or (2) an investment plan, managed by two of the largest investment firms, that consists of decreasing one-year term insurance, with the difference invested in an aggressively managed blue-chip common stock stock fund? If we use October 18, 1987, to evaluate the two programs, the second alternative, term insurance and an aggressive blue-chip stock plan, would be the winner. This picture changed considerably, however, with the stock market crash of October 19, 1987. The net rate of investment income for all life insurers for 1986 was 9.35 percent.[13] This rate gives some indication of the ability of insurers to provide investment returns to their policyholders.

---

[13] *Life Insurance Fact Book Update, 1987* (Washington, D.C.: American Council of Life Insurance).

Impact of Regulation

Given the many new types of policies, it has become more difficult to make generalizations about regulations dealing with insurance policies. Life insurance policies are subject to state regulations that promote conservatism, safety of principal and financial integrity, and limit the ability of the insurer to take investment risks.

State regulations place limitations on how an insurance company can invest its assets. Generally speaking, an insurer must invest an amount equal to its minimum required capital and surplus in obligations of the U.S. government and securities issued by the state in which it is domiciled. An amount equal to liabilities to policyholders may be invested in U.S., state, and local obligations; corporate bonds; preferred stock; certain types of mortgages; and real estate. Only after minimum capitalization and policyholder-supplied funds have been invested can the insurer acquire common stocks and other assets that are considered more risky. These regulations and portfolio management decisions resulted in the following allocation of assets of U.S. life insurers during 1986:[14]

Government Securities	15.4%
Corporate Bonds	36.5
Common Stocks	9.7
Mortgages	20.7
Real Estate	3.3
Policy Loans	5.7
Other Assets	8.7
	100.0%

New Products

At the current rate of change, the traditional level-premium whole life policy may become a product of the past. The life insurance industry introduced interest-sensitive variable rate products in the late 1970s, and since that time there has been an explosion in their growth, both in new types of policies and the amount of policies issued. Between 1982 and 1985, the universal and variable life contracts went from 7 percent of all ordinary life sales to 31 percent.[15]

An example of a new product, introduced in early 1988, is a special type of *variable universal life policy*.[16] This policy offers three guarantees and an option to invest the "sum available for investment" in six investment accounts similar to mutual funds: (1) capital growth bond, (2) balanced assets, (3) emerging growth equity, (4) money market, (5) common stocks, and (6) real estate securities. Built into this policy are three guarantees: (1) a certain death benefit regardless of fund performance, (2) an interest account with a 4 percent floor, and (3) an optional 5.5 percent rate guarantee to age sixty-five. This is a far cry from the traditional

---

[14] *Life Insurance Fact Book Update—1987.*

[15] *Life Insurance Fact Book, 1986.*

[16] Linda Koco, "Manufactures VUL Offers Three Guarantees, Six Funds," *National Underwriter, Life & Health*, 1 Feb. 1988, p. 13.

whole life policy with fixed premiums and a fixed face value and is more attractive than traditional universal life policies.

Because of the ability of the computer to perform numerous and complex calculations, the industry can unbundle the mortality charges from the investment aspects of policies and track the investments. There are few limitations on new contracts; this permits the policyholder to make changes from one period to another in such things as the amount of death protection or the annual premium. Some of these products allow policyholders to select the investment medium in which reserves will be invested. If the policyholder elects an equity investment, the attendant risk must also be assumed by the policyholder.

Tax Implications

Life insurance proceeds payable to a named beneficiary are exempt from federal income tax. There are also settlement options and loan provisions that provide further tax advantages for life insurance. It is beyond the scope of this chapter to discuss complicated income and estate tax planning problems. Many life insurance products presently available are designed to solve these and other business problems, with little regard for insurance as an investment alternative.

Summary

The following general statements can be made about life insurance policies:

1. Individuals have some needs which can be met only by life insurance policies. There is no alternative product which can provide a large death benefit or estate for the average individual. The debate regarding the two primary ways to accomplish this will continue: (a) buy pure term insurance and create an increasing estate with investments other than insurance policies, or (b) use one of the new life insurance policies to provide both a death benefit and an investment portfolio.

2. The cost of pure mortality must be paid, and although quite inexpensive in the younger years, it becomes prohibitively expensive in the later years of one's life.

3. If a policyholder prefers investment guarantees over many years, the return on the savings/reserve portion of a policy can be no greater than that on the underlying portfolio of the insurer.

4. If the policy permits investments in speculative or risky alternatives, this risk of loss or gain is assumed by the policyholder.

5. The cost of life insurance is not uniform among providers. An entire chapter could be written about the question How does one determine the best life insurance to buy? This topic is beyond the scope of this text.[17]

6. Life insurance enjoys certain tax advantages not available to other investments.

---

[17] For a comprehensive discussion, however, see Kenneth Black and Harold Skipper Jr., *Life Insurance*, 11th ed., Prentice Hall, Englewood Cliffs, N.J., 1987.

INSURANCE PRODUCTS VERSUS TRADITIONAL INVESTMENTS

Investment can be defined as the outlay of money for income or profit. *Life insurance* is defined as the business of providing people coverage by contract whereby the insurer undertakes to indemnify or guarantee another against loss by death. As these definitions indicate, the primary purposes of these two activities are fundamentally different. There are arguments, however, that attempt to classify life insurance as an investment. This section of the chapter will review some of these arguments. This section will also attempt to explain logically some of the problems of evaluating life insurance as an investment. An analysis will be presented that answers the question, What is the rate of return on invested funds for an insurance policy?

Determining the Sum Available for Investment

In a traditional analysis, the investment principal consists of the total dollars available for investment in various alternatives designed to produce the investment return. Investment alternatives include common stocks, bonds, real estate, governmental securities, and others discussed in this text. Simplistically, the investment return is determined by deducting the expenses from the gross return; the difference is the net return on investment. The only expense factor recognized in this view is the expenses involved in keeping the investment principal productively employed.

To put life insurance on the same level as the investment principal for comparison purposes also requires consideration of the mortality factor. The net investment return is defined as gross return less expenses. The net investment return expressed as a percentage of investment principal represents the net rate of return on investment. Life insurance alternatives, however, must consider the dollars available for investment *and* the costs of mortality and loading. The difference can then be expressed as a percentage of dollars available for investment.

The following example illustrates these concepts:

INVESTMENT		LIFE INSURANCE
$1000	Original investment principal	$1000
$ 70	Expenses (assumed to be 7% of principal)	$ 70
0	Mortality*	$ 145
$1000	Funds available for investment	($1000 − $145) = $855
$ 100	Gross Investment Return (assumed to be 10%)	$ 85.50
$100/1000 = 10%	Gross Rate of Return	$85.50/855 = 10%

* An initial $1000 premium will purchase $68,900 of whole life at age 35, with a pure mortality cost of $2.11 per $1000 that year (68.9 × $2.11 = $145).

In both of the above cases, expenses are ignored in computing the gross rate of return. The life insurance alternative deducts the additional cost of mortality, which is not present in the investment alternative. This assumption indicates that of the original $1000 principal, the life insurance alternative provides only $855 for investment purposes. To compute the return on the life insurance alternative on the basis of the $1000 original principal would greatly distort the rate of return.

The Whole Life Contract

Life insurance was not originally intended to be an investment product, competing with real estate, common stocks, and other investment alternatives. The insurance industry, however, has made some persuasive arguments that cash-value life policies are competitive when the tax advantages and risk characteristics are considered. The primary purpose of life insurance is to create an immediate estate at the time of death. To make life insurance economically feasible or affordable for the masses, the *level-premium* concept was adopted. This concept provides that there will be a charge in excess of the pure or one-year-term cost of mortality. This excess charge is the *policy reserve* and is accumulated at compound interest. An important issue for this procedure is What rate of return does the policyholder earn on these reserves? Until very recently, most insurers were quite conservative and set the rate at 3 to 6 percent. Now there are arguments that current rates may be too liberal for the new generation of interest-sensitive products. As a very simplistic explanation, this reserve must equal the face of the policy by the end of the mortality period, which is actuarially set at some advanced age such as ninety-five or one hundred. This must be the case because, by definition, every mortal must die. If investment products guarantee this estate amount from the beginning of the policy, then a death benefit equal to the difference between the savings accumulated and this targeted estate amount must be considered. To discuss the life insurance product as an investment alternative intelligently, the premise must be that there is a fixed sum (face of policy) that will be paid at death and that the insurer must be able to guarantee this sum. By accepting this premise, a comparison of life insurance with investment alternatives can be made.

The above discussion leads to the conclusion that when an investment alternative and life insurance product are compared, the cost of mortality must first be deducted from the total cost of the insurance product.

Difference in Philosophy

In examining any insurance product as an investment alternative, certain comparisons must be made. This brings up issues such as rate of return, safety of principal, liquidity, and risk tolerance of the investor. Before any discussion of those matters is attempted, it must be assumed that a provision for mortality has been segregated from the investment discussion. Very simply stated, the mortality cost is determined by actuarial procedures in which well-trained statisticians compute how much it will cost the individual that year, as part of a large group, for the number of likely deaths. In the insurance industry, this mortality cost is represented by the cost of one-year or temporary insurance for a given age.

The discipline of finance recognizes that there is a wide range of attitudes and risk preferences for investors. Some investors are very risk averse, while others are willing to assume a great deal of risk.

The attitude in the investment philosophy of life insurance companies has been quite risk averse or conservative. This conservatism has been forced upon the industry in no small degree by statutes relating to reserve requirements, types of investments, and premium rates. Permanent life insurance carries long-term guarantees in which safety of principal is paramount. Some of the new variable contracts do allow the insured to take some of the same risks, within certain limits, as for an investor.

EMPIRICAL FINDINGS: THE RATE OF RETURN

There is good reason to believe that the public has decided to put less of its insurance dollar into permanent life insurance. A study published in 1985 discussed the fact that the percentage of savings going into cash-value life insurance has declined significantly over the past thirty years.[18] As a percentage of income, savings going into cash value insurance have declined from 1.14 percent in the period 1952–56 to .70 percent in the period 1977–81. The author of this study related this decline to the decline in the after-tax rate of return for life insurance investments, compared with alternative savings opportunities with similar risk characteristics. The decreasing rate of return provided by insurance companies was blamed on changes in tax regulations that have been detrimental to life insurance savings. The decrease in life insurance savings has occurred at a time when the demand for life insurance has been growing substantially, as measured by the face value of policies in force.

The rate of return is largely dependent upon the methodology used. In a 1983 study which examined the *differential premium*, it was found that an amount equal to the difference between a participating and nonparticipating premium (i.e., differential premium) had a return of 14–20 percent, depending on the age of the insured.[19] The study covered the period 1959–1978. The rate of return on common stocks, represented by the S&P 500, over the same twenty years was only 6.53 percent. This study might have been pertinent to certain older level-premium policies over the past twenty years, but it did not really compare the rates of return of investment portfolios and newer life insurance products.

A far different conclusion was reached in a study comparing the performance of sixty universal life contracts with a diversified investment portfolio.[20] The study concluded: "Under the assumptions made, it appears that the investor would be better off paying for term insurance in the open market and investing the balance of what would have been spent on an annual universal life premium in an individually created diversified financial market account with no or low expense loads. This consideration seems to hold up even in light of tax considerations and potential transaction costs."[21]

---

[18] Mark Warshawski, "Life Insurance Savings and the After-Tax Rate of Return," *Journal of Risk and Insurance* (December 1985): pp. 585–606.

[19] Phyllis S. Myers and S. Travis Pritchett, "Rate of Return on Differential Premiums for Selected Participating Life Insurance Contracts," *Journal of Risk and Insurance* (December 1983): pp. 569–86.

[20] Anthony C. Cherin and Robert C. Hutchins, "The Rate of Return on Universal Life Insurance," *Journal of Risk and Insurance* (December 1987): pp. 691–711.

[21] Cherin and Hutchins, p. 709.

TABLE 25.5 COMPARISON OF UNIVERSAL/VARIABLE LIFE WITH MONEY MARKET ACCOUNTS, BONDS, AND STOCKS*

	MONEY MARKET						
YEAR	UVLF, mmf	UVLB, mmf	BTID, mmf	IRA, mmf	BTID, mb		
7	$ 6,554	$ 6,852	$ 6,830	$ 6,705	$ 6,884		
15	16,990	18,220	16,552	16,264	16,841		
30	43,065	48,390	37,052	43,547	38,697		

	BOND INVESTMENT						
	UVLF, BOND	UVLB, BOND	BTID, BOND	IRA, BOND	BTID, ddb	BTID, da	BTID, mb
7	$ 7,722	$ 7,995	$ 7,900	$ 7,723	$ 7,665	$ 4,857	$ 8,010
15	23,892	26,324	22,871	23,243	21,950	21,338	23,601
30	114,730	129,337	82,426	124,578	74,468	112,230	88,970

	EQUITY INVESTMENT						
	UVLF, STOCK	UVLB, STOCK	BTID, STOCK	IRA, STOCK			
7	$ 8,324	$ 8,633	$ 8,505	$ 8,312			
15	29,022	32,106	27,142	28,222			
30	193,389	218,104	126,863	213,206			

* UVLF = Universal/variable life, front loaded
  UVLB = Universal/variable life, back loaded
  BTID = Buy term and invest difference
  IRA = Individual Retirement Account
  mb = Municipal bonds
  mmf = Money market fund
  da = Deferred annuity
  ddb = Deep discount bonds

SOURCE: Adapted from Stephen P. D'Arcy and Keun C. Lee, "Universal/Variable Life Insurance versus Similar Unbundled Strategies," *Journal of Risk and Insurance* (September 1987): pp. 453–77. Reproduced by permission.

A fourth study compared the rate of return on the savings component of ordinary whole life policies of seventy-three of the largest life insurers with the rates of return on eight alternatives over the period 1959–1979.[22] The alternatives ranged from bank savings deposits to a portfolio of the thirty common stocks composing the DJIA. This study found that the returns were very similar on an after-tax basis, after considering transaction costs. The new interest-sensitive and variable (equity) policies do give a better return than the products of a decade ago. It may be a bit early, however, to make judgments concerning their probable performance in the long run.

A 1987 study by D'Arcy and Lee concluded that universal/variable policies could provide a better after-tax rate of return than a number of alternative investments.[23] Their analysis is summarized in Table 25.5. One of the critical factors

[22] Ravindra Kamath, "A Performance Evaluation of Whole Life Insurance Policies," *CLU Journal* (October 1982): pp. 42–50.

[23] Stephen P. D'Arcy and Keun Chang Lee, "Universal/Variable Life Insurance versus Similar Unbundled Investment Strategies," *Journal of Risk and Insurance* (September 1987): pp. 452–77.

identified by the study was the length of the holding period; on average, eight years were required for the return on a universal/variable life policy to exceed the return on investment alternatives. The two universal/variable life policies provided $100,000 of death protection; one was "front loaded" and the other "back loaded," with a load fee of $1,000. The total investment horizon was 30 years, representing an individual between the ages of 30 and 60. These two policies were compared to three investment alternatives: money market securities, fixed-income securities, and equity securities. In each instance term insurance was to be purchased equal to that in force in the universal/variable policy ($100,000). After the cost of pure death protection was deducted, the remaining funds were invested in the three investment accounts. The rates of return (see Table 25.5) for each of the three investment alternatives: money market return = 6.50 percent; fixed income return = 11.35 percent; equity return = 14 percent.

These investment returns were used to compare investment alternatives with the insurance products for holding periods from 1 to 30 years. The values in the table, shown for 7-, 15-, and 30-year holding periods, represent the end of period values for each alternative. For example, when comparing a money market fund, mmf, investment with a universal/variable life policy with a front load, UVLF, after 7 years, the end-of-period value is $6,554. For each of the five money market/insurance strategies, the largest end-of-period value (the best alternative) occurred for the strategy of buying term insurance and investing the difference in a short-term municipal bond fund, BTID, mb ($6,884).

In summary, the empirical studies discussed above concluded that

1. A smaller percentage of insurance dollar expenditures by individuals were going into permanent life insurance when the demand for life insurance was increasing.

2. The return on pre-1980 permanent life insurance has not been competitive with similar conservative investment alternatives, by most measures.

3. The after-tax rate of return on some current universal and variable life products appeared to be somewhat competitive with a number of conservative investment alternatives.

SUMMARY

Pension funds constitute the largest investor in common stocks and fixed-income securities. Pension funds are important because of their impact on financial markets and their investment strategies. Obviously, pension funds are not investment alternatives for individuals. For individuals covered by a pension fund, however, their vested benefits may be their largest single asset.

Individuals should be familiar with the pension funds offered by their employers. These details provide a basis for determining the retirement benefits that the fund may provide. This analysis is important in developing the overall financial and investment plans of the individual. A recent study also indicates that individuals in higher income brackets will be more dependent on pension funds and private savings to provide adequate retirement income.

This chapter also presented a brief discussion of traditional and new products offered by insurance companies. The purpose of this discussion has been to stress that insurance products are likely to play a role in the overall financial and investment plans of individuals.

This chapter briefly addressed the question, Are life insurance policies good investment alternatives? The answer depends upon many interrelated variables. The same thing might be said of other investment alternatives, such as U.S. government securities: Are they a good investment alternative? Certainly it can be said unequivocally that Treasury securities are safe. We cannot, however, say that they should be used in all investment portfolios. The same logic should be applied in deciding whether insurance products are an appropriate addition to an individual's portfolio.

QUESTIONS

1. Compare and contrast a defined benefit versus a defined contribution pension plan.

2. Suppose you are attempting to determine the benefits that will be provided by your company's pension plan. If the plan is a defined benefit plan, explain how the retirement benefits can be estimated. If the plan is a defined contribution plan, explain how the benefits can be estimated.

3. Should an individual be concerned about default risk for his or her private pension plan? Explain.

4. Suppose your pension plan is a defined contribution plan and you are concerned about the investment performance of the plan. Should this concern influence how you manage your own personal retirement savings?

5. Explain how the management of a corporate pension plan can affect the common stockholders of the sponsoring corporation.

6. In efficient capital markets, do you think the effects of well-managed and poorly managed corporate pension plans would be reflected in the companies' stock prices?

7. Table 25.4 provides statistics on retirement income replacement ratios and the importance of Social Security, private savings, and retirement plans in providing retirement income. Explain why the statistics indicate that percentage retirement benefits from Social Security decline rapidly relative to pre-retirement income.

8. Compare and contrast term life, ordinary whole life, endowment life, universal life, and variable life insurance policies.

9. Explain how insurance companies are able to offer an ordinary whole life policy with a death benefit (face value) far in excess of the initial premium cost.

10. Based on the empirical studies reviewed in this chapter, do you think that the risk-return characteristics of some of the newer insurance products compare favorably with traditional stock and bond investments?

11. In your opinion, should insurance products be viewed as an investment alternative? Explain.

12. Do you think that all individuals need life insurance coverage, regardless of their personal financial circumstances?

REFERENCES

Arnott, Robert D. "The Pension Sponsor's View of Asset Allocations." *Financial Analysts Journal* (September-October 1985): pp. 17–23.

Black, Fischer. "The Investment Policy Spectrum: Individuals, Endowment Funds and Pension Funds." *Financial Analysts Journal* (January-February 1976): pp. 23–30.

Black, Kenneth, and Harold Skipper Jr. *Life Insurance.* 11th ed., Prentice Hall, Englewood Cliffs, N.J., 1987

Bodie, Zvi, Jay O. Light, Randall Morch, and Robert A. Taggart, Jr.. "Corporate Pension Policy: An Empirical Investigation." *Financial Analysts Journal* (September-October 1985): pp. 10–16.

Bookstaber, Richard, and Jeremy Gold. "In Search of the Liability Asset." *Financial Analysts Journal* (January-February 1988): pp. 62, 70–80.

Broveman, Samuel. "The Rate of Return on Life Insurance and Annuities." *Journal of Risk and Insurance* (September 1986): pp. 419–34.

Chen, K. C., and Stephen P. D'Arcy. "Market Sensitivity to Interest Rate Assumptions in Corporate Pension Plans." *Journal of Risk and Insurance* (June 1986): pp. 209–25.

Cherin, Anthony C., and Robert C. Hutchins. "The Rate of Return on Universal Life Insurance." *Journal of Risk and Insurance* (December 1987): pp. 691–711.

D'Arcy, Stephen P., and Keun Chang Lee. "Universal/Variable Life Insurance versus Similar Unbundled Investment Strategies." *Journal of Risk and Insurance* (September 1987): pp. 452–77.

Ezra, D. Don, and Keith P. Ambachtsheer. "Pension Funds: Rich or Poor?" *Financial Analysts Journal* (March-April 1985): pp. 43–56.

Good, Walter R. "Accountability for Pension Fund Performance." *Financial Analysts Journal* (January-February 1984): pp. 39–42.

Joehnk, Michael D., ed. *Asset Allocation for Institutional Portfolios.* Homewood, Ill.: Dow Jones-Irwin, 1987.

Kamath, Ravindra. "A Performance Evaluation of Whole Life Insurance Policies." *CLU Journal* (October 1982): pp. 42–50.

Kantor, Michael. "Pension Multiplier Revisited." *Financial Analysts Journal* (January-February 1988): pp. 14, 15, 47.

Kittell, Cathryn E., ed. *The Challenges of Investing for Endowment Funds.* Homewood, Ill: Dow Jones-Irwin, 1987.

Koco, Linda. "Manufactures VUL Offers Three Guarantees, Six Funds." *National Underwriter, Life and Health,* Financial Services ed., 1 February 1988, pp. 13, 15.

Life Insurance *Fact Book Update—1987.* Washington D.C.: American Council of Life Insurance.

Malley, Susan L., and Susan Jayson. "Why Do Financial Executives Manage Pension Funds the Way They Do?" *Financial Analysts Journal,* (November-December 1986): pp. 56–62.

McKenna, Fred W., and Yong H. Kim. "Managerial Risk Preferences, Real Pension Costs, and Long-run Corporate Pension Fund Investment Policy." *Journal of Risk and Insurance* (March 1986): pp. 29–48.

Michel, Allen, and Israel Shaked. "Industry Influence on Pension Funding." *Journal of Portfolio Management* (Spring 1986): pp. 71–77.

Myers, Phyllis S., and S. Travis Pritchett. "Rate of Return on Differential Premiums for Selected Participating Life Insurance Contracts." *Journal of Risk and Insurance* (December 1983): pp. 569–86.

Regan, Patrick J. "The Relationship between Unfunded Pension Liabilities and Share Prices." *Financial Analysts Journal* (March-April 1981): pp. 18, 66.

———. "Overfunded Pension Plans." *Financial Analysts Journal* (November-December 1985): pp. 10–12.

Skipper, Harold Jr. "Replacement Vulnerability of Older Nonparticipating Ordinary Life Policies." *Journal of Risk and Insurance* (December 1980): pp. 691–712.

VanDerhei, Jack L. "The Effect of Voluntary Termination of Overfunded Pension Plans on Shareholder Wealth." *Journal of Risk and Insurance* (March 1987): pp. 131–56.

Warshawski, Mark. "Life Insurance Savings and the After-Tax Rate of Return." *Journal of Risk and Insurance* (December 1985): pp. 585–606.

Weiss, Stuart. "The Remarkable Recuperation of Pension Funds." *Business Week*, 22 March 1985, pp. 218–26.

West, Richard R. "When Is a GIC Not a GIC?" *Financial Analysts Journal* (January-February 1983): pp. 24–26.

CHAPTER 26

PERSONAL INVESTMENT MANAGEMENT

INTRODUCTION

The purpose of this chapter is to integrate much of the material that has been presented, in terms of personal investment management. The viewpoint used throughout the book has been that of the individual investor. Decisions facing individual investors include (1) formulating investment goals; (2) developing a financial plan to achieve the goals; (3) analyzing alternative investments; (4) analyzing the portfolio, including the asset mix and overall level of diversification, and (5) evaluating and revising the portfolio. This chapter will not attempt to repeat or summarize the discussion that has been presented concerning each of these decisions. Rather, the chapter presents an illustration that further demonstrates the importance of personal portfolio diversification and provides an example of a basic financial plan.

The second major topic covered in the chapter is the use of professionals in the areas of financial planning and portfolio management. This material is relevant to individuals who might be interested in pursuing careers in these areas. The discussion can also be helpful to individuals who might decide that they need professional advice in formulating their investment strategies and financial plans.

PERSONAL PORTFOLIO DIVERSIFICATION

Overview

The importance of portfolio diversification has been stressed throughout this text. Diversification can be accomplished by including an adequate number of assets in the portfolio and by including more than one class of assets in the portfolio. For example, if common stocks are included in the portfolio, it is important to recall that naive diversification requires, on average, ten to fifteen stocks to eliminate the majority of unsystematic or diversifiable risk. However, the portfolio is still subject to the systematic risk inherent in common stocks. The level of systematic risk introduced to the portfolio by common stocks can be reduced by including other classes of assets in the portfolio, such as money market securities, bonds, and possibly real assets such as real estate and precious metals. In summary, diversification can be accomplished by including an adequate number of securities from each classification and more than one type of asset in the portfolio.

This section of the chapter illustrates these principles by presenting a portfolio analysis that includes eleven investment alternatives, ranging from money market securities to real estate. The analysis is based on the annual ex-post holding period returns, *HPR*s, and risk measures for these alternatives over the period 1978–1987. In this sense, the analysis uses hindsight to identify mean-variance efficient portfolios. The composition of efficient portfolios for the 1990s, however, may be quite different from that for the 1980s.

The illustration is therefore, designed to illustrate the principles and importance of personal portfolio diversification. It is not designed to suggest portfolio strategies or appropriate portfolio compositions for the future. These decisions must be based on a careful analysis and forecast for the economy and the investment environments for alternative investments.

Table 26.1 provides summary statistics for the eleven types of investments that will be included in the portfolio analysis. Notice that five of the eleven categories represent mutual funds with different investment objectives. The use of *HPR*s for mutual funds has several implications for the portfolio analysis. First, mutual funds provide diversification in the number of securities they hold. It is likely that individual funds will invest in over one hundred securities. Their *HPR*s therefore reflect a diversified portfolio. Second, mutual funds (with the exception of index funds) represent actively managed portfolios. Their *HPR*s reflect the skills of the portfolio managers. Third, each of the five categories of mutual funds in Table 26.1 represents essentially all of the funds in each particular category. In this sense, the *HPR*s represent the average performance of the funds in the category. Finally, the use of mutual fund data is not intended to suggest that individual investors should invest only in bonds, stocks, and other alternatives through mutual funds.

With the exception of the mutual funds and gold, silver, and wheat futures contracts, the remaining *HPR*s in Table 26.1 reflect the performance of a portfolio or index for each type of investment. For example, the long-term Treasury bond alternative represents a sample of bonds with maturities longer than ten years. The *HPR*s for stocks, in general, are based on an index of common stocks as represented by the S&P 500. Finally, the *HPR*s for real estate are based on an index that includes residential, commercial, and industrial properties. The real estate *HPR*s therefore represent a diversified portfolio in the types and number of properties.

Several interesting observations can be made from the data in Table 26.1. Notice that silver bullion provided the highest average annual *HPR* (29.06 percent) of the eleven alternatives. Its standard deviation, however, was also the highest (120.15 percent). The coefficient of variation for silver, however, was below that of the wheat futures contracts. The relative risk of the wheat futures contracts was the highest of the eleven categories. This occurred because the average *HPR* for wheat futures contracts was only 2.56 percent, while the standard deviation was 18.32 percent.

It is also interesting to note that the *HPR*s and standard deviations for the three domestic common stock alternatives were similar and had the expected relationships. The return performance of international stock mutual funds exceeded that of domestic stocks. The returns for small-company stocks and "growth-company" stocks were relatively close, but the standard deviation of the *HPR*s for small-company stocks was somewhat higher than that for growth stocks. The returns and risk for stocks in general (S&P 500), as expected, were below those of small-company and growth-company stocks.

The *HPR*s and risk measures for bonds were somewhat unusual. Notice that the average *HPR* for Treasury bonds (10.72 percent) was above the average for corporate bonds (9.73 percent). Two factors caused this apparent reverse risk-return relationship. First, the *HPR*s for corporate bonds were measured using mutual funds. Management fees, transaction costs, and other expenses incurred by the funds reduced the *HPR*s. Also, mutual funds often attempt to manage default and interest rate risk by making portfolio revisions. The *HPR*s, therefore, did not result from a buy-and-hold strategy using long-term corporate bonds.

The second reason that the average *HPR* on corporate bonds was less than that on Treasury bonds is the behavior of interest rates over the period 1978–1987.

TABLE 26.1 EX-POST RETURNS AND RISK FOR ELEVEN TYPES OF INVESTMENTS: 1978–1987

	AVERAGE ANNUAL HPR, $\overline{HPR}$	VARIANCE OF HPR, σ^2	STANDARD DEVIATION OF HPR, σ	COEFFICIENT OF VARIATION[1]
1. International Stock Mutual Funds	20.32%	369.47%	19.22%	.95
2. Money Market Mutual Funds	9.88	11.55	3.40	.34
3. Growth-Company Stock Mutual Funds	16.25	199.33	14.12	.87
4. Corporate Bond Mutual Funds	9.73	110.34	10.50	1.08
5. Long-Term Treasury Bonds	10.72	268.73	16.39	1.53
6. Small-Company Stock Mutual Funds	17.02	330.72	18.19	1.07
7. Gold Bullion	17.01	1,911.44	43.72	2.57
8. Silver Bullion	29.06	14,436.02	120.15	4.13
9. Wheat Futures Contracts	2.56	335.62	18.32	7.16
10. S&P 500 Stock Index	15.69	149.33	12.22	.78
11. Real Estate Index	12.50	31.36	5.60	.45

[1] Coefficient of variation calculated as $\sigma/\overline{HPR}$.

SOURCE: Annual HPRs obtained from several sources, including Salomon Brothers, Standard & Poor's Corporation, Frank Russell Company, and Shearson Lehman.

As discussed in Chapter 16, higher-quality bonds have larger betas and longer durations than lower-quality bonds. During periods of declining yields, the *HPR*s on higher-quality bonds will be larger than those for lower-quality bonds. This occurred during 1982 and 1985–86, when yields were generally falling. During periods of stable yields, however, the *HPR*s on corporate bonds will be larger than those on Treasury bonds.

Portfolio Analysis

One simple way to check for possible diversification benefits that can occur by including more than one category or type of investment in a portfolio is to calculate the correlation coefficients between each pair of alternatives, using annual *HPR*s. Table 26.2 provides the correlation coefficients for the eleven categories of assets in Table 26.1.

The most significant observation that Table 26.2 provides is that seventeen of the sixty-six correlation coefficients are negative. Investment alternatives with negative correlation coefficients are most effective in reducing the risk of the portfolio. On the other hand, alternatives with positive correlation coefficients close to 1 are less effective in reducing portfolio risk. Notice from Table 26.2 that the *HPR*s from small-company stocks and growth-company stocks are highly correlated (.96) with each other and with the S&P 500 (.80 and .88, respectively). International stock *HPR*s, however, are not as highly correlated with the S&P 500, growth-company stocks, and small-company stocks.

The next step in the portfolio analysis is to identify portfolios that form the efficient frontier. Recall from Chapter 6 that efficient frontier portfolios are mean-variance efficient—offer the highest return for any given level of risk. Since eleven investment alternatives are considered, a computer program based on Markowitz' principles of diversification was used to identify efficient frontier portfolios. Table 26.3 provides information about nine portfolios that are on the efficient frontier. The formulation for the computer solution did not allow short sales, since the portfolio weights must be 0 or greater and less than or equal to 1 $(0 < X_J \leq 1)$.

The portfolios in Table 26.3 are listed in descending order of risk and return, with the first portfolio being the maximum return portfolio, MRP. The last portfolio in the table has the smallest risk and return and is the minimum variance portfolio, MVP. As expected, the MRP portfolio consists entirely of one asset, silver, since it had the largest average *HPR*. Portfolios 2–4 in Table 26.3 include only two types of investments: international stocks and silver. Their relatively high *HPR*s and negative correlation coefficient $(-.21)$ are characteristics that cause them to be included in efficient frontier portfolios.

Real estate is an important part of portfolios 5–7. Real estate's relatively attractive *HPR* and low standard deviation, combined with the negative correlation coefficients with international and growth-company stocks, make it an attractive addition to "medium-risk" efficient portfolios.

Portfolio 7 is interesting because it includes six of the eleven categories of investments. Real estate, however, is the most important of the six, since 57.26 percent of the portfolio funds are invested in real estate. The remaining five categories in portfolio 7 are all financial assets: international and growth-company stocks, money market securities, and corporate and Treasury bonds.

TABLE 26.2 CORRELATION COEFFICIENTS BETWEEN HPRs OF ELEVEN TYPES OF INVESTMENTS

	(1) INTERNATIONAL STOCK MUTUAL FUNDS	(2) MONEY MARKET MUTUAL FUNDS	(3) GROWTH STOCK MUTUAL FUNDS	(4) CORPORATE BOND MUTUAL FUNDS	(5) LONG-TERM TREASURY BONDS	(6) SMALL-COMPANY STOCK MUTUAL FUNDS	(7) GOLD BULLION	(8) SILVER BULLION	(9) WHEAT FUTURES CONTRACTS	(10) S&P 500 INDEX	(11) REAL ESTATE INDEX
1. International Stock Mutual Funds	1.00										
2. Money Market Mutual Funds	−0.56	1.00									
3. Growth Stock Mutual Funds	0.38	0.02	1.00								
4. Corporate Bond Mutual Funds	−0.07	0.01	0.14	1.00							
5. Long-Term Treasury Bonds	0.07	−0.10	0.15	0.97	1.00						
6. Small-Company Stock Mutual Funds	0.30	0.13	0.96	0.14	0.11	1.00					
7. Gold Bullion	0.03	−0.17	0.51	−0.27	−0.17	0.46	1.00				
8. Silver Bullion	−0.21	−0.01	0.38	−0.22	−0.16	0.38	0.93	1.00			
9. Wheat Futures Contracts	0.03	−0.30	0.38	−0.60	−0.60	0.40	0.67	0.61	1.00		
10. S&P 500 Index	0.54	−0.18	0.88	0.34	0.37	0.80	0.21	0.06	0.14	1.00	
11. Real Estate Index	−0.20	0.60	0.34	−0.37	−0.43	0.47	0.30	0.38	0.39	0.04	1.00

TABLE 26.3 EFFICIENT FRONTIER PORTFOLIOS

PORTFOLIO NUMBER	HPR_p	σ_p	X_1	X_2	X_3	X_4	X_5	X_6	X_7	X_8	X_9	X_{10}	X_{11}
1.	29.06%	120.15%	0	0	0	0	0	0	0	1.0000	0	0	0
2.	26.41	82.66	.3035	0	0	0	0	0	0	.6966	0	0	0
3.	23.76	46.23	.6067	0	0	0	0	0	0	.3934	0	0	0
4.	21.11	18.52	.9099	0	0	0	0	0	0	.0902	0	0	0
5.	18.46	12.77	.6289	0	.0816	0	0	0	0	.0444	0	0	.2452
6.	15.81	7.42	.3225	0	.1582	0	0	0	0	.0117	0	0	.5077
7.	13.16	3.61	.1062	.1022	.1018	.0780	.0393	0	0	0	0	0	.5726
8.	10.51	2.00	.1041	.7289	0	.1030	0	0	0	.0010	.0631	0	0
9.	10.03	1.73	.0798	.7008	0	.1284	0	0	0	0	.0911	0	0

(1) Portfolio weight, X_j, corresponds to the categories of investments identified in Table 26.2. For example, X_1 = proportion of portfolio funds in international stocks, X_2 = proportion of portfolio funds in money market mutual funds, etc.

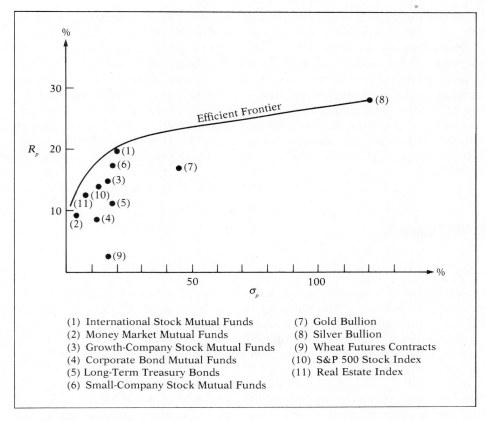

(1) International Stock Mutual Funds
(2) Money Market Mutual Funds
(3) Growth-Company Stock Mutual Funds
(4) Corporate Bond Mutual Funds
(5) Long-Term Treasury Bonds
(6) Small-Company Stock Mutual Funds
(7) Gold Bullion
(8) Silver Bullion
(9) Wheat Futures Contracts
(10) S&P 500 Stock Index
(11) Real Estate Index

FIGURE 26.1   Efficient frontier

The MVP consists of 70.08 percent money market securities, with the remaining funds invested in international stocks, corporate bonds, and wheat futures. The risk of this portfolio ($\sigma_p = 1.73\%$) is considerably less than the risk of money market mutual funds ($\sigma_2 = 3.40\%$). The *HPR* of the MVP ($R_p = 10.03\%$) is also above the *HPR* of money market mutual funds ($HPR_2 = 9.88\%$).

Figure 26.1 provides a graph of the efficient frontier and indicates the *HPR*s and standard deviations of the eleven categories included in the analysis. With the exception of the MRP, the efficient frontier portfolios dominate the individual assets in terms of risk and return. Again, this provides strong evidence concerning the advantages of diversification by asset type.

Implications and Summary

The main purpose of the previous example of portfolio analysis is to demonstrate the significant and tangible benefits that can result from diversifying by asset type. The importance of diversifying by the number of securities of each type in the portfolio was not shown, since the *HPR*s for each asset category were calculated based on an average or index for that category.

As the chapters in the book indicate, there are many different investment alternatives; each must be analyzed using appropriate techniques. Not all alternatives are appropriate investments for every individual. The investment goals and objectives and risk-return preferences of the individual indicate which alternatives are appropriate.[1] The portfolio analysis example also illustrates that portfolios consisting of 2–5 categories of assets provide efficient diversification. None of the efficient frontier portfolios identified in Table 26.3 contain all eleven categories.

As indicated earlier, ex-post efficient portfolios may not be ex-ante efficient portfolios. Depending on financial and economic developments, additional categories or different portfolio weights may be needed to form ex-ante efficient portfolios.

INVESTING FOR RETIREMENT

Overview

The importance of developing investment objectives has been stressed throughout this book. An individual investor may have a number of different investment objectives—for example, to start a new business, to purchase a home, and to provide retirement income. Therefore, different investment strategies are appropriate for each objective. Essentially, the individual would have a separate portfolio for each objective.

This section of the chapter discusses investment strategies that are appropriate for retirement investing. Generally, these strategies involve a long investment horizon, are designed to take advantage of favorable tax treatments, and should be somewhat conservative in terms of their risk-return trade-offs.

Tax-Sheltered Retirement Plans

There are several features in the tax laws that provide significant tax benefits for retirement investments. The two most important tax breaks allow contributions to be made to the retirement plan on a before-tax basis and defer taxes on investment returns until retirement. The significance of these tax breaks suggests that most individuals should use tax-sheltered plans to the fullest extent possible before considering other plans. The plans that offer favorable tax treatments to individual investors are discussed below.

1. INDIVIDUAL RETIREMENT ACCOUNTS, IRAs This popular and well-known plan allows individuals to contribute up to $2,000 per year to the plan, or $2,250 for a spousal IRA if the spouse does not work. Beginning in 1987, the full $2,000 contribution is deductible if the individual is not covered by an

---

[1] According to Capital Market Theory all individuals would invest in the market portfolio (a combination of all investment alternatives) in combination with the risk-free asset. The lack of the availability of a true market portfolio and other market imperfections require individuals to select individual alternative investments.

employer-maintained retirement plan. If the individual is covered by a pension plan, the full deduction is still allowed if annual income is less than $25,000 ($40,000 for joint income). Partial deductions are allowed for incomes between $25,000–$35,000 ($40,000–$50,000 for joint income), but no deductions are allowed for incomes above $35,000 ($50,000 for joint income). Although tax reform eliminated the tax deductibility of IRA contributions for some individuals, the tax liability on IRA earnings can still be deferred.

2. KEOGH PLANS Keogh plans are attractive to self-employed individuals. A Keogh plan is essentially a profit-sharing plan that can be used to shelter self-employment income. If the business has employees in addition to the owner, they must be included in the plan. The annual contribution limit to the plan is 25 percent of self-employment net income, up to a maximum of $30,000. The larger deductible annual contributions make Keogh plans more attractive than IRAs for higher-income individuals. Individuals who are employed but who also have their own business can have an employer-sponsored pension plan and a Keogh plan for their self-employment income.

3. 401(K) PLANS A 401(K) plan differs from an IRA or Keogh plan; it allows annual contributions from both the employee and the employer. Contributions by the employee are made on a before-tax basis, and employer contributions are tax deductible. In one sense, a 401(K) plan is basically a deferred compensation plan for employees. Annual contributions are limited to $7,000 per year and are further reduced by any amount contributed to an IRA. Individuals may use a "catch-up" provision that allows contributions of up to $15,000 per year if the maximum allowable annual contribution has not been made in the past.

ILLUSTRATION OF FINANCIAL PLANNING

This section provides a basic illustration of financial planning for the Drane family. As discussed in Chapter 1, the Dranes have three major concerns: (1) having enough money to pay for a college education for their children; (2) accumulating enough wealth to retire at age sixty; and (3) maintaining their standard of living.

The following is a brief summary of the information about the Dranes presented in Chapter 1:

a. Ages: Bob = 49; Barbara = 49; Doug = 20; Marsha = 17; Todd = 15.

b. Doug is a senior finance major; Marsha and Todd plan to attend college after high school.

c. Current family earnings: $68,000 per year from family-owned carpet business.

d. Major assets: home with fair market value of $130,000 and fixed-rate mortgage of $8,300; savings account balance of $62,000; 50 percent ownership of common stock of carpet business.

e. Annual savings: $6,000.

Doug, the oldest child wanted to help his parents analyze their present financial situation and began to develop a plan that could be used to accomplish their goals. Doug had recently completed an investments course at the university and wanted to apply some of the things he learned. His parents, while initially skeptical, agreed to let Doug analyze their situation and recommend a course of action.

Doug prepared the analysis presented in Table 26.4. This analysis projects the family's income and expenses over the next ten years and assumes his parents will retire at age sixty. Since his father and mother do not have a pension plan through the business, Doug realized that the first priority was to establish a plan to take advantage of the favorable tax laws. His plan assumes that a 401(K) plan, funded by contributions from the carpet business, would be appropriate. Because the business does not have any significant earnings after paying salaries, Doug assumed that his father would reduce his salary by $6,000 per year and have the business contribute this amount to the 401(K) plan. This would not have an impact on the taxes or cash flows of the business. His father, however, would benefit because he would be saving $6,000 before taxes rather than the $6,000 presently saved from after-tax income.

Based on his investments class, Doug was convinced that the financial markets are efficient and that it is unlikely that investors can earn risk-adjusted excess returns. Using the data in Table 26.1, he decided to use the average *HPR*s over the last ten years as a reasonable estimate of future returns. Since his parents' savings are needed to pay for college expenses, he decided a conservative portfolio with liquidity was appropriate. Based on his economic forecast and the investment

TABLE 26.4 A FINANCIAL PLAN FOR THE DRANES

	CURRENT YEAR	1	2	3	4
After-tax earnings[1]	$68,000	$62,000	$65,100	$68,355	$71,773
Expenses[2]	62,000	62,000	64,480	67,059	69,742
Savings	$ 6,000	0	$ 620	$ 1,296	$ 2,031
College Expense:[3]					
Doug	$ 7,000				
Marsha		$ 7,560	$ 8,164	$ 8,818	$ 9,523
Todd				8,818	9,523
Total	$ 7,000	$ 7,560	$ 8,164	$17,636	$19,046
Savings:					
Beginning of year	$62,000	$68,930	$70,186	$71,599	$64,416
College expense	(7,000)	(7,560)	(8,184)	(17,636)	(19,046)
Annual savings (withdrawal)	6,000	–	620	1,296	2,031
Investment income[4]	7,930	8,816	8,977	9,157	8,239
End of Year	$68,930	$70,186	$71,599	$64,416	$55,640
401(K) Retirement Plan:					
Beginning of year	–	–	$ 6,000	$12,776	$20,429
Annual contributions (withdrawal)	–	$ 6,000	6,000	6,000	6,000
Investment income[5]	–	–	776	1,653	2,643
End of year	–	$ 6,000	$12,776	$20,429	$29,072

[1] Assumes an annual growth rate of 5%
[2] Assumes an annual growth rate of 4%
[3] Assumes college costs will increase 8% per year
[4] Rate of return assumed to be 12.79% earned on beginning of year balance.
[5] Rate of return assumed to be 12.94% earned on beginning of year balance.

environment, he decided to invest 50 percent of the funds in a money market mutual fund at a 9.88 percent yield and 50 percent in an index mutual fund that attempts to match the performance of the S&P 500. According to Table 26.1, the average annual *HPR* over the last ten years on the S&P 500 was 15.69 percent. The savings balances, therefore, will be invested in a portfolio expected to provide a return of 12.79 percent [.5(9.88%) + .5(15.69%)].

Doug decided that the funds for the 401(K) plan should also be conservatively invested. Because of the longer investment horizon and his economic forecast, he decided that 20 percent of the funds should be in a money market mutual fund, 30 percent in an international common stock mutual fund, and 50 percent in a corporate bond fund. Using the average *HPR*s in Table 26.1, the *HPR* on this portfolio is estimated as

$$E(R)_p = .2(9.88\%) + .3(20.32\%) + .5(9.73\%) = 12.94\%$$

He used these estimated rates of return to calculate the amount his parents should have in their savings and retirement accounts at age sixty.

Using the most recent estimates of the percentage of pre-retirement income that will be needed during retirement, Doug calculated that his parents would need 68 percent of their pre-retirement income (see Chapter 25). Applying this

REMAINING WORKING YEARS						RETIREMENT YEARS	
5	6	7	8	9	10	11	12
$75,361	$79,129	$83,086	$87,240	$91,602	$96,182	$65,404	$68,674
72,531	75,432	78,450	81,588	84,851	88,245	65,404	68,674
$ 2,830	$ 3,697	$ 4,636	$ 5,652	$ 6,751	$ 7,937	–	–
$10,285	$11,108						
$10,285	$11,108						
$55,640	$55,301	$54,963	$66,629	$80,803	$ 97,889	$118,346	$116,847
(10,285)	(11,108)	–	–	–	–	–	–
2,830	3,697	4,636	5,652	6,751	7,937	(16,635)	(16,635)
7,116	7,073	7,030	8,522	10,335	12,520	15,136	14,945
$55,301	$54,963	$66,629	$80,803	$97,889	$118,346	$116,847	$115,157
$29,072	$38,834	$49,859	$62,311	$76,374	$ 92,257	$110,195	$108,824
6,000	6,000	6,000	6,000	6,000	6,000	(15,630)	(15,630)
3,762	5,025	6,452	8,063	9,883	11,938	14,259	14,082
$38,834	$49,859	$62,311	$76,374	$92,257	$110,195	$108,824	$107,276

percentage to the estimate of earnings for the year before retirment ($96,182) indicated income needs of $65,404. Using the statistics in Chapter 25, Doug also assumed that 51 percent, or $33,356, of the retirement income had to come from a retirement plan or individual savings.

If his parents' savings account equals $118,346 at retirement, as indicated in Table 26.4, they should be able to withdraw a maximum of $16,635 per year for twenty years, using a present value annuity procedure:

$$\$118,346 = A \left[\frac{1 - \dfrac{1}{(1.1279)^{20}}}{.1279} \right]$$

$$A = \$16,635$$

A similar calculation for the 401(K) retirement plan results in a maximum annual withdrawal of $15,630. Without considering Social Security benefits, his parents' annual retirement income would be

Savings withdrawals	$16,635
401(K) withdrawals	15,630
Total	$32,265

Based on this analysis, Doug concluded that his plan would not allow his parents to retire early with the level of income they are likely to need. He decided to discuss this initial plan with his parents and suggest that they may have to consider delaying their retirement, so that they would be entitled to full Social Security benefits. He also wanted to discuss the possibility of selling the common stock in the business at their retirement. Doug realized that his plan did not answer all of the questions raised by his parents and that additional work, possibly using a professional planner, was needed.

FINANCIAL SERVICES INDUSTRY

The financial services industry has undergone significant changes since the early 1970s. Prior to this time, the functions provided by the industry were available from a diverse group of professionals such as tax attorneys, CPAs, insurance agents, and stockbrokers. Advice from these professionals is still available, but many financial services firms now provide all of these services within a single organization. These firms can offer a comprehensive list of services, including tax planning, legal advice, investment and financial research, and brokerage services; in addition, they offer other products to satisfy the needs of the client.

Individuals acting as investment advisors and/or financial planners must register with the SEC under the requirements of the Investment Advisors Act of 1940. This act requires each advisor to inform the SEC of his or her experience, education, type of advice, and fees for services. Because of the broad definition of "investment advisor," however, many individuals act as advisors without registering. Since registration is not strictly enforced, there is essentially no legal barrier to anyone entering the investment advisory profession.

Because of the rapid growth of the financial services industry, many colleges and universities are offering programs of study in this area. Since a financial planner is likely to be a generalist, courses are offered in areas such as investments, security analysis, insurance, taxes, and employee benefits.

Because of the growing complexity of investment products, the investment environment, and tax laws, the investment advisory industry is likely to continue its rapid growth. Many individual investors may decide that they do not have the time or expertise to effectively manage their portfolio and that professional help is needed. If these trends continue, the industry will offer an increasing number of jobs to individuals who have the necessary knowledge and skills.

Investment advisors and financial planners may charge a fee or receive their compensation in commissions on products or services that they sell. The fee can be based on a percentage of the market value of the portfolio that is being managed. Typically, the fee would be 1–2 percent per year for portfolios $100,000 or larger. Many established money managers will not accept a client unless the portfolio is at least $100,000. A second alternative is to base the fee on the time devoted to the client. Fees for established advisors and planners often exceed $100 per hour.

The majority of financial planners receive their compensation from commissions on products. This practice, while common in the industry, raises the issue of the objectivity of the planner in making recommendations. The client may wonder if the advisor is suggesting a particular product or service because of the potential commission or because the planner thinks the product or service is best for the client.

An individual who is interested in using an advisor or planner should inquire about charges and fees. In certain cases, especially for individuals with small portfolios, it might be appropriate to seek an advisor/planner who bases compensation on commissions. In other cases, a fee arrangement may be more appropriate. Recognizing this possibility, some advisors/planners use a combination of fees and commissions. In addition to charges, a potential client should carefully check the training and experience of the advisor/planner. The following section briefly discusses three widely recognized professional designations that can be achieved by financial analysts and planners.

PROFESSIONAL INVESTMENT COUNSELING

Overview

Many individuals claim to be experts in financial planning and investment management. Unfortunately, some of these individuals earn more money by selling advice than by following their own recommendations. The purpose of this section is to discuss three professional designations for individuals offering financial planning and investment counseling. That an individual possesses one of these designations, however, is no guarantee that his or her advice and recommendations are always correct. Rather, the designation indicates that the individual has met certain standards and is knowledgeable about financial planning, investment selection, and investment management. Knowledge of these professional designations may be useful for individuals considering a career in investments and personal financial planning or for individuals attempting to select an investment planner or advisor.

Chartered Financial Analyst

1. HISTORY The professional designation of Chartered Financial Analyst, CFA, was first offered in the early 1960s by the Institute of Chartered Financial Analysts, ICFA. The CFA designation is considered the most prestigious and the most difficult designation to obtain.

    The idea of developing a certification process for financial analysts was first proposed by Benjamin Graham in the 1920s. Graham thought that there was a need to develop an accreditation program because of the lack of legal or industry regulations for financial analysts. Because of Graham's advocacy, a committee was formed in 1959 to develop an accreditation program. The committee contacted Professor Ezra Solomon, who developed the basic requirements of what is now the CFA designation.

    The early organization continued to grow, and the ICFA was incorporated in Virginia in January 1962. The University of Virginia provides educational and logistical support, but the ICFA is an independent organization with headquarters in Charlottesville, Virginia. The ICFA first offered an examination for the CFA designation in 1963. Since the CFA study and examination program began in 1963, approximately 57,000 examinations have been given, and 10,500 CFA designations have been awarded.[2]

2. OBJECTIVES OF THE ICFA

    a. To develop and keep current a "body of knowledge" applicable to the investment decision-making process;

    b. To administer a study and examination program for eligible candidates, with the objectives of assisting candidates in mastering and applying the body of knowledge and testing the candidates' competency;

    c. To award the CFA designation to those candidates who have passed the three levels of examinations, who meet the stipulated standards of professional conduct, and who otherwise are eligible for membership in the ICFA;

    d. To provide a program of continuing education, through seminars, publications, and other means, to keep members aware of changes and the expanding body of knowledge; and

    e. To sponsor and enforce a Code of Ethics and Standards of Professional Conduct that apply to candidates and members.

3. REQUIREMENTS FOR CFA The process leading to the CFA designation takes a minimum of three years and varies with the background of the individual. There are three requirements for becoming a CFA candidate:

    a. Hold a bachelor's degree from an accredited academic institution or have equivalent work experience;

    b. Submit three character references; and

    c. Pay the indicated fees of approximately $550.

---

[2] *The CFA Candidate Study and Examination Program Review, 1987*, (Charlottesville, Va. Institute of Chartered Financial Analysts, 1987), p. 1.

Once an individual is admitted as a CFA candidate, the following three requirements must be met before the CFA designation can be awarded:

a. Have a least three years' experience as a financial analyst;

b. Comply with the Code of Ethics and Standards of Professional Conduct of the ICFA; and

c. Pass the Level I, II, and III examinations.

Preparing for the three written examinations is accomplished largely by a program of self-study, using materials provided by the ICFA. Each of the three examinations is increasingly complex, and the major topics covered on the examinations are

a. Portfolio management

b. Equity securities analysis

c. Fixed-income securities analysis

d. Economics

e. Financial accounting

f. Code of Ethics and Standards of Professional Conduct

g. Quantitative methods

Only one exam can be taken each year, and exams must be taken and passed in order (i.e., Level I, Level II, Level III). Therefore, it takes a minimum of three years to complete the examination requirements. A candidate is given a maximum of seven years to pass all three exams. The following statistics apply to the June 1987 examinations:[3]

| | EXAM LEVEL | | | |
	I	II	III	OVERALL
Candidates taking exam	3,095	1,555	1,052	5,702
Passed	1,782	995	775	3,532
Pass rate	58%	64%	72%	62%
1978–87 Average Pass Rate	60%	70%	76%	66%

4. ADDITIONAL INFORMATION Additional information and application forms are available from the ICFA:

The Institute of Chartered Financial Analysts
Post Office Box 3668
Charlottesville, Virginia 22903
Telephone: (804) 977-6600

The ICFA also offers a number of investment publications, such as *CFA Digest*, *CFA Newsletter*, and *Institute of Chartered Financial Analysts: A Twenty-five Year History*. A large number of other publications are available as part of the self-study program designed by the ICFA.

---

[3] *1987 Annual Report* (Charlottesville, Va.: Institute of Chartered Financial Analysis, 1987), p. 9.

Chartered Financial Consultant

A second professional designation that indicates training and knowledge in the area of investments and financial planning is the Chartered Financial Consultant, ChFC. This program is available through the American College, located in Bryn Mawr, Pennsylvania. This program traditionally offered training to individuals in the insurance industry but recently has been expanded to include all aspects of personal financial planning.

The ChFC program is more generalized than the CFA program and prepares candidates to provide financial counseling and financial services management to clients.

Candidates must complete courses and a program of study that covers the following topics:

(1) Financial services environment

(2) Income taxation

(3) Financial statement analysis/individual insurance benefits

(4) Investments

(5) Estate and gift tax planning

(6) Financial and estate planning applications

(7) Economics

(8) Employee benefits

(9) Wealth accumulation planning

(10) Planning for business owners and professionals

In addition to passing examinations in the areas listed above, candidates must have three years of business experience and comply with the college's Code of Ethics. Depending on the background of the candidate, the program can be completed in 2–5 years. Additional information can be obtained from the American College:

The American College
Post Office Box 1513
Bryn Mawr, Pennsylvania 19010
Telephone: (800) 441-9466

Certified Financial Planner

A third professional designation, Certified Financial Planner, CFP, is offered by the College of Financial Planning, located in Denver, Colorado. The objectives of this program are to (1) advance the knowledge of individuals in the financial planning and counseling field, (2) provide learning opportunities through programs of study, and (3) develop and administer examinations for candidates.

Candidates must earn five "credits" before they can be admitted to the program. Credits can be earned in the following ways:

(1) One credit for each year of relevant work experience

(2) One credit for a bachelor's degree

(3) One credit for a graduate degree

Once a candidate is accepted into the program, the following requirements must be met to earn the CFP designation:

(1) Adhere to the Code of Ethics;

(2) Demonstrate a commitment to continuing education; and

(3) Pass six comprehensive three-hour examinations over the following topics:

    a.   Financial planning

    b.   Risk management

    c.   Investments

    d.   Tax planning and management

    e.   Retirement planning and employee benefits

    f.   Estate planning

On average, the program requires two years to complete. Additional information about the CFP designation is available from the College of Financial Planning:

The Institute of Certified Financial Planners
Two Denver Highlands
10065 East Harvard Avenue, Suite 320
Denver, Colorado 80231
Telephone: (303) 751-7600

There are a number of similarities and differences between the CFA, ChFC, and CFP designations. The CFA is considered the most specialized and rigorous of the programs and is highly regarded in the business and academic communities. The CFP is also becoming a prestigious designation and is earning credibility in the financial planning industry. The majority of individuals who have earned the ChFC designation are involved with the insurance industry and often hold other designations such as Chartered Life Underwriter, CLU.

Individuals who are considering hiring an investment advisor should research the credentials of potential advisors. In addition to professional designations, the education, experience, and specialization of the advisor should be investigated. Many financial planners who charge fees also receive commissions on products that they sell, such as insurance and mutual funds.

SUMMARY

This chapter provided some additional insights into personal investment management. A comprehensive portfolio analysis example was provided that vividly illustrated the importance of diversification by categories or types of investments. Many of the investment alternatives discussed in this book were included in the example. Essentially, this approach illustrates the advantages of viewing one's entire net worth as a household portfolio that includes both financial and real assets.

Despite those advantages, specific investment strategies are appropriate for different segments of the overall portfolio. For example, the segment devoted to building a retirement nest egg should take advantage of the favorable tax treatment offered by IRAs, Keogh plans, and 401(K) plans.

Many individuals rely on professional financial counselors. In selecting a counselor, however, it is important to consider how their compensation is determined and their professional qualifications. The three major professional designations for advisor/planners are the Chartered Financial Analyst, CFA, Chartered Financial Consultant, ChFC, and Certified Financial Planner, CFP. These designations do not guarantee that the advisor's advice will always be correct, but they do indicate the minimum level of training and experience the advisor has achieved. Individuals considering a career as an investment analyst/counselor should consider earning one of these professional designations.

QUESTIONS

1. Discuss the advantages of including several classes or categories of assets in a portfolio. Are there disadvantages to this type of diversification?

2. Explain the difference in diversification by the number of securities in a portfolio versus different classes or categories of assets in the portfolio. Which form of diversification is necessary to reduce the unsystematic risk of the portfolio? Which form of diversification is likely to protect the portfolio from the effects of inflation?

3. Use the data in Table 26.1 to answer the following questions:

   a. Provide an explanation of why wheat futures contracts provided a "low" average *HPR* over the period 1978–1987 but had a relatively high variance. Do you think wheat futures contracts are appropriate in a long-term or short-term investment strategy?

   b. Why is the coefficient of variation for money market mutual funds lower than the other ten categories of assets in the table?

4. International stock mutual funds and silver bullion are both considered risky investments because of the variability in their *HPR*s. Explain how these two categories of assets can be combined into a portfolio that will have considerably less risk than either of the investments individually.

5. Chapter 13 on market efficiency cited several studies that indicate that portfolios consisting of the common stock of "small" companies offer risk-adjusted excess returns. The efficient frontier portfolios identified in Table 26.3, however, do not include an investment in small-company stock. What explanation can you offer for this apparent contradiction?

6. An investment in gold is often recommended as a hedge against inflation. Over the period 1978–1987, the annual rate of inflation as measured by the CPI was 6.47 percent. Does the information about gold bullion in Table 26.1 indicate that it provided an inflationary hedge? Why was gold bullion not included in the efficient frontier portfolios identified in Table 26.3?

7. Explain why ex-post efficient portfolios may not be ex-ante efficient.

8. Compare and contrast IRAs, Keogh plans, and 401(K) plans. Discuss the two major tax advantages that make these plans attractive for retirement investing.

9. Discuss the similarities and differences in the CFA, CFP, and ChFC designations. Which professional designation appears to be most difficult to obtain? If an individual is interested in becoming a security analyst, which professional designation would be most appropriate?

10. Define the *financial services* industry. What trends appear to be emerging in this industry?

11. What recommendations would you make to improve the financial plan presented in Table 26.4? Do you think it is possible to develop a plan that will permit the Dranes to achieve all of their financial goals?

REFERENCES

Arndt, Sheril. "401(K) Pension Plans Gaining in Popularity." *National Underwriter* 1 February 1988, pp. 1, 31.

Arnott, Robert D. "The Future for Quantitative Investment Products." *Journal of Portfolio Management* (Winter 1988): pp. 52–56.

Benari, Yoav. "An Asset Allocation Paradigm." *Journal of Portfolio Management* (Winter 1988): pp. 47–51.

Black, Fischer. "The Investment Policy Spectrum: Individuals, Endowment Funds and Pension Funds." *Financial Analysts Journal* (January-February 1976): pp. 23–30.

Bogan, Elizabeth C., and Thomas R. Bogan. "Individual Retirement Accounts and Pre-retirement Savings Goals." *Financial Analysts Journal* (November-December 1982): pp. 45–47.

Bustable, C. W., and D. H. Bao. "IRAs vs. Unsheltered Investments: A Quantitative Analysis." *Journal of Accountancy* (March 1984): pp. 119–21.

Institute of Chartered Financial Analysts. *The CFA Candidate Study and Examination Program Review, 1987.* Charlottesville, Va.: Institute of Chartered Financial Analysts, 1987.

Maginn, John L., and Donald L. Tuttle, eds. *Managing Investment Portfolios: A Dynamic Process.* New York: Warren, Gorham & Lamont, 1983.

———. *Managing Investment Portfolios: A Dynamic Process, 1985–1986 Update.* New York: Warren, Gorham & Lamont, 1985.

Malkiel, Burton G. *A Random Walk Down Wall Street.* 4th ed. New York: W. W. Norton, 1985.

Milne, Robert D. "Determination of Portfolio Policies: Individual Investors." In *Managing Investment Portfolios: A Dynamic Process*, edited by John L. Maginn and Donald L. Tuttle. New York: Warren, Gorham & Lamont, 1983.

Reed, Stanley. "Better than IRAs? 401(K) Pension Plans Generate Interest." *Barron's*, 23 August 1982, pp. 34–36.

Rosenberg, Hilary. "Funds Strive to Secure Self-Directed IRAs." *Barron's*, 18 February 1985, p. 55.

APPENDIXES

APPENDIX A1

TIME VALUE OF MONEY CONCEPTS

TIME VALUE OF MONEY FORMULAS

A. Future value of $

$$P_n = P_0(1 + i)^n$$

B. Present value of $1

$$P_0 = \frac{P_n}{(1 + i)^n}$$

C. Future value of an annuity

$$FVA_n = A\sum_{t=0}^{n-1} (1 + i)^t = A\left[\frac{(1 + i)^n - 1}{i}\right]$$

D. Present value of an annuity

$$PVA_n = A\sum_{t=1}^{n} \frac{1}{(1 + i)^t} = A\left[\frac{1 - \dfrac{1}{(1 + i)^n}}{i}\right]$$

EXAMPLES OF ADJUSTING HOLDING PERIOD RETURNS

I. Annualizing Holding Period Returns
  A. To convert an *HPR* calculated for a holding period less than one year to an annualized *HPR:*

$$AHPR = (1 + HPR)^{N/n} - 1$$

  where $n =$ actual length of the holding period in days, weeks, months, or other units of time

  $N =$ total number of days, weeks, months, or other units of time in one year

  For example, if the weekly *HPR* = .003, then the *AHPR* assuming weekly compounding is:

$$AHPR = (1 + .003)^{52/1} - 1 = .1686$$

  B. Example of converting an *HPR* calculated for a holding period longer than one year to an annualized *HPR*. Assume an *HPR* of .18 occurred over a 16-month holding period. With annual compounding, the annualized *HPR* is:

$$AHPR = (1 + .18)^{12/16} - 1 = .1322$$

II. Calculating an Effective Holding Period Return
  A. The effective annual *HPR* can be calculated as:

$$EAHPR = (1 + HPR/m)^m - 1$$

  where $EAHPR =$ effective annual holding period return

  $HPR =$ stated *HPR*

  $m =$ number of compounding periods in one year

  For example, the *EAHPR* for a *HPR* of 10% per year compounded monthly is:

$$EAHPR = (1 + .1/12)^{12} - 1 = .1047$$

  B. The effective *HPR* for a holding period less than one year can be calculated as:

$$EHPR = (1 + HPR)^{1/m} - 1$$

  For example, assume the annual *HPR* is .1. The effective *quarterly HPR* would be:

$$EQHPR = (1 + .1)^{1/4} - 1 = .0241$$

TABLE A1.1 FUTURE VALUES OF ONE DOLLAR (FVIF)

Period n	1%	2%	3%	4%	5%	6%	7%	8%	9%	10%	11%	12%
1	1.0100	1.0200	1.0300	1.0400	1.0500	1.0600	1.0700	1.0800	1.0900	1.1000	1.1100	1.1200
2	1.0201	1.0404	1.0609	1.0816	1.1025	1.1236	1.1449	1.1664	1.1881	1.2100	1.2321	1.2544
3	1.0303	1.0612	1.0927	1.1249	1.1576	1.1910	1.2250	1.2597	1.2950	1.3310	1.3676	1.4049
4	1.0406	1.0824	1.1255	1.1699	1.2155	1.2625	1.3108	1.3605	1.4116	1.4641	1.5181	1.5735
5	1.0510	1.1041	1.1593	1.2167	1.2763	1.3382	1.4026	1.4693	1.5386	1.6105	1.6851	1.7623
6	1.0615	1.1262	1.1941	1.2653	1.3401	1.4185	1.5007	1.5869	1.6771	1.7716	1.8704	1.9738
7	1.0721	1.1487	1.2299	1.3159	1.4071	1.5036	1.6058	1.7138	1.8280	1.9487	2.0762	2.2107
8	1.0829	1.1717	1.2668	1.3686	1.4775	1.5938	1.7182	1.8509	1.9926	2.1436	2.3045	2.4760
9	1.0937	1.1951	1.3048	1.4233	1.5513	1.6895	1.8385	1.9990	2.1719	2.3579	2.5580	2.7731
10	1.1046	1.2190	1.3439	1.4802	1.6289	1.7908	1.9672	2.1589	2.3674	2.5937	2.8394	3.1058
11	1.1157	1.2434	1.3842	1.5395	1.7103	1.8983	2.1049	2.3316	2.5804	2.8531	3.1518	3.4785
12	1.1268	1.2682	1.4258	1.6010	1.7959	2.0122	2.2522	2.5182	2.8127	3.1384	3.4985	3.8960
13	1.1381	1.2936	1.4685	1.6651	1.8856	2.1329	2.4098	2.7196	3.0658	3.4523	3.8833	4.3635
14	1.1495	1.3195	1.5126	1.7317	1.9799	2.2609	2.5785	2.9372	3.3417	3.7975	4.3104	4.8871
15	1.1610	1.3459	1.5580	1.8009	2.0789	2.3966	2.7590	3.1722	3.6425	4.1772	4.7846	5.4736
16	1.1726	1.3728	1.6047	1.8730	2.1829	2.5404	2.9522	3.4259	3.9703	4.5950	5.3109	6.1304
17	1.1843	1.4002	1.6528	1.9479	2.2920	2.6928	3.1588	3.7000	4.3276	5.0545	5.8951	6.8660
18	1.1961	1.4282	1.7024	2.0258	2.4066	2.8543	3.3799	3.9960	4.7171	5.5599	6.5436	7.6900
19	1.2081	1.4568	1.7535	2.1068	2.5270	3.0256	3.6165	4.3157	5.1417	6.1159	7.2633	8.6128
20	1.2202	1.4859	1.8061	2.1911	2.6533	3.2071	3.8697	4.6610	5.6044	6.7275	8.0623	9.6463
21	1.2324	1.5157	1.8603	2.2788	2.7860	3.3996	4.1406	5.0338	6.1088	7.4002	8.9492	10.804
22	1.2447	1.5460	1.9161	2.3699	2.9253	3.6035	4.4304	5.4365	6.6586	8.1403	9.9336	12.100
23	1.2572	1.5769	1.9736	2.4647	3.0715	3.8197	4.7405	5.8715	7.2579	8.9543	11.026	13.552
24	1.2697	1.6084	2.0328	2.5633	3.2251	4.0489	5.0724	6.3412	7.9111	9.8497	12.239	15.179
25	1.2824	1.6406	2.0938	2.6658	3.3864	4.2919	5.4274	6.8485	8.6231	10.835	13.585	17.000
26	1.2953	1.6734	2.1566	2.7725	3.5557	4.5494	5.8074	7.3964	9.3992	11.918	15.080	19.040
27	1.3082	1.7069	2.2213	2.8834	3.7335	4.8223	6.2139	7.9881	10.245	13.110	16.739	21.325
28	1.3213	1.7410	2.2879	2.9987	3.9201	5.1117	6.6488	8.6271	11.167	14.421	18.580	23.884
29	1.3345	1.7758	2.3566	3.1187	4.1161	5.4184	7.1143	9.3173	12.172	15.863	20.624	26.750
30	1.3478	1.8114	2.4273	3.2434	4.3219	5.7435	7.6123	10.063	13.268	17.449	22.892	29.960
35	1.4166	1.9999	2.8139	3.9461	5.5160	7.6861	10.677	14.785	20.414	28.102	38.575	52.800
40	1.4889	2.2080	3.2620	4.8010	7.0400	10.286	14.974	21.725	31.409	45.259	65.001	93.051
45	1.5648	2.4379	3.7816	5.8412	8.9850	13.765	21.002	31.920	48.327	72.890	109.53	163.99
50	1.6446	2.6916	4.3839	7.1067	11.467	18.420	29.457	46.902	74.358	117.39	184.56	289.00

(continued)

TABLE A1.1 (Continued)

13%	14%	15%	16%	17%	18%	19%	20%	25%	30%	35%	40%	50%
1.1300	1.1400	1.1500	1.1600	1.1700	1.1800	1.1900	1.2000	1.2500	1.3000	1.3500	1.4000	1.5000
1.2769	1.2996	1.3225	1.3456	1.3689	1.3924	1.4161	1.4400	1.5625	1.6900	1.8225	1.9600	2.2500
1.4429	1.4815	1.5209	1.5609	1.6016	1.6430	1.6852	1.7280	1.9531	2.1970	2.4604	2.7440	3.3750
1.6305	1.6890	1.7490	1.8106	1.8739	1.9388	2.0053	2.0736	2.4414	2.8561	3.3215	3.8416	5.0625
1.8424	1.9254	2.0114	2.1003	2.1924	2.2878	2.3864	2.4883	3.0518	3.7129	4.4840	5.3782	7.5938
2.0820	2.1950	2.3131	2.4364	2.5652	2.6996	2.8398	2.9860	3.8147	4.8268	6.0534	7.5295	11.391
2.3526	2.5023	2.6600	2.8262	3.0012	3.1855	3.3793	3.5832	4.7684	6.2749	8.1722	10.541	17.086
2.6584	2.8526	3.0590	3.2784	3.5115	3.7589	4.0214	4.2998	5.9605	8.1573	11.032	14.758	25.629
3.0040	3.2519	3.5179	3.8030	4.1084	4.4355	4.7854	5.1598	7.4506	10.604	14.894	20.661	38.443
3.3946	3.7072	4.0456	4.4114	4.8068	5.2338	5.6947	6.1917	9.3132	13.786	20.107	28.925	57.665
3.8359	4.2262	4.6524	5.1173	5.6240	6.1759	6.7767	7.4301	11.642	17.922	27.144	40.496	86.498
4.3345	4.8179	5.3503	5.9360	6.5801	7.2876	8.0642	8.9161	14.552	23.298	36.644	56.694	129.75
4.8980	5.4924	6.1528	6.8858	7.6987	8.5994	9.5964	10.699	18.190	30.288	49.470	79.371	194.62
5.5348	6.2613	7.0757	7.9875	9.0075	10.147	11.420	12.839	22.737	39.374	66.784	111.12	291.93
6.2543	7.1379	8.1371	9.2655	10.539	11.974	13.590	15.407	28.422	51.186	90.158	155.57	437.89
7.0673	8.1372	9.3576	10.748	12.330	14.129	16.172	18.488	35.527	66.542	121.71	217.80	656.84
7.9861	9.2765	10.761	12.468	14.426	16.672	19.244	22.186	44.409	86.504	164.31	304.91	985.26
9.0243	10.575	12.375	14.463	16.879	19.673	22.901	26.623	55.511	112.46	221.82	426.88	1477.9
10.197	12.056	14.232	16.777	19.748	23.214	27.252	31.948	69.389	146.19	299.46	597.63	2216.8
11.523	13.743	16.367	19.461	23.106	27.393	32.429	38.338	86.736	190.05	404.27	836.68	3325.3
13.021	15.668	18.822	22.574	27.034	32.324	38.591	46.005	108.42	247.06	545.77	1171.4	4987.9
14.714	17.861	21.645	26.186	31.629	38.142	45.923	55.206	135.53	321.18	736.79	1639.9	7481.8
16.627	20.362	24.891	30.376	37.006	45.008	54.649	66.247	169.41	417.54	994.66	2295.9	11223.
18.788	23.212	28.625	35.236	43.297	53.109	65.032	79.497	211.76	542.80	1342.8	3214.2	16834.
21.231	26.462	32.919	40.874	50.658	62.669	77.388	95.396	264.70	705.64	1812.8	4499.9	25251.
23.991	30.167	37.857	47.414	59.270	73.949	92.092	114.48	330.87	917.33	2447.2	6299.8	37877.
27.109	34.390	43.535	55.000	69.345	87.260	109.59	137.37	413.59	1192.5	3303.8	8819.8	56815.
30.633	39.204	50.066	63.800	81.134	102.97	130.41	164.84	516.99	1550.3	4460.1	12348.	85223.
34.616	44.693	57.575	74.009	94.927	121.50	155.19	197.81	646.23	2015.4	6021.1	17287.	*
39.116	50.950	66.212	85.850	111.06	143.37	184.68	237.38	807.79	2620.0	8128.5	24201.	*
72.069	98.100	133.18	180.31	243.50	328.00	440.70	590.67	2465.2	9727.9	36449.	*	*
132.78	188.88	267.86	378.72	533.87	750.38	1051.7	1469.8	7523.2	36119.	*	*	*
244.64	363.68	538.77	795.44	1170.5	1716.7	2509.7	3657.3	22959.	*	*	*	*
450.74	700.23	1083.7	1670.7	2566.2	3927.4	5988.9	9100.4	70065.	*	*	*	*

*Interest factors exceed 99.999.

TABLE A1.2 FUTURE VALUES OF AN ANNUITY OF ONE DOLLAR (FVIFA)

Period n	1%	2%	3%	4%	5%	6%	7%	8%	9%	10%	11%	12%
1	1.0000	1.0000	1.0000	1.0000	1.0000	1.0000	1.0000	1.0000	1.0000	1.0000	1.0000	1.0000
2	2.0100	2.0200	2.0300	2.0400	2.0500	2.0600	2.0700	2.0800	2.0900	2.1000	2.1100	2.1200
3	3.0301	3.0604	3.0909	3.1216	3.1525	3.1836	3.2149	3.2464	3.2781	3.3100	3.3421	3.3744
4	4.0604	4.1216	4.1836	4.2465	4.3101	4.3746	4.4399	4.5061	4.5731	4.6410	4.7097	4.7793
5	5.1010	5.2040	5.3091	5.4163	5.5256	5.6371	5.7507	5.8666	5.9847	6.1051	6.2278	6.3528
6	6.1520	6.3081	6.4684	6.6330	6.8019	6.9753	7.1533	7.3359	7.5233	7.7156	7.9129	8.1152
7	7.2135	7.4343	7.6625	7.8983	8.1420	8.3938	8.6540	8.9228	9.2004	9.4872	9.7833	10.089
8	8.2857	8.5830	8.8923	9.2142	9.5491	9.8975	10.260	10.637	11.028	11.436	11.859	12.300
9	9.3685	9.7546	10.159	10.583	11.027	11.491	11.978	12.488	13.021	13.579	14.164	14.776
10	10.462	10.950	11.464	12.006	12.578	13.181	13.816	14.487	15.193	15.937	16.722	17.549
11	11.567	12.169	12.808	13.486	14.207	14.972	15.784	16.645	17.560	18.531	19.561	20.655
12	12.683	13.412	14.192	15.026	15.917	16.870	17.888	18.977	20.141	21.384	22.713	24.133
13	13.809	14.680	15.618	16.627	17.713	18.882	20.141	21.495	22.953	24.523	26.212	28.029
14	14.947	15.974	17.086	18.292	19.599	21.015	22.550	24.215	26.019	27.975	30.095	32.393
15	16.097	17.293	18.599	20.024	21.579	23.276	25.129	27.152	29.361	31.772	34.405	37.280
16	17.258	18.639	20.157	21.825	23.657	25.673	27.888	30.324	33.003	35.950	39.190	42.753
17	18.430	20.012	21.762	23.698	25.840	28.213	30.840	33.750	36.974	40.545	44.501	48.884
18	19.615	21.412	23.414	25.645	28.132	30.906	33.999	37.450	41.301	45.599	50.396	55.750
19	20.811	22.841	25.117	27.671	30.539	33.760	37.379	41.446	46.018	51.159	56.939	63.440
20	22.019	24.297	26.870	29.778	33.066	36.786	40.995	45.762	51.160	57.275	64.203	72.052
21	23.239	25.783	28.676	31.969	35.719	39.993	44.865	50.423	56.765	64.002	72.265	81.699
22	24.472	27.299	30.537	34.248	38.505	43.392	49.006	55.457	62.873	71.403	81.214	92.503
23	25.716	28.845	32.453	36.618	41.430	46.996	53.436	60.893	69.532	79.543	91.148	104.60
24	26.973	30.422	34.426	39.083	44.502	50.816	58.177	66.765	76.790	88.497	102.17	118.16
25	28.243	32.030	36.459	41.646	47.727	54.865	63.249	73.106	84.701	98.347	114.41	133.33
26	29.526	33.671	38.553	44.312	51.113	59.156	68.676	79.954	93.324	109.18	128.00	150.33
27	30.821	35.344	40.710	47.084	54.669	63.706	74.484	87.351	102.72	121.10	143.08	169.37
28	32.129	37.051	42.931	49.968	58.403	68.528	80.698	95.339	112.97	134.21	159.82	190.70
29	33.450	38.792	45.219	52.966	62.323	73.640	87.347	103.97	124.14	148.63	178.40	214.58
30	34.785	40.568	47.575	56.085	66.439	79.058	94.461	113.28	136.31	164.49	199.02	241.33
35	41.660	49.994	60.462	73.652	90.320	111.43	138.24	172.32	215.71	271.02	341.59	431.66
40	48.886	60.402	75.401	95.026	120.80	154.76	199.64	259.06	337.88	442.59	581.83	767.09
45	56.481	71.893	92.720	121.03	159.70	212.74	285.75	386.51	525.86	718.90	986.64	1358.2
50	64.463	84.579	112.80	152.67	209.35	290.34	406.53	573.77	815.08	1163.9	1668.8	2400.0

(continued)

TABLE A1.2 (Continued)

13%	14%	15%	16%	17%	18%	19%	20%	25%	30%	35%	40%	50%
1.0000	1.0000	1.0000	1.0000	1.0000	1.0000	1.0000	1.0000	1.0000	1.0000	1.0000	1.0000	1.0000
2.1300	2.1400	2.1500	2.1600	2.1700	2.1800	2.1900	2.2000	2.2500	2.3000	2.3500	2.4000	2.5000
3.4069	3.4396	3.4725	3.5056	3.5389	3.5724	3.6061	3.6400	3.8125	3.9900	4.1725	4.3600	4.7500
4.8498	4.9211	4.9934	5.0665	5.1405	5.2154	5.2913	5.3680	5.7656	6.1870	6.6329	7.1040	8.1250
6.4803	6.6101	6.7424	6.8771	7.0144	7.1542	7.2966	7.4416	8.2070	9.0431	9.9544	10.946	13.188
8.3227	8.5355	8.7537	8.9775	9.2068	9.4420	9.6830	9.9299	11.259	12.756	14.438	16.324	20.781
10.405	10.730	11.067	11.414	11.772	12.142	12.523	12.916	15.073	17.583	20.492	23.853	32.172
12.757	13.233	13.727	14.240	14.773	15.327	15.902	16.499	19.842	23.858	28.664	34.395	49.258
15.416	16.085	16.786	17.519	18.285	19.086	19.923	20.799	25.802	32.015	39.696	49.153	74.887
18.420	19.337	20.304	21.321	22.393	23.521	24.709	25.959	33.253	42.619	54.590	69.814	113.33
21.814	23.045	24.349	25.733	27.200	28.755	30.404	32.150	42.566	56.405	74.697	98.739	171.00
25.650	27.271	29.002	30.850	32.824	34.931	37.180	39.581	54.208	74.327	101.84	139.23	257.49
29.985	32.089	34.352	36.786	39.404	42.219	45.244	48.497	68.760	97.625	138.48	195.93	387.24
34.883	37.581	40.505	43.672	47.103	50.818	54.841	59.196	86.949	127.91	187.95	275.30	581.86
40.417	43.842	47.580	51.660	56.110	60.965	66.261	72.035	109.69	167.29	254.74	386.42	873.79
46.672	50.980	55.717	60.925	66.649	72.939	79.850	87.442	138.11	218.47	344.90	541.99	1311.7
53.739	59.118	65.075	71.673	78.979	87.068	96.022	105.93	173.64	285.01	466.61	759.78	1968.5
61.725	68.394	75.836	84.141	93.406	103.74	115.27	128.12	218.04	371.52	630.92	1064.7	2953.8
70.749	78.969	88.212	98.603	110.28	123.41	138.17	154.74	273.56	483.97	852.75	1491.6	4431.7
80.947	91.025	102.44	115.38	130.03	146.63	165.42	186.69	342.94	630.17	1152.2	2089.2	6648.5
92.470	104.77	118.81	134.84	153.14	174.02	197.85	225.03	429.68	820.22	1556.5	2925.9	9973.8
105.49	120.44	137.63	157.41	180.17	206.34	236.44	271.03	538.10	1067.3	2102.3	4097.2	14962.
120.20	138.30	159.28	183.60	211.80	244.49	282.36	326.24	673.63	1388.5	2839.0	5737.1	22443.
136.83	158.66	184.17	213.98	248.81	289.49	337.01	392.48	843.03	1806.0	3833.7	8033.0	33666.
155.62	181.87	212.79	249.21	292.10	342.60	402.04	471.98	1054.8	2348.8	5176.5	11247.	50500.
176.85	208.33	245.71	290.09	342.76	405.27	479.43	567.38	1319.5	3054.4	6989.3	15747.	75752.
200.84	238.50	283.57	337.50	402.03	479.22	571.52	681.85	1650.4	3971.8	9436.5	22047.	*
227.95	272.89	327.10	392.50	471.38	566.48	681.11	819.22	2064.0	5164.3	12740.	30867.	*
258.58	312.09	377.17	456.30	552.51	669.45	811.52	984.07	2580.9	6714.6	17200.	43214.	*
293.20	356.79	434.75	530.31	647.44	790.95	966.71	1181.9	3227.2	8730.0	23222.	60501.	*
546.68	693.57	881.17	1120.7	1426.5	1816.7	2314.2	2948.3	9856.8	32423.	*	*	*
1013.7	1342.0	1779.1	2360.8	3134.5	4163.2	5529.8	7343.9	30089.	*	*	*	*
1874.2	2590.6	3585.1	4965.3	6879.3	9531.6	13203.	18281.	91831.	*	*	*	*
3459.5	4994.5	7217.7	10436.	15090.	21813.	31515.	45497.	*	*	*	*	*

*Interest factors exceed 99,999

TABLE A1.3 PRESENT VALUES OF ONE DOLLAR (PVIF)

Period n	1%	2%	3%	4%	5%	6%	7%	8%	9%	10%	11%	12%
1	.9901	.9804	.9709	.9615	.9524	.9434	.9346	.9259	.9174	.9091	.9009	.8929
2	.9803	.9612	.9426	.9246	.9070	.8900	.8734	.8573	.8417	.8264	.8116	.7972
3	.9706	.9423	.9151	.8890	.8638	.8396	.8163	.7938	.7722	.7513	.7312	.7118
4	.9610	.9238	.8885	.8548	.8227	.7921	.7629	.7350	.7084	.6830	.6587	.6355
5	.9515	.9057	.8626	.8219	.7835	.7473	.7130	.6806	.6499	.6209	.5935	.5674
6	.9420	.8880	.8375	.7903	.7462	.7050	.6663	.6302	.5963	.5645	.5346	.5066
7	.9327	.8706	.8131	.7599	.7107	.6651	.6227	.5835	.5470	.5132	.4817	.4523
8	.9235	.8535	.7894	.7307	.6768	.6274	.5820	.5403	.5019	.4665	.4339	.4039
9	.9143	.8368	.7664	.7026	.6446	.5919	.5439	.5002	.4604	.4241	.3909	.3606
10	.9053	.8203	.7441	.6756	.6139	.5584	.5083	.4632	.4224	.3855	.3522	.3220
11	.8963	.8043	.7224	.6496	.5847	.5268	.4751	.4289	.3875	.3505	.3173	.2875
12	.8874	.7885	.7014	.6246	.5568	.4970	.4440	.3971	.3555	.3186	.2858	.2567
13	.8787	.7730	.6810	.6006	.5303	.4688	.4150	.3677	.3262	.2897	.2575	.2292
14	.8700	.7579	.6611	.5775	.5051	.4423	.3878	.3405	.2992	.2633	.2320	.2046
15	.8613	.7430	.6419	.5553	.4810	.4173	.3624	.3152	.2745	.2394	.2090	.1827
16	.8528	.7284	.6232	.5339	.4581	.3936	.3387	.2919	.2519	.2176	.1883	.1631
17	.8444	.7142	.6050	.5134	.4363	.3714	.3166	.2703	.2311	.1978	.1696	.1456
18	.8360	.7002	.5874	.4936	.4155	.3503	.2959	.2502	.2120	.1799	.1528	.1300
19	.8277	.6864	.5703	.4746	.3957	.3305	.2765	.2317	.1945	.1635	.1377	.1161
20	.8195	.6730	.5537	.4564	.3769	.3118	.2584	.2145	.1784	.1486	.1240	.1037
21	.8114	.6598	.5375	.4388	.3589	.2942	.2415	.1987	.1637	.1351	.1117	.0926
22	.8034	.6468	.5219	.4220	.3418	.2775	.2257	.1839	.1502	.1228	.1007	.0826
23	.7954	.6342	.5067	.4057	.3256	.2618	.2109	.1703	.1378	.1117	.0907	.0738
24	.7876	.6217	.4919	.3901	.3101	.2470	.1971	.1577	.1264	.1015	.0817	.0659
25	.7798	.6095	.4776	.3751	.2953	.2330	.1842	.1460	.1160	.0923	.0736	.0588
26	.7720	.5976	.4637	.3607	.2812	.2198	.1722	.1352	.1064	.0839	.0663	.0525
27	.7644	.5859	.4502	.3468	.2678	.2074	.1609	.1252	.0976	.0763	.0597	.0469
28	.7568	.5744	.4371	.3335	.2551	.1956	.1504	.1159	.0895	.0693	.0538	.0419
29	.7493	.5631	.4243	.3207	.2429	.1846	.1406	.1073	.0822	.0630	.0485	.0374
30	.7419	.5521	.4120	.3083	.2314	.1741	.1314	.0994	.0754	.0573	.0437	.0334
35	.7059	.5000	.3554	.2534	.1813	.1301	.0937	.0676	.0490	.0356	.0259	.0189
40	.6717	.4529	.3066	.2083	.1420	.0972	.0668	.0460	.0318	.0221	.0154	.0107
45	.6391	.4102	.2644	.1712	.1113	.0727	.0476	.0313	.0207	.0137	.0091	.0061
50	.6080	.3715	.2281	.1407	.0872	.0543	.0339	.0213	.0134	.0085	.0054	.0035

(*continued*)

TABLE A1.3 (*Continued*)

13%	14%	15%	16%	17%	18%	19%	20%	25%	30%	35%	40%	50%
.8850	.8772	.8696	.8621	.8547	.8475	.8403	.8333	.8000	.7692	.7407	.7143	.6667
.7831	.7695	.7561	.7432	.7305	.7182	.7062	.6944	.6400	.5917	.5487	.5102	.4444
.6931	.6750	.6575	.6407	.6244	.6086	.5934	.5787	.5120	.4552	.4064	.3644	.2963
.6133	.5921	.5718	.5523	.5337	.5158	.4987	.4823	.4096	.3501	.3011	.2603	.1975
.5428	.5194	.4972	.4761	.4561	.4371	.4190	.4019	.3277	.2693	.2230	.1859	.1317
.4803	.4556	.4323	.4104	.3898	.3704	.3521	.3349	.2621	.2072	.1652	.1328	.0878
.4251	.3996	.3759	.3538	.3332	.3139	.2959	.2791	.2097	.1594	.1224	.0949	.0585
.3762	.3506	.3269	.3050	.2848	.2660	.2487	.2326	.1678	.1226	.0906	.0678	.0390
.3329	.3075	.2843	.2630	.2434	.2255	.2090	.1938	.1342	.0943	.0671	.0484	.0260
.2946	.2697	.2472	.2267	.2080	.1911	.1756	.1615	.1074	.0725	.0497	.0346	.0173
.2607	.2366	.2149	.1954	.1778	.1619	.1476	.1346	.0859	.0558	.0368	.0247	.0116
.2307	.2076	.1869	.1685	.1520	.1372	.1240	.1122	.0687	.0429	.0273	.0176	.0077
.2042	.1821	.1625	.1452	.1299	.1163	.1042	.0935	.0550	.0330	.0202	.0126	.0051
.1807	.1597	.1413	.1252	.1110	.0985	.0876	.0779	.0440	.0254	.0150	.0090	.0034
.1599	.1401	.1229	.1079	.0949	.0835	.0736	.0649	.0352	.0195	.0111	.0064	.0023
.1415	.1229	.1069	.0930	.0811	.0708	.0618	.0541	.0281	.0150	.0082	.0046	.0015
.1252	.1078	.0929	.0802	.0693	.0600	.0520	.0451	.0225	.0116	.0061	.0033	.0010
.1108	.0946	.0808	.0691	.0592	.0508	.0437	.0376	.0180	.0089	.0045	.0023	.0007
.0981	.0829	.0703	.0596	.0506	.0431	.0367	.0313	.0144	.0068	.0033	.0017	.0005
.0868	.0728	.0611	.0514	.0443	.0365	.0308	.0261	.0115	.0053	.0025	.0012	.0003
.0768	.0638	.0531	.0443	.0370	.0309	.0259	.0217	.0092	.0040	.0018	.0009	.0002
.0680	.0560	.0462	.0382	.0316	.0262	.0218	.0181	.0074	.0031	.0014	.0006	.0001
.0601	.0491	.0402	.0329	.0270	.0222	.0183	.0151	.0059	.0024	.0010	.0004	.0001
.0532	.0431	.0349	.0284	.0231	.0188	.0154	.0126	.0047	.0018	.0007	.0003	.0001
.0471	.0378	.0304	.0245	.0197	.0160	.0129	.0105	.0038	.0014	.0006	.0002	.0000
.0417	.0331	.0264	.0211	.0169	.0135	.0109	.0087	.0030	.0011	.0004	.0002	.0000
.0369	.0291	.0230	.0182	.0144	.0115	.0091	.0073	.0024	.0008	.0003	.0001	.0000
.0326	.0255	.0200	.0157	.0123	.0097	.0077	.0061	.0019	.0006	.0002	.0001	.0000
.0289	.0224	.0174	.0135	.0105	.0082	.0064	.0051	.0015	.0005	.0002	.0001	.0000
.0256	.0196	.0151	.0116	.0090	.0070	.0054	.0042	.0012	.0004	.0001	.0000	.0000
.0139	.0102	.0075	.0055	.0041	.0030	.0023	.0017	.0004	.0001	.0000	.0000	.0000
.0075	.0053	.0037	.0026	.0019	.0013	.0010	.0007	.0001	.0000	.0000	.0000	.0000
.0041	.0027	.0019	.0013	.0009	.0006	.0004	.0003	.0000	.0000	.0000	.0000	.0000
.0022	.0014	.0009	.0006	.0004	.0003	.0002	.0001	.0000	.0000	.0000	.0000	.0000

TABLE A1.4 PRESENT VALUES OF AN ANNUITY OF ONE DOLLAR (PVIFA)

Period n	1%	2%	3%	4%	5%	6%	7%	8%	9%	10%	11%	12%
1	0.9901	0.9804	0.9709	0.9615	0.9524	0.9434	0.9346	0.9259	0.9174	0.9091	0.9009	0.8929
2	1.9704	1.9416	1.9135	1.8861	1.8594	1.8334	1.8080	1.7833	1.7591	1.7355	1.7125	1.6901
3	2.9410	2.8839	2.8286	2.7751	2.7232	2.6730	2.6243	2.5771	2.5313	2.4869	2.4437	2.4018
4	3.9020	3.8077	3.7171	3.6299	3.5460	3.4651	3.3872	3.3121	3.2397	3.1699	3.1024	3.0373
5	4.8534	4.7135	4.5797	4.4518	4.3295	4.2124	4.1002	3.9927	3.8897	3.7908	3.6959	3.6048
6	5.7955	5.6014	5.4172	5.2421	5.0757	4.9173	4.7665	4.6229	4.4859	4.3553	4.2305	4.1114
7	6.7282	6.4720	6.2303	6.0021	5.7864	5.5824	5.3893	5.2064	5.0330	4.8684	4.7122	4.5638
8	7.6517	7.3255	7.0197	6.7327	6.4632	6.2098	5.9713	5.7466	5.5348	5.3349	5.1461	4.9676
9	8.5660	8.1622	7.7861	7.4353	7.1078	6.8017	6.5152	6.2469	5.9952	5.7590	5.5370	5.3282
10	9.4713	8.9826	8.5302	8.1109	7.7217	7.3601	7.0236	6.7101	6.4177	6.1446	5.8892	5.6502
11	10.368	9.7868	9.2526	8.7605	8.3064	7.8869	7.4987	7.1390	6.8052	6.4951	6.2065	5.9377
12	11.255	10.575	9.9540	9.3851	8.8633	8.3838	7.9427	7.5361	7.1607	6.8137	6.4924	6.1944
13	12.134	11.348	10.635	9.9856	9.3936	8.8527	8.3577	7.9038	7.4869	7.1034	6.7499	6.4235
14	13.004	12.106	11.296	10.563	9.8986	9.2950	8.7455	8.2442	7.7862	7.3667	6.9819	6.6282
15	13.865	12.849	11.938	11.118	10.380	9.7122	9.1079	8.5595	8.0607	7.6061	7.1909	6.8109
16	14.718	13.578	12.561	11.652	10.838	10.106	9.4466	8.8514	8.3126	7.8237	7.3792	6.9740
17	15.562	14.292	13.166	12.166	11.274	10.477	9.7632	9.1216	8.5436	8.0216	7.5488	7.1196
18	16.398	14.992	13.754	12.659	11.690	10.828	10.059	9.3719	8.7556	8.2014	7.7016	7.2497
19	17.226	15.678	14.324	13.134	12.085	11.158	10.336	9.6036	8.9501	8.3649	7.8393	7.3658
20	18.046	16.351	14.877	13.590	12.462	11.470	10.594	9.8181	9.1285	8.5136	7.9633	7.4694
21	18.857	17.011	15.415	14.029	12.821	11.764	10.836	10.017	9.2922	8.6487	8.0751	7.5620
22	19.660	17.658	15.937	14.451	13.163	12.042	11.061	10.201	9.4424	8.7715	8.1757	7.6446
23	20.456	18.292	16.444	14.857	13.489	12.303	11.272	10.371	9.5802	8.8832	8.2664	7.7184
24	21.243	18.914	16.936	15.247	13.799	12.550	11.469	10.529	9.7066	8.9847	8.3481	7.7843
25	22.023	19.523	17.413	15.622	14.094	12.783	11.654	10.675	9.8226	9.0770	8.4217	7.8431
26	22.795	20.121	17.877	15.983	14.375	13.003	11.826	10.810	9.9290	9.1609	8.4881	7.8957
27	23.560	20.707	18.327	16.330	14.643	13.211	11.987	10.935	10.027	9.2372	8.5478	7.9426
28	24.316	21.281	18.764	16.663	14.898	13.406	12.137	11.051	10.116	9.3066	8.6016	7.9844
29	25.066	21.844	19.188	16.984	15.141	13.591	12.278	11.158	10.198	9.3696	8.6501	8.0218
30	25.808	22.396	19.600	17.292	15.372	13.765	12.409	11.258	10.274	9.4269	8.6938	8.0552
35	29.409	24.999	21.487	18.665	16.374	14.498	12.948	11.655	10.567	9.6442	8.8552	8.1755
40	32.835	27.355	23.115	19.793	17.159	15.046	13.332	11.925	10.757	9.7791	8.9511	8.2438
45	36.095	29.490	24.519	20.720	17.774	15.456	13.606	12.108	10.881	9.8628	9.0079	8.2825
50	39.196	31.424	25.730	21.482	18.256	15.762	13.801	12.233	10.962	9.9148	9.0417	8.3045

(continued)

TABLE A1.4 (*Continued*)

13%	14%	15%	16%	17%	18%	19%	20%	25%	30%	35%	40%	50%
0.8850	0.8772	0.8696	0.8621	0.8547	0.8475	0.8403	0.8333	0.8000	0.7692	0.7407	0.7143	0.6667
1.6681	1.6467	1.6257	1.6052	1.5852	1.5656	1.5465	1.5278	1.4400	1.3609	1.2894	1.2245	1.1111
2.3612	2.3216	2.2832	2.2459	2.2096	2.1743	2.1399	2.1065	1.9520	1.8161	1.6959	1.5889	1.4074
2.9745	2.9137	2.8550	2.7982	2.7432	2.6901	2.6386	2.5887	2.3616	2.1662	1.9969	1.8492	1.6049
3.5172	3.4331	3.3522	3.2743	3.1993	3.1272	3.0576	2.9906	2.6893	2.4356	2.2200	2.0352	1.7366
3.9975	3.8887	3.7845	3.6847	3.5892	3.4976	3.4098	3.3255	2.9514	2.6427	2.3852	2.1680	1.8244
4.4226	4.2883	4.1604	4.0386	3.9224	3.8115	3.7057	3.6046	3.1611	2.8021	2.5075	2.2628	1.8829
4.7988	4.6389	4.4873	4.3436	4.2072	4.0776	3.9544	3.8372	3.3289	2.9247	2.5982	2.3306	1.9220
5.1317	4.9464	4.7716	4.6065	4.4506	4.3030	4.1633	4.0310	3.4631	3.0190	2.6653	2.3790	1.9480
5.4262	5.2161	5.0188	4.8332	4.6586	4.4941	4.3389	4.1925	3.5705	3.0915	2.7150	2.4136	1.9653
5.6869	5.4527	5.2337	5.0286	4.8364	4.6560	4.4865	4.3271	3.6564	3.1473	2.7519	2.4383	1.9769
5.9176	5.6603	5.4206	5.1971	4.9884	4.7932	4.6105	4.4392	3.7251	3.1903	2.7792	2.4559	1.9846
6.1218	5.8424	5.5831	5.3423	5.1183	4.9095	4.7147	4.5327	3.7801	3.2233	2.7994	2.4685	1.9897
6.3025	6.0021	5.7245	5.4675	5.2293	5.0081	4.8023	4.6106	3.8241	3.2487	2.8144	2.4775	1.9931
6.4624	6.1422	5.8474	5.5755	5.3242	5.0916	4.8759	4.6755	3.8593	3.2682	2.8255	2.4839	1.9954
6.6039	6.2651	5.9542	5.6685	5.4053	5.1624	4.9377	4.7296	3.8874	3.2832	2.8337	2.4885	1.9970
6.7291	6.3729	6.0472	5.7487	5.4746	5.2223	4.9897	4.7746	3.9099	3.2948	2.8398	2.4918	1.9980
6.8399	6.4674	6.1280	5.8178	5.5339	5.2732	5.0333	4.8122	3.9279	3.3037	2.8443	2.4941	1.9986
6.9380	6.5504	6.1982	5.8775	5.5845	5.3162	5.0700	4.8435	3.9424	3.3105	2.8476	2.4958	1.9991
7.0248	6.6231	6.2593	5.9288	5.6278	5.3527	5.1009	4.8696	3.9539	3.3158	2.8501	2.4970	1.9994
7.1016	6.6870	6.3125	5.9731	5.6648	5.3837	5.1268	4.8913	3.9631	3.3198	2.8519	2.4979	1.9996
7.1695	6.7429	6.3587	6.0113	5.6964	5.4099	5.1486	4.9094	3.9705	3.3230	2.8533	2.4985	1.9997
7.2297	6.7921	6.3988	6.0442	5.7234	5.4321	5.1668	4.9245	3.9764	3.3254	2.8543	2.4989	1.9998
7.2829	6.8351	6.4338	6.0726	5.7465	5.4509	5.1822	4.9371	3.9811	3.3272	2.8550	2.4992	1.9999
7.3300	6.8729	6.4641	6.0971	5.7662	5.4669	5.1951	4.9476	3.9849	3.3286	2.8556	2.4994	1.9999
7.3717	6.9061	6.4906	6.1182	5.7831	5.4804	5.2060	4.9563	3.9879	3.3297	2.8560	2.4996	1.9999
7.4086	6.9352	6.5135	6.1364	5.7975	5.4919	5.2151	4.9636	3.9903	3.3305	2.8563	2.4997	2.0000
7.4412	6.9607	6.5335	6.1520	5.8099	5.5016	5.2228	4.9697	3.9923	3.3312	2.8565	2.4998	2.0000
7.4701	6.9830	6.5509	6.1656	5.8204	5.5098	5.2292	4.9747	3.9938	3.3317	2.8567	2.4999	2.0000
7.4957	7.0027	6.5660	6.1772	5.8294	5.5168	5.2347	4.9789	3.9950	3.3321	2.8568	2.4999	2.0000
7.5856	7.0700	6.6166	6.2153	5.8582	5.5386	5.2512	4.9915	3.9984	3.3330	2.8571	2.5000	2.0000
7.6344	7.1050	6.6418	6.2335	5.8713	5.5482	5.2582	4.9966	3.9995	3.3332	2.8571	2.5000	2.0000
7.6609	7.1232	6.6543	6.2421	5.8773	5.5523	5.2611	4.9986	3.9998	3.3333	2.8571	2.5000	2.0000
7.6752	7.1327	6.6605	6.2463	5.8801	5.5541	5.2623	4.9995	3.9999	3.3333	2.8571	2.5000	2.000C

APPENDIX A2

THE STANDARD NORMAL CUMULATIVE PROBABILITY FUNCTION

Table A2.1 provides cumulative probabilities for the standard normal cumulative probability function. To use the table, the random variable must be standardized (i.e., mean = 0, standard deviation = 1)

$$Z = \frac{X - \mu}{\sigma}$$

where Z = standard normal random variable

X = value of random variable

μ = mean of random variable

σ = standard deviation of random variable

As shown in the first and last rows of Table A2.1, values for Z range from -3.9 to 3.9. The numbers in the table represent the probability that $P(X \le Z)$. For example, $P(X \le -1.65) = .0495$ and $P(X \le 2.26) = .9881$.

Also notice that values for Z that are calculated to two decimal places are provided for $-2.99 \le Z \le 2.99$ but for only one decimal place for $-3.0 \le Z \le 3.0$.

TABLE A2.1 VALUES OF THE STANDARD NORMAL CUMULATIVE PROBABILITY FUNCTION

z	0	1	2	3	4	5	6	7	8	9
−3.	.0013	.0010	.0007	.0005	.0003	.0002	.0002	.0001	.0001	.0000
−2.9	.0019	.0018	.0017	.0017	.0016	.0016	.0015	.0015	.0014	.0014
−2.8	.0026	.0025	.0024	.0023	.0023	.0022	.0021	.0021	.0020	.0019
−2.7	.0035	.0034	.0033	.0032	.0031	.0030	.0029	.0028	.0027	.0026
−2.6	.0047	.0045	.0044	.0043	.0041	.0040	.0039	.0038	.0037	.0036
−2.5	.0062	.0060	.0059	.0057	.0055	.0054	.0052	.0051	.0049	.0048
−2.4	.0082	.0080	.0078	.0075	.0073	.0071	.0069	.0068	.0066	.0064
−2.3	.0107	.0104	.0102	.0099	.0096	.0094	.0091	.0089	.0087	.0084
−2.2	.0139	.0136	.0132	.0129	.0126	.0122	.0119	.0116	.0113	.0110
−2.1	.0179	.0174	.0170	.0166	.0162	.0158	.0154	.0150	.0146	.0143
−2.0	.0228	.0222	.0217	.0212	.0207	.0202	.0197	.0192	.0188	.0183
−1.9	.0287	.0281	.0274	.0268	.0262	.0256	.0250	.0244	.0238	.0233
−1.8	.0359	.0352	.0344	.0336	.0329	.0322	.0314	.0307	.0300	.0294
−1.7	.0446	.0436	.0427	.0418	.0409	.0401	.0392	.0384	.0375	.0367
−1.6	.0548	.0537	.0526	.0516	.0505	.0495	.0485	.0475	.0465	.0455
−1.5	.0668	.0655	.0643	.0630	.0618	.0606	.0594	.0582	.0570	.0559
−1.4	.0808	.0793	.0778	.0764	.0749	.0735	.0722	.0708	.0694	.0681
−1.3	.0968	.0951	.0934	.0918	.0901	.0885	.0869	.0853	.0838	.0823
−1.2	.1151	.1131	.1112	.1093	.1075	.1056	.1038	.1020	.1003	.0985
−1.1	.1357	.1335	.1314	.1292	.1271	.1251	.1230	.1210	.1190	.1170
−1.0	.1587	.1562	.1539	.1515	.1492	.1469	.1446	.1423	.1401	.1379
−.9	.1841	.1814	.1788	.1762	.1736	.1711	.1685	.1660	.1635	.1611
−.8	.2119	.2090	.2061	.2033	.2005	.1977	.1949	.1922	.1894	.1867
−.7	.2420	.2389	.2358	.2327	.2297	.2266	.2236	.2206	.2177	.2148
−.6	.2743	.2709	.2676	.2643	.2611	.2578	.2546	.2514	.2483	.2451
−.5	.3085	.3050	.3015	.2981	.2946	.2912	.2877	.2843	.2810	.2776

(*continued*)

TABLE A2.1 (Continued)

z	0	1	2	3	4	5	6	7	8	9
−3.	.0013	.0010	.0007	.0005	.0003	.0002	.0002	.0001	.0001	.0000
−.4	.3446	.3409	.3372	.3336	.3300	.3264	.3228	.3192	.3156	.3121
−.3	.3821	.3783	.3745	.3707	.3669	.3632	.3594	.3557	.3520	.3483
−.2	.4207	.4168	.4129	.4090	.4052	.4013	.3974	.3936	.3897	.3859
−.1	.4602	.4562	.4522	.4483	.4443	.4404	.4364	.4325	.4286	.4247
−.0	.5000	.4960	.4920	.4880	.4840	.4801	.4761	.4721	.4681	.4641
.0	.5000	.5040	.5080	.5120	.5160	.5199	.5239	.5279	.5319	.5359
.1	.5398	.5438	.5478	.5517	.5557	.5596	.5636	.5675	.5714	.5753
.2	.5793	.5832	.5871	.5910	.5948	.5987	.6026	.6064	.6103	.6141
.3	.6179	.6217	.6255	.6293	.6331	.6368	.6406	.6443	.6480	.6517
.4	.6554	.6591	.6628	.6664	.6700	.6736	.6772	.6808	.6844	.6879
.5	.6915	.6950	.6985	.7019	.7054	.7088	.7123	.7157	.7190	.7224
.6	.7257	.7291	.7324	.7357	.7389	.7422	.7454	.7486	.7517	.7549
.7	.7580	.7611	.7642	.7673	.7703	.7734	.7764	.7794	.7823	.7852
.8	.7881	.7910	.7939	.7967	.7995	.8023	.8051	.8078	.8106	.8133
.9	.8159	.8186	.8212	.8238	.8264	.8289	.8315	.8340	.8365	.8389
1.0	.8413	.8438	.8461	.8485	.8508	.8531	.8554	.8577	.8599	.8621
1.1	.8643	.8665	.8686	.8708	.8729	.8749	.8770	.8790	.8810	.8830
1.2	.8849	.8869	.8888	.8907	.8925	.8944	.8962	.8980	.8997	.9015
1.3	.9032	.9049	.9066	.9082	.9099	.9115	.9131	.9147	.9162	.9177
1.4	.9192	.9207	.9222	.9236	.9251	.9265	.9278	.9292	.9306	.9319
1.5	.9332	.9345	.9357	.9370	.9382	.9394	.9406	.9418	.9430	.9441
1.6	.9452	.9463	.9474	.9484	.9495	.9505	.9515	.9525	.9535	.9545
1.7	.9554	.9564	.9573	.9582	.9591	.9599	.9608	.9616	.9625	.9633
1.8	.9641	.9648	.9656	.9664	.9671	.9678	.9686	.9693	.9700	.9706
1.9	.9713	.9719	.9726	.9732	.9738	.9744	.9750	.9756	.9762	.9767
2.0	.9772	.9778	.9783	.9788	.9793	.9798	.9803	.9808	.9812	.9817
2.1	.9821	.9826	.9830	.9834	.9838	.9842	.9846	.9850	.9854	.9857
2.2	.9861	.9864	.9868	.9871	.9874	.9878	.9881	.9884	.9887	.9890
2.3	.9893	.9896	.9898	.9901	.9904	.9906	.9909	.9911	.9913	.9916
2.4	.9918	.9920	.9922	.9925	.9927	.9929	.9931	.9932	.9934	.9936
2.5	.9938	.9940	.9941	.9943	.9945	.9946	.9948	.9949	.9951	.9952
2.6	.9953	.9955	.9956	.9957	.9959	.9960	.9961	.9962	.9963	.9964
2.7	.9965	.9966	.9967	.9968	.9969	.9970	.9971	.9972	.9973	.9974
2.8	.9974	.9975	.9976	.9977	.9977	.9978	.9979	.9979	.9980	.9981
2.9	.9981	.9982	.9982	.9983	.9984	.9984	.9985	.9985	.9986	.9986
3.	.9987	.9990	.9993	.9995	.9997	.9998	.9998	.9999	.9999	1.000

APPENDIX A3

MATHEMATICAL TERMS, SYMBOLS, AND KEY FORMULAS

MATHEMATICAL TERMS AND SYMBOLS
KEY FORMULAS

MATHEMATICAL TERMS AND SYMBOLS

α_j (alpha)	Vertical intercept from characteristic line used to estimate security j's beta. Also used to indicate risk-adjusted excess returns
β_j (beta)	Slope of characteristic line; indicates the level of systematic risk for security or portfolio j
b	Earnings retention rate
C_t	Dollar coupon for a bond in period t
$Cov(x, y)$	Covariance between variables x and y; also written as $COV_{x,y}$ and $\sigma_{x,y}$
CV_j	Coefficient of variation for security j
D_j	Duration for security j
D_t	Dividends per share for period t
E_t	Earnings per share for period t
$E(X)$	Expected value of random variable X
e^x	Antilog of base e logarithm where $e = 2.7182 \ldots$
$E(HPR_j)$	Expected holding period return for security j
FVIF	Future value interest factor
FVIFA	Future value interest factor for an annuity
g	Annual growth rate in dividends or earnings per share
HPR_t	Holding period return for period t
$\overline{HPR}_j$	Mean holding period return for security j
i_j	Yield to maturity on security j
K_j	Required rate of return on security j
λ_j (lambda)	Market price of risk (risk premium) for risk factor j
$ln(X)$	Natural or base e logarithm
M_N	Maturity or face value of a bond at time period N
N	Term-to-maturity of a bond or period when last cash flow is received
$N(Z)$	Cumulative normal probability
π (Pi)	Symbol used to indicate that variables in an equation should be multiplied
P_j	Probability that event j will occur
PVIF	Present value interest factor
PVIFA	Present value interest factor for an annuity
R^2	Coefficient of determination or square of the correlation coefficient
r_j	Return on equity for firm j
$\rho_{x,y}$ (rho)	Correlation coefficient between variables x and y; also denoted as R
R_F	Risk-free rate of return
S	Striking or exercise price on a call or put option
Σ (sigma)	Symbol used to indicate that variables in an equation should be summed
σ_A (sigma)	Standard deviation of random variable A
σ_A^2	Variance of random variable A
$U(X)$	Level of utility associated with investment X
V_0	Intrinsic value of a security today
$\bar{X}_A$	Mean of random variable A
X_j	The weight or relative importance of asset j in a portfolio
$\hat{Y}_t$	Estimate of dependent variable Y usually calculated using regression equation constants and specified values for the independent variables.

KEY FORMULAS

I. Bond valuation
   A. Zero coupon bond

   $$V_0 = \frac{M_N}{(1 + i)^N}$$

   B. Perpetuity (consol)

   $$V_0 = \frac{C}{i}$$

   C. Finite maturity

   $$V_0 = C\left[\frac{1 - \dfrac{1}{(1 + i)^n}}{i}\right] + \frac{M_N}{(1 + i)^N}$$

II. Bond risk measures
   A. Duration

   $$D_j = \frac{C\left[\dfrac{(1 + i)^{N+1} - (1 + i) - iN}{i^2(1 + i)^N}\right] + \dfrac{M_N N}{(1 + i)^N}}{C\left[\dfrac{1 - \dfrac{1}{(1 + i)^N}}{i}\right] + \dfrac{M_N}{(1 + i)^N}}$$

   B. Beta

   $$\beta_j = \frac{Cov(r_j, r_m)}{\sigma_m^2}$$

III. Common Stock Valuation
   A. Zero Dividend Growth

   $$V_0 = \frac{D}{K}$$

   B. Constant Dividend Growth

   $$V_0 = \frac{E(1 - b)(1 + br)}{K - br} = \frac{D_0(1 + g)}{K - g} = \frac{D_1}{K - g}$$

   C. Two-Phase Model

   $$V_0 = D_0(1 + g_1)\left(\frac{1 + g_1}{1 + K}\right)\left(\frac{(1 + K)^{A-1} - 1}{K}\right) + \frac{\dfrac{D_0(1 + g_1)^A(1 + g_2)}{K - g_2}}{(1 + K)^A}$$

   D. *H*-Model

   $$V_0 = \frac{D_0}{K - g_2}\left[(1 + g_2) + \frac{A + B}{2}(g_1 - g_2)\right]$$

E. CEPS Model

$$V_0 = \frac{CEPS(1 + g_{CEPS})}{K - g_{CEPS}}$$

F. Inflation Adjustment Model

$$V_0 = \frac{D(1 + g)(1 + fI)}{(K + g) + (h - f)I}$$

IV. Preferred Stock Valuation

$$V_0 = \frac{D}{K}$$

I. Option Valuation
  A. Call Option

  $$V_c = P_s N(d_1) - Se^{-rt}N(d_2)$$

  B. Put Option

  $$V_p = P_t e^{-rt} + V_c - P_s$$

VI. Risk Measures for Securities
  A. Range

  $$Range = \text{maximum } HPR - \text{minimum } HPR$$

  B. Variance

  1. Equal probabilities

  $$\sigma_j^2 = 1/n \sum_{t=1}^{n} (HPR_t - \overline{HPR})^2$$

  2. Unequal Probabilities

  $$\sigma_j^2 = \sum_{j=1}^{n} (P_j)(HPR_j - \overline{HPR})^2$$

  C. Coefficient of Variation

  $$CV_j = \frac{\sigma_j}{\overline{HPR_j}}$$

  D. Covariance

  $$COV_{ij} = 1/n \sum_{t=1}^{n} (HPR_{it} - \overline{HPR_i})(HPR_{jt} - \overline{HPR_j})$$

  $$COV_{ij} = \rho_{ij}\sigma_i\sigma_j$$

  E. Correlation

  $$\rho_{ij} = \frac{1/n \sum_{t=1}^{n} (HPR_{it} - \overline{HPR_i})(HPR_{jt} - \overline{HPR_j})}{\sigma_i\sigma_j}$$

  $$\rho_{ij} = \frac{COV_{ij}}{\sigma_i\sigma_j}$$

F. Beta

$$\beta_j = \frac{COV_{jm}}{\sigma_m^2}$$

VII. Risk Measures for Portfolios

A. Variance for a two-security portfolio

$$\sigma_p^2 = X_1^2\sigma_1^2 + X_2^2\sigma_2^2 + 2X_1X_2COV_{1,2}$$

B. Variance for a three-security portfolio

$$\sigma_p^2 = X_1^2\sigma_1^2 + X_2^2\sigma_2^2 + X_3^2\sigma_3^2 + 2X_1X_2COV_{1,2} + 2X_1X_3COV_{1,3} \\ + 2X_2X_3COV_{2,3}$$

C. Variance for n-security portfolio

$$\sigma_p^2 = \sum_{i=1}^{n}\sum_{j=1}^{n} X_iX_jCOV_{i,j}$$

D. Beta for a portfolio

$$\beta_p = \sum_{j=1}^{n} X_j\beta_j$$

E. Duration for a portfolio

$$D_p = \sum_{j=1}^{n} X_jD_j$$

VIII. Asset Pricing Models

A. Capital asset pricing model

$$E(R_j) = R_f + \beta_j[E(R_m) - R_f]$$

B. Arbitrage pricing model

$$E_i = \lambda_0 + \lambda_1 b_{i1} + \lambda_2 b_{i2} + \ldots + \lambda_k b_{ik}$$

NAME INDEX

CORPORATION AND ORGANIZATION NAME INDEX

SUBJECT INDEX